Colin Mackenzie

Mackenzie's Ten Thousand Receipts in all the Useful and Domestic Arts

Colin Mackenzie

Mackenzie's Ten Thousand Receipts in all the Useful and Domestic Arts

ISBN/EAN: 9783337306854

Printed in Europe, USA, Canada, Australia, Japan

Cover: Foto ©Lupo / pixelio.de

More available books at **www.hansebooks.com**

MACKENZIE'S
TEN THOUSAND RECEIPTS,

IN ALL THE

USEFUL AND DOMESTIC ARTS;

CONSTITUTING

A COMPLETE AND PRACTICAL LIBRARY,

RELATING TO

AGRICULTURE, ANGLING, BEES, BLEACHING, BOOK-KEEPING, BREWING, COTTON CULTURE, CROCHETING, CARVING, CHOLERA, COOKING, CALICO PRINTING, CONFECTIONERY, CEMENTS, CHEMICAL RECEIPTS, COSMETICS, DISEASES, DAIRY, DENTISTRY, DIALYSIS, DECALCOMANIA, DYEING, DISTILLATION, ENAMELLING, ENGRAVING, ELECTRO-PLATING, ELECTROTYPING, FISH CULTURE, FARRIERY, FOOD, FLOWER GARDENING, FIREWORKS, GAS METRES, GILDING, GLASS, HEALTH, HORSEMANSHIP, INKS, JEWELLERS' PASTE, KNITTING, KNOTS, LITHOGRAPHY, MERCANTILE CALCULATIONS, MEDICINE, MISCELLANEOUS RECEIPTS, METALLURGY, MEZZOTINTS, OIL COLORS, OILS, PAINTING, PERFUMERY, PASTRY, PETROLEUM, PICKLING, POISONS AND ANTIDOTES, POTICHOMANIA, PROOF-READING, POTTERY, PRESERVING, PHOTOGRAPHY, PYROTECHNICS, RURAL AND DOMESTIC ECONOMY, SUGAR RAISING, SILVERING, SCOURING, SILK AND SILK-WORMS, SORGHUM, TOBACCO CULTURE, TANNING, TREES, TELEGRAPHING, VARNISHES, VEGETABLE GARDENING, WEIGHTS AND MEASURES, WINES, ETC., ETC.

BEING AN ENTIRELY NEW EDITION

CAREFULLY REVISED AND RE-WRITTEN,

AND

Containing the Improvements and Discoveries up to last Date of Publication.

JANUARY, 1867.

BY A

CORPS OF EXPERTS.

Again Revised to Date of Present Issue, April 25th, 1867, with Addition of Special Articles upon the Rinderpest and Trichinæ.

ALSO,

REPORT AND AWARD OF THE TRIAL OF AGRICULTURAL IMPLEMENTS AT THE GREAT NATIONAL FIELD TRIAL HELD AT AUBURN, N. Y., IN JULY, 1866.

PHILADELPHIA:
T. ELLWOOD ZELL & COMPANY,
Nos. 17 & 19 SOUTH SIXTH STREET.
1867.

Entered according to Act of Congress, in the year 1867, by

T. ELLWOOD ZELL,

In the Clerk's Office of the District Court of the United States for the Eastern District of Pennsylvania.

J. FAGAN & SON,
STEREOTYPERS,
PHILADELPHIA.

PRINTED BY SHERMAN & CO.

PREFACE

TO THE NEW AND REVISED EDITION

OF OCTOBER, 1865.

In preparing a new edition of this popular work, the Editors have endeavored to incorporate all the improvements in the various branches, which have been introduced, since the publication of the last edition. Much of the work has been entirely re-written, and new articles have been added on Photography, Pyrotechnics, Angling, Pisciculture, etc. The matter has not been simply scissored from newspapers, but carefully digested from standard authorities, the scientific journals, and from the practical knowledge of the Editors and contributors. The Editors have to acknowledge valuable assistance from gentlemen, eminent in the departments of Agriculture, Horticulture, Wine-making, Perfumery, Cements, Engraving, Photography, Angling, Tanning, etc. The work, it is believed, will be found more reliable and thorough than any one of its class now in print. The Miscellaneous department is almost entirely new, and contains much valuable and interesting information. Some matters properly belonging under other heads, but received too late, have been transferred to it. The reader is especially requested to refer to the index, when seeking information.

OPINIONS OF THE PRESS.

FROM THE PHILA. NORTH AMERICAN, DEC. 22, 1865.

The vast amount of useful knowledge bearing on every-day life which constantly flits through the world, has often led to efforts for gathering and rendering it available by those who want it, when they want it. Mr. Zell having made a previous successful effort in this direction, has enlarged the field of his usefulness by a new edition of his work, which will be exceedingly useful to all, and almost indispensable to some. He has gathered the formulæ and directions of all the most recent discoveries in the useful and domestic arts, and has made it as nearly complete as possible. Though the work is designed for popular rather than scientific use, it contains much that will interest scientific men, as well as general readers. Agriculture, horticulture, domestic economy, farriery, medicine, brewing, distillation, dyeing, paints and varnishes, metallurgy, photography, engraving, pottery, weights and measures—these are among the subjects treated very fully, and which are of first importance. There is no effort to prepare treatises upon any of these. The kernel alone is retained, and that in the best form for use by practical men. There is a great body of what may be termed the cream of useful knowledge, under the general head of agriculture, which it were well all farmers should have for perusal at leisure moments. Manures, crops, drainage, and the care of animals, are all treated in a condensed manner, with directions and information which cannot fail to advantage readers. The gardener, poulterer, and apiarian, are provided with excellent receipts. The half-hundred pages devoted to medicine will be useful where a physician cannot be procured; and under the miscellaneous head there are a variety of facts on horsemanship and knitting, gunpowder and book-keeping, dogs and crocheting, which could not readily be found elsewhere. A great deal of the information hitherto published in this form has been of doubtful use, and has discredited honest efforts to aid the community. The counterfeit only proves the worth of what is genuine, and this really careful and useful *vade mecum* ought not to suffer from the reputation of the trash which it seeks to supplant. The index—an essential in such a compilation—has been carefully arranged, at much length. There are diagrams and illustrations where they are needed, and the whole forms a volume which ought to be very widely circulated, and which will repay its cost in almost any family within a year.

FROM THE PHILA. SUNDAY DISPATCH, NOV. 26, 1865.

Mackenzie's Ten Thousand Receipts, containing new discoveries and processes in use up to October, 1865. 487 pages. To describe this volume properly would require the space given to a catalogue, and the volubility of an auctioneer. We find in it almost everything that can be conceived as an object of inquiry involving the special preparation of materials or the management of processes. Agriculture, chemistry, cooking, manufactures, medicine, the decorative arts, household management, and a thousand other things which defy classification, are embraced in this closely-printed book, which, in the way of condensation, contains enough to stock a library with volumes printed in fashionably large type. We could not undertake to recite the whole title-page, which is of itself prodigious, affording but a feeble idea of what is within. Suffice it to say, that almost anything that anybody wants to know how to do will be found in this volume properly described, and illustrated in some cases by useful engravings. It has been re-written by a corps of scientific gentlemen, and is really a book which should be found in every house.

FROM THE GERMANTOWN (PA.) TELEGRAPH, NOV. 22, 1865.

The editor and publisher of this extremely well gotten-up edition, has been many months in its preparation, having employed in this time a corps of able experts, in order that the work might be brought out not only in a style hitherto unapproached, but with intrinsic claims upon the community which cannot but be acknowledged. Truthfully, these "Ten Thousand Receipts in the Domestic Arts," constitute a "complete and practical library," relating to the hundreds of subjects treated of, connected with the indispensable every-day affairs of family life. The clearness of the print, the arrangement of the receipts, with the comprehensive index, render recourse to it at all times as easy almost as turning over the pages of a magazine, and obtaining from it the information sought in plain language and in condensed form, so that all can quickly see and readily understand. But this is not a work designed exclusively for domestic purposes, as the word "Domestic" is most generally understood; but it contains valuable suggestions and advice upon almost every practical pursuit. There is scarcely anything omitted in which any considerable number of people are interested.

FROM THE PHILA. PRESS, NOV. 24, 1865.

This is a domestic cyclopædia, of nearly 500 pages, in new type, small but clear. We are assured that two years' labor, by very competent gentlemen, has been bestowed upon this large and improved edition, and can well believe it. There is scarcely a subject connected with the useful and domestic arts about which a seeker for information cannot find what he wants in this book. The most recent improvements and discoveries, up to October, 1865, when the work was stereotyped, have been included. The quantity of information in this volume is very great—so far as we have tested it we can vouch for its accuracy. As a work of reference, it has been made complete by the addition of a copious index.

FROM THE PHILA. SUNDAY TRANSCRIPT, DEC. 10, 1865.

It is one of the most remarkable books of the day, containing, as it does, a reference to every conceivable subject under the sun. In itself it is a complete and practical library, so arranged as to be invaluable in the household, on the farm, and in the counting-room. Pastry and petroleum, agriculture and knitting, receive equal attention, while the entire volume presents a fund of information not accessible in any other form. The thrifty housekeeper can pick up numerous capital receipts for pies, or can learn the art of carving, which is treated as one of the exact sciences; the merchant will find mercantile calculations; the artist will find a dissertation upon oil colors, water colors, and mezzotints; the farmer will learn something about gardening. In fact, there is no branch of trade but can be benefited by a perusal of this book. Although the receipts are quoted as 10,000, judging from the book they will double that figure.

FROM THE PHILA. INQUIRER, NOV. 24, 1865.

The present issue of this useful work by Mr. Zell, is a new and improved edition, carefully revised and re-written by a corps of gentlemen eminently qualified for the peculiar task. To it has been likewise added all the improvements and discoveries in the useful and domestic arts up to the date of publication, October, 1865. Two years of labor have been necessary to bring the book out in the present improved shape.

FROM THE PHILA. EVENING TELEGRAPH, DEC. 23, 1865.

Mr. Zell maintains his position among the first-class houses of our land, principally through his agencies and the few well-selected works to which he has given life. Principal among the latter is "Mackenzie's Ten Thousand Receipts," a work of universal information. In it are found, in fact, all the useful knowledge of the age compressed into this universal compendium of information. If a man be familiar with all the contents of this book, he will be an accomplished gentleman, a practical doctor, and in many respects a professional man. The work is one we can recommend as likely to be every day useful. We understand it is prepared by a gentleman well known in the world of science; it bears the impress of a well-informed mind. It is specific in its directions, and illustrated by numerous wood-cuts. Too much credit cannot be given to both the compiler and publisher for the remarkable care and skill exercised in compressing into one volume, and that so carefully printed, so great an amount of useful information.

FROM THE PHILA. EVENING BULLETIN, DEC. 12, 1865.

This work has been thoroughly re-written, and comprises all manner of improvements and discoveries, brought up to October of this year. It forms a complete library of valuable knowledge upon almost every imaginable subject connected with the useful and domestic arts, and is a most important volume of reference for the manufacturer, agriculturalist and housekeeper.

PREFACE

TO THE LATEST LONDON EDITION.

As the object of all study, and the end of all wisdom, is practical utility, so a collection of the most approved Receipts, in all the arts of Domestic and Social Life, may be considered as a volume containing nearly the whole of the wisdom of man, worthy of preservation. In truth, the present volume has been compiled under the feeling, that if all other books of Science in the world were destroyed, this single volume would be found to embody the results of the useful experience, observations, and discoveries of mankind during the past ages of the world.

Theoretical reasonings and historical details have, of course, been avoided, and the object of the compiler has been to economize his space, and come at once to the point. Whatever men do, or desire to do, with the materials with which nature has supplied them, and with the powers which they possess, is here plainly taught and succinctly preserved; whether it regard complicated manufactures, means of curing diseases, simple processes of various kinds, or the economy, happiness, and preservation of life.

The best authorities have been resorted to, and innumerable volumes consulted, and wherever different processes of apparently equal value, for attaining the same end, have been found, they have been introduced.

Among the works consulted have been,

The Monthly Magazine, 56 vols.	Thomas's Practice of Physic.
The Repertory of Arts and Sciences, 60 vols.	Cooper's Dictionary of Surgery.
The London Journal of Arts and Sciences.	Thornton's British Herbal.
The Transactions of the Society of Arts, 30 vols.	Waller's British Herbal.
The Magazine of Trade and Manufactures, 6 vols.	Imison's School of Arts.
	Handmaid to the Arts.
The Gazette of Health, 9 vols.	Smith's Laboratory of the Arts.
The Series of the Horticultural Society, 5 vols.	Hamilton on Drawing.
The Series of the Agricultural Society, 30 vols.	The Editor's Thousand Experiments in Manu-
The Farmer's Magazine, 16 vols.	factures and Chemistry.
Young's Farmer's Calendar.	Davy's Agricultural Chemistry.
Loudon on Gardening, 1 vol.	Henry's Elements of Chemistry.
Jennings's Domestic Cyclopædia, 2 vols.	Chaptal's Chemistry applied to the Arts.
Tingrey on Varnishing.	Gregory's Cyclopædia.
Richardson on the Metallic Arts.	The English and other Cyclopædias.

Besides innumerable treatises on special subjects, minor journals, and a great variety of manuscript communications from friends and connections of the editor and publisher.

A general, rather than a scientific, arrangement has been adopted, because the object of the work is popular and universal, and, though likely to be useful to men of science, it is more especially addressed to the public at large. In like manner, as far as possible, technical and scientific language has been avoided, and popular names and simple descriptions have been preferred.

Every care has been taken in the printing to avoid errors in quantities, as well as to select the best receipts of each kind; but notices of errors, omissions, or experimental improvements, will be thankfully received by the publisher, for the use of future editions.

The Index will render it easy to refer to every article of importance.

PREFACE

TO THE EARLY AMERICAN EDITION.

In fulfilling the duty of preparing for the press a new and enlarged edition of the valuable work of Mackenzie, the Editor has steadily borne in mind its evident aim at general practical utility; and consequently he has submitted both alterations and additions to its rules. While the former will be found but few—a circumstance arising from the nature of the book; the latter are both numerous and important—amounting to about fifty pages, exclusive of those contained in the Miscellaneous Department and the Appendix.

The Medical part has been condensed, simplified, and adapted to the climate and diseases of the United States. A short, but complete manual of "Directions for rearing the Silk Worm, and the Culture of the White Mulberry Tree," together with an extensive article on the Diseases of the Horse, may be noticed as among the important additions. The Culinary art has not been neglected — the numerous *original* receipts from the best modern authorities of the "Kitchen," for preparing various delicacies of the animal and vegetable kingdom, including Pastry, Puddings, etc., will no doubt prove acceptable to American housekeepers. The man of family, the Sportsman, the Artist, the Mechanic, and the Farmer, have all been remembered. And an unusually large and correct Index gives every facility of reference that could be wished.

The attention of the Reader is called to the "Miscellaneous Receipts." In this portion, which is very copious, numerous receipts have been placed, which could not with propriety be elsewhere arranged. It has also been made the receptacle of much valuable matter obtained from several kind female friends, and the fruit of researches into many curious and rare books; and which was prepared at too late a period for insertion in the appropriate departments. The Appendix of "Instructions in the Art of Carving," with its numerous wood cuts, will, it is hoped, prove acceptable and useful to our country readers, for whose accommodation this work was originally designed.

The Editor more especially notices the following works, as sources from which he has derived considerable assistance: The Franklin Journal; Willich's Domestic Encyclopædia, by Professor Cooper; a Tract published by the Pennsylvania Society for the Rearing of Silk-Worms, etc.; and the curious work of Colonel Hanger, of sporting memory.

In conclusion, the publishers beg leave to state, that neither time nor expense has been considered in endeavoring to render this edition cheaper and better than any other which has been published, and at the same time worthy of the patronage which is solicited for it. They have availed themselves of the services of a gentleman as Editor, who has been for a considerable time engaged in the preparatory researches. The type, though small, is very legible and distinct; and in the selection of the paper, whilst regard has been had to the color, it has been deemed of main importance that it should be sufficiently durable to resist the frequent usage into which a work of this description must necessarily be called.

CONTENTS.

[FOR DETAILS, SEE INDEX, AT CLOSE OF THE VOLUME.]

	PAGE
AGRICULTURE	9
Manure	11, 18
Wheat	27
Drainage	49
Sugar	52
Cotton and Tobacco	53
Silk-Worm	54
HORTICULTURE	60
Budding and Grafting	54
Fruit	67
Insects and Diseases of Trees	76
Keeping Fruit	86
Flower Gardening	88
RURAL AND DOMESTIC ECONOMY	91
Dairy Work	91
Management of Bees	98
FARRIERY	104
Diseases of Horses	105
" Dogs	115, 449
" Hogs	116
" Sheep	117
" Cattle	120
MEDICINE	122
Diseases	122
Cholera	162
Accidents	143
Wounds	144
Fractures	146
Dislocations	148
Amputations	150
Drowning	151, 180
Poisons	152
Medicines	154
Diseases of Females	165
Diseases of Children	169
Domestic Medicines	173
Hygiene	178
Rules for Health	184
Teeth	186
CULINARY ARTS	188
Cooking	188
Confectionery	232
Pickling	238
Preserving	239
Carving	241
Food	247

CONTENTS.

	PAGE
BREWING	251
Cider	263
Wines	265
DISTILLATION	277
Essential Oils	289
Waters	292
Vinegar	296
Artificial Waters	300
PERFUMERY	303
BLEACHING AND SCOURING	309
DYEING	315
Staining	325
PAINTS AND COLORS	327
VARNISHES	339
Lacquers	345
CEMENTS	352
Glue	355
INKS	358
METALLURGY	362
Assaying	363
Parting	367
Alloys	368
Foils	373
Electro-plating	374
Gilding	376
Iron and Steel	381
PYROTECHNY	384
Matches	386
TANNING	386
ENAMELLING	390
POTTERY	394
GLASS	399
PHOTOGRAPHY	409
Philolithography	417
ENGRAVING	419
Lithography	424
WEIGHTS AND MEASURES	427
Specific Gravity	429
Gas Meters	430
Value of Coins	431
CHEMICAL RECEIPTS	432
Boiler Encrustations	433
Artificial Cold	435
Antiseptics and Disinfectants	435
WEATHER PROGNOSTICS	439
ANGLING	443
Pisciculture	445
MISCELLANEOUS	446
To Tie Knots	446
Knitting	447
Canary Birds	448
Dogs	449
Insects	449
Petroleum	451
Electric Telegraph	451
Book-keeping	452
Proof-reading	452
Rowing	453
Domestic Receipts	455–458–464
Medical Receipts	460–463–464
Dialysis	463
Horsemanship	463
Decalcomania	464
Gunpowder	466
Farm Seed	466
INDEX	467–487

MACKENZIE'S
TEN THOUSAND RECEIPTS.

AGRICULTURE.

THE MODERN THEORY OF AGRICULTURE.

Liebig and other chemists have, within the last twenty-five years, endeavored to establish a science of agriculture, based upon a knowledge of the constitution of plants and of soils, and their mutual relations. We propose to give a very condensed account of the general conclusions arrived at.

Food of Plants.

Plants derive their food from the *air* as well as from the earth; the former by their leaves, the latter by their roots. Elements most necessary to them are *carbon*, *hydrogen*, *oxygen*, and *nitrogen*, with various mineral substances present in the soil. Carbon is the most abundant. This is to a large extent extracted from the atmosphere by the leaves of plants, during the day-time. Hydrogen and oxygen are in the water contained in the earth and air; and oxygen is in the air mixed with nitrogen. Plants do not seem able, however, to separate much nitrogen from the air as such, but more readily obtain it by the decomposition of *ammonia* (composed of hydrogen and nitrogen), which is formed in the atmosphere, and washed down into the earth by rain-water, so as to reach the roots. All ordinary waters, it must be remembered, contain substances dissolved in them. Irrigation of land does not act only by the water itself, but by that which is dissolved or diffused in it. Davy calculated that, supposing one part of sulphate of lime to be contained in every two thousand parts of river water, and every square yard of dry meadow land to absorb eight gallons of water, then, by every flooding, more than one and a half hundred weight of gypsum per acre is diffused by the water — a quantity equal to that generally used in spreading gypsum as a manure or fertilizer; and so, if we allow only twenty-five parts of animal and vegetable remains to be present in a thousand parts of river water, we shall find that every soaking with such water will add to the meadow nearly two tons per acre of organic matter. The extraordinary fertility of the banks and delta of the river Nile is due to the natural annual overflow of the river, extended by artificial irrigation. In China also, the principle of irrigation is carried out very largely, and it is applicable, on a large or small scale, in any country. The water of lakes is usually charged with dissolved or suspended substances even more abundantly than that of rivers.

Humus.

Soils contain a great amount of matter which results from the decay of vegetables and animals; to a compound of which with earthy material the name of *humus* is given. This was once incorrectly supposed to give the whole nutriment of the plant. Trees and plants, instead of *abstracting* carbon from the earth, really, by taking it from the air, and subsequently dying and decaying, annually by their leaves, and finally altogether, *give* carbon and other atmospheric elements to the soil. As above said, all plants by their leaves absorb carbonic acid from the air, and retain carbon, giving out oxygen. It is evident, therefore, that the leaves are of great importance to the plant. So are the roots, for their absorbing office. Thus it is true that the growth of a plant is always proportioned to the *surface* of its roots and leaves together. Vegetation, in its simplest form, consists in the abstraction of carbon from carbonic acid, and hydrogen from water; but the taking of nitrogen also, from ammonia especially, is important to them, and most of all, to those which are most nutritious, as the wheat, rye, barley, &c., whose seeds contain gluten and other nitrogenous principles of the greatest value for food. Plants will grow well in pure charcoal, if supplied with rain-water, for rain-water contains ammonia.

Animal substances, as they putrefy, always evolve ammonia, which plants need and absorb. Thus is explained one of the benefits of manuring, but not the only one, as we shall see presently. Animal manure, however, acts chiefly by the formation of ammonia. The quantity of gluten in wheat, rye, and barley is very different; and they contain nitrogen in varying proportions. Even in samples of the same seed the quantity varies; and why? Evidently because one variety has been better fed with its own appropriate fertilizer than another which has been reared on a soil less accurately adapted by artificial means for its growth. French wheat contains 12 per cent. of gluten; Bavarian 24 per cent. Sir H. Davy obtained 19 per cent. from winter, and 24 from summer wheat; from Sicilian 21, from Barbary wheat 19 per cent. Such great differences must be owing to some cause, and this we find in the different methods of cultivation. An increase of animal manure gives rise not only to an increase in the *number* of seeds, but also to a remarkable difference in the propor-

(9)

tion of gluten which those seeds contain. Among manures of animal origin there is great diversity. Cow dung contains but a small proportion of nitrogen. One hundred parts of wheat, grown on a soil to which this material was applied, afforded only 11 parts of gluten and 64 of starch; while the same quantity of wheat, grown on a soil fertilized with *human urine*, yielded 35 per cent. of gluten, and of course a smaller proportion of less valuable ingredients. During the putrefaction of urine, ammoniacal salts are formed in large quantity, it may be said, exclusively; for under the influence of warmth and moisture, the most prominent ingredient of urine is converted into carbonate of ammonia.

Guano.

Guano consists of the excrements of sea-fowl, collected during long periods on certain islands in the South Sea. A soil which is deficient in organic matter is made much more productive by the addition of this manure. It consists of ammonia, combined with uric, phosphoric, oxalic, and carbonic acids, with some earthy salts and impurities.

The urine of men and animals living upon flesh contains a large quantity of nitrogen, partly in the form of urea. Human urine is the most powerful manure for all vegetables which contain nitrogen; that of horses and horned cattle contains less of this element, but much more than the solid excrements of those animals. In the face of such facts as these, is it not pitiable to observe how the urine of the stable or cow-shed is often permitted to run off, to sink uselessly into the earth, or to form a pool in the middle of a farm-yard, from which, as it putrefies, the ammonia formed in it rapidly escapes into the atmosphere?

Cultivated plants need more nitrogen than wild ones, being of a higher and more complex organization. The result of forest growth is chiefly the production of carbonaceous woody fibre; of garden or field culture, especially the addition of as much nitrogen as the plant can be made to take up.

Solid Manure.

The solid excrements of animals do not contain as much nitrogen as those which are voided in a liquid form, and do not constitute so powerful a fertilizing material. In urine, moreover, ammonia loses a good deal of its volatility by being combined and dissolved in the form of salts. In an analogous manner, one of the uses of sulphate of lime or gypsum, as a manure, is to fix the ammonia of the atmosphere. Charcoal and *humus* have a similar property.

Mineral Matter in Plants.

Besides the substances already mentioned, others are needed by plants as part of their food, to form their structure. The firmness of straw, for example, is due to the presence in it of *silica*, the principal constituent of sand and flints. Potassa, soda, lime, magnesia, and phosphoric acid, are contained in plants, in different proportions. All of these they must obtain from the soil. The alkalies above-named (potassa and soda) appear to be essential to the perfect development of the higher vegetable forms. Some plants require them in one mode of combination, and some in another; and thus the soil that is very good for one, may be quite unfit for others. Firs and pines find enough to support them in barren, sandy soil.

The proportion of silicate of potash (necessary for the firmness of wheat straw) does not vary perceptibly in the soil of grain-fields, because what is removed by the reaper, is again replaced in putrefying straw. But this is not the case with meadow-land. Hence we never find a luxuriant crop of grass on sandy and limestone soils which contain little potash, evidently because one of the constituents indispensable to the growth of the plants is wanting. If a meadow be well manured, we remove, with the increased crop of grass, a greater quantity of potash than can, by a repetition of the same manure, be restored to it. So, grass-land manured with gypsum soon ceases to feel its agency. But if the meadow be strewed from time to time with wood ashes, or soap-boilers' lye made from wood ashes, then the grass thrives as luxuriantly as before. And why? The ashes are only a means of restoring the necessary potash for the grass stalks. So oats, barley, and rye may be made for once to grow upon a sandy heath, by mixing with the scanty soil the ashes of the heath-plants that grow upon it. Those ashes contain soda and potash, conveyed to the growing furze or gorse by rain-water. The soil of one district consists of sandstone; certain trees find in it a quantity of alkaline earths sufficient for their own sustenance. When felled, and burnt, and sprinkled upon the soil, oats will grow and thrive that without such aid would not vegetate.

The most decisive proof of the absurdity of the indiscriminate use of any strong manure was obtained at Bingen, a town on the Rhine, where the produce and development of vines were highly increased by manuring them with animal matters, such as shavings of horn. After some years, the formation of the wood and leaves decreased perceptibly. Such manure had too much hastened the growth of the vines: in two or three years they had exhausted the potash in the formation of their fruit leaves and wood; so that none remained for the future crops, as shavings of horn contain no potash. Cow-dung would have been better, and is known to be better.

Conditions of Vegetation.

The sun's heat and light, air, water, and the common elements of the earth are necessary to the *existence* of plants. But a greater or less abundance of certain elements, and their existence in more or less favorable states of combination, determines the magnitude and fertility, or, in a word, the whole productiveness, of the vegetable growth.

The rules of agriculture should then, if rationally perfected, enable us to give to each plant what it requires for the attainment of the special object of its culture; namely, the *increase of certain parts* which are used as food for men and animals.

One instance may illustrate this idea. The means to be resorted to for the production of fine pliable *straw* for hats and bonnets are the very opposite to those which would tend to produce the greatest possible amount of seed or *grain* from the same plant.

Sand, clay, and lime, as has been said, are the principal constituents of soils. Clay and marl always contain potash and soda. Pure sand, or pure limestone, would alone constitute absolutely barren soils. All arable land contains an admixture of clay, although an excess of it, in proportion, is of course disadvantageous.

Rotation of Crops.

The *exhaustion of alkalies* in a soil by successive crops is the true reason why practical farmers *suppose* themselves *compelled* to suffer land to lie fallow. It is the greatest possible mistake to think that the temporary diminution of fertility in a field is chiefly owing to the loss of the decaying vegetable matter it previously contained: it is principally the consequence of the exhaustion of potash and soda, which are restored by the slow process of the more complete disintegration of the materials of the soil. It is evident that the careful tilling of fallow land must accelerate and increase this further breaking up of its mineral ingredients. Nor is this repose of the soil always necessary. A field, which has become unfitted for a certain kind of produce, may not, *on that account,* be unsuitable for another; and upon this observation a system of agriculture has been gradually formed, the principal object of which is to obtain the greatest possible produce in a succession of years, with the least outlay for manure. Because plants require for their growth different constituents of soil, changing the crop from year to year will maintain the fertility of that soil (provided it be done with judgment) quite as well as leaving it at rest or fallow. In this we but imitate nature. The oak, after thriving for long generations on a particular spot, gradually sickens; its entire race dies out; other trees and shrubs succeed it, till, at length, the surface becomes so charged with an excess of dead vegetable matter, that the forest becomes a peat moss, or a surface upon which no large tree will grow. Generally long before this can occur, the operation of natural causes has gradually removed from the soil substances, essential to the growth of oak, leaving others favorable and necessary to the growth of beech or pine. So, in practical farming, *one crop, in artificial rotation with others, extracts from the soil a certain quantity of necessary materials; a second carries off, in preference, those which the former has left.*

One hundred parts of wheat straw yield 15½ of ashes; the same quantity of barley straw, 8½; of oat straw, only 4; and the ashes of the three are, chemically, of about the same composition. Upon the same field, which will yield only one harvest of wheat, two successive crops of barley may be raised, and three of oats. We have in these facts a clear proof of what is abstracted from the soil, and the key to the *rational* mode of supplying the deficiency.

Since wheat consumes a large amount of silicate of potassa from the soil, the plants which should succeed or alternate with it must be such as require but little potassa, as potatoes or turnips. After three or four years the same lands may well bear wheat; because, during the interval, the soil will have been, by the action of the atmosphere, and the solution of vegetable and animal substances decaying upon or in it, again rendered capable of yielding what the wheat requires. Whether this process can be *artificially anticipated,* by supplying the exhausted ingredient to the soil, is a further and most interesting and important inquiry.

We could keep our fields in a constant state of fertility by replacing, every year, as much as is removed from them by their produce. An *increase* of fertility may be expected, of course, only when *more* is added of the *proper* material to the soil than is taken away. Any soil will partially regain its strength by lying fallow. But any soil, under cultivation, must at length (without help) lose those constituents which are removed in the seeds, roots and leaves of the plants raised upon it. To remedy this loss, and also increase the productiveness of the land, is the object of the use of proper *manures.*

Land, when not employed in raising food for animals or man, should, at least, be applied to the purpose of raising manure for itself; and this, *to a certain extent,* may be effected by means of green crops, which, by their decomposition, not only add to the amount of vegetable mould contained in the soil, but *supply the alkalies that would be found in their ashes.* That the soil should become richer by this burial of a crop, than it was before the seed of that crop was sown, will be understood by recollecting that *three-fourths* of the whole organic matter we bury *has been derived from the air:* that by this process of ploughing in, the vegetable matter is more equally diffused through the whole soil, and therefore more easily and rapidly decomposed; and that by its gradual decomposition, ammonia and nitric acid are certainly generated, though not so largely as when animal matters are employed. He who neglects the green sods, and crops of weeds that flourish by his hedgerows and ditches, overlooks an important natural means of wealth. Left to themselves, they ripen their seeds, exhausting the soil, and sowing them annually in his fields: collected in compost heaps, they add materially to his yearly crops of corn.

Organic Manures.

The following conclusions may be regarded as scientifically sustained, as well as confirmed by practical experience:

1. That fresh human urine yields nitrogen in greater abundance to vegetation than any other material of easy acquisition; and that the urine of animals is valuable for the same purpose, but not equally so.

2. That the mixed excrements of man and animals yield (if carefully preserved from further decomposition), not only nitrogen, but other invaluable saline and earthy matters that have been already extracted in food from the soil.

3. That animal substances which, like urine, flesh, and blood, decompose rapidly, are fitted to operate *immediately* and powerfully on vegetation.

4. That *dry* animal substances, as horn, hair, or woollen rags, decompose slowly, and (weight for weight) contain a greater quantity of organized as well as unorganized materials, manifesting their influence it may be for several seasons.

5. That bones, acting like horn, in so far as their animal matter is concerned, and like it for a number of seasons more or less, according as they have been more or less finely crushed, may ameliorate the soil by their earthy matter for a long period (even if the jelly they contain have been injuriously removed by the size maker), permanently improving the condition and adding to the natural capabilities of the land.

Uses of Guano.

This manure is a powerful stimulant to vegetable development generally; it is especially available in raising wheat, corn, potatoes, garden vegetables, and tobacco. If the land needs it, it may be put on as often as a crop is to be raised; though not, it is said, as a top dressing. For wheat, 150 to 200 pounds of guano may be used to the acre; for Indian corn, 300 to 400 pounds; unless it is put directly in the hills, when 100 pounds per acre will do. For potatoes, 300 to 400 pounds, in a drill, with bone dust. The addition of the latter makes the good effects of the guano more durable.

Mineral Fertilizers.

Simple lime, although an important constituent of plants, is rarely suitable as an application to them in its pure state. Carbonate of lime (represented by chalk, &c.) is a natural ingredient in very many soils. The sulphate of lime (gypsum, plaster of Paris) is often used for fertilizing purposes. It is less easily decomposed than the carbonate. The precise conditions which make it most advantageous, are not positively determined yet. Phosphate of lime is a very important constituent of plants; and, as it exists also in the bones of animals, a double relation follows: namely, that it should be abundant in soil on which plants are raised for food of men and animals; and, on the other hand, that animal bones contribute it to the soil when they decay upon it.

Wood ashes contain a large amount of carbonate of potassa, with also the sulphate and silicate of that alkali. Peat ashes vary in different regions, but always are found useful as manure. Kelp, or the ashes of sea-weeds, are often employed in the same way; they contain soda in considerable amount. Nitrate of potassa (nitre, or saltpetre) is said to quicken vegetable action when added to the soil, and to give the leaves a deeper green. A hundred pounds to the acre of grass or young corn, have been reported to produce a beneficial effect. In localities far inland, common salt, chloride of sodium, is indispensable to the soil, although a small amount of it will suffice. Animal manures contain it. An excess of salt will render land barren; as was well known to the ancients.

Conclusions.

We may take it for granted that every thinking, practical mind, will admit it as proved, that *there must be an exact adaptation and fitness between the condition of any given soil and the plants intended to be raised upon it;* and, further, that if this mutual fitness does not naturally exist, a knowledge of its requirements will enable us to supply it artificially. The great difficulty is, to obtain this knowledge fully and accurately. It must be confessed that, at present, much is wanting to render it complete and directly available. Industrious observation and experiment may, hereafter, make it so; and thus give us a system of truly scientific agriculture.

A few statements only remain to be added to what has been said. The best natural soils are those where the materials have been derived from the breaking up and decomposition, not of one stratum or layer, but of many—divided minutely by air and water, and minutely blended together; and in improving soils by artificial additions, the farmer cannot do better than imitate the processes of nature.

We have spoken of soils as consisting mostly of *sand, lime,* and *clay,* with certain saline and organic substances in smaller and varying proportions; but the examination of the ashes of plants shows that a *fertile* soil must of necessity contain an appreciable quantity of at least *eleven* different substances, which in most cases exist in greater or less relative abundance in the soil of cultivated plants; and of these the *proportions* are not by any means immaterial. In general, the soils which are made up of the most various materials are called *alluvial;* having been formed from the depositions of floods and rivers. Many of them are extremely fertile. Soils consist of two parts; of an *organic* part, which can readily be burned away when the surface-soil is heated to redness; and of an *inorganic* part, which remains fixed in the fire, consisting of earthy and saline substances; from which, if carbonic acid or any elastic gas be present, it may, however, be driven by the heat. The *organic* part of soils is derived chiefly from the remains of vegetables and animals which have lived and died in and upon the soil, which have been spread over it by rivers and rains, or which have been added by the industry of man for the purposes of increased fertility.

This *organic* part varies much in quantity, as well as quality, in different soils. In peaty soils it is very abundant, as well as in some rich, long cultivated lands. In general, it rarely amounts to one-fourth, or 25 per cent., even in our best arable lands. Good wheat soils contain often as little as eight parts in the hundred of organic animal or vegetable matter; oats and rye will grow in a soil containing only 1½ per cent.; and barley when only two or three parts per cent. are present.

The *inorganic* portion of any given soil, again, is divisible into two portions; that part which is *soluble* in water, and thus easily taken up by plants, and a much more bulky portion which is *insoluble.*

Sir Humphrey Davy found the following to be the composition of a good productive soil. In every 9 parts, 8 consisted of siliceous sand; the remaining (one-ninth) part was composed, in 100 parts, as follows:

Carbonate of lime (chalk), . . . 63 grains.
Pure silex, ... 15 grains.
Pure alumina, or the earth of clay, . 11 grains.
Oxide (rust) of iron, . . . 3 grains.
Vegetable and other saline matter, . 5 grains.
Moisture and loss, ... 3 grains.
—
100

Thus the whole amount of *organic* matter in this instance is only 1 part in 200, or one-half of one per cent.; a fact which, in itself, would demonstrate the fallacy of supposing that decomposed animal and vegetable matter in the soil form the exclusive supply to growing plants.

In another instance, soil was taken from a field in Sussex, remarkable for its growth of flourishing oak trees. It consisted of 6 parts of sand, and 1 part of clay and finely-divided matter. One hundred grains of it yielded, in chemical language—

Of silica (or silex), ... 54 grains.
Of alumina, ... 28 grains.
Carbonate of lime, ... 3 grains.
Oxide of iron, ... 5 grains.
Vegetable matter in a state of decomposition, ... 4 grains.
Moisture and loss, ... 6 grains.
—
100

To *wheat soils,* the attention of the practical farmer will be most strongly directed. An excellent wheat soil from West Drayton, in England, yielded 3 parts in 5 of silicious sand; and the remaining two parts consisted of carbonate of lime, silex, alumina, and a minute proportion of decomposing animal and vegetable remains.

Of these soils, the last was by far the most, and the first the least, coherent in texture. In all cases, the constituent parts of the soil which give tenacity and stiffness, are the finely-divided portions; and they possess this quality in proportion to the quantity of alumina (or earth of clay) they contain.

The varying power of soils to *absorb* and retain *water* from the air, is much connected with their fertility. This absorbent power is always greatest in the most fertile lands. Their productiveness is also much influenced by the nature of the subsoil on which they rest; for, when soils are situated immediately upon a bed of rock or stone, they dry sooner by the sun's agency than when the subsoil is clay or marl.

A great deal more might be said upon other

kindred points. But, as has been already remarked, agricultural science is, as yet, imperfect. It is a mistake for the practical farmer to contemn "book farming," as if it were something visionary or useless; while, on the other hand, the agricultural chemist and vegetable physiologist must submit all their inductions and conclusions to the test of careful and repeated trials. The one can seldom analyze soils, and the other can rarely attend to raising crops; so they must help each other, and, together, aid in advancing the oldest of human arts, and one of the most beautiful of the sciences—that of the earth's culture.

PRACTICAL FARMING.
Component parts of Soil.

The principal component parts of the soil, whatever may be the color, are clay, lime, sand, water, and air. The primitive earths, argil, lime, and sand, contain each, perhaps in nearly equal degrees, the food of plants; but in their union the purposes of vegetation are most completely answered. The precise quantities of each necessary to make this union perfect, and whether they ought to be equal, it is not very easy to ascertain, since that point is best determined in practice, when the soil proves to be neither too stiff nor adhesive, from the superabundance of clay, nor of too loose and weak a texture, from an over quantity of sand in its composition. The medium is undoubtedly best; but an excess towards adhesion is obviously most safe. A stiff or strong soil holds the water which falls upon it for a long time, and, being capable of much ploughing, is naturally well qualified for carrying the most valuable arable crops. A light sod, or one of a texture feeble and easily broken, is, on the contrary, soon exhausted by aration, and requires renovation by grass; or otherwise it cannot be cultivated to advantage.

To distinguish Clayey Soils.

A clayey soil, though distinguished by the color which it bears, namely black, white, yellow, and red, differs from all other soils, being tough, wet, and cold, and consequently requiring a great deal of labor from the husbandman before it can be sufficiently pulverized, or placed in a state for bearing artificial crops of corn or grass. Clay land is known by the following qualities, or properties.

It holds water like a cup, and once wetted does not soon dry. In like manner, when thoroughly dry, it is not soon wetted; if we except the varieties which have a thin surface, and are the worst of all to manage. In a dry summer, clay cracks and shows a surface full of small chinks, or openings. If ploughed in a wet state, it sticks to the plough like mortar, and in a dry summer, the plough turns it up in great clods, scarcely to be broken or separated by the heaviest roller.

To manage Sandy Soils.

Soils of this description are managed with infinitely less trouble, and at an expense greatly inferior to what clays require; but at the same time, the crops produced from them are generally of smaller value. There are many varieties of sand, however, as well as of clay; and in some parts of the country, the surface is little better than a bare barren sand, wherein artificial plants will not take root unless a dose of clay or good earth is previously administered. This is not the soil meant by the farmer when he speaks of sands. To speak practically, the soil meant is one where sand is predominant, although there be several other earths in the mixture. From containing a great quantity of sand, these soils are all loose and crumbling, and never get into a clod, even in the driest weather. This is the great article of distinction betwixt sand and sandy loams. A sandy loam, owing to the clay that is in it, does not crumble down, or become loose like a real sand, but retains a degree of adhesion after wetness or drought, notwithstanding the quantity of sand that is mixed with it. Perhaps a true sandy loam, incumbent upon a sound subsoil, is the most valuable of all soils. Upon such, every kind of grain may be raised with advantage, and no soil is better calculated for turnips and grass.

The real sands are not favorable to the growth of wheat, unless when preceded by clover, which binds the surface, and confers a temporary strength for sustaining that grain. Much of the county of Norfolk, in England, is of this description; and it is well known that few districts of the kingdom yield a greater quantity of produce. Till Norfolk, however, was invigorated by clay and marl, nearly one-half of it was little better than waste; but by the success which accompanied the use of these auxiliaries, a new soil was in a manner created; which, by a continuation of judicious management, has given a degree of fame to the husbandry of that country, far surpassing that of other districts naturally more fertile.

Gravelly Soils.

The open porous nature of these soils disposes them to imbibe moisture, and to part with it with great facility: from the latter of which circumstances they are subject to burn, as it is termed, in dry seasons. The main difference between gravel and sand is, that the former is chiefly composed of small soft stones; though in some instances the stones are of a silicious or flinty nature, and, in others, of the calcareous or chalky. From these constitutional circumstances arises the propriety of deepening gravelly soils by coats of marl or earth, and of keeping them fresh by frequent returns of grass, and repeated applications of manure. Gravelly soils, from the lightness of their texture, are not expensive or difficult in the means of cultivation. All the necessary business required for gravels may be carried forward with ease and expedition; and such soils are, in general, soon brought into a proper state for the reception of crops.

The constitutional qualities of gravels point out the propriety of ploughing them deep, so that the surface soil may be augmented, and greater room given to the growth of the plants cultivated on them. A shallow-ploughed gravel can stand no excess of weather, however enriched by manure. It is burnt up by a day or two of drought, and it is almost equally injured by an excessive fall of rain, unless the pan or firm bottom, which such soils easily gain, be frequently broken through by deep ploughing.

Uses of different Soils.

Clayey soils, when sufficiently enriched with manures, are naturally well qualified for carrying crops of wheat, oats, beans, and clover; but are not fitted for barley, turnips, potatoes, etc., or even for being kept under for grass longer than one year. Such soils ought to be regularly summer-fallowed once in six, or at least once in eight years, even when they are comparatively in a clean state, as they contract a sourness and adhesion from wet ploughing, only to be removed by exposure to the sun and wind during the dry months of summer. Soils of this kind receive little benefit from winter ploughing, unless so far as their surface is thereby presented to the frost, which mellows and reduces them in a manner infinitely superior to what could be accomplished by all the operations of man. Still they are not cleaned or made free of weeds by winter ploughing; and therefore this operation can only be considered as a good means for procuring a seed-bed, in which the seeds of the future crop may be safely deposited. Hence the necessity of cleansing clay soils during the summer months, and of having always a large part of every clay farm under summer fallow. All clayey soils require great industry and care, as well as a considerable portion of knowledge in dressing or management, to keep them in good condition; yet when their natural toughness is got the better of, they always yield the heaviest and most abundant crops. One thing requisite for a clayey soil, is to keep it rich and full of manure; a poor clay being the most ungrateful of all soils, and hardly capable of repaying the expense of labor, after being worn out and exhausted. A clayey soil also receives, comparatively, small benefit from grass; and when once allowed to get into a sterile condition, the most active endeavors will with difficulty restore fertility to it after the lapse of many years.

Upon light soils the case is very different. These flourish under the grass husbandry; and bare summer fallow is rarely required, because they may be cleaned and cropped in the same year, with that valuable esculent, turnip. Upon light soils, however, wheat can seldom be extensively cultivated; nor can a crop be obtained of equal value, either in respect to quantity or quality, as on clay sand loams. The best method of procuring wheat on light lands, is to sow upon a clover stubble, when the soil has got an artificial solidity of body and is thereby rendered capable of sustaining the grain till it arrives at maturity. The same observation applies to soils of a gravelly nature; and upon both barley is generally found of as great benefit as wheat.

Thin clays and peat earths are more friendly to the growth of oats than of other grains, though in favorable seasons a heavy crop of wheat may be obtained from a thin clayey soil, when it has been completely summer-fallowed and enriched with dung. A first application of calcareous manure is generally accompanied with great advantage upon these soils; but when once the effect of this application is over, it can hardly be repeated a second time, unless the land has been very cautiously managed after the first dressing. Neither of these soils is friendly to grass, yet there is a necessity of exercising this husbandry with them, because they are incapable of standing the plough more than a year or two in the course of a rotation.

Wheat ought to be the predominant crop upon all the rich clays and strong loams, and light soils of every kind are well qualified for turnips, barley, etc. Upon the thin and moorish soils, oats must necessarily preserve a prominent rank, and grass seeds may be cultivated upon every one of them, though with different degrees of advantage, according to the natural and artificial richness of each soil, or to the qualities which it possesses for encouraging the growth of clover, in the first instance, and preserving the roots of the plant afterwards.

Operation of Tillage.

Tillage is an operation whereby the soil is either cleared from noxious weeds, or prepared for receiving the seeds of plants cultivated by the husbandman. When this operation is neglected, or even partially executed, the soil becomes foul, barren, and unproductive; hence, upon arable farms, tillage forms the prominent branch of work; and, according to the perfection or imperfection with which it is executed, the crops of the husbandman, whether of corn or grass, are in a great measure regulated.

Tillage, in the early ages, was performed by hand labor; but, in modern times, the plough has been the universal instrument used for executing this necessary and important branch of rural work. In no other way can large fields be turned over, because the expense of digging with the spade, the only other method of turning over the ground, would much exceed any profit that can be reaped. Stones lying above or below the surface are the most formidable obstruction to perfect tillage. On stony ground, the work is not only imperfectly executed, but in many cases the implement is broken to pieces, and a considerable portion of time lost before it is repaired and put in order. The removal of stones, therefore, especially of such as are below the surface, ought to be a primary object with every agriculturist; because a neglect of this kind may afterwards occasion him considerable loss and inconvenience.

To drain the ground, in other words, to lay it dry, also facilitates tillage exceedingly; for ploughing cannot be performed with advantage where either the surface or subsoil is wet.

Best Mode of Tillage.

The only sure and certain way by which the soil is cleaned or rendered free of weeds, is by ploughing in the summer months, when the ground is dry, and when, by the influence of the sun and air, the weeds may be destroyed with facility. Seldom at any other period is the soil much benefitted by ploughing, unless so far as a seed-bed is thus procured for the succeeding crop; and though the situation or state of the ground, when these intermediate ploughings are bestowed, is of importance in judging of their utility, yet the radical process of summer fallow cannot, by any means, be altogether dispensed with. Though, if the winter and spring ploughings are executed under favorable circumstances, and plenty of manure is at hand, it may be delayed for a greater number of years than is otherwise practicable, if good husbandry is to be maintained.

Without summer fallow, or, which is the same thing, without working the ground in the summer months, perfect husbandry is unattainable on all heavy or cold soils, and upon every variety incumbent on a close or retentive bottom.

To keep his land clean will always be a principal object with every good farmer; for if this is neglected, in place of carrying rich crops of grain or grass, the ground will be exhausted by crops of weeds. Where land is foul, every operation of husbandry must be proportionably non-effective; and even the manures applied will, in a great measure, be lost.

The necessity of summer fallow depends greatly upon the nature and quality of the soil; as, upon some soils, a repetition of this practice is less frequently required than upon others. Wherever the soil is incumbent upon clay or till, it is more disposed to get foul, than when incumbent upon a dry gravelly bottom; besides, wet soils, from being ploughed in winter, contract a stiffness which lessens the pasture of artificial plants, and prevents them from receiving sufficient nourishment. When land of a dry gravelly bottom gets foul, it may easily be cleaned without a plain summer fallow; since crops, such as turnips, etc., may be substituted in its place, which, when drilled at proper intervals, admit of being ploughed as often as necessary; whereas wet soils, which are naturally

IMPLEMENTS.   15

unfit for carrying such crops, must be cleaned and brought into good order by frequent ploughings and harrowings during the summer months.

To Conduct a Fallow.

Upon all clayey soils (and upon such only is a complete summer fallow necessary) the first ploughing ought to be given during the winter months, or as early in the spring as possible; which greatly promotes the rotting of the sward and stubble. This should be done by gathering up the ridge, which both lays the ground dry and rips up the furrows. As soon as seed-time is over, the ridge should be cloven down, preparatory to cross ploughing; and after lying a proper time, should be harrowed and rolled repeatedly, and every particle of quickens that the harrows have brought above, should be carefully picked off with the hand. It is then proper to ridge or gather it up immediately, which both lays the land in proper condition for meeting bad weather, and opens up any fast land that may have been missed in the furrows when the cross ploughing was given. After this harrow, roll, and gather the root weeds again; and continue so doing till the field is perfectly clean.

To Prepare the Ground.

The above object is most completely accomplished, when the ground is ploughed deep and equal, while the bottom of the furrow immediately above the subsoil is perfectly loosened and turned equally over with the part which constitutes the surface. In many places these properties are altogether neglected, the ground being ploughed in a shallow way, while the bottom of the ploughed land remains something like the teeth of a saw, having the under part of the furrow untouched, and consequently not removed by the action of the plough. While these things are suffered, the object of tillage is only partially gained. The food of plants can only be imperfectly procured; and the ground is drenched and injured by wetness; these ridges, or pieces of land, which are not cut, preventing a descent of the moisture from above to the open furrows left for carrying it off. Where the seed-bed is prepared by one ploughing, the greatest care ought to be used in having it closely and equally performed. When two are given, they should be in opposite directions, so that any firm land left in the first may be cut up in the second ploughing. It is not profitable to plough twice one way, if it can be safely avoided. Another important point towards procuring good tillage, is never to plough the land when in a wet state; because encouragement is thus given to the growth of weeds, while a sourness and adhesion is communicated to the ground, which is rarely got the better of till the operations of a summer fallow are again repeated.

All soils ought not to be wrought or ploughed in one manner. Each kind has its particular and appropriate qualities; and, therefore, each requires a particular and appropriate mode of tillage. Ploughing, which is the capital operation of husbandry, ought, on these accounts, to be administered according to the nature of the soil which is to be operated upon, and not executed agreeably to one fixed and determined principle. On strong clays and loams, and on rich gravels and deep sands, the plough ought to go as deep as the cattle are able to work it; whereas, on thin clays and barren sands the benefit of deep ploughing is very questionable; especially when such are incumbent on a till bottom, or where the subsoil is of a yellow-ochre nature; such, when turned up, being little better than poison to the surface, unless highly impregnated with alluvial compost, the effect of which expels the poisonous substance contained in this kind of subsoil, and gives a fertility to the whole mass, more decisively permanent than would follow a heavy application of the best rotten dung.

Two sets of Ploughs required for perfect Tillage.

On clayey soils, where the ridges are so that the ground may be preserved in something like a dry condition, the plough used for tillage ought to have a mould-board considerably wider set than is required for light soils, in order that the furrow may be close cut below, and only turned over. The method of constructing the plough necessarily makes a heavier draught than would be the case were the mould-board placed differently; though if good and sufficient work be wanted, the necessity of constructing the implement in the way mentioned, is absolute and indispensable. The plough to be used on light soils, or on all soils that admit of what is technically called crown and furrow ploughing, may be made much straighter below, and yet be capable of executing the work in a perfect manner. On every farm, consisting of mixed soils, two sets of ploughs ought to be kept, otherwise proper work cannot be performed. All land ought to be ploughed with a shoulder, and the advantages of ploughing in this way are, that, if ploughed before winter, the surface is enabled to resist the winter rains, and afterwards present a face on which the harrows can make a proper impression, when the seed process is to be executed. This deserves particular attention when old grass fields are broken up; as, by neglecting it, the harrows are often unable to cover the seed. It is perfectly practicable to plough land with a tolerably broad furrow, say 10, 11, or 12 inches, and yet to plough it clean, provided the implement used is properly constructed; but, then, care must be taken that the furrow be of proportionate deepness, otherwise it will be laid on its back, instead of being deposited at an angle proper for undergoing the harrowing process.

The use of *subsoilers* is now common, to turn up the depth of the soil. In sandy earth, beneath a ten-inch furrow, a subsoiler may go ten inches deeper; but this is not easy or possible in all soils.

Implements of Husbandry. *

No country in the world is better provided with implements for executing rural labor than Great Britain; and to this superiority may, in some measure, be attributed the increased and increasing perfection of agriculture over the whole island. American ingenuity has gone still further in the same direction. We have ploughs of all the different kinds that ever were constructed: as for wheel carriages, the variety is immense; whilst harrows, and other common implements, of various constructions and dimensions, are equally numerous. But it is in the articles more properly allied to machinery, that the superiority of American rural implements is most conspicuous. Drills for sowing grain and small seeds with regularity, have been constructed upon scientific principles; and machines for separating grain from straw, have been invented, and brought to a degree of perfection which few people expected when these machines were first introduced.

The double Michigan plough is an important improvement on the old plough. Instead of a coulter it has a small plough attached to the beam in front of the other, which takes a slice from the sod, and makes cleaner work for the plough. Steam ploughs have also been invented.

* See page 470.

The universal Sowing Machine.

This machine, whether made to be worked by hand, drawn by a horse, or fixed to a plough, and used with it, is extremely simple in its construction, and not liable to be put out of order; as there is but one movement to direct the whole. It will sow wheat, barley, oats, rye, clover, coleseed, hemp, flax, canary, rape, turnip; besides a great variety of other kinds of grain and seeds, broadcast, with an accuracy hitherto unknown. It is equally useful when fixed to a plough; it will then drill a more extensive variety of grain, pulse, and seed (through every gradation, with regard to quality), and deliver each kind with greater regularity than any drill plough whatever.

Among many other valuable and peculiar properties, it will not only sow in the broadcast way with a most singular exactness, but save the expense of a seedsman; the seed being sown (either over or under furrow at pleasure), and the land ploughed at the same operation.

Another advantage attending the use of this machine is, that the wind can have no effect on the falling of the seed.

The machine, when made to be used without a plough, and to be drawn by a horse, may be of different lengths. The upper part contains the hoppers, from which the grain or seed descends into the spouts. The several spouts all rest upon a bar, which hangs and plays freely by two diagonal supporters; a trigger, fixed to this bar, bears a catch wheel: this being fixed on the axle, occasions a regular and continued motion, or jogging of the spouts, quicker or slower in proportion to the space the person sowing with it drives. At the bottom of the machine is placed an apron or shelf, in a sloping position, and the corn or seed, by falling thereon from the spouts above, is scattered about in every direction.

To sow the corn or seed in drills, there are movable spouts, which are fixed on or taken off at pleasure, to direct the seed from the upper spout to the bottom of the furrow.

Harrows.

These beneficial implements are of various sizes and dimensions; but the harrow most commonly used consists of four bulls, with cross-mortised sheaths, each bull containing five teeth, of from five to seven inches in length below the bulls, the longest being placed forwards. Harrows of this kind, drawn by one horse, are generally used on most farms for all purposes, though on others large brake-harrows, consisting of five bulls, each containing six teeth, and worked by two horses, are employed during the fallow process, and for reducing rough land. Some of these brake-harrows are constructed with joints, so as to bend and accommodate their shape to the curvature of ridges. A small harrow, with short teeth, is also used for covering grass seeds, though we have rarely seen any detriment from putting grass seeds as deep into the ground as the teeth of ordinary sized harrows are capable of going.

The best methods of Harrowing.

When employed to reduce a strong obdurate soil, not more than two harrows should be yoked together, because they are apt to ride and tumble upon each other, and thus impede the work, and execute it imperfectly. On rough soils, harrows ought to be driven as fast as the horses can walk; because their effect is in the direct proportion to the degree of velocity with which they are driven. In ordinary cases, and in every case where harrowing is meant for covering the seed, three harrows are the best yoke, because they fill up the ground more effectually, and leave fewer vacancies, than when a smaller number is employed. The harrowman's attention, at the seed process, should be constantly directed to prevent these implements from riding upon each other, and to keep them clear of every impediment from stones, lumps of earth, or clods, and quickens or grass roots; for any of these prevents the implement from working with perfection, and causes a mark or trail upon the surface, always unpleasing to the eye, and generally detrimental to the vegetation of the seed. Harrowing is usually given in different directions, first in length, then across, and finally in length as at first. Careful husbandmen study, in the finishing part of the process, to have the harrows drawn in a straight line, without suffering the horses to go in a zigzag manner, and are also attentive that the horses enter fairly upon the ridge, without making a curve at the outset. In some instances, an excess of harrowing has been found very prejudicial to the succeeding crop; but it is always necessary to give so much as to break the furrow, and level the surface, otherwise the operation is imperfectly performed.

Rollers.

The roller is an implement frequently used for smoothing the surface of land when in tillage, especially when the processes of summer fallow are going forward. Several kinds of rollers are used in America. Some are of stone, others of wood or iron, according to the nature of the operation intended to be performed. The only material difference in rollers is their weight; but it should be attended to, when a roller is made of large diameter, that its weight ought to be the greater, for in proportion to the largeness of its diameter will be the extent of surface upon which the roller rests. The weight of a roller ought therefore to be in proportion to its diameter, otherwise its effect will be proportionably diminished.

Rolling, however, is a modern improvement, and used for different purposes. In the first place, it is of great advantage to roll young grasses after the ground is stoned, because the scythe can then be placed nearer the surface, and the crop cut more equally than when the operation is neglected. 2dly. Land on which turnips are to be cultivated can rarely be made fine enough, without the repeated use of this implement. And 3dly. The process of summer fallow, upon strong soils, is much advanced by rolling, because without its aid the large and obdurate clods cannot be reduced or couch-grass eradicated. From these circumstances it will readily appear, that rollers of various sizes and dimensions are required on every farm, for accomplishing different purposes. Wooden rollers, drawn by one horse, answer very well for grass and turnip land; but massy stone rollers, drawn either by two or three horses, are absolutely necessary on clay soils.

It is obvious, that when a large field is to be rolled, a number of rollers ought at once to be set at work, otherwise an opportunity may be lost, never to be regained. The deficiency is most conspicuous when barley is taken after turnips in a dry season. From poaching the ground with carts, in order to carry off the crop, and even by the treading of sheep, a degree of stiffness is contracted, which requires the use of the roller before grass seeds can be sown.

On all occasions it is most beneficial to roll across, because, when going in length, the implement is of small benefit to the furrows, the slightest acclivation of the ridges preventing the work from being equally performed. The expedition which takes place when rollers are used, compared with the tedious and expensive process of breaking clods with malls, formerly the general custom, sufficiently proves the importance of these implements, though it deserves to be remarked, that, when rolling is bestowed upon a spring-sown field, harrowing it afterwards is of great advantage. By harrowing when the clods are reduced, the earth stands the effects of rain better afterwards, and does not consolidate so firmly as when that process is neglected.

Mowers and Reapers.*

These machines are of great value, especially to those with large farms. One machine, the mower, can be made to perform duty both with grass and grain; but reapers are constructed especially for the latter. *Weeders* are also in use in some parts of the country, drawn by horse power.

The Thrashing Machine.

The thrashing machine is the most valuable implement in the farmer's possession, and one which adds more to the general produce of the country, than any invention hitherto devised. The saving of manual labor thereby obtained is almost incalculable; while the work is performed in a much more perfect manner than was formerly practicable, even when the utmost care and exertion were bestowed. In fact, had not the thrashing machine been invented, it is hardly possible to conceive what would have been the rate of expense of thrashing, or even whether a sufficient number of hands could, at any rate of expense, have been obtained for thrashing the grain of the country.

Since the invention of this machine, Mr. Meikle and others have progressively introduced a variety of improvements, all tending to simplify the labor, and to augment the quantity of the work performed. When first erected, though the grain was equally well separated from the straw, yet as the whole of the straw, chaff, and grain, was indiscriminately thrown into a confused heap, the work could only with propriety be considered as half executed. By the addition of rakes, or shakers, and two pairs of fanners, all driven by the same machinery, the different processes of thrashing, shaking, and winnowing are now all at once performed, and the grain immediately prepared for the public market. When it is added, that the quantity of grain gained from the superior powers of the machine is fully equal to a twentieth part of the crop, and that, in some cases, the expense of thrashing and cleaning the grain is considerably less than what was formerly paid for cleaning it alone, the immense saving arising from the invention will at once be seen.

The expense of horse labor, from the increased value of the animal and the charge of his keeping, being an object of great importance, it is recommended that, upon all sizable farms, that is to say, where two hundred acres, or upwards, of grain are sown, the machine should be worked by wind, unless where local circumstances afford the conveniency of water.

Where coals are plenty and cheap, steam may be advantageously used for working the machine.

Method of Treading Grain.

In some countries wheat is trodden out by horses, nearly in the same way as it was formerly done in Palestine by oxen.

The treading floors are generally from sixty to 100 feet in diameter; but the larger their diameter is, the easier is the work to the horses. The track, or path, on which the sheaves are laid, and on which the horses walk, is from twelve to twenty-four feet wide, or more. The floors are commonly enclosed by fences; and the horses are generally driven between them promiscuously and loose, each pressing to be foremost, so that fresh air may be obtained,—biting, jostling, and kicking each other with the greatest fury. The labor in this way is extremely severe. Upon some small floors a centre-stick is placed, to which hangs a rope, or a pole and swivel, and four or five horses being fastened together, travel round upon the sheaves with the utmost regularity. Previously to laying down the wheat sheaves, the state of the air, and the probability of its continuing dry through the day, is fully considered. If they resolve to tread, the morning is suffered to pass away till the dew is removed. A row of sheaves is first laid upon the floors with the heads and butts in a line across the track of it, as a bolster for receiving other sheaves; and these sheaves range with the path, or circle, the butts resting on the floor. Other sheaves are ranged in like manner, with the heads raised on the former, till the whole floor is filled, when it appears to be filled with nothing but ears of wheat, sloping a little upwards. Upon laying down each sheaf, the band thereof is cut with a knife. A west wind is always desirable while treading is going on, as when wind is from the eastward dampness generally prevails.

In some instances, twenty-four horses are formed at some distance from the floor into four ranks; and when the floor is ready laid, the word is given to advance. For the sake of order and regular work, a boy mounted on one of the foremost horses advances in a walk with the whole rank haltered or tied together, and enters upon the bed of wheat, walking the horses slowly over it; another rank is ordered to follow as soon as the first is supposed to have obtained a distance equal to a fourth part of the circumference of the bed, and in the same manner the other ranks proceed. They are forbidden to go past a walk, till they have proceeded five or six rounds, when the word is given to move at a sober trot, and to keep their ranks at a full distance from each other, regularity and deliberate movement being necessary for preventing confusion. The gentle trot is continued till it may be supposed the horses have travelled eight or nine miles, which is the extent of their first journey; they are then led off to be foddered and watered, when the trodden light straw is taken off as deep as the place where the sheaves lie close, and are but partially bruised.

As soon as this first straw is removed, one-third of the width of the bed is turned over on the other two-thirds from the inner side or circle of the bed, which narrows the neck of the next journey. The horses are again led on, and trot out their second journey, till the straw be clear of wheat. The outer part of the bed is then turned upon the middle part, when the horses take another journey. The loose straw being then taken off, the whole remaining bed is turned up from the floor, and shaken with forks, and handles of rakes, after which the horses give another tread, which finishes the work. The grain is then shoved up from the floor with the heads of rakes turned downwards, and put into heaps of a conical form, in which situation it often remains exposed to the weather for several days. The correct American agriculturists, however, have houses adjoining the treading floor, where the grain is deposited till it is cleared from the chaff and offal; though, as most of them continue treading, if the weather be favorable, till the whole crop is separated from

---

* See page 470.

the straw, it is pretty obvious that the grain stands a considerable chance of being damaged before the several processes are concluded.

Fanners.

If thrashing machines are of much advantage to the public, by separating grain completely from the straw, the introduction of fanners, or the machine by which grain is cleansed from chaff, and all sorts of offal, may, with justice, be considered as of equal benefit to the practical agriculturist.

Since thrashing machines were introduced, fanners almost in every case are annexed to them, and in some instances, where powerful machines are used, fitted internally with suitable riddles, it is perfectly practicable to measure and market the grain immediately as it comes from the machine.

Manures.

The term manure is applied indiscriminately to all substances, which are known from experience either to enrich the different soils, or contribute in any other way to render them more favorable to vegetation.

In an agricultural point of view, the subject of manures is of the first magnitude. To correct what is hurtful to vegetation in the different soils, and to restore what is lost by exhausting crops, are operations in agriculture which may be compared to the curing of diseases in the animal body, or supplying the waste occasioned by labor.

To manage Dung upon Light Lands.

For soils of this description, where turnips are taken as a first crop, dung can hardly be too well prepared; because the nature of the crop to which it is applied renders a complete incorporation with the ground absolutely necessary; without which the young plants might be starved at their very entrance into life. In the best farmed English counties, dung is often kept more than a year, in order that it may be perfectly rotted.

In general there is not much difficulty in preparing dung upon turnip farms; because, in the driest season, from the nature of the food used, such a quantity of liquid passes from the animals, as to prevent burning, provincially fire-fanging, the greatest obstacle to the rotting of dung that can be experienced. If turnip dung is regularly removed, if it is properly mixed with the horse litter and other excrementitious matter accumulated upon the farm, it will be found an easy task to prepare all that is made by the middle of April, at which time the fold-yard should be cleared. What is produced after that time should be stored up separately, receive waterings if the weather is dry, and be reserved for clover-stubbles, or other fields that are to be dunged in autumn.

The middle of April is a good time for clearing the fold-yard; but this does not prevent the work from going partially forward through the winter, when suitable opportunities occur.

When driven out of the fold-yard, the dung should be laid up in a regular heap or pile, not exceeding six quarters, or four feet and a half in height; and care should be taken not to put either horse or cart upon it, which is easily avoided by backing the cart to the pile, and laying the dung compactly together with a grape or fork. It is also useful to face up the extremities with earth, which keeps in the moisture, and prevents the sun and wind from doing injury. Perhaps a small quantity of earth strewed upon the top might also prove useful. Dung, when managed in this manner, generally ferments very rapidly; but if it is discovered to be in a backward state, a complete turn over, about the 1st of May, when the weather becomes warm, will quicken the process; and the better it is shaken asunder, the sooner will the object in view be accomplished.

A secluded spot of ground, not much exposed to wind, and perfectly secure from being floated with water, ought always to be chosen for the site of such piles or heaps. If the field to which it is to be applied is at hand, a little after-trouble may be saved by depositing it there in the first instance. But it is found most convenient to reserve a piece of ground adjacent to the homestead for this purpose. There it is always under the farmer's eye, and a greater quantity can be moved in a shorter time than when the situation is more distinct. Besides, in wet weather (and this is generally the time chosen for such an operation), the roads are not only cut up by driving to a distance, but the field on which the heap is made, may be poached and injured considerably.

Upon Heavy Lands.

Upon clay soils, where wheat forms a principal part of the crop, where great quantities of beans are cultivated, and few turnips sown, unless for the use of milch cows, the rotting of dung is not only a troublesome but an expensive affair. Independent of what is consumed by the ordinary farm stock, the overplus of the straw must, somehow or other, be rotted, by lean cattle kept in the fold-yard, who either receive the straw in racks, or have it thrown across the yard, to be eaten and trodden down by them. According to this mode of consumption, it is evident that a still greater necessity arises for a frequent removal of this unmade dung; otherwise, from the trampling of beasts, and the usual want of moisture, it would compress so much as altogether to prevent putrefaction. To prepare dung sufficiently upon farms of this description is at all times an arduous task, but scarcely practicable in dry seasons; for if it once gets burnt (fire-fanged), it is almost physically impossible to bring it into a suitable state of preparation afterwards; and, at all events, its virtues are thereby considerably diminished.

Straw flung out in considerable portions to the fold-yard, after being compressed by the trampling of cattle, becomes rather like a well-packed stack, than a mass of dung in a preparatory state. The small quantity of water and dung made by the animals is barely sufficient to cause a slight fermentation; and this slight fermentation, when the heap gets into a compressed state, is sure to bring on fire-fang, as already said, after which its original powers can rarely be restored. To prevent such an injury, no measure can be so successfully used as a frequent removal of this unmade dung, especially if the weather is wet at the time. If people can stand out to work, there cannot be too much wetness while executing this operation; for there is always such a quantity of the straw that has not passed through the entrails of the cattle, as renders it almost impossible to do injury, in the first instance, by an excess of moisture.

It is therefore recommended, upon every clay-land farm, especially those of considerable size, that the fold-yard be frequently cleared; and that the greatest care be taken to mix the stable or horse-dung in a regular way with what is gathered in the fold-yard, or made by other animals, in order that a gradual heat or fermentation may be speedily produced. Where the materials are of the sorts now described (that is, a small quantity of dung, or excrementitious matter, and a large store of unrotten straw, only partially moistened), no damage can ensue from putting horses and carts upon the heap; nay, a positive benefit will be gained from this slight compression.

The heap or pile, in the case of turnip dung, should be formed in a secluded spot, if such can be got at hand; because the less it is exposed to the influence of the sun and wind, the faster will fermentation proceed. It should be constructed on a broad basis, which lessens the bounds of the extremities, and separate heaps are necessary, so that too much may not be deposited at once. By shifting the scene frequently, and allowing each covering or coat to settle and ferment before laying on any more, the most happy effects will follow, and these heaps (at least all such as are completed before the first of May), may reasonably be expected to be in a fit condition for applying to the summer-fallow fields, in the end of July, or first of August. If the external parts get dry at any time during the process, it will be proper to water them thoroughly, and in many cases to turn over the heap completely. It may be added, that much benefit has been experienced from laying a thick coating of snow upon such heaps, as by the gradual melting thereof the whole moisture is absorbed, and a strong fermentation immediately follows.

Upon large farms, where the management of manure is sufficiently understood and practised, it is an important matter to have dunghills of all ages, and ready for use whenever the situation of a field calls for a restorative. No method of application to clay soils, however, is so beneficial as during the year of summer fallow, though in such a situation a greater stock of manure is often gathered than is required for the fields under this process.

As to the proper quantity of dung to be used, no greater quantity ought to be given at one time than is sufficient to fructify the grounds; in other words, to render it capable of producing good crops, before the time arrives when a fresh dose can be administered.

The Spreading of Dung.

The increased attention now bestowed, in all the cultivated districts, to the spreading of dung, originated from the measure of limiting the quantity applied. When forty, fifty, nay even sixty double loads were applied to an acre, it was not very difficult to cover its surface, even with an imperfect separation, though it certainly was impracticable to bury the big lumps with a furrow of ordinary size; but when the quantity was brought down to eighteen and twenty loads, and, still more, when twelve or fourteen loads were thought sufficient, a different conduct became absolutely necessary. Another improvement also followed, viz., spreading dung when raw or green, that is, immediately after the carts; in which way, at least during summer, it will be separated at one-half the expense, and to much better purpose, than when it is suffered to lie in the heap for a day or two. In short, it is a sure mark of a slovenly farmer to see dung remain unspread in a field, unless it be in the winter months, when it may happen that hands cannot be got for carrying on such operations with the usual regularity. At that time the injury sustained by losing a few days is not great, though as a general rule it will be found that the expense is always smallest when the carts are regularly followed up.

Application of Dung to Turnips.

When turnip husbandry forms the chief branch of fallow process, dung is naturally of a superior quality, and requires little artificial management for bringing it to a proper state of preparation. In the greater part of Scotland, and even in England, where the drill and horse-hoeing system is practised, the common, and undoubtedly the most approved way of applying dung to turnips, is by laying it in the intervals of the drills or small ridges, which are previously made up by a bout, or two furrows of the plough. These drills or ridges are formed at a distance of from twenty-four to thirty inches from the centre of each; and by driving the horses and cart along the middle one of the space intended to be manured, the dung is drawn out either by the carter, or by another man specially appointed for that purpose, in such proportions as the poverty of the soil, or the disposition of the occupier, may reckon necessary. If the breadth of the drills is only taken at a time, the dung stands a better chance of being regularly administered; for it often happens, that when a greater number are included in one space, the two outside drills receive a less quantity than the intervening ones. Those, therefore, who limit themselves to three drills, generally divide the spreaders; as it requires six hands, women or boys, to follow up what is usually called a head of carts, the number of carts to a head being regulated by the distance of the dunghill, or the kind of road over which it is to be carried.

The quantity of dung usually given for turnips is from twelve to fifteen double cart loads, of one and a half cubic yards each, to a Scots acre. In some cases only ten loads are given; but the land ought to be in high condition where such a small quantity is bestowed. In fact, no soil can be made too rich for turnips or other green crops, peas excepted; but the object to be attended to in this, and every other case, is an allotment of the manure collected on the premises, in such a way as that the greatest possible return over the whole farm, not from a particular field, may be gained by the occupier.

Application of Dung to Potatoes.

The culture is in several respects similar to that of turnips, but in others it differs materially. Potatoes are planted earlier in the season than turnips; the ground rarely receives so much work; the soils upon which they are cultivated are more variable; and the dung considered to be most suitable for promoting their growth, does not require such high preparation. Many farmers, notwithstanding these circumstances, follow out the same process as described under the head of turnips. After the ground receives three, or at most four ploughings, the drills are made up, dung deposited in the intervals, the seed planted above the dung, and the drills reversed; after which, say at the distance of two or three weeks, a slight harrowing is given. They avoid making up drills, but dung the ground in what may be called the broadcast way; and, entering the plough, plant the seed in every third furrow, into which only the dung is raked; and so on till the whole is finished. Before the young plants appear, or even after they are above the surface, a complete harrowing is given, which is considered as equal to a hand-hoeing; and from the dung being completely covered, scarce any of it is dragged up, while the seed, being undermost, none of it is disturbed by the operation. Some farmers do not dung their potato fields; but, reserving the manure till the crop is removed, find the remainder of the rotation greatly benefited. Potatoes scourge severely, and, in general cases, require a larger quantity of dung than turnips; but, as the extent of land under this culture is not great in common farming, few people grudge this extra quantity, because, except in a few favored situations, a good crop cannot otherwise be reasonably expected.

AGRICULTURE.

To Manure Clayey Soils.

Upon all soils incumbent on a wet or close bottom, whether characterized as clay, loam, or moor, it may be laid down as a primary principle, that dung cannot be so profitably applied, as while the ground is under the process of summer fallow.

When the ground is under the process of summer fallow, it is then the best and most appropriate time for applying manure to clayey soils. When under this process, the soil, comparatively speaking, is reduced into minute particles, which affords an opportunity of conveying the virtues of manure through the veins or pores of all its parts. The soil, at that time, is also freed from its aboriginal inhabitants, quickens and other root-weeds, which claim a preferable right of support; hence the artificial plants, afterwards cultivated, possess, without a rival, such supplies as have been granted, without any deduction whatever. In short, without laying any stress upon elementary effects during the process, it does not admit of a doubt, that the same quantity of manure, bestowed upon the ground when summer-fallowed, will produce a greater return to the occupier, than if it had been applied at any other stage of the rotation.

Dung should not be laid upon fallows before they are completely cleaned; though, no doubt, in wet summers, that operation is not easily accomplished.

To make sure work, the fallows, if possible, should be early stirred, and no opportunity slipped of putting them forward with the utmost expedition; for it rarely happens that much good can be done towards the destruction of root-weeds after the month of July. Before that time a judicious farmer will have his fallow dressed up, and in a suitable state for receiving dung. It should be well harrowed, if the weather is favorable, previous to the dung being laid on; and if rolled, or made smooth, the spreaders will be enabled to perform their task with much more precision.

At the proper season every other operation ought to be laid aside, so that dung may be expeditiously spread out. To do it in wet weather is attended with pernicious effects; the horses are oppressed, a longer time is required, the land is poached, and in some measure deprived of all benefit from the previous fallow. These circumstances will be reflected upon by the attentive farmer; they will stimulate him not to lose a moment when the weather is favorable, and prevent him from forcing on the work, when injury, rather than benefit, may be expected. After all, seasons are so perverse as to render every rule nugatory. These must, however, be taken as they come, avoiding at such times to break the land down, acclivating the ridges sufficiently, and keeping the water-furrows completely clear.

Quantity of Dung for Fallows.

The quantity of dung usually applied to fallows in ordinary condition is from fourteen to twenty double loads per acre; though often good crops are reaped when twelve loads only have been given. Much, however, depends upon the condition of the land, upon the quality of the dung, and the way in which the carts are loaded. A decent load may contain one cubic yard and three-fourths, and weigh a ton, or thereabouts. It also deserves notice, that less dung will serve some lands than others, especially if they have lately been ploughed from grass; but, at all events, sixteen such loads as are mentioned will answer for any sort of soil, unless it has been previously quite wrought out. Even if it were in this forlorn state, it is better management to dung upon the stubble of the first crop than to give an over-dose when under summer fallow.

Time of Spreading the Dung.

All dung laid upon summer fallow ought to be spread the moment it is pulled out of the cart. It can at no other time be done so well, or so cheaply, though on many farms, small ones especially, where a full supply of hands is wanting, this beneficial practice is much neglected. Four spreaders, boys or girls, with an attentive overs-man to follow up and supply any omissions, are sufficient for one head of carts; the number included in a head being regulated by the distance of the field from the dunghill. Some farmers employ a person on whom they can depend to draw the dung from the cart, who has judgment to proportion it according to circumstances, and is responsible for any failure in the execution; but the carter is the person usually employed, though, unless a boy is given him to drive, a regular distribution can hardly be expected. To insure accuracy in laying down, fields are sometimes thrown into a dam-broad figure; and, a heap being drawn into each square, you could have nearly ascertained the quantity required for the whole. The great object, after a regular and economical distribution, is to shake and part the whole completely; as, by minute attention to this circumstance, a much greater effect is necessarily produced.

Intermediate Dunging.

After the fallows are dunged, the remainder in hand is reserved for what may be called the intermediate dunging, generally bestowed either upon clover stubbles, upon wheat stubbles previously to taking beans, or upon bean stubbles before the seed furrow is given for wheat. It is obvious, that the farmer must be regulated, in this intermediate dunging, by the weather at the time, though it rarely happens but that dung may be got out upon clover stubbles at one time of the winter or other. When applied to beans, a beneficial practice, the dung, as we said above, is by some people laid upon the wheat stubble, and ploughed down before winter; hence it is in full action in the spring, when the seed furrow is given. Others make up drills at seed time, depositing the dung in the intervals, as for turnips or potatoes; but it seldom occurs that weather can then be got, at least on real bean soils, for executing this management.

Many arable farms, under the strictest economy, are unable to furnish supplies for an intermediate dunging, at least to its full extent; but persons so circumstanced have it always in their power to overcome the defect, and preserve a regular rotation, by keeping certain fields longer in grass, which of course will yield weightier crops when broken up, and stand less in need of manure during the after rotation. As, for instance, in a rotation of six, and it is here that the greatest shortcoming is felt, grass seeds to a certain extent, say a half, may be thrown in with the crop of wheat taken after fallow, which is the second year of the rotation; this part may be pastured for three years, and broken up in the sixth for oats, which concludes the course. Again, in a rotation of eight, grass seeds, in like manner, may be sown with a part of the fallow wheat, which part can be pastured for three years, then broken up for oats, succeeded by beans and wheat. By such arrangements, made according to circumstances, it is an easy matter to preserve a regular rotation, and to proportion the corn crops to the quantity of manure collected upon the premises.

MANURES.

To increase the Quantity of Dung by Soiling.

The practice of soiling, or feeding horses or cattle in the house or farm yard, is eminently calculated to increase the quantity of manure upon every farm, and improve its quality. The soiling of horses, in the summer months, on green clover and rye-grass, is a practice which prevails in many grain districts where farm labor is regularly executed. The utility of the practice does not need the support of argument, for it is not only economical to the farmer, but saves much fatigue to the poor animal; besides, the quantity of dung thereby gathered is considerable.

Oxen and cows of all sorts, might be supported and fed in like manner, during the whole of the grass season. It is well known that milch-cows have, in several instances, been so kept; but it has rarely happened that other descriptions of cattle have been fed for the butcher according to this mode, though it is perfectly practicable.

The chief benefit of soiling may be considered as arising from the immense quantity of fine dung which would thus be accumulated, and which can be returned to the ground in the succeeding season, after being properly fermented and prepared. In all grain-farms, at least those of clayey soils, it is a work of great difficulty to rot the straw produced upon it; and much of it is misapplied, in consequence of such soils being naturally unfit for raising green winter-crops.

If a numerous stock of cattle were kept either in the house or in separate divisions of the fold yard, all the straw threshed in the summer months might be immediately converted into dung, the quality of which would be equal, if not superior, to what is made from turnips consumed at the stake. Dung is the mother of good crops; and it appears that no plan can be devised by which a large quantity can be so easily and cheaply gathered, or by which straw can be so effectually rotted and rendered beneficial to the occupier of a clay-land farm, as the soiling of grass in the summer season. In a word, the dung of animals fed upon green clover, may justly be reckoned the richest of all dung. It may, from the circumstances of the season, be rapidly prepared, and may be applied to the ground at a very early period, much earlier than any other sort of dung can be used with advantage.

To make Composts.

The use of manure, in the shape of compost, or ingredients of various qualities, mixed together in certain proportions, has long been a favorite practice with many farmers: though it is only in particular situations that the practice can be extensively or profitably executed. The ingredients used in these composts are chiefly earth and lime, sometimes dung, where the earth is poor; but lime may be regarded as the main agent of the process, acting as a stimulus for bringing the powers of the heap into action. Lime, in this view, may be considered as a kind of yeast, operating upon a heap of earth as yeast does upon flour or meal. It is obvious, therefore, that unless a sufficient quantity is given, the heap may remain unfermented, in which case little benefit will be derived from it as a manure.

The best kind of earth for compost is that of the alluvial sort, which is always of a rich greasy substance, often mixed with marl, and in every respect calculated to enrich and invigorate barren soils, especially if they are of a light and open texture. Old yards, deep headlands, and scourings of ditches, offer themselves as the basis of compost middens; but it is proper to summer-fallow them before hand, so that they may be entirely free of weeds. When the lime is mixed with the soil of these middens, repeated turnings are necessary, that the whole may be suitably fermented, and some care is required to apply the fermented mass at a proper time to the field on which it is to be used. The benefit of such a compost in nourishing soils is even greater than what is gained by dressing them with dung.

Lord Meadowbank's Directions for making Composts of Peat-moss.

Let the peat-moss, of which compost is to be formed, be thrown out of the pit for some weeks or months, in order to lose its redundant moisture. By this means, it is rendered the lighter to carry, and less compact and weighty when made up with fresh dung for fermentation; and, accordingly, less dung is required for the purpose, than if the preparation is made with peat taken recently from the pit. The peat taken from near the surface, or at a considerable depth, answers equally well.

Take the peat-moss to a dry spot convenient for constructing a dunghill to serve the field to be manured. Lay the cart-loads of it in two rows, and of the dung in a row betwixt them. The dung thus lies nearly on an area of the future compost dunghill, and the rows of peat should be near enough each other, that workmen, in making up the compost, may be able to throw them together by the spade. In making up, let the workmen begin at one end, and, at the extremity of the row of dung (which should not extend quite so far at that end as the rows of peats on each side of it do), let them lay a bottom of peat, six inches deep and fifteen feet wide, if the grounds admit of it, then throw forward, and lay on, about ten inches of dung above the bottom of peat; then add from the side rows about six inches of peat; then four or five of dung, and then six more of peat; then another thin layer of dung; and then cover it over with peat at the end where it was begun, at the two sides, and above. The compost should not be raised above four feet, or four feet and a half high; otherwise it is apt to press too heavily on the under parts, and check the fermentation. When a beginning is thus made, the workmen will proceed working backwards, and adding to the columns of compost, as they are furnished with the three rows of materials directed to be laid down for them. They must take care not to tread on the compost, or render it too compact; and, in proportion as the peat is wet, it should be made up in lumps, and not much broken.

In mild weather, seven cart-loads of common farm-dung, tolerably fresh made, is sufficient for twenty-one cart-loads of peat-moss; but in cold weather, a larger proportion of dung is desirable. To every twenty-eight carts of the compost, when made up, it is of use to throw on, above it, a cart-load of ashes, either made from coal, peat, or wood; half the quantity of slacked lime, the more finely powdered the better.

The compost, after it is made up, gets into a general heat, sooner or later, according to the weather, and the condition of the dung. In summer, in ten days or sooner; in winter, not perhaps for many weeks, if the cold is severe. In the former season, a stick should be kept in it in different parts, to pull out and feel now and then; for, if it approaches blood-heat, it should either be watered or turned over; and, on such an occasion, advantage may be taken to mix with it a little fresh moss. The heat subsides after a time, and with great variety, according to the weather, the dung, and the perfection of the compost; which should then be allowed to be untouched, till within three weeks of using, when it should be turned over upside down, and outside in, and all lumps broken: then

AGRICULTURE.

it comes into a second heat, but soon cools, and should be taken out for use. In this state the whole, except bits of the old decayed wood, appears a black free mass, and spreads like garden mould. Use it weight for weight, as farm-yard dung; and it will be found, in a course of cropping, fully to stand the comparison.

Peat, nearly as dry as garden-mould in seed-time, may be mixed with the dung, so as to double the volume. Workmen must begin with using layers; but, when accustomed to the just proportions, if they are furnished with peat moderately dry, and dung not lost in litter, they throw it up together as a mixed mass, and make a less proportion of dung serve for the preparation.

The rich coarse earth, which is frequently found on the surface of peat, is too heavy to be admitted into this compost; but it makes an excellent top-dressing, if previously mixed and turned over with lime.

Dr. Rennie's Method of Converting Moss into Manure.

The importance of moss as a manure is now generally admitted by all who have had an opportunity of making experiments on that subject. The Rev. Dr. Rennie, of Kilsyth, having proved the utility of filtration, has recommended, in private letters, to water the collected heap of moss for about ten days, once each day, very copiously; and when that is done, to trim it up to a compact body, allow it to dry, and to receive a gentle degree of heat. The degree of heat necessary for accomplishing that end, is sufficient, though not discoverable by the hand. If it only affects the thermometer a little, it is declared to be a manure. The doctor also declares, that moss can be converted by filtering steam through it; and more expeditiously still, by exposing it to a running stream of water. If the water penetrates the moss, it expels its poisonous qualities sooner and more effectually than any other mode ever devised. When it is sufficiently purified by any of these means, it must be laid up to dry, and is in a short time ready for applying to the land.

Use of Lime as Manure.

This mineral, after undergoing the process of calcination, has long been applied by husbandmen as a stimulus to the soil, and, in consequence of such an application, luxuriant crops have been produced, even upon soils apparently of inferior quality, and which would have yielded crops of trifling value had this auxiliary been withheld. In fact, the majority of soils cannot be cultivated with advantage till they are dressed with lime; and whether its beneficial effect shall be considered as an alterative, or as a stimulant, or as a manure, it will be found to be the basis of good husbandry, and of more use than all other manures put together. Wherever lime has been properly applied, it has constantly been found to prove as much superior to dung, as dung is to the rakings of roads, or the produce of peat-mire.

In respect of operation, it is immaterial whether lime be used upon grass land or summer-fallow. Upon old grass land, it is perhaps best to plough first, and to summer-fallow in the second year, when lime can be applied. On new and clean grass land, it may be limed at the outset, that is before the plough is admitted.

To lime moorish soils is a hazardous business, unless dung is likewise bestowed: but to repeat the application upon such soils, especially if they have been severely cropped, is almost a certain loss; a compost of lime and rich earth is, in such cases, the only substitute.

Strong loams and clays require a full dose to bring them into action; such soils being capable of absorbing a greater quantity of calcareous matter. Lighter soils, however, require less lime to stimulate them, and may be injured by administering a quantity that would prove moderately beneficial to those of a heavy nature.

Upon fresh land, or land in a proper state for a calcareous application, lime is much superior to dung. Its effects continue for a longer period; while the crops produced are of a superior kind and less susceptible of injury from the excesses of drought and moisture. Finally, the ground, particularly what is of a strong nature, is much easier wrought; and, in many instances, the saving of labor would almost tempt a judicious farmer to lime his land, were no greater benefit derived from the application than the opportunity thereby gained of working it in a perfect manner.

It may be added, that though strong soils require to be animated with a strong dose of lime, those of a light texture will do well with little more than half the quantity requisite on the others, especially if they are fresh, or have not already received an application of calcareous matter.

Application of Marl.

In many places the value of land has been much augmented by the application of marl. Treating of this article in a practical way, it may be divided into shell-marl and earth-marl. Shell-marl is composed of animal shells dissolved; earth-marl is also fossil. The color of the latter is various; its hardness being sometimes soft and ductile, like clay; sometimes hard and solid, like stone; and sometimes it is extended into thin beds, like slate. Shell-marl is easily distinguished by the shells, which always appear in it; but the similarity betwixt earth-marl and many other fossil substances, renders it difficult to distinguish them.

Shell-marl is very different in its nature from clayey and stone marls, and, from its effects upon the soil, is commonly classed among the animal manures: it does not dissolve with water as the other marls do. It sucks it up, and swells with it like a sponge. Dr. Home says, that it takes six times more of acids to saturate it than any of the other marls which he had met with. But the greatest difference betwixt the shell-marl and the other marls consists in this, the shell-marl contains oils.

This marl, it would seem from the qualities which it possesses, promotes vegetation in all the different ways. It increases the food of plants; it communicates to the soil a power of attracting this food from the air; it enlarges the pasture of plants; and it prepares the vegetable food for entering their roots.

Shelly Sand.

The shelly sand, often found deposited in beds in the crevices and level parts of the sea-coasts, is another substance capable of being employed, both as a manure and stimulant, not only on account of its containing calcareous matter, in greater or less proportions, but also from the mixture of animal and vegetable substances that are found in it. The portion of calcareous matter contained in these substances must vary according to circumstances; but, when the quantity is any way large, and in a reduced or attenuated state, the quality is so much the more valuable. On that account the quantity which ought to be applied to the soil, must be regulated by the extent of calcareous matter, supposed, or found, upon trial, to be contained in the article.

Clayey and Stone Marls.

The clayey and stone marls are distinguished by their colors, viz., white, black, blue, and red. The white, being of a soft, crumbly nature, is considered to be the best for pasture land; and the blue, which is more compact and firm, for grain land. In the districts where marl is much used, these distinctions of management are attended with advantage, if the following rules are adhered to:

If marl is of the blue kind, or of any kind that is compact or firm, lay it upon the land early in the season, so as the weather may mellow it down before the last plough; and, if on pasture land, let it also be early laid on, and spread very thin, breaking any lumps afterwards which are not completely separated by the first spreading. If marl is of the white, or any of the loose or crumbling sorts, it need not be laid on so early; because these varieties break and dissolve almost as soon as exposed to the weather.

Sea-weed.

Sea-weed is driven ashore after storms, and is found to be an excellent article for manuring light and dry soils, though of little advantage to those of a clayey description. This article may be applied on the proper soil with advantage to any crop, and its effects are immediate, though rarely of long continuance. As the coast-side lands of Great Britain are, in every case, of superior fertility to those that are inland, we may attribute this superior fertility to the great quantity of manure found upon their shores after every storm or high tide, whereby the resources of the ocean are in a manner brought forward for the enrichment of the lands locally situated for participating in such benefits. The utmost attention has long been paid to the gathering and laying on of this valuable manure.

Application of Sea-weed.

Sea-weed is applied at all seasons to the surface, and sometimes, though not so profitably, it is mixed with untrodden dung, that the process of putrefaction may be hastened. Generally speaking, it is at once applied to the soil, which saves labor, and prevents that degree of waste which otherwise would necessarily happen. Sea-weed is, in one respect, preferable to the richest dung, because it does not produce such a quantity of weeds. The salt contained in sea-weed, and applied with it, is the real cause of the after-cleanliness. This may be inferred from the general state of coast-side lands, where sea-weed is used. These lands are almost constantly kept in tillage, and yet are cleaner and freer from weeds than those in the inland situations, where grain crops are not so often taken.

When a coast-side farm contains mixed soils, the best management is exercised, by applying sea-weed to dry, and dung to clay-land. In this way, the full advantage of manure may be obtained, and a form so circumstanced is of infinitely greater value, with respect to manuring and laboring, than the one which contains no such variety.

Burning the Surface.

The practice of burning the surface, and applying the ashes as manure to the soil that remains, has been long prevalent in Britain; and is considered as the most advantageous way of bringing in and improving all soils, where the surface carried a coarse sward, and was composed of peat-earth, or other inactive substances. The burning of this surface has been viewed as the best way of bringing such soils into action; the ashes, furnished by the burning, serving as a stimulant to raise up their dormant powers, thereby rendering them fertile and productive in a superior degree to what could otherwise be accomplished.

Mr. Curwen's Method of Burning Surface Soil and Clay.

Mounds of seven yards in length, and three and a half in breadth, are kindled with seventy-two Winchester bushels of lime. First, a layer of dry sods or parings, on which a quantity of lime is spread, mixing sods with it, then a covering of eight inches of sods, on which the other half of the lime is spread, and covered a foot thick, the height of the mound being about a yard.

In twenty-four hours it will take fire. The lime should be immediately from the kiln. It is better to suffer it to ignite itself, than to effect it by the operation of water. When the fire is fairly kindled, fresh sods must be applied. I should recommend obtaining a sufficient body of ashes before any clay is put on the mounds. The fire naturally rises to the top. It takes less time, and does more work to draw down the ashes from the top, and not to suffer it to rise above six feet. The former practice of burning in kilns was more expensive; did much less work; and, in many instances, calcined the ashes.

I think it may fairly be supposed that the lime adds full its worth to the quality of the ashes. Where limestone can be had, I should advise the burning of a small quantity in the mounds, which would be a great improvement to the ashes, and, at the same time, help to keep the fire in.

The general adopting of the system of surface and soil clay-burning, is likely to be an important discovery for the interests of agriculture.

To burn Moss with the Ashes.

The following directions for burning moss along with the ashes are of considerable importance: Begin the fire with dry faggots, furze, or straw, then put on dried moss finely minced and well beaten with a clapper; and when that is nearly burnt through, put on moss less dry, but well minced and clapped, making holes with a prong to carry on the fire, and so adding more moss till a hill of ashes, something of the size of a wagon load, is accumulated, which, when cold, carry to the bins, or store heaps, before the ashes get wet.

Mr. Roscoe's Method of Improving Moss Land.

The best method of improving moss land is by the application of a calcareous substance in a sufficient quantity to convert the moss into a soil, and by the occasional use of animal or other extraneous manures, such as the course of cultivation and the nature of the crops may be found to require.

After setting fire to the heap and herbage on the moss, and ploughing it down as far as practicable, Mr. Roscoe ploughs a thin sod or furrow with a very sharp horse plough, which he burns in small heaps and dissipates; considering it of little use but to destroy the tough woods of the ediophorus, nardus stricta, and other plants, whose matted roots are almost imperishable. The moss being thus brought to a tolerably dry and level substance, then plough it in a regular furrow six inches deep, and as soon as possible after it is turned up, set upon it the necessary quantity of marl, not less than 200 cubic yards to the acre. As the marl begins to crumble and fall with the sun or frost, it is spread over the land with considerable exactness, after which put in a crop as early as possible, sometimes by the plough, and at others with the horse-scuffle, or searifier, according to the nature of the crop, a quantity of manure, setting on about twenty tons to the acre.

Moss-land, thus treated, may not only be advantageously cropped the first year with green crops, as potatoes, turnips, etc., but with any kind of grain.

Peat and Peat Ashes used as Manure.

In the county of Bedford, England, peat ashes are sold as manure, and are used as a top dressing for clovers, and sometimes for barley, at the rate of from forty to sixty bushels per acre. They are usually spread during the month of March, on clover, and on the surface of the barley-lands after the seed is sown. Peat ashes are also admirably useful as manure for turnips, and are easily drilled with or over the seed, by means of a drill-box connected with a loaded cart.

After the quantity required has been cast, a portion sufficient to kindle a large heap (suppose two cart-loads), is dried as much as if intended for winter's use. A conical pile is then built and fired, and as soon as the flame or smoke makes its appearance at any of the crevices, it is kept back by fresh peat, just sufficiently dry to be free from water; and thus the pile is continually increased, until it has burnt thirty or forty loads, or as much more as may be required. The slower the process the better; but, in case of too languid a consumption, the heap should be stirred by a stick, whenever the danger of extinction seems probable.

In case of rain, the workmen should be prepared with some coarse thick turf, with which to cover the surface of the cone.

Coal Ashes used as Manure.

Coal ashes may likewise be made a most useful article of manure, by mixing with every cart-load of them one bushel of lime in its hottest state, covering it up in the middle of the heap for about twelve hours, till the lime be entirely slacked, and incorporating them well together; and, by turning the whole over two or three times, the cinders, or half-burnt parts of the coal, will be reduced to as fine a powder as the lime itself. The coal-ashes should, however, be carefully kept dry; this mixture will be found one of the best improvers of moorish and benty land.

Method of Burning Lime without Kilns.

The practice of lime-burners in Wales has formerly been to burn lime in broad shallow kilns, but lately they have begun to manufacture that article without any kiln at all.

They place the limestone in large bodies, which are called coaks, the stones not being broken small as in the ordinary method, and calcine these heaps in the way used for preparing charcoal. To prevent the flame from bursting out at the top and sides of those heaps, turfs and earth are placed against them, and the aperture partially closed; and the heat is regulated and transfused through the whole mass, that notwithstanding the increased size of the stones, the whole becomes thoroughly calcined. As a proof of the superior advantage that lime burnt in these clamps or coaks has over lime burnt in the old method, where farmers have an option of taking either lime at the same price, a preference is invariably given to that burned in heaps. This practice has long prevailed in Yorkshire and Shropshire, and is also familiar in Scotland.

Mr. Craig's Improved Method of Burning Clay.

Make an oblong enclosure, of the dimensions of a small house — say fifteen feet by ten — of green turf-seeds, raised to the height of three and a half or four feet. In the inside of this enclosure air-pipes are drawn diagonally, which communicate with holes left at each corner of the exterior wall. These pipes are formed of sods put on edge, and the space between so wide only as another sod can easily cover. In each of the four spaces left between the air-pipes and the outer wall, a fire is kindled with wood and dry turf, and then the whole of the inside of the enclosure or kiln filled with dry turf, which is very soon on fire; and, on the top of that, when well kindled, is thrown on the clay, in small quantities at a time, and repeated as often as necessary, which must be regulated by the intensity of the burning. The air-pipes are of use only at first, because if the fire burns with tolerable keenness, the sods forming the pipes will soon be reduced to ashes. The pipe on the weather side of the kiln only is left open, the mouths of the other three being stopped up, and not opened except the wind should veer about. As the inside of the enclosure or kiln begins to be filled up with clay, the outer wall must be raised in height, at least fifteen inches higher than the top of the clay, for the purpose of keeping the wind from acting on the fire. When the fire burns through the outer wall, which it often does, and particularly when the top is over-loaded with clay, the breach must be stopped up immediately, which can only be effectually done by building another sod wall from the foundation opposite to it, and the sods that formed that part of the first wall are soon reduced to ashes. The wall can be raised as high as may be convenient to throw on the clay, and the kiln may be increased to any size by forming a new wall when the previous one is burnt through.

The principal art in burning consists in having the outer wall made quite close and impervious to the external air, and taking care to have the top always lightly, but completely, covered with clay; because if the external air should come in contact with the fire, either on the top of the kiln or by means of its bursting through the sides, the fire will be very soon extinguished. In short, the kilns require to be well attended, nearly as closely as charcoal-pits. Clay is much easier burnt than either moss or loam — it does not undergo any alteration in its shape, and on that account allows the fire and smoke to get up easily between the lumps — whereas moss and loam, by crumbling down, are very apt to smother the fire, unless carefully attended to. No rule can be laid down for regulating the size of the lumps of clay thrown on the kiln, as that must depend on the state of the fire. After a kiln is fairly set going, no coal or wood, or any sort of combustible, is necessary, the wet clay burning of itself, and it can only be extinguished by intention, or the carelessness of the operator, the vicissitudes of the weather having hardly any effect on the fires, if properly attended to. When the kiln is burning with great keenness, a stranger to the operation may be apt to think that the fire is extinguished. If, therefore, any person, either through impatience or too great curiosity, should insist on looking into the interior of the kiln, he will certainly retard, and may possibly extinguish, the fire; the chief secret consisting, as before-mentioned, in keeping out the external air.

The above method of burning clay may be considered as an essential service rendered to agriculture; as it shows farmers how to convert, at a moderate expense, the most worthless barren subsoil into excellent manure.

To decompose Green Vegetables for Manure.

The following process for the decomposition of green vegetables, for manure, has been practised with great success in the counties of Norfolk and Suffolk, England:—

Place a layer of vegetable matter a foot thick,

MANURES.

then a thin layer of lime, alternately; in a few hours the decomposition will begin, and, unless prevented by sods, or a fork full of vegetables, will break out into a blaze; this must be guarded against; in twenty-four hours the process will be completed. Weeds of every description will answer for vegetables; two pounds' worth of lime will produce manure for four acres. Use the vegetables as soon after cutting as possible, and the lime fresh from the kiln, as distance will allow.

Bone Manure.

Mills are constructed for the purpose of bruising (not pounding) bones; and the dust riddled therefrom is reckoned a still stronger manure. The same person selects the best bones, which are sawn into pieces, for button-moulds and knife-handles: and the saw-dust from this operation is particularly useful in gardens and hot-beds. It suits every vegetable, hot-house, or green-house plant.

Bone manure is best adapted for cold and light sandy land. The usual quantity per acre is seventy bushels, when used alone; but when mixed with ashes, or common manure of any sort, thirty bushels per acre is thought quite enough. It is applied at the same periods as other manure, and has been found in this way to remain seven years in the ground. The rough part of this manure, after being five years in the ground, has been gathered off one field and thrown upon another of a different soil, and has proved, even then, good manure.

The bones which are best filled with oil and marrow are certainly the best manure; and the parts generally used for buttons and knife-hafts are the thigh and shank bones. The powdered bones are dearer, and generally used for hot-beds in gardens, being too expensive for the field, and not so durable as bruised bones, yet, for a short time, more productive.

A dry, light, or gentle soil, is best adapted for the use of bone-manure; as it is supposed that, in land which retains wet, the nutritive part of the bone washes to the surface of it and does not incorporate sufficiently with the soil.

Bruised bones are better when mixed with ashes or any other manure, as the juice of the bone is then more equally spread over the field. Bone manure ought to be ploughed into the land in tillage. On the grass the powder should be sown in the hand.

Super-Phosphate of Lime.

To Liebig is due the greatest credit for the theory that the organic matter of plants is supplied abundantly by nature from air and water; that the ashes of plants exhibit the mineral matters most needed for a fertile soil; that the ashes of the most valuable parts, such as the husk of wheat, especially show what matters are required for the most abundant production of those parts; that soils are most frequently deficient in phosphoric acid, which should be supplied in the form of bones, guano, and more especially as a more or less soluble phosphate of lime. Long and extensive experience has proved the great value of a fertilizer which contains a portion of so-called super-phosphate of lime; that is, a bone-phosphate of lime, which is treated with sulphuric acid, so that more or less of the phosphate will dissolve in water. Of course a true chemical super-phosphate would wholly dissolve, but such a one is impracticable in use; moreover it is found by practice that a few per cent. of phosphoric acid in a fertilizer is sufficient to insure its promotion of fertility. Hence some fertilizers in commerce consist almost wholly of a phosphate of lime mixed with a little sulphate of lime (plaster), resulting from the action of the sulphuric acid, so that it contains 15 to 20 per cent. phosphoric acid, one-third or one-fourth of which readily dissolves in water. These fertilizers are found to yield excellent results when applied to the soil.

The superiority of these nitrogenous superphosphated fertilizers over all others may be summed up in a few words. They surpass stable manure in their extremely small bulk and weight for the same fertilizing effect, and consequently in the greater ease and less expense of their handling, hauling and spreading, and yet further in their never fouling land by the seeds of weeds and noxious plants. They excel bones and phosphatic guano in their more rapid action and their yielding a quicker return. They excel Peruvian guano in continuing their fertilizing effects for a longer period of time, in their being less violent at first, and yet sufficiently energetic to yield a return the first season of their application. Most of our land is either poor by nature or through exhaustive cropping, and there is nothing that will more rapidly restore and increase their fertility than the ammoniated super-phosphates. It may be yet further observed, that there is scarcely any soil to which their application will not prove a decided benefit, and scarcely a crop which they will not improve, whether grain, vegetables, cotton, tobacco, fruits, etc.

Various Substances used as Manure.

J. B. Bailey, Esq., presented to the Agricultural Society of Manchester, the following enumeration of substances which may be applied usefully as manures instead of stable dung, viz., mud, sweepings of the streets, and coal-ashes, night-soil, bones, refuse matters, as sweepings and rubbish of houses, etc., sea-weeds, sea-shells, and sea-gravel, river-weeds, sweepings of roads, and spent tanner's bark to mix with lime. Peat or moss, decayed vegetables, putrid water, the ashes of weeds, etc., the refuse of bleacher's ashes, soap suds, or lye, peat ashes, water indiluting, refuse salt.

The use of liquid manure, so long common in China and Japan, is gaining in favor with agriculturists everywhere. Peruvian guano is one of the important discoveries of modern times; with its use ground almost barren may be made productive; it is available for almost all kinds of crops.

Plaster of Paris used as Manure.

Plaster of Paris is used as a manure in Pennsylvania and elsewhere. The best kind is imported from hills in the vicinity of Paris: it is brought down the Seine, and exported from Havre de Grace. The lumps composed of flat shining spicula are preferred to those which are formed of round particles like sand; the simple method of finding out the quality is to pulverize some, and put it dry into an iron pot over the fire, when that which is good, will soon boil, and great quantities of the fixed air escape by ebullition. It is pulverized by first putting it in a stamping-mill. The finer its pulverization the better, as it will thereby be more generally diffused.

It is best to sow it on a wet day. The most approved quantity for grass is six bushels per acre. No art is required in sowing it more than making the distribution as equal as possible on the sward of grass. It operates altogether as a top manure, and therefore should not be put on in the spring until the principal frosts are over and vegetation has begun. The general time for sowing in America is in April, May, June, July,

AGRICULTURE.

August, and even as late as September. Its effects will generally appear in ten or fifteen days; after which the growth of the grass will be so great as to produce a large burden at the end of six weeks after sowing.

It must be sown on dry land, not subject to be overflown. It has been sown on sand, loam, and clay, and it is difficult to say on which it has best answered, although the effect is sooner visible on sand. It has been used as a manure in this state for twelve years; for, like other manure, its continuance very much depends on the nature of the soil on which it is placed.

Mode of Applying Blubber as a Manure.

This is a very rich ingredient, as well for arable as pasture lands, when mixed at the rate of one ton of blubber to twenty loads of mould, and one chaldron of lime, per acre. It must be turned over and pulverized; and when it has lain in this state three or four months, it will become fit for use, and may be put upon the land in such quantities as the quality of the land to be manured requires. It is a very strong manure, and very excellent.

Application of Manures to Land.

Early in autumn, after the hay crop is removed, is the most convenient and least objectionable period for the purpose. The common practice is to apply manures during the frost, in the winter. But the elastic fluids being the greatest supports of vegetation, manures should be applied under circumstances that favor their generation. These will occur in spring, after the grass has, in some degree, covered the ground, the dung being then shaded from the sun. After a frost much of the virtues of the dung will be washed away by the thaw, and its soluble parts destroyed, and in a frosty state the ground is incapable of absorbing liquids.

Management of Arable Land.

Alternate husbandry, or the system of having leguminous and culmiferous crops to follow each other, with some modifications, is practicable in every soil. According to its rules, the land would rarely get into a foul and exhausted state; at least, if foul and exhausted under alternate husbandry, matters would be much worse were any other system followed. The rotation may be long or short, as is consistent with the richness of the soil, on which it is executed, and other local circumstances. The crops cultivated may be any of the varieties which compose either of the two tribes, according to the nature of soil and climate of the district where the rotation is exercised, and where circumstances render ploughing not so advantageous as pasturing, the land may remain in grass, till those circumstances are obviated, care being always taken, when it is broken up, to follow alternate husbandry during the time it is under tillage.

In this way we think it perfectly practicable to follow the alternate system in every situation; nor do we consider the land being in grass for two, three, or four years, as a departure from that system, if called for by a scarcity of manure, poverty of soil, want of markets for corn, or other accidental circumstances. The basis of every rotation we hold to be either a bare summer fallow, or a fallow on which drill turnips are cultivated, and its conclusion to be with the crop taken in the year preceding a return of fallow or drilled turnips, when, of course, a new rotation commences.

First Rotation of Crops.

According to this rotation, wheat and drilled beans are the crops to be cultivated, though clover and rye-grass may be taken for one year, in place of beans, should such a variety be viewed as more eligible. The rotation begins with summer fallow, because it is only on strong deep lands that it can be profitably practised; and it may go on for any length of time, or so long as the land can be kept clean, though it ought to stop the moment that the land gets into a contrary condition. A considerable quantity of manure is required to go on successfully; dung should be given to each bean crop; and if this crop is drilled and attentively horse-hoed, the rotation may turn out to be one of the most profitable that can be exercised.

Second Rotation.

Upon loams and clays, where it may not be advisable to carry the first rotation into execution, a different one can be practised, according to which labor will be more divided, and the usual grains more generally cultivated; as, for instance:
1. Fallow, with dung. 2. Wheat. 3. Beans, drilled and horse-hoed. 4. Barley. 5. Clover and rye-grass. 6. Oats, or wheat. 7. Beans, drilled and horse-hoed. 8. Wheat.

This rotation is excellently calculated to insure an abundant return through the whole of it, provided dung is administered upon the clover stubble. Without this supply the rotation would be crippled, and inferior crops of course produced in the concluding years.

Third Rotation.

This rotation is calculated for clays and loams of an inferior description to those already treated of:
1. Fallow, with dung. 2. Wheat. 3. Clover and rye-grass. 4. Oats. 5. Beans, drilled and horse-hoed. 6. Wheat.

According to this rotation, the rules of good husbandry are studiously practised, while the sequence is obviously calculated to keep the land in good order, and in such a condition as to insure crops of the greatest value. If manure is bestowed either upon the clover stubble or before the beans are sown, the rotation is one of the best that can be devised for the soils mentioned.

Fourth Rotation.

On thin clays gentle husbandry is indispensably necessary, otherwise the soil may be exhausted, and the produce unequal to the expense of cultivation. Soils of this description will not improve much while under grass, but unless an additional stock of manure can be procured, there is a necessity of refreshing them in that way, even though the produce should, in the meantime, be comparatively of small value. The following rotation is an excellent one:
1. Fallow, with dung. 2. Wheat. 3. Grass, pastured, but not too early eaten. 4. Grass. 5. Grass. 6. Oats.

This rotation may be shortened or lengthened, according to circumstances, but should never extend further in point of ploughing, than when dung can be given to the fallow break. This is the keystone of the whole, and if it is neglected the rotation is rendered useless.

Fifth Rotation.

Peat-earth soils are not friendly to wheat unless aided by a quantity of calcareous matter. Taking them in a general point of view, it is not advisable to cultivate wheat, but a crop of oats may almost be depended upon, provided the previous management has been judiciously executed. If the sub-soil of peat-earth lands be retentive of moisture, the process ought to commence with a bare summer fallow; but if such are incumbent on free and open bottoms, a crop of turnips may

be substituted for fallow, according to which method the surface will get a body which naturally it did not possess. Grass, on such soils, must always occupy a great space of every rotation, because physical circumstances render regular cropping utterly impracticable.
1. Fallow, or turnips, with dung. 2. Oats, of an early variety. 3. Clover, and a considerable quantity of perennial rye-grass. 4. Pasture for several years, till circumstances permit the land to be broken up, when oats are to be repeated.

Sixth Rotation.

Light soils are easily managed, though to procure a full return of the profits which they are capable of yielding, requires generally as much attention as is necessary in the management of those of a stronger description. Upon light soils a bare summer fallow is seldom called for, as cleanliness may be preserved by growing turnips and other leguminous articles. Grass also is of eminent advantage upon such soils, often yielding a greater profit than what is afforded by culmiferous crops.
1. Turnips. 2. Spring wheat, or barley. 3. Clover and rye-grass. 4. Oats, or wheat.

This rotation would be greatly improved, were it extended to eight years, whilst the ground by such an extension, would be kept fresh, and constantly in good condition. As for instance, were seeds for pasture sown in the second year, the ground kept three years under grass, then broken up for oats in the sixth year, drilled with beans and peas in the seventh, and sown with wheat in the eighth, the rotation would be complete; because it included every branch of husbandry, and admitted a variety in management generally agreeable to the soil, and always favorable to the interest of cultivators. The rotation may also consist of six crops, were the land kept only one year in grass, though few situations admit of so much cropping, unless additional manure is within reach.

Seventh Rotation.

Sandy soils, when properly manured, are well adapted to turnips, though it rarely happens that wheat can be cultivated on them with advantage, unless they are dressed with alluvial compost, marl, clay, or some such substance, as will give a body or strength to them which they do not naturally possess. Barley, oats, and rye, the latter especially, are, however, sure crops on sands; and, in favorable seasons, will return greater profit than can be obtained from wheat.
1. Turnips, consumed on the ground. 2. Barley. 3. Grass. 4. Rye or oats.

By keeping the land three years in grass, the rotation would be extended to six years, a measure highly advisable.

From what has been stated, every person capable of judging will at once perceive the facility of arranging husbandry upon correct principles, and of cropping the ground in such a way as to make it produce abundant returns to the occupier, whilst at the same time it is preserved in good condition, and never impoverished or exhausted. All these things are perfectly practicable under the alternate system, though it is doubtful whether they can be gained under any other.

It may be added, that winter-sown crops, or crops sown on the winter furrow, are most eligible on all clayey soils.

Ploughing, with a view to clean soils of the description under consideration, has little effect unless given in the summer months. This renders summer fallow indispensably necessary; and, without this radical process, none of the heavy and wet soils can be suitably managed, or preserved in a good condition.

To adopt a judicious rotation of chopping for every soil, requires a degree of judgment in the farmer, which can only be gathered from observation and experience. The old rotations were calculated to wear out the soil, and to render it unproductive; but the modern rotations, such as those which we have described, are founded on principles which insure a full return from the soil, without lessening its value, or impoverishing its condition. Much depends, however, upon the manner in which the different processes are executed; for the best-arranged rotation may be of no avail, if the processes belonging to it are imperfectly and unreasonably executed.

To cultivate Wheat.

On soils really calculated for wheat, though in different degrees, summer fallow is the first and leading step to gain a good crop or crops of that grain. The first furrow should be given before winter, or as early as the other operations of the farm will admit; and every attention should be used to go as deep as possible; for it rarely happens that any of the succeeding furrows exceed the first one in that respect. The number of after-ploughings must be regulated by the condition of the ground and the state of the weather; but, in general, it may be observed, that ploughing in length and across, alternately, is the way by which the ground will be most completely cut, and the intention of fallowing accomplished.

Varieties of Seed.

Wheat may be classed under two principal divisions, though each of these admits of several subdivisions. The first is composed of all the varieties of red wheat. The second division comprehends the whole varieties of white wheat, which again may be arranged under two distinct heads, namely, thick-chaffed and thin-chaffed.

The thick-chaffed varieties were formerly in greatest repute, generally yielding the whitest and finest flour, and, in dry seasons, not inferior in produce to the other; but since 1799, when the disease called mildew, to which they are constitutionally predisposed, raged so extensively, they have gradually been going out of fashion.

The thin-chaffed wheats are a hardy class, and seldom mildewed, unless the weather be particularly inimical during the stages of blossoming, filling, and ripening, though some of them are rather better qualified to resist that destructive disorder than others. In 1799, thin-chaffed wheats were seriously injured; and instances were not wanting to show, that an acre of them, with respect to value, exceeded an acre of thick-chaffed wheat, quantity and quality considered, not less than fifty per cent. Since that time, therefore, their culture has rapidly increased; and to this circumstance may, in a great measure, be attributed the high character which thin-chaffed wheats now bear.

Method of Sowing.

Sowing in the broadcast way may be said to be the mode universally practised. Upon well prepared lands, if the seed be distributed equally, it can scarcely be sown too thin; perhaps two bushels per acre are sufficient; for the heaviest crops at autumn are rarely those which show the most vigorous appearance through the winter months. Bean stubbles require more seed than summer fallows, because the roughness of their surface prevents such an equal distribution; and clover leas ought to be still thicker sown than bean stubbles. Thin sowing in spring ought not to be practised, otherwise the crop will be late, and imperfectly ripened. No more harrowing should be given to fields that have been fallowed, than what is necessary to cover the seed, and level the surface sufficiently. Ground, which is to lie in a broken-down state through the winter, suffers severely when an excessive harrowing is given, especially if it is incumbent on a close bottom; though, as to the quantity necessary, none can give an opinion, except those who are personally present.

To sow Grain by Ribbing.

The ribbing of grain crops was introduced into Great Britain in the year 1810. The process is as follows: Suppose the land in fallow, or turnips eat off, let it be gathered into ridges of twelve feet each; then harrow it well, particularly the furrows of the ridges; after which take a narrow-bottomed swing plough, five inches and a half broad at the heel, with a narrow-winged sock, drawn by one horse; begin in the furrow, as if you intended to gather two ridges together, which will make a rib exactly in the middle of the furrow; then turn back up the same furrow you came down, keeping close to the rib made; pursue the same mode on the other side, and take a little of the soil which is thrown over by the mouldboard from the back of each rib, and so on till you come near the furrow, when you must pursue the same mode as at first. In water furrowing you will then have a rib on each side of the furrow, distance between the rib, ten or twelve inches. The seed to be sown from the hand, and, from the narrowness or sharpness of the top of the ridges, the grain will fall regularly down, then put on a light harrow to cover the seed. In wet soils the ridges ought to be twice gathered, as ribbing reduces them.

It will answer all kinds of crops, but not all soils. Strong clayey soils cannot be pulverized sufficiently for that purpose; nor can it be effected in clover-lea, unless it be twice ploughed and well harrowed. Ribbing is here esteemed preferable to drilling, as you have the same opportunity of keeping the land clean, and the grain does not fall so close together as by drilling.

The farmer may hand or horse-hoe his crops, and also hoe in his clover-seed, which is considered very advantageous. It is more productive of grain, especially when it is apt to lodge, and, in all cases, of as much straw; and ribbing is often the means of preventing the corn lodging.

In a wet season ribbing is more favorable to harvesting, because the space between the ribs admits the air freely, and the corn dries much sooner. The reapers also, when accustomed to it, cut more and take it up cleaner.

Improved Method of Drilling Wheat.

The drill contains three coulters, placed in a triangular form, and worked by brushes, with cast-iron nuts, sufficient for one horse to draw, and one man to attend to. It will drill three acres per day of wheat, barley or oats, at five inches asunder; and five acres per day of beans, peas, etc., at twelve inches asunder. The general practice is to drill crossways, and to set the rows five or six inches, and never exceeding seven inches, apart, it being found that if the distance is greater they are too long filling up in the spring, that they afford a greater breadth for the growth of weeds, are more expensive to hoe, and more liable to be laid in the summer. In drilling wheat never harrow after the drill if it can be avoided, the drill generally leaving the corn sufficiently covered; and by this plan the vegetation is quickened, and the ridges of soil between each two rows preserve the plants in winter, and render the operation of harrowing in the spring much more efficacious. The spring harrowing is performed the contrary way to that of the drilling, as the harrow working upon the ridges does not pull up the plants, and leaves the ground mouldy for the hoe. This point should be particularly attended to. The harrowing after the drill evidently leaves the ground in a better state to the eye, but the advantages in the produce of the crop are decidedly in favor of the plan of leaving the land in the rough state already described, as the operation of the winter upon the clods causes them to pulverize, and furnishes an abundant nutrition to the plants in the spring; and followed by the hoe about the time the head or ear is forming, it makes the growth of the plant more vigorous, and greatly improves the size of the head or ear. The drilling for wheat should generally commence about the latter end of September, at which time the farmer may drill about two bushels per acre. As the season advances, keep increasing the quantity to three bushels per acre, being guided by the quality of the soil and other circumstances. A great loss has frequently arisen through drilling too small a quantity of seed, as there can be none spared in that case for the rooks and grubs: and a thick, well-planted crop will always yield more abundantly than a thin stooling crop, and ripen sooner.

The drill system would have been in more general practice, if its friends had also recommended the use of a larger quantity of seed to the acre, and the rows to be planted nearer together. It is impossible to obtain so great a produce per acre by the broadcast system as by the drill system at the same expense, for the land ever so free from weeds. Fifty bushels per acre may be raised by the drill, but never more than forty bushels by sowing broadcast. The wheat crops should generally be top-dressed in winter with manure compost, or some other dressing in frost, or when you can cart upon the land; but if that operation is rendered impracticable, souting in March, or any other dressing of that description, hoed in at the spring, is preferable to a dressing laid on in the autumn and ploughed in.

The advantages of the drill over the broadcast system are numerous and decisive, as it enables the farmer to grow corn without weeds, is sooner ready for stacking after the scythe or sickle, produces a cleaner and more regular sample for the market, and hence obtains a better price, leaves the land in a better state for a succeeding crop, and materially increases the quantity of food for human consumption.

To Pickle the Seed.

This process is indispensably necessary on every soil, otherwise smut, to a greater or less extent, will, in nine cases out of ten, assuredly follow. Stale urine may be considered as the safest and surest pickle, and where it can be obtained in a sufficient quantity, is commonly resorted to. The mode of using it does not however seem to be agreed upon, for while one party contends that the grain ought to be steeped in the urine, another party considers it sufficient to sprinkle the urine upon it. But whatever difference of opinion there may be as to the kind of pickle that ought to be used, and the mode of using it, all admit the utility of mixing the wetted seed with hot lime fresh slaked; and this, in one point of view, is absolutely necessary, so that the seed may be equally distributed. It may be remarked that experience justifies the utility of all these modes, provided they are attentively carried into execution. There is some danger from the first, for if the seed steep-

INDIAN CORN, SORGHUM.

ed in urine is not immediately sown, it will infallibly lose its vegetative power. The second, viz., sprinkling the urine on the seed, seems to be the safest if performed by an attentive hand, whilst the last may do equally well, if such a quantity of salt be incorporated with the water as to render it of sufficient strength. It may also be remarked, that this last mode is often accompanied with smut, owing no doubt to a deficiency of strength in the pickle; whereas a single head with smut is rarely discovered when urine has been used.

To cultivate Indian Corn.

The land should be a loamy sand, very rich. In April the grains should be set like hops, at three to four feet distance, three to six grains in a hill, each grain about an inch deep in the ground. The seed from New England is the best. In May the alleys should be hoed and the hills weeded and earthed up higher; many good farmers plough three times after planting. At the latter end of that month all the superfluous stalks should be taken away, and only three stems of corn left in each hill. By the middle of June, it will cover the alley. It grows much like bulrushes, the lower leaves being like broad flags, three or four inches wide, and as many feet in length; the stems shooting upwards, from seven to ten feet in height, with many joints, casting off flag-leaves at every joint. Under these leaves and close to the stem grows the corn, covered over by many coats of sedgy leaves, and so closed in by them to the stem, that it does not show itself easily till there bursts out at the end of the ear a number of strings that look like tufts of horse-hair, at first of a beautiful green, and afterwards red or yellow, the stem ending in a flower. The corn will ripen in October or early November; but the sun at that season not having strength enough to dry it, it must be laid upon racks or thin open floors in dry rooms, and frequently turned, to avoid moulding; the grains are about as big as peas, and adhere in regular rows round a white pithy substance, which forms the ear. An ear contains from two to four hundred grains, and is from six to ten inches in length. They are of various colors, blue, red, white and yellow. The manner of gathering them is by cutting down the stems and breaking off the ears. The stems are as big as a man's wrist, and look like bamboo cane; the pith is full of a juice that tastes as sweet as sugar, and the joints are about a foot and a half distant. The increase is upwards of five hundred fold. Upon a large scale the seed may be drilled in alleys like peas, and to save digging, the ground may be ploughed and harrowed, which will answer very well. It will grow upon all kinds of land. The ears which grow upon dry sandy land are smaller, but harder and riper. The grain is taken from the husk by hand, and when ground upon stones, makes an excellent flour, of which it yields much more, with much less bran, than wheat does, and exceeds it in crust, pancakes, puddings, and all other uses except bread; but a sweetness peculiar to it, which in all other cases makes it agreeable, is here less so. It is excellent for feeding horses, poultry and hogs, and fattens them much better and sooner than peas or barley. The stems make better hedges for kitchen gardens than reeds do. It clears the ground from weeds, and makes a good season for any other kind of grain. It was the only bread-grain known in America when first discovered by the Spaniards, and is there called maize.

Sorghum.

This, also called Chinese sugar-cane, is now attracting attention, especially in the West. It may be cultivated almost precisely like maize, and is more profitable. It is cut off when it is ripe and beginning to fade slightly, or sometimes earlier than this. It may then be ground like sugarcane. This is often done in a mill like a ciderpress. The syrup is then boiled at once, in large shallow kettles. It is said that sorghum should be grown on a sandy soil, not too rich; if the earth is rich, it grows too strong and fibrous, with less sugar in the stem.

Diseases of Wheat.

Wheat is subject to more diseases than other grains, and, in some seasons, especially in wet ones, heavier losses are sustained from those diseases than are felt in the culture of any other cuniferous crop with which we are acquainted. Wheat may suffer from the attack of insects at the root; from blight, which primarily affects the leaf or straw, and ultimately deprives the grain of sufficient nourishment; from mildew on the ear, which operates thereon with the force of an apoplectic stroke; and from gum of different shades, which lodges on the chaff or cups in which the grain is deposited.

Blight.

Blight originates from moist or foggy weather, and from hoar-frost, the effects of which, when expelled by a hot sun, are first discernible on the straw, and afterwards on the ear, in a greater or less degree, according to local circumstances. Let a field be examined in a day or two after such weather, and a careful observer will soon be satisfied that the fibres and leaves of plants are contracted and enfeebled, in consequence of what may be called a stoppage of perspiration. This disorder may take place either earlier or later, but is most fatal when it appears at the time the grain is forming in the ear. It may appear at an earlier stage; and though the productive powers of the plant will thereby be lessened, yet, if circumstances are afterwards favorable, the quality of the grain produced may not be much impaired; or it may appear after the grain is fully formed, and then very little damage will be sustained, except by the straw.

Mildew.

Mildew may be ranked as a disease which affects the ear, and is brought on by causes somewhat similar to those which occasion blight, though at a more advanced period of the season. If this disorder comes on immediately after the first appearance of the ear the straw will also be affected, but if the grain is nearly or fully formed then injury on the straw is not much discernible. We have seen a crop that carried wheat that was mildewed where the straw was perfectly fresh, though, indeed, this rarely happens. A severe mildew, however, effectually prevents both grain and straw from making any further progress, the whole plant apparently going backward every day till existence in a manner ceases altogether. Something akin to mildew is the gum which, in all warm moist seasons, attaches itself to the ear, and often occasions considerable damage. All these different disorders are generally accompanied by insects, and by minute parasitic vegetable growths, considered by many to be the authors of the mischief that follows. Their appearance, however, may justly be attributed to the diseased state of the plant; for wherever putrefaction takes place, either in animal or vegetable substances, the presence of these parasites will never be wanting.

Rust.

Another disorder which affects wheat and is by several people denominated the real rust, is brought on by excessive heat, which occasions the plants to suffer from a privation of nourishment, and become sickly and feeble. In this atrophic state a kind of dust gathers on the stalks and leaves, which increases with the disease, till the plant is in a great measure worn out and exhausted. The only remedy in this case, and it is one that cannot easily be administered by the hand of man, is a plentiful supply of moisture, by which, if it is received before consumption is too far advanced, the crop is benefited in a degree proportional to the extent of nourishment received, and the stage at which the disease has arrived.

Impropriety of Sowing Mildewed Wheat.

Some people have recommended the sowing of blighted and mildewed wheat, because it will vegetate; though certainly the recommendation, if carried into practice, would be attended with imminent danger to those who attempted it. That light or defective wheat will vegetate and produce a plant we are not disposed to contradict, but that it will vegetate as briskly, or put out a stem of equal strength, and capable of withstanding the severe winter blasts as those produced from sound seed we must be excused for not believing. Let it only be considered that a plant of young wheat, unless when very early sown, lives three or four months, in a great measure, upon the nourishment which it derives from the parent seed; and that such nourishment can, in no view of the subject, be so great when the parent is lean and emaciated as when sound, healthy and vigorous. Let it also be remembered that a plant produced from the best and weightiest seed must, in every case, under a parity of other circumstances, have a stronger constitution at the outset, which necessarily qualifies it to push on with greater energy when the season of growth arrives. Indeed, the economy of nature would be overturned should any other result follow. A breeder of cattle or sheep would not act more foolishly, who trusted that a deformed diminutive bull or ram would produce him good stock, than the corn farmer does who uses unsound or imperfect seed.

To remove the Mildew on Wheat.

A solution of common salt in water, in the proportion of a pound to a gallon, is an excellent remedy for the mildew on grain. After sprinkling three or four days, the mildew will disappear, leaving only a discoloration on the straw where it was destroyed. The best and most expeditious way of applying the mixture is with a flat brush, such as is used by whitewashers. The operator having a pail of the mixture in one hand, with the other he dips the brush into it, and makes his regular casts as when sowing grain broadcast; in this way he will readily get over ten acres in the day, and with an assistant a great deal more. About two hogsheads of the mixture will suffice for an acre. Wherever the mixture touches the mildew immediately dies.

To prevent Mildew in Wheat.

Dissolve three ounces and two drachms of sulphate of copper, copperas, or blue vitriol, in three gallons and three quarts, wine measure, of cold water, for every three bushels of grain that is to be prepared. Into another vessel capable of containing from fifty-three to seventy-nine wine gallons, throw from three to four bushels of wheat, into which the prepared liquid is poured, until it rises five or six inches above the grain. Stir it thoroughly; and carefully remove all that swims on the surface. After it has remained half an hour in the preparation, throw the wheat into a basket that will allow the water to escape, but not the grain. It ought then to be immediately washed in rain, or pure water, which will prevent any risk of its injuring the germ, and afterwards the seed ought to be dried before it is sown. It may be preserved in this shape for months. Another method, which has been tried in Russia, is to expose the seed for one or two weeks to a dry heat of about 80° or 90°.

To prevent the Smut in Wheat.

Liming the seed by immersion is recommended by a French writer, as the only preventive warranted by science and sanctioned by experience, and the following is given as the method in which the process is best performed:

To destroy the germs of the blight in four and a half bushels or 256 pounds of grain, about six or seven gallons of water must be used, as grain may be more or less dry, and from thirty-five to forty-two ounces avoirdupois of quick-lime, according as it may be more or less caustic, and according as the seed may have more or less of the blight. Boil part of the water, black the lime with it, and then add the rest. When joined the heat of the water should be such that the hand can with difficulty bear it. Pour the lime water upon the corn placed in a tub, stirring it incessantly, first with a stick, and afterwards with a shovel. The liquid should, at first, cover the wheat, three or four fingers' breadth; it will soon be absorbed by the grain. In this state let it remain covered over for twenty-four hours, but turn it over five or six times during the day. Such parts of the liquor as will drain off may then be separated, when the corn, after standing a few hours, in order that it may run freely out of the hand, may be sown. If not intended to be used immediately, the limed wheat should be put in a heap, and moved once or twice a day till dry. Experience has proved that limed grain germinates sooner than unlimed; and, as it carries with it moisture sufficient to develop the embryo, the seed will not suffer for want of rain; insects will not attack it, the acrid taste of the lime being offensive to them; and, as every grain germinates, a less quantity is requisite. In fact, the grain being swelled, the sower filling his hand as usual, will, when he has sown sixty-five handsful of limed corn, have in reality only used fifty-two. As blighted grains preserve for a long time the power of germinating, the careful farmer, whose grain has been touched, should carefully sweep out the crevices in the walls and cracks in the floors of his barn, and take great pains to clean them thoroughly. Dry heat, as above spoken of, may be worth trying.

Another Method.

A tub is used that has a hole at bottom for a spigot and faucet, fixed in a wisp of straw, to prevent any small pieces of lime passing (as in brewing). To seventy gallons of water add a bushel of unslaked lime, stir it well till the whole is mixed, let it stand thirty hours, run it off into another tub (as practised in beer); add forty-two pounds of salt, which, with stirring, will soon dissolve; this is a proper pickle for brining and liming seed wheat without any obstacle, and greatly facilitates the drilling.

Steep the wheat in a broad-bottomed basket, twenty-four inches in diameter and twenty inches deep, running in the grain gradually in small quantities, from ten to twelve gallons; stirring the same. What floats skim off, and do not sow; then draw up the basket, to drain the pickle for a few minutes; this may be performed in half an hour, and when sufficiently pickled proceed as before. The wheat will be fit for sowing in twenty-four hours, if required; but for drilling two hours pickled will be best, and prepared four or five days before.

Mr. Henderson's Method of preventing Smut in Wheat.

Take of best soft green soap, made from fish-oil, one pound, and of scalding water four gallons. Put the soap into a glazed vessel with a small portion of the water; continue stirring it, and add the water as it dissolves, till the whole is a perfect lye. It should be used at about ninety degrees of Fahrenheit's thermometer or new-milk warm. Put the wheat into a tub, and pour on it a quantity of the liquor sufficient to cover it completely, and throw a blanket over it to preserve the heat. Stir it every ten minutes, and take off the scum. When it has remained in this manner for an hour, drain the liquor from the wheat through a sieve, or let the tub be furnished with a drain-bottom like a brewing vat. Let the liquor which was drawn off stand a few minutes to subside, and then pour it off the sediment. Repeat the operation till the whole quantity is steeped, only observe to add each time as much hot lye as was observed by the former steeping. Dry the wheat with quick-lime, and sow as soon as convenient. It will keep ten days after steeping; but should be spread thin on a dry floor.

If a tub with a drain-bottom is used, such as a hogshead with a spigot to draw off the lye, four ounces of soap and one gallon of water, scalding hot, will preserve a stock of warm lye sufficient for any quantity of wheat. The operation should be performed in a clean place, at a distance from barns and granaries, the roofs of which may be observed hanging full of smut. The refuse of smutted wheat should be buried deep in the earth, and not thrown to the dunghill, from which it would be conveyed to the field.

Advantages of Reaping Grain before being Perfectly Ripe.

M. Cadet de Vaux has recommended, as an important and useful innovation, the reaping of grain before it is perfectly ripe. This practice originated with M. Salles, of the Agricultural Society of Beziers: grain thus reaped (say eight days before it is ripe) is fuller, larger, and finer, and is never attacked by the weevil. This was proved by reaping one half of a field as recommended, and leaving the other till the usual time. The early-reaped portion gave a hectolitre (about three bushels) of grain more for an acre of land than the later-reaped. An equal quantity of flour from each was made into bread; that made from the grain reaped green gave seven pounds of bread more than the other in two bushels. The weevil attacked the ripe grain but not the green. The proper time for reaping is when the grain, pressed between the fingers, has a doughy appearance, like bread just hot from the oven when pressed in the same way.

To Manage the Wheat Harvest.

It is advantageous to cut wheat before it is fully ripe; but, in ascertaining the proper state, it is necessary to discriminate between the ripeness of the straw and the ripeness of the grain; for, in some seasons, the straw dies upwards, under which circumstance a field, to the eye, may appear to be completely fit for the sickle, when, in reality, the grain is imperfectly consolidated, and perhaps not much removed from a milky state. Though it is obvious that under such circumstances no further benefit can be conveyed from the root, and that nourishment is withheld the moment that the roots die, yet it does not follow that grain so circumstanced should be immediately cut, because, after that operation is performed it is in a great measure necessarily deprived of every benefit from the sun and air, both of which have greater influence in bringing it to maturity so long as it remains on foot than when cut down, whether laid on the ground or bound up in sheaves. The state of weather at the time also deserves notice, for as in moist or even variable weather every kind of grain, when cut prematurely, is more exposed to damage than when completely ripened. All these things will be studied by the skilful husbandman, who will also take into consideration the dangers which may follow were he to permit his wheat crop to remain uncut till completely ripened. The danger from wind will not be lost sight of, especially if the season of the equinox approaches; even the quantity dropped in the field and in the stack-yard, when wheat is over ripe, is an object of consideration. Taking all these things into view, it seems prudent to have wheat cut before it is fully ripe, as less damage will be sustained from acting in this way than by adopting a contrary practice.

If the weather be dry and the straw clean, wheat may be carted to the stack-yard in a few days; indeed, if quite ripe it may be stacked immediately from the sickle, especially when not meant for early threshing. So long, however, as any moisture remains in the straw, the field will be found to be the best stack-yard; and where grass or weeds of any kind are mixed with the crop, patience must be exerted till they are decayed and dried, lest heating be occasioned.

Barley.

Next to wheat the most valuable grain is barley, especially on light and sharp soils.

It is a tender grain and easily hurt in any of the stages of its growth, particularly at seed time; a heavy shower of rain will then almost ruin a crop on the best prepared land; and in all the after processes greater pains and attention are required to insure success than in the case of other grains. The harvest process is difficult, and often attended with danger; even the threshing of it is not easily executed with machines, because the awn generally adheres to the grain, and renders separation from the straw a troublesome task. Barley, in fact, is raised at greater expense than wheat, and generally speaking is a more hazardous crop. Except upon rich and genial soils, where climate will allow wheat to be perfectly reared, it ought not to be cultivated.

Varieties of Barley.

Barley may be divided into two sorts, fall and spring; to which may be added a bastard variety, called bear or bigg, which affords similar nutriment or substance, though of inferior quality. The spring is cultivated like oats; the fall, like fall wheat. Early barley, under various names, was formerly sown in Britain upon lands that had been previously summer-fallowed, or were in high condition.

The most proper seed season for spring barley is any time in March or April, though we have seen good crops produced, the seed of which was sown at a much later period.

To prepare the Ground.

Barley is chiefly taken after turnips, sometimes after peas and beans, but rarely by good farmers either after wheat or oats, unless under special circumstances. When sown after turnips it is generally taken with one furrow, which is given as fast as the turnips are consumed, the ground thus receiving much benefit from the spring frosts. But often two or more furrows are necessary for the fields last consumed, because when a spring drought sets in the surface from being poached by the removal or consumption of the crop, gets so hardened as to render a greater quantity of ploughing, harrowing and rolling necessary than would otherwise be called for. When sown after beans and peas, one winter and one spring ploughing are usually bestowed; but when after wheat or oats, three ploughings are necessary, so that the ground may be put in proper condition. These operations are very ticklish in a wet and backward season, and rarely in that case is the grower paid for the expense of his labor. Where land is in such a situation as to require three ploughings before it can be seeded with barley, it is better to summer-fallow it at once than to run the risks which seldom fail to accompany a quantity of spring labor. If the weather be dry, moisture is lost during the different processes, and an imperfect braird necessarily follows; if it be wet, the benefit of ploughing is lost, and all the evils of a wet seed time are sustained by the future crop.

Quantity of Seed.

The quantity sown is different in different cases, according to the quality of the soil and other circumstances. Upon very rich lands eight pecks per acre are sometimes sown; twelve is very common, and upon poor land more is sometimes given.

By good judges a quantity of seed is sown sufficient to insure a full crop, without depending on its sending out offsets; indeed, where that is done few offsets are produced, the crop grows and ripens equally, and the grain is uniformly good.

M'Curtney's Invention for Hummelling Barley.

This invention is extremely simple, and the cost small. It is a bit of notched stick or bar, lined on one side with a thin plate of iron, and just the length of the rollers, fixed by a screw-bolt at each end to the inside of the cover of the drum, about the middle of it, so that the edge of the said notched stick is about one-eighth of an inch from the arms of the drum as it goes round. Two minutes are sufficient to put it on, when its operation is wanted, which is when putting through the second time, and it is easily taken off. It rubs off the awns or spikes to admiration, and by putting the grain another time through the mill, it will rub the husk off the ends of the pickle so entirely, that it is unnecessary to sow it afterwards.

To harvest Barley.

More care is required in the harvesting of barley than of any of the other white crops, even in the best of seasons; and in bad years it is often found very difficult to save it. Owing to the brittleness of the straw after it has reached a certain period, it must be cut down, as when it is suffered to stand longer much loss is sustained by the breaking of the heads. On that account it is cut at a time when the grain is soft, and the straw retains a great proportion of its natural juices, consequently requires a long time in the field before either the grain is hardened or the straw sufficiently dry. When put into the stack too soon it is apt to heat, and much loss is frequently sustained. It is a custom with many farmers to have an opening in the middle of their barley stacks, from top to bottom. This opening is generally made by placing a large bundle of straw in the centre of the stack when the building commences, and in proportion as it rises, the straw is drawn upwards, leaving a hollow behind, which, if one or two openings are left in the side of the stack near the bottom, insures so complete a circulation of air as not only to prevent heating, but to preserve the grain from becoming musty.

Varieties of Oats.

Of this grain the varieties are more numerous than of any other of the culmiferous tribe. Those varieties consist of what is called the common oat, the Angus oat, which is considered as an improved variety of the other, the Poland oat, the Friesland oat, the red oat, the dun oat, the Tartar or Siberian oat, and the potato oat. The Poland and potato varieties are best adapted to rich soils; the red oat for late climates; and the other varieties for the generality of soils of which the British isles are composed. The Tartar or Siberian kind, though very hardy and prolific, is much out of use, being of a coarse substance, and unproductive of meal. The dun oat has never been much cultivated, and the use of Poland and Friesland is now much circumscribed, since potato oats were introduced; the latter being considered, by the most discerning agriculturists, as of superior value in every respect where the soil is rich and properly cultivated.

To prepare the Ground.

Oats are chiefly sown after grass; sometimes upon land not rich enough for wheat, that has been previously summer-fallowed, or has carried turnips; often after barley, and rarely after wheat, unless cross-cropping, from particular circumstances, becomes a necessary evil. One ploughing is generally given to the grass lands, usually in the month of January, so that the benefit of frost may be gained, and the land sufficiently mellowed for receiving the harrow. In some cases a spring furrow is given, when oats succeed wheat or barley, especially when grass seeds are to accompany the crop. The best oats, both in quantity and quality, are always those which succeed grass; indeed, no kind of grain seems better qualified by nature for foraging upon grass land than oats; as a full crop is usually obtained in the first instance, and the land left in good order for succeeding crops.

Quantity of Seed.

From twelve to eighteen pecks of seed are generally allowed to the acre of ground, according to the richness of the soil and the variety that is cultivated. Here it may be remarked that land sown with potato oats requires much less seed, in point of measure, than when any of the other sorts are used; because potato oats both tiller well, much better than Poland, and have not an awn or tail like the ordinary varieties. On that account, a measure contains many more seeds of them than of any other kind. If land is equally well cultivated, there is little doubt but that the like quantity of seed given when barley is cultivated, may be safely trusted to when potato oats are to be raised.

To harvest Oats.

Oats are a hardy grain, and rarely get much damage when under the harvest process, except from high winds or from shedding, when opened out after being thoroughly wetted. The early varieties are much more liable to these losses than the late ones, because the grain parts more easily from the straw, an evil to which the best of grain is at all times subject. Early oats, however, may be cut a little quick, which, to a certain extent, lessens the danger to which they are exposed from high winds; and if the sheaves be made small the danger from shedding after rains is considerably lessened, because they are thus sooner ready for the stack. Under every management, however, a greater quantity of early oats will be lost during the harvest process than of late ones; because the latter adhere firmly to the straw, and consequently do not drop, so easily as the former.

To cultivate Rye.

Rye ought never to be sown upon wet soils, nor even upon sandy soils where the subsoil is of a retentive nature. Upon downs, links, and all soft lands which have received manure, this grain thrives in perfection, and, if once covered in, will stand a drought afterwards that would consume any other of the culmiferous tribe. The several processes may be regarded as nearly the same with those recommended for wheat, with the single exception of pickling, which rye does not require. Rye may be sown either in winter or spring, though the winter-seeded fields are generally bulkiest and most productive. It may succeed either summer fallow, clover or turnips; even after oats good crops have been raised, and where such crops are raised the land will always be found in good condition.

To cultivate Beans.

Beans naturally succeed a culmiferous crop, and we believe it is not of much importance which of the varieties is followed, provided the ground be in decent order, and not worn out by the previous crop. The furrow ought to be given early in winter, and as deep as possible, that the earth may be sufficiently loosened, and room afforded for the roots of the plant to search for the requisite nourishment. The first furrow is usually given across the field, which is the best method when only one spring furrow is intended; but as it is now ascertained that two spring furrows are highly advantageous, the one in winter ought to be given in length, which lays the ground in a better situation for resisting the rains, and renders it sooner dry in spring than can be the case when ploughed across. On the supposition that three furrows are to be given, one in winter and two in spring, the following is the most eligible preparation:

Approved Modes of Drilling.

The land being ploughed in length as early in winter as is practicable, and the gaw and headland furrows sufficiently digged out, take the second furrow across the first as soon as the ground is dry enough in spring to undergo the operation; water-furrow it immediately, and dig again the gaw and headland furrows, otherwise the benefit of the second furrow may be lost. This being done, leave the field for some days, till it is sufficiently dry, when a cast of the harrows becomes necessary, so that the surface may be levelled. Then enter with the ploughs and form the drills, which are generally made up with an interval of twenty-seven inches. In the hollow of this interval deposit the seed by a drill-barrow, and reverse or slit out the drills to cover the seed, which finishes the process for the time. In ten or twelve days afterwards, according to the state of the weather, cross-harrow the drills, thereby levelling the field for the hoeing process. Water-furrow the whole in a neat manner, and spade and shovel the gaw and the headland furrows, which concludes the whole process.

This is the most approved way of drilling beans. The next best is to give only one spring furrow, and to run the drill-barrow after every third plough, in which way the intervals are nearly of the same extent as already mentioned. Harrowing is afterwards required before the young plants reach the surface, and water-furrowing, etc., as above described.

Dung is often given to beans, especially when they succeed wheat which has not received manure. The best way is to apply the dung on the stubble before the winter furrow is given, which greatly facilitates the after process. Used in this way, a fore stock must be in hand; but where the farmer is not so well provided spring dunging becomes necessary, though evidently of less advantage. At that season it may either be put into the drills before the seed is sown or spread upon the surface and ploughed down, according to the nature of the drilling process which is meant to be adopted. Land dunged to beans, if duly hoed, is always in high order for carrying a crop of wheat in succession. Perhaps better wheat, both in respect to quantity and quality, may be cultivated in this way than in any other mode of sowing.

Drilling Machines.

Different machines have been invented for drilling beans, but the most common and handy is one of the narrow form. This hand drill is pushed forward by a man or woman, and will, according as the brush or director is lowered or heightened, sow thicker or thinner, as may be expedient and necessary. Another machine, drawn by a horse, and sowing three drills at a time, has been constructed, and upon flat lands will certainly distribute the seed with the most minute exactness. Upon unequal fields, and even on those laid out in high ridges, the use of this machine is attended with a degree of inconvenience sufficient to balance its advantages. The hand-drill, therefore, in all probability, will be retained for general use, though the other is capable of performing the work with minuter regularity.

Quantity of Seed.

Less than four bushels ought not to be hazarded if a full crop is expected. We seldom have seen thin beans turn out well, unless the soil is particularly rich; nay, unless the rows close, weeds will get away after the cleaning process is finished, thereby disappointing the object of drilling and rendering the system of little avail towards keeping the ground in good condition.

Hoeing Process.

Beans are cleaned in various ways: 1st. By the hand-hoe. 2d. By the scraper, or Dutch hoe. 3d. By a plough of small dimensions, but constructed upon the principles of the approved swing plough. Ploughs with double mould-boards are likewise used to earth them up, and with all good managers the weeds in the drills which cannot be touched by the hoe are pulled out by the hand; otherwise no field can be considered as duly cleaned.

In treating of the cleaning process we shall confine ourselves to the one most suited to the generality of bean soils. About ten or twelve days after the young plants have appeared above the surface, enter with the scraper, and loosen any weeds that may have vegetated. At this time the wings or cutters of the implement ought to be particularly sharp, so that the scraper may not run too deep and throw the earth upon the plants.

In about ten days after the ground is scraped, according to the state of the weather, and other circumstances, use the small swing plough to lay the earth away from the sides of the rows, and in doing so go as near to the plants as possible, taking care at the same time not to loosen their roots. If any weeds stand in the rows pull them out with the hand, afterwards earth-up the plants with the small swing plough, or run the scraper in the intervals, as may seem expedient.

To manage the Harvest.

Before beans are cut the grain ought to be tolerably well ripened, otherwise the quality is impaired, whilst a long time is required to put the straw in such a condition as to be preserved in the stack. In an early harvest, or where the crop is not weighty, it is an easy matter to get beans sufficiently ripened: but, in a late harvest, and in every one where the crop takes on a second growth, it is scarcely practicable to get them thoroughly ripened for the sickle. Under these circumstances it is unnecessary to let beans stand uncut after the end of September or the first of October, because any benefit that can be gained afterwards is not to be compared with the disadvantages that accompany a late wheat seed time. Beans are usually cut with the sickle and tied in sheaves, either with straw ropes or with ropes made from peas sown along with them. It is proper to let the sheaves lie untied several days, so that the winding process may be hastened, and, when tied, to set them up on end, in order that full benefit from air may be obtained and the grain kept off the ground. In building bean stacks it is a useful measure for preserving both grain and straw from injury, to keep an opening in the centre, and to convey air from the extremity by a hole or funnel. Beans, on the whole, are a troublesome crop to the farmer, though of great utility in other respects. Without them heavy soils can scarcely be managed with advantage, unless summer fallow is resorted to once in four years, but by the aid derived from drilled beans summer fallow may be avoided for eight years, whilst the ground at that period will be found in equal, if not superior condition.

To cultivate Peas.

Peas are partially sown with beans to great advantage, and when cultivated in this way the same system of preparation, etc., described under the head of beans is to be adopted. Indeed, upon many soils not deep enough for beans, a mixture of peas to the extent of one-third of the seed sown proves highly advantageous. The beans serve as props to the peas, and the latter being thus kept off the ground and furnished with air and other atmospheric nutriment, blossom and pod with much greater effect than when sown according to the broadcast system.

Peas agree well with lime and other analogous stimulants, and can hardly be reaped in perfection where these are wanting. The varieties cultivated are numerous, but those adapted to field culture may be divided into two kinds, namely, early and late, though these branch out again into several varieties. We have white peas both early and late, and likewise gray peas, possessed of similar properties. The nomenclature is entirely arbitrary, and therefore not to be illustrated. As a general rule the best seed time for late peas is in the early spring, though early ones, such as the Extra Early and Blue Imperial pea, may be sown successfully later in the season.

Peas ought to be sown tolerably thick, so that the ground may be covered as early as possible.

To cultivate Tares.

The tare is a plant of a hardy growth, and when sown upon rich land will return a large supply of green fodder for the consumption of horses or for fattening cattle. When intended for this use, the seed ought to be sown tolerably thick, perhaps to the extent of four bushels per acre, though when intended to stand for seed a less quantity is required, because otherwise the thickness of the crop will prevent the plants from blossoming and podding in a sufficient way. When meant for seed early sowing ought to be studied, otherwise the return will be imperfect; but when for green food any time betwixt the first of April and the latter end of May will answer well, provided crops in succession from the first to the last mentioned period be regularly cultivated. Instances are not wanting of a full crop being obtained even when the seed was sown so late as the middle of June, though sowing so late is a practice not to be recommended. After the seed is sown and the land carefully harrowed, a light roller ought to be drawn across, so that the surface may be smoothed, and the scythe permitted to work without interruption. It is proper also to guard the field for several days against the depredations of pigeons, who are remarkably fond of tares, and will pick up a great part of the seed unless constantly watched.

Horses thrive very well upon tares, even better than they do upon clover and rye-grass; and the same remark is applicable to fattening cattle, who feed faster upon this article of green fodder than upon any kind of grass or esculent with which we are acquainted. Danger often arises from their eating too many, especially when podded; as colics and other stomach disorders are apt to be produced by the excessive loads which they devour.

Potatoes.

Potatoes, as an article of human food, are, next to wheat, of the greatest importance in the eye of a political economist. From no other crop that can be cultivated will the public derive so much food as from this valuable esculent; and it admits of demonstration that an acre of potatoes will feed double the number of people that can be fed from an acre of wheat. Very good varieties are the Gleason, Calico, and Early Goodrich.

To prepare the Ground.

To reduce the ground till it is completely free from root-weeds, may be considered as a desideratum in potato husbandry; though in many seasons these operations cannot be perfectly executed, without losing the proper time for planting, which never ought to be beyond the first of May, if circumstances do not absolutely interdict it. Three ploughings, with frequent harrowings and rollings, are necessary in most cases before the land is in suitable condition. When this is accomplished form the drills as if they were for turnips; cart the manure, which ought not to be sparingly applied, plant the seed above the manure, reverse the drills for covering it and the seed, then harrow the drills in length, which completes the preparation and seed process.

Quantity of Seed.

It is not advantageous to cut the seed into small slips, for the strength of the stem at the outset depends in direct proportion upon the vigor and power of the seed-plant. The seed-plant, therefore, ought to be large, rarely smaller than the fourth-part of the potato; and if the seed is of small size, one-half of the potato may be profitably used. At all events, rather err in giving over large seed than in making it too small; because, by the first error, no great loss can ever be sustained; whereas, by the other, a feeble and late crop may be the consequence. When the seed is properly cut, it requires from ten to twelve hundredweight of potatoes to plant an acre of ground, where the rows are twenty-seven inches apart; but this quantity depends greatly upon the size of the potatoes used; if they are large, a greater weight may be required, but the extra quantity will be abundantly repaid by the superiority of crop which large seed usually produces.

Advantageous Method of raising them.

The earth should be dug twelve inches deep, if the soil will allow it; after this, a hole should be opened about six inches deep, and horse-dung or long litter should be put therein, about three inches thick; this hole should not be more than twelve inches in diameter. Upon this dung or litter a potato should be planted whole, upon which a little more dung should be shaken, and then the earth should be put thereon. In like manner the whole plot of ground must be planted, taking care that the potatoes be at least sixteen inches apart. When the young shoots make their appearance they should have fresh mould drawn around them with a hoe; and if the tender shoots are covered, it will prevent the frost from injuring them; they should again be earthed when the shoots make a second appearance, but not covered, as in all probability the season will be less severe.

A plentiful supply of mould should be given them, and the person who performs this business should never tread upon the plant, or the hillock that is raised round it, as the lighter the earth is, the more room the potato will have to expand.

A gentleman obtained from a single root, thus planted, very nearly forty pounds weight of large potatoes; and from almost every other root upon the same plot of ground from fifteen to twenty pounds weight; and, except the soil be stony or gravelly, ten pounds or half a peck of potatoes may generally be obtained from each root by pursuing the foregoing method.

But note—cuttings or small sets will not do for this purpose.

Mode of Taking up and Storing the Crop.

Potatoes are generally dug up with a three-prong grape or fork, but at other times, when the weather is dry, the plough is used, which is the most expeditious implement. After gathering the interval, the furrow taken by the plough is broken and separated, in which way the crop may be more completely gathered than when taken up by the grape. The potatoes are then stored up for winter and spring use; and as it is of importance to keep them as long through summer as possible, every endeavor ought to be made to preserve them from frost, and from sprouting in the spring months. The former is accomplished by covering them well with straw when lodged in a house, and by a thick coat of earth when deposited in a pit, and the latter, by picking them carefully at different times, when they begin to sprout, drying them sufficiently by exposure to the sun, or by a gentle toast of a kiln.

Method of Cultivating Potatoes in Ireland.

The drill system, in the cultivation of potatoes in Ireland, is particularly recommended by Lord Farnham, in a letter to Sir John Sinclair. The small farmers and laborers plant them in lazy-beds, eight feet wide. This mode is practised on account of the want of necessary implements for practising the drill system, together with a want of horses for the same purpose. They are cut into sets, three from a large potato; and each set to contain at least one eye. The sets are planted at the distance of seven inches asunder, six and a quarter cwt. are considered sufficient seed for an English acre. Lord Farnham recommends rotten dung in preference to any fresh dung. If not to be procured, horse-dung, hot from the dunghill. In any soil he would recommend the dung below the seed.

When the potatoes are vegetated ten inches above the surface, the scuffler must be introduced, and cast the mould from the potato. If any weeds are found in the drills they must be hand-hoed; in three days afterwards they must be moulded up by the double-breasted plough, as high as the neck of the potato. This mode must be practised twice, or in some cases three times, particularly if the land is foul. I do not (says Lord Farnham) consider any mode so good as the drill system.

General Observations.

To prepare for the drill system either oat or wheat stubble, it should be ploughed in October or the beginning of November; to be ploughed deep and laid up for winter dry. In March let it be harrowed, and give it three clean earths. Be very particular to eradicate the couch grass. The drills to be three feet asunder; drill deep the first time that there is room in the bottom of the furrow to contain the dung. The best time to begin planting the potatoes is about the latter end of April by this system. It is as good a preparation for wheat as the best fallows.

Three feet and a half for drills are preferable to four feet. Mr. Curwen prefers four feet and a half. He says the produce is immense. Potatoes ought to be cut at least from two to three weeks before being planted; and if planted very early whole potatoes are preferable to cut ones, and dung under and over. Some agriculturists lately pay much attention to raising seedling potatoes, with the hope of renewing the vigor of the plant.

To produce early Potatoes in great Quantity.

Early potatoes may be produced in great quantity by resetting the plants, after taking off the ripe and large ones. A gentleman at Dumfries has replanted them six different times in one season, without any additional manure; and, instead of falling off in quantity, he gets a larger crop of ripe ones at every raising than the former ones. His plants have still on them three distinct crops, and he supposes they may still continue to vegetate and germinate until they are stopped by the frost. By this means he has a new crop every eight days, and has had so for a length of time.

To grow Potatoes constantly on the same piece of Ground.

Let the cuttings be made from the finest potatoes instead of the smallest and worst, usually employed for the purpose; and it will be found, contrary to what is supposed by farmers, that they will not degenerate. The same will happen with respect to the seeds of the watery squash, early peas, and several other kinds of vegetables.

To preserve Potatoes from Frost.

This is best done by filling completely the place where they are deposited, whether it be a house or a pit, and allowing the place to remain shut during the winter. But this cannot be done easily with a potato-house, as it cannot be completely packed or filled like a pit. Besides, some potatoes are generally wanted daily, and thus air is admitted and a greater vacuity constantly making, both which are very likely to be the means of proving injurious or destructive to what potatoes may be in the house when a severe frost sets in. There is no such thing in nature as a vacuum; therefore, if a place is not filled with some substance or other, it will be filled with air. For this reason, pits are better for preserving potatoes from frost than a house, because a pit can be more effectually filled: and, by opening a pit when potatoes are wanted, and removing the whole into some part of a house, and still keeping over them a covering of straw or turf, the potatoes are kept close. A potato-house, however, is very useful, and what every farmer ought to have, as in this house he may still keep a small quantity of his crop for daily use by emptying a pit occasionally, and keeping them always well covered with straw, as has been already mentioned.

The potato-house ought to be well plastered with clay, and perfectly dry before using it.

Potato-pits should be made upon ground that has a southern exposure, a deep soil, and declining to a considerable distance from the pit. In a deep soil the pits can be made sufficiently deep before reaching any cold bottom, and the declivity carries away water. When the pits have been fully finished and covered, a sod should be cut out all the way round the potatoes, and the cut continued a little way as the descent points out. A pit of about ten feet deep, six wide and ten long, will hold from four to six cart loads of potatoes. The covering should consist of straw, fern, rushes, etc. next the potato, then the whole of the earth dug out should be thrown upon the heap; and, last of all, a covering of earth, if done in the best way. This covering will be about two feet thick.

Another Method.

The best and easiest way of preserving potatoes is for the farmer to drive all his potatoes home, and to lay them upon dry ground without breaking the surface, and as near the stables as possible, putting them in heaps of about three or four carts, then covering them with straw, and above that with turf, where it can be commanded, or with a neat thatching of straw. Then let a quantity of stable dung, of the roughest kind and the newest, be laid upon each heap, to remain during the winter, but which must be removed in the spring. As the weather appears severe, the quantity of dung may be increased at pleasure. If this practice were adopted few or no potatoes would be penetrated by the frost, as none would be in hazard except one pit, or part of it, when it was removing or placed in the potato-house during the winter season.

To remove Frost from Potatoes.

The weather which soonest injures and destroys potatoes, is when the atmosphere is depressed with cold to such a degree that it congeals water; then potatoes, unless covered, will be frosted; and the cover proper to preserve them ought to be proportioned to the intenseness of the weather.

Potatoes, when slightly frosted, so as to have acquired a slight sweet taste only, are often found quite wet. When they are in this state, in order to recover them, and bring them to a proper taste, the whole quantity infected should be turned over, and a quantity of mill-seeds thrown among them as they are turned over; this both extracts and absorbs the injured moisture from the body of the potatoes infected. But there is still a more powerful remedy than simply mixing them with mill-seeds, and that is a small quantity of slaked lime, perfectly dry, mixed among the seeds to be used, which has a very wonderful effect in recovering potatoes that have been considerably injured by frost.

When frosted potatoes are to be used, either at the table, or given to horses, black cattle or swine, plunging them in cold water, about half a day before using them, is of great advantage; and if put into running water so much the better, as it has been proved to be more powerful in extracting the frost, on account of its alterative quality and superior purity.

Another Method.

Another way of removing frost from potatoes, when they are to be prepared for the table, is to strip them of their skins, and, if large, to cut them into two or more pieces; then to plunge them into cold water for a considerable time, with a handful of salt in the water; and, when put on to be boiled, put as much salt into the water as possible, not to make them too salt when boiled.

This is a powerful way of making the potato throw off the bad taste and spoiled quality lodged in its substance.

When prepared for horses, black cattle, and swine:—Salt put among the potatoes and boiled together, will destroy any injurious quality which frost has lodged or brought on. Chaff or oats bruised in a mill, boiled with the frosted potatoes, when designed for horses or cattle, tend to destroy the bad effects of the frost.

Uses to which Frosted Potatoes may be beneficially applied.

When potatoes have acquired a disagreeable taste by means of frost, they will make good and wholesome bread by boiling them, as has been mentioned, with salt, mashing or bruising them small, then kneading them together with oatmeal. Not less than two-thirds should consist of meal, which will destroy the sweet taste, and the dry and generous quality of the meal will effectually correct and destroy anything noxious to the injured roots.

Horses, swine, dogs, etc., may all be fed with potatoes, though frosted, by boiling them and mixing them with oats coarsely ground, or with oat-meal, always adding a good quantity of salt in the mixture. Poultry also may be fed with potatoes very much frosted, if mixed with oat-meal in about equal proportions, without salt, as this species of animal cannot admit of it.

Further uses of Frosted Potatoes.

Potatoes frosted, when three times distilled, produce a spirit from hydrometer proof to ten per cent. over proof; therefore a principal purpose and use to which they may be turned, is the making of alcohol, more particularly as that article is useful for many purposes where strength is its principal recommendation. The ordinary strength that spirits are run preparatory to converting them into alcohol, is from forty to fifty per cent. over proof, which, re-distilled from calcined carbonate of potash, will produce alcohol at 825, water being 1000.

When potatoes are frosted to such a degree as to be useless for food from their sweet taste, they are very useful to weavers in dressing their yarn, and particularly cotton. They are prepared for this purpose by boiling them well, then mash or beat them small; then put them into a vessel, adding a little barm, drippings of ale or porter barrels, allowing them to stand two or three months to ferment.

Shoemakers may use it also; only as their paste requires more solidity and greater strength, flour is generally mixed along with the fermented potatoes in about equal proportions.

Bookbinders also may use this paste, alum being mixed to assist the strength of the composition. And it may be beneficially used by paper stainers and upholsterers, when made up with a mixture of flour and alum.

When potatoes are so penetrated with frost that they have become quite soft, they are useless for man or beast, but make excellent manure for light, sharp soils, and for this purpose are worth about one-fifth or sixth of their original value. In places where it is a great object to get straw turned into dung, the value of the frosted potato is still greater, as it assists the farmer in that operation.

To make Starch from Frosted Potatoes.

Potatoes much frosted will make very good starch, though it is a shade darker in color. All coarse clothes requiring to be stiffened, where whiteness is no object, may be done with starch made from potatoes greatly penetrated with frost. The best method of making potatoes into starch is to grate them down into water, then to take out all the refuse with the hand, and next to strain the whole of the water in which the potatoes have been grated through a thin cloth, rather coarse, or fine sieve, and afterwards frequently putting on and pouring off water until it comes clear from the starch, which is always allowed to settle or fall to the bottom of the vessel in which the operation is performed. An experiment was tried with a few potatoes that were put out to frost. They were grated down and made into starch powder. The produce of the fresh potato weighed ·876 grains, while that of the frosted was only 412, being less than half the quantity.

The refuse of the potato, when taken from the sieve, possesses the property of cleansing woollen cloths without hurting their colors, and the water decanted from the starch powder is excellent for cleansing silks without the smallest injury to their color. In making hair-powder it has long been used, and is therefore well known.

Turnips.

The benefits derived from turnip husbandry are of great magnitude; light soils are cultivated with profit and facility; abundance of food is provided for man and beast; the earth is turned to the uses for which it is physically calculated, and by being suitably cleaned with this preparatory crop, a bed is provided for grass seeds, wherein they flourish and prosper with greater vigor than after any other preparation.

To prepare the Ground.

The first ploughing is given immediately after harvest, or as soon as the wheat seed is finished, either in length or across the field, as circumstances may seem to require. In this state the ground remains till the oat seed is finished, when a second ploughing is given to it, usually in a contrary direction to the first. It is then repeatedly harrowed, often rolled between the harrowings, and every particle of root-weeds carefully picked off with the hand; a third ploughing is then bestowed, and the other operations are repeated. In this stage, if the ground has not been very foul, the seed process generally commences, but often a fourth ploughing, sometimes a fifth is necessary before the ground is sufficiently clean. Less labor, however, is necessary now than in former times, when a more regular mode of cropping was commonly followed.

To sow the Seed.

The next part of the process is the sowing of the seed; this may be performed by drilling machines of different sizes and constructions, though all acting on the same principle. A machine drawn by a horse in a pair of shafts, sows two drills at a time and answers extremely well, where the ground is flat, and the drills properly made up. The weight of the machine insures a regularity of sowing hardly to be gained by those of a different size and construction. From two to three pounds of seed are sown upon the acre, though the smallest of these quantities will give many more plants in ordinary seasons than are necessary; but as the seed is not an expensive article the greater part of farmers incline to sow thick, which both provides against the danger of part of the seed perishing, and gives the young plants an advantage at the outset.

Turnips are sown from the beginning to the end of June; but the second and third weeks of the month are, by judicious farmers, accounted the most proper time. Some people have sown as early as May, and with advantage; but these early fields are apt to run to seed before winter, especially if the autumn be favorable to vegetation. As a general rule it may be laid down that the earliest sowings should be on the latest soils; plants on such soils are often long before they make any great progress, and, in the end, may be far behind those in other situations, which were much later sown. The turnip plant, indeed, does not thrive rapidly till its roots reach the dung, and the previous nourishment afforded them is often so scanty as to stunt them altogether before they get so far.

Cleaning Process.

The first thing to be done in this process is to run a horse-hoe, called a scraper, along the intervals, keeping at such a distance from the young plants that they shall not be injured; this operation destroys all the annual weeds which have sprung up, and leaves the plants standing in regular stripes or rows. The hand-hoeing then commences, by which the turnips are all singled out, at a distance of from eight to twelve inches, and the redundant ones drawn into the spaces between the rows. The singling out of the young plants is an operation of great importance, for an error committed in this process can hardly be afterwards rectified. Boys and girls are always employed as hoers; but a steady and trusty man-servant is usually set over them to see that the work is properly executed.

In eight or ten days, or such a length of time as circumstances may require, a horse-hoe of a different construction from the scraper is used. This, in fact, is generally a small plough, of the same kind with that commonly wrought, but of smaller dimensions. By this implement, the earth is pared away from the sides of the drills, and a sort of new ridge formed in the middle of the former interval. The hand-hoers are again set to work, and every weed and superfluous turnip is cut up; afterwards the horse-hoe is employed to separate the earth, which it formerly threw into the furrows, and lay it back to the sides of the drills. On dry lands this is done by the scraper, but where the least tendency to moisture prevails, the small plough is used, in order that the furrows may be perfectly cleaned out. This latter mode, indeed, is very generally practised.

To cultivate the Yellow Turnip.

This variety, as now cultivated in the field, is quite different from the yellow garden turnip, being larger in size, containing more juice, or nutritive substance, much easier cultivated, and preserving its power till the middle of May, when the grass-season may be expected. Upon ordinary soils it is superior to ruta baga, because it will grow to a considerable weight, where the other would be stunted or starved; and it stands the frost equally well. No farmer who keeps stock to any extent should be without it. The mode of culture required is in every respect similar to what is stated concerning common turnips, with these exceptions, that earlier sowing is necessary, and that the plants need not be set out so wide as they do not swell to such a size.

Ruta Baga or Swedish Turnip.

The process of management is precisely the same with that of turnips, with this addition, that more dung is required, and that seed-time ought to be three or four weeks earlier. Rich soil, however, is required for this article; for it will not grow to any size worthwhile, on soils of middling quality, whatever quality of dung may be required.

Ruta baga is of great advantage in the feeding of horses, either when given raw or boiled, or with broken corn. If a sufficient quality were cultivated a great deal of grain might be saved, while the health and condition of the working stock would be greatly invigorated and augmented. An evening feed of this nutritious article would be of incalculable benefit; most horses are fond even of the common turnip in a raw state; and it is a subject well worthy of every farmer's attention, whether it would not be for his interest to raise these esculents in such a quantity as to serve them during the long period when grass cannot be obtained. That the health of the animals would thereby be benefited is unquestionable; and the saving of grain would greatly exceed the trouble occasioned by furnishing a daily supply of these roots.

To destroy the Fly on Turnips.

Lime sown by the hand, or distributed by a machine, is an infallible protection to turnips against the ravages of the fly. It should be applied as soon as the turnips come up, and in the same daily rotation in which they were sown. The lime should be slaked immediately before it is used; if the air be not sufficiently moist to render that operation unnecessary.

Another Method. — Let the farmer carefully watch his turnips as they come up, and whenever the fly makes its appearance, take a certain quantity of brimstone, about two and a half or three pounds to an acre; put this into a kettle, and melt it in the turnip-field, in a situation the most eligible for the wind to carry the fume over the ground; then take any combustible matter calculated to make a considerable smoke, which, being dipped in the liquid brimstone, must be strewn all over the field in a state of ignition, and so close together that the fumes of the burning matter may completely cover every part of the ground. The decoction of the bitter almond is more fatal to the lives of insects and worms than almost any other vegetable or mineral poison. It is made by infusing the bitter almond powder (the ground cakes that remain after expressing the oil) in warm water for twenty-four hours; twenty-eight pounds will make forty gallons, a sufficient quantity for a large garden.

Remedy against the Bite of the Turnip Fly.

It is upon the principle of creating an offensive smell that turnip seed is recommended to be steeped in train oil before it is sown. This has been found to be a perfect security against the bite of the turnip fly.

To prevent the Fly in Turnips.

Sow good and fresh seed in well-manured and well-prepared ground.

To prevent the increase of Pismires in Grass Lands newly laid down.

Make a strong decoction of walnut-tree leaves, and after opening several of the pismire's sandy habitations, pour upon them a quantity of the liquor, just sufficient to fill the hollow of each heap; after the middle has been scooped, throw in the contents from the sides, and press down the whole mass with the foot, till it becomes level with the rest of the field. This, if not found effectual at first, must be repeated a second or a third time, when they will infallibly be destroyed.

To preserve Growing Crops from the Devastation of Vermin.

The good effects of elder in preserving plants from insects and flies are experienced in the following cases:—

1. For preventing cabbages and cauliflower plants from being devoured and damaged by caterpillars.
2. For preventing blights, and their effects on fruit trees.
3. For preserving corn from yellow flies and other insects.
4. For securing turnips from the ravages of flies.

The dwarf elder appears to exhale a much more fetid smell than the common elder, and therefore should be preferred.

To Check the Ravages of the Turnip Fly.

Suppose that the farmer had no objection to bestow five pounds of seed per acre, in order to secure his crop of turnips. If he sows broad cast, let him medicate one half of the seed, in the manner to be afterwards explained, leaving the other half unprepared. The latter may be sown one day, and the medicated a day or two after, so as to give a start to the other. The medicated will, in that case, escape from the attacks of the fly or beetle. If the slug, however, does appear, rolling in the night is necessary. If the farmer drills his turnips after the land is prepared for the drill, two and a half pounds of the unmedicated seed should be sown broadcast, and a day or two afterwards the medicated seed sown in the drills. In this way a crop may be obtained, at least by the industrious farmer who does not grudge a little trouble to secure a good one. He will find that the plants sown broadcast will give full employment to the fly, till the less savory plants in the drill pass the moment of danger. As to preparing or medicating the seed, sulphur is so obnoxious to the whole insect tribe, and at the same time so favorable to vegetation, that it seems entitled to a preference. The turnip seed may be a little damped, and then mixed with the flour of sulphur, at the rate of two ounces of sulphur to one pound of seed; or let the seed be steeped in a liquor formed by boiling three parts of lime to one of sulphur, and 100 parts of water. This steep is much approved of for all such purposes. It is not improbable that the same liquid in which wheat is commonly pickled would prove a preservative against the fly. It may be proper to add, that when the season is very dry, it has been found a most useful practice to moisten the dung well before it is inserted into the drill, to spread the dung very rapidly in the rows, and instantly to sow, at the rate of four pounds of turnip seed per acre, upon the dung. The ground should then be gathered up into bouts twenty-seven inches wide, by the going and returning of the plough.

TO DESTROY WEEDS AND INSECTS.

The seeds are thus put in contact with the wet dung. Many perish, but a sufficient number escape to produce a good crop. In this case, the sowing any unmedicated seed broadcast may be dispensed with.

To cultivate San-foin.

Chalky loams and gravelly soils on a calcareous bottom, are most proper for this grass. It is more adapted to hay than pasture, and much heavier crops of this grass are obtained from thin lands than when clover is sown. San-foin is a hardy kind of grass, well worth the attention of cultivators in upland districts where the soil is obdurate and shallow, and where clover and rye-grass can with difficulty be raised to such a height as to stand the scythe. When sown, fresh seed ought constantly to be used, as the vegetation of old seed cannot be depended upon. Four bushels may be used for an acre, and great care ought to be taken to cover the seed well, and to put it deeper into the ground than the seeds of other grasses.

To preserve Grain from Vermin.

To preserve rye and secure it from insects and rats, nothing more is necessary than not to winnow it after it is threshed, and to stow it in the granaries mixed with the chaff. In this state it has been kept for more than three years, without experiencing the smallest alteration, and even without the necessity of being turned to preserve it from humidity and fermentation. Rats and mice may be prevented from entering the barn by putting some wild vine or hedge plants upon the heaps; the smell of this wood is so offensive to these animals that they will not approach it.

To prevent the Destruction of Corn by Insects.

In laying the floors of a granary let Italian poplars be made use of for the timber. Many experiments show that granaries, after laying down this flooring, will no longer be infested with weevils, etc.

To destroy Slugs upon Wheat.

Collect a number of lean ducks, keep them all day without food, and turn them into the fields towards evening; each duck would devour the slugs much faster than a man could collect them, and they would soon get very fat for market.

To prevent the Ravages of Mice in Corn Stacks.

The following simple remedy against the depredations of mice in corn stacks, has lately been recommended for its undoubted efficacy. Sprinkle from four to six bushels of dry white sand upon the root of the stack before the thatch is put on. The sand is no detriment to the corn, and stacks thus dressed have remained without injury. So very effective is the remedy, that nests of dead young mice have been found where the sand has been used, but not a live mouse could be seen.

To clear Barns and Out-houses from Mites and Weevils.

The following method is practised in Germany, for granaries infested with mites and weevils. Let the walls and rafters, above and below, of such granaries be covered completely with quick-lime slaked in water, in which trefoil, wormwood, and hyssop have been boiled. This composition should be applied as hot as possible. A farmer who had the granaries empty in June last, collected quantities of the largest sized ants in sacks, and scattered them about the places infested with weevils. The ants immediately fell upon and devoured them all.

To destroy Slugs on Land.

Procure some fresh lime, and after throwing as much water upon it as will reduce it to a powder, sow the lime in a hot state upon the land that is overrun with the vermin, at the rate of about twelve bushels to the acre. The lime should be sown towards the wind, and falling upon them in a fermented state, it will instantly kill them.

Usefulness of the Hedgehog.

This little animal, the object of persecution, not only to little boys but to the farmer and gamekeeper, on account of its supposed mischievous propensities, is in fact one which the agriculturist should endeavor to preserve, as it is the most effectual destroyer of snails, worms, and insects, on which it almost entirely subsists. A garden in which a hedgehog is kept, will, in the course of two or three nights, be entirely freed from slugs; and that enemy to fruit, the millepede, is a favorite food to him. The London gardeners are so aware of this, as often to purchase hedgehogs to put in their grounds. If it ever has been found eating poultry or game, as has by some been asserted, they must previously have been killed by rats, weasels, or some more ferocious animal than the hedgehog, whose habits are those of gentleness and timidity, who is not formed for attack, and whose sole mode of defense is rolling itself up in a ball and opposing its strong prickles to the enemy. This statement is given in the hope of rescuing a harmless and useful creature from the general abhorrence in which it is held, and the unmerciful treatment it meets with.

Birds.

Farmers should be friendly to birds, as they are of the greatest service in destroying worms and insects, and thus preserving the crops and fruits. The small amount of vegetable food they consume is thus much more than compensated for. Sparrows are especially useful in this way.

To destroy Weeds.

To clear the ground of weeds is an operation no less necessary in husbandry than the disposing it to produce vegetables of any kind in plenty. *Annual weeds*, or such as spring from seed and die the same year, are most easily destroyed. For this purpose, it will be sufficient to let them spring up till near the time of ripening their seed, and then plough them down before it comes to maturity. It is also of service to destroy such weeds as grow in borders or neglected corners, and frequently scatter their seeds to a great distance; such as the thistle, dandelion, rag-weed, etc.; for these propagate their species through a deal of ground, as their seeds are carried about with the wind to very considerable distances. A farmer ought also to take care that the small seeds of weeds, separated from corn in winnowing, be not sown again upon the ground; for this certainly happens when they are thrown upon a dunghill, because, being the natural offspring of the earth, they are not easily destroyed. The best method of preventing any mischief from this cause is to burn them.

Perennial weeds are such as are propagated by the roots, and last for a number of years. They cannot be effectually destroyed but by removing the roots from the ground, which is often a matter of some difficulty. The only method that can be depended upon in this case is frequent ploughing to render the ground as tender as possible, and harrowing with a particular kind of harrow, in order to collect these pernicious roots. When collected, they ought to be dried and burnt, as the only effectual method of insuring their doing no farther mischief.

AGRICULTURE.

To destroy Broom, Furze and Thorns.

Besides those kinds of weeds which are of an herbaceous nature, there are others which are woody, and grow to a very considerable size; such as broom, furze and thorns. The first may be destroyed by frequent ploughing and harrowing, in the same manner as other perennial weeds are. Another method of destroying broom is by pasturing the field where it grows with sheep.

The best method of extirpating furze is to set fire to it in frosty weather, for frost has the effect of withering and making them burn readily. The stumps must then be cut over with a hatchet, and when the ground is well softened by rain it may be ploughed up, and the roots taken out by a harrow adapted to that purpose. If the field is soon laid down to grass they will again spring up; in this case, pasturing with sheep is an effectual remedy. The thorn, or bramble, can only be extirpated by ploughing up the ground and collecting the roots.

Usefulness of Mowing Weeds.

In the month of June weeds are in their most succulent state, and in this condition, after they have lain a few hours to wither, hungry cattle will eat greedily almost every species. There is scarcely a hedge, border, or a nook, but what at that season is valuable; and it certainly must be good management to embrace the transient opportunity, for in a few weeks they will become nuisances.

To banish Crows from a Field.

Machinery of various kinds, such as wind-mills in miniature, horse-rattles, etc., to be put in motion by the wind, are often employed to frighten crows; but with all of these they soon become familiar, when they cease to be of any use whatever.

The most effectual method of banishing them from a field, as far as experience goes, is to combine with one or other of the scarecrows in vogue the frequent use of the musket. Nothing strikes such terror into these sagacious animals as the sight of a fowling-piece and the explosion of gunpowder, which they have known so often to be fatal to their race. Such is their dread of a fowling-piece, that if one is placed upon a dyke or other eminence, it will for a long time prevent them from alighting on the adjacent grounds. Many persons now, however, believe that crows, like most other birds, do more good by destroying insects and worms, etc., than harm by eating grain.

To cultivate Carrots.

To command crops of this root, manure the land with twenty-five or thirty loads of dung per acre, pretty rotten, plough it in, and then cover the seed by harrowing. The dung neither injures the taste of the carrot, makes them grow deformed, nor causes the canker. A farmer's object is to produce as great a quantity as possible from every acre, which must undoubtedly be accomplished by manure. In confirmation of this opinion the following statement is given:

Unmanured Carrots, sown March 31.

	Ton.		lbs.
Roots	9		1918 per acre.
Tops	4		336 do.

Manured after Potatoes, sown April 7.

	Ton.		lbs.
Roots	12		1582 per acre.
Tops	5		994 do.

The soil in both was exactly the same, and the dung half rotten. The preceding crop had in both instances been potatoes, and the quality of the carrots was similar in both cases. An extensive collection of such well authenticated experiments is better calculated to extend the boundaries of agricultural knowledge than all the theories and mere reasonings upon them yet published.

Mode of Cultivating Parsnips in Guernsey.

Although this root is cultivated in almost all the soils of that island, that is esteemed the best which consists of a good light loam, the deeper the better. If the loamy soil is not deep, the under soil at least should be opened, to allow of the free penetration of the roots.

If the land is not perfectly clear from couch grass and other weeds, it is pared with the paring-plough in October, and harrowed to remove the weeds. About the middle of February the land is prepared for sowing by means of two ploughs. A small plough precedes and opens the furrow to the depth of four inches, and is followed by a large plough drawn by four or six oxen and as many horses, which deepens the furrow to ten or fourteen inches. As soon as the clods are capable of being broken the harrowing commences, and is repeated till the soil is pulverized, and reduced nearly to the state of garden mould. All of the processes are intended to loosen the soil to as great a depth as possible.

The seed should not be more than a year old, as it is uncertain when of a greater age. It is sown broadcast, and on a day just so windy as to insure its regular spreading over the surface. The seed is then covered by the harrow. The quantity sown is from two to four quarts.

As soon as the plants are sufficiently strong, they are hand-weeded and thinned, and this operation must be repeated at least three times during the summer. The distance between the plants is ultimately about nine inches; and to save a portion of the labor a harrowing is sometimes given between the first and second weedings.

The first weeding is performed about the middle of May, and repeated when necessary till the beginning of July.

The roots are dug up about the middle of August, when they are thought to be most nutritious, and to fatten animals better than after the leaves are decayed. The quantity dug up at this season is not more than is required for two or three days' consumption. It is only in October that the root is fully ripe, when it may be dug up with forks and preserved dry in sheds during the winter; but it is usually left in the ground in Guernsey, where frost is rare, and taken up as it is wanted.

The parsnip is considered by the Guernsey farmers to be the most nutritious root known, superior even to the carrot and the potato. When small it is given to the animals whole, but when large it is sliced longitudinally. Hogs prefer this root to all others, and it makes excellent pork. Horses are equally fond of the parsnip, although from eating it with too much avidity it sometimes sticks in the throat. But this may easily be prevented by cutting the roots into pieces before they are given.

To cultivate Hemp.

The Soil.

The soils most suited to the culture of this plant are those of the deep, black, putrid vegetable kind, that are low, and rather inclined to moisture, and those of the deep mellow, loamy, or sandy descriptions. The quantity of produce is generally much greater on the former than on the latter; but it is said to be greatly inferior in quality. It may, however, be grown with success on lands of a less rich and fertile kind, by proper care and attention in their culture and preparation.

To prepare the Ground.

In order to render the grounds proper for the reception of the crop, they should be reduced into a fine mellow state of mould, and be perfectly cleared from weeds, by repeated ploughings. When it succeeds grain crops, the work is mostly accomplished by three ploughings, and as many harrowings: the first being given immediately after the preceding crop is removed, the second early in the spring, and the last, or seed earth, just before the seed is to be put in. In the last ploughing, well rotted manure, in the proportion of fifteen or twenty, or good compost, in the quantity of twenty-five or thirty-three horse-cart loads, should be turned into the land; as without this it is seldom that good crops can be produced. The surface of the ground being left perfectly flat, and as free from furrows as possible; as by these means the moisture is more effectually retained, and the growth of the plants more fully promoted.

Quantity of Seed, etc.

It is of much importance in the cultivation of hemp crops that the seed be new, and of a good quality, which may in some measure be known by its feeling heavy in the hand, and being of a bright shining color.

The proportion of seed that is most commonly employed, is from two to three bushels, according to the quality of the land; but, as the crops are greatly injured by the plants standing too closely together, two bushels, or two bushels and a half may be a more advantageous quantity.

As the hemp plant is extremely tender in its early growth, care should be taken not to put the seed into the ground at so early a period, as that it may be liable to be injured by the effects of frost; nor to protract the sowing to so late a season, as that the quality of the produce may be affected. The best season, on the drier sorts of land, in the southern districts, is as soon as possible after the frosts are over in April, and, on the same descriptions of soil, in the more northern ones, towards the close of the same month, or early in the ensuing one.

Method of Sowing.

The most general method of putting crops of this sort into the soil is the broadcast, the seed being dispersed over the surface of the land in as even a manner as possible, and afterwards covered in by means of a very light harrowing. In many cases, however, especially when the crops are to stand for seed, the drill method in rows, at small distances, might be had recourse to with advantage; as, in this way, the early growth of the plants would be more effectually promoted, and the land be kept in a more clean and perfect state of mould, which are circumstances of importance in such crops. In whatever method the seed is put in, care must constantly be taken to keep the birds from it for some time afterwards.

This sort of crop is frequently cultivated on the same piece of ground for a great number of years, without any other kind intervening; but, in such cases, manure must be applied with almost every crop, in pretty large proportions, to prevent the exhaustion that must otherwise take place. It may be sown after most sorts of grain crops, especially where the land possesses sufficient fertility, and is in a proper state of tillage.

After Culture.

As hemp, from its tall growth and thick foliage, soon covers the surface of the land, and prevents the rising of weeds, little attention is necessary after the seed has been put into the ground, especially where the broadcast method of sowing is practised; but, when put in by the drill machine, a hoeing or two may be had recourse to with advantage in the early growth of the crop.

In the culture of this plant, it is particularly necessary that the same piece of land grows both male and female, or what is sometimes denominated simple hemp. The latter kind contains the seed.

When the grain is ripe (which is known by its becoming of a whitish-yellow color, and a few of the leaves beginning to drop from the stems); this happens commonly about thirteen or fourteen weeks from the period of its being sown, according as the season may be dry or wet (the first sort being mostly ripe some weeks before the latter), the next operation is that of taking it from the ground; which is effected by pulling it up by the roots, in small parcels at a time, by the hand, taking care to shake off the mould well from them before the handsful are laid down. In some districts, the whole crop is pulled together, without any distinction being made between the different kinds of hemp; while, in others, it is the practice to separate and pull them at different times, according to their ripeness. The latter is obviously the better practice; as by pulling a large proportion of the crop before it is in a proper state of maturity, the quantity of produce must not only be considerably lessened, but its quality greatly injured by being rendered less durable.

After being thus pulled, it is tied up in small parcels, or what are sometimes termed baits.

Where crops of this kind are intended for seeding, they should be suffered to stand till the seed becomes in a perfect state of maturity, which is easily known by the appearance of it on inspection. The stems are then pulled and bound up, as in the other case, the bundles being set up in the same manner as grain, until the seed becomes so dry and firm as to shed freely. It is then either immediately threshed out upon large cloths for the purpose in the field, or taken home to have the operation afterwards performed.

Process of Grassing Hemp.

The hemp, as soon as pulled, is tied up in small bundles, frequently at both ends.

It is then conveyed to pits, or ponds of stagnant water, about six or eight feet in depth, such as have a clayey soil being in general preferred, and deposited in beds, according to their size, and depth; the small bundles being laid both in a straight direction and crosswise of each other, so as to bind perfectly together; the whole, being loaded with timber, or other materials, so as to keep the beds of hemp just below the surface of the water.

It is not usual to water more than four or five times in the same pit, till it has been filled with water. Where the ponds are not sufficiently large to contain the whole of the produce at once, it is the practice to pull the hemp only as it can be admitted into them, it being thought disadvantageous to leave the hemp upon the ground after being pulled. It is left in these pits four, five, or six days, or even more, according to the warmth of the season and the judgment of the operator, on his examining whether the hempy material readily separates from the reed or stem; and then taken up and conveyed to a pasture field which is clean and even, the bundles being loosened and spread out thinly, stem by stem, turning it every second or third day, especially in damp weather, to prevent its being injured by worms or other insects. It should remain in this situation for two, three, four, or more weeks, according to circumstances, and be then collected together when in a perfectly dry state, tied up into large bundles, and placed in some secure building until an opportunity is afforded for breaking it, in order to separate the hemp. By this means the process of grassing is not only shortened, but the more expensive ones of breaking, scutching, and bleaching the yarn, rendered less violent and troublesome.

After the hemp has been removed from the field it is in a state to be broken and swingled, operations that are mostly performed by common laborers, by means of machinery for the purpose, the produce being tied up in stones. The refuse collected in the latter process is denominated sheaves, and is in some districts employed for the purposes of fuel. After having undergone these different operations, it is ready for the purposes of the manufacturer.

To cultivate Flax.

The soils most suitable for flax, besides the alluvial kind, are deep friable loams, and such as contain a large proportion of vegetable matter in their composition. Strong clays do not answer well, nor soils of a gravelly or dry sandy nature. But whatever be the kind of soil, it ought neither to be in too poor nor too rich a condition, because in the latter case the flax is apt to grow too luxuriant and produce a coarse sort, and in the former case, the plant, from growing weakly, affords only a small produce.

To prepare the Ground.

When grass land is intended for flax, it ought to be broken up as early in the season as possible, so that the soil may be duly mellowed by the winter frosts, and in good order for being reduced by the harrows, when the seed process is attempted. If flax is to succeed a corn crop, the like care is required to procure the aid of frost, without which the surface cannot be rendered fine enough for receiving the seed. Less frost, however, will do in the last than in the first case, therefore the grass land ought always to be earliest ploughed. At seed time, harrow the land well before the seed is distributed, then cover the seed to a sufficient depth, by giving a close double time of the harrows. Water-furrow the land, and remove any stones and roots that may remain on the surface, which finishes the seed process.

Quantity of Seed.

When a crop of seed is intended to be taken, thin sowing is preferable, in order that the plants may have room to fork or spread out their leaves, and to obtain air for the blossoming and filling seasons. But it is a mistake to sow thin when flax is intended to be taken, for the crop then becomes coarse, and often unproductive. From eight to ten pecks per acre is a proper quantity in the last case; but when seed is the object, six pecks will do very well.

To save the Flax and Seed.

Flax should be pulled when the lower part of the plant begins to turn yellow, and when, on opening the pods, the most forward of the seeds are found in a soft state, and the middle of the seeds is green; while the seed is quite soft, the flax should be spread on the ground in bundles of about as much as a woman can grasp with both hands, and it should remain so till the upper part is dry; in fine weather it will be dry in twenty-four or forty-eight hours; the bundles should be then made up, with the dry part inside, and set up in stocks of ten bundles each, to stand on the ground till the whole is dry, pods and all; the seed will then be ripe and the flax in the best state, and may be stacked, housed, or worked; great care should be taken to keep the root ends even.

Method of Watering.

When flax is pulled it ought to be immediately put into the water, so that it may part with the rind and be fit for the manufacturer. Standing pools, for many reasons, are most proper for the purpose, occasioning the flax to have a better color, to be sooner ready for the grass, and even to be of superior quality in every respect. When put into the water it is tied up in beets, or small sheaves, the smaller the better, because it is then most equally watered. These sheaves ought to be built in the pool, in a reclining upright posture, so that the weight placed above may keep the whole firmly down. In warm weather, ten days of the watering process are sufficient; but it is proper to examine the pools regularly after the seventh day, lest the flax should putrefy or rot, which sometimes happens in very warm weather. Twelve days will answer in any sort of weather; though it may be remarked, that it is better to give rather too little of the water than too much, as any deficiency may be easily made up by suffering it to lie longer on the grass, whereas an excess of water admits of no remedy. After lying on the grass for a due time, till any defect of the watering process is rectified, the flax is taken up, tied when dry in large sheaves, and carried to the mill to be switched and prepared for the hackle.

Dressing Flax.—Instructions for Using the Machinery.

The process is divided into two parts: the first part is intended for the farmer, or flax-grower, to bring the flax into a fit state for general or common purposes. This is performed by three machines: one for threshing out the seed, one for breaking and separating the wood from the fibre, and one for further separating the broken wood and matter from the fibre. In some cases the farmers will perhaps thrash out the seed in their own mill, and therefore, in such cases, the first machine will be, of course, unnecessary.

The second part of the process is intended for the manufacturer to bring the flax into a state for the very finest purposes, such as lace, cambric, damask, and very fine linen. This second part is performed by the refining machine only.

The Threshing Machine.

Take the flax in small bundles, as it comes from the field or stack, and holding it in the left hand, put the seed end between the threshing machine and the bed or block against which the machine is to strike; then take the handle of the machine in the right hand, and move the machine backward and forward, to strike on the flax, until the seed is all threshed out.

The Breaking Machine.

Take the flax in small handsful in the left hand, spread it flat between the third and little finger, with the seed end downwards, and the root-end above, as near the hand as possible; then put it between the beater of the breaking machine, and beat it gently till the three or four inches, which have been under the operation of the machine, appear to be soft; then remove the flax a little higher in the hand, so as to let the soft part of the flax rest upon the little finger, and continue to beat it till all is soft, and the wool is separated from the fibre, keeping the left hand close to the block and the flax as flat upon the block as possible. The other end of the flax is then to be turned, and the end which has been beaten is to

HOPS.

be wrapped round the little finger, the root end flat, and beaten in the machine till the wood is separated, exactly in the same way as the other end was beaten.

The Cleansing Machine.

It is to be used in the same way, in all respects, as the breaking machine, first cleansing one end of the flax, and then turning the other, keeping the flax all the while flat in the hand.

To Huckle.

A common hackle will be found useful in this stage for opening the ends, and may be placed for greater convenience at the side of the breaking and cleansing machine.

This concludes the first process of the machinery intended for the farmer or flax-grower. The second, or manufacturer's process, requires

The Refining Machine.

Take a small piece of flax as it comes from the breaking or cleansing machine, pass the seed end through the fluted rollers of the refining machine, and bring it round, laying it flat on the root-end of the flax, forming it into a skein. A few fibres of the end brought round, and looped in the flax on which it is laid, will keep the skein together. It must be kept flat and even on the machine, which may continue to go round and work the flax till it is brought to any degree of fineness that may be required, and this will not require more than from two to six minutes.

Washing or Whitening.

The flax, when prepared by these machines, without having been water-steeped, or dew-rotted, may be washed in small quantities at a time, either in water only or with soap and water, without any other mixture, and brought by these simple means to the purest white. It is to be wrung several times in water till the water becomes no longer colored from the matter, and care is to be taken that the flax is laid flat like tape, and then spread upon the grass, but it is recommended that the flax should be spun in the yellow state, and then washed in warm water and soap, or boiled with care in water and soap from ten to fifteen minutes, so that, when dried, it will be perfectly white. If the weather should be favorable it would be well to have it dried on the grass.

As to the labor required, the machines are easily wrought by women or girls, and without any assistance from men.

The Produce.

As to the produce of different degrees of fineness from a given weight of the raw material, we subjoin the following statement:

112 lbs. of flax from the stack, after the seed was threshed out, produced 30 lbs. in the state No. 1; refined to No. 3 it produced 20 lbs. of flax and 3 lbs. of common tow; 20 lbs. of No. 3 produced 14½ lbs. of No. 4. The loss in weight is caused by the discharge of matter; there is no loss of fibre.

An average crop will produce about two tons to the acre after the seed is threshed out. This will produce one-fourth fibre, making ten cwt. to the acre No. 1.

To cultivate Hops.—The Soil, &c.

The hop is planted on various soils, and chiefly in valleys. Hops are generally of the best quality from strong clay land. The crop, however, is there very precarious. Those on peat are much more productive, but are liable to be affected by the mould in some seasons, which reduces their value considerably. The best plantations are on a deep, loamy soil, where the produce of the latter and the quality of the former are sometimes obtained. Those which are grown on sandy and gravelly lands are seldom remarkable for either great produce or superior quality.

The plant is extremely liable to disasters from its first putting up in the spring until the time of picking the crop, which is in September. Snails or slugs, ants and flies, are formidable enemies in the first instance. Frosts are inimical to its growth, and the vines are frequently blighted even after they have reached the top of the poles. Small green flies and other insects which make their appearance in the months of May and June, when the wind is about northeast, often greatly injure them, and they are subject to take damage by high winds from the southwest. The best situation for a plantation, therefore, is a southern aspect, well shaded on three sides either by hills or planting, which is supposed to be the chief protection that can be given them.

To plant Hops.

In the winter time provide the soil and manure for the hop-ground against the following spring. If the dung be rotten, mix it with two or three parts of common earth, and let it incorporate together till there is occasion to make use of it in making the hop-hills; but if it be new dung, then let it be mixed as before till the spring in the next year, for new dung is very injurious to hops. Hops require to be planted in a situation so open that the air may freely pass round and between them to dry up and dissipate the moisture, which often destroys the middle of large plantations, while the outsides remain unhurt.

The hills should be eight or nine feet asunder. If the ground be intended to be ploughed with horses between the hills, it will be best to plant them in squares, chequerwise; but if the ground is so small that it may be done with the breast-plough, or spade, the holes should be ranged in a quincunx form. Which way soever is made use of, a stake should be stuck down at each of the places where the hills are to be made.

To choose Hops.

Be very particular in the choice of the plants as to kind, for if the hop-garden be planted with a mixture of several sorts of hops that ripen at several times, it will cause much trouble and great detriment.

The two best sorts are the white and the gray bind; the latter is a large, square hop, more hardy, bears more abundantly, but ripens later than the former. There is another sort of the white bind, which ripens a week or ten days before the common; but this is a tenderer and a less plentiful bearer, though it has this advantage, that it comes first to market. If there be a sort of hop you value, and would wish to increase, the superfluous binds may be laid down when the hops are tied, cutting off the tops and burying them in the hill, or when the hops are dressed all the cuttings may be saved, for almost every part will grow and become a good set the next spring.

Seasons of Planting.

English planters approve the months of October and March. The most usual time of procuring the cuttings is in March, when the hops are cut and dressed. As to the manner of planting the sets, there should be five good sets planted in every hill, one in the middle, and the rest round about, sloping. Let them be pressed close with the hand and covered with fine earth; a stick should be placed on each side of the hill to secure it.

To form a New Plantation.

The best method is to have cuttings from approved stock, planted out the year before they are wanted, in the hop-ground; as the use of plants instead of cuttings not only gains a year, but the former are more certain to flourish. A small piece of moist land is sufficient to raise plants for many acres, and at little expense. If the ground be in grass, pare and dig in the pods; work the land with a spade, and set it out into ridges of three and a half yards wide, and two yards between each; having a strip of grass (called a pillar) next every ridge, and an open drain between every two pillars, the depth of which must vary according to the soil, some being less than one foot, and others nearly four feet in depth. Three rows of plants, or, as they are termed, hills, are made upon each ridge, which should intersect each other; they are generally two yards distant in the rows, so that about 1300 is the usual number of hills in a statute acre. Small sticks are proper to tie the binds up to the first year, then small poles for a year or two; the size of which should be gradually increased. Some set two poles to every hill, which is proper for ground producing luxuriant binds; but on clay land three poles are set in a triangular form to the hills on the two outside rows of each ridge, and only two in the middle row. Many additional poles, longer than the rest, called catch-poles, are also set to take the binds as they run beyond the lesser poles. Where the bind is weak, three heads are commonly trained up each pole; though two are better, if strong. If the ground intended for a new plantation is not clean from couch-grass, a complete fallow is essential, whether it be grass or stubble; and a crop of turnips may be taken to advantage, if the land is proper for their growth, and can be made clean, as hops are planted in March.

To take up Hop-Ground.

The following are termed the annual orders:—Digging the ground completely over; hoeing the earth from the hills, and cutting off the stock a little above the root, which are called pickling and cutting; poling, which is carrying the poles from the stacks, and setting them down to the hills with a round implement, shod with iron, and called a poy, having a crutch at the top, and a peg through the middle to tread upon; tying the binds round the poles with rushes, and pulling up the superfluous binds; hoeing the ground all over with a hoe of large dimensions; wheeling and laying manure upon every hill; covering the manure with the soil, which is done by scraping the ground over with a hoe, and is called billing; and stacking, which is carrying and setting up the poles into heaps or stacks, after the crop has been taken.

Extra-works.

As the preceding are termed the ordinary, so the following are called the extra-works, as not being included in the yearly bargain with the men by the generality of planters, and some of them are done only by the very best managers. On clayey ground, either the earth ought to be bared off the hills, and a covering of good manure applied to them previous to digging, which will require from twelve to fifteen tons per acre; or from twenty to twenty-five tons of manure, or a greater quantity of fresh earth (when the ground wants condition) should be wheeled and spread all over the ridges. It is not improper, in some cases, to pursue these methods alternately; but on boggy and very rich ground the earth only can be applied with advantage. The drains should be scoured out yearly on very wet ground; and what is thrown out is always intermixed with the soil in digging; on drier soils this is done every second or third year, and on very dry land it is scarcely necessary to do it at all. Recruiting the stock by planting, where any hills have failed, is done at little cost in well-managed plantations, as there are seldom many at once in those. If there is any couch-grass, it should be dug out with three-pronged forks in March, and carried off the ground. The renewal of poles requires from one to two hundred per acre every year. If, when the binds first appear, they are beaten by slugs, a handful of malt culm or saw-dust is sometimes laid round each hill, which they cannot travel over; and should flies or ants attack them, soot is the best preventive. The carrying in and setting catch-poles varies much as to number, as some set fewer than one hundred, and others five or six hundred per acre. Moving the drains and pillars is generally done once, but twice moving is better (whether the grass be made into fodder, or is suffered to fall into the drains for manure), as then no seeds scatter on the ground. Extra-hoe once before the billing, and once after. After high winds many poles are broken down, which should be set up again soon

Manure proper for Hop-Culture.

As to the manure most proper for the hop-culture, good stable dung is much used, and is preferred to the manure made by beasts at pasture, as the latter encourages ants on strong ground. Woollen rags are the best for forcing a luxuriant bind, and if used with judgment, are excellent for clayey ground; but they are apt to make the hops small, if too many are used. Malt culm and dove manure are excellent, and one complete dressing with lime is very serviceable for strong ground.

To pick Hops.

When the crop is ripe, a proper number of pickers is procured, for whom are provided light wooden frames, called binges; they are clothed with hop-bagging, into which the hops are picked off the poles by women and children, having them brought by men, who take them up by cutting the binds about a foot above the ground, and drawing up the poles by an instrument called a dragon. Each binge has from four to six pickers, and a man attends to one or two binges, according to the crop; he strips the binds from the poles as they are picked, and lays them in heaps ready for stocking; he also carries the hops to the kilns, if near; or to a cart, as they are measured from the binge. The number of binges employed vary with the crop and kiln-room; about one to an acre is usual. The hops are taken out of the binge with a basket which holds six pecks.

Another Method.

The most convenient way of picking them is into a long square frame of wood, with a cloth hanging on center-hooks within it, to receive the hops as they are picked.

They must be picked very clean, free from leaves and stalks; and as there shall be occasion, two or three times in a day, the frame must be emptied into a hop-bag made of coarse linen cloth, and carried immediately to the oast or kiln, in order to be dried: for if they should be too long in the bag they will be apt to heat and be discolored. If the weather be hot, there should no more poles be drawn than can be picked in an hour, and they should be gathered in fair weather, if it can be, and when the hops are dry; this will save some expense in firing, and preserve their color better when they are dried.

HOPS, MADDER.

To dry Hops.

The best method of drying hops is with charcoal on an oast or kiln, covered with hair-cloth of the same form and fashion that is used for drying malt. The kiln ought to be square, and may be ten, twelve, fourteen, or sixteen feet across at the top, where the hops are laid, as the plantation requires and the room will allow. There ought to be a due proportion between the height and breadth of the kiln, and the steddle where the fire is kept, viz., if the kiln be twelve feet square on the top, it ought to be nine feet high from the fire, and the steddle ought to be six feet and a half square, and so proportionable in other dimensions.

The hops must be spread even upon the oast, a foot thick or more, if the depth of the curb will allow it; but care is to be taken not to overload the oast if the hops are green or wet. The oast ought to be first warmed with a fire before the hops are laid on, and then an even steady fire must be kept under them, it must not be too fierce at first lest it scorch them, nor must it be suffered to sink or slacken, but rather be increased, till the hops are nearly dried, lest the moisture or sweat which the fire has raised, fall back or discolor them.

When they have lain about nine hours they must be turned, and in two or three hours more they may be taken off. It may be known when they are well dried, by the brittleness of the stalks and the easy falling off of the hop-leaves.

To bag Hops.

As soon as the hops are taken off the kiln, lay them in a room for three weeks or a month to cool, give, and toughen; for if they are bagged immediately they will powder, but if they lie awhile (and the longer they lie the better, provided they are covered close with blankets to secure them from the air), they may be bagged with more safety, as not being liable to be broken to powder in treading; and this will make them bear treading the better, and the harder they are trodden the better they will keep.

To dress Hops.

When the ground is dug in January or February, the earth about the hills and very near them, should be taken away with the spade. About the end of February, if the hops were planted the spring before, or if the ground be weak, they ought to be dressed in dry weather; but if the ground be strong and in perfection, the middle of March will be a good time; and if it is apt to produce over-rank binds, the beginning of April may be soon enough. Then having with an iron picker cleared away all the earth out of the hill, so as to clean the stock to the principal roots, with a sharp knife cut off all the shoots which grew with the binds the last year; and also all the young suckers, that none may be left to run in the alley and weaken the hill. It will be proper to cut one part of the stock lower than the other, and also to cut that part low that was left highest the preceding year. In dressing those hops that have been planted the year before, cut off both the dead tops and the young suckers which have sprung up from the sets, and also cover the stocks with fine earth, a finger's length in thickness.

To pole Hops.

About the middle of April the hops are to be poled; when the shoots begin to sprout up, the poles must be set to the hills deep in the ground, with a square iron picker or crow, that they may the better endure the wind; three poles are sufficient for one hill. These should be placed as near the hill as possible, with their bending tops turned outwards from the hill, to prevent the binds from entangling; and a space between two poles ought to be left open to the south, to admit the sunbeams.

To tie Hops.

The buds that do not clasp of themselves to the nearest pole when they are grown to three or four feet high, must be guided to it by the hand, turning them to the sun, whose course they will always follow. They must be bound with withered rushes, but not so close as to hinder them from climbing up the pole. This continue to do till all the poles are furnished with binds, of which two or three are enough for a pole; and all the sprouts and binds that there are no occasion for, are to be plucked up; but if the ground is young, then none of these useless binds should be plucked up, but should be wrapped up together in the middle of the hill.

To gather Hops.

About the beginning of July hops begin to blow, and will be ready for gathering the last of August. A judgment may be made of their ripeness by their strong scent, their hardness, and the brownish color of their seed. When by these tokens they appear to be ripe they must be picked with all the expedition possible, for if at this time a storm of wind should come, it would do them great damage, by breaking the branches and bruising and discoloring the hops; and it is very well known that hops, being picked green and bright, will sell for a third more than those which are discolored.

To cultivate the Madder Plant.

The ground is ploughed deep in autumn, and again in March, and then laid up in ridges eighteen inches asunder, and about a foot high. About the beginning of April the ground is opened where the old roots are planted, and the side shoots taken off, which are transplanted immediately upon the new ridges, at about a foot distance, where they remain two seasons; at Michaelmas, when the tops of the plants are decayed, the roots are taken up. This method of planting in ridges is only necessary in wet land. If all the horizontal roots are destroyed from time to time, it will cause the large downright roots to be much bigger, in which the goodness of this plant chiefly consists. After the roots, the only parts of the madder used by dyers, are taken up, they are kiln-dried, and then reduced to powder by a mill. Previously to the grinding they are carefully assorted.

The fine quality of madder is distinguished by its being of a bright, lively, light color, well ground, without any coarse parts proceeding from the peelings. Fresh is always more valuable than old madder. It should be kept close to prevent the access of air, as its virtue evaporates when exposed.

Madder is principally cultivated in Holland, Germany, and France, especially the former place, where it grows in greater abundance than in any other part of the world. The turkey madder root is principally cultivated about Smyrna. This plant may be propagated either by offsets or seeds. On a light thin soil the culture cannot be carried on to any profit; that soil in which the plant delights is a rich sandy loam, three feet or more in depth.

The ground being first made smooth, is divided into beds four feet wide, with alternate alleys half as broad again as the beds. In each alley is a shallow channel for irrigating the whole field, etc., that part of the alley that is not otherwise engaged may be sown with legumes. The madder seed is sown broadcast in the proportion of from twenty-five to thirty pounds per acre about the end of April. In a fortnight or three weeks the young plants begin to appear, and from this time to the month of September care must be taken to keep the ground well watered and free from weeds. If the plants are examined in autumn they will be found to be surrounded with small yellow offsets at the depth of two inches, and early in September the earth from the alleys is to be dug out and laid over the plants of madder to the height of two or three feet. With this the first year's operation finishes.

The second year's work begins in May with giving the beds a thorough weeding; and care must be taken to supply them with plenty of water during summer. In September the first crop of seed will be ripe, at which time the stems of the plants may be mown down, and the roots covered a few inches with earth taken as before out of the alleys.

The weeding should take place as early as possible in the spring of the third year; and the crop, instead of being left for seeds, may be cut three times during summer for green fodder, all kinds of cattle being remarkably fond of it. In October the roots are taken up, the offsets are carefully separated, and immediately used to form a new plantation; and the roots, after being dried, are sold either without further preparation or ground to a coarse powder and sprinkled with an alkaline lye. The roots lose four-fifths of their weight in drying, and the produce of an acre is about 2000 pounds of dry salable madder.

Use of Madder.

The principal use of madder is in dyeing. It gives out its color both to water and rectified spirits; the watery tincture is of a dark dull red, the spirituous of a deep bright one. It imparts to woollen cloth, prepared with alum and tartar, a very durable, though not a very beautiful red dye. As it is the cheapest of all red drugs that give a durable color, it is the principal one commonly made use of for ordinary stuffs. Sometimes its dye is heightened by the addition of Brazil-wood, and sometimes it is employed in conjunction with the dearer reds, as cochineal, for demi-scarlets and demi-crimsons. Madder-root is sometimes employed in medicine as an emmenagogue. When the madder is given to animals with their food it produces a curious phenomenon, namely, tinging their bones with red. The bones of young pigeons will be thus tinged of a rose-color in twenty-four hours, and of a deep scarlet in three days; but the bones of adult animals will be a fortnight in acquiring a rose-color.

Best Method of Hay-making.

Instead of allowing the hay to lie, as usual in most places, for some days in the swath after it is cut, never cut hay but when the grass is quite dry, and then make the gatherers follow close upon the cutters; put it up immediately into small cocks about three feet high each, and of as small a diameter as they can be made to stand with; always giving each of them a slight kind of thatching, by drawing a few handsful of the hay from the bottom of the cock all round and laying it lightly upon the top, with one of the ends hanging downwards. This is done with the utmost ease and expedition; and when once in that state the hay is, in a great measure, out of danger; for unless a violent wind should arise immediately after the cocks are put up, nothing else can hurt the hay; as no rain, however violent, can penetrate into these cocks but for a very little way; and if they are dry put up they never sit together so closely as to heat, although they acquire, in a day or two, such a degree of firmness as to be in no danger of being overturned by wind after that time, unless it blows a hurricane.

In these cocks allow the hay to remain until, upon inspection, the farmer judges it will keep in pretty large tramp-cocks (which is usually in a week or two, according as the weather is more or less favorable), when two men, each with a long-pronged pitchfork, lift up one of these small cocks between them with the greatest ease, and carry them one after another to the place where the tramp-cock is to be built; and in this manner proceed over the field till the whole is finished.

Mode of Hay-making in England.

The clover is cut, and after it has lain four or five days in the swath, till it is sufficiently dry, the hay-maker, with a rake, rolls up a sufficient quantity to form a ripple, which is set up in the form of a cone. Taking a few of the longest straws he twists them round the top, which forms the point of the cone, keeps the ripple compact, and shoots off the rain. In taking up the clover from the swath and forming the ripple, it is necessary to keep the upper or dry part inwards: by that means it is much sooner dry, and in a fit state for the stack. It is generally necessary for clover to remain five or six days in the ripple before it is put into the stack; but that depends on the state of the weather. There is no occasion to untie the ripples. The method of rippling is not so expensive as cocking; it is much superior both in wet and dry seasons—not so liable to be injured by the wet—much sooner dry, and of course of a better quality and more nourishing for cattle. Each ripple will weigh, when dry, about four or five pounds. They should not be made too large. Except where meadow grass is very long it would not be practicable to ripple it. The practice of rippling is simple, attended with little trouble or expense, and whenever tried will recommend itself.

To manage Cut Grass for Hay.

Grass, when cut for hay, ought to be quickly raked, in order that its powers may neither be exhausted by the sun nor dissipated by the air. In the first stage small cocks are preferable, and on after days these may be gathered into large ones or hand-ricks, by which method the hay is equally made and properly sweetened. After standing eight or ten days in these ricks, according to the nature of the weather, hay may be carted home and built in stacks of sufficient size for standing through the winter months.

Buckwheat.

This thrives among mountains better than on lowlands. Sow in July. It grows ripe with frost; the seeds grow black after a frost.

Importance of Straw in Husbandry.

This is a subject that has not always been so much attended to as its importance deserves.

Though many useful observations on straw are occasionally introduced in agricultural writings, and though its value, as the basis of future crops, is fully admitted by every intelligent farmer, yet the subject has seldom been professedly treated of at any length: we shall endeavor, therefore, to compress the most important particulars connected with it under the following heads:

1. The weight of straw produced on an average of the different crops of grain and pulse per statute acre.

2. The value of the different kinds of straw, and

STRAW.

3. The various uses to which each kind of straw is applicable.

Weight of Straw produced by the different Crops.

The quantity of straw per acre differs according to a variety of circumstances; as, 1. The species of grain, whether wheat, barley, oats, etc. 2. The different kinds of the same grain. 3. The season, for in dry seasons the quantity is less than in moist. 4. The soil, for in fertile soils the straw is more abundant than in poor ones. 5. The season when the seed is sown, for spring-sown wheat has less straw than the winter-sown. And, 6. The manner in which the straw is cut, for an inch or two at the root-end of the straw makes a great addition to the dunghill.

From a statement by Mr. Young it would appear that the average produce in straw of all the different crops, stubble included, may be calculated at 1 ton, 7 cwt. per acre, but that is rejecting the weaker soils.

It is calculated by Mr. Brown, of Markle, that on an average of years, the produce of straw in good land and under tolerable management, will be nearly in the following proportion per acre:

	lbs.
Wheat,	2240
Beans and peas,	1820
Oats,	1820
Barley,	1400
Total,	7280

Or, at an average of these crops, 130 stone per acre, 22 lbs. avoirdupois per stone; in all 2860 lbs., or 1 ton, 5 cwt., 2 quarters and 4 lbs.

It may be safely estimated that on an average of years well cultivated and fertile soils, when the crop is carefully cut down, will annually produce, on the average of the crops above mentioned, 1 ton, 5 cwt. per acre.

Value of the different kinds of Straw.

The intrinsic value of straw must vary materially, according to its leading properties, the quantity of manure into which it may be converted by littering, or its fitness to be employed as thatch, these being the chief uses to which it is applicable; but in general its price depends on its vicinity to large towns. It is only in situations where foreign manure can be procured easily and at a cheaper rate than by converting the straw raised upon the farm into dung that the sale of straw is ever permitted. Two loads of wheat-straw per acre are reckoned a tolerable crop.

As straw is rarely permitted to be sold, being usually employed in maintaining winter stock, the real value of the article to the farmer is but inconsiderable, depending upon the quantity and quality of the dung it produces. So little is it thought necessary accurately to ascertain the value of straw, that in several cases it has been given by the outgoing to the incoming tenant as an equivalent for the expense of harvesting, threshing and marketing the last crop. It is often thought insufficient to cover even that expense, and a further abatement is allowed on the price of the grain.

Various purposes to which Straw is applicable.

The subject of feeding with straw will be better understood by considering the specific properties of the different kinds of straw employed in feeding stock, and the rules that ought to be observed when stock are fed with that material.

Wheat Straw.

This kind of straw, from its strength, is considered to be peculiarly calculated both for litter and threshing, and indeed wherever the practice of cutting straw into chaff for mixing with grain for horses prevails, wheat straw is preferred. When given to cattle or horses, it is sometimes cut into chaff, and either given raw in that state, or what is greatly preferred, steamed with other food, in particular with potatoes.

In order to improve wheat straw as fodder, it is the practice in some parts of England to cut the grain rather green, which preserves more of the natural juices, and consequently makes the fodder better. Some of the best farmers are accustomed to cut wheat much earlier than common in their respective districts. One of these was a miller in Norfolk, who occupied a large farm, where he always cut his wheat several days before any one else thought of beginning, well knowing the good consequences in the value of the grain. It must then be less apt to be injured by shaking or harvesting.

Oat Straw.

Among the culmiferous grains, the straw of the oat is considered to be the best fodder, when given uncut. It is well known, indeed, that oat straw, during the winter season, is almost universally given instead of hay, in all the best cultivated counties of Scotland during the winter months, though that of peas and beans is certainly preferred where both are grown.

In some districts farmers cut oats in the straw into a species of fodder, which is called "cut meat." This is given not only to horses, but to cattle, especially fattening cattle. It is thought to give not only fatness but a fineness of skin to all sorts of stock.

Bean Straw.

If well harvested this straw forms a very hearty and nutritious kind of food for cattle in the winter season. Both oxen and horses, when duly supplied with oats in proportion to the work they have to execute, thrive well on it, and the reduced parts, or what is termed in England the coving-chaff, is found valuable as a manger food for the laboring teams; when blended with other substances it is probable that, in particular cases, the stems might be cut into chaff with advantage, but when made use of in these methods it should be used as fresh as possible after being threshed. A mixture of bean straw (which by itself is rather dry), and of peas-haum, which is sweet and nourishing, makes excellent fodder.

But though this straw, more especially when mixed with peas-haum, is of great value as fodder to the working stock of the farm, it does not suit well with riding-horses, as it is apt to hurt their wind. In some horses both bean-straw and peas-haum are apt to occasion colic pains, or the disease which is called botts, probably occasioned by flatulency. For this disease, about half an ounce or a tablespoonful of laudanum is found to be a good remedy.

Pea Straw.

In Scotland the haum of peas is used as fodder for working-horses instead of hay, and when well harvested forms a very excellent provender, insomuch that it is considered to be of almost equal value to the grain itself.

Tare-straw or Hay.

This is an article strongly recommended by some farmers; for when the land has been dunged and the seed good, the produce is considerable. The crop should be cut as soon as the blossoms begin to fall off or the pod to form, and the whole, converted into hay-tares, require a great deal of sun to cure, and rain is very injurious to them. It would be a good plan to mix them with dry straw, which would improve both.

Rules regarding the consumption of Straw in feeding Cattle.

Straw is much used in the feeding of cattle in Scotland, and there can be no doubt that oxen will feed well on straw and turnips, if the straw be good. It is recommended in all cases that for a month or six weeks after a bullock is put to turnips, straw only should be given with them. But in the more advanced stages of fattening, hay is so much superior, that it should if possible be supplied. It is certain, at the same time, that hay is a very expensive food for stock, and ought to be saved as much as possible where it can prudently be done. It is well known that a full allowance of turnips and straw, during the winter months, will fatten better than a small allowance of hay in place of the straw. In the spring, hay, which retains its nutritive juices longer than straw, is much more valuable, both for fattening stock and feeding horses, and it is therefore the practice to reserve hay for about three months' consumption of these kinds of stock, and for no others.

Rules for Feeding Horses with Straw.

In regard to horses, hay may very often be more or less scarce or dear; but with straw and the oats, which must always be given them whether they get straw or hay, they not only plough three-fourths of an acre per day, or work from seven to eight hours at other labor, but are actually full of flesh and vigor when sowing commences. They must, however, have hay instead of straw, when the severe labor of spring takes place.

When, therefore, farmers' horses are so much reduced in condition as to be unable to go through the severe labor of spring, it is owing to their not having got a sufficient quantity of oats or corn. Pea and bean-straw certainly make the best fodder, when not injured by rain; but if that kind of straw is damaged in harvest, white straw is to be preferred.

Rules for Feeding Sheep with Straw.

There is no food of which sheep are fonder than pea-straw. The soil of pastoral districts being rarely of a kind calculated for peas, any extensive cultivation of that grain is impracticable; but where circumstances are favorable to that crop, peas ought to be cultivated, were it merely for the straw, as it would enable the store-farmers to carry on their system of sheep-farming with much more advantage. Indeed, the same plan might be advisable in other districts. It might be proper to add, that for ewes at yeaning time, lentil-hay is better than tare-hay or even pea-haum.

Miscellaneous Rules and Observations regarding the Consumption of Straw.

On turnip farms it is the usual practice to feed horses till March, where the labor is not severe, and cows through the winter, with oat-straw, whilst the fattening and straw-yard cattle got the straw of wheat and barley. If any peas or beans be cultivated on the farm, that straw being given to the horses, a part of the oat-straw may be left for the fattening and straw-yard cattle. Upon turnip farms, it is not thought profitable to cut the greater part of the clovers for hay. These are usually eaten by sheep, and no more hay saved than what may serve the horses, cows, and fattening stock for eight or ten weeks, immediately before grass, with a small quantity occasionally given to the sheep fed on turnips.

The expense of feeding even the horses alone, for eight months, on hay, would be more than a farmer can well afford; at the same time it is a rule with the best farmers to give hay to their horses in the early part of winter; then peas or bean-straw till seed-time commences in the spring; and afterwards hay.

Straw keeps much better unthreshed, in a large stack, than in a barn. Straw in general, more especially white straw, is found to lose its value as fodder, in whatever way it may be kept, after the sharp dry breezes of the spring months have set in.

It is a general rule that straw, when intended to be used as food for stock, should be given as speedily as possible after it is threshed. The threshing separates and exposes it so much, that if kept long it is, comparatively speaking, of little value as fodder. Lisle, an intelligent writer on agriculture, and a practical farmer, states, that he found cows did not eat straw so well on a Monday morning as they did the rest of the week, because the straw was not fresh from the flail. Straw, therefore, should be constantly made use of, as soon after it is threshed as possible: for by keeping it becomes either musty or too dry, and cattle do not eat it, or thrive on it so well. It cannot be doubted that air has a very injurious effect upon all kinds of fodder, and the more it can be kept from the influence of the sun and the atmosphere, the better. It is seldom given as fodder, unless to straw-yard cattle, after the month of March.

When clover is sown with grain crops, the clover has often arrived at such a length as to mix with the straw in cutting the crop. This certainly improves the straw in good harvests; but as little clover as possible should be cut with the straw, as it makes it very difficult to secure the crop, unless it be left upon the ground for several days.

Straw as applicable to Litter.

Straw, when mixed with the dung and the urine of cattle, horses, etc. etc., is a rich and excellent manure; but even alone, when ploughed in, or decomposed by pure simple water, it is of use. All the various sorts of straw answer the purposes of litter. Some farmers contend that rye-straw is the best litter; others prefer the straw of wheat, which absorbs, it is said, so much urine and moisture, that a cart of wheat-straw is supposed equal in value to three carts of well-made dung. In England the straw of peas and beans is extremely valuable, forming, it is said, when well broken by threshing, a desirable litter for working-horses, hogs, and other stock; but in Scotland it is never used as litter, unless it has been spoilt by bad management or a most unseasonable season in harvest, as its feeding properties there are so well known. Littering is of use, not only for converting straw into manure, but for keeping the animals warm and dry. In fact cattle cannot be soiled on clover, or fed on turnips, without abundance of litter.

There are four modes of converting straw into dung by littering stock:—1. In stalls or stables; 2. In hammels; 3. In fold-yards; and 4. In open folds, where sheep are littered with straw.

The quantity of dung produced from a given quantity of straw depends a good deal upon the kind of straw that is used (as some kinds absorb much more moisture than others), and upon the degree of care employed in preparing the dung. Speaking generally, the original weight of straw may be tripled, if the manufacturing process be properly conducted, and the dung applied to the ground before its powers are lessened or exhausted. The quantity of dung which may be made from an acre, especially if the dung arising from clover, turnips, and hay, consumed on a farm, is included in the general stock, will be something more than four tons; consequently, any farm of decent soil may be manured at the rate of twelve tons per acre, every third year, from its own produce, provided the corn crops are cut with accuracy and the straw manufactured into dung in a husbandman-like manner.

Straw as applicable to Thatching.

For many ages straw was the common material for roofing farm-buildings and cottages, and was formerly made use of even in towns. The expense of a thatched roof is not great, in so far as respects labor; and the value of the straw is, to the grower, either the price he could obtain for it, or that of the dung that could be made from it, as the kind used for thatch is seldom used as fodder. Where economy must be attended to in the building of cottages, straw is taken as the least costly material; but in these days, when manure is so extremely valuable, as little straw as possible should be spared for other purposes.

The durability of a thatched roof is likewise maintained. A good coat of thatch will need very little repair during an ordinary lease. But care must be taken that the straw is very clean threshed. If it is not, the grain left will soon spring, and introduce putrefaction and encourage vermin. The threshing-mill renders straw less fit for thatch than when it is threshed by the flail.

In Great Britain, wheat is seldom threshed with the straw, but the ears are cut off, and the straw, bound in sheaves, and tied very light, is used for thatching.

Miscellaneous Uses of Straw.

It is well known that various articles are manufactured from straw, such as bonnets, and other ornaments for the ladies. Even in remote counties in England, the straw manufacture is carried on. The straw is prepared in London, and the plait is returned to that market. Straw-plaiting is the principal manufacture in Bedfordshire. The quantity thus used is very considerable, and it furnishes employment for numbers of persons who might otherwise with difficulty find the means of subsistence.

In some districts straw mixed with clay is used for building the walls of houses or gardens, and with the same mixture for the roofs of houses, instead of the common mode of thatching.

In districts on the sea-shore, it is common for experienced farmers to keep in reserve a considerable proportion of their wheat or barley straw, and to make it into a dunghill, alternately with the sea-ware, stratum upon stratum, till both are exhausted. This is an excellent plan where the sea-weed cannot be immediately applied, but it is the best system to plough it in, when obtained.

In some places great quantities of bean-haum, as well as common straw, are bought up at potash manufactories, and burnt for the ashes.

Straw is also used for stuffing beds. For this purpose the chaff of oats is found to be a material not much inferior to ordinary feathers; and being so much cheaper, chaff beds are almost universally used by the lower orders in Scotland.

Another purpose to which straw is applied, is that of packing; and it is proper to observe that the quantity used in packing china and stoneware, in the districts where these manufactories prevail, is found to be a serious injury to the farmer.

Rev. James Hall has ascertained that every bean-stalk, according to its size, contains from twenty to thirty-five filaments, which are of a nature among the strongest and most durable hitherto discovered. He calculates that on an average there are about 200 lbs. weight of such filaments on an acre, capable of being applied to various useful purposes, where durability and strength, rather than fineness and delicacy, are required. A tolerable paper is now made of straw.

To under-drain Clay Lands.

This operation is always best performed in spring or summer, when the ground is dry. Main drains ought to be made in every part of the field where a cross-cut or open drain was formerly wanted; they ought to be cut four feet deep, upon an average. This completely secures them from the possibility of being damaged by the treading of horses or cattle, and being so far below the small drains, clears the water finely out of them. In every situation, pipe-turfs for the main drains. If they can be had, are preferable. If good stiff clay, a single row of pipe-turf; if sandy, a double row. When pipe-turf cannot be got conveniently, a good wedge drain may answer well, when the subsoil is a strong, stiff clay; but if the subsoil be only moderately so, a thorn drain, with couples below, will do still better; and if the subsoil is very sandy, except pipes can be had, it is in vain to attempt under-draining the field by any other method. It may be necessary to mention here that the size of the main drains ought to be regulated according to the length and declivity of the run, and the quantity of water to be carried off by them. It is always safe, however, to have the main drains large, and plenty of them; for economy here seldom turns out well.

Having finished the main drains, proceed next to make a small drain in every furrow of the field, if the ridges formerly have not been less than fifteen feet wide. But if that should be the case, first level the ridges, and make the drains in the best direction, and at such a distance from each other as may be thought necessary. If the water rises well in the bottom of the drains, they ought to be cut three feet deep; and in this case would dry the field sufficiently well, although they were from twenty-five to thirty feet asunder; but if the water does not draw well to the bottom of the drains, two feet will be a sufficient deepness for the pipe-drain, and two and a half feet for the wedge-drain. In no case ought they to be shallower where the field has been previously levelled. In this instance, however, as the surface water is carried off chiefly by the water sinking immediately into the top of the drains, it will be necessary to have the drains much nearer each other — say from fifteen to twenty feet. If the ridges are more than fifteen feet wide, however broad and irregular they may be, follow invariably the line of the old furrows, as the best direction for the drains; and, where they are high-gathered ridges, from twenty to twenty-four inches will be a sufficient depth for the pipe-drain, and from twenty-four to thirty inches for the wedge-drain. Particular care should be taken in connecting the small and main drains together, so that the water may have a gentle declivity, with free access into the main drains.

When the drains are finished, the ridges are cleaved down upon the drains by the plough; and where they had been very high formerly, a second clearing may be given; but it is better not to level the ridges too much, for by allowing them to retain a little of their former shape,. the ground being lowest immediately where the drains are, the surface water collects upon the top of the drains; and, by shrinking into them, gets freely away. After the field is thus finished, run the new ridges across the small drains, making them about nine or ten feet broad, and continue afterwards to plough the field in the same manner as dry land.

It is evident from the above method of draining that the expense will vary very much, according to the quantity of main drains necessary for the field, the distance of the small drains from each other, and the distance the turf is to be carried.

The advantage resulting from under-draining, is very great; for besides a considerable saving annually of water furrowing, cross cutting, etc., the land can often be ploughed and sown to advantage, both in the spring and in the fall of the year, when otherwise it would be found quite impracticable; every species of drilled crops, such as beans, potatoes, turnips, etc., can be cultivated successfully; and every species, both of green and white crops, is less apt to fail in wet and untoward seasons.

To drain Lands.

Wherever a burst of water appears in any particular spot, the sure and certain way of getting quit of such an evil is to dig hollow drains to such a depth below the surface as is required by the fall or level that can be gained, and by the quantity of water expected to proceed from the burst or spring. Having ascertained the extent of water to be carried off, taken the necessary levels, and cleared a mouth or leading passage for the water, begin the drain at the extremity next to that leader, and go on with the work till the top of the spring is touched, which probably will accomplish the intended object. But if it should not be completely accomplished, run off from the main drain with such a number of branches as may be required to intercept the water, and in this way disappointment will hardly be experienced. Drains, to be substantially useful, should seldom be less than three feet in depth, twenty or twenty-four inches thereof to be close packed with stones or wood, according to circumstances. The former are the best materials, but in many places are not to be got in sufficient quantities; recourse, therefore, must often be made to the latter, though not so effectual or durable.

It is of vast importance to fill up drains as fast as they are dug out; because, if left open for any length of time, the earth is not only apt to fall in, but the sides get into a broken, irregular state, which cannot afterwards be completely rectified. It also deserves attention, that a proper covering of straw or sod should be put upon the top of the materials, to keep the surface earth from mixing with them; and where wood is the material used for filling up, a double degree of attention is necessary, otherwise the proposed improvement may be effectually frustrated.

Pit Draining.

The pit method of draining is a very effectual one, if executed with judgment. When it is sufficiently ascertained where the bed of water is deposited, which can easily be done by boring with an auger, sink a pit into the place of a size which will allow a man freely to work within its bounds. Dig this pit of such a depth as to reach the bed of the water meant to be carried off; and when this depth is attained, which is easily discerned by the rising of the water, fill up the pit with great land-stones and carry off the water by a stout drain to some adjoining ditch or mouth, whence it may proceed to the nearest river.

Mr. Bayley's directions for Draining Land.

First make the main drains down the slope or fall of the field. When the land is very wet, or has not much fall, there should in general be two of these to a statute acre; for the shorter the narrow drains are, the less liable they are to accidents. The width of the trench for the main drains should be thirty inches at top, but the width at the bottom must be regulated by the nature and size of the materials to be used. If the drain is to be made of bricks ten inches long, three inches thick, and four inches in breadth, then the bottom of the drain must be twelve inches; but if the common sole bricks are used, then the bottom must be proportionably contracted. In both cases there must be an interstice of one inch between the bottom bricks and the sides of the trench, and the vacuity must be filled up with straw, rushes, or loose mould. For the purpose of making these drains the bricks should be moulded ten inches long, four broad and three thick, which dimensions always make the best drain.

To construct Main Drains.

When the ground is soft and spongy the bottom of the drain is laid with bricks placed across. On these, on each side, two bricks are laid flat, one upon the other, forming a drain six inches high and four broad, which is covered with bricks laid flat. When stones are used instead of bricks, the bottom of the drain should be about eight inches in width; and in all cases the bottom of main drains ought to be sunk four inches below the level of the narrow ones, whose contents they receive, even at the point where the latter fall into them.

The main drains should be kept open or uncovered till the narrow ones are begun from them, after which they may be finished; but before the earth is returned upon the stones or bricks, it is advisable to throw in straw, rushes or brushwood, to increase the freedom of the drain. The small narrow drains should be cut at the distance of sixteen or eighteen feet from each other, and should fall into the main drain at very acute angles, to prevent any stoppage. At the point where they fall in, and eight or ten inches above it, they should be made firm with brick or stone. These drains should be eighteen inches wide at the top and sixteen at bottom.

To fill Drains.

The completest method yet known is to cut the strongest willows, or other aquatic brushwood, into lengths of about twenty inches, and place them alternately in the drain, with one end against one side of the bottom and the other leaning against the opposite side. Having placed the strong wood in this manner, fill up the space between them, on the upper side, with the small brushwood, upon which a few rushes or straw being laid, as before mentioned, the work is done. Willow, alder, asp or beach boughs, are exceedingly durable if put into the drain green, or before the sap is dried; but if they are suffered to become dry, and then laid under ground, a rapid decay is the consequence.

As in some situations it is an object of great importance to save the expense of materials commonly used in filling drains, a variety of devices have, with that view, been adopted. One of these is of the following nature:—A drain is first dug to the necessary depth, narrow at bottom. Into the trench is laid a smooth tree or cylindrical piece of wood, twelve feet long, six inches in diameter at the one end and five at the other, having a ring fastened into the thickest end. After strewing a little sand upon the upper side of the tree, the clay, or toughest part of the contents of the trench, is first thrown in upon it, and after that the remainder of the earth is fully trodden down. By means of the ring, the tree is then drawn out to within a foot or two of the smaller or hinder end; and the same operation is repeated till the whole drain is complete. Such a drain is said to have conducted a small run of water a considerable way under ground for more than twenty years without any sign of failure.

To water Meadows.

The water should be set on in the month of October, and also as early in that month as possible. The effects of this watering are very important in strengthening the roots and stalks of the plants, and preparing them for shooting up strong and vigorous next spring; and the blades that now rise form a rough coat against winter, protecting the vital powers of the plants from the severity of that season. It sometimes happens, also, that by delaying the watering process too long, early frosts supervene, and very much impede or prevent the operation. The floods of autumn are very enriching to meadows; but this benefit is lost sight of to a certain degree when the process of watering is delayed too long. Indeed, the latter pasturage of meadows may generally be consumed early in October; and what may then remain is of no importance compared with the advantages to be derived from early watering. Besides, if the meadow must be watered in separate divisions, and at different periods, it must happen, that by delaying the operation till November, some parts of the meadow may receive no water sooner than December or January; and if these months are very severe, it may be wholly impracticable to complete the process at that season.

If the land is fine and rich, it will generally be found that three weeks may be sufficient for the first turn; if sour and coarse, four weeks may be necessary. The verdure will then be fine, and the soil rich and yielding. If scum appear on the grass, the water must be instantly removed.

Should the water not overflow properly, stops must be placed in the small feeders. These are either of stones or stakes, which are firm and durable. Sods rise and float away, and boards are seldom firm enough, though at times they may answer well. If the water, after all, does not flow properly over, notches must be cut, in order to make passages for it.

Separate divisions of meadow occupy the water in succession throughout winter; during which they ought all to receive one turn of the water, as above recommended, if not given in later than autumn.

In severe frosts, it is not very safe to remove the water, as it operates so far to protect the grass; and if exposed wet to frost, it might be greatly injured. If it be necessary to alter the water in such weather, let it be done in the morning of a dry day.

In spring every division of the meadow requires to be again watered; and the fine rich verdure that appears, with the soft unctuous tread of the soil, are indications of advantage being obtained; but the appearance of a white scum warns the floater instantly to remove the water.

To form Inclosures.

Inclosures, with some trifling exceptions, are formed in Great Britain by building stone walls, or planting thorn hedges. In this country rail fences are most used, but wire is becoming common. According to the first method, the walls are either of dry stone, or of stone and lime; and in the last instance lime is either used only in bedding the outer part of the wall, or applied to the whole of it, as circumstances may render necessary. These walls are either coped with sod, or have a cope which tapers to the top, closely built with stone and lime, or the coping is executed with large irregular stones, according to the taste and disposition of the persons by whom they are erected. A wall built with stone and lime is undoubtedly the preferable fence; but the expense far exceeds the value of the interest a tenant generally has in the premises. Such walls ought, therefore, in every case, to be erected by the proprietor, who thus increases the value of his property, in a direct proportion with the increased value given to the land, by the erection of such fences.

To render a stone wall useful as a fence, its height ought never to be less than five feet three inches, otherwise it will not keep in many of the breeds of sheep which prevail in the country. In erecting the fence great care ought to be taken to build upon a solid foundation, otherwise the wall is apt to incline to a side, and gradually to fall down. The coping should be made close, for if the water gets down the inside of the wall, it will bulge out, and finally go to ruin.

To plant Thorn Hedges.

When a thorn hedge is to be planted, it is of advantage to fallow the ground a year beforehand; and if the soil is poor, to dress it with dung, so that the young plants may not be oppressed with weeds, or stunted for want of food, when weak and unable to send forth their fibres in search of nourishment. These things being attended to, and the hedge planted, an annual cleaning ought to be given; sometimes two cleanings are necessary before the hedge will thrive. It is also necessary to fence it at the back with paling, that beasts may be restrained from going over it, and to switch it over when two or three years of age, in order that it may be kept close at the bottom. As the hedge grows up, repeated cuttings are necessary, so that a wide bottom may be gained, without which no hedge can be considered as a suitable fence; and some attention is required to give a proper shape to the top, which is a matter of much importance to the welfare of the hedge. When thorns are allowed to grow to unequal heights, the strong plants are sure to smother the weak ones; and when the hedge becomes broad at the top, it retains water and snow to the great injury of the plant. All these evils may be avoided by proper management: though twelve years must elapse before the best-managed hedge can be considered as a sufficient fence.

To protect Young Thorn Hedges.

The expense of protecting young hedges from cattle, by paling and railing, have always appeared to be too great, and, at the same time, an unnecessary consumption of wood and nails. It occurred to Mr. Moore, steward to the Marquis of Bute, that a more economical protection might be effected by forming a small earthen dike upon the side of the ditch, opposite the line of thorns, sufficiently high to prevent cattle getting into the ditch. Accordingly, some years ago, he tried the experiment, and found it completely to answer his expectation.

The materials of this sort of a protection being always on the ground, it is attended with no expense but the workmanship, and the want of the use of the land occupied by this small ditch, for the time required will be much more than compensated by the saving of paling, railing, workmanship, and nails. Mr. Moore has also practised with success, in parts where dead thorns, or brush for cooking, are scarce, the placing of stones across the top of the dike, instead of the usual cocking. These stones, after having served their purpose, will be useful for drains or dikes where improvements are carrying on.

To form a Plantation.

When a plantation of timber is to be formed, the first step necessary is to fence the ground that is to be planted, so that cattle of all kinds may be kept from making inroads. The ground to be planted ought to be completely fallowed the preceding year, and, if in a rough or waste state, two years fallowing will be useful. If wet or boggy, open drains are to be dug through all the hollow places, so that superfluous moisture may be removed. These operations being performed, the planting may proceed, in executing which great care should be taken to make the pits of a proper size; and, in filling them up, that the best earth be returned nearest the roots. A mixture of timber, in the same plantation, is always advantageous, and thick planting is eligible for the purpose of affording shelter. As the plantation gets forward, attention must be paid to thinning and pruning the trees, removing always those first that are either sickly or debilitated; and, in this way, and by exercising constant attention in the management, timber trees will advance with much more rapidity, than when neglected and overlooked.

Much expense is often incurred in planting trees, which is afterwards lost by neglecting to train them up. Trees indeed are, in most cases, put into the earth, and then left to themselves to grow or die; whereas with them, as with all other plants, the fostering hand of man is indispensably called for in every stage of growth, otherwise they will rarely arrive at perfection, or make that return to the owner which may be reasonably expected when the several processes of planting, pruning, and thinning are duly exercised.

Planting trees in hedge-rows is not only prejudicial to fences, but of great detriment to grain crops cultivated in fields surrounded by these hedge-rows, especially if the fields are of a small size. If shelter is wanted for a field, the best way of procuring it is to form belts, or strips of planting, from fifty to sixty feet wide; for timber trees thrive much better than when planted in rows, or narrow strips. All cold or moorish soils are greatly benefited by being inclosed in this way; though it may be remarked that small inclosures ought to be avoided, because they occasion a great waste of ground without affording a benefit in other respects proportioned to the heavy expense entailed upon the proprietor or tenant, for supporting such a number of unnecessary fences.

The best method of raising Oaks.

The Dutchess of Rutland received the gold medal of the Society for the Encouragement of Arts, Manufactures, and Commerce, for experiments in raising oaks. After five several experiments, her grace is of opinion that the best method is "to sow the acorns where they are to remain, and, after hoeing the rows two years, to plant potatoes, one row only between each row of oaks, for three years. The benefit to the oaks from planting potatoes is incalculable; for, from the said experiments and from others made at the same time, and with the same seedling oaks, planted with a mixture of larch, spruce, beech, birch, and other forest trees, and also with oaks only — in all cases she has found that potatoes between the rows are so superior to all other methods that the oaks will actually grow as much the first four years with them as in six without them. "It appears," she observes, "that the great secret in raising plantations of oaks is to get them to advance rapidly the first eight years from seed, or the first five years from planting, so that the heads of the trees are completely united, and become a smothering crop; after this is effected the trees will appear to strive to outgrow each other, and will advance in height rapidly; they will be clean straight trees, to any given height: experiments have proved the fact, which may be verified by viewing Belvoir."

Sugar-Cane.

The best climate for the sugar-cane is that of tropical or sub-tropical regions. Although sometimes grown in South Carolina, Tennessee, and Kentucky, it cannot be depended upon as a crop farther north than Louisiana. The principal varieties of the plant are the Creole, called also Malabar, the Otaheite, and the Batavian.

The plants are, in our Southern States, put in between January and March; October is the season for gathering the crop. At that time the slips or cuttings are selected for setting out, as the cane is never grown from seed. On general principles we venture to suggest that final deterioration is probable in any plant which is never renewed from seed.

For planting, after breaking up the land, furrows are run four, six or eight feet apart; in these the slips, each having several joints, are laid, from two to five feet apart, and covered not very deeply. The spaces between the rows are ploughed or hoed well. In Louisiana three crops will successively follow from a single planting; in the West Indies one laying will last from ten to twenty years. The yield of sugar to the acre is from 500 to 5000 or more lbs. to the acre; never more than 2000 in this country.

When ripe the canes are cut down close to the ground and stripped of the leaves, which are left to shelter the roots through the winter. This trash is now and then burned or ploughed under. The lowest part of the cane is richest in sugar. All parts of the plant make good fodder.

As soon as cut the canes should be taken to the mill, before fermentation sets in. There are many kinds of mills in use, from the simplest to the most powerful steam apparatus. In them all the canes are crushed repeatedly, so that the juice runs out below; but a great deal of sugar yet remains in the *bagasse*. The crude syrup contains various impurities, and should be at once strained through copper or iron wire into the clarifying vessels. Then it is boiled for concentration, lime being added in just sufficient quantity to neutralize the free acid, which is known by its no longer reddening litmus paper. The heat used should not be more than is necessary for boiling. In about twenty-four hours crystalization begins. The molasses is then drained out from hogsheads bored at the bottom. This process requires from three to six weeks before it is fit for shipping, but it continues to deposit or drip molasses for some time afterwards. Refining or whitening the sugar is performed in various ways, the most useful agent for the purpose being animal-charcoal or bone-black.

Maple Sugar.

This is obtained by tapping the sugar-maple tree in the spring, while the sap is ascending vigorously. The trees grow in groves or orchards in New England, New York, Pennsylvania, Michigan, and Canada, as well as farther south. In February and March persons go to the maple groves and bore the trees with augers, two holes in each tree, near each other, two feet above the ground and only half an inch beyond the bark into the white wood. Tubes of split elder are then introduced, and the sap allowed to flow into troughs prepared for it. The sap is poured into kettles and boiled briskly, the scum being removed as it forms. When it becomes a thick syrup it is cooled and filtered through woollen cloth. After a second boiling it is left for granulation in moulds made of birch bark. Maple sugar may be refined so as to be perfectly white, but is generally eaten in the crude state. A good deal of it is sold in small cakes in the northern cities.

Beet-Root Sugar.

In France and Belgium this is quite largely manufactured. The fresh root of the sugar beet contains from five to twelve per cent. of sugar. The juice is obtained by pressure, after a kind of tearing or grating process has broken up the fibres and cells. The liquor is then boiled with lime, filtered, concentrated by evaporation, and granulated much as cane-sugar.

Tobacco.

The tobacco plant will flourish as far north as Southern Ohio and Pennsylvania. Even in Connecticut large quantities of it are now raised for market. The most suitable soil for it is a light, rich, sandy soil; the finest qualities grow on newly cleared land. Tobacco consumes the strength of the soil more than most crops. The best fertilizer for it is Peruvian guano.

Having selected a lot of newly cleared land, in the early part of March lay a large quantity of brush, leaves, etc., over the ground, and burn it thoroughly, then plough and pulverize the earth well, raking in as much ashes as possible. When the bed has been made smooth and firm, sow your seed about the middle of March, and then tramp it in, being careful to tramp the surface equally.

A few days before the plants are ready for transplanting, the ground should be thrown into ridges with the plough, by throwing two furrows together about two feet apart, and then raking down to from two to three inches above the general level of the surface. A time of wet weather is the best for transplanting. Set the plants about eighteen inches or two feet apart in the rows. This work is generally done from the middle of May to the middle of June.

Cultivate the plants as you would a corn crop, being careful to keep the ground well stoned and clean from weeds. The greatest enemy to contend with is the tobacco worm, which must be often and well looked for and destroyed. These worms will sometimes devour a large plant in a few hours. Some planters keep large flocks of turkeys, and train them to the tobacco field, in order that they may devour the worms; this answers well, and saves a good deal of manual labor.

When the plant makes buds for seed, they must be broken off, or it will make small leaves.

After the plant seems fully grown and assumes a yellowish cast, it is then ripe and fit for housing, which must be done by cutting it off at the ground and piercing with split sticks about four feet long, putting as many plants on each stick as it will hold without pressing them too closely together. If a free circulation of air be prevented the plants will mould. When thus done, hang them up in an airy house, made for the purpose, to dry. It is better to wilt the plants in the sun before housing, if it can be done.

When housed it requires nothing further until it has become seasoned. Then, in damp weather, while the leaves are pliable, strip them off, noting the different qualities as you proceed. Tobacco is generally, at this stage, divided into four qualities —the *ground* leaves, the *bright* red, the *dull* red, and the *tail ends*, or top leaves. When there are large quantities to handle, it is best to have a stripper for each quality, the first taking off the ground leaves, then passing the plant to the next to take off the bright red, and so on until the leaves are all taken off. The stripper should hold them in his hand till he has as many as he can well carry; then he takes a leaf and ties around the stock ends of the bunch, and ties them fast. The bunches of leaves are then to be well packed in heaps, and to remain so until they begin to *heat*. Then they must be shaken out and again hung on the sticks and put up in the house as before. When the bunches are packed in bulk to heat, the pack must be examined every twelve hours, lest it get too hot and spoil.

After the bunches have undergone the fermenting process they are to be tightly packed by hand in hogsheads and powerfully pressed, putting from 800 to 1000 pounds in a hogshead. It is then ready for market.

Cotton.

The most suitable soil for the cotton plant is a rich loam. It cannot be too rich, and it is a poor crop on poor land. Cotton has been raised with success in Delaware, and even in Pennsylvania, but the finest long-staple cannot be produced so far north.

The seed are planted in hills, the rows three or three and a half feet asunder, and the plants about two feet apart in the row. After springing it should be thinned to one plant in a hill. The season for planting is as early in the spring as the ground can be prepared. The soil should be well cultivated and kept clean from weeds.

In the fall, when the pods open, it must be gathered every day and stowed away until there is a sufficiency to run through the cotton gin, which cleans it of seed. It is then packed in bales, when it is ready for market. The yield of cotton per acre is from 500 to 1000 pounds, according to soil, cultivation, season, etc.

DIRECTIONS FOR THE REARING OF SILK WORMS.

Procure eggs in February and March, and choose those of a pale slate or clay color; avoid all which are yellow, as they are imperfect. Keep them in a cold, dry place (where water will, however, not freeze,) until the leaf buds of the mulberry begin to swell. If the eggs be soiled, dip the paper or cloth to which they adhere in water once or twice, to wash off the coat with which they are covered, and which will impede the hatching of the worms. It is not necessary to scrape off the eggs from the paper or cloth on which they have been deposited. Dry them quickly in a draught of air, and put them in one or more shallow boxes lined with paper, which place, if possible, in a small room of the temperature of 64°, and keep it up to that degree for the first two days by means of a fire in the chimney, or, still better, in a brick, tile, or porcelain stove, or for want of these in a iron stove, and use tanners' waste-brok turf, or charcoal for fuel, to promote and keep up a regular bent day and night. The third day increase the heat to 66°, the fourth to 68°, the fifth to 71°, the sixth to 73°, the seventh to 75°, the eighth to 77°, the ninth to 80°, the tenth, eleventh and twelfth to 82°. It is impossible to expect regularity in hatching, if reliance be placed upon our variable weather, and it is the regularity of the worms coming forth which will ensure their uniform growth, save much trouble in feeding and attending those of various ages, and cause the whole, or the greater part, to form their cocoons at the same time, provided proper care be given during their progress.

When the eggs assume a whitish hue the worm is formed; cover the eggs with white paper (never use a newspaper,) pierced full of holes the size of a large knitting needle; the worms when hatched will creep through them; turn up the edges of the paper to prevent their crawling off. Lay twigs of the mulberry, having two or three dry and young leaves on the paper, to collect the worms, and more as they continue to mount. For want of mulberry leaves feed for a short time upon lettuce leaves, perfectly dry; if large they should be cut in strips and the mid rib thrown away, or, still better, feed with the twigs of the white mulberry tree cut up fine. The worms first hatched are the strongest, nevertheless, if only a few come out on the first day, give them away to save trouble, and depend upon those which appear on the second and third days. Give away also the produce of the fourth day, and then the whole stock will go on regularly. If it be wished to rear all that are hatched, endeavor to keep the produce of each day separate, by numbering the boxes and shelves. When the leaves on the twigs are loaded with worms, they are to be gently placed on clean, stout, white paper laid on frames with crossed rattans, giving them plenty of room. The shelves over which these frames should slide may be four feet square and fixed to upright posts; they may be multiplied as required. Whether a distinct building or apartment in a dwelling-house be devoted to a large parcel, it is absolutely necessary to secure the command of a gentle circulation of air by having ventilators in the windows, floors, and doors.

One or more tin circular ventilators in place of panes of glass would always ensure a regular circulation in the apartment; they may be stopped when their motion is not required. Red ants are deadly enemies to silk worms; to prevent their attacks the posts containing fixed shelves must not touch the ceiling, nor must the shelves reach the walls; the lower part of the posts should be smeared with thick molasses. If the worms are fed on tables or movable frames, their legs may also be smeared with molasses or put in a dish of water; guard also against cockroaches, mice, and other vermin.

The worms being all hatched, whether they are to remain in the first apartment or be removed to another room or distinct building, the heat must be reduced to 75°, for as the worms grow older they require less heat.

It is impossible to insure the regular hatching of the worms without the use of a thermometer.

First Age—that is, until the Worms have passed their First Moulting or changed their First Skin.

The apartment must be light, but the sun must not shine on the worms in any stage.

Feed the worms with the most tender leaves four times a day, allowing six hours between each meal; give the smallest quantity for the first feeding, and gradually increase it at each meal between the moultings.

In about an hour and a half, the silk-worms devour their portion of leaves, and then remain more or less quiet. Whenever food is given, widen the spaces for them; scattered food may be swept into its place.

Experiments may be made as to the comparative advantages of using chopped or whole young leaves. If chopped, a sharp knife must be used, to prevent the leaves from being bruised, and thereby causing the exudation of water from them, which would prove injurious. On the fourth day the skin becomes of a hazel color and looks shining, their heads enlarge and assume a silvery bright appearance; these are marks of their approaching first change. Their food on this day, therefore, may be diminished, or when these appearances take place, but not before. Enlarge the spaces as the worms increase in size. The leaves ought to be gathered a few hours before they are used, that they may lose their sharpness: they keep very well in a cool cellar three days. The leaves ought to be gathered over night for the morning's meal, to prevent the danger of collecting them in rainy weather. The leaves must be pulled carefully, and not bruised. On the fourth day the appetites of the worms begin to decrease, preparatory to their first moulting, and their food must be diminished in proportion as the previous meal has not been completely eaten. If the precarious heat of the weather has been depended upon, the first change may not appear until the sixth or seventh day.

In the course of the fifth day all the worms become torpid; during this period, and in the subsequent moultings, they must on no account be disturbed. A few begin to revive at the close of the fifth day; some leaves may be then given. After the first moulting the worms are of a dark ash color.

Second Age.

As the worms are fond of the young twigs, some of these should be spread over them with the leaves attached, upon which the worms will immediately fasten, and they may then be removed to a clean paper; or lay a strip of chopped leaves near the worms, and they will leave the old food.

The litter is to be taken away; but as some of the worms often remain among the old leaves, they ought to be examined. To this end the litter should be removed to another room, spread out on a table, and a few twigs placed over it, on which the worms, if any, will mount, when they may be added to the others. This rule must be attended to after every moulting. Ten per cent. is generally allowed for loss of young worms. The first two meals of the first day should be less plentiful than the last two, and must consist of the most tender leaves; these must be continued for food until after the third moulting.

If between the moultings any worms should appear sick and cease to eat, they must be removed to another room, where the air is pure and a little warmer than that they have left, put on clean paper, and some fresh leaves, chopped fine, given to them; they will soon recover, and then may be added to the others.

On the third day the appetite of many worms will be visibly diminished, and in the course of it many will become torpid; the next day all are torpid; on the fifth day they will all have changed their skins and will be roused.

The color of the worms in the second age becomes a light grey, the muzzle is white, and the hair hardly to be seen.

It must never be forgotten, that during the time the worms are occupied in moulting the food should be greatly diminished, and no more given than will satisfy those which have not yet become torpid on the first day, or those which have changed their skins before the others.

Third Age.

During this age the thermometer must range between 71° and 73°. The revived worms are easily

SILK WORMS.

known by their new aspect. The latest worms should be placed apart, as their next moulting will be a day later also, or they may be put in the hottest part of the room to hasten their growth. This rule must be observed in the next moulting—increase the spaces.

The second day the first two meals are to be the least copious, the last two the greatest, because towards the close of the day the worms grow very hungry. The third day will require about the same quantity as the preceding last meals; but on the fourth day, as the appetites of the worms sensibly diminish, not more than half the former feed will be required. The first meal is to be the largest: feed those that will eat at any time of the day. The fifth day still less will suffice, as the greatest part are moulting; the sixth day they begin to rouse. Remove the litter, or even before they are moulted, if the worms are numerous.

Fourth Age.

The thermometer should range between 68° and 71°. If the weather be warm, and the glass rise several degrees higher, open the ventilators, exclude the sun, and make a slight blaze in the chimney, to cause a circulation of the air. Widen the spaces for the worms. The leaves must now be regularly chopped in a straw-cutting box, or with a chopping-knife. The food is to be greatly increased on the second, third, and fourth days. On the fifth less will be required, as in the course of this day many become torpid; the first meal on this day should therefore be the largest. On the sixth they will want still less, as nearly the whole will be occupied in effecting their last change of skin. Renew the air in the apartment by burning straw or shavings in the chimney, and open the ventilators. If the evenings be cool, after a hot day, admit the external air for an hour. None but full grown leaves should be hereafter given to the worms, and they must be all chopped; avoid the fruit, as they would prove injurious, and add greatly to the litter. On the seventh day all the worms will have roused, and thus finish their fourth age. The litter must be again removed.

Fifth Age, or until the Worms prepare to Mount.

The thermometer should be about 68°. The constitution of the worms being now formed, they begin to elaborate the silk-vessels, and fill them with the silky material, which they decompose, and form from the mulberry leaves. Give abundance of room: do not let the worms lie so close as to touch one another, for their respiration will be thereby impeded. Continue to feed regularly and fully, as the appetite of the worms now becomes voracious: give food rather five times a day than four; even six meals will not be too many. The last meal should be late at night, and the first the next day in the morning, at an early hour. The worms are not again to be moved, and the hurdles or feeding frames must be cleaned. On the seventh day of the fifth age they have attained their largest size, viz., three inches long, and begin to grow shining and yellow. The appetites of some diminish, but that of others continues, and must be supplied, to hasten their maturity. The litters must be removed every two days during the fifth age, but not when the worms are moulting, unless it can be done without disturbing them.

The preservation of the proper temperature of the apartment at this stage cannot be too seriously impressed upon the cultivator. If sudden and great heat in the weather should take place, as often happens at this time, serious loss may be suffered, without proper precautions. The increased heat to which the worms are exposed causes them to cease eating, to leave their feeding shelves, and to wander about the room in order to find corners and places to form their cocoons in before the silk fluid has been fully elaborated or matured; thus defeating, in a great measure, all the care previously bestowed upon them. In the summer of the year 1825 vast numbers of worms were killed by hot weather in Mansfield, Connecticut. To guard against sudden heat in the weather, close the window shutters while the sun is beating on them, and keep the ventilators in the ceiling or other parts of the room open; and. if possible, tubs of ice should be brought into the apartment until the thermometer shows a diminution of temperature to the proper degree. The windows must also be kept open every evening, and until sunrise next morning, and water sprinkled on the floor to promote evaporation, and consequently a freshness in the air. If the worms should become diseased during the fourth or fifth ages, oak leaves may be given to them. These are stated to have been found very beneficial; but the species of oak is not mentioned. The white oak may be tried.

Of the rearing of Silk Worms in the last period of the Fifth Age; that is, until the Cocoon is Perfected.

The fifth age can only be looked on as terminated when the cocoon is perfect.

The cleanliness of the feeding frames in these last days of the fifth age requires great attention to preserve the health of the silk worms. About the tenth day of the fifth age the worms attain perfection, which may be ascertained by the following indications:

1st. When on putting some leaves on the wickers, the insects get upon the leaves without eating them, and rear their heads as if in search of something else.

2d. When looking at them horizontally the light shines through them, and they appear of a whitish-yellow transparent color.

3d. When numbers of the worms which were fastened to the inside of the edges of the wickers, and straightened, now get upon the edges and move slowly along, instinct urging them to seek change of place.

4th. When numbers of worms leave the centre of the wickers, and try to reach the edges and crawl upon them.

5th. When their rings draw in and their greenish color changes to a deep golden hue.

6th. When their skins become wrinkled about the neck, and their bodies have more softness to the touch than heretofore, and feel like soft dough.

7th. When in taking a silk worm in the hand, and looking through it, the whole body has assumed the transparency of a ripe yellow plum. When these signs appear in any of the insects, everything should be prepared for their rising, that those worms which are ready to rise may not lose their strength and silk in seeking for the support they require. Handle the worms at this stage with the greatest gentleness, as the slightest pressure injures them. When moved, they should be left on the twigs or leaves to which they are fastened, to prevent their being hurt by tearing them off. A blunt hook should be used to take up those not adhering to leaves or twigs.

Preparation of the Hedge.

A week or ten days before the worms are ready to mount, bundles of twigs of chestnut, hickory, oak, or of the birch of which stable-brooms are made, must be procured, prepared, and arranged in bunches, so that the worms may easily climb up them to work their cocoons. As soon as it is observed that the worms want to rise, the bundles of twigs must be arranged on the feeding trays, leaving fifteen inches between them. The top branches should touch the lower part of the tray above that on which they are placed, so as to form an arch — and be placed a little aslant, that the worms, when climbing, may not fall off. The branches should be spread out like fans, that the air may penetrate through all parts and the worms work with ease. When the worms are too near one another they do not work so well, and form double cocoons, which are only worth half a single round cocoon. Leave openings at the tops of the curves for the worms to form their cocoons in.

As soon as the worms are prepared to rise, the feeding frames should be cleaned thoroughly and the apartment well ventilated. Put the worms which are ready to rise near the hedges, and give a few leaves to those that are still inclined to eat. After they have begun to rise, those that are weak and lazy do not yet seem to be inclined to rise, and remain motionless on the leaves. These should be taken away, and put in a clean dry room of at least 75° of heat, where there are hurdles covered with paper, and the hedge prepared for them. The increased heat will cause them to rise directly. All the silk worms being off the hurdles, they should be immediately cleaned. The temperature of the room should be between 68° and 71°. When the worms are forming their cocoons the utmost silence must be preserved in the room, as they are very sensible to noise, and, if disturbed, will for a moment cease to spin; thus the continuity of the thread will be interrupted, and the value of the cocoon diminished. When the cocoons have attained a certain consistency, the apartment may be left quite open.

Sixth Age, beginning in the Chrysalis State, and ending when the Moths Appear.

The following are the necessary things to be done:

I. To gather the cocoons.
II. To choose the cocoons which are to be preserved for the eggs.
III. Preservation of cocoons until the appearance of the moth.

I. Gathering of the Cocoons.

Strong, healthy, and well managed silk worms will complete their cocoons in three days and a half at farthest, reckoning from the moment when they first begin casting the floss. This period will be shorter if the silk worms spin the silk in a higher temperature than that which has been indicated, and in very dry air.

It will be better not to take off the cocoon before the eighth or ninth day, reckoning from the time when the silk-worm first rose. They may be taken off on the seventh, if the laboratories have been conducted with such regularity that the time may be known with certainty, when this may be done.

Begin on the lower tier of hurdles and take the cabins down gently, giving them to those who are to gather the cocoons; place a basket between two of the gatherers to receive the cocoons; another person should receive the stripped bushes, which may be laid by for another year. All the cocoons that want a certain consistency, and feel soft, should be laid aside, that they may not be mixed with the better. Empty the baskets upon hurdles or trays placed in rows, and spread the cocoons about four fingers deep, or nearly to the top of the feeding frame. When the cocoons are detached, the down or floss in which the silk-worms have formed the cocoon should be taken off. If the cocoons are for sale, weigh them and send them to the purchaser. The baskets, the floor and all things used, should be cleaned.

When gathering the cocoons, make four assortments: 1st. Those designed for breed. 2d. The dupions, or double ones. 3d. The firmest of those which are to be reeled. 4th. Those of a looser texture.

II. Choosing the Cocoons for the Production of Eggs.

About two ounces of eggs may be saved out of one pound and a half of male and female cocoons. The small cocoons of a straw color, with hard ends, and fine webs, and which are a little depressed in the middle, as if tightened by a ring or circle, are to be preferred. There are no certain signs to distinguish the male from the female cocoons; the best known are the following:

The small cocoons sharper at one or both ends, and depressed in the middle, generally produce the male. The round full cocoons without ring or depression in the middle, usually contain the female.

These may be distinguished from the dupions by the extra size, the clumsy shape, rather round than oval, of the latter. As however all marks may fail, an extra number may be kept, of the best of those which are spun double; and when the moths come out, the males and females being easily distinguished, an addition can be made from them to the defective side.

By shaking the cocoon close to the ear, we may generally ascertain whether the chrysalis be alive. If it be dead, and loosened from the cocoon, it yields a sharp sound. When dead it yields a muffled sound, more confined in the cocoon.

III. Preservation of Cocoons intended for Seed, or until the Appearance of the Moth.

Experience shows that where the temperature of the room is above 73° the transition of the chrysalis to the moth state will be too rapid, and the coupling will not be productive; if below 66° the development of the moth is tardy, which is also injurious. Damp air will change it into a weak and sickly moth; the apartment should, therefore, be kept in an even dry temperature, between 66° and 73°. When collected spread the cocoons on a dry floor, or on tables, and strip them clean of down or floss, to prevent the feet of the moth from being entangled in it when coming out. While cleaning them, all those that appear to have any defect should be luid aside; this is the time, also, to separate the male and female cocoons, as far as we can distinguish them.

Select an equal number of males and females, and keep the cocoons of the same day's mounting separate, that the moths may pierce them at the same time. If the good cocoons taken from the whole parcel, are all first mixed, and the selection for those intended for breeding be made from this general heap, many will be set aside, which were formed by worms that had mounted upon different days, and which will be pierced by the moths unequally, and hence there will not be an equal number of males and females produced at the same time; this irregular appearance may cause the loss of a great many moths, or of several thousand eggs.

When the selection has been made, the sorted cocoons must be put on tables, in layers of about two inches, allowing the air to pass freely through them, that it may not be necessary to stir them frequently; but it is beneficial to stir them round once a day, if the air be moist. When the seed cocoons are not very numerous, they may be strung upon threads, and hung against a wall, or suspended from a beam. Just so much of the middle of the cocoon is to be pierced with a needle as is sufficient to attach it to the thread. The middle is chosen, because it cannot be ascertained at which end the moth will pierce the cocoon. Place a male and female cocoon alternately upon the thread, that they may be near each other when they come out.

If the heat of the apartment is above 73°, every method of diminishing the heat should be tried: such as keeping all the apertures to the sunny side carefully closed, to cause thorough drafts of air to dry the humidity that exhales from the chrysalides. Should the temperature rise to 78° or 82°, the cocoons must be put in a cooler place, as a dry cellar.

Seventh Age of the Silk Worm.

The seventh, and the last age of the silk worm, comprises the entire life of the moth.

The formation of the moth, and its disposition to issue from the cocoon, may be ascertained when one of its extremities is perceived to be wet, which is the part occupied by the head of the moth. A few hours after, and sometimes in one hour after, the moth will pierce the cocoon and come out; occasionally the cocoon is so hard, and so wound in silk, that the moth in vain strives to come forth, and dies in the cocoon. Sometimes the female deposits some eggs in the cocoon before she can get out, and often perishes in it; this circumstance has induced some to extract the chrysalis from the cocoon by cutting it, that the moth may have only to pierce its thin envelope; but the experienced Dandolo disapproves of the practice (although he has performed the operation with success) because it is tedious; and should the moth be put on a plain surface, five in a hundred will not be able to get out, but will drag the envelope along, and at last die, not being able to disencumber themselves. If the surface be not smooth, the moths will issue with greater ease; it is very favorable to the moths when they put forth their head and first legs, to find some substance to which they may fasten, and thus facilitate clearing out of the cocoon by the support. For this reason they should be spread out very thin on tables covered with a muslin or linen cloth. The life of the moth lasts, in Italy, ten, eleven, or twelve days, according to the strength of its constitution, and the mildness of the atmosphere. With Mr. Dusar, of Philadelphia, the moths lived from five to eight days; a hot temperature accelerates their operations and the drying which precedes their death.

Hatching of the Moths, and their Preservation.

Cocoons kept in a temperature of 66° begin to be hatched after fifteen days; those kept in a heat between 71° and 73°, begin to come forth after eleven or twelve days. The room in which the moths are produced should be dark, or at least there should be only sufficient light to distinguish objects. This is an important rule, and must be carefully attended to. The moths do not come forth in great numbers the first or the second day, but are chiefly hatched on the fourth, fifth, sixth, and seventh days, according to the degree of heat in which the cocoons have been kept. The hours when the moths burst the cocoons in the greatest numbers, are the three and four hours after sunrise, if the temperature is from 64° to 66°. The male moths, the very moment they come out, go eagerly in quest of the female; when they are united, they must be placed on frames covered with linen, and made in such a manner as to allow the linen to be changed when soiled. Much care must be taken in raising the united moths; they must be held by the wings in order not to separate them. When one small table is filled with moths in a state of union, they are to be carried into a small room, sufficiently airy and fresh, and which can be made very dark. Having employed the first hours of the day in selecting and carrying the united moths, the males and females which are found separate on the tables are to be brought into contact, put on frames and carried into the dark room. It is easy to ascertain if there are more females than males. The body of the female is nearly double the size of that of the male; besides, the male which is single, beats about its wings at the least approach of light; the hour must be noted at which the tables containing the united moths are placed in the dark room.

If, after this operation is over, there still remain some moths of each sex, they are to be placed in a small box with a perforated cover, until the moment favorable for their union arrives. From time to time they must be looked at, to see if they separate, in order that they may be brought anew into contact.

When any thing is to be done in the dark chamber, as little light as possible must be admitted, only sufficient to distinguish objects. The more light there is the more the moths are disturbed and troubled in their operations, as light is too stimulating for them. The boxes are very convenient to keep quiet the males which remain, and thus prevent the fine powder adhering to their wings from flying about, and the destruction of their wings, and consequently their vital power. The cocoons must be removed as fast as they are pierced by the moth, for being moist they communicate their humidity to those which are still entire. The paper also on the trays, when soiled, is to be removed, and fresh supplied. Constant attention is required during the whole day, as there is a succession in the process of hatching, and union of the moths, which occasionally vary in relative proportion to one another. Instead of a frame paper may be used for receiving the eggs. A few good cocoons will not produce moths, owing to their hardness, which prevents the moth from making a hole by which to come forth.

Separation of the Moth and laying the Eggs.

If there be an excess of males they must be thrown away; if of females, males must be allotted to them, which have already been in a state of union. Great care must be taken when the couples are separated not to injure the males. The male ought not to remain united more than six hours; after the lapse of that time take the moths by the wings and body and separate them gently. All the males which are no longer in union must be placed upon a frame, the most vigorous afterwards selected and united with those females which have not yet had a mate. Other vigorous males must be preserved in a separate box, and kept in darkness. When there is a want of males let them remain united to the female the first time only five hours instead of six; the females are not injured by waiting for the male even many hours; the only loss sustained is that of some eggs, which are not impregnated. Before separating the two sexes prepare in a cool, dry, airy chamber the linen on which the moth is to deposit its eggs.

Six hours, as just said, is the usual time for the moths to remain united, for in that time the eggs of the female will be fully impregnated. It is also the general practice not to use the male another female, but Mr. Delonchamps assures us that in the event of having more female than male moths, the latter may be again used to profit. In the year 1824 he raised many worms from eggs the produce of a sixth coupling, which were fully equal to those produced from those at the first; the union continued never less than from twenty to twenty-four hours; the male after a sixth union appeared as lively and as brisk as at first, but he had no more females. The eggs from even a thirteenth union of the same male with different females had all the characters of those of the best quality. In these cases the disunion of the pair was, moreover, never spontaneous, but always required to be effected by the hands.

The following is the manner in which the cloth must be arranged:

At the bottom of a tressel or frame, which must be proportioned to the number of moths, place horizontally on each side of the length two boards, so arranged that one of their sides may be nailed to the tressel about five inches and a half high above the ground, and that the other side of the board shall be a little higher and project outwards. Upon the tressel lay a cloth, so that it may hang equally on each side. The ends of the cloth must cover the boards below; the more perpendicular the lateral parts of the tressel are the less soiled will be the cloth by the evacuation of the liquid from the moths. The moths which have been united six hours are then to be gently separated, the females placed on the frame and carried to the tressel and placed on the cloth, one over another, beginning at the top and going downwards. Note the time at which the moths are placed on the cloth, and keep those which are placed afterwards separate, to avoid confusion.

The females that have had a virgin mate must be treated in the same manner as those which have been united with one that had been coupled previously five hours. The females should be left on the cloth thirty-six or forty hours without being touched; at this time if it be observed that the linen has not been well stocked with eggs, other females must be placed upon it, in order that the eggs may be equally distributed. When the heat of the room is 77° or 79°, or when at 63° or 65°, the eggs will be yellow, that is unimpregnated, or of a reddish color, that is imperfectly impregnated, and will not produce worms; the temperature of the room must therefore be kept between these extremes. Sometimes a female moth will escape from its mate before impregnation and produce many worthless eggs.

The female cocoons, as before noted, are generally larger than the males and not so much pointed as these are, and are without the ring or depression in the middle, which commonly distinguishes the cocoons containing the latter.

Eight or ten days after the deposition of the eggs the jonquil color peculiar to them will change to a reddish gray, and afterwards into a pale clay hue; they are of a lenticular form, and on both surfaces there is a slight depression.

Preservation of the Eggs.

Collect the eggs which have fallen on the cloth covering the shelves of the tressel, when quite dry, and put them in a box, and, if numerous, in layers not more than half the breadth of the finger. The cloths raised from the tressel when quite dry are to be folded and placed in a dry room, the temperature of which does not exceed 65°, nor below the freezing point, 32°.

During the summer the cloths must be examined every month, to remove insects, and to preserve the cloths always in fresh air; if the quantity be large, place them on a frame of cord attached to the ceiling or a rafter. A barrel-hoop crossed with stout pack-thread will make a good frame. A small quantity may be kept in a tin case. If a board box be used the joints and edges of the top should be pasted with paper to exclude ants.

There exists a notion that every two or three years the eggs should be changed. It requires little to be said on this egregious error. To suppose that the good cocoons of a cultivator, after a few years, are no longer fit to produce seed, and yet that these cocoons can give good seed for the use of another, would be to admit a superstitious contradiction, which reason, practice, and science alike condemn. A change of seed can only be necessary when, from great neglect for a series of years of the worms, a diminutive race has been produced. Worms properly treated will never degenerate. On the subject of the degeneracy of silk-worms, in the United States, the most positive information can be given.

Mr. Samuel Alexander, of Philadelphia, says: "I am convinced that silk worms cultivated in Pennsylvania, instead of degenerating, improve; proof of which I possess, in comparing the cocoons of four years since with those of the last year. I can say, with truth, the worms hatched from the eggs I brought from the south of Europe have produced annually better silk." The testimony of Mr. Sharrod M'Call, of Florida, is still more decisive.

A sample of beautiful sewing-silk, sent with his communication to the Secretary of the Treasury, was part of a parcel produced by worms, the stock of which he has had thirty years; and they were obtained from a maternal ancestor, who had possessed them many years before.

During all this long period no degeneracy has been observed. Let proper care be taken of silkworms, and no deterioration will take place.

The time has passed when the idle reveries of Buffon, Robertson, De Pauw, and others, respecting the tendency of nature "to belittle" and degenerate everything foreign in the new world, were received as truths. Facts, proud facts, demonstrate not only the absurdity of their positions, but the superiority of many American animals and vegetables, when compared with similar productions in the old world.

To bake Cocoons.

Cocoons reel more readily, and yield silk of a superior quality, without killing the insect by either steam of hot water, or by baking them; but those who have not the means of reeling off their cocoons in two or three days after they are formed, or of selling them, must kill the insects they contain, or they will eat through, and spoil the cocoons by breaking the continuity of the thread. The easiest way to do this is to bake them in an oven, which must be about as hot as when bread has been taken out of it. After picking out all the spotted cocoons, put the rest in flat baskets, filling them within an inch of the top; cover them with paper, and a wrapper over it; put these baskets in the oven, and after an hour draw them out and cover them with a woollen rug, leaving the wrapper as it was. Let them stand five or six hours, to keep in the heat and stifle the chrysalis. Then spread them in thin layers on shelves, and move them every day (to prevent their becoming mouldy) until perfectly dry. It may be important to state that the birth of the moth may be prolonged a month, by keeping the cocoons in a very cold dry cellar. If the cocoons are kept over summer, they must be protected from ants, mice, and cockroaches.

On the Culture of the White Mulberry Tree.

The proper soils for this tree are dry, sandy, or stony; the more stony the better, provided the roots can penetrate them. The situation should be high: low, rich, and moist lands never produce nourishing leaves, however vigorously the trees may grow. They are always found to be too watery. The same remark may be made upon the leaves of young seedling plants, which will not produce good or abundant silk, and are only proper when the worms are young, say in their first two ages. It may be useful to have a parcel of these growing in a warm situation, that they may come forward before large trees, and serve for early food.

Mulberry trees may be propagated by—1st, seed; 2d, grafting; 3d, budding; 4th, layers; 5th, cuttings; 6th, suckers.

The ripe fruit may be sown in drills, in ground previously prepared; or the seeds may be washed out of the pulp, and mixed with an equal quantity of sand or fine mould, and then sown. They should be covered about a quarter of an inch deep. The seeds will soon vegetate, if the ground be rich, and will live through the winter, unless the cold should be unusually severe. A quantity of plants from seeds thus treated lived through the coldest winters in the Middle States. In very cold weather the young plants may be covered with straw or long manure. The following spring thin the plants, so that they may stand one foot apart at least. Seeds intended to be sown in the spring, or to be kept, should be washed out, as they are apt to heat or to mould, if permitted to remain in the fruit. Land destined for spring sowing should be dug or ploughed in the preceding autumn, left rough all winter, and be harrowed or raked fine, as soon as the season will permit, and the seed sown in drills. The young plants must be watered in dry weather, and weeds carefully kept down. Weeds will not only stint the growth of the plants, but cause disease in them, which may affect the future vigor and health of the tree. In the second year transplant them to two feet distance from one another, to give room for cleansing and dressing the land. When transplanting, cut off some of the roots, especially those that are ragged or decayed, and the tap-root, to force out lateral roots; and also the tops, at six or seven inches from the ground. When the plants in the nursery have sprung, strip off the side buds, and leave none but such as are necessary to form the head of the tree. The buds which are left should be opposite to one another. If the plants in the nursery do not shoot well the first year, in the month of March following cut them over, about seven inches from the ground, and they will grow briskly. They should be watered with diluted barn-yard water.

When the plants have grown to the size of one inch in diameter, plant them out in fields or places where they are to remain, and make the hole six feet square; trim the roots, and press the earth on the roots as the holes are filled. During the first year of planting out, leave all the buds which the young trees have pushed out on the top till the following spring, when none are to be left but three or four branches to form the head of the tree. The buds on these branches should be on the outside of them, that the shoots may describe a circle round the stem, and that the interior of the tree may be kept open; and as the buds come out rub off all those on the bodies of the trees. For several years after, every spring open the heads of the trees when to: thick of wood, and cut off any branch which crosses or takes the lead of the rest, leaving two buds on the outside of every trimmed branch. Count Verri, of Italy, an experienced cultivator of the mulberry tree, recommends to leave only one bud at the end of every branch, preferring those which are outside and opposite to each other; and when three buds appear together to leave the middle one, which is always most vigorous, and to detach the two on each side of it. If the superior buds do not push well, the two next lower ones must be left. Every farmer knows the very great importance of dressing ground round young trees twice in the course of a year, and of securing them to stakes, to insure an upright, straight growth, and to prevent their being shaken by winds or levelled by storms. The trees may be planted at the usual distances of apple trees. The intervals may be cultivated in cabbages, turnips, or mangel wurtzel. The attendance necessary to Indian corn would endanger the young trees.

It is so much the practice in the United States to let trees take their chance for growing, after they have been planted, or sprung up from seeds or stones, that these particular directions may be disregarded. But let a comparative experiment be made with mulberry trees permitted to grow at will, and others treated as here directed, and the difference in their beauty and growth will be obvious. The advantage, in these respects, will be decidedly in favor of trees which have been attended to.

Without deciding upon the superiority of the various modes of propagating mulberry trees, it is thought proper to mention the great advantage of the mode of budding. In the year 1826, Mr Millington, of Missouri, "budded the white mulberry on stocks of native trees; and such as were done before July were forced out immediately by cutting off the stocks above the buds. Some of these buds made limbs more than two feet long by the 27th of October. The buds put in after the middle of July he did not intend to force out until the following spring. He thinks budding more expeditious and surer than engrafting, and when it fails does not injure the stock so much as this mode. Native stocks, to engraft or bud on, can be procured with ease; and the trees thus raised would not be liable to disease in their roots, like foreign trees: and these engrafted or budded trees would grow much faster, and furnish leaves much sooner, and of a larger size, and better quality. This will not be doubted by those who have observed how much faster an engrafted tree grows, and how much larger its leaves are than those of a seedling tree."

Experience has fully shown that the leaves of the native mulberry tree produce good and strong silk; although not so fine as that from the white mulberry. Those, therefore, who have only the native tree, may begin their operations with it; and they will acquire a knowledge of the business of rearing silk worms, while the foreign species is growing.

It must be added that experience in the raising of the mulberry silk worm has led to much disappointment in this country. Recently, the ailanthus silk worm (bombyx or attacus cynthia) has been introduced, and affords promise of success. Dr. Stewardson, of Philadelphia, and Rev. Mr. Morris, of Baltimore, report very favorably of its hardiness and productiveness. Fabrics made of its silk are very durable. The U. S. Agricultural Department, at Washington, will furnish the eggs for trial.

HORTICULTURE.

To choose the best Soil for a Garden.

Prefer a sandy loam, not less than two feet deep, and good earth not of a binding nature in summer, nor retentive of rain in winter; but of such a texture that it can be worked without difficulty in any season of the year. There are few sorts of fruit-trees or esculent vegetables, which require less depth of earth to grow in than two feet to bring them to perfection, and if the earth of the kitchen-garden be three or more feet deep, so much the better; for when the plants are in a state of maturity, if the roots even of peas, spinach, kidney beans, lettuce, etc., be minutely traced, they will be found to penetrate into the earth, in search of food, to the depth of two feet, provided the soil be of a nature that allows them; if it can be done, a garden should be made on land whose bottom is not of a springy wet nature. If this rule can be observed, draining will be unnecessary, for when land is well prepared for the growth of fruit trees and esculent vegetables, by trenching, manuring, and digging, it is by these means brought into such a porous temperament, that the rains pass through it without being detained longer than necessary. If the land of a garden be of too strong a nature, it should be well mixed with sand, or scrapings of roads, where stones have been ground to pieces by carriages.

To make Gravel Walks.

The bottom should be laid with lime-rubbish, large flint stones, or any other hard matter, for eight or ten inches, to keep weeds from growing through, and over this the gravel is to be laid six or eight inches thick. This should be lain rounding up in the middle, by which means the larger stones will run off to the sides, and may be raked away; for the gravel should never be screened before it is laid on. It is a common mistake to lay these walks too round, which not only makes them uneasy to walk upon, but takes off from their apparent breadth. One inch in five feet is a sufficient proportion for the rise in the middle; so that a walk twenty feet wide should be four inches higher at the middle than at the edges, and so in proportion. As soon as the gravel is laid, it should be raked, and the large stones thrown back again; then the whole should be rolled both lengthwise and crosswise; and the person who draws the roller should wear shoes with flat heels that he may make no holes, because holes made in a new walk are not easily remedied. The walks should always be rolled three or four times after very hard showers, from which they will bind more firmly than otherwise they could ever be made to.

To prepare Hot-beds, Manures, and Composts.

Stable-dung is in the most general use for forming hot-beds, which are masses of this dung after it has undergone its violent fermentation.

Bark is preferable to dung because the substance which undergoes the process of putrid fermentation requires longer time to decay. Hence it is found useful in the bark pits of hot-houses, as requiring to be less often moved or renewed than dung or any other substance.

Leaves, and especially oak leaves, come the nearest to bark, and have the additional advantage that when perfectly rotten like dung they form a rich mould or excellent manure.

The object of preparation in these three substances being to get rid of the violent heat which is produced when the fermentation is most powerful, it is obvious that preparation must consist in facilitating the process. For this purpose a certain degree of moisture and air in the fermenting bodies are requisite, and hence the business of the gardener is to turn them over frequently and apply water when the process appears impeded, and exclude rain when chilled with too much water.

Recent stable-dung generally requires to lie a month in ridges or beds, and be turned over in that time thrice before it is fit for cucumber-beds of the common construction; but for McPhail's hot-beds, or for linings, or for frames with movable bottoms, three weeks, a fortnight, or less, will suffice, or no time at all need be given, but the dung formed at once into linings. Tan and leaves require in general a month. Fermentation is always most rapid in summer, and if the materials are spread abroad during the frost, it is totally impeded. In winter the process of preparation generally goes on under the back sheds, which situation is also the best in summer, as full exposure to the sun and wind dries too much the exterior surface; but where sheds cannot be had, it will go on very well in the open air. Some cultivators have devised plans to economize heat by fermenting dung in vineries which are just beginning to be forced, or in vaults under pine pits, or plant stoves.

To form Dung Beds.

In general such beds are formed on a level surface, but Mr. T. A. Knight's plan is to form a surface of earth as a basis, which shall incline to the horizon to the extent of 15°; on this he forms the dung-bed to the same inclination, and finally the frame, when placed on such a bed, if as is usual, it be deepest behind, will present its glass at an angle of 20°, instead of six or eight, which is undoubtedly of great advantage in the winter season.

Ashes are often mixed with the dung of hot-beds, and are supposed to promote the steadiness and duration of their heat, and at least to revive it if somewhat decayed. Tan leaves have also been used for the same purpose, and it is generally found that about one-third of tan and two-thirds of dung will form a more durable and less violent bent than a bed wholly of dung. The heat of dung-beds is revived by linings or collateral and surrounding walls or banks of fresh dung, the old dung of the bed being previously cut down close to the frames, and in severe weather the sides of the beds are often protected by bundles of straw or faggots.

The residuum of heats, properly reduced by keeping, is a good simple manure for most fruit trees, and excellent in a compost; but where the soil is naturally cold a little ashes of coals, wood, straw, or burnt turf, or a minute proportion of soot, ought to be incorporated with it. Hog-dung has a peculiar virtue in invigorating weak trees Rotten turf, or any vegetable refuse, is a general manure, excellent for all soils not already too rich. One of the best correctives of too rich a soil is drift sand. For an exhausted soil, where a fruit-tree that has been an old, profitable occupant is wished to be continued, a dressing of animal matter is a powerful restorative, such as hogs' or bul-

COMPOSTS FOR MANURES.

locks blood, offal from the slaughter-house, refuse of skins and leather, decomposed carrion, etc. The drainings of dung laid on as mulch are highly serviceable.

It is very proper to crop the ground among now planted orchard trees for a few years, in order to defray the expense of hoeing and cultivating it, which should be done until the temporary plants are removed and the whole be sown down in grass. As the trees begin to produce fruit, begin also to relinquish cropping. When by their productions they defray all expenses, crop no longer.

To make Composts for Manure.

During hot weather, says Knight, I have all the offals in the garden, such as weeds, leaves of strawberries and other vegetables, short grass, peas, and asparagus haum, with the foliage of trees and shrubs when newly shed, carefully collected into a heap. These are all turned over and mixed during the winter, that they may be sufficiently rotted to mix with the dung against the end of summer. I have also another heap formed with the prunings from gooseberry and currant bushes, fruit-trees, raspberry shoots, clippings of box-edgings, and lappings from shrubs; also the roots of greens and cabbages, which are generally burnt at two different periods in the year, viz., in spring and autumn, but previous to each burning I endeavor to pare up all the coarse grasses around the garden, with a portion of the soil adhering thereto, and whenever these are sufficiently dried have them collected to the heap intended to be burnt. The fire is kindled at a convenient distance from the heaps, and a portion of such as burn most easily is first applied, until the fire has gained a considerable power. After this the process of burning is continued by applying lighter and heavier substances alternately, that the one may preserve the action of the fire, and the other prevent it from reducing them too much to ashes. When the whole are thus consumed a quantity of mould is thrown over the heap to prevent the fire from breaking through, and whenever it can be broken into with safety it is then mixed up into a dunghill with the rotted vegetables, moss-earth and stable-yard dung in such proportions as is likely to insure a moderate fermentation, which is generally completed in three or four weeks, at which time it is most advantageously applied in having it carried to the ground and instantly dug in.

To make Composts for Moulds.

Composts are mixtures of several earths, or earthy substances, or dungs, either for the improvement of the general soil under culture or for the culture of particular plants.

In respect to composts for the amendment of the general soil of the garden, their quality must depend upon that of the natural soil; if this be light, loose, or sandy, it may be assisted by heavy loams, clays, etc., from ponds and ditches, cleanings of sewers, etc. On the other hand, heavy clayey and all stubborn soils may be assisted by light composts of sandy earth, drift, and sea-sand, the shovellings of turnpike roads, the cleansing of streets, all kinds of ashes, rotten tanner's bark, rotten wood, saw dust, and other similar light opening materials that can be most conveniently procured.

To make Composts for Plants.

These may be reduced to light sandy loam from old pastures: strong loam approaching nearly to brick earth from the same source; peat earth, from the surface of heaths or commons; bog earth, from bogs or morasses; vegetable earth, from decayed leaves, stalks, cow-dung, etc.; sand, either sea-sand, drift-sand, or powdered stone, so as to be as free as possible from iron; lime-rubbish; and, lastly, common garden earth. There are no known plants that will not grow or thrive in one or other of these earths, alone or mixed with some other earth, or with rotten dung or leaves. Nurserymen have seldom more than three sorts of earth: loam, approaching to the qualities of brick-earth; peat or bog-earth, and the common soil of their nursery. With these and the addition of a little sand for striking plants, some sifted lime-rubbish for succulents, and some well-rotted cow-dung for bulbs, and some sorts of trees, they continue to grow thousands of different species in as great or greater perfection as in their native countries, and many, as the pine, vine, camellia, rose, etc., in a superior manner.

To prepare Composts.

The preparation necessary for heavy and light composts for general enrichment, and of the above different earths, consists in collecting each soil in the compost ground, in separate ridges of three or four feet broad, and as high, turning them every six weeks or two months for a year or a year and a half before they are used. Peat earth, being generally procured in the state of turves full of the roots and tops of heath, requires two or three years to rot; but, after it has lain one year, it may be sifted, and what passes through a small sieve will be found fit for use. Some nurserymen use both these loams and peats as soon as procured, and find them answer perfectly for most plants; but for delicate flowers, and especially bulbs, and all florists' flowers, and for all composts in which manures enter, not less than one year ought to be allowed for decomposition, and what is called sweetening.

To make a Green-House or Conservatory.

The depth of green-houses should never be greater than their height in the clear; which, in small or middling houses may be sixteen or eighteen feet, but in large ones from twenty to twenty-four feet; and the length of the windows should reach from about one foot and a half above the pavement, and within the same distance of the ceiling.

The floor of the green-house, which should be laid either with Bremen squares, Purbeck stone, or flat tiles, must be raised two feet above the surface of the adjoining ground, or, if the situation be damp, at least three feet; and if the whole is arched with low brick arches under the floor, they will be of great service in preventing damp; and under the floor, about two feet from the front, it will be very advisable to make a flue of ten inches wide, and two feet deep; this should be carried the whole length of the house, and then returned back along the binder part, and there be carried up into funnels adjoining to the tool-house, by which the smoke may be carried off. The fire-place may be contrived at one end of the house, and the door at which the fuel is put in, as also the ash-grate, may be contrived to open into the tool-house.

Whilst the front of the green-house is exactly south, one of the wings may be made to face the southeast, and the other the southwest. By this disposition the heat of the sun is reflected from one part of the building to the other all day, and the front of the main green-house is guarded from the cold winds. These two wings may be so contrived as to maintain plants of different degrees of hardiness, which may be easily effected by the situation and extent of the fire-place, and the manner of conducting the flues.

The sloping glasses of these houses should be made to slide and take off, so that they may be drawn down more or less in warm weather to admit air to the plants; and the upright glasses in the front may be so contrived as that every other may open as a door upon hinges, and the alternate glasses may be divided into two; the upper part of each should be so contrived as to be drawn down like a sash, so that either of them may be used to admit air in a greater or less quantity, as there may be occasion. As to the management of plants in a green-house, open the mould about them from time to time, and sprinkle a little fresh mould in them, and a little warm dung on that; also water them when the leaves begin to wither and curl, and not oftener, which would make them fade and be sickly; and take off such leaves as wither and grow dry.

To propagate Vegetables.

Plants are universally propagated by seed, but partially also by germs or bulbs, suckers, runners, slips, and offsets, and artificially by layers, in-arching, grafting, budding, and cutting.

The propagation by seed is to make sure of live seeds; for some lose their vitality very early after being gathered, while others retain it only for one or perhaps two seasons; some seeds also are injured, and others improved by keeping. The size of seeds requires also to be taken into consideration, for on this most frequently depends the depth which they require to be buried in the soil; the texture of their skin or covering must be attended to, as on this often depends the time they require to be buried in the soil previously to germination. On the form and surface of the outer coating of seeds sometimes depends the mode of sowing, as in the carrot, and on their qualities in general depends their liability to be attacked by insects. The nature of the offspring expects it, and the proper climate, soil, and season, require also to be kept in view in determining how, where, when, and in what quantity any seed must be sown.

Germs or bulbs, cauline or radical, require in general to be planted immediately, or soon after removal from the parent plant, in light earth, about their own depth from the surface. Matured bulbs may be preserved out of the soil for some months, without injury to the vitality; but infant bulbs are easily dried up and injured when so treated.

Slips are shoots which spring from the collar or the upper part of the roots of herbaceous plants, as in auricular, and under shrubs, as thymes, etc. The shoot, when the lower part from whence the roots proceed begins to ripen or acquire a firm texture, is to be slipped or drawn from the parent plant, so far as to bring off a heel or claw of old wood, stem, or root, on which generally some roots, or rudiments of roots, are attached. The ragged parts and edges of this claw or rough section are then to be smoothed with a sharp knife, and the slip to be planted in suitable soil and shaded till it strikes root afresh.

The division of the plant is adopted in many species, as in grasses, the daisy, polyanthus, and a great variety of others. The plant is taken up, the earth shaken from its roots; the whole is then separated, each piece containing a portion of root and stem, which may be planted without further preparation.

With certain species taking runners is a convenient and sure mode of propagation. All that is requisite is to allow the plantlet on the shoot or runner to be well rooted before being separated from the parent. It may then be planted where it is finally to remain.

Suckers are merely runners under ground; some run to a considerable distance, as the acacia, narrow-leaved elm, sea-lime grass, etc.; others again are more limited in their migrations, as the lilac, syringa, Jerusalem artichoke, saponaria, etc. All that is necessary is to dig them up, cut off each plantlet with a portion of root, after which its top may be reduced by cutting off from one-fourth to one-half of the shoot, in order to fit it to the curtailed root, and it may then be planted, either in the nursery department or, if a strong plant, where it is finally to remain.

Propagation by Layering.

In general the operation of layering in trees and shrubs is commenced before the ascent of the sap, or delayed till the ascent is fully up. The shoot, or extremity of the shoot, intended to become a new plant, is half separated from the parent plant, at a few inches distance from its extremity, and, while this permits the ascent of the sap at the season of its rising, the remaining half of them, being cut through and separated, forms a dam or sluice to the descending sap, which, thus interrupted in its progress, exudes at the wound, in the form of a granulous protuberance, which throws out roots. If the cut or notch in the stem does not penetrate at least half way through, some sorts of trees will not form a nucleus the first season; on the other hand, if the notch be cut nearly through the shoot, a sufficiency of alburnum, or soft wood, is not left for the ascent of the sap, and the shoot dies. In delicate sorts it is not sufficient to cut a notch merely, because in that case the descending sap, instead of throwing out granulated matter, in the upper side of the wound, would descend by the entire side of the shoot; therefore, besides a notch formed by cutting out a portion of bark and wood, the notched side is slit up at least one inch, separating it by a bit of twig, or small splinter of stone or potsherd. The operation of layering is performed on herbaceous plants, as well as trees; and the part to become the future plant is, in both cases, covered with soil about a third of its length.

When the layers are rooted, which will generally be the case by the autumn after the operation is performed, they are all cleared from the stools or main-plants, and the head of each stool, if to be continued for furnishing layers, should be dressed; cutting off all decayed scraggy parts, and digging the ground round them. Some fresh rich mould should also be worked in, in order to encourage the production of the annual supply of shoots for layering.

Propagation by In-arching.

A sort of layering, by the common or slit process, in which the talus or heel, intended to throw out fibres, instead of being inserted in the soil, is inserted in the wood, or between the wood and bark of another plant, so as to incorporate with it. It is the most certain mode of propagation with plants difficult to excite to a disposition for rooting; and, when all other modes fail, this, when a proper description of stock or basis is to be found, is sure to succeed.

The stocks designed to be in-arched, and the tree from which the layer or shoot is to be bent or arched towards them, and put in or united, must be placed, if in pots, or planted if in the open soil, near together. Hardy trees of free-growing kinds should have a circle of stocks planted round them every year in the same circumference, every other one being in-arched the one year, and when removed their places supplied by others. If the branches of the tree are too high for stocks in the ground, they should be planted in pots, and eler─ied on posts or stands, or supported from the tree, etc.

To perform the operation, having made one of the most convenient branches or shoots approach the stock, mark, on the body of the shoot, the part where it will most easily join to the stock; and in that part of each shoot pare away the bark and part of the wood two or three inches in length, and in the same manner pare the stock in the proper place for the junction of the shoot; next make a slit upwards in that part of the branch or shoot, as in layering, and make a slit downward in the stock to admit it. Let the parts be then joined, slipping the tongue of the shoot into the slit of the stock, making both join in an exact manner, and tie them closely together with bags. Cover the whole afterward with a due quantity of tempered or grafting clay or moss. In hot-houses care must be taken not to disturb the pots containing the plants operated on.

By Budding.

Budding, or, as it is sometimes called, grafting, by germs, consists in taking an eye or bud attached to a portion of the bark of a ligneous vegetable, of various size and form, and generally called a shield, and transplanting it to another or a different ligneous vegetable. Nursery-men now generally prefer budding to any other mode of propagation. The object in view is precisely that of grafting, and depends on the same principle; all the difference between a bud and a scion being that a bud is a shoot or scion in embryo. Budded trees are two years later in producing their fruit than grafted ones; but the advantage of budding is that, where a tree is rare, a new plant can be got from every eye, whereas by grafting it can only be got from every three or four eyes. There are also trees which propagate much more readily by budding than grafting; and others, as most of the stone fruits, are apt to throw out gum when grafted. Budding is formed from the beginning of July to the middle of August, the criterion the formation of the buds in the axillæ of the leaf of the present year.

The buds are known to be ready by the shield, or portion of bark to which they are attached, easily parting with the wood.

Shield Budding

Is performed as follows: Fix on a smooth part on the side of the stem, rather from than towards the sun, and of a height depending, as in grafting, on whether dwarf, half, or whole standard trees are desired; then, with the budding-knife, make a horizontal cut across the rind, quite through the firm wood; from the middle of this transverse cut make a slit downward perpendicularly, an inch or more long, going also quite through to the wood. Proceed with expedition to take off a bud; holding the cutting or scion in one hand, with the thickest end outward, and with the knife in the other hand, enter it about half an inch or more below a bud, cutting nearly half-way into the wood of the shoot, continuing it, with one clean slanting cut, about half an inch or more above the bud, so deep as to take off part of the wood along with it, the whole about an inch and a half long; then directly with the thumb and finger, or point of the knife, slip off the woody part remaining to the bud; which done, observe whether the eye or germ of the bud remains perfect; if not, and a little hole appears in that part, the bud has lost its root, and another must be prepared. This done, place the back part of the bud or shield between the lips, and with the flat haft of the knife separate the bark of the stock on each side of the perpendicular cut clear to the wood, for the admission of the bud, which directly slip down, close between the wood and bark, to the bottom of the slit. Next cut off the top part of the shield even with the horizontal cut, in order to let it completely into its place, and to join exactly the upper edge of the shield with the transverse cut, that the descending sap may immediately enter the back of the shield, and protrude granulated matter between it and the wood, so as to effect a living union. The parts are to be bound round with a ligament of fresh bass, previously soaked in water, to render it pliable and tough. Begin a little below the bottom of the perpendicular slit, proceeding upward closely round every part, except just over the eye of the bud, and continue it a little above the horizontal cut, not too tight, but just sufficient to keep the hole close, and exclude the air, sun, and wet.

Another Method of Budding.

Trees are generally budded by making a transverse section in the bark of the stock, and a perpendicular slit beneath it; the bud is then pushed down to give it the position which it is to have. This operation is not always successful, and it is better to employ an inverse or contrary method by making the vertical slit above the transverse section or cut, and pushing the bark containing the bud upwards into its proper position. This method very rarely fails of success, because as the sap descends by the bark, the bud placed above the transverse section receives abundance, whereas if it be placed below the section very little sap can ever get to it to promote the growth of the bud. Oil rubbed upon the stems and branches of fruit trees destroys insects and increases the fruit-buds. Used upon the stems of carnations, it guards them against the depredations of the ear-wig. The coarsest oil will suit, and only a small quantity is required.

To bud with Double Ligatures.

This is an expeditious mode of budding by Mr. T. A. Knight. The operations are performed in the manner above stated, but instead of one ligature two are applied, one above the bud, inserted upon the transverse section, through the bark; the other applied below in the usual way. As soon as the buds have attached themselves the lower ligatures are taken off, but the others are suffered to remain. The passage of the sap upwards is in consequence much obstructed, and the inserted buds begin to vegetate strongly in July (being inserted in June), and when these have afforded shoots about four inches long the remaining ligatures are taken off, to permit the excess of sap to pass on, and the young shoots are nailed to the wall. Being there properly exposed to light, their wood will ripen well, and afford blossoms in the succeeding spring.

To graft Trees.

This is a mode of propagation applicable to most sorts of trees and shrubs, but not easily to very small under-shrubs, as heath, or herbaceous vegetables. It is chiefly used for continuing varieties of fruit trees. A grafted tree consists of two parts, the scion and the stock; their union constitutes the graft, and the performance of the operation is called grafting.

The end of grafting is, first, to preserve and multiply varieties and sub-varieties of fruit-trees, endowed accidentally or otherwise with particular qualities, which cannot be with certainty transferred to their offspring by seeds, and which would be multiplied too slowly or ineffectually by any other mode of propagation.

Second, to accelerate the fructification of trees,

barren as well as fruit bearing; for example, suppose two acorns of a new species of oak received from a distant country; sow both, and after they have grown one or two years cut one of them over and graft the part cut off on a common oak of five or six years' growth; the consequence will be that the whole nourishment of this young tree of five years' growth being directed towards nourishing the scion of one or two years, it will grow much faster, and consequently arrive at perfection much sooner than its fellow, or its own root left in the ground.

The third use of grafting is to improve the quality of fruits, and the fourth to perpetuate varieties of ornamental trees or shrubs.

Materials used in Grafting.

Procure a strong pruning-knife for cutting off the heads of the stocks previous to their preparation by the grafting-knife for the scion, a small saw for larger stocks, and a penknife for very small scions, chisel and mallet for cleft grafting, bass ribbons for ligatures, and grafting clay.

To prepare Grafting-Clay.

Grafting-clay is prepared either from stiff yellow or blue clay, or from clayey loam or brick earth; in either case adding thereto about a fourth part of fresh horse dung, free from litter, and a portion of cut hay, mixing the whole well together and adding a little water; then let the whole be well beaten with a stick upon a floor or other hard substance, and as it becomes too dry apply more water, at every beating turning it over, and continue beating it well at top till it becomes flat and soft. This process must be repeated more or less according as the nature of the clay may require to render it ductile, and yet not so tough as to be apt to crack in dry weather.

Whip Grafting.

Whip, or as it is sometimes called tongue grafting, is the most generally adopted in nurseries for propagating fruit-trees. To effect this mode in the best style, the top of the stock and the extremity of the scions should be nearly of equal diameter. Hence this variety admits of being performed on smaller stocks than any other. It is called whip-grafting, from the method of cutting the stock and scions sloping on one side so as to fit each other, and thus tied together in the manner of a whip-thong to the shaft or handle.

The scion and stock being cut off obliquely, at corresponding angles, as near as the operator can guess, then cut off the tip of the stock obliquely, or nearly horizontally; make now a slit nearly in the centre of the sloped face of the stock downwards and a similar one in the scion upwards. The tongue or wedge-like process forming the upper part of the sloping face of the scion, is then inserted downwards in the cleft of the stock, the inner barks of both being brought closely to unite on one side, so as not to be displaced in tying, which ought to be done immediately with a rib-band of bass, brought in a neat manner several times round the stock, and which is generally done from right to left, or in the course of the sun. The next operation is to clay the whole over an inch thick on every side from about half an inch or more below the bottom of the graft to an inch over the top of the stock, finishing the whole coat of clay in a kind of oval globular form, rather longways up and down, closing it effectually about the scion and every part, so as no light, wet, nor wind may penetrate, to prevent which is the whole intention of claying.

Cleft Grafting.

This is resorted to in the case of strong stocks, or in heading down and re-grafting old trees. The head of the stock or branch is first cut off obliquely, and then the sloped part is cut over horizontally near the middle of the slope; a cleft nearly two inches long is made with a stout knife or chisel in the crown downward, at right angles to the sloped part, taking care not to divide the pith. This cleft is kept open by the knife. The scion has its extremity for about an inch and a half, cut into the form of a wedge; it is left about the eighth of an inch thicker on the outer side, and brought to a fine edge on the inside. It is then inserted into the opening prepared for it, and the knife being withdrawn the stock closes firmly upon it.

Crown Grafting.

This is another mode adopted for thick stocks, shortened branches, or headed down trees. It is sometimes called grafting in the bark or rind, from the scion being inserted between the bark and wood. This mode of grafting is performed with best effect somewhat later than the others, as the motion of the sap renders the bark and wood of the stock much more easily separated for the admission of the scions.

In performing this operation, first cut or saw off the head of the stock or branch horizontally or level, and pare the top smooth; then having the scions cut one side of each flat and somewhat sloping, an inch and a half long, forming a sort of shoulder at the top of the slope, to rest upon the crown of the stock; and then raise the rind of the stock with the ivory wedge forming the handle of the budding knife, so as to admit the scion between that and the wood two inches down, which done, place the scion with the cut side next the wood, thrusting it down far enough for the shoulder to rest upon the top of the stock; and in this manner may be put three, four, five or more scions in one large stock or branch. It is alleged as a disadvantage attending this method in exposed situations, that the ingrafted shoots for two or three years are liable to be blown out of the stock by violent winds; the only remedy for which is tying long rods to the body of the stock or branch, and tying up each scion and its shoots to one of the rods.

Side Grafting.

This method resembles whip grafting, but differs in being performed on the side of the stock, without bending down. It is practised on wall trees to fill up vacancies, and sometimes in order to have a variety of fruits upon the same tree. Having fixed upon those parts of the branches where wood is wanting to furnish the bend or any part of the tree, then slope off the bark and a little of the wood, and cut the lower end of the scions to fit the part as nearly as possible, then join them to the branch, and tie them with bass and clay them over.

Saddle Grafting.

This is performed by first cutting the top of the stock into a wedge-like form, and then splitting up the end of the scion and thinning off each half to a tongue-shape; it is then placed on the wedge, embracing it on each side, and the inner barks are made to join on one side of the stock, as in cleft grafting. This is a very strong and handsome mode for standard trees, when grafted at the standard height. It is also desirable for orange-trees and rose-standards, as it makes a handsome finish, covering a part of the stock, which, by the other methods, long remains a black scar, and sometimes never becomes covered with bark. The stocks for this purpose should not be much thicker than the scions, or two scions may be inserted.

Shoulder or Chink Grafting.

This is performed with a shoulder, and sometimes also with a stay at the bottom of the slope. It is chiefly used for ornamental trees, where the scion and stock are of the same size.

Root Grafting.

Root grafting is sometimes performed in nurseries on parts of the roots of removed trees, when the proper stocks are scarce; in which case the root of the white thorn has been resorted to as a stock both for the apple and pear. In general, however, a piece of the root of the tree of the same genus is selected, well furnished with fibres, and a scion placed on it in any of the ordinary ways for small stocks. Thus united, they are planted so deep as to cover the ball of clay, and leave only a few eyes of the scion above ground.

In a month after grafting it may be ascertained whether the scion has united with the stock by observing the progress of its buds; but, in general, it is not safe to remove the clay for three months or more, till the graft be completely cicatrized. The clay may generally be taken off in July or August, and at the same time the ligatures loosened where the scion seems to require more room to expand: a few weeks afterwards, when the parts have been thus partially inured to the air, and when there is no danger of the scion being blown off by winds, the whole of the ligatures may be removed.

To choose Scions.

Scions are those shoots which, united with the stock, form the graft. They should be gathered several weeks before the season for grafting arrives. It is desirable that the sap of the stock should be in brisk motion at the time of grafting; but by this time the buds of the scion, if left on the parent tree, would be equally advanced, whereas the scions, being gathered early, the buds are kept back, and ready only to swell out when placed on the stock. Scions of pears, plums and cherries, are collected in the end of January or beginning of February. They are kept at full length sunk in dry earth, and out of the reach of frost till wanted, which is sometimes from the middle of February to the middle of March. Scions of apples are collected any time in February, and put in from the middle to the end of March. In July grafting the scions are used as gathered.

To choose Cuttings.

In respect to the choice of cuttings, those branches of trees and shrubs which are thrown out nearest the ground, and especially such as recline, or nearly so, on the earth's surface, have always the most tendency to produce roots. Even the branches of resinous trees, which are extremely difficult to propagate by cuttings, when reclining on the ground, if accidentally or otherwise covered with earth in any part, will there throw out roots, and the extremity of the lateral shoot will assume the character of a main stem, as may be sometimes seen in the larch, spruce and silver fir.

The choice of cuttings then is to be made from the side shoots of plants rather than from their summits or main stems, and the strength and health of side shoots being equal, those nearest the ground should be preferred. The proper time for taking cuttings from the mother plant is when the sap is in full motion, in order that, in returning by the bark, it may form a callus or protruding ring of granular substance between the bark and wood, whence the roots proceed. As this callus or ring of spongy matter is generally best formed in ripened wood, the cutting, when taken from the mother plant, should contain a part of the former year, or in plants which grow twice a year, of the wood of the former growth; or in the case of plants which are continually growing, as most evergreen exotics, such wood as has begun to ripen or assume a brownish color. This is the true principle of the choice of cuttings as to time; but there are many sorts of trees, as willow, elder, etc., the cuttings of which will grow almost at any season, and especially if removed from the mother plant in winter, when the sap is at rest.

These ought always to be cut across, with the smoothest and soundest section possible at an eye or joint. And as buds are in a more advanced state in wood somewhat ripened or fully formed than in forming wood, this section ought to be made in the wood of the growth of the preceding season; or as it were in the point between the two growths. It is a common practice to cut off the whole or a part of the leaves of cuttings, which is always attended with bad effects in evergreens, in which the leaves may be said to supply nourishment to the cutting till it can sustain itself. This is very obvious in the case of striking from buds, which, without a leaf attached, speedily rot and die. Leaves alone will even strike root, and form plants in some instances, and the same may be stated of certain flowers and fruits.

Piping.

This is a mode of propagation by cuttings, and is adopted with plants having jointed tubular stems, as the dianthus tribe; and several of the grasses and the arundines may be propagated in this manner. When the shoot has nearly done growing, its extremity is to be separated at a part of the stem where it is nearly indurated or ripened. This operation is effected by holding the root end between the finger and thumb of one hand, below a pair of leaves, and with the other pulling the top part above the pair of leaves, so as to separate it from the root part of the stem at the socket, formed by the axillæ of the leaves, leaving the stem to remain with a tubular termination. These pipings are inserted without any further preparation in finely sifted earth to the depth of the first joint or pipe.

To insert Cuttings.

Cuttings, if inserted in a mere mass of earth, will hardly throw out roots, while, if inserted at the sides of the pots so as to touch the pot in their whole length, they seldom fail to become rooted plants. The art is to place them to touch the bottom of the pot; they are then to be plunged in a bark or hot-bed and kept moist.

To manage Cuttings.

No cutting requires to be planted deep, though the large ought to be inserted deeper than such as are small. In the case of evergreens the leaves should be kept from touching the soil, otherwise they will damp or rot off; and in the case of tubular-stalked plants, which are in general not very easily struck, owing to the water lodging in the tube and rotting the cutting, both ends may be advantageously inserted in the soil, and besides a greater certainty of success, two plants will be produced. Too much light, air, water, heat or cold, are alike injurious. To guard against these extremes in tender sorts, the means hitherto devised is that of inclosing an atmosphere over the cuttings by means of a hand or bell-glass, according to their delicacy. This preserves a uniform stillness and moisture of atmosphere. Immersing the pot in earth has a tendency to preserve a steady, uniform degree of moisture at the roots; and shading, or planting the cuttings if in the open air in a shady situation, prevents the bad effects of excess of light. The only method of regulating the heat is by double or single coverings of glass or mats, or both. A hand-glass placed over a bell-glass will preserve, in a shady situation, a very constant degree of heat.

What the degree of heat ought to be is decided by the degree of heat requisite for the mother plant. Most species of the erica, dahlia, and geranium, strike better when supplied with rather more heat than is requisite for the growth of these plants in green-houses. The myrtle tribe and camellias require rather less; and in general a lesser portion of heat, and of everything else proper for plants, in their rooted and growing state, is the safest.

To sow Seeds with Advantage.

This is the first operation of rearing. Where seeds are deposited singly, as in rows of beans or large nuts, they are said to be planted; where dropped in numbers together, to be sown. The operation of sowing is either performed in drills, patches or broadcast. Drills are small excavations formed with the draw-hoe, generally in straight lines parallel to each other, and in depth and distance apart varying according to the size of the seeds. In these drills the seeds are strewed from the hand of the operator, who, taking a small quantity in the palm of his hand and fingers, regulates its emission by the thumb. Some seeds are very thinly sown, as the pea and spinach; others thick, as the cress and small salading. Patches are small circular excavations made with the trowel; in these seeds are either sown or planted, thicker or thinner, and covered more or less, according to their natures. This is the mode adopted in sowing in pots, and generally in flower borders.

In broadcast sowing the operator scatters the seed over a considerable breadth of surface, previously prepared by digging, or otherwise being minutely pulverized. The seed is taken up in portions in the hand and dispersed by a horizontal movement of the arm to the extent of a semicircle, opening the hand at the same time and scattering the seeds in the air so that they may fall as equally as possible over the breadth taken in by the sower at once, and which is generally six feet—that being the diameter of the circle in which his hand moves through half the circumference. In sowing broadcast on beds and narrow strips or borders, the seeds are dispersed between the thumb and fingers by horizontal movements of the hand in segments of smaller circles.

Dry weather is essentially requisite for sowing, and more especially for the operation of covering in the seed, which in broadcast sowing is done by treading or gently rolling the surface, and then raking it; and in drill-sowing by treading in the larger seeds, as peas, and covering with the rake; smaller seeds, sown in drills, are covered with the same implement without treading.

To plant Shrubs and Trees.

Planting, as applied to seeds or seed-like roots, as potatoes, bulbs, etc., is most frequently performed in drills or in separate holes made with the dibbler; in these the seed or bulb is dropped from the hand, and covered with or without treading, according to its nature. Sometimes planting is performed in patches, as in pots or borders, in which case the trowel is the chief instrument used.

Quincunx is a mode of planting in rows, by which the plants in the one row are always opposed to the blanks in the other, so that when a plot of ground is planted in this way the plants appear in rows in four directions.

Planting, as applied to plants already originated, consists generally in inserting them in the soil of the same depth, and in the same position as they were before removal, but with various exceptions. The principal object is to preserve the fibrous roots entire, to distribute them equally around the stem among the mould or finer soil, and to preserve the plant upright. The plant should not be planted deeper than it stood in the soil before removal, and commonly the same side should be kept towards the sun. Planting should as much as possible be accompanied by abundant watering, in order to consolidate the soil about the roots; and where the soil is dry, or not a stiff clay, it may be performed in the beginning of wet weather, in gardens; and in forest planting, on dry soils, in all open weather during autumn, winter and spring.

To water Gardens.

Watering becomes requisite in gardens for various purposes, as aliment to plants in a growing state, as support to newly-transplanted plants, for keeping under insects, and keeping clean the leaves of vegetables. One general rule must be ever kept in mind during the employment of water in a garden, that is, never to water the top or leaves of a plant when the sun shines. All watering should be carried on in the evening or early in the morning, unless it be confined to watering the roots, in which case transplanted plants, and others in a growing state, may be watered at any time; and if they are shaded from the sun, they may also be watered over their tops. Watering over the tops is performed with the rose, or dispenser attached to the spout of the watering-pot, or by the syringe or engine. Watering the roots is best done with the rose; but in the case of watering pots in haste, and where the earth is hardened, it is done with the naked spout. In new-laid turf, or lawn of a loose, porous soil, and too mossy surface, the water-barrel may be advantageously used.

Many kitchen crops are lost, or produced of very inferior quality, for want of watering. Lettuces and cabbages are often hard and stringy, turnips and radishes do not swell, onions decay, cauliflowers die off; and, in general, in dry soils, copious waterings in the evenings, during the dry season, would produce that fullness of succulency, which is found in the vegetables produced in the low countries, and in the Marsh Gardens at Paris; and in this country at the beginning and latter end of the season.

The watering of the foliage of small trees, to prevent the increase of insects, and of strawberries and fruit shrubs, to swell the fruit, is also of importance.

To water the Foliage of Wall Trees.

Water is to be supplied to a garden from a reservoir, situated on an eminence, a considerable height above the garden walls. Around the whole garden, four inches below the surface of the ground, a groove, between two and three inches deep, has been formed in the walls, to receive a three-quarter inch pipe for conducting the water. About fifty feet distant from each other, are apertures through the wall, two and a half feet high, and ten inches wide, in which a cock is placed, so that on turning the handle to either side of the wall, the water issues from that side. The nozzles of the cocks have screws on each side, to which is attached at pleasure a leathern pipe, with a brass cock and director; roses, pierced with holes of different sizes, being fitted to the latter.

By this contrivance, all the trees, both inside and outside the wall, can be most effectually watered and washed, in a very short space of time, and with little trouble. One man may go over the whole in two hours. At the same time the borders, and even a considerable part of the quarters, can be watered with the greatest ease, when required.

To transplant.

Transplanting consists in removing propagated plants, whether from seeds, cuttings, or grafts, according to their kinds and other circumstances, to a situation prepared to receive them. Transplanting, therefore, involves three things: first, the propagation of the soil, to which the plant is to be removed; secondly, the removal of the plant; thirdly, the insertion in the prepared soil.

The preparation of the soil implies, in all cases, stirring, loosening, mixing, and comminution; and, in many cases, the addition of manure or compost, according to the nature of the soil and plant to be inserted, and according as the same may be in open grounds, or pots, or hot-houses.

The removal of the plant is generally effected by loosening the earth around it, and then drawing it out of the soil with the hand; in all cases avoiding as much as possible to break, or bruise, or otherwise injure the roots. In the case of small seedling plants, merely inserting the spade, and raising the portion of earth in which they grow will suffice; but in removing larger plants, it is necessary to dig a trench round the plant.

In some cases, the plant may be lifted with a ball of earth, containing all its roots, by means of the trowel; and in others, as in large shrubs or trees, it may be necessary to cut the roots at a certain distance from the plant, one year before removal, in order to furnish them with young fibres, to enable them to support the change. In pots less care is necessary, as the roots and ball of earth may be preserved entire.

To accelerate Plants in Hot-Houses.

There are two leading modes of accelerating plants in these buildings; the first is by placing them there permanently, as in the case of the peach, vine, etc., planted in the ground; and the second is by having the plants in pots, and introducing or withdrawing them at pleasure. As far as respects trees, the longest crops, and with far less care, are produced by the first method; but in respect to herbaceous plants and shrubs, whether culinary, as the strawberry and kidney-bean, or ornamental, as the rose and the pink, the latter is by far the most convenient method. Where large pots are used, the peach, cherry, fig, etc., will produce tolerable crops. Vines and other fruit trees, when abundantly supplied with water and manure in a liquid state, require but a very small quantity of mould.

To protect Vegetables from injuries by means of Straw Ropes.

This is effected by throwing the ropes in different directions over the trees, and sometimes depositing their ends in pails of water. It has been tried successfully on wall-trees, and on potatoes and other herbaceous vegetables. As soon as the buds of the trees become turgid, place poles against the wall, in front of the trees, at from four to six feet asunder, thrusting their lower ends into the earth, about a foot from the wall, and fastening them at the top with a strong nail, either to the wall or coping. Then procure a quantity of straw or hay-ropes, and begin at the top of one of the outer poles, making fast the end, and pass the rope from pole to pole, taking a round turn upon each, until the end is reached, when, after securing it well, begin about eighteen inches below, and return in the same manner to the other end, and so on till within two feet of the ground. Straw-ropes have also been found very useful in protecting other early crops from the effects of frost, as peas, potatoes, or kidney-beans, by fixing them along the rows with pins driven into the ground.

The same by Nets.

The net should be placed out at the distance of fifteen or eighteen inches from the tree, being kept off by looped sticks, with their butts placed against the wall, and at a distance of about a yard from each other. In order to make them stand firmly, the net should be first stretched tightly on, and be fastened on all sides. If the nets were doubled or trebled, and put on in this way, they would be a more effectual screen, as the meshes or openings would, in that case, be rendered very small. Woollen nets are deemed the best, and are now in general use in Scotland. In screening with nets of any kind, they are always to be left on night and day, till all danger be over.

The same by Canvas Screens.

This is effected either by placing movable canvas screens over or around detached trees, portable hand-cases over herbaceous plants, tents or open sheds over the forests' productions, or frames or sheets against trees trained on walls. In all cases they should be placed clear of the tree or plant, either by extended, forked or hooked sticks, or any other obvious resource.

To raise and manage Fruit Trees.

In the removal or transplantation of trees, gardeners and nurserymen are generally very careless and inattentive in taking them up, and care not how much the roots are broken or lessened in number, provided they have enough left to keep the tree alive; the consequence is that although the branches left on remain alive, there is so great a deficiency of sap, from the loss of roots, that the vessels cannot be filled the following spring.

The roots are broken or cut off at random, and generally diminished more than one-half, or they are doubled back and distorted, and if there be enough left to keep the plant alive, it is thought quite sufficient, and by these means the appearance of blossoms and fruit being prematurely produced, those stinted and deformed plants are sold as half or full-trained trees for four times the price of others, and when sold they are again taken up and the roots treated and diminished in the same careless manner.

When the soil of a garden wherein fruit-trees are to be planted is not naturally comfortable or congenial to the first principle, it must be made so. The top of a wall should be so formed as to throw off water, for otherwise it will generally be damped, which renders the trees unhealthy, and when the substance against which the branches are fixed is dry, the temperature on all sides will be more equal.

In preparing beds or borders, due attention must be paid both to the soil and subsoil, as each equally affects the health and fruitfulness of trees, and principally as it retains or discharges water, stagnant water being at all times particularly detrimental to the fructification of trees.

For peaches, nectarines, etc., a border of ten or twelve feet wide will generally prove sufficient. In cases where the soil has been too close and retentive, and the roots apt to grow deep on the substratum, lay a stratum of six inches of the common soil of the garden and then form a stratum of about six inches for the roots to run and repose in, composed of two-third parts of fine drift sand (the scrapings of a public road that has been made or repaired with flints), and one-third part of rich vegetable mould, well mixed together; and the better way to perform this is, first to lay on about three inches of the composition, and on this place the roots of the plant, and over them spread the other three inches, and cover the whole down with from nine to twelve inches of the common soil of the place.

Where it is not found necessary to form an artificial substratum, it will be sufficient to remove the soil to the depth of fifteen or eighteen inches, and there form the stratum of the roots, covering it down with a foot or nine inches of the common soil.

General mode of planting Trees.

The operation of inserting plants in the soil is performed in various ways; the most general mode recommended by Marshal and Nicol is pitting, in which two persons are employed, one to operate on the soil with a spade, and the other to insert the plant and hold it till the earth is put round it, and then press down the soil with the foot.

The pit having been dug for several months, the surface will therefore be incrusted by the rains or probably covered with weeds. The man first strikes the spade downwards to the bottom two or three times, in order to loosen the soil, then poaches it, as if mixing mortar for the builder; he next lifts up a spadeful of the earth, or if necessary two spadesful, so as to make room for all the fibres without their being anywise crowded together; he then chops the rotten turf remaining in the bottom and levels the whole. The boy now places the plant perfectly upright an inch deeper than when it stood in the nursery, and holds it firm in that position. The man trindles in the mould gently; the boy gently moves the plant, not from side to side, but upwards and downwards, until the fibres be covered. The man then fills in all the remaining mould, and immediately proceeds to chop and pounch the next pit, leaving the boy to set the plant upright and to tread the mould about it. This in stiff, wet soil he does lightly, but in sandy or gravelly soil he continues to tread until the soil no longer retains the impression of his foot. The man has by this time got the pit ready for the next plant; the boy is also ready with it in his hand, and in this manner the operation goes on.

One general rule, and one of considerable importance in transplanting, is to set the plant or tree no deeper in the ground than it was originally; deep planting very often causes a delay, if not sudden destruction.

More expeditious method.

The following mode has been practised for many years on the Duke of Montrose's estate, in Scotland: The operator with his spade makes three cuts twelve or fifteen inches long, crossing each other in the centre at an angle of 60°, the whole having the form of a star. He inserts his spade across one of the rays, a few inches from the centre, and on the side next himself; then bending the handle towards himself, and almost to the ground, the earth opening in fissures from the centre in the direction of the cuts which had been made, he at the same instant inserts his plant at the point where the spade intersected the ray, pushing it forward to the centre and assisting the roots in rambling through the fissures. He then lets down the earth by removing his spade, having pressed it into a compact state with his heel; the operation is finished by adding a little earth with the grass side down, completely covering the fissures for the purpose of retaining the moisture at the root, and likewise as a top-dressing, which greatly encourages the plant to put fresh roots between the swards.

German method of forcing Trees.

With a sharp knife make a cut in the bark of the branch which is meant to be forced to bear, and not far from the place where it is connected with the stem, or if it is a small branch or shoot, near where it is joined to the large bough; the cut is to go round the branch, or to encircle it, and penetrate to the wood. A quarter of an inch from this cut make a second like the first, round the branch, so that by both encircling the branch a ring is formed upon the branch a quarter of an inch broad between the two cuts. The bark between these two cuts is taken clean away with a knife down to the wood, removing even the fine inner bark, which lies immediately upon the wood, so that no connexion whatever remains between the two parts of the bark, but the bare and naked wood appears white and smooth; but this bark ring, to compel the tree to bear, must be made at the time when the buds are strongly swelling or breaking out into bloom.

The Apple.

The best soil for the apple is a dry, loamy, rich soil, with a light clay subsoil that the roots can easily penetrate to a considerable depth; with an easterly or southern exposure. The best fertilizers are barn-yard manure, lime, and bone-dust. Care should be taken to apply the manure generally over the surface.

The best varieties for cultivation are the following, which ripen in succession: the Early Harvest; Red Astrachan; Summer Rose; American Summer Pearmain; Large Early Bough; Gravenstein; Maiden's Blush; Fall Pippin; Smokehouse; Rambo; Esopus; Spitzenberg; Boston Russet; Rhode Island Greening; Baldwin; Wine-sap.

The apple-tree is subject to several diseases. The best preventive of them is heading low, so that the trunk of the tree will be shaded from the hot sun, and washing the tree occasionally with soap-suds,—a pint of soft soap to a gallon of water.

The Pear.

The best soil for the pear is a moderately heavy, sandy, and dry soil, with a sub-soil of light clay which is easily penetrated by the roots to a great depth; a moderate portion of iron in the soil is desirable. The best situation is an undulating eastern or southern exposure. The best fertilizers, as in the case of the apple, are barn-yard manure, lime, and bone-dust. Iron cinders are a good application when there is a deficiency of that element in the soil.

The most desirable varieties for general culture as standards to ripen in succession are as follows: Doyenne d'Été; Bloodgood; Dearborn's Seedling; Beurre Giffard; Bartlett; Sickel; Tyson; Howell; Belle Lucrative; Buffum; Blemish Beauty; Beurre Bose; Doyenne Boussock; Beurre d'Anjou; Sheldon; Beurre Clairgeau; Lawrence.

The best varieties for dwarf pears, on quince stocks, are Beurre d'Anjou; Duchesse d'Angouléme; Glou Morceau; Vicar of Wakefield.

The most serious disease of the pear is the blight. The remedy is, to cut the blight off well down into the second wood.

The Peach.

The soil most suitable for the peach-tree is a dry, light, sandy, undulating soil, with a light clay subsoil, and an eastern or southern exposure. The best fertilizer for the peach is Peruvian guano. Among the best varieties to ripen in succession are, of clearstones, the Early York; Early Tillotson; George the Fourth; Oldmixon Freestone; Columbian; Crawford's Late. Of clingstones,—Large White; Oldmixon Cling; Heath. The principal diseases of the peach are, the yellows, and worms which prey upon the crown roots near the surface of the ground. The most effectual preventive for the yellows is, to be careful to get healthy trees, and to plant them well above the surface of the ground, by throwing up ridges with the plough, say fifteen or twenty feet apart; then plant the tree on the ridge, also making a slight mound to cover the roots. If the tree shows signs of weakness, dig the earth well from the crown roots, scrape the worms away if any, and then sprinkle in the hole around the roots a handful or two of guano, and fill it up with earth. Worms may be prevented, also, by coating the bark of each tree, for three or four inches next to the ground, with coal or gas tar; which will not allow the parent insect to deposit its eggs. Only a short distance must be so coated, as to cover the whole trunk would kill the tree. A kind of coat made of the gas-soaked felt used for roofs will answer the same purpose.

All orchard trees require good cultivation, but especially the peach. Ashes are said by some to be a good addition to its manure.

The Plum.

The plum-tree is hardy, and requires but little attention; it bears abundantly, and may be considered a sure crop when the soil suits. The best for it is a stiff clay, which is not suitable to the habits of the curculio, the great enemy of the plum.

The best varieties are, the Green Gage, Purple Gage, and Prince's Yellow Gage.

The Blackberry.

For the cultivated blackberry the soil should be rich, dry, and mellow. Barn-yard manure and bone-dust are its best fertilizers; it is a good plan to mix them with half-rotten straw, or some such thing. They should be planted three feet apart in the rows; the rows being six feet asunder. The most approved variety is the Lawton or Rochelle; its fruit is very large, beautiful, and luscious, when allowed to become fully ripe on the bush. The Dr. Warder, Dorchester and Marshall Winter varieties are also very fine. Immense numbers of cultivated blackberries are now sold annually in the markets of our cities.

The Raspberry.

The best soil for the raspberry is a rich, light, deep soil. Plant them in rows six feet apart and three feet asunder in the row. It is well occasionally to throw up the earth around them so as to protect the roots which keep near the surface from the hot sun. The most desirable varieties are, the American Black; Hudson River Antwerp; Improved American Black; Brinckle's Orange.

The Strawberry.

For this fruit the most suitable soil is light and sandy. It may be enriched by ashes, bone, barn-yard manure, etc. The plants should be set one foot apart, in rows two feet from each other. Put in the young plants from the middle of August to the middle of September. Keep the ground mellow and free from weeds. In the following spring manure and hoe the ground well, to keep it moist and free from weeds. With such care a quart of fruit has sometimes been picked from one plant, the next season after planting. Some cultivators prefer to cut off all the blossoms the first spring, so as to strengthen the plants for growth. The best varieties of strawberry are, Wilson's Albany; Hovey's Seedling; Triomphe de Gand; Bartlett; McAvoy's Superior.

The Cranberry.

This is a hardy trailing shrub, growing wild in many parts of the country. It is easily cultivated, and when once established in the soil requires very little attention; it produces large crops, and the fruit commands high prices. The best soil is that of swampy, sandy meadows or bogs, which are unfit for any other purpose. This fruit is well worthy of the attention of any one who has wet, swampy land. It will flourish from Maine to middle Virginia.

To plant Small Fruits.

Currants and gooseberries are often planted in lines, by the side of the walks or alleys of the garden; but it is a better method to plant them in quarters by themselves, and to make new plantations every sixth or seventh year.

Raspberries produce the finest fruit when young; that is, about the third or fourth year after planting, if properly managed.

It is proper to plant some of all the above fruits on a north border, or other shaded situation, in order to prolong the season of them, if that be an object, besides planting them out in quarters as hinted above.

From four to six feet square, according to the quality of the soil, may be deemed a proper distance at which to plant the above fruits; that is, in good land six feet, in middling land five, and in poor land four feet apart. Some may also very properly be planted against vacant places on any of the walls, pales or espaliers. Antwerp raspberries, in particular, and some kinds of gooseberries, are highly improved in size and flavor if trained to a south wall.

To choose Plants.

No better mode exists at present than having recourse for trees to the most reputable nurseries; and, with McPhail and Nicol, we would recommend, instead of maiden plants, "to make choice of those not very young, but such as are healthy, and have been transplanted several times, and been in a state of training for two or three years at least." A safe mode is to plant partly maiden and partly trained plants, by which means those which come early into fruit, should they prove bad sorts, may be replaced by others.

To manage Orchards.

The whole ground of an orchard should be dug in the autumn and laid up in a rough state for the winter, giving it as much surface as possible in order that the weather may fully act upon and meliorate the soil; thus following it as far as the case will admit. Observe to dig carefully near to the trees, and so as not to hurt their roots and fibres. If the soil be shallow, and if these lie near to the surface, it would be advisable to dig with a fork instead of the spade.

Crop to within two feet of the trees the first year, a yard the second, four feet the third, and so on until finally relinquished; which, of course, would be against the eighth year, provided the trees were planted at thirty or forty feet apart, with early-bearing sorts between. By this time, if the kinds have been well chosen, the temporary trees will be in full bearing, and will forthwith defray every necessary expense.

Let a small basin or hollow be made round the stem of each tree, a foot or eighteen inches in diameter and two or three inches deep, according to the extent of its roots. Fill this basin with dung to the thickness of five or six inches, over which sprinkle a little earth, just enough to keep it from being blown about. This both nourishes the young fibres, and keeps the ground about them moist in hot weather if wetted freely once a week.

To clothe the Stems of Standard Trees.

This is done by an envelope of moss or short grass; or litter wound round with shreds of matting is of great use the first year after planting to keep the bark moist, and thereby aid the ascent and circulation of the sap in the alburnum. This operation should be performed at or soon after planting, and the clothing may be left on till by decay it drops off of itself. It is of singular service in very late planting, or when, from unforeseen circumstances, summer-planting becomes requisite.

To prune Orchard Trees.

The object in pruning young trees is to form a proper head. The shoots may be pruned in proportion to their lengths, cutting clean away such as cross one another, and fanning the tree out towards the extremities on all sides, thereby keeping it equally poised, and fit to resist the effects of high winds. When it is wished to throw a young tree into a bearing state, which should not be thought of, however, sooner than the third or fourth year after planting, the leading branches should be very little shortened and the lower or side branches not at all, nor should the knife be used, unless to cut out such shoots as cross one another.

The season for pruning orchards is generally winter or early in spring. A weak tree ought to be pruned directly at the fall of the leaf. To prune in autumn strengthens a plant, and will bring the blossom buds more forward; to cut the wood late in spring tends to check a plant, and is one of the remedies for excessive luxuriance.

To recover Deformed Trees.

Where a tree is stinted or the head ill-shaped from being originally badly pruned, or barren from having overborne itself, or from constitutional weakness, the most expeditious remedy is to head down the plant within three, four or five eyes (or inches, if an old tree) of the top of the stem, in order to furnish it with a new head. The recovery of a languishing tree, if not too old, will be further promoted by taking it up at the same time and pruning the roots: for as, on the one hand, the depriving of too luxuriant a tree of part even of its sound, healthy roots, will moderate its vigor, so, on the other, to relieve a stinted or sickly tree of cankered or decayed roots, to prune the extremities of sound roots, and especially to shorten the dangling tap-roots of a plant affected by a bad subsoil, is, in connection with heading down, or very short pruning, and the renovation of the soil, and draining if necessary of the subsoil, the most availing remedy that can be tried.

To cure Diseases of Orchard Trees.

A tree often becomes stinted from an accumulation of moss, which affects the functions of the bark and renders the tree unfruitful. This evil is to be removed by scraping the stem and branches of old trees with the scraper, and on young trees a hard brush will effect the purpose. Abercrombie and Nicol recommend the finishing of this operation by washing with soap-suds, or a medicated wash of some of the different sorts for destroying the eggs of insects.

Wherever the bark is decayed or cracked it ought to be removed.

The other diseases to which orchard trees are subject are chiefly the canker, gum, mildew and blight, which are rather to be prevented by such culture as will induce a healthy state than to be remedied by topical applications. Too much lime may bring on the canker, and if so, the replacing a part of such soil with alluvial or vegetable earth would be of service.

The gum may be constitutional, arising from offensive matter in the soil; or local, arising from external injury. In the former case improve the soil, in the latter employ the knife.

The mildew may be easily subdued at its first appearance, by scattering flour of sulphur upon the infected parts.

For the blight and caterpillars, Forsyth recommends burning of rotten wood, weeds, potato-haulm, with straw, etc., on the windward side of the trees, when they are in blossom. He also recommends washing the stems and branches of all orchard trees with a mixture of "fresh cow dung with wine and soap-suds," as a whitewasher would wash the ceiling or walls of a room. The promised advantages are, the destruction of insects and fine bark, more especially when it is found necessary to take off all the outer bark.

To preserve Apple, Cherry, and Plum-trees from Frost, as practised in Russia.

The severity of the winters at St. Petersburg is so great that few fruit trees will survive it, even with careful matting; to prevent the loss which is thus usually sustained, the following mode of training has been attended with complete success. It consists in leading the branches of the trees on horizontal trellises only ten or twelve inches from the ground. When the winter sets in, there are heavy falls of snow, and as the frost increases, the snow generally augments, by which the trees are entirely buried, and receive no injury from the most intense frost.

Another very great advantage of training trees in the above method consists in the growth of the wood, it being of equal strength, and the fruit produced being all alike, the blooms come out much earlier, and the crop ripens sooner. The trees are always clean and free from insects.

The only cherry that does not succeed in that way is the Black-heart; this is attributed to the damps which affect the early blossoms, but in a milder climate this injury would be obviated by placing the trellis higher from the ground. When the trellis decays under the apples, it is never renewed, as the trees keep always (from the strength of their branches) their horizontal position.

There are other advantages of treating fruit trees in this manner; they come sooner into bearing, and their fruit is not affected by high winds. The apples are never gathered, but suffered to drop off, for the distance they fall is not sufficient to bruise them.

To preserve and pack Roots, etc.

Roots, cuttings, grafts, and perennial plants in general, are preserved, till wanted, in earth or moss, moderately moist, and shaded from the sun. The same principle is followed in packing them to be sent to a distance. The roots, or root ends of the plants, or cuttings, are enveloped in balls of clay or loam, wrapped round with moist moss, and air is admitted to the tops. In this way orange-trees are sent from Genoa to any part of Europe and North America in perfect preservation; and cuttings of plants sent to any distance which can be accomplished in eight months, or even longer with some kinds. Scions of the apple, pear, etc., if enveloped in clay, and wrapt up in moss or straw, and then placed in a portable icehouse, so as to prevent a greater heat than 32° from penetrating to them, would keep for a year, and might thus be sent from England to China. The buds of fruit trees may be preserved in a vegetating state, and sent to a considerable distance by reducing the half-stalks to a short length, and enclosing the shoot in a double fold of cabbage-leaf, bound close together at each end, and then enclosing the package in a letter. It is of advantage to place the under surface of the cabbage-leaf inwards, by which the enclosed branch is supplied with humidity, that being the porous surface of the leaf, the other surface being nearly or wholly impervious to moisture.

Screen for protecting Wall Trees.

It consists of two deal poles, on which is nailed thin canvas, previously dipped in a tanner's bark pit, to prevent its being mildewed when rolled up wet. At the top the ends of the poles fit into double iron loops, projecting a few inches from the wall, immediately under the coping; and at the bottom they are fixed by a hole at the end of each pole, upon a forked iron coupling which projects about fourteen inches from the wall, thereby giving the screen a sufficient inclination to clear the branches. When it is wished to uncover the trees, one of the poles is disengaged, and rolled back to the side of the other, where it is fastened as before. The most violent winds have no injurious effect upon shades of this kind; a wall is very expeditiously covered and uncovered, and there is not any danger of damaging the blossoms in using them; they occupy very little space when rolled up, are not liable to be out of order; and, although rather expensive at first, seem to be very durable. From the facility with which the screen is put up, it may be beneficially used in the seasons when fruit ripens to secure a succession, by retarding the crop of any particular tree.

The lower ends of the poles are advantageously retained in their place by means of a small iron spring key, attached to the coupling by a short chain.

To protect Fruits from Insects.

Some species, as wasps, flies, etc., are prevented from attacking ripe fruits by gauze or nets, or by inclosing the fruit, as grapes, in bags.

The blossoms of the hoya carnosa drives wasps from grapes in hot-houses; and the fruit of the common yew-tree the same in open air.

To manage Pineries.

The culture of Pine-apples (says Nicol), is attended with a heavier expense than that of any other fruit under glass, especially if they be grown in lofty stoves; but, independent of this, pine-apples may certainly be produced in as great perfection, if not greater, and with infinitely less trouble and risk, in fluid pits, if properly constructed, than in any other way.

The pinery should, therefore, be detached from the other forcing-houses, and consists of three pits in a range; one for crowns and suckers, one for succession, and one for fruiting plants. The fruiting pit to be placed in the centre, and the other two right and left, forming a range of one hundred feet in length, which would give pine-apples enough for a large family.

The fruiting pit to be forty feet long, and ten wide, over walls; and each of the others to be thirty feet long, and nine feet wide also over walls. The breast-wall of the whole to be on a line, and to be eighteen inches above ground. The back-wall of the centre one to be five feet, and of the others to be four and a half feet higher than the front. The front and end flues to be separated from the bark bed by a three inch cavity, and the back flues to be raised above its level.

The furnaces may either be placed in front or at the back, according to convenience; but the strength of the heat should be first exhausted in front, and should return in the back flues. The fruiting pit would require two small furnaces in order to diffuse the heat regularly, and keep up a proper temperature in winter; one to be placed at each end; and either to play first in front and return in the back; but the flues to be above, and not alongside of one another. The under one to be considered merely as an auxiliary flue, as it would be wanted occasionally. None of these flues need be more than five or six inches wide, and nine or ten deep. Nor need the furnaces be so large, by a third or a fourth part, as those for large forcing houses; because there should be proper oil-cloth covers for the whole, as guards against severe weather, which would be a great saving of fuel. The depth of the pits should be regulated so that the average depth of the bark-beds may be a yard below the level of the front flues, as to that level the bark will generally settle, although made as high as their surfaces when new stirred up. If leaves, or a mixture of leaves with dung, are to be used instead of bark, the pits will require to be a foot or half a yard deeper.

General Mode of Cultivating the Pine.

The culture of this plant generally commences in a common hot-bed frame, heated by dung; at the end of six or nine months it is removed to a larger framed hot-bed or pit, generally called a succession-bed; and after remaining here from three to twelve months, it is removed to its final destination, the fruiting-bed. Here it shows its fruit, continues in a growing state during a period of from six to twelve months, according to the variety grown, mode of culture, etc., and finally ripens its fruit and dies, leaving the crown or terminal shoot of the fruit, and one or more suckers or side-shoots as successors. The production of a single pine-apple, therefore, requires a course of exotic culture, varying from eighteen months to three years.

Soil.

The pine-apple plant will grow in any sort of rich earth taken from a quarter of the kitchen garden, or in fresh sandy loam taken from a common pastured with sheep, etc. If the earth be not of a rich, sandy quality, of darkish color, it should be mixed well with some perfectly rotten dung and sand, and if a little vegetable mould is put with it, it will do it good, and also a little soot. Though pine-plants will grow in earth of the strongest texture, yet they grow most freely in good sandy loam not of a binding quality.

Heat.

Pines do not require so strong a bottom-heat as many keep them in; yet there is something in a mild tan-heat so congenial to their natures, that they thrive much better in pots plunged in a bark-bed, if properly managed, than when planted out on a bed of earth that is heated, and often scorched by under-flues. The tan or bark-pits are, therefore, essential to the pinery. Bark-pits are filled with tan which has previously undergone a course of draining and sweating. The heat thus produced will last from three to six months, when it is sifted and again put in a state of fermentation, by replacing the deficiency occasioned by decay, and a separation of the dust by sifting with new tan. In this way the bark-bed is obliged to be stirred, turned, refreshed, or even renewed, several times a year, so as to produce and retain at all times a bottom-heat of from 75° to 85° in each of the three departments of pine culture.

Propagation of the Pine.

The pine is generally propagated by crowns and suckers, though, in common with every other plant, it may be propagated by seed.

To separate Crowns and Suckers.

When the fruit is served at table, the crown is to be detached by a gentle twist, and returned to the gardener, if it be wanted for a new plant. Fruit stalk suckers are taken off at the same period. Suckers at the base of the herb are commonly fit for separation when the fruit is mature; though, if the stool be vigorous, they may be left on for a month after the fruit is cut, the stool receiving plentiful waterings on their account. The fitness of a sucker to be removed is indicated, at the lower part of the leaves, by a brownish tint; on the appearance of which, if the lower leaf be broken off, the sucker is easily displanted by the thumb.

If the old fruiting-plant offers only small bottom suckers, or fails to furnish any, good suckers may be thus brought out: having waited till the fruit is cut, take the old plant in its pot out of the bark-bed; strip off the under-leaves near the root, and with the knife cut away the leaves to six inches from the bottom. Take out some of the stale mould from the pot, fill up with fresh, and give a little water. Plunge the old plant into a bed with a good growing heat. Let the routine culture not be neglected, and the old plants will soon send out good suckers; allow these to grow till they are four inches long or more, and on the signs of fitness detach them.

As soon as either crowns or suckers are detached, twist off some of the leaves about the base; the vacancy thus made at the bottom of the stem is to favor the emission of roots. Pare the stump smooth; then lay the intended plants on a shelf in a shaded part of the stove or any dry apartment. Let crowns and fruit off-sets lie till the part that adhered to the fruit is perfectly healed; and root suckers in the same manner till the part which was united to the old stock is become dry and firm. They will be fit to plant in five or six days.

Treatment of the Plants.

Keep the plants growing gently, and have the pots, in general, completely filled with the roots by the time at which it is intended to excite them into blossom. From the middle of February to the 1st of March is a good time to have the main crop in flowers; as the prospective season is the finest. About a month before it is expected to see fruit dress the plants by taking away two inches in depth from the top of the mould. Twist off some of the lower leaves. Fill up with fresh compost, round the stem, to the remaining leaves. The bark-bed should be revived at the same time, so as to make it lively; but no new tan should be used till the time for the fullest heat arrives. It is desired to ripen eminently large fruit, destroy the suckers on their spring, by twisting out their hearts with an iron sharp-pointed instrument formed for the purpose. Apply this to the heart of the sucker; and, turning it round, bring the heart away; on the other hand, when the multiplication of the stock is a principal object, the suckers must not be extirpated. A yet further advantage may be given to the swelling of the fruit, by having a few of the lower leaves of the plant taken off, and by putting a rim of tin, or anything else in the form of a hoop, round the top of the pot, sufficient to raise the mould three or four inches. The mould should be of the best quality, and constantly kept in a moderately moist state; this may be done by having the surface kept covered with moistened moss. The roots of the pine-plant, especially those produced from the part of the stem just under the leaves, will then make a surprising progress, and the fruit will be greatly benefited by this expedient.

To cut Ripe Pines.

The indications of maturity are a diffusive fragrance, accompanied by change in the color of the fruit; most sorts becoming yellow or straw color; others dark green, or yellowish tinged with green. Cut pine-apples before they are dead ripe, or the spirit of the flavor will be dissipated. Bring away with the fruit above five inches of stalk, and leave the crown adhering to the top. If pine-apples be not cut soon after they begin to color, they fall greatly off in flavor and richness, and that sharp luscious taste, so much admired, becomes insipid.

To destroy Insects in Pines.

If the plants by proper culture be kept healthy and vigorous, insects will not annoy, but leave them. The coccus hesperides seems to delight in disease and decay, as flies do in carrion. The following recipe may safely be applied to pine-apples in any state, but certainly best to crowns and suckers, at striking them in August; to others it may, at any rate, be used in the March shifting, when they are shaken out of their pots:

Take of soft soap, 1 pound; flowers of sulphur, 1 pound; tobacco, half a pound; nux vomica, 1 ounce; soft water, 4 gallons. Boil all these together till the liquor is reduced to three gallons, and set it aside to cool. In this liquor immerse the whole plant, after the roots and leaves are trimmed for potting. Plants in any other state, placed in the bark-bed, may safely be watered over head with the liquor reduced in strength by the addition of a third part of water. As the bug harbors most in the angles of the leaves, there is the better chance that the medicated water will be effectual, because it will there remain the longest, and there its sediment will settle. The above is a remedy for every species of the coccus; and for most insects, on account of its strength and glutinous nature. Its application will make the plants look dirty; therefore, as soon as the intended effects may be supposed to have followed, whatever remains of the liquor on the leaves should be washed off with clean water. It would be improper to pour a decoction charged with such offensive materials, over fruiting plants.

Other Methods.

Turn the plants out of the pots, and clean the roots; then keep them immersed for twenty-four hours in water in which tobacco stalks have been infused. The bugs are then to be rubbed off with a sponge, and plants, after being washed in clean water and dipped, are to be repotted.

In the "Caledonian Horticultural Transactions," a similar mode is described, only in the place of tobacco-juice flowers of sulphur are directed to be mixed with the water. With a bit of bass-mat, fixed on a small stick and dipped in water, displace as many of the insects as can be seen. Then immerse the plants in a tub of water, containing about one pound of flowers of sulphur to each garden potful. Let them remain covered in the water twenty-four hours, then lay them with their tops downwards to dry, and re-pot them in the usual manner.

The experience of Hay, one of the best practical gardeners in Scotland, leads him to conclude that even moderate moisture is destructive to these insects. For many years he regularly watered his pine plants over head with the squirt during the summer months. This was done only in the evening. It never injured the plants, and the bug never appeared upon them.

The Grape.

For the grape, the best soil is a light, loamy, dry, limestone soil, with a high and warm exposure, especially to the south. The earth should be kept well cultivated and free from weeds. The most useful fertilizers for the grape are well-rotted barn-yard manure, bone, and lime. For ordinary cultivation the best varieties are, the Isabella, Catawba, Diana, Delaware, Concord, Clinton, and the Rebecca when you have a sheltered situation. Some of the finer foreign wine-grapes, of France, Italy, and the Rhine region, may be naturalized with success in some parts of the United States; but it is hardly yet determined which are best suited for the purpose.

To plant Vines.

Vines are often either trained against the back wall or on a trellis under a glass roof. In the former case the plants are always placed inside the house; but in the latter, there are two opinions among practical men, one in favor of planting them outside, and the other inside the parapet wall.

Abercrombie says: "Let them be carefully turned out of the pots, reducing the balls a little and singling out the matted roots. Then place them in the pits, just as deep in the earth as they were before, carefully spreading out the fibres and filling in with fine sifted earth or with vegetable mould. Settle all with a little water, and let them have plenty of free air every day, defending them from very severe frost or much wet; which is all the care they will require till they begin to push young shoots.

Composts for Vines.

The following are the materials and proportions of a good compost, recommended by Abercrombie: Of top-spit sandy loam, from an upland pasture, one-third part; unexhausted brown loam from a garden, one-fourth part; scrapings of roads, free from clay, and repaired with gravel or slate, one-sixth part; vegetable mould, or old tan reduced to earth, or rotten stable-dung, one-eighth part; shell marl or mild lime, one-twelfth part. The borders to be from three to five feet in depth, and, where practicable, not less than four feet wide in surface within the house, communicating with a border outside of the building not less than ten feet wide.

To choose the Plants.

Vines are to be had in the nurseries, propagated either from layers, cuttings, or eyes; and, provided the plants be well rooted, and the wood ripe, it is a matter of indifference from which class the choice is made.

Speedy Mode of Storing a New Grape House.

This mode is only to be adopted where a vinery previously exists in the open air, or where there is a friend's vinery in the neighborhood.

In the end of June or beginning of July, when the vines have made new shoots from ten to twelve feet long, and about the time of the fruit setting, select any supernumerary shoots, and loosening them from the trellis, bend them down so as to make them form a double or flexure in a pot filled with earth, generally a mixture of loam and vegetable mould, taking care to make a portion of last year's wood, containing a joint, pass into the soil in the pot. The earth is kept in a wet state, and at the same time a moist warm air is maintained in the house. In about ten days roots are found to have proceeded plentifully from the joint of last year's wood, and these may be seen by merely stirring the surface of the earth, or sometimes they may be observed penetrating to its surface. The layer may now be safely detached; very frequently it contains one or two bunches of grapes, which continue to grow and come to perfection. A layer cut off in the beginning of July generally attains, by the end of October, the length of fifteen or twenty feet. A new grape-house, therefore, might in this way be as completely furnished with plants in three months, as by the usual method, above described, in three years.

Another Mode.

A mode of more general utility than the foregoing, is to select the plants in the nursery a year before wanted, and to order them to be potted into very large pots, baskets, or tubs, filled with the richest earth, and plunged into a tan bed. They will thus make shoots which, the first year after removal to their final destination, will, under ordinary circumstances, produce fruit.

To prune and train Vines.

The methods of pruning established vines admit of much diversity, as the plants are in different situations. Without reckoning the cutting down of young or weak plants alternately to the lowermost summer shoot, which is but a temporary course, three different systems of pruning are adopted.

The first is applicable only to vines out of doors, but it may be transferred to plants in a vinery without any capital alteration. In this method one perpendicular leader is trained from the stem, at the side of which, to the right and left, the ramifications spring. Soon after the growing season has commenced, such rising shoots as are either in fruit or fit to be retained, or are eligibly placed for mother-bearers next season, are laid in either horizontally, or with a slight diagonal rise at something less than a foot distance, measuring from one bearing shoot to the next. The rising shoots, intended to form young wood, should be taken as near the origin of the branch as a good one offers, to allow of cutting away, beyond the adopted lateral, a greater quantity of the branch, as it becomes old wood; the new-sprung laterals, not wanted for one of these two objects, are pinched off. The treatment of those retained during the rest of the summer thus differs: As the shoots in bearing extend in growth, they are kept stopped about two eyes beyond the fruit. The coronate shoots, cultivated merely to enlarge the provision of wood, are divested of embryo bunches, if they show any, but are trained at full length as they advance during the summer, until they reach the allotted bounds. In the winter pruning there will thus be a good choice of mother-bearers. That nearest the origin of the former is retained, and the others on the same branch are cut away; the rest of the branch is also taken off, so that the old wood may terminate with the adopted lateral. The adopted shoot is then shortened to two, three, four, or more eyes, according to its place on the vine, its own strength, or the strength of the vine. The lower snoots are pruned in the shortest, in order to keep the means of always supplying young wood at the bottom of the tree.

Second method.

The second method is to head the natural leader so as to cause it to throw out two, three, or more principal shoots; those are trained as leading branches, and in the winter-pruning are not reduced, unless to shape them to the limits of the house, or unless the plant appears too weak to sustain them at length. Laterals from these are cultivated about twelve inches apart, as mother-bearers; those in fruit are stopped in summer, and after the fall of the leaf are cut into one or two eyes. From the appearance of the mother-bearers, thus shortened, this is called spur-pruning.

Third method.

The third plan seems to flow from taking the second as a foundation, in having more than one aspiring leader, and from joining the superstructure of the first system immediately to this in reserving well-placed shoots to come in as bearing wood. Thus, supposing a stem which has been headed to send up four vigorous competing leaders, two are suffered to bear fruit and two are divested of such buds as break into clusters, and trained to the length of ten, twelve, fifteen feet or more, for mother-bearers, which have borne a crop, are cut down to within two eyes of the stool or legs, according to the strength of the plant, while the reserved shoots lose no more of their tops than is necessary to adjust them to the trellis.

To prune Vines to advantage.

In pruning vines leave some new branches every year, and take away (if too many) some of the old, which will be of great advantage to the tree, and much increase the quantity of fruit. When you trim your vine, leave two knots and cut them off the next time, for usually two buds yield a bunch of grapes. Vines thus pruned have been known to bear abundantly, whereas others that have been cut close to please the eye have been almost barren of fruit.

To mature Grapes by Incision of the Vine Bark.

It is not of much consequence in what part of the tree the incision is made, but in case the trunk is very large the circles ought to be made in the smaller branches. All shoots which come out from the root of the vine or from the front of the trunk, situated below the incision, must be removed as often as they appear, unless bearing wood is particularly wanted to fill up the lower part of the wall, in which case one or two shoots may be left.

Vines growing in forcing houses are equally improved in point of size and flower, as well as made to ripen earlier, by taking away circles of bark. The time for doing this is when the fruit is set, and the berries are about the size of small shot. The removed circles may here be made wider than on vines growing in the open air, as the bark is sooner renewed in forcing houses, owing to the warmth and moisture in those places. Half an inch will not be too great a width to take off in a circle from a vigorous growing vine, but I do not recommend the operation to be performed at all in weak trees.

This practice may be extended to other fruits, so as to hasten their maturity, especially figs, in which there is a most abundant flow of returning sap, and it demonstrates to us why old trees are more disposed to bear fruit than young ones. Miller informs us that vineyards in Italy are thought to improve every year by age till they are fifty years old. For as trees become old the returning vessels do not convey the sap into the roots with the same facility they did when young. Thus by occasionally removing circles of bark we only anticipate the process of nature. In both cases a stagnation of the true sap is obtained in the fruiting branches, and the redundant nutriment then passes into the fruit.

It often happens after the circle of bark has been removed, a small portion of the inner bark adheres to the alburnum. It is of the utmost importance to remove this, though ever so small, otherwise in a very short space of time the communication is again established with the roots, and little or no effect is produced. Therefore, in about ten days after the first operation has been performed, look at the part from whence the bark was removed, and separate any small portion which may have escaped the knife the first time.

To prevent the Dropping off of Grapes.

Make a circular incision in the wood, cutting away a ring of bark about the breadth of the twelfth of an inch. The wood acquires greater size about the incision, and the operation accelerates the maturity of the wood, and that of the fruit likewise. The incision should not be made too deep and further than the bark, or it will spoil both in the wood and the fruit.

To retard the Sap.

At certain periods preventing or retarding the mounting of the sap tends to produce and ripen the fruit. An abundance of sap is found to increase the leaf buds and decrease the flower buds. A process to retard sap has long been employed in the gardens of Montreuil. The practice is to divaricate the sap as near the root as may be, by cutting off the main stem and training two lateral branches, from which the wall is to be filled. Another process of interrupting the rising of the sap by separating the bark has been long in practice in vine-forcing houses; this is done when the grapes are full grown, and is found to assist the bark in diminishing the aqueous and increasing the saccharine juice.

To destroy Insects in Vines.

The red spider is the grand enemy to the vine; after every winter's pruning and removal of the outward rind on the old wood, anoint the branches, shoots and trellis with the following composition, the object of which is the destruction of their eggs or larvæ:

Soft soap, 2 lbs.; flour of sulphur, 2 lbs.; leaf of roll tobacco, 2 lbs.; nux vomica, 4 oz.; turpentine, 1 English gill.

Boil the above in 8 English gallons of soft river water till it is reduced to six.

Lay on this composition, milk-warm, with a painter's brush; then with a sponge carefully anoint every branch, shoot and bud, being sure to rub it well into every joint, hole and angle. If the house is much infected the walls, flues, rafters, etc., are also to be painted over with the same liquor. Watering over the leaves and fruit at all times, except the ripening season, is the preventive recommended, and which all gardeners approve.

To protect Grapes from Wasps.

Plant near the grapes some yew-trees, and the wasps will so far prefer the yew-tree berries as wholly to neglect the grapes.

To take off Superfluous Suckers from Shrubs.

Many flowering shrubs put out strong suckers from the root, such as lilacs, syringa, and some of the kinds of roses which take greatly from the strength of the mother plant, and which, if not wanted for the purpose of planting the following season should be twisted off or otherwise destroyed.

FRUIT-TREES.

To renovate old Apple-Trees.

Take fresh made lime from the kiln, slake it well with water and well dress the tree with a brush, and the insects and moss will be completely destroyed, the outer rind will fall off and a new, smooth, clear, healthy one will be formed, and the tree will assume a most healthy appearance and produce the finest fruit.

Treatment of Apple-Trees.

The limbs of apple-trees are recommended by some to be brushed all over in the midst of summer, but it is difficult to brush the branches of trees when the fruit is upon them. Instead of brushing the trees in summer, as soon as the leaves have fallen every tree should be carefully and freely pruned; this will open a passage to the sun and air, and will contribute to health in the future season. In addition to this, says a correspondent of the Monthly Magazine, I should recommend brushing off the moss and cutting out the cankered parts at any season this is convenient, and I further recommend the tree to be anointed some feet from the ground with a composition of sulphur and goose oil, and unless the orchard is ploughed, the soil should be opened at the roots.

To render New Pippins Productive.

To render it more hardy, the farina of the pippin should be introduced to the flower of the Siberian crab, whereby a mule is produced, which ripens in cold and exposed situations, yet retains the rich flavor of the other parent. But these hybrid or mule productions in a few generations return to the character of the one or the other variety. A most excellent variety ot this apple, called the Downton Pippin, has been obtained by introducing the farina of the golden to the female flower of the Orange Pippin, and the progeny is more hardened than either parent.

To obtain Early Fruit by Exhibiting the Trees.

Mr. Knight having trained the branches of an apple-tree against a southern wall in winter, loosened them to their utmost, and in spring, when the flower-buds began to appear, the branches were again trained to the wall. The blossoms soon expanded and produced fruit, which early attained perfect maturity, and, what is more, the seeds from their fruits afforded plants which, partaking of the quality of the parent, ripened their fruit very considerably earlier than other trees raised at the same time from seeds of the same fruit, which had grown in the orchard.

To hasten the Ripening of Wall Fruit.

Painting the wall with black paint or laying a composition of the same color, produces not only more in quantity, in the proportion of five to three, but the quality is also superior in size and flavor to that which grows against the wall of the natural color. But the trees must be clear of insects, or they will thrive, from the same cause, more than the fruit.

To preserve Plants from Frost.

Before the plant has been exposed to the sun or thawed, after a night's frost, sprinkle it well with syringe water in which sal-ammoniac or common salt has been infused.

To engraft the Coffee-Tree.

Plant in small hampers during the rainy season young plants raised by seed, when they are from twelve to eighteen inches high. Place them in the shade until they are quite recovered, then remove them in the hampers, respectively, to the foot of the coffee trees chosen for the mother plants, which ought to be of the most healthy and productive kind.

These latter ought to be cut down to within three or four inches of the ground, to make them throw out new wood near their roots. It is those shoots which are grafted when they are about a foot or fifteen inches long upon the seedling plants in the hampers placed round the mother plants. The hampers should be in part buried in the ground to preserve the earth within them moist.

There are several ways of performing the operation of grafting, but we shall give only the two following, which seem most likely to answer the purpose, without calling upon the cultivator to pursue too complex a process:

1st Draw together the stem of the plant in the hamper and one of the branches of the mother plant. Then make a longitudinal incision on each of them of the same length; bring the two incisions together, so that one wound covers the other; bind them closely together and finally cover them with a mixture of clayey earth and cow dung. It would be useful to cut off the top of the plant in the hamper, in order to force the sap into the branch of the mother plant.

2d. Draw together the tree in the hamper and the branch of the mother plant as before, and take off from three to eight inches of the head of the former. Then make a triangular incision upon this cut, and a similar one on the branch of the mother plant, to unite the two wounds; make them fast together and cover them with the same composition as before; then place the branch upright by means of a prop. When the parts are firmly knit together, cut the branch away from the mother plant, and the engrafting is completed.

Young trees thus engrafted, after remaining one or two years in the nursery, should be removed to the plantation they are designed for. This method is highly useful to the fruit trees which do not propagate with all their best qualities by means of seed. In the same manner excellent varieties of spice trees may be raised from plants propagated by seed.

To preserve Fruit Trees in Blossom from Frost.

Surround the trunk of the tree in blossom with a wisp of straw or hemp. The end of this sink by means of a stone tied to it in a vessel of spring water at a little distance from the tree. One vessel will conveniently serve two trees, or the cord may be lengthened so as to surround several before its end is plunged into the water. It is necessary that the vessel should be placed in an open situation out of the reach of any shade, so that the frost may produce all its effects on the water by means of the cord communicating with it.

Chinese Mode of Propagating Fruit Trees.

Strip a ring of bark about an inch in width from a bearing branch; surround the place with a ball of fat earth or loam, bound fast to the branch with a piece of matting, over this they suspend a pot or horn with water, having a small hole in the bottom just sufficient to let the water drop, in order to keep the earth constantly moist. The branch throws new roots into the earth just above the place where the ring of bark was stripped off. The operation is performed in the spring, and the branch is sawn off and put into the ground at the fall of the leaf. The following year it will bear fruit.

This mode of propagating, not only fruit trees but plants of every description, received particular attention from the editor while in China, and has since been practised by him in this country with never-failing success. The mode he has adopted is this:—A common tin cup has a round hole punched in the bottom, a little larger than will admit the stem of the branch it is intended to receive. A slit is then to be made from the edge down one side and along the bottom to the central aperture. The two sides can thus be separated so as to let in the branch without injury; it is then closed up, the cup filled with loam mixed with chopped moss, and another cup or gourd pierced with a small hole suspended from a branch above. This is to be kept filled with water. The time to do this is in the spring just before the sap rises. In the fall the limb, as before stated, is to be taken off below the cup and planted, with all the earth that adheres to the roots.

To heal Wounds in Trees.

Make a varnish of common linseed oil, rendered very drying by boiling it for the space of an hour, with an ounce of litharge to each pound of oil, mixed with calcined bones, pulverized and sifted to the consistence of an almost liquid paste. With this paste the wounds are to be covered by means of a brush, after the bark and other substance have been pared, so as to render the whole as smooth and even as possible. The varnish must be applied in dry weather, in order that it may attach itself properly.

Composition for Healing Wounds in Trees.

Take of dry pounded chalk three measures, and of common vegetable tar one measure; mix them thoroughly, and boil them with a low heat till the composition becomes of the consistency of beeswax; it may be preserved for use in this state for any length of time. If chalk cannot conveniently be got, dry brick-dust may be substituted. After the broken or decayed limb has been sawed off, the whole of the saw-cut must be very carefully pared away, and the rough edges of the bark, in particular, must be made quite smooth : the doing of this properly is of great consequence; then lay on the above composition hot, about the thickness of half a dollar, over the wounded place, and over the edges of the surrounding bark; it should be spread with a hot trowel.

To propagate Herbs by Slips and Cuttings.

Many kinds of pot-herbs may, in July, be propagated by cuttings or slips, which may be planted out to nurse on a shady border for a few weeks, or till they have struck root, and may then be planted out where they are to remain. If made about the middle or end of the month, they will be ready for transplanting before the end of August, and in that case will be well established before the winter. The kinds are marjoram, mint, sage, sorrel, tansy, tarragons and thyme.

To prevent the growth of Weeds round Young Fruit-Trees.

To diminish the growth of weeds round fruit trees, spread on the ground round the fresh transplanted trees, as far as the roots extend, the refuse stalks of flax after the fibrous parts have been separated. This gives them very surprising vigor, as no weeds will grow under flax refuse, and the earth remains fresh and loose. Old trees treated in the same manner, when drooping in an orchard, will recover and push out vegerian shoots. In place of flax stalks the leaves which fall from trees in autumn may be substituted, but they must be covered with waste twigs or anything else that can prevent the wind from blowing them away.

To avoid the bad effects of Iron Nails, etc., on Fruit-Trees.

It often happens that some of the limbs of fruit-trees, trained against a wall, are blighted and die, while others remain in a healthy and flourishing state. This has hitherto been erroneously attributed to the effects of lightning; but from closer observation, and from several experiments, it has been found to arise from the corroding effects of the nails and cramps with which trees in this situation are fastened. To avoid this inconvenience, therefore, it requires only to be careful in preventing the iron from coming in contact with the bark of the trees.

To destroy Moss on Trees.

Remove it with a hard scrubbing brush in February and March, and wash the trees with cow-dung, urine and soap-suds.

To protect Trees and Shrubs from the attack of Hares.

Take three pints of melted tallow to one of tar, and mix them well together over a gentle fire. In November take a small brush and go over the rind or bark of the trees with the mixture, in a milk-warm state, as thin as it can be laid on with the brush. This coating will not hinder the juices or sap expanding in the smallest degree. Its efficacy has been proved by applying the liquid to one tree and missing another, when the latter has been attacked and the former left. During five years' experience, of those besmeared the first two years not one was injured afterwards. If all the bark were properly gone over with the mixture, they probably would not need any more for some years.

To prevent the Propagation of Insects on Apple-Trees.

Let a hard shoe-brush be applied to every infected limb, as if it were to coach harness, to get off the dirt, after which, with the tin box and brush, give the limbs a dressing, leaving them exposed to the sun to increase the efficacy of the application. This should be repeated occasionally during the summer, choosing always a dry time, and warm, clear sunshine.

To prevent the Ravages of the Gooseberry Caterpillar.

The only remedy is placing something about the stem or among the branches of the bush, the smell of which is obnoxious to flies, and which they will not approach. The smell of coal-tar or petroleum is said to keep off the caterpillars: the fact is, that it keeps off the fly. The practice is to wrap a beam or twist of seed, strongly impregnated with this strong-scented bitumen, round the stem of the bush, and no caterpillar will touch a leaf.

Other remedies are used, such as soap-suds thrown over the bushes, lime, chimney-soot, and a strong decoction of elder-leaves; but who can eat gooseberries and currants after they have been besmeared with such filthy materials? Keeping off the fly by the smell of something which is disagreeable to it goes to the root of the evil at once, and there is nothing in the smell of coal-tar which can excite a prejudice in the most delicate stomach.

Another Method.

A few small pits or holes, from twelve to fifteen inches deep, being dug among the bushes, at convenient distances, all the surface mould immediately under and near to the bushes, wherein the greatest quantity of shells is likely to be deposited, is taken off with a common garden hoe and buried in these holes or pits; after which the whole surface is carefully dug over to a considerable depth. Wherever these operations are properly performed, no apprehension of loss from this kind of caterpillar need be entertained.

FRUIT-TREES.

To cure the Disease in Apple-Trees.

Brush off the white down, clear off the red stain underneath it, and anoint the places infected with a liquid mixture of train oil and Scotch snuff.

Another Method.

Orchards are occasionally much injured by an insect appearing like a white efflorescence; when bruised between the fingers it emits a blood-red fluid. Mix a quantity of cow-dung with human urine, to the consistence of paint, and let the infected trees be anointed with it, about the beginning of March.

To cure the Canker in Apple-Trees.

The only means of preventing the canker worm, which destroys the young fruit, and endangers the life of the tree, when discovered, and which, in many instances, has proved to be effectual, is encircling the tree, about knee-high, with a streak of tar, early in the spring, and occasionally adding a fresh coat.

In other Trees.

Cut them off to the quick, and apply a piece of sound bark from any other tree, and bind it on with a flannel roller. Cut off the canker, and a new shoot will grow strong, but in a year or two you will find it cankered.

To cure Ulcers in Elm-Trees.

The remedy consists in boring every tree attacked by the disease, at the ulcer itself; and in applying a tube to the hole occasioned by the borer, penetrating about nine lines in depth. The sound trees, which are also bored, afford no liquor, whereas those that are ulcerated afford it in great abundance, increasing particularly in fine weather, and when the wound is exposed to the south. Stormy weather and great winds stop the effusion. In this manner the ulcers dry and heal in forty-eight hours.

To cleanse Orchard Trees by Lime.

The use of lime has been highly recommended in the dressing of old moss-eaten orchard trees. Some fresh made lime being slaked with water, and some old worn out apple-trees well dressed with it with a brush, the result was that the insects and moss were destroyed, the outer rind fell off, and a new, smooth, clear, healthy one formed; the trees, although twenty years old, assuming a most healthy appearance.

To cure Blight in Fruit Trees.

A smothering straw-fire should be made early in October, in calm weather, under each tree, and kept up during an hour or more. This done, scrape the moss and other impurities from the trunk, and from every obscure hole and corner; set your ladders to the branches, carefully cleaning them in the same way, taking from the remaining leaves every web or nidus of insects. If need be, wash the trunk, and all the larger wood, with a solution of lime and dung. Last of all, it is necessary to destroy the insects or eggs, which may have dropped upon the ground, and it may be useful to loosen the soil in the circumference. In the spring, or early blighting season, apply your ladders, make a careful survey of every branch, and act accordingly; repeat this monthly, picking off all blights by hand, and using the water-engine, where ablution may be necessary. To those who have fruit, or the market profit thereof, every orchard or garden, little or great, will amply repay such trouble and expense.

Another Method.

Trees newly transplanted, in general, escape its attack, when other trees, of the same kind of fruit, grown in the same situation, are nearly destroyed. Peach and nectarine trees should be dug up once in every five or six years, and replanted with fresh mould. By this method, a larger quantity of fruit of a superior kind will be obtained. The covering of trees with mats, by almost totally depriving them of light, has a tendency to create blight, which often attends an excess of heat or cold.

To preserve Apple-Trees from Blight.

Washing the branches with quick-lime will preserve the trees from blight, and insure a crop; those which escape washing suffer from the blight, whilst the others produce a good crop.

To prevent the Blight or Mildew from injuring Orchards.

Rub tar well into the bark of the apple-trees, about four or six inches wide round each tree, and at about one foot from the ground. This effectually prevents blight, and abundant crops are the consequence.

To prevent Mildew on Fruit-Trees.

Take one quart of whiskey, two pounds of powdered sulphur, two ounces of copperas, and a small quantity of camphor. Dissolve first the camphor, reduced to powder, gradually in the spirit, then dissolve also the copperas in it; then rub gradually the powdered sulphur into the solution, when the whole will form a mixture of a thickish consistence. The fruit-trees, in the spring of the year, immediately after being cleaned and tied up, are to have their trunks and all their branches completely covered with this mixture, by means of a large paint-brush.

To prevent Mildew on Peach-Trees.

In the months of January and February, if the trees are in a stunted or sickly state, take away all the old mould from the roots as carefully as possible, and put in its place fresh rotten turf from an old pasture, without any dung; and the trees will not only recover their health, but produce a crop of fine fruit.

To prevent Gumming in Fruit-Trees.

To prevent gumming, or the spontaneous exudation of gum from the trunks of fruit trees, which injures to a considerable extent the growth and strength of the tree,—

Take of horse dung any quantity, mix it well up with a quantity of clay and a little sand, so as to make a composition; then add a quantity of pitch-tar (which is put upon cart-wheels), and form a wettish composition of the whole. The fruit trees, in the spring of the year, after they are cleaned and tied up, are to have their trunks and stems completely bedaubed or covered with this mixture.

To cultivate the Cucumber.

To produce cucumbers at an early season, is an object of emulation with every gardener; and there is scarcely any person who has not a cucumber-bed in his garden. Cucumbers are forced in hot-beds, pits, and hot-houses, and the heat of fire, steam, and dung have been applied to their culture; but dung is the only thing yet found out, by the heat of which the cucumber may be advantageously cultivated.

Soil.

Cucumbers, like every other plant, will grow in any soil, though not with the same degree of vigor, provided they be supplied with a sufficiency of heat, light, water, and air.

For Early Forcing.

Abercrombie recommends a mould or compost of the following materials One-third of rich top-spit earth, from an upland pasture, one-half of vegetable mould, and one-sixth of well decomposed horse dung, with a small quantity of sand.

McPhail used vegetable mould made from a mixture of the leaves of elm, lime, beech, sycamore, horse and sweet chestnut, spruce and Scotch fir, walnut, laurel, oak, evergreen, oat, ash, etc., and among them withered grass, and weeds of various sorts. This vegetable mould is preferable to any other.

Compost used in Kew Garden.

Of light loam, a few months from the common, one-third part; the best rotten dung, one-third part; leaf mould, and heath earth, equal parts, making together one-third part; the whole well mixed for use.

To form the Seed.

If one light frame will be large enough for ordinary purposes, choose a dry sheltered part of the melon ground, and form a bed. When high winds are suffered to blow against a cucumber bed, they have a very powerful effect on it; therefore, when a cucumber bed is about to be formed, the first object of consideration should be to have it sheltered from the high winds and boisterous stormy weather. Having put on the frame, and waited till the bed is fit for moulding, lay in five or six inches depth of the proper earth or compost.

Sowing.

Abercrombie sows some seeds in the layer of the earth, which he spreads over the bed, putting them in half an inch deep. He also sows some seeds in two, three, or more small pots of the same kind of earth, which may be plunged a little into that of the bed.

To raise Plants from Cuttings.

Instead of raising cucumber plants from seed, they may be raised from cuttings, and thus kept on from year to year, in the following manner: Take a shoot which is ready for stopping, cut it off below the joint, then cut smooth the lower end of the shoot or cutting, and stick it into fine leaf or other rich mould, about an inch deep, and give it plenty of heat, and shade it from the rays of the sun till it be fairly struck. By this method cucumber plants may readily be propagated.

Treatment till removed to the Fruiting Bed.

After sowing continue the glasses on the frame; giving occasional vent above for the steam to evaporate. The plants will be up in a few days, when it will be proper to admit air daily, but more guardedly at the upper ends of the lights. In frosty weather hang part of a mat over the aperture. When the plants are a little advanced, with the seed-leaves about half an inch broad, take them up and prick some in small pots of light earth, previously warmed by the heat of the bed. Put three plants in each pot, and insert them a little slopingly, quite to the seed-leaves. Plunge the pots into the earth; and prick some plants also into the earth of the bed. Give a very little water just to the roots; the water should be previously warmed to the temperature of the bed. Draw on the glasses; but admit air daily, to promote the growth of the plants, as well as to give vent to the steam rising in the bed, by tilting the lights behind from half an inch to an inch or two high, in proportion to the heat of the bed and the temperature of the weather. Cover the glasses every night with garden mats and remove them timely in the morning. Give twice a week, once in two days, or daily, according to the season, a very light watering. Keep up a moderate lively heat in the bed by requisite linings of hot dung to the sides.

To guard the Seeds from Mice.

Lay a pane of glass over the pot or pan till they have come up, and afterwards at night cover with a pot of equal size till the seed-leaves have expanded and the husks have dropped; for, until then, the plants are liable to be destroyed. The cover, however, should always be removed by sunrise, and replaced in the evening. It is at night these vermin generally commit their depredations. No air need be admitted till the heat begins to rise, and steam begins to appear; but after that the light should be tilted a little every day, in whatever state the weather may be, until the plants break ground. Air must then be admitted with more care; and if frosty, or very chill, the end of a mat should be hung over the opening, that the air may sift through it, and not immediately strike the plants.

To transplant Cucumbers.

As soon as the seed-leaves of the plants are fully expanded, transplant them singly into pots of the 48th size, and give a little water and air night and day. The temperature for seedlings is from 65° to 75°. With this heat and water, as the earth in the pots becomes dry, and a little air night and day so as to keep the internal air in the frame sweet and fluctuating between the degrees of heat above-mentioned, the plants will be fit for finally transplanting out in one month, that is, by the 14th of November, into the fruiting frames.

To form the Fruiting Bed.

Begin to make preparations for the fruiting bed, about three weeks before the plants are ready to be planted out for good. The dung collected, after being well worked, is made up into a bed about four or five feet high, and the frames and lights set upon it. It is afterwards suffered to stand for a few days to settle, and until its violent heat be somewhat abated, and when it is thought to be in a fit state for the plants to grow in, its surface is made level, and a hill of mould laid in just under the middle of each light, and when the mould gets warm the plants are ridged out in it. After this, if the bed has become perfectly sweet, and there be heat enough in it, and the weather proves fine, the plants will grow finely.

To Plant Out.

When the temperature is ascertained to be right, bring the plants in their pots; turn over the hills of mould, forming them again properly, and then proceed to planting. Turn them in pots clean out one at a time, with the ball of earth whole about the roots; and thus insert one patch of three plants which have grown together, with the ball of earth entire into the middle of each hill, earthing them nearly around the stems. Also any not in pots having been pricked into the earth of the bed, if required for planting, may be taken up with a small ball of earth and planted similarly. With water warmed to the air of the bed, give a very light watering about the roots, and shut down the glasses till next morning. Shade the plants a little from the mid-day sun a few days, till they have taken root in the hills, and cover the glasses every evening with large mats, which should be taken off in the morning.

Mr. Phail's Method of Covering the Frames.

First, lay clean single mats on the lights in length and breadth, nearly to cover the sashes, taking care not to suffer any part of the mats to hang over the sashes on or above the linings, for that would be the means of drawing the steam into the frames in the night time. On these mats spread equally a covering of soft hay, and on the hay lay another covering of single mats, upon which are laid two, and sometimes three or four, rows of boards to prevent the covering from being blown off by the winds. The mats laid on next to the glass are merely to keep the seeds and dust which may happen to be in the hay from getting into the frames among the plants. If the bed be high, in covering up, steps or short ladders must be used by those whose office it is to cover and uncover; and great care must be taken not to break or injure the glass.

Setting the Fruit.

The cucumber bears male and female blossoms distinctly on the same plant. The latter only produce the fruit, which appears first in miniature close under the case, even before the flower expands. There is never any in the males; but these are placed in the vicinity of the females, and are absolutely necessary, by the dispersion of their farina, to impregnate the female blossom; the fruit of which will not, otherwise, swell to its full size, and the seeds will be abortive. The early plants under the glass, not having the full current of the natural air, nor the assistance of bees and other winged insects to convey the farina, the artificial aid of the cultivator is necessary to effect the impregnation.

At the time of fructification watch the plants daily, and, as soon as a female flower and some male blossoms are fully expanded, proceed to set the fruit the same day. Take off a male blossom, detaching it with part of the foot-stalk; hold this between the finger and thumb; pull away the flower-leaf close to the stamens and central part, which apply close to the stigma of the female flower, twirling it a little about, to discharge thereon some particles of the fertilizing powder. Proceed thus to set every fruit, as the flowers of both sorts open, while of a lively full expansion; and generally perform it in the early part of the day, using a fresh male, if possible, for each impregnation, as the males are usually more abundant than the female blossoms. In consequence, the young fruit will soon be observed to swell freely. Cucumbers attain the proper size for gathering in about fifteen or twenty days from the time of setting; and often, in succession, for two or three months or more, in the same bed, by good culture. The above artificial operation will be found both necessary and effectual in forcing the cucumber, between the decline of autumn and May, while the plants are mostly shut under glass. In plants more fully exposed to the free air the impregnation is effected mostly or wholly by nature.

To save the Seed.

Select some best summer fruit, from good productive plants, which permit to continue in full growth till they become yellow. Then cut them from the vine, and place them upright on end, in the full sun, for two or three weeks, when they may be cut open, and, the seed being washed out from the pulp, spread it to dry and harden; then put it up in papers or bags for future sowing. It will remain good many years; and seed of three or four years' keeping is preferable for early frame crops.

Insects and Diseases.

The thrips sometimes attack early cucumbers, and are to be destroyed by fumigation. The red spider rarely makes its appearance; when it does water must have been improperly withheld. Some soils produce canker in the shoots, especially where they branch from the main stem. When this is the case, the only resource is to renew the soil and the plants.

To grow Cucumbers under Hand-Glasses.

The following method is given by McPhail as that generally practised: The seeds are sown about the middle of April, in a cucumber or melon bed, add when they come up they are potted out into small pots, two or three plants in each, and kept properly watered, and stopped at the first or second joint. About the middle of May a warm situation, where the mould is very rich, is pitched on, and a trench dug out about two feet deep, three broad, and the length proportioned according to the number of lights it is intended for. This breach is filled with good warm dung. and when the dung is come to its full heat it is covered over with eight, ten, or twelve inches deep of rich mould. The glasses are then set upon it about three feet distant from each other, and when the mould gets warm under them the plants are turned out of the pots, with their balls whole, and plunged in the mould under the glasses, and a little water given them to settle the mould about their roots, the glasses set over them; and, after they have made roots and begin to grow, in fine days they are raised a little on one side to let the plants have free air; and, as the weather gets warmer, air is given more plentifully, to harden the plants, so that they may be able to bear the open air and run from under the glasses. When the plants begin to fill the glasses, they are trained out horizontally, and the glasses set upon bricks to bear them from the plants. After this the plants require nothing more than to be supplied with water when the summer showers are not sufficient, and to stop them when they run too thin of branches, and thin them of leaves or branches when they are likely to be overcrowded.

In warm summers and in warm situations, by this mode of management, the plants will bear plentifully for about two months, provided they be not attacked by insects or weakened by diseases.

To prevent the Irregular Growth of Melons.

Melons frequently, in certain situations, lose their circular form and grow larger on one side than the other, and these misshapen fruits are always bad. To remedy this, take a small forked stick, in proportion to the size of the melon, and thrust it into the ground as nearly as possible to the tail of the fruit, taking the precaution to lay a little moss between the two prongs, and suspend the melon to the fork. In a few days the melon will resume its form, when the fork may be removed, and the operation is finished. The quality of the fruit remains undiminished.

To produce Mushrooms.

If the water wherein mushrooms have been steeped or washed be poured upon an old bed, or if the broken part of mushrooms be strewed thereon, there will speedily arise great numbers.

To produce New Potatoes throughout the Winter Months.

Prepare a proper quantity of red sand, of a rather loamy nature, and mix it up with a portion of lime in powder, viz., about one-third, about fourteen days before using it. This soil is to be spread about three inches thick at the bottom of any old wooden box, or on a very dry brick cellar floor. The cellar ought not to be exposed to the frost, nor yet too much confined from the air. Procure a measure or two of large potatoes of a prior year's growth; the sorts preferred are the red-apple potatoes and the pink-eyes of purple potatoes. Set these on the soil whole, about three inches apart, with the crown or the principal eye to the soil in preference; but put no soil over them. Plant about the 20th of September, which allows from ten to twelve weeks for their growth; the old potatoes also throw out numerous sprouts or stalks, with many potatoes growing on them. The original potatoes for planting whole, for sets in September, should be such as were of perfect growth in the October of the preceding year, and well preserved during the winter. The sprouts which shoot from them should be removed by the end of April; and these sprouts, which will be from six to twenty-six inches long, may be planted with all their fibres in a garden, for a first crop; about June 15 the potato sets may be sprit again, and the sprouts planted for a second crop; and in September the potato sets may be sprit a third time, and the sprouts of the last produce thrown away as useless. At the end of September the original or seed potato is to be gently placed on the soils, as before mentioned for a Christmas crop. At the end of three months at furthest the old potatoes should be carefully twisted from the new ones, and the sprouts taken off the old potato, and the old potato is then to be placed on its bottom or side, on a fresh bed of soil prepared as before, and left to produce another crop from fresh eyes placed next the soil; as you are to observe that the old potato should not be set or placed twice on the same side, and you must take care at that time to remove the sprouts, to prevent the moisture from rotting the old potato. By the above method may be had four crops of new potatoes from one potato, exclusive of those produced from the sprouts planted in the garden in April and June, from which may be obtained two crops of well-grown potatoes in September and October, weighing from ten to twelve ounces each. The crops were very plentiful, in proportion to the quantity planted.

The potatoes are remarkably well flavored, and may be kept longer without prejudice after gathering, before dressed, than potatoes grown in the natural ground.

To raise Peas in Autumn.

The purple-flowered peas are found to answer best for a late crop in autumn, as they are not so liable to be mildewed as many of the other sorts, and will continue flowering till the first crop stops them. These peas may be sown in July, August, or so late as the first week in September, if sown in a warm, sheltered situation, and in a soil inclining to sand. Soak the peas in warm milk, and after you have drawn the drills water them before you sow the peas; it is best to sow them towards the evening. If the autumn should prove very dry they will require frequent watering. When peas are sown before winter or early in spring, they are very apt to be eaten by mice. To prevent this, soak the peas for a day or two in train oil before you sow them, which will encourage their vegetation and render them so obnoxious to the mice that they will not eat them.

To sow Peas in Circles instead of Straight Rows.

It is a great error in those persons who sow the rows of tall-growing peas close together. It is much better in those sorts which grow six or eight feet high to have only one row, and then to leave a bed ten or twelve feet wide for onions, carrots, or any crops which do not grow tall. The advantages which will be derived are, that the peas will not be drawn up so much, will be stronger, will flower much nearer the ground, and in wet weather can be more easily gathered without wetting you. But instead of sowing peas in straight rows, if you will form the ground into circles of three feet diameter, with a space of two feet between each circle, in a row thirty feet long, you will have six circles of peas, each nine feet, in all fifty-four feet of peas instead of thirty, on the same extent of ground. If you want more than one row of circles leave a bed of ten or twelve feet before you begin another. For the very tall sorts four feet circles will afford more room for the roots to grow in, and care must be taken by applying some tender twigs or other support, to prevent the circles from joining each other. This method is equally applicable for scarlet beans.

To prevent Mice from Destroying early-sown Peas.

The tops of furze, or whins, chopped and thrown into the drills, and thus covered up, by goading them in their attempts to scratch, is an effectual preventive. Sea sand strewed pretty thickly upon the surface has the same effect. It gets in their ears and is troublesome.

To cultivate Common Garden Rhubarb.

It is not enough to give it depth of good soil, but it must be watered in drought, and in winter must be well covered with straw or dung. If this be attended to, your rhubarb will be solid when taken out of the ground, and your kitchen, if a warm one, will soon fit it for use.

To force Rhubarb.

Cover plants of the rheum hybridum with common garden-pots (number twelve), having their holes stopped. These are covered with fermenting dung and the plants come very fine and quickly, but are much broken by the sides and tops of the pots. After it is all well up the dung and pots are entirely taken off and large hand-glasses are substituted in their stead, thickly covered with mats every night and in dull weather. This process greatly improves their flavor, and gives a regular supply till that in the open air is ready for use.

Another Method.

Inclose and cover the bed with open framework, around and on which place the dung, and with this treatment the rhubarb will come up very regularly, be of excellent quality and want far less attention than is required by the former method, for the frame-work renders hand-glasses or any other cover unnecessary. Care should be taken to lay the dung in such a manner that the top may be partly or wholly taken off at any time for the purpose of gathering or examination without disturbing the sides.

This is a superior method of forcing the rheum hybridum, but still the forcing by pots will answer very well for any of the smaller-growing species.

Third Method.

To those who dislike the trouble of either frames or pots, it may be useful to know that rhubarb will come in much quicker by being covered about six inches thick with light litter; care should be taken in putting it on and removing it that no injury be done to the plants.

To dry Rhubarb.

The best method of drying rhubarb is to strip it off its epidermis. This is a long operation, but both time and expense are spared in the end by the promptness and regularity of the drying. Many cultivators of rhubarb on a large scale have repeated the experiment and have met with the most decisive results.

To cure Rhubarb.

The method of curing the true rhubarb is as follows: Take the roots up when the stalks are withering or dying away, clean them from the earth with a dry brush, cut them in small pieces of about four or five inches in breadth and about two in depth, taking away all the bark, and make a hole in the middle and string them on pack thread, keeping every piece apart, and every morning, if the weather is fine, place them in the open part of the garden on stages erected by placing small posts about six feet high in the ground and six feet asunder, into which fix horizontal pegs about a foot apart, beginning at the top, and the rhubarb being sprung crosswise on small poles, place them on these pegs, so that if it should rain you could easily remove each pole with the suspended pieces into any covered place. Never suffer them to be out at night, as the damp moulds them.

To cultivate Onions.

Never use the hoe to the plant except it be for clearing the ground from weeds. When the onions have shot out their leaves to their full size, and when they begin to get a little brown at the top, clear away all the soil from the bulb down to the ring, from whence proceed the fibres of the roots, and thus form a basin round each bulb, which catches the rain and serves as a receptacle for the water from the watering-pot. The old bulbs will then immediately begin to form new ones, and if they are kept properly moist and the soil is good the clusters will be very large and numerous. This is not the only advantage of this mode of treatment, as the bulbs thus grown above ground are much sounder than those formed beneath the surface, and will keep quite as well as any other sort, which was not the case until this plan was adopted.

By a particular mode of culture, the onion in this country may be grown nearly in form and size like those from Spain and Portugal. The seeds of the Spanish or Portugal onion should for this purpose be sown at the usual period in the spring, very thickly, and in poor soil, under the shade of apple or pear-trees. In autumn the bulbs will not be much larger than peas, when they should be taken from the soil and preserved until the succeeding spring, and then planted at some distance from each other, in a good soil, and exposed to the sun. The bulbs will often exceed five inches in diameter, and will keep throughout the winter much better than those cultivated in the usual manner.

The Portuguese Mode of Cultivating Onions.

They must first be raised on a nursery-bed, in the warmest and most sheltered part of the garden, as early in the month of February as the season will permit; as soon as the plants are strong enough to bear removal, that is to say, when they are about the thickness of a goose-quill, let some puddle be prepared with garden mould and water, with a small proportion of soot, the whole to be of the consistence of thick cream; as the plants are drawn from the seed-bed, let their roots be instantly immersed in the puddle, and there remain till they are transplanted, where they are permanently to continue. The plants should be set out about six inches apart, and the ground kept perfectly clear of weeds, and regularly refreshed with water in hot and dry weather. On this latter circumstance will very much depend their size and mildness; to this is owing the superiority of onions grown in Portugal, which are all cultivated in the way here recommended. By keeping the roots in puddle, if it were only for a few minutes, during the interval between the taking up and transplanting, they are prevented from receiving the slightest check from the access of the atmospheric air, and will require no immediate watering when first transplanted.

To obtain a good Crop of Onions.

In order to obtain a good crop of onions it is proper to sow at different seasons, viz., in light soils, in August, January, or early in February; and, in heavy wet soils, in March, or early in April. Onions, however, should not be sown in January, unless the ground be in a dry state, which is not often the case at so early a period of the season: but if so, advantage should be taken of it.

To cultivate Asparagus.

That part of the garden which is longest exposed to the sun, and least shaded by shrubs and trees, is to be chosen for the situation of the asparagus quarter. A pit is then to be dug five feet in depth, and the mould which is taken from it must be sifted, taking care to reject all stones, even as low in size as a filbert nut. The best parts of the mould must then be laid aside for making up the beds.

The materials of the beds are then to be laid in the following proportion and order:—

Six inches of common dunghill manure; eight inches of turf; six inches of dung as before; six inches of sifted earth; eight inches of turf; six inches of very rotten dung; eight inches of the best earth.

The best layer of earth must then be well mixed with the last of dung. The addition of salt to the earth of asparagus beds, especially in places far from the sea, is suggested by the natural habits of the plant.

The quarter must now be divided into beds five feet wide, by paths constructed of turf, two feet in breadth, and one in thickness. The asparagus must be planted about the end of March, eighteen inches asunder. In planting them, the bud or top of the shoot is to be placed at the depth of an inch and a half in the ground, while the roots must be spread out as widely as possible, in the form of an umbrella. A small bit of stick must be placed as a mark at each plant, as it is laid in the ground. As soon as the earth is settled and dry, a spadeful of fine sand is to be thrown on each plant, in the form of a mole-hill. If the asparagus plants should have begun to shoot before their transplantation, the young shoots should be cut off, and the planting will, with these precautions, be equally successful, though it should be performed in this country even as late as July. Should any of the plants originally inserted have died, they also may be replaced at this season. The plants ought to be two years old when they are transplanted; they will even take at three, but at four they are apt to fail.

In three years the largest plants will be fit to cut for use. If the buds be sufficiently large to furnish a supply in this manner, the asparagus shoots should be cut as fast as they appear; otherwise they must be left till the quantity required has pushed forth; in which case the variety in color and size prevents them from having so agreeable an appearance. An iron knife is used for this purpose.

The asparagus-bed now described will generally last thirty years; but if they be planted in such abundance as to require cutting only once in twenty-seven years, half the bed being always in a state of reservation, it will last a century or more. The turf used in making the beds should be very free from stones.

Another Method.

Make the bed quite flat, five feet wide, of good soil, without any dung, long or short; sow it with onions. Then sow two asparagus seeds (lest one should fail) about one inch deep, near each other; twelve inches each way sow two more; and if the spring is cold and dry let the weeds grow until rain comes. In October cover the bed with manure or rotten hot-bed. The next spring remove the weakest of the two plants, and keep the bed free from weeds. To raise seed, select the thickest stems; after blossoming enough, take off the tops, to make the seed strong. This is also the best way to raise double ten-weeks and Brompton stocks. Six pounds are sufficient for any strong plant; setting them to flower near double ones is of no use. The excess in petal arises from cultivation, and transplanting into rich soil; wild flowers are seldom double. Keep all small seeds in the pod until you sow them.

To force Asparagus.

The pits in which succession pines are kept in the summer have at bottom a layer of leaves about eighteen inches deep, covered with the same thickness of tan, which becomes quite cold when the pines are removed. In one of the pits should be spread over the entire surface of the old tan a quantity of asparagus roots, and cover it with six inches more of tan, and apply linings of hot dung, and successively renew it round the sides, keeping up thereby a good heat. The above mode was practised in the middle of December by Mr. William Ross, and in five weeks the crop was fit for use. As soon as the shoots made their appearance, and during the day-time he took off the lights, introducing as much air as possible, which gave them a good natural color, and the size was nearly as large as if they had been produced in the open ground, at the usual season.

To insure perfect success, it is expedient to have good roots to place in the bed; the usual plan of taking them from the exhausted old beds of the garden is bad. If they are past their best and unfit to remain in the garden, they cannot be in a good state for forcing. Young roots, four years old from the seed, are much preferable: they are costly if they are to be purchased every year; but where there is sufficient space a regular sowing for this particular purpose should be made annually, and thus a succession of stock secured.

To render Asparagus more Productive.

In the formation of beds the male plants only should be selected, which may easily be done by not planting from the seed-bed until they have flowered. When the plants are one year old transplant them into the other beds, at six inches distance; let them remain there until they flower, which will be in most of them in the second year; put a small stick to each male plant to mark it, and pull up the females, unless it is wished to make a small plantation with one of them to prove the truth of the experiment.

Towards the end of July, especially if it be rainy weather, cut down the stalks of the asparagus, fork up the beds, and rake them smooth. If it be dry, water them with the draining of a dunghill; but, instead of leaving them round, leave them rather flat or hollow in the middle, the better to retain the water or rain. In about twelve or fourteen days the asparagus will begin to appear, and if it be dry weather continue watering once or twice a week. By this method asparagus may be cut about the end of September; at which time the hot-beds will succeed this, so that by making five or six hot-beds during the winter, a regular succession of it may be had every month of the year.

To raise Capsicum and make Cayenne Pepper.

Capsicum pepper is produced from the capsicum, which is raised for ornament, with many other annual flowers, or for pickling the green pods, and is the seed and pod when ripe. In March or April procure some pods of any of the sorts of capsicums, as there are many varieties of them of different shapes; take out the seeds, and sow them on a bed not too thick. When they are about four inches high prick them out on the hot-bed at six inches asunder, or put each into a small pot, or three into a large one, and keep them still under the glasses. In June, when the weather is settled, plant them all in a warm situation in a rich earth, where they are to remain, some on the borders of the flower garden and some into larger pots, which you can shelter in bad weather.

To cultivate the Alpine Strawberry.

The process consists of sowing the seed on a moderate hot-bed in the beginning of April, and removing the plants, as soon as they have acquired sufficient strength, to beds in the open ground. They will begin to blossom after midsummer, and afford an abundant late autumnal crop. This strawberry ought always to be treated as our annual plants.

To cultivate Sea Kail.

The seed is to be sown in the month of April in drills, on a good light dry soil; as the plants rise, thin them and keep them clean. The first winter earth them up to protect them from the frost; the following summer thin them to about eighteen inches distance, leaving the best plants. At Christmas take away the decayed leaves and cover up each plant with a large deep pan or flower-pot, upon which lay a quantity of the leaves of trees, to keep off the frost and create heat to the plants. Stable litter is sometimes used instead of leaves, but it is apt to give the plants a rank taste. In the following month of April the pots will be quite full of fine tender blanched shoots, which may be cut over by the ground (but not too near) and the stumps covered up again for a second crop. This may be repeated with the same plants two or three times during the spring, before the plants are left for summer's growth. With this treatment the sea kail, if sufficiently boiled in two waters, will be found equal to any asparagus or broccoli, and may be eaten with butter, or butter and vinegar and pepper, as may suit the taste. The plant being a perennial one, will last for any length of time with proper culture.

To cultivate Radishes to have them at all Seasons.

Take seeds of the common radish and lay them in rain water to steep for twenty-four hours; then put them quite wet into a small linen bag, well tied at the mouth with a packthread. If you have steeped a large quantity of seeds, you may divide them into several bags. Then expose the bags in a place where they will receive the greatest heat of the sun for about twenty-four hours, at the end of which time the seed will begin to grow, and you may then sow it in the usual manner in earth well exposed to the heat of the sun. Prepare two small tubs to cover each other exactly. These may be easily provided by sawing a small cask through the middle, and they will serve in winter; in summer one will be sufficient for each kind of earth that has been sown. As soon as you have sown your seeds you must cover them with your tub, and at the end of three days you will find radishes of the size and thickness of young lettuces, having at their extremities two small round leaves, rising from the earth, of a reddish color. These radishes, cut or pulled up, will be excellent if mixed with a salad, and they have a much more delicate taste than the common radishes which are eaten with salt.

By taking the following precautions you may have them in the winter, and even during the hardest frosts. After having steeped the seeds in warm water, and exposed them to the sun as already directed, or in a place sufficiently hot to make them shoot forth, warm the two tubs; fill one of them with earth well dunged; sow your seeds, thus prepared, in one of them, and cover it with the other tub; you must then be careful to sprinkle it with warm water as often as may be necessary. Then carry the two tubs closely joined, taking care they cover each other, into a warm vault or cellar, and at the end of fifteen days you may gather a fine salad.

To increase Potage Herbs.

The manzel worzel would, if permitted to run up, grow to a great height, and afford a good plucking of potage vegetables twice a week in winter (only). It must be planted late, but may continue in the ground two or three years, when its roots will be wasted, the herbage become dwarfish, and it must be renewed by seed.

To guard Cabbages from the Depredations of Caterpillars.

Sow with hemp all the borders of the ground wherein the cabbage is planted; and, although the neighborhood be infested with caterpillars, the space inclosed by the hemp will be perfectly free, and not one of these vermin will approach it.

To banish the Red Spider.

Cut off the infected leaf. The leaf once attacked soon decays and falls off; but in the mean time the animals remove to another, and the leaf, from the moment of attack, seems to cease to perform its office; but persevere in the amputation, and the plants become healthy.

To stop the Ravages of Caterpillars from Shrubs, Plants, and Vegetables.

Take a chafing-dish with lighted charcoal, and place it under the branches of the tree or bush whereon are the caterpillars; then throw a little brimstone on the coals. The vapor of the sulphur, which is mortal to these insects, and the suffocating fixed air arising from the charcoal, will not only destroy all that are on the tree, but will effectually prevent the shrubs from being, at that season, infested with them. A pound of sulphur will clear as many trees as grow on several acres.

Another method of driving these insects off fruit trees is to boil together a quantity of rue, wormwood, and common tobacco (of each equal parts), in common water. The liquor should be very strong. Sprinkle this on the leaves and young branches every morning and evening during the time the fruit is ripening.

To destroy Insects on Plants.

Tie up some flowers of sulphur in a piece of muslin or fine linen, and with this the leaves of young shoots of plants should be dusted, or it may be thrown on them by means of a common swansdown puff, or even by a dredging box.

Fresh assurances have repeatedly been received of the powerful influence of sulphur against the whole tribe of insects and worms which infest and prey on vegetables. Sulphur has also been found to promote the health of plants on which it was sprinkled; and that peach-trees in particular were remarkably improved by it, and seemed to absorb it. It has been likewise observed that the verdure and other healthful appearances were perceptibly increased; for the quantity of new shoots and leaves formed subsequently to the operation, and having no sulphur on their surfaces, served as a kind of comparative index, and pointed out distinctly the accumulation of health.

To cultivate the Sunflower.

The sunflower, kidney-beans, and potatoes, mixed together, agree admirably, the neighborhood of the sunflower proving advantageous to the potato. It is a well-authenticated fact that, with careful attention, the sunflower will make excellent oil.

The marc or refuse of the sunflower, after the oil is expressed, may be prepared as a light viand for hogs and goats, pigeons and poultry, which will banquet on it to satiety. Query, would it not make good oil-cakes for fattening pigs? if brought into notice it might become an object of magnitude. Forty-eight pounds of sunflower will produce twelve pounds of oil. In fine, I esteem it as worthy of consideration; for 1. In the scale of excellence, it will render the use of grain for feeding hogs, poultry, pigeons, etc. completely unnecessary. 2. As it resembles olive oil, would it not be found, on examination, competent to supply its place? Whatever may be the points of difference, it certainly may be serviceable in home consumption and manufactures. 3. Its leaves are to be plucked as they become yellow, and dried. 4. It affords an agreeable and wholesome food to sheep and rabbits. To goats and rabbits the little branches are a delicious and luxurious gratification, as is also the disc of the pure flower, after the grains have been taken out. Rabbits eat the whole, except the woody part of the plant, which is well adapted for the purpose of fuel. 5. Its alkaline qualities appear to deserve notice: forty-eight quintals yield eighty pounds of alkali, a produce four times superior to that of any other plant we are acquainted with, maize excepted. 6. Might it not be used as a lye? And minuter observation might convert it into soap, the basis of both being oil.

Dig and trench about it, as both that and the potato love new earths. Let the rows be twenty-nine inches distant from each other, and it will be advantageous, as the turnsole loves room.

Three grains are to be sown distant some inches from each other, and, when their stems are from eight to twelve inches high, the finest of the three only to be left. Two tufts of French beans to be planted with potatoes. The French beans will climb up the side of the sunflower, which will act and uniformly support like sticks, and the sunflower will second this disposition, by keeping off the great heat from the potato, and produce more than if all had been planted with potatoes.

Each sunflower will produce one or two pounds, and the acre will bring in a vast amount, or contain one thousand pounds, being one-third more than grain.

To economize the Sunflower.

The cultivation of the annual sunflower is recommended to the notice of the public, possessing the advantage of furnishing abundance of agreeable fodder for cattle in their leaves. When in flower bees flock from all quarters to gather honey. The seed is valuable in feeding sheep, pigs, and other animals; it produces a striking effect in poultry, as occasioning them to lay more eggs, and it yields a large quantity of excellent oil by pressure. The dry stalks burn well, the ashes affording a considerable quantity of alkali.

To remove Herbs and Flowers in the Summer.

If you have occasion to transplant in the summer season, let it be in the evening, after the heat is passed. Plant and water the same immediately, and there will be no danger from the heat next day; but be careful in digging up the earth you do not break any of the young shoots, or the sap will exude out of the same, to the great danger of the plants.

Method of Growing Flowers in Winter.

In order to produce this effect the trees or

shrubs, being taken up in the spring, at the time when they are about to bud, with some of their own soil carefully preserved among the roots, must be placed upright in a cellar till Michaelmas; when, with the addition of fresh earth, they are to be put into proper tubs or vessels, and placed in a stove or hot-house, where they must every morning be moistened or refreshed with a solution of half an ounce of sal-ammoniac in a pint of rain-water. Thus, in the month of February, fruits or roses will appear; and, with respect to flowers in general, if they are sown in pots at or before Michaelmas, and watered in a similar manner, they will blow at Christmas.

To preserve Wood from Insects.

In the East Indies aloes are employed as a varnish to preserve wood from worms and other insects; and skins, and even living animals, are anointed with it for the same reason. The havoc committed by the white ants, in India, first suggested the trial of aloe juice to protect wood from them, for which purpose the juice is either used as extracted, or in solution by some solvent.

To preserve Young Shoots from Slugs and Earwigs.

Earwigs and slugs are fond of the points of the young shoots of carnations and pinks, and are very troublesome in places where they abound; to prevent them they are sometimes insulated in water, being set in cisterns or pans. If a pencil dipped in oil was drawn round the bottom of the pots once in two days, neither of these insects or ants would attempt them. Few insects can endure oil, and the smallest quantity of it stops their progress.

Vegetable Liquor to hasten the Blowing of Bulbous-Rooted Flowers.

Take nitre, 3 ounces; common salt, 1 ounce; potash, 1 ounce; sugar, ½ ounce; rain-water 1 pound. Dissolve the salts in a gentle heat, in a glazed earthen pot, and when the solution is complete add the sugar, and filter the whole. Put about eight drops of this liquor into a glass jar, filled with rain or river-water. The jars must be kept always full, and the water removed every ten or twelve days, adding each time a like quantity of the liquor. The flowers also must be placed on the corner of a chimney-piece, where a fire is regularly kept. The same mixture may be employed for watering flowers in pots, or filling the dishes in which they are placed, in order to keep the earth, or the bulbs or plants which they contain, in a state of moisture.

To restore Flowers.

Most flowers begin to droop and fade after being kept during twenty-four hours in water; a few may be revived by substituting fresh water, but all (the most fugacious, such as poppy, and perhaps one or two others excepted,) may be restored by the use of hot water. For this purpose place the flowers in scalding hot water, deep enough to cover about one-third of the length of the stem; by the time the water has become cold the flowers will have become erect and fresh; then cut off the coddled ends of the stems and put them into cold water.

To preserve Flower Seeds.

Those who are curious about saving flower seeds must attend to them in the month of August. Many kinds will begin to ripen apace, and should be carefully sticked and supported to prevent them from being shaken by high winds, and so partly lost. Others should be defended from much wet, such as asters, marygolds, and generally those of the class syngenesia, as from the construction of their flowers they are apt to rot, and the seeds to mould in bad seasons. Whenever they are thought ripe, or sooner in wet weather, they should be removed to an airy shed or loft, gradually dried and rubbed or beat out at convenience. When dried wrap them up in papers or in tight boxes containing powdered charcoal.

To improve all sorts of Seeds.

Charles Miller, son of the celebrated botanist, published a recipe for fertilizing seed, and tried it on wheat, by mixing lime, nitre and pigeon's dung in water, and therein steeping the seed. The produce of some of these grains is stated at sixty, seventy and eighty stems, many of the ears five inches long, and fifty corns each, and none less than forty.

To preserve Seeds for a long time.

When seeds are to be preserved longer than the usual period, or when they are to be sent to a great distance, sugar, salt, cotton, saw-dust, sand, paper, etc., have been adopted with different degrees of success. Chinese seeds, dried by means of sulphuric acid, in Leslie's manner, may be afterwards preserved in a vegetating state for any necessary length of time by keeping them in an airy situation in any common brown paper, and occasionally exposing them to the air on a fine day, especially after damp weather. This method will succeed with all the larger mucilaginous seeds. Very small seeds, berries and oily seeds may probably require to be kept in sugar, or among currants or raisins.

To preserve Exotic Seeds.

Five years ago, says a correspondent of the Monthly Magazine, I had a collection of seeds sent me from Scrampoore, in the East Indies, which have been since that period kept in small bottles in a dry situation, without corks; last spring some of them were sown, and produced strong, healthy plants, under the following system; but if taken from the bottles and sown in the ordinary way I have found them either to fail altogether or to produce germination so weak that the greatest care can never bring them to any perfection.

I have long observed that oxygen is necessary to animal and vegetable life, and that soil which has inbibed the greatest proportion of that air or gas yields the strongest germination, and with the least care produces the best and most healthy plants; under that impression I prepare the soil by adding to it a compost made from decayed vegetables, night soil and fresh earth, well mixed together and turned several times; but should the weather be dry I have generally found the compost better by adding water to keep it moist. On the evening before I intended to sow the seeds I have immersed them in a weak solution of chlorine, and suffered them to remain until they begun to swell.

By pursuing this treatment even with our English annual seeds, I am gratified with an earlier germination and with generally stronger and more healthy plants.

To dry Flowers.

They should be dried off as speedily as possible, the calyces, claws, etc., being previously taken off; when the flowers are very small the calyx is left, or even the whole flowering spike, as in the greatest portion of the labiate flowers; compound flowers with pappous seeds, as coltsfoot, ought to be dried very high and before they are entirely opened, otherwise the slight moisture that remains would develope the pappi, and these would form a kind of cottony nap, which would be very hurtful in infusions, by leaving irritating particles in the throat. Flowers of little or no smell may be dried in a heat of 75° to 100° Fahr.; the succulent petals of the liliaceous plants, whose odor is very fugaceous, cannot well be dried; several sorts of flowering tops, as those of lesser centaury, lily of the valley, wormwood, mellilot, water germander, etc., are tied up in small parcels and hung up, or exposed to the sun, wrapped in paper cornets, that they may not be discolored. The color of the petals of red roses is preserved by their being quickly dried with heat, after which the yellow anthers are separated by sifting; the odor of roses and red pinks is considerably increased by drying.

To dry Tops, Leaves, or Whole Herbs.

They should be gathered in a dry season, cleansed from discolored and rotten leaves, screened from earth or dust, placed on handles covered with blotting paper and exposed to the sun or the heat of a stove, in a dry, airy place. The quicker they are dried the better, as they have less time to ferment or grow mouldy; hence they should be spread thin and frequently turned; when dried they should be shaken in a large meshed sieve to get rid of the eggs of any insects. Aromatic herbs ought to be dried quickly with a moderate heat, that their odor may not be lost. Cruciferous plants should not be dried, as in that case they lose much of their antiscorbutic qualities. Some persons have proposed to dry herbs in a water bath, but this occasions them, as it were, to be half boiled in their own water.

To dry Roots.

They should be rubbed in water to get rid of the dirt and also some of the mucous substance that would otherwise render them mouldy; the larger are then to be cut, split, or peeled, but in most aromatic roots, the odor residing in the bark, they must not be peeled; they are then to be spread on sieves or hurdles and dried in a heat of about 120° Fahr. either on the top of an oven, in a stove, or a steam closet, taking care to shake them occasionally to change the surface exposed to the air. Thick and juicy roots, as rhubarb, briony, peony, water-lily, etc., are cut in slices, strung upon a thread and hung in a heat of about 90° to 100° Fahr. Squills are scaled, threaded and dried round the tube of a German stove, or in a hot closet. Rhubarb should be washed to separate that mucous principle which would otherwise render it black and soft when powdered. Potatoes are cut in slices and dried.

To preserve Roots.

These are preserved in different ways, according to the object in view. Tuberous roots, as those of the dahlia, paeonia, tuberose, etc., intended to be planted in the succeeding spring, are preserved through the winter in dry earth, in a temperature rather under than above what is natural to them. So may the bulbous roots of commerce, as hyacinths, tulips, onions, etc., but for convenience, these are kept either loose, in cool dry shelves or lofts, or the finer sorts in papers, till the season of planting.

Roots of all kinds may be preserved in an ice-house till the return of the natural crop.

After stuffing the vacuities with straw, and covering the surface of the ice with the same material, place on it cases, boxes, baskets, etc., and fill them with turnips, carrots, beet-roots, and in particular potatoes. By the cold of the place vegetation is so much suspended that all these articles may be thus kept fresh and uninjured till they give place to another crop in its natural season.

To gather Vegetables.

This is, in part, performed with a knife, and in part by fracture or torsion with the hand. In all cases of using the knife, the general principle of cutting is to be attended to, leaving also a sound section on the living plant. Gathering with the hand ought to be done as little as possible.

To preserve Vegetables.

This is effected in cellars or sheds, of any temperature, not lower nor much above the freezing-point. Thus cabbages, endive, chicory, lettuce, etc., taken out of the ground with their main roots, in perfectly dry weather, at the end of the season, and laid on, or partially immersed in sand or dry earth, in a close shed, cellar, or ice-cold room, will keep through the winter, and be fit for use till spring, and often till the return of the season of their produce in the garden.

Time for Gathering Fruits.

This should take place in the middle of a dry day. Plums readily part from the twigs when ripe; they should not be much handled, as the bloom is apt to be rubbed off. Apricots may be accounted ready when the side next the sun feels a little soft upon gentle pressure with the finger. They adhere firmly to the tree, and would overripen on it and become mealy. Peaches and nectarines, if moved upwards, and allowed to descend with a slight jerk, will separate, if ready; and they may be received into a tin funnel lined with velvet, so as to avoid touching with the fingers or bruising.

A certain rule for judging of the ripeness of figs is to notice when the small end of the fruit becomes of the same color as the large one.

The most transparent grapes are the most ripe. All the berries in a bunch never ripen equally; it is therefore proper to cut away unripe or decayed berries before presenting the bunches at table.

Autumn and winter pears are gathered, when dry, as they successively ripen.

Immature fruit never keeps so well as that which nearly approaches maturity. Winter apples should be left on the trees till there be danger of frost; they are then gathered on a dry day.

To gather Orchard Fruits.

In respect to the time of gathering, the criterion of ripeness, adopted by Forsyth, is their beginning to fall from the tree. Observe attentively when the apples and pears are ripe; and do not pick them always at the same regular time of the year, as is the practice with many. A dry season will forward the ripening of fruit, and a wet one retard it so that there will sometimes be a month's difference in the proper time for gathering. If this is attended to the fruit will keep well, and be plump, and not shrivelled, as is the case with all fruit that is gathered before it is ripe.

The art of gathering is to give them a lift, so as to press away the stalk, and if ripe, they readily part from the tree. Those that will not come off easily should hang a little longer; for when they come off hard they will not be so fit to store; and the violence done at the foot-stalk may injure the bud there formed for the next year's fruit.

Let the pears be quite dry when pulled, and in handling avoid pinching the fruit, or in any way bruising it, as those which are hurt not only decay themselves, but presently spread infection to those near them; when suspected to be bruised, let them be carefully kept from others, and used first; as gathered, lay them gently in shallow baskets

To preserve Green Fruits.

Green fruits are generally preserved by pickling or salting, and this operation is usually performed by some part of the domestic establishment.

To preserve Ripe Fruit.

Such ripe fruit as may be preserved is generally laid up in lofts and bins, or shelves, when in large quantities, and of baking qualities; but the better sorts of apples and pears are now preserved in a system of drawers, sometimes spread out in them; at other times wrapped up in papers, or placed in pots, cylindrical earthen vessels, among sand, moss, paper, chaff, hay, saw-dust, etc., or sealed up in air-tight jars or casks, and placed in the fruit-cellar.

To preserve Pears.

Having prepared a number of earthen-ware jars, and a quantity of dry moss, place a layer of moss and pears alternately till the jar is filled, then insert a plug, and seal around with melted rosin. These jars are sunk in dry sand to the depth of a foot; a deep cellar is preferable for keeping them to any fruit-room.

Another Method.

Choice apples and pears are preserved in glazed jars, provided with covers. In the bottom of the jars, and between each two layers of fruit, put some pure pit-sand, which has been thoroughly dried. The jars are kept in a dry, airy situation, as cool as possible, but secure from frost. A label on the jar indicates the kind of fruit, and when wanted it is taken from the jar and placed for some time on the shelves of the fruit-room.

In this way Colmarts, and other fine French pears may be preserved till April; the Terling till June; and many kinds of apples till July, the skin remaining.

To preserve Apples and Pears.

The most successful method of preserving apples and pears is by placing them in glazed earthen vessels, each containing about a gallon, and surrounding each fruit with paper. These vessels being perfect cylinders, about a foot each in height, stand very conveniently upon each other, and thus present the means of preserving a large quantity of fruit in a very small room; and if the space between the top of one vessel and the base of another be filled with a cement composed of two parts of the curd of skimmed milk, and one of lime, by which the air will be excluded, the later kinds of apples and pears will be preserved with little change in their appearance, and without any danger of decay, from October till February or March. A dry and cold situation, in which there is little change of temperature, is the best for the vessels; but the merits of the pears are greatly increased by their being taken from the vessels about ten days before they are wanted for use, and kept in a warm room, for warmth at this, as at other periods, accelerates the maturity of the pear.

To preserve various sorts of Fruit.

By covering some sorts of cherry, plum, gooseberry and currant trees, either on walls or on bushes with mats, the fruit of the red and white currant, and of the thicker-skinned gooseberry-trees, may be preserved till Christmas and later. Grapes, in the open air, may be preserved in the same manner; and peaches and nectarines may be kept a month hanging on the trees after they are ripe.

Arkwright, by late forcing, retains plump grapes on his vines till the beginning of May, and even later, till the maturity of his early crops. In this way grapes may be gathered every day in the year.

Another Method.

But the true way to preserve keeping-fruit, such as the apple and pear, is to put them in air-tight vessels, and place them in the fruit cellar, in a temperature between thirty-two and forty degrees. In this way all the keeping sorts of these fruits may be preserved in perfect order for eating for one year after gathering.

To store Fruit.

Those to be used first, lay by singly on shelves or on the floor, in a dry southern room, on clean dry moss or sweet dry straw, so as not to touch one another. Some, or all the rest, having first laid a fortnight singly, and then nicely culled, are to be spread on shelves or on a dry floor. But the most superior way is to pack in large earthen, China or stone jars, with very dry long moss at the bottom, sides, and also between them if possible. Press a good coat of moss on the top, and then stop the mouth close with cork or otherwise, which should be rosined round about with a twentieth part of beeswax in it. Baked saw-dust will do as well. As the object is effectually to keep out air (the cause of putrefaction), the jars, if earthen, may be set on dry sand, which put also between, round and over them, to a foot thick on the top. In all close storing, observe there should be no doubt of the soundness of the fruit. Guard in time from frost those that lie open. Jars of fruit must be soon used after unsealing.

To keep Apples and Pears for Market.

Those who keep their fruit in storehouses for the supply of the London and other markets, as well as those who have not proper fruit-rooms, may keep their apples and pears in baskets or hampers, putting some soft paper in the bottoms and round the edges of the baskets, etc., to keep the fruit from being bruised; then put in a layer of fruit, and over that another layer of paper; and so on, a layer of fruit and of paper alternately, till the basket or hamper be full. Cover the top with paper three or four times thick to exclude the air and frost as much as possible. Every different sort of fruit should be placed separately; and it will be proper to fix a label to each basket or hamper, with the name of the fruit that it contains, and the time of its being fit for use.

Another Way.

Another way of keeping fruit is to pack it in glazed earthen jars. The pears or apples must be separately wrapped up in soft paper, then put a little well-dried bran in the bottom of the jar, and over the bran a layer of fruit; then a little more bran to fill up the interstices between the fruit, and to cover it; and so on, a layer of fruit and bran alternately, till the jar be full; then shake it gently, which will make the fruit and bran sink a little; fill up the vacancy at top with a piece of bladder to exclude the air; then put on the top or cover of the jar, observing that it fits as closely as possible. These jars should be kept in a room where there can be a fire in wet or damp weather.

Nicol considers it an error to sweat apples previously to storing them. The fruit ever after retains a bad flavor. It should never be laid in heaps at all; but if quite dry when gathered should be immediately carried to the fruit-room, and be laid, if not singly, at least twin on the shelves. If the finer fruits are placed on anything else than a clean shelf, it should be on fine paper. Brown paper gives them the flavor of pitch. The fine larger kinds of pears should not

TO PACK FRUIT.

be allowed even to touch one another, but should be laid quite single and distinct. Apples, and all ordinary pears, should be laid thin; never tier above tier. Free air should be admitted to the fruit-room always in good weather, for several hours every day; and in damp weather a fire should be kept in it. Be careful at all times to exclude frost from the fruit, and occasionally to turn it when very mellow.

To preserve Fruits or Flowers.

Mix one pound of nitre with two pounds of sal ammoniac and three pounds of clean common sand. In dry weather take fruit of any sort not fully ripe, allowing the stalks to remain, and put them one by one into an open glass, till it is quite full; cover the glass with oiled cloth, closely tied down; put the glass three or four inches into the earth in a dry cellar, and surround it on all sides, to the depth of three or four inches, with the above mixture. This method will preserve the fruit quite fresh all the year round.

To preserve Walnuts.

Walnuts for keeping should be suffered to drop of themselves, and afterwards laid in an open airy place till thoroughly dried; then pack them in jars, boxes or casks, with fine clean sand that has been well dried in the sun, in an oven, or before the fire, in layers of sand and walnuts alternately; set them in a dry place, but not where it is too hot. In this manner they have been kept good till the latter end of April. Before sending them to table wipe the sand clean off; and if they have become shrivelled, steep them in milk and water for six or eight hours before they are used; this will make them plump and fine, and cause them to peel easily.

To preserve Chestnuts and Filberts.

The chestnut is to be treated like the walnut after the husk is removed, which in the chestnut opens of itself. Chestnuts and walnuts may be preserved during the whole winter by covering them with earth, as cottagers do potatoes.

Filberts may always be gathered by hand, and should afterwards be treated as the walnut. Nuts intended for keeping should be packed in jars or boxes of dry sand.

To preserve Medlars and Quinces.

The medlar is not good till rotten ripe. It is generally gathered in the beginning of November, and placed between two layers of straw to forward its maturation. Others put medlars in a box on a three-inch layer of fresh bran, moistened well with soft warm water; then strew a layer of straw between them, and cover with fruit two inches thick, which moisten also, but not so wet as before. In a week or ten days after this operation they will be fit for use.

Quinces are gathered in November, when they are generally ripe. After sweating in a heap for a few days, they are to be wiped dry and placed on the fruit-shelf, at some distance from each other.

To pack Fruit for Carriage.

If fruit is to be sent to any considerable distance, great care should be taken in packing it. It should not be done in baskets, as they are liable to be bruised among heavy luggage, and the fruit of course will be impaired. Forsyth, therefore, recommends boxes made of strong deal, of different sizes, according to the quantity of fruit to be packed. The following are the dimensions of the boxes in which fruit used to be sent by the coach to Windsor and Weymouth, for the use of the royal family:

The larger box is two feet long, fourteen inches broad, and the same in depth. The smaller box is one foot, nine inches long, one foot broad, and the same in depth. These boxes are made of inch deal, and well secured with three iron clamps at each corner; they have two small iron handles, one at each end, by which they are fastened to the roof of the coach. In these boxes are sent melons, cherries, currants, pears, peaches, nectarines, plums and grapes; they are first wrapped in pine leaves, and then in paper. The cherries and currants are first packed in a flat tin box one foot four inches long, ten inches broad and four deep.

In packing, proceed thus: First put a layer of fine, long, dry moss in the bottom of the tin box, then a layer of currants or cherries, then another layer of moss, and so on alternately fruit and moss until the box is so full that when the lid is hasped down the fruit may be so finely packed as to preserve them from friction. Then make a layer of fine moss and short, soft, dry grass, well mixed, in the bottom of the deal box; pack in the melons with some of the same, tight in between all the rows, and also between the melons in the same row, till the layer is finished, choosing the fruit as nearly of a size as possible, filling up every interstice with the moss and grass. When the melons are packed, put a thin layer of moss and grass over them, upon which place the tin box with the currants, packing it firmly all round with moss to prevent it from shaking; then put a thin layer of moss over the box and pack the pears firmly (but so as not to bruise them) on that layer in the same manner as the melons, and so on with the peaches, nectarines, plums, and lastly the grapes, filling up the box with moss, that the lid may shut down so tight as to prevent any friction among the fruit. The boxes should have locks and two keys, which may serve for them all, each of the persons who pack and unpack the fruit having a key. The moss and grass should always be returned in the boxes, which, with a little addition, will serve the whole season, being shaken up and well aired after each journey, and keeping it sweet and clean. After the wooden box is locked cord it firmly.

If fruit is packed according to the above directions, it may be sent to great distances by coaches or wagons with perfect safety.

Other Methods of Packing Fruit.

Fruits of the most delicate sorts are sent from Spain and Italy to England, packed in jars with saw-dust from woods not resinous or otherwise ill tasted. One large branch of grapes is suspended from a twig or pin laid across the mouth of the jar, so that it may not touch either the bottom or sides; saw-dust or bran is then strewed in, and when full the jar is well shaken to cause it to settle; more is then added till it is quite full, when the supporting twig is taken away, and the earthen cover of the jar closely fitted and sealed, generally with fine stucco.

In the same way grapes may be sent from the remotest part of Scotland or Ireland to the metropolis. When the distance is less they may be sent enveloped in fine paper and packed in moss. The simplest mode for short distances is to wrap each bunch in fine, soft paper, and lay them on a bed of moss in a broad, flat basket with a proper cover.

Cherries and plums may be packed in thin layers, with paper and moss between each.

Peaches, apricots, and the finer plums may each be wrapped separately in vine or other leaves, or fine paper, and packed in abundance of cotton, flax, fine moss, or dried short grass. Moss is up-

To preserve Grapes.

Where there are several bunches in one branch, it may be cut off, leaving about six inches in length or more of the wood, according to the distance between the bunches, and a little on the outside of the fruit at each end; seal both ends with common bottle wax, then hang them across a line in a dry room, taking care to clip out with a pair of scissors any of the berries that begin to decay or become mouldy, which, if left, would taint the others. In this way grapes may be kept till February, but if cut before the bunches are too ripe, they may be kept much longer.

Grapes may be kept by packing them in jars (every bunch being first wrapped up in soft paper), and covering every layer with bran well dried, laying a little of it in the bottom of the jar, then a layer of grapes, and so on, a layer of bran and of grapes alternately till the jar is filled; then shake it gently and fill it to the top with bran, laying some paper over it and covering the top with a bladder tied firmly on to exclude the air; then put on the top or cover of the jar, observing that it fits close. These jars should be placed in a room where a fire can be kept in wet, damp weather.

French Method of Preserving Grapes.

Take a cask or barrel inaccessible to the external air, and put into it a layer of bran dried in an oven, or of ashes well dried and sifted. Upon this place a layer of bunches of grapes, well cleaned, and gathered in the afternoon of a dry day, before they are perfectly ripe. Proceed thus with alternate layers of bran and grapes till the barrel is full, taking care that the grapes do not touch each other, and to let the last layer be of bran; then close the barrel, so that the air may not be able to penetrate, which is an essential point. Grapes thus packed will keep nine or even twelve months. To restore them to their freshness, cut the end of the stalk of each bunch of grapes and put that of white grapes into white wine and that of black grapes into red wine, as flowers are put into water to revive or to keep them fresh.

To pack Young Trees for Exportation.

The long, white moss of the marshes, sphagnum palustre, may be applied for this purpose. Squeeze one part of the moisture from the moss, and lay courses of it about three inches thick, interposed with other courses of the trees, shortened in their branches and roots, stratum above stratum, till the box is filled; then let the whole be trodden down and the lid properly secured. The trees will want no care even during a voyage of ten or twelve months, the moss being retentive of moisture, and appearing to possess an antiseptic property which prevents fermentation or putrefaction. Vegetation will proceed during the time the trees remain inclosed, shoots arising both from the branches and roots, which, however, are blanched and tender, for want of light and air, to which the trees require to be gradually inured. This moss is very common in most parts of Europe and America.

How to dry Sweet Corn.

When the corn is in good condition for eating, the grains being fully grown, boil a quantity of ears just enough to cook the starch, and then let them dry a few hours, and then shell or cut off the grains and spread them in the sun till dried. The best way to dry the corn is to nail a piece of cloth of very open texture on a frame, which, if two feet wide and five long, will be of a convenient size to handle. If the corn is spread thinly upon this cloth it will dry quickly without souring. It should be covered with a mosquito netting to keep off the flies. Another person gives the following directions for drying sweet corn: As soon as the corn is fit for the table, husk and spread the ears in an open oven or some quickly-drying place. When the grains loosen shell the corn, or shell as soon as you can; then spread upon a cloth to dry in the sun, or on paper in a warm oven; stir often, that it may dry quickly, and not overheat. It more resembles the undried by its being whole, is sweeter and retains more of its natural flavor by drying faster. When wholly dried expose it to the wind by turning it slowly from dish to dish; the wind blows off all the troublesome white chaff.

Flower Gardening.

Autumn is the best time to manure a flower garden. It should be done once a year, and better in spring (April) than not at all. Lay on four inches deep of well-rotted manure, and dig it in at once. During the summer the earth will need now and then to be stirred with a hoe or rake; but in May it should always be thoroughly dug over with a spade, avoiding of course the plants in the bed. In May transplanting, setting of bulbs, or bedding plants and sowing seeds may be done.

Weeding can be best done by hand, early in the morning; letting the sun kill the weeds that are pulled up.

Never water, unless the soil evidently requires it. Clayey soils seldom need it; loose and sandy more often. Use always a watering-pot, with a rose, to sprinkle gently, without pouring or dashing. Rain-water is the best; it may be collected in a hogshead from a roof-spout. Very cold water should never be used for flowers; better too warm than too cold.

Shade-trees spoil a garden, but it should be protected from a strong wind.

Shrubbery.

To plant shrubs, dig for each a hole two or three feet in diameter; fill with rich loam; set the shrub or small tree in the middle, and tread it firm. If it droop, syringe or sprinkle it at night, or set a flower-pot near the root and fill it with water to soak down.

Prune shrubs only to avoid too great irregularity of shape or to remove dead parts.

For the winter, tender plants require to be tied up in cedar boughs or straw, in November. The covering should be taken off in April.

Favorite shrubs are the following: the June Berry, Flowering Acacia, Flowering Almond, Lilacs, Laburnum, Siberia Tree-pea, Tree Pæonies, Magnolias, Azaleas, Fringe Tree, Althea, Tartarean Honeysuckle, Spiræus, Syringa, Pyrus Japonica, Cranberry Tree.

Climbers, which are both hardy and ornamental, are the Trumpet-flower (Bignonia radicans) Virginia Creeper, Clematis, Glycene, and the Honeysuckles, Coral, Evergreen, etc.; and the climbing roses, as the Baltimore Belle, Queen of the Prairie, Superba, and Greville Rose.

Rhododendrons are highly ornamental when they thrive. So is the Kalmia, or common laurel; and the evergreen Ledum.

Roses.

These require a rich, well-mixed soil, in pots or

in the garden. Loam, or leaf mould, with half as much manure, and a little fine sand, will do the best. Roses which require to be taken up and kept in house for the winter should be well pruned at that time. Do not water roses so as to make the soil sodden around the roots. A little broken charcoal about them will aid the brilliancy of their blooming.

Roses are chiefly of the China, Tea, and Bourbon varieties. Of the first these are much admired: Agrippina (crimson), Eel's Blush (a great bloomer), Common Daily, White Daily, Madame Bosanquet, Sanguinea (crimson), Louis Philippe (dark crimson), Eugene Hardy (nearly white), and Eugene Beauharnois (fragrant).

Tea Roses are more delicate. The following are preferred: Odorata, Devoniensis, Caroline, Triomphe de Luxembourg, Safrano (beautiful buds), Clara Sylvain (pure white), Bougère, Madame Desprez (white), and Pactole (lemon yellow).

Bourbon Roses are hardy in our Middle and Southern States. Of them we would choose Gloire de Dijon, Souvenir de la Malmaison, Hermosa, and Paul Joseph; though there are many other fine kinds.

Pinks.

Carnations and picotees are most admired, but the double crimson Indian pink is very pretty and easily raised. The pinks do best in a soil of three parts loam, one part cow manure, and sandy peat one part, with a little old plaster, sifted. Pinks do not bear a great deal of moisture. They are raised either from layers or pipings, or from seed. Pipings are superfluous shoots cut off and potted in compost surrounded by moist sand. The seeds may be sown in spring, in similar pots or pans, or in open beds. In the Northern States they need potting for the winter as early as October.

Geraniums.

These require a strong loam for soil; the top of a pasture will do, with a little sand and charcoal. Geraniums require a good deal of light and air, and should not be crowded. They bloom in spring and summer, not often flowering in winter even in pots. Horseshoe or scarlet geranium is very popular; so are the rose, oak, and nutmeg geraniums. They all bear pruning very well. Large-flowered geraniums (pelargoniums) are beset by the green fly. Once in a week or two in warm weather they should be smoked, to get rid of the flies, and syringed every day or two.

Verbenas.

These repay care well: having variety of color, blooming freely, and being easily cultivated. It is easy to raise new varieties from seed. All colors but blue and a handsome yellow have been produced. They are often raised from cuttings. The soil for verbenas should be about two parts loam, two leaf mould, and a little sand. Cuttings of young shoots may be taken from old plants early in February. After rooting for a few weeks in sandy loam, they may be potted; bedded out when warm weather comes, and repotted in September. You may take cuttings from choice plants in August, root them for two weeks, then pot, and repot them when the roots touch the sides of the pot. This is, by the way, proper as a rule with any plants.

Verbenas are native to dry, hilly ground, and need but moderate watering. Favorites are, Giant of Battles, Admiral Dundas, General Simpson, Celestial, Defiance, Lord Raglan, Glory of America.

Heliotrope.

This gives a delightful fragrance, and is not hard to cultivate. It may be managed just as the verbena, but should be repotted often, and allowed to grow large, being trimmed for shape only.

What is called the lemon verbena is another plant, a half-hardy shrub, grown for the sweet scent of its leaves. It should be kept in a cellar all winter and planted out in the spring.

Of biennial and perennial flowering plants there are many of great beauty for the garden, of which we have no room to give more than the names. They require little care beyond loosening the earth round them in the spring. The spring is the time for transplanting them. In the summer prune away weak stems; in the fall cover them with coarse manure; if evergreen, shelter with cedar or pine boughs. They may be propagated by division of the root early in the spring or after the summer bloom is over. The following are choice kinds: Lily of the Valley, Larkspur (Delphinum Formosum), Phlox (*Phlox Drummondii* is a beautiful annual), Canterbury Bell, Foxglove, Hemerocallis, Iris or Flag, Everlasting Pea, Spirea (several varieties are very beautiful), Sweet William, Alyssum.

If one has a greenhouse, large or small, he may enjoy also, with good management, in winter as well as summer, the following: Camellias, Orange and Lemon trees, Daphne, Azalea, Oleander, Erica, Fuchsia, Salvia, Tropæolum (common nasturtium is Tropæolum majus), Abutilon, Cactus, Calla, Cuphæa, Achænia, Maranta, Pittosporum, Jasmines (white and yellow, very sweet), Calceolaria, Chinese Primrose, Laurestinus, Wax-plant, Begonia, Chrysanthemums (good garden bloomers in autumn), and the various bulbous plants, namely, Oxalis, Hyacinths, Tulips (grown beautifully in beds), Crocuses, Snowdrops, Jonquils, Narcissus. The Tuberose, and the Gladiolus are universally admired. The latter is gaining recently especially in favor. There are twenty or thirty varieties, which may be bought for three or four dollars a dozen. When grown from seed they bloom the third year. Finest varieties of Gladiolus are, Penelope, Brenchleyensis, Count de Morny, Vesta, Calypso.

Though not here exactly in place, we may name the periwinkles, larger and smaller, as beautiful in leaf and flower, for the border of a bed or about the fence of a garden; and Ivy as the most permanently beautiful of vines for a wall. The Parlor Ivy is a great grower, in baskets or elsewhere, and a pretty plant; not a true ivy, however, neither is the Kenilworth Ivy.

Annuals.

These are either hardy or half-hardy. The former may be sown in the fall to bloom the next summer, or early in spring. The latter are sown early in spring to bloom in the summer. These are also either for the hot-bed only, or for the garden. Many plants which are annual in the open air, in a temperate climate, may become perennial in a conservatory.

Tuberous annuals, kept through the winter to plant out again, are the Four-o-clock, Scarlet Bean, etc.

The following must be sown where they are to remain: Annual Larkspurs, Poppy, Mignonette, Lupin, Sweet Pea. They may be started in pots, however.

In sowing annuals, let the depth be according to the size of the seed; very shallow for the small kinds. Thin out the weakest as they come up. August or April will do to sow the hardy kinds; the beginning of May for the other sorts. In the fall pull up the old stalks.

Besides those named above, desirable annuals

are, Asters, Coreopsis, Sweet Alyssum, Escholtzia, Portulacca (a fine bloomer in a good place), Canna Indica, Zinnia, and Cypress Vine. The last should have a light frame for it to climb on.

Lilies and tiger-lilies have, in the above outline of garden-culture, been overlooked. They can only be named as having great beauty and variety. Dahlias are going out of fashion; they are not fragrant, and not superior in beauty in proportion to the pains formerly taken with them.

For artificial heating, the structures in use are: the Stove, where the temperature is from 70° to 120° Fahr., with copious moisture; the Hot house being a more common name for the same; the Green-house, of glass, kept at from 40° to 70°, for care and rearing of plants; and the Conservatory, used more for their display when in perfection. A Pit is an excavation of six or eight feet in depth, covered with a glass roof. This is very useful, and not costly.

On a small scale, all that can be done in a green-house may be accomplished in a parlor or chamber, with a Ward Case or a Walton Case. The Hanging-Basket and the Aquarium are also delightful sources of enjoyment to those who acquire skill in their management.

Insects.

Red spider is killed by water; syringing will dispose of it. Mealy bug and scale are to be searched for and destroyed by hand; but sponging, especially with soap-suds, may suffice. The green fly is best gotten rid of by smoking. Put the plant under a barrel in which tobacco is burning; or burn tobacco-leaves or smoking tobacco under the plant in its place.

Soil for Window Gardening.

Loam, or common garden earth, brown or black, got from old pastures, left to crumble; peat, or black earth from damp woods or meadows; leaf-mould, the top soil of old woods; manure, well rotted by time, as in an old hot-bed; and common or silver sand, free from salt; these, in different proportions will do for all plants. For potting, good authority (C. S. Rand, Parlor and Garden) recommends two parts leaf-mould, one part manure, one-half part loam, one-half part peat, and one part sand.

Potted plants seldom need manure. Liquid manure or guano should, if used for them, be diluted and not often applied.

PRACTICAL DIRECTIONS FOR GARDENERS.

1. Perform every operation in the proper season.
2. Perform every operation in the proper manner.

This is to be acquired in part by practice, and partly also by reflection. For example, in digging over a piece of ground, it is a common practice with slovens to throw the weeds and stones on the dug ground, or on the adjoining alley or walk, with the intention of gathering them off afterwards. A better way is to have a wheel-barrow or a large basket, in which to put the weeds and extraneous matters, as they are picked out of the ground. Some persons, in planting or weeding, whether in the open air, or in hot-houses, throw down all seeds, stones, and extraneous matters on the paths or alleys, with a view to pick them up, or sweep or rake them together afterwards; it is better to carry a basket or other utensil, either common or subdivided, in which to hold in one part the plants to be planted, in another the extraneous matters, etc.

3. Complete every part of an operation as you proceed.
4. Finish one job before beginning another.
5. In leaving off working at any job, leave the work and tools in an orderly manner.
6. In leaving off work for the day, make a temporary finish, and carry the tools to the tool-house.
7. In passing to and from the work, or on any occasion, through any part of what is considered under the charge of the gardener, keep a vigilant look out for weeds, decayed leaves, or any other deformity, and remove them.
8. In gathering a crop, remove at the same time the roots, leaves, stems, or whatever else is of no farther use, or may appear slovenly, decaying, or offensive.
9. Let no crop of fruit or herbaceous vegetables go to waste on the spot.
10. Cut down the flower-stalks on all plants.
11. Keep every part of what is under your care perfect in its kin l.

Attend in spring and autumn to walls and buildings, and get them repaired, jointed, glazed, and painted where wanted. Attend at all times to machines, implements, and tools, keeping them clean, sharp, and in perfect repair. See particularly that they are placed in their proper situations in the tool-house. House every implement, utensil, or machine not in use, both in winter and summer. Allow no blanks in edgings, rows, single specimens, drills, beds, and even, where practicable, in broadcast sown pieces. Keep edgings and edges cut to the utmost nicety. Keep the shapes of the wall trees filled with wood according to their kind, and let their training be in the first style of perfection. Keep all walks in perfect form, whether raised or flat, free from weeds, dry, and well rolled. Keep all the lawns, by every means in your power, of a close texture, and dark green velvet appearance. Keep water clear and free from weeds, and let not ponds, lakes, or artificial rivers, rise to the brim in winter, nor sink very far under it in summer.

RURAL and DOMESTIC ECONOMY.

To make good Bread.

Place in a large pan twenty-eight pounds of flour; make a hole with the hand in the centre of it like a large basin, into which strain a pint of brewers' yeast; this must be tested, and if too bitter a little flour sprinkled into it, and then strained directly; then pour in two quarts of water of the temperature of 100°, or blood heat, and stir the flour round from the bottom of the hole formed by the hand till that part of the flour is quite thick and well mixed, though all the rest must remain unwetted; then sprinkle a little flour over the moist part and cover it with a cloth; this is called *sponge*, and must be left to rise. Some leave it only half an hour, others all night.

When the sponge is light, however, add four

quarts of water of the same temperature as above, and well knead the whole mass into a smooth dough. This is hard work if done well. Then cover the dough and leave it for an hour. In cold weather both sponge and dough must be placed on the kitchen hearth, or in some room not too cold, or it will not rise well. Before the last water is put in two tablespoonsful of salt must be sprinkled over the flour. Sometimes the flour will absorb another pint of water.

After the dough has risen it should be made quickly into loaves; if much handled the bread will be heavy. It will require an hour and a half to bake, if made into four-pound loaves. The oven should be well heated before the dough is put into it. To try its heat, throw a little flour into it; if it brown *directly*, it will do.

To make Butter.

Let the cream be at the temperature of 55° to 60°, by a Fahrenheit thermometer; this is very important. If the weather be cold put boiling water into the churn for half an hour before you want to use it; when that is poured off strain in the cream through a butter cloth. When the butter is coming, which is easily ascertained by the sound, take off the lid, and with a small, flat board scrape down the sides of the churn, and do the same to the lid; this prevents waste. When the butter is come the butter-milk is to be poured off and spring water put into the churn, and turned for two or three minutes; this is to be then poured away and fresh added, and again the handle turned for a minute or two. Should there be the least milkiness when this is poured from the churn, more must be put in.

The butter is then to be placed on a board or marble slab and salted to taste; then with a cream cloth, wrung out in spring water, press all the moisture from it. When dry and firm make it up into rolls with flat boards. The whole process should be completed in three-quarters of an hour.

In hot weather pains must be taken to keep the cream from reaching too high a heat. If the dairy be not cool enough, keep the cream-pot in the coldest water you can get; make the butter early in the morning, and place cold water in the churn for a while before it is used.

The cows should be milked near the dairy; carrying the milk far prevents its rising well. In summer churn twice a week. Wash the churn well each time with soap or wood-ashes.

To cure Hams.

For each ham of twelve pounds weight: Two pounds of common salt; 2 ounces of saltpetre; ¼ pound of bay salt; ¼ pound of coarse sugar.

This should be reduced to the finest powder. Rub the hams well with it; female hands are not often heavy enough to do this thoroughly. Then place them in a deep pan, and add a wineglassful of good vinegar. Turn the hams every day; for the first three or four days rub them well with the brine; after that time it will suffice to ladle it over the meat with a wooden or iron spoon. They should remain three weeks in the pickle. When taken from it wipe them well, put them in bags of brown paper and then smoke them with *wood* smoke for three weeks.

TO MANAGE A DAIRY.
Directions to the Cow-Feeder.

Go to the cow-stall at six o'clock in the morning, winter and summer; give each cow half a bushel of the mangel-wurtzel, carrots, turnips, or potatoes, cut; at seven o'clock, the hour the dairy-maid comes to milk them, give each some hay, and let them feed till they are all milked. If any cow refuses hay, give her something she will eat, such as grains, carrots, etc., during the time she is milking, as it is absolutely necessary the cow should feed whilst milking. As soon as the woman has finished milking in the morning, turn the cows into the airing ground, and let there be plenty of fresh water in the troughs; at nine o'clock give each cow three gallons of this mixture: to eight gallons of grain add four gallons of bran or pollard; when they have eaten that put some hay into the cribs; at twelve o'clock give each three gallons of the mixture as before; if any cow looks for more give her another gallon; on the contrary, if she will not eat what you gave her, take it out of the manger, for never at one time let a cow have more than she will eat up clean. Mind and keep the mangers clean, that they do not get sour. At two o'clock give each cow half a bushel of carrots, or turnips; look the turnips, etc., over well before giving them to the cows, as one rotten turnip will give a bad taste to the milk, and most likely spoil a whole dairy of butter. At four o'clock put the cows into the stall to be milked; feed them on hay as at milking-time in the morning, keeping in mind that the cow whilst milking must feed on something. At six o'clock give each cow three gallons of the mixture as before. Rack them up at eight o'clock. Twice in a week put into each cow's feed at noon a quart of malt-dust. Corn or mill feed (offal from grinding flour from wheat) is still better. One-half peck of corn, or a little more, mill-feed twice a day, mixed with chopped straw or hay, *wet* and *mashed*.

Directions to the Dairy-Maid.

Go to the cow-stall at 7 o'clock; take with you cold water and a sponge, and wash each cow's udder clean before milking; dowse the udder well with cold water, winter and summer, as it braces and repels heats. Keep your hands and arms clean. Milk each cow as dry as you can, morning and evening, and when you milk each cow as you suppose dry, begin again with the cow you first milked and drip them each, for the principal reason of cows failing in their milk is from negligence in not milking the cow dry, particularly at the time the calf is taken from the cow. Suffer no one to milk the cow but yourself, and have no gossiping in the stall. Every Saturday night give in an exact account of the quantity each cow has given in the week.

To make Oats prove Doubly Nutritious to Horses.

Instead of grinding the oats, break them in a mill, and the same quantity will prove doubly nutritious. Another method is to boil the corn and give the horses the liquor in which it has been boiled; the result will be, that instead of six bushels in a crude state, three bushels so prepared will be found to answer, and to keep the animals in superior vigor and condition.

Cheap Method of Rearing Horned Cattle.

After having expressed the oil from the linseed, make up the remaining husks or dross into round balls of the size of a fist, and afterwards dry them; infuse and dissolve two or three of these balls in hot water, and add in the beginning a third or fourth part of fresh milk, but afterwards, when the calves are grown, mix only skim milk with the infusion.

To rear Calves.

The best method of rearing calves is to take them from the cows in three weeks or a month, and to give them nothing but a little fine hay until they begin through necessity to pick a little; then cut some of the hay and mix it with bran or oats in a trough, and slice some turnips about the size of a dollar, which they will soon by licking learn to eat; after which give them turnips enough.

To rear Calves without Milk.

In two or three days after they are calved take the calves from the cows, put them in a house by themselves, then give them a kind of water gruel, composed of about one-third barley and two-thirds of oats ground together very fine, then sift the mixture through a very fine sieve, put it into the quantity of water below mentioned, and boil it half an hour, when take it off the fire, and let it remain till it is milk-warm; then give each calf about a quart in the morning, and the same quantity in the evening, and increase it as the calf grows older. It requires very little trouble to make them drink it; after the calves have had this diet about a week or ten days, tie up a little bundle of hay and put it in the middle of the house, which they will by degrees come to eat; also put a little of the meal above mentioned in a small trough for them to eat occasionally; keep them in this manner until they are of proper age to turn out to grass, before which they must be at least two months old.

Another Method.

Make an infusion of malt, or fresh wort as a substitute for milk; in summer it may be given to the calves cold, but in winter it must have the same degree of warmth as the milk just coming from the cow; the quantity is the same as the milk commonly given at once to a calf, and to be increased in proportion as the calf grows.

To Fatten Poultry.

An experiment has been tried of feeding geese with turnips cut in small pieces like dice, but less in size, and put into a trough of water; with this food alone the effect was that six geese, each when lean weighing only nine pounds, actually gained twenty pounds each in about three weeks' fattening.

Malt is an excellent food for geese and turkeys; grains are preferred for the sake of economy, unless for immediate and rapid fattening; the grains should be boiled afresh.

Other cheap articles for fattening are oatmeal and treacle; barley-meal and milk; boiled oats and ground malt.

Corn before being given to fowls should always be crushed and soaked in water. The food will thus go further, and it will help digestion. Hens fed thus have been known to lay during the whole of the winter months.

Turkeys are very tender while young, afterwards quite hardy. Put them in large and open coops; they may be well raised with hens, and ramble less so. When hatched some put a grain of black pepper down their throats as a sort of cordial. The best food for ducks when hatched is bread and milk; in a few days barley-meal, wetted into balls as big as peas.

To choose a Milch Cow.

As to a choice of breeds for a private family, none (says Mr. Lawrence) probably combine so many advantages as the Suffolk dun cows. They excel both in quantity and quality of milk; they feed well after they become barren; they are small-sized, and polled or hornless; the last a great convenience. The horns of cows which butt and gore others, should be immediately broad tipped. There is a breed of polled Yorkshire or Holderness cows, some of them of middling size, great milkers, and well adapted to the use of families where a great quantity of milk is required, and where price is no object and food in plenty. If richer milk and a comparison of the two famous breeds be desired, one of each may be selected, namely, the last mentioned and the other of the midland county, or long-horned species. Color is so far no object, that neither a good cow nor a good horse can either be of a bad color; nevertheless, in an ornamental view, the sheeted and pied stock of the Yorkshire short-horns make a picturesque figure in the grounds.

The Alderney cows yield rich milk upon less feed than larger stock, but are seldom large milkers, and are particularly scanty of produce in the winter season. They are, besides, worth little or nothing as barreners, not only on account of their small size, but their inaptitude to take on fat, and the ordinary quality of their beef.

To determine the Economy of a Cow.

The annual consumption of food per cow, if turned to grass, is from one acre to an acre and a half in summer, and from a ton to a ton and a half of hay in the winter. A cow may be allowed two pecks of carrots per day. The grass being cut and carried will economize it full one-third. The annual product of a good, fair dairy cow during several months after calving, and either in summer or winter, if duly fed and kept in the latter season, will be an average of seven pounds of butter per week, from five to three gallons of milk per day. Afterwards a weekly average of three or four pounds of butter from barely half the quantity of milk. It depends on the constitution of the cow, how nearly she may be milked to the time of her calving, some giving good milk until within a week or two of that period, others requiring to be dried eight or nine weeks previously. I have heard (says Mr. Lawrence) of twenty pounds of butter, and even twenty-two pounds, made from the milk of one long-horned cow in seven days, but I have never been fortunate enough to obtain one that would produce more than twelve pounds per week, although I have had a Yorkshire cow which milked seven gallons per day, yet never made five pounds of butter in one week. On the average, three gallons of good milk will make one pound of butter.

To fatten Hogs.

The Shakers have proved that ground corn is one-third better than unground, and nineteen pounds of cooked meal are equal to fifty pounds raw. Boiled and slightly fermented vegetables are also very fattening to swine.

To breed Pheasants.

Eggs being provided, put them under a hen that has kept the nest three or four days, and if you set two or three hens on the same day you will have the advantage of shifting the good eggs. The hens having set their full time, such of the young pheasants as are already hatched put in a basket, with a piece of flannel, till the hen has done hatching. The brood now come put on let a frame with a net over it, and a place for the hen, that she cannot get to the young pheasants, but that they may go to her, and feed them with boiled egg cut small, boiled milk and bread, alum curd, a little of each sort, and often. After two or three days they will be acquainted with the call of the hen that hatched them, may have their liberty to run on the grass plat, or elsewhere, observing to shift them with the sun and out of the cold winds; they need not have their liberty in the morning till the sun is up, and they must be shut up with the hen in good time in the evening. You must be very careful in order to guard against the distemper to which they are liable, in the choice of a situation for breeding the birds up, where no poultry, pheasants, or turkeys, etc., have ever been kept, such as the warm side of a field, orchard. or pleasure-ground, or garden, or even on a common, or a good green lane, under circumstances of this kind, or by a wood side; but then it is proper for a man to keep with them under a temporary hovel, and to have two or three dogs chained at a proper distance, with a lamp or two at night.

The birds going on as before mentioned should so continue till September or (if very early bred) the middle of August. Before they begin to shift the long feathers in the tail, they are to be shut up in the basket with the hen regularly every night. For such young pheasants as are chosen for breeding stock at home, and likewise to turn out in the following spring, provide a new piece of ground, large and roomy for two pens, where no pheasants, etc., have been kept, and there put the young birds in as they begin to shift their tails. Such of them as are intended to be turned out at a future time, or in another place, put into one pen netted over, and leave their wings as they are, and those wanted for breeding put in the other pen, cutting one wing of each bird. The gold and silver pheasants pen earlier, or they will be off. Cut the wing often, and when first penned feed all the young birds with barley-meal, dough, corn, plenty of green turnips, and alum curd, to make which take new milk, as much as the young birds require, and boil it with a lump of alum, so as not to make the curd hard and tough, but custard-like.

A little of this curd twice a day, and ants' eggs after every time they have had a sufficient quantity of the other food. If they do not eat heartily, give them some ants' eggs to create an appetite, but by no means in such abundance as to be considered their food.

Not more than four hens should be allowed in the pens to one cock. Never put more eggs under a hen than she can well and closely cover, the eggs being fresh and carefully preserved. Short broods to be joined and shifted to one hen; common hen pheasants in close pens, and with plenty of cover, will sometimes make their nests and hatch their own eggs; but they seldom succeed in rearing their brood, being so naturally shy; whence should this method be desired, they must be left entirely to themselves, as they feel alarm even in being looked at. Eggs for setting are generally ready in April. Period of incubation the same as in the pheasant as in the common hen. Pheasants, like the pea-fowl, will clear grounds of insects and reptiles, but will spoil all wall-trees within their reach, by pecking off every bud and leaf.

Strict cleanliness to be observed, the meat not to be tainted with dung, and the water to be pure and often renewed. Food for grown pheasants, barley or wheat; generally the same as for other poultry. In a cold spring, hemp seed, or other warming seeds, are comfortable, and will forward the breeding stock.

To manage Young Chickens.

The chickens first hatched are to be taken from the hen, lest she be tempted to leave her task unfinished. They may be secured in a basket of wool or soft hay, and kept in a moderate heat; if the weather be cold, near the fire. They will require no food for twenty-four hours, should it be necessary to keep them so long from the hen. The whole brood being hatched, place the hen under a coop abroad, upon a dry spot, and, if possible, not within reach of another hen, since the chickens will mix, and the hens are apt to maim and destroy those which do not belong to them. Nor should they be placed near young fowls, which are likely to crush them, being always eager for their small meat.

The first food should be split grits, afterwards tail wheat; all watery food, soaked bread or potatoes, being improper; corn or mill screenings (before the wheat is ground) will do. Eggs boiled hard, or curds chopped small, are very suitable as first food. Their water should be pure, and often renewed, and there are pans made in such forms, that the chickens may drink without getting into the water, which, by wetting their feet and feathers, numbs and injures them; a basin in the middle of a pan of water will answer the end; the water running around it. There is no necessity for cooping the brood beyond two or three days, but they may be confined as occasion requires, or suffered to range, as they are much benefited by the foraging of the hen. They should not be let out too early in the morning, whilst the dew lies upon the ground, nor be suffered to range over wet grass, which is a common and fatal cause of disease in fowls. Another caution requisite is to guard them against unfavorable changes of the weather, particularly if rainy. Nearly all the diseases of fowls arise from cold moisture.

For the period of the chickens' quitting the hen there is no general rule; when she begins to roost, if sufficiently forward, they will follow her; if otherwise, they should be secured in a proper place till the time arrives when they are to associate with the other young poultry, since the larger are sure to overrun and drive from their food the younger broods.

Access to a barn-yard for worms is good for them. A warm house for shelter in winter is very important for chickens.

To hatch Chickens in the Egyptian Mode.

The mamals or ovens of Egypt are scarcely above nine feet in height, but they have an extent in length and breadth which renders them remarkable, and yet they are more so in their internal structure. The centre of the building is a very narrow gallery, usually about the width of three feet, extending from one end of the building to the other, the height of which is from eight to nine feet; the structure for the most part of brick. The entrance into the oven is through the gallery, which commands the whole extent of it, and facilitates the several operations that are necessary to keep the eggs to the proper degree of heat. The oven has a door, not very wide, and only as high as it is broad; this door, and many others in use in the mamals, are commonly no more than round holes.

The gallery is a corridor, with this difference from our common corridors, which have only one row of rooms, whereas that of the mamal has always two rows of them on both sides: namely, one on the ground floor, and another above. Every one upon the ground floor has one above, perfectly equal, both in length and breadth. The rooms of each row on the ground floor, are all equal, in length, breadth, and height. Reaumur observes, "We know of no other rooms in the world so low as these, being only three feet in height." Their breadth, which is in the same direction with the length of the gallery, is four or five feet; they are very narrow in proportion to their length, which is twelve or fifteen feet.

Every one of these rooms has its door or round aperture, about a foot and a half in diameter, opening into the gallery, the hole being wide enough for a man to creep through. All the eggs to be hatched are first ranged in these rooms. Four or five thousand eggs are put into each of them. These are the real ovens, so that the whole edifice, which is denominated a chicken oven, is an assemblage of many ovens set together, side by side, opposite and over each other, and in the course of the process a part of the eggs are warmed in the upper rooms, after having been previously in the lower.

Forty or fifty thousand eggs are hatched at once, or another account extends the number to eighty thousand. The eggs are spread on mats, flocks or flax, in each room upon the ground floor, where they contract their first and general warmth, during a certain number of days.

The heat of the air in the inferior rooms, and consequently that of the eggs, would rise to an excessive degree, were the fire in the gutter incessantly kept up. They keep it up only an hour in the morning, and an hour at night, and they style these heatings the dinner and supper of the chickens; they receive, however, two more meals, that is, luncheon and afternoon meal, the fire being lighted four times a day.

On the day on which they cease to light the fires, some of the eggs of each inferior room are always conveyed into the room above. The eggs had been too much heaped in the former, and it is now time to extend and give them more room.

The proper number of eggs from each inferior room having been removed into the room above, all the apertures of the rooms and of the gallery are closely and exactly stopped with bungs of tow, excepting, perhaps, half the apertures in the arches or ceilings of the upper rooms, which are left open in order to procure there a circulation of air. This precaution is sufficient to preserve in the ovens, for many days together, the temperature which has been obtained; which indeed would be the case with ovens upon so considerable a scale in any country, more especially one so hot as Egypt.

Three hundred and eighty-six ovens are kept in Egypt annually, during four or six months, allowing more time than is necessary to hatch eight successive broods of chickens, ducks and turkeys, making on the whole yearly three thousand and eighty-eight broods. The number in different hatchings is not always the same, from the occasional difficulty of obtaining a sufficient number of eggs, which may be stated at a medium between the two extremes of forty and eighty thousand to each oven.

The overseer contracts to return, in a living brood, to his employer, two-thirds of the number of eggs set in the ovens—all above being his own perquisite, in addition to his salary for the season, which is from eighty to forty crowns, exclusive of his board. According to report, the crop of poultry thus artificially raised in Egypt was seldom, if ever, below that ratio, making the enormous annual amount of ninety-two million six hundred and forty thousand.

The chickens are not sold from the stove by tale, but by the bushel or basket full!

Excellent Substitute for Candles.

Procure meadow-rushes, such as they tie the hop shoots to the poles with. Cut them when they have attained their full substance, but are still green. The rush, at this age, consists of a body of pith with a green skin on it. Cut off both ends of the rush and leave the prime part, which, on an average, may be about a foot and a half long. Then take off all the green skin except for about a fifth part of the way round the pith. Thus it is a piece of pith all but a little strip of skin in one part all the way up, which is necessary to hold the pith together.

The rushes being thus prepared, the grease is melted, and put, in a melted state, into something that is as long as the rushes are. The rushes are put into the grease, soaked in it sufficiently, then taken out and laid in a bit of bark taken from a young tree, so as not to be too large. This bark is fixed up against the wall by a couple of straps put round it, and there it hangs for the purpose of holding the rushes.

The rushes are carried about in the hand; but to sit by, to work by, or to go to bed by, they are fixed in stands made for the purpose, some of which are high to stand on the ground, and some low to stand on a table. These stands have an iron part something like a pair of pliers to hold the rush in, and the rush is shifted forward from time to time, as it burns down to the thing that holds it.

These rushes give a better light than a common small dip candle, and they cost next to nothing, though the laborer may with them have as much light as he pleases.

Petroleum or kerosene is now cheaper than candles, and gives a beautiful light.

To cultivate Mustard.

A yard square of ground, sown with common mustard, the crop of which may be ground for use in a little mustard-mill as wanted, will save some money. The mustard will look brown instead of yellow, but the former color is as good as the latter; and, as to the taste, the real mustard has certainly a much better taste than that of the drugs and flour which sometimes go under the name of mustard. Let any one try it, and he will never use the latter again. The drugs, if taken freely, leave a burning at the pit of the stomach, which the real mustard does not.

To cure Herrings, Pilchards, Mackerel, Sprats, etc.

Reservoirs of any size, vats or casks, perfectly water-tight, should be about half filled with brine made by dissolving about twenty-eight parts of solid salt in seventy-two of fresh water. The fish, as fresh as possible, gutted or not, must be plunged into this fully-saturated brine in such quantity as nearly to fill the reservoir; and, after remaining quite immersed for five or six days, they will be fit to be packed as usual, with large-grained solid salt, and exported to the hottest climates. As brine is always weakest at the upper part, in order to keep it of a uniform saturation, a wooden lattice-work frame, of such size as to be easily let into the inside of the reservoir, is sunk an inch or two under the surface of the brine, for the purpose of suspending upon it lumps of one or two pounds, or larger, of solid salt, which effectually saturates whatever moisture may exude from the fish; and thus the brine will be continued of the utmost strength so long as any part of the salt remains undissolved. The solidity of the lumps admits of their being applied several times, or whenever the reservoirs are replenished with fish; and the brine, although repeatedly used, does not putrefy; nor do the fish, if kept under the surface, ever become rancid.

All provisions are best preserved by this method, especially bacon, which, when thus cured, is not so liable to become rusty as when done by the usual method of rubbing with salt.

Portable Ice-House.

Take an iron-bound butt or puncheon and knock out the head; then cut a very small hole

TO MAKE ICE.

In the bottom, about the size of a wine-cork. Place inside of it a wooden tub, shaped like a churn, resting it upon two pieces of wood, which are to raise it from touching the bottom. Fill the space round the inner tub with pounded charcoal, and fit to the tub a cover with a convenient handle, having inside one or two small hooks, on which the bottles are to be hung during the operation. Place on the lid a bag of pounded charcoal, about two feet square, and over all place another cover, which must cover the head of the outer cask.

When the apparatus is thus prepared let it be placed in a cold cellar, and buried in the earth above four-fifths of its height; but, though cold, the cellar must be dry; wet ground will not answer, and a sandy soil is the best. Fill the inner tub, or nearly so, with pounded ice; or, if prepared in winter, with snow well pressed down, and the apparatus will be complete.

Whenever it is wished to make ices take off the upper cover, then the sack or bag of pounded charcoal, and suspend the vessel containing the liquid to be frozen to the hooks inside of the inner cover; then close up the whole as before for half an hour, when the operation will be complete, provided care be taken to exclude external air.

To produce Ice for Culinary Purposes.

Fill a gallon stone bottle with hot spring water, leaving about a pint vacant, and put in two ounces of refined nitre; the bottle must then be stopped very close and let down into a deep well. After three or four hours it will be completely frozen, but the bottle must be broken to procure the ice. If the bottle is moved up and down so as to be sometimes in and sometimes out of the water, the consequent evaporation will hasten the process. The heating of the water assists the subsequent congelation; and experience has proved that hot water in winter will freeze more rapidly than cold water just drawn from a spring.

To make Ice.

The following is a simple and speedy method of congealing water:

Into a metal vase half filled with water pour very gently an equal quantity of ether, so that no mixture may take place of the two liquids. The vase is placed under the receiver of an air-pump, which is so fixed upon its support as to remain quite steady when the air is pumped out.

At the first strokes of the piston the ether becomes in a state of ebullition; it is evaporated totally in less than a minute, and the water remains converted into ice.

To procure Ice from a Powder.

This is made by pulverizing and drying the shivery fragments of porphyritic trap, which will absorb one-fifth of its own weight of water. Two quarts of it, spread in a large dish, will, in a few minutes, in an exhausted receiver, freeze half of three quarters of a pound of water, in a cup of porous earthenware. This is a cheap substitute for the still more powerful freezing mixtures mentioned in chemical works.

To char Peats at the Moss.

The best method of charring peats where they are dug is, when the peats are properly dried, wheel to the outside of the moss a single horse-cart load of them. Level a spot of ground, about seven feet in diameter, near to a drain, and drive a stake of wood into the ground about five feet long; roll some dry heather or pol (the refuse of flax) round the stake, and lay some also upon the ground where the peats are to be placed; then set the peats upon and all round the stake, inclining to the centre, with a little dry heather or pol between each two floors of peat, until near the top or last course: then they are laid in a horizontal direction; and the stack, when finished, is in the form of a bee-hive. The next operation is to set the stack on fire, which is done at the bottom all round. The fire will soon run up the post in the centre, and, when the heather or pol is all consumed, the space forms a chimney, and occasions the stack to burn regularly. If the windward side should burn too fast, apply some wet turf. When the peats are thought to be sufficiently burnt, which is easily known from the appearance of the smoke, apply wet turf and water from the adjoining drain as fast as possible until the whole is extinguished. The charcoal may be removed upon the following day.

To char Peats for Family Use.

When charcoal is required for cookery, or any other purpose in the family, take a dozen or fifteen peats and put them upon the top of the kitchen fire upon edge; they will soon draw up the coal fire, and become red in a short time. After being turned about once or twice, and done with smoking, they are charred, and may be removed to the stoves. If more char is wanted, put on another supply of peats. By following this plan the kitchen fire is kept up, and thus, with very little trouble, a supply of the best charred peat is obtained, perfectly free from smoke, and the vapor by no means so noxious as charcoal made from wood. Peats charred in this way may be used in a chafer in any room, or even in a nursery, without any danger arising from the vapor. It would also be found very fit for the warming of beds, and much better than live coals, which are in general used full of sulphur, and smell all over the house.

Peats charred in a grate, and applied to the purpose of charcoal immediately, without being extinguished, make the purest and best char, and freest of smoke. When peats are charred in a large quantity, and extinguished, any part of the peat that is not thoroughly burnt in the heart will imbibe moisture, and when used will smoke and have a disagreeable smell, which would at once hinder charred peat from being used in a gentleman's family.

To make a Cheap Fuel.

Mix coal, charcoal, or sawdust, one part; sand, of any kind, two parts; marl or clay, one part; in quantity as thought proper. Make the mass up wet, into balls of a convenient size, and when the fire is sufficiently strong place these balls, according to its size, a little above the top bar, and they will produce a heat considerably more intense than common fuel, and insure a saving of one-half the quantity of coals. A fire then made up will require no stirring, and will need no fresh food for ten hours.

To clean Water-casks.

Scour the inside well out with water and sand, and afterwards apply a quantity of charcoal dust. Another and better method is to rinse them with a pretty strong solution of oil of vitriol and water, which will entirely deprive them of their foulness.

To preserve Eggs.

Apply with a brush a solution of gum arabic to the shells, or immerse the eggs therein; let them dry, and afterwards pack them in dry charcoal dust. This prevents their being affected by any alterations of temperature.

Another Method.

Mix together in a tub or vessel one bushel of quick-lime; thirty-two ounces of salt; eight ounces of cream of tartar, with as much water as will reduce the composition to a sufficient consistence to float an egg. Then put and keep the eggs therein, which will preserve them perfectly sound for two years at least.

A Substitute for Milk and Cream.

Beat up the whole of a fresh egg in a basin, and then pour boiling tea over it gradually, to prevent its curdling. It is difficult from the taste to distinguish the composition from rich cream.

To cure Butter.

Take two parts of the best common salt, one part of sugar, and one-half part of saltpetre; beat them up and blend the whole together. Take one ounce of this composition for every sixteen ounces of butter, work it well into the mass, and close it up for use.

Butter cured this way appears of a rich, marrowy consistence and fine color, and never acquires a brittle hardness, nor tastes salt. It will likewise keep good three years, only observing that it must stand three weeks or a month before it is used.

To remove the Turnip Flavor from Milk and Butter.

Dissolve a little nitre in spring-water, which keep in a bottle, and put a small teacupful into eight gallons of milk, when warm from the cow.

To make Butter, Dumbarton Method.

First scald the churn with boiling water to insure cleanliness; then, having put in the cream, work it till the butter is separated from the milk, and put the former into a clean vessel. Next draw a corn sickle several times cross-ways through it, for the purpose of extracting any hairs or superfluities which may adhere to it. Let the butter be put into spring-water during this operation, which will prevent its turning soft, and which will clear it likewise from any remnants of milk. Next mix with every stone of butter ten ounces of salt. Incorporate it well, otherwise the butter will not keep. In May and June each stone of butter will take one ounce more of salt, but after the middle of August one ounce less will suffice. When made put it into a well-seasoned kit, and shake a handful of salt on the top, which will preserve it from mouldiness. In this way continue to make and salt the butter, placing one cake upon the other until the kit is full. Observe that the kit does not leak, as the liquor oozing through would occasion the butter to spoil.

To make Cheshire Cheese.

It is necessary in making the best cheese to put in the new milk without skimming, and if any overnight's milk be mixed with it, it must be brought to the same natural warmth; into this put as much rennet as is just sufficient to come to the curd, and no more; for on this just proportion the mildness of the cheese is said to depend; a piece dried of the size of a worn dime, and put into a teacupful of water with a little salt, about twelve hours before it is wanted, is sufficient for eighteen gallons of milk. The curd is next broken down, and, when separated from the whey, is put into a cheese-vat, and pressed very dry; it is next broken very small by squeezing it with the hands. New curd is mixed with about half its quantity of yesterday's, and which has been kept for that purpose. When the curds have been thus mixed, well pressed and closed with the hands in a cheese-vat, till they become one solid lump, it is put into a press for four or five hours, then taken out of the cheese-vat and turned, by means of a cloth put into the same for this purpose, and again put into the press for the night. It is then taken out, well salted, and put into the press again till morning, when it is taken out and laid upon a flag or board till the salt is quite melted, then it is wiped, put into a dry room, and turned every day, till it becomes dry enough for the market.

To correct Damaged Grain.

Put the injured article into an oven, from which the bread has been just drawn. Spread it in a bed of from three to four inches in thickness, and stir it frequently with a shovel or rake to facilitate the disengagement of the vapor. In ten or fifteen minutes, according to its humidity, withdraw it; when perfectly cool and aired, it will be restored to its wholesome qualities.

Another Method.

Musty grain, totally unfit for use, and which can scarcely be ground, may be rendered perfectly sweet and sound by simply immersing it in boiling water, and letting it remain till the water becomes cold. The quantity of water must be double that of the corn to be purified. The musty quality rarely penetrates through the husk of the wheat; and in the very worst cases, it does not extend through the amylaceous matter which lies immediately under the skin. In the hot water, all the decayed or rotten grains swim on the surface, so that the remaining wheat is effectually cleaned from all impurities, without any material loss. It is afterwards to be dried, stirring it occasionally on the kiln.

To improve New Seconds Flour of bad quality.

Mix common carbonate of magnesia well, in proportion of from twenty to forty grains to a pound of flour; calcined magnesia will improve the bread, but not nearly to the same extent as the carbonate. It will improve the color of bread made from new seconds flour, while it impairs the color of bread from fine old and new flour.

To preserve Flour.

Attach a number of lofts to every mill, so that the flour, in place of being thrust into sacks, the moment it escapes from the friction of the stones, may be taken up by the machinery, and spread out to cool in the most careful manner. The violent friction of the stones necessarily creates a great heat and steam; and if flour is thrust into sacks in this state, a chemical action will make it moist, soft, and clammy.

To preserve Wheat.

Kiln dry it and put it in cubical cases of earthenware, glazed on the outside, and filled full as possible; cover them with a piece of the same ware made to fit close, and secured with a mixture of pitch, tar, and hemp cloth, till the whole be made air-tight. A case of this kind might be made which would hold four bushels or a quarter of wheat.

To correct Moist Flour.

In preparing the dough, let one-third of the flour be kept unmixed, till the dough begins to rise, then add a little of the flour, and when it rises again add a little more, and so on for four or five hours, till the whole of the flour is used. In this manner the mixture, which occasions a glistening appearance in the dough, will be taken up, and the bread, as is already mentioned, will be highly improved.

To remove Flies from Rooms.

Take half a teaspoonful of black pepper, in powder, one teaspoonful of brown sugar, and one tablespoonful of cream; mix them well together, and place them in the room, on a plate where the flies are troublesome, and they will soon disappear.

To make Excellent Bread.

Mix seven pounds of best flour with three pounds of pared boiled potatoes. Steam off the water, and leave them a few minutes on the fire, mash them fine, and mix them whilst quite warm in the flour, with a spoonful or more of salt. Put a quart of water, milk warm, with three large spoonsful of yeast, gradually to the potatoes and flour. Work it well into a smooth dough, and let it remain four hours before it is baked.

To make Bread with a very small quantity of Yeast.

Put one bushel of flour into the trough, mix three-quarters of a pint of warm water, and one teaspoonful of thick yeast well together; pour a small quantity in a hole made in the centre of the flour large enough to contain two gallons of water; then stir with a stick, about two feet long, some of the flour, until it is as thick as pudding batter. Strew some of the dry flour over it, and let it rest for an hour, then pour about a quart more water, and having stirred it as before, leave it for two hours, and then add a gallon more of warm water. Stir in the flour again, and in about four hours more, mix up the dough, and cover it warm; in about four hours more you may put it in the oven, and as light bread will be obtained as though a pint of yeast had been used.

To prepare Bread in the Method of the London Bakers.

Sift a sack of flour into the kneading-trough; add six pounds of salt, dissolve them separately in a pailful of water (cooled to 90° Fahr.) with two quarts of yeast. Stir it well, and strain it through a cloth or sieve; afterwards mix it with the flour into a dough, next cover it up with cloths and shut down the trough-lid close to retain the heat. In two hours more mix in another pailful of warm water with the sponge, and again cover it up for two hours. After this knead it for more than an hour, with three pailsful of warm water. Return the dough to the trough, sprinkle it with dry flour, and in four hours' time knead it well for about half an hour, when it will be fit to mould into loaves.

To prepare Household Bread.

Mix four ounces of salt, three quarts of water, a pint of yeast, and a peck of seconds flour, in a trough. When properly fermented, knead and divide it into loaves. Sometimes a portion of rye-meal, rice, flour, or boiled potatoes, are mixed with the flour previous to the kneading; the two former serve to bind the bread, the latter cause it to be open and spongy.

To produce one-third more Bread from a given Quantity of Wheat.

Boil a bushel of the coarsest bran in seven gallons of water for one hour; keep stirring it, that it may not stick to the bottom; then pour it off into a trough or tub full of holes, over which lay a coarse cloth or sieve. On the top of the whole put a wooden cover, with a weight sufficiently heavy to press out the liquor from the bran, which will sink to the bottom of the tub in a thick pulp. This liquor will contain the essential oil of the grain, and when kneaded in with a proper proportion of flour it will yield one-third more than the same quantity would made with water in the usual way.

To make French Bread.

Put a pint of milk into three quarts of water. In winter let it be scalding hot, but in summer little more than milk warm. Put in salt sufficient. Take a pint and a half of good ale yeast, free from bitterness, and lay it in a gallon of water the night before. Pour off the yeast into the milk and water, and then break in rather more than a quarter of a pound of butter. Work it well till it is dissolved; then beat up two eggs in a basin, and stir them in. Mix about a peck and a half of flour with the liquor, and in winter make the dough pretty stiff, but more slack in summer; mix it well, and the less it is worked the better. Stir the liquor into flour, as for pie-crust, and after the dough is made cover it with a cloth, and let it lie to rise while the oven is heating. When the loaves have lain in a quick oven about a quarter of an hour, turn them on the other side for about a quarter of an hour longer. Then take them out, and chip them with a knife, which will make them look spongy, and of a fine yellow, whereas rasping takes off this fine color, and renders their look less inviting.

To make wholesome Mixed Bread.

Take of rice 3 pounds; boil it in a sufficient quantity of water till reduced to a soft pulp, then rub it with 6 pounds of mealy potatoes, cooked by steam, and, when well blended, add 6 pounds of flour. Make the whole into a dough with water, and ferment with yeast, in the usual manner.

To make Bran Bread.

To four pounds of best household flour put two tablespoonsful of small beer yeast and a half pint of warm water. Let it stand two hours in a warm place. Add half a pound of bran and a teaspoonful of salt; make the dough with skim-milk or warm water; cover it up and let it stand an hour. Put the loaves into warm dishes, and let them stand twenty minutes before they go into the oven.

Another Method.

Mix with half a peck of flour, containing the whole of the bran, a quarter of a pint of small-beer yeast, and a quart of lukewarm water; stir it well with a wooden spoon until it becomes a thick batter, then put a napkin over the dough and set it about three feet from the fire, until it rises well. Add, if requisite, a little more warm water, strew over it a tablespoonful of salt, and make the whole into a stiff paste. Put it to the fire, and when it rises again knead it into the dough. If baked in tins the loaves will be improved.

To make Leaven Bread.

Take about two pounds of dough of the last making, which has been raised by barm; keep it in a wooden vessel covered well with flour. This will become leaven when sufficiently sour. Work this quantity into a peck of flour with warm water. Cover the dough close with a cloth or flannel, and keep it in a warm place; further mix it next morning with two or three bushels of flour, mixed up with warm water and a little salt. When the dough is thoroughly made cover it as before. As soon as it rises knead it well into loaves. Observe in this process, that the more leaven is put to the flour the lighter the bread will be, and the fresher the leaven the less sour it will taste.

To make Four Quartern Loaves for Family Use.

Procure a peck of flour, with which mix a handful of salt to three quarts of water, and add half a pint of good fresh yeast. Work the whole well together, and set it to rise at a moderate distance from the fire from two to three hours. Then divide it into four equal parts, put it into tins, and send it to the baker's.

The London bakers, to give their flour a factitious whiteness, boil alum in the water; but such means will not be resorted to in any private family.

To make Cheap Bread.

Take pumpkins and boil them in water until it is quite thick, and with the decoction mix flour so as to make dough. This makes an excellent bread. The proportion is increased at least one-fourth, and it keeps good a length of time.

Another Method.

Birkenmayer, a brewer of Constance, has succeeded in manufacturing bread from the farinaceous residue of beer. Ten pounds of this species of paste, one pound of yeast, five pounds of ordinary meal, and a handful of salt produce twelve pounds of black bread, both savory and nourishing.

To make Bread of Iceland Moss and Flour.

This vegetable may be used alone or with flour in the making of bread. Boil seven pounds of lichen meal in 100 pints of water, and afterwards mix the same with 69 pounds of flour, and when baked the product will be 160 pounds of good household bread; whereas, without this addition, the flour would not produce more than 79 pounds of bread. To prepare it, use 1 pound of lichen meal, in the form of paste, to about 3¾ pounds of flour.

To make Bread on Mr. Cobbett's Plan.

Suppose the quantity to be a bushel of flour. Put this flour into a trough that people have for the purpose, or it may be in a clean smooth tub of any shape, if not too deep and sufficiently large. Make a pretty deep hole in the middle of this heap of flour. Take (for a bushel) a pint of good fresh yeast; mix it and stir it well up in a pint of soft water, milk warm. Pour this into the hole in the heap of flour. Then take a spoon and work it round the outside of this body of moisture, so as to bring into it by degrees flour enough to make it form a thin batter, which must be stirred about well for a minute or two. Then take a handful of flour and scatter it thinly over the head of this batter, so as to hide it; then cover the whole over with a cloth to keep it warm; and this covering, as well as the situation of the trough, as to distance from the fire, must depend on the nature of the place and state of the weather, as to heat and cold. When the batter has risen enough to make cracks in the flour, begin to form the whole mass into dough, thus: Begin round the hole containing the batter, working the flour into the batter, and pouring in as it is wanted to make the flour mix with the batter, soft water, milk warm, or milk. Before beginning this, scatter the salt over the heap, at the rate of half a pound to a bushel of flour. When the whole is sufficiently moist, knead it well. This is a grand part of the business; for, unless the dough be well worked, there will be little round lumps of flour in the loaves; and besides the original batter, which is to give fermentation to the whole, will not be duly mixed. It must be rolled over, pressed out, folded up, and pressed out again, until it be completely mixed, and formed into a stiff and tough dough.

When the dough is made it is to be formed into a lump in the middle of the trough, and, with a little dry flour thinly scattered over it, covered over again to be kept warm and to ferment, and in this state, if all be done rightly, it will not have to remain more than about fifteen or twenty minutes.

The oven should be hot by the time that the dough has remained in the lump about twenty minutes. When both are ready take out the fire and wipe the oven clean, and at nearly the same moment take the dough out upon the lid of the baking trough, or some proper place, cut it up into pieces and make it up into loaves, kneading it again in these separate parcels, shaking a little flour over the board to prevent the dough adhering to it. The loaves should be put into the oven as quickly as possible after they are formed; when in the oven lid or door should be fastened up very closely, and if all be properly managed loaves of about the size of quartern loaves will be sufficiently baked in about two hours. But they usually take down the lid and look at the bread in order to see how it is going on.

To detect Adulteration in Bread.

Run into the crumb of a loaf one day old the blade of a knife considerably heated, and if adulterated with alum it will show its unwholesome adherences on the surface, and it may further be detected by the smell. Bone-dust or plaster of Paris may be discovered by slicing the soft part of a loaf thin and soaking it in a large quantity of water in an earthen vessel placed over a slow fire three or four hours. Then having poured off the water and pap the obnoxious matter will be found at the bottom.

To preserve Houses from Vermin.

Bugs, in particular, may readily be destroyed by dissolving half a drachm of corrosive sublimate in a quarter of an ounce of spirit of salts, mixing it with one quart of spirit of turpentine. Shake these well together, dip a brush in it and wash those places where bugs are supposed to resort, and this will remove them with greater certainty than any other mode now practised.

To make Hominy.

Indian corn is now generally made into hominy by a kind of mill or machine. In the country, however, it is often made by soaking the corn for a short time, merely enough to soften and loosen the outer hull of the grain, so that it can be broken off by beating it in a mortar.

To make a mortar large enough a log of wood is chosen, on top of which a large fire is lit, and allowed to burn out a sufficiently deep cavity; or else with a saw and hatchet an edge or shoulder is cut on four sides of the log, against which shingles are fastened upright, projecting above the top of the log far enough to make a receptacle.

After beating, as above mentioned, the grain is put into water, when the loosened hulls can easily be separated. Some add lye to the water for the preparatory soaking, because it softens the hull sooner, but it injures the flavor of the hominy.

MANAGEMENT OF BEES.

To work Bees in Glass Hives.

To produce the finest virgin honey without the cruel practice of destroying the bees, and having the opportunity of seeing them at their labors, a double-topped straw hive has been invented by Mr. John Molton, and is so constructed as to support four glasses, which may be removed with safety, and the bees kept warmer and more secure than in any other hives.

Hive a swarm in the lower part of the hive in the usual way. The board at the top must be kept close by taking care to secure the openings; this is done by turning the top board by means of a thumb screw, so that when first hived the holes of both boards shall not correspond, and by thus turning the upper board it will prevent the bees from passing through while hiving. At night bring the hive into the bee-house, or where it is intended to stand; in about two days after place on the glasses (which should be clean) over their respective openings, and stop them round with mortar, after which turn the board to admit the bees to ascend for the purpose of working; cover the glasses with the small upper hive, and do not look at them for a few days. Indeed, nothing will then be necessary but to ascertain when they are filled, which is known by the cell being sealed over, which may be expected in about twenty days after a swarm has been hived.

When the honey is to be taken and all the glasses removed, it will be requisite first to turn the board to exclude the bees; then with a thin knife loosen them from the adapter; leave them thus for about an hour; then carry the glasses inverted a short distance from the hive into the shade, or raise the glasses with a small wedge, and what few bees remain will readily leave and return to their original hive. This, if effected early in the season, will afford the opportunity of immediately replacing the same, or another set of glasses to be again filled.

Observe, if wanted at any time to take only one or two of the glasses with honey, do not turn the board, as by so doing the combs are disunited, and the bees themselves will then empty the remaining glasses (although afterwards re-fill them), which might occasion a loss of time in the best part of the season for working; to simplify which, only loosen such glasses as are wished to be removed with a thin knife, set them on a divider, and replace others in their stead. The middle of a fine day is the best time to remove glasses.

It will not be advisable to take any honey from the hive after the end of July, as the remaining part of the season might not prove favourable to their gathering enough for their winter support; therefore, it will be necessary about this time, or early in August, to remove all the glasses and turn the board, to finally shut them up.

Those glasses only partly filled with combs should be carefully set aside, to be placed on again the following April; if, however, the stock will require feeding, leave one or more of the glasses with honey for that purpose, which is by far the best mode.

Thus much for the swarm which is left till the following April — the time to commence again working the glasses, as hives are now full of combs and brood; should the season prove favorable, work the glasses twice or more, and equal success will attend every subsequent corresponding year, but the first season a swarm cannot be expected to fill the glasses more than once, which will produce eight pounds of the finest honey. This method of management will not prevent the bees from swarming.

The honey thus obtained being fresh from the hive, will be of the finest quality, pure, perfectly free from the young brood, of remarkably fine fragrance, clear in color, and very far superior to any produced from common hives; it may also be taken at pleasure without injury to the bees, especially without being obliged to resort at any time to the painful and execrable process of smothering these industrious and valuable insects.

To work Bees in Straw Hives.

The double cottage straw hive will answer many purposes in the keeping of bees, as either a glass or a small straw hive may be worked on the top of it, which gives it an advantage over the common hive, although the method of management is simple and the price easy.

Prepare this hive for a swarm by spreading mortar round the crown of it, to carry the adapter to support a glass or small straw hive, as it may be worked with either. Hive the swarm as usual, taking care to secure the opening at the top; after removing it to its appointed place let the swarm work for ten days, then clear the opening at top, and affix either a glass or a small straw hive; the bees will then ascend for working. Stop the upper hive around with mortar to the adapter, and darken it with a common hive; in the course of from fifteen to twenty days examine it, and if full take the honey as here directed: Pass a knife or wire between the adapter and small hive to separate the combs, after which remove the small hive of honey on a divider (a brass plate about twelve inches square); it will then be immediately necessary to place a small hive on the adapter, or stop the opening till another hive is to be worked. Carry the small hive now on the divider a short distance away, or rather into a darkened room; invert it and place over it a small, empty hive of the same size; keep them steady, and, by tapping round the bottom hive the bees in a few minutes will ascend to the hive above; carry them to within about two yards of their original stock, shake them out, and they will enter again as usual.

To work Bees in a Box Hive.

This elegant box hive consists of three divisions, and is so ingeniously constructed that the finest honey may be taken without destroying the bees; you may work a glass hive on the top, and inspect the whole of their curious and interesting labors without disturbing them.

When a swarm is placed in this hive shut the slider of the adapter; tie a small cord round to secure the parts; hive the swarm in the usual manner; at night bring it into the bee-house or place appointed; open the entrance at bottom and remove the cord; if a glass hive is worked on the top place it on the same evening, stop it round, then draw back the slider to clear the grate, leave it a few minutes, and the bees will ascend for working. Then raise the two upper divisions to be able to remove the bottom division, and by the compression the bees are obliged to work in the glass hive, which should be darkened with its proper cover and left for a few days without being looked at; it will be necessary to replace the unemployed division at the bottom four or five days previous to the removal of the glass of honey: in removing which shut the slider and leave it in this state for one hour; then follow those plain directions laid down for the removal of glass hives.

If more honey is wanted from this hive than the glass affords, examine the divisions early in September; if the three are full, viz., the two upper hives of honey and the bottom of combs, and not otherwise, proceed to remove the fillets of the top division and pass the brass divider between those parts, where it should remain for an hour; then raise the division with a wedge and draw back the slider of the adapter to let the bees out, and when clear, which will be in a few minutes, remove this division and place the adapter to the next division, and by withdrawing the divider it will fit close down; when the combs of honey are taken out from this division it should be replaced at the bottom; consequently, every year or once in two years gives them, as it were, a fresh division or part of a hive to rebuild in, which keeps the bees constantly at work and the combs in a good state of preservation.

To work Bees in a Hexagon Box Hive and Straw Hive.

This box hive is admirably constructed with slider and grating, having large glass windows, and supporting a glass hive on the top, that, when well supplied with bees, affords the pleasing opportunity of viewing the progress of their labors, and exhibits a very interesting and beautiful appearance.

To hive a swarm it is only necessary to shut the slider over the grating, and then proceed as before directed. (When a glass hive is to be worked follow the instructions given with the superior box hive.) This hive is the best calculated to work bees from other hives, especially when they are in a state of decay, particularly the common hive. It is effected merely by withdrawing the slider clear of the grate and placing the common hive over it in the evening, taking care to stop the entrance of the former with mortar. The bees will of course then enter at bottom, and when they have worked the bottom hive nearly full, which is ascertained by means of the windows, carefully lift them up and place them under another hexagon hive; consequently this colony consists of three hives, and it will not be safe to remove the upper hive unless the bees have worked combs into the bottom hive, which, if effected at the end of the season, the common hive may be safely taken with its contents.

To work Bees in the Common Hive.

This hive being in such general use in this country for many years, requires but little observation, except on some essential points, which, to benefit the cultivator, ought to be attended to. First, care should be taken to have the hive made of clean and good straw, and manufactured of a suitable thickness. Some hives are so thin and loose as to require many days of the most valuable time of the swarm to render the hive fit for their use.

Secondly, a hive should be chosen in proportion to the size of the swarm; and when a good hive is obtained, and a swarm placed in it, which should fill it to within a rim or two of the bottom, shelter it from cold winds and rain; for, if once the wet penetrates a hive it affects the combs, and the bees getting a distaste for their home, will work very slowly, and often desert it altogether; whereas, if they have a hive to their liking leave them unmolested, and they will soon furnish it with combs and honey. It is not material in what aspect the stock stands, provided the sun shines on the hive once in the course of the day. Well peopled hives, kept dry, will thrive in most situations.

One of those fatal accidents to which this hive is subject, occurs through covering it with a hackle or turf, by which their great enemy, the mouse, is enticed, who will make a nest on the top, and ultimately eat its way through the crown of the hive, and destroy both combs and bees. About August the robbing commences by bees and wasps, which is but little regarded; an important benefit will be derived by destroying the queen wasp, seen about April, which is the mother of thousands; much therefore depends on the preservation of those hives which are to stand the winter. To protect them apply the guard invented by Mr. Espinasse, which is calculated to prove highly beneficial in its effects.

In September attention should be directed to weigh the stocks; none of those of less than from fifteen to twenty pounds in weight can safely be relied on to stand the winter without feeding; and stop all hives down to the board with mortar.

To establish an Apiary.

The best time to establish an apiary is about February, as the stocks have passed through the winter in safety. The combs are then empty of brood, light of honey, and the removal safe and easy. Stocks should be selected by a competent judge, as the weight alone cannot always be relied on; but such as weigh twelve pounds and upwards — the number of bees must also be observed, and that they are well combed to near the bottom — these may be safely chosen.

When they are brought home set them in the bee-house, being particularly careful to keep them dry. The next day plaster the hive to the board, leaving an entrance the size of the little finger.

If this season has passed, purchase the first and early swarms; for late ones or casts are not worth keeping, unless two or three have been united.

To remove stocks, the evening is the best time; the hive should be raised by wedges some hours previous, unless the floor be also moveable with the hive — otherwise many bees will remain on the floor at the time, and prove very troublesome. But when the door is moveable, plaster the hive with mortar to the board; pin a card pierced with holes before the entrance, securing the hive to the board firmly; in this way it would travel any distance.

Swarms purchased should be brought home the same evening; for if delayed for a day or two, combs will be worked, and subject to be broken in removing.

To cultivate Bee-Flowers.

Bees are most fond of those places where their favorite flowers are to be found; therefore beekeepers should encourage the growth of such shrubs and flowers as are known to supply honey and wax in the greatest abundance; in most situations bees do not fly far for food, generally not more than half a mile; they may be observed to return with great precipitation to the hive when rain or a storm approaches. The following are the most favorable for pasturage, and those which blossom early are the most desirable:

Shrubs, etc.	Flowers.
Gray willow.	Mignonette.
Tulip poplar.	Lemon thyme.
Persimmon.	Garden and wild thyme
Gooseberry.	Buckwheat.
Raspberry.	Winter savory.
Apricot and all other fruit-trees.	Hyssop.
	Mustard.
American linden.	Turnips. } when
Locust.	Cabbage. } left for
Broom.	White clover. } seed.
Alder.	Scarlet and other beans.

Mignonette, borage, and lemon thyme are the principal, as they continue very long in bloom, and afford the finest honey. Rosemary is also a great favorite, but seldom supplies much honey in this country, unless the weather proves very hot and dry when it is in blossom, yet it is worth cultivating, especially in a southern aspect, being one of the principal aromatic plants from which the bees in the neighborhood of Narbonne collect their honey, which is esteemed the finest in Europe. Fields of beans, white clover, and buckwheat are of great benefit. Rivers or streams of water are also very beneficial, as bees make use of a great deal of water.

To swarm Bees.

Swarming depends on the increase of bees, and a queen being ready to lead them. Their breeding begins sooner or later, according to the forwardness of the spring, the fruitfulness of the queen, and the populousness of the hive. When bees carry in farina or pellets on their thighs, it denotes they have commenced breeding, which may be as early as February, and not finish till

October; and when their numbers are much increased they show indications of swarming, by their clustering in great quantities below the resting-board. They never rise but on a fine day, and sometimes will settle, and for some cause return to the stock, probably for want of a queen being with them. Some hives will cast three times, but mostly only twice. The second cast may be expected within three or four days, and never later than ten days after the first. Should a stock overswarm itself it will perish, unless strengthened; this may be ascertained by observing the quantity of bees afterwards seen to enter. It is necessary in the swarming season, from April to July, particularly in May and June, to observe the hives on a fine day; in general the bees issue forth about noon — from nine to two o'clock, or about three in the afternoon.

To hive Bees.

Bee-keepers should have square hives by them, prepared to hive the bees as soon as they are settled; for should the sun shine hot upon the swarm it may take another flight, and may possibly be lost entirely. The manner of hiving them must be regulated by the nature of the place on which they settle. The custom of preparing hives varies; a clean new hive only requires the loose straw to be rubbed off with a cloth; if any dressing be used, fennel dipped in ale and sugar will best answer the purpose. Having ready a cloth whereon to place the hive, and a wedge to raise it; if the swarm should settle on a branch, shake the best part of it into the hive, place it on the cloth on the ground, and continue to disturb the swarm where it is settled, and the hive being left underneath, they will all go in, or cut the branch off, and gently place it in the hive. Should the bees settle on the ground, place the hive over them; and though bees are not apt to sting at this time, the hiving should be performed quietly. Avoid talking and breathing on them, and if any of them are crushed, they will resent it; therefore, to prevent accident, invariably use the bee-dress, which will give confidence. All swarms are to be sheltered and left near to where they settle till the evening; thence to be removed very gently to the appointed place.

To unite Swarms, and reinforce Stocks.

It is essential when there are weak swarms of bees, that they should be strengthened. The idea, so prevalent, of the greatest number of hives producing the most honey and wax, is erroneous; for a great part of the bees is necessarily employed in rearing the young, and therefore the number of those who are occupied in collecting honey is not near so great as has been imagined; for every swarm, the least as well as the greatest, is provided with a queen, equal in fecundity to the queen of the larger stock, and as the brood she brings continually demands the labor and attendance of nearly half the bees, this circumstance renders the other moiety, from the smallness of their number, unable to accumulate a large quantity of honey in the short time it mostly abounds, and therefore honey cannot be obtained in glass hives or otherwise, but from a strongly-peopled hive.

Have the swarms or casts in the usual way, and at about eight o'clock the same evening spread a cloth on the ground, near to the hive required to be reinforced; bring the new swarm, and strike it down rather hard, flat on the ground. The bees will then fall in a cluster; quickly place over them the stock to be reinforced; in ten minutes they will have united and become as one family, to be removed the same evening to its former situation.

Or, each cast or swarm may be hived separately. In the evening, turn the crown of the hive into a pail, and set the other hive exactly over it; in the morning the bees from the bottom hive will have ascended.

The system of uniting, so very important, is but little practised, and has been overlooked by many cultivators; but it is absolutely necessary to have the hives well peopled and completely sheltered from wet, which are the principal and main objects to be particularly attended to in the art of bee-keeping; and the advantages of uniting swarms will be found particularly beneficial on working the glasses with the newly invented double-topped hives.

To feed Bees.

With the aid of feeding it is perfectly easy to bring any hive of bees through the winter; but to ensure the success of a very light stock, it is essential to keep it also very warm and dry. Feeding is absolutely necessary when more honey has been taken than the hive can afford, by means of small hives or glasses. Such stocks as are intended to be kept through the winter should weigh twenty pounds or upwards at the end of September; but casts and late swarms seldom attain this weight, unless two or more should have been united. The composition for feeding consists of moist sugar and new beer, the proportion of one pound of sugar to a pint of beer, simmered to the consistency of treacle; to be inserted into the hives by means of small troughs, at night, and removed the next morning early. Should a hive be very poor and weak, it is better to feed in larger quantities each time.

Another Method.

Have a thick wooden hoop, about six inches deep, to set upon the board when the hive is taken up, and set honey-combs with the natural honey in them, or filled with sugar a little moistened, and set the hive upon it. A piece of an old hive will make a good hoop. Old empty combs should be carefully kept covered up with a piece of thin linen or muslin, in a very clean place for feeding the bees. Weak hives should be removed at a distance from the rest, when they must be fed; if near the strong will rob them. Remove them in the following manner: Take up the board with the hive, tie a cloth firm over it, and with a handbarrow carry it gently between two where it is intended to be placed. Troughs of pithy wood, filled with moistened sugar or honey, and thrust in at the aperture of the hive, is a good method of feeding. Be sure when raising a hive from the board, to fix it down again with plaster lime.

Be not hasty in concluding a hive is dead though the bees seem inactive. Expose them at mid-day, turned upon a white sheet, where the sun is most powerful, for half an hour; then house them in a warm place, where neither noise, bad smells, nor light can annoy them.

If wanted to purchase a hive defer it till May. Set careful persons to watch at several stalls that they may reckon, by watch time, every loaded bee that comes in for ten or fifteen minutes. That which has most laborers should be the choice. All the refuse honey, after draining the best in jars, should be kept in a clean place for feeding the bees.

Improved Machine for feeding Bees.

Prepare a board a little larger than the bottom of the hive, in the centre of which make an opening about ten inches diameter; then form a frame of half inch deal, to consist of four sides, each about twelve inches by three inches; make the angles firm with small wooden blocks, to which affix the before-mentioned board. A door should then be made in a side of the frame sufficiently large to admit a deep plate, or small dish, to contain the food. By the use of this machine the bees are fed quietly, and protected from the cold weather and the intrusion of other bees. It is scarcely necessary to observe further, that the door of the machine should face such part of the bee-house as best suits convenience. The dish of food to be placed under should be covered with a piece of thick paper the size of the plate or dish, pierced in holes through which the bees will feed; and a quantity of short pieces of straw also put into the dish will prevent the bees from daubing themselves. They should be fed at night, and the dish only taken away early on the following morning, to do this the face and hands should be covered. The autumn and early part of the spring are times proper to examine if any hives require feeding; but always commence before the stock is in absolute want of food, otherwise the bees will be so poor and weak as to be unable to come down.

To manage Honey.

To judge of the best honey, it should be of a bright pale color, thick, and a little aromatic. To obtain it from the combs in its pure state, it must be left to run from them without pressing. The color shows whether it is fine or inferior. If wanted to press some in the comb, choose the fairest and such as have not been broken; wrap each comb in white paper, and as lines the blue cover of loaf sugar. Set it edgeways as it stood in the hive, and it may be preserved many months. The combs meant to be drained, must be cut in slices. Lay them on a hair-search, supported by a rack over the jar, in which the honey is to remain; for the less it is stirred after draining the better it keeps. Fill the jar to the brim, as a little scum must be taken off when it has settled. A bladder, well washed in lukewarm water, ought to be laid over the double fold of white paper with which it is covered.

To take the Honey without destroying the Bees.

The following easy method of taking the honey without destroying the bees, is generally practised in France. In the dusk of the evening, when the bees are quietly lodged, approach the hive, and turn it gently over. Having steadily placed it in a small pit, previously dug to receive it, with its bottom upwards, cover it with a clean new hive, which has been properly prepared, with a few sticks across the inside of it, and rubbed with aromatic herbs. Having carefully adjusted the mouth of each hive to the other, so that no aperture remains between them, take a small stick and beat gently round the sides of the lower hive for about ten minutes or a quarter of an hour, in which time the bees will leave their cells in the lower hive, ascend, and adhere to the upper one. Then gently lift the new hive, with all its little tenants, and place it on the stand from which the other hive was taken. This should be done some time in the week preceding midsummer day, that the bees may have time, before the summer flowers are faded, to lay in a new stock of honey, which they will not fail to do for their subsistence through winter.

To manage Bees generally.

The best situation for bees is to the north, with a range of hills wooded on the summit, and toward the base, enriched with heather, skirted to the east with a stream from the rocks. To confine this rivulet, the bee-master should sow the sandy beech with the seed of furze, and cover it with a light surface of earth. The furze would soon vegetate; and blooming, in the course of three years, overpay his labor by providing the bees with pasture on soil otherwise barren, and the margin of the brook would gradually rise to restrain its encroachment on fertile lands. Suppose a white clover field to the south of the hills, and south from the field a large garden, where hardy winter greens have been allowed to flower as early food for the bees. White mustard should also be sown very early in patches near the hive; but not nearer than one yard. A few dwarf flowers may come within two feet, but tall grown ones would assist insects to get up. To the west it would be desirable to have a shrubbery, a wood, a broom common, or heather moor.

The stations for the hives must be six yards asunder, and never nearer than three yards. The board on which they are placed ought to be of one piece; or, if joined, the under side of the joining should be lined with a thinner board fixed closely with wooden pins. The edges of this rounded standard should project four inches all round from the hive. Place it on three wooden pillars sixteen inches long, ten inches above the ground; but six inches of its length should be firmly thrust into the earth; in all, its length to be sixteen inches. The pillar in front should be an inch shorter than the other two, and the three pillars should be within twelve or fourteen inches of the outer edge of the board to, exclude rats and mice. For the same reason no tall-growing plant, no wall, nor any means for ascent should be within three or four feet of the hive. In fine weather the entrance to the hive must be four inches long and an inch and a half in depth.

Fowls do not eat bees, but are useful to them by destroying worms. Ducks sometimes eat them and are killed thereby.

In the beginning of the fine season, when the bees can get food, or have stores remaining, the bee-master has nothing to do but to keep the ground about the hives clear from weeds and from whatever might enable vermin to climb there. Yet as a thriving stock inclines very soon to swarm, the hives must be frequently looked after, from eight in the morning till five in the afternoon. The symptoms are generally thus:— The little city seems crowded with inhabitants; they are continually in motion during the day; and after working-time they make loud noises. The drones may be seen flying about in the heat of the day, and the working bees go with a reeling motion and busy hum. When the bees come regularly out of the hives let no noise, no interruption incommode them; but if they fly long, as if they were unsettled, some tinkling noise or the loud report of a gun will make the fugitives repair to the nearest lodgings. If there is an empty hive with combs and some honey in it they will readily go there. If a new hive is used, remember to smooth it well within and singe off loose straws. Perpendicular sticks should never be employed. Four cross sticks at equal distances will support the combs. Old hives do very well for late swarms that are not to be preserved through the winter; but box hives are best for them, as the bees work fastest there. They are not, however, fit for being kept through the cold seasons.

The *first* spontaneous swarming is only to be anticipated by finding the royal cells sealed up.

It is to be observed that great haste in forcing a swarm into the hive may disperse them. Give them time to settle undisturbed, though keep a steady eye on their motions; but whenever they gather into a cluster lose no time in placing the hive over them. If the swarm rest on anything that can be brought to the ground, spread a clean linen cloth; lay two sticks on it, two feet asunder; lay the body on which the swarm have fixed gently on the sticks, covering it with the hive by a motion the least perceptible, and taking care that the edges of the hive rest upon the sticks. Cover hive and all with a cloth, for the sun might allure the bees to rise again. When they have gone into the hive, cover it with its own board and carry it cautiously to its station. Bees are apt to leave their hive even after they begin to work, so they must be watched till evening and throughout the ensuing day. Whenever they are sure to remain, fix the hive to its board with a little lime round the edges, and crown it with green sods to keep out too great heat or rain.

If a hive divides into two swarms it is a sign that each swarm has a queen. Put each into old hives or boxes; but they must be kept separate. If a cluster of bees about the size of a small plum is seen together, the queen will generally be found there. Separate them, and with a drinking glass turned down you may seize the queen. Put her and a score or two of her subjects into a box full of holes, large enough to admit air, and yet not to allow the bees to escape. Feed her with honey combs, and keep her in reserve in case of the death of a queen in one of the hives. When a hive ceases to work it is a sure sign the queen is no more. Then the bee-master may wait an hour and not see a loaded bee enter the habitation. But if the spare queen be taken late in the evening, wetting her wings to prevent her escape, and introduce her to the desponding society, they will receive her gladly and begin to work.

If the bees of a hive fight among themselves, be assured there are two queens: and they will destroy each other if one is not taken away to keep.

When bees are to swarm a second or more times, they do not come out in clusters, but they make a sound called bellings, which may be heard, ceasing for a little, and renewed again and again. If there are different tones it is certain there are several young queens in the hive. It is only by putting the ear close to it that the sound can be heard distinctly.

To keep large Hives for Winter.

They must not be more than three years old and well stocked with bees. A hive for preserving should weigh from thirty to forty pounds. Place them in October where they are to remain, observing the usual precautions against vermin or winds, and giving them if possible a distance of six or eight yards asunder, that they may not rob each other. Set the hive after sunset. Plaster the edge firmly round with plaster lime, all except the entrance. Fit a piece of hard wood to the aperture, cut two holes a quarter of an inch square, and fix the board as a door with plaster lime. Cover the hive with drawn straw tied together at the top, and fix it with straw ropes around. Cut the straw a quarter of an inch below the board, for a few lengths may conduct vermin into the torpid community. Once in four or five weeks raise the hive from the board after sunset. Scrape the board clean and brush away dead bees. Observe when turning them up if they move their wings; if not, bring them into a warmer situation, free from noise, and the light excluded. Keep them there till the extreme rigor of the season is past, and then return them to their old situation after sunset.

Sunshine in snow is destructive to bees if they get out. Put a planting of twigs across the holes to give air and yet confine the inmates. Never confine them more than eight or ten days; and except in snow in the sunshine, their own sagacity will direct when it is safe to go out. It is absolutely necessary for their health to have leave for going in and out in tolerably mild weather.

To manage Bee-Hives of Mr. Thorley's Construction.

The bottom part is an octangular bee-box, made of deal boards about an inch in thickness, the cover of which is externally seventeen inches in diameter but internally only fifteen inches, and its height ten. In the middle of the cover of this octangular box is a hole, which may be opened or shut at pleasure by means of a slider. In one of the panels is a pane of glass, covered with a wooden door. The entrance at the bottom of the box is about three and a half inches broad and half an inch high. Two slips of deal, about half an inch square, cross each other in the centre of the box, and are fastened to the panel by means of small screws: to these slips the bees fasten their combs. In this octangular box the bees are hived after swarming in the usual manner, and then suffered to continue till they have built their combs and filled them with honey, which may be known by opening the door and viewing their works through the glass pane, or by the weight of the hive. When the bee-master finds his laborious insects have filled their habitation, he is to place a common bee-hive of straw, made either flat on the top or in the common form, on the octangular box, and drawing out the slider a communication will be opened between the box and the straw hive; in consequence of which the bees will fill this hive also with the product of their labors.

When the straw-hive is well filled the slider may be pushed in, and the hive taken away and another placed in its room, with the slider drawn out. This new hive will also be filled in the same manner.

Mr. Thorley assured the Society of Arts that he had taken three successive hives filled with honey and wax from a single hive during the same summer, and that the food still remaining in the octangular box was sufficient for the support of the bees during the winter. He says that if this method were pursued in every part of the kingdom, instead of the cruel method of destroying these useful insects, he is persuaded, from long experience, that wax would be collected in such plenty that candles made with it might be sold as cheap as those of tallow are sold at present.

Mr. Thorley has also added another part to his bee-hive, consisting of a glass reservoir eighteen inches high, eight inches in diameter at the bottom and in the greatest part thirteen; this receiver has a hole at the top about one inch in diameter, through which a square piece of deal is extended nearly to the bottom of the vessel, having two cross bars, to which the bees fasten their combs. Into the other end of this square piece is screwed a piece of brass, which serves as a handle to the receiver or glass hive. When the bees have filled their straw hive, which must have a hole in the centre, covered with a piece of tin, Mr. Thorley places the glass receiver upon the top of the straw hive and draws out the piece of tin. The bees, now finding their habitation enlarged, pursue their labors with such alacrity that they fill their glass hives likewise with their stores, the whole progress of their works. It will, however, be necessary to cover the glass with an empty hive of straw, or at least with a cloth, lest too much light prevent their working. In this way Mr. Thorley in a good season has had a glass hive filled in thirty days, containing thirty-eight pounds of fine honey. When the glass is completely filled slide a tin plate between the hive or box, so as to cover the passage, and in half an hour the glass may be taken away with safety. The few bees that remain will readily go to their companions.

Mr. Thorley has added a glass window to his straw hives, in order to observe the progress of the bees, and this contrivance is useful, especially if one hive is to be removed whilst the season continues favorable for their collecting of honey, for when the combs are filled with honey the cells are scaled up, and the bees forsake them, and reside mostly in the hives in which their works are chiefly carried on. Observing also that the bees were apt to extend their combs through the passage or communication into the upper hive, which rendered it necessary to divide the comb when the upper hive was taken away, he puts in the passage a wire screen or netting, the meshes of which are large enough for a loaded bee to pass easily through them, and thus he prevents the junction of the combs from one box to the other, and consequently obviates the necessity of cutting them and of spilling some honey, which, running down among a crowd of bees, incommoded them much.

Langstroth's patent hive is now much recommended. In it each comb has a separate frame. You can cut the queen cells in the spring and thus prevent swarming. A hive ought not to be used for more than eight years. But the bees need not be destroyed; you may *drive* them from one hive to another by *rapping* on the occupied one.

To manage Bees on Mr. Cobbett's plan.

The best hives are those made of clean, unblighted rye-straw. A swarm should always be put into a new hive, and the sticks should be new that are put into the hive for the bees to work on, for if the hive be old it is not so wholesome, and a thousand to one but it contains the embryos of moths and other insects injurious to bees. Over the hive itself there should be a cap of thatch, made also of clean rye-straw, and it should not only be new when first put on the hive, but a new one should be made to supply the place of the former one every three or four months, for when the straw begins to get rotten, as it soon does, insects breed in it, its smell is bad, and its effect on the bees is dangerous.

The hives should be placed on a bench, the legs of which mice and rats cannot creep up. Tin round the legs is best. But even this will not keep down ants, which are mortal enemies to bees. To keep them away if they infest the hive, take a green stick and twist it round the leg of the bench, and at a few inches from it, and cover this stick with tar. This will keep away the ants.

Besides the hive and its cap there should be a sort of shed, with top, back and ends, to give additional protection in winter, though in summer hives may be kept too hot, and in that case the bees become sickly and the produce light. The situation of the hive is to face the southeast, or at any rate to be sheltered from the north and the west. From the north always, and from the west in winter. If it be a very dry season in summer it contributes greatly to the success of the bees to place clear water near their home in a thing that they can conveniently drink out of, for if they have to go a great way for drink they have not much time for work.

It is supposed that bees live only a year; at any rate it is best never to keep the same stall or family over two years, except it be wanted to increase the number of hives. The swarm of this summer should be always taken in the autumn of the next year. If you save the bees when the honey is taken, they must be fed, and if saved they will die of old age before the next fall, and though young ones will supply the place of the dead, this is nothing like a good swarm put up during the summer.

A good stall of bees, that is to say the produce of one, is always worth about two bushels of good wheat. The cost is nothing to the laborer. He must be a stupid countryman, indeed, who cannot make a bee-hive, and a lazy one, indeed, if he will not if he can. In short, there is nothing but care demanded, and there are very few situations in the country where a laboring man may not have half a dozen stalls of bees to take every year. The main things are to keep away insects, mice and birds, and especially a little bird called the bee-bird, and to keep all clean and fresh as to the hives and coverings. Never put a swarm into an old hive. If wasps or hornets annoy you, watch them home in the day time, and in the night kill them by fire or by boiling water.

The new Italian bee is more industrious than the common bee. It has, too, a larger proboscis, and can suck the red clover. It is more docile than the common bee. A new queen can be best introduced into a hive in a small cage of wire gauze, with about a hundred bees of her own kind, or else she may be put in while unhatched in the royal cell.

FARRIERY.

[Attention is called to valuable articles upon RINDERPEST and TRICHINÆ, on pages 467, 468, 469, which could not be finished in time to insert here, owing to delay in receiving the latest European information (May 15, 1866).]

The Teeth of a Horse.

At five years of age the horse has forty teeth—twenty-four molar or jaw teeth, twelve incisor or front teeth and four tusks or canine teeth between the molars and incisors, but usually wanting in the mare.

At birth only the two nippers or middle incisors appear.

At one year old the incisors are all visible of the first or milk set.

Before three years the permanent nippers have some through.

At four years old the permanent dividers next to the nippers are out.

At five the mouth is perfect, the second set of teeth having been completed.

At six the hollow under the nippers, called the *mark*, has disappeared from the nippers, and diminished in the dividers.

At seven the mark has disappeared from the dividers, and the next teeth, or corners, are level, though showing the mark.

At eight the mark has gone from the corners, and the horse is said to be aged. After this time, indeed good authorities say after five years, the age of a horse can only be conjectured. But the teeth gradually change their *form*, the incisors becoming round, oval, and then triangular. Dealers sometimes *bishop* the teeth of old horses; that is, scoop them out, to imitate the mark; but this can be known by the absence of the white edge of enamel which always surrounds the real mark, by the shape of the teeth, and other marks of age about the animal.

When a Horse is Unsound.

Any of the following defects constitute unsoundness in a horse:

Lameness, of all kinds and degrees. Diseases of any of the internal organs. Cough of all kinds, *as long as it exists*. Colds or catarrhs, while they last. Roaring; broken wind; thick wind; grease; mange; farcy and glanders; megrims or staggers; founder; convex feet; contracted feet; spavins and ringbones; enlargements of the sinews or ligaments; cataracts and other defects of the eyes, impairing sight.

The following may or may not occasion unsoundness, according to the state or degree in which they exist: Corns, splints, thrushes, bogspavins, throughpins, wind-galls, crib-biting. Curbs are unsoundness unless the horse has worked with them for some months without inconvenience.

Cutting, particularly speedy cutting, constitutes unsoundness when it cannot be remedied by care and skill. Quidding, when a confirmed habit, injures the soundness of a horse.

Defects, called blemishes, are: Scars, from broken knees; capped hocks, splints, bog-spavins, and throughpins; loss of hair, from blisters or scars; enlargements from blows or cutting; specks or streaks on the corner of the eye.

Vices are: Restiveness, shying, bolting, running away, kicking, rearing, weaving or moving the head from side to side, stringhalt, quidding, slipping the halter.

Wounds in Horses or Cattle.

When horses, cattle, or any of our domestic animals are wounded, the treatment may be very simple, and much the same as in the human race. It is extremely improper to follow a practice that is common in many parts of the country among farriers, cow-doctors, and even shepherds — that of applying to the wound, or putting into the sore part, common salt, powder of blue vitriol, or tar, or cloths dipped in spirits, as brandy, rum, etc., or turpentine, or any other stimulant articles; for all such very much increase the pain, and, by irritating the sore, may increase the inflammation, even to the length of inducing mortification. Though the treatment may be varied according to circumstances, yet, in most cases, it may be sufficient to take notice of the following particulars: It will be proper to wash away any foulness or dirt about the part, and to examine particularly its condition.

To stop the Bleeding.

Should any large bloodvessel be cut, and discharging copiously, it will be right to stop it, by some lint or sponge, with moderate compression or bandaging, at the same time, and not taking it off for two or three days. Should the pressure fail of effect, caustic applications, such as the lunar caustic, or even the actual cautery, the point of a thick wire, sufficiently heated, may be tried; or, if a surgeon be at hand, the vessel may be taken up by the crooked needle, with waxed thread, and then tied.

Adhesive Plaster and Sewing.

Where there is no danger of excessive bleeding, and a mere division of the parts, or a deep gash or cut, it will be right to adjust the parts, and keep them together by a strip of any common adhesive plaster; or, when this will not do by itself, the lips of the wound, especially if it be a clean cut, may be closed by one or more stitches, with a moderately coarse needle and thread, which in each stitch may be tied, and the ends left of a proper length, so that they can be afterwards removed, when the parts adhere. It is advised to tie the threads, because sometimes the wounded part swells so much that it is difficult to get them cut and drawn out, without giving pain and doing some mischief.

Bandages.

If the part will allow a roller or bandage to be used, to keep the lips of it together, this may likewise be employed; for, by supporting the sides of the wound, it would lessen any pain which the stitches occasion. With this treatment the wound heals often in a short time, or in a few days, rarely exceeding five or six, and sooner in the young and healthy than in the old and relaxed, and sooner in the quiet and motionless than in the restless and active.

Should the wound be large and inflammation, with the discharge of matter, likely to take place, it may still be proper, by gentle means, to bring the divided parts near to each other, and to retain them in their natural situation by means of a bandage. This should not be made too tight, but merely to support the part. In this way, and by avoiding stimulant applications, the wound will heal more readily than otherwise, and the chance of any blemishes following will be diminished. Washes of spirits, brandy, and the like, Friar's balsam, spirit of wine and camphor, turpentine, or any other such irritating applications, are highly improper, and sometimes makes a fresh, clean wound (that would readily heal almost of itself) inflame and perhaps mortify, or become a bad sore.

Sores and Bruises.

Over the whole sore, or where the part is bruised or where there is a tendency to suppuration, a poultice should be applied and kept on by suitable bandages. The poultice may be made of any kind of meal, fine bran, bruised linseed, or of mashed turnips, carrots, etc. The following has been found useful as a common poultice: "Fine bran, 1 quart; pour on a sufficient quantity of boiling water to make a thin paste; to this add of linseed powder enough to give it a proper consistence." The poultice may be kept on for a week or ten days, or even longer, if necessary, changing it once or twice a day, and cleaning the wound, when the poultice is removed, by washing it by means of a soft rag or linen cloth, with water not more than blood warm (some sponges are too rough for this purpose); or, where the wound is deep, the water may be injected into it by a syringe, in order to clean it from the bottom.

Ointment.

In the course of a few days, when the wound, by care and proper management with the poultices, begins to put on a healthy appearance, and seems to be clean and of a reddish color, not black or bloody, then there may be applied an ointment made of tallow, linseed oil, beeswax, and hogs' lard, in such proportions as to make it of a consistence somewhat firmer than butter. The ointment should be spread on some soft clean tow, and when applied to the sore it ought never to be tied hard upon it (which is done too frequently and very improperly), but only fixed by a bandage of a proper length and breadth (for a mere cord is often improper), so close and securely as to keep it from slipping off. This application may be changed once a day, or, when nearly well and discharging but little, once in two days.

Green Ointment for Wounds.

Put into a well-glazed earthen vessel 2 ounces of beeswax; melt it over a clear fire, and add 2 ounces of resin; when that is melted, put in half a pound of hogs' lard; to this put 4 ounces of turpentine; keep stirring all the time with a clean stick or wooden spatula. When all is well mixed, stir in 1 ounce of finely powdered verdigris. Be careful it does not boil over. Strain it through a coarse cloth, and preserve it in a gallipot. This ointment is very good for old and recent wounds, whether in flesh or hoof; also galled backs, cracked heels, mallenders, sallenders, bites, broken knees, etc.

Treatment, according to Appearance of the Part.

When the wounded part begins to discharge a whitish, thick matter, and is observed to fill up, the general treatment and dressings to the sore now mentioned should be continued; and in the course of the cure the animal, when free of fever, may be allowed better provision, and may take gentle exercise. If the animal be feeble from the loss of blood originally, or from the long continuance of a feverish state, produced by the inflammation attending the wound, or from weakness arising from confinement, or connected with its constitution naturally, and if the wound appear to be in a stationary state, very pale and flabby on its edges, with a thin discharge, then better food may be given to it; and if still no change should be observed, along with the better food, the wound may be treated somewhat differently from what has been already advised. The ointment may be made more stimulant, by adding to it some resin and less beeswax, or, what would be more stimulant still, some common turpentine; for it is only in very rare cases that oil of turpentine can be requisite. The effects of an alteration in the mode of treatment should be particularly remarked, and stimulants should be laid aside, continued, or increased, according as may be judged proper. Before changing the dressings applied to the wound, or before rendering them more stimulant and active by using heating applications, the effect of closer bandaging may be tried; for sometimes, by keeping the parts a little more firmly together, the cure is promoted.

Food and Regimen.

In case of severe wounds attention should be paid to the condition of the animal in other respects. There being always when such happen a tendency to violent inflammation and fever, that may end fatally, means should be employed to moderate both. The apartment should be cool and airy, and so quiet that the animal should not be disturbed; the drink should not be warm, but rather cold, and given freely, though not in too large quantities at a time; the food should be sparingly given, and of a lighter quality than usual, and should be rather succulent and laxative, than dry or apt to produce costiveness. Bleeding may be employed, either generally from a vein, or in some cases, when it can be done, by cupping from the hurt part, as in the case of a bruise (though this last will seldom be requisite or found convenient). Laxative medicines also ought to be given and repeated, as there may be occasion.

Abscesses.

These are swellings containing matter, that make their appearance in different parts of the body. The remedies are, to wash the swollen part with a quart of vinegar, in which are dissolved two ounces of sal ammoniac and half an ounce of sugar of lead. If the swelling does not abate in two or three days, apply the suppurating poultice. When the tumor becomes soft and points, open it with a lancet, and let out the matter. Then dress it with basilicon ointment.

Aubury or Wart.

Tie a strong silk, or two or three horse-hairs, round the neck of the wart, tightening it gradually till it falls away. Then dip a piece of tow in alumwater and bind it on the spot for a whole day. Heal the sore with the green ointment.

Balls for Horses.

These should always be made fresh for using, lest they become too hard. They should be about three-eighths of an inch in diameter, and from two and a half to four inches long.

Inflamed Bladder.

Make the animal drink largely of flaxseed tea, barley or rice water, or any mucilaginous liquid, and inject a portion of the same frequently. Bleeding is sometimes useful, and a dose of castor oil is never to be omitted. After the oil has operated, give the following ball every sixth hour: Powdered nitre, half an ounce; camphor, 1 drachm; liquorice powder, 3 drachms; honey sufficient to form the ball. Should these means not relieve the animal, omit the ball, and give 1 drachm of opium twice a day.

Bog Spavin.

This is an enlargement of the hock-joint, with fluid, common in young horses, from violent exercise.

Clip off the hair from the swelling, and rub all round outside of the swelling with a piece of hard brown soap, then apply to the swelling a blister made of the following

Blistering Ointment.

Hogs' lard, half an ounce; beeswax, 3 drachms; Spanish flies, 2 drachms. Mix them all well, and spread it on white leather, and apply it to the spavin.

Oil of cantharides, with four times its weight of olive oil, may be used, instead of the ointment. The blistered surface should be dressed with simple cerate.

Bone Spavin.

This may be treated like the former; it is, however, generally incurable. The operation of firing (which should be done by a professed farrier), and turning to grass, afford the only reasonable chances of relief.

The lameness in this disease of the hock is peculiar; the limb being drawn with great celerity.

Bots.

Several kinds of worms infest the bowels of horses. The bot infests the stomach and intestine; it is a small, reddish worm, with a large head, and may be frequently observed in the dung.

The truncheon is short and thick, with a blackish head, and is found in the maw, where, if suffered to remain, it sometimes pierces through, and thus is many a fine horse destroyed.

The maw-worm is of a pale red color, resembling an earth-worm, from two to three inches long, occupying, also, the maw.

Symptoms of Worms in Horses.

Stamping forcibly on the ground with either of his fore-feet, and frequently striking at his belly with his hind ones. Belly projecting and hard — looking frequently behind him, and groaning as if in great pain.

Remedies for Worms.

Keep the horse from all kinds of food for one day; at night give him a small quantity of warm bran mash, made as usual, and directly after, a

DISEASES OF HORSES.

ball made of 1 scruple of calomel, 1 scruple of turpeth mineral, and as much crumb of bread and honey as will form the mass. Next evening give him a pint of castor, and half a pint of linseed oil. The animal is then to be fed as usual for two or three days, and the same plan again to be employed.

In the fall, when the horses are first taken from grass, bots may often be expelled by giving them brine (four or five ounces of salt to one quart of water) following a drench of sweetened milk. Oil of turpentine is also a powerful vermifuge; four ounces may be given in a pint of gruel, fasting previously. An almost certain cure for bots is the nux vomica, called vulgarly dog-buttons. Rasp the whole of one of the nuts, and pour upon it a pint of boiling water. Let it cool to blood-heat, and then drench the horse with it; having, about half an hour before, bled him in the mouth, so that he would swallow the blood, which draws the worms into the stomach from the mucous membrane, into which they fasten themselves.

Inflammation of the Bowels.

This not very common, but when it does occur dangerous, disorder is of two kinds. The first or peritoneal inflammation begins with an appearance of dullness and uneasiness in the animal; appetite diminished or totally gone; constant pawing with the fore feet; he lies down, rises suddenly, looks round to his flanks — countenance strongly expressive of pain; urine small, high colored, and voided with great pain; pulse quick and small; legs and ears cold; profuse sweats; mortification and death.

The second species of the disorder is when the inflammation attacks the internal coat of the intestines, and is generally accompanied by a violent purging and some fever — the symptoms of the latter, however, are much less violent, nor does the animal appear to be in so much pain.

Treatment.

In the first or peritoneal inflammation, the only dependence is on early and large bleeding. In addition to this rub the whole belly well with the mustard embrocation, clothe the animal warmly (with fresh sheep-skins if possible), insert several rowels about the chest and belly, putting into them the blistering ointment. As the horse is generally costive give him a pint of castor oil, and inject clysters of warm flaxseed tea, give him warm water or thin gruel or flaxseed tea to drink, rub his legs with the hands well, and see that he has plenty of clean fresh litter. If in six hours the disease is not relieved, bleed him again, and should the costiveness continue, repeat the oil and clysters. If, after giving all these remedies a faithful and continued trial, the pain should continue, recourse may be had to the anodyne clyster.

In the second species of this disorder, bleeding need not be resorted to unless the febrile symptoms run high. Clothe the horse warnly, use the mustard embrocation freely, and omit the oil. Give him frequently, by means of a bottle (if he will not drink it), quantities of very thin gruel or flaxseed tea. If, in spite of this, the disease continue, use the anodyne clyster; if that fail, the astringent draught. The pain occasioned by physicking, is to be relieved by large clysters of thin gruel or flaxseed, which produce copious evacuations and relief.

Broken Wind.

This is an incurable disease; all that can be done is to relieve the animal for a time so as to enable him to perform a day's work. To do this make the following:

Paste-Ball for Broken-Winded Horses.

Assafœtida, 2 ounces; powdered squills, 2 drachms; linseed powder, 1 ounce; honey, as much as will make the mass. Divide it into four balls, and give one, morning and evening. Much benefit may result from bleeding in this disorder at an early period of the complaint. His food should be carrots or turnips. The hay, oats, or whatever is given, should be in small quantities at a time, and always sprinkled with clean, soft water.

Broken Knees.

Apply a poultice of bread and milk or bread and warm water to reduce the inflammation, then dress the wound with basilicon.

Burns or Scalds.

If slight, apply cold lead water: if extensive, a liniment made of equal parts of linseed oil and lime water. If there is much fever, bleed.

Canker.

Cut away freely all the diseased parts, and if necessary draw the frogs, then apply the

Liniment for Canker.

Warm 6 ounces of tar, mix with it drop by drop 1 oz. by measure of oil of vitriol, then add 1 oz. of oil of turpentine. Bind this firmly on the part, destroying all the diseased protuberances with lunar caustic. When the wound looks healthy, dress it with the green ointment.

Chapped Hocks.

If the swelling proceed from a bruise or a blow, bathe it three or four times a day with salt and vinegar made warm. If it threaten abscess, apply the suppurating poultice, and when matter is formed let it out, then use the green ointment.

Cold.

Take a quart of blood from the neck, then give warm mashes with a scruple of nitre in them. Purge with castor and linseed oil, and keep the stable warm.

Convulsions.

Symptoms.—The horse raises his head higher than usual and pricks up or thrusts back his ears—neck stiff and immovable, skin tight. He stands in a straddling posture, pants and breathes with difficulty.

Cure.—Bleed him if his strength will permit it, and his pulse is high, eye red, etc., otherwise not. If you observe bots or any other kind of worms, pursue the treatment recommended for them.

Acute Cough.

Take a quart of blood from the neck, and give the following

Ball for Cough.

Half an ounce of Venice soap, half an ounce of nitre, ten grains of tartar emetic, and ten grains of opium. Make these into a ball with honey, and give one every other night. Keep the horse warm and remedy costiveness by castor oil.

Corns.

Let the farrier cut them out with a sharp knife. Should they show a disposition to grow again, touch them with oil of vitriol or caustic and dress them with green ointment. Be careful in shoeing not to let the shoe press on the corn.

Curb.

This is a swelling, from sprain, in the back and lower part of the hock. Cauterize the curb in a line down its middle or apply the blistering ointment; or iodine ointment.

Cracked Heels.

Poultice the parts with carrots or turnips boiled

soft, three or four times, then anoint them with yellow basilicon mixed with a little green ointment.

The Gripes.

As soon as the disease is observed, give the draught below, and a clyster composed of 8 oz. common salt in six quarts of water gruel or warm water. If there is great pain with quick pulse, take away three quarts of blood. The belly should be well rubbed with the mustard or other stimulating embrocation. If no relief is obtained in two hours repeat the draught and embrocation, and should even this fail give him a pint of castor oil with one and a half ounces of laudanum. If castor oil cannot be had a pint and a quarter of linseed oil may be used.

Draught for Gripes.

Balsam copaiva 1 ounce, oil of juniper 1 drachm, spirit of nitrous ether half an ounce, mint water 1 pint. Mix for one dose.

Another.—Allspice, bruised, ½ pound; brandy, 2 quarts. Dose, 2 to 4 ounces, in water, ale, or mint tea.

Diabetes.

This disorder, which consists in an involuntary discharge of the urine, which is pale and thin, frequently proves fatal. To treat it, give the following

Ball for Diabetes.

Peruvian bark 4 drachms, ginger 1 drachm, if costive after it, give a pint of castor oil. Repeat if necessary.

Eyes.

Inflammation of the eye is often cured by scarifying with a lancet the inside of the upper and lower brow, and the distended vessels of the eye itself. It is to be remembered that in treating an inflammation of this important organ, we should proceed precisely as if treating a human being laboring under the same complaint and keep the animal on short allowance, prevent costiveness, keep the stable cool and dark.

Soreness or weakness of the eye is cured by bleeding from the neck and using the following

Eye-water.

To 1 quart of water put 3 drachms of the sugar of lead or two drachms of white vitriol. When dissolved let it settle and pour off the clear liquor for use. A drop may be put into each eye three times a day with a feather.

Film or Cataract.

There is no remedy for this but an operation by a surgeon. There is a variety of washes, etc., recommended by various authors, but they are useless.

Farcy.

This disease commences in small hard knots, which soon become soft and ulcerous, generally situated on the lymphatic vessels and extending upwards. It not unfrequently ends in the glanders.

Cure for Farcy.

Open the ulcers and touch the inside of the edges slightly with powdered verdigris, by means of a camel's hair pencil. At the same time give the following ball: White arsenic 8 grains, or corrosive sublimate 6 grains, powdered and mixed with flour or bread or any other vehicle that will form a ball with molasses. Keep the animal warm, mix chopped carrots with his mashes. Intermit one day and give a similar ball—if it purge add 10 grains of opium to it. Attend constantly to the ulcers; wash them with warm soap-suds, and keep the animal by himself—if the disease gains the nostrils and head, and becomes glanders there is no remedy.

Grease.

This is a white offensive discharge from the skin of the heels. Wash the part well with warm soap-suds twice a day, and if the swelling be great apply a poultice to it, when the sores are cleansed touch them with a rag or feather dipped in a solution of chloride of zinc, 1 grain to the ounce of water.

Foundered Feet.

This is known by the contraction of the hoof, which will appear considerably smaller than the sound one. The horse just touches the ground with the toe of the foundered foot on account of pain, and stands in such a tottering way that you may shove him over with your hand.

Cure.—Take off the shoe, bleed freely from the thigh vein, and purge two or three times. Keep the hair close trimmed and the parts clean.

Hoof-bound.

Cut down several lines from the coronet to the toe all round the hoof and fill the cuts with tallow and soap mixed. Take off the shoes and (if you can spare him) turn the animal into a wet meadow, where his feet will be kept moist. Never remove the sole nor burn the lines down, as this increases the evil.

Lampas.

This consists in a swelling of the first bar of the upper palate. It is cured by rubbing the swelling two or three times a day with half an ounce of alum and the same quantity of double refined sugar mixed with a little honey. In young horses it hardly amounts to a disease.

Laxity.

Never attempt to stop the discharge too suddenly or too soon; this common but erroneous practice has killed many fine horses. To begin the cure give him the following

Mild Purging Ball.

Rhubarb in powder 1 ounce; magnesia half an ounce; calomel 1 scruple; oil of aniseed 1 drachm. Mix up a ball with honey and liquorice powder. Next day give the horse 1 fluidounce of laudanum in a pint of water. On the third day repeat the drench until the animal is well.

Inflammation of the Lungs.

Bleed the animal copiously as soon as the complaint is perceived, and repeat it in six hours if the fever, quickness of breathing, etc., do not abate. Blister his sides, rowel the chest, and give the following ball, which is to be taken morning and evening until the staling is considerably increased; one a day will then be sufficient. Grass or bran mashes should be the food.

The Ball.

Powdered nitre 6 drachms; camphor 1 drachm; as much syrup and linseed oil as will form the ball; or, a drachm of tartar emetic, 3 drachms of nitre and 1 drachm of digitalis.

Mallenders.

This is a scabby eruption in the bend of the knee-joint, causing lameness. Wash the cracks well with warm soap-suds and a sponge, and then with the vulnerary water twice every day; wipe the parts dry and apply the citrine ointment, or white lead cerate.

Mange.

This is a kind of itch. Wash with soap-suds

and purge with castor oil, and then apply strong sulphur ointment freely and repeatedly. Feed the horse well, and work him moderately.

Molten Grease, or Dysentery.

Bleed and purge moderately, feed regularly on a diminished allowance, and use back-raking and large injections.

Pollevil.

This is a swelling of the back of the head from a bruise. Bring the swelling to a head, as any other tumor, by the suppurating poultice, which is made as follows:

Suppurating Poultice.

Take four handsful of bran and three middling sized turnips, boil them till soft, beat them well together; then boil them again in milk to a thick poultice, adding to it 2 ounces of linseed and half a pound of hog's lard.

Quittor.

Quittor is a severe bruise of the coronet by the other foot, followed after by suppuration. Make an opening for the matter to descend from all the neighboring sinuses. Keep the parts well cleaned with warm soap-suds, then inject alum water into the sinuses. If there be a core, touch it with caustic; when this is discharged dress with the green ointment.

Ring Bone.

If recent, blister the part; if an old affection, recourse must be had to firing.

Sand-Crack.

Remove the shoe and ascertain carefully the extent of the injury; if the crack be superficial, fill it with the composition below, and keep the foot cool and moist. If the crack has extended to the sensible parts, and you can see any fungous flesh, with a small drawing knife remove the edges of the cracked horn that press upon it. Touch the fungus with caustic, dip a roll of tow or linen in tar and bind it firmly over it. The whole foot is to be kept in a bran poultice for a few days, or until the lameness is removed. A shoe may then be put on, so as not to press on the diseased part. The pledget of tow may now be removed, the crack filled with the composition, and the animal turned into some soft meadow.

Composition for Sand-Crack.

Beeswax 4 ounces; yellow rosin 2 ounces; common turpentine 1 ounce; tallow or suet ½ ounce. To be melted together.

Sit-fasts

Are horny substances on the back, under the saddle. Take hold of them with a pair of pincers and cut them out radically; leave no part behind, or they will grow again. Dress the wound with the green ointment.

Sallenders

Require the same treatment as mallenders, which see. They differ only in being at the bend of the hock-joint.

Staggers.

Three disorders often receive this name: *mad staggers*, or inflammation of the brain; *megrims*, or epilepsy, and *stomach staggers*, or palsy of the stomach. In the *first* the animal is very violent; young horses are most frequently affected. Bleeding is the usual treatment. *Megrims* is attended by the signs of vertigo and confusion, lasting for a few minutes at a time. Moderate feeding and gentle purgation are recommended for it. *Stomach staggers* generally proceeds from distension of the stomach with indigestible food, especially when the horse is otherwise in a bad condition. The great object of treatment must be to empty the alimentary canal by the use of cordial purgatives and clysters, as of salt and water, used repeatedly.

Drench for Staggers.

Barbadoes aloes 6 drachms; calomel 2 drachms; oil of peppermint 20 drops; warm water 1 pint; tincture of cardamons 2 ounces. Mix for one dose.

Another.

Common salt 4 ounces; ginger 2 drachms carbonate of soda 1 ounce; water 1 quart.

Strains.

In whatever part of the body this accident occurs, the treatment should be perfect rest, moderate bleeding and purging till the inflammation is reduced, when any stimulating embrocation may be used.

Strangury.

Take away a quart of blood and throw up a laxative clyster: then give one ounce of saltpetre and one fluidounce of sweet spirits of nitre in a pint of water.

Strangles.

This is known by a swelling between the jawbone and the root of the tongue. If a large tumor appear under the jaw, apply the suppurating poultice. When it is ripe open it, squeeze out the matter and apply a warm poultice. In a few days it will run off. Give warm bran mashes and gentle exercise.

Thrush.

Remove the shoe and pare off all the ragged parts so as to expose the diseased parts; after cleaning the frog nicely apply a solution of blue vitriol, and shortly after pour some melted tar ointment into the cleft of the frog, and cover its whole surface with tow soaked in the same, and on the tow a flat piece of wood about the width of the frog, one of its ends passing under the toe of the shoe, the other extending to the back part of the frog and bound down by cross pieces of wood, the ends of which are placed under the shoe. Repeat the dressing every day.

Vives.

This is a disease most common to young horses, and consists in a long swelling of the parotid gland, beginning at the root of the ears and descending downwards. If it is painful and inflamed, apply the poultice; if it suppurates, open the lump, let out the matter and dress with the green ointment. If it is hard and indolent apply strong mercurial ointment to disperse it and bleed moderately.

Wind Galls.

These swellings appear on each side of the back sinew, above the fetlock. It is dangerous to puncture them as is sometimes done, as it may produce an incurable lameness. Tight bandages and moistening the parts frequently with a strong solution of sal ammoniac in vinegar may do some good.

Wounds.

All the rules laid down in this book for the treatment of wounds in the human subject, apply strictly to horses. As in simple cuts, however, sticking plaster cannot be used, the edges of the wound should be neatly stitched together. Much can be done also by the judicious application of bandages. Farriers, generally, are in the habit of pursuing such absurd, cruel, and fatal practices in these cases, either by cutting off a part that appears to be partly torn from its connection, or by using stimulating applications, that it becomes necessary to repeat again that all the rules laid down for the treatment of wounds in this work as applicable to man are equally so to the noble animal of which we are speaking. Read over these rules. Substitute the word "horse" for "patient" and you will be at no loss how to proceed.

Bleeding in General.

Bleeding is often the most useful and efficacious means of curing diseases in horses, etc. In inflammatory affections it is generally the first remedy resorted to, and its immediate salutary effects are often surprising. But it is often abused by being practised where it is not required, or where the animal is too weak to bear it, or by being done too largely or too often in the same case. It is a great error to suppose that all diseases or cases of diseases require bleeding.

When it is necessary to lessen the whole quantity of blood in the system, open the jugular or neck vein. If the inflammation is local, bleed where it can be conveniently done, either from the part affected, or in its vicinity, as by opening the plate vein, superficial vein of the thigh, or temporal arteries.

In fevers of all kinds in the horse, and when inflammation attacks any important organ, as the brain, eyes, lungs, stomach, intestines, liver, kidneys, bladder, etc., bleeding is of the greatest use. It diminishes the quantity of blood in the body; and by this means prevents the bad consequences of inflammation. The quantity of blood to be taken varies according to the age, size, condition, and constitution of the horse, and urgency of the symptoms.

From a large strong horse, four or six quarts will generally be requisite, and this may be repeated in smaller quantities if symptoms demand it. The blood, in these diseases, must flow from a large orifice made in the vein. A horse should never be suffered to bleed upon the ground, but into a measure in order that the proper quantity may be taken. Young horses, also, while shedding their teeth, have sometimes much constitutional irritation, which bleeding relieves. But in these affections it is very rarely necessary to bleed to the same extent as in fevers, etc.; two or three quarts generally suffice to be taken away.

Fullness of Blood.

Moderate bleeding, as from two to three or four quarts, is also used to remove fullness of habit, or plethora, attended with slight inflammatory symptoms. In this case the eyes appear heavy, dull, red or inflamed, frequently closed as if asleep; the pulse small and oppressed; the heat of the body somewhat increased; the legs swell; the hair also rubs off. Horses that are removed from grass to a warm stable, and full fed on hay and corn, and not sufficiently exercised, are very subject to one or more of these symptoms. Regulating the quantity of food given to him, proper exercise, and occasional laxatives, as the following powder, will be commonly found sufficient after the first bleeding, and operation of an aloetic purge. In slight affections of this kind, a brisk purge will often alone be sufficient.

Laxative and Diaphoretic Powder.

Take of nitre, cream of tartar, and flower of sulphur, of each, 4 ounces.

Powder and mix them well together for use.

One tablespoonful of this mixture may be given every night and morning, in as much scalded bran, or a feed of corn moistened with water, that the powders may adhere thereto.

This powder will be found excellent for such horses as are kept on dry food, whether they be in the stable, or travel on the road; also for stallions in the spring of the year, as they not only keep the body cool and open, but cause him to cast his coat, and make his skin appear as bright as silk.

Purging.

In obstinate grease and swellings of the legs, accompanied with lameness of the joints, dry coughs, worms, diseases of the skin, farcy, apoplexy or staggers, affections of the liver, and several other diseases treated of in this book, mercurial purges are of the greatest service. They purge; destroy worms; generally increase the flow of urine; operate upon the skin, liver, and other viscera in a peculiar manner; cause a healthful action in these parts; and remove many chronic complaints incident to the horse. Great caution is necessary during their operation, lest the horse take cold. The water given him must be warm, and when exercised he should be properly clothed.

Horses that are kept on dry food, and are full fed, with little or no exercise, require regular purging every six months.

To prepare Horses for Physic.

Previously to administering a purge, the body should be prepared.

The proper method of preparing a horse for physic is to give him two or three mashes of the scalded bran and oats and warm water, for three or four days together. This will soften the fæces, and promote the operation of the medicine. But if a strong purge be given to a horse of costive habit, without preparation, it will probably occasion a violent inflammation.

Often the bran mashes will move the bowels sufficiently, without other physic. The mash is made by pouring boiling water on fresh sweet bran in a pail, so that the mixture, when stirred, may be of about the consistence of a soft poultice.

Purgative Balls for Horses.

Take of Barbadoes aloes, 7½ ounces; Castile soap, 1½ ounces; powder ginger, 1½ ounces; oil of aniseed, 5 drachms; syrup, a sufficient quantity to make 6 balls, each of which is a dose.

Drink to check Over-purging.

Take of prepared chalk, ginger, and aniseeds, in powder, each 1 ounce; essential oil of peppermint, 15 drops; rectified spirit of wine, ½ an ounce.

Mix the whole in a pint and a half of warm linseed gruel, and give it.

Another.

Take of prepared chalk, 2 ounces; aniseeds, and caraway seeds, in powder, each, 1 ounce; opium, ½ a drachm. Mix, and give it in a pint of linseed gruel.

Astringent Drink after Looseness.

If the looseness continue, after the above drink has been administered for two or three days, the following astringent drink may be given:—

Take of pomegranate shell, in powder, and prepared testaceous powder, each, 1 ounce; Dover's powders, and ginger powdered, each 2 drachms. Mix, and give in a pint of warm gruel, and repeat twice a day.

Cough Drink.

Take of Barbadoes tar and gum ammoniac, each, 1 ounce. Incorporate them with the yolk of an egg, then add, nitre 1 ounce; ginger half an ounce; tincture of opium 1 ounce. Mix them together.

Let this drink be gradually mixed in a pint of warm ale or linseed tea, and give it in the morning fasting; let the horse stand without food for two hours after, then give him a mash of scalded

DISEASES OF HORSES.

bran and oats and warm water. Repeat every other morning, for three or four times.

Fever Ball for Horses.

Take of antimonial powder, tartarized antimony, and camphor, each 1 drachm; nitre and Castile soap, each 2 drachms; Barbadoes aloes, 2 drachms. Mix, and beat them into a ball with syrup of buckthorn.

Let this ball be given to the horse about two hours after bleeding; and in six hours after giving him the ball, let him have the following

Purgative Drink.

Take of Epsom salts, 4 ounces; nitre, ½ an ounce; coarse sugar, two tablespoonsful. Dissolve them in a quart of gruel; then add 10 ounces of castor oil. Mix, and give it while new-milk warm.

After the first ball is given the aloes may be left out, and then the ball and drink may be given once a day (one in the morning and the other in the evening), until a proper passage be obtained.

Powerful Mixture for Fevers.

If the fever still continue to increase it will be proper to take a little more blood from him, and then to have recourse to the following fever powder:

Take of tartar emetic, 1 ounce; calcined hartshorn, 1 ounce. Mix, and grind them in a mortar to a fine powder; then put them in a bottle for use; two drachms of these powders are a proper dose for a horse.

A dose of this powder, with one ounce of nitre, may be given twice or three times a day in a pint of warm gruel, or be made into a ball with conserve of roses. If the fever be violent, and the horse in a raging state, ¼ an ounce of tincture of opium may be added to each dose of powders.

Drink for an Inflammatory Fever.

Take of tartar emetic, 1 drachm; camphor, 1 drachm, rubbed into powder, with a few drops of spirit of wine.

This drink is excellent for all kinds of inflammatory fevers; especially such as are attended with imminent danger. It may be given every four hours, or three times a day, in a pint of water-gruel.

Purging Ball for Jaundice.

Take of Barbadoes aloes, from 4 to 5 drachms; white antimonial powder and Castile soap, each 2 drachms; calomel, 1 drachm. Mix, and beat them into a ball with a sufficient quantity of syrup of buckthorn.

The horse should have a couple of mashes the day before this ball is given, by way of preparation, and the ball should be given fasting the morning following; let him fast for two hours after, then give him a mash of scalded bran and oats with warm water, and treat him in the same manner as for other physic.

Restorative Balls after Jaundice.

Take of gentian and caraway seeds, in powder, of each 8 ounces; powdered ginger, 6 drachms; Castile soap, 1½ ounces; and honey sufficient to form into 6 balls.

One of these balls should be given every other day for some time.

Pectoral Balls for Broken Wind.

Take of Barbadoes tar, Venice turpentine, and Castile soap, each 2 ounces; squills, in powder, 1 ounce. Beat them well together; then add nitre, 2 ounces; aniseeds and caraway seeds, fresh powdered, each 1 ounce. Beat them into a mass with honey and liquorice powder, and divide into ten balls.

Alterative Balls for Surfeit, Mange, etc.

Take of precipitated sulphur of antimony, gentian root, and socotrine aloes, each 1 ounce in fine powder; nitre, 2 ounces; calomel, in powder, 2 drachms. Mix, and make them into a mass for balls with honey or treacle. Each ball to weigh 1 ounce and a half.

These balls will be found sometimes useful in many diseases; such as surfeit, hidebound, mange, grease or swelled legs, lameness of the joints, molten-grease, inflammation of the eyes; and, indeed, in all lingering and obstinate diseases. One ball may be given every other morning for a week together.

Astringent Ball for Profuse Staling.

Take of galls, in fine powder, 2 drachms; Peruvian bark, ½ ounce. Make into a ball with honey or treacle.

It will be proper to repeat this ball every morning, and, if the disease is obstinate, every night and morning, and continue until the urine is diminished to about its natural quantity.

Restorative Balls for Profuse Staling.

Take of gentian root, in powder, ½ an ounce; ginger, powdered, 2 drachms; alum, 1 drachm; treacle, sufficient to make into a ball.

Mercurial Ball for Worms.

Take of calomel and Castile soap, each 1 drachm; wormseed, in powder, ¼ an ounce. Beat them into a ball with syrup of buckthorn.

This ball should be given at night, and the following drink, or purging ball, the next morning:

Drink for Worms.

Take of Barbadoes aloes, from 3 to 6 drachms (according to their size and strength); wormseed and gentian, in powder, each ½ an ounce; caraway seeds, in powder, 1 ounce. Mix, and give in a pint of strong decoction of wormwood, and repeat in about four or five days; but omit giving the mercurial ball after the first time.

Purging Ball for the Worms.

Take of Barbadoes aloes, 8 drachms; ginger, Castile soap, and oil of savin, each 2 drachms; syrup of buckthorn, sufficient to make them into a ball.

This purge is calculated for a strong horse; but it may be made weaker by lessening the quantity of aloes to 6 or 7 drachms, which are, in general, sufficient after a mercurial ball. The horse should have mashes, warm water, and proper exercise.

Stomach Drink after the Expulsion of the Worms.

Take of aromatic spirit of ammonia and sweet spirit of nitre, each 1 ounce; gentian root, in powder, 1½ ounces; Peruvian bark and hiera picra, in powder, each ½ an ounce; horse-spice, 2 ounces. Mix the whole in three pints of ale, and divide into three parts, and give one every morning fasting.

Two hours after give him a mash and warm water. The virtues of this drink deserve the highest commendation in restoring those horses which have been much reduced by some long-continued disease; as in lowness of spirits, debility and relaxation of the solids, a loss of appetite, and for such also as are over-ridden, either in the field or on the road.

Clyster for Convulsions.

Take of linseed and valerian root, each 4 ounces; boil them in 3 quarts of water to 4 pints; add Epsom salts, 4 ounces; assafœtida, ½ ounce; opium, 2 drachms. Dissolve the whole in the above while hot, and apply it new milk-warm.

This is a most powerful clyster in all disorders of the intestines, that are attended with pain and convulsions or spasms in those parts, such as a violent attack of the colic, proceeding from an obstruction in the urinary passage.

To cure Gripes in Horses.

This disorder goes by different names in different districts of the country; as fret, from the uneasiness attending it; bots, from its being thought to arise from these animals or worms, etc. The animal looks dull and rejects his food; becomes restless and uneasy, frequently pawing; voids his excrements in small quantities, and often tries to stale; looks round, as if towards his own flank or the seat of complaint; soon appears to get worse, often lying down, and sometimes suddenly rising up, or at times trying to roll, even in the stable, etc. As the disorder goes on the pain becomes more violent, he appears more restless still, kicks at his belly, groans, rolls often, or tumbles about, with other marks of great agitation; becomes feverish, and has a cold moisture at the roots of his ears and about his flanks, and when he lies at rest a little space begins to perspire strongly, and to get covered with sweat more or less profuse.

In most cases of ordinary gripes signs of flatulence, or of the presence of air confined in the bowels, occur and constitute a part of the disease, or increase it. The removal of it is, therefore, an object to which the attention of most grooms has been in a chief degree directed; and as it can frequently be got rid of, and the disease cured, by exciting the powerful action of the intestines, cordial and stimulating medicines are had recourse to, and, no doubt, in many have afforded relief. Some farriers, indeed, without much care in distinguishing cases, almost exclusively rely upon such, and employ them too freely. This, however, should not be done; for it sometimes happens that disorders not unlike flatulent colic or gripes do occur, when there is neither pent-up air present nor any relaxation or want of energy and action in the intestines themselves, and stimulating medicines might then do no good, but often much mischief.

When the disorder is early discovered, or has newly come on, it will be proper to lose no time to get ready a clyster, and likewise a medicinal draught for removing the wind and abating the pain. After removing with the hand any excrement in the great gut that can be reached by it, a clyster, made of five or six quarts of water, or water-gruel, blood warm, and six or eight ounces of common salt, may be injected; and one or other of the following draughts may be given, before or about the same time.

Draught for the Same.

Take of table-beer, a little warmed, 1½ pints (English); common pepper or powdered ginger, 1 teaspoonful; gin, whiskey, or rum, from 2 to 4 ounces, or from 1 to 2 glassesful. These mixed together for one dose.

Another.—Oil of turpentine, 1 ounce, and water-gruel, 1½ pints (English). Mixed for a dose.

Another.—Take of opium, 1 ounce; cloves, bruised, 2 ounces; ginger, 3 ounces; brandy, rum, or gin, 1 quart. Digest these in a corked bottle, shaking it every day, for 3 weeks; then strain through blotting paper. Dose, 2 ounces.

These and the like preparations may be given either out of a bottle or drench-horn, one or two persons raising and keeping properly up the horse's head; while another, who administers the medicine, pulls out and a little aside the tongue, with his left hand, and with the other pours in the draught.

Further Treatment.

Cordial drenches of the kinds recommended, with the clyster, will have the effect in ordinary cases to relieve the disorder; but should this not be the case, after waiting an hour or two (longer or shorter, according to the severity of the ailment or the period since its commencement), then the medicine should be repeated, but in a less dose than at first—perhaps one-half or two-thirds of the former quantity. The horse should be occasionally walked out, properly covered with clothes, lest the chill air bring on shivering and give rise to feverishness; and his belly should be now and then rubbed a considerable time at once — five or ten minutes—but with intervals of rest, so that he may have time to stale or dung. If the disorder does not yield to these remedies, then others must be employed of a more active nature. Some persons recommend castor oil, in the proportion of half a pint to a pint, with an ounce or two of laudanum, or tincture of opium, mixed with water-gruel, in the quantity of a pint or rather less. In case the horse has lain down, and continued so for some time, and is covered with sweat when he rises, two or more persons should be employed to rub him dry, and he should also be kept well clothed. The stable should be airy, moderately cool, and his place in it roomy and well littered, to keep him from hurting himself should he roll about.

White's Ball for Gripes.

Draughts of liquid medicine operate more speedily than any other form; but as the disorder may attack a horse during a journey, where such cannot readily be procured, Mr. White has given a receipt for a ball for the convenience of those who travel; and if it be wrapped up closely in a piece of bladder it may be kept a considerable time without losing its power. The ball is composed of the following ingredients, viz., Castile soap, 3 drachms; camphor 2 drachms; ginger, 1 drachm and a half; and Venice turpentine, 6 drachms. To be made into a ball for one dose.

Laudanum Draught.

Laudanum may be used in cases of urgency, especially in the wet or lax gripes. Take a quart of beer, and make it a very little warmer than blood heat; then put a tablespoonful of powdered ginger into it, and a small wineglassful of laudanum, just before it is given to the horse. This, in most cases, will give ease in a short time; but if the complaint is exceedingly violent, give about half the above quantity in fifteen or twenty minutes. As soon as the pain seems to be abated, if the belly is costive, give the horse a purgative. In case of looseness no purgative must be given; the laudanum, which is of a binding nature, will correct it.

When pain is occasioned by inflammation, it is seldom proper to employ opium or any medicine of that kind; but when it depends upon spasm or irritation, no medicines are so beneficial. In inflammation of the bowels, for example, opium might do injury, but in flatulent or spasmodic colic, or gripes, it seldom fails of success.

Another Anodyne Medicine.

When horses are affected with colic, or where the use of anodynes is requisite, the following preparation may be given, namely: opium, 1 drachm, or 60 grains; Castile soap, 2 drachms; and powdered aniseed, ½ ounce, or 4 drachms. To be made into a ball with syrup, for one dose.

In speaking of the medicines for gripes, or the

DISEASES OF HORSES.

flatulent colic, sometimes termed fret, Mr. White mentions, domestic remedies may be employed when proper medicines cannot be procured in time. For this purpose a draught may be readily made up of a pint of strong peppermint water, with about four ounces of gin, and any kind of spice.

Another.—A pint of port wine, with spice or ginger.

Another.—Half a pint of gin diluted with 4 ounces of water and a little ginger.

Another.—Take of Epsom salt, 6 ounces; Castile soap, sliced, 2 ounces. Dissolve them in 1½ pints of warm gruel; then add tincture of opium, ½ ounce; oil of juniper, 2 drachms. Mix, and give them new-milk warm.

This drink may be repeated every four or five hours till the symptoms begin to abate.

The Same when on a Journey.

Take of tincture of opium and oil of juniper, each, 2 drachms; sweet spirit of nitre, tincture of benzoin, and aromatic spirit of ammonia, each ½ ounce. Mix them together in a bottle for one drink, and give it in a pint of warm gruel.

For the colic, flatulency, and colicky pains of the intestines this drink will be found a valuable cordial. It may be repeated every two hours until the symptoms abate.

Another.—The complaint may be removed by warm beer and ginger, or a cordial ball, mixed with warm beer.

It is necessary to repeat the caution given respecting the necessity of distinguishing the flatulent, or windy, or spasmodic colic from the inflammatory one, and from that which depends on costiveness. It is always necessary to empty the bowels by means of clysters, and should the horse have appeared dull and heavy previous to the attack, it will be advisable to bleed. If costiveness attends it, give a laxative drench after the paroxysm, which will prevent its return.

Diuretic Balls for Horses.

Mix together 1 ounce of oil of juniper; 1 ounce of balsam of sulphur; 2 ounces of Venice turpentine; 4 ounces of sal prunella; 1 pound of black resin.

Melt all together gently over a slow fire, in an iron pot, and make up into balls of the size of a nutmeg.

Another.—Take of nitre, 3 pounds; resin, 3 pounds; soap, 1½ pounds; juniper berries, 1 pound; oil of juniper 1½ ounces.

To be made up into balls of the common size, with spirits of turpentine.

To cure Diseases in Horses' Feet.

Every person may see, upon turning up the bottom of a horse's foot, an angular projection pointing towards the toe, termed the frog and its bars, the remainder or hollow part being technically termed the sole, though the entire bottom of the foot might better receive this name. It is certain, however, that "the frog and sole" require pressure—a congenial kind of pressure without concussion—that shall cause the sensible, inside, or quick-sole to perform its functions of absorbing the serous particles secreted or deposited therein by the blood vessels. If the frog and its bars are permitted to remain in such a state as to reach the ground, wherever the sod happens to be soft or yielding the hollow part of the sole receives its due proportion of pressure laterally, and the whole sole or surface of the foot is thereby kept in health.

8

Prevention.

Every veterinarian of sense will perceive the necessity of keeping the heels apart, yet although the immediate cause of their contracting is so universally known and recognized, the injudicious method (to call it by no harsher name) of paring away the frog and sole, which prevents the bars from ever touching the ground, is still continued to an alarming extent.

So much for prevention. When disease comes on, which may be accelerated by two other species of mismanagement, another course is usually followed not less injudicious than the first mentioned original cause of all the mischief.

Horses' hoofs are of two distinct kinds or shape, the one being oval, hard, dark-colored and thick, the other round, palish, and thin in the wall, or crust of the hoof. The first has a different kind of frog from the latter, this being broad, thick and soft, whilst the oval hoof has a frog that is long, acute and hard. The rags, which hard work and frequent shoeing occasion on the horny hoof of the round foot, produce ragged frogs also, both being thus pared away to make a fair bottom to receive the shoe (burning hot!), the whole support is so far reduced, and the sensible sole coming much nearer the ground, becomes tender and liable to those painful concussions which bring on lameness—principally of the fore feet. Contraction of those kinds of heels which belong to the cart-horse, and pommice-foot, are the consequence.

The oval foot pertains to the saddle-horse, the hunter, and bit of blood-kind whose bold projecting frogs the farriers remove, and these being compelled to perform long and painful journeys ever starting or going off with the same leading-leg, and continuing the same throughout, lameness is contracted in that foot, which none can account for, nor even find out whereabout it may be seated. Applications of "the oyals" (that egregious compound of folly, ignorance and brutality), follow the first appearance of lameness, and are made alike to the shoulder, the leg, and the sole, under the various pretences of rheumatism, strain in the shoulder, and founder. The real cause, however, is not thought of, much less removed, but, on the contrary, the evil is usually augmented by removing the shoe and drawing the sole to the quick nearly in search of suppositious corns, surbatings, etc.—pretended remedies that were never known to cure, but which might have been all prevented by the simplest precautions imaginable. These are:

1st. Let the frog and sole acquire their natural thickness.

2d. Lead oft sometimes with one leg, sometimes with the other.

3d. Stuff the hollow of the hoofs (all four of them) with cow-dung, or tar ointment, changing it entirely once a day. In every case it is advisable that he be worked moderately, for it is useless to talk to the owners of horses about giving the afflicted animal an entire holiday at grass.

Should the proprietor of the beast be a sordid customer, the farrier can expect no fee for such simple advice as is here given, so he must procure a phialful of water, and putting therein a little saltpetre and a little coloring matter, to be either mixed with the stuffing, or to wash the sole clean daily, though the remedy will do as well (nearly) without such addition. A more efficacious auxiliary will be found in procuring a patch of clay, to be kneaded on the ground, on which the animal (which is worth so much trouble) may be allowed to stand, and if a small patch be made for each foot, the horse himself will prove their value (in most cases) by feeling for them as it were, and showing by his manner how gratified he is at the coldness they afford to his heated feet. Herein it must be observed that stuffing with clay is not recommended, this being one of the numerous blunders of those farriers who, having found the benefit of any application or remedy, push it to a ridiculous extremity.

Remedy for Lameness in Horses.

Mr. Sewell, of the Veterinary College, stated his having discovered a method of curing horses which are lame in the fore-feet. It occurred to him that this lameness might originate in the nerves of the foot, near the hoof, and in consequence he immediately amputated about an inch of the diseased nerve, taking the usual precaution of guarding the arteries and passing ligatures, etc. By this means the animal was instantly relieved from pain, and the lameness perfectly cured.

To cure the Thrush in Horses' Feet.

Simmer over the fire till it turns brown equal parts of honey, vinegar, and verdigris, and apply it with a feather or brush occasionally to the feet. The horse at the same time should stand hard, and all soft dung and straw be removed.

Shoeing Horses in Winter.

In Canada, where the winter is never of a less duration than five months, they shoe their horses in the following manner, which serves for the whole winter: The smith fixes a small piece of steel on the fore part of each shoe, not tempered too hard, which turns up about a quarter of an inch, in the shape of a horse's lancet; the same to the hinder part of the shoe, turned up a little higher than the fore part, tempered in the same manner. In going up a hill the fore part gives a purchase that assists the horse, and in going down prevents him sliding forwards.

Shoes having a number of downward *points* are still better, though more expensive.

To prevent the Feet of Horses from Balling with Snow.

If the frog in the hoofs of horses and the fetlock be cleaned, and well rubbed with soft soap, previously to their going out in snowy weather, it will effectually prevent their falling from what is termed balling with snow. A number of accidents might be prevented by this simple precaution.

Ointment for the Mange.

Take of common turpentine 1 pound; quicksilver, 4 ounces; hogs' lard, ½ a pound; flour of sulphur, 4 ounces; train-oil, ½ a pint.

Grind the silver with the turpentine, in a marble mortar, for five or six hours, until it completely disappears, and add a little oil of turpentine to make it rub easier; then add the remainder, and work them all well together till united.

This ointment must be well rubbed on every part affected, in the open air, if the sunshine and the weather be warm; but if it be winter, take the horse to a blacksmith shop, where a large bar of iron must be heated, and held at a proper distance over him, to warm the ointment.

Liniment for the Mange.

Take of white precipitate, 2 ounces; strong mercurial ointment, 2 ounces; flowers of sulphur, ¼ a pound; rape-oil, 2 quarts.

First grind the white precipitate in a little oil; afterwards add the remainder, taking care that they are well mixed.

This liniment must be well rubbed in with a hard brush, in the open air, provided the day be fine and the weather warm. If the horse draws in a team the inside of the collar must be washed, or the inside of the saddle, if a saddle-horse, for the disease is highly contagious.

Eye-water.

Take of camphor, 2 drachms, dissolved in 2 ounces of rectified spirit of wine; Goulard's extract, 1 ounce; rose-water, 1 quart.

Shake all together in a bottle for use.

Let the eye and the eyelids be well bathed three or four times a day, with a clean linen rag dipped in the eye-water.

For Inflammation of the Lungs.

Take of white antimonial powder, 2 drachms; nitre, ½ an ounce; Castile soap, 2 drachms; aromatic confection, ¼ an ounce.

Beat them into a ball.

This ball must be given to the horse as soon as it can be prepared, after he has been bled; and continue it two or three times a day as long as the inflammation continues. About six hours after, give him a purging drink, and repeat it every night and morning until a passage is obtained, or the bowels are sufficiently opened.

Embrocation for Sprains.

Take of soap liniment and camphorated spirit of wine, of each, 8 ounces; oil of turpentine, ½ an ounce.

Mix and shake when used.

This evaporating and discutient embrocation is well calculated to remove pain and inflammation, which is generally effected in the course of a fortnight or three weeks. During that time the horse should not be allowed to go out of the stable or farm-yard.

Bracing Mixture for Sprains.

After the above embrocation the following bracing mixture must be rubbed on the part once a day:

Take of Egyptiacum (liniment of verdigris), 2 ounces; oil of turpentine, 1 ounce.

Shake well together; then add camphorated spirit of wine and compound tincture of benzoin, each 2 ounces; vinegar, 11 ounces.

Mix, and shake well together every time they are used.

Paste to stop Bleeding.

Take of fresh nettles 1 handful; bruise them in a mortar; add blue vitriol, in powder, 4 ounces; wheaten flour, 2 ounces; wine vinegar, ½ ounce; oil of vitriol, ¼ ounce.

Beat them all together into a paste.

Let the wound be filled up with this paste, and a proper pledget of tow laid over the mouth, in order to prevent it from falling out, and then bandage it on with a strong roller. This dressing must remain in the wound ten or twelve hours.

Ointment for Scratched Heels.

Take of hog's lard, 1 pound; white lead, 4 ounces; white vitriol, 1 ounce; sugar of lead, ½ ounce; olive oil, 3 ounces.

Grind all the powders in a marble mortar with the oil, or on a marble slab; then add the lard, and work the whole together till united.

This is a neat composition, and very proper to keep in the stable during the winter. It will not only be found useful for greasy and scratched heels, but also for stubs and treads of every description. A small quantity must be rubbed on the part affected every night and morning, in slight cases; but in treads, or wounds upon the heels, it will be best to spread the ointment on pledgets of tow, and secure them with bandages.

DISEASES OF HORSES.

Ointment for Greasy Heels.

Take of white ointment, 1 pound; white vitriol, blue vitriol, and sugar of lead, in powder, each, ½ ounce.

Mix well together.

This ointment, when used, must be spread on strong brown paper, and applied over the part that greases, and bandaged on with listing. The horse may, after dressing, be turned into a drystraw yard, and a few diuretic balls given to him; one may be given every third day. Once dressing is, in general, sufficient to perform a cure; if not, it may be repeated in a week after.

Astringent Embrocation for Strains in Different Parts.

Take of camphor 2 drachms, dissolved in ½ an ounce of strong rectified spirit of wine; nitre, 1 ounce, dissolved in ½ a pint of wine vinegar; spirits of turpentine, 4 ounces; white lead, or armenian bole, in powder, ½ an ounce; aqua fortis, 1 ounce.

Mix, and shake them all together in a bottle for use.

Mixture for Canker in the Mouth.

Take of wine vinegar, ½ a pint; burnt alum and common salt, each 1 ounce; armenian bole, ½ an ounce.

Mix, and shake them together in a bottle for use. It will be proper to dress the horse's mouth with this mixture, every morning and evening, in the following manner: Take a small cane, or a piece of whalebone, half a yard long, and tie a linen rag, or a little tow round one end; then dip it into the mixture, and pass it up his mouth, and gently remove it to all the affected parts; let him champ it well about in his mouth: after which let him fast an hour, then give him food as usual.

Glanders.

This disease is contagious, destructive, and seldom cured. It is known by a discharge from one or both nostrils, and a swelling of the gland under the jaw; coming on thick slowly, and followed after a time by ulceration. Catarrh or influenza may be mistaken for it; but this is a much more rapid disorder. Ozœna is a disease attended with an offensive discharge; in glanders the discharge is not offensive unless at an advanced stage. In doubtful cases, sometimes, the inoculation of a donkey with the matter is used as a test. Glanders may be communicated to a human being; and is then also fatal and seldom cured. Every horse suspected of glanders should be kept carefully apart from all others. If the disorder is slow in its progress, and the animal can be prevented from giving it to others, he may be kept for moderate work, upon good feeding, in some instances, for several years. If hard worked, ill-fed or exposed, a glandered horse will run down very fast.

Tetanus, or Lock-Jaw.

This may follow punctured wounds of the foot, as in shoeing, or docking, nicking, or gelding; occurring two or three weeks after the accident or operation. Sometimes it has followed violent exertion; and it is not unfrequently produced by cold. If the stiffness of the muscles be confined to the head or neck, it is much more curable than when general. Two or three out of five out of all the cases are said to get well under good treatment. Mild purgatives, sheep-skin clothing, clysters containing from a quarter to half an ounce of opium, repeated according to the symptoms, and nourishing injections, if the jaws cannot be opened so as to swallow, constitute the best means of management.

Rupture in the Horse.

Rupture or hernia is the protrusion of a bowel or some other part from its proper cavity. It is sometimes congenital, and may then be reduced at the same time that castration is performed. At other times rupture may be produced by blows, kicks, or falls. A hernia is dangerous to life when it becomes strangulated or compressed by a stricture at the orifice of protrusion. Skilful surgical aid should always be obtained in any such case at once. But, sometimes, in the absence of a veterinarian, any one may restore the gut by introducing the hand into the bowel and drawing it up; the other hand, at the same time, making gentle pressure upon the swelling in the abdomen. No violence should ever be used in attempting this: and the bowels should first be emptied by a clyster, to which, sometimes, to relax the parts, half an ounce or an ounce of tobacco is added. Too large a quantity of the latter would be dangerously prostrating.

Purging Ball—Dogs.

Take of jalap, in powder, 1 scruple; Barbadoes aloes, 1 drachm; ginger, in powder, 10 grains; conserve of hips, or syrup, enough to form a ball.

Liniment for the Mange.

Take of flowers of sulphur, 4 ounces; white precipitate, 1 ounce; strong mercurial ointment, 1 ounce; Cape aloes, in powder, ½ ounce; neat's-foot oil, 1½ pints.

First rub the powders together in a mortar; then put in the ointment, and gradually add the oil; it must be stirred when used. The affected part must be well anointed with this liniment, every third day, for three or four times.

Mercurial Liniment for the Red Mange.

Take of mild mercurial ointment, 4 ounces; oil of turpentine, 3 ounces; Cape aloes, in powder, ½ ounce.

Mix well together, and anoint the parts every third day for three or four times. Many sportsmen have their dogs regularly dressed with this liniment two or three weeks before the hunting season commences; it is supposed to improve their scent, and make them more fit for the chase.

Mild Ointments for the Mange.

Take of oil of vitriol, ½ an ounce; hog's lard, 8 ounces. Mix, and anoint the dog every day for three or four times, or oftener if required.

This ointment is used in surfeit, and slight cases of mange.

Lotion for the Mange.

Take of white hellebore root, bruised, 2 ounces; water, 3 pints, boil down to 2 pints and strain; sal ammoniac, 2 drachms; sublimate, 1 drachm; Cape aloes, half an ounce.

Dissolve the sal ammoniac and other ingredients in the decoction.

This lotion is sometimes used to cure the mange, when greasy applications are objected to.

Distemper in Dogs.

The following prescriptions are each about a dose for a full-grown pointer. They must, of course, be increased or diminished in proportion to the size and strength of the dog.

Take of opium, 3 grains; tartar emetic, 5 grains. To be given at night.

Repeat the dose every third night, till the dog is recovered; taking care to keep him in a warm place, and always feed with a warm liquid diet, such as broth, gruel, etc.

If the nostrils should discharge, have them washed or syringed twice a day, with a lotion of alum or sugar of lead; putting about half an ounce of either to a pint of water.

Another.—For a Half-Grown Pointer.

Take of jalap powder, 25 grains; calomel, 5 grains. Made into a pill with a little gum-water.

For a Full-Grown Pointer.

Take of jalap powder, 30 grains; calomel, 8 grains. Mixed as above.

One of these doses, mixed with butter, or in a small piece of meat, should be given to the dog, every morning, on an empty stomach. The food should be light, and easy to digest; and the lotion, if required for the nostrils, should be observed here, as before mentioned.

Distemper among Cattle.

Examine your cow's mouth, though she appears very well; and if you find any pimple in it, or on the tongue, or if you perceive any within the skin ready to come out, immediately house her, keep her warm, and give her warm tar-water. To a large beast give a gallon; to a small one three quarts. Give it four times every day; but not every time the quantity you first gave. Lessen the dose by degrees; but never give less than two quarts to a large beast, nor less than three pints to a small one; and house her every night for some time, and give her warm gruel and malt mash.

To make Tar-Water for Cows.

Take one quart of tar, put to it 4 quarts of water, and stir it well ten or twelve minutes; let it stand a little while, and then pour it off for use. You must not put water to the same tar more than twice. Let the first dose be made of fresh tar. Continue to give it till the beast is well. Don't let her go too soon abroad.

For the Garget in Cows.

This disorder is very frequent in cows after ceasing to be milked; it affects the glands of the udder with hard swellings, and often arises from the animal not being clean milked. It may be removed by anointing the part three times a day with a little ointment, composed of camphor and blue ointment. Half a drachm or more of calomel may be given in warm beer, from a horn or bottle, for three or four mornings, if the disorder is violent.

To cure the Redwater in Cattle.

Take 1 ounce of armenian bole, half an ounce of dragon's blood, 2 ounces of Castile soap, and 1 drachm of alum. Dissolve these in a quart of hot ale or beer, and let it stand until it is blood-warm; give this as one dose, and if it should have the desired effect, give the same quantity in about twelve hours after. This is an excellent medicine for changing the water, and acts as a purgative; every farmer that keeps any number of cattle, should always have doses of it by him.

To cure the Scouring in Cattle.

The following composition has been found to succeed in many cases which were apparently drawing to a fatal termination.

Take of powdered rhubarb, 2 drachms; castor oil, 1 ounce; prepared chalk, 1 teaspoonful.

Mix well together in a pint of warm milk. If the first dose does not answer, repeat it in thirty-six or forty-eight hours. If the calf will suck, it will be proper to allow him to do it.

Cure for Cattle swelled with Green Food.

When any of your cattle happen to get swelled with an over-feed of clover, frosty turnips, or such like, instead of the usual method of stubbing in the side, apply a dose of train oil, which, after repeated trials, has been found completely successful. The quantity of oil must vary according to the age or size of the animal. For a grown-up beast, of an ordinary size, the quantity recommended is about a pint, which must be administered to the animal with a bottle, taking care, at the same time, to rub the stomach well, in order to make it go down. After receiving this medicine, it must be made to walk about until such time as the swelling begins to subside.

Lung Fever.

This affection is epidemic among horses as well as cattle; airy stables and great cleanliness are important. There is no specific remedy. The same may be said of *typhoid* fever; known by great uneasiness, scouring, and nervous twitchings, with fever.

Treatment of Cattle and Fowls.

The experiment has often been tried of the benefit derived to horses from being well combed and kept clean. It has been found that a horse neglected as to cleanliness will not be so well conditioned, either for fatness or strength, though he gets abundance of corn; at least, it is certain that it would be worth trying. This everybody knows, that the most neglected of the horse race are kept cleaner than the cleanest of the horned cattle, particularly those shut up in houses.

"I have two hints to give," says a contemporary writer; "as the expense can be nothing and the advantage may be great; I read in a description of Norway, that when the cows drink at the hot springs they give more milk than those that drink cold water. Cows drink so much at a time that there is no doubt, when the water is nearly at freezing, they must feel sensibly cooled all over, which will naturally affect their produce of milk. I would therefore propose the experiment of warming the water for milch cows in cold weather."

The next proposal is that the corn given to fowls should be crushed and soaked in water; this helps the digestion, and hens will lay in winter when so fed that they would not otherwise.

In a time of scarcity, and when the food of man is dear, such experiments as proposed are well worth making; and the practice proposed with the fowls ought to become general, as it costs nothing.

To cure the Measles in Swine.

It sometimes happens, though seldom, that swine have the measles; while they are in this state their flesh is very unwholesome food, having been ascertained to produce tape-worm in those who feed upon it, especially if not well cooked. This disorder is not easily discovered while the animal is alive, and can only be known by its not thriving or fattening as the others. After the animal is killed and cut up its fat is full of little kernels about the size of the roe or eggs of a salmon. When this is the case, put into the food of each hog, once or twice a week, as much crude pounded antimony as will lie on a shilling. A small quantity of the flour of brimstone, also, may be given with their food when they are not thriving, which will be found of great service to them. But the best method of preventing disorders in swine is to keep their sties perfectly clean and dry, and to allow them air, exercise and plenty of clean straw.

Kidney Worm.

The sign of this is dragging of the hind legs; which, in the hog, never occurs otherwise unless from an injury. An experienced farmer asserts that arsenic will always cure it. Give as much as a dime will hold, in dough or any other vehicle. If once is not sufficient, the dose may be repeated.

Rupture in Swine.

Where a number of swine are bred, it will frequently happen that some of the pigs will have what is called a 'rupture,' i. e. a hole broken in the rim of the belly, where part of the guts comes out and lodges betwixt the rim of the belly and the skin, having an appearance similar to a swelling in the testicles. The male pigs are more liable to this disorder than the females. It is cured by the following means:

Geld the pig affected, and cause it to be held up with its head downwards; flay back the skin from the swollen place, and from the situation in which the pig is held the guts will naturally return to their proper place. Sew up the hole with a needle, which must have a square point, and also a bend in it, as the disease often happens between the hinder legs, where a straight needle cannot be used. After this is done, replace the skin that was flayed back and sew it up, when the operation is finished. The pig should not have much food for a few days after the operation, until the wound begins to heal.

Sore Throat in Swine.

This is a swelling of the glands of the throat, attended by wheezing, and general weakness of the animal. Indigo is useful for it; a piece as large as a hickory nut mashed up in water and poured down. Once is generally enough.

Hog Cholera.

Though usually incurable when it occurs, it may nearly always be prevented by putting ashes in the trough with the food once a week.

For the Foot-Rot in Sheep.

Take a piece of alum, a piece of green vitriol, and some white mercury — the alum must be in the largest proportion; dissolve them in water, and after the hoof is pared anoint it with a feather and bind on a rag over all the foot.

Another.—Pound some green vitriol fine, and apply a little of it to the part of the foot affected, binding a rag over the foot as above. Let the sheep be kept in the house a few hours after this is done, and then turn them out to a dry pasture. This is the most common way of curing the foot rot in Middlesex.

Another.—Others anoint the part with a feather dipped in aqua fortis or weak nitrous acid, which dries in at once. Many drovers that take sheep to market-towns, carry a little bottle of this about with them, which, by applying to the foot with a feather, helps a lame sheep by hardening its hoof and enabling it to travel better. Some may think aqua fortis is of too hot a nature, but such a desperate disorder requires an active cure, which, no doubt, is ever to be used cautiously.

Another.—Spread some slacked quick-lime over a house floor pretty thick; pare the sheep's feet well, and turn them into this house, where they may remain for a few hours, after which turn them into a dry pasture. This treatment may be repeated two or three times, always observing to keep the house clean, and adding a little more quick-lime before putting them in.

The foot must be often dressed, and the sheep kept as much as possible upon dry land. Those animals that are diseased should be kept separate from the flock, as the disorder is very infectious.

Prevention and Cure of the Foot-Rot in Sheep.

On suspected grounds, constant and careful examination ought to take place; and when any fissures or cracks, attended with heat, make their appearance, apply oil of turpentine and common brandy. This, in general, produces a very beneficial effect, but where the disease has been long seated, and becomes, in a manner, confirmed—after cleaning the foot, and paring away the infected parts, recourse is had to caustics, of which the best seem to be sulphuric acid and the nitrate of mercury. After this pledgets are applied, the foot bound up, and the animal kept in a clean, dry situation, until its recovery is effected.

But it often happens, where the malady is inveterate, that the disease refuses to yield to any or all of the above prescriptions.

The following mode of treatment, however, if carefully attended to, may be depended upon as a certain cure. Whenever the disease makes its appearance, let the foot be carefully examined, and the diseased part well washed, and pared as close as possible, not to make it bleed; and let the floor of the house, where the sheep are confined, be strewn three or four inches thick with quick-lime hot from the kiln; and let the sheep, after having their feet dressed in the manner above described, stand in it during the space of six or seven hours.

In all cases, it is of great importance that the animal be afterwards exposed only to a moderate temperature — be invigorated with proper food — and kept in clean, easy, dry pasture; and the disease will be effectually remedied in the course of a few days.

To prevent Sheep from catching Cold after being Shorn.

Sheep are sometimes exposed to cold winds and rains immediately after shearing, which exposure frequently hurts them. Those farmers who have access to the sea should plunge them into the salt water; those who have not that opportunity, and whose flocks are not very large, may mix salt with water and rub them all over, which will in a great measure prevent any mishap befalling the animal after having been stripped of its coat.

It is very common in the months of June and July, for some kinds of sheep, especially the fine Leicester breed, which are commonly thin-skinned about the head, to be struck with a kind of fly, and by scratching the place with their feet, they make it sore and raw. To prevent this, take tar, train oil, and salt, boil them together, and when cold, put a little of it on the part affected. This application keeps off the flies, and likewise heals the sore. The salt should be in very small quantity, or powdered sulphur may be used instead of it.

To prevent the Scab.

Separating the wool, lay the before-mentioned ointment in a strip, from the neck down the back to the rump; another strip down each shoulder, and one down each hip; it may not be unnecessary to put one along each side. Put very little of the ointment on, as too much of it may be attended with danger.

To destroy Maggots in Sheep.

Mix with 1 quart of spring water, a table spoonful of the spirits of turpentine, and as much of the sublimate powder as will lie upon a dime. Shake them well together, and cork it up in a bottle, with a quill through the cork, so that the liquid may come out of the bottle in small quantities at once. The bottle must always be well shaken when it is to be used. When the spot is observed where the maggots are, do not disturb them, but pour a little of the mixture upon the spot, as much as will wet the wool and the maggots. In a few minutes after the liquor is applied the maggots will all creep to the top of the wool, and in a short time drop off dead. The sheep must, however, be inspected next day, and if any of the maggots remain undestroyed, shake them off, or touch them with a little more of the mixture.

A little train oil may be applied after the maggots are removed, as sometimes the skin will be hard by applying too much of the liquid. Besides, the fly is not so apt to strike when it finds the smell of the oil, which may prevent a second attack.

This method of destroying maggots is superior to any other, and it prevents the animal from being disfigured by clipping off the wool, which is a common practice in some countries.

Cure for the Scab in Sheep.

The simplest and most efficacious remedy for this disease, was communicated to the Society for the Encouragement of Arts, etc., by the late Sir Joseph Banks; and is as follows:

Take 1 pound of quicksilver, ½ a pound of Venice turpentine, ½ a pint of oil of turpentine, 4 pounds of hog's lard.

Let them be rubbed in a mortar till the quicksilver is thoroughly incorporated with the other ingredients. For the proper mode of doing which, it may be right to take the advice or even the assistance of some apothecary, or other person used to make such mixtures.

The method of using the ointment is this: Beginning at the head of the sheep, and proceeding from between the ears, along the back, to the end of the tail; the wool is to be divided in a furrow, till the skin can be touched, and as the furrow is made, the finger, slightly dipped in the ointment, is to be drawn along the bottom of it, where it will leave a blue stain on the skin and adjoining wool.

From this furrow, similar ones must be drawn down the shoulders and thighs to the legs, as far as they are woolly; and if the animal is much infected, two more should be drawn along each side, parallel to that on the back, and one down each side, between the fore and hind legs.

Immediately after being dressed, it is usual to turn the sheep among other stock, without any fear of the infection being communicated; and there is scarcely an instance of a sheep suffering any injury from the application. In a few days the blotches dry up, the itching ceases, and the animal is completely cured. It is generally, however, thought proper not to delay the operation beyond Michaelmas.

The hippobosca ovina, called in Lincolnshire Sheep-fagg, an animal well known to all shepherds, which lives among the wool, and is hurtful to the thriving of sheep, both by the pain its bite occasions, and the blood it sucks, is destroyed by this application, and the wool is not at all injured. Our wool-buyers purchase the fleeces on which the stain of the ointment is visible, rather in preference to others, from an opinion, that the use of it having preserved the animal from being vexed, either with the scab or faggs, the wool is less liable to the defects of joints or knots; a fault observed to proceed from very sudden stop in the thriving of the animal, either from want of food, or from disease.

To cure the Water in the Heads of Sheep.

"Of all the various operations by which this distemper may be eradicated, I must, from experience, give the preference to one which will, perhaps, astonish such readers as form their opinions more from theory than practice. A number of medical men have already controverted the fact, and, with the utmost presumption, disputed my veracity to my face, after I had witnessed its efficacy in a thousand instances. It is no other than that of putting a sharpened wire up the nostril quite through the middle of the brain, and by that means perforating the bag which contains the fluid causing the disease. This is, of all other methods, the most certain to succeed; but it has this unpleasant appendage annexed to it, if it do not cure, it is certain to kill.

This method of cure is not only the most expedient, but it is in every shepherd's power, and one which he can scarcely perform amiss, if he attend to the following plain directions:

The operation must be performed with a stiff steel wire, such as is used for knitting the coarsest stockings. It must be kept clean, and free of rust, oiled, and sharpened at the point. Care must be taken, however, that its point be only one-eighth of an inch in length, for if it is tapered like a needle, it is apt to take a wrong direction in going up the nostrils, fix in the gristle below the brain, and torment the animal to no purpose. If blunt in the point, it often fails to penetrate the bladder, which is of considerable toughness, shoving it only a little to one side; the safest way, of course, is to have the point of the wire sharp and short.

The shepherd must first feel with his thumbs for the soft part in the skull, which invariably marks the seat of this disease. If that is near the middle of the head above, where, in two cases out of three at least, it is sure to be, let him then fix the animal firm betwixt his knees, hold the head with one hand, laying his thumb upon the soft or diseased part, and with the other hand insert the wire through the nostril, on a parallel with the seat of the distemper, aiming directly at the point where his thumb is placed. The operation is performed in one second, for if he feels the point of the wire come in contact with his thumb, let him instantly set the animal to its feet, and if the weather is at all cold, let it stand in the house over-night.

If the disease is seated exactly in that part where the divisions of the skull meet, and consequently in a right line with the top of the nose, he must probe both nostrils, when, should he miss the bulb on the one side, he will be sure to hit it on the other. If the seat of the disease cannot at all be found, and if the animal have all the symptoms of the malady the water is then enclosed among the ventricles in the middle of the brain, and must be treated as above. Nothing can be done in the last case save with the wire, but it is hard to cure when so affected. I have found, on dissection, the fluid contained in many little cells in the centre of the brain, and though the wire had penetrated some of these cells, it had missed others.

By this simple operation alone I have cured hundreds, and though I never kept an exact register, I think I have not known it to fail above once in four times as an average in all the instances which have come under my observation, and some of these I knew to be injudiciously performed, the disease not being seated in a point which the wire could reach. I have at times cured a dozen, and ten, in regular succession, without failing once, and I have again in some cold seasons of the year, killed three or four successively.

Sir George M'Kenzie has insinuated in his book on sheep that I was the inventor of this mode of cure, but it is by no means the case. The practice, I understand, has been in use among shepherds for ages past, but they were often obliged to perform it privately, their masters, like the professors about Edinburgh, always arguing that the piercing of the brain must necessarily prove fatal. Sir George has, however, misunderstood my account in this matter in the Highland Society's Transactions; I did not mean to insinuate that it was with pleasure I discovered the art of curing them in this way, but only my success in that art. I mentioned in these Transactions that when I was a shepherd boy, for a number of years I probed the skull of every sturdied sheep that I could lay my hands on, without any regard to whom they belonged, and likewise took every opportunity of visiting my patients as often as possible; and, as the country around me swarmed with them every spring and summer, my practice, of course, was of prodigious extent. It was several years before I was sensible of failing in one instance, which, however, it was often impossible to ascertain, they having left the spot sometimes before I could again go that way: but many a valuable young sheep I cured for different owners without ever acknowledging it, having no authority to try such experiments.

The following symptoms, after the operation, may be depended on: If the animal becomes considerably sick, it is a good sign that it will recover. If it continues to grow sicker and abstains from feeding for the space of two days, it is likely to die, and if in a condition to be fit for family use ought to be killed forthwith. The flesh of the animal is nothing the worse for this disease; on the contrary, it is universally supposed by the country people that their flesh is sweeter, more delicate and palatable than any other. This, I suppose, must be owing to their tender age, it being unusual to kill any sheep so young, save lambs.

The first symptom of recovery is their bleating. If once they begin to bleat occasionally, they are sure to recover, however stupid they may appear at that time. It seems that they are then becoming sensible of the want of society, the only thing which causes sheep to bleat, and which, for a long time previous to that they had totally disregarded.

I must mention here that the most successful curer of this distemper I ever knew, performed the operation in a different manner from the one practised by me, and above recommended. Instead of a wire he carried always a large corking-pin in his bonnet, and, like me, tapped every sturdied sheep he found, but always above, putting the point of the pin through the skull at the place where it was most soft, in the same manner as the trocar is used. As this does not at all endanger the sheep's life, I frequently tried this plan previous to that of probing with the wire; but, as far as I can recollect, I never cured one by that means. I remember once conversing with him on the subject, when he told me that he seldom or never failed in curing them upon their own farms, but that in sundry neighboring farms he rarely cured any. From this it would appear that on different soils the animals are differently affected. I am now convinced that he must generally have inserted the pin so far as to penetrate the bottom of the sac, which I never had the sense to try, and which, if we reason from analogy must prove as effective and less hazardous than the other, for it appears to me that in order to insure a recovery it is necessary that the bottom or lowest part of the sac be penetrated.

Undoubtedly the best mode of curing this disease would be to extract the sac and all that it contains entirely. There is little doubt but that if this were performed by gentle and skilful hands, it would prove the most effectual cure; but as it is I can attest that it seldom proves successful. The shepherds have not skill and ingenuity sufficient to close the skull properly up again, or in such a manner as is requisite to defend it from external injury; of course I would rather recommend the mode in which they cannot easily go wrong, and which I have seen prove most beneficial, when performed by men of like acquirements themselves."—*Farmer's Magazine.*

To prevent the "Sturdy" or Water in the heads of Sheep.

With regard to the causes inducing water in the head of sheep, there is but one opinion entertained among shepherds, which is that it is occasioned by a chilliness in the back of the animal, on account of its being exposed to the winds, and the sleety showers of winter. These cause it to acquire a kind of numbness and torpidity, which, if often repeated, are apt to terminate in an affection to giddiness, and finally in a water in the head.

That the disease is occasioned solely by a chilliness in the back, appears from the following facts:

1. It is always most general after a windy and sleety winter.

2. It is always most destructive on farms that are ill sheltered, and on which the sheep are most exposed to those blasts and showers.

3. It preys only on sheep rising their first year, the wool of whom separates above, leaving the back quite exposed to the wet and to the cold.

4. If a piece of cloth or hide is sewed to the wool, so as to cover the back, such a sheep will not be affected with the disease. The experiment is a safe, a cheap, and an easy one; and, exclusive of its good effects in preventing the fatal disease under consideration, it is more beneficial to a young sheep that is not over-high in condition, and administers more to its comfort during the winter than any other that I know of. It keeps the wool from opening, and the sheep always dry and warm on the back; which, exposed to cold, either in man or beast, it is well known, affects the vitals materially. When thus shielded, the young sheep will feed straight in the wind on the worst days, without injury, and, indeed, without much regarding the weather. This covering keeps them from the rain, prevents them from being shelled and loaded with frozen snow, and from destruction by cold, by leanness, and the water in the head. The expense attending it is so trifling, that it is scarcely worth mentioning. One pair of old blankets will furnish coats for forty sheep; and if these are carefully taken off on the return of spring, and laid aside, they will serve the same purpose for two or three successive years.

Practice of the Spanish Shepherds.

The first care of the shepherd on coming to the spot where his sheep are to spend the summer, is to give to his ewes as much salt as they will eat. For this purpose he is provided with twenty-five quintals of salt for every thousand head, which is consumed in less than five months; but they eat none on their journey or in winter. The method of giving it to them is as follows: The shepherd places fifty or sixty flat stones about five steps distance from each other. He strews salt upon each stone, then leads his flock slowly through the stones, and every sheep eats at pleasure. This is frequently repeated, observing not to let them eat on those days in any spot where there is limestone. When they have eaten the salt they are led to some argillaceous spots, where, from the craving they have acquired, they devour everything they meet with, and return again to the salt with redoubled ardor.

Cure of Dropsy in the Crops of Young Turkeys.

"This kind of dropsy is announced by a dull

look, paleness of the head, loss of appetite, and aversion to food. The birds allow themselves to be approached and seized with facility, and they are without strength. Very soon a slight swelling of the crop is added to these symptoms, which in ten days becomes very considerable. I have taken nearly a pint of water from one. By pressing upon the crops of some of them a certain quantity of matter is discharged by the bill, but never enough entirely to ease the crop. All these symptoms increase, and the bird dies at the end of fifteen or eighteen days' illness.

I sought after the cause of this disorder, and it was easy to find that it was occasioned by the stagnant water of which these animals had drunk; in the course of the year the heat had been great, and there was little rain. The heat had hatched a vast swarm of small red worms, resembling ascarides. It is quite certain that these insects must have been swallowed by the turkeys, and from this cause, and the bad quality of the water which they had drunk a great degree of inflammation in the crop would ensue, with a stoppage of the passage which conducts to the gizzard. I divided the turkeys into two classes; for those who were still sound I ordered grain and good water; with all that were diseased I practised the operation of tapping with a lancet, in the lowest part of the crop. I injected at the opening, by means of a small syringe, a slight decoction of Jesuit's bark, mixed with a little brandy; which was repeated twice in the course of the day. Next day the wound was better marked. I made again the same injection, and two hours after, I forced them to eat a little of the yolk of an egg, mixed with some crumbs of bread. At the end of three days the wound in the crop was closed; which I might have prevented, but finding a natural opening in the bill, I made them take, during eight days, in their drink the same substance which had been injected; and they were, by degrees, put on their diet. I need not add that clear water was instead of that of the standing pools. [*] imals had died before my arrival; [d]uring the treatment, and the rest [st]ck, which might be about forty, either [esca]ped the disease or were cured."—*M. Ligneau.*

To cure Colds of every description in Cattle.

The first attempt should be to remove the cause, by giving to the animal a warm cordial drink; which, acting as a stimulant on the stomach and intestines, will give fresh motion to these parts, and enable nature to resume her former course.

Take of sweet fennel-seeds and cummin-seeds, each 2 ounces, in powder; long pepper, turmeric, ginger each 1 ounce, in powder. Mix for one drink. The method of giving this drink is as follows: Put it into a pitcher with 2 ounces of fresh butter and 2 tablespoonsful of treacle or coarse sugar; then pour one quart of boiling ale upon the whole; cover them down till new-milk warm, and then give the drink to the beast.

In two hours after giving the drink let the animal have a good mash made of scalded bran, or ground malt, with a handful or two of ground oats or barley meal added to it, and warm water that day. In slight colds, during the summer, these drinks may be given to cattle while in their pasture; and, where it can be made convenient, let them fast two hours after, and then graze as usual. It is also necessary to examine the sick animals every day, to watch them while they both dung and stale, and to see whether the body be of a proper heat and the nose or muzzle of a natural breeze.

If these be regular there is not much danger. If, however, feverish symptoms should appear (which frequently happens), the animal will become costive. In such cases give one of the following:

Purging Drink.

Take of Glauber salts, 1 pound; ginger, in powder, 2 ounces; treacle, 4 ounces.

Put all the ingredients into a pitcher and pour 3 pints of boiling water upon them. When new-milk warm give the whole for one dose.

Another.

Take of Epsom salts, 1 pound; anise-seeds and ginger, in powder, each 2 ounces; treacle, 4 ounces.

Let this be given in the same manner as the preceding.

In most cases these drinks will be sufficient to purge a full-grown animal of this kind. By strict attention to the above method of application, a fever may be prevented, and the animal speedily restored.

If the fever continue, after the intestines have been evacuated (which is seldom the case), it will be proper to take some blood from the animal, and the quantity must be regulated according to the disease and habit of body.

To cure the Yellows or Jaundice in Neat Cattle.

As soon as the disease makes its first appearance, it may, for the most part, be removed by administering the following drink:

Reduce to powder cummin-seeds, anise-seeds, and turmeric root, each 2 ounces; grains of paradise, and salt of tartar, each 1 ounce.

Now slice 1 ounce of Castile soap, and mix it with 2 ounces of treacle; put the whole into a pitcher, then pour a quart of boiling ale upon the ingredients, and cover them down till new-milk warm, then give the drink. It will often be proper to repeat this, two or three times, every other day, or oftener if required. If the beast be in good condition, take away from two to three quarts of blood; but the animal should not be turned out after bleeding that day, nor at night, but the morning following it may go to its pasture as usual. After this has had the desired effect, let the following be given:

Take of balsam copaiva, 1 ounce; salt of tartar, 1 ounce; Castile soap, 2 ounces. Beat them together in a marble mortar; and add of valerian root, in powder, 2 ounces; ginger root and Peruvian bark, in powder, each 1 ounce; treacle, 2 ounces. Mix for one drink.

Let this drink be given in a quart of warm gruel, and repeated if necessary every other day. It will be proper to keep the body sufficiently open through every stage of the disease; for if costiveness be permitted, the fever will increase, and if not timely removed, the disorder will terminate fatally.

Frenzy, or Inflammation of the Brain,

Is sometimes occasioned by wounds or contusions in the head, that are attended with violent inflammations of the vessels, and if not speedily relieved, may terminate in a gangrene or a mortification, which is very often the case, and that in a few days.

Method of Cure.

In the cure of this disease, the following method must be attended to:—First lessen the quantity of blood by bleeding, which may be repeated if required, and by which the great efflux of blood upon the temporal arteries will be lessened and much retarded. The following purgative drink will be found suitable for this disease, and likewise for most fevers of an inflammatory nature.

Take of Glauber salts, 1 pound; tartarized antimony, 1 drachm; camphor, 2 drachms; treacle, 4 ounces.

Mix, and put the whole into a pitcher, and pour 3 pints of boiling water upon them.

When new-milk warm add laudanum, half an ounce, and give it all for one dose.

This drink will in general operate briskly in the space of 20 or 24 hours; if not, let one half of the quantity be given to the beast every night and morning, until the desired effect be obtained.

To cure Hoven or Blown in Cattle.

This complaint is in general occasioned by the animal feeding for a considerable time upon rich succulent food, so that the stomach becomes overcharged, and they, through their greediness to eat, forget to lie down to ruminate or chew their cud. Thus the paunch or first stomach is rendered incapable of expelling its contents; a concoction and fermentation take place in the stomach, by which a large quantity of confined air is formed in the part that extends nearly to the anus, and for want of vent at that part, causes the animal to swell even to a state of suffocation, or a rupture of some part of the stomach or intestines ensues. As sudden death is the consequence of this; the greatest caution is necessary in turning cattle into a fresh pasture, if the bite of grass be considerable; nor should they be suffered to stop too long at a time in such pastures before they are removed into a fold yard, or some close where there is but little to eat, in order that the organs of rumination and digestion may have time to discharge their functions.

If this be attended to several times, it will take away that greediness of disposition, and prevent this distressing complaint.

Treatment.

As soon as the beast is discovered to be either hoven or blown, by eating too great a quantity of succulent grasses, let a purging drink be given; this will, for the most part, check fermentation in the stomach, and in a very short time force a passage through the intestines.

Paunching.

This is a method frequently resorted to in dangerous cases. The operation is performed in the following manner:—Take a sharp penknife and gently introduce it into the paunch between the haunch bone and the last rib on the left side. This will instantly give vent to a large quantity of fetid air; a small tube of a sufficient length may then be introduced into the wound, and remain until the air is sufficiently evacuated; afterwards, take out the tube, and lay a pitch plaster over the orifice. Wounds of this kind are seldom attended with danger; where it has arisen, it has been occasioned by the injudicious operator introducing his knife into a wrong part. After the wind is expelled, and the body has been reduced to its natural state, give an opiate drink.

To cure Swimming in the Head.

This disease mostly attacks animals that have been kept in a state of poverty and starvation during the winter season; and which have in the spring of the year been admitted into a fertile pasture; hence is produced a redundancy of blood and other fluids, pressing upon the contracted vessels, while the animal economy, on the other hand, is using its utmost endeavor to restore reduced nature to its original state. If it be not checked in its infancy by bleeding, evacuating, etc., inflammation in all probability must take place; in which case the beast is attended with all the symptoms of one that is raving mad.

The cure must first be attempted by taking from two to three or four quarts of blood from the animal, according to size and strength; two or three hours after, give a purging drink.

Purging is generally necessary in this disease.

Age of Cattle, etc.

The age of the ox or cow is told chiefly by the teeth, and less perfectly by the horns. The temporary teeth are in part through at birth, and all the incisors are through in twenty days; the first, second and third pairs of temporary molars are through in thirty days; the teeth have grown large enough to touch each other by the sixth month; they gradually wear and fall in eighteen months; the fourth permanent molars are through at the fourth month; the fifth at the fifteenth; the sixth at two years. The temporary teeth begin to fall at twenty-one months, and are entirely replaced by the thirty-ninth to the forty-fifth month. The development is quite complete at from five to six years. At that time the border of the incisors has been worn away a little below the level of the grinders. At six years, the first grinders are beginning to wear, and are on a level with the incisors. At eight years, the wear of the first grinders is very apparent. At ten or eleven years, used surfaces of the teeth begin to bear a square mark surrounded by a white line; and this is pronounced on all the teeth by the twelfth year; between the twelfth and the fourteenth year this mark takes a round form. The rings on the horns are less useful as guides. At ten or twelve months the first ring appears; at twenty months to two years the second; at thirty to thirty-two months the third ring; at forty to forty-six months the fourth ring; at fifty-four to sixty months the fifth ring, and so on. But, at the fifth year, the three first rings are indistinguishable, and at the eighth year all the rings. Besides, the dealers file the horns.

Age of the Sheep.

In the sheep, the temporary teeth begin to appear in the first week, and fill the mouth at three months; they are gradually worn, and fall at about fifteen or eighteen months. The fourth permanent grinders appear at three months, and the fifth pair at twenty to twenty-seven months. A common rule is, "two broad teeth every year." The wear of the teeth begins to be marked about six years.

Age of the Pig.

The age of the pig is known up to three years by the teeth; after that there is no certainty. The temporary teeth are complete in three or four months; about the sixth month the premolars between the tusks and the first pair of molars appear; in six to ten months the tusks and posterior incisors are replaced; in twelve months to two years the other incisors; the fourth permanent molars appear at sixth months; the fifth pair at ten months; and the sixth and last at eighteen months.

MEDICINE.

General Rules for treating Diseases.

Rule 1.—In every complaint, whatever it may be called, if you find the pulse quick, hard, full, and strong, the head aching, tongue foul, skin hot, or those marks which denote it to be of an inflammatory nature, remember the plan is to reduce excitement by purging, low diet, drinking plentifully of cold water and lemonade, rest, etc.

Rule 2.—If, on the contrary, the pulse be small, soft, feeble, and intermitting, the tongue dark, and great debility or weakness is evident, reverse the whole plan; the diet must be generous and nourishing, the bowels opened with gentle laxatives, and the strength supported by bark, sulphate of quinine, wine, and tonics of various kinds.

It is necessary, however, to be careful in distinguishing the weakness which is here meant, from that state of debility which arises from excessive action, from the stuffing up of the vessels, and which requires the lancet. As a mistake might prove fatal, attention should be paid to the pulse, by which they can be known. In that state which requires tonics, the pulse is small, soft—sometimes like a thread, and quick. In the other, it is slower and full, giving considerable resistance to the pressure of the finger.

Rule 3.—If, in addition to those symptoms mentioned in the second rule, the tongue be covered with a black coat—foul, dark-looking sores form about the gums and insides of the cheeks—the breath be offensive, etc., the same class of remedies is to be vigorously employed, with a free use of acids and other antiseptic articles.

Rule 4.—Severe local pains, as in the head, side, etc., may require the use of the lancet, purging, and blisters to the part.

Rule 5.—Incessant and earnest entreaties on the part of the sick for, or longing after, any particular article of diet, if steadily persevered in, may be safely indulged, whether the use of it agrees or not with our preconceived ideas on the subject.

Rule 6.—In all fevers, where the pulse is quick, full and strong, the skin burning to the touch, and there is no perspiration, apply gently cold water over the head and limbs of the patient, wipe him dry and cover him in bed. If, in consequence of this, a chill be experienced, and the pulse sink, give warm wine, etc., and omit the water for the future. Should a pleasant glow, over the whole frame, follow the affusion, and the patient feel relieved by it, repeat it as often as may be necessary.

Rule 7.—Observe carefully, the effects of various articles of food, as well as physic, upon your own body, and choose those which experience proves to agree best with you. It is a vulgar, but true saying, that "What is one man's meat is another's poison." When, however, the stomach is out of order, do not conclude hastily that a particular article is injurious; as, at such a time, everything may seem to disagree, and the simplest things are then the best.

Rule 8.—Keep a sick room always well ventilated. Plenty of fresh air is an important remedial agent in all diseases.

It is not meant by this that the patient should be exposed to a direct current of air, which should be always avoided by well and sick.

OF THE PULSE.

The pulse is nothing more than the beating of an artery. Every time the heart contracts, a portion of blood is forced into the arteries, which dilate or swell to let it pass, and then immediately regain their former size, until by a second stroke of the same organ, a fresh column of blood is pushed through them, when a similar action is repeated. This swelling and contracting of the arteries then constitutes the pulse, and consequently it may be found in every part of the body where those vessels run near enough to the surface to be felt. Physicians look for it at the wrist from motives of convenience.

The strength and velocity of the pulse vary much in different persons, even in a state of perfect health. It averages about seventy beats a minute in adults. It is much more frequent in children than in adults; and in old men it grows more slow and feeble, owing to the decreased energy of the heart. The pulse is increased both in strength and velocity by running, walking, riding, and jumping; by eating, drinking, singing, speaking, and by joy, anger, etc. It is diminished, in like manner, by fear, want of nourishment, melancholy, excessive evacuations, or by whatever tends to debilitate the system.

In feeling the pulse, then, in sick persons, allowance should be made for these causes, or, what is better, we should wait until their temporary effects have ceased.

A full, tense, and strong pulse is when the artery swells boldly under the finger, and resists its pressure more or less; if, in addition to this, the pulsation be very rapid, it is called quick, full, and strong; if slow, the contrary.

A hard, corded pulse is that in which the artery feels like the string of a violin, or a piece of tightened cat-gut, giving considerable resistance to the pressure of the finger.

The soft and intermitting pulses are easily known by their names. In cases of extreme debility, on the approach of death, and in some particular diseases, the artery vibrates under the finger like a thread.

In feeling the pulse, three or four fingers should be laid on it at once. The most convenient spot to do this, as already mentioned, is the wrist, but it can be readily done in the temple, just before, and close to the ear, in the bend of the arm, at the under part of the lower end of the thing, among the hamstrings, and on the top of the foot.

There are two kinds of large blood-vessels in the human body: arteries and veins. The arteries carry the blood from the heart to the extremities of the body, where they are connected through the capillaries with the veins which bring it back again. An artery pulsates or beats; a vein does not.

OF FEVER.

Fever is by far the most common complaint to which the human body is subject. It may be briefly described as a combination of heat, loss of appetite, weakness, and inability to sleep. It makes its appearance in two ways: either suddenly and violently, or gradually and gently. When it comes on in the first manner, a cold shaking, attended with sickness at the stomach, or vomiting, marks its access; the cold is more severe than in the latter, as is also the pain in the head, and other symptoms. When its attack is gradual, a feeling of soreness over the whole body such as is experienced after a hard day's work by one not accustomed to it, shows its approach. Nausea, pains in the head, chills, and more or less heat and thirst soon follow.

As these symptoms vary infinitely in their degrees of violence, the treatment to be pursued must differ accordingly. Thus the same directions that are given for simple inflammatory fever must be adhered to, in one whose symptoms are lighter, though similar, only there is no necessity for pushing them to so great an extent.

Simple Inflammatory Fever.

Symptoms.— Chills, flushed face, skin hot, eyes red, pulse quick, full, strong, and regular, great thirst, tongue white, urine high-colored and small in quantity, bowels costive, breathing quick, etc.

Causes.—Cold, violent exercise while exposed to the heat of the sun, intemperance, the indulgence of unruly passions.

Treatment.—Bleed the patient, if he be robust, at the very beginning of the attack. The quantity of blood to be taken should be regulated by the strength and age of the person, and the violence of the symptoms. In this country, where diseases are very acute, from twelve to fifteen ounces is an average quantity for a robust man. If there be great pain in the head, shave it and apply a blister, or cloths wrung out of iced vinegar and water, frequently renewed. The bowels are to be freely opened with Epsom salts or citrate of magnesia, and the diet should consist of plenty of cold water, rice water, or lemonade. If the heat of the body be excessive and burning to the touch, and there is no perspiration, let cold water be applied with a sponge to his head and limbs, and then wipe him dry and cover him in bed. If there be intense pain in the head or side, apply a blister. The saline mixture, below, will be found useful throughout. An emetic, at the very onset, sometimes cuts short the disease. The room should be kept quiet, cool, and dark, every source of excitement being removed.

Saline Mixture.— Carbonate of potassa, 2 drachms; water, 6 ounces. When the salt is dissolved, add by degrees portions of fresh lemon juice till it ceases to effervesce. A tablespoonful may be taken every half hour.

Intermittent, or Fever and Ague.

Of this fever, there are several varieties, which differ from each other only in the length of time that elapses between their attacks. There is one called *quotidian,* in which it comes on every twenty-four hours; another named *tertian,* in which it arrives every forty-eight hours, and the third *quartan,* because the intermission lasts seventy-two hours.

Symptoms. — The symptoms of fever and ague are, unfortunately, too well known among us, commencing with yawning, stretching and uneasiness; this is succeeded by slight chills or shiverings, that end in a violent or convulsive shaking of the whole body. This is the cold fit, and is immediately followed by the fever or hot fit. The pulse rises, the skin becomes hot, with pain in the head, tongue white, and all the marks of fever, terminating in a profuse sweat, which gradually subsiding, leaves the patient in his natural state, though somewhat weakened.

Treatment.—On the first alarm that is given by a chill, or any of those feelings indicative of its approach, take 50 or 60 drops of laudanum in a glass of warm wine, with a little sugar and a few drops of the essence of peppermint, get into bed, and cover yourself with several blankets; this seldom fails to cut short the disease. If the cold fit, however, has passed by, the next accession should be carefully watched, and the same remedy resorted to. If the inflammatory symptoms seem to require it, open the bowels with senna and salts; when this is done, in the *intervals* use a quinine pill of one grain every hour; if it cannot be procured take as large doses Peruvian bark as the stomach will bear; in addition to this, endeavor during the cold fit to bring on the hot one, as speedily as possible, by warm drinks, bladders or bottles filled with warm water applied to the soles of the feet and the stomach. *Weak* whiskey punch answers this purpose very well, it also is of use by inducing sweat when the hot stage is formed. If the disease resists this treatment, try six drops of Fowler's Solution of Arsenic three times a day, with the bark, gradually increasing it to nine or ten drops at each dose. As this is a powerful remedy, care must be taken to watch its effects; if it produce sickness at the stomach, headache, or swelling of the face, it must be laid aside. To restore the tone of the system when getting better, remove to a healthy pure air, use gentle and daily exercise, with a generous diet, iron and bitters. If the liver or spleen become affected, recourse may sometimes be had to mercury.

Much mischief is done by giving either the quinine or the bark too early in the disease, and before its inflammatory stage is passed. It should never be employed until the bowels have been well opened and the excitement reduced.

Remittent Fever.

This is a kind of fever which occasionally abates, but does not entirely cease, before a fresh attack comes on, so that the patient is never completely free from it. The most usual form of it is called bilious fever, or bilious remittent.

Bilious Fever.

Symptoms. — In this disease all the marks of great excitement and a superfluity of bile are visible; the skin is hot, the pulse tense and full, tongue white in the commencement, changing to brown, as the fever increases, breathing hurried and anxious, bowels very costive, and skin of a yellowish hue. In bad cases, there is great pain in the head, delirium, the patient picks at the bed clothes, a convulsive jerking of the tendons at the wrist, tongue black and furred, a deep yellow skin, vomiting, and hiccup.

Causes.—A peculiar poisonous vapor from ponds, marshes, and decaying vegetable matter.

Treatment. — This must be conducted on our general principles. As the inflammatory and bilious symptoms are the most prevalent at the commencement, bleed the patient if he be robust. The next step is to open his bowels. Ten grains of calomel, combined with a portion of jalap, may be given in molasses, and repeated or followed by a saline purgative, until copious evacuations are produced. If the pain in the head be very great, shave it and apply a blister. Should the skin be very hot, and great thirst and restlessness prevail, apply cold water over the body, as directed in simple inflammatory fever. The diet should consist of rice-water, lemonade, etc., taking care to keep up a moderate discharge from the bowels by purgatives, during the whole of the disease.

If, however, in spite of all endeavors to the contrary, the complaint seems advancing, the patient should be brought carefully under the influence of quinine. As soon as symptoms of exhaustion or a typhoid state make their appearance, no mercury should be given internally; on the contrary, bark, wine, acids, etc., are necessary to support the patient, who should be kept clean, cool, and comfortable, excluding all noise. The extreme irritability of the stomach, which is frequently found in bilious fever, may be overcome by the saline draught, in a state of effervescence (to be found on page 123), and in the latter stage of it, when the pulse flags, and the system appears sinking, the quinine mixture, below, has been found extremely useful. Blisters and mustard poultices may also be applied in this case to the ankles, thighs, and wrists. The internal use of the quinine is an invaluable remedy in all such cases, and should never be omitted.

There are in fact two distinct stages in this disease that require two different plans of treatment. The first is bilious and inflammatory, and should be met by bleeding, vomiting, purging with calomel, blisters to the head, and the affusion of cold water.

The second is typhoid and bilious, and must be treated by wine, brandy, the quinine mixture, sound porter, and the peculiar plan recommended in typhoid fever.

Quinine Mixture.

Sulphate of quinine 32 grains; elixir of vitriol 1 drachm; peppermint water 4 ounces. The dose is a teaspoonful every hour or two.

Typhoid or Low Nervous Fever.

Symptoms.—Languor, debility, dejection of mind, alternate flushes of heat and chills, bleeding at the nose, loathing of food, confusion of ideas. These are succeeded by vertigo, pain in the head, cough, frequent weak and sometimes intermitting pulse, the tongue dry and covered with a brown fur, the teeth and gums being encrusted with the same, the forehead is covered with sweat, while the hands are dry and glow with heat, the patient talks wildly. There is diarrhœa and swelling of the abdomen.

Causes.—Grief, home-sickness, whatever tends to weaken the system, a poor diet, living in close, filthy apartments. Distinguish it from typhus fever by the attack coming on more gradually, and by the greater mildness of the symptoms and the want of those marks mentioned in the former.

Treatment.—If the bowels be costive give some gentle laxative, as rhubarb or castor oil. As soon as this has operated, or even before (if the weakness of the patient seem to require it), exhibit wine whey and beef-tea, always remembering that if the strength of the patient be not supported by these means, he may die of debility. Applying cold water gently over the body is a remedy in this disease, of great value. If delirium or insensibility come on, shave the head and apply a blister to it, or cloths wrong out of iced vinegar and water. If a copious purging ensue it must be stopped, or it will prove fatal; this may be done by the mixture No. 1, or by opium. Musk mixture, No. 2, and the camphor mixture, No. 3, will also be found useful. Great reliance is sometimes placed upon the sulphate of quinine, which may be taken in doses of two or three grains four times a day, dissolved in a little gum arabic tea, or in pills.

The order of remedies, then, in typhoid fever, is to open the bowels with the mildest laxatives, to use wine or sometimes brandy, to apply cold water over the body, to give milk, chicken water, jellies, tapioca, sago, etc.; to check purging, keep the room cool and clean, use the quinine mixture, one or all of the different mixtures of camphor or musk, and if delirium come on to apply blisters to the head. Bleeding is, at best, a doubtful remedy in typhoid, and should never be allowed without being ordered by a physician; nine times out of ten it is certain death to the patient.

No. 1. *Astringent Mixture.*—Chalk mixture 4 ounces; tincture of kino 1 drachm; lavender compound 1 drachm; laudanum 30 drops. Dose, a tablespoonful every two or three hours, as may be required.

No. 2. *Musk Mixture.*—Musk 1 drachm; gum arabic, powdered, 1 drachm; loaf sugar the same; water 6 ounces. Rub up the musk and sugar, adding the water very gradually. The dose is a tablespoonful every two hours.

No. 3. *Camphor Mixture.*—Camphor 30 grains; powdered gum arabic 2 drachms; loaf sugar 1½ drachms, peppermint water 6 ounces. Moisten the camphor with a few drops of spirits of wine, and rub it to a powder. The gum arabic and sugar heat to a paste, add the camphor, and pour in the water gradually. The dose is a tablespoonful every two or three hours.

Typhus Fever.

Symptoms.—Severe chills, astonishing and sudden loss of strength, countenance livid and expressive of stupor, the skin sometimes burning to the touch, at others the heat is moderate, the pulse is quick, small and rarely hard, violent pain in the head, redness of the eyes, low, muttering delirium, the tongue is covered with a dark brown or black-looking crust, blackish sores form about the gums, the breath is very offensive, and, in the latter stage, the urine also, which deposits a dark sediment; in extremely bad cases blood is poured out under the skin, forming purple spots, and breaks out from the nose and different parts of the body, the pulse flutters and sinks, hiccup comes on, and death closes the horrid scene.

Treatment.—As severe cases of this disease are apt to run their career with fatal rapidity, no time should be lost; bleeding is not admissible, the loss of a few ounces of blood being equivalent to a sentence of death. The first medicine given may be a *mild* purgative; castor oil will answer the purpose. If the heat of the patient's body be great, sponge him with vinegar and water. This practice produces the happiest results. As soon as he is wiped dry, and has taken the wine if chilled, give four drops of nitro-muriatic acid in a wine glass of the cold infusion of bark every four hours. Wine and water should generally be liberally given in this disease as soon as the typhus symptoms show themselves. Liquid food, as milk or beef tea, should be given at short intervals. The sulphate of quinine in the same doses as mentioned in typhoid is a valuable remedy.

As a wash for the mouth, nothing is better than an ounce of alum dissolved in a pint of water. Rest at night must be procured by opium, if necessary. If towards the end of the complaint there arise a gentle looseness, accompanied with a moisture on the skin, that seems likely to prove critical, it should not be meddled with; but otherwise it must be stopped by astringents. As this is a contagious disease, all unnecessary communication with the sick should be forbidden. The chamber should be kept cool, clean, and frequently sprinkled with vinegar, and all nuisances be immediately removed. Much advantage will result from taking the patient, on the very commencement of the attack, into a new and healthy atmosphere.

Hectic Fever.

This is never a primary disease, but is always found as a symptom of some other one, as consumption.

Symptoms.—Night sweats, bowels costive at first, then loose, alternate chills and flushes, a circumscribed spot on the cheeks, especially in the afternoon, a peculiar delicacy of complexion, and emaciation to so great a degree that the patient sometimes looks like a living skeleton.

Treatment. — Remove the cause, if possible, by curing the disease of which it is a symptom; and support the strength of the patient.

Inflammation of the Brain.

Symptoms. — Intense pain in the head, the eyes incapable of bearing the light, delirium, face flushed, oppression at the breast, the pulse hard and very rapid, tongue at first of a fiery red, then yellow, brown or black.

Causes. — Exposure to excessive heat of the sun, blows on the head, intense application to study, intemperance. Distinguish it from inflammatory fever by the pulse, which in the one is full, strong and regular, in the other hard, quick and corded, and by the raving delirium. From typhus by the two latter marks.

Treatment. — Bleed the patient (as quickly as possible) until he nearly faints. Upon the resolute employment of the lancet in the onset we must place our chief dependence. The bowels should be freely opened with Epsom salts, the head shaved, and a blister or cloths dipped in iced vinegar and water, or pounded ice, be applied to it, and the room kept perfectly cool, dark and quiet. Rice-water, lemonade, or cold water is to be the only diet. Should the violence of the disease not give way to these remedies, repeat the purging, blistering, etc., as often as may be necessary. The most vigorous measures to reduce the inflammation are required, or death will be the consequence. Quietness of mind and body is also essential throughout the attack.

Headache.

Causes. — Some particular disorder of which it is a symptom. Indigestion, a foul stomach, tight cravats or shirt collars, exposure to the heat of the sun, a rushing of blood into the head, neuralgia, etc.

Treatment. — This will vary according to the cause. If it arises from indigestion, that must be attended to. A foul stomach is one of the most usual causes of headache. In this case, from three to six grains of blue mass may be administered, which, at a day's or night's interval, should be followed by a purgative. If from the beating of the artery in the temples, and a sense of fulness in the head, we suspect it to originate from an undue determination to that part, bleed freely, or cup or leech, and apply cloths dipped in cold water to it. Long-continued and obstinate headache has been frequently benefited by a seton on the back of the neck.

Inflammation of the Eye.

Symptoms. — Pain, heat and swelling of the parts, which appear bloodshot, the tears hot and scalding, fever, intolerance of light; sometimes when the lids are affected the edges become ulcerated.

Causes. — External injuries, as blows, particles of sand, etc., getting into them, exposure to cold, a strong light, intemperance.

Treatment. — If the complaint is caused by foreign bodies, they must be removed with the point of a paint brush, or the end of a piece of wire covered with lint, or washed out by injecting warm milk and water into the eye with a small syringe. If particles of iron stick in it they may be drawn out by a magnet. From whatever circumstance it may originate, the inflammation is to be subdued by taking blood from the neighborhood of the eye by a dozen or more leeches. The bowels should be freely opened with Epsom salts, and a cold lead-water poultice, enclosed in a piece of thin gauze, be laid over the part. The room should be perfectly dark and the diet extremely low. Rose-water may be used as a lotion. If the pain is very severe, a small quantity of equal parts of laudanum and water may be dropped into the eye. If the eye-lids are ulcerated, touch them with the white vitriol ointment. Bathing the eye frequently with clear cold water is a refreshing and useful practice. If the eye-ball be ulcerated over the pupil, lead-water must be avoided; as, in that case, it might cause opacity.

There are many other diseases incident to the eyes, but none that can be managed by any but a physician or surgeon. When, therefore, any alteration in the structure of the eye is perceived, no time should be lost in having recourse to the one or the other.

Inflammation of the Ear.

Symptoms. — Pain in the ear, which at last either gradually ceases, or matter is discharged through the opening.

Causes. — The accumulation of hard wax, insects getting into it, injuries from blows, etc.

Treatment. — A little warm olive oil or glycerin, with an equal part of laudanum, dropped into the ear, and retained there by a piece of wool or cotton, will frequently procure almost instant relief. If it be caused by hard wax, inject warm soapsuds or salt water to soften it, and then, with care, endeavor to extract it, when the oil and laudanum may again be employed. In cases of great severity a blister may be applied behind the ear. A temporary deafness frequently results from this complaint, and sometimes, when matter is formed, the bones of the organ are destroyed, and hearing is lost forever.

Bleeding from the Nose.

Causes. — Fullness of blood, violent exercise, particular positions of the body, blows, etc.

Treatment. — Keep the patient erect or sitting, with his head thrown a little backwards, take off his cravat, unbutton his shirt collar, and expose him freely to the cold air; apply ice or cold vinegar and water to the back of his neck. If the pulse be full, bleed him from the arm. If these are not sufficient, moisten a plug of linen or cotton with brandy, roll it in powdered alum, and screw it up the nostril. A piece of catgut may also be passed through the nostril into the throat, drawn out at the mouth, and a bit of sponge be fastened to it and drawn back again, so as to make the sponge block up the posterior nostril. In doing this it is necessary to leave a piece of the catgut so as to be got hold of, in order to withdraw the sponge. It is seldom, however, that the first remedies will not answer the purpose. The patient should avoid removing the clots which form until the bleeding has entirely ceased.

Polypus.

The nose is subject to two species of this tumor, the pear-shaped or pendulous polypus, and a flattened, irregular excrescence, which is extremely painful and is of a cancerous nature. As soon as any affection of this kind is suspected, apply to a surgeon.

Cancer of the Lip.

This kind of cancer generally commences in a small crack, which, after a while, becomes exquisitely painful. If closely examined, this crack is found to be seated in a small, hard tumor, which soon ulcerates, and, if not checked, extends the disorder to the throat, thereby endangering life.

Treatment. — The knife is the only remedy for this, as well as every other species of cancer, and no time should be lost in resorting to a surgeon.

Mercurial Ulcers in the Mouth.

Large, dark-looking ulcers in the mouth are a common effect of the abuse of mercury. They may be known by the horrid smell of the breath, by the teeth being loosened from the gums, and by a coppery taste in the mouth.

Treatment.—Omit all mercurial preparations, wash the mouth frequently with sage tea or brandy and water, and keep the bowels open with sulphur.

Ulcers and Pimples on the Tongue.

Small pimples are occasionally found on the tongue, which at last form ulcers. Sometimes they are occasioned by the rough and projecting edge of a broken or decayed tooth: when this is the cause, the part must be rounded by a file or the tooth extracted, when the sore will heal without further trouble. Whitish-looking specks, which seem inclined to spread, are also met with on the inside of the cheeks and lips. They are easily removed by touching their surfaces with burnt alum.

Cancer of the Tongue.

Cancer of the tongue commences like that of the lip, being a crack or fissure in a small, hard, deep-seated tumor on the side of the tongue.

Treatment.—No time should be lost in useless attempts to cure it by medicines. The only safety for the patient is in the knife, and that at an early period.

Enlargement of the Uvula.

The uvula is that little tongue-like appendage that hangs down from the middle of the fleshy curtain which divides the mouth from the throat. It is very subject to inflammation, the consequence of which is that it becomes so long that its point touches, and sometimes even lies along the tongue, which creates considerable uneasiness, and is now and then the cause of a constant cough, which finally ends in consumption. It is commonly called the falling of the palate.

Treatment.—Strong gargles of vinegar and water, or a decoction of black-oak bark, or a watery solution of alum, will frequently cure the complaint. It happens very frequently, however, that in consequence of repeated attacks it becomes permanently lengthened, and then the only resource is to cut off the end of it. If you are near a physician apply to him; if not, the operation is so simple that any man of common dexterity can perform it, particularly as little or no blood follows the incision. All that is requisite is to seat the patient, seize the part with a hook, or a slender pair of pincers, draw it a little forward, and snap off its point with a pair of scissors.

Swelling of the Tonsils.

The tonsils are two glands situated in the throat, one on each side, which are very apt to swell from inflammation by colds. They sometimes become so large as to threaten suffocation.

Treatment.—In the commencement this is the same as directed for inflammatory sore throat, which see. If it does not succeed, apply to a surgeon to take them away.

Inflammatory Sore Throat.

Symptoms.—Chills and flushes of heat succeeding each other; fever; the inside of the mouth, the throat and tonsils much inflamed; swallowing is painful; hoarseness; beat and darting pains in the throat.

Causes.—Cold; sitting in damp clothes; wet feet; excessive exertions of voice.

Distinguish it from diphtheria by the fever being inflammatory, the absence of ash-colored patches near the tonsils, etc.

Treatment.—An emetic taken at a very early stage of this disorder will frequently prevent it from forming. The next step is to leech the patient freely and give him a large dose of Epsom salts. A mustard poultice or blister to the throat is an invaluable application, and should never be neglected. The room should be kept cool and quiet, and the diet consist of barley or rice-water. The throat may be gargled several times in the day with alum and water; inhaling the steam of hot water from the spout of a tea pot is of use.

Putrid Sore Throat or Diptheria.

Symptoms.—Difficulty of swallowing; respiration hurried; breath hot; skin dry and burning; a quick, weak and irregular pulse; scarlet patches break out about the lips, and the inside of the mouth and throat is of a fiery red color. About the second or third day, upon examining the throat, a number of specks or patches between an ash and a dark brown color are observed on the palate, uvula, tonsils, etc.; a brown fur covers the tongue; the lips are covered with little vesicles or bladders, which burst and give out a thin, acrid matter that produces ulceration wherever it touches. In bad cases the inside of the mouth and throat become black, and are covered with foul spreading ulcers, and all the symptoms that characterize low fever ensue.

Distinguish it from scarlet fever by the fever being a typhus and not inflammatory, and by the peculiar sore throat, and from measles by the absence of cough, sneezing, watering of the eyes, etc.

Treatment.—Bleeding in this disease is absolutely forbidden. The same may be said of active or strong purgatives. The bowels, however, should be kept open by mild laxatives or clysters. Emetics are used in the beginning with advantage, but the great and evident indication is to prevent and counteract the disposition to putrescency, and to support the strength. For this purpose the cold infusion of bark, or bark in substance, with ten or twelve drops of muriatic acid and eight or nine drops of laudanum, should be taken frequently, and in large doses. Chlorate of potassa is a valuable article; it may be taken in solution, twenty grains for an adult every two hours, in a teaspoonful of water. To cleanse the throat, gargle frequently with vinegar or muriatic acid and water or glycerin. The diet should consist of milk, arrow-root, jelly, panada, tapioca and gruel, and the drink of wine whey, wine and water, etc., increasing the quantity of the wine according to the weakness and age of the patient. The greatest cleanliness is to be observed in the chamber. As this disease is thought by some to be contagious, all unnecessary communication with the sick room should be prevented.

Strictures in the Throat.

Symptoms.—The first mark of an obstruction or stricture in the throat is a slight difficulty in swallowing solids, which continues increasing for months, or until the passage becomes so contracted that the smallest particle of food cannot pass, but having remained an instant in the strictured part is violently rejected. If the obstacle is not removed the patient starves.

Treatment.—Meddle not with the complaint yourself, for you can do nothing to relieve it, but apply with all speed to a surgeon, and remember that life is at stake.

Catarrh or Cold.

Symptoms.—A dull pain in the head; swelling and redness of the eyes; the effusion of a thin, acrid mucus from the nose; hoarseness; cough; fever, etc.

Treatment.—If the symptoms be violent, bleed and give twenty drops of hartshorn in half a pint of warm vinegar whey. Hoarhound and boneset tea, taken in large quantities, are very useful. The patient should be confined to his bed, and be freely purged. If there is great pain in the breast, apply a blister to it. To ease the cough take one teaspoonful of No. 1 every thirty minutes, or till relief is obtained.

The Influenza is nothing more than an aggravated and epidemic state of catarrh, and is to be cured by the same remedies. No cough or cold is too light to merit attention. Neglected colds lay the foundations for diseases that every year send thousands to the grave.

No. 1. *Cough Mixture.*—Paregoric ½ in ounce; syrup of squills 1 ounce; antimonial wine 2 drachms; water 6 ounces. Dose is one teaspoonful every thirty minutes, or at longer intervals, till the cough abates.

Asthma.

Symptoms.—A tightness across the breast; frequent short breathing, attended with a wheezing, increased by exertion and when in bed. It comes on in fits or paroxysms.

Treatment.—If the cough be violent and frequent, with great pain in the breast, and the patient be young and robust, it may be necessary to bleed or cup him. In old people it should be resorted to with caution. The tincture* of lobelia is highly recommended in asthma. It should be taken in doses of a very few drops at first, and cautiously increased. If the pulse sinks under it, or nausea, giddiness, etc., is produced, it must be laid aside. In fact, it is hardly prudent to take this active and dangerous article, except under a physician's care. The dried roots of the thorn-apple and skunk-cabbage are sometimes smoked through a pipe for the same purpose, soaked in a solution of nitre and dried. Asthma is a disease that is seldom completely cured by art; nature, however, occasionally effects it.

Pleurisy.

Symptoms.—A sharp pain or stitch in the side, increased upon breathing, inability to lie on the affected side, pulse hard, quick and corded, tongue white.

Treatment.—Take away at once from twelve to fifteen ounces of blood, place a large blister over the side, and give a full dose of Epsom salts. Follow the bleeding by cups if relief is not obtained; and afterwards a blister. All the remedies for the reduction of inflammation must be actively employed. The patient should be confined to his bed, with the head and shoulders a little elevated, and if pain be severe, especially at night, 10 grains of Dover's powder may be given. The diet should always consist of rice or barley-water, gruel, etc.

Spitting of Blood.

Symptoms.—Blood of a bright red color, often frothy, brought up by coughing.

Causes.—Consumption, a fulness of blood, rupture of a blood vessel from any cause. Distinguish it from vomiting of blood by its bright color, and being brought up with coughing.

Treatment.—Give the patient at once a tablespoonful of common salt, and direct him to swallow it slowly. If the pulse be full, and he be robust, bleed him. The sugar of lead has much reputation in this complaint: two or three grains of it, with from a half to a whole grain of opium, may be taken every three or four hours, and in severe cases, where the blood flows rapidly, five or six grains, with two of opium, may be taken at once. The most perfect rest should be strictly enjoined, and the diet should be cooling and simple.

Consumption.

Symptoms.—A short, dry cough, languor and gradual loss of strength, pulse small, quick, and soft, pain in the breast, expectoration of a frothy matter, that at last becomes solid and yellow, the breathing grows more anxious and hurried, the emaciation and pain increase, hectic fever, night sweats, and a looseness of the bowels come on, and the patient, unsuspicious of danger, dies.

Causes.—Neglected colds, dissipation, hereditary tendency, etc. Distinguish it by the long-continued cough, pain in the breast, and great emaciation, by the substance thrown up containing pus, in common language, matter. It is known by its being opaque, mixing with water, and heavier than it, so that if thrown into a vessel containing that fluid it sinks to the bottom. When thrown upon hot coals it yields an offensive odor.

Treatment.—In a confirmed state of consumption, nothing that art has hitherto been able to do can afford us any solid hopes of a cure. When once the disease is firmly seated in the lungs all that is possible is to smooth the passage to the grave, and perhaps for a while to retard it. If, however, the disease is taken in its very bud, much may be done by a change of climate, a milk diet, cod-liver oil, moderate daily exercise on horseback, and by carefully avoiding cold and all exciting causes. A removal to a warm climate should be the first step taken, if practicable; if not, a voyage to sea or a long journey on horseback. A complete suit of flannel, worn next the skin, is an indispensable article for every one who is even inclined to this most fatal disorder.

Palpitation of the Heart.

The symptoms of this complaint must be obvious from its name. When it arises from organic disease of the heart or its vessels, nothing can be done to cure it. The patient should be careful to avoid a full habit of body, and abstain from violent exercise and sexual indulgences. He should live low, and keep as quiet and composed as possible. A fit of anger, or any imprudence, may cost him his life. There is a milder kind of this disease, resulting from debility, nervousness, indigestion, etc., which must be remedied by restoring the strength of the general system. It is also symptomatic of other diseases, and must be treated accordingly.

Dropsy of the Chest.

Symptoms.—Great difficulty of breathing, which is increased by lying down, oppression and weight at the breast, countenance pale or livid, and extremely anxious, great thirst, pulse irregular and intermitting, cough, violent palpitation of the heart, the patient can lie on one side only, or cannot lie down at all, so that he is obliged to sleep sitting, frightful dreams, a feeling of suffocation, etc.

Treatment.—All that can be done is to follow the same plan that is laid down for the treatment of dropsy in general, which consists of purging and diuretics. When the water appears to be confined to one cavity of the chest, and the oppression cannot be borne, some relief may be obtained by a surgical operation.

Inflammation of the Stomach.

Symptoms.—A fixed, burning pain in the stomach, small, very quick hard pulse, sudden and

---

* Take a sufficient quantity of the leaves, stem and pods of the plant, put them into a bottle and fill it up with brandy or spirits, and let it remain for a few days.

great weakness, the pain in the stomach increased on the slightest pressure, vomiting, hiccup.

Causes.—Cold suddenly applied to the body or stomach, drinking largely of cold water while very warm. The striking in of eruptions, poisons, gout, rheumatism. Distinguish it from inflammation of the bowels by the seat of the pain, which is just below the breast bone, in what is called the pit of the stomach, the burning heat and pain there, by the hiccup and vomiting.

Treatment.—The softness of the pulse is here no rule to go by, for it is caused by the disease. The rule is to bleed or leech over the pit of the stomach. From ten to twenty ounces may be taken in a full stream from a robust man at the beginning. As soon as he is bled, or while the blood is flowing, put him into a warm bath, and have a large blister prepared, which, after he has remained some time in the bath, should be applied directly over the stomach. A warm laxative clyster is now to be thrown up, and when the stomach will retain it, give him small quantities of arrow root jelly or gum arabic tea from time to time, with a few drops of laudanum. The most rigid diet must be observed, and the patient kept very quiet. When the inflammation is reduced, and the stomach will bear it, a grain of solid opium may be given occasionally with advantage. If the disease has been brought on by poison taken into the stomach, apply the remedies directed in such cases. If mortification ensues, death is the inevitable consequence. It is known to exist when from the state of torture we have just described there is a sudden change to one of perfect ease.

Cramp in the Stomach.

Symptoms.—Violent spasmodic pain in the stomach, which is so severe as nearly to occasion fainting.

Treatment.—Give thirty to sixty drops of laudanum, in a teaspoonful of ether, with a little hot wine. Apply a mustard plaster over the stomach, bladders or bottles filled with warm water to the soles of the feet, or put the patient into the warm bath. If the first dose of laudanum does not relieve the pain, repeat it.

Hiccups.

Symptoms.—A spasmodic affection of the stomach and diaphragm, producing the peculiar noise which gives rise to the name.

Treatment.—When hiccups occur at the close of any disease, they may be considered the harbingers of death; they, however, frequently arise from acidity in the stomach and other causes. A long draught of cold water, a sudden surprise or fright puts an end to them. A blister over the stomach may be applied for the same purpose. I have succeeded in relieving a violent case of hiccups, that resisted every other remedy, by the oil of amber, in doses of five drops every ten minutes. It may be taken in a little mint-water. Camphor is also useful.

Heartburn.

This common and distressing affection is generally connected with indigestion. To relieve it for the moment, magnesia, soda, or Seltzer water, or water acidulated with sulphuric acid, may be employed. To cure the complaint requires the digestive powers to be strengthened by tonics, bitters, and the different preparations of iron, etc., as directed for indigestion. The application of a blister over the stomach may be of use. The white oxide of bismuth in six grain doses, three times a day, taken in milk, has been found of service.

Indigestion, or Dyspepsia.

Symptoms.—Want of appetite; low spirits; pains and fullness in the stomach; belching; a sour water rising in the mouth; heartburn; the bowels irregular and generally costive; weakness and emaciation; pulse small and slow; pain in the head; skin dry; great uneasiness after eating.

Causes.—All those which induce debility; eating too rapidly, without chewing the food; excessive indulgence in the pleasures of the table, or intemperance in any way; a sedentary life, or want of exercise; a diseased liver.

Treatment.—In every case of indigestion, the first thing the patient should do is to abstain from whatever may have tended to produce it. The diet should consist of animal food that is light, nourishing, and easily digested. Roasted beef or mutton is perhaps preferable to any other. Country air and constant exercise on horseback are invaluable remedies in this disease, which, as it is generally occasioned by a departure from natural habits and employments, must be relieved by a return to them. Flannel should be worn next the skin, and care taken to avoid cold or exposure to wet. A wine-glass of the infusion of bark and quassia (made by placing one ounce of powdered bark and one of ground quassia in a close vessel, to which is added a quart of boiling water; to be kept simmering near the fire until the whole is reduced to a pint), with ten or twelve drops of the elixir of vitriol, should be regularly taken, three times a day, for months. The bowels are to be kept open by some warm laxative as rhubarb, and the whole frame braced by the daily use of the cold bath. Weak spirits and water, or a single glass of sound old Madeira may be taken at dinner. Much benefit has been found to result from a long-continued use of the wine of iron (made by taking iron-filings 4 ounces, and pouring on it 4 pints of Madeira wine; let it stand for a month, shaking it frequently), a glass of which may be taken twice a day. If the complaint arise from a diseased liver, recourse must be had to the plan laid down for its cure.

An attack of temporary indigestion may be treated by abstinence, rest, and a teaspoonful of magnesia, if the bowels be costive, otherwise a quarter of a teaspoonful of the bicarbonate of soda.

Vomiting of Blood.

Symptoms.—A flow of dark blood from the stomach, preceded by a sense of weight and oppression in that organ. The blood is generally mixed with particles of food, etc.

Distinguish it from spitting of blood, by its dark color, and being mixed with food.

Treatment.—If the accompanying symptoms be inflammatory, bleed or cup, and use some cooling purge; if otherwise, try fifteen drops of the muriated tincture of iron, with six of laudanum, in a glass of water, every hour till the bleeding ceases. If the cause be a diseased liver, or tumor in the neighborhood, treat it accordingly.

Inflammation of the Liver.

Symptoms.—A dull pain in the right side below the rib, which is more sensible on pressure; an inability to lie on the left side; pain in the right shoulder; a sallow complexion. Such are the symptoms of an acute attack of this disease. There is another species of it called chronic, in which its approaches are so gradual that it is a difficult matter to determine its nature. It commences with all the symptoms of indigestion, and ends in jaundice or dropsy.

Causes.—Long-continued fever and ague; drunkenness, or a free use of spirituous liquors is a very common cause; injuries from blows, etc.

Distinguish it from pleurisy by the pain not

being so severe, and by its extending to the top of the shoulder; by not being able to rest on the left side.

Treatment.—Bleed or cup the patient according to his age, strength, and the violence of the pain, and, if necessary, apply a blister over the part, which may be kept open by dressing it with the savin ointment. The bowels should be opened by Epsom salts or calomel and jalap. If this does not abate the symptoms in a few days, give a calomel pill of one-half grain every five hours, or rub a drachm of the strongest mercurial ointment into the side until the gums are found to be a little sore, when the frictions or pills must be discontinued until the mouth is well, and then again resorted to as before. If an abscess points outwardly, apply bread and milk poultices to the tumor, omit the mercury, use wine, bark, and a generous diet. As soon as matter is to be felt within it, open it at its lowest and most projecting part with the point of a sharp lancet, and let out its contents very slowly, taking care not to close the wound till this is completely effected. The nitromuriatic acid, in doses of four drops, three times a day, steadily persevered in, will sometimes produce a cure. A tea made of the root or leaves of the dandelion is sometimes medicinal in liver complaint.

Jaundice.

Symptoms.—Languor; loathing of food; a bitter taste in the mouth; vomiting; the skin and eyes of a yellow color; the stools clayey, and the urine giving a yellow tinge to rags dipped in it. There is a full pain in the right side, under the last rib, which is increased by pressure. When the pain is severe, there is fever; the pulse hard and full, etc.

Causes.—An interruption to the regular passage of the bile, which is retained in or carried into the blood. It may be occasioned by gall-stones, a diseased liver, etc. Intemperance is a very common cause, hence tipplers are more subject to it than others.

Treatment.—If the pulse be full and hard, the pain great, and other inflammatory symptoms be present, blood is to be taken away as freely as the age and strength of the patient, and the violence of the pain, seems to demand. He should then be placed in a warm bath, and allowed to remain there some time; when removed to bed, a grain or two of opium may be given every few hours until the pain is relieved. Bladders partly filled with warm water, or cloths wrung out of hot decoctions of herbs, may also be applied to the seat of the pain. If the stomach be so irritable as not to retain anything on it, try fomentations and the effervescing mixture, or a blister to the part. As soon as some degree of ease is obtained by these means, purgatives must be employed, and steadily persevered in; calomel and jalap or Epsom salts, in the ordinary doses, answer very well. If, however, this cannot be done, and, from the pain being acute at one particular spot, there is reason to suppose that a gall-stone is lodged there, the following remedy may be tried, of which one-fifth or a little less may be taken every morning, drinking freely of chicken broth, flaxseed tea, or barley water after it.

Ether 3 drachms; spirits of turpentine, 2 drachms. Mix them.

The diet ought to be vegetable, and should the disease have arisen from a neglected inflammation of the liver, it must be treated accordingly. (See Inflammation of the Liver.) Regular exercise (on horseback, if possible) should never be neglected by persons subject to this disease in its chronic form.

Ague Cake.

This is the vulgar appellation for an enlarged spleen, and expresses, with much brief meaning, the cause of the complaint, as it generally results from ill-treated or obstinate intermittents. It is, however, not productive of much uneasiness, and frequently disappears of itself. The plan of treatment, if there is acute pain in the part, is to purge and blister. If it remains enlarged after this, mercury may be carefully resorted to, as directed in chronic inflammation of the liver.

Inflammation of the Intestines.

Symptoms.—Sharp pain in the bowels, which shoots round the navel, and which is increased by pressure, sudden loss of strength, vomiting of dark-colored, sometimes excrementitious matter, costiveness, small, quick, and hard pulse, high-colored urine.

Distinguish it from colic, by the pain being increased by pressure, whereas in colic it is relieved by it.

Treatment.—This is another of those formidable diseases that require the most actively reducing measures in the onset. From ten to twenty ounces of blood ought to be taken away at once, and the patient placed in a warm bath, after which a large blister should be applied to the belly. Emollient and laxative clysters may be injected from time to time, and if the vomiting and irritability of the stomach permit it to be retained, give a dose of castor oil. If this be rejected too, the oil mixture No. 1. This, however, though one of great importance, is a secondary consideration; to subdue the inflammation, by bleeding or leeching, being the great object. The diet should consist of barley or rice-water only. If in the latter stages of the disease, when the inflammation has somewhat subsided, an obstinate costiveness be found to resist all the usual remedies, dashing cold water over the belly will sometimes succeed.

Remember that this complaint frequently runs its course in a day or two, and that, unless treatment be promptly employed in the very beginning, mortification and death will ensue. If a strangulated rupture occasion the disease, the same, and, if possible, still stronger reasons exist for bleeding, previously to any attempts at reduction. When certain quantities are mentioned, it is always to be understood that they are applicable to robust men. Common sense will dictate the necessity of diminishing them, as the patient may fall more or less short of this description. If strangulated rupture be feared, surgical aid should be early obtained.

No. 1. *Oil Mixture.*—The yolk of one egg; castor oil, 2 ounces. Mix them well, and add lavender compound, 2 drachms; sugar, 1 ounce; water, 5 ounces. Mix them well. The dose is a tablespoonful every hour till it operates, or half the quantity at once; the remainder, in divided doses, if no passage is obtained after a space of four hours.

Cholera Morbus

Symptoms.—A violent vomiting and purging of bile, preceded by a pain in the stomach and bowels; quick, weak, and fluttering pulse; heat, thirst, cold sweats, hiccups, and sometimes death in a few hours.

Treatment.—Bladders or bottles containing hot water should be applied to the feet, and flannel cloths wrung out of hot spirits, or a mustard plaster, be laid over the stomach. When it is supposed that the stomach is sufficiently cleared, give two grains of solid opium in a pill, and repeat half the quantity every few hours, as the case may require. If the weakness be very great, and the spasms so alarming as to cause a fear of the immediate result, the quantity of opium may be increased carefully. If the pill will not remain in the stomach, give eighty or ninety drops of laudanum, in a tablespoonful of thin starch, by clyster, and repeat it as often as may be necessary. Fifty or sixty drops of laudanum in a small quantity of strong mint tea, or the effervescing draught, will frequently succeed in allaying the irritation. If all these means fail, apply a blister to the stomach. For thirst, give ice; a little at once. To complete the recovery, and to guard against a second attack, a complete casing of flannel is requisite, together with the use of vegetable bitters and tonics. Persons subject to this disease should be cautious in their diet and avoid exposure to moist, cold air.

Dysentery.

Symptoms.—Fever; frequent small stools, accompanied by griping, bearing down pains, the discharge consisting of pure blood or blood and matter, sometimes resembling the shreds or washings of raw flesh; a constant desire to go to stool.

Distinguish it from diarrhœa or lax by the fever, griping pains, and the constant desire to evacuate the bowels, by the discharge itself being blood, or matter streaked with blood, etc.

Treatment.—As dysentery or bloody flux is almost always in this country connected with considerable inflammation, it will be proper, in some cases, to bleed the patient at the beginning of the attack. Whether it be thought prudent to bleed or not, an early dose of castor oil, with clysters of the same, and the application of blisters to the belly should never be omitted. The stomach and bowels may be cleansed by barley or rice-water taken by the mouth and in clysters. As soon as this is effected give half a grain of opium with half a grain of ipecac every two, three or four hours. The diet should consist of gum arabic dissolved in milk, arrow-root jelly, barley-water, etc. Clysters of the same articles, with the addition of an ounce of olive oil and twenty drops of laudanum, may be likewise injected. Towards the latter end of the complaint, opium and astringents are proper, and indeed necessary. I say the latter end of it, for in the commencement they would be hurtful. In this stage of it also, if a severe tenesmus (or constant desire to go to stool) remains, anodyne clysters, as of forty to eighty drops of laudanum in an ounce of starch will be found useful, or what is more effectual, a couple of grains of opium placed just within the fundament. The various astringents which are proper for dysentery in its latter stages, are found below, and may be used, with port wine and water, as a drink:

Astringents.—Acetate of lead 1 scruple; opium 10 grains. Divide into twenty pills. Take one every two, three or four hours.

Tincture of catechu 2 ounces. Take two teaspoonsful in a little port wine every hour, or oftener if required; or,

Extract of logwood 20 grains; cinnamon water 2 ounces; tincture of kino 1 drachm; sugar 2 drachms. To be taken at once.

Diarrhœa or Lax.

Symptoms.—Repeated and large discharges of a thin excrementitious matter by stool, sometimes attended with griping and a rumbling noise in the bowels.

Treatment.—If the disease arises from cold, a few doses of the chalk mixture, No. 1, will frequently put an end to it. It is, however, sometimes necessary to begin with an emetic of twenty grains of ipecacuanha, and then open the bowels by some mild purgative, as castor oil or rhubarb. Bathing the feet in warm water, and copious draughts of boneset tea, will be found of great benefit if it originate from suppressed perspiration. For the same purpose, also, from six to ten grains of Dover's powder may be taken at night, being careful not to drink much for some time after it. If worms are the cause, treat it as directed. When it is occasioned by mere weakness, and in the latter stages of it (proceed from what it may), when every irritating matter is expelled, opium, combined with astringents, is necessary as in the similar period of dysentery. The diet should consist, in the beginning, of rice, arrow-root, sago, etc., and subsequently of roasted chicken. Weak brandy and water, or port wine and water, may accompany the chicken for a common drink. Persons subject to complaints of this kind should defend their bowels from the action of cold by a flannel shirt; the feet and other parts of the body should also be kept warm.

No. 1. *Chalk Mixture.*— Prepared chalk 2 drachms; loaf sugar 1 drachm. Rub them well together in a mortar, and add gradually of mucilage of gum arabic 1 ounce; water 6 ounces; lavender compound 2 drachms; laudanum 30 drops. The dose is a tablespoonful every hour, or oftener. Shake the bottle well before pouring out the liquid, or the chalk will be at the bottom.

Colic.

Symptoms.—Violent shooting pain that twists round the navel; the skin of the belly drawn into balls; obstinate costiveness; sometimes a vomiting of excrement.

Distinguish it from inflammation of the bowels by the pain being relieved by pressure, and from other diseases by the twisting round the navel, the skin being drawn into balls, etc.

Treatment.—The first thing to be done in this disease is to give a dose of oil or magnesia with laudanum in a little peppermint water, and apply a mustard poultice over or below the navel. Forty, sixty or seventy drops of laudanum may be given at once, as the pain is more or less violent, and the dose may be repeated in a half hour, or less time, if ease is not procured. During this time, if the first doses of laudanum are found ineffectual in reducing the pain, and it is very great, eighty or ninety drops may be given as a clyster in a gill of gruel or warm water. One great rule in the treatment of colic, where the pain is excessive, is to continue the use of opium in such increased doses as will relieve it. When this result is obtained, castor oil by the mouth and clyster must be employed to open the bowels.

In bilious colic, when there is vomiting of bile, the effervescing draught, with thirty drops of laudanum, may be taken to quiet the stomach, to which flannels wrung out of warm spirits may be applied. When the vomiting has abated, the oil mixture or the pills below should be taken until a free discharge is procured. If, notwithstanding our endeavors, the disease proceeds to such an extent as to induce a vomiting of excrement, the tobacco clyster must be tried, or an attempt be made to fill the intestines with warm water. This is done by forcibly injecting it in large quantities, at the same time the patient swallows as much as he is able. In this way, with a proper syringe, two gallons have been successfully introduced. In all cases of colic, when there is obstinate costiveness, an examination of the fundament should be made with the finger. If there are any hard, dry pieces of excrement there, they may be removed either by the finger or the handle of a spoon. Examination of the groin and navel should also be made, to see if there be a rupture which may be strangulated.

Those who are subject to colic should avoid fermented liquors and much vegetable food; be always well clothed, and take care not to expose themselves to cold and wet. The bowels should never be allowed to remain costive.

Purgative Pills.—Of calomel and jalap each 10 grains; opium 1½ grain; tartar emetic ½ a grain; oil of aniseed 1 drop. Make the whole into a mass. To be taken at once, or divided into pills, if the patient prefer it.

Painter's Colic.

Symptoms.—Pain and weight in the belly; belching; constant desire to go to stool, which is ineffectual; quick, contracted pulse; the belly becomes painful to the touch, and is drawn into knots; constant colic pains; the patient sits in a bent position: after a while palsy of part or of the whole body.

Treatment.—This disease is too apt to end in palsy, leaving the hands and limbs contracted and useless. In every case of colic, whose symptoms resemble the above, if the person has been exposed to lead in any of its shapes, all doubt on the subject vanishes.

Give laudanum in moderate doses, and rub the belly well with warm spirits, and place him in a bath as hot as he can bear. As soon as he is well dried, and has rested in bed a few minutes, take him up and dash a bucket of cold water over his belly and thighs, or mix an ounce of sulphate of magnesia in a pint of water, and give a wineglassful every half hour until ease is obtained. If this, with castor oil by the mouth and in clysters will not produce a stool, apply a large blister to the belly. As soon as the symptoms are somewhat abated, castor oil or laxative clysters may be resorted to for the purpose of keeping the bowels open, and to guard against a return small doses of opium should be taken from time to time. Bitters, the different preparations of iron, bark, etc., are necessary to restore the strength of the system.

Worms.

Symptoms.—Intolerable itching at the nose, sometimes at the fundament, disagreeable breath; grinding of the teeth and starting during sleep; hardness of the belly; gradual emaciation; colic, and sometimes convulsions.

Treatment.—This will vary according to the kind of worm that is to be destroyed. They are of three kinds:

The White Thread-Worm

Resembles a small piece of white thread, and is usually found near the fundament, at the lower end of the guts, where it produces a contraction of the parts, and a most intolerable itching. Clysters of lime-water will frequently bring the whole nest of them away, and procure instant relief. The tincture of aloes below, however, is one of the best remedies known for not only this, but the round worm.

Tincture of Aloes.—Socotrine aloes 1 ounce; liquorice 2 ounces; coriander-seed ½ an ounce; gin 1 pint. Digest in a bottle for a week, shaking the bottle frequently; then strain. The dose for a child is a teaspoonful every morning; for an adult two tablespoonsful, with half the quantity of a strong decoction of the Carolina pink root.

Santonin suppositories (three grains to a sufficient amount of cacao butter) are a certain cure for seat-worms.

The Round Worm

Occupies the small intestines, and sometimes the stomach. It is of various lengths, from three to eight or more inches. If the tincture of aloes fail to remove it, the pink root may be taken in decoction, or in powder, in doses of sixty or eighty grains, to be followed after three or four days by ten or fifteen grains of calomel. Cowhage, in molasses or honey, with a dose of castor oil every third day, has been very highly extolled. In cases where all other means have failed, tobacco leaves, pounded with vinegar and applied to the belly, have produced the desired effect. They are dangerous, however, especially with young children.

The Tape-Worm.

Inhabits the whole of the internal canal, and sometimes defies all our efforts to get him out of it. Large doses of spirits of turpentine, from one to two ounces, in barley water, have been advantageously employed for this purpose. If the spirits of turpentine be tried, large quantities of gruel or barley water should be used with it in order to prevent its irritating the stomach and kidneys. Pumpkin seeds, taken largely on an empty stomach, will often expel the worm.

By whatever means these troublesome guests are got rid of, the patient should be careful to strengthen his system and bowels by a course of the barks, bitters, wine, etc., and to use a great proportion of animal food in his diet. Repeated purging with calomel is, perhaps, as effectual a remedy for worms as we have, particularly if succeeded by the pink root tea.

Inflammation of the Kidneys.

Symptoms.—Deep seated pain in the small of the back; urine high-colored and small in quantity, sometimes bloody; sickness at the stomach; vomiting.

Treatment.—This will depend upon the cause. If it proceed from gravel, the plan to be pursued will be detailed under that head. If it arise from any other, cup the back freely, repeat it in ten or twelve hours, if necessary, and put him into a warm bath. Twenty grains or more of the uva ursi, with half a grain of opium three times a day, accompanied by small quantities of warm barley or rice-water, is one of the most valuable remedies we are in possession of. The diet during the attack should consist of mucilaginous drinks only, which must be frequently taken, notwithstanding they may be rejected by vomiting.

Gravel.

Symptoms.—A fixed pain in the loins; numbness of the thigh; constant vomiting; retraction of the testicle; urine small in quantity, voided with pain and sometimes bloody. As the gravel passes from the kidney into the bladder the pain is so acute as to occasion fainting, etc.

Treatment.—Put him into a warm bath, where he should remain some time. Meanwhile an emollient and anodyne clyster should be got ready, which must be given to him as soon as he leaves it. Cloths wrung out of decoctions of herbs or spirits and water should be applied to the part, and small quantities of warm gum arabic tea or barley-water be taken frequently. A grain of opium every two hours will be found useful. Bicarbonate of soda in twenty-grain doses every three hours, often gives great relief. Strong coffee, without sugar or cream, sometimes acts like a charm in soothing the pain; twenty drops of the spirits of turpentine taken on a lump of sugar every half hour, is said by high authority to do the same. If the irritation of the stomach is very great, the effervescing draught, with thirty or forty drops of laudanum, may be tried. When the pain, etc., is somewhat abated, the bowels should be opened with castor oil. The uva ursi, as before mentioned, is one of the most valuable remedies in all diseases of the kidneys that we have. Blisters in all such cases are never to be applied. Persons subject to this distressing complaint should be careful to avoid acids and fermented liquors of all kinds, including the red wines, beer, pickles, etc. For a common drink soft water, or the seltzer and soda waters, are to be preferred. When any threatening symptoms are perceived, recourse should be had to the soda and uva ursi, with half a grain of opium three times a day, to be continued for weeks.

Inflammation of the Bladder.

Symptoms.—Pain and swelling of the bladder, the pain increased by pressure; a frequent desire to make water, which either comes away in small quantities, or is totally suppressed.

Treatment.—Cup the patient freely, according to his age and strength, and put him into the warm bath. Inject mucilaginous and laxative clysters, and pursue the exact plan of treatment that is recommended for the cause from which it may proceed. See Suppression of Urine, etc.

Difficulty of Urinating, etc.

Symptoms.—A frequent desire to make water, attended with pain, heat, and difficulty in doing so; a fullness in the bladder.

Treatment.—If it arise from simple irritation by blisters, etc., plentiful draughts of warm liquids, as gum arabic or barley-water, will be sufficient to remove it; if from any other cause, a bladder half filled with warm water, or cloths wrung out of a warm decoction of herbs, should be kept constantly applied over the parts, and occasionally clysters of thin starch with laudanum be injected.

Retention of Urine.

Symptoms.—Pain and swelling of the bladder; violent and fruitless attempts to make water, attended with excruciating pain, etc.

Treatment.—As a total retention of urine is always attended with considerable danger, there should be no delay in endeavoring to remove it. The first step is to place the patient immediately in the warm bath. While he is there a laxative and anodyne clyster must be got ready, which is to be given as soon as he leaves it, and soon repeated. In the mean time the warm fomentations and bladder of hot water must be kept applied, and the mixture below be taken every three or four hours. If there be any difficulty in procuring it, twenty drops of laudanum in a little warm barley or rice-water, or a decoction of the dandelion, will answer instead. Warm sweet oil or milk and water may be injected up the urethra, and three or four grains of camphor, in a little milk, be taken every hour.

If no relief is obtained by these means, leech the perineum, apply snow or ice to the bladder, or make the patient stand on a cold brick or stone pavement, and dash cold water over his thighs, and, if this fail, try the tobacco clyster, which sometimes succeeds after everything else has been resorted to in vain. If a catheter can be procured, try gently to pass it into the bladder while in the bath. If the patient himself cannot do it, let a handy friend attempt it; if foiled in one position, try another. Success is of the utmost importance, for there is nothing but an operation, in the event of its not being obtained, that can save life.

In every case of retention of urine the order of remedies then is: the warm bath, laxatives and anodyne clysters, fomentations or bladders half filled with warm water over the lower belly, camphor and milk every hour or every three hours, passing the catheter, leeching, dashing cold water over the thighs and legs, or applying snow or ice to the bladder, and, lastly, the tobacco clyster.

Mixture.—Mucilage of gum arabic, 1½ ounces; olive oil, 2 drachms. Rub them well together, and add ether, 1 drachm; laudanum, 30 drops.

Incontinence of Urine.

Symptoms.—An involuntary dribbling or flow of urine.

Treatment.—If it arises from a relaxation or weakness of the parts, use the cold bath daily. Apply blisters between the fundament and the bag, and have recourse to bark and the different tonics, as iron, etc., recommended in indigestion. Twenty or thirty grains of the uva ursi, twice or three times a day, with half a pint of lime-water after each dose, may also be tried. If the disease is occasioned by a palsy of the parts, the tincture of Spanish flies may be of service. If a stone in the bladder is the cause, apply to a surgeon to cut it out. In the mean time some kind of vessel should be attached to the yard, to receive the urine, in order to prevent it from excoriating the parts.

Stone in the Bladder.

Symptoms.—A frequent desire to make water, which comes away in small quantities at a time, and is often suddenly interrupted, the last drops of it occasioning pain in the head of the yard; riding over a rough road, or any irregular motion or jolting, causes excruciating pain and bloody urine, accompanied with a constant desire to go to stool; itching of the fundament; a numbness in the thighs, etc; retraction or drawing up of the testicle.

Treatment.—Cutting out or crushing the stone is the only remedy.

Diabetes, or an Immoderate Flow of Urine.

Symptoms.—Frequent discharges of large quantities of urine, which is sometimes of a sweet taste; skin dry, bowels costive, appetite voracious, weakness, and gradual emaciation of the whole body.

Treatment.—The principal remedy for the cure of this disease consists in confining the patient to a diet composed almost exclusively of animal food. Blisters may, also, be applied over the kidneys, and kept open with the savin ointment. The prescription below has proved sometimes successful. The carbonate of ammonia, in doses of 11 or 12 grains three times a day, is strongly recommended, upon high authority. In addition to these, opium in liberal doses, exercise on horseback, the fleshbrush, and flannel next the skin, are not to be neglected. The bowels should be kept open by rhubarb.

Prescription.—Peruvian bark, uva ursi, of each 20 grains; opium, ½ grain. Make a powder, to be taken three times a day with lime-water.

Dropsy of the Belly.

Symptoms.—A swelling of the belly, from water contained in it, preceded by a diminution of urine, dry skin, and oppression at the breast.

Treatment.—One of the most valuable remedies for dropsy is found in the elaterium, one-fourth of a grain of which is a dose. As it is a most active article, it is proper to begin with one-sixteenth of a grain daily, which may be cautiously increased to a fourth, or till it is found to exert its full powers by bringing away large watery stools. From an ounce to an ounce and a half of cream of tartar, dissolved in water, and taken daily, has frequently succeeded in removing the complaint. A tea made by stewing an ounce of bruised juniper berries in a pint of water may be freely drunk with advantage. Bathing the feet before going to bed, and taking immediately after 20 grains of Dover's powder, by producing copious sweating, has produced the same effect.

Dropsy is, notwithstanding, a difficult disease to cure. It must be attempted, however, by the use of such articles as we have mentioned, beginning with the first, and, if it fail, proceeding to the next and so on. If the swelling increases to such an extent as to be absolutely insupportable, send for a surgeon to draw off the water. At the decline of the disease the strength must be supported and restored by bark, wine, and the tonic plan recommended for indigestion. Elaterium or other purgatives must not be resorted to, if the patient be debilitated.

Tympany.

Symptoms. — The symptoms of tympany, or a collection of air either in the intestines themselves, or in the cavity of the belly, are more or less gradual in their approach. When the disease lies within the intestines, it commences with wind in the stomach and bowels, which keeps up a constant rumbling, belching. etc., colic, costiveness, diminution of urine, want of appetite, etc. When it is in the cavity of the belly, and outside the intestines, the swelling is much greater, and very elastic, when it is struck, giving a hollow sound like a drum; there is no belching, etc.

Treatment. — If the complaint is within the intestines, keep the nozzle of a clyster-pipe up the fundament, to permit the wind to pass through it, in order to diminish the pressure on the bowels. Warm mint tea, ginger, horseradish, ether, Cayenne pepper, spices and essential oils, with laxative medicines and clysters, should be freely used, with a moderately tight broad bandage round the belly. If these means do not answer the end, warm and active purges must be resorted to, such as the compound tincture of senna or jalap. Rubbing with turpentine may also prove useful. It is very apt to terminate in death.

Gonorrhœa, or Clap.

Symptoms. — A tingling sensation at the end of the yard, which swells, looks red and inflamed, followed by a discharge of matter that stains the linen, first of a whitish. then of a yellow or green color, a scalding pain in making water, involuntary and painful erections.

Treatment. — There are two kinds of this affection, the mild and the virulent. The first is of so trivial a nature, that plentiful draughts of any soothing liquid, as barley-water or flaxseed tea, with a low diet, are sufficient to remove it. The second produces effects more or less violent on different persons, and occasionally resists for months every remedy that can be thought of. If there be much pain and inflammation in the penis, apply a bread and milk poultice to it, take a dose of salts, and lose some blood. This is the more necessary if, in consequence of the swelling of the foreskin. it cannot be drawn back, or being back, cannot be drawn forward. In the meantime, take pretty large doses of the balsam copaiva daily. A very low diet should be adhered to, and the patient should remain perfectly quiet.

A painful incurvation of the yard, called a chordee, may be relieved by dipping it into cold water, or surrounding it with cloths soaked in laudanum. To prevent it, take fifty or sixty drops of the latter article, or two or three grains of camphor on going to bed.

If, in consequence of violent exercise, or strong injections, the testicles swell, confine the patient on his back, leech and purge him. Pounded ice or snow, or cloths dipped in cold vinegar or water, or lead-water should also be applied to the parts, and a very low diet strictly observed. If, from the same cause, the glands in the groin are enlarged, treat them in like manner.

Gleet.

Symptoms. — The weeping of a thin glairy fluid, like the white of an egg, from the penis, caused by a long-continued clap.

Treatment. — A gleet is exceedingly difficult to get rid of, and frequently defies every effort that is made for that purpose. It must be attempted, however, by the daily use of the cold bath, and thirty drops of the muriated tincture of iron, taken three times a day, for months, in a glass of the cold infusion of bark. The best advice to be given in this case is to apply at once to an intelligent surgeon, who will prescribe injections of alum, sulphate of zinc, or nitrate of silver.

Involuntary Emissions.

Symptoms. — An involuntary emission of semen during sleep, inducing great emaciation and debility.

Treatment. — Abstain from all sexual indulgence and lascivious ideas or books, sleep on a hard bed, use the cold bath daily, with a generous and nourishing diet. Chalybeate water and all the different preparations of iron, with the cold infusion of bark and elixir of vitriol, as directed for indigestion, should be freely employed.

Strictures.

Symptoms. — A difficulty in passing water, which, instead of flowing in a full stream, either dribbles away, twists like a corkscrew, or splits and forks in two or three directions. They are occasioned by strong injections, long-continued or ill-treated clap. The cause, however, is not always to be satisfactorily ascertained.

Treatment. — Procure several bougies of different sizes. Take the largest one, dip it in sweet oil, and pass it into the urethra till it meets with the stricture, then make a mark on the bougie, so that when it is withdrawn you can tell how far down the passage the obstruction exists, and having ascertained this, take the smallest one, well oiled, and endeavor to pass it an inch or two beyond the stricture. If this can be accomplished, let it remain so a few minutes. This must be repeated every day, letting the instrument remain somewhat longer each time it is passed, and after a few days using one a little larger, and so on progressively until the largest one can be introduced. If this fails, apply to a surgeon, who may destroy it with caustic or the knife.

Syphilis, or Pox.

Symptoms. — Chancres and buboes are among the first symptoms of this dreadful malady, which, if not checked, goes on to cause an ulcerated throat, nodes, a destruction of the bones and cartilages of the nose, and the palate. The voice is lost, the hair falls off, foul spreading ulcers show themselves all over the body, the stench of which is insupportable, and before he dies the miserable victim to it becomes a loathsome mass of corruption.

A chancre at first resembles a pimple, with a little pit or depression containing matter, which soon becomes an ulcer, with an irregular thickened edge, covered with a tough, ash-colored matter. the basis of which is hard and surrounded by inflammation. It is generally found on the foreskin or head of the yard.

A bubo is an enlargement of a gland in the groin, beginning in a small hard lump, not bigger than a bean, and increasing to the size of a hen's egg.

A node is a hard tumor formed on a bone.

Treatment.—Apply at once to an intelligent physician. If this be impossible, confine the patient to a simple diet, and keep the part clean. Two or three grains of blue mass may be used daily, and all stimulating substances must be avoided. Every one has some infallible receipt to cure this disorder; but in nine cases out of ten the remedy proves worse than the disease. As for the chancres, touch them freely with lunar caustic, and apply a little piece of rag to them, smeared with red precipitate ointment. If they are situated under the foreskin, which is held over the head of the yard by a permanent phymosis, it (the foreskin) may have to be slit up. If there is a bubo, apply thirty leeches. If this does not prevent its increasing, and the formation of matter is inevitable, apply poultices to it, and as soon as a fluctuation can be felt, let out its contents by several small punctures through the skin with a sharp lancet. To assist in the evacuation, press a soft sponge gently on the tumor.

Cancer of the Yard.

Symptoms.—A small tumor, like a wart, upon the head of the yard or foreskin, followed by inflammation and ulceration, which discharges a thin, disagreeable fluid; after a time a cancerous fungus is produced, attended by a most intolerable burning and darting pain.

Treatment.—Apply at once to a surgeon, who will cut it out; death is the only alternative.

Venereal Warts.

Crops of these animal mushrooms sometimes spring up round the head of the yard or on the foreskin. If flat, they may be destroyed by caustic or nitric acid; if mounted on a stem or foot-stalk, by tying a piece of thread tightly round it.

Dropsy of the Bag.

Symptoms.—A collection of water, which is first perceived at the bottom of the bag, increasing in size as it advances upwards, and forming a tumor of the shape of a pear. If examined as directed for dropsy of the belly, the wavy motion may be felt, and if a candle be placed behind it, it becomes partly transparent.

Treatment.—The only certain cure is an operation, for which, as there is no pressing danger, apply to a surgeon. There are three species of this dropsy, in one of which the water is contained within the lining of the bag; another, within the covering of the spermatic cord; and the third, in the cellular membrane of the bag. The first we have mentioned. The second occurs most frequently in children; it sometimes, however, is found in adults, and very much resembles a rupture. The treatment is the same as in the first. The third may be distinguished by a doughy feel and irregular shape. It is to be cured by punctures to let out the water, and by suspending the testicle.

Enlarged Spermatic Vein.

Symptoms.—A hard knotty and irregular swelling of the vein, which sometimes increases to a large size. When lying down the swelling diminishes, which distinguishes it from a dropsy of the parts.

Treatment.—Suspend the testicles, or keep the patient on his back, apply lotions of lead-water to the parts; the cold bath.

Cancer of the Testicle.

Symptoms.—The testicle is enlarged, hardened, craggy and unequal in its surface, painful on being handled, with irregular pains shooting up the groin, into the back, without any previous inflammation, disease, or external violence.

Treatment.—Apply immediately to a surgeon. Castration, and that at an early state of the disease, is the only remedy that can save life. Be careful, however, to distinguish it from simple swelling of the testicle by inflammation, blows, etc., which see.

Impotency.

This is of three kinds. The first arises from an original defect in the organs of generation. The second, from local debility of the parts, brought on by excessive venery, self-abuse, or some preceding disease, while the third originates from fear, excess of passion, or want of confidence at the moment of coition.

The first is incurable. The second must be treated by the general principles and remedies pointed out for restoring the strength of the system, consisting of the cold bath, preparations of iron, bark, elixir of vitriol, generous diet, exercise, and by steadily avoiding the causes which may have produced it. The remedies for the third must be sought for in calming excessive agitation, and acquiring, by habits of intimacy, that confidence they are sure to produce.

Gout.

Symptoms.—Pain in the small joints, generally in the ball of the great toe, the parts swollen and red, the attack coming on in the night. Such are the striking symptoms of this disease, and generally the first that are noticed. It is occasionally, however, preceded by all those attendant on indigestion. In the advanced stages chalky lumps are formed in the joints.

Treatment.—If the patient be young, vigorous, having the disease for the first time, bleed and purge him, confine him to a low diet, and treat it exactly as an inflammation arising from any other cause. To procure sweating, Dover's powder may be taken on going to bed. As soon as the inflammation, by these means, is reduced, use the cool or cold bath, and take strong exercise on foot daily; avoid high-seasoned food, feather beds, wine, acids and fermented liquors, for the remainder of your life! Gout is the child of indolence and intemperance, and to avoid it the above means must be employed and steadily persevered in.

If, however, the patient is old or infirm, and subject to regular fits of it, he must not be handled so roughly. The most perfect rest should be observed, and the parts lightly covered with fleecy hosiery, and flannel cloths wetted with the lotion below, made milk-warm, or with pure laudanum. The bowels should be opened with some warm laxative. Then give the alkaline mixture below. The degree of warmth that is applied to the part must be regulated by the feelings of the patient, who, if weak, may use a nourishing diet, if strong, a more abstemious one.

If from any cause the disease leaves the extremities and flies to the stomach, apply mustard poultices and blisters to the soles of the feet and ankles, give large doses of ether and laudanum, hot wine, brandy, etc., and endeavor by all such means (including the hot bath) to send it back again.

If the head be the part it is transferred to, and apoplexy is produced by it, take away fifteen or twenty ounces of blood immediately, and give active purgatives, as 10 or 15 grains of calomel, followed by senna tea or Epsom salts. If, in a few hours, the patient is not relieved, the head continuing confused and painful, and the pulse full and throbbing, cup him to the amount of eight or ten ounces, and apply cold vinegar and water constantly to the part.

Gout Lotion.—Alcohol 3 ounces; camphor mixture 9 ounces. Render the whole milk-warm by adding a sufficient quantity of boiling water.

Alkaline Mixture.—Carbonate of potassa 2½ drachms; wine of colchicum root 1½ fluidrachms; water 6 ounces. Take a tablespoonful three times daily.

Inflammatory Rheumatism.

Symptoms.—Pain; swelling and inflammation in some one (or several) of the larger joints, the pain shifting from one part to another; all the symptoms of fever, pulse full and hard, tongue white, bowels costive, and urine high-colored.

Treatment.—First purge with salts and magnesia; then give the alkaline mixture as above, but without the colchicum, if the patient be not of a gouty habit. The Dover's powder should be taken to procure sweating, and a low diet should be strictly observed. In severe cases I have known it necessary to bleed. When the disease is overcome, if in consequence of the bleeding, etc., the patient is left very low and weak, wrap him up in blankets, give him warm, nourishing food, wine, etc., etc.

Chronic Rheumatism.

Symptoms.—A chronic rheumatism is nothing more than one of long standing. It is unaccompanied by fever, and makes its attacks on every change of weather, on getting wet, etc., etc. It is frequently caused by inflammatory rheumatism, and sometimes seems to exist as a primary affection.

Treatment.—I have found no one plan of treatment in this species of the disease so effectual as the following: Purge moderately with senna and salts, rub the parts well with the volatile liniment, and use Cayenne pepper and mustard at dinner in large quantities, and on going to bed thirty drops of laudanum with a teaspoonful of the tincture of guaiacum. It is to be recollected that this is applicable only to chronic cases; if there is fever, etc., it will do much damage. Should there be any cause to suspect that a venereal taint is connected with it, have recourse to the iodide of potassium, five or ten grains thrice daily, in water. Warm liniments are useful. A large blister frequently relieves the whole of the symptoms in the course of a night. The best safeguard against the complaint is the use of flannel next to the skin, winter and summer.

Hip-joint Disease.

Symptoms.—Excruciating pain in the hip-joint and knee; the leg becomes longer, then shorter than its fellow; when lying down the foot rolls outwards, the buttocks appearing flatter than usual; lameness; after a while abscesses in various parts of the thigh; hectic fever, etc.

Treatment.—Apply blisters to the part, and if there be much inflammation leech or cup; make a caustic tissue in the little hollow at the top and outside of the thigh, and use all the remedies directed for scrofula. The diet should be nourishing, and the limb kept at rest. Cod-liver oil, from a teaspoonful to a tablespoonful thrice daily, may be given. When matter is formed, bark, wine and a generous diet must be employed. It often proves incurable.

Dropsy of the Knee-joint.

Symptoms.—The joint swells, the skin remaining of a natural color. By placing the hand on one side of it, and striking it gently on the other, the wavy or fluctuating motion is perceptible; steady pressure on one side will raise the other above its natural level.

Treatment.—Keep a perpetual blister on the joint, or make a caustic issue below it, on the inside of the leg; cold water from the spout of a tea-kettle is a useful application. Camphorated mercurial ointment to the knee, and iodine taken internally, have sometimes been of service.

White Swelling.

Symptoms.—Deeply seated pains in the knee, unattended at first by swelling, which at last comes on with increase of pain. After a while the joint enlarges, matter is sometimes discharged, hectic fever follows, and cuts off the patient.

Treatment.—If from scrofula, use the general remedies directed for that disease, and apply a blister to the part, which may be kept open by the savin ointment for months; if from blows, apply the blister as before; leech and purge freely, and act as directed in cases of similar accidents. If in spite of these precautions the disease continues to advance, amputation may be the only resource.

Pieces of Cartilage in the Joints.

Portions of cartilage are sometimes displaced in the joints, when they act like any other foreign body of a similar texture. While in the hollows of the part they give no uneasiness, but as they frequently slip in between the ends of the bones, causing excruciating pain, it is sometimes, though rarely, necessary to cut them out. For this purpose apply to a surgeon. As all openings into the cavities of the joints are attended with much danger, unless the pain be insupportable it is better to endure the inconvenience than to run the risk of the operation.

Scrofula, or King's Evil.

Symptoms.—Hard and indolent swellings of the glands of the neck, that when ripe, instead of matter discharge a whitish curd. It mostly occurs in persons of a fair complexion, blue eyes, and delicate make. In bad cases the joints swell with great pain, the limbs waste away, the ligaments and bones are destroyed, when hectic fever soon relieves the patient from his misery.

Treatment.—Sea-water is generally considered a great remedy in scrofula. It is to be used daily as a bath. Made milk warm it forms one of the most excellent local applications that we have. When the swellings break, a very strong decoction of hemlock may be advantageously used for the same purpose. The diet should be nourishing. After a fair trial of the waters of the ocean, recourse should be had to iodine and cod-liver oil. The former may be taken in *Lugol's Solution*, the dose of which is from three to six drops, according to age, twice or thrice daily.

Inflamed Glands.

Every gland in the body is subject to inflammation. Whenever one of them is perceived to be in this state, which may be known by the swelling and pain, measures should be taken to reduce it. Leeches, blisters and all the remedies directed for such purposes, should be actively employed, among which purging and a low diet must not be neglected.

Scirrhus.

Symptoms.—A hard tumor, unequal on its surface, and not very sensible, giving but little or no pain on being handled.

Treatment.—Do not meddle with the tumor, but apply to a surgeon as soon as possible.

Cancer.

Symptoms.—A tumor, differing from the preceding one, by being surrounded with enlarged veins. It is, also, more painful, the skin being sometimes discolored and puckered. The whole tumor is particularly heavy, and at last breaks into a malignant ulcer, or sore, whose edges are raised, ragged, uneven, and curl over like the leaves of a flower; white streaks or bands cross it from the centre to the circumference. Acute and darting pains accompany both this and the preceding stage of the disease.

Treatment. — There is but one remedy that can be depended on for the cure of this painful and inveterate complaint, and even that should be resorted to early, in order to ensure success. All the diseased parts must be cut out. Arsenic, corrosive sublimate, phosphate of iron, and a thousand other articles have been recommended, both externally and internally, but without any effectual advantage. To relieve the pain, opium may be taken in large doses. The sore should be defended from the air, by some mild ointment. Powdered chalk, scraped carrots, fresh hemlock leaves and powdered charcoal may be used for the same purpose.

Goitre.

Symptoms. — A tumor in the fore part of the throat, seated in a gland close to the projection called "Adam's apple."

Treatment. — Goitre is sometimes incurable. When taken at the very beginning of the complaint, however, and in young persons, it is said to have been dispersed by a course of iodine joined to frictions of the part, with strong mercurial ointment. As it seldom causes any inconvenience, and is always unattended by pain, it is not a matter of much consequence. The inhabitants of the Alps consider it a mark of beauty, and there are some cantons where every man, woman and child is adorned with a tumor of this nature, of which they would feel very sorry to be deprived. It cannot be cut out, on account of the great number of blood-vessels of which it is composed.

Fainting.

Causes. — Sudden and violent emotions of the mind; bleeding; diseases of the heart and its great vessels.

Treatment. — Lay the person on his back, take off his cravat, then open the doors and windows, and sprinkle cold water in his face. Smelling salts may be held to his nose.

Apoplexy.

Symptoms. — Falling without sense or motion, profound sleep; face livid or flushed; eyes wide open or half closed, and immovable; breathing slow, laboring, and irregular; pulse full and slow.

Causes. — A rushing of blood to the head, excessive fat in persons with a short neck, gluttony, violent exercise, intense heat, anger, hearty meat suppers, blows on the head, intoxication, etc., etc.

Treatment. — If the pulse remains full, the face flushed, etc., take away twenty ounces or more of blood on the spot, remove the cravat, unbutton the shirt-collar, and place the patient in bed, with his head and shoulders a little elevated. The windows and doors must be thrown open, and no more persons than are necessary, be allowed to remain in the room. The head is to be shaved and cupped, a blister applied to the back of the neck and the head, and mustard poultices to the feet. An active purgative should always be administered as soon as the patient is bled, and its operation assisted by repeated clysters. If the patient cannot swallow pills, try liquids, if neither, have recourse to a strong purgative clyster. If, by these means, the breathing is not easier, and the pulse softer, bleed again, or cup the back of the neck.

If, however, the patient is old and infirm, and the attack has come on more gradually, if the pulse is weak, and the face pale, bleed moderately, or not at all, and give immediately a warm purgative, apply the blisters, etc. If it arises from swallowing vegetable poisons, give an active emetic, as thirty grains of white vitriol, and act as directed in cases of similar accidents. In this second kind of apoplexy, stimulants, as hartshorn to the nose, etc., may be used; in the first they are very injurious, and should never be employed.

Stroke of the Sun.

This proceeds from exposure to the sun's rays, and exhibits the same symptoms as apoplexy, commencing with vertigo, loss of sight, ringing in the ears, etc., and must be treated by cupping or bleeding, and in every other respect as directed for apoplexy. Extreme heat sometimes, however, produces a state of prostration without head symptoms; for which cold affusion and rest are the best remedies.

Epilepsy.

Symptoms. — A fit, in which the patient falls to the ground in a convulsion; the eyes are distorted and turned up, hands clenched, foaming at the mouth, convulsions, the whole ending in a deep sleep.

Treatment. — Keep the patient from hurting himself, by holding gently his hands, legs, and particularly his head, which he is apt to dash violently against the ground, or surrounding objects. A piece of soft wood should be placed between his teeth, to prevent his tongue from being bitten. This is, in general, all that can be done during the fit. If, however, there are symptoms of great determination of blood to the head, bleeding should not be neglected. White vitriol, the mistletoe, carbonate of iron, etc., etc., have been recommended and tried for the cure of this complaint, but in vain.

The valerianate of zinc may, however, be tried. It is taken in pills of a grain each, one three times a day, gradually increasing this dose to five at a time. To reap any benefit from this medicine, it is necessary to persevere in it for months. If it fails, iron or some other tonic may be resorted to. Large doses of spirits of turpentine are said to have afforded relief. The diet, in all cases, should be vegetable, and if symptoms of fulness of blood be present, it will be proper to bleed. Persons subject to these fits, should never be left alone, or ride on horseback, for obvious reasons. It should be known that sexual excesses often produce or keep up this complaint.

Palsy.

Symptoms. — A partial or complete loss of the powers of motion, and the sensibility of particular parts of the body; the pulse soft and slow.

Treatment. — In a young and robust person, it may be proper to bleed, and give an active purgative. In old people, or where the powers of the body are much weakened, warm laxative medicines, with stimulating applications, as the flesh-brush, blisters, mustard poultices, and rubbing the spine with the volatile liniment, form the best plan of treatment. If it affect different parts of the body at once, horseradish, mustard, and Cayenne pepper should be used liberally, as they are prepared for table. If a swelling or tumor be found on the back-bone, or any injury has been done it, which may have caused the disease, caustic issues may be placed on each side of it, and as near the injured part as possible. The diet should be light and nourishing. The warm bath must not be neglected.

Tetanus.

There are several very long and very learned names affixed to this disease, as it may happen to attack one part of the body or another. When it is confined to the muscles of the neck and jaws, lock-jaw is the common and expressive term for it. The affection, however, is always the same, requires similar treatment, and consists in an involuntary contraction and stiffening of a part of the muscles, the senses remaining perfect.

Lock-jaw.

Symptoms.—A stiffness in the back of the neck, which renders it first painful, and at last impossible to turn the head round; difficulty in swallowing; pain in the breast, shooting to the back; the lower jaw becomes stiff and gradually closes.

Treatment.—If the disease is supposed to arise from a wounded nerve, or from an injury done to tendinous parts, by a pointed instrument, enlarge the wound with a sharp lancet or penknife, and pour laudanum or turpentine into it, as directed for similar accidents. Give 2 or 3 grains of opium at once, and repeat it every two hours, increasing the dose according to the violence of the symptoms and the effects produced by it, without too much regarding the quantity that has been taken. Cases are on record where 60 grains (a drachm) of solid opium have been taken at once, and with the happiest effect. This, however, is a large dose, and should never be ventured on but under the most desperate and alarming circumstances. Active purging with castor oil and senna tea must not be omitted, and if the power of swallowing be lost, laudanum, etc., most be given in clysters. Drawing a tooth is generally recommended by physicians in those cases where the jaws are firmly closed, for the purpose of transmitting medicines and food to the stomach. This has always appeared to me as every way calculated to increase the evil. If no opening exists between the teeth, access can always be obtained by clysters, and in this way nourishment and remedies may be injected. It is always proper, however, when the disease is perceived to be coming on, to place two small pieces of soft wood between the grinders of the upper and lower jaw, one on each side, so that they may be kept asunder.

Madeira wine, in doses of a wineglassful every hour, continued for several days, and combined with the internal use of opium and the warm bath, has been found of great service. Cold water dashed freely over the patient every two or three hours may likewise be tried. After every affusion he should be well wiped and put into a warm bed, when a large dose of laudanum in warm Madeira wine should be given. The tobacco clyster has sometimes succeeded when everything else has failed. So has chloroform by inhalation. Blistering the whole length of the spine, and caustic issues on its sides, as nearly on a line with the parts affected as possible, are strongly recommended.

Although a valuable addition to our means of cure, the tobacco clyster is not to be employed lightly, or on common occasions. It should always be reserved to the last moment, never using it until everything else has failed. The prostration of the system, and other alarming symptoms it sometimes causes, renders this caution necessary.

Painful Affection of the Nerves of the Face.

This disease is also called tic-douloureux, neuralgia, etc.

Symptoms.—A very severe pain darting in particular directions, not lasting more than a second, but very rapidly repeated, and excited by the slightest touch; during the intervals there is no pain whatever. There is no inflammation or swelling of the cheek, as in toothache, nor does the pain seem so deeply seated.

Treatment.—Blisters, tincture of aconite, mercurial ointment, opium, iron, and Fowler's Solution of Arsenic, with many other remedies of the same class, have been all recommended and used for the cure of this most painful of all the affections to which the human body is subject. Where the pains are so excessive as not to be borne, one or two grains of the extract of belladonna may be taken every three hours. When the pain is somewhat relieved, this quantity must be diminished. For a cure apply to a skilful surgeon, who may divide the nerves.

Angina Pectoris.

Symptoms.—An acute pain at the lower end of the breast-bone, shooting into the left arm; great difficulty of breathing; anxiety; palpitation of the heart; a feeling of suffocation. It usually comes on while ascending a hill or going up stairs.

Treatment.—During the fit place the patient's feet in a hot mustard foot-bath, and apply mustard plasters to the chest and back. Give one or two teaspoonfuls of Hoffmann's anodyne, in water, or forty drops of laudanum. If fainting, dash cold water in his face. Strips of linen, moistened with the solution below, applied several times a day to the breast-bone for a month, are said to have effected complete cures. They act by producing a crop of pimples, on the appearance of which the disease sometimes declines.

Persons subject to this complaint should avoid all fermentable food, and excess in eating or drinking, taking care to live quietly and to keep the bowels open. Cupping and purging, followed by opium, to lessen the spasm, with the warm bath, and a perpetual blister or plaster of the tartar emetic ointment to the chest, are perhaps the best remedies that can be employed.

Tartar emetic, 1 drachm; spirits of camphor, ½ an ounce; boiling water, 1 pint. Mix.

Dance of St. Vitus.

Symptoms.—Irregular and convulsive motions of the limbs and head, usually occurring in children. It varies, however, in different persons, and is frequently counterfeited by beggars.

Treatment.—The daily use of the cold bath, with the Peruvian bark, has often succeeded in curing the complaint in young subjects. In addition to these, any of the preparations of iron combined with moderate doses of musk, opium, camphor, etc., may be tried. The disease is generally recovered from.

Scarlet Fever.

Symptoms.—Chills, heat, thirst, headache; the skin is marked with large red or scarlet patches, which at last unite, disappearing in a kind of branny scurf; sore throat.

Distinguish it from measles by the spots coming out on the second day of the fever. In measles they seldom appear until the fourth day. By their color, which is that of a boiled lobster, whereas in measles it is of a dark red.

Treatment.—An emetic (ipecacuanha) may be given on the first appearance of the disease, to be followed by a dose of salts, or eight grains of calomel, with as many of rhubarb. If the pulse is full and strong, the head aches, and the heat is great, draw blood, and apply cold water over the body freely and frequently. There is no disease in which the advantages of cold affusion are more striking. In order to reap the full benefit of it, however, it must be freely employed, that is, as often as heat, etc., seem to require it, or eight or ten times in the twenty-four hours. The saline mixture, p. 123, is of great use. If there is any soreness of the throat, the gargles recommended for that complaint should be used, and a mustard poultice be applied to the parts. If symptoms of putrescency appear, have recourse to the plan recommended for putrid sore throat. As scarlet fever is undoubtedly contagious, the usual precautions should of course be adopted.

Writers on this subject generally consider scarlet fever as consisting of three kinds, viz., the simple fever, the fever with sore throat, and the malignant fever. The treatment of the first should be like that of any other inflammatory fever; that of the second has been detailed in speaking of inflammatory sore throat; and the last is precisely that of putrid sore throat.

Erysipelas, or St. Anthony's Fire.

Symptoms.— Fever, delirium, vomiting; pulse strong or weak, as the fever inclines to the inflammatory or typhous kind. On the fourth day — sometimes on the second or third — the skin in some one part becomes red and inflamed, which is soon extended to others, the parts affected being swollen and of a bright scarlet. If the face is attacked, it spreads itself on the scalp, and the eyelids sometimes swell so as to prevent the patient from seeing. After a longer or shorter period, the eruption ends in small watery vesicles, or in branny scales. At this period the fever sometimes abates; at others, drowsiness or delirium comes on, which increases it, and destroys the patient by the eleventh day.

Treatment.— This disease is of two kinds, one of which is principally confined to the skin, while the other affects the whole system. If the accompanying fever is inflammatory bleeding will be proper, otherwise not. This operation is to be cautiously employed in erysipelas, as it sometimes runs into a typhous state. If, however, the patient is robust, his head aches, and great marks of fullness and inflammation are evident, which is generally the case in this country, bleeding, purging with salts, and cooling drinks should be employed, to which, also, may be added Dover's powders, boneset tea, etc., to produce sweating. The room should be kept cool. If, on the contrary, the fever is typhous, or the patient is of a weak and irritable habit of body, bleeding should never be resorted to. Opium, wine, bark, elixir of vitriol, and tincture of chloride of iron (20 drops every three hours) are necessary in this case, to guard against mortification, which sometimes ensues.

As local applications, bathing the parts with laudanum or lead-water, or dusting them with rye meal or wheat flour, are the best. Should the disease evidently be confined to the skin, the application of a blister will sometimes put an end to it. If it affect the face, it may be prevented from extending to the scalp, by painting a line just beyond the eruption quite thickly with tincture of iodine. If abscesses form, large openings must be made, to let out the matter and the dead parts. When the first or inflammatory kind prevails, the diet should be barley, sago, or panada, etc., with lemonade, tamarind water, etc., for drink; and, on the contrary, when the second or typhous form of it (especially if accompanied by putrid symptoms) shows itself, a more generous diet, with a moderate quantity of wine, etc., must be employed.

It may not be useless again to observe, that in the United States erysipelas often calls for reducing and cooling measures. Among the various articles which are employed in this, as well as all inflammatory diseases, none ranks higher than lemonade, which should always, if possible, be made from the fresh fruit. When taken cold, and in liberal quantities, it is not only delicious to the palate of the patient, but tends powerfully to cure the complaint.

Measles.

Symptoms. — Inflammatory fever; dry cough and hoarseness; sneezing, watering of the eyes, which itch; a running from the nose; great drowsiness. On the fourth day small red points break out, first on the face, and then gradually over the body. They are in clusters, and, on passing the hand over them, are found to be a little raised. On the fifth or sixth day the vivid red is changed to a brown, and the eruption goes off.

Distinguish it from small-pox and all other diseases by the dry cough and hoarseness, by the appearance of the eyes, which are red, swollen, and loaded with tears.

Treatment.—The patient must be confined to a low diet, and kept in bed, with as much covering, but no more, as may be agreeable to his feelings. The room should be cool, and, if there is much fever and pain in the head, bleeding may be necessary. Should there be pain and oppression at the breast, apply a blister. The bowels may be opened by salts. The mild form of measles ought to be treated like any other inflammatory complaint, taking care, however, not to repel the eruption by cold. If this happens, place the patient in a warm bath, give him warm wine, etc., internally, and apply mustard poultices and blisters to the feet and ankles.

There is another and more dangerous kind of this disease, which may be known by the fever being typhous, and by all the symptoms showing a depressing tendency. The moment this is perceived have recourse to bark wine, muriatic acid, etc., etc., as directed in typhus fever.

Chicken-Pox.

Symptoms.—Fever; inability to sleep; pain in different parts of the body; a crop of small pimples or points on the back, which, by the second day, are changed into little blisters, which are ripe on the third and disappear before the fifth day, without forming true pus or matter, and leaving no marks or pits behind them.

Distinguish it from small-pox by the eruption coming out on the back, by the mildness of the fever, by the fluid contained in the vesicles or blisters not being true pus, and by the whole falling off in scales on the fifth day.

Treatment.—Confine the patient to his bed, keep him cool and quiet, and give him a dose of salts. This is all that is necessary.

Cow-Pox.

Symptoms.—A pimple at the spot where the matter was inserted, which gradually undergoes certain regular changes that characterize the complaint.

Changes of genuine Cow-Pox.—On the fourth day, or sooner, from the time of the operation, a small speck of inflammation is to be perceived, which, on the fifth day is a pimple, surrounded by a circle of inflammation. On the sixth this pimple changes to a vesicle containing a thin fluid. On the seventh this vesicle is more perfect, its margin forming a regular circle; it is also a little flattened on the top, the centre of which is of a dark color. On the eighth or ninth day slight chills, flushes of heat, etc., are sometimes felt, accompanied by swelling of the pustule and pains shooting up into the arm-pit, the glands or kernels of which occasionally swell.

On the tenth or eleventh day the pustule is surrounded by a circular, vivid, inflammatory blush that is very beautiful. This is regarded as a decisive proof of the presence of the genuine cowpox. On the eleventh day the centre of the pustule begins to grow of a dark color, which gradually increases to a brown or mahogany one by the end of the second week, when it begins to leave the skin, from which it is finally separated.

Treatment.—If the pain, inflammation and swelling are excessive, reduce them by cold applications, a dose of salts, low diet and rest.

Small-Pox.

Symptoms.—Inflammatory fever; drowsiness; pain in the pit of the stomach, increased by pressure; pain in the back; vomiting; on the third day the eruption breaks out on the face, neck and breast in little red points that look like flea-bites, and which gradually appear over the whole body. On the fifth day little round vesicles filled with a transparent fluid appear on the top of each pimple. The eruptive fever now declines. On the ninth day the pustules are perfectly formed, being round and filled with a thick, yellow matter, the head and face also swelling considerably. On the eleventh day the matter in the pustules is of a dark yellow color, the head grows less, while the feet and hands begin to swell. The secondary fever now makes its appearance. The pustules break and dry up in scabs and crusts, which at last fall off, leaving pits, which sufficiently mark the cause.

Such are the symptoms of the distinct or mild small-pox, but it frequently assumes a more terrible shape, in what is called the confluent. In the latter all the symptoms are more violent from the beginning. The fever is typhous; there is delirium, preceded by great anxiety, heat, thirst, vomiting, etc. The eruption is irregular, coming out on the second day in patches, the vesicles of which are flatted in; neither does the matter they contain turn to a yellow, but to a brown color. Instead of the fever going off on the appearance of the eruption, it is increased after the fifth day, and continues throughout the complaint. The face swells in a frightful manner, so as to close the eyes; sometimes putrid symptoms prevail from the commencement.

Treatment.—Place the patient in a cool, airy room, and let him be but lightly covered with bed clothes. Purge him moderately with salts, and give him thirty drops of laudanum every night. The diet should consist of panada, arrow-root, etc., and his drink consist of lemonade or water. If from any cause the eruption strikes in, put him into a warm bath, give a little warm wine whey, or the wine alone, and apply blisters to the feet. Obstinate vomiting is to be quieted by the effervescing draught, with the addition of a few drops of laudanum.

In the confluent small-pox the treatment must be varied as it inclines more or less to the inflammatory or putrid type. If it inclines to the first, act as directed for the distinct kind; if to the last, employ all those means directed in typhus fever. If the eyes are much affected, it will be necessary to bathe them frequently with warm milk, and to smear the lids with some simple ointment.

Itch.

Symptoms.—An eruption of small pimples between the fingers, on the wrists, and over the whole body, which form matter, and are attended with an intolerable itching.

Treatment.—The remedy is sulphur. It should be used internally with cream of tartar, so as to purge moderately, and at the same time be applied externally in the form of an ointment. The following practice is said to be effectual: Take of flour of sulphur 2 ounces, and mix it well with 2 drachms of nitre; throw the mixture into a warming-pan containing live coals, and pass the pan between the sheets in the usual manner. The patient, stripped to his skin, now gets into bed (taking care not to let the fumes escape), when the clothes should be tucked in all round him. Repeat the process ten or twelve times. The sulphur ointment, applied after a prolonged tepid bath, will generally answer.

Herpes.

Symptoms.—Broad, itchy spots of a reddish or white color breaking out in different places, which at last run into each other, forming extensive ulcers; after a time they become covered with scales, which fall off, leaving the surface below red; while the disease heals in one part it breaks out in another.

Treatment.—The ointment of the oxide of zinc is a very common application. Washing the part with a solution of corrosive sublimate in water, one grain to the ounce, is, however, to be preferred. The citrine ointment may also be tried. If these fail, apply a strong solution of blue vitriol to the ulcers, and take a grain of calomel morning and evening. The decoction of sarsaparilla and guaiacum may be used with them. If the disease resists the mercury, try Fowler's Solution of Arsenic in doses of five drops three times a day, to be cautiously increased as directed for intermitting fevers. The warm bath should never be neglected in cutaneous complaints.

Scald-Head.

Symptoms.—Inflammation of the skin of the head, which ends in a scabby eruption that extends over the whole scalp.

Causes.—Want of cleanliness, putting on the hat, using the comb, or sleeping in the bed of a person who has it.

Treatment.—Shave the head close, wash it well with warm soap and water, and cover it thickly with fresh powdered charcoal. The bowels must be kept open by magnesia or Epsom salts. If this fails, try the citrine or tar ointment to the parts, with a liberal use of the compound decoction of sarsaparilla. The diet should be wholesome and nourishing, avoiding spirituous liquors and salted meats. The warm bath should not be neglected.

Ringworm.

Symptoms.—An eruption running in curved lines, generally in a circle, that itches when rubbed, or when the body is heated.

Treatment.—Into one ounce of water throw more blue vitriol than it will dissolve, so as to form what is technically called a saturated solution. Touching the ulcerated parts with this liquid several times through the day, will alone frequently cure it. If this fails, apply the citrine or tar ointments. In very obstinate cases, recourse may be had to the usual doses of Fowler's Solution. If it affects the head, shave it. In this, as well as all other diseases of the skin, the greatest cleanliness is necessary.

Nettle-Rash.

Symptoms.—An eruption similar to that caused by the stinging of nettles, whence its name. On rubbing the skin which itches, the eruption will suddenly appear, remain for a moment, and then vanish, breaking out in some other spot. The parts affected are swolled, at one time presenting the appearance of welts, as from the stroke of a whip-lash, and at another, that of white solid lumps.

Treatment.—A few doses of magnesia or Epsom salts, and a little attention to the diet, which should be mild, are generally sufficient to remove it. If it proceed from eating poisonous fish, or any unwholesome food, take an emetic, etc., as directed in such cases.

Blotched-Face.

Symptoms.—An eruption of hard, distinct tubercles or pimples, generally appearing on the face, but sometimes on the neck, breast, and shoulders.

Treatment.—There are a great many varieties of this affection, some of which have been separately treated of by Wilson and other writers on diseases of the skin, to whom I would refer any one who is particularly interested therein. Notwithstanding all that has been said on the subject, there is no disease more difficult to get rid of than this. Where it arises from suppressed perspiration, high-seasoned food, or intemperance, it may indeed be relieved by the warm bath, by sweating, purging, and a low diet; but when it exists in persons who have always led temperate lives, and in whom it seems constitutional, medicine has but little effect on it. In all cases, however, the following plan may be adopted: Take a dose of Epsom salts once or twice a week, use the warm bath daily, live on mush and milk exclusively, and drink nothing but water. The parts may be touched frequently with the lotion below. If, after a trial of several months, this should not succeed, try Fowler's solution, or the pills for scald head, with the decoction of guaiacum and sarsaparilla. The various cosmetics and astringent applications recommended for these affections are always prejudicial, for although they sometimes repress the eruption, they occasion more severe and dangerous complaints.

Lotion.—Take of corrosive sublimate, 4 grains; of spirits of wine, ½ an ounce; when the salt is dissolved, add of common gin and of water, each, 3 ounces.

Scurvy.

Symptoms.—Bleeding of the gums, teeth loose, spots of various colors on the skin, generally livid, debility, countenance pale and bloated, pulse small, quick, and intermitting. In its advanced stage the joints swell, and blood bursts out from different parts of the body.

Treatment.—Remove the patient to a new and healthy situation, where the air is dry and pure, give him plenty of fresh vegetables, such as potatoes, spinach, lettuce, beets, carrots, and scurvygrass. A small proportion of fresh animal food should be taken with them. This, with oranges, lemons and sugar, or lemonade, spruce-beer, with wine and water, are generally sufficient to cure the complaint. If there is much pain in the bowels, laudanum must be used to relieve it. If the breathing is difficult, or there is much pain in the breast, apply a blister to it, for on no account should blood be drawn in scurvy. A teaspoonful of charcoal, well mixed with half a pint of vinegar, forms an excellent gargle to clean the gums and ulcers in the mouth. Those on the body may be washed with the same, or lemon-juice, pure, or mixed with water. The yeast or charcoal poultice may also be applied to them with advantage. To restore the tone of the system, recourse must be had to the Peruvian bark, with the elixir of vitriol, the muriated tincture of iron, exercise, etc., etc.

Of Tumors.

By the word tumor is meant a swelling of any part of the body. They are of different kinds, arise from various causes, and are more or less dangerous, according to the nature of their contents, and the spot they occupy. Unless cancerous, they are generally not dangerous to life.

Of Ruptures.

Ruptures are tumors caused by the protrusion of a part of the bowels through certain natural openings. They are divided into reducible, irreducible, and strangulated. They mostly occur in men in the groin and bag.

Causes.—Straining in any way, as at stool, vomiting, lifting heavy weights, violent exercise, as jumping, running, etc.; a natural weakness of the parts.

Reducible Ruptures.

Symptoms.—A small swelling, free from pain, and generally soft, the color of the skin over it remaining unaltered. While standing up the swelling increases, on lying down it decreases, the patient being able to return the parts himself, while in that position. The swelling is also increased by coughing, sneezing, or straining as if at stool. If he is flatulent, a rumbling sensation may be felt in it.

Treatment.—The patient should place himself on his back, with his head and shoulders a little elevated. Draw up his knees to his belly, and (if in this position the parts do not return of themselves) endeavor to push or knead them gently up into the belly, through the opening at which they come out, and which, if the tumor be in the groin or bag, is an oval ring or slit in the groin, at the precise spot where the swelling first appeared. When this is effected, he should remain quiet until a truss can be procured, the spring of which must be passed round his body, the pad be applied directly over the spot just mentioned, and held there with one hand, while the other passes the strap into the buckle and draws it sufficiently tight. Having done this, he should get up and walk about. If the swelling no longer appears, the truss is properly applied; if otherwise, take it off, return the parts as before, and apply it again; when, if, on rising, walking about, slightly coughing, etc., the parts are found to be well kept up, he may resume his ordinary business. The truss should be worn night and day, as long as he lives.

Irreducible Ruptures.

Symptoms.—A rupture in which there is no pain, yet that cannot be returned into the belly, caused by an increased bulk of the parts, or their having formed adhesions, or grown fast to adjoining parts.

Treatment.—A rupture thus situated must be simply supported by a bag or bandage, and left to itself. The patient should be extremely cautious in his diet, and in avoiding costiveness, by the use of clysters, or, if necessary, laxative medicines. He should also be very careful to protect the tumor from blows, always recollecting that it is in danger of strangulation.

Strangulated Ruptures.

Symptoms.—The first mark of a rupture being strangulated, or of pressure being made on it, is costiveness. The tumor, which before was insensible, becomes painful, the pain being most severe at the spot where the strangulation or stricture exists, and extending from thence across the belly, which becomes swollen and hard. The pain resembles that which the patient would suppose to arise if a cord was drawn tightly across it. The pain continues to increase, and is augmented by pressure; sneezing, coughing, nausea, and vomiting, first of the contents of the stomach, and afterwards of the intestines, ensue; great anxiety, restlessness, and a quick hard pulse. Hiccups, cold clammy sweats, weakened respiration, and a pulse so feeble as hardly to be perceived, announce the approach or presence of mortification.

Treatment.—Lose not a moment in sending for the best medical aid that may be within reach. In the mean time, having placed the patient as directed for reducible ruptures, apply both hands on the tumor with gentle pressure, or grasp the tumor gently but steadily with one hand, while with the fingers of the other you endeavor to knead or push up the parts nearest the ring in the groin, applying the pressure in the same course the parts have taken in their descent. If this fails, seize the tumor between the finger and thumb of the left hand, close to where it enters the belly, and carry them downwards, with a moderate pressure, so as to dislodge any excrement which may be there, while with the right you endeavor to push in the gut.

If you cannot succeed in two or three attempts, place the patient in a warm bath and try it again. If still foiled (you have no time to waste in unavailing attempts) cover the tumor with pounded ice, snow, or any very cold application. Should this fail, bleed the patient until he nearly faints, regardless of the small thready pulse; if fainting actually occurs, seize that moment to return the parts, as before directed.

Should the rupture still remain irreducible, there are but two resources left, the tobacco clyster and an operation. One-half of the clyster should be injected; if it occasions sickness and a relaxation of the parts, endeavor to return them. If the first half does not produce these effects, throw up the remainder of it, and when relaxation comes on endeavor, as before, to push up the gut. As regards the operation, no one should ever attempt it but a surgeon. Large doses of laudanum allay vomiting, and are otherwise beneficial; in all cases of this kind they should never be omitted.

Remarks.—Ruptures are liable to be confounded with some other diseases, as dropsy of the bag, enlarged spermatic vein, etc. The modes of distinguishing them have already been pointed out, although it must be confessed that with respect to the latter considerable difficulty exists. If the disease is a rupture, by placing the patient on his back, returning the tumor, and holding the fingers firmly over the opening, and then desiring him to rise, the swelling will not appear. If, on the contrary, it is an enlarged spermatic vein, it will be found to be greater than ever. The latter has also a peculiar ropy feel, as if a bundle of cords were in the bag.

Aneurism.

Symptoms.—At first a small tumor without pain or redness, attended by a peculiar throbbing; it disappears on pressure, and returns the moment it is removed. As the tumor increases in size, the throbbing or beating of the artery grows less perceptible. It is generally found in the ham, thigh, neck, groin, and arm. Distinguish it by the beating or throbbing, which is diminished by pressing on the artery above the tumor, and by the latter disappearing on pressure, and returning when it is removed.

Treatment.—In the early stage apply a soft and elastic cushion to the tumor, and bind it tightly over it by a bandage. If the patient is of a full habit he should be bled and purged. This plan, steadily and vigorously pursued for a long time, has sometimes effected complete cures. There is nothing, however, but an operation that can be depended on; wherefore, as soon as any swelling of this nature is perceived, no time should be lost in procuring surgical assistance. If the tumor is left to itself it will finally burst, and death be the inevitable consequence.

Fleshy Tumors.

Symptoms.—Small warty projections, which, as they increase in size, drag down the skin from the neighboring parts, which forms a kind of stem or foot-stalk, on which the tumor hangs. They are hard, full of vessels, and are neither painful nor inflamed.

Treatment.—When very small, they may be frequently touched with caustic, which will destroy them; if large, the ligature or knife must be employed, for which purpose have recourse to a surgeon.

Steatomatous Tumors.

Symptoms.—A small, fatty swelling, which gradually increases, and sometimes grows to an enormous size. It is soft and free from pain, the color of the skin remaining unaltered.

Treatment.—These tumors, technically called steatomatous, are merely inconvenient from their bulk. They can only be removed by the ligature or knife, for which purpose apply to a surgeon.

Encysted Tumors.

Symptoms.—A distinct, hard, circumscribed swelling, gradually growing larger until a slight inflammation comes on, when it becomes a little painful, soon after which a fluctuation is distinctly to be perceived. As it progresses the vessels become enlarged; it seldom exceeds the size of an egg.

Treatment.—Apply to a surgeon.

Ganglion.

Symptoms.—A small, movable, elastic swelling, with little or no pain, or alteration in the skin, situated under or between tendons or sinews, and generally near to a joint; it sometimes hinders the motions of the part.

Treatment.—Apply pressure, blisters or frictions of strong camphorated mercurial ointment to the tumor. If these are of no avail, make a small puncture in it with the point of a sharp lancet, let out its contents and apply pressure to the part, so as to make the two sides of the sack or bag grow together.

Boils.

Symptoms.—A hard, circumscribed, inflamed and very painful tumor, of a conical shape, seldom exceeding in size a pigeon's egg.

Treatment.—If the patient is of a full habit, bleed and purge him with Epsom salts. A soft poultice of warm bread and milk, or rye or flaxseed meal, should always be applied to the boil, and frequently changed. If the pain is excessive, a teaspoonful of laudanum may be mixed with each one. In a few days matter will be formed, when it may be let out with a sharp lancet.

Carbuncle.

A deeply seated, hard, immovable and circumscribed tumor, which appears generally on the back, shoulders, etc. About the middle it is of a dark red or purple color, being much paler or mottled round its edges. It is attended with an intolerable itching and burning pain, and at last becomes a kind of sloughing ulcer.

Treatment.—This will depend upon the state of the constitution. Most generally there is great weakness, in which case the diet must be generous. Bark, with the elixir of vitriol and opium, to relieve the pain, are to be frequently employed. As a local remedy, a blister ranks very high. It should be placed directly on the part. After being cut, it may be succeeded by a basilicon plaster. A modern writer strongly recommends the solution of arsenic as a local remedy in this disease. Pledgets of linen dipped in the liquor, are to be laid on the swelling and frequently renewed. When matter begins to form, apply a bread and milk poultice, and treat it in every respect as a common ulcer. Surgeons mostly advise the early use of deep incisions of carbuncle entirely across it, in two directions, at right angles to each other.

Whitlow, or Felon.

Symptoms.—An inflamed tumor at the end of the finger. It is of three kinds. The first is situated immediately under the skin, around the nail; the second in the cellular membrane, the pain and swelling of which is much greater than in the first, and the matter much longer in forming; the third lies under the sheath or covering of the tendons of the fingers, and is infinitely more violent, painful and dangerous than either of the others.

Treatment.—If of the first description, open the little abscess with a needle and let out the matter, which should be prevented from forming, if possible, by bathing the part with camphorated spirits. The second should be dispersed by purging, and by leeches and blisters. If the inflammation is not reduced by these means, with a very sharp penknife make an early and free incision in the middle of the last joint of the finger down to the bone. Suffer the blood to run for a few minutes, and then treat it as a common cut. The same practice should be followed with regard to the third.

Piles.

Symptoms.—A pain in the fundament when going to stool; on examination small tumors are perceived to project beyond its verge. They are of two kinds—the blind and bleeding. They may also be internal and external.

Blind Piles.

Treatment.—A diet of rye mush and milk, strictly adhered to for a length of time, will very frequently cure the disease. If they project, are swelled and painful, apply twenty or thirty leeches to them, and cold applications. The common gall ointment is a very soothing application. Balsam copaiva in doses sufficiently large to purge freely is also highly recommended. A radical cure, however, is only to be sought for in the knife or ligature, for which apply to a surgeon. If the pain is very great, laudanum may be taken to ease it.

Bleeding Piles.

Treatment.—If the bleeding is considerable, inject a solution of alum or a decoction of oak bark, or make pressure upon the vessels by introducing a sheep's gut, tied at one end, into the fundament, and then filling it with any astringent fluid by a clyster pipe. This evacuation is sometimes salutary, and it often requires much judgment to know if it should be stopped or not.

Of Abscess.

Symptoms.—The formation of matter under the skin, or in any part of the body, preceded by inflammation, and marked by a dull, heavy weight; by the pain becoming more acute and darting; by a peculiar throbbing; by the swelling becoming more elevated and soft to the touch. If the tumor is not opened it bursts.

Treatment.—Apply a soft and warm bread and milk or linseed poultice to the part, and endeavor to hasten the formation of matter. When this is evident, let it out with a sharp lancet. If the patient is weak, let him have a generous diet, with wine, porter, bark, etc.

Psoas Abscess.

Symptoms.—A weakness across the loins, accompanied by a dull pain. After a while the pain shifts from the back to the thigh and hip, becoming more darting and severe. The glands in the groin swell, and at last a soft tumor is perceived at the lower edge of the groin, or by the side of the fundament; the swelling increases to a large size, and sometimes extends itself down the thigh.

Treatment.—In the early stage purge the patient; keep him on a low diet and apply a large blister over the lower part of the back. Confinement in bed is absolutely necessary. When matter is formed make an opening into the tumor in the following manner: Push a sharp lancet first through the skin, then obliquely upwards under it, and then, by depressing the point, pierce the swelling itself. In this way the abscess is opened without the danger that attends wounds of large cavities. If it is small, the whole of the matter may be allowed to flow away at once; if large, after drawing a pint, close the wound for a few hours, and then finish the operation. The lips of the wound must be kept together by sticking plaster. As there are many vessels of importance in the groin, care must be taken to avoid wounding them, and, if a surgeon can be had, he should always be applied to for this purpose.

Of Fistula.

Symptoms.—An abscess or ulcer in the neighborhood of the fundament, preceded by an inflamed swelling, which gives much pain. If there is no communication between the gut and the sore, it is called an incomplete, if there is, a complete fistula.

Treatment.—As the tumor is often taken for piles, attention should be paid to distinguish them. In all cases apply forty or fifty leeches to the part, keep the bowels perfectly loose by a diet of rye mush, and confine the patient to his bed. If, however, the formation of matter cannot be hindered, the swelling must be opened early and a poultice applied to it, when the disease occasionally heals like any other sore; but nine times out of ten it forms a callous winding abscess, through which (if it is complete) excrement, etc., often passes. When it arrives at this point, nothing but an operation can ever be of any service.

There is another species of fistulous opening, which follows the obstruction caused by strictures, etc., in the urinary passage. The water not being able to flow through the natural canal, makes its way out between the bag and the fundament, constituting what is called fistula in perineo. It may almost be called an incurable disease; at all events, none but a surgeon can do anything to relieve it.

Of Ulcers.

By ulcers are meant holes or sores in the skin and flesh, which discharge matter. They are divided into inflamed, fungous, sloughing, and indolent ulcers in the neighborhood of carious bone, and those attended by a peculiar diseased action.

Inflamed Ulcers.

Symptoms.—The margin of the sore is ragged, the skin ending in a sharp edge round it. The neighboring parts are red, swelled and painful, the bottom of the ulcer is uneven and covered with a white spongy substance. In place of healthy yellow matter, it discharges a thin fluid; the surface of it bleeds on the slightest touch.

Treatment.— Confine the patient to bed, purge him occasionally, let his diet be low, and apply a soft bread and milk or linseed poultice to the ulcer. When healthy yellow matter is formed, omit the poultice, keep the sore very clean, and apply a plaster of simple ointment.

Fungous Ulcers.

Symptoms.— The presence of large round granulations, rising above the level of the adjoining parts, or what is commonly called proud flesh, marks this species of ulcer.

Treatment.— Sprinkle red precipitate over the proud flesh, or touch it with lunar caustic, apply dressings of simple cerate to the sore, and pass a bandage tightly over the whole. Burnt alum and blue vitriol may also be used to destroy the proud flesh. Pressure by adhesive plaster or a bandage will often succeed when all other means fail.

Sloughing Ulcer.

Symptoms.— The death of parts of an ulcer which mortify and fall off, generally attended by fever and pain.

Treatment.— The diet should be generous, laudanum must be taken to relieve pain, and bark, wine, porter, etc., to strengthen the system. The carrot poultice is the best local application. The sore may also be washed with a solution of bromine, or of nitric acid, fifty drops to the pint of water. When the dead portions have all fallen off, treat it as a simple ulcer, paying attention, however, to the state of the system.

Indolent Ulcer.

Symptoms.— The edges of the skin are thick, raised, smooth and shining. The points of new flesh are glossy, and the appearance of the whole ulcer is that of an old one in which the healing process is at a stand.

Treatment.— Touch the whole surface, sides and edges of the sore with caustic, blue vitriol, or powder it with Spanish flies or red precipitate, and endeavor in this way to rouse the parts to action. If one article fails, try another. Strips of sticking plaster may be passed over the ulcer, about an inch apart, so as to draw its edges nearer together, and a long bandage be applied over the whole.

Carious Ulcer.

Symptoms.— Ulcers situated over or near carious (or dead) bones, are thereby prevented from healing; they frequently penetrate deep into the parts, forming a canal with hard and indolent sides, that discharges an offensive, unhealthy matter.

Treatment.— Keep the sore clean, repress any proud flesh that may arise, and pay attention to the general health of the patient, taking care that his strength be kept up, if necessary, by wine, bark, porter, etc., etc. The ulcer will not heal until all the pieces of dead bone are thrown off. This process sometimes lasts for years, in which case patience is the only remedy and nature the best physician.

Cases of ulceration frequently occur, proceeding from various causes, whose ravages seem to bid defiance to medical power. In all cases of ulceration, too much stress cannot be laid upon the necessity of keeping the parts clean.

OF ACCIDENTS.

If, in consequence of a broken bone or other injury, the patient is unable to walk, take a door from its hinges, lay him carefully on it, and have him carried by assistants to the nearest house. If no door or sofa can be procured, two boards, sufficiently long and broad, should be nailed to two cross pieces, the ends of which must project about a foot, so as to form handles. If in the woods, or where no boards can be procured, a litter may be formed from the branches of trees. In this way a hand-barrow may be constructed in a few minutes, on which the sufferer may be properly carried.

If he has been wounded and bleeds, the bleeding must be stopped before he is removed.

Having reached a house, lay him on a bed, and undress him with care and gentleness. If any difficulty arises in getting off his coat or pantaloons, rip up the seams rather than use force. This being done, proceed to ascertain the nature of the injury.

This may be either simple or compound; that is, it may be a contusion or bruise, a wound, fracture, or dislocation, or it may be two or all of them united in one or several parts.

A contusion is the necessary consequence of every blow, and is known by the swelling and discoloration of the skin.

Wounds are self-evident.

Fractures are known by the sudden and severe pain, by the misshapen appearance of the limb, sometimes by its being shortened, by the patient being unable to move it without excruciating pain, but most certainly, by grasping the limb above and below the spot where the fracture is supposed to exist, and twisting it different ways, when a grating will be felt, occasioned by the broken ends of the bone rubbing against each other. If the swelling, however, is very great, this experiment should not be made until it is reduced.

Dislocations, or bones being out of joint, are known by the deformity of the joint when compared with its fellow, by the pain and inability to move the limb, by its being longer or shorter than usual, and by the impossibility of moving it in particular directions.

Of Sprains.

Plunge the part sprained into very cold water, and hold it there as long at a time as you can bear it — for several hours — then rub it well with camphorated spirits. If the accident has happened to a joint, as in the ankle, and it remains weak, pour cold water on it from the spout of a tea-kettle, held at a distance, several times in the day.

Of Contusions.

If slight, bathe the part frequently with cold vinegar and water for a few hours, and then rub it well with brandy, or spirits of any kind. Should it be very great, or so as to affect the whole body, which may be known by a general soreness, bleed and purge the patient, and confine him to a diet of rice-water, lemonade, panada, etc. If fever comes on, repeat the purging, etc. In all cases of this nature, be sure the water is regularly evacuated, for it sometimes happens that in consequence of the nerves of the bladder being palsied by the blow, the patient feels no desire to pass it, though the bladder be full. If a suppression ensues, pass a catheter, if possible, or procure assistance for that purpose. The most serious effects, however, resulting from contusion, are when the blow is applied to the head, producing either concussion or compression of the brain.

Concussion of the Brain.

Symptoms.—The patient is stunned, his breathing slow, drowsiness, stupidity, the pupil of the eye rather contracted, vomiting. After a time he recovers.

Treatment.—Apply cloths dipped in cold vinegar and water to his head, and when the stupor is gone and the pulse rises, bleed him, and open his bowels with Epsom salts. He should be confined to bed, kept on a low diet, in a quiet situation, and every measure taken to prevent an inflammation of the brain, which, if it comes on, must be treated by bleeding, blisters, etc.

Compression of the Brain.

Symptoms.—Loss of sense and motion, slow, noisy, and laborious breathing, pulse slow and irregular, the muscles relaxed, as in a person just dead, the pupil of the eye enlarged and will not contract even by a strong light, the patient lies like one in an apoplectic fit, and cannot be roused.

Treatment.—Open a vein and draw off sixteen or twenty ounces of blood, shave the head, and if possible, procure surgical assistance without delay, as there is nothing, unless an operation, that can be of any avail.

Of Wounds.

Wounds are of three kinds, viz., incised, punctured, and contused; among the latter are included gun-shot wounds. The first step in all wounds, is

To Stop the Bleeding.

If the flow of blood is but trifling, draw the edges of the wound together with your hand, and hold them in that position some time, when it will frequently stop. If, on the contrary, it is large, of a bright red color, flowing in spirts or with a jerk, clap your finger on the spot it springs from, and hold it there with a firm pressure, while you direct some one to pass a handkerchief round the limb (supposing the wound to be in one) above the cut, and to tie its two ends together in a hard knot. A cane, whip-handle, or stick of any kind, must now be passed under the knot (between the upper surface of the limb and the handkerchief), and turned round and round until the stick is brought down to the thigh, so as to make the handkerchief encircle it with considerable tightness. You may then take off your finger; if the blood still flows, tighten the handkerchief by a turn or two of the stick, until it ceases. The patient may now be removed (taking care to secure the stick in its position) without running any risk of bleeding to death by the way.

As this apparatus cannot be left on for any length of time, without destroying the life of the parts, endeavor as soon as possible to secure the bleeding vessels, and take it off. Having waxed together three or four threads of a sufficient length, cut the ligature they form into as many pieces as you think there are vessels to be taken up, each piece being about a foot long. Wash the parts with warm water, and then with a sharp hook, or a slender pair of pincers in your hand, fix your eye steadfastly upon the wound, and direct the handkerchief to be relaxed by a turn or two of the stick; you will now see the mouth of the artery from which the blood springs, seize it with your hook or pincers, draw it a little out, while some one passes a ligature round it, and ties it up tight with a double knot. In this way take up in succession every bleeding vessel you can see or get hold of.

If the wound is too high up in a limb to apply the handkerchief, don't lose your presence of mind, the bleeding can still be commanded. If it is the thigh, press firmly in the groin; if in the arm, with the hand end or ring of a common door key, make pressure above the collar bone, and about its middle against the first rib which lies under it. The pressure is to be continued until assistance is procured, and the vessel tied up.

If the wound is on the head, press your finger firmly on it, until a compress can be brought, which must be bound firmly over the artery by a bandage. If the wound is in the face, or so situated that pressure cannot be effectually made, or you cannot get hold of the vessel, and the blood flows fast, place a piece of ice directly over the wound, and let it remain there till the blood coagulates, when it may be removed, and a compress and bandage be applied.

Incised Wounds.

By an incised wound is meant a clean cut. Having stopped the bleeding, wash away all dirt, etc, that may be in it with a sponge and warm water, then draw the sides of the wound together, and keep them in that position by narrow strips of sticking plaster, placed on at regular distances, or from one to two inches apart. A soft compress of old linen or lint may be laid over the whole.

Should much inflammation follow, remove the strips, and purge the patient (who should live very low, and be kept perfectly quiet) according to the exigency of the case. If it is plain that matter must form before the wound will heal, apply a soft poultice or wet lint (water dressing) until that event takes place, when dressing of some simple ointment may be substituted for it.

Although narrow strips of linen, spread with sticking-plaster, form the best means of keeping the sides of a wound together, when they can be applied, yet in the ear, nose, tongue, lips, and eye-lids, it is necessary to use stitches, which are made in the following manner: Having armed a common needle with a double waxed thread, pass the point of it through the skin, at a little distance from the edge of the cut, and bring it out of the opposite one at the same distance. If more than one stitch is required, cut off the needle, thread it again, and proceed as before, until a sufficient number are taken, leaving the threads loose until all the stitches are passed, when the respective ends of each thread must be tied in a hard double knot, drawn in such a way that it bears a little on the side of the cut. When the edges of the wound are partly united, cut the knots carefully, and withdraw the threads.

From what has been said, it must be evident that in all wounds, after arresting the flow of blood and cleansing the parts, if necessary, the great indication is to bring their sides into contact throughout their whole depth, in order that they may grow together as quickly as possible, and without the intervention of matter. To obtain this very desirable result, in addition to the means already mentioned, there are two things to be attended to, the position of the patient and the application of the bandage. The position of the patient should be such as will relax the skin and muscles of the part wounded, thereby diminishing their tendency to separate.

A common bandage of a proper width, passed over the compresses moderately tight, not only serves to keep them in their place, but also tends by its pressure to forward the great object already mentioned. If, however, the wound is so extensive and painful that the limb or body of the patient cannot be raised for the purpose of applying or removing it, the best way is to spread the two ends of one or two strips of linen or leather with sticking-plaster, which may be applied in place of the bandage, as follows: Attach one end of a strip to the sound skin, at a short distance from the edge of the compress, over which it is to be drawn with moderate firmness, and secured in a similar manner on its opposite side. A second or third may, if necessary, be added in the same way.

In all wounds, if violent inflammation come on, reduce it by bleeding, purging, etc., but if there is reason to fear lock-jaw, give wine, porter, brandy, opium, and a generous diet.

Punctured Wounds.

These are caused by sharp pointed instruments,

as needles, awls, nails, etc. Having stopped the bleeding, withdraw any foreign body, as part of a needle, splinters, bit of glass, etc., that may be in it, provided it can be done easily; and if enlarging the wound a little will enable you to succeed in this, do so. Though it is not always necessary to enlarge wounds of this nature, yet in hot weather it is a mark of precaution which should never be omitted. As soon as this is done, apply wet lint or soft linen, covered with oiled silk, or cover the wound with a poultice, moistened with laudanum. This practice may prevent lock-jaw, which is but too frequent a consequence of wounds of this description. When matter forms, cover the part with mild dressings, as a common sore. Laudanum may be given in large doses to relieve pain, and should the inflammation be excessive, bleed and purge. In hot weather, however, or in feeble persons, bleeding should be avoided.

Contused Wounds.

Wounds of this nature are caused by round or blunt bodies, as musket-balls, clubs, stones, etc. They are in general attended by but little bleeding; if, however, there should be any, it must be stopped. If it arises from a ball which can be easily found and withdrawn, it is proper to do so, as well as any piece of the clothing, etc., that may be in it; or if the ball can be distinctly felt directly under the skin, make an incision across it, and take it out, but never allow of any poking in the wound to search for such things; the best extractor of them, as well as the first and best application in contused wounds, proceed from what they may, being a soft bread and milk poultice.

Should the inflammation be great, bleed and purge. Pain may be relieved by laudanum, and if the parts assume a dark look, threatening a mortification, cover them with a carrot poultice.

If the wound is much torn, wash the parts very nicely with warm water, and then (having secured every bleeding vessel) lay them all down in as natural a position as you can, drawing their edges gently together, or as much so as possible, by strips of sticking-plaster, or stitches if necessary. A soft poultice or water dressing is to be applied over the whole.

Poisoned Wounds from bites of Mad Dogs, Rattlesnakes, etc.

The instant a person is bitten either by a mad dog, rattlesnake, or any rabid animal or reptile, he should apply a ligature by means of the stick, above the wound, as tightly as he can well bear it, and without hesitation or delay, cut out the parts bitten, taking along with them a portion of the surrounding sound flesh. The wound should then be freely touched with caustic, or have turpentine poured into it. A decoction of Spanish flies in turpentine may also be applied to the skin surrounding the wound. By these means inflammation will be excited, and suppuration follow, which may prevent the usual dreadful consequences of such accidents. As soon as the parts are cut out take off the ligature.

Should the patient be too timid to allow the use of the knife apply a cupping-glass, and then burn the wound very freely with caustic, and place in it a tuft of tow or cotton, well moistened with the above decoction. The discharge of matter that follows should be kept up for some time. The only reasonable chance for safety is found in the above plan, all the vegetable and mineral productions that have been hitherto recommended as internal remedies, being of very doubtful, if of any, efficacy.

It is asserted, however, that not more than one in ten persons bitten by mad dogs have the hydrophobia. When it occurs it is incurable; but nervous symptoms produced by fear are sometimes mistaken for it. Rattlesnake bites are now commonly treated by giving the sufferer intoxicating doses of whiskey. Ammonia, locally applied immediately after the bite, may be of some use; and the same has been said of iodine and bromine. (Bibron's Antidote.)

Stings of Bees and Wasps, Bites of Musquitoes, etc.

Nothing relieves the pain arising from the sting of a hornet, bee, or wasp so soon as plunging the part in extremely cold water, and holding it there for some time. Water of ammonia may antagonize the poison. A cold lead-water poultice is also a very soothing application. If a number of these insects have attacked you at once, and the parts stung are much swollen, lose some blood, and take a dose of salts.

Musquito-bites may be treated in the same manner, although I have found a solution of common salt and water, made very strong, speedy and effectual in relieving the pain. Camphorated spirits, vinegar, etc., may also be used for the same purpose. A solution of Prussian blue in soft water, with which the parts are to be kept constantly moist, is a highly celebrated remedy for the stings of bees, wasps, etc., etc.

Wounds of the Ear, Nose, etc.

Wash the parts clean, and draw the edges of the wound together by as many stitches as are necessary. If the part is even completely separated, and has been trodden under feet, by washing it in warm water, and putting it accurately in the proper place, by the same means, it may still adhere; and so may teeth that have been knocked out, if replaced.

Wounds of the Scalp.

In all wounds of the scalp it is necessary to shave off the hair. When this is done, wash the parts well, and draw the edges of the wound together with sticking-plaster. If it has been violently torn up in several pieces, wash and lay them all down on the skull again, drawing their edges as nearly together as possible by sticking-plaster, or, if necessary, by stitches. Cover the whole with a soft compress, smeared with simple cerate, or with water dressing.

Wounds of the Throat.

Seize and tie up every bleeding vessel you can get hold of. If the windpipe is cut only partly through, secure it with sticking-plaster. If it is completely divided, bring its edges together by stitches, taking care to pass the needle through the loose membrane that covers the windpipe, and not through the windpipe itself. The head should be bent on the breast, and secured by bolsters and bandages in that position, to favor the approximation of the edges of the wound.

Wounds of the Chest.

If it is a simple incised wound, draw the edges of it together by sticking-plaster, cover it with a compress of wet linen, and pass a bandage round the chest. The patient is to be confined to his bed, kept on a very low diet, and to be bled and purged in order to prevent inflammation. If the latter comes on, reduce it by bleeding.

Should the wound be occasioned by a bullet, extract it and any pieces of cloth, etc., that may be lodged in it, if possible, and cover the part with a piece of linen smeared with some simple ointment, taking care that it is not drawn into the chest. If a portion of the lung protrudes, return it without any delay, but as gently as possible.

Wounds of the Belly.

Close the wound by strips of sticking-plaster,

and stitches passed through the skin, about half an inch from its edges, and cover the whole with a soft compress, secured by a bandage. Any inflammation that may arise is to be reduced by bleeding, purging, and a blister over the whole belly.

Should any part of the bowels come out at the wound, if clean and uninjured, return it as quickly as possible; if covered with dirt, clots of blood, etc., wash it carefully in warm water previous to so doing. If the gut is wounded, and only cut partly through, draw the two edges of it together by a stitch, and return it; if completely divided, connect the edges by four stitches at equal distances, and replace it in the belly, always leaving the end of the ligature to project from the external wound, which must be closed by sticking-plaster. In five or six days, if the threads are loose, withdraw them gently and carefully.

Wounds of Joints.

Bring the edges of the wound together by sticking-plaster, without any delay, keep the part perfectly at rest, bleed, purge, and live very low, to prevent inflammation. Should it come on, it must be met at its first approach by bleeding or leeching to as great an extent as the condition of the patient will warrant. If a permanent stiffening of the joint seems likely to ensue, keep the limb in that position which will prove most useful, that is, the leg should be extended, and the arm bent at the elbow. Wounds of joints are always highly dangerous, and frequently terminate in death.

Wounds of Tendons.

Tendons or sinews are frequently wounded and ruptured. They are to be treated precisely like any other wound, by keeping their divided parts together. The tendon which connects the great muscle forming the calf of the leg, with the heel, called the tendon of Achilles, is frequently cut with the adze, or ruptured in jumping from heights. This accident is to be remedied by drawing up the heel, extending the foot, and placing a splint on the fore part of the leg, extending from the knee to beyond the toes, which being secured in that position by a bandage, keep the foot in the position just mentioned. The hollows under the splint must be filled up with tow or cotton. If the skin falls into the space between the ends of the tendon, apply a piece of sticking-plaster, so as to draw it out of the way. It takes five or six weeks to unite, but no weight should be laid on the limb for several months.

OF FRACTURES.

The signs by which fractures may be known having been already pointed out with sufficient minuteness, it will be unnecessary to dwell thereon; it will be well, however, to recollect this general rule: In cases where, from the accompanying circumstances and symptoms, a strong suspicion exists that the bone is fractured, it is proper to act as though it were positively ascertained to be so.

Fractures of the Bones of the Nose.

The bones of the nose from their exposed situation are frequently forced in. Any smooth article that will pass into the nostril should be immediately introduced with one hand, to raise the depressed portions to the proper level, while the other is employed in moulding them into the required shape. If violent inflammation follow, bleed, purge, and live on a low diet.

Fractures of the Lower Jaw.

This accident is easily discovered by looking into the mouth, and is to be remedied by keeping the lower jaw firmly pressed against the upper one by means of a bandage passed under the chin and over the head. If it is broken near the angle, or that part nearest the ear, place a cushion or roll of linen in the hollow behind it, over which the bandage must pass, so as to make it push that part of the bone forward. The parts are to be confined in this way for twenty days, during which time all the nourishment that is taken should be sucked between the teeth. If, in consequence of the blow, a tooth is loosened, do not meddle with it, for if let alone, it will grow fast again.

Fractures of the Collar-Bone.

This accident is a very common occurrence, and is known at once by passing the finger along it, and by the swelling, etc. To reduce it, seat the patient in a chair, without any shirt, and place a pretty stout compress of linen, made in the shape of a wedge, under his arm, the thick end of which should press against the arm-pit. His arm, bent to a right angle at the elbow, is now to be brought down to his side, and secured in that position by a long bandage, which passes over the arm of the affected side and round the body. The forearm is to be supported across the breast by a sling. It takes from four to five weeks to re-unite.

Fractures of the Arm.

Seat the patient on a chair, or the side of a bed. Let one assistant hold the sound arm, while another grasps the wrist of the broken one and steadily extends it in an opposite direction, bending the forearm a little, to serve as a lever. You can now place the bones in their proper situation. Two splints of shingle or stout pasteboard, long enough to reach from below the shoulder to near the elbow, must be then well covered with tow or cotton, and laid along each side of the arm, and kept in that position by a bandage. The forearm is to be supported in a sling. Two small splints may, for better security, be laid between the first ones, that is, one on top and the other underneath the arm, to be secured by the bandage in the same way as the others.

Fractures of the Bones of the Forearm.

These are to be reduced precisely in the same way, excepting the mode of keeping the upper portion of it steady, which is done by grasping the arm above the elbow. Apply two splints, one extending to the palm and one to the back of the hand, and over them a bandage. When the splints and bandage are applied, support it in a sling.

Fractures of the Wrist.

This accident is of rare occurrence. When it does happen the injury is often so great as to require amputation. If you think the hand can be saved, lay it on a splint well covered with tow; this extends beyond the fingers. Place another splint opposite to it, lined with the same soft material, and secure them by a bandage. The hand is to be carried in a sling.

The bones of the hand are sometimes broken. When this is the case fill the palm with soft compresses or tow, and then lay a splint on it long enough to extend from the elbow to beyond the ends of the fingers, to be secured by a bandage, as usual.

When a finger is broken, extend the end of it until it becomes straight, place the fractured portion in its place, and then apply two small pasteboard splints, one below and the other above, to be secured by a narrow bandage or adhesive straps. The top splint should extend from the end of the finger over the back of the hand. It may sometimes be proper to have two additional splints for the sides of the finger.

Fractures of the Ribs.

When, after a fall or blow, the patient complains of a pricking in his side, we may suspect a rib is broken. It is ascertained by placing the tips of two or three fingers on the spot where the pain is, and desiring the patient to cough, when the grating sensation will be felt. All that is necessary is to pass a broad bandage round the chest, so tight as to prevent the motion of the ribs in breathing, and to observe a low diet.

Fractures of the Thigh.

This bone is frequently broken, and hitherto has been considered the most difficult of all fractures to manage. To the ingenuity, however, of the late Dr. J. Hartshorne, of this city, the world is indebted for an apparatus which does away the greatest impediments that have been found to exist in treating it, so as to leave a straight limb, without lameness or deformity. Nor is it the least of its merits, that any man of common sense can apply it nearly as well as a surgeon.

It consists of two splints made of half or three-quarter inch well-seasoned stuff, from eight to ten inches wide, one of which should reach from a little above the hip to fifteen or sixteen inches beyond the foot, while the other extends the same length from the groin. The upper end of the inner splint is hollowed out and well padded or stuffed. Their lower ends are held together by a cross-piece, having two tenons, which enter two vertical mortices, one in each splint, and secured there by pins. In the centre of this cross-piece (which should be very solid) is a female screw. Immediately above the vertical mortices are two horizontal ones of considerable length, in which slide the tenons of a second cross-piece, to the upper side of which is fastened a foot-block, shaped like the sole of a shoe, while in the other is a round hole for the reception of the head of the male screw, which passes through the female one just noticed. On the top of this cross-piece, to which the foot-block is attached, are two pins, which fall into grooves at the head of the screw, thereby firmly connecting them. The foot-block, as before observed, is shaped like the sole of a shoe. Near the toe is a slit, through which passes a strap and buckle. Near the heel are a couple of straps, with two rings, arranged precisely like those of a skate, of which, in fact, the whole foot-block is an exact resemblance. A long male screw, of wood or other material, completes the apparatus.

To apply it, put a slipper on the foot of the broken limb, and lay the apparatus over the leg. By turning the screw the foot-block will be forced up to the foot in the slipper, which is to be firmly strapped to it, as boys fasten their skates. By turning the screw the contrary way, the padded extremity of the inner splint presses against the groin, and the foot is gradually drawn down, until the broken limb becomes of its natural length and appearance, when any projection or little inequality that may remain can be felt and reduced by a gentle pressure of the hand.

The great advantages of this apparatus, I again repeat, are the ease with which it is applied, and the certainty with which it acts. The foot once secured to the block, in a way that every schoolboy understands, nothing more is required than to turn the screw until the broken limb is found to be of the same length as the sound one. It is right to observe that this should not be effected at once, it being better to turn the screw a little every day, until the limb is sufficiently extended.

As this apparatus may not always be at hand, it is proper to mention the next best plan of treating the accident. It is found in the splints of Desault, improved by Dr. Physick, consisting of four pieces. The first has a crutch head, and extends from the arm-pit to six or eight inches beyond the foot. A little below the crutch are two holes, and near the lower end, on the inside, is a block, below which there is also a hole. The second reaches from the groin, the same length with the first, being about three inches wide above and two below. Two pieces of stout pasteboard, as many handkerchiefs or bands of muslin, with some tow or raw cotton, and a few pieces of tape, form the catalogue of the apparatus.

It is applied as follows. Four or five pieces of tape are to be laid across the bed, at equal distances from each other. Over the upper two is placed one of the short pasteboard splints, well covered with tow. The patient is now to be carefully and gently placed on his back, so that his thigh may rest on the splint. One of the handkerchiefs, or a strong soft band, is to be passed between the testicle and thigh of the affected side, and its ends held by an assistant standing near the head of the bed. The second handkerchief is to be passed round the ankle, crossed on the instep, and tied under the sole of the foot. Instead of this, a number of long strips of adhesive plaster, two inches wide, may be applied to the ankle and up the leg, and tied together below the foot. By steadily pulling these two handkerchiefs, the limb is to be extended, while, with the hand, the broken bones are replaced in their natural position. The long splint is now to be placed by the side of the patient, the crutch in the arm-pit (which is defended with tow), while the short one is laid along the inside of the thigh and leg. The ends of the first handkerchief, being passed through the upper holes, are to be drawn tight and secured by a knot, while the ends of the second one pass over the block before mentioned, to be fastened in like manner at the lower one. All that remains is the short pasteboard splint, which, being well covered with tow, is to be laid on the top of the thigh. The tapes being tied so as to keep the four splints together, completes the operation.

Tow or raw cotton is to be everywhere interposed between the splints and the limb, and a large handful of it placed in the groin, to prevent irritation from the upper or counter extending band. It is necessary to be careful, while tying the two handkerchiefs, that they are not relaxed, so that if the operation is properly performed, the two limbs will be nearly of an equal length.

The superior advantages of Hartshorne's apparatus over this, as well as all others, must be evident to every one acquainted with the difficulty of keeping up that constant extension which is so absolutely necessary to avoid deformity and lameness, and which is so completely effected by the screw. Next to that, however, stands the one just described, which can be made by any carpenter in a few minutes, and which, if carefully applied, will be found to answer extremely well. While waiting for apparatus, the thigh may be kept extended by attaching a weight of a few pounds to the extending band below the foot, and suspending it beyond the foot of the bed.

Fractured thighs and legs generally reunite in six or eight weeks; in old men, however, they require three or four months.

In cases of fracture of the thigh or leg, the patient should always, if possible, be laid on a mattress, supported by boards instead of the sacking, which, from its elasticity and the yielding of the cords, is apt to derange the position of the limb.

Fractures of the Knee-pan.

This accident is easily ascertained on inspection. It may be broken in any direction, but is most generally so across or transversely. It is reduced by bringing the fragments together, and keeping them in that position by a long bandage passed carefully round the leg, from the ankle to the knee, then pressing the upper fragment down so as to meet its fellow (the leg being extended), and placing a thick compress of linen above it, over which the bandage is to be continued.

The extended limb is now to be laid on a broad splint, extending from the buttock to the heel, thickly covered with tow to fill up the inequalities of the leg. For additional security, two strips of muslin may be nailed to the middle of the splint, and one on each side, and passed above the joint, the one below, the other above, so as to form a figure of eight. In twenty or thirty days the limb should be moved a little to prevent stiffness. But it usually requires two or three months for perfect union of this bone.

If the fracture is through its length, bring the parts together, place a compress on each side, and keep them together with a bandage, leaving the limb extended and at rest. Any inflammation in this or other fracture is to be combated by bleeding, low diet, etc., etc.

Fractures of the Leg.

From the thinness of the parts covering the principal bone of the leg, it is easy to ascertain if it be broken obliquely. If, however, the fracture be directly across, no displacement will occur, but the pain, swelling, and the grating sensation will sufficiently decide the nature of the accident.

If the fracture is oblique, let two assistants extend the limb, while the broken parts are placed by the hand in their natural position. Two splints, that reach from a little above the knee to nine or ten inches below the foot, having near the upper end of each four holes, and a vertical mortice near the lower end, into which is fitted a cross-piece, are now to be applied as follows:—Lay two pieces of tape about a foot long on each side of the leg, just below the knee-joint, and secure them there by several turns of a bandage; pass a silk handkerchief round the ankle, cross it on the instep, and tie it under the sole of the foot. The two splints are now placed one on each side of the leg, the four ends of the pieces of tape passed through the four holes and firmly tied, and the cross-piece placed in the mortice. By tying the ends of the handkerchief to this cross-piece the business is finished.

If the fracture is across, and no displacement exists, apply two splints of stout pasteboard, reaching from the heel to the knee, and well covered with tow, one on each side of the leg, securing them by a bandage passing round the limb, and outside the splints. Instead of splints, however, a fracture-box is often used, made by fastening, with hinges, to a bottom-piece rather longer than the leg, two side-pieces about six inches high, and reaching above the knee. The leg may rest in this on a pillow. A footboard fastened to the bottom-piece may serve to fix the foot by the aid of a bandage.

In cases of oblique fracture of the leg close to the knee, Hartshorne's apparatus for fractured thighs may be applied, as already directed.

Fractures of the Bones of the Foot.

The bone of the heel is sometimes, though rarely, broken. It is known by a crack at the moment of the accident, a difficulty in standing, by the swelling, and by the grating noise on moving the heel. To reduce, take a long bandage, lay the end of it on the top of the foot, carry it over the toes under the sole, and then by several turns secure it in that position.

The foot being extended as much as possible, carry the bandage along the back of the leg above the knee, where it is to be secured by several turns, and then brought down on the front of the leg, to which it is secured by circular turns. In this way the broken pieces will be kept in contact, and in the course of a month or six weeks will be united.

Fractures of the foot, toes, etc., are to be treated like those of the hand and fingers.

Of Dislocations.

The signs by which a dislocation may be known have been already mentioned. It is well to recollect that the sooner the attempt is made to reduce it the easier it will be done. The strength of one man, properly applied, at the moment of the accident, will often succeed in restoring the head of a bone to its place, which in a few days would have required the combined efforts of men and pulleys. If after several trials with the best apparatus that can be mustered, you find you cannot succeed, make the patient drink strong solution of tartar emetic until he is very sick. In this way, owing to the relaxed state of the muscles, a very slight force will often be sufficient, where a very great one has been previously used without effect.

If any objections are made to this proceeding, or if the patient will not consent to it, having your apparatus (which is presently to be mentioned) all ready, make him stand up, and bleed him in that position until he faints; the moment this happens, apply your extending and counter-extending forces. Another important rule is to vary the direction of the extending force. A slight pull in one way will often effect what has been in vain attempted by great force in another.

Dislocation of the Lower Jaw.

This accident, which is occasioned by blows or yawning, is known by an inability to shut the mouth, and the projection of the chin. To reduce it, seat the patient in a chair, with his head supported by the breast of an assistant, who stands behind him. Your thumbs being covered with leather, are then to be pushed between the jaws, as far back as possible, while with the fingers outside you grasp the bone, which is to be pressed downwards at the same time that the chin is raised. If this is properly done, the bone will be found moving, when the chin is to be pushed backwards and the thumbs slipped between the jaws and the cheeks. If this is not done, they will be bitten by the sudden snap of the teeth as they come together. The jaws should be kept closed by a bandage for a few days, and the patient live on soup.

Dislocation of the Collar-bone.

This bone is rarely dislocated. Should it occur, apply the bandages, etc., directed for a fracture of the same part.

Dislocation of the Shoulder.

Dislocations of the shoulder are the most common of all the accidents of the kind. It is very easily known by the deformity of the joint, and the head of the bone being found in some unnatural position. To reduce it, lay the patient on the ground, place your heel in his arm-pit, and steadily and forcibly extend the arm by grasping it at the wrist. The same thing may be tried in various positions, as placing yourself on the ground with him, laying him on a low bed, while you are standing near the foot of it, etc.

If this fails, pass a strong band over the shoulder, carry it across the breast, give the ends to assistants, or fasten them to a staple in the wall; the middle of a strong band or folded towel is now to be laid on the arm above the elbow, and secured there by numerous turns of a bandage. The two ends of the towel being then given to assistants, or connected with a pulley, a steady, continued, and forcible extension is to be made for a few moments, while with your hands you endeavor to push the head of the bone into its place.

Dislocation of the Elbow.

If the patient has fallen on his hands, or holds his arm bent at the elbow, and every endeavor to straighten it gives him pain, it is dislocated backwards. Seat him in a chair, let one person grasp the arm near the shoulder and another the wrist, and forcibly extend it, while you interlock the fingers of both hands just above the elbow, and pull it backwards, remembering that under those circumstances, whatever degree of force is required, should be applied in this direction. The elbow is sometimes dislocated sideways or laterally. To reduce it, make extension by pulling at the wrist, while some one secures the arm above, then push the bone into its place, either inwards or outwards, as may be required. After the reduction of a dislocated elbow keep the joint at perfect rest for five or six days, and then move it gently. If inflammation comes on, bleed, purge, etc., etc. Dislocation of the elbow is often accompanied by fracture, in which case it will not bear violence.

Dislocation of the Wrist, Fingers, etc.

Dislocations of the wrist, fingers and thumb are readily perceived on examination; they are all to be reduced by forcibly extending the lower extremity of the part, and pushing the bones into their place. If necessary, small bands may be secured to the fingers by a narrow bandage to facilitate the extension. These accidents should be attended to without delay, for if neglected for a little time they become irremediable.

Dislocation of the Thigh.

Notwithstanding the hip-joint is the strongest one in the body, it is sometimes dislocated. As a careful examination of the part, comparing the length and appearance of the limb with its fellow, etc., sufficiently mark the nature of the accident, we will proceed to state the remedy.

Place the patient on his back upon a table covered with a blanket. Two sheets, folded like cravats, are then to be passed between the thigh and testicle of each side, and their ends (one half of each sheet passing obliquely over the belly to the opposite shoulder, while the other half passes under the back in the same direction) given to several assistants, or what is much better, tied very firmly to a hook, staple, post, or some immovable body. A large, very strong napkin, folded as before, like a cravat, is now to be laid along the top of the thigh, so that its middle will be just above the knee, where it is to be well secured by many turns of a bandage. The two ends are then to be knotted. If you have no pulleys, a twisted sheet or rope may be passed through the loop formed by the napkin. If you can procure the former, however, fasten the loop over the hook of the lower block and secure the upper one to the wall, directly opposite to the hooks or men that hold the sheets that pass between the thighs. A steadily increasing and forcible extension of the thigh is then to be made by the men who are stationed at the pulleys or sheet while you are turning and twisting the limb to assist in dislodging it from its unnatural situation. By these means, properly applied, the head of the bone will frequently slip into the socket with a loud noise.

If, however, you are foiled, change the direction of the extending force, recollecting always that it is not by sudden or violent jerks that any benefit can be attained, but by a steady, increasing and long-continued pull. Should all your efforts prove unavailing (I would not advise you to lose much time before you resort to it), make the patient, as before directed, very sick or drunk, and when he cannot stand apply the pulleys. If this fails, or is objected to, bleed him till he faints, and then try it again.

Dislocation of the Knee-pan.

When this little bone is dislocated it is evident on the slightest glance. To reduce it, lay the patient on his back, straighten the leg, lift it up to a right angle with his body, and in that position push the bone back to its place. The knee should be kept at rest for a few days.

Dislocation of the Leg.

As these accidents cannot happen without tearing and lacerating the soft parts, but little force is required to place the bones in their natural situation. If the parts are so much torn that the bone slips again out of place, apply Hartshorne's or Desault's apparatus, as for a fractured thigh.

Dislocation of the Foot.

The foot is seldom dislocated. Should it happen, however, let one person secure the leg and another draw the foot, while you push the bone in the contrary way to that in which it was forced out. The part is then to be covered with compresses dipped in lead-water and a splint applied on each side of the leg that reaches below the foot. Accidents of this nature are always dangerous; all that can be done to remedy them consists in the speedy reduction of the bone, keeping the parts at rest and subduing the inflammation by bleeding, low diet, etc., etc.

Of Compound Accidents.

Having spoken of the treatment to be pursued for a bruise, wound, fracture, and dislocation, as happening singly, it remains to state what is to be done when they are united.

We will suppose that a man has been violently thrown from a carriage. On examination, a wound is found in his thigh, bleeding profusely, his ankle is out of joint, with a wound communicating with its cavity, and the leg broken.

In the first place stop the bleeding from the wound in the thigh, reduce the dislocation next, draw the edges of the wounds together with sticking plaster, and lastly, apply Hartshorne's or Desault's apparatus to remedy the fracture.

If, instead of a wound, fracture, and dislocation, there is a concussion or compression of the brain, a dislocation and fracture, attend to the concussion first, the dislocation next, and the fracture the last.

Of Amputation.

As accidents sometimes happen at sea, or in situations where it is impossible to obtain a surgeon, and which require the immediate amputation of a limb, it is proper to say a few words on that subject. To perform the operation is one thing, to know when it ought to be performed is another. Any man of common dexterity and firmness can cut off a leg, but to decide upon the necessity of doing so, requires much judgment, instances having occured where, under the most seemingly desperate circumstances, the patient through fear or obstinacy has refused to submit to the knife, and yet afterwards recovered.

Although in many cases much doubt may exist in determining whether it is proper to amputate or not, yet in others, all difficulty vanishes, as when a ball has carried away an arm. Supposing for a moment while rolling in a heavy sea, during a gale, the lashings of a gun give way, by which a man has his knee, leg, or ankle completely mashed, or that either of those parts is crushed by a fall from the topgallant yard, a falling tree, etc. The great laceration of blood vessels, nerves, and tendons, the crushing and splintering of the bones, almost necessarily resulting from such accidents, render immediate amputation an unavoidable and imperious duty.

If there are none of the regular instruments at hand, you must provide the following, which are always to be had, and which answer extremely well — being careful to have the knives as sharp and smooth as possible.

Instruments.— The handkerchief and stick, a carving or other large knife, with a straight blade, a penknife, a carpenter's tenon or mitre saw, a slip of leather or linen, three inches wide and eighteen or twenty long, slit up the middle to the half of its length, a dozen or more ligatures, each about a foot long, made of waxed thread, bobbin, or fine twine, a hook with a sharp point, a pair of slender pincers, several narrow strips of sticking-plaster, dry lint, a piece of linen, large enough to cover the end of the stump, spread with simple ointment or lard, a bandage three or four yards long, the width of your hand; sponges and warm water.

Amputation of the Arm.

Operation.— Give the patient ninety drops of laudanum, or let him breathe ether from a large sponge till sound asleep, and seat him on a narrow and firm table or chest, of a convenient height, so that some one can support him, by clasping him round the body, the handkerchief and stick have not been previously applied, place it as high up on the arm as possible (the stick being very short) and so that the knot may pass on the inner third of it. Your instruments having been placed regularly on a table or waiter, and within reach of your hand, while some one supports the lower end of the arm, and at the same time draws down the skin, take the large knife and make one straight cut all round the limb, through the skin and fat only, then with the penknife separate as much of the skin from the flesh above the cut, and all round it, as will form a flap to cover the face of the stump; when you think there is enough separated, turn it back, where it must be held by an assistant, while with the large knife you make a second straight incision round the arm and down to the bone, as close as you can to the doubled edge of the flap, but taking great care not to cut it. The bone is now to be passed through the slit in the piece of linen before mentioned, and pressed by its ends against the upper surface of the wound by the person who holds the flap, while you saw through the bone as near to it as you can. With the hooks or pincers, you then seize and tie up every vessel that bleeds, the largest first, and smaller ones next, until they are all secured. When this is done, relax the stick a little; if an artery springs, tie it as before. The wound is now to be gently cleansed with a sponge and warm water, and the stick to be relaxed. If it is evident that the arteries are all tied, bring the flap over the end of the stump, draw its edges together with strips of sticking-plaster, leaving the ligature hanging out at the angles, lay the piece of linen spread with ointment over the straps, a pledget of lint over that, and secure the whole by the bandage, when the patient may be carried to bed, and the stump laid on a pillow.

The handkerchief and stick are to be left loosely round the limb, so that if any bleeding happens to come on, it may be tightened in an instant by the person who watches by the patient, when the dressings must be taken off, the flap raised, and the vessel be sought for and tied up, after which, every thing must be placed as before.

It may be well to observe that in sawing through the bone, a long and free stroke should be used, to prevent any hitching, as an additional security against which, the teeth of the saw should be well sharpened and set wide.

There is also another circumstance, which it is essential to be aware of: the ends of divided arteries cannot at times be got hold of, or being diseased their coats give way under the hook, so that they cannot be drawn out; sometimes also, they are found ossified or turned into bone. In all these cases, having armed a needle with a ligature, pass it through the flesh round the artery, so that when tied, there will be a portion of it included in the ligature along with the artery. When the ligature has been made to encircle the artery, cut off the needle and tie it firmly in the ordinary way.

The bandages, etc., should not be disturbed for five or six days, if the weather is cool; if it is very warm, they may be removed in three. This is to be done with the greatest care, soaking them well with warm water until they are quite soft, and can be taken away without sticking to the stump. A clean plaster, lint, and bandage are then to be applied as before, to be removed every two days. At the expiration of ten or fifteen days the ligatures generally come away; and in three or four weeks, if every thing goes on well, the wound heals.

Amputation of the Thigh.

This is performed in precisely the same manner as that of the arm, care being used to prevent the edges of the flap from uniting until the surface of the stump has adhered to it.

Amputation of the Leg.

As there are two bones in the leg which have a thin muscle between, it is necessary to have an additional knife to those already mentioned, to divide it. It should have a long narrow blade, with a double-cutting edge, and a sharp point; a carving or case knife may be ground down to answer the purpose, the blade being reduced to rather less than half an inch in width. The linen or leather strip should also have two slits in it instead of one. The patient is to be laid on his back, on a table covered with blankets or a mattress, with a sufficient number of assistants to secure him. The handkerchief and stick being applied on the upper part of the thigh, one person holds the knee, and another the foot and leg as steadily as possible, while with the large knife the operator makes an oblique incision round the limb, through the skin, and beginning at five or six inches below the knee pan, and carrying it regularly round in such a manner that the cut will be lower down on the calf than in front of the leg. As much of the skin is then to be separated by the penknife as will cover the stump. When this is turned back, a second cut is to be made all round the limb and down to the bones, when, with the narrow-bladed knife just mentioned, the flesh between them is to be divided. The middle piece of the leather strip is now to be pulled through between the bones, the whole being held back by the assistant, who supports the flap while the bones are sawed, which should be so managed that the smaller one is completely cut through by the time the other is only half so. The arteries are then to be taken up, the flap brought down and secured by adhesive plasters, etc. as already directed.

Amputation of the Forearm.

As the forearm has two bones in it, the narrow bladed knife, and the strip of linen with three tails, are to be provided. The incision should be straight round the part, as in the arm, with this exception, complete it as directed for the preceding case.

Amputation of Fingers and Toes.

Draw the skin back, and make an incision round the finger, a little below the joint it is intended to remove, turn back a little flap to cover the stump, then cut down to the joint, bending it so that you can cut through the ligaments that connect the two bones, the under one first, then that on the side. The head of the bone is then to be turned out, while you cut through the remaining soft parts. If you see an artery spirt, tie it up, if not, bring down the flap and secure it by a strip of sticking-plaster, and a narrow bandage over the whole.

Remarks. — To prevent the troublesome consequences of secondary bleeding, before the strips of plaster are applied over the edges of the flap, give the patient, if he is faint, a little wine and water, and wait a few minutes to see whether the increased force it gives to the circulation, will occasion a flow of blood; if it does secure the vessel it comes from. If there is a considerable flow of blood from the hollow of the bone, place a small cedar plug in it. Should violent spasms of the stump ensue, have it carefully held by assistants, and give the patient large doses of laudanum; it may in fact be laid down as a general rule, that after every operation of the kind, laudanum should be given in greater or less doses, as the patient may be in more or less pain.

Of Suspended Animation.

From Drowning.—The common methods of rolling the body of a drowned person on a barrel, or holding it up by the heels, etc., are full of danger, and should never be permitted. If a spark of life should happen to remain, this violence would extinguish it forever. As soon, therefore, as the body is found, convey it as gently as possible to the nearest house, strip it of the wet clothes, dry it well, and place it on a bed between warm blankets. First draw the tongue out for a few moments while the body is prone to open the windpipe. Every part is now to be well rubbed with flannels dipped in warm brandy, or spirits of any kind, while a warming-pan, hot bricks, or bottles or bladders filled with warm water, are applied to the stomach, back, and soles of the feet. During these operations a certain number of the assistants (no more persons are to be allowed in the room than are absolutely necessary) should try to inflate the lungs by blowing through the nozzle of a common bellows, or a pipe of any kind, placed in one nostril, while the other with the mouth is kept being done at intervals about sixteen times a minute. Raising both arms forward and upward, over the head, at the same time and at the same intervals, will aid in expanding the chest. If a warm bath can be procured, place the body in it. Clysters of warm brandy and water, salt and water, or peppermint-water may be injected.

All these operations, particularly rubbing the body, and trying to inflate the lungs should be continued for six or eight hours, and when the patient has come to himself, small quantities of warm wine, wine whey, brandy and water, etc., may be given to him from time to time. If, after he has recovered, a stupor or drowsiness remains (but not before) bleed him very moderately.

Should the accident occur in winter, and the body feel cold, as if frozen, previously to applying warmth, rub it well with snow, ice, or very cold water. Above all things remember that perseverance for many hours in the remedies pointed out, may give you the unspeakable pleasure of restoring a fellow creature to life.

From Cold.—Take the body into a room, the doors and windows of which are open, and where there is no fire, and rub it with snow or cold water; if this can be procured in plenty, the patient, with the exception of his face, which should be left out, may be completely covered with it to the thickness of two feet. After a while, friction with flannels and hot spirits is to be used, as in the preceding case, and warmth very gradually applied. The lungs are to be inflated, as directed in cases of drowning, and when the patient is able to swallow, warm wine, etc., may be given in small quantities.

If a limb is frost-bitten, the cold applications should be continued longer, and warmth be more gradually applied than when the whole body is frozen. Care should be taken to handle the parts carefully, so as not to break off the ear, tip of the nose, etc.

From Hanging.—The remedies for this accident are the same as in drowning, with the addition of taking away a small quantity of blood, by cupping glasses, from the neck, or by opening the jugular vein.

From Foul Air.—Throw open the doors and windows, or take the patient into the open air, and seat him, undressed, well wrapped in a blanket, in a chair, leaning a little to the right side, place his feet or whole body in a bath, and sprinkle his stomach with cold vinegar or water, and rub it immediately with flannels dipped in oil. Clysters of vinegar and water are to be injected, and when animation returns, continue the frictions, and give warm mint tea, etc.

Of Swallowing Poisons.

The first thing to be done when a person is discovered to have swallowed poison is to ascertain what it is he has taken, the next to be speedy in resorting to its appropriate remedies. If any one of these cannot be had, try some other without loss of time. An emetic is generally safe and proper.

Acids.

Oil of vitriol, aqua fortis, muriatic acid, oxalic acid.

Symptoms.—A burning heat in the mouth, throat, and stomach, stinking breath, an inclination to vomit, or vomiting various matters mixed with blood, hiccups, costiveness, or stools more or less bloody, pain in the belly, so great that the weight of a sheet cannot be borne, burning thirst, difficulty of breathing, suppression of urine, etc.

Remedies.—Mix an ounce of calcined magnesia with a pint of water and give a glassful every two minutes. If it is not at hand, use flaxseed tea, rice-water, or water alone, in large quantities, until the former can be procured. If it cannot be obtained, dissolve an ounce of soap in a pint of water and take a glassful every two minutes; chalk or whiting may also be taken by the mouth, and clysters of milk be frequently injected. If the patient will not vomit, put him in the warm bath, bleed him freely and apply leeches and blisters over the parts pained. If the cramps and convulsions continue, give him a cup of common tea, with an ounce of sugar, forty drops of Hoffman's Anodyne, and fifteen or twenty of laudanum, every quarter or half hour. No nourishment but sweetened rice-water is to be taken for several days. In these cases never give tartar emetic, ipecacuanha, or tickle the throat with a feather—they only increase the evil. For oxalic acid, some preparation of lime is the antidote.

Alkalies.

Caustic potash, caustic soda, volatile alkali.
Symptoms.—These substances occasion the same effects as acids.
Remedies.—Take two tablespoonsful of vinegar or lemon-juice in a glass of water at once; follow it up by drinking large quantities of water. Pursue the same treatment otherwise as in poisoning from acids.

Mercury.

Corrosive sublimate, red precipitate, vermilion.
Symptoms.—Constriction and great pain in the throat, stomach and bowels, vomiting of various matters mixed with blood, unquenchable thirst, difficulty of urine, convulsions.
Remedies.—Mix the whites of a dozen or fifteen eggs with two pints of cold water, and give a glassful every two minutes, with as much milk as can be swallowed, and large doses of ipecacuanha. If after the egg mixture is all taken the vomiting does not stop, repeat the dose, with the addition of more water. Leeches, the warm bath, blisters, etc., are to be used to reduce the pain and inflammation, as before directed.

Arsenic.

Symptoms.—These are the same as produced by the mercurial poisons.
Remedies.—Give large quantities of warm water until a plentiful vomiting is induced, to assist which ipecacuanha may be taken in considerable doses at the same time. The antidote for arsenic is hydrated peroxide of iron. It may be prepared by adding spirits or water of ammonia to solution of persulphate of iron. The hydrated peroxide may be given *freely* after straining out the liquid in a bag. If it cannot be had, magnesia will be useful as a partial antidote. Barley, rice-water, flaxseed tea, milk, etc., should afterwards be employed. Oil is never to be used in this case until the symptoms have considerably abated, or the poison has been ejected.

Copper.

The symptoms occasioned by swallowing verdigris are nearly the same as those of the mercurial poisons. The great remedy is large quantities of the white of eggs. In addition to this use all the means recommended for corrosive sublimate, etc.

Antimony.

Antimonial wine, tartar emetic, butter of antimony, etc.
Symptoms.—Excessive vomiting, pain and cramp in the stomach, convulsions, etc.
Remedies.—Encourage the vomiting by warm water, and if after awhile it does not stop, give a grain of opium in a glass of the sweetened water every fifteen minutes. To relieve the pain, apply leeches to the stomach, throat, or parts affected. Infusion of galls may be given also quite freely.

Salts of Tin.

Give as much milk as can be got down, and if it is not at hand use large quantities of cold water to induce vomiting. If the symptoms do not abate, pursue the plan directed for acids.

Salts of Bismuth, Gold and Zinc.

Pursue the plan recommended for copper.

Lunar Caustic.

Dissolve two tablespoonsful of common table salt in two pints of water; a few glasses of this will induce vomiting. If not relieved, drink flaxseed tea, apply leeches, etc., as for acids.

Saltpetre.

Pursue the plan recommended for copper.

Sal Ammoniac.

Symptoms.—Vomiting; pain in the belly; a stiffness of the whole body; convulsions.
Remedies.—Introduce your finger or a feather into the throat to induce vomiting, and give plenty of sweetened water. To relieve the convulsions, give the tea, laudanum, etc., as for acids, or the laudanum alone, and to ease the pain in the belly apply leeches, etc.

Phosphorus.

The symptoms and remedies are the same as by poisons from acids, with the addition of olive oil or lard oil by the tablespoonful.

Spanish Flies.

Symptoms.—Great pain in the stomach, with obstinate and painful erections, accompanied by a difficulty or suppression of urine, or if any is passed it is bloody; a horror of swallowing liquids; frightful convulsions.
Remedies.—Make the patient swallow as much sweet oil as he can possibly get down. Milk and sugared water are also to be freely used. In addition to the plan recommended for acids, solutions of gum arabic or flaxseed tea are to be injected into the bladder. If no vomiting is induced, put him in the warm bath, continue the sweetened water, and rub his thighs and legs with two ounces of warm oil, in which a quarter of an ounce of camphor has been dissolved. Eight or ten grains of camphor may be mixed with the yolk of an egg and taken internally. If there is acute pain in the bladder, apply leeches over it.

Powdered Glass.

Stuff the patient with thick rice, bread, potatoes, or any other vegetable; then give him five grains of tartar emetic to vomit him, after which use milk freely, clysters and fomentations to the belly, with the warm bath; leeches, etc., are not to be neglected.

Lead.

Sugar of lead, extract of saturn, white lead, litharge, minium.
Symptoms.—A sweet, astringent taste in the mouth; constriction of the throat; pain in the stomach; bloody vomiting, etc.
Remedies.—Dissolve a handful of Epsom or Glauber salts in a pint of water, and give it at once; when it has vomited him use gum-water. If the symptoms continue, act as directed for acids.

Opium, or Laudanum.

Symptoms.—Stupor; an insurmountable inclination to sleep; delirium; convulsions, etc.
Remedies.—Endeavor to excite vomiting by two grains of tartar emetic, or four grains of blue or thirty of white vitriol. Thrust a feather down the throat for the same purpose, or use the stomach pump. Never give vinegar or other acids until the poison is altogether or nearly evacuated. After this has taken place, give repeatedly a cup of very strong coffee. The coffee, etc., are to be continued until the drowsiness is gone off, which, if it continues and resembles that of apoplexy, must be relieved by bleeding. The patient is to be forcibly kept in constant motion. The galvanic battery and artificial respiration are sometimes necessary.

MEDICINE.

Toadstools.

Remedies.—Give the patient immediately two grains of tartar emetic, twenty-five or thirty of ipecacuanha, and an ounce of salts, dissolved in a glass of water, one-third to be taken every fifteen minutes, until he vomits freely. Then purge with castor oil. If there is great pain in the belly, apply leeches, blisters, etc.

Tobacco, Hemlock, Nightshade, Spurred Rye, etc.

Remedies.—An emetic as directed for opium. If the poison has been swallowed some time, purge with castor oil. Brandy or ammonia may be required for stimulation in tobacco poisoning.

Poisonous Fish.

Remedies.—An emetic. If it has been eaten some time, give castor oil by the mouth and clyster. After these have operated, twenty drops of ether may be taken on a lump of sugar.

Foreign Bodies in the Throat.

Persons are frequently in danger of suffocation from fish-bones, pins, etc., which stick in the throat. The moment an accident of this kind occurs, desire the patient to be perfectly still, open his mouth, and look into it. If you can see the obstruction, endeavor to seize it with your finger and thumb, or a long slender pair of pincers. If it cannot be got up, or is not of a nature to do any injury in the stomach, push it down with the handle of a spoon, or a flexible round piece of whalebone, the end of which is neatly covered with a roll of linen, or anything that may be at hand. If you can get it neither up nor down, place two grains of tartar emetic in the patient's mouth. As it dissolves, it will make him excessively sick, and in consequence of the relaxation, the bone, or whatever it may be, may descend into the stomach or be ejected from the mouth.

If a pin, button, or other metallic or pointed body has been swallowed (or pushed into the stomach), make the patient eat plentifully of thick rice pudding, and afterwards give him a dose of castor oil, to carry it off by the bowels.

Of Burns and Scalds.

There are three kinds of remedies generally employed in accidents of this nature. Cooling applications, such as pounded ice, snow, cold water, lime-water and oil. Stimulants, as warm spirits of turpentine, and carded or raw cotton.

Any one of these articles that happens to be nearest at hand may be tried, although the preference is due to the lime-water and linseed or sweet oil, equal parts, applied on strips of soft linen or muslin, and laid over the parts burned, and covered with oiled silk. Raw cotton may be used if the burn is extensive but not deep. Sprinkling wheat, rye, or starch flour is preferred by some; fresh lard by others, or glycerin. Equal parts of lime-water and linseed oil, well mixed, form one of the most soothing of all applications. Should the system seem to sink, wine, bark, etc. must be employed.

Of Mortification.

From what has been already stated, it is evident that in treating wounds, etc., as well as diseases, one great and important indication is to repress excessive inflammation, which, if allowed to proceed to a certain point, sometimes produces mortification or death of the parts.

If the fever and pain suddenly cease; if the part which before was red, swollen and hard becomes purple and soft, abandon at once all reducing measures, lay a blister over the whole of the parts, and give wine, porter, bark. etc., freely and without delay. If the blisters do not put a stop to the disease, and the parts become dead and offensive, cover them with the charcoal or fermenting poultice until nature separates the dead parts from the living, during which process a generous diet, bark, etc., must be allowed. A wash of dilute solution of nitric acid, 50 drops to a pint, may be poured over the parts daily; or a dressing of solution of bromine.

There is a particular kind of mortification which comes of itself, or without any apparent cause. It attacks the small toes of old people, and commences in a small bluish or black spot, which spreads to different parts of the foot. To remedy it place a blister over the spot, and give two grains of opium night and morning, taking care to keep the bowels open by castor oil, and to diminish the quantity of opium, if it occasions any unpleasant effects.

In extensive mortifications of the forearm it is necessary to amputate. This, however, should never be done, until by the repeated application of stimulating poultices or washes to the sound parts adjoining the mortified ones, they are disposed to separate, which may be easily known by inspection.

Directions for Bleeding.

Tie up the arm, placing the bandage at least two inches above the projection of the elbow joint, and then feel for the pulse at the wrist. If it is stopped, the bandage is too tight, and must be relaxed. Select the most prominent vein, and feel with the tip of your finger if an artery lies near it. If you feel one pulsating so close to the vein that you are fearful of wounding it, choose another. Having set your lancet (I allude, of course, to the spring lancet, the only one that can be used with safety), bend the arm in the precise position it is to be kept in while the blood flows. The cutting edge of the lancet is now to be placed on the vein, while you depress the handle or frame just as much as you wish the cut to be deep. By touching the spring on the side with your thumb, the business is done. To stop the bleeding, relax the bandage, press the two edges of the wound together, place a little compress of linen on it, and bind up the whole with a bandage passing round the joint in a figure of eight.

Directions for Passing the Catheter.

Take the penis of the patient near its head between the finger and thumb of your left hand (standing beside him), while with your right you introduce the point of the instrument into the urinary passage, its convex side towards his knees. While you push the catheter down the urethra, endeavor, at the same time to draw up the penis on it. When you first introduce it the handle will of course be near the belly of the patient, and as it descends will be thrown further from it, until it enters the bladder, which will be known by the flow of the urine. If you cannot succeed while the patient is on his back, make him stand up, or place him with his shoulders and back on the ground, while his thighs and legs are held up by assistants. If still foiled, place him again on his back, and, when you have got the catheter as far down as it will go, introduce the forefinger, well oiled, into the fundament, and endeavor to push its point upwards, while you still press it forward with the other hand. Force is never, on any account, to be used. Vary your position as often as you please; let the patient try it himself; but always remember it is by humoring the instrument, and not by violence, that you can succeed.

Directions for Passing Bougies.

Take the penis between your finger and thumb, and pass the point of the instrument (which should be well oiled) down the urethra, as directed for the catheter. When it has entered three or four inches, depress the penis a little, and, by humoring the bougie with one hand and the penis with the other, endeavor to pass it as far as may be wished. The patient himself will frequently succeed, when every one else fails.

MISCELLANEOUS ARTICLES.

To diminish Inordinate Inflammation.

Mix 1 drachm of Goulard's extract of lead, or solution of sugar of lead in water, with 4 ounces of rectified spirit, and 6 ounces of distilled water. Make a lotion, which is to be applied to those surfaces where inflammation is very rapid.

Another Method. — Dissolve 2 drachms of sulphate of zinc (white vitriol) in a pint of distilled water. To be applied as above.

Marsh-mallow Fomentation.

Boil together for a quarter of an hour 1 ounce of dried marsh-mallow root, with ½ an ounce of chamomile flowers, in a pint of water; strain through a cloth. The fomenting flannels should be sprinkled with spirits just before they are applied to the inflamed part.

Fomentation of Poppies.

Bruise 4 ounces of dried poppy heads, and then boil them in 6 pints of water, until a quart only remains after straining. This fomentation is to be applied to inflamed parts, where there is much pain, but which are required to suppurate.

Refrigerant Lotion.

Mix together equal parts of acetated water of ammonia and tincture of camphor, which apply to the inflamed joint or other part.

Another. — Dissolve 1 ounce of muriate of ammonia in 4 ounces of common vinegar, and add 10 ounces of water. To be applied with or without a cloth to inflamed surfaces.

Another. — Mix together 2 ounces of rectified spirit, and 5 ounces of acetated water of ammonia.

Sedative Lotion.

Dissolve half a drachm of sugar of lead in 4 ounces of distilled vinegar, and then add 1 ounce of common spirits with a pint of water. Linen cloths dipped in this lotion are to be applied to inflamed joints, etc.

Cold and Sedative Cataplasm.

Take of goulard water, 1½ drachms; rectified spirits, 2 ounces; water, 1 pint. These are to be mixed with a sufficient quantity of the crumb of a new loaf to form a cataplasm. To be applied at night to inflamed parts.

Another. — Mix with crumb of bread as above, one drachm of goulard water (or solution of sugar of lead) and a pint of common water that has been boiled.

Cataplasm to hasten Suppuration.

Make two quarts of finely-powdered bran, and one part of linseed meal, into a poultice, with boiling water. A little oil should be spread over the surface just before it is applied.

Another. — Take of crumb of bread and linseed meal equal parts; make them into a poultice with boiling milk.

Linseed Cataplasm.

Stir linseed flour into boiling water in sufficient quantity to form a cataplasm of proper consistency, and before application smear the surface with a little olive or linseed oil. If irritation, with great pain and tension, or hardness should prevail, it will be necessary to substitute a decoction of poppy heads for the common water. This poultice is in general use in all the hospitals.

Embrocation for Sprains.

Shake in a phial until they become white like milk, 10 drachms of olive oil, with 2 drachms of spirits of hartshorn (water of ammonia); then add 4 drachms of oil of turpentine. When properly mixed, they may be directly used as an embrocation for sprains and bruises.

Where weakness remains in consequence of a sprain, cold water ought to be pumped on the part every morning; and a long calico roller should be bound firmly (but not too tightly) round it immediately after. By these means strength will soon be restored.

Another. — Digest fifteen ounces of white hard soap scraped with a knife, in four pints of spirits of wine, and one pint of water of ammonia, or hartshorn (liquor ammoniæ), previously mixed in a large bottle. When dissolved, add five ounces of camphor. When this last is entirely dissolved the embrocation is fit for use.

This excellent and powerful stimulant was selected from the Pharmacopœia of the Middlesex Hospital: for private use the above quantities of the ingredients are to be reduced in proportion to each other, according to the quantity likely to be used in a family. If one-third only is required, use five ounces of soap, one of camphor, sixteen ounces of spirit of wine, and four ounces of water of ammonia.

Application of Leeches.

In the applying of leeches to the human body, success is rendered more certain by previously drying them, or allowing them to creep over a dry cloth. To attract them the part should be moistened with cream, sugar, or blood, and if this should be insufficient, the leech may be cooled by touching it with a cloth dipped in cold water. The escape of leeches from the part is to be prevented by covering them with a wineglass or tumbler.

Cataplasm for Ulcers.

Boil any quantity of fresh carrots until they are sufficiently soft to be beaten up into a smooth pulp. This cataplasm is equally beneficial in the cure of sloughing, as well as scorbutic ulcers. The latter are known by a brown color, the discharge being thin and corroding, whilst the fungous excrescences which shoot out, bleed on the slightest touch. The ulcer is surrounded by a livid ring, or areola, in which small spots are frequently observed. The former are known by their very dark and flabby surface, from several parts of which offensive matter exudes. They are attended by prostration, and have a fetid discharge.

Another. — Boil any quantity of the bottom leaves of the common meadow sorrel, until they are sufficiently soft, then beat them into a smooth pulp, which is to be applied as a cataplasm to ulcers of the above-mentioned nature.

Another. — Poultices of the pulp of apples have been successfully employed on the continent for these ulcers. They are made by mixing two ounces of the pulp of boiled apples with the same weight of the crumb of bread.

Lotion for Scorbutic Ulcers.

Mix from one to two drachms of muriatic acid (spirit of salt) with a pint of water. This lotion is very useful in cleansing and stimulating the above-mentioned ulcers.

Another. — Make a lotion by dissolving half an ounce of nitrate of potass (saltpetre) in half a pint of common vinegar; with which cleanse the ulcers in question.

Lotion for Cancerous Ulcers.

Mix together an ounce and a half of the tincture of muriate of iron, with seven ounces of distilled water. Apply as a lotion.

Contagious Ulcer peculiar to Soldiers and Seamen.

This ulcer generates a poison capable of converting other healthy ulcers into its own nature. It generally appears on the inner side of the leg, near the ankle. It exhales a putrid smell, whilst a thin acrimonious humor is discharged, which excoriates the neighboring parts; and fungous excrescences frequently shoot out. The limb becomes much swelled and very painful, whilst the sore bleeds on the slightest touch. If not checked the most fatal consequences are to be apprehended.

Treatment. — The following remedies have been found most efficacious, viz., the carrot and yeast poultice as mentioned before; a lotion of tincture of myrrh, 1 ounce, with 7 ounces of decoction of bark, in equal parts; 1 scruple of sulphate of copper, or blue vitriol, in solution with distilled water, or with 8 ounces of lime-water; camphorated spirit of wine; camphorated vinegar; the cold salt water bath; and the application of the juice of limes. If the sores remain irritable and painful, the hemlock and poppy fomentations are to be used; accompanied with the internal administration of Peruvian bark, and other tonic remedies.

Ulcers and Sore Legs of Poor People.

Pure lime-water is one of the best dressings for ulcers.

The lotion made according to the following recipe, has been found very beneficial in cases of foul ulcers and sore legs of poor people. It has also succeeded (applied warm) in curing a fistulous ulcer: Take of green vitriol, ¾ ounce; alum, ½ ounce; verdigris, ¼ drachm; crude sal ammoniac, 2 scruples.

After reducing them to powder, put them into a new glazed pipkin, holding about a quart. Set it upon a slow fire, and increase by degrees till the ingredients boil up to the top two or three times. Then take it from the fire and set it to cool. Break the pipkin to get the stone out. Stir them round all the time they are on the fire with a lath. The dust and the smoke should not come near the eyes, nose, or mouth. Put a piece of the stone, the size of a walnut, to a quart bottle of soft water. To use, shake the bottle and wet a piece of fine linen four times doubled. Lay it upon a new burn or old ulcer. The linen should always be kept wet with it. [For this receipt the late Emperor of France gave 10,000 louis-d'ors, after it had been approved of in his hospitals.]

Malt Poultice.

Mix as much ground malt with half a pint of yeast as will make a cataplasm of moderate consistence. This poultice is gently stimulating, and very serviceable in destroying the fetid and disagreeable smell which arises from foul ulcers and gangrenous wounds.

Another. — A similar poultice, and for the same purpose, is prepared by stirring into an infusion of malt as much oatmeal as may be required to make it of a proper thickness, and afterwards adding about a spoonful of yeast.

Strong Beer Poultice.

Stir into half a pint of ale, or strong beer-grounds, as much oatmeal or linseed-meal as will make a cataplasm of proper thickness. This will prove an excellent stimulant and antiseptic for foul ulcers. It should be applied as warm as the parts will bear, and should be renewed every six hours.

Yeast Poultice.

Mix well together 1 pound of linseed-meal, and a pint of ale yeast. Expose this cataplasm to a gentle heat until a certain degree of fermentation takes place. This poultice is excellent for stimulating and cleansing foul ulcers.

Charcoal Poultice.

To half a pound of the common oatmeal cataplasm, add two ounces of fresh burnt charcoal finely pounded and sifted. Mix the whole well together, and apply it to foul ulcers and venereal sores; the fetid smell and unhealthy appearance of which it speedily destroys.

Treatment of Whitlow.

This is a small tumor which appears under or around the finger nail; it is attended with redness and pain, and very quickly advances to suppuration. After the abscess is evacuated of the white matter contained in it, it very soon heals of itself. The loss of the nail, however, is sometimes, through improper management, the consequence of the disease.

In order to check the inflammation in the first instance, at once stop the fissure, it will be proper frequently to apply the following lotion, that is, until the pain and heat are abated: Dissolve one ounce of sal ammoniac in two ounces of common vinegar; adding one of rectified spirit, and twelve ounces of distilled water.

Another Application. — It sometimes happens that the ulcer, which remains after the discharge of the matter, is very indolent and difficult to heal. In such a case the following application will be of great service: Rub ½ an ounce of camphor, in a mortar, with an ounce of olive oil. Now melt over a gentle fire 8 ounces of olive oil, with 4 ounces of yellow wax, and stir it in ½ an ounce of a solution of sugar of lead (liquor plumbi acetatis); when this mixture is cold, pour the camphor and oil in the mortar into it, taking care to stir the whole well until quite cold. If suppuration should ensue, marked by a white prominent spot, an opening should immediately be made, that the matter may escape.

Whitlow at the extremity of the Finger.

This kind of whitlow being more deeply seated than that of the nail, is more severe, and is attended by throbbing and acute pain. The matter, likewise, often insinuates itself beneath the nail. To prevent suppuration it will be proper to keep the finger immersed for a long time in warm water, and to apply the lotion, recommended for the same purpose in common whitlow. If these fail in effecting a resolution of the tumor, an early and free incision should be made through the integuments, and carried to the bottom of the diseased part; after which the blood may be allowed to flow for some time; the opening is to be treated afterwards as a common wound, viz., by the application of adhesive plaster.

Another Remedy. — Dr. Balfour, of Edinburgh, has found the application of pressure in incipient cases of whitlow to succeed in preventing the formation of matter, and speedily to cure the disease. He applies compression with the hand in a degree which the patient can easily bear, with the view of preventing extensive suppuration, and then a narrow fillet. This operation, in severe cases, is repeated three or four times in the course of the day, when the pain and swelling disappear, leaving a single speck of pus at the point of the thumb immediately under the skin. If vent be given to this by the slightest touch of the lancet, the wound will heal up immediately.

White Swelling.

Dr. Kirkland recommends a volatile plaster for this disease, made after the following manner: Melt together in an iron ladle, or earthern pipkin, two ounces of soap and half an ounce of litharge plaster. When nearly cold, stir in one drachm of sal ammoniac in fine powder: spread upon leather, and apply to the joint as above.

If the above method fail, and ulceration take place, a surgeon should be applied to without delay.

Ointment for Chaps and Eruptions of the Skin.

Simmer ox marrow over the fire, and afterwards strain it through a piece of muslin into gallipots. When cold rub the part affected.

Ringworm.

Mr. T. G. Graham, of Cheltenham, recommends the lime-water which has been used for purifying gas, as a very efficacious remedy in the above troublesome disease. The head is to be well cleaned, morning and evening, with soap and water, and afterwards washed with the lime-water from the gas works. The above lime water is a very heterogeneous compound, so that it is impossible to say which of its ingredients is effectual. It contains lime, ammonia, sulphuretted hydrogen, volatile oil, and probably several other compounds of a more complex nature.

Scald Head.

Take of sulphur, 1 ounce; lard, 1 ounce; sal ammoniac, 2 drachms: Mix for an ointment, to be rubbed upon the part affected two or three times a day.

Ointment for Scald Head, Ringworm, etc.

The following ointment for scald head, ringworm, and tetter, has uniformly succeeded in speedily effecting a cure.

Take of subacetate of copper (in very fine powder), ½ a drachm; prepared calomel, 1 drachm; fresh spermaceti ointment, 1 ounce. Mix well together. To be rubbed over the parts affected every night and morning. This ointment is also very efficacious in cases of foul and languid ulcers.

Leprous Affections of the Skin.

Dr. Hufeland praises the excellent effects of the oil of the walnut kernel in leprous and other cutaneous complaints. It is one of the safest, simplest, and most efficacious external remedies that can be employed, as it mitigates the pains, and that burning sensation, sometimes almost insupportable, which accompany these obstinate diseases; it never seems to have any ill effect, if attention be given to the eruption suddenly disappearing, or diving, as it is said, by repulsion—a circumstance which frequently happens by the application of of metallic ointments, and which is often attended with much danger to the constitution; although it cures the cutaneous affection in a short time, it is not followed by any bad consequences, provided the eruption does not originate in any obstinate internal or general disease. In a child, which was almost covered with chronic and suppurating pimples, against which internal remedies, baths and mercurial ointments had been employed without producing a perfect cure, the oil of walnut kernel was used with complete success. It is likewise an excellent remedy in small cutaneous eruptions that are now and then observed in children. The oil ought to be fresh, expressed without heat, and applied to the affected places twice or thrice a day.

Itch Ointment.

Take of flowers of sulphur 1 ounce; essence of lemon 1 ounce; hogs' lard 2 ounces. Make it into an ointment. Smear all the joints for three nights with this; wash it off in the morning with soap and water. Repeat the smearing three times at the interval of two days, and the most inveterate itch is certain to disappear. It will be well at the same time to take night and morning a teaspoonful of an electuary of flowers of sulphur, mixed with honey or treacle.

To remove Chilblains.

Take an ounce of white copperas dissolved in a quart of water, and occasionally apply it to the affected parts. This will ultimately remove the most obstinate blains. This application must be used before they break, otherwise it will do injury.

Another Method.

Take a piece of fresh wood of the fir, made flat and smooth, and hold it to the fire until it becomes moderately warm, and all the turpentine begins to exude; then place the part affected upon this board and keep it there as long as it can well be borne, after which let the part be washed with warm water, wrapped up in flannel and kept free from cold. This application is improper if the chilblains be broken, but if applied before it has arrived at that stage, it has never failed in removing the complaint after two or three applications.

Another.—Crude sal ammoniac 1 ounce; vinegar ½ a pint; dissolve, and bathe the part, if not yet broken, two or three times a day. If sal ammoniac is not at hand, alum or common salt will do, but not so effectually. If the chilblains are of very long continuance and obstinate, touch them with equal parts of liquid opodeldoc (*linimentum saponis*) and tincture of Spanish flies, or rather less of the latter. If the chilblains break, poultice or dress them with basilicon, and add turpentine if necessary.

Another.—The following ointment for this annoying disease has been attended with the most beneficial effect: Take of citron ointment 1 ounce; oil of turpentine 2 drachms; olive oil 4 drachms. Mix. To be well rubbed over the parts affected every night and morning.

Another.—The following has also been found very beneficial in the cure of chilblains both in the incipient or inflammatory stage or when advanced to ulceration. When in the former state, the part should be well rubbed over with it by means of a warm hand, and afterwards kept covered with soft, thin leather. When ulcerated it should be applied on lint sufficiently large to cover the surrounding inflammation: Take of spermaceti ointment 6 drachms; prepared calomel 2 scruples; rectified oil of turpentine 1 drachm. Mix. Pure glycerin is a very good mild application for chilblains.

Treatment of Corns.

When small in size they are to be removed either by stimulants or escharotics, as the application of nitrate of silver (lunar caustic), merely by wetting the corn and touching it with a pencil of the caustic every evening. Previous to this the skin may be softened by immersion of the feet in warm water.

Another Mode.

Rub together in a mortar 2 ounces of powder of savin leaves, ½ an ounce of verdigris and ½ an ounce of red precipitate. Put some of this powder in a linen rag and apply it to the corn at bed-time.

Removal by Cutting, etc.

If the corn has attained a large size, removal by cutting, or by ligature, will be proper; if it hangs by a small neck, the latter method is preferable. It is done by tying a silk thread round the corn, and on its removal next day tying another still tighter, and so on till completely removed. When the base is broad, a cautious dissection of the corn from the surrounding parts by means of a sharp knife or razor is necessary. This is done by paring gently until the whole is removed. In all cases of cutting corns the feet ought to be previously washed, as in case of making a wound in the toe great danger may result from want of cleanliness in this respect. Mortification has in some instances been the effect of such neglect.

Prevention, etc.—Corns should be secured from pressure by means of a thick adhesive plaster, in the centre of which a hole has been made for the reception of the projecting part. This, with frequent immersion in water and occasional paring, has often been found to remove them, and always prevents their enlargement. An effectual mode of extirpation is by the application of a small blister, the effect of which will be, generally, to raise them with the skin out of their bed. When rest from labor can be obtained, this is an excellent method. Dress the blister (which need not exceed the size of a silver dime) with hog's lard, or simple wax ointment.

To remove Warts.

Nitrate of silver (lunar caustic) cures those troublesome excrescences called warts in an extremely simple and harmless manner. Caustic potassa is still more certain.

The method of using it is to dip the end of the caustic in a little water and to rub it over the warts. After doing so a few times they will be gone. The muriate of ammonia (sal ammoniac) is likewise a very useful remedy. "Out of twenty years' practice," says a medical correspondent in the Monthly Magazine, "I never knew the above remedies to fail."

Ward's Paste for the Piles.

Pulverize finely in an iron mortar 1 ounce of black pepper, 1 ounce of elecampane root and three ounces of fennel seed, and mix them intimately together. Now melt together over a clear fire 2 ounces of sugar and 2 ounces of clarified honey, so as to form a clear syrup, which add to the mixed powder in the mortar, and heat the whole into a mass of uniform consistence. This medicine is to be taken when the irritation of piles runs so high as to threaten fistula. The dose is a piece of the size of a nutmeg, to be taken three times a day: this is to be washed down by a glass of cold water, or white wine.

Extraneous Bodies in the Ear.

These are to be extracted by means of a small forceps, or by syringing the ear with warm or tepid water. But should such means prove unsuccessful, they may be suffered to remain without danger, if they do not produce pain, as in a very short time they will be forced out by the accumulating wax. Insects may be killed by filling the ear with oil and afterwards removed by syringing with warm water.

To check Hæmorrhage consequent upon the Extraction of Teeth.

A good surgeon recommends the following method for the treatment of the above frequent and sometimes serious accident: "Take a small, fine phial cork, of a size adapted to the socket whence the tooth has been extracted and the hæmorrhage proceeds; then with a small dossil of lint wet with tincture of chloride of iron, and put on the smallest end of the cork, push the cork into the bleeding orifice, pressing it firmly in till it be, as it were, wedged in the socket, and keep it there as long as may be necessary, desiring the patient to press against it with the teeth of the opposite jaw till the bleeding be stopped, which is almost instantly. This acts as a tourniquet, and gives time to use whatever other means may be deemed requisite; but it is seldom that anything else is required." Solution of persulphate of iron, alum, and powder of tannin are also good styptics.

Remedies for Diseases of the Teeth.

If hollow or decayed, apply compound tincture of benzoin, or some essential oil, on cotton, to the part; or pills with camphor and opium: or chew the roots of pellitory of Spain. Some burn the nerve with sulphuric or nitric acid, or a hot iron.

Collyria, or Eye-waters. [See page 125.]

Take of extract of lead, 10 drops; rose-water, 6 ounces. Mix, and wash the eyes night and morning.

Another.—Take of extract of lead, 10 drops; spirit of camphor, 20 drops; rose-water. ½ a pint. Mix. This eye-water is extremely useful in ophthalmia, attended with much inflammation.

Another.—Take of opium, 10 grains; camphor, 6 grains; boiling water, 12 ounces. Rub the opium and camphor with the boiling water and strain. This collyrium abates the pain and irritation attendant on severe cases of inflammation of the eyes.

Another.—Take of white vitriol, ½ drachm; spirits of camphor, 1 drachm; warm water, 2 ounces; rose-water, 4 ounces. Dissolve the vitriol in the warm water, and add the spirit of camphor and rose-water. This is a useful collyrium in the chronic state of ophthalmia, or what is generally called weakness of the eyes after inflammation.

Another.—Dissolve 10 grains of soft extract of opium in 6 ounces of warm distilled water; strain through fine linen, and then add 2 ounces of liquor of acetate of ammonia, Where the pain is great, this collyrium will be productive of great relief.

Another.—Make a lotion for the inflamed eyes with 20 drops of tincture of camphor, 10 drops of solution of sugar of lead, 1 of Goulard's extract, and 7 ounces of distilled water. If the pain is very distressing, a drop of the vinous tincture of opium may be conveyed twice a day into the eye by means of a feather. This is an effectual means of obtaining relief.

Another.—Mix together 1 ounce of the liquor of acetate of ammonia, and 7 ounces of distilled rose-water.

Another.—When the eye is merely weak, frequent ablution with cold water, by means of an eye-cup of green glass, will be of great use. Still better is the application to the lids, very frequently, of lead-water, with a camel's hair pencil. At night a very cooling cataplasm, or poultice, may be made of crumb of bread soaked in a pint and a half of cold water, in which a drachm of alum has previously been dissolved. This is to be applied over the eyes in a handkerchief when going to bed.

For Inflammation of the Eyelids.

The following ointment has been found exceedingly beneficial in inflammation of the eyeball and edges of the eyelids, which has become very prevalent. Take of prepared calomel, 1 scruple; spermaceti ointment, ½ an ounce. Mix them well together in a glass mortar; apply a small quantity to each corner of the eye, every night and morning, and also to the edges of the lids, if they are affected. Another good ointment is composed of carbonate of lead, 2 drachms; simple cerate, an ounce. If this should not eventually remove the inflammation, the following lotion may be applied three or four times a day, by means of an eye-cup. The bowels should be kept in a laxative state, by taking occasionally ¼ of an ounce of the Rochelle or Epsom salts.

Lotion to be used at the same time.

Take of acetated zinc, 6 grains; rose-water (fresh), 6 ounces. Mix. Before the ointment is applied to the corners of the eyes, wash them with this lotion. These remedies have succeeded in almost every case of inflammation of the eyes to which they have been applied.

Treatment of Styes.

These are small abscesses seated in the edge of the eyelid, and produced by the obstruction of very minute glands. They are often attended with much heat and pain, and always with great inconvenience. The application of ice to the part will sometimes check them in the beginning. If they do not suppurate quickly, a small poultice of bread and milk is to be applied warm. When the matter is formed, an opening should be made with the point of a lancet, or a needle, and a small portion of weak citrine ointment is afterwards to be applied.

Infusion of Senna.

Take of senna, 3 drachms; lesser cardamom seeds, husked and bruised, ½ drachm; boiling water, as much as will yield a filtered infusion of 6 ounces. Digest for an hour, and filter, when cold.

This is a well contrived purgative infusion, the aromatic correcting the drastic effects of the senna. It is of advantage that it should be used fresh prepared, as it is apt to spoil very quickly.

Electuary of Senna.

Take of senna, 8 ounces; coriander seeds, 4 ounces; liquorice, 4 ounces; figs, 1 pound; pulp of tamarinds, cassia fistula, and prunes, of each, ¼ pound; double refined sugar, 2½ pounds. Powder the senna with the coriander seeds, and sift out 10 ounces of the mixed powder; boil the remainder with the figs and liquorice, in 4 pounds of water, to one-half; express, and strain the liquor, which is then to be evaporated to the weight of about 1½ pounds; dissolve the sugar in it, add this syrup, by degrees, to the pulps; and, lastly, mix in the powder.

This electuary is a very convenient laxative, and has long been in common use among practitioners. Taken to the size of a nutmeg, or more, as occasion may require, it is an excellent laxative for loosening the belly in costive habits.

Compound Colocynth Pills.

Take of pith of colocynth, cut small, 6 drachms; hepatic aloes, 1½ ounces; scammony, ¼ an ounce; lesser cardamom seeds, husked and bruised, 1 drachm; Castile soap, softened with warm water, so as to have a gelatinous consistence, 3 drachms; warm water, 1 pint. Digest the colocynth in the water, in a covered vessel, with a moderate heat, for 4 days. To the liquor, expressed and filtered, add the aloes and scammony, separately, reduced to powder; then evaporate the mixture to a proper thickness for making pills, having added, towards the end of the evaporation, the soap-jelly and powdered seeds, and mix all the ingredients thoroughly together.

These pills are much used as warm and stomachic laxatives; they are well suited for costiveness, so often attendant on people of sedentary lives, and, upon the whole, are among the most useful articles in the materia medica.

Aloetic Pills.

Take of socotrine aloes, powdered, 1 ounce; extract of gentian, ½ ounce; oil of caraway seeds, 2 scruples; syrup of ginger, as much as is sufficient. Beat them together. The dose is from five to ten grains.

Compound Aloetic Pills.

Take of hepatic aloes, 1 ounce; ginger root, in powder, 1 drachm; soap, ½ an ounce; essence of peppermint, ½ a drachm. Powder the aloes with the ginger, then add the soap and the oil, so as to form an intimate mixture. This is an excellent purge for costive habits, in the dose of from 5 to 10 grains.

Compound Rhubarb Pills.

Take of rhubarb, in powder, 1 ounce; socotrine aloes, 6 drachms; myrrh, ½ ounce; volatile oil of peppermint, ½ drachm. Make them into a mass, with a sufficient quantity of syrup of orange peel. These pills are intended for moderately warming and strengthening the stomach, and gently opening the bowels. A scruple of the mass may be taken night and morning.

Purgative Powder, formerly called Hiera Picra.

Take of socotrine aloes, 1 pound; white canella, 3 ounces. Powder them separately, and then mix them. The spicy canella acts as a corrigent to the aloes; but the compound is more adapted to be formed into pills than to be used in the state of powder. It is a convenient medicine for costive habits, not subject to the piles. Dose from 10 grains to a scruple at bed-time.

Mild Purgative Emulsion.

Take of manna and oil of almonds, each 1 ounce; carbonate of potassa, 12 grains; cinnamon and rose-water, each 3 ounces. Mix carefully the oil, potassa and manna together, gradually pouring the liquids to form an emulsion, of which take two tablespoonsful night and morning.

Electuary for the Piles.

Take of the electuary of senna, 1½ ounces; washed flowers of sulphur, 4 drachms; syrup of roses, as much as is sufficient. Make into an electuary, of which take the size of a nutmeg, going to bed, as may be required. This is an excellent remedy for persons who have the piles, or are subject to their return.

Castor Oil Clyster.

Take of castor oil, 2 ounces; 1 egg; mix them well, and then add gruel, 8 ounces; which will operate very mildly, and is efficacious in case of worms.

Purging Clyster.

Take of manna, 1 ounce. Dissolve in 10 ounces by measure, of compound decoction of chamomile; then add of olive oil, 1 ounce; sulphate of magnesia, ½ ounce. Mix and let it be given directly.

REMEDIES FOR COUGHS AND COLDS.

Paregoric Elixir, or Camphorated Tincture of Opium.

Take of hard purified opium, in powder, benzoic acid, each 1 drachm; camphor, 2 scruples; essential oil of aniseed, 1 drachm; proof spirit of wine, 2 pints. Digest for ten days and strain. In this formula, the virtues of the opium and the camphor are combined. It derives an agreeable flavor from the acid of benzoin and essential oil. The latter will also render it more stimulating. It was originally prescribed under the title of elixir asthmaticum, which it does not ill deserve. It contributes to allay the tickling which provokes frequent coughing, and at the same time, it soothes the breast, and gives greater liberty of breathing.

It is given to children against the chincough, etc. in doses of from 5 drops to 20; to adults, from 20 to 100. Half an ounce, by measure, contains about a grain of opium.

Expectorant Pills.

Take of dried root of squills, in fine powder, 1 scruple; gum ammoniac, lesser cardamom seeds, in powder, extract of liquorice, each 1 drachm. Form them into a mass with simple syrup. This is an elegant and commodious form for the exhibition of squills, whether for promoting expectoration, or for the other purposes to which that medicine is applied. The dose is from 10 grains to 1 scruple, three times a day.

Napoleon's Pectoral Pills.

The following recipe was copied from one in the possession of the late Emperor of France, and was a very favorite remedy with Napoleon for difficulty of breathing, or oppression of the chest, arising from a collection of mucus in the air cells and vessels of the lungs, and in the gullet. Considerable benefit has been derived from it in many similar cases. Take of ipecacuanha root, in powder, 30 grains; squill root, in powder, gum ammoniac, in powder, each 2 scruples; mucilage of gum arabic, sufficient to form a mass. To be divided into 24 pills; two to be taken every night and morning.

Dr. Ratcliff's Cough Mixture.

Mix together 4 drachms of syrup of squills; 4 drachms of elixir of paregoric; 4 drachms of syrup of poppies. Of this take a teaspoonful in a little tea or warm water, as occasion requires.

Dr. Munro's Cough Medicine.

Take 4 drachms of paregoric elixir; 2 drachms of sulphuric ether; 2 drachms of tincture of tolu. Mix, and take a teaspoonful night and morning, or when the cough is troublesome, in a little milk-warm water.

Simple Remedy for Coughs.

Take of boiling water, half a pint; black currant jelly, a desertspoonful; sweet spirits of nitre, a teaspoonful. Mix the jelly in the water first, till it is quite dissolved, and add the nitre last. Take a desertspoonful of the mixture at night, going to bed, or when the cough is troublesome. The mixture should be made and kept in a teapot, or other covered vessel.

Remedy for Chronic Cough.

The following is very serviceable in common obstinate coughs, unattended with fever. Take of tincture of tolu, 3 drachms; elixir of paregoric, ½ an ounce; tincture of squills, 1 drachm. Two teaspoonsful to be taken in a tumbler of barley-water going to bed, and when the cough is troublesome.

For Coughs in Aged Persons.

In the coughs of aged persons, or in cases where there are large accumulations of purulent or viscid matter, with feeble expectoration, the following mixture will be found highly beneficial: Pour gradually 2 drachms of nitric acid, diluted in half a pint of water, on 2 drachms of gum ammoniac, and triturate them in a glass mortar, until the gum is dissolved. A tablespoonful to be taken, in sweetened water, every two or three hours.

Cough Emulsion.

Take of oil of almonds, 6 drachms; milk of almonds, 5 ounces; rose water, gum arabic, and purified sugar, equal parts, 2 drachms. Let these be well rubbed together, and take two tablespoonsful four times a day, and a teaspoonful upon coughing. This is far preferable to the common white emulsions formed by an alkali, which, uniting with the oil, produces a kind of soap, and readily mingling with the water, forms the white appearance observed, and is commonly disgusting to patients, and unpleasant to the stomach; whereas this suits every palate, and removes that tickling in the throat so very distressing to patients.

Emulsion for a Cold, etc.

Take of milk of almonds, 1 ounce; syrup of tolu, 2 drachms; rose-water, 2 drachms; tincture of squills, 16 drops. Make into a draught. Four to be taken during the day. This is an admirable remedy in colds, and also in chronic cough, as well as in asthma.

Gargle for Thrush.

Thrush or aphthæ in the mouth, will be greatly benefited by the frequent use of the following gargle: Mix together 20 drops of muriatic acid (spirits of salts); 1 ounce of honey of roses; and 4 ounces of decoction of barley.

Another.—Make a gargle of 2 drachms of borax; 1 ounce of honey of roses, and 7 ounces of rose-water. To be used three or four times a day.

Gargle for Sore Throat.

Take of decoction of bark, 7 ounces; tincture of myrrh, 2 drachms; purified nitre, 3 drachms. Make into a gargle. This is a sovereign method to disperse a tumefied gland, or common sore throat. By taking upon such occasions a small lump of purified nitre, putting it into the mouth, and letting it dissolve there, then removing it, and applying it again in a few seconds, and swallowing the saliva, I have, says Dr. Thornton, for many years prevented a sore throat from forming.

For Putrid Sore Throat.

Take of decoction of bark, 6 ounces; diluted muriatic acid, 1 drachm; honey of roses, 1 ounce. Make into a gargle. To be used, mixed with port wine, frequently during the day.

For Inflammatory Sore Throat.

Take of nitre, 2 drachms; honey, 4 drachms; rose-water, 6 ounces. Mix. To be used frequently.

Another.—Dissolve 2 teaspoonsful of alum in 1 pint of sage tea.

Another.—Take of muriatic acid, 20 drops; glycerin, 1 ounce; water, 3 ounces. Mix.

For Ulcerated Sore Throat.

The chlorate of potassa, in cases of putrid ulcerated sore throat, has been used with the most decisive success. Its internal exhibition more effectually allays thirst and abates fever than any other medicine; and, when applied as a gargle to inflamed or ulcerated sore throats, it has been found to disperse the inflammation and to deterge the ulcers more effectually than the infusion of rose-leaves with the sulphuric acid, the gargle generally resorted to in those cases. The chlorate of potassa may be given in the dose of from 20 to 30 grains in a half glass of water, three or four times a day. For the purpose of gargling the throat, 4 drachms of the chlorate may be added to half a pint of water.

MEDICINE FOR WORMS.

The Male Fern.

The root of male fern has long been esteemed a powerful remedy for worms; and its powder has been sold under a fictitious name as an infallible specific for the broad or tape-worm. Sometimes it has been ordered to be taken without any mixture; at other times gamboge, scammony mercury, and other purgative medicines have been ordered to be taken with it.

In the year 1755 the king of France purchased, for a large sum of money, the recipe of a medicine which was said to be an effectual cure for the tape-worm, from the widow of a surgeon in Switzerland, whose husband used to administer it. On discovery it proved to be fern-root reduced to powder, which is to be taken in the following manner: The day before the patient is to begin to take the fern he is to take a dose of some opening medicine, and after its operation to make a very light supper. Next morning he is to take 3 drachms of the powder of the fern-root, in a cup of lime-flower water, and after it a little orange-peel, or some other grateful aromatic, and, if he vomits it up, to take soon after another full dose of the powder of the fern-root. Two hours after this is swallowed the following purging powders are to be taken, viz., 12 grains of resin of scammony, mixed with as much of the panacea mercurialis (calomel digested in spirit of wine), and 5 grains of gamboge, in powder; the dose being made stronger or weaker, according to the strength of the patient. Soon after taking this dose, the patient is to drink tea, and as soon as the physic begins to operate, if he perceives that the tænia is coming away, he is to remain on the close-stool till it has entirely passed. If the purgative should prove too weak, the patient is to take a dose of Epsom salts, and to drink freely of broth. If the first dose of the fern powder and of the purging medicine has not the desired effect, the powder and purge are to be repeated next day; and if at any time the tænia is observed to be coming away, the greatest care must be taken not to break it.

Worm-seed.

Worm-seed is one of the oldest and most common anthelmintics, especially in the lumbrici of children. On account of its essential oil, it is heating and stimulating. It is given to children to the extent of ten grains or half a drachm, finely powdered, and strewed on bread and butter; or made into an electuary with honey or treacle; or candied with sugar; or diffused through milk, and taken in the morning when the stomach is empty. After it has been used for some days, it is customary to give a cathartic; or it is combined from the beginning with rhubarb, jalap, or calomel.

To destroy Ascarides.

Take of socotrine aloes, 2 drachms; new milk, 8 ounces. Rub them together for a clyster. This is useful to destroy the ascarides, or little seat-worm. Still more effectual are suppositories containing each 3 grains of santorin, in a sufficient amount of cacao butter.

Powder of Tin.

In a teaspoonful of honey, or currant jelly, mix a drachm of powder of tin, and take it twice a day for six successive mornings and evenings, making altogether 12 drachms, or 1½ ounces of the tin. A little rhubarb, or any mild aperient medicine, may be taken each alternate night of the six. This is the quantity for an adult person, but would not prove too much for a child, we apprehend, as the tin does not act upon the bowels, but upon the worm itself.

Oil of Turpentine.

Dr. Gibney, of Cheltenham, observes that the oil of turpentine is almost a specific in every species of worms, and its failure, in the practice of many physicians, he attributes to the improper exhibition of it. When the dose is not sufficiently large, it affects the kidneys and skin, and produces no effect on the worm or intestinal canal. He prescribes 1 or 2 drachms, at intervals, for children of three years of age, and 6 drachms for older children, and more for adults. He directs it to be taken when the stomach is most empty, and enjoins strict abstinence during its use. Begin with a good dose early in the morning, and repeat it every hour for three or four hours, as circumstances may indicate. Combine with it mucilage of gum arabic, simple cinnamon water, and syrup. And, in case it should not operate on the bowels as an aperient, take a dose of castor oil. This treatment is renewed about every four or five days, for some time after the evacuation of worms, or until the fæces become healthy.

Essence of Bergamot.

An Italian physician, of great eminence, has found the "*essentia de cedra*" (essence of bergamot), in the dose of one or two drachms, mixed with honey, more efficacious in destroying the tape, and also the long round worm, than the oil of turpentine or naphtha.

For Tape-worm in Children.

Beat up 5½ drachms of rectified oil of turpentine with the yolk of an egg and some sugar and water, or common syrup. Give this to a child having tape-worms. Two doses are sure of expelling them. Pumpkin seeds, made into an electuary with honey or molasses, and taken rather copiously on an empty stomach, will generally kill and remove tape-worm.

For the Long, Round Worm.

Take of pink-root and senna each ½ an ounce, and infuse two hours in hot water. Take one or two glasses each morning on an empty stomach.

MEDICINES FOR INDIGESTION.

Gentian Wine.

Take gentian root and dried lemon-peel, fresh, of each 1 ounce, 2 drachms of long pepper and 2 pints of light wine; infuse without heat for a week and strain out the wine for use. In complaints of the stomach arising from weakness or indigestion, a glass of this wine may be taken an hour before dinner and supper.

Chalybeate Wine.

Take 2 ounces of filings of iron, cinnamon and mace, each 2 drachms, and 2 pints of Rhenish wine. Infuse for three or four weeks, frequently shaking the bottle; then pass the wine through a filter. This wine is a remedy for obstruction of the menses. The dose is half a wine glass taken twice or thrice a day. Lisbon wine, if sharpened with half an ounce of cream of tartar, is also beneficial.

Powerful Tonic.

Take of decoction of bark 6 ounces; compound tincture of bark 1 ounce; bark in powder 1 drachm; calcined magnesia 1 drachm. Form a mixture. Two tablespoonsful are to be given three times a day.

For Debility of the Stomach.

Take of chamomile flowers, lemon-peel, orange-peel, each 4 drachms; boiling water 1 pint. Let them remain for four hours, and strain. To the strained liquor add syrup of ginger 6 drachms. The dose is a wineglassful in the morning early and repeat an hour before dinner for habits debilitated by drinking or natural weakness of the stomach.

Stomachic Aperient Pills.

The pills made according to the following recipe have been long prescribed as a dinner pill with success: Take of rhubarb-root powdered 1½ drachms; Turkey myrrh 1 drachm; socotrine aloes ½ a drachm; extract of chamomile flowers 2½ drachms; essential oil of chamomile flowers 16 drops. Mix well together, and divide into 80 pills. Two or three to be taken about an hour before dinner.

Tonic Draught in cases of General Debility.

Take of the decoction of bark 12 drachms; tincture of bark 1 drachm; syrup of Tolu ½ drachm; aromatic sulphuric acid 8 drops. Make into a draught, to be taken three times a day.

Abernethy's Prescription for Indigestion.

Take of calomel (or proto-chloride of mercury), precipitated sulphuret of antimony, each 1 scruple; powder of gum guaiacum 2 scruples; Spanish soap as much as will be sufficient to form into twenty pills, which are to be taken night and morning.

For Indigestion and Costiveness.

The following remedies for indigestion, attended with heartburn and costiveness, were prescribed by Dr. Gregory, of Edinburgh: Take of carbonate of potassa 4 drachms; simple cinnamon-water, pure water, each 6 ounces; compound tincture of gentian ¾ of an ounce. Mix. Three large spoonsful are to be taken twice a day.

Accompanying Purgative.

Take of compound pill of aloes, with colocynth, 2 drachms. To be divided into 24 pills, two to be taken twice a week.

Remedy for Flatulency.

Take of bay-berries 6 drachms; grains of paradise 2 scruples; socotrine aloes and filings of iron each 2 scruples; oil of turpentine 2 drachms; simple syrup sufficient to form an electuary.

Dr. Reese's Remedy for Flatulence and Cramp in the Stomach.

Take of carbonate of soda 1 drachm; compound tincture of rhatany 1 ounce; compound tincture of ginger and chamomile 3 drachms; camphorated julep 7 ounces. Mix. Three tablespoonsful are to be taken twice a day.

Night-mare.

Great attention is to be paid to regularity and choice of diet. Intemperance of every kind is hurtful, but nothing is more productive of this disease than drinking bad wine. Of eatables those which are most prejudicial are all fat and greasy meats and pastry. These ought to be avoided, or eaten with caution. The same may be said of salt meats, for which dyspeptic patients have frequently a remarkable predilection, but which are not on that account the less unsuitable.

Moderate exercise contributes in a superior degree to promote the digestion of food and prevent flatulence; those, however, who are necessarily confined to a sedentary occupation, should particularly avoid applying themselves to study or bodily labor immediately after eating. If a strong propensity to sleep should occur after dinner, it will be certainly better to indulge it a little, as the process of digestion frequently goes on much better during sleep than when awake.

Going to bed before the usual hour is a frequent cause of night-mare, as it either occasions the patient to sleep too long or to lie long awake in the night. Passing a whole night or part of a night without rest likewise gives birth to the disease, as it occasions the patient, on the succeeding night, to sleep too soundly. Indulging in sleep too late in the morning, is an almost certain method to bring on the paroxysm, and the more frequently it returns, the greater strength it acquires; the propensity to sleep at this time is almost irresistible. Those who are habitually subject to attacks of the night-mare ought never to sleep alone, but should have some person near them, so as to be immediately awakened by their groans and struggles, and the person to whom this office may be entrusted should be instructed to rouse the patient as early as possible, that the paroxysm may not have time to gain strength.

Digestive Pills.

Take of soft extract of quassia, 1 drachm; essential oil of peppermint, 1 drop. Make into 12 pills, of which take 3 an hour before dinner. These pills are excellent to create digestion in habits injured by hard drinking.

To improve Digestion.

Eat a small crust of bread every morning, fasting, about an hour before breakfast.

To restore the Appetite.

Take of shavings of quassia, 2 drachms; boiling water, 1 pint. Let this remain in a close vessel until cold, then strain off, and add to the strained liquor, compound tincture of cardamoms, 2 ounces; spirit of lavender, 4 drachms; powder of rhubarb, 1 scruple. Take three tablespoonfuls an hour before dinner to create an appetite.

Aloetic and Assafœtida Pills.

Take of socotrine aloes, in powder, assafœtida, soap, equal parts. Form them into a mass with mucilage of gum arabic. These pills, in doses of about 10 grains twice a day, produce the most salutary effects in cases of dyspepsia, attended with hysteria, flatulence, and costiveness.

For Heartburn.

This complaint is an uneasy sensation in the stomach, with anxiety, a bent more or less violent, and sometimes attended with oppression, faintness, an inclination to vomit, or a plentiful discharge of clear lymph, like saliva.

This pain may arise from various causes; such as wind, sharp humors, and worms gnawing the coats of the stomach; also from acrid and pungent food; likewise from rheumatic and gouty humors, or surfeits, and from too free a use of tea.

The diet should be of a light animal kind; the drink brandy and water, toast and water, Bristol water; no vegetables should be allowed; very little bread, and that well toasted.

If heartburn has arisen from acidity in the stomach, it will be necessary to take two tablespoonfuls of the following mixture three times a day:—3 drachms of magnesia, 1 scruple of rhubarb, in powder; 1 ounce of cinnamon water, ½ a drachm of spirits of lavender, and 4 ounces of distilled water.

For Heartburn, attended by Pain and Flatulence.

Mix together 12 grains of prepared chalk, ½ an ounce of peppermint water, 1 ounce of pure water, 2 drachms of spirits of pimento, and 12 drops of tincture of opium. This draught is to be taken three times a day.

Another.—Mix together 10 grains of bicarbonate of soda, 1 fluidrachm of compound tincture of cardamom, 20 drops of paregoric, and a tablespoonful of water. Take this occasionally.

For Heartburn, attended by Costiveness.

In this case, gentle laxatives, combined with carminatives, are to be administered, until the cause is entirely removed. Take of confection of senna, 2 ounces; jalap, in powder, 2 drachms; compound powder of cinnamon, 20 grains; cream of tartar, 1 drachm, and syrup of ginger as much as will form an electuary; of which the bulk of a walnut is to be taken every night on going to bed.

DIARRHŒA, GOUT, RHEUMATISM, Etc.

To check Diarrhœa, or Looseness.

Take of the soft extract of bark, 15 grains; purified alum, in powder, 5 grains; tincture of opium, 6 drops. Make into a bolus, to be taken three times a day, in half a glass of red wine.

Another Method.

Take of tincture of opium, 15 drops; chalk mixture, 6 ounces; cinnamon water, 1 ounce. Make into a mixture, of which take a large tablespoonful every six hours.

Another.—Take of powder of rhubarb, 10 grains; powder of chalk, with opium, 1 scruple; powder of chalk without opium, 1 drachm. Make into four papers, of which take one night and morning.

Another.—Take of tincture of opium, 20 drops; chalk mixture, 4½ ounces; tincture of cinnamon, ½ ounce; cinnamon water, 2 ounces. Make a mixture, of which take two tablespoonsful after every liquid motion. Given in diarrhœa, and the looseness often attendant upon consumption.

Treatment of Obstinate Diarrhœa.

Take of tannin, 1 drachm; opium, 10 grains. Divide into 20 pills, one to be taken three or four times a day. This is excellent in obstinate diarrhœa, first evacuating with rhubarb and columbo, equal parts, 3 grains every four hours.

Anodyne Clyster.

Take of tincture of opium, ½ drachm; decoction of barley, 8 ounces. Make a clyster, to be thrown up directly, to stop diarrhœa and remove spasm.

Opiate Enema.

Take of milk of assafœtida, 8 ounces; tincture of opium, ½ drachm. To be injected as a clyster at bed-time. This is useful in disorders of the anus, which induce insufferable pain.

Remedy for Piles.

Take of galls, in powder, 2 drachms; hogs' lard, ½ an ounce. Make into an ointment, to be applied by means of lint to the external piles, or even pressed somewhat up the fundament every night. This has done wonders in the piles, taking, at the same time, the following: Take of quassia, in raspings, 2 drachms; boiling water, 1 pint. Let it remain three hours, strain; to 7 ounces of the strained liquor, add aromatic confection, 1 drachm; ginger, in powder, 2 scruples. Take of this mixture, two tablespoonsful at twelve and seven every day.

Pills for Rheumatism.

Take of guaiacum (gum resin) in powder, soap, equal parts, 1 drachm; essential oil of juniper berry, 4 drops. Make into 28 pills; take two four times a day. This is an admirable remedy.

Ointment for the same.

In America, an ointment of stramonium, made by gently boiling 6 ounces of the recent leaves (bruised) in a pound and a half of fresh hog's lard, till they become crisp, is in high repute as a remedy for this disease. The size of a nutmeg, Dr. Turner, of Philadelphia, has found to remove rheumatic pains, after electricity and powerful liniments, with internal remedies, had totally failed; and Dr. Zollickoffer says, that he has known the stramonium ointment to succeed in cases of rheumatism, after the internal exhibition of the tincture of stramonium had failed. For internal use he prefers a tincture of the leaves (made in the proportion of an ounce and a half of the dried leaves to a pint of proof spirit) to the extract.

Draught for Lumbago and Sciatica.

At a meeting of the Medical Society of London, oil of turpentine was strongly recommended, as being almost a panacea for acute rheumatism, etc. The formula in which it was administered is as follows:—Oil of turpentine, 20 drops; decoction of bark, 1½ ounces. To be taken every four hours. The use of the lancet and purgatives were generally premised. No sensible operation ensued from the medicine; but the patients were quickly relieved of the complaint.

Rheumatic Pains in the Face.

M. Double has administered the sulphate of quinia in several cases of acute pains in the face, approaching to tic douloureux, with complete success. He advises it to be given in the dose of 6 grains, dissolved in camphorated jalap, three times a day. This dose, however, is large.

Friction, Compression, and Percussion.

Not only rheumatism, but the cramp and gout, which bear affinity to each other, have long been greatly relieved by friction, wherever it was bearable, but some cures were performed upon patients slightly attacked, by pertinaciously rubbing the parts day after day; to this method of obtaining relief, Dr. Balfour has recently added those of compression and percussion, with complete success. Percussion at the sole of the foot relieves pain there and higher up the limb, and compression affords a certain degree of ease. Compression, alone upon the tendon of the heel (grasping by the warm hand between the finger and thumb), is sure to afford relief, as long as the pressure is continued, at least so far as the knee. A bandage round the thigh gives instant relief to that part of the member; grasping, or repeated pinchings, leave the patient in comparative ease. Percussion, by the patient himself, with his crutch, upon the spot most affected, is very beneficial. Dr. Balfour "pummels" the same part daily, until the cure is effected.

Tremor, caused by lifting up the limb, is always to be checked by passing a bandage round the ancle; and the reason assigned for this whole series of remedies is the excitement of certain nerves to action, or arresting that of others. This practice is by no means a novelty; it has long been employed by the negroes upon their European masters, by whom it is termed "shampooing."

Remedy for the Gout.

Wine of colchicum root, 15 drops; carbonate of potassa, 15 grains, in a tablespoonful of water, thrice daily.

Another.— Take of rhubarb, powdered, guaiac gum, nitrate of potass, flowers of sulphur, each, 1 ounce; treacle, 1 pound. Mix well together. From one to two teaspoonsful (according to its aperient effects) to be taken every night, with a little warm gin and water.

The Chelsea Pensioner's remedy for Gout and Rheumatism.

Gum guaiacum, 2 drachms; rhubarb, pulverized, ½ drachm; flowers of sulphur, ½ ounce; cream of tartar, 2 drachms; nutmeg, or ginger powder, ¼ drachm. Made an electuary with treacle, and two teaspoonsful taken night and morning.

CHOLERA.

History.

This disease, sometimes confounded with cholera morbus, is an epidemic; that is, it occurs at certain times, and moves from place to place; some parts of the world never having been visited by it. It prevails especially in cities; and follows the routes of travel, from India, where it is an annual scourge, westward across the globe, once in a number of years. It is not contagious from person to person, but is always propagated by human or other animal filth, in the air or water. An absolutely clean and pure locality will always be free from cholera.*

Symptoms.

After watery diarrhœa, generally, of a few hours' duration, vomiting begins, of a clear colorless fluid; which, as well as the copious passages from the bowels, resembles rice-water. There is, also, coldness of the skin, which gradually increases; with cramps, thirst, great feebleness of the pulse, and general prostration, deepening into collapse. In this last condition the patient is blue all over, with the skin shrunken, and the pulse at the wrist imperceptible; sometimes the breath is cold. Few recover from this state.

Treatment.

Medical men vary infinitely in their mode of management of this disease; as no specific remedy for it has been discovered. Considerable experience with it, in 1849, 1850, and 1854, enables the writer of this article to express a confident opinion in favor of the following mode of practice; by which, although it cannot be claimed to be infallible, he believes that he has saved a number of lives.

Apply a large mustard-plaster over the abdomen, and another on the back. Rub the limbs well with brandy mixed with Cayenne pepper. If the cramps continue, substitute for the mustard-plaster over the abdomen, a poultice of hops steeped in hot-water. Let the patient have, very frequently, small pieces of ice to dissolve in the mouth; and, *every five minutes*, a dose of the following anodyne and cordial tincture:—

Take of aromatic spirits of ammonia, laudanum, chloroform, and spirits of camphor, each, 1½ fl. drs.; creasote, 8 drops; oil of cinnamon, 2 drops; alcohol, enough to make 1 oz. of the tincture. Put 1 teaspoonful of this into a wineglassful of ice-water, and give 1 teaspoonful of the solution every five minutes until the patient decidedly improves; then lengthen the intervals by degrees till the symptoms all abate.

It is important to know that epidemic cholera is not a disease of the bowels or stomach particularly, but of the whole system. In this it differs from common cholera morbus. When an epidemic of cholera is prevailing, it is not well to live on a thin or weak diet, of rice, etc., as this will not promote immunity from the disease. Neither is it prudent to indulge at such a time in spirituous or other stimulants, as intemperance increases the danger. The true plan is, to live regularly, according to one's usual habits and needs, so as to keep the system steadily *up to par* in every way, without *excess* or *reduction*.

Another important fact is, that the diarrhœa, which commonly, though not invariably, precedes an attack of cholera, may be checked often by very mild means. During a cholera epidemic no one should neglect even a slight looseness of the bowels. Paregoric, in doses varying from 20 drops to 1 dr., at intervals, according to the case, will usually be suitable; or the following mixture, used much in Turkey, will be found serviceable: tincture of opii, camphor, and rhubarb, each 2 fluid-drs. Dose, 18 to 20 drops every two hours in a little sugar-water. But medical advice should be early obtained.

FUMIGATION AND VENTILATION.
To Purify the Air in Halls, Hospitals, etc.

Dr. Van Marum has discovered a very simple method, proved by repeated experiments, of preserving the air pure in large halls, theatres, hospitals, etc. The apparatus for this purpose is nothing but a common lamp, made according to Argand's construction, suspended from the roof of the hall, and kept burning under a funnel, the tube of which rises above the roof without, and is furnished with a ventilator. For his first experiment he filled his large laboratory with the smoke of oak shavings. In a few minutes after he lighted his lamp, the whole smoke disappeared, and the air was perfectly purified.

Simple mode of Ventilation.

Ships' holds are well ventilated when there is wind, by means of a sail, rigged out from the deck to below like a funnel, whose largest orifice points to leeward. But in some situations, as prisons, where foul air stagnates, this method cannot be adopted. Therefore, the plan has been adopted of making two holes in the side of the building or ship, communicating with the open air by a tin tube. Two pair of bellows are fitted up, the nozzle of one being introduced air-tight into one of the tin tubes, and a leathern pipe nailed on the wall, over the other tube, to which it may be fastened by wax thread. The other end of this pipe is to be made fast to the clicker-hole of the second pair of bellows; a luting of plaster of Paris, rendering both ends air-tight. A common blacksmith's forge-bellows will thus empty a space containing thirty hogsheads of foul air, and supply its place with good fresh air in a very few minutes.

Air-Pipes for Ventilating Ships, etc.

Air-pipes are used for drawing foul air out of ships, or other close places, by means of fire. One extremity is placed in a hole in the side of a furnace (closed in every part excepting the outlet for the smoke); the other in the place which it is designed to purify. The rarefaction produced by the fire, causes a current of air to be determined to it, and the only means by which the air can arrive at the fire being through the pipe, a quick circulation in the place where the extremity of the pipe may be situated, is consequently produced.

The Air Trunk.

This apparatus was contrived by Dr. Hales, to prevent the stagnation of putrid effluvia in jails and other places, where a great number of people are crowded together. It consists merely of an oblong trunk open at both ends, one of which is inserted into the ceiling of the room, the air of which is to be kept pure: and the other extends a good way beyond the roof. Through this trunk a continued circulation is carried on; and the reason why vapors of this kind ascend more swiftly through a long trunk than a short one is, that the pressure of fluids is always according to their different depths, without regard to the diameter of their basis, or of the vessel that contains them. When the column of putrid effluvia is long and narrow, the difference between the column of atmosphere pressing on the upper end of the trunk, and that which presses on the lower end, is much greater than if the column of putrid effluvia was short and wide; and consequently the ascent is much swifter. One pan of a single pair of scales, which was two inches in diameter, being held within one of these trunks over the House of Commons, the force of the ascending air made it rise so as to require four grains to restore the equilibrium, and this when there was no person in the house; but when it was full, no less than twelve grains were requisite to restore the equilibrium; which clearly shows that these trunks must be of real and very great efficacy.

German Method of Cooling and Purifying the Air in Summer.

In the hot days of summer, especially in houses

---

* "The discharges of cholera patients contain the generative principle of cholera."—*European Cholera Conference, Constantinople, May 21, 1866.* Hence utensils and water-closets used by cholera patients should be carefully scalded, or disinfected with chloride of lime or copperas. See Index for Disinfectants.

exposed to the meridian sun, a capacious vessel filled with cold water is placed in the middle of a room, and a few green branches (or as many as it will hold) of lime, birch, or willow-tree, are plunged with the lower ends into the fluid. By this easy expedient the apartment is, in a short time, rendered much cooler; the evaporation of the water producing this desirable effect in sultry weather without any detriment to health. Besides, the exhalation of green plants, under the influence of the solar rays, greatly tends to purify the air; but care must be taken that they do not remain in the apartment after night-fall, or in the shade.

To Fumigate Foul Rooms.

To one tablespoonful of common salt, and a little peroxide of manganese, in a glass cup, add four or five different times, a quarter of a wine-glass of strong sulphuric acid. Place the cup on the floor and go out, taking care to shut the door. The vapor will come in contact with the malignant miasma and destroy it. Prepared chloride of lime will do as well.

Caution in Visiting Sick Rooms.

Never venture into a sick room in a violent perspiration (if circumstances require a continuance there for any time), for the moment the body becomes cold it is in a state likely to absorb the infection and receive the disease. Nor visit a sick person (especially if the complaint be of a contagious nature) with an empty stomach, as this disposes the system more readily to receive the infection. In attending a sick person, stand where the air passes from the door or window to the bed of the diseased, not betwixt the diseased person and any fire that is in the room, as the heat of the fire will draw the infectious vapor in that direction, and danger would occasionally arise from breathing in it.

Fumigating Powder.

Take of cascarilla reduced to a coarse powder, chamomile flowers, aniseed, each equal parts, two ounces. Put some hot cinders in a shovel, sprinkle this gradually on it, and fumigate the chambers of the sick. It takes away all smell, and keeps off infection.

Disinfecting Liquid.

Make a strong solution either of nitrate or acetate of lead; and sprinkle with it the floor and walls of a foul apartment. The first of the above is Ledoyen's liquid.

Preparation of Acetic Acid.

Put 4 ounces of acetate of lead, in powder, into a tubulated glass retort, and pour over it 4 ounces of sulphuric acid. Place the retort in a sand-bath, the heat of which should be kept as uniform as possible. Adapt a common receiver, over which there must be constantly kept a piece of wet flannel or cotton for the condensation of the gas as it comes over. Sometimes sulphurous acid gas will be found to adulterate the acetic acid; this is easily known by the suffocating odor which it emits. The best way to prevent this is by a slow distillation; or the whole may be distilled a second time. The acetic acid possesses a very pungent odor, owing to its volatility; consequently it should be kept in a well stopped phial. It is used as the basis of all the aromatic vinegars.

Aromatic Vinegar.

Acetic acid may be mixed with camphor and aromatics, as in Henry's Aromatic Vinegar, in a quantity sufficient for a small smelling bottle, at no great expense. But it is the acetic acid which is useful in preventing infection, and not the aromatics, which are added for the pleasure of the perfume.

Cheap Aromatic Vinegar for Purifying large Buildings, Manufactories, &c.

Take of common vinegar any quantity; mix powdered chalk or common whiting with it, as long as bubbles of carbonic acid gas arise. Let the white matter subside, and pour off the insipid supernatant liquor; afterwards let the white powder be dried either in the open air or by a fire. When dry pour upon it, in a glass or stone vessel, sulphuric acid as long as white acid fumes continue to ascend. This product is similar to the acetic acid known in the shops by the name of Aromatic Vinegar. The simplicity of this process points it out as a very useful and convenient one for purifying prisons, hospital ships, and houses where contagion is presumed or suspected, the white acid fumes diffusing themselves quickly around.

To prevent and Destroy the Mephitism of Plastered Walls.

Wherever a number of people are assembled, either in health or sickness, the walls become insensibly impregnated with infectious exhalations. Currents of air, when admitted, sweep and cleanse the atmosphere, but do not carry away the miasmata concealed in the porosity of the walls, which retain the infectious humidity of the perspiration of bodies, gradually condensing on their surface. Quick-lime may be substituted to destroy such mephitism of walls, and also to prevent the evil. The most infected tans and sieves lose their smell when mixed with the whiting or size of lime. Lime enters whitewashing, and may become the principal substance of it, by substituting it for Spanish white. When made the principal ingredient of whitewashing, it will prevent walls from being impregnated with infectious miasmata. The addition of milk and oil are requisite, for lime has no adhesion on walls, nor can a body or substance be given to the layer. The slightest rubbing with a pencil brush will rub it off, and leave the wall naked. The cheesy part of the milk, with the addition of oil, which makes a soapy body with lime, form, after the evaporation of the humidity, a dense coherent layer, or sort of varnished plaster, which overcomes the porosity of stone, plaster, brick, and wood. This wash has another advantage, that of checking the nitrification of walls, which the painting of them in water colors has a tendency to accelerate.

To deodorize Privies.

Chloride of lime (bleaching powder) will effect this. So will chloride of zinc, or sulphate of iron. The first is the most convenient, although the last is also used, with fifteen times its weight of water

Ridgewood's Disinfectant.

In 100 parts, use of carbolic acid 5 to 8 per cent.; lime from magnesia limestone, 5 per cent.; fuller's earth, 70 to 80 per cent.; with a little sulphate of potash and sulphate of soda.

To disinfect Letters.

A common method of disinfecting letters, and other articles coming from places that are supposed to be visited by the plague, is to expose them to the fumes of burning sulphur, mixed with saltpetre. A high temperature, short of combustion, will answer the same purpose.

CAUTIONS TO GLAZIERS, PAINTERS, AND PLUMBERS.

The following medical cautions were recommended by the physicians and surgeons of the Bath Hospital, to those who have received benefit by the use of the Bath waters, in cases where the poison of lead is concerned, as plumbers, glaziers,

DISEASES OF FEMALES.

painters, and other artificers, who work in trades which expose them to similar hazards from the same cause; to be observed by them at their return to the exercise of their former occupation.

1. To maintain the strictest temperance, particularly respecting distilled spirits, which had better be altogether forborne.

2. To pay the strictest attention to cleanliness; and never suffer paint to remain upon their hands; and particularly never to eat their meals, or go to rest, without washing their hands and face with soap, perfectly clean.

3. Not to eat or drink in the room or place wherein they work; and much less to suffer any food or drink to remain unused, even for the shortest space of time, in any part of a room while painting, or where color stands; and not to work on an empty stomach.

4. As the clothes of persons in this line (painters, particularly) are generally much soiled with color, it is recommended for them to perform their work in frocks of ticking, which may be frequently washed, and conveniently laid aside when the workmen go to their meals, and again put on when they resume their work.

5. Every business which can, in these branches, should be performed with gloves on their hands. Painters, in performing clean light work, would find gloves an inconvenience; but to avoid the evil here mentioned, the handle of the brush should be often scraped. Woollen or worsted gloves are recommended, as they may and should be often washed, after being soiled with the paint, or even with much rubbing against the metal.

6. Caution is necessary, in mixing, or even in unpacking, the dry colors, that the fine powder do not get into their mouths, or be drawn in by the breath. A crape covering over the face might be of service; but care should be taken to turn always the same side of the crape towards the face, and to clean or wash it frequently.

7. All artificers should avoid touching lead when hot; and this caution is especially necessary for printers or compositors, who have often lost the use of their limbs by handling the types when drying by the fire, after being washed.

8. Glaziers' putty should never be made or moulded by the hand. An iron pestle and mortar would work the ingredients together, at least equally as well, and without hazard. It is necessary in working putty to handle it, nor is it usually pernicious. Cleanliness is therefore the best recommendation.

9. If any persons, in any of the above employments, should feel pain in the bowels, with costiveness, they should immediately take 20 drops of laudanum, and when the pain is abated 2 tablespoonsful of castor oil, or ½ an ounce of Epsom salts, dissolved in warm chamomile tea. If this does not succeed, a pint or two pints of warm soapsuds should be thrown up as a clyster.

10. As a preventive, ten or fifteen drops of aromatic sulphuric acid (elixir of vitriol), is likely to be of service, if taken daily.

DISEASES PECULIAR TO FEMALES.

Hysteric Fits.

This complaint, called also the hysteric passion, appears under various shapes, and is often owing to a lax, tender habit, obstruction of the menses, fluor albus, etc.

In the fit the patient is seized with an oppression in the breast, and difficult respiration, accompanied with a sensation of something like a ball ascending into the throat, which puts her under great apprehensions of being suffocated. There is a loss of speech, and generally violent convulsive motions. These, with a train of hypochondriac symptoms, are sufficient to determine the disease; to which may be added frequent laughing and crying, and various wild, irregular actions: after which a general soreness all over the body is felt; the spirits are low; the feet are cold. The urine is clear and limpid, and discharged in great quantity. The hysteric fit may be easily distinguished from fainting; for in this the pulse and respiration are entirely stopped; in that they are both perceivable.

Cure and Prevention.

Nothing recovers a person sooner out of the hysteric fit than putting the feet and legs in warm water.

When low spirits proceed from a suppression of the piles or the menses, these evacuations must be encouraged, or repeated cuppings substituted. When they take their origin from long-continued grief, anxious thoughts, or other distresses of mind, nothing has done more service, in these cases, than agreeable company, daily exercise, and especially long journeys, and a variety of amusements.

Regimen.—A light animal food, red wine, cheerful company, and a good clear air, with moderate exercise, are of great importance in this disorder. Drinking tea, and such like tepid relaxing fluids, should be but moderately indulged in.

The cure consists in whatever tends to strengthen the solids, and the whole habit in general; and nothing will effect this more successfully than a long-continued use of the mineral chalybeate waters, and riding on horseback. Assafœtida pills, 3 grains each, are often temporarily useful.

Anti-hysteric Spirits.

Take of proof spirit, 1 pint; sal ammoniac, 2 ounces; assafœtida, 6 drachms; potash, 3 ounces. Mix them, and draw off, by distillation, 1 pint, with a slow fire.

The spirit is pale when newly distilled, but acquires a considerable tinge by keeping. The dose is a teaspoonful, in some water, during hysterics, and the same to be taken occasionally.

Anti-hysteric Pills.

Take of compound pills of galbanum, 2 drachms; rust of iron, 4 scruples; syrup of ginger, as much as is sufficient. Form a mass, which is to be made into 40 pills, of which take 4 at noon and at seven in the evening every day, drinking after them half a glass of port wine. These pills are good in hysteric affections.

Fœtid Enema.

This is made by adding to the ingredients of the common clyster 2 drachms of the tincture of assafœtida.

In cases of hysterics and convulsions, the fœtid enema is of singular use.

Opiate Draught.

Mix together cinnamon water, 1 ounce; spirit of caraways, ½ an ounce; sulphuric ether, ½ a drachm; tincture of castor, ½ a drachm. Let this draught be taken every six hours, if the stomach should be affected by cramp. If the feet are cold, bottles filled with warm water should be applied to them.

Tonic for Debility in Females.

Take of soft extract of bark, 2 drachms; columbo and rust of iron, each 1 drachm; simple syrup, as much as is sufficient. Make into fifty pills; take two, and gradually increase to five, three times a day.

Compound Galbanum Pills.

Take of galbanum, myrrh, sagapenum, each 1 ounce; assafœtida, ¼ an ounce; syrup of saffron, as much as is sufficient. Beat them together. These pills are excellent as anti-hysterics and emmenagogues; from five grains to half a scruple may be taken every night, or oftener.

Compound Spirit of Lavender.

Take of spirit of lavender, 3 pounds; spirit of rosemary, 1 pound; cinnamon, ½ an ounce; nutmeg, the same; red sanders, 3 drachms. Digest for ten days and then strain off. This is often taken upon sugar, and is a salutary cordial, far preferable to drams, which are too often had recourse to by persons feeling a great sinking or depression of the spirits.

Infusion of Senna, with Tamarinds.

Add to the infusion of senna, before it is strained, an ounce of tamarinds; then strain. This forms a mild and useful purge, excellently suited for delicate stomachs and inflammatory diseases. The taste of the senna is well covered by the aromatic sugar, and by the acidity of the tamarinds. An ounce is a convenient purge.

Mild Purgative.

Take of manna, 2 ounces; tamarinds, 1 ounce; rose-water, 1 ounce. Boil the rose-water and tamarinds together for a quarter of an hour, then add the manna. Three tablespoonfuls to be taken every three hours, until a motion is obtained. Less is to be given to a child.

Fluor Albus, or Whites.

The fluor albus is a flux of thin matter, of a pellucid or white color; sometimes it is greenish or yellow, sharp and corroding, often foul and fœtid, especially if it be of any long standing.

Tedious labors, frequent miscarriages, immoderate flowings of the menses, profuse evacuations, poor diet, an inactive and sedentary life, are the causes which generally produce this disease.

Regimen, etc. — The diet should be nourishing: milk, jellies, sago, broths and light meats, red port wine in moderation, chalybeate waters, moderate exercise, and frequent ablution of the parts should be recommended. A standing posture of body long continued, violent dancing, or much walking, must be forbidden.

Astringent Injection.

To restore tone to the parts, it will be necessary three or four times a day to inject a portion of the following mixture by means of a syringe:

Rub together in a mortar white vitriol, 1 drachm; sugar of lead, 10 grains; water, 2 drachms. Mix the whole with a pint of distilled water.

Another.—Mix together 1 drachm of powdered alum with 1 pint of decoction of oak-bark. Inject as above.

Tonic and Astringent Pills.

Take of gum kino, and extract of Peruvian bark, each, 1 drachm; grated nutmeg, 1 scruple; powdered alum, ½ drachm; syrup, in sufficiency to form a mass, which is to be divided into 36 pills. Three of these are to be taken at eleven, forenoon, and five in the afternoon; being taken two hours before dinner, three hours afterwards washed down by a glassful of good port wine. Recourse may, at the same time, be had to tincture of Peruvian bark, to preparations of steel, and mineral waters.

Prevention. — Females afflicted with this disorder should by no means indulge in the too free use of tea, or other warm slops of a relaxing nature. They should sleep on a mattress, rise early, and take such exercise as may be convenient, and, if possible, on horseback. Cold bathing should also be used as often as convenient. In winter a flannel shift ought to be worn.

Immoderate Flow of the Menses.

When the menses continue too long, or come on too frequently for the strength of the patient, they are said to be immoderate, and are generally occasioned by weak vessels, thin blood, or a plethoric habit. This often happens in delicate women, who use enervating liquids too freely, especially tea. It also arises in consequence of abortion, and sometimes attends women who are obliged to work hard.

Where the hæmorrhage is excessive, opiates are of great use. Tincture of the chloride of iron may be given, 20 drops three times daily in water.

Astringent Fomentations.

Astringent fomentations may often be very properly prescribed. Cloths dipped in decoction of oak or Peruvian bark, with the addition of a small quantity of brandy, or red wine and vinegar, will answer the purpose extremely well.

Astringent Injection.

Where the hæmorrhage is profuse, and resists the usual means now recommended, it will be necessary to throw up the following astringent injection into the uterus from time to time. Take of decoction of bark, 1 pint; alum, in powder, 3 drachms. Mix, and use as an injection, three times if necessary.

Regimen, etc. — To confirm the cure, and prevent a relapse, the body should be strengthened by proper exercise, mineral waters, a light but nourishing diet; such as light broths, red port wine in moderation, and an easy cheerful mind.

When an immoderate flux of the menses, or floodings after abortion, is either attended with or preceded by acute pain, not inflammatory, in the lower part of the back or belly, and returns with greater violence, as the discharge comes on, opium will, in such a case, answer better than astringents, and may be given in clysters, composed of water or 3 ounces of infusion of roses, with ½ a drachm of laudanum.

Green Sickness.

This disease is commonly attended with listlessness to motion, a heaviness, paleness of complexion, and pain in the back and loins, also hæmorrhages at the nose, pains in the head, with a great sense of weight across the eyes, loathing of food, a quick and weak pulse, fluor albus, hectic heats, coughs, and hysteric fits.

There is often indigestion and costiveness, with a preternatural appetite for chalk, lime and other absorbents.

Regimen, etc.—The diet ought to be nutritive and generous, with a moderate use of wine. Exercise ought also to be daily used, and particularly on horseback. The mind should likewise be kept amused by associating with agreeable company.

Chalybeate Pills.

Mix together extract of bark and sulphate of iron (green vitriol), each 1 scruple; sub-carbonate of soda 15 grains; powdered myrrh 30 grains. Add syrup of ginger to form the whole into a mass, which divide into thirty-four pills. After the stomach has been cleansed by a gentle emetic, two of these are taken two or three times a day, taking care to wash them down with nearly a wineglassful of the following

Tonic Draught.

Mix together compound tincture of Peruvian bark and compound tincture of cardamoms, each 1 ounce; compound infusion of gentian 1 pint.

Chalybeate Draught.

Pour fifteen drops of tincture of muriate of iron

into a glassful of cold water, or a decoction of Peruvian bark. Drink this twice or thrice a day, an hour before or two hours after eating.

Tincture of Iodine.

In many cases of green sickness, attended with symptoms of approaching consumption, and also in incipient phthisis, the saturated tincture of iodine may be administered with great effect. When taken internally it is very beneficial in dispersing wen. Ten drops of the saturated tincture taken three times a day, may effectually remove the complaint in the course of five or six weeks. The Lugol's Solution of Iodine will do as well as the above for the same uses. Dose five or six drops twice daily.

Cessation of the Menses.

The constitution undergoes a very considerable change at the critical period when menstruation ceases, and it often happens that chronic, and sometimes fatal complaints arise, if care is not taken when this natural discharge terminates. It seldom stops all at once, but gradually ceases, being irregular both as to quantity and time.
Regimen, etc.—When the disappearance is sudden in females of a plethoric habit, malt liquors, wine and animal food ought for a time to be excluded from their diet. They should likewise avoid all liquors of a spirituous nature. Regular exercise should be taken and the body constantly kept open by the tincture of senna, Epsom salts, or any other mild laxative medicine.

If giddiness and occasional pain in the head affect the patient, or if there be a visible fulness in the vessels, the application of leeches to the temple will be found very beneficial, and if ulcers should break out in the legs, etc., they ought by no means to be healed up, unless a salutary drain by means of an issue be established in some other part.

Dropsy.

Dissolve an ounce of acetate of potassa in a pint of cold water; take a wineglassful every morning and evening.

For Vomiting during Pregnancy.

The morning sickness is one of the most painful feelings attendant on the pregnant state, and it is one of those which medicine commonly fails to relieve. A cup of chamomile or peppermint tea taken when first waking, and suffering the patient to be still for an hour, will sometimes alleviate the distressing sickness, but should it recur during the day these means seldom succeed.

Two or three teaspoonfuls of the following mixture should then be taken, either occasionally or when the vomiting and heartburn are more continual immediately after every meal: Take of calcined magnesia 1 drachm; distilled water 6 ounces; aromatic tincture of rhatany 6 drachms; water, pure ammonia, 1 drachm. Mix.

Another.—Dr. Scellier extols the following mixture as a remedy for nausea and vomiting during the period of pregnancy: Take of lettuce-water 4 ounces; gum arabic 1 scruple; syrup of white poppies, syrup of marsh-meadow root, each 2 ounces; Prussic acid 4 drops. Let an apothecary prepare the mixture. A tablespoonful is to be taken every half hour when the vomiting is present.

If the lettuce-water cannot be obtained, 8 grains of the inspissated white juice (lactuarium) dissolved in 4 ounces of water, may be substituted for it.

Another.—The saline mixture in a state of effervescence, with a pill of one or two grains of lactuarium, is by some preferred to the above composition. When the matter brought up is acid, a weak solution of the carbonate of soda may be substituted for the saline mixture.

To relieve Sickness and Qualms in Pregnancy.

Take of infusion of quassia, 1 ounce; cinnamon-water, 4 drachms; aromatic spirit of ammonia, 2e drops; prepared oyster-shells, 2 grains. To be taken at a draught, at twelve and seven o'clock every day.

For Heartburn during Pregnancy.

Take of solution of ammonia, calcined magnesia, each 1 drachm; cinnamon-water 2 ounces; common water 6 ounces. The dose is a tablespoonful as often as required.

Head-ache.

When head-ache or drowsiness proves troublesome to a pregnant woman of robust habit, a few ounces of blood should be taken from the arm. If she be of a weak or irritable habit, leeches ought to be applied to the temples. In both cases the bowels should be opened by magnesia, rhubarb, or some other gentle laxative medicine.

Hysteria.

When hysteria or fainting occurs, the pregnant patient should be placed in a horizontal position in the open air. When she is a little recovered a glass of wine in a little cold water should be administered, or what is perhaps better, a few drops of the spirits of hartshorn in a glass of water.

Costiveness and Piles.

To prevent these, women in a pregnant state should make frequent use of the following electuary:

Mix together in a marble mortar 2 ounces of the electuary of senna, ½ a drachm of powder of jalap; 2 drachms of cream of tartar, and ½ an ounce of syrup of roses. Half a teaspoonful to be taken every night at bed-time, or oftener, as long as the above complaints continue.

Pregnant women should be particularly careful not to use aloes as a purgative, this medicine being very apt to increase the piles. The same caution is necessary with respect to Anderson's and Scott's pills, the basis of both of which is aloes. If the piles should prove so very troublesome as to prevent the patient from sitting comfortably, leeches ought to be applied to the part; in all other cases simple ablution with cold water, with the use of purgatives as above directed, will be sufficient.

Troublesome Itchings.

Cooling laxatives are likewise proper in this place; also frequent ablution with cold or lukewarm water. If the itching does not speedily abate, a lotion is to be applied to the parts twice a day, consisting of a drachm of sugar of lead in a pint of distilled water.

Swelling of the Feet and Ankles.

Pregnant women are usually free from this complaint in the morning, but suffer a good deal from it towards night.

Prevention.— In the commencement it will be merely requisite for the patient to use a footstool, when sitting, so that her feet may never be in a hanging position for any length of time.

Remedy. — If there should be great distension, so as to give the sensation of almost bursting, slight scarification may be made with the edge of a lancet; and flannels, wrung out of a hot fomentation of chamomile, are soon after to be applied. A teaspoonful of cream of tartar mixed in water may be taken once or twice daily, to act on the kidneys. It is almost unnecessary to state that this complaint invariably disappears at the period of delivery.

Cramp of the Legs and Thighs.

This complaint may be speedily relieved by rubbing the part affected with the following liniment: Mix together (by shaking in a phial) laudanum, ½ an ounce; tincture of camphor, 1 ounce; and sulphuric ether, ½ an ounce.

Cramp in the Stomach.

This is to be avoided by proper attention to diet, which should not be of a flatulent nature, or too hard of digestion. Attention is likewise to be paid to the state of the bowels.

Distention and Cracking of the Skin.

This is very apt to occur in the latter months of gestation, accompanied sometimes with considerable soreness. It is to be relieved by frequent friction with warm oil.

Distention of Veins.

The veins of the legs, thighs, and belly are apt to become enlarged in the latter stages of pregnancy. Although no bad consequences ever attend this, it will be necessary sometimes to relieve it by moderate bleeding, and by repeated small doses of infusion of senna, mixed with Epsom salts; at the same time using a spare diet. The distended vein may frequently be relieved by the application of a pretty tight bandage.

Incontinence of Urine.

This very uncomfortable complaint is to be relieved by a frequent horizontal position, but cannot be entirely remedied except by delivery. Strict attention, however, ought to be paid to cleanliness, and much comfort will be felt by the use of a large sponge properly fastened.

Restlessness and Want of Sleep.

In this case, cooling laxative medicines, as the infusion of senna, with Epsom salts, ought frequently to be used. If relief be not soon obtained, small quantities of blood are to be taken from the patient. Opiates ought seldom to be used, as they tend sometimes to increase the febrile state of the patient.

Convulsions.

When a female is disposed to this complaint from a plethoric habit, there will be great fullness and giddiness in the head, in the latter months of gestation; also drowsiness, with a sensation of weight in the forehead when she stoops, or bends forward, accompanied sometimes by imperfect vision, and the appearance of atoms floating before the eyes. In such a case, ten or twelve ounces of blood ought to be taken from the arm, and the bowels are afterwards to be kept open by frequent and small doses of infusion of senna, mixed with cream of tartar, until the above symptoms entirely disappear. Wine, spirituous and malt liquors, and solid or animal food are likewise to be avoided.

When convulsions have occurred, and when there is reason to believe that they are owing to irritation, rather than plethora, it will likewise be necessary to bleed the patient in a small degree, both from the arm, and by the application of leeches to the temples. The bowels are also to be kept perfectly open, and a common clyster, containing from half a drachm to a drachm of laudanum, is to be administered. The warm bath is likewise exceedingly useful; at the same time taking care to strengthen the habit as much as possible.

The Milk Fever.

This fever generally arises about the third or fourth day after delivery. The symptoms are pain and distention of the breasts, shooting frequently towards the arm-pit. Sometimes the breasts become hard, hot, and inflamed. It generally continues a day or two, and ends spontaneously by copious sweats, or a large quantity of pale urine.

Remedies.—If it should prove violent, especially in young women of a plethoric constitution, we should abate the inflammation by bleeding; this, however, is rarely necessary. But, in every constitution, the body must be kept open by gentle cooling laxatives, or clysters. The breasts should be often drawn either by the child, or, if the mother does not design to give suck, by some proper person. If the breasts are hard, very turgid, or inflamed, emollient fomentations ought to be applied to them. The common poultice of bread and milk, with the addition of a little oil, may be used on this occasion; and warm milk, or a decoction of elder flowers, for a fomentation.

Regimen.—The patient should use a simple diet, consisting only of panada, or some other farinaceous substances. Her drink may be barley-water, milk and water, gruel, or the like.

Inflamed Breasts.

When the breasts tumefy, and begin to be uneasy, a few days after delivery, from the milk stagnating, gentle diaphoretics and purgatives are to be used, and camphorated spirits of wine is to be applied, or warm cloths dipped in brandy, are to be put to the arm-pits. Should pain with inflammation come on, apply a poultice of bread, milk and oil, and an emollient fomentation; and in case suppuration cannot be prevented, it must be opened with a lancet. The ulcer is afterwards to be treated according to the common rules for disorders of that kind.

If there be only a hardness in the breast, from coagulated milk, emollient cataplasms and fomentations are to be used, likewise fresh linseed oil, by way of liniment.

Sore Nipples.

Chapped or sore nipples are very frequent with those who give suck. In this case the olive oil is a very proper application; or fresh cream spread upon fine linen; or a solution of gum arabic in water. Collodion, applied with a camel's hair pencil, is the most effectual remedy.

It is almost needless to observe that, whatever applications be made use of to the nipples, they ought to be washed off before the child is permitted to suck. This is not always necessary with collodion.

Puerperal Fever.

Puerperal fever commonly begins with a rigor, or chilliness, on the first, second, or third day after delivery; followed by a violent pain and soreness over the belly. There is much thirst; pain in the head, chiefly in the forehead and parts about the eyebrows; a flushing in the face; anxiety; a hot, dry skin; quick and weak pulse, though sometimes it will resist the finger pretty strongly; a shortness in breathing; high-colored urine, and a suppression of the natural discharge. Sometimes a vomiting and purging attend from the first, but in general, in the beginning, the belly is costive; however, when the disease proves fatal, a diarrhœa generally supervenes, and the stools at last become involuntary.

The cause of this fever has been commonly ascribed either to a suppression of the natural discharge, an inflammation in the womb, or a retention of the milk.

Remedies.—If the belly be costive, an emollient opening clyster is to be administered; and, if stools and an abatement of the pain be not procured thereby, immediate recourse is to be had to cathartics, and bleeding from the arm. Those to be recommended are, infusion of senna, or castor oil: either in sufficient quantity.

After the intestinal canal is sufficiently cleared, a gentle diaphoresis is to be encouraged by such medicines as at the same time promote the relief of pain. This intention is best answered by small doses of ipecacuanha, tartar emetic, or antimonial wine, combined with opium in pill or laudanum, and given about four times in the course of the twenty-four hours. In the intermediate spaces of time, interpose saline draughts. It is proper to state, that when child-bed fever is epidemic, especially in cities or hospitals, it is more malignant and prostrating, and will not bear reducing treatment.

Regimen.—The patient's drink should consist of pure water with toast in it; barley-water, either by itself or with the addition of a little nitre; whey made with rennet or vinegar; milk and water; lemonade; a slight infusion of malt; and mint or sage tea.

MANAGEMENT AND DISEASES OF CHILDREN.

Infant Nursing.

A child, when it comes into the world, should be laid (for the first month) upon a thin mattress rather longer than itself, which the nurse may sometimes keep upon her lap, that the child may always lie straight, and only sit up as the nurse slants the mattress. To set a child quite upright before the end of the first month is hurtful. Afterwards the nurse may begin to set it up and dance it by degrees; and it must be kept as dry as possible.

Friction.

The clothing should be very light, and not much longer than the child, that the legs may be got at with ease, in order to have them often rubbed in the day with a warm hand or flannel, and in particular the inside of them. Rubbing a child all over, takes off scurf, and makes the blood circulate.

Rubbing the anklebones and inside of the knees will strengthen those parts, and make the child stretch its knees and keep them flat.

Position.

A nurse ought to keep a child as little in her arms as possible, lest the legs should be cramped, and the toes turned inwards. Let her always keep the child's legs loose. The oftener the posture is changed the better.

Exercise.

By slow degrees the infant should be accustomed to exercise, both within doors and in the open air; but he never should be moved about immediately after sucking or feeding; it will be apt to sicken him. Exercise should be given by carrying him about and gently dandling him him in his mother or nurse's arms; but dancing him up and down on the knee is very fatiguing for a young child.

To prevent Distortion.

Tossing a child about, and exercising it in the open air in fine weather, is of the greatest service. In cities children are not to be kept in hot rooms, but to have as much air as possible. Want of exercise is the cause of rickets, large heads, weak joints, a contracted breast, and diseased lungs, besides a numerous train of other evils.

Rendering Children Hardy.

Endeavor to harden the body, but without resorting to any violent means. All attempts to render children hardy, must be made by gradual steps. Nature admits of no sudden transitions. For instance, infants should, by imperceptible degrees, be inured to the cool, and then to the cold bath; at the same time attention must be paid to their previous management. If they have hitherto been accustomed to an effeminating treatment, and should be suddenly subjected to an opposite extreme, such a change would be attended with danger. When children have once been accustomed to a hardy system of education, such a plan must be strictly adhered to.

Cleanliness and Bathing.

The child's skin is to be kept perfectly clean by washing its limbs morning and evening, and likewise its neck and ears; beginning with warm water, till by degrees he will not only bear, but like to be washed with cool or cold water.

After he is a month old, if he has no cough, fever, or eruption, the bath should be colder and colder (if the season be mild), and gradually it may be used as it comes from the fountain. After carefully drying the whole body, head and limbs, another dry soft cloth, a little warmed, should be used gently to take all the damp from the wrinkles or fat parts that fold together. Then rub the limbs; but when the body is rubbed, take special care not to press upon the stomach or belly. On these parts the hand should move in a circle, because the bowels lie in that direction. If the skin is chafed, starch-powder is to be used. The utmost tenderness is necessary in drying the head, and no binding should be made close about it. Squeezing the head, or combing it roughly, may cause dreadful diseases, and even the loss of reason. A small soft brush, lightly applied, is safer than a comb. Clean clothes every morning and evening will tend greatly to a child's health and comfort.

Dress.

With regard to the child's dress in the day, let it be a shirt, a petticoat of fine flannel, reaching two or three inches below the child's feet, with a dimity top (commonly called a *bodice-coat*), to tie behind. Over this put a robe or frock or whatever may be convenient, provided it is fastened behind, and not reaching much below the child's feet, that his motions may be strictly observed.

Caps are, as a general rule, undesirable. The head should be kept cool.

The dress for the night may be a shirt, a blanket to tie on, and a thin gown to tie over the blanket.

The Act of Dressing.

Some people in dressing an infant seem in such haste as to toss him in a way that must fatigue and harass him. The most tender deliberation should be observed. In addition to this hurried dressing, his clothes are often so tight that he frets and roars. Pins should never be used in an infant's clothes; and every string should be so loosely tied that one might get two fingers between it and the part where it is fixed. Bandages round the head should be strictly forbidden. Many instances of idiocy, fits, and deformity, are owing to tight bandages.

Sleep.

Infants cannot sleep too long; and it is a favorable symptom, when they enjoy a calm and long-continued rest, of which they should by no means be deprived, as this is the greatest support granted to them by nature. A child lives comparatively much faster than an adult; its blood flows more rapidly; and every stimulus operates more powerfully. Sleep promotes a more calm and uniform circulation of the blood, and it facilitates assimilation of the nutriment received. The horizontal posture, likewise, is the most favorable to the growth and bodily development of the infant.

Duration of, and time for Sleep.

Sleep ought to be in proportion to the age of the infant. After an uninterrupted rest of nine months in the womb, this salutary refreshment should continue to fill up the greater part of a child's existence. A continued wakefulness of twenty-four hours would prove destructive. After the age of six months, the periods of sleep, as well as all other animal functions, may in some degree be regulated; yet, even then, a child should be suffered to sleep the whole night, and several hours both in the morning and afternoon. Mothers and nurses should endeavor to accustom infants from the time of their birth, to sleep in the night preferably to the day, and for this purpose they ought to remove all external impressions which may disturb their rest, such as noise, light, etc., but especially they should not obey every call for taking them up and giving food at improper times. After the second year of their age, they will not instinctively require to sleep in the forenoon, though after dinner it may be continued till the third and fourth year, if the child shows a particular inclination to repose; because till that age, the full half of its time may safely be allotted to sleep. From that period, however, it ought to be shortened for the space of one hour with every succeeding year; so that a child seven years old may sleep about eight, and not exceeding nine hours; this proportion may be continued to the age of adolescence, and even manhood.

Awaking Suddenly.

To awaken children from their sleep with a noise, or in an impetuous manner, is extremely injudicious and hurtful, nor is it proper to carry them from a dark room immediately into a glaring light, against a dazzling wall; for the sudden impression of light debilitates the organs of vision, and lays the foundation of weak eyes, from early infancy. In fact it is a sound precept, *never to waken a young child from sleep at all.*

Restlessness at night.

An infant is sometimes very restless at night, and it is generally owing either to cramming him with a heavy supper, tight night-clothes, or over-heating by too many blankets. It may also proceed from putting him to sleep too early. Undressing and bathing will weary and dispose him for sleep, and the universal stillness will promote it. This habit and all others depend on attention at first. Accustom him to regular hours, and if he has a good sleep in the forenoon and afternoon, it will be easy to keep him brisk all the evening. It is right to offer him drink when a young infant; and more solid, though simple food, when he is going to bed, after he is two or three months old, but do not force him to receive it; and never let anything but the prescription of a physician in sickness, tempt the nurses to give him wine, spirits, or any drug to make him sleep. Milk and water, whey, or thin gruel, is the only fit liquor for little ones, even when they can run about. The more simple and light their diet and drink, the more they will thrive. In the night a drink of water will often do better than the breast. Such food will keep their bowels regular, and they cannot be long well if that essential point be neglected.

Amusements, etc.

The bodily education of boys and girls ought in every respect to be uniform. A great difference usually prevails in the education of the sexes during infancy. Parents being too anxious for the accomplishment of girls, imagine that they must be kept under a certain restraint. Boys, in general, are not laced, but girls are compressed tight enough to suffocate them; because it is erroneously supposed, that this injudicious practice contributes to an elegant shape, though, ultimately, the contrary effect is obvious; as it is the surest way of making children round shouldered and deformed. Girls are, from their cradles, compelled to a more sedentary life; and with this intention, dolls, and other playthings, are early procured; yet boys are permitted to take more frequent exercise. Thus, girls are confined in their apartments, while boys amuse themselves in the open air. Such absurd constraints impede the free and progressive evolution of the different faculties and powers.

The Yellow Gum.

The yellow gum is known by a yellow tinge of the skin, with languor and a tendency to sleep. It is to be relieved by giving a teaspoonful or more of castor oil, to clear the intestines. When the disease does not give way to this treatment, give half a grain of calomel, or 4 grains of rhubarb.

Vomiting.

When the food is vomited in an unaltered state, it is generally a sign of over-feeding; but when the vomiting is bilious, or when the food is partly digested, the diet ought to be changed, and the bowels opened by 1 grain of calomel, given in sugar. This is to be followed by a teaspoonful of castor oil on the following morning. If the vomiting should still continue, give lime-water or the calomel powder (containing 1 or 2 grains, according to the age) a second time. If there be much irritation, apply a spice-plaster to the stomach, and, if possible, give a teaspoonful of the saline medicine, in a state of effervescence, and containing 1 or 2 drops of laudanum.

Hiccups.

These generally arise from acidity in the stomach, and may be remedied by the administration of 6 grains of prepared chalk with 2 grains of powdered rhubarb, given in a little syrup or gruel. If very severe, the stomach is to be rubbed with a little soap liniment, or opodeldoc, to which a little laudanum has been added.

Griping and Flatulency.

These are known by continual crying, restlessness, and drawing up of the legs. When attended by diarrhœa and green stools, it is to be relieved, in general, by the administration of a few grains of rhubarb and magnesia. If sour belchings, etc. still continue, it will be proper to give a teaspoonful every quarter of an hour, of equal parts of camphor-water and cinnamon-water. After this, particularly if there be any purging, it will be proper to give a little rhubarb and magnesia again, and now and then a little chalk mixture.

Absorbent Mixture.

If the pains are very great so as to make the child scream violently, two teaspoonsful of the following mixture, with 1 or 2 drops of laudanum, may be given directly: Mix together, prepared chalk, 1 scruple; tincture of caraway seeds, 3 drachms; compound spirits of lavender, 1 drachm, and of peppermint-water, 2 ounces.

As soon as there is diminution of pain, a purgative should be given, particularly if the bowels happen to be in a costive state. The best will be castor oil. The above mixture may afterwards be occasionally continued, but without the laudanum.

DISEASES OF CHILDREN.

Diarrhœa.

This may, in general, if the stools are green, be relieved by a brisk purgative, of from 1 to 2 grains of calomel, with 4 or 5 grains of rhubarb, according to the age of the child. The absorbent mixture is then to be given as before directed.

Further Remedies.

When the stools are very frequent, and are either slimy or tinged with blood, it will be proper to give 5 grains of rhubarb every six hours, the food being beef tea, sago, isinglass in milk or calfsfoot jelly, the body being wrapped in warm flannel. A spice plaster may likewise be applied to the belly, and a dessertspoonful of the following tonic and astringent mixture is to be given every six hours. Mix together chalk mixture, 2 ounces; laudanum, 12 drops; and cinnamon water, 1 ounce.

Opiate Clyster.

If the fluid stools are ejected with great force a clyster should be given composed of half a teacupful of boiled starch, and 2 to 5 drops of laudanum. This may be repeated at intervals of eight hours, if the symptoms do not abate.

Excoriations of the Skin.

Children are apt to be chafed between the thighs, behind the ears, and in the wrinkles of the neck, from want of proper attention to cleanliness. In such cases it will be necessary to bathe the parts twice a day (or every time that the child's things are changed) with a little warm milk and water, and to apply a puff with a little powder of pure starch, arrow-root, or ryemeal, immediately afterwards, so as to keep the parts dry. When discharges take place behind the ears they must not be dried up too suddenly, as such a circumstance might produce a diversion to the brain. In such cases it will be always best to give frequent doses of castor oil, or calomel, every other night, in the proportion of 1 grain to 3 grains of rhubarb.

Cutaneous Eruptions.

No real danger attends these eruptions, which are generally known by the names of red-gum, nettle-rash, etc. All that is required to be done is to keep the bowels open by such means as are prescribed in the foregoing article, and to guard against cold, which might drive the eruption inwardly, and so produce internal inflammations of a critical nature. If the milk or food be considered the cause, the nurse or diet ought to be changed; and if sickness and vomiting should prevail, it will be proper to give the absorbent mixture mentioned under the head of Griping and Flatulency.

The Thrush.

This disease makes its appearance with little ulcerations in the mouth, tongue, etc., of a white color, and sometimes of a yellow appearance. They are generally owing to acidities in the stomach, etc.

In this disorder nothing avails more than an emetic at first, and then a little magnesia and rhubarb (if there be diarrhœa), with thin chickenwater as drink. Chlorate of potassa, or the absorbent mixture (see Griping and Flatulency), will also be proper. If there is no looseness, it will be proper to give a grain or two of calomel, with 3 or 4 grains of rhubarb. The mouth and throat should at the same time be cleansed by gargles.

Syrup of Black Currants.

Take of the juice of black currants, strained, 1 pint; double refined sugar, 24 ounces. Dissolve the sugar, and boil to make a syrup.

A teaspoonful of this may be given to children in the thrush.

Falling Down of the Fundament.

This happens frequently to children who cry much, or who have had a diarrhœa, or from straining on going to stool. If it proceed from costiveness, give lenitive clysters. In case the gut be swelled or inflamed, foment with warm milk, or decoction of oak bark, or wash frequently with cold water. The protruded parts are now to be replaced by the finger, and supported by a truss or bandage. The internal use of tonics will be proper. A child subject to this should not be allowed to sit on a low vessel or chair when the bowels are moved.

Dentition.

When children are about cutting their teeth they slaver much, are feverish, hot, and uneasy; their gums swell, and are very painful; they are sometimes loose in the bowels, and at other times costive; now and then convulsions come on.

Leeches are often of use applied behind the ears; also blisters.

Scarifying the Gums.

Instead of giving narcotics to children cutting their teeth, it is strenuously recommended to have the tumid gums divided by a lancet down to the tooth; an operation at once safe and unattended with pain. If done in time, from removing the cause of the complaint, all the symptoms will disappear of themselves. Instead of giving preparations of opium, it will be found, in the majority of cases far better to administer calomel, in minute doses, as this medicine is well known to possess peculiar efficacy in promoting absorption in these parts. The bowels, if costive, should be kept regularly open, and if there should be looseness of the bowels, it should by no means be discouraged. Instead of coral or any other hard body, let the child nibble at a ring of gum-elastic.

Convulsions.

Children are particularly liable to convulsions at the period of teething, small pox, measles, and other eruptive diseases; sometimes, also, from external causes, such as tight clothes, bandages, etc. When they proceed from any of these, bathing the feet, or the whole body, in warm water, of 92° or 94°, and administering a mild clyster, will almost immediately relieve them. To shorten the duration of the fit, cold water should be poured over the face and neck, while the rest of the body is in the bath. Afterwards a mustard plaster, weakened with flour, may be applied for a short time to the back.

The return of convulsions is to be prevented only by the removal of the cause of the existing irritation; but, in general, when the body is kept carefully open, there will be little cause to fear a return.

Inward Fits.

In these fits the infant appears as if asleep; the eyelids, however, are not quite closed, but frequently twinkle, and show the whites turned upwards. The muscles of the face are sometimes slightly distorted, the mouth having the appearance of a laugh or smile. The breath is sometimes very quick, and at others stops for a time; while the eyelids and lips are pale and dark alternately. The infant startles on the least noise, and sighs deeply or breaks wind. This relieves him for a little, but he soon relapses into a doze. Whenever the above-mentioned symptoms are observed, it will be right to awaken the infant, by stirring or otherwise, and to rub its back and belly well before the fire, until wind escapes. At the same time it will be proper to give half a teaspoonful of drink or pap, containing 2 drops of oil of anise or caraways. As soon after as possible, a purgative of castor oil, or a grain or two of calomel (according to the age), with 2 or 3 grains of rhubarb, is to be given, to empty the bowels of whatever crude matter may occasion the disorder.

The Rickets.

This disorder affects the bones of children, and causes a considerable protuberance, incurvation, or distortion of them. It may arise from various causes, but more particularly when proper care has not been taken with children; when they have been too tightly swathed in some parts, and too loosely in others; keeping them too long in one and the same position; and not keeping them clean and dry. Sometimes it may proceed from a lax habit, at others from costiveness.

It usually appears about the eighth or ninth month and continues to the sixth or seventh year of the child's age. The head becomes large and the fontanel keeps long open; the countenance is full and florid; the joints knotty and distorted, especially about the wrists, less near the ankles. The ribs protuberate and grow crooked; the belly swells; cough and disorder of the lungs succeed, and there is, withal, a very early understanding, and the child moves but weakly, and waddles in walking.

Regimen, etc.—The regimen should be light and properly seasoned; the air dry and clear; exercise and motion should be encouraged, and bandages as well as instruments contrived to keep the limbs in a proper situation; but we should take care that they be so formed as not to put the child to pain or restrain it too much.

Cold sea-bathing is of infinite use, after which friction should be used, and the child placed between two blankets, so as to encourage perspiration. The back should be well rubbed with opodeldoc or good old rum every night. Chalybeates are also very serviceable.

A decoction of Peruvian bark is also good, with red wine; it is to be used with moderation in the forenoon and after dinner.

Distortion of the Spine.

Dr. Weitch, an eminent physician of Berlin, has published in Hufeland's journal a simple remedy for weakness of the back-bone of infants, and which he considers capable of preventing distortion. This method consists, first, in frequent and close examination of the child's back-bone, and secondly, on the slightest trace of any distortion, to wash the same with brandy every morning and night, and to pay the strictest attention to the child's keeping a straight posture both sleeping and waking, and if it can be bathed from time to time it will be so much the better.

Jelly from the Raspings of Ivory.

The raspings of ivory impart to boiling water a very pleasant jelly, which has been found more easy of digestion and more nutritious than that of the hartshorn shavings or isinglass. Mixed with the jelly of the arrow-root in the proportion of one part to seven, it has been recommended for weakly and rickety children and consumptive or emaciated invalids.

Ringworm and Scald Head.

It is well known that these disorders, which are in many respects similar, are contagious; therefore no comb or hair-brush used by a child affected by them is to be used by another child either in a school or in the same family. Nor should the hat or cap of such a child be worn by any other.

Treatment.—The intractableness of most children, when attempted to be controlled or governed by the accustomed mode of treatment, proves in most instances a material obstacle in the way of curing this malignant disease, and the quickness with which the hair of the scalp grows in children, has hitherto in many instances rendered every effort ineffectual. It was a constant failure under these inauspicious circumstances that led Mr. Barlow, a medical professor in Lancashire, to adopt the subjoined lotion: Take of sulphate of potassa, recently prepared, 3 drachms; Spanish white soap 1½ drachms; lime-water 7½ ounces, and spirits of wine 2 drachms. Mix by shaking well in a phial.

By bathing the affected head with this lotion a few times, morning and evening, and suffering the parts to dry without interruption, the scabs will loosen and peel off from the scalp, and leave the parts underneath perfectly healed, without torturing the patient by shaving the head, though the hair should be kept short.

Ointment for the same.

Take of spermaceti ointment 1 ounce; tar ointment 1 ounce; powdered angustura bark 3 drachms. Rub the whole well in a marble mortar and apply to the parts affected.

Alterative Medicines.

In six cases out of ten this disease is aggravated by a scrofulous taint of system, and when this is the case the following alterative medicines accelerates the cure:

Iodide of potassium 1 drachm; water 6 ounces. Give a teaspoonful night and morning.

Instead of the above 1 grain of calomel may be given going to rest, and repeated every night for a few nights; also, the use of arsenic and of salt water, externally and internally as an alterative, has been found very useful.

In all cases the bowels ought to be kept open, and the diet should consist of wholesome and nutritive food, avoiding fish and salt meats. Cleanliness and occasional use of the warm bath will likewise be of service.

Hooping Cough.

This convulsive cough is occasioned by a viscid matter which cannot be easily expectorated. The poor infant, in endeavoring to bring it up, strains violently, till he becomes almost suffocated and convulsed.

Remedies.—In this complaint, next to occasional vomiting, the daily use of the warm bath is most useful. Bleeding may sometimes be used to prevent inflammation of the internal membranes, or cupping between the neck and shoulders. Gentle emetics may be given early.

Give a tablespoonful of milk of assafœtida every four hours, or half as much, with five or ten drops of wine of ipecac, or, in violent cases, 2 or 3 grains of musk as often.

To the above may be added, as auxiliaries, a Burgundy pitch plaster on the pit of the stomach, a flannel waistcoat or shirt next the skin, and a change of air when practicable. The diet should be light and easy of digestion, avoiding everything of a fat and oily nature.

Embrocation for Hooping Cough.

Take of tartar emetic 2 drachms; boiling water 2 ounces; tincture of cantharides 1 drachm; oil of thyme 3 drachms. Mix. A dessertspoonful to be rubbed upon the chest every night and morning till it becomes sore.

Regimen, etc., for Hooping Cough.

A frequent change of air is exceedingly useful in hooping cough, particularly short voyages at sea; at the same time flannel is to be worn next the skin. Young children should lie with their heads and shoulders raised, and when the cough occurs they ought to be placed on their feet and bent a little forward, to guard against suffocation. The diet should be light and the drink warm and mucilaginous.

The Croup.

This disease is almost peculiar to children, and sometimes fatal, if care is not taken in the commencement. It commonly approaches with the usual signs of a catarrh, but sometimes the peculiar symptoms occur at the first onset; namely, a hoarseness, with a shrill ringing sound both in speaking and coughing, as if the noise came from a brazen tube. At the same time there is a sense of pain about the larynx, and some difficulty of respiration, with a whizzing sound in inspiration, as if the passage of air was diminished, which is actually the case. The cough is generally dry, but if anything is spit up, in the worst cases it is a matter, sometimes resembling small portions of a membrane. There is also a frequent pulse, restlessness, and an uneasy sense of heat. The inside of the mouth is sometimes without inflammation, but frequently a redness, and even a swelling, exists. Sometimes there is an appearance of matter on them, like that ejected by coughing.

Remedies.—As soon as possible a brisk emetic should be administered, for the purpose of freeing the patient from the congulable lymph which is already secreted. The powder, wine or syrup of ipecac will generally answer. In obstinate cases a teaspoonful of alum powder with one of ipecac is recommended. Topical bleeding, by means of leeches, should immediately succeed, and the discharge be encouraged. As soon as it diminishes, a blister so large as to cover the whole throat should be applied, and suffered to lie on for thirty hours or longer. Then warm steam should be inhaled, and the bowels should be evacuated by calomel.

As soon as the emetic has operated sufficiently, 1 grain doses of calomel with 5 grains of nitre may be administered, by which means the breathing will in general be soon relieved; but should it become more difficult in the course of a few hours the emetic is to be again repeated, and after its operation the opium again employed. This practice is to be alternately used till such time as the patient is out of danger, which will in general be in the course of three or four days. The child should be kept nearly upright in bed.

The warm bath is very useful in this complaint. As an adjunct, apply an ointment to the breast, composed of 5 grains of tartar emetic, and 5 grains of powdered opium, to a drachm of spermaceti cerate, until eruptions are excited on the skin.

USEFUL DOMESTIC MEDICINES.

Dover's Sudorific Powder.

Take of ipecacuanha in powder, opium (purified), each 1 part; sulphate of potass, 8 parts. Triturate them together into a fine powder.

The dose is from two to five or ten grains, repeated according as the patient's stomach and strength can bear it. It is proper to avoid much drinking immediately after taking it, otherwise it is very apt to be rejected by vomiting before any other effects are produced. Perspiration should be kept up by diluents.

Aloetic Powder with Iron.

Take of socotrine aloes, powdered, 1½ ounces; myrrh, powdered, 2 ounces; extract of gertian and sulphate, each in powder, 1 ounce. Mix them.

In this powder we have an aloetic and chalybeate conjoined. It is a useful medicine, and is particularly employed in cases of obstructed menstruation.

Compound Assafœtida Pills.

Take of assafœtida, galbanum and myrrh, each 1 ounce; rectified oil of amber, 1 drachm. Beat them into a mass with simple syrup.

These pills are anti-hysteric and emmenagogue, and are very well calculated for answering those intentions. Half a scruple, a scruple, or more, may be taken every night or oftener.

Compound Aloetic Pills.

Take of hepatic aloes, 1 ounce; ginger powder, 1 drachm; soap, ½ ounce; essential oil of peppermint, ½ drachm.

Let the aloes and the ginger be rubbed well together, then add the soap and the oil, so as to form a mass.

These pills may be advantageously used for obviating the habitual costiveness of sedentary persons. The dose is from ten to fifteen grains.

Aloetic and Myrrh Pills.

Take of socotrine aloes, 4 drachms; myrrh, 2 drachms; saffron, 1 drachm. Beat them into a mass with simple syrup.

These pills have been long employed to stimulate and open the bowels in chlorotic, hypochondriacal, and long-diseased habits. The dose is from ten grains to a scruple, twice a day.

Plummer's Pills.

These pills are alterative, diaphoretic, purgative, and beneficial in cutaneous eruptions, etc.

Take of calomel, 1 drachm; sulphate of antimony, 1 drachm; gum guaiacum, 2 drachms.

Mix these assiduously with mucilage, and divide into sixty pills, two pills forming the dose. To be taken at night.

Compound Soap Liniment.

Take of camphor, 1 ounce; soap, 3 ounces; spirit of rosemary, 1 pint.

Digest the soap in the spirit of rosemary until it be dissolved, and add to it the camphor. This is useful to excite action on the surface, and is used to disperse scrofulous enlargements, and to moisten flannel which is applied to the throat in cases of quinsy.

Cajeput Opodeldoc.

Take of almond soap, 2 ounces; alcohol, 1 pint; camphor, 1 ounce; cajeput oil, 2 ounces.

First dissolve the soap and camphor in the alcohol in a retort, by means of a sand heat, and when the solution is about to congeal, or becomes nearly solid, add the oil of cajeput: shake them well together, and put it into bottles to congeal.

This composition is a great improvement on the opodeldocs in general use, and in cases of rheumatism, paralytic numbness, chilblains, enlargements of joints, and indolent tumors, where the object is to rouse the action of absorbent vessels, and to stimulate the nerves, it is a very valuable external remedy.

In several cases of lumbago and deep-seated rheumatic pains, it has been known to succeed in the almost immediate removal of the disease.

Liniment of Ammonia.

Take of water of ammonia, ½ an ounce; olive oil, 1½ ounces.

Shake them together in a phial till they are mixed.

In the inflammatory quinsy, a piece of flannel, moistened with this mixture, applied to the throat, and renewed every four or five hours, is one of the most efficacious remedies. By means of this warm stimulating application, the neck, and sometimes the whole body, is put into a sweat, which, after bleeding, either carries off or lessens the inflammation. Where the skin cannot bear the acrimony of this mixture, a larger proportion of oil may be used.

Eau-de-luce.

Ten or 12 grains of white soap are dissolved in 4 ounces of rectified spirit of wine; after which the solution is strained. A drachm of rectified oil of amber is then added, and the whole filtered. With this solution should be mixed such a proportion of the strongest volatile spirit of ammonia, in a clear glass bottle, as will, when sufficiently shaken, produce a beautiful milk-white liquor. If a kind of cream should settle on the surface, it will be requisite to add a small quantity of the spirituous solution of soap. Those who may wish to have this liquor water perfumed, may employ lavender or Hungary water instead of the spirit of wine.

This composition is, however, seldom obtained in a genuine state when purchased at the shops. Its use as an external remedy is very extensive; for it has not only been employed for curing the bites of vipers, wasps, bees, gnats, ants, and other insects, but also for burns, and even the bite of a mad dog, though not always with uniform success. Besides, it affords one of the safest stimulants in cases of suffocation from mephitic vapors, and in that state of apoplexy which is termed serous, as likewise after excessive intoxication, and in all those paralytic complaints where the vessels of the skin or the muscular fibre require to be excited into action.

Simple Ointment.

Take of olive oil, 5 ounces; white wax 2 ounces. This is a useful emollient ointment for softening the skin.

Ointment of Hog's Lard.

Take of prepared hog's lard, 2 pounds; rose-water, 3 ounces. Beat the lard with the rose-water until they be mixed; then melt the mixture with a slow fire, and set it apart that the water may subside; after which, pour off the lard from the water, constantly stirring until it be cold.

This ointment may be used for softening the skin, and healing the chaps.

Lip Salve.

Melt together 2½ ounces of white wax; 3 ounces of spermaceti; 7 ounces oil of almonds; 1 drachm of balsam of Peru; and 1½ ounces of glycerin wrapped up in a linen bag.

Pour the salve into small gallipots or boxes, and cover with bladder and white leather.

Basilicon, or Yellow Resinous Ointment.

Take of yellow resin, 1 pound; yellow wax, 1 pound; olive oil, 1 pint. Melt the resin and wax with a gentle heat; then add the oil, and strain the mixture while yet warm.

This plaster is employed for the dressing of broken chilblains, and other sores that require stimulating; it is also used to drive milk away, being placed over the tumid breasts when the child is weaned.

Turners' Cerate.

This ointment is known by the vulgar name of Turners' cerate, as curing the wounds of Turners. It is generally used for broken chilblains.

Take of prepared calamine, yellow wax, each ½ pound; olive oil, 1 pint.

Melt the wax with the oil, and as soon as they begin to thicken, sprinkle in the prepared calamine and keep it stirring till the cerate is cool.

Savin Ointment.

Take of fresh savin leaves, separated from the stalks, and bruised, ½ pound; prepared hog's lard, 2 pounds; yellow wax, ½ pound. Boil the leaves in the lard until they become crisp; then filter with expression; lastly, add the wax, and melt them together.

This is an excellent issue ointment, being, in many respects, preferable to that of cantharides. It is mixed with equal parts of blistering ointment, in order to keep up a discharge.

Mercurial Ointment.

Take of mercury, and mutton suet, each, 1 part; hogs' lard, 3 parts. Rub the mercury diligently in a mortar with a little of the hogs' lard, until the globules disappear; then add the remainder of the lard, and rub until the ointment is completely prepared.

One drachm of this ointment contains twelve grains of mercury.

The preparation of mercurial ointment requires much labor, care, and patience. During the trituration, the mercury is mechanically divided into minute globules, which are prevented from running together again by the viscosity of the fat. These globules at length disappear, being oxidized, or rendered black by intimate mixture with the lard. Whatever tends to favor this (for instance, a slight degree of rancidity of the lard) shortens the time, and lessens the labor required for the preparation of the ointment. It is not uncommon, however, to use other means, which are not admissible, to facilitate the process, such as the use of sulphur or turpentine. The first may be detected by the very black color of the ointment, and also by the sulphurous odor exhaled when a paper covered with a little of it is held over the flame of a candle. The turpentine is detected by its odor also, when the ointment containing it is treated in the same manner.

When newly prepared, mercurial ointment has a light gray or bluish color, owing to its containing some unoxidized metal, which separates in globules when it is liquefied by a gentle heat; when kept for some time the color is much deepened, and less metallic mercury is seen, owing to the more complete oxidizement of the metal.

Cerate of Spanish Flies.

Take of cerate of spermaceti, softened with heat, 6 drachms; Spanish flies, finely powdered, 1 drachm. Mix them by melting over a gentle fire.

Under this form cantharides may be made to act to any extent that is requisite. . It may supply the place either of the blistering plaster or ointment, and there are cases in which it is preferable to either. It is particularly more convenient than the plaster of cantharides, where the skin to which the blister is to be applied is previously much affected, as in cases of small-pox, and in supporting a drain under the form of issue it is less apt to spread than the softer ointment.

Compound Burgundy Pitch Plaster.

Take of Burgundy pitch 2 pounds; labdanum 1 pound; yellow resin and yellow wax each 4 ounces; expressed oil of mace 1 ounce.

To the pitch, resin and wax melted together, add first the labdanum and then the oil of mace.

After a long-continued cough in the winter, a Burgundy pitch plaster should be put over the breast-bone.

Compound Labdanum Plaster.

Take of labdanum 3 ounces; frankincense 1

ounce; cinnamon, powdered, expressed oil of mace, each ½ an ounce; essential oil of mint 1 drachm.

To the melted frankincense add first the labdanum, softened by heat, then the oil of mace. Mix these afterwards with the cinnamon and oil of mint and beat them together in a warm mortar into a plaster. Let it be kept in a close vessel.

This has been considered as a very elegant stomach plaster. It is contrived so as to be easily made occasionally (for such compositions, on account of their volatile ingredients, are not fit for keeping), and to be but moderately adhesive, so as not to offend the skin, also that it may without difficulty be frequently renewed, which these applications, in order to their producing any considerable effect, require to be. They keep up a perspiration over the part affected, and create a local action, which diverts inflammation; consumption from colds in delicate habits is by such means frequently obviated.

Adhesive Plaster.

Take of common, or litharge plaster, 5 parts, white resin, 1 part.

Melt them together, and spread the liquid compound thin on strips of linen by means of a spatula or table knife.

This plaster is very adhesive, and is used for keeping on other dressings, etc.

Court-Plaster.

Bruise a sufficient quantity of fish glue, and let it soak for twenty-four hours in a little warm water; expose it to heat over the fire, to dissipate the greater part of the water, and supply its place by colorless brandy, which will mix the gelatine of the glue. Strain the whole through a piece of open linen; on cooling it will form a trembling jelly.

Now extend a piece of black silk on a wooden frame, and fix it in that position by means of tacks or pack thread. Then with a brush made of badger's hair apply the glue, after it has been exposed to a gentle heat to render it liquid. When this stratum is dry, which will soon be the case, apply a second, and then a third if necessary, to give the plaster a certain thickness; as soon as the whole is dry cover it with two or three strata of a strong tincture of balsam of Peru.

This is the real English court-plaster; it is pliable and never breaks, characters which distinguish it from so many other preparations sold under the same name.

Compound Tincture of Rhubarb.

Take of rhubarb, sliced, 2 ounces; liquorice root, bruised, ½ ounce; ginger, powdered, saffron, each 2 drachms; distilled water, 1 pint; proof spirits of wine, 12 ounces by measure.

Digest for 14 days, and strain. Dose, ½ an ounce as an aperient, or 1 ounce in violent diarrhœa.

Tincture of Ginger.

Take of ginger, in coarse powder 2 ounces; proof spirit, 2 pints.

Digest in a gentle heat for 7 days, and strain.

This tincture is cordial and stimulant, and is generally employed as a corrective to purgative draughts.

Compound Tincture of Senna.

Take of senna leaves, 2 ounces; jalap root, 1 ounce; coriander seeds, ½ ounce; proof spirits, 2½ pints.

Digest for 7 days, and to the strained liquor add 4 ounces of sugar candy.

This tincture is a useful carminative and cathartic, especially to those who have accustomed themselves to the use of spirituous liquors; it often relieves flatulent complaints and colics where the common cordials have little effect; the dose is from one to two ounces. It is a very useful addition to castor oil, in order to take off its mawkish taste; and, as coinciding with the virtues of the oil, it is therefore much preferable to brandy, shrub, and such like liquors, which otherwise are often found necessary to make the oil sit on the stomach.

Solution of Citrate of Magnesia.

Take of magnesia, 120 grains; citric acid, 450 grains; bicarbonate of potassa, 40 grains; dissolve the citric acid in 4 fluidounces of water, and, having added the magnesia, stir until it is dissolved. Filter the solution into a strong twelve-ounce bottle, into which has been poured 2 fluidounces of syrup of citric acid. Then add the bicarbonate of potassa, and enough water almost to fill the bottle, which must be closed with a cork, and this secured with twine. Shake moderately till all is dissolved. This is a very pleasant drink, and in the dose of a tumblerful a pretty active and cooling purgative.

Duffy's Elixir.

Take of senna, 2 pounds; rhubarb shavings, 2 pounds; jalap root, 1 pound; caraway seeds, 1 pound; aniseeds, 2 pounds; sugar, 4 pounds; shavings of red sanders-wood, ½ pound.

Digest these in 10 gallons of spirits of wine for 14 days, and strain for use.

This elixir possesses almost the same qualities as the Compound Tincture of Senna. The above quantities may be reduced to as small a scale as may be required.

The Black Drop.

Take ½ a pound of opium, sliced; 3 pints of good verjuice; 1½ ounces of nutmeg; and ½ an ounce of saffron; boil them to a proper thickness, then add a ¼ of a pound of sugar and 2 spoonsful of yeast. Set the whole in a warm place near the fire for 6 or 8 weeks, then place it in the open air until it becomes of the consistence of a syrup; lastly, decant, filter, and bottle it up, adding a little sugar to each bottle. Dose, 5 to 15 drops.

The above ought to yield about two pints of the strained liquor.

Godfrey's Cordial.

Dissolve ½ an ounce of opium, 1 drachm of oil of sassafras, in 2 ounces of spirits of wine. Now mix 4 pounds of treacle with 1 gallon of boiling water, and when cold mix both solutions. This is often used to soothe the pains of children, etc. It must be employed with caution, however, as it contains opium. It is an injurious error to keep children quiet by stupifying them constantly or frequently with opiates, or other narcotics.

Balsam of Honey.

Take of balsam of Tolu, 2 ounces; gum storax, 2 drachms; opium, 2 drachms; honey, 8 ounces. Dissolve these in a quart of spirits of wine.

This balsam is exceedingly useful in allaying the irritation of cough. The dose is 1 or 2 teaspoonsful in a little tea or warm water.

Tincture of the Balsam of Tolu.

Take of balsam of Tolu, 1 ounce; alcohol, 1 pint. Digest until the balsam be dissolved, and then strain the tincture through a paper.

This solution of the balsam of Tolu possesses all the virtues of the balsam itself. It may be taken internally, with the several intentions for which that balsam is proper, to the quantity of a teaspoonful or two in any convenient vehicle.

Mixed with simple syrup it forms an agreeable balsamic syrup.

Tincture of Peruvian Bark.

Take of Peruvian bark, 4 ounces; proof spirit, 2 pints. Digest for 10 days and strain.

It may be given from a teaspoonful to ½ an ounce, or an ounce, according to the different purposes it is intended to answer.

Huxham's Tincture of Bark.

Take of Peruvian bark, powdered, 2 ounces; the peel of Seville oranges, dried, 1½ ounces; Virginian snakeroot, bruised, 3 drachms; saffron, 1 drachm: cochineal, powdered, 2 scruples; proof spirit, 20 ounces. Digest for 14 days and strain.

As a corroborant and stomachic, it is given in doses of 1 to 3 drachms; but when employed for the cure of intermittent fevers, it must be taken to a greater extent.

Tincture of Guaiacum.

Take of guaiacum, 4 ounces; rectified spirits of wine, 2 pints. Digest for 7 days and filter.

What is called gum guaiacum is, in fact, a resin, and perfectly soluble in alcohol. This solution is a powerful stimulating sudorific, and may be given in doses of about ½ an ounce in rheumatic and asthmatic cases.

Ammoniated Tincture of Guaiacum.

Take of resin of guaiacum, in powder, 4 ounces; ammoniated alcohol, in powder, 1½ pounds. Digest for 7 days and filter through a paper.

This is a very elegant and efficacious tincture; the ammoniated spirit readily dissolving the resin, and, at the same time, promoting its medical virtues. In rheumatic cases, a tea, or even tablespoonful, taken every morning and evening, in any convenient vehicle, particularly in milk, has proved of singular service.

Compound Tincture of Benzoin.

Take of benzoin, 3 ounces; purified storax, 2 ounces; balsam of Tolu, 1 ounce; socotrine aloes, ½ an ounce; rectified spirits of wine, 2 pints. Digest for 7 days and filter.

This preparation may be considered as an elegant simplification of some very complicated compositions, which were celebrated under different names; such as Baume de Commandeur, Wade's Balsam, Friar's Balsam, Jesuit's Drops, etc. These, in general, consisted of a confused farrago of discordant substances. The dose is a teaspoonful in some warm water four times a day, in chronic bronchitis and spitting of blood. It is useful, also, when applied on lint, to recent wounds, and serves the purpose of a scab, but must not be soon removed. Poured on sugar it sometimes checks spitting of blood immediately.

Tincture of Catechu.

Take of extract of catechu, 3 ounces; cinnamon, bruised, 2 ounces; diluted alcohol, 2 pints. Digest for seven days, and strain through paper.

The cinnamon is a very useful addition to the catechu, not only as it warms the stomach, but likewise as it covers its roughness and astringency.

This tincture is of service in all kinds of defluxions, catarrhs, looseneses, and other disorders where astringent medicines are indicated. From one to three teaspoonsful may be taken every now and then, in red wine, or any other proper vehicle

Godbold's Vegetable Balsam.

A pound of sugar candy, dissolved by heat, in a quantity of white wine vinegar, and evaporated to the measure of 1 pint, during which operation as much garlic as possible is dissolved with it, answers all the purposes of Godbold's Vegetable Balsam, and is probably the same medicine.

Spirit of Nutmeg.

Take of bruised nutmegs, 2 ounces; proof spirit, 1 gallon; water sufficient to prevent burning. Distil off a gallon.

This is used to take off the bad flavor of medicine, and is a grateful cordial.

Lavender Water.

The common mode of preparing this, is to put 3 drachms of the essential oil of lavender, and a drachm of the essence of ambergris, into 1 pint of spirit of wine.

Water of pure Ammonia.

Take of sal ammoniac, 1 pound; quick-lime, 2 pounds; water, 1 gallon. Add to the lime two pints of the water. Let them stand together an hour; then add the sal ammonia, and the other six pints of water, boiling, and immediately cover the vessel. Pour out the liquor when cold, and distil off, with a slow fire, one pint. This spirit is too acrimonious for internal use, and has therefore been chiefly employed for smelling in faintings, etc., though, when properly diluted, it may be given inwardly with safety.

Water of Acetated Ammonia.

Take of ammonia, by weight, 2 ounces; distilled vinegar, 4 pints; or as much as is sufficient to saturate the ammonia.

This is an excellent diaphoretic saline liquor. Taken warm in bed, it proves commonly a powerful sudorific; and as it operates without heat, it is used in febrile and inflammatory disorders, where medicines of the warm kind, if they fail of procuring sweat, aggravate the distemper. Its action may likewise be determined to the kidneys, by walking about in cool air. The common dose is half an ounce, either by itself, or along with other medicines adapted to the intention. Its strength is not a little precarious, depending on that of the vinegar.

Black Pectoral Lozenges.

Take of extract of liquorice, gum arabic, each, 4 ounces; white sugar, 8 ounces.

Dissolve them in warm water, and strain; then evaporate the mixture over a gentle fire till it be of a proper consistence for being formed into lozenges, which are to be cut out of any shape.

White Pectoral Lozenges.

Take of fine sugar, 1 pound; gum arabic, 4 ounces; starch, 1 ounce; flowers of benzoin, ¾ of a drachm.

Having beaten them all in a powder, make them into a proper mass with rose-water, so as to form lozenges.

These compositions are very agreeable pectorals, and may be used at pleasure. They are calculated for promoting expectoration, and allaying the tickling in the throat, which provokes coughing.

Syrup of Ginger.

Take of ginger, bruised, 4 ounces; boiling distilled water, 3 pints.

Macerate four hours, and strain the liquor; then add double refined sugar, and make into a syrup.

This syrup promotes the circulation through the extreme vessels; it is to be given in torpid and phlegmatic habits, where the stomach is subject to be loaded with slime, and the bowels distended with flatulency. Hence it enters into the compound tincture of cinnamon and the aromatic powder.

Dyspeptic patients, from hard drinking, and those subject to flatulency and gout, have been known to receive considerable benefit from the use of ginger tea, taking two or three cupfuls for breakfast, suiting it to their palate.

USEFUL DOMESTIC MEDICINES.

Syrup of Poppies.

Take of the heads of white poppies, dried, 3½ pounds; double refined sugar, 6 pounds; distilled water, 8 gallons.

Slice and bruise the heads, then boil them in the water to three gallons, and press out the decoction. Reduce this, by boiling, to about four pints, and strain it while hot through a sieve, then through a thin woollen cloth, and set it aside for twelve hours, that the grounds may subside. Boil the liquor poured off from the grounds to three pints, and dissolve the sugar in it, that it may be made a syrup.

This syrup, impregnated with the narcotic matter of the poppy-head, is given to children in doses of two or three drachms, and to adults of from half an ounce to one ounce and upwards, for easing pain, procuring rest, and answering the other intentions of mild medication. Particular care is requisite in its preparation, that it may be always made, as nearly as possible, of the same strength.

Syrup of Violets.

Take of fresh flowers of the violet, 1 pound; boiling distilled water, 3 pints.

Macerate for twenty-five hours, and strain the liquor through a cloth, without pressing, and add double refined sugar, to make the syrup. This is an agreeable laxative medicine for young children.

Syrup of Squills.

Take of vinegar of squills, 2 pounds; double refined sugar, in powder, 3¼ pounds.

Dissolve the sugar with a gentle heat, so as to form a syrup.

This syrup is used chiefly in doses of a spoonful or two for promoting expectoration, which it does very powerfully. It is also given as an emetic to children.

Oxymel of Squills.

Take of clarified honey, 3 pounds; vinegar of squills, 2 pints.

Boil them in a glass vessel, with a slow fire, to the thickness of a syrup.

Oxymel of squills is a useful aperient, detergent, and expectorant, and of great service in humoral asthmas, coughs, and other disorders where thick phlegm abounds. It is given in doses of two or three drachms, along with some aromatic water, as that of cinnamon, to prevent the great nausea which it would otherwise be apt to excite. In large doses it proves emetic.

Vinegar of Squills.

Take of squills, recently dried, 1 pound; vinegar, 6 pints; proof spirit, ½ pint.

Macerate the squills with the vinegar, in a glass vessel, with a gentle heat, for twenty-four hours, then express the liquor, and set it aside until the fæces subside. To the decanted liquor add the spirit.

Vinegar of squills is a medicine of great antiquity. It is a very powerful promoter of secretion, and hence it is frequently used with great success as a diuretic and expectorant. The dose of it is from a drachm to half an ounce. Where crudities abound in the first passages, it may be given at first in a larger dose, to evacuate them by vomiting. It is most conveniently exhibited along with cinnamon, or other agreeable aromatic waters, which prevent the nausea it would otherwise, even in small doses, be apt to occasion.

Tar-water.

Take of tar, 2 pints; water, 1 gallon. Mix, by stirring them with a wooden rod for a quarter of an hour, and, after the tar has subsided, strain the liquor, and keep it in well-corked phials.

Tar-water should have the color of white wine, and an empyreumatic taste. It is frequently used as a remedy in chronic bronchitis. It acts as a stimulant, raising the pulse and increasing the discharge by the skin and kidneys. It may be drunk to the extent of a pint or two in the course of a day.

Decoction of Sarsaparilla.

Take of sarsaparilla root, cut, 6 ounces; distilled water, 8 pints.

After macerating for two hours with a heat about 195°, then take out the root and bruise it; add it again to the liquor, and macerate it for two hours longer; then boil down the liquor to 4 pints, and strain it. The dose is from 4 ounces to half a pint, or more, daily.

Compound Decoction of Sarsaparilla.

Take of sarsaparilla root, cut andbruised, 6 ounces; the bark of sassafras root, the shavings of guaiacum wood, liquorice root, each 1 ounce; the bark of mezereon root, 3 drachms; distilled water, 10 pints.

Digest with a gentle heat for six hours; then boil down the liquor to one-half (or five pints), adding the bark of the mezereon root towards the end of boiling. Strain off the liquor. The dose is the same as the last, and for the same purposes.

These decoctions are of use in purifying the blood, and resolving obstructions in scorbutic and scrofulous cases; also in cutaneous eruptions, and many other diseases. Obstinate swellings, that had resisted the effects of other remedies for above twelve months, have been said to be cured by drinking a quart of decoction of this kind daily for some weeks. Decoctions of sarsaparilla ought to be made fresh every day, for they very soon become quite fetid, and unfit for use, sometimes in less than twenty-four hours, in warm weather.

Decoction of the Woods.

Take of guaiacum raspings, 3 ounces; raisins, stoned, 2 ounces; sassafras root, sliced, liquorice root, bruised, each 1 ounce; water, 10 pounds.

Boil the guaiacum and raisins with the water, over a gentle fire, to the consumption of one-half, adding, towards the end, the sassafras and liquorice, and strain the decoction without expression.

This decoction is of use in some rheumatic and cutaneous affections. It may be taken by itself, to the quantity of a quarter of a pint, twice or thrice a day, or used as an assistant in a course of mercurial or antimonial alteratives; the patient in either case keeping warm, in order to promote the operation of the medicine.

Water-gruel.

Put a large spoonful of oatmeal into a pint of water, stir it well together, and let it boil 3 or 4 minutes, stirring it often. Then strain it through a sieve, put in some salt according to taste, and, if necessary, add a piece of fresh butter. Stir with a spoon until the butter is melted, when it will be fine and smooth. Raisins are often added to it.

Panada.

Put a blade of mace, a large piece of the crumb of bread, and a quart of water, in a clean saucepan. Let it boil two minutes, then take out the bread, and bruise it very fine in a basin. Mix with it as much of the warm water as it will require, pour away the rest, and sweeten it to the taste of the patient. If necessary, put in a piece of butter of the size of a walnut, but add no wine. Grate in a little nutmeg if requisite.

Isinglass Jelly, etc.

Put an ounce of isinglass and half an ounce of cloves into a quart of water. Boil it down to a pint, strain it upon a pound of loaf sugar, and when cold add a little wine, when it will be fit for use. A very nourishing beverage may be made by merely boiling the isinglass with milk, and sweetening with lump sugar.

Wine Whey.

Boil a pint of milk, and put into it a glass of sherry or Madeira wine. Set it over the fire till it boils again; then put it aside till the curd has settled; then strain it, and sweeten to taste.

Beef-tea.

Cut a pound of lean beef into small pieces, pour over it a pint of cold water, and let it soak two hours; then boil it half an hour. Remove the scum that rises and all the fat or oil from the top. Pour off, and season with salt, but do not strain it.

Beef-essence.

Put a pound of lean beef, cut into pieces, into a porter bottle, without water; cork it loosely, and place it in a pot of water, which should be made to boil around it for an hour. The essence of the meat will thus be drawn out in the liquid state.

Transparent Soup for Convalescents.

Cut the meat from a leg of veal into small pieces, and break the bone into several bits. Put the meat into a very large jug, and the bones at top, with a bunch of common sweet herbs, a quarter of an ounce of mace, and half a pound of Jordan almonds, finely blanched and beaten. Pour on it 4 quarts of boiling water, and let it stand all night covered, close by the fireside. The next day put it into a well-tinned saucepan, and let it boil slowly, till it is reduced to 2 quarts. Be careful, at the time it is boiling, to skim it, and take off the fat as it rises. Strain into a punch-bowl, and when settled for two hours pour it into a clean saucepan, clear from the sediments, if any. Add 3 ounces of rice or 2 ounces of vermicelli, previously boiled in a little water. When once more boiled, it will be fit for use.

Seidlitz Powders.

Take of Rochelle salts, 1 drachm; carbonate of soda, 25 grains; tartaric acid, 20 grains.

Dissolve the two first in a tumbler of water; then add the latter, and swallow without loss of time.

SALUTARY CAUTIONS.

Purification of Water by Charcoal.

Nothing has been found so effectual for preserving water sweet at sea, during long voyages, as charring the insides of the casks well before they are filled. Care ought at the same time to be taken that the casks should never be filled with sea-water, as sometimes happens, in order to save the trouble of shifting the ballast, because this tends to hasten the corruption of the fresh water afterwards put into them. When the water becomes impure and offensive at sea, from ignorance of the preservative effect produced on it by charring the casks previous to their being filled, it may be rendered perfectly sweet by putting a little fresh charcoal, in powder into each cask before it is tapped, or by filtering it through fresh-burnt and coarsely powdered charcoal.

Cleanliness.

To preserve seamen in health and prevent the prevalence of scurvy and other diseases, it will be further necessary to keep the ship perfectly clean and to have the different parts of it daily purified by a free admission of air when the weather will admit of it, and likewise by frequent fumigations. This precaution will more particularly be necessary for the purification of such places as are remarkably close and confined.

Prevention of Dampness and Cold.

The coldness and dampness of the atmosphere are to be corrected by sufficient fires. Cleanliness on board of a ship is highly necessary for the preservation of the health of seamen, but the custom of frequent swabbings or washings between the decks, as is too frequently practised, is certainly injurious, and greatly favors the production of scurvy and other diseases by a constant dampness being kept up.

Exercise and Amusements.

The men should be made to air their hammocks and bedding every fine day; they should wash their bodies and apparel often, for which purpose an adequate supply of soap ought to be allowed, and they should change their linen and other clothes frequently. In rainy weather, on being relieved from their duty on deck by the succeeding watch, they should take off their wet clothes instead of keeping them on and lying down in them, as they are too apt to do. Two sets of hammocks ought to be provided for them. In fine, pleasant weather, and after their usual duty is over, they should be indulged in any innocent amusement that will keep their minds as well as bodies in a state of pleasant activity, and perhaps none is then more proper than dancing. This makes a fiddle or a pipe and tabor desirable acquisitions on board of every ship bound on a long voyage.

Effects of Climate, etc.

In warm climates the crews of ships are healthier at sea when the air is dry and serene, and the heat moderated by gentle breezes, than when rainy or damp weather prevails; and they usually enjoy better health when the ship is moored at a considerable distance from the shore, and to windward of any marshy ground or stagnant waters, than when it is anchored to leeward of these and lies close in with the land. Masters of vessels stationed at or trading to any parts between the tropics, will therefore act prudently when they have arrived at their destined port, to anchor at a considerable distance from the shore, and as far to windward of all swamps, pools and lakes as can conveniently be done, as the noxious vapors which will be wafted to the crew when the ship is in a station of this nature will not fail to give rise to disease among them.

Caution to be observed when on Shore.

When unavoidably obliged to submit to such an inconvenience, some means ought to be adopted to prevent disagreeable consequences from ensuing. For this purpose a large sail should be hoisted at the foremast, or most windward part of the ship, so as to prevent the noxious vapors from coming abaft; the cabin, steerage and between the decks should be fumigated now and then, and the seamen allowed to smoke tobacco moderately.

Unless absolutely necessary it will be improper to permit any of the crew to sleep from on board when stationed off an unhealthy shore, but when necessity obliges them to do so for the purpose of wooding or watering, a tent or marquee should be erected, if a proper house cannot be procured, and this should be pitched on the dryest and highest spot that can be found, being so situated as that the door shall open towards the sea. Under cover of this a sufficient number of hammocks are to be suspended for the accommodation of the men by night, as they should by no means be suffered to sleep on the open ground.

If the tent happens unfortunately to be in the neighborhood of a morass, or has unavoidably been pitched on flat, moist ground, it will be advisable to keep up a constant fire in it by day as well as by night, and as a further preventive against those malignant disorders which are apt to arise in such situations, the men should be directed to smoke moderately of tobacco, and to take a half or a quarter of a wineglassful of the compound tincture of Peruvian bark every morning on an empty stomach, and the same quantity again at night.

Cautions when in Tropical Climates.

In tropical climates the healthiness of seamen will much depend upon avoiding undue exposure to the sun, rain, night air, long fasting, intemperance, unwholesome shore duties, especially during the sickly season, and upon the attention paid to the various regulations and preventive measures. The bad effects of remaining too long in port at any one time (independent of irregularities of harbor duties, particularly after sunset, as well as during his meridian power) cannot be too strongly adverted to by the commander of every ship, and therefore a measure of the highest importance in the navy is the employment of negroes and natives of the country, or at least men accustomed to the torrid zone, in wooding, watering, transporting stores, rigging, clearing, careening ships, etc., and in fine in all such occupations as might subject the seamen to excessive heat or noxious exhalations, which cannot fail to be highly dangerous to the health of the unacclimated seaman.

The practice of heaving down vessels of war in the West Indies, in the ordinary routine of service at least, cannot be too highly deprecated, as well from the excessive fatigue and exertion it demands as because it is a process which requires for its execution local security, or in other words a land that is locked, and therefore generally an unhealthy harbor. The instances of sickness and mortality from the effects of clearing a foul hold in an unhealthy harbor are too numerous to be specified.

Intoxication.

A very productive source of disease in warm climates among seamen is an immoderate use of spirituous and fermented liquors, as they are too apt, whilst in a state of intoxication, to throw themselves on the bare ground where, perhaps, they lie exposed for many hours to the influence of the meridian sun, the heavy dews of the evening or the damp, chilling air of the night. The commander of a ship who pays attention to the health of his crew, will therefore take every possible precaution to prevent his men from being guilty of an excess of this nature, and likewise from lying out in the open air when overcome by fatigue and hard labor.

The different voyages of that celebrated navigator, Captain Cook, as well as that of the unfortunate La Perouse, incontestibly prove that by due care and a proper regimen seamen may be preserved from the scurvy and other diseases which have formerly been inseparable from long sea voyages, and that they can thus support the fatigues of the longest navigations in all climates and under a burning sun. It has been thoroughly proved, also, that grog is not at all necessary, or, in the long run, beneficial to seamen. In times of the greatest exposure and fatigue, as during severe storms, hot coffee has been found a more effectual stimulant than spirits, without the dangers connected with the use of the latter.

Noxious Vapors.

Smoking or fumigating ships with charcoal or sulphur, is the most effectual means of killing all kinds of vermin, and is therefore always resorted to; but it is recommended that no sailor or boy be allowed to go under the decks until the hatches, and all the other openings, have been for three hours uncovered; in that time all noxious vapors will be effectually dissipated.

Captain Cook's Rules for Preserving the Health of Seamen.

1. The crew to be at three watches. The men will by this means have time to shift and dry themselves, and get pretty well refreshed by sleep before called again to duty. When there is no pressing occasion, seamen ought to be refreshed with as much uninterrupted sleep as a common day laborer.

2. To have dry clothes to shift themselves after getting wet. One of the officers to see that every man, on going wet from his watch, be immediately shifted with dry clothes, and the same on going to bed.

3. To keep their persons, hammocks, bedding, and clothes clean and dry. This commander made his men pass in review before him one day in every week, and saw that they had changed their linen, and were as neat and clean as circumstances would admit. He had also every day the hammocks carried on the booms, or some other airy part of the ship, unlashed, and the bedding thoroughly shaken and aired. When the weather prevented the hammocks being carried on deck, they were constantly taken down, to make room for the fires, the sweeping, and other operations. When possible, fresh water was always allowed to the men to wash their clothes, as soap will not mix with sea-water, and linen washed in brine never thoroughly dries.

4. To keep the ship clean between decks.

5. To have frequent fires between decks, and at the bottom of the well. Captain Cook's method was to have iron pots with dry wood, which he burned between decks, in the well, and other parts of the ship; during which time some of the crew were employed in rubbing, with canvas or oakum, every part that had the least damp. Where the heat from the stoves did not readily absorb the moisture, loggerheads, heated red hot, and laid on sheets of iron, speedily effected the purpose.

6. Proper attention to be paid to the ship's coppers, to keep them clean and free from verdigris.

7. The fat that is boiled out of the salt beef or pork, never to be given to the men.

8. The men to be allowed plenty of fresh water, at the ship's return to port; the water remaining on board to be started, and fresh water from the shore to be taken in its room.

By means of the above regulations (in addition to rules relative to temperance, and supplying the crews as much as possible with fresh meat and vegetables), this celebrated navigator performed a voyage of upwards of three years, in every climate of the globe, with the loss of only one man.

To obtain Fresh Water from the Sea.

The method of obtaining fresh water from the sea by distillation, was introduced into the English navy in the year 1770, by Dr. Irving, for which he obtained a parliamentary reward of £5000.

In order to give a clear notion of Dr. Irving's method, let us suppose a teakettle to be made without a spout, and with a hole in the lid in the place of the knob; the kettle being filled with sea-water, the fresh vapor, which arises from the water as it boils, will issue through the hole in the lid; into that hole fit the mouth of a tobacco pipe, letting the stem have a little inclination downwards, then will the vapor of fresh water take its course through the stem of the tube, and may be collected by fitting a proper vessel to its end.

This would be an apt representation of Dr. Irving's contrivance, in which he has luted or adapted a tin, iron, or tinned copper tube, of suitable dimensions, to the lid of the common kettle used for boiling the provisions on board a ship; the fresh vapor which arises from boiling sea-water in the kettle passes, as by common distillation, through this tube into a hogshead, which serves as a receiver; and in order that the vapor may be readily condensed, the tube is kept cool by being constantly wetted with a mop dipped in cold sea-water. The waste water running from the mop may be carried off by means of two boards nailed together, like a spout. Dr. Irving particularly remarks, that only three-fourths of the sea-water should be distilled; the brine is then to be let off and the copper replenished, as the water distilled from the remaining concentrated brine is found to have a disagreeable taste, and as the farther continuation of the distillation is apt to be injurious to the vessels. When the water begins to boil, likewise, the vapor should be allowed to pass freely for a minute; this will effectually cleanse the tube and upper part of the boiler.

To render Sea-water capable of Washing Linen.

It is well known that sea-water cannot be employed for washing clothes. It refuses to dissolve soap, and possesses all the properties of hard water.

This is a great inconvenience to seamen, whose allowance of fresh water is necessarily limited, and it prevents them from enjoying many of those comforts of cleanliness which contribute not a little to health. The method of removing this defect is exceedingly simple, and by no means expensive. It was pointed out by Dr. Mitchell, of New York:—Drop into sea-water a solution of soda or potash. It will become milky, in consequence of the decomposition of the earthy salts, and the precipitation of the earths. This addition renders it soft, and capable of washing. Its milkiness will have no injurious effect.

PRESERVATION FROM DROWNING AND SHIPWRECK.

When a Man falls Overboard.

The instant an alarm is given that a man is overboard, the ship's helm should be put down, and she should be hove in stays; a hen-coop or other object that can float should also be thrown overboard as near the man as possible, with a rope tied to it, and carefully kept sight of, as it will prove a beacon towards which the boat may pull as soon as lowered down. A primary object is, having a boat ready to lower down at a moment's notice, which should be hoisted up at the stern if most convenient; the lashings, tackle, etc., to be always kept clear, and a rudder, tiller, and spare spar to be kept in her. When dark, she should not be without a lantern and a compass.

There should also be kept in her a rope with a running bowline, ready to fix in or to throw to the person in danger. Coils of small rope, with running bowlines, should also be kept in the chains, quarters and abaft, ready to throw over, as it most generally occurs that men pass close to the ship's side, and have often been miraculously saved by clinging to ropes.

Upsetting of a Boat.

If a person should fall out of a boat, or the boat upset by going foul of a cable, etc., or should he fall off the quays, or indeed fall into any water, from which he cannot extricate himself, but must wait some little time for assistance—had he presence of mind enough to whip off his hat, and hold it by the brim, placing his fingers within side of the crown (top upwards), he would be able, by this method, to keep his mouth above water till assistance should reach him. It often happens that danger is apprehended long before we are involved in the peril, although there may be time enough to prepare this, or adopt any other method. Travellers, in fording rivers at unknown fords, or where shallows are deceitful, might make use of this method with advantage.

Cork Waistcoats.

Provide a cork waistcoat, composed of four pieces, two for the breast, and two for the back, each pretty near in length and breadth to the quarters of a waistcoat without flaps; the whole is to be covered with coarse canvas, with two holes to put the arms through. There must be a space left between the two back pieces, and the same betwixt each back and breast piece, that they may fit the easier to the body. By this means the waistcoat is open only before, and may be fastened on the wearer by strings; or if it should be thought more secure, with buckles and leather straps. This waistcoat may be made up at a small expense.

If those who use the sea occasionally, and especially those who are obliged to be almost constantly there, were to use these waistcoats, it would be next to impossible that they should be drowned.

Further means.

It will likewise be proper to prepare an oil-skin bag, on going to sea, for a temporary supply of provisions, in case of shipwreck. If suddenly plunged into the water, and unable to swim, it will be necessary to keep the hands and arms under the water—few animals being capable of drowning, owing to their inability to lift their fore legs over their heads.

The legs, therefore, being necessarily immersed in the water, the difference between the specific gravity of the animal and the water is sufficient to enable it to keep its nostrils and mouth above the water, and therefore it is not suffocated by the fluid, but breathes freely. But man, on the contrary, being able to lift his hands over his head, and generally doing so in case of this accident, his hands and arms make up the difference in specific gravity, and his head, impelled by the weight of his hands and arms below the water, his body fills, and he is consequently choked and suffocated. The remedy therefore is, in all such cases, to keep down the hands and arms, and as a further security, to act with them under and against the water, it will then be impossible to sink, unless the weight of clothes or other circumstances operate to the contrary.

The Marine Spencer.

The marine spencer is made in the form of a girdle, of a proper diameter to fit the body, and six inches broad, composed of about 500 old tavrn corks, strung upon a strong twine, well lashed together with lay-cord, covered with canvas, and painted in oil so as to make it water-proof. Two tapes or cords, about two feet long, are fastened to the back of the girdle with loops at the ends. Another tape or cord of the same length, having a few corks strung to the middle of it, is covered with canvas painted. A pin of hard wood, three inches long, and half an inch in diameter, is fastened to the front of the girdle by a tape or cord, about three inches long. To use the spencer, it should be slipped from the feet close up to the arms, the tapes or cords are to be brought one over each shoulder, and fastened by the loops to the pin; those between the legs are to be fastened to the other pin. A person thus equipped, though unacquainted with swimming, may safely trust himself to the waves; for he will float, head and shoulders above water, in any storm, and by paddling with his hands, may easily gain the shore. Such a spencer may also be made of cork shavings put into a long canvas bag.

It has also been suggested, that every part of the usual dress of the sailor should be made with a view to preserving his life, in cases of accident; and for this purpose that a quantity of cork shavings or clippings should be quilted into his jacket about the collar and neck, between the outside and inside lining; or as a belt of considerable breadth across the back and shoulders, then principally omitted under the arms, and resumed over the chest and stomach, yet not so much as to create inconvenience. If in these, and other parts of his dress, so much cork could be conveniently worked, as would give the sailor an opportunity of recovering himself, and making use of his own powers in cases of contingency, many valuable lives might be saved.

Bamboo Habit.

The bamboo habit is an invention of the Chinese, by the use of which a person, unskilled in the art of swimming, may easily keep himself above water. The Chinese merchants, when going on a voyage, are said always to provide themselves with this simple apparatus, to save their lives in cases of danger from shipwreck. It is constructed by placing four bamboos horizontally, two before, and two behind the body of each person, so that they project about twenty-eight inches; these are crossed on each side by two others, and the whole properly secured, leaving an intermediate space for the body. When thus formed, the person in danger slips it over his head, and ties it securely to the waist, by which simple means he cannot possibly sink.

To extricate Persons from broken Ice.

Let two or more persons hold a rope or ropes, at both ends, stretched over the broken ice; so that the drowning person may catch hold of it.

The Life-Boat.

The life-boat is generally thirty feet long, and in form much resembles a common Greenland boat, except the bottom, which is much flatter. She is lined with cork, inside and outside of the gunwale, about two feet in breadth, and the seats underneath are filled with cork also.

She is rowed by ten men, double banked, and steered by two men with oars, one at each end, both ends being alike. Long poles are provided for the men, to keep the boat from being driven broadside to the shore, either in going off or landing. About six inches from the lower poles, it increases in diameter, so as to form a flat surface against the sand. The weight of the cork used in the boat seven hundredweight.

She draws very little water, and when full is able to carry twenty people. The boat is able to contend against the most tremendous sea and broken water; and never, in any one instance, has she failed in bringing the crew in distress into a place of safety. The men have no dread in going off with her in the highest sea and broken water; cork jackets were provided for them; but their confidence in the boat is so great, that they do not use them.

The success attending this expedient for diminishing the number of unhappy individuals almost daily lost in a watery grave appears to have been more than equal to the most sanguine expectations formed of its utility; and the great object in view, viz., the safety of those persons who hazard their own security to preserve others, has been fully accomplished.

Safe and readily constructed Life-boat.

In London Eng. a model of a life-boat was exhibited before the Royal Humane Society, which may be put together in the space of half an hour, in any case of shipwreck, and which cannot sink or overset, let the sea run ever so high. All that is necessary to be provided is a keel or plank of any convenient length, and a few pigs of iron, such as vessels usually carry out for ballast. The officers of the ship are to take care to keep two or three empty water-casks, perfectly tight, the bungholes corked up, and a piece of tin or leather nailed over them. These casks are to be lashed with ropes to the keel, along with the pigs of iron for ballast; and any spare poles or spars may be also lashed to the sides, so as to give the raft the form of a vessel, and at each end make a lodgement for the men. Any of the square sails of the ship will form a lug-sail, and may speedily be adapted to the new life-boat, and a strong and broad spar may be lashed on as a rudder.

Another.—Let a quantity of ballast, even more than what is commonly used for sailing, be laid in the bottom of the boat; over this lay bags filled with cork, prepared for the purpose, and numbered according to their places, and if considerably higher than the gunwales, so much the better. A sail or part of one, folded, may be thrown over from stem to stern, to combine and unite the several parts; and, lastly, the whole is to be secured together by passing ropes by so many turns as may be deemed sufficient round and round over the gunwales and under the keel, and these, if necessary, may be hitched by a turn or two taken lengthwise.

Every person either on board or holding by the boat, so prepared, may be absolutely certain of being carried safe through any beach whatever.

When no such preparation of cork has been made, the following is proposed as a substitute:

Let a quantity of ballast, as coals in canvas, be secured in its place, as well as circumstances will admit; then take an empty water-cask (beer-cask, or any others that are tight) and fill the boat with them, and if the bilge of the cask rises considerably higher than the gunwales, it will be so much the better; let a sail then be thrown in to jam the cask and ballast in their places, as well as to combine and unite the several parts by covering all fore and aft; and, lastly, let the whole be lashed and secured together, in the manner above stated. It is believed the boat in this trim would always continue upright on her keel, be lively and buoyant on the water, and have sufficient efficacy to support the crew of any ordinary vessel, till drifted within their own depth.

It frequently happens that after men have gained the shore, they perish of cold for want of dry clothes. As a remedy for this, every man should try to secure one or two flannel or woollen shirts, by wrapping them up tightly in a piece of oiled cloth or silk; and, to guard against tearing, the last might be covered with canvas, or inclosed in a tin box.

Further Method of Preservation in Cases of Shipwrecks.

It being the great object, in cases of shipwreck, to establish a communication betwixt the vessel and the shore with the least possible delay, various methods have been invented and pointed out for this purpose.

A common paper kite launched from the vessel, and driven by the wind to the shore, has been supposed capable of conveying a piece of packthread, to which a larger rope might be attached and drawn on board.

A small balloon, raised by rarefied air, might be made to answer the same purpose.

A sky-rocket, of a large diameter, has also been considered as capable of an equal surface, and, indeed, this method seems the best; for, besides the velocity of the discharge, could it be brought to act during the night, it must both point out the situation of the ship, and the direction that the line took in flying ashore.

Useful Hints when a Leak is Sprung.

When a vessel springs a leak near her bottom, the water enters with all the force given by the weight of the column of water without, which force is in proportion to the difference of the level between the water without and that within. It enters at first therefore with more force, and in greater quantity than it can afterwards, when the water within is higher. The bottom of the vessel, too, is narrower, so that the same quantity of water, coming into that narrow part, rises faster than when the space for it is larger. This helps to terrify; but, as the quantity entering is less and less as the surfaces without and within become more nearly equal in height, the pumps that could not keep the water from rising at first, might afterwards be able to prevent its rising higher, and the people might remain on board in safety, without hazarding themselves in an open boat on the wide ocean.

Besides the equality in the height of the two surfaces, there may sometimes be other causes that retard the farther sinking of a leaky vessel. The rising water within may arrive at quantities of light wooden works, empty chests, and particularly empty water-casks, which, fixed so as not to float themselves, may help to sustain her. Many bodies which compose a ship's cargo may be specifically lighter than water. All these, when out of water, are an additional weight to that of the ship, and she is in proportion pressed deeper in the water, but as soon as these bodies are immersed, they weigh no longer on the ship; but, on the contrary, if fixed, they help to support her, in proportion as they are specifically lighter than the water.

Temporary Nautical Pump.

Captain Leslie, in a voyage from North America to Stockholm, adopted an excellent mode of emptying water from his ship's hold, when the crew were insufficient to perform that duty. About ten or twelve feet above the pump he rigged out a spar, one end of which projected overboard, while the other was fastened, as a lever, to the machinery of the pump. To the end which projected overboard was suspended a water-butt, half full, but corked down; so that when the coming wave raised the butt-end, the other end depressed the piston of the pump; but at the retiring of the wave this was reversed, for, by the weight of the butt, the piston came up again, and with it the water. Thus, without the aid of the crew, the ship's hold was cleared of the water in a few hours.

Another.—When a vessel springs a leak at sea, which cannot be discovered, instead of exhausting the crew by continual working at the pumps, they may form, with very little trouble, a machine to discharge the water, which will work itself, without any assistance from the hands on board.

Let a spar, or spare top-mast, be cut to the length of eight or ten feet, or more, according to the size of the vessel; mortise four holes through the thickest end, through which run four oars, fixing them tight, exactly in the middle. To the four handles nail on four blades (made of staves), the size of the other ends, which will form a very good water-wheel, if the oars be strong; then fix into the opposite end what is commonly called a crank: the iron handle of a grindstone would suit extremely well; if this is not to be had, any strong bar of iron may be bent into that form, wedging it tight to prevent its twisting round. Then nail up a new pair of chaps on the fore part of the pump, for a new handle to be fixed in, which will point with its outer end to the bow of the vessel. This handle will be short on the outside, but as long on the inside as the diameter of the bore of the pump will admit, in order that the spear may be plunged the deeper, and of course the longer stroke. The handle must be large enough to have a slit sawed up it, sufficient to admit a stave edgeways, which must be fastened with a strong iron pin, on which it may work. The lower end of the stave must be bored to admit the round end of the crank; then fix the shaft, with the oars (or arms) over the gunwale, on two crotchets, one spiked to the gunwale, and the other near the pump, cutting in the shaft a circular notch, as well to make it run easier, by lessening the friction, as to keep the whole steady. A bolt is now to be fixed in each crutchet close over the shaft, to keep it from rising. As soon as the wheel touches the water it will turn round, and the crank, by means of the stave fixed on its end, will work the handle of the pump.

To render the Sinking of a Ship Impossible.

According to the present plan of ship-building, in case of a leak at sea, which cannot be kept under by pumping, the ship and crew must inevitably be lost, to the great affliction and loss of thousands of families. In order to prevent such accidents in future, which hitherto have been too common, a gentleman of the name of Williams suggests an easy arrangement which, if universally adopted, even under the worst circumstances, will enable the crew to save not only themselves, but the ship and cargo likewise:

It is that every ship should be divided into four equal compartments, with partitions of sufficient strength; the probability in case of a leak is that it would take place in one of them, and, allowing it to fill, the safety of the ship would not be endangered, for three-fourths of the cargo would remain undamaged. To prove this we will suppose a vessel of 100 tons so divided (though the plan is as applicable to a ship of 1000 tons as to a canal boat), and that one of the compartments filled with water; this would not increase her weight more than from six to eight tons from the cargo previously occupying the space and reducing her buoyancy about one-third. The same effect would take place was she sent out of port with only one-fourth of her hull above water, though vessels are commonly sent out with one-third, and even more. Packets, as they carry little or no cargo, may with safety be divided into three compartments. In cases of fire the advantage is equally obvious, as any of the quarters might be inundated with safety.

BATHING.
The Art of Swimming.

It has been observed before that men are drowned by raising their arms above water, the unbuoyed weight of which depresses the head; all other animals have neither motion nor ability to act in a similar manner, and therefore swim naturally. When a man therefore falls into deep water, he will rise to the surface and continue there if he does not elevate his hands. If he move his hands under the water in any manner he pleases his head will rise so high as to allow him liberty to breathe, and if he move his legs as in the act of walking (or rather of walking upstairs), his shoulders will rise above the water, so that he may use less exertion with his hands, or apply them to other purposes. These plain directions are recommended to the attention of those who have not learned to swim in their youth, and they will, if attended to, be found highly advantageous in preserving life.

If a person falls into the water or gets out of his depth and cannot swim, and if he wishes to drown himself, let him kick and splash as violently as possible, and he will soon sink. On the contrary, if impressed with the idea that he is lighter than the water, he avoids all violent action and calmly but steadily strives to refrain from drawing his breath while under the water, and keeps his head raised as much as possible, and gently but constantly moves his hands and feet in a proper direction, there will be a great probability of his keeping afloat until some aid arrives.

Cramp in Bathing.

For the cure of the cramp when swimming, Dr. Franklin recommends a vigorous and violent shock of the part affected by suddenly and forcibly stretching out the leg, which should be darted out of the water into the air if possible.

Precautions in Bathing.

Never venture into cold water when the body is much exhausted or relaxed with heat.

Dr. Franklin relates an instance within his own knowledge of four young men who, having worked at harvest in the heat of the day, with a view of refreshing themselves plunged into a spring of cold water; two died upon the spot, a third the next morning, and the fourth recovered with great difficulty.

Be very careful where you bathe, even though ever so good a swimmer, lest there should be weeds to entangle the feet, or any thing else to endanger life. It is by the neglect of this precaution that many good swimmers expose themselves to greater danger than those who cannot swim at all, their very expertness thus becoming fatal to them by tempting them into places where their destruction is inevitable.

Sea-bathing.

The use of the tepid salt water bath, or indeed of sea-bathing itself, when the water is warm, (that is) between 60° and 70° of heat, is in many cases beneficial, when a colder temperature would be decidedly injurious.

It may be satisfactory to know that in situations distant from the shore, where sea-water cannot be had, artificial sea-water, made by dissolving 4 pounds of bay-salt in 16 gallons of fresh water, possesses all the properties of the water of the sea, a small portion of sulphate of magnesia excepted.

The Shower-bath.

The cold shower-bath is less alarming to nervous persons and less liable to produce cramps than cold immersion; it may be considered as the best and safest mode of cold bathing, and is recommended in many nervous complaints.

It has also afforded relief in some cases of insanity.

Substitute for a Shower-bath.

Where the saving of expense is an object, it may be effectually answered by filling a common watering pot with cold water. Let the patient sit undressed upon a stool, which may be placed in a large tub, and let the hair, if not cut short, be spread over the shoulders as loosely as possible. Now pour the water from the pot over the patient's head, face, neck, shoulders, and all parts of the body, progressively down to the feet, until the whole has been thoroughly wetted.

A large sponge may, in some measure, be substituted for the shower bath; particularly in affections of the head which arise from intemperance, night-watching, study, or other perplexity. Headache, from these causes, will be greatly alleviated by wiping the top and fore-part of the head with a sponge frequently dipped in water. The cold thus produced will check the determination of blood to the head, and has often been known to prevent delirium and insanity.

The Tepid-bath.

On immersing the body in a tepid-path, which takes its range from 85° to 90°, no striking sensation either of heat or cold is felt. But a person much chilled, will on entering the tepid-bath feel the water warm, while another who has been heated by exercise, will find it insensibly cold.

The tepid-bath is attended with several advantages: the surface of the skin is by it freed from that scaly matter, which always collects more or less on the healthiest person; the pores of the skin thus being free, the natural perspiration is promoted, the limbs are rendered supple, and any stiffness which may have been produced by exertion or fatigue, is removed. Such immersion has been found to allay thirst; a proof that a quantity of water is absorbed, and enters the body through the skin.

The tepid-bath seems the best adapted to the purposes of cleanliness and healthy exercise. To delicate females and young children, it is of primary importance. Nothing can be more absurd than the common practice of mothers and nurses in washing children, no matter how sickly or unwell, with cold water, under the idea of bracing the constitution: whereas the use of tepid water alone, is not only the most agreeable, but the most proper fluid to excite the energies of the system in young children.

Affusion with tepid water has generally the same result, except, that if the body continue exposed to the air after the affusion, a sensation of cold is produced, which ought to be avoided by wiping dry the upper part of the body whilst the lower extremities are still covered with water.

There can be little doubt that human existence, by tepid bathing, temperance, and proper exercise, may be made more agreeable and also be prolonged.

GENERAL RULES FOR PRESERVING LIFE AND HEALTH.
Sir R. Phillip's Rules.

1. Rise early, and never sit up late.
2. Wash the whole body every morning with

cold water, by means of a large sponge, and rub it dry with a rough towel, or scrub the whole body for ten or fifteen minutes with flesh brushes.

3. Drink water generally, and avoid excess of spirits, wine, and fermented liquors.

4. Keep the body open by the free use of the syringe, and remove superior obstructions by aperient pills.

5. Sleep in a room which has free access to the open air.

6. Keep the head cool by washing it when necessary with cold water; and abate feverish and inflammatory symptoms when they arise by persevering stillness.

7. Correct symptoms of plethora and indigestion by eating and drinking less per diem for a few days.

8. Never eat a hearty supper, especially of animal food; and drink wine, spirits, and beer, if these are necessary, only after dinner.

Dr. Boerhaave's Rules.

This great man left, as a legacy to the world, the following simple and unerring directions for preserving health; they contained the sum and substance of his vast professional knowledge during a long and useful life:—" Keep the feet warm, the head cool, and the body open." If these were generally attended to the physician's aid would seldom be required.

Clothing.

To adapt the dress with a scrupulous nicety to the fluctuations of temperature every day, would indeed require such minute attention as hardly any person can bestow; but every person may comply with the general rules of clothing, as far as not to lay aside too early the dress of the winter, nor to retain that of the summer too late: from a neglect of which precaution thousands of lives are every year sacrificed to mortality. The perfection of dress, considered merely as such, is to fit without fettering the body.

Air.

Nothing is more pernicious than the air of a place where a numerous body of people is collected together within doors, especially if to the breath of the crowd there be added the vapors of a multitude of candles, and the consumption of the vital air by fires in proportion. Hence it happens that persons of a delicate constitution are liable to become sick or faint in a place of this kind. These ought to avoid, as much as possible, the air of great towns; which is also peculiarly hurtful to the asthmatic and consumptive, as it is likewise to hysteric women and men of weak nerves. Where such people cannot always live without the verge of great towns, they ought at least to go out as often as they can into the open air, and if possible pass the night in the wholesome situation of the suburbs.

Ventilation.

Air that has long stagnated becomes extremely unwholesome to breathe, and often immediately fatal. Such is that of mines, wells, cellars, etc. People ought therefore to be very cautious in entering places of this description which have been long shut up. The air of some hospitals, jails, ships, etc., partakes of the same unwholesome and pernicious nature, and they ought never to be destitute of ventilators—those useful contrivances for expelling foul and introducing fresh air into its place. The same may be said of all places where numbers of people are crowded together; or where fires, especially charcoal fires, are burning.

It is found that most plants have the property of correcting bad air within a few hours, when they are exposed to the light of the sun; but that on the contrary, during the night or when flowering they corrupt the common air of the atmosphere. Hence it is an unwholesome practice to have shrubs in an apartment that is slept in, at least when in bloom.

Ventilation of Churches.

Both in public and private buildings there are errors committed which affect in an extraordinary degree the salubrity of the air. Churches are seldom open during all the week; they are never ventilated by fires, and rarely by opening the windows, while, to render the air of them yet more unwholesome, frequently no attention is paid to keeping them clean. The consequence of which is that they are damp, musty, and apt to prove hurtful to people of weak constitutions; and it is a common remark that a person cannot pass through a large church or cathedral, even in summer, without a strong feeling of chilliness.

Ventilation of Houses.

The great attention paid to making houses close and warm, though apparently well adapted to the comfort of the inhabitants, is by no means favorable to health, unless care be taken every day to admit fresh air by the windows. Sometimes it may be proper to make use of what is called pumping the room, or moving the door backward and forward for some minutes together. The practice of making the beds early in the day, however it may suit convenience or delicacy, is doubtless improper. It would be much better to turn them down and expose them to the influence of the air admitted by the windows.

For many persons to sleep in one room, as in the ward of a hospital, is hurtful to health; and it is scarcely a less injurious custom, though often practised by those who have splendid houses, for two or more to sleep in a small apartment, especially if it be very close.

Houses situated in low marshy countries, or near lakes of stagnant water, are likewise unwholesome; as they partake of the putrid vapors exhaled in such places. To remedy this evil, those who inhabit them, if they study their health, ought to use a more generous diet than is requisite in more dry and elevated situations. It is very important, too, in such localities to dry the house with a fire whenever the air is damp, even in the summer.

Burying in Churches, etc.

It was formerly, and is now, too common to have church-yards in the middle of populous towns. This is not only reprehensible in point of taste, but, considering how near to the surface of the earth the dead bodies in many places are deposited, there must necessarily arise putrid vapors, which, however imperceptible, cannot fail to contaminate the air. The practice of burying in churches is still more liable to censure; and not many years ago, the pernicious effects of this custom were so severely felt in France, as to occasion a positive edict against it.

To Dissipate Noxious Vapors in Wells, etc.

Procure a pair of smith's bellows, affixed on a wooden frame, so as to work in the same manner as at the forge. This apparatus being placed at the edge of the well, one end of a leathern tube (the nose of a fire engine), should be closely adapted to the nose of the bellows, and the other end thrown into the well, reaching within one foot of the bottom.

If the well be even so infected, that a candle will not burn at a short distance from the top; after blowing with the bellows only half an hour, the candle will burn brightly at the bottom; then, without further difficulty, proceed in the work.

It is obvious, that in cleaning vaults, or working in any subterraneous place subject to damps, the same method must be attended with the like beneficial effects.

Persons whose business requires them to attend upon large quantities of fermenting liquors, or to work in close places with lighted charcoal, frequently experience headache, giddiness, and other disagreeable effects from the noxious vapors which these exhale, and often have their health impaired, or their lives endangered by a continuance in the employment. In some cases, the danger, perhaps, cannot be avoided, except by going into the open air, as soon as headache or giddiness begins, and drinking a glass of cold water, or washing the face and neck with the same. In the case of persons whose work requires charcoal fires, their dangerous effects may be prevented, by taking care not to sit near the fire when burning, or to burn it in a chimney, and when there is none, to keep the door open, and place a large tub of lime-water in the room.

To Protect Gilders, Jewellers, and others from the Pernicious Effects of Charcoal.

It is advisable for all those who are exposed to the vapors of charcoal, particularly gilders, jewellers, refiners of metal, etc., to place a flat vessel, filled with lime-water, near the stove in which the charcoal is burnt.

The lime combines with the carbonic acid gas evolved by the ignited charcoal, and preserves the purity of the air. When the surface of the water becomes covered with a film, or pellicle, it must be changed for a fresh quantity.

To Prevent Lamps from proving Pernicious to Asthmatic People.

The smoking of lamps is frequently disregarded in domestic life; but the fumes ascending from oil, especially if it be tainted or rancid, are highly pernicious, when inhaled into the lungs of asthmatic persons. To prevent this, let a sponge, three or four inches in diameter, be moistened with pure water, and in that state be suspended by a string or wire, exactly over the flame of the lamp, at the distance of a few inches; this substance will absorb all the smoke emitted during the evening or night, after which it should be rinsed in warm water, by which means it will be again rendered fit for use.

To Disinfect Substances or Places.

Put a saucer full of chloride of lime on the floor of the room, and renew it every two or three days. Or, sprinkle Labarraque's solution of chloride of soda over the floor or walls. Ledoyen's solution of nitrate of lead will at once remove the odor of most foul air. But the only absolutely certain method of disinfection is by heat; for example, let every person be removed from the tainted building or vessel, and then, by means of stoves, keep up a temperature of 140° Fahr., for two or three days.

To Protect Gilders from the Pernicious Effects of Mercury.

They should have two doors in their work room, opposite to each other, which they should keep open, that there may be a free circulation of air. They should likewise have a piece of gold applied to the roof of the mouth, during the whole time of the operation. This plate will attract and intercept the mercury as they breathe, and when it grows white they must cast it into the fire, that the mercury may evaporate, and replace it when it is cool again. They should, indeed, have two pieces of gold, that one may be put into the mouth whilst the other is purifying and cooling; by these means they will preserve themselves from the diseases and infirmities which mercury occasions.

Riding and Walking.

For preserving health, there is no kind of exercise more proper than walking, as it gives the most general action to the muscles of the body; but, for valetudinarians, riding on horseback is preferable. It is almost incredible how much the constitution may be strengthened by this exercise, when continued for a considerable time; not so much in the fashionable way of a morning ride, but of making long journeys, in which there is the farther advantage of a perpetual change of air. Numbers of people, reduced to a state of great weakness, have, by this means, acquired a degree of vigor and health, which all the medical prescriptions in the world could not otherwise have procured. But it is of importance, in travelling for health, that one should not employ his mind in deep reflections, but enjoy the company of an agreeable companion, and gratify his sight with the prospect of the various objects around him. In this exercise, as well as in every other, we ought always to begin gently, and to finish gradually, never abruptly; and proportion the exertion to the strength.

Exercise after Meals.

Exercise is hurtful immediately after meals, particularly to those of nervous and irritable constitutions, who are thence liable to heartburn, eructations, and vomiting. Indeed, the instinct of the inferior animals confirms the propriety of this rule; for they are all inclined to indulge themselves in rest after food. At all events, fatiguing exercise should be delayed till digestion is performed, which generally requires three or four hours after eating a full meal.

Reading aloud.

This is a species of exercise much recommended by the ancient physicians: and to this may be joined that of speaking. They are both of great advantage to those who have not sufficient leisure or opportunities for other kinds of exercise. To speak very loud, however, is hurtful to weak lungs. Singing, as by the vibratory motion of the air it shakes the lungs and the bowels of the abdomen or belly, promotes, in a remarkable degree, the circulation of the blood. Hence, those sedentary artificers or mechanics, who from habit almost constantly sing at their work, unintentionally contribute much to the preservation of their health.

Wind Instruments.

All these are more or less hurtful to the lungs, which they weaken, by introducing much air, and keeping that organ too long in a state of distention. On this account, persons of weak lungs, who play much on the flute, hautboy, or French horn, are frequently afflicted with spitting of blood, cough, shortness of breath, and pulmonary consumption. Blowing those instruments likewise checks the circulation of the blood through the lungs, accumulates it towards the head, and disposes such persons to apoplexy.

Friction.

One of the most gentle and useful kinds of exercise is friction of the body, either by the naked hand, a piece of flannel, or, what is still better, a flesh-brush. This was in great esteem among the ancients, and is so at present in the East Indies. The whole body may be subjected to this mild operation, but chiefly the belly, the spine, or backbone, and the arms and legs. Friction clears the skin, resolves stagnating humors, promotes perspiration, strengthens the fibres, and increases the warmth and energy of the whole body. In rheumatism, gout, palsy, and green sickness, it is an excellent remedy. To the sedentary, the hypochondriac, and persons troubled with indigestion, who have not leisure to take sufficient exercise, the daily friction of the belly, in particular, cannot be too much recommended as a substitute for other means, in order to dissolve the thick humors which may be forming in the bowels, by stagnation, and to strengthen the vessels. But, in rubbing the belly, the operation ought to be performed in a circular direction, as being most favorable to the course of the intestines, and their natural action. It should be performed in the morning, on an empty stomach, or, rather, in bed before getting up, and continued at least for some minutes at a time.

Getting Wet.

This accident is at all times less frequent in towns than in the country, owing to the almost universal use of the umbrella in the former.

When a person is wet he ought never to stand, but to continue in motion till he arrives at a place where he may be suitably accommodated. Here he should strip off his wet clothes, to be changed for such as are dry, and have those parts of his body which have been wetted, well rubbed with a dry cloth. The legs, shoulders, and arms, are generally the parts most exposed to wet; they should, therefore, be particularly attended to. It is almost incredible how many diseases may be prevented by adopting this course. Catarrhs, inflammations, rheumatisms, diarrhœas, fevers, and consumptions, are the foremost among the train which frequently follow an accident of this kind.

Precautions in removing from a Hot to a Cold Situation.

It should be a determined rule to avoid all rapid transitions from one extreme to another, and never to remove from a room highly heated to a fresh or cold air while the body remains warm, or till the necessary change to a warmer dress has been previously made. If, at any time, the body should be violently heated, during the warm weather, it is sure to suffer by going into vaults, cellars, ice-houses, by cold bathing, or by sitting on cold stones, or damp earth; many lingering and incurable maladies have been brought on by such imprudence, nay, present death has, in some instances, been the consequence of such transgression. Pulmonary consumption, which makes annually such dreadful ravages among the young and middle aged, has been frequently induced by such apparently trifling causes.

To keep the Feet Dry.

One method that has been found to succeed in keeping the feet dry is to wear, over the foot of the stocking, a sock made of oiled silk. To keep it in its proper place, it will be necessary to wear over it a cotton or worsted sock. India-rubber overshoes or boots are now generally worn. But they or oiled silk, as they prevent the evaporation of the insensible perspiration, and thus obstruct the pores of the skin, should never be worn long at a time.

To preserve the Eye-sight.

1. Never sit for any length of time in absolute gloom, or exposed to a blaze of light. The reason on which this rule is founded proves the impropriety of going hastily from one extreme to the other, whether of darkness or of light, and shows us that a southern aspect is improper for those whose sight is weak and tender.

2. Avoid reading small print, and straining the eyes by looking at minute objects.

3. Do not read in the dusk, nor, if the eyes be disordered, by candle-light.

4. Do not permit the eyes to dwell on glaring objects, more particularly on first waking in the morning; the sun should not of course be suffered to shine in the room at that time, and a moderate quantity of light only should be admitted. For the same reasons, the furniture, walls, and other objects of a bed-room should not be altogether of a white or glaring color; indeed, those whose eyes are weak, would find considerable advantage in having green for the furniture, and as the prevailing color of their bed-chambers. Nature confirms the propriety of this direction, for the light of the day comes on by slow degrees, and green is the universal color she presents to our eyes.

5. Those individuals who are rather long-sighted should accustom themselves to read with the book somewhat nearer to the eye than what they naturally like; while others, that are rather short-sighted, should use themselves to read with the book as far off as possible. By these means, both will improve and strengthen their sight, while a contrary course increases its natural imperfections. It is well to read or sew with the light above or behind, rather than in front of the face, or with a shade to protect the eyes from glare.

Use of Spectacles.

From whatever cause the decay of sight arises, an attentive consideration of the following rules will enable any one to judge for himself when his eye-sight may be assisted or preserved by the use of proper glasses:

1. When we are obliged to remove small objects to a considerable distance from the eye in order to see them distinctly.

2. If we find it necessary to get more light than formerly, as, for instance, to place the candle between the eye and the object.

3. If on looking at and attentively considering a near object it fatigues the eye and becomes confused, or if it appears to have a kind of dimness or mist before it.

4. When small, printed letters are seen to run into each other, and on looking steadfastly at them appear double or treble.

5. If the eyes are so fatigued by a little exercise that we are obliged to shut them from time to time, so as to relieve them by looking at different objects.

When all these circumstances concur, or any of them separately takes place, it will be necessary to seek assistance from glasses, which will ease the eyes, and in some degree check their tendency to become worse, whereas if they be not assisted in time the weakness will be undoubtedly increased and the eyes be impaired by the efforts they are compelled to make. When weakness of the sight is not remedied by glasses, it will be necessary to avoid all use of the eyes which gives pain or causes fatigue, especially at night.

Cosmetics.

To set off the complexion with all the advantage it can attain, nothing more is requisite than to wash the face with pure water, or if anything farther be occasionally necessary, it is only the addition of a little soap. [See pages 306, 465.]

THE TEETH.

An object very subservient to health, and which merits due attention, is the preservation of the teeth, the care of which, considering their importance in preparing the food for digestion, is, in general, far from being sufficiently attended to. Many persons neglect to wash their mouths in the morning, which ought always to be done. Indeed this ought to be practised at the conclusion of every meal, where either animal food or vegetables are eaten, for the former is apt to leave behind it a rancid acrimony, and the latter an acidity, both of them hurtful to the teeth. Washing the mouth frequently with cold water is not only serviceable in keeping the teeth clean, but in strengthening the gums, the firm adhesion of which to the teeth is of great importance in preserving them sound and secure. The addition of a few drops of tincture of myrrh to the water will make it more cleansing and sweeter to the breath.

Tooth Powders.

Many persons, while laudably attentive to the preservation of their teeth, do them hurt by too much officiousness. They daily apply to them some dentifrice powder, which they rub so hard as not only to injure the enamel by excessive friction, but to hurt the gums even more than by the abuse of the the toothpick. The quality of some of the dentifrice powders advertised in newspapers is extremely suspicious, and there is reason to think that they are not altogether free from a corrosive ingredient. One of the safest and best compositions for the purpose is a mixture of two parts of prepared chalk, one of Peruvian bark, and one of hard soap, all finely powdered, which is calculated not only to clean the teeth without hurting them, but to preserve the firmness of the gums.

Besides the advantage of sound teeth for their use in mastication, a proper attention to their treatment conduces not a little to the sweetness of the breath. This is, indeed, often affected by other causes existing in the lungs, the stomach, and sometimes even in the bowels, from a rotten state of the teeth, both from the putrid smell emitted by carious bones and the impurities lodged in their cavities, never fails of aggravating an unpleasant breath wherever there is a tendency of that kind. [See pages 307, 308.]

Loose Teeth.

When the teeth are loosened by external violence, by falls and blows, or by the improper use of instruments in pulling diseased teeth in the neighbourhood of sound ones, they may again be made tolerably fast by pressing them as firmly as possible into their sockets, and preserving them so with ligatures of cat-gut, Indian weed or waxed silk, and keeping the patient upon spoon-meat till they are firm. When looseness of the teeth is owing to decay, nothing will fasten them till the cause be removed, and this ought to be done early, otherwise it will have no effect. Frequently the teeth become loose from a sponginess of the gums, often attributed to scurvy. The best remedy is scarifying the gums deeply, and allowing them to bleed freely; this should be repeated till they are fully fastened. Mild astringents, as tincture of bark, are here attended with good effects, though those of a strong nature will certainly do harm. The mouth should be frequently washed with cold water strongly impregnated with these, and the patient should not use the teeth which have been loose till they become firm again. The loosening of the teeth in old age cannot be remedied, as it is owing to the wasting of their sockets, from which the teeth lose their support.

Foul Teeth.

The teeth sometimes become yellow or black without any adventitious matter being observed on them; at other times they become foul, and give a taint to the breath, in consequence of the natural mucus of the mouth, or part of the food remaining too long about them. The most frequent cause of foul teeth is the substance called tartar, which seems to be a deposition from the saliva, and with which the teeth are often almost entirely encrusted. When this substance is allowed to remain, it insinuates itself between the gums and the teeth, and then gets down upon the jaw in such a manner as to loosen the teeth. When they have been long covered with this or with any other matter, it is seldom they can be cleaned without the assistance of instruments. But when once they are cleaned they may generally be kept so by rubbing them with a thin piece of soft wood made into a kind of brush and dipped into distilled vinegar, after which the mouth is to be washed with common water.

Cleaning the Teeth.

When the teeth are to be cleaned with instruments, the operator ought, with a linen cloth or with a glove, to press against the points of the teeth, so as to keep them firm in their sockets with the fingers of the one hand while he cleans them with the necessary instruments held in the other, taking care not to scrape them so hard as to loosen them, or to rub off the enamel. This being done, the teeth should be rubbed over with a small brush or a piece of sponge dipped in a mixture of cream of tartar and Peruvian bark. The same application may be made to the teeth for a few days, when afterwards they may be kept clean as already directed.

The teeth are sometimes covered over with a thin dark colored scurf, which has by some been mistaken for a wasting of the enamel, but which is only an extraneous matter covering it. By perseverance this may be cleaned off as completely as where the teeth are covered with tartar; but it is apt, after some time, to appear again. When this is observed the same operation must be repeated.

For the purpose of applying powders or washes to the teeth, a hard or soft brush is commonly employed; the latter is supposed preferable, as being in less danger of wearing down the enamel or of separating the teeth.

Toothache.

Toothache may be of either of three kinds: from irritation of the nerve, exposed in the hollow of a decaying tooth; from inflammation of the jaw, with or without a gathering at the root of a tooth; and from neuralgia. For the first of these, there is a certain cure; but it requires care in the application. Wrap a small pledget of raw cotton around the point of a knitting or darning needle, and dip it in creasote; then insert the point with the cotton directly into the hollow of the aching tooth. If it reach the nerve, it will give relief instantly. The cotton may be left in for a while, covered by a dry piece. Care is needed not to let the creasote drop or run upon the lips or gums, on which it will act as a caustic. If a drop should escape, however, little or no harm will follow if the mouth be at once washed well with cold water.

Weights and Measures.

By the following tables it will be seen that in the

Measures of Fluids.

1 gallon measure	contains 8 pints
1 pint	" 16 ounces,
1 ounce	" 8 drachms,
1 drachm	" 60 minims.

Weight of Dry Substances.

1 pound	contains 12 ounces,
1 ounce	" 8 drachms,
1 drachm	" 60 grains,
1 scruple	" 20 grs. or
1-3 of a drachm.	

It is customary to distinguish quantities of fluids from dry substances, by prefixing the letter f. (fluid) when an ounce or drachm is mentioned in medical works, but in the foregoing prescriptions or formulæ, this was considered to be unnecessary, as the slightest acquaintance with the substances to be used will point out what is implied.

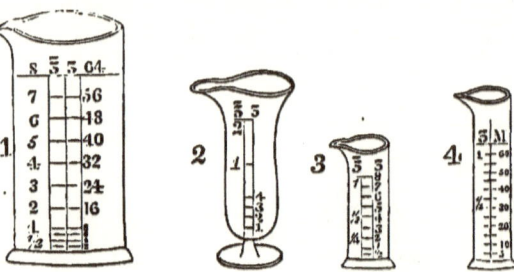

Measuring-Glasses

In order to measure quantities of fluids, glasses, graduated on their sides (according to the above figures), will be found useful in all families and private laboratories:

No. 1, Represents a glass calculated to measure any quantity from two drachms to eight ounces.
No. 2, From one drachm to two ounces.
No. 3, From half a drachm to one ounce; and
No. 4, Any quantity from five minims (or drops) to one drachm.

Scale of Medicinal Doses.

The following table of the gradations of doses of medicines for different ages, will in general be found pretty correct, and ought never to be deviated from, except by professional advice.

If at the age of manhood the dose be one drachm, the proportions will be at

From 14 to 21 years, 2 scruples; 7 to 14 years, half a drachm; 4 to 7 years, 1 scruple; 4 years, 15 grains; 3 years, half a scruple; 2 years, 8 grains; 1 year, 5 grains; 6 months, 3 grains; 3 months, 2 grains; 1 month, 1 grain.

CULINARY ARTS.

PLAIN COOKERY.

To Boil Meats, etc.

The most simple of culinary processes is not often performed in perfection, though it does not require so much nicety and attendance as roasting; to skim the pot well, and to keep it moderately boiling, and to know how long the joint requires, comprehends the most useful point of this branch of cookery. The cook must take especial care that the water really boils all the while she is cooking, or she will be deceived in the time. An adept cook will manage with much less fire for boiling than she uses for roasting, and it will last all the time without much mending. When the water is coming to a boil there will always rise from the cleanest meat a scum to the top, this must be carefully taken off as soon as it appears, for on this depends the good appearance of a boiled dinner. When you have skimmed it well, put in a little cold water, which will throw up the rest of it. If left alone it soon boils down and sticks to the meat, which, instead of looking white and healthful, will have a coarse and uninviting appearance.

Many cooks put in milk to make what they boil look white, but this does more harm than good; others wrap the meat in a cloth; but if it is well skimmed it will have a much more delicate appearance than when it is muffled up.

Put the meat into cold water in the proportion of about a quart to every pound of meat; it should remain covered during the whole process of boiling, but only just so. Water beyond what is absolutely necessary renders the meat less savory and weakens the broth.

The water should be gradually heated according to the thickness, etc., of the article boiled; for instance, a leg of mutton of ten pounds' weight should be placed over a moderate fire, which will gradually heat the water without causing it to boil, for about forty minutes. If the water boils much sooner, the meat will be hardened, and shrink up as if it were scorched. Reckon the time from its first coming to a boil; the slower it boils the tenderer, the plumper, and whiter it will be. For those who choose their food thoroughly cooked, twenty minutes to a pound will not be found too much for gentle simmering by the side of the fire. Fresh killed meat will take much longer time boiling than that which has been kept till what the butchers call ripe; if it be fresh killed it will be tough and hard if stewed ever so long, and ever so gently. The size of the boiling pots should be adapted to what they are to contain; in small families we recommend block-tin saucepans, etc., as lightest and safest, taking care that the covers fit close, otherwise the introduction of smoke may be the means of giving the meat a bad taste. Beef and mutton a little underdone is not a great fault, but lamb, pork, and veal are uneatable and truly unwholesome, if not thoroughly boiled. Take care of the liquor in which poultry or meat has been boiled, as an addition of peas, herbs, etc., will convert it into a nourishing soup.

To Bake Meats, etc.

This is one of the cheapest and most convenient

ways of dressing a dinner in small families, and although the general superiority of roasting must be allowed, still certain joints and dishes, such as legs and loins of pork, legs and shoulders of mutton, and fillets of veal, will bake to great advantage if the meat be good. Besides those joints above-mentioned, we shall enumerate a few baked dishes which may be particularly recommended.

A pig when sent to the baker prepared for baking, should have its ears and tail covered with buttered paper, and a bit of butter tied up in a piece of linen to baste the back with, otherwise it will be apt to blister. If well baked it is considered equal to a roast one.

A goose prepared the same as for roasting, or a duck placed upon a stand and turned, as soon as one side is done upon the other, are equally good.

A buttock of beef, prepared as follows, is particularly fine: After it has been put in salt about a week, let it be well washed and put into a brown earthen pan with a pint of water; cover the pan tight over with two or three thicknesses of cap paper, and give it four or five hours in a moderately heated oven.

A ham, if not too old, put in soak for an hour, taken out and baked in a moderately heated oven, cuts fuller of graver, and of a finer flavor, than a boiled one.

Codfish, haddock, and mackerel should have a dust of flour and some bits of butter spread over them. Eels, when large and stuffed, herrings and sprats are put in a brown pan, with vinegar and a little spice, and tied over with paper.

A hare, prepared the same as for roasting, with a few bits of butter and a little milk, put into the dish and basted several times, will be found nearly equal to roasting. In the same manner, legs and shins of beef will be equally good with proper vegetable seasoning.

To Roast Meats, etc.

The first thing requisite for roasting is to have a strong, steady fire, or a clear brisk one, according to the size and weight of the joint that is put down to the spit. A cook, who does not attend to this, will prove herself totally incompetent to roast victuals properly. All roasting should be done open to the air, to ventilate the meat from its gross fumes; otherwise it becomes baked instead of roasted. The joint should be put down at such a distance from the fire as to imbibe the heat rather quickly; otherwise its plumpness and good quality will be gradually dried up, and it will turn shrively, and look meagre. When the meat is first put down, it is necessary to see that it lies level in the pan, otherwise the process of cooking will be very troublesome. When it is warm, begin to baste it well, which prevents the nutritive juices escaping; and, if required, additional dripping must be used for that purpose.

As to sprinkling with salt while roasting, most able cooks dispense with it, as the penetrating particles of the salt have a tendency to draw out the animal juices. However, a little salt thrown on, when first laid down, is sometimes necessary, with strong meats. When the smoke draws towards the fire, and the dropping of the clear gravy begins, it is a sure sign that the joint is nearly done. Then take off the paper, baste well, and dredge it with flour, which brings on that beautiful brownness which makes roasted meats look so inviting.

With regard to the time necessary for roasting various meats, it will vary according to the different sorts, the time it has been kept, and the temperature of the weather. In summer twenty minutes may be reckoned equal to half an hour in winter. A good screen, to keep off the chilling currents of air, is essentially useful. The old housewife's rule is to allow rather more than a quarter of an hour to each pound, and in most instances it proves practically correct.

In roasting mutton or lamb, the loin, the chine, and the saddle, must have the skin raised, and skewered on, and, when nearly done, take off this skin, and baste and flour to froth it up.

Veal requires roasting brown, and, if a fillet or loin, be sure to paper the fat, that as little of it may be lost as possible. When nearly done baste it with butter and dredge with flour.

Pork should be well done. When roasting a loin, cut the skin across with a sharp knife, otherwise the crackling is very awkward to manage. Stuff the knuckle part with sage and onion, and skewer it up. Put a little drawn gravy in the dish, and serve it up with apple-sauce in a tureen. A spare-rib should be basted with a little butter, a little dust of flour, and some sage and onions shred small. Apple-sauce is the only one which suits this dish.

Wild fowls require a clear brisk fire, and should be roasted till they are of a light brown, but not too much; yet it is a common fault to roast them till the gravy runs out, thereby losing their fine flavor.

Tame fowls require more roasting, as the heat is longer in penetrating. They should be often basted, in order to keep up a strong froth, and to improve their plumpness. The seasoning of the dressing or stuffing of a fowl is important to its flavor. The dressing should consist of bread crumbs, seasoned with black pepper, salt, and no herb but thyme.

Pigs and geese should be thoroughly roasted before a good fire, and turned quickly.

Hares and rabbits require time and care, especially to have the ends sufficiently done, and to remedy that raw discoloring at the neck, etc., which proves often so objectionable at table.

To regulate Time in Cookery.

Mutton.— A leg of 8 pounds will require two hours and a half. A chine or saddle of 10 or 11 pounds, two hours and a half. A shoulder of 7 pounds, one hour and a half. A loin of 7 pounds, one hour and three quarters. A neck and breast, about the same time as a loin.

Beef.— The sirloin of 15 pounds, from three hours and three-quarters to four hours. Ribs of beef, from 15 to 20 pounds, will take three hours to three hours and a half.

Veal.—A fillet, from 12 to 16 pounds, will take from four to five hours, at a good fire. A loin, upon the average, will take three hours. A shoulder, from three hours to three hours and a half. A neck, two hours. A breast, from an hour and a half to two hours.

Lamb.— Hind quarter of 8 pounds will take from an hour and three-quarters to two hours. Fore quarter of 10 pounds, about two hours. Leg of 5 pounds, from an hour and a quarter to an hour and a half. Shoulder or breast, with a quick fire, an hour.

Pork.— A leg of 8 pounds will require about three hours. Griskin, an hour and a half. A spare-rib of 8 or 9 pounds will take from two hours and a half to three hours to roast it thoroughly. A bald spare-rib of 8 pounds, an hour and a quarter. A loin of 5 pounds, if very fat, from two hours to two hours and a half. A sucking pig, of three weeks old, about an hour and a half.

Poultry.—A very large turkey will require about three hours; one of 10 pounds two hours; a small one an hour and a half.

A full-grown fowl, an hour and a half; a moderate sized one an hour and a quarter.
A pullet, from half an hour to forty minutes.
A goose, full grown, two hours.
A green goose, forty minutes.
A duck, full size, from an hour and a quarter to one hour and three-quarters.

Venison.— A buck haunch which weighs from 20 to 25 pounds will take about four hours and a half roasting; one from 12 to 18 pounds will take three hours and a quarter.

To Broil.

This culinary branch is very confined, but excellent as respects chops or steaks, to cook which in perfection the fire should be clear and brisk, and the grid-iron set on it slanting, to prevent the fat dropping in it. In addition, quick and frequent turning will insure good flavor in the taste of the article cooked.

To Fry Meats, etc.

Be always careful to keep the frying-pan clean, and see that it is properly tinned. When frying any sort of fish, first dry them in a cloth, and then flour them. Put into the pan plenty of dripping, or hog's lard, and let it be boiling hot before putting in the fish. Butter is not so good for the purpose, as it is apt to burn and blacken, and make them soft. When they are fried, put them in a dish or hair-seive, to drain, before they are sent to table. Olive oil is the best article for frying, but it is very expensive, and bad oil spoils every thing that is dressed with it. Steaks and chops should be put in when the liquor is hot, and done quickly, of a light brown, and turned often. Sausages should be done gradually, which will prevent their bursting.

Corned Beef.

Fifty pounds of beef, three pounds of coarse salt, one ounce of saltpetre, three-quarters of a pound of sugar, two gallons of water. Mix the above ingredients together and pour over the meat. Cover the tub closely.

To Pot Beef.

Cut it small, add to it some melted butter, two anchovies boned and washed, and a little of the best pepper, beat fine. Put them into a marble mortar, and beat them well together till the meat is yellow; put it into pots and cover with clarified butter.

To Pot Leg of Beef.

Boil a leg of beef till the meat will come off the bone easily; then mix it with a cow heel, previously cut into thin pieces, and season the whole with salt and spice; add a little of the liquor in which the leg of beef was boiled, put it into a cheese-vat, or cullender, or some other vessel that will let the liquor run off; place a very heavy weight over it, and it will be ready for use in a day or two. It may be kept in souse made of bran boiled in water, with the addition of a little vinegar.

Dried Beef.

Have the rounds divided, leaving a piece of the sinew to hang up by; lay the pieces in a tub of cold water for an hour; then rub each piece of beef that will weigh fifteen or twenty pounds, with a handful of brown sugar and a tablespoonful of saltpetre, pulverized, and a pint of fine salt; sprinkle fine salt in the bottom of a clean tight barrel, and lay the pieces in, strewing a little coarse salt between each piece; let it lie two days; then make the brine in a clean tub, with cold water and ground alum salt — stir it well; it must be strong enough to bear an egg half up; put in half a pound of best brown sugar and a tablespoonful of saltpetre to each gallon of the salt and water, pour it over the beef, put a clean large stone on the top of the meat to keep it under the pickle (which is very important), put a cover on the barrel, examine it occasionally to see that the pickle does not leak, and if it should need more, add of the same strength. Let it stand six weeks, then hang it up in the smoke-house, and after it has drained, smoke it moderately for ten days, it should then hang in a dry place. Before cooking let it soak for twenty-four hours; a piece that weighs fifteen or twenty pounds should boil two hours — one half the size, one hour; and a small piece should soak six or twelve hours, according to size.

Potted Lobster or Crab.

This must be made with fine hen lobsters when full of spawn, boil them thoroughly; when cold, pick out all the solid meat, and pound it in a mortar; it is usual to add, by degrees, (a very little) finely powdered mace, black or Cayenne pepper, salt, and, while pounding, a little butter. When the whole is well mixed, and beat to the consistence of paste, press it down hard in a preserving-pot, pour clarified butter over it, and cover it with wetted bladder.

To Pot Shad.

Clean the shad, take off the tail, head, and all the fins, then cut it in pieces, wash and wipe it dry. Season each piece well with salt and Cayenne pepper. Lay them in layers in a stone-jar, place between each two layers some allspice, cloves, and stick-cinnamon. Cover them with good cider-vinegar, tie thick paper over the jar, place them in a moderate oven, and let them remain three or four hours.

To make Bologna Sausages.

Take a pound of beef suet, a pound of pork, a pound of bacon fat and lean, and a pound of beef and veal. Cut them very small. Take a handful of sage leaves chopped fine, with a few sweet herbs. Season pretty high with pepper and salt, take a large well-cleaned gut and fill it. Set on a saucepan of water, and when it boils, put it in, first pricking it to prevent its bursting. Boil it one hour.

To make Oxford Sausages.

Take 1 pound of young pork, fat and lean, without skin or gristle; 1 pound of beef suet, chopped fine together; put in ½ pound of grated bread; half the peel of a lemon, shred; a nutmeg grated; 6 sage leaves, chopped fine; a teaspoonful of pepper; and 2 of salt; some thyme, savory, and marjoram, shred fine. Mix well together and put it close down in a pan till used. Roll them out the size of common sausages, and fry them, in fresh butter, of a fine brown, or broil them over a clear fire, and send them to table hot.

To make Epping Sausages.

Take 6 pounds of young pork, quite free from skin, gristle, or fat; cut it small, and beat it fine in a mortar. Chop 6 pounds of beef suet very fine, shred a handful of sage leaves fine, spread the meat on a clean dresser, and shake the sage over it. Shred the rind of a lemon very fine, and throw it with sweet herbs on the meat. Grate 2 nutmegs, to which put a teaspoonful of pepper, and a tablespoonful of salt. Throw the suet over it, and mix all well together. Put it down close in the pot, and when used, roll it up with as much egg as will make it smooth.

Hog's Head Cheese.

Take off the ears and noses of four heads, and

pick out the eyes, and lay them in salt and water all night, then wash and put them on to boil, take out the bones carefully, chop and season them well, and pack it in bowls; they will turn out whole, and may be eaten cold with vinegar, or fried as sausage.

Bouilli.

Take the thin ends of prime ribs; bubble them slowly with a little salt, pepper, 3 bay leaves, 1 onion stuck with cloves, and a bunch of sweet herbs. Remove all the scum, and bubble till a skewer will penetrate without force.

Scrapple.

Take 8 pounds of scraps of pork, that will not do for sausage, boil it in 4 gallons of water; when tender, chop it fine, strain the liquor and pour it back into the pot; put in the meat, season it with sage, summer savory, salt and pepper to taste, stir in a quart of corn meal; after simmering a few minutes, thicken it with buckwheat flour very thick; it requires very little cooking after it is thickened, but must be stirred constantly.

To Stew Oysters.

Put your oysters with all their liquor into a saucepan; no water; to every dozen add a lump of butter size of a walnut, salt, black pepper, a blade of mace, two bay leaves; bubble for five minutes, add a little cream, shake all well together, and turn them out, grating a little nutmeg on each oyster as it lies in the sauce.

Stewed Oysters.

One hundred oysters, ½ a pint of cream, 2 ounces of butter, beat the butter smooth with a *little* flour. Put the oysters in a pan over the fire; when they become hot, stir in the cream, butter, and flour. Season to your taste with salt, mace, and pepper. They should be served as soon as they are taken off the fire.

Oysters Roasted.

Roast your oysters over a quick fire till they are done dry, but not scorched; turn them out on the plate of a brazier, without any of their liquor; add a large lump of butter. Set the plate over the lamp when the butter is melted, add a gill of Madeira, a little salt and Cayenne.

Another Mode.

Put the oysters alive in the shell upon a good fire and leave them till their shells open *a little*; then take them off, open them on a plate, and season with salt and pepper *only*. Thus they are excellent for delicate stomachs.

Scalloped Oysters.

One hundred oysters, a baker's loaf crumbed, four eggs boiled hard; salt and cayenne pepper to taste. Chop the eggs very fine and mix with the crumbs, which season highly with cayenne and salt. Cover the bottom of a deep pie-dish with the eggs and crumbs; then with a fork, place a layer of oysters with two or three small pieces of butter, and so continue until all are in, reserving sufficient crumbs for the cover. For those who like it, a little mace may be added. Bake in a quick oven three-quarters of an hour. Serve hot.

Fried Oysters.

Take fine large oysters, free them from all the small particles of shell, then place them on a clean towel and dry them. Have ready some crackers made very fine, which season with a little salt, black and cayenne pepper of equal proportions. Beat as many eggs and cream mixed, as will moisten all the oysters required, then with a fork dip each one in the egg and lay them on the cracker, and with the back of a spoon pat the cracker close to the oyster; lay them on a dish, and so continue until are done. Put in a frying-pan an equal portion of butter and lard or sweet oil boiling hot, then put in as many oysters as the pan will hold without allowing them to touch, and fry quickly a light brown on both sides. A few minutes will cook them. Send to table hot.

Panned Oysters.

Take fifty large oysters, remove every particle of shell which may adhere to them, put them into a colander and pour over a little water to rinse them. After letting them drain, put them into a stewpan with a quarter of a pound of butter, salt, black and red pepper to taste. Put them over a clear fire, and stir while cooking. As soon as they commence to shrink remove them from the fire, and send to table hot in a well (covered) heated dish.

Codfish-Cakes.

Wash the fish, and after remaining in water all night, boil it. Take out all the bones, cut up very fine and mix with an equal quantity of potatoes; add a piece of butter, cayenne, and a little more salt, if necessary. Then make it out into small round cakes, and fry in butter or beef drippings, a light brown on both sides.

To Boil Lobsters.

The medium sized are best; put them alive into a kettle of boiling water which has been salted, and let them boil from half an hour to three-quarters, according to their size. When done take them out of the kettle, wipe them clean, and rub the shell with a little sweet oil, which will give a clear red appearance. Crack the large claws without mashing them, and with a sharp knife split the body and tail from end to end. Send to table and dress as follows: after mincing it very fine add salt, cayenne pepper, mustard, salad oil, and vinegar to taste, observing to mix all well together.

To Pickle Oysters.

Drain off the liquor from one hundred oysters, wash them and put to them a table-spoonful of salt and a tea-cup of vinegar; let them simmer over the fire about ten minutes, taking off the scum as it rises; then take out the oysters and put to their own liquor a tablespoonful of whole black pepper and a teaspoonful of mace and cloves; let it boil five minutes, skim and pour it over the oysters in a jar.

To Spice Oysters.

One hundred oysters, one dozen cloves, two dozen allspice, mace, cayenne pepper, and salt to taste. Strain the liquor through a sieve, put it in a saucepan, and add the oysters, spice, pepper, salt, and half a pint of cider vinegar. Place them over a slow fire, and as soon as they boil take them off. Pour them into a large bowl and set them away to cool. When cold cover them close.

Flounders—a la crème.

Scale, clean, and wrap your fish in a cloth, boil it gently in plenty of water well salted; when done drain it carefully without breaking, lay it on your dish and mask it with cream or white onion sauce.

French Stew of Peas and Bacon.

Cut about one-quarter of a pound of fresh bacon into thin slices, soak it on the fire in a stewpan until it is almost done; then put about a quart of peas to it, a good bit of butter, a bunch of parsley, and two spoonfuls of catsup; simmer on a slow fire and reduce the sauce; take out the parsley and serve the rest together.

New England Chowder.

Have a good haddock, cod, or any other solid fish; cut it in pieces three inches square, put a pound of fat salt pork in strips into the pot, set it on hot coals and fry out the oil; take out the pork and put in a layer of fish, over that a layer of onions in slices, then a layer of fish with slips of fat salt pork, then another layer of onions; and so on alternately until your fish is consumed; mix some flour with as much water as will fill the pot, season with black pepper and salt to your taste, and boil it for half an hour. Have ready some crackers (Philadelphia pilot bread if you can get it) soaked in water till they are a little softened, throw them into your chowder five minutes before you take it up. Serve in a tureen.

Daniel Webster's Chowder.

Four tablespoonfuls of onions, fried with pork; a quart of boiled potatoes well mashed; 1½ pounds of sea biscuit broken; 1 teaspoonful of thyme, mixed with one of summer savory: ½ bottle of mushroom catsup; one bottle of port or claret; ¼ of a nutmeg, grated; a few cloves, mace, and allspice; 6 pounds fish (sea-bass or cod), cut into slices; 25 oysters, a little black pepper, and a few slices of lemon. The whole put in a pot and covered with an inch of water, boiled for an hour and gently stirred.

Soup Maigre.

Take of veal, beef cut into small pieces, and scrag of mutton, 1 pound each; put them into a saucepan, with 2 quarts of water; put into a clean cloth 1 ounce of barley, an onion, a small bundle of sweet herbs, 3 or 4 heads of celery cut small, a little mace, 2 or 3 cloves, 3 turnips pared and each cut in two, a large carrot cut into small pieces, and a young lettuce. Cover the pot close, and let it stew very gently for six hours. Then take out the spice, sweet herbs, and onion, and pour all into a soup-dish, seasoned with salt.

Another Soup Maigre.

Quarter of a pound of butter placed in a stew-pan, add to it 2 tablespoonsful of flour, ½ pint of milk. Then add cold vegetables chopped very fine, and stew together a quarter of an hour. Before sent up, beat the yolks of two eggs, add ¼ of a pint of cream, and a little pepper and salt to taste.

Portable Soup.

Cut into small pieces 3 large legs of veal, 1 of beef, and the lean part of a ham; lay the meat in a large cauldron, with a quarter of a pound of butter at the bottom, 4 ounces of anchovies, and 2 ounces of mace. Cut small 6 heads of clean washed celery, freed from green leaves, and put them into the cauldron, with 3 large carrots cut thin. Cover all close, and set it on a moderate fire. When the gravy begins to draw, keep taking it off till it is all extracted. Then cover the meat with water, let it boil gently for four hours, then strain it through a hair-sieve into a clean pan, till it is reduced to one-third. Strain the gravy drawn from the meat into a pan, and let it boil gently, until it be of a glutinous consistence. Take care and skim off all the fat as it rises. Watch it when it is nearly done, that it does not burn; next season it with Cayenne pepper, and pour it on flat earthen dishes, a quarter of an inch thick. Let it stand till the next day, and then cut it out by round tins larger than a silver dollar. Set the cakes in dishes in the sun to dry, and turn them often. When fully dried, put them into a tin box with a piece of clean white paper between each, and keep them in a dry place. If made in frosty weather it will soon become solid. This kind of soup is exceedingly convenient for private families, for by putting one of the cakes in a saucepan with about a quart of water, and a little salt, a basin of good broth may be made in a few minutes. It will likewise make an excellent gravy for roast turkeys, fowls, and game.

Asparagus Soup.

Put a small broiled bone to 1½ pints of peas, and water in proportion, a root of celery, a small bunch of sweet herbs, a large onion, Cayenne pepper, and salt to taste; boil it briskly for five hours, strain and pulp it; then add a little spinach-juice, and asparagus boiled and cut into small pieces. A teaspoonful of walnut soy, and a teaspoonful of mushroom catsup, answers as well as the bone.

Giblet Soup.

Take 4 pounds of gravy beef, 2 pounds of scrag of mutton, and 2 pounds of scrag of veal; boil them in 2 gallons of water, stew them gently till it begins to taste well, pour it out and let it stand till cold, skim off all the fat. Take 2 pair of giblets well scalded, put them to the broth, and simmer them till they are very tender. Take them out and strain the soup through a cloth. Put a piece of butter rolled in flour into the stewpan, with some fine chopped parsley, chives, a little pennyroyal, and sweet marjoram. Place the soup over a slow fire, put in the giblets, fried butter, herbs, a little Madeira wine, some salt, and Cayenne pepper; when the herbs are tender, send the soup and giblets intermixed to table. This forms a very savory dish.

Charitable Soup.

Take the liquor of meat boiled the day before, with the bones of leg and shin of beef; add to the liquor as much as will make 130 quarts, also the meat of 10 stones of leg and shin of beef, and 2 ox-heads, all cut in pieces; add 2 bunches of carrots, 4 bunches of turnips, 2 bunches of leeks, ½ a peck of onions, 1 bunch of celery, ½ a pound of pepper, and some salt. Boil it for six hours. Either oatmeal or barley may be put in to thicken it, if thought necessary. This soup may be used at any gentleman's table.

Veal Gravy Soup.

Garnish the bottom of the stewpan with thin pieces of lard, then a few slices of ham, slices of veal cutlet, sliced onions, carrots, parsnips, celery, a few cloves upon the meat, and a spoonful of broth; soak it on the fire in this manner till the veal throws out its juice; then put it on a stronger fire, till the meat catches to the bottom of the pan, and is brought to a proper color; then add a sufficient quantity of light broth, and simmer it on a slow fire till the meat is thoroughly done; add a little thyme and mushrooms. Skim and sift it clear for use.

Beef Gravy Soup.

Cut slices of lean beef, according to the quantity wanted, which place in a stew-pan, upon sliced onions and roots, adding two spoonsful of fat broth; soak this on a slow fire for half an hour, stirring it well; when it catches a proper color add thin broth made of suitable herbs, with a little salt over it.

A Cheap Rice and Meat Soup.

Put a pound of rice and a little pepper and broth herbs into two quarts of water, cover them close, and simmer very softly; put in a little cinnamon, two pounds of good ox-cheek, and boil the whole till the goodness is incorporated by the liquor.

Another Cheap Soup.

Take an ox-cheek, 2 pecks of potatoes, ¼ of a peck of onions, ⅔ of a pound of salt, and 1½ ounces of pepper — to be boiled in 90 pints of water, on a slow fire until reduced to 60. A pint of this soup, with a small piece of meat, is a good meal for a hearty working man. Some of every vegetable, with a few herbs, may be added.

Herring Soup.

Take 8 gallons of water, and mix it with 5 pounds of barley-meal. Boil it to the consistence of a thick jelly. Season it with salt, pepper, vinegar, sweet herbs, and, to give it a gratifying flavor, add the meat of 4 red herrings pounded.

To prepare a Nutritious Soup.

A pound of Scotch barley, with sufficient time allowed in the cooking, will make a gallon of water into a tolerable pudding consistency. A pint basin filled with it will hold a spoon upright, when at its proper degree of warmth for eating. Thoroughly steeped, it will produce a rich pulp, the form of the grains being nearly lost. Five hours' exposure, in a moderately heated oven, will be sufficient; and it may be improved by an hour or two more.

Amongst other means for such preparation, when a baker's oven has been emptied of its bread, a pan of 1 gallon size may be put in to steep its contents during the preceding night, and then renew the usual baking in the morning. What has been lost by evaporation, may be restored by the addition of warm water. All the seasoning requisite to make it as savory as plain family dishes generally are, will be about 3 large onions, 1 ounce of salt, and ⅛ of an ounce of pepper. This seasoning should be put in before sending it to the oven.

Scotch Broth.

Set on the fire 4 ounces of pearl barley, with 6 quarts of salt water; when it boils skim it, and add what quantity of salt beef or fresh brisket you choose, and a marrow-bone or a fowl, with 2 pounds of either lean beef or mutton, and a good quantity of leeks, cabbages, or savoy, or you may use turnips, onions, and grated carrots; keep it boiling for at least 4 or 5 hours; but, if a fowl be used, let it not be put in till just time enough to bring it to table when well done, for it must be served separately.

A Vegetable Soup.

Take 1 onion, 1 turnip, 2 pared potatoes, 1 carrot, 1 head of celery; boil them in 3 pints of water till the vegetables are cooked; add a little salt; have a slice of bread toasted and buttered, put it into a bowl, and pour the soup over it. Tomatoes, when in season, form an agreeable addition.

Pea Soup.

Leave 1 pint of peas in the pot with the water they were boiled in; make a thickening of flour, milk and butter, seasoned with salt, pepper, parsley and thyme; toast 2 or 3 slices of bread; cut it up in the tureen; and when the soup has boiled about 10 minutes, pour it over.

Children are mostly fond of pea soup, and it seldom disagrees with them. A few slices of fat ham will supply the place of butter.

Corn Soup.

To each quart of young corn, cut from the cob, allow 3 pints of water. Put the corn and water on to boil, and as soon as the grains are tender, have ready 2 ounces of sweet butter mixed with 1 tablespoonful of flour. Stir the flour and butter into the corn and water, and let it boil 10 or 15 minutes longer. Just before the soup is taken out of the pot beat up an egg, and stir into it, with salt and pepper to your taste.

Noodles for Soup.

Beat up an egg, and to it add as much flour as will make a very stiff dough. Roll it out in a thin sheet, flour it, and roll it up closely, as you would do a sheet of paper. Then with a sharp knife cut it in shavings about like cabbage for slaw; flour these cuttings to prevent them from adhering to each other, and add them to your soup whilst it is boiling. Let them boil 10 minutes.

Pepperpot.

Cut in small pieces 3 pounds of tripe, put it on to boil in as much water as will cover it, allowing a teaspoonful of salt to every quart of water. Let it boil 3 hours, then have ready 4 calves'-feet, which have been dressed with the tripe, and add as much water as will cover them; also 3 onions sliced, and a small bunch of sweet herbs chopped fine. Half an hour before the pepperpot is done add four potatoes cut in pieces; when these are tender add 2 ounces of butter rolled in flour, and season the soup highly with Cayenne pepper. Make some dumplings of flour and butter and a little water — drop them into the soup; when the vegetables are sufficiently soft, serve it.

The calves'-feet may be served with drawn butter. Any kind of spice may be added. If allspice or cloves are used, the grains should be put in whole.

Clam Soup.

Wash the shells and put them in a kettle. Put the kettle where it will be hot enough to cause a steam from the clams, which will open them. To 1 quart of clams put 2 quarts of water, and then proceed as for oyster soup.

Oyster Soup.

To 1 quart of oysters add 1 quart of water. Pour the water on the oysters and stir them. Then take them out one at a time, so that no small particles of shell may adhere to them. Strain the liquor through a sieve, put it in a stew-pan over the fire with a little mace, and season with red pepper and salt to your taste. When this boils put in your oysters. Let them boil again; then add ½ pint of cream and serve hot.

Chicken Soup.

Clean and wash a large fat chicken, put it on to boil in about 4 quarts of water, to which add ½ a teacupful of rice, 1 onion cut fine, 4 or 5 turnips pared and cut into small pieces, 1 dessertspoonful of white sugar (a little sugar, not more than a tablespoonful to 3 or 4 quarts, may be added, scorched brown, to any soup while boiling, with advantage), a little sweet marjoram, with salt and red-pepper to taste. After boiling over a slow fire for rather more than an hour, put in 6 white potatoes, pared, washed, and cut in quarters, which, as soon as done, add a little parsley minced fine. When done, if not sufficiently seasoned, more may be added. Place the chicken on a dish, which garnish with sprigs of double parsley, the soup in a tureen, and send to table hot.

Chicken Broth.

Take a nice tender chicken, and after cleaning it very nicely, cut it into quarters, and put it into a soup-kettle with 3 quarts of water, 2 tablespoonsful of rice, or pearl-barley, and salt to taste. Let it boil slowly, and as the scum rises remove it. When thoroughly done place the chicken on a dish, garnish with double parsley, and eat with drawn butter, and serve the broth in a deep-covered china bowl or tureen, and send to table hot.

Mutton Broth.

Take 3 pounds of the scrag-end of a neck of very fresh mutton, cut it into several pieces, wash them in cold water, and put them into a stewpan with 2 quarts of cold spring-water; place the stewpan on the fire to boil, skim it well, and then add a couple of turnips cut into slices, a few branches of parsley, a sprig of green thyme, and a little salt. When it has boiled gently by the side of the stove for an hour and a half, skim off the fat from the surface, and then let it be strained through a lawn sieve into a basin and kept for use.

Drawn Butter.

Half pint of boiling water, 2 teaspoonsful of flour, and 2 ounces of butter. Mix the flour and butter together until they are perfectly smooth. Stir this into the boiling water, and add salt to taste. If made with milk in place of water, less butter will answer.

Common Sauce.

Soak slices of veal, ham, onions, parsnips, 2 cloves of garlic, 2 heads of cloves, then add broth, a glass of white wine, and 2 slices of lemon; simmer it over a slow fire, skim it well, and sift it.

Miser's Sauce.

Chop 5 or 6 large onions, mix a little verjuice, or vinegar, pepper, salt, and a little butter; serve it up either warm or cold.

Parson's Sauce.

Chop lemon-peel very fine, with 2 or 3 pickled cucumbers, a bit of butter, salt, and coarse pepper; a little flour, with 2 spoonsful of catsup, and stew it on the fire without boiling.

Nonpareil Sauce.

Take a slice of boiled ham, as much breast of roasted fowl, a pickled cucumber, a hard yolk of an egg, one anchovy, a little parsley, and a head of shallot, chopped very fine: boil it a moment in good catsup, and use it for meat or fish.

Nivermoise Sauce.

Put in a small stewpan a couple of slices of ham, a clove of garlic, 2 cloves, a laurel-leaf, sliced onions, and roots; let it catch the fire a little. Then add a small quantity of broth, 2 spoonsful of catsup, and a spoonful of the best vinegar. Simmer it for an hour on the side of the stove, then sift it in a sieve, and serve it for a high-flavored sauce.

Gravy Cakes.

Chop 2 legs of beef in pieces, put them into a pot of water, stew it over a slow fire a day and a night; then add onions, herbs, and spices as for gravy; continue stewing it till the meat is off the bones, and the gravy quite out; then strain the liquor into a milk-pan, to which quantity it should be reduced; when cold, take off the fat, put it into a saucepan, and add whatever is required to flavor it; simmer it on a slow fire till reduced to about 12 saucers two-thirds full, put them in an airy place till as dry as leather, put them in paper bags, and keep in a dry place.

Sailor's Sauce.

Chop a fowl's liver with 2 or 3 shallots, and a couple of truffles or mushrooms; simmer these in a spoonful of oil, 2 or 3 spoonsful of gravy, a glass of wine, a little salt and coarse pepper; simmer it about half an hour, and skim it very well before using.

Queen's Sauce.

Simmer crumbs of bread in good gravy, until it is quite thick, take it off the fire, and add a few sweet almonds pounded, 2 hard yolks of eggs, and a breast of fowl roasted, all pounded very fine; boil a sufficient quantity of cream to your sauce, and sift all together, then add pepper and salt; and warm it without boiling.

Tomato Catsup.

Boil tomatoes, full ripe, in their juice, to nearly the consistence of a pulp, pass them through a hair sieve, and add salt to the taste. Aromatize it sufficiently with clove, pepper, and nutmegs.

Catsup for Sea-stores.

Take a gallon of strong stale beer, a pound of anchovies washed from the pickle, the same of shallots peeled; ½ an ounce of mace, ½ an ounce of cloves, ¼ of an ounce of whole pepper, 3 or 4 large races of ginger, and 2 quarts of large mushroom flaps, rubbed to pieces. Cover these close, and let it simmer till half wasted. Then strain it through a flannel bag; let it stand till quite cold, and then bottle it. This may be carried to any part of the world; and a spoonful of it to a pound of fresh butter melted, will make a fine fish sauce, or will supply the place of gravy sauce. The stronger and staler the beer the better will be the catsup.

Another.—Chop 24 anchovies, having first boned them; put to them 10 shallots cut small, and a handful of scraped horse-radish, ¼ of an ounce of mace, a quart of white wine, a pint of water, and the same quantity of red wine; a lemon cut into slices, ½ a pint of anchovy liquor, 12 cloves, and the same number of peppercorns. Boil them together till it comes to a quart, then strain it off, cover it close, and keep it in a cold dry place. Two spoonsful of it will be sufficient for a pound of butter. It is a good sauce for boiled fowls, or, in the room of gravy, lowering it with hot water, and thickening it with a piece of butter rolled in flour.

Fish Sauce.

Take 1 pound of anchovies, a quart of claret, ¾ of a pint of white wine vinegar, ½ an ounce of cloves and mace, 2 races of ginger sliced, a little black pepper, the peel of a lemon, a piece of horse-radish, a large onion, a bunch of thyme and savory; set all these over a slow fire to simmer an hour, then strain it through a sieve; when cold put it in a bottle with the spice, but not the herbs. To a large coffee-cupful cold, put a pound of butter; stir it over the fire till it is as thick as cream; shake the bottle when used, and put no water to the butter.

Cream Sauce for a Hare.

Run the cream over the hare or venison just before frothing it, and catch it in a dish; boil it up with the yolks of two eggs, some onion, and a piece of butter rolled in flour and salt. Half a pint of cream is the proportion for two eggs.

Apple Sauce.

Pare and core tart apples, cut them in slices, rinse and put them in an earthern stewpan, set them on the fire, do not stir them until they burst and are done; mash them with a spoon, and when perfectly cool sweeten with white sugar to taste.

Sweet Sauce.

Mix 2 glasses of red wine, one of vinegar, 3 teaspoonsful of cullis, a bit of sugar, 1 sliced onion, a little cinnamon, and a laurel-leaf; boil them a quarter of an hour.

Nun's Butter.

Four ounces of butter; six ounces of sugar; as much wine as the butter will take. Beat the butter and sugar together, and gradually add the wine and a little nutmeg.

Brown Sauce.

Mix together one tablespoonful of moist sugar,

two of French vinegar, three of salad oil, a teaspoonful of mixed mustard, some pepper and salt, and serve.

A Dish of Macaroni.

Boil 4 ounces of macaroni till it is quite tender, then lay it on a sieve to drain, and put it into a stewpan with about a gill of cream, and a piece of butter rolled in flour; stew it five minutes and pour it on a plate. Lay Parmesan cheese toasted all over it, and send it up in a water-plate.

Cole-Slaw.

Get a fresh cabbage, take off the outside leaves, cut it in half, and with a sharp knife shave it into fine slips. Put it into a deep dish, and pour over it a dressing prepared in the following manner: Beat up 2 eggs, add to it 1 gill of vinegar and water mixed; place it on the range; when it begins to thicken stir in a piece of butter the size of a small walnut, a little salt; when cold pour it over the cabbage and stir it together; and before sending to table sprinkle with a little black pepper.

To boil Peas.

Early peas require about half an hour to boil, and the later kinds rather longer; the water should boil when they are put in; when they are tough and yellow, they may be made tender and green by putting in a little pearl-ash or ashes tied up in a bag, just before they are taken up; this will tender all green vegetables, but do not put too much; when done dip them out; drain and season them with butter, pepper and salt; put a bunch of parsley in the middle of the dish.

String Beans.

These, to be tender, should be boiled from three to four hours, after the strings have been very carefully removed. Add a little butter, salt and black pepper when they are dished.

Potatoes.—Fourteen ways of Dressing Them.

General Instructions. — The vegetable kingdom affords no food more wholesome, more easily prepared, or less expensive than the potato; yet, although this most useful vegetable is dressed almost every day, in almost every family—for one plate of potatoes that comes to table as it should, ten are spoiled.

Be careful in your choice of potatoes; no vegetable varies so much in color, size, shape, consistence and flavor.

Choose those of a large size, free from blemishes, and fresh, and buy them in the mould; they must not be wetted till they are cleaned to be cooked. Protect them from the air and frost by laying them in heaps in a cellar, covering them with mats, or burying them in sand or in earth. The action of frost is most destructive; if the considerable, the life of the vegetable is destroyed, and the potato speedily rots.

1. *Potatoes boiled.* — Wash them, but do not pare or cut them unless they are very large; fill a saucepan half full of potatoes of equal size (or make them so by dividing the larger ones), put to them as much cold water as will cover them about an inch; they are sooner boiled, and more savory than when drowned in water; most boiled things are spoiled by having too little water, but potatoes are often spoiled by too much; they must merely be covered, and a little allowed for waste in boiling, so that they may be just covered at the finish.

Set them on a moderate fire till they boil, then take them off, and set them by the side of the fire to simmer slowly till they are soft enough to admit a fork (place no dependence on the usual test of their skin cracking, which, if they are boiled fast, will happen to some potatoes when they are not half done, and the inside is quite hard); then pour the water off (if you let the potatoes remain in the water a moment after they are done enough they will become waxy and watery), uncover the saucepan, and set it at such a distance from the fire as will secure it from burning; their superfluous moisture will evaporate, and the potatoes will be perfectly dry and mealy.

You may afterwards place a napkin, folded up to the size of the saucepan's diameter, over the potatoes, to keep them hot and mealy till wanted.

This method of managing potatoes is in every respect equal to steaming them; and they are dressed in half the time.

There is such an infinite variety of sorts and sizes of potatoes, that it is impossible to say how long they will take to cook; the best way is to try them with a fork. Moderate sized potatoes will generally be done in fifteen or twenty minutes.

2. *Cold Potatoes Fried.* — Put a bit of clean dripping into a fryingpan; when it is melted, slice in your potatoes with a little pepper and salt, put them on the fire, keep stirring them; when they are quite hot they are ready.

3. *Potatoes Boiled and Broiled.* — Dress your potatoes as before directed, and put them on a gridiron over a very clear and brisk fire; turn them till they are brown all over, and send them up dry, with melted butter in a cup.

4. *Potatoes Fried in Slices or Shavings.* — Peel large potatoes, slice them about a quarter of an inch thick, or cut them in shavings round and round as you would peel a lemon; dry them well in a clean cloth, and fry them in lard or dripping. Take care that your fat and fryingpan are quite clean; put the pan on a quick fire, watch it, and as soon as the lard boils, and is still, put in the slices of potatoes, and keep moving them till they are crisp; take them up and lay them to drain on a sieve; send them up with a very little salt sprinkled over them.

5. *Potatoes Fried Whole.* —When nearly boiled enough, as directed in No. 1, put them into a stewpan with a bit of butter, or some nice clean beef drippings; shake them about often (for fear of burning them) till they are brown and crisp; drain them from the fat.

It will be an improvement to the three last receipts, previously to frying or broiling the potatoes, to flour them and dip them in the yolk of an egg, and then roll them in fine sifted bread-crumbs.

6. *Potatoes Mashed.* — When your potatoes are thoroughly boiled, drain dry, pick out every speck, etc., and while hot rub them through a colander into a clean stewpan; to a pound of potatoes put about half an ounce of butter, and a tablespoonful of milk; do not make them too moist; mix them well together.

7. *Potatoes Mashed with Onions.*—Prepare some boiled onions, by putting them through a sieve, and mix them with potatoes. In proportioning the onions to the potatoes, you will be guided by your wish to have more or less of their flavor.

8. *Potatoes Escaloped.* — Mash potatoes as directed in No. 6, then butter some nice clean scallop shells, or patty-pans; put in your potatoes, make them smooth at the top, cross a knife over them, strew a few fine bread-crumbs on them, sprinkle them with a paste brush with a few drops of melted butter, and then set them in a Dutch oven; when they are browned on the top, take them carefully out of the shells, and brown the other side.

9. *Colcannon.* — Boil potatoes and greens, or

spinach, separately; mash the potatoes, squeeze the greens dry, chop them quite fine, and mix them with the potatoes with a little butter, pepper and salt; put it into a mould, greasing it well first; let it stand in a hot oven for ten minutes.

10. *Potatoes Roasted.* — Wash and dry your potatoes (all of a size), and put them in a tin Dutch oven, or cheese toaster; take care not to put them too near the fire, or they will get burnt on the outside before they are warmed through.

Large potatoes will require two hours to roast them.

11. *Potatoes Roasted under Meat.* — Half boil large potatoes, drain the water from them, and put them into an earthern dish, or small tin pan, under meat that is roasting, and baste them with some of the dripping; when they are browned on one side, turn them and brown the other; send them up round the meat, or in a small dish.

12. *Potato Balls.* — Mix mashed potatoes with the yolk of an egg, roll them into balls, flour them, or egg and bread-crumb them, and fry them in clean drippings, or brown them in a Dutch oven.

13. *Potato Snow.* — The potatoes must be free from spots, and the whitest you can pick out; put them on in cold water; when they begin to crack strain the water from them, and put them into a clean stewpan by the side of the fire till they are quite dry and fall to pieces; rub them through a wire sieve on the dish they are to be sent up in, and do not disturb them afterwards.

14. *Potato Pie.* — Peel and slice your potatoes very thin into a pie dish; between each layer of potatoes put a little chopped onion (three-quarters of an ounce of onion is sufficient for a pound of potatoes), between each layer sprinkle a little pepper and salt, put in a little water, and cut about two ounces of fresh butter into little bits, and lay it on the top, cover it close with puff paste. It will take about an hour and a half to bake it.

To Broil Tomatoes.

Wash and wipe the tomatoes, and put them on the gridiron over live coals, with the stem down. When that side is brown turn them and let them cook through. Put them on a hot dish and send quickly to table, to be there seasoned to taste.

To Bake Tomatoes.

Season them with salt and pepper; flour them over, put them in a deep plate with a little butter, and bake in a stove.

To Steam Potatoes.

Put them clean-washed, with their skins on, into a steam saucepan, and let the water under them be about half boiling; let them continue to boil rather quickly, until they are done. If the water once relaxes from its heat the potato is sure to be affected, and to become soddened, let the quality be ever so good. A too precipitate boiling is equally disadvantageous, as the higher parts to the surface of the root begin to crack and open, while the centre part continues unheated and undecomposed.

Mushrooms.

Be careful in gathering mushrooms that you have the right kind: they are pink underneath and white on the top, and the skin will peel off easily, but it sticks to the poisonous ones; and the smell and taste of the good ones are not rank. After you have peeled them, sprinkle them with salt and pepper, and put them in a stewpan, with a little water and a lump of butter. Let them boil fast ten minutes, and stir in a thickening of flour and cream. They may be fried in butter, or broiled on a gridiron. They are sometimes very abundant in the fall, on ground that has not been ploughed for several years; they appear after a warm rain. They may be peeled, salted, and allowed to stand for some hours before cooking.

Chicken Pot-pie.

Take a pair of tender, fat chickens, singe, open, and cut them into pieces, by separating all the joints. Wash them through several waters, with eight or ten pared white potatoes, which put into a pan, and, after seasoning highly with salt and black pepper, dredge in three tablespoonsful of flour. Stir well together; then line the sides (half way up) of a medium-sized stew-kettle with paste made with two pounds of flour and one of butter. Put the chicken and potato into the kettle, with water just sufficient to cover them. Roll out some paste for a cover, the size of the kettle, and join it with that on the sides; cut a small opening in the centre, cover the kettle, and hang it over a clear fire or set it in the oven, as most convenient; turn the kettle round occasionally, that the sides may be equally browned. Two hours over a clear fire, or in a quick oven, will cook it. When done, cut the top crust into moderate-sized pieces, and place it round a large dish; then, with a perforated skimmer, take up the chicken and potatoes and place in the centre; cut the side crust and lay it on the top; put the gravy in a sauce-tureen, and send all to table hot.

Oatmeal Gruel.

Boil a handful of raisins in a pint of water for ten minutes. Mix 2 tablespoonsful of good oatmeal with a little cold water, and pour it into a saucepan, and boil fifteen or twenty minutes. Salt a little, and sweeten to taste.

Arrow-root.

Mix 2 tablespoonsful of arrow-root (Bermuda is the best) in a little water to a paste. Add a little lemon or orange peel to a pint of boiling water, and stir in the arrow-root while boiling. Cook it till clear, and season with nutmeg and sugar to taste, and wine, if desired. Half milk and half water, or all milk, may be used instead of water.

Tapioca.

Cover 3 tablespoonsful of tapioca with water, and soak it two or three hours. Add a little water to it, and boil till clear. Sweeten to taste, and eat alone or with cream.

Tapioca Jelly.

Wash thoroughly 2 tablespoonsful of tapioca; pour over it a pint of water, and soak for three hours. Place it then over a slow fire and simmer till quite clear. If too thick, add a little boiling water. Sweeten with white sugar, and flavor with a little wine.

Apple Tapioca.

Pare, core, and quarter 8 apples; take ½ tablespoonful tapioca which has been all night soaking in water; add ½ teacupful white sugar, and a little nutmeg or cinnamon. Put the tapioca into a stewpan to simmer 10 minutes; then add the apples, and simmer ten minutes more. When cold it will form a jelly around the apples.

To make Dr. Kitchener's Pudding.

Beat up the yolks and whites of 3 eggs; strain them through a sieve, and gradually add to them about a quarter of a pint of milk. Stir these well together. Mix in a mortar 2 ounces of moist sugar and as much grated nutmeg as will lie on a sixpence; stir these into the eggs and milk; then put in 4 ounces of flour, and beat it into a smooth batter; stir in, gradually, 8 ounces of very fine-chopped suet and 3 ounces of bread-crumbs. Mix all thoroughly together, at least half an hour before putting the pudding into the pot. Put it into an earthenware mould that is well buttered, and tie a pudding-cloth over it.

Nottingham Pudding.

Peel 6 good apples; take out the cores with the point of a small knife, but be sure to leave the apples whole; fill up where the core was taken from with sugar, place them in a pie-dish, and pour over them a nice light batter, prepared as for batter pudding, and bake them an hour in a moderate oven.

To make Yorkshire Pudding.

This nice dish is usually baked under meat, and is thus made. Beat 4 large spoonsful of flour, 2 eggs, and a little salt for fifteen minutes; put to them 3 pints of milk, and mix them well together; then butter a dripping-pan, and set it under beef, mutton, or veal, while roasting. When it is brown, cut it into square pieces, and turn it over, and, when the under side is browned also, send it to the table on a dish.

Dutch Pudding.

Cut a round piece out of the bottom of a Dutch loaf, and put that and the piece that was cut out into a quart of cold new milk, in the evening, and let it stand all night. If the milk is all soaked up by the morning, add some more. Put the piece in the bottom again, tie the loaf up in a cloth, and boil it an hour. Eat it with sugar, or with melted butter, white wine, and sugar sauce.

To make a Dish of Frumenty.

Boil an approved quantity of wheat; when soft, pour off the water, and keep it for use as it is wanted. The method of using it is to put milk to make it of an agreeable thickness; then, warming it, adding some sugar and nutmeg.

To make a Windsor Pudding.

Shred half a pound of suet very fine, grate into it half a pound of French roll, a little nutmeg, and the rind of a lemon. Add to these half a pound of chopped apples, half a pound of currants, clean washed and dried, half a pound of jar raisins, stoned and chopped, a glass of rich sweet wine, and 5 eggs, beaten with a little salt. Mix all thoroughly together, and boil it in a basin or mould for three hours. Sift fine sugar over it when sent to table, and pour white-wine sauce into the dish.

A Cheshire Pudding.

Make a crust as for a fruit pudding, roll it out to fourteen or fifteen inches in length and eight or nine in width; spread with raspberry jam or any other preserve of a similar kind, and roll it up in the manner of a collared eel. Wrap a cloth round it two or three times, and tie it tight at each end. Two hours and a quarter will boil it.

To make a Plain Pudding.

Weigh three-quarters of a pound of any odd scraps of bread, whether crust or crumb, cut them small, and pour on them a pint and a half of boiling water to soak them well. Let it stand till the water is cool, then press it out, and mash the bread smooth with the back of a spoon. Add to it a teaspoonful of beaten ginger, some moist sugar, and three-quarters of a pound of currants. Mix all well together, and lay it in a pan well buttered. Flatten it down with a spoon, and lay some pieces of butter on the top. Bake it in a moderate oven, and serve it hot. When cold it will turn out of the pan, and eat like good plain cheesecakes.

Transparent Pudding.

Beat up 8 eggs, put them into a stew-pan with half a pound of sugar, the same of butter, and some grated nutmeg, and set it on the fire, stirring it till it thickens; then pour it into a basin to cool. Set a rich paste round the edge of your dish, pour in your pudding, and bake it in a moderate oven. A delicious and elegant article.

A Potato Rice Pudding.

Wash a quarter of a pound of whole rice; dry it in a cloth and bent it to a powder. Set it upon the fire, with a pint and a half of new milk, till it thickens, but do not let it boil. Pour it out, and let it stand to cool. Add to it some cinnamon, nutmeg, and mace, pounded; sugar to the taste; half a pound of suet shred very small, and 8 eggs well beaten with some salt. Put to it either half a pound of currants, clean washed and dried by the fire, or some candied lemon, citron, or orange peel. Bake it half an hour with a puff crust under it.

Swiss Pudding.

Butter your dish; lay in it a layer of bread-crumbs, grated very fine; then boil 4 or 5 apples very tender; add a little butter. nutmeg, and fine-sifted sugar. Mix all up together, and lay on the bread-crumbs, then another layer of the crumbs; then add pieces of fresh butter on the top, and bake in a slow oven for a quarter of an hour, until it becomes a delicate brown. It may be eaten hot or cold.

Carrot Pudding.

Take ¼ peck of carrots, boil and mash them well; then add ½ pound flour, ½ pound currants, ½ pound raisins, ½ pound suet chopped fine, ½ cup of sugar, 2 tablespoonsful of cinnamon, 1 teaspoonful of allspice. Boil four hours, and serve hot with sauce flavored with Madeira wine.

Plain Rice Pudding.

One quart of milk, ½ a teacupful of rice, 2 teaspoonsful of sugar, ⅓ of a nutmeg, grated; a small piece of butter, size of hickory-nut. Pick and wash the rice; add all the ingredients. Stir all well together, and put in a slack oven one and a half to two hours. When done pour it in a pudding-dish, and serve when cold. If baked in an oven, take off the brown skin before it is poured in the pudding-dish, and replace it on the top of the pudding as before.

Indian Pone.

Put on one quart of water in a pot; as soon as it boils stir in as much Indian meal as will make a very thin batter. Beat it frequently while it is boiling, which will require ten minutes; then take it off, pour it in a pan, and add one ounce of butter, and salt to taste. When the batter is lukewarm, stir in as much Indian meal as will make it quite thick. Set it away to rise in the evening; in the morning make it out in small cakes, butter your tins, and bake in a moderate oven. Or the more common way is to butter pans, fill them three parts full, and bake them.

This cake requires no yeast.

Blackberry Mush.

Put your fruit in a preserving kettle; mash it to a pulp, with sugar enough to make it quite sweet. Set it over the fire, and, as soon as it begins to simmer, stir in very gradually two teaspoonsful of flour to a quart of fruit. It should be stirred all the time it is boiling. Serve it either warm or cold, with cream.

Raspberries may be cooked in the same way.

Potato Pudding.

Take 5 potatoes, boil, and mash them through a colander, with a little salt and 1 teacupful of milk or cream; ¼ pound of butter, ½ pound of sugar, beaten to a cream. Beat 4 eggs, and stir them with the batter; then add the mashed potatoes when cool. Season with 1 tablespoonful of brandy and 1 nutmeg, grated, with a little cinnamon. Bake in a quick oven.

Bread Pudding.

Take a pint measure of bread broken small or crumbed; boil a quart of milk, with a little salt, and pour it over the bread; cover and let the bread swell till it can be mashed smooth. Beat 4 eggs and stir into it, with 4 tablespoonsful of flour. Sprinkle a bag inside with flour, pour in the pudding, tie loosely, and boil one hour.

To make Oldbury Pudding.

Beat 4 eggs well, have ready a pint basin floured and buttered, pour in the eggs, and fill it up with new milk previously boiled, and when cold beat them together; put a white paper over the basin, cover with a cloth, and boil it twenty minutes. Send it up with wine and butter sauce.

Quince Pudding.

Scald the quinces tender, pare them thin, scrape off the pulp, mix with sugar very sweet, and add a little ginger and cinnamon. To a pint of cream put three or four yolks of eggs, and stir it into the quinces till they are of a good thickness. Butter the dish, pour it in, and bake it.

To make Raspberry Dumplings.

Make a puff paste, and roll it out. Spread raspberry jam, and make it into dumplings. Boil them an hour; pour melted butter into a dish, and strew grated sugar over it.

To make Raspberry and Cream Tarts.

Roll out thin puff paste, lay it in a patty-pan; put in raspberries, and strew fine sugar over them. Put on a lid, and when baked, cut it open, and put in ½ a pint of cream, the yolks of 2 eggs well beaten, and a little sugar.

To make Paste for Tarts.

Put an ounce of loaf sugar, beat and sifted, to 1 pound of fine flour. Make it into a stiff paste, with a gill of boiling cream, and 3 ounces of butter. Work it well, and roll it very thin.

Pie Crust.

Sift a pound and a half of flour, and take out a quarter for rolling, cut in it a quarter of a pound of lard, mixed with water and roll it out; cut half a pound of butter, and put it in at two rollings with the flour that was left out.

For making the bottom crust of pies, put half a pound of lard into a pound of flour, with a little salt, mix it stiff, and grease the plates before you make pies; always make your paste in a cool place, and bake it soon. Some persons prefer mixing crust with milk instead of water.

To make a good Paste for Large Pies.

Put to a peck of flour 3 eggs, then put in half a pound of suet and a pound and a half of butter. Work it up well and roll it out.

Another method. Take a peck of flour, and 6 pounds of butter, boiled in a gallon of water, then skim it off into the flour, with as little of the liquor as possible. Work it up well into a paste, pull it into pieces till cold, then make it into the desired form.

Puff Paste.

Sift a pound of flour. Divide 1 pound of butter into four parts, cut one part of the butter into the flour with a knife; make it into dough with water, roll it, and flake it with part of the butter. Do this again and again till it is all in. This will make enough crust for at least ten puffs. Bake with a quick heat, for ten or fifteen minutes.

To make a Puff Paste.

Take a quarter of peck of flour, and rub it into a pound of butter very fine. Make it up into a light paste with cold water just stiff enough to work it up. Then lay it out about as thick as a silver dollar; put a layer of butter all over, then sprinkle on a little flour, double it up, and roll it out again. Double and roll it with layers of butter three times, and it will be fit for use.

Mince Pies, not very rich.

Take 4 pounds of beef after it has been boiled and chopped, 1 pound of suet, 2 pounds of sugar, 2 pounds of raisins, and 4 pounds of chopped apples, mix these together with a pint of wine and cider, to make it thin enough; season to your taste with mace, nutmeg, and orange peel; if it is not sweet enough, put in more sugar. Warm the pies before they are eaten. Where persons are not fond of suet, put butter instead, and stew the apples instead of so much cider.

To make a Short Crust.

Put 6 ounces of butter to 8 ounces of flour, and work them well together; then mix it up with as little water as possible, so as to have it a stiffish paste; then roll it out thin for use.

Lemon Pudding.

Cut off the rind of 3 lemons, boil them tender, pound them in a mortar, and mix them with a quarter of a pound of Naples biscuits, boiled up in a quart of milk or cream; beat up 12 yolks and 6 whites of eggs. Melt a quarter of a pound of fresh butter, and put in half a pound of sugar, and a little orange flower water. Mix all well together, stir it over the fire till thick, and squeeze in the juice of half a lemon. Put puff paste round the dish, then pour in the pudding; cut candied sweetmeats, and strew over, and bake it for three quarters of an hour.

Batter Pudding.

Take 6 ounces of fine flour, a little salt and 3 eggs, beat up well with a little milk, added by degrees till the batter is quite smooth, make it the thickness of cream, put into a buttered pie-dish, and bake three quarters of an hour, or into a buttered and floured basin tied over tight with a cloth, boil one and a half or two hours.

Newmarket Pudding.

Put on to boil a pint of good milk, with half a lemon peel, a little cinnamon, boil gently for five or ten minutes, sweeten with loaf sugar, break the yolks of 5 and the whites of 3 eggs into a basin, beat them well, and add the milk, beat all well together, and strain through a fine hair sieve, have some bread and butter cut very thin, lay a layer of it in a pie dish, and then a layer of currants, and so on till the dish is nearly full, then pour the custard over it, and bake half an hour.

Newcastle, or Cabinet Pudding.

Butter a half melon mould, or quart basin, and stick all round with dried cherries, or fine raisins, and fill up with bread and butter, etc., as in the above, and steam it an hour and a half.

Vermicelli Pudding.

Boil a pint of milk, with lemon peel and cinnamon, sweeten with loaf sugar, strain through a sieve, and add a quarter of a pound of vermicelli, boil ten minutes, then put in the yolks of 5 and the whites of 3 eggs, mix well together, and steam it one hour and a quarter; the same may be baked half an hour.

Bread Pudding.

Make a pint of bread crumbs, put them into a

stewpan with as much milk as will cover them, the peel of a lemon, and a little nutmeg grated, a small piece of cinnamon; boil about ten minutes; sweeten with powdered loaf sugar; take out the cinnamon, and put in 4 eggs; beat all well together, and bake half an hour, or boil rather more than an hour.

Suet Pudding.

Suet, quarter of a pound; flour, 3 tablespoonfuls; eggs, 2; and a little grated ginger; milk, half a pint. Mince the suet as fine as possible, roll it with the rolling pin so as to mix it well with the flour; beat up the eggs, mix them with the milk, and then mix all together; wet your cloth well in boiling water, flour it, tie it loose, put into boiling water, and boil an hour and a quarter.

Custard Pudding.

Boil a pint of milk, and a quarter of a pint of good cream; thicken with flour and water, made perfectly smooth, till it is stiff enough to bear an egg on it; break in the yolks of 5 eggs, sweeten with powdered loaf sugar, grate in a little nutmeg, and the peel of a lemon; add half a glass of good brandy, then whip the whites of the 5 eggs till quite stiff, and mix gently all together; line a pie dish with good puff paste, and bake half an hour.

Ground rice, potato flour, panada, and all puddings made from powders, are, or may be, prepared in the same way.

Boiled Custards.

Put a quart of new milk into a stewpan, with the peel of a lemon cut very thin, a little grated nutmeg, a small stick of cinnamon; set it over a quick fire, but be careful it does not boil over; when it boils, set it beside the fire, and simmer ten minutes; break the yolks of 8, and the whites of 4 eggs into a basin, beat them well, then pour in the milk a little at a time, stirring it as quick as possible to prevent the eggs curdling; set it on the fire again, and stir well with a wooden spoon; let it have just one boil; pass it through a fine sieve; when cold, add a little brandy, or white wine, as may be most agreeable to palate; serve up in glasses, or cups.

Pumpkin Pudding.

Two and a half pounds of pumpkin, 6 ounces of butter, 6 eggs, 1 tablespoonful of wine, 2 tablespoonfuls of brandy, sugar to taste, 1 teaspoonful of cinnamon, and half a teaspoonful of ginger. Cut the pumpkin in slices, pare it, take out the seeds and soft parts; cut it into small pieces, and stew it on very little water, until it becomes tender, then press it in a colander until quite dry, turn it out in a pan, put in the butter and a little salt, mash it very fine. When cool, whisk the eggs until thick and stir in; then add sugar to taste, with the brandy, wine, and spice. This is sufficient for three or four puddings. Line your plates with paste, and bake in a quick oven.

Boiled Pudding.

One quart of milk, 5 eggs, 12 large tablespoonsful of flour.

Whisk the eggs very light, then put in the flour; add a little of the milk, and beat the whole perfectly smooth. Then pour in the remainder of the milk and enough salt, just to taste. Rinse your pudding-bag in cold water and flour it well inside. Pour in the mixture and allow a vacancy of from two to three inches at the top of the bag as the pudding will swell as soon as it begins to boil.

Be careful to tie the bag tight, and put it immediately in a large kettle of boiling water. Let it boil for two hours. As soon as it is taken out of the kettle, dip it for an instant into a pan of cold water. This prevents the pudding from adhering to the bag. Serve it immediately, as it would spoil by standing. It may be eaten with wine sauce, or any other sauce which may be preferred.

Indian Meal Pudding.

One quart of milk, 4 tablespoonfuls of very fine Indian meal, 3 ounces of butter, 5 eggs, ¼ of a pound of sugar, a little salt, half a gill of brandy, half a grated nutmeg, a little cinnamon. Boil the milk and stir in the meal, as if for mush.

Let it boil fifteen minutes, and beat it perfectly smooth.

Add the salt and butter while it is hot. As soon as it becomes cool stir in the eggs, which have been beaten very thick, and then the other ingredients. If the quarter of a pound of sugar does not make the mixture sufficiently sweet, more may be added.

Bake in a light paste like other puddings.

Rhubarb Pies.

Take off the skin from the stalks, cut them into small pieces; wash and put them to stew with no more water than that which adheres to them; when done, mash them fine and put in a small piece of butter, and when cool sweeten to taste and add a little nutmeg. Line your plates with paste, put in the filling, and bake in a quick oven. When done sift white sugar over.

Apple Dumplings.

Pare and core large tart apples. An apple-corer is better than a knife to cut out the seeds, as it does not divide the apple. Make a paste of 1 pound of flour and ¼ pound of butter; cover the apples with the paste, tie them in cloths, but do not squeeze them tightly.

Tender apples will boil in three quarters of an hour. Send to the table hot. Eat with butter and molasses, or sugar and cream.

Pancakes.

One pound of flour, 3 eggs beaten very light, as much milk as will make it as thick as cream, a little salt. Add the eggs to the flour with the milk; salt to taste. Stir all well together until perfectly smooth. Put in the pan a piece of lard about the size of a chestnut; as soon as it is hot put in two table spoonsful of the batter, and move the pan about to cause the batter to spread. When done on one side turn it over. Serve them hot with any sauce you please.

Fritters.

One pound and a quarter of flour, 3 half pints of milk, 4 eggs. Beat the eggs until thick, to which add the milk. Pass the flour in a pan and by degrees stir in the egg and milk, beating the whole until very smooth. Salt to taste. With a tablespoon drop them into hot lard, and fry a light brown on both sides. Send to table hot, and eat with nun's butter, or butter and molasses.

Cold Custard.

Take ¼ of a calf's rennet, wash it well, cut it in pieces and put it into a decanter with a pint of Lisbon wine. In a day or two it will be fit for use. To one pint of milk add a teaspoonful of the wine. Sweeten the milk and warm it a little and add the wine and nutmeg, stirring it slightly. Pour it immediately into a dish, move it gently to avoid place, and in a few minutes it will become a custard. It makes a tremor curd to put in the wine until the sugar. It may be eaten with sugar and cream.

Green Gooseberry Cheese.

Take 5 pounds of unripe rough gooseberries, cut off the blossoms and stems, and put them in cold water for an hour or two; then take them out, bruise them in a marble mortar, and put them into a brass pan or kettle over a clear fire, stirring them till tender; then add 4½ pounds of lump sugar pounded, and boil it till very thick and of a fine green color, stirring it all the time.

Ale Posset.

Take a small piece of white bread, put it into a pint of milk and set it over the fire. Then put some nutmeg and sugar into a pint of ale, warm it, and when the milk boils pour it upon the ale. Let it stand a few minutes to clear.

Coffee for Thirty People.

Put 1 pound of best coffee into a stewpan sufficiently large to hold 7 quarts of water; put it on the fire to dry, or roast the coffee (be sure to shake it for fear it should burn); then take it off the fire and put the whites of two eggs into it, stir it till it is mixed, then pour on it 6 quarts of water *boiling;* let it stand ½ of an hour covered closely, then strain it through a jelly-bag, or let it stand awhile to settle; pour into an urn and serve hot for use.

Cocoa.

Grind one teacupful of cocoa into a coffee-mill. Put it in a small bag made of very thin muslin, tie it close; put it in a pot with three half pints of boiling water and 1 pint of boiling milk. Boil the whole for half an hour, then pour it into another pot and send it to table. This will be found to suit invalids much better than chocolate, as it contains no butter.

Wine Whey.

Boil a pint of milk and pour into it a gill of wine (Madeira or Sherry), and let it boil again; take it from the fire and stand a few moments without stirring. Remove the curd and sweeten the whey.

Milk Punch.

Into a tumbler full of milk put 1 or 2 tablespoonsful of brandy, whiskey, or Jamaica rum. Sweeten it well, and grate nutmeg on the top.

Egg and Wine.

Beat a fresh raw egg well, and add 1 or 2 tablespoonsful of wine. Sweeten to taste.

Icing for Cakes.

Put 1 pound of fine sifted, treble-refined sugar into a basin, and the whites of three new-laid eggs; beat the sugar and eggs up well with a silver spoon until it becomes very white and thick; dust the cake over with flour and then brush it off, by way of taking the grease from the outside, which prevents the icing from running; put it on smooth with a palette knife, and garnish according to fancy; any ornaments should be put on immediately, for if the icing gets dry it will not stick on.

A Plain Poundcake.

Beat 1 pound of butter and 1 pound of sugar in an earthen pan until it is like a fine thick cream, then beat in 9 whole eggs till quite light. Put in a glass of brandy, a little lemon-peel shred fine, then work in 1¼ pound of flour; put it into the hoop or pan and bake it for an hour. A pound plum-cake is made the same with putting 1½ pound of clean washed currents, and ½ pound of candied lemon-peel.

Plain Gingerbread.

Mix 3 pounds of flour with 4 ounces of moist sugar, ½ ounce of powdered ginger, and 1¼ pounds of warm molasses; melt ½ pound of fresh butter in it, put it to the flour and make it a paste; then form it into nuts or cakes, or bake it in one cake.

Another Method.

Mix 6 pounds of flour with 2 ounces of caraway seeds, 2 ounces of ground ginger, 2 ounces of candied orange-peel, the same of candied lemon peel cut in pieces, a little salt, and 6 ounces of moist sugar; melt 1 pound of fresh butter in about ½ a pint of milk, pour it by degrees into 4 pounds of molasses, stir it well together, and add it, a little at a time, to the flour; mix it thoroughly, make it into a paste; roll it out rather thin and cut it into cakes with the top of a dredger or wine glass; put them on floured tins, and bake them in rather a brisk oven.

Gingerbread Poundcake.

Six eggs, 1 pint molasses, ½ pound sugar, ½ pound butter, wineglass of brandy, 1 lemon, 1 nutmeg, 3 tablespoonsful of ginger, 2 teaspoonfuls of ground cloves, 1 tablespoonful of cinnamon, 1 teaspoonful of soda. Flour enough to make a stiff batter.

Bath Cakes.

Mix well together ½ pound of butter, 1 pound of flour, 5 eggs, and a cupful of yeast. Set the whole before the fire to rise, which effected add a ¼ of a pound of fine powdered sugar, 1 ounce of caraways well mixed in, and roll the paste out into little cakes. Bake them on tins.

Shrewsbury Cakes.

Mix ½ pound of butter well beaten like cream, and the same weight of flour, 1 egg, 6 ounces of beaten and sifted loaf sugar, and ½ ounce of caraway seeds. Form these into a paste, roll them thin, and lay them in sheets of tin; then bake them in a slow oven.

Portugal Cakes.

Mix into a pound of fine flour a pound of loaf sugar, beaten and sifted, and rub it into a pound of butter, till it is thick, like grated white bread; then put to it 2 tablespoonfuls of rose-water, 2 of sack, and 10 eggs; work them well with a whisk, and put in 8 ounces of currants. Butter the tin pans, fill them half full, and bake them.

Ginger Cakes without Butter.

Take 1 pound of sugar, ¼ of a pound of ginger, 1 pint of water, 2 pounds of flour, and 8 caps of orange-peel. Pound and sift the ginger, and add 1 pint of water; boil it 5 minutes, then let it stand till cold. Pound the preserved orange-peel, and pass it through a hair-sieve; put the flour on a pasteboard, make a wall, and put in the orange-peel and ginger with the boiled water; mix this up to a paste and roll it out, prick the cakes before baking them.

Savoy Cakes.

To 1 pound of fine sifted sugar put the yolks of 10 eggs (have the whites in a separate pan), and set it, if in summer, in cold water, if there is any ice set the pan on it, as it will cause the eggs to be beat finer. Then beat the yolks and sugar well with a wooden spoon for 20 minutes, and put in the rind of a lemon grated; beat up the whites with a whisk, until they become quite stiff and white as snow. Stir them into the batter by degrees, then add ¾ of a pound of well-dried flour; finally, put it in a mould in a slack oven to bake.

Rice Cakes.

Beat the yolks of 15 eggs for nearly ½ an hour with a whisk, mix well with them 10 ounces of fine sifted loaf sugar, put in ½ a pound of ground rice, a little orange-water or brandy, and the rinds of 2 lemons grated, then add the whites of 7 eggs well beaten, and stir the whole together for ¼ of an hour. Put them into a hoop and set them in a quick oven for ½ an hour, when they will be properly done.

Banbury Cakes.

Take 1 pound of dough made for white bread, roll it out, and put bits of butter upon the same as for puff-paste, till 1 pound of the same has been worked in; roll it out very thin, then cut it into bits of an oval size, according as the cakes are wanted. Mix some good moist sugar with a little brandy, sufficient to wet it, then mix some clean washed currants with the former, put a little upon each bit of paste, close them up, and put the side that is closed next the tin they are to be baked upon. Lay them separate, and bake them moderately, and afterwards, when taken out, sift sugar over them. Some candied-peel may be added, or a few drops of the essence of lemon.

Cream Cakes.

Beat the whites of 9 eggs to a stiff froth, stir it gently with a spoon lest the froth should fall, and to every white of an egg grate the rinds of 2 lemons; shake in gently a spoonful of double refined sugar sifted fine, lay a wet sheet of paper on a tin, and with a spoon drop the froth in little lumps on it near each other. Sift a good quantity of sugar over them, set them in the oven after the bread is out, and close up the mouth of it, which will occasion the froth to rise. As soon as they are colored they will be sufficiently baked; lay them by 2 bottoms together on a sieve, and dry them in a cool oven.

Crumpets.

Set 2 pounds of flour with a little salt before the fire till quite warm; then mix it with warm milk and water till it is as stiff as it can be stirred; let the milk be as warm as it can be borne with the finger, put a cupful of this with 3 eggs well beaten, and mixed with 3 teaspoonfuls of very thick yeast; then put this to the batter and beat them all well together in a large pan or bowl, add as much milk and water as will make it into a thick batter; cover it close and put it before the fire to rise; put a bit of butter in a piece of thin muslin, tie it up, and rub it lightly over the iron hearth or frying-pan, then pour on a sufficient quantity of batter at a time to make one crumpet; let it do slowly, and it will be very light. Bake them all the same way. They should not be brown, but of a fine yellow.

Muffins.

Mix a quartern of fine flour, 1½ pints of warm milk and water, with ¼ of a pint of good yeast, and a little salt; stir them together for ½ of an hour, then strain the liquor into ¼ of a peck of fine flour; mix the dough well and set it to rise for an hour, then roll it up and pull it into small pieces, make them up in the hand like balls and lay a flannel over them while rolling, to keep them warm. The dough should be closely covered up the whole time; when the whole is rolled into balls, the first that are made will be ready for baking. When they are spread out in the right form for muffins, lay them on tins and bake them, and as the bottoms begin to change color turn them on the other side.

Another Recipe.

One quart of milk, 1 ounce of butter, 3 eggs, 4 tablespoonfuls of yeast; salt to taste; flour sufficient to make a thick batter. Warm the milk and butter together; when cool, whisk the eggs, and stir in. Then put 1½ pounds of flour in a pan, to which add the milk and eggs gradually. If not sufficiently thick for the batter to drop from the spoon, more flour may be added until of proper consistence, after beating well; then add the salt and yeast. Cover, and set the batter to rise in a warm place; when light, grease the muffin-rings and griddle, place the rings on, and fill them half-full of batter; when they are a light-brown, turn them over, ring and muffin together. The griddle should not be too hot, or else the muffin will be sufficiently browned before cooked through. Send to table hot; split open, and eat with butter.

Flannel Cakes.

One pint of fine Indian meal, 1 pint of wheat flour, 1 teaspoonful of salt, 2 gills of yeast. Mix the wheat and Indian meal together, with as much tepid water as will make it into a batter, not quite as thin as for buckwheat cakes; then add the salt and yeast, and set them in a moderately warm place to rise. When light, bake them on a griddle; butter, and send to table hot.

Common Buns.

Rub 4 ounces of butter into 2 pounds of flour, a little salt, 4 ounces of sugar, a dessertspoonful of caraways, and a teaspoonful of ginger; put some warm milk or cream to 4 tablespoonsful of yeast; mix all together into a paste, but not too stiff; cover it over and set it before the fire an hour to rise, then make it into buns, put them on a tin, set them before the fire for ¼ of an hour, cover over with flannel, then brush them with very warm milk and bake them of a nice brown in a moderate oven.

Cross Buns.

Put 2½ pounds of fine flour into a wooden bowl, and set it before the fire to warm; then add ½ a pound of sifted sugar, some coriander seed, cinnamon and mace, powdered fine; melt ½ a pound of butter in ½ a pint of milk; when it is as warm as the finger can bear, mix with it 3 tablespoonfuls of very thick yeast, and a little salt; put it to the flour, mix it to a paste, and make the buns as directed in the last receipt. Put a cross on the top, not very deep.

Rusks.

Beat up 7 eggs, mix them with ½ a pint of warm new milk, in which ¼ of a pound of butter has been melted, add ¼ of a pint of yeast, and 3 ounces of sugar; put them gradually into as much flour as will make a light paste nearly as thin as batter; let it rise before the fire ½ an hour, add more flour to make it a little stiffer, work it well and divide it into small loaves or cakes, about 5 or 6 inches wide, and flatten them. When baked and cold put them in the oven to brown a little. These cakes, when first baked, are very good buttered for tea; they are very nice cold.

Buckwheat Cakes.

One quart of buckwheat meal, 1 pint of wheat flour, ½ a teacupful of yeast; salt to taste. Mix the flour, buckwheat and salt with as much water, moderately warm, as will make it into a thin batter. Beat it well, then add the yeast; when well mixed, set it in a warm place to rise. As soon as they are very light, grease the griddle, and bake them a delicate brown, butter them with good butter, and eat while hot.

Sugar Biscuit.

Three pounds of flour; three-quarters of a pound of butter; one pound of sugar; one quart of sponge. Rub the flour, butter and sugar together, then add the sponge, with as much milk as will make a soft dough. Knead well and replace it in the pan to rise. This must be done in the afternoon; next morning knead lightly, make it into small cakes about the size of a silver dollar, and half an inch in thickness; place them on slightly buttered tins, one inch apart each way, set them in a warm place to rise; when light bake them in a quick oven; when done wash them over with a little water, not having the brush too wet, and let them remain on the tins until cool.

Dried Rusks.

Take sugar biscuits which have been baked the day previous; cut them in half between the upper and under crusts with a sharp knife. Place them on tins, and soon after the fire has ignited in the oven put them in, and as the heat increases they become gradually dried through. When a light brown they are done. These are universally liked by the sick.

English Macaroons.

One pound of sweet almonds; 1 pound and a quarter of sugar; 6 whites of eggs; and the raspings of 2 lemons. Pound the almonds very fine with 6 whites of eggs, feel the almonds, and if they are free from lumps they will do; then add the powdered sugar, and mix it well with the lemon raspings. Dress them in wafer paper of the required shape; bake them in a moderate heat, then let them stand till cold, cut the wafer paper round them, but leave it on the bottoms.

Sponge Biscuits.

Beat the yolks of 12 eggs for half an hour; then put in 1½ p unds of beaten sifted sugar, and whisk it till it rises in bubbles; beat the whites to a strong froth, and whisk them well with the sugar and yolks; work in 14 ounces of flour, with the rinds of 2 lemons grated. Bake them in tin moulds buttered, in a quick oven, for an hour; before they are baked sift a little fine sugar over them.

Bread Cheesecakes.

Slice a penny loaf as thin as possible; pour on it a pint of boiling cream, and let it stand two hours. Beat together 8 eggs, half a pound of butter, and a grated nutmeg; mix them into the cream and bread with half a pound of currants, well washed and dried, and a spoonful of white wine or brandy. Bake them in patty-pans, on a raised crust.

Rice Cheesecakes.

Boil 4 ounces of rice till it is tender, and then put it into a sieve to drain; mix with it 4 eggs well beaten up, half a pound of butter, half a pint of cream, 6 ounces of sugar, a nutmeg grated, a glass of brandy or ratafia water. Beat them all well together, then put them into raised crusts, and bake them in a moderate oven.

Apple Cakes.

Take half a quartern of dough, roll it out thin; spread equally over it 5 ounces each of coffee and sugar, a little nutmeg or allspice, and 2 ounces of butter; then fold and roll it again two or three times, to mix well the ingredients. Afterwards roll it out thin, and spread over it 4 rather large apples, pared, cored, and chopped small; fold it up, and roll until mixed. Let it stand to rise after. Half a pound of butter may be added.

Bread Cakes.

Take 1 quart of milk; stir in enough bread-crumbs to make a thin batter. Beat 3 eggs well and stir them in, adding a little salt; add 2 tablespoonfuls of flour. Bake them on the griddle and serve hot.

Waffles.

One quart of milk; 5 eggs; 2 ounces of butter. Warm the milk sufficiently to melt the butter; when cool separate the eggs and beat the yolks in the milk, with as much flour as will make it into a thick batter, then salt to taste; lastly, beat the whites until stiff and dry, which stir in, half at a time, very lightly. Bake in irons. This method is very good; by it they may be made in a short time.

Sally Lunn.

Rub 3 ounces of butter into a pound of flour; then add 3 eggs beaten very light, a little salt, 1 gill of yeast, and as much milk as will make it into a soft dough. Knead it well. Put it in a buttered pan, cover it, and set it in a warm place to rise. Bake in a moderate oven, and send to table hot. To be eaten with butter.

A Cheap Fruit-Cake.

Take 4 pounds of flour, 3 of butter, 3 of sugar, 2 of raisins, 1 of currants, 2 dozen eggs, an ounce of mace, 3 nutmegs, and a half pint of brandy. If you want it dark put in a little molasses. Mix the ingredients together, and bake it from two to three hours.

Common Jumbles.

Take a pound of flour, half a pound of butter, and three-quarters of a pound of sugar, 3 eggs, a little nutmeg, and rose brandy. Mix the butter and sugar together, and add the flour and eggs; mould them in rings, and bake them slowly.

Ginger-Nuts.

Half a pound of butter, half a pound of sugar, 1 pint of molasses, 2 ounces of ginger, half an ounce of ground cloves and allspice mixed, 2 tablespoonfuls of cinnamon, as much flour as will form a dough. Stir the butter and sugar together; add the spice, ginger, molasses, and flour enough to form a dough. Knead it well, make it out in small cakes, bake them on tins in a very moderate oven. Wash them over with molasses and water before they are put in to bake.

TO MAKE PUNCH.

For a gallon of punch take six fresh Sicily lemons; rub the outsides of them well over with lumps of double-refined loaf-sugar, until they become quite yellow; throw the lumps into the bowl; roll your lemons well on a clean plate or table; cut them in half and squeeze them with a proper instrument over the sugar; bruise the sugar, and continue to add fresh portions of it, mixing the lemon pulp and juice well with it. Much of the goodness of the punch will depend upon this. The quantity of sugar to be added should be great enough to render the mixture without water pleasant to the palate even of a child. When this is obtained, add gradually a small quantity of hot water, just enough to render the syrup thin enough to pass through the strainer. Mix all well together, strain it, and try if there be sugar enough; if at all sour add more. When cold put in a little cold water, and equal quantities of the best cognac brandy and old Jamaica rum, testing its strength by that infallible guide the palate. A glass of calves'-foot jelly added to the syrup when warm will not injure its qualities.

The great secret of making good punch may be given in a few words: *a great deal of fresh lemon-juice—more than enough of good sugar—a fair proportion of brandy and rum, and very little water.*

To make Nectar.

Put half a pound of loaf sugar into a large porcelain jug; add one pint of cold water; bruise and stir the sugar till it is completely dissolved; pour over it half a bottle of hock and one bottle of Madeira. Mix them well together, and grate in half a nutmeg, with a drop or two of the essence of lemon. Set the jug in a bucket of ice for one hour.

TO MAKE COFFEE.

The best coffee is imported from Mocha. It is said to owe much of its superior quality to being kept long. Attention to the following circumstances is likewise necessary. 1. The plant should be grown in a dry situation and climate. 2. The berries ought to be thoroughly ripe before they are gathered. 3. They ought to be well dried in the sun; and 4. Kept at a distance from any substance (as spirits, spices, dried fish, etc.) by which the taste and flavor of the berry may be injured.

To drink coffee *in perfection*, it should be made from the best Mocha or Java, or both mixed, carefully roasted, and after cooling for a few minutes, reduced to powder, and immediately infused; the decoction will then be of a superior description. But for ordinary use, Java, Laguayra, Maracaibo, Rio and other grades of coffee may be used. An equal mixture of Mocha, Java and Laguayra make an excellent flavor. We have been recently shown (1865) some samples of African coffee from Liberia, which is said to possess a very superior flavor. The following mode of preparing it may be adopted:

1. The berries should be carefully roasted, by a gradual application of heat, browning, but not burning them.

2. Grinding the coffee is preferable to pounding, because the latter process is thought to press out and leave on the sides of the mortar some of the richer oily substances, which are not lost by grinding.

5. A filtrating tin or silver pot, with double sides, between which hot water must be poured, to prevent the coffee from cooling, as practised in Germany, is good. Simple decoction, in this implement, with boiling water, is all that is required to make a cup of good coffee; and the use of isinglass, the white of eggs, etc., to fine the liquor, is quite unnecessary. By this means, also, coffee is made quicker than tea.

Generally, too little powder of the berry is given. It requires about one small cup of ground coffee to make four cups of decoction for the table. This is at the rate of an ounce of good powder to four common coffee cups. When the powder is put in the bag, as many cups of boiling water are poured over it as may be wanted, and if the quantity wanted is very small, so that after it is filtrated it does not reach the lower end of the bag, the liquor must be poured back three or four times, till it has acquired the necessary strength.

Another Method.—Pour a pint of boiling water on an ounce of coffee; let it boil five or six minutes, then pour out a cupful two or three times, and return it again; put two or three isinglass chips into it, or a lump or two of fine sugar; boil it five minutes longer. Set the pot by the fire to keep hot for ten minutes, and the coffee will be beautifully clear. Some like a small bit of vanilla. Cream or *boiled* milk should always be served with coffee.

In Egypt, coffee is made by pouring boiling water upon ground coffee in the cup; to which only sugar is added. For those who like it extremely strong, make only eight cups from three ounces. If not fresh roasted, lay it before a fire till hot and dry; or put the smallest bit of fresh butter into a preserving-pan; when hot throw the coffee into it, and toss it about till it be freshened.

Coffee most certainly promotes wakefulness, or, in other words, it suspends the inclination to sleep.

A very small cup of coffee, holding about a wineglassfull, called by the French *une demi tasse*, drunk after dinner very strong, without cream or milk, is apt to promote digestion.

Persons afflicted with asthma have found great relief, and even a cure, from drinking very strong coffee, and those of a phlegmatic habit would do well to take it for breakfast. It is of a rather drying nature, and with corpulent habits it would also be advisable to take it for breakfast.

Arabian Method of Preparing Coffee.

The Arabians, when they take their coffee off the fire, immediately wrap the vessel in a wet cloth, which fines the liquor instantly, makes it cream at the top, and occasions a more pungent steam, which they take great pleasure in snuffing up as the coffee is pouring into the cups. They, like all other nations of the East, drink their coffee without sugar.

People of the first fashion use nothing but Sultana coffee, which is prepared in the following manner: Bruise the outward husk or dried pulp, and put it into an iron or earthen pan, which is placed upon a charcoal fire; then keep stirring it to and fro, until it becomes a little brown, but not of so deep a color as common coffee; then throw it into boiling water, adding at least the fourth part of the inward husks, which is then boiled together in the manner of other coffee. The husks must be kept in a very dry place, and packed up very close, for the least humidity spoils the flavor. The liquor prepared in this manner is esteemed preferable to any other. The French, when they were at the court of the king of Yemen, saw no other coffee drank, and they found the flavor of it very delicate and agreeable. There was no occasion to use sugar, as it had no bitter taste to correct. Coffee is less unwholesome in tropical than in other climates.

In all probability the Sultana coffee can only be made where the tree grows; for, as the husks have little substance if they are much dried, in order to send them to other countries, the agreeable flavor they had when fresh is greatly impaired.

Improvement in making Coffee.

The process consists in simmering over a small but steady flame of a lamp. To accomplish this a vessel of peculiar construction is requisite. It should be a straight-sided pot, as wide at the top as at the bottom, and inclosed in a case of similar shape, to which it must be soldered air-tight at the top. The case to be above an inch wider than the pot, and descending somewhat less than an inch below it. It should be entirely open at the bottom, thus admitting and confining a body of hot air round and underneath the pot. The lid to be double, and the vessel, of course, furnished with a convenient handle and spout.

The extract may be made either with hot water or cold. If wanted for speedy use, hot water, not actually boiling, will be proper, and the powdered coffee being added, close the lid tight, stop the spout with a cork, and place the vessel over the lamp. It will soon begin to simmer, and may remain unattended, till the coffee is wanted. It may then be strained through a bag of stout, close linen, which will transmit the liquid so perfectly clear as not to contain the smallest particle of the powder.

Though a fountain lamp is preferable, any of the common small lamps, seen in every tin shop, will answer the purpose. Alcohol, pure spermaceti oil, or some of the recent preparations of petroleum are best, and if the wick be too high, or the oil not good, the consequence will be smoke, soot, and extinction of the aroma. The wick should be little more than one-eighth of an inch high. In this process, no trimming is required. It may be left to simmer, and will continue simmering all night without boiling over, and without any sensible diminution of quantity.

Parisian Method of making Coffee.

In the first place, let coffee be of the prime quality,

grain small, round, hard, and clear; perfectly dry and sweet; and at least three years old—let it be gently roasted until it be of a light brown color; avoid burning, for a single scorched grain will spoil a pound. Let this operation be performed at the moment the coffee is to be used; then grind it while it is yet warm, and take of the powder an ounce for each cup intended to be made; put this along with a small quantity of shredded saffron into the upper part of the machine, called a *grecque* or biggin; that is, a large coffee-pot with an upper receptacle made to fit close into it, the bottom of which is perforated with small holes, and containing in its interior two movable metal strainers, over the second of which the powder is to be placed, and immediately under the third: upon this upper strainer pour boiling water, and continue doing so gently until it bubbles up through the strainer; then shut the cover of the machine close down, place it near the fire, and so soon as the water has drained through the coffee, repeat the operation until the whole intended quantity be passed. Thus all the fragrance of its perfume will be retained with all the balsamic and stimulating powers of its essence; and in a few moments will be obtained — without the aid of isinglass, whites of eggs, or any of the substances with which, in the common mode of preparation, it is mixed—a beverage for the gods. This is the true Parisian mode of preparing coffee; the invention of it is due to M. de Belloy, nephew to the Cardinal of the same name.

A coffee-pot upon an entirely new plan, called the Old Dominion, and made in Philadelphia, Pa., is very much liked by some. Perhaps, however, the old mode of boiling and clearing with egg, or the French mode, with the biggin or strainer, is the best.

Sufficient attention is not, however, paid to the proper roasting of the berry, which is of the utmost importance; to have the berry done just enough and not a grain burnt. It is customary now in most large cities for grocers to keep coffee ready roasted, which they have done in large wire cylinders, and generally well done, but not always fresh.

Coffee Milk.

Boil a dessertspoonful of ground coffee in about a pint of milk a quarter of an hour; then put in it a shaving or two of isinglass, and clear it; let it boil a few minutes, and set it on the side of the fire to fine. Those of a spare habit, and disposed towards affections of the lungs, would do well to use this for breakfast, instead of ordinary coffee.

COOKERY.

It was the intention in our article on Cookery to divide it into two parts, separating fine from plain, every-day receipts; but this was found impracticable, no two judgments agreeing upon the proper division, hence our abandonment of the plan, and leaving to each reader his or her own judgment.

To make a Savory Dish of Veal.

Cut some large scallops from a leg of veal, spread them on a dresser, dip them in rich eggy batter; season them with cloves, mace, nutmeg, and pepper beaten fine; make force-meat with some of the veal, some beef suet, oysters chopped, sweet herbs shred fine; strew all these over the collops, roll and tie them up, put them on skewers and roast them. To the rest of the force-meat add two raw eggs, roll them in balls and fry them. Put them into the dish with the meat when roasted; and make the sauce with strong broth, an anchovy or a shallot, a little white wine and some spice. Let it stew, and thicken it with a piece of butter rolled in flour. Pour the sauce into the dish, lay the meat in with the force-meat balls, and garnish with lemon.

Lamb's Kidneys, au vin.

Cut your kidneys lengthways, but not through, put 4 or 5 on a skewer, lay them on a gridiron over clear, lively coals, pouring the red gravy into a bowl each time they are turned; five minutes on the gridiron will do. Take them up, cut them in pieces, put them into a pan with the gravy you have saved, a large lump of butter, with pepper, salt, a pinch of flour, glass of Madeira (champagne is better), fry the whole for two minutes, and serve very hot.

Breast of Veal, glacée.

Cut your breast as square as possible; bone it and draw the cut pieces together with a thread; put it into a pan with a ladle of veal bouillon, cover it with slices of salt pork and a buttered paper, previously adding 2 carrots in bits, 4 onions in slices, 2 bay leaves, 2 cloves, pepper and salt; put some coals on the lid as well as below; when two-thirds done take out the vegetables, reduce your gravy to jelly, turn your meat, and set on the cover till done; it takes in all two hours and a half over a gentle fire.

Shoulder en Galantine.

Bone a fat, fleshy shoulder of veal, cut off the ragged pieces to make your stuffing, viz., 1 pound of veal to 1 pound of salt pork minced extremely fine, well seasoned with salt, pepper, spices, and mixed with 3 eggs, spread a layer of this stuffing well minced over the whole shoulder to the depth of an inch; over this mushrooms, slips of bacon, slices of tongue, and carrots in threads, cover this with stuffing as before, then another layer of mushrooms, bacon, tongue, etc., when all your stuffing is used, roll up your shoulder lengthways, tie it with a thread, cover it with slips of larding and tie it up in a clean white cloth; put into a pot the bones of the shoulder, 2 calves'-feet, slips of bacon, 6 carrots, 10 onions, 1 stuck with 4 cloves, 4 bay leaves, thyme, and a large bunch of parsley and shallots, moisten the whole with bouillon; put in your meat in the cloth and boil steadily for three hours. Try if it is done with the larding needle; if so, take it up, press all the liquor from it and set it by to grow cold; pass your jelly through a napkin, put 2 eggs in a pan, whip them well and pour the strained liquor on them, mixing both together, add peppercorns, a little of the 4 spices, a bay leaf, thyme, parsley; let all boil gently for half an hour, strain it through a napkin, put your shoulder on its dish, pour the jelly over it and serve cold.

Shoulder of Mutton.

Bone the larger half of your shoulder, lard the inside with well seasoned larding, tie it up in the shape of a balloon, lay some slips of bacon in your pan, on them your meat, with 3 or 4 carrots, 5 onions, 3 cloves, 2 bay leaves, thyme, and the bones that have been taken out moisten with bouillon, set all on the fire and simmer for three hours and a half; garnish with small onions.

Sheep's Tongues.

Fifteen tongues are sufficient for a dish : wash and clean them well, throw them into hot water for twenty minutes, wash them again in cold water, drain, dry and trim them neatly, lard them with seasoned larding and the small needle; lay in your pan slips of bacon, 4 carrots in pieces, 4 onions, 1 stuck with 2 cloves, slips of veal, 2 bay leaves, thyme, and a faggot of shallots and parsley; put your tongues in, cover them with slips of larding, moisten the whole with bouillon, and let it simmer five hours.

To make an Excellent Ragout of Cold Veal.

Either a neck, loin, or fillet of veal will furnish this excellent ragout, with a very little expense or trouble.

Cut the veal into handsome thin cutlets: put a piece of butter or clean dripping into a fryingpan; as soon as it is hot, flour and fry the veal of a light brown; take it out, and if you have no gravy ready, put a pint of boiling water into the fryingpan, give it a boil up for a minute, and strain it into a basin while you make some thickening in the following manner: Put about an ounce of butter into a stewpan; as soon as it melts, mix with it as much flour as will dry it up; stir it over the fire for a few minutes, and gradually add to it the gravy you made in the fryingpan; let them simmer together for ten minutes (till thoroughly incorporated); season it with pepper, salt, a little mace, and a wineglass of mushroom catsup, or wine; strain it through a tammy to the meat: and stew very gently till the meat is thoroughly warmed. If you have any ready boiled bacon, cut it in slices, and put it to warm with the meat.

To make Veal Cake.

Take the best end of a breast of veal, bone and cut it into three pieces; take the yolk out of eight eggs boiled hard, and slice the whites, the yolks to be cut through the middle, two anchovies, a good deal of parsley chopped fine, and some lean ham cut in thin slices; all these to be well seasoned separately with Cayenne, black pepper, salt and a little nutmeg; have ready a mug the size of the intended cake, with a little butter rubbed on it, put a layer of veal on the bottom, then a layer of egg and parsley, and ham to fancy; repeat it till all is in, lay the bones on the top and let it be baked three or four hours; then take off the bones and press down the cake till quite cold. The mug must be dipped in warm water and the cake turned out with great care, that the jelly may not be broken which hangs round it.

To make Dry Devils.

These are usually composed of the broiled legs and gizzards of poultry, fish bones, or biscuits, *sauce piquante*. Mix equal parts of fine salt, Cayenne pepper and curry powder, with double the quantity of powder of truffles; dissect a brace of woodcocks rather under roasted, split the heads, subdivide the wings, etc., etc., and powder the whole gently over with the mixture; crush the trail and brains along with the yolk of a hard boiled egg, a small portion of pounded mace, the grated peel of half a lemon and half a spoonful of soy, until the ingredients be brought to the consistence of a fine paste; then add a tablespoonful of catsup, a full wineglass of Madeira and the juice of two Seville oranges; throw the sauce along with the birds into a stew-dish, to be heated with spirits of wine; cover close up, light the lamp and keep gently simmering, and occasionally stirring until the flesh has imbibed the greater part of the liquid. When it is completely saturated, pour in a small quantity of salad oil, stir all once more well together, put out the light and serve it round instantly.

To make an Olio.

Boil in a broth pot a fowl, a partridge, a small leg of mutton, five or six pounds of large slices of beef and a knuckle of veal; soak all these without broth for some time, turn the meat to give it a good color, and add boiling water; when it has boiled about an hour, add all sorts of best broth herbs; this broth, when good, is of a fine brown color.

To make Beef a la Mode.

Take 11 pounds of the mouse buttock, or clod of beef, cut it into pieces of 3 or 4 ounces each; put 2 or 3 large onions and 2 ounces of beef dripping into a large, deep stewpan; as soon as it is quite hot flour the meat and put it into the stewpan; fill it sufficiently to cover the contents with water and stir it continually with a wooden spoon; when it has been on a quarter of an hour, dredge it with flour, and keep doing so till it has been stirred as much as will thicken it; then cover it with boiling water. Skim it when it boils, and put in 1 drachm of black ground pepper, 2 of allspice and 4 bay leaves; set the pan by the side of the fire to stew slowly about 4 hours. This is at once a savory and economical dish.

Beef a la Mode.

Take out the bone from a round, and with a sharp knife cut many deep incisions in the meat. Then wash and season well with salt and pepper. Crumb the soft part of a loaf of bread, to which add one teaspoonful of sweet marjoram, the same of sweet basil, one small onion minced fine, two or three small blades of mace finely powdered, with sufficient salt and pepper to season it. Rub all well together with five ounces of fresh butter. Mix all these ingredients well together. With this dressing fill all the incisions and fasten well with skewers. Tie a piece of tape round the meat to keep it in shape. Cut 3 or 4 thin slices of pickled pork, which place in a large stewkettle with 3 half-pints of water; put in the meat, stick 6 or 8 cloves over the top; cover the kettle very close and set it in a quick oven. It will take several hours to cook, as it requires to be well done. When sufficiently cooked place it on a heated dish, remove the pork from the kettle, and, if not sufficient gravy, add a little boiling water and dredge in sufficient flour to make the gravy of a proper thickness; then stir in 1 dessertspoonful of sugar browned a very dark color, and season to taste. As soon as it comes to a boil add 1 gill of Madeira wine. After letting it simmer a short time put it in a sauce tureen, remove the skewers and tape from the meat, pour over the top 2 or 3 tablespoonfuls of gravy and send all to table hot.

Bouilli en Matelotte.

Peel a handful of small onions, fry them in butter till they are of a light brown, throw in a handful of flour, shake the pan well, add a glass of red wine, a pint of (bouillon) mace, salt, pepper, thyme, and 2 bay leaves; bubble the whole gently till the onions are tender, and pour it over slices of cold bouilli. Set all in a saucepan well covered on hot *ashes*, to stand for 15 minutes. Take care it does not boil.

Beef en Daube.

Prepare a round or rump as for beef a la mode, well larded with the largest needle; put it into your pot with a spoonful of lard. Set the pot on hot coals, dust it with flour, turn your beef till it is well browned on both sides; have ready a kettle of boiling water, cover your meat, add in bits 6 large onions, 2 bunches of carrots and an egg plant in slices. Put on your lid and bubble slowly but steadily for 4 hours (for 16 pounds of beef, longer if heavier) or till the skewer will pass easily into it. About half an hour before serving throw in a pint of small mushrooms, season with pepper and salt, a dozen bay leaves and all kinds of spice. Set your beef in a deep dish and cover with the sauce.

Beef's Tongue aux Champignons.

Wash your tongue well and boil for half an hour; season some larding with salt, pepper, all kinds of spice, shallots and chopped parsley; lard your tongue across; put it in a stewpan with a few slices of bacon and beef, carrots, onions, thyme, 3 bay leaves, 3 cloves; cover with bouillon and stew very gently for 4 hours; when done, skin your tongue and cut it up lengthways in the middle and under part, *but not through*, so that you can bend it up and lay it on your dish in the shape of a heart. *Have ready* a quantity of button mushrooms fried in butter, with a sprinkle of lemon juice moistened with bouillon, and bubbled to a proper consistence. Pour it over your tongue and serve hot.

Fish en Matelotte.

Almost every kind of fish answers for this dish. Scale, clean and cut them in pieces; put them into a pan with a handful of small onions previously fried *whole* in butter, two bay leaves, a bunch of shallots and parsley, small mushrooms, thyme, salt and pepper; pour over the whole as much red wine as will cover it; set your pan on a quick fire; when the wine is one-half gone, mix a spoonful of flour with a lump of butter, roll it in little balls and put them one by one into your sauce, stirring it the whole time. Arrange your fish handsomely on a deep dish, pour over it the sauce and garnish with slices of lemon.

To Fry Sweetbreads.

Boil them in salt and water about a quarter of an hour; then take them out and let them cool. Skin and cut them in half, season with pepper and salt, and dust a little flour over and fry them slowly in equal portions of butter and lard. When of a fine brown, place them on a dish; then dust a little flour into the pan with the fat they were fried in; stir it well and pour in about a gill of hot water; season the gravy to your taste with salt and pepper, and as soon as it boils pour it over the sweetbreads and serve them hot.

Veal Cutlets.

Pound them well with a rolling-pin or potato-masher; then wash and dry them on a clean towel, and season with pepper and salt. Have ready ½ a pint of fine powdered cracker, which season with salt and pepper. Whisk 2 eggs with 1 gill of milk, and pour over the cutlets; then take 1 at a time and place in the crumbs, pat well with the back of a spoon, in order to make the cracker adhere close to the meat. Put them into hot lard, and fry slowly until well done and handsomely browned on both sides.

Steak a la Soyer.

The rump-steak to be broiled, and to be dressed with pepper, salt, Cayenne and flour, all in a dredge-box together; keep constantly turning the steak and dredging it; chop up 1 small shallot, put it in a stewpan with a little catsup; when the steak is sufficiently done add a little butter to it; strain the sauce through a small sieve, and serve up very hot.

Kidneys a la Brochette.

Let your kidneys steep 5 minutes in cold water to soften the skin; remove it and split each; through the middle put a wooden or silver skewer, if you have it; when they are skewered, season them with pepper and salt. Dip each into oil or melted butter, and broil them on a gridiron. Before you serve remove the skewers, unless they are of silver, and serve them on a dish with butter and fine herbs.

Beef Sanders.

Mince cold beef small with onions, add pepper and salt and a little gravy; put into a pie-dish or scallop-shells, until about 3 parts full. Then fill up with mashed potatoes. Bake in an oven or before the fire until done a light brown. Mutton may be cooked in the same way.

Timbale of Macaroni, with Chicken and Ham.

Simmer ½ pound macaroni in plenty of water, and a tablespoonful of salt till it is tender; but take care not to have it *too soft*; strain the water from it; beat up 5 yolks and the whites of 2 eggs; take ½ a pint of the best cream, and the breast of a fowl and some slices of ham. Mince the breast of the fowl and some slices of ham; add them, with from 2 to 3 tablespoonful of finely grated Parmesan cheese, and season with pepper and salt. Mix all these with the macaroni, and put into a pudding-mould, well buttered. Let it strain in a stewpan of boiling water about 1 hour, and serve quite hot, with rich gravy It is very good cold.

Sweetbreads, French Style.

Take 3 large sweetbreads, put them into hot water, and let them boil 10 minutes; when cool, skin, but do not break them. Season with salt and pepper, and dredge over a little flour; then fry them slowly in butter a light brown on both sides. When done, place them on a dish, and remove all the brown particles from the pan (retaining the butter); then pour in, while off the fire, 1 gill of boiling water, and dredge in 1 dessert-spoonful of browned flour, stirring it all the time. Then season with salt and water to taste; mix well, and, just before removing it from the fire, stir in gradually 2 tablespoonsful of Madeira wine. After dredging in the flour, and seasoning the gravy, as soon as it comes to a boil, stir in the wine; while boiling hot, pour it over the sweetbreads, and send to table in a well-heated (covered) dish.

Boiled Leg of Mutton a l'Anglaise.

Select a leg of mutton, rather fat, and not kept above 3 or 4 days; trim it, and put it on to boil in a stock-pot or braizing-pan, filled up with cold water; when it boils, remove the scum, and put it on the side of the stove to continue gently boiling for about 2½ hours; a handful of salt and a couple of turnips and carrots should be put into the pot to boil with the leg. When the mutton is done, drain and dish it up, garnish it round with mashed turnips, dressed with a little sweet cream, a pat of butter, pepper and salt; mould the mashed turnips in the shape of large eggs, with a tablespoon, and place these closely round the leg of mutton, introducing between each spoonful of mashed turnips a carrot nicely turned, that has been boiled, either with the mutton, or in some broth separately; pour some gravy under it, put a paper ruffle on the bone, and send it to table, accompanied with a sauce-boat of caper-sauce.

Roasted Sucking-Pig a l'Anglaise.

In selecting a sucking-pig for the table, those of about 3 weeks old are generally preferred, their meat being more delicate than when allowed to grow larger. Let the pig be prepared for dressing in the usual way, that is, scalded, drawn, etc., pettitoes cut off, and the paunch filled with stuffing previously prepared for the purpose as follows: chop 2 large onions, and 12 sage-leaves, boil them in water for 2 minutes, and after having drained the sage and onions on to a sieve, place it in a stewpan with a pat of butter, pepper and salt, and set the whole to simmer gently for 10 minutes on a very slow fire; then add a double handful of bread-crumbs, 2 pats of butter, and the yolks of 2 eggs; stir the whole over the fire for 5 minutes, and then use the stuffing as before directed. When the sucking-pig is stuffed, sew the paunch up with twine; spit the pig for roasting, carefully fastening it on the spit at each end with small iron skewers, which should be run through the shoulders and hips to secure it tightly, so that it may on no account slip round when down to roast. The pig will require about 2 hours to roast thoroughly, and should be frequently basted with a paste-brush dipped in salad oil. Oil is better adapted for this purpose than either dripping or butter, giving more crispness to the skin; when basted with oil, the pig will, while roasting, acquire a more even and a finer color. When done, take it up from the fire on the spit, and immediately cut the head off with a sharp knife, and lay it on a plate in the hot closet. Next, cut the pig in two, by dividing it first with a sharp knife straight down the back to the spine, finishing with a meat-saw; a large dish should be held under the pig while it is thus being divided, into which it may fall when completely cut through; place the two sides back to back on the dish, without disturbing the stuffing, split the head in two; put the brains in a small stewpan, trim off the snout and jaws, leaving only the cheeks and ears, place these one at each end of the dish, surround the remove with a border of small potatoes, fried of a light color, in a little clarified butter; pour under some rich brown gravy, and send to table with the following sauce: to the brains, put into a small stewpan as before directed, add a spoonful of blanched chopped parsley, pepper and salt, a piece of glaze the size of a large walnut, some well-made butter-sauce, and the juice of a lemon; stir the whole well together over the fire, and when quite hot, send it to table separately, in a boat, to be handed round with the sucking-pig.

Braized Ham, with Spinach, etc.

When about to dress a ham, care must be taken after it has been trimmed, and the thigh-bone removed, that it be put to soak in a large pan filled with cold water; the length of time it should remain in soak depending partly upon its degree of moisture, partly upon whether the ham be new or seasoned. If the ham readily yields to the pressure of the hand, it is no doubt new, and this is the case with most of those sold in the spring season; for such as these a few hours' soaking will suffice; but when hams are properly seasoned, they should be soaked for 24 hours. Foreign hams, however, require to be soaked much longer, varying in time from 2 to 4 days and nights. The water in which they are soaked should be changed once every 12 hours in winter, and twice during that time in summer; it is necessary to be particular also in scraping off the slimy surface from the hams, previously to replacing them in the water to finish soaking.

When the ham has been trimmed and soaked, let it be boiled in water for an hour, and then scraped and washed in cold water; place it in a braizing-pan with 2 carrots, as many onions, 1 head of celery, 2 blades of mace, and 4 cloves; moisten with sufficient common broth to float the ham, and then set it on the stove to braize very gently for about four hours. To obtain tenderness and mellowness, so essential in a well-dressed ham, it must never be allowed to boil, but merely to simmer very gently by a slow fire. This rule applies also to the braizing of all salted or cured meats. When the ham is done, draw the pan in which it has braized away from the fire, and set it to cool in the open air, allowing the ham to remain in the braize. By this means it will retain all its moisture; for when the ham is taken out of the braize as soon as done, and put on a dish to get cold, all its richness exudes from it. The ham having partially cooled in its braize, should be taken out and trimmed, and afterwards placed in a braizing-pan with some of its own stock; and about three-quarters of an hour before dinner put either in the oven or on a slow fire. When warmed through place the ham on a baking-dish in the oven to dry the surface, then glaze it; replace it in the oven again for about three minutes to dry it, and glaze it again; by that time the ham, if properly attended to, will present a bright appearance. Put it now on its dish, and garnish it with well-dressed spinach, placed round the ham in tablespoonfuls, shaped like so many eggs, pour some sauce round the base, put a ruffle on the bone, and serve.

Note.— Any of our home-cured hams, dressed according to the foregoing directions, may also be served with a garnish of asparagus-peas, young carrots, green peas, broad beans, French beans or Brussels sprouts.

Roast Turkey, a l'Anglaise.

Stuff a turkey with some well-seasoned veal stuffing, let it be trussed in the usual manner, and previously to putting it down to roast cover it with thin layers of fat bacon, which should be secured on with buttered paper tied round the turkey, so as entirely to envelop it on the spit; then roast it, and when done dish it up, garnish with stewed chestnuts and small pork sausages, nicely fried; pour a rich sauce round it, glaze the turkey, and send to table.

Plain Rump Steak.

The steak should be cut rather thick, neatly trimmed, seasoned with a little pepper and salt, and broiled over a clear fire; when done remove it carefully from the gridiron, in order to preserve the gravy which collects on its upper surface. Place the steak on its dish, rub a small pat of fresh butter over it, garnish round with grated horse-radish, and send some beef gravy separately in a sauce-boat. Epicures, however, prefer the gravy which runs out of a juicy steak when well broiled to any other addition. Small ribs of beef, and especially steaks cut from between the small ribs, form an excellent substitute for rump steaks; both, when nicely broiled, may be served with cold *Maitre d'Hôtel* butter, anchovy ditto.

Beef Steak, a la Française.

Cut one pound of trimmed fillet of beef across the grain of the meat into three pieces; flatten these with the cutlet-bat, and trim them of a round or oval form; then cut and trim three pieces of suet, half the size of the former: dip the steaks in a little clarified butter, season with pepper and salt, and place them on the gridiron over a clear fire to broil; when done glaze them on both sides, dish them up on two ounces of cold *Maitre d'Hôtel* butter, garnish round with fried potatoes, and serve. These potatoes must be cut or turned in the form of olives, and fried in a little clarified butter.

Hashed Beef, Plain.

Slice the beef up in very thin pieces, season with pepper and salt, and shake a little flour over it. Next chop a middle-sized onion, and put it into a stewpan with a tablespoonful of Harvey sauce, and an equal quantity of mushroom catsup; boil these together for two minutes, and then add half a pint of broth or gravy; boil this down to half its quantity, throw in the beef, set the hash to boil on the stove fire for five minutes longer, and then serve with sippets of toasted bread round it.

Slices of Braized Beef, a la Claremont.

Take braized beef remaining from a previous day's dinner, and cut in rather thin round or oval slices, placed in a saucepan in neat order, and warmed with a gravyspoonful of good stock; these must then be dished up in a circle, overlapping each other closely; pour some sauce over them, and serve.

Note.—Slices of braized beef warmed and dished up, as in the foregoing case, may be greatly varied by being afterwards garnished with macaroni prepared with grated cheese, a little glaze and tomato-sauce, also with all sharp sauces, with purées of vegetables, and with vegetable garnishes.

Bubble and Squeak.

Cut some slices (not too thin) of cold boiled round or edge-bone, of salt beef; trim them neatly, as also an equal number of pieces of the white fat of the beef, and set them aside on a plate. Boil two summer or Savoy cabbages, remove the stalks, chop them fine, and put them into a stewpan with four ounces of fresh butter and one ounce of glaze; season with pepper and salt. When about to send to table, fry the slices of beef in a sauce or fryingpan, commencing with the pieces of fat; stir the cabbage on the fire until quite hot, and then pile it up in the centre of the dish; place the slices of beef and the pieces of fat round it, pour a little brown sauce over the whole, and serve.

Mutton Cutlets, Plain.

Choose a neck of mutton that has been killed at least four days, saw off the scrag end, and as much of the rib-bones as may be necessary in order to leave the cutlet-bones not more than three inches and a half long; the spine-bones must also be removed with the saw, without damaging the fillet. Next cut the neck of mutton thus trimmed into as many cutlets as there are bones; detach the meat from the upper part of each bone, about three-quarters of an inch, then dip them in water and flatten them with a cutlet-bat, trim away the sinewy part, and any superfluous fat. The cutlets must then be seasoned with pepper and salt, passed over with a paste-brush dipped in clarified butter, and nicely broiled over or before a clear fire. When they are done dish them up neatly, and serve with plain brown gravy under them.

Cutlets prepared in this way may also be served with either of the following sauces: Poor-man's, Poivrade; for which see another page.

Mutton Cutlets, Bread-crumbed and Broiled with Shallot Gravy.

Trim the cutlets in the usual manner, and season them with pepper and salt; then egg them slightly over with a paste-brush dipped in two yolks of eggs, beaten upon a plate for the purpose; pass each cutlet through some fine bread-crumbs; then dip them separately in some clarified butter, and bread-crumb them over once more; put them into shape with the blade of a knife, and lay them on a gridiron to be broiled over a clear fire, of a light-brown color; then glaze and dish them up, and serve them with plain or shallot gravy. These cutlets may also be served with any of the sauces directed to be used for plain broiled cutlets.

Sweetbreads Larded with Stewed Peas.

Three heart sweetbreads generally suffice for a dish. They must be procured quite fresh, otherwise they are unfit for the table, and should be steeped in water for several hours, and the water frequently changed; the sweetbreads are then to be scalded in boiling water for about 3 minutes, and immersed in cold water for half an hour, after which they must be drained upon a napkin, trimmed free from any sinewy fat, and put between two dishes to be slightly pressed flat, and then closely larded with strips of bacon in the usual manner. The sweetbreads must next be placed in a deep saucepan on a bed of thinly-sliced carrots, celery and onions, with a garnished faggot of parsely and green onions placed in the centre and covered with thin layers of fat bacon. Moisten with about a pint of good stock, place a round of buttered paper on the top, cover with the lid, and after having put the sweetbreads to boil on the stove-fire, remove them to the oven or on a moderate fire (in the latter case live embers of charcoal must be placed on the lid) and allow them to braize rather briskly for about twenty minutes, frequently basting them with their own liquor. When done remove the lid and paper covering and set them again in the oven to dry the surface of the larding; glaze them nicely and dish them up on some stewed peas (which see).

Sweetbreads prepared in this way may also be served with dressed asparagus, peas, French beans, scallops of cucumbers, braized lettuce, celery, and also with every kind of vegetable purée. To raise the sweetbreads above the garnish, or sauce served with them, it is necessary to place as many foundations as there are sweetbreads in the dish; these may be made either by boiling some rice in broth until it becomes quite soft, then working it into a paste; after this has been spread on a dish about an inch thick, a circular tin cutter must be used to stamp it out. They may also be prepared from veal force-meats, or even fried croûtons of bread will serve the purpose.

Lamb Cutlets Bread-crumbed, with Asparagus-Peas.

Trim the cutlets, season with pepper and salt, rub them over with a paste-brush dipped in yolks of eggs and roll them in bread crumbs; then dip them in some clarified butter and bread-crumb them over again; put them in shape with the blade of a knife and place them in neat order in a saucepan with some clarified butter. When about to send to table fry the cutlets of a light color, drain them upon a sheet of paper, glaze and dish them up; fill the centre with asparagus-peas, pour some thin sauce around them and serve.

Pork Cutlets Plain-broiled, with Gravy, etc.

These cutlets must be cut from the neck or loin of dairy-fed pork, not too fat; they should be trimmed but very little, the rough part of the chine-bone only requiring to be removed; the skin must be left on and scored in six places. Season the cutlets with pepper and salt, and broil them on a gridiron over a clear fire; coke makes a better fire than coal for broiling, as it emits no gas and causes less smoke. Take care that they are thoroughly done and not scorched; dish them up with any of the following gravies or sauces, and serve: Sage and onion, shallot, onion, fine herbs, gravies, or essences, tomato sauce.

Venison Scallops.

Venison for this purpose ought to be kept until it has become quite tender; a piece of the end of the neck may be used. Cut the fillet from the bone, with all the fat adhering to it; remove the outer skin, and then cut it into scallops, taking care not to trim off more of the fat than is necessary; place them in a saucepan with clarified butter, season with pepper and salt, and fry them brown on both sides; pour off all the grease, add some scallops of mushrooms, a piece of glaze and a glass of Port wine; simmer the whole together over a stove-fire for about 3 minutes, and then pour in some Poivrade sauce; toss the scallops in the sauce on the fire until quite hot, and then dish them up with a border of quenelles of potatoes and serve. These scallops may also be served with sweet sauce, in which case the mushrooms must be omitted.

Venison Chops.

Cut the chops about an inch thick from the end of the haunch or the best end of the neck, flatten them a little with a cutlet-bat, trim them without waste, season with pepper and salt and broil them on a gridiron over a clear fire of moderate heat, turning them over every 3 minutes while on the fire; when done through with their gravy in them, lift them carefully off the gridiron without spilling the gravy that may be swimming on the surface, dish them up with a little rich brown gravy under them, and serve some currant jelly or venison sweet sauce separately in a boat.

Fricassee of Chickens with Mushrooms, etc.

Procure 2 fat, plump chickens, and after they have been drawn singe them over the flame of a charcoal fire, and then cut up into small members or joints in the following manner: First remove the wings at the second joint, then take hold of the chicken with the left hand, and with a sharp knife make 2 parallel cuts lengthwise on the back about an inch and a half apart, so as partly to detach or at least to mark out where the legs and wings are to be removed; the chicken must next be placed upon its side on the table, and after the leg and fillet (with the pinion left on the upper side) have been cut, the same must be repeated on the other, and the thigh-bones must be removed. Then separate the back and breast, trim these without waste and cut the back across into 2 pieces; steep the whole in a pan containing clear tepid water for about 10 minutes, frequently squeezing the pieces with the hand to extract all the blood. Next strew the bottom of a stewpan with thinly-sliced carrot, onion and a little celery, 3 cloves, 12 pepper-corns, a blade of mace and a garnished faggot of parsley; place the pieces of chicken in close and neat order upon the vegetables, etc.; moisten with about a quart of boiling broth from the stockpot, or failing this, with water; cover with the lid and set the whole to boil gently by the side of the stove-fire for about half an hour, when the chicken will be done. They must then be strained in a sieve and their broth reserved in a basin; next immerse the pieces of chicken in cold water, wash and drain them upon a napkin, and afterward trim them neatly and place them in a stewpan in the larder. Then put 2 ounces of fresh butter to melt in a stewpan; to this add 2 tablespoonfuls of flour, and stir the mixture over the fire for 3 minutes without allowing it to acquire any color; it should then be removed from the stove, and the chicken broth being poured into it the whole must be thoroughly mixed together into a smooth sauce; throw in some trimmings of mushrooms and stir the sauce over the fire until it boils, then set it by the side to continue gently boiling to throw up the butter and scum. When the sauce has boiled half an hour skim it; reduce it by further boiling to its proper consistency, and then incorporate with it a leason of 4 yolks of eggs mixed with a pat of butter and a little cream; set the leason in the sauce by stirring it over the fire until it nearly boils, then pass it through a tammy into the stewpan containing the pieces of chicken, and add thereto half a pottle of prepared button-mushrooms. When about to send to table warm the fricassee without allowing it to boil, and dish it up as follows: First put the pieces of the back in the centre of the dish, place the legs at the angles, the bones pointed inwardly; next place the fillets upon these, and then set the pieces of breast on the top; pour the sauce over the *entrée*, and place the mushrooms about the fricassee in groups; surround the *entrée* with eight or ten glazed *croûtons* of fried bread cut in the shape of hearts, and serve.

Note.—Truffles cut into scallops, or shaped in the form of olives, crayfish-tails, button-onions, or artichoke-bottoms cut into small pointed quarters, may also be served with a fricassee of chickens.

Pigeons a la Gauthier.

Procure 4 young, fat pigeons; draw, singe and truss them with their legs thrust inside; next put a half-pound of fresh butter into a small stewpan with the juice of a lemon, a little mignonette, pepper, and salt; place this over a stove-fire, and when it is melted put the pigeons with a garnished faggot of parsley in it, cover the whole with thin layers of fat bacon and a circular piece of buttered paper, and set them to simmer very gently on a slow fire for about 20 minutes, when they will be done. The pigeons must then be drained upon a napkin, and after all the greasy moisture has been absorbed place them in the dish in the form of a square, with a large quenelle of fowl (decorated with truffles) in between each pigeon; fill the centre with a ragout of crayfish-tails; pour some of the sauce over and round the pigeons, and serve.

Rabbits a la Bourguignonne.

Cut the rabbits up into small joints, season with pepper and salt, and fry them slightly over the fire without allowing them to acquire much color; adding half a pint of button-onions previously parboiled in water, a very little grated nutmeg, and half a pottle of mushrooms; toss these over the fire for five minutes, then add a tumblerfull of French white wine (Chablis or Sauterne), and set this to boil sharply until reduced to half the quantity; next add 2 large gravyspoonsful of Poivrade sauce (which see), simmer the whole together gently for ten minutes longer, and finish by incorporating a leason of 4 yolks of eggs, the juice of ½ a lemon, and a dessertspoonful of chopped parboiled parsley; dish up the pieces of rabbit in a pyramidal form, garnish the *entrée* with the onions, etc., placed in groups round the base, pour the sauce over it and serve.

Salmis of Wild Duck.

Roast a wild duck before a brisk fire for about 25 minutes, so that it may retain its gravy, place it on its breast in a dish to get cool, then cut it up into small joints comprising 2 fillets, 2 legs with the breast and back each cut into 2 pieces, and place the whole in a stewpan. Put the trimmings into a stewpan with ½ pint of red wine, 4 shallots, a sprig of thyme, a bay-leaf, the rind of an orange free from pith, the pulp of a lemon, and a little Cayenne; boil these down to half their original quantity then add a small ladleful of sauce, allow the sauce to boil, skim it and pass it through a tammy on to the pieces of wild duck. When about to send to the table warm the salmis without boiling, dish it up, pour the sauce over it, garnish the entrée with 8 heart-shaped *croûtons* of fried bread nicely glazed, and serve.

Roast Hare.

Skin and draw the hare, leaving on the ears, which must be scalped and the hairs scraped off; pick out the eyes and cut off the feet or pads just above the first joint, wipe the hare with a clean cloth, and cut the sinews at the back of the hind-quarters and below the fore legs. Prepare some veal stuffing and fill the paunch with it, sew this up with string or fasten it with a wooden skewer, then draw the legs under as if the hare was in a sitting posture, set the head between the shoulders and stick a small skewer through them, running also through the neck to secure its position; run another skewer through the fore legs gathered up

14

under the paunch, then take a yard of string, double it in two, placing the centre of it on the breast of the hare and bring both ends over the skewer, cross the string over both sides of the other skewer and fasten it over the back. Split the hare and roast it before a brisk fire for about three-quarters of an hour, frequently basting it with butter or dripping. Five minutes before taking the hare up throw on a little salt, shake some flour over it with a dredger, and baste it with some fresh butter; when this froths up and the hare has acquired a rich brown crust take it off the spit, dish it up with water-cresses round it, pour some brown gravy under, and send some currant jelly in a boat to be handed round.

Roast Pheasant.

Draw the pheasant by making a small opening at the vent, make an incision along the back part of the neck, loosen the pouch, etc., with the fingers and then remove it; singe the body of the pheasant and its legs over the flame of a charcoal fire or with a piece of paper, rub the scaly cuticle off the legs with a cloth, trim away the claws and spurs, cut off the neck close up to the back leaving the skin of the breast entire, wipe the pheasant clean, and then truss it in the following manner: Place the pheasant upon its breast, run a trussing-needle and string through the left pinion (the wings being removed), then turn the bird over on its back and place the thumb and fore-finger of the left hand across the breast, holding the legs erect; thrust the needle through the middle joint of both thighs, draw it out and then pass it through the other pinion and fasten the strings at the back; next pass the needle through the legs and body and tie the strings tightly; this will give it an appearance of plumpness. Spit and roast the pheasant before a brisk fire for about half an hour, frequently basting it; when done send to table with brown gravy under it and bread sauce (which see) separately in a boat.

Wild Fowl, en Salmis.

Cut up a cold roast duck (wild), goose, brant, or whatever it may be. Put into a bowl or soup-plate (to every bird) a dessertspoonful of well made mustard, a sprinkle of cayenne and black pepper, with about a gill of red wine; mix them well together, set your pan on the fire with a lump of butter, when it melts add gradually the wine, etc., let it bubble a minute; put in your duck and bubble it for a few minutes. If your duck has proved tough when first cooked, use a saucepan and let it bubble till tender, taking care there is enough gravy to keep it from burning. Serve on dry toast very hot.

Pigeons.

Pigeons may be broiled or roasted like chicken. They will cook in three-quarters of an hour. Make a gravy of the giblets, season it with pepper and salt, and thicken it with a little flour and butter.

Terrapins.

Plunge them into boiling water till they are dead, take them out, pull off the outer skin and toe-nails, wash them in warm water and boil them with a teaspoonful of salt to each middling-sized terrapin till you can pinch the flesh from off the bone of the leg, turn them out of the shell into a dish, remove the sand-bag and gall, add the yolks of 2 eggs, cut up your meat, season pretty high with equal parts of black and cayenne pepper and salt. Put all into your saucepan with the liquor they have given out in cutting up, but not a drop of water; add ¼ of a pound of butter with a gill of Madeira to every 2 middle-sized terrapins; simmer gently till tender, closely covered, thicken with flour and serve hot.

To Stew Terrapins.

Wash 4 terrapins in warm water, then throw them in a pot of boiling water, which will kill them instantly; let them boil till the shells crack, then take them out and take off the bottom shell, cut each quarter separate, take the gall from the liver, take out the eggs, put the pieces in a stewpan, pour in all the liquor and cover them with water; put in salt, cayenne, and black pepper and a little mace, put in a lump of butter the size of an egg and let them stew for half an hour; make a thickening of flour and water which stir in a few minutes before you take it up with two glasses of wine. Serve it in a deep covered dish, put in the eggs just as you dish it.

Chicken Stewed with New Corn.

Cut up the chickens as for pies, season them well, have green corn cut off the cob, put a layer of chicken in the bottom of a stewpan and a layer of corn, and so till you fill all in; sprinkle in salt, pepper and parsley and put a piece of butter in, cover it with water and put on a crust with slits cut in it, let it boil an hour; when done lay the crust in a deep dish. Dip out the chicken and corn and put it on the crust, stir in the gravy a thickening of milk and flour; when this boils up pour it in with the corn and chicken. Chicken and corn boiled together in a pot make very nice soup with dumplings.

Mayonnaise.

A cold roast fowl divided into quarters; young lettuce cut in quarters and placed on the dish with salad dressing; eggs boiled hard and cut in quarters, placed round the dish as a garnish; capers and anchovies are sometimes added.

Salmon Curry.

Have 2 slices of salmon, weighing about 1 pound each, which cut into pieces of the size of walnuts; cut up 2 middling-sized onions, which put into a stew-pan with 1 ounce of butter and a clove of garlic cut in thin slices; stir over the fire till becoming rather yellowish, then add a teaspoonful of curry powder, and half that quantity of curry paste. Mix all well together with a pint of good broth; beat up and pass through a tammy into a stewpan; put in the salmon, which stew about half an hour; pour off as much of the oil as possible. If too dry, moisten with a little more broth, mixing it gently; and serve as usual, with rice separate. Salmon curry may also be made with the remains left from a previous dinner, in which case reduce the curry sauce until rather thick before putting in the salmon, which only requires to be made hot in it. The remains of a turbot may also be curried in the same way, and so may any other kind of fish.

Pigeon Pie.

Truss half a dozen fine large pigeons, as for stewing; season them with pepper and salt, and fill them with veal stuffing or some parsley chopped very fine, and a little pepper, salt, and 3 ounces of butter mixed together. Lay at the bottom of the dish a rump steak of about a pound weight, cut into pieces and trimmed neatly, seasoned and beat out with a chopper; on it lay the pigeons, the yolks of 3 eggs boiled hard, and a gill of broth or water; wet the edge of the dish, and cover it over with puff-paste; wash it over with yolk of egg, and ornament it with leaves of paste, and the feet of the pigeons. Bake it an hour and a half in a moderate-heated oven. Before it is sent to table make an aperture in the top, and pour in some good gravy, quite hot.

Giblet Pie.

Clean well, and half stew 2 or 3 sets of goose

giblets; cut the leg in 2, the wing and neck into 3, and the gizzard into 4 pieces. Preserve the liquor, and set the giblets by till cold; otherwise the heat of the giblets will spoil the paste you cover the pie with; then season the whole with black pepper and salt, and put them into a deep dish; cover it with paste, rub it over with yolk of egg, ornament, and bake it an hour and a half in a moderate oven. In the mean time take the liquor the giblets were stewed in, skim it free from fat, put it over a fire in a clean stewpan, thicken it a little with flour and butter, or flour and water, season it with pepper and salt and the juice of half a lemon; add a few drops of browning, strain it through a fine sieve, and, when you take the pie from the oven, pour some of this into it through a funnel. Some lay in the bottom of the dish a moderately thick rump-steak. If you have any cold game or poultry, cut it in pieces, and add it to the above.

Rump Steak Pie.

Cut 3 pounds of rump steak, that has been kept till tender, into pieces half as big as your hand; trim off all the skin, sinews, and every part which has not indisputable pretensions to be eaten, and beat them with a chopper. Chop very fine half a dozen eschalots, and mix them with half an ounce of pepper and salt mixed; strew some of the mixture at the bottom of the dish, then a layer of steak, then some more of the mixture, and so on till the dish is full; add half a gill of mushroom catsup, and the same quantity of gravy, or red wine; cover it as in the preceding receipt, and bake it two hours.

Large oysters parboiled, bearded, and laid alternately with the steaks, their liquor reduced and substituted instead of the catsup and wine, will be a variety.

Chicken Pie.

Parboil and then cut up neatly two young chickens; dry them; set them over a slow fire for a few minutes. Have ready some veal stuffing or forcemeat; lay it at the bottom of the dish, and place in the chickens upon it, and with it some pieces of dressed ham; cover it with paste. Bake it from an hour and a half to two hours. When sent to table add some good gravy, well seasoned and not too thick.

Duck pie is made in like manner, only substituting duck stuffing instead of the veal.

The above may be put into a raised French crust, and baked. When done take off the top, and put a ragout of sweetbread to the chicken.

Rabbit Pie.

Made in the same way, but make a forcemeat to cover the bottom of the dish, by pounding a quarter pound of boiled bacon with the livers of the rabbits; some pepper and salt, some pounded mace, some chopped parsley, and an eschalot, thoroughly beaten together; and you may lay some thin slices of ready-dressed ham or bacon on the top of your rabbits.

Raised French Pie.

Make about 2 pounds of flour into a paste, as directed; knead it well, and into the shape of a ball; press your thumb into the centre, and work it by degrees into any shape (oval or round is the most general) till about five inches high; put it on a sheet of paper, and fill it with coarse flour or bran; roll out a covering for it about the same thickness as the sides; cement its sides with the yolk of egg; cut the edges quite even, and pinch it round with the finger and thumb; yolk-of-egg it over with a paste-brush, and ornament it in any way as fancy may direct, with the same kind of paste. Bake it of a fine brown color, in a slow oven, and when done cut out the top, remove the flour or bran, brush it quite clean, and fill it up with a fricassee of chicken, rabbit, or any other entrée most convenient. Send it to table with a napkin under.

Raised Ham Pie.

Soak four or five hours a small ham; wash and scrape it well; cut off the knuckle, and boil it for half an hour; then take it up and trim it very neatly. Take off the rind and put it into an oval stewpan, with a pint of Madeira or Sherry, and enough veal stock to cover it. Let it stew for two hours, or till three-parts done; take it out and set in a cold place; then raise a crust as in the foregoing receipt, large enough to receive it; put in the ham, and around it the veal forcemeat; cover and ornament. It will take about one hour and a half to bake in a slow oven. When done take off the cover, glaze the top, and pour round the following sauce, viz.: take the liquor the ham was stewed in; skim it free from fat; thicken with a little flour and butter mixed together, a few drops of browning, and some cayenne pepper.

The above is a good way of dressing a small ham, and has a good effect cold for a supper.

Raised Pork Pie.

Make a raised crust, of a good size, with paste, about four inches high; take the rind and chinebone from a loin of pork, cut it into chops, beat them with a chopper, season them with pepper and salt and powdered sage, and fill your pie; put on the top and close it, and pinch it round the edge; rub it over with yolk of egg, and bake it two hours, with a paper over to prevent the crust from burning. When done, pour in some good gravy, with a little ready-mixed mustard and a teaspoonful of catsup.

Scotch Minced Collops.

Take 2 pounds of the fillet of beef, chopped very fine; put it in a stewpan, and add to it pepper and salt and a little flour; add a little good gravy, with a little catsup and Harvey sauce, and let it stew for twenty minutes over a slow fire. Serve up very hot, garnished with fried sippet of bread. This quantity of beef makes a good-sized dish.

Beefsteak Pudding.

Get rump steaks, not too thick; beat them with a chopper; cut them into pieces about half the size of your hand, and trim off all the skin, sinews, etc.; have ready an onion peeled and chopped fine, likewise some potatoes peeled and cut into slices a quarter of an inch thick; rub the inside of a basin or an oval plain mould with butter, sheet it with paste as directed for boiled puddings; season the steaks with pepper, salt, and a little grated nutmeg; put in a layer of steak, then another of potatoes, and so on till it is full, occasionally throwing in part of the chopped onion; add to it half a gill of mushroom catsup, a tablespoonful of lemon pickle, and half a gill of water or veal broth; roll out a top, and close it well to prevent the water getting in; rinse a clean cloth in hot water, sprinkle a little flour over it, and tie up the pudding; have ready a large pot of water boiling, put it in, and boil it two hours and a half; take it up, remove the cloth, turn it downwards in a deep dish, and when wanted take away the basin or mould.

Vol au Vent.

Roll off tart paste till about the eighth of an inch thick; then with a tin cutter made for that purpose (about the size of the bottom of the dish you intend sending to table), cut out the shape, and lay it on a baking plate with paper, rub it over with yolk of egg; roll out good puff-paste an inch thick, stamp it with the same cutter, and lay it on the tart paste, then take a cutter two sizes smaller, and press it in the centre nearly through the puff paste; rub the top with yolk of egg and bake it in a quick oven about twenty minutes, of a light brown color; when done take out the paste inside the centre mark, preserving the top, put it on a dish in a warm place, and when wanted, fill it with a white fricassee chicken, rabbit, ragout of sweetbread, or any other *entrée* you wish.

To make a Perigord Pie.

Take half a dozen partridges, and dispose of their legs in the same manner as is done with chickens, when intended to be boiled. Season them well with pepper, salt, a small quantity of cloves, and mace beaten fine. Cut 2 pounds of lean veal, and 1 pound of fat bacon into small bits, and put them into a stewpan with ½ a pound of butter, together with some shallots, parsley, and thyme, all chopped together. Stew these till the meat appears sufficiently tender. Then season it in the same manner as directed for the partridges. Strain and pound the meat in a mortar till it is perfectly smooth, then mix the pulp in some of the liquor in which it has been stewed. The pie-crust being raised, and ready to receive the partridges, put them in with the above-mentioned forcemeat over them, and over that lay some thin slices of bacon. Cover the pie with a thick lid, and be sure to close it well at the sides, to prevent the gravy from boiling out at the place where the joining is made, which would occasion the partridges to eat dry. This sized pie will require three hours' baking, but be careful not to put it in a fierce heated oven. A pound of fresh truffles will add considerably to the merits of this excellent pie.

Beefsteak and Oyster Pie.

Cut 3 pounds of fillet of beef or rump steaks into large scallops, fry them quickly over a very brisk fire so as to brown them before they are half done; then place them on the bottom of the dish, leaving the centre open in two successive layers; fill the centre with four dozen oysters, previously parboiled and bearded, season with pepper and salt, and pour the following preparation over the whole. When the scallops of beef have been fried in a sauce or fryingpan, pour nearly all the grease out, and shake a tablespoonful of flour into it; stir this over the fire for one minute, and then add a pint of good gravy or broth, two tablespoonsful of mushroom catsup, and an equal quantity of Harvey sauce, and the liquor of the oysters; stir the whole over the fire, and keep it boiling for a quarter of an hour. Half an hour after this sauce has been poured into the pie, cover it with puff paste in the usual way, bake it for an hour and a half, and serve.

Chicken Pie, a la Reine.

Cut 2 chickens into small members, as for fricassee; cover the bottom of the pie-dish with layers of scallops of veal and ham placed alternately; season with chopped mushrooms and parsley, pepper and salt, then add a little white sauce; next place in the dish the pieces of chicken in neat order, and round these put a plover's egg in each cavity; repeat the seasoning and the sauce, lay a few thin slices of dressed ham neatly trimmed on the top; cover the pie with puff paste, ornament this with pieces of the same cut into the form of leaves, etc., egg the pie over with a paste-brush, and bake it for one hour and a half. A very good chicken pie may be made by omitting the plover's eggs, mushrooms, ham, and the sauce; substituting for these the yolk of eggs boiled hard, chopped parsley, bacon, and a little mushroom catsup, some common gravy, or even water.

Beefsteak and Oyster Pudding.

Line a two-quart pudding basin with some beef-suet paste; fill this lining with a preparation similar to that described for making beefsteak and oyster pie, except that the sauce must be more reduced. When the pudding is filled, wet the edges of the paste round the top of the basin with a paste-brush dipped in water, cover it with a piece of suet-paste rolled out to the size of the basin, fasten it down by bearing all round the edge with the thumb, and then with the thumb and forefinger, twist the edges of the paste over and over so as to give it a corded appearance. This pudding must be either steamed or boiled three hours; when done turn it out of the basin carefully, pour some rich brown gravy under it and serve.

Kidney Pudding.

Cut two pounds of sheep's or lamb's kidneys into scallops, put them into a basin with some chopped parsley, shallot, and a little thyme, and season with pepper and salt; then add a large gravyspoonful of good sauce, and the juice of half a lemon; mix these ingredients well together. Line a basin with suet-paste, and fill the pudding with the foregoing preparation; cover it in the usual way, steam or boil it for two hours and a half, and when sent to table pour under it some rich brown gravy, to which has been added a little Indian soy, and serve.

Eggs, au Gratin.

Boil the eggs hard, and when done take off the shells, cut them in slices, and set them aside on a plate. Next, put a large tablespoonful of white sauce into a stewpan to boil over the stove fire, and when it is sufficiently reduced, add 2 ounces of grated Parmesan cheese, a small pat of butter, a little nutmeg, pepper, the yolks of 4 eggs, and the juice of half a lemon; stir this quickly over the stove until it begins to thicken, and then withdraw it from the fire. Place the eggs in close circular rows, in the dish, spread some of the preparation in between each layer, observing that the whole must be dished up in the form of a dome; smooth the surface over with the remainder of the sauce, strew some fried bread-crumbs mixed with grated Parmesan cheese over the top, put some fried *croûtons* of bread or pastry round the base, and set them in the oven to bake for about ten minutes, then send to table.

Omelet, with fine Herbs.

Break 6 eggs in a basin, to these add ½ a gill of cream, a small pat of butter broken in small pieces, a spoonful of chopped parsley, some pepper and salt; then put 4 ounces of fresh butter in an omelet-pan on the stove fire; while the butter is melting, whip the eggs, etc., well together until they become frothy; as soon as the butter begins to fritter, pour the omelet into the pan, and stir the omelet as the eggs appear to set and become firm; when the whole has become partially set, roll the omelet into the form of an oval cushion, allow it to acquire a golden color on one side over the fire, and then turn it out on its dish; pour a little thin sauce, or half glaze under it, and serve.

Omelet, with Parmesan Cheese.

Break 6 eggs into a basin, then add a gill of cream, 4 ounces of grated Parmesan cheese, some pepper, and a little salt; beat the whole well together, and finish the omelet as previously directed.

Eggs a la Dauphine.

Boil 10 eggs hard, take off the shells, and cut each egg into halves, lengthwise; scoop the yolks out and put them into the mortar, and place the whites on a dish. Add 4 ounces of butter to the yolks of eggs, also the crumb of a French-roll soaked in cream, some chopped parsley, grated nutmeg, pepper and salt, and 2 ounces of grated Parmesan cheese; pound the whole well together, and then add 1 whole egg and the yolks of 2 others; mix these well together by pounding, and use this preparation for filling the whites of eggs kept in reserve for the purpose, smooth them over with the blade of a small knife dipped in water, and as they are filled place them on a dish. Next, with some of the remaining part of the preparation, spread a thin foundation at the bottom of the dish, and proceed to raise the eggs up in 3 or 4 tiers, to a pyramidal form, a single egg crowning the whole; 4 hard-boiled yolks of eggs must then be rubbed through a wire-sieve, over the *entremêts* for them to fall upon in shreds, like vermicelli; place a border of fried *croûtons* of bread round the base, and set the eggs in the oven for about twenty minutes, that they may be baked of a bright yellow color; when done withdraw them, pour some thin Béchamel round the *entremêts*, and serve.

Pontiff's Sauce.

Soak slices of veal, ham, sliced onions, carrots, parsnips, and a white head of celery; add a glass of white wine, as much good broth, a clove of garlic, 4 shallots, 1 clove, a little coriander, and 2 slices of peeled lemons. Boil on a slow fire till the meat is done; skim it and sift in a sieve; add a little catsup, and a small quantity of fine chopped parsley, just before it is used.

Nun's Sauce.

Put slices of veal and ham in a stewpan, with a spoonful of oil, 2 mushrooms, a bunch of parsley, a clove of garlic, 2 heads of cloves, ½ a leaf of laurel; let it catch a little on the fire; then add some good broth, a little gravy, and some white wine, simmer it for some time, skim it well, and sift in a sieve. When ready add 2 or 3 green shallots, and a dozen of pistachio-nuts, whole.

Sauce Piquante.

Put a bit of butter with 2 sliced onions into a stewpan, with a carrot, a parsnip, a little thyme, laurel, basil, 2 cloves, 2 shallots, a clove of garlic, and some parsley; turn the whole over the fire until it be well colored; then shake in some flour, and moisten it with some broth, and a spoonful of vinegar. Let it boil over a slow fire; skim and strain it through a sieve. Season it with salt and pepper, and serve it with any dish required to be heightened.

Sauce for Veal.

Take the bones of cold roast or boiled veal, dredge them well with flour, and put them into a stewpan, with a pint and a half of broth or water, a small onion, a little grated or finely minced lemon-peel, or the peel of a quarter of a small lemon pared as thin as possible, half a teaspoonful of salt, and a blade of pounded mace; to thicken it, rub a tablespoonful of flour into half an ounce of butter; stir it into the broth, and set it on the fire, and let it boil very gently for about half an hour, strain through a tammis or sieve, and it is ready to put to the veal to warm up, which is to be done by placing the stewpan by the side of the fire. Squeeze in half a lemon, and cover the bottom of the dish with toasted bread sippets cut into triangles, and garnish the dish with slices of ham or bacon.

Béchamel, or White Sauce.

Cut in square pieces, half an inch thick, 2 pounds of lean veal, ½ a pound of lean ham, melt in a stewpan 2 ounces of butter; when melted let the whole simmer until it is ready to catch at the bottom (it requires great attention, as, if it happen to catch at the bottom of the stewpan, it will spoil the look of your sauce), then add to it 3 tablespoonsful of flour; when well mixed, add to it 3 pints of broth or water, pour a little at a time, that the thickening be smooth, stir it until it boils, put the stewpan on the corner of the stove to boil gently for two hours, season it with 4 cloves, 1 onion, 12 peppercorns, a blade of mace, a few mushrooms, and a fagot made of parsley, a sprig of thyme, and a bay-leaf. Let the sauce reduce to a quart, skim the fat off, and strain it through a tammis cloth.

Kitchener's (Dr.) Sauce, Superlative.

Claret or Port wine, and mushroom catsup, a pint of each; ½ a pint of walnut or other pickle liquor; pounded anchovies, 4 ounces; fresh lemon-peel, pared very thin, 1 ounce; peeled and sliced shallots, the same; scraped horse-radish, 1 ounce; allspice and black pepper powdered, ½ an ounce each; Cayenne, 1 drachm, or curry powder, 3 drachms; celery-seed, bruised, a drachm. All avoirdupois weight. Put these into a wide mouth bottle, stop it close, shake it up every day for a fortnight, and strain it, when some think it improved by the addition of a quarter pint soy, or thick browning, and you will have a "delicious double relish."

Sauce Italienne.

Put a piece of butter into a stewpan, with mushrooms, onion, parsley, and ½ of a laurel-leaf, all cut fine; turn the whole over the fire for some time, and shake in a little flour; moisten it with a glass of white wine, and as much good broth; add salt, pepper, and a little mace; beat all fine. Let it boil half an hour; then skim away all the fat, and serve it up. A fine flavor may be given to it whilst boiling, by putting in a bunch of sweet herbs, which take out before the dish is served up.

Ragout of Asparagus.

Scrape 100 of grass clean; put them into cold water; cut them as far as is good and green; chop small 2 heads of endive, 1 young lettuce, and 1 onion. Put ¼ of a pound of butter into the stewpan, and when it is melted, put in the grass with the other articles. Shake them well, and when they have stewed 10 minutes, season them with a little pepper and salt; strew in a little flour, shake them about, and then pour on ½ a pint of gravy. Stew the whole till the sauce is very good and thick, and then pour all into the dish. Garnish with a few of the small tops of the grass.

Ragout of Mushrooms.

Broil on a gridiron some large peeled mushrooms, and clean off the inside; when the outside is brown, put them into a stewpan with a sufficient quantity of water to cover them; when they have stewed 10 minutes, put to them 1 spoonful of white wine, the same of browning, and a little vinegar. Thicken it with butter and flour, give a gentle boil, and serve it up with sippets round the dish.

Ragout of Artichoke Buttons.

Soak them in warm water for two or three hours, changing the water; then put them into the stewpan with some good gravy, mushroom catsup or powder. Add a little Cayenne pepper and salt when they boil; thicken them with a little flour, put them into the dish with sauce over them, and serve them hot.

Ragout of Calves' Sweetbreads.

Scald 2 or 3 sweetbreads, cut each into 3 or 4 pieces, and put them into a stewpan with mushrooms, butter, and a fagot of sweet herbs; soak these together a moment, then add broth and gravy; simmer on a slow fire, skim the sauce well, and reduce it; season with pepper, salt and lemon-juice when ready.

Ragout of Roots.

Cut carrots and parsnips to the length of a finger, and of much the same thickness; boil them till half done in water, put them into a stewpan with small bits of ham, chopped parsley, and shallots, pepper and salt, a glass of wine and broth; let them stew slowly until the broth is reduced pretty thick, and add the squeeze of a lemon when ready to serve. For maigre, instead of ham, use mushrooms, and make a mixture beat up with yolks of eggs and maigre broth. Celery is done much the same, only it is cut smaller. If these roots are to be served in a boat for sauce, boil them tender in the broth-pot, or in water, cut them into the desired length, and serve with a good gravy or white sauce.

Cottage Cheese.

Take 1 or more quarts of sour milk, put it in a warm place, and let it remain until the whey separates from the curd; then pour it into a three-cornered bag, hang it up, and let it drain until every particle of whey has dripped from it; then turn it out, and mash with a spoon until very fine, after which add a little milk or cream, with salt to taste; before sending to table (if liked) dredge a little black pepper over the top.

Maître d'Hôtel Butter.

Put ¼ of a pound of fresh butter upon a plate, the juice of two lemons, and 2 large tablespoonsful of chopped parsley, ½ a teaspoonful of salt, and half that quantity of black pepper; mix all well together, and keep in a cool place for use.

Mushroom Catsup.

Clean the mushrooms by wiping them, and cutting off the ends of the stems. Put them in a deep pan, and sprinkle salt over each layer. Let them remain for 2 days. Then put them in a sieve, and strain off all the juice. Pour it into your preserving-kettle, allow 12 cloves, 12 allspice, 2 or 3 pieces of mace, and ½ of a small nutmeg, grated. Let it boil for fifteen minutes, remove it from the fire, and let it stand for two or three days. Strain and bottle for use.

Tomato Catsup.

Take ½ a peck of tomatoes, wash and slice them; put them in your preserving-kettle, and let them stew gently until quite soft, but do not stir them. Strain the juice through a sieve, pour it back into the kettle. Add 24 cloves, ½ an ounce of allspice, ¼ an ounce of mace; salt and Cayenne to your taste. Set it on the fire, and let it boil until reduced to half the original quantity. The next day strain out the spice, and to every pint of juice add ½ gill of vinegar, and bottle for use.

Wine Sauce.

Two ounces of butter, 2 teaspoonsful of flour, ½ a pint of boiling water, 1 gill of Madeira wine, ¼ a pound of sugar, ½ a grated nutmeg. Mix the flour and butter together; pour in the boiling water; let it boils a few minutes; then add the sugar and wine. Just before going to table add the nutmeg. Serve hot.

Cream Béchamel Sauce.

Put 6 ounces of fresh butter into a middle-sized stewpan; add 4 ounces of sifted flour, some nutmeg, a few peppercorns, and a little salt; knead the whole well together; then cut 1 carrot and 1 onion into very thin slices, throw them into the stewpan, and also a bouquet of parsley and thyme, tied together; next moisten these with a quart of white broth and a pint of cream; and having stirred the sauce over the stove-fire for about ½ an hour, pass it through the tammy into the basin for use. This sauce is not expensive, neither does it require much time or trouble to make. It is useful as a substitute for other white sauces, and also for many other purposes.

Poor Mou's Sauce.

Chop an onion very fine, put it into a stewpan with a small piece of butter, and gently fry the onion on the fire until it assumes a light-brown color; then add a tablespoonful of white-wine vinegar, and a pinch of pepper; allow these to simmer for 3 minutes, and then add a small ladleful of blond of veal or *consommé*; let the whole be reduced to half the original quantity; and, just before using the sauce, throw in a spoonful of chopped and blanched parsley.

Poivrade Sauce.

Take 1 carrot, 1 onion, and 1 head of celery; cut them into very small dice, and place them in a stewpan, with 2 ounces of raw lean of ham cut similarly, some thyme, and 1 bay-leaf, 1 blade of mace, a few peppercorns, and some parsley; fry these with a little butter, of a light-brown color; moisten with 2 glasses of sherry and 1 of French vinegar; reduce the above to one-half its quantity, and then add a small ladleful of brown sauce and a little *consommé*; stir the sauce till it boils, and then set it by the side to clear itself; skim it, and pass it through a tammy to keep ready for use.

Indian Curry Sauce.

Take 2 large onions, 1 carrot, and 1 head of celery, and slice them very thin; place these with 2 ounces of fresh butter in a stewpan, and fry them over a slow fire till the onions are nearly melted, but without becoming brown; add 3 blades of mace, some thyme, and 1 bay-leaf, 1 bouquet of parsley, and 2 tablespoonsful of Cooks' or Bruce's meat curry paste, 1 tablespoonful of curry powder, and as much browning or flour as may be required to thicken the quantity of sauce needed; moisten with some good broth or *consommé*, and stir the sauce on the fire till it boils; then set it by the side to clear itself of the butter, etc. Having skimmed and reduced the sauce to a proper consistency, pass it through a tammy (extracting the parsley), as for a *purée*, and take it up ready for use, or add it to whatever kind of meat is prepared for the curry; observing that the broth thereof should be used for making the sauce.

Brown Oyster Sauce.

Prepare this precisely as the last sauce, but, instead of the cream, use an equal quantity of brown gravy. Brown oyster sauce is a very desirable accessory to beefsteaks, beef-pudding, beefsteak pie, broiled slices of cod-fish, and various other plain dressed dishes.

German Sweet Sauce.

Stew 6 ounces of dried cherries in 2 glasses of red wine, together with some bruised cinnamon, cloves and lemon-peel, for 20 minutes on a slow fire; pass the whole through a tammy, and put it into a stewpan with a little reduced brown sauce and 6 ounces of stewed prunes.

This sauce is in great request for German dishes; it improves the flavor of braized venison in its varied forms of preparation, and is preferred by many for that purpose to Poivrade or Piquante sauce.

Cherry Sauce.

Put a pot of black currant jelly into a stewpan, together with 6 ounces of dried cherries, a small stick of cinnamon, and 12 cloves tied up in a piece of muslin; moisten with ½ pint of red wine, and set the whole to simmer gently on a slow fire for 10 minutes; then take out the cinnamon and cloves, and send to table.

This kind of sauce is well adapted for roast hare or venison.

Red Currant Jelly Sauce for Venison.

Bruise 1 stick of cinnamon and 12 cloves, and put them into a small stewpan with 2 ounces of sugar, and the peel of one lemon pared off very thin, and perfectly free from any portion of white pulp; moisten with 3 glasses of Port wine, and set the whole to simmer gently on the fire for ¼ of an hour; then strain it through a sieve into a small stewpan, containing a pot of red currant jelly. Just before sending the same to table set it on the fire to boil, in order to melt the currant jelly, so that it may mix with the essence of spice, etc.

Fried Bread Sauce.

Mince a little lean ham, and put it into a small stewpan, with 1 chopped shallot, some grated nutmeg, mignonette pepper, and ½ a pint of good gravy; simmer the whole on the stove-fire till reduced to half, then strain it with pressure through a tammy into another small stewpan, containing 4 tablespoonfuls of fried bread-crumbs of a light-brown color, and some chopped parsley, and a little essence of chicken, and the juice of ½ a lemon; stir the sauce till it boils, and serve. This kind of sauce is appropriate for all small birds, such as wheat-ears, ortolans, ruffs and reeves, etc., etc.

Brown Gravy for Roast Veal.

Place 4 ounces of fresh butter in a stewpan and knead it with a good tablespoonful of flour; add a ladleful of good brown gravy, some essence of mushrooms or mushroom catsup, a little grated nutmeg, and pepper; stir the sauce on the stove, and keep it gently boiling for ten minutes. If it becomes too thick add a little more gravy, so as to keep it of the same consistency as any other sauce; finish with a little lemon-juice. If there is no gravy or essence of mushrooms at hand, use in their stead a ladleful of water, a piece of glaze, some mushroom catsup, and a little Indian soy; these will answer nearly the same purpose.

Plain Curry Sauce.

Put 2 ounces of fresh butter into a stewpan, together with rather more than an ounce of flour and a good tablespoonful of curry-paste or powder; knead these well together, then add a little shred carrot, celery and onions; moisten with about a pint of good strong consommé; stir the sauce on the fire until it boils, and after having kept it boiling for about twenty minutes, pass it through the tammy, as for a purée; then remove the sauce into a bain-marie or stewpan, to be used when required. This economical method of making curry sauce should only be resorted to in cases of emergency or necessity, otherwise it is desirable to follow the directions contained in Indian Curry Sauce.

Caper Sauce for Boiled Mutton.

To about half a pint of good butter sauce add a tablespoonful of capers, with a little pepper and salt.

Mayonnaise Sauce.

Place two raw yolks of eggs in a round-bottomed basin, and set this in a deep saucepan containing some pounded ice; add a little pepper and salt to the yolks, and proceed to work them quickly with the back part of the bowl of a wooden spoon, moistening at intervals with salad-oil and vinegar, which must, however, be sparingly used at first, and gradually increased as you proceed, until by this means the quantity of sauce desired is produced; add a little lemon-juice to make the sauce white.

Boar's Head Sauce.

Grate a stick of horse-radish, and place it in a basin with 4 ounces of red currant-jelly, a spoonful of mixed mustard, the grated rind of an orange and lemon, together with the juice of both; 2 ounces of pounded sugar, a tablespoonful of vinegar, and 2 tablespoonfuls of salad-oil. Mix these ingredients thoroughly together and serve.

Mullaga-tawny Soup.

Cut 4 pounds of a breast of veal into pieces, about two inches by one; put the trimmings into a stewpan with 2 quarts of water, 12 corns of black pepper, and the same of allspice; when it boils skim it clean, and let it boil an hour and a half, then strain it off; while it is boiling, fry of a nice brown in butter the bits of veal and 4 onions; when they are done put the broth to them, and put it on the fire; when it boils skim it clean, let it simmer half an hour, then mix 2 spoonfuls of curry and the same of flour with a little cold water, and a teaspoonful of salt; add these to the soup, and simmer it gently till the veal is quite tender, and it is ready; or bone a couple of fowls or rabbits, and stew them in the manner directed above for the veal; and you may put in a bruised shallot, and some mace and ginger, instead of black pepper and allspice.

A Tureen of Hodge-Podge of Different Sorts.

Take either a brisket of beef, mutton, steaks, whole pigeons, rabbits cut in quarters, veal or poultry; boil a long time over a slow fire in a short liquid, with some onions, carrots, parsnips, turnips, celery, a bunch of parsley, green shallots, 1 clove of garlic, 3 of spices, a laurel leaf, thyme, a little basil, large thick sausages, and thin broth or water; when done drain the meat and place it upon a dish intermixed with roots, sift and skim the sauce, reduce some of it to a glaze, if desired; glaze the meat with it, then add some gravy on the same stewpan, and broth sufficient to make sauce enough with pepper and salt; sift it in a sieve, and serve upon the meat. If brisket of beef is used, let it be half done before putting in the roots, which should be scalded first, as it makes the broth more palatable.

Hotch-Potch. — (Meg Dod's Recipe.)

Make the stock of sweet fresh mutton. Grate the zest of 2 or 3 large carrots, slice down also young turnips, young onions, lettuce and parsley. Have a full quart of these things when sliced, and another of green peas, and sprays of cauliflower. Put in the vegetables, withholding half the peas till near the end of the process. Cut down 4 pounds of ribs of lamb into small chops trimming off superfluous fat, and put them into the soup. Boil well and skim carefully; add the remaining peas, white pepper and salt, and when thick enough serve the chops in the tureen with the hotch-potch.

Winter Soup.

Make a good brown stock of a small shin of

beef, with vegetables, carrots, turnips, onions and celery; when sufficiently boiled the vegetables must be taken out *whole*, and the soup seasoned with pepper and salt and a little Cayenne to taste, also a little Harvey sauce and cat-up; then fry some mutton cutlets, the quantity required for the number, a pale brown, add them to the soup with the vegetables cut up small.

Vermicelli and Vegetable Soup.

Five pounds of lean beef, 2 heads of celery, 2 carrots, 2 turnips, 4 onions, 1 bunch of sweet herbs (in a muslin bag), ½ an ounce of white pepper, ½ an ounce of allspice, a little salt, 5 pints of water. To be boiled *six hours*, well skimmed and strained from the vegetables, etc. Next day 1 carrot, 1 turnip, the hearts of the 2 heads of celery, to be boiled in water after being cut into dice, and added to the soup with ¾ of a pound of vermicelli.

Liebig's Broth.

Cut ½ a pound of freshly-killed beef or chicken into small pieces. Add to it 1⅛ pounds of water, in which are dissolved 4 drops of muriatic acid and ¾ of a drachm of salt. Mix all well together, and let them stand for an hour. Then strain through a hair sieve, but without pressing or squeezing. Pour it again and again through the sieve until clear. Pour ½ a pound of pure water over what is left on the sieve. This broth is to be given cold to the sick.

Curry.

Take the skin off 2 chickens; carve, wash and dry them; put them in a stewpan with a teacupful of water, salt, and a few onions, and stew them with a few green peas, or the egg-plant, till tender; then take a lump of butter the size of a pigeon's egg, a little mace, Cayenne pepper to taste, a teaspoonful each of fresh turmeric and cardamoms, pounded with a shallot in a marble mortar; roll these ingredients with a little flour in the butter, and dissolve them in the stew. If the curry is to be brown, it must be fried a little before the curry-ball is added to the gravy.

Another.—Carve a pair of fat young fowls with a sharp knife, precisely as if at table; dust them with flour, fry them in butter till they are well browned, lay them in a stewpan, with slips of 4 large onions; add boiling water to the browning, etc., left in the pan, give it a boil, and pour the whole over your chicken; if not liquor enough to rather more than cover it, add hot water; put on the lid of your pan and set it on hot coals. In half an hour take out a cup of the gravy, mix it well with a tablespoonful of curry powder, and throw it again into the pan; stir it well round; taste and see if your gravy is warm, if not add Cayenne; bubble the whole quietly till the fowls are tender, serve in a deep dish with boiled rice.

Malay's Curry.

Proceed as above; fry the onions, pieces of fowls, and a couple of egg-plants in slices: put the whole in your stewpan with the milk of 2 cocoa-nuts; grate the flesh, put it into a linen bag and squeeze out the juice, which put in the saucepan likewise; add the curry and finish as above.

Curry Powder.

Coriander seed, 3 ounces; turmeric, 5 ounces; black pepper, mustard and ginger, each 1 ounce; lesser cardamom seeds, ½ an ounce; Cayenne pepper, ½ an ounce; cinnamon and cummin seed, ¼ of an ounce each. Dry them well; reduce them separately to a powder; pass them through a fine sieve, and mix them well. It should be kept in a closely-stopped bottle in a dry place.

White Soup.

Stew a knuckle of veal and a scrag of mutton three or four hours, with spice; strain it; blanch ½ a pound of sweet almonds; beat them with a spoonful or two of cream to prevent their oiling; put them with a pint of cream into the soup, stir it and give it a boil; strain it through a cloth, squeeze the almonds as dry as possible, heat it again, and thicken it as a custard with eggs; put a toasted roll in the tureen, and pour the soup over it. If there is a breast of cold fowl or veal, less almonds will do. If the meat be stewed and strained the day before, it does much better.

To make Jelly Broth.

Put into the stewpan slices of beef, veal fillet, a fowl, and one or two partridges, according to the quantity required. Put it on the fire without liquid until it catches a little, and add the meat now and then. To give it a proper color, add some good clear boiling broth and scalded roots, as carrots, turnips, parsnips, parsley roots, celery, large onions, two or three cloves, a small bit of nutmeg and whole pepper. Boil it on a slow fire about four or five hours with attention, and add a few cloves of garlic or eschalots, and a small fagot or bunch of parsley and thyme tied together. When it is of a good yellow color, sift it; it serves for sauces, and adds strength to the soups.

Preparation of Calf's Udder.

The udder is an elongated piece of fat-looking substance attached to the inner part of a leg of veal. It is easily separated from the meat by a knife, and should then be bound round with twine in the shape of a sausage, so as to prevent it from falling to pieces on taking it out of the stockpot; the udder so tied up is then put into the stockpot to boil. Having allowed the dressed udder time to cool and get firm, either on the ice or otherwise, pare off the outside with a knife, cut it into small pieces, and pound it in a mortar; then rub it through a wire sieve with a wooden spoon, and put it on a plate upon the ice to cool, in order that it may be quite firm when required for use.

Note.—The two foregoing preparations being the basis of a great variety of forcemeats, it is essential that they should be well understood before attempting the following more complicated amalgamations. It should also be observed, that all meat and fish intended for *quenelles* must be forced through a wire sieve by rubbing it vigorously with the back of a wooden spoon, and then be kept on ice till used.

Forcemeat of Liver and Ham, for Raised Pies.

Take the whole or part of a light-colored calf's liver, or several fat livers of any kind of poultry, if to be obtained. If calf's liver be used, cut it into rather small square pieces, and, if time permit, steep them in cold spring-water, in order to extract the blood, so that the forcemeat may be whiter. Take the pieces of liver out of the water, and place them upon a clean rubber, to drain the water from them. Meanwhile cut some fat ham or bacon (in equal proportion to the liver) into square pieces, put them into a sauce-pan on a brisk fire to fry; after which add the pieces of liver, and fry the whole of a light-brown color; season with Cayenne pepper and salt, and a little prepared aromatic spice, some chopped mushrooms, parsley, and three shallots. After this take the pieces of liver and ham out of the pan, lay them on a chopping-board, and chop them fine; then put them into a mortar with the remaining contents of the pan; pound the whole thoroughly, and rub it through a wire sieve on to an earthen dish. This kind of forcemeat, or farce, is an excellent ingredient in making raised pies.

Spring Soup.

Take 4 carrots and as many turnips, scraped and washed; scoop them into the form of small olives or peas, with a vegetable scoop of either shape; add the white part of 2 heads of celery, 24 small onions (without the green stalk), and 1 head of firm white cauliflower, cut into small flowerets. Blanch or parboil the foregoing in boiling water for three minutes, strain them on a sieve, and then throw them into 3 quarts of bright *consommé* of fowl. Let the whole boil gently for half an hour by the side of the stove fire; then add the white leaves of 2 cabbage-lettuces (previously stamped out with a round cutter the size of a shilling), a handful of sorrel-leaves, snipped or cut like the lettuces, a few leaves of tarragon and chervil, and a small piece of sugar. Let these continue to boil gently until done. When about to send the soup to table, put into the tureen half a pint of young green peas, an equal quantity of asparagus-heads boiled green, and a handful of small *croûtons à la duchesse*, prepared in the following manner: Cut the crust off a rasped French roll into strips; stamp or cut out these with a round tin or steel cutter into small pellets, about the size of a dime, and dry them in the oven to be ready for use. Before sending the soup to table, taste it to ascertain whether it be sufficiently seasoned.

Julienne Soup.

Take 3 red carrots of a large size, as many sound turnips, and the white parts of the same number of leeks, heads of celery, and onions. Cut all these vegetables into fine shreds an inch long; put them into a convenient-sized stewpan, with 2 ounces of fresh butter, a little salt, and a teaspoonful of pounded sugar. Simmer these vegetables on a slow stove fire, taking care they do not burn. When they become slightly brown add 3 quarts of veal gravy or light-colored *consommé*; let the soup boil, skim all the butter off as it rises to the surface, and, when the vegetables are done, throw in the leaves of two cabbage-lettuces and a handful of sorrel, shred like the carrots, etc.; add a few leaves of tarragon and chervil. Boil the whole for ten minutes longer, taste the soup in order to ascertain whether the seasoning is correct, and serve.

Scotch Broth.

Take a neck of fresh mutton; trim it the same as for cutlets; take the scrag and trimmings, with 2 carrots, 3 turnips, 2 heads of celery, 2 onions, a bunch of parsley, and a sprig of thyme, and with these make some mutton broth, filling up with either broth from the common stockpot or with water. While the mutton broth is boiling, cut up the neck of mutton, previously trimmed for the purpose, into chops, which should have the superfluous skin and fat pared away, and place them in a three-quart stewpan, together with the red or outer part of 2 carrots, 3 turnips, 2 leeks, 1 onion, and 2 heads of celery — the whole of these to be cut in the form of very small dice; add 6 ounces of Scotch barley, previously washed and parboiled, and then pour on to the whole the broth made from the scrag, etc, when strained and the fat removed. Allow the soup thus far prepared to boil gently until the chops and vegetables be thoroughly done. Five minutes before sending the soup to table throw into it a tablespoonful of chopped and blanched parsley. Be sparing in the use of salt, so as not to overpower the simple but sweet flavor which characterizes this broth.

Hodge-Podge.

Make the mutton broth as shown in the preceding directions, and in addition to its contents add a pint and a half of green peas (either marrowfats or Prussian-blues). Allow the soup to boil gently until the ingredients be thoroughly done, then mix in with them one pint of purée of green spinach and parsely; taste to ascertain that the seasoning be correct, and serve.

Lettuce and Whole-Pea Soup.

Pick, wash and blanch a dozen white-heart cabbage-lettuces; cut them open and spread them on a clean napkin; season them with pepper and salt; then put two together face to face and proceed to tie them up with twine. Cover the bottom of a stewpan with thin layers of fat bacon and place the lettuce thereon; pour over them some broth from the boiling stockpot, over which lay a round of buttered paper, place the lid on the stewpan, start them to boil on the fire, and then place them on a slackened stove to simmer gently for about an hour, after which drain the lettuces on a clean napkin, untie them, and after having cut them into inch lengths lay them in the soup-tureen, together with a pint of young green peas boiled for the purpose and a small pinch of pepper. Take every particle of fat off the broth in which the lettuces have been braized and add it to the lettuces and peas already in the tureen, over which pour 2 quarts of bright, strong consommé of fowl; ascertain that the soup is palatable, and having thrown in a handful of duchess's crusts, send to table.

Turtle Soup.

Procure a fine, lively, fat turtle, weighing about 120 pounds, fish of this weight being considered the best, as their fat is not liable to be impregnated with that disagreeable, strong flavor objected to in fish of larger size. On the other hand, turtles of very small size seldom possess sufficient fat or substance to make them worth dressing. When time permits kill the turtle overnight, that it may be left to bleed in a cool place till the next morning, when at an early hour it should be cut up for scalding, that being the first part of the operation. If, however, the turtle is required for immediate use, to save time the fish may be scalded as soon as it is killed. The turtle being ready for cutting up, lay it on its back, and with a large kitchen-knife separate the fat or belly-shell from the back by making an incision all round the inner edge of the shell; when all the fleshy parts adhering to the shell have been carefully cut away, it may be set aside. Then detach the intestines by running the sharp edge of a knife closely along the spine of the fish, and remove them instantly in a pail to be thrown away. Cut off the fins and separate the fleshy parts, which place on a dish by themselves till wanted. Take particular care of every particle of the green fat, which lies chiefly at the sockets of the fore-fins, and more or less all round the interior of the fish, if in good condition. Let this fat, which, when in a healthy state, is elastic and of a bluish color while raw, be steeped for several hours in cold spring-water, in order that it may be thoroughly cleansed of all impurities; then with a meat-saw divide the upper and under shells into pieces of convenient size to handle, and having put them with the fins and head into a large vessel containing boiling water, proceed quickly to scald them; by this means they will be separated from the horny substance which covers them, which will then be easily removed. They must then be put into a larger stockpot nearly filled with fresh hot water and left to continue boiling by the side of the stove-fire until the glutinous substance separates easily from the bones. Place the pieces of turtle carefully upon clean dishes and put them in the larder to get cold; they should then be cut up into pieces about an inch and a half square, which pieces are to be finally put into the soup when it is nearly finished. Put the bones back into the broth to boil an hour longer, for the double purpose of extracting all their savor and to effect the reduction of the turtle broth, which is to be used for filling up the turtle stockpot hereafter. In order to save time, while the above is in operation the turtle stock or *consommé* should be prepared as follows: With 4 ounces of fresh butter spread the bottom of an 18 gallon stockpot; then place in it 3 pounds of raw ham cut in slices; over these put 10 pounds of leg of beef and knuckles of veal, 4 old hens (after having removed their fillets, which are to be kept for making the *quenelles* for the soup); to these add all the fleshy pieces of the turtle (excepting those pieces intended for *entrées*), and then place on the top the head and fins of the turtle; moisten the whole with a bottle of Madeira and 4 quarts of good stock; add a pottle of mushrooms, 12 cloves, 4 blades of mace, a handful of parsley roots and a good sized bouquet of parsley tied up with 2 bay leaves, thyme, green onions and shallots. Set the *consommé* thus prepared on a brisk stove fire to boil sharply, and when the liquid has become reduced to a glaze fill the stockpot up instantly, and as soon as it boils skim it thoroughly, garnish with the usual complement of vegetables, and remove it to the side of the stove to boil gently for 5 hours. Remember to probe the head and fins after they have been boiled 2 hours, and as soon as they are done drawn them on a dish, cover them with a wet napkin well saturated with water to prevent it from sticking to them, and put them away in a cool place with the remainder of the glutinous parts of the turtle already spoken of. The stockpot should now be filled up with the turtle broth reserved for that purpose as directed above. When the turtle stock is done strain it off into an appropriate sized stockpot, remove every particle of fat from the surface, and then proceed to thicken it with a proportionate quantity of flour to the consistency of thin sauce. Work this exactly in the same manner as practised in brown sauce, in order to extract all the butter and scum, so as to give it a brilliant appearance. One bottle of old Madeira must now be added, together with a *purée* of herbs of the following kinds, to be made as here directed: Sweet basil must form one third proportion of the whole quantity of herbs intended to be used; winter savory, marjoram and lemon thyme in equal quantities, making up the other two thirds; add to these a double handful of green shallots and some trimmings of mushrooms; moisten with a quart of broth, and having stewed these herbs for about an hour rub the whole through the tammy into a *purée*. This *purée* being added to the soup, a little Cayenne pepper should then be introduced. The pieces of turtle, as well as the fins, which have also been cut into small pieces and the larger bones taken out, should now be allowed to boil in the soup for a quarter of an hour, after which carefully remove the whole of the scum as it rises to the surface. The degree of seasoning must be ascertained, that it may be corrected if faulty. To excel in dressing turtle it is necessary to be very accurate in the proportions of the numerous ingredients used for seasoning this soup. Nothing should predominate, but the whole should be harmoniously blended. Put the turtle away in four quart sized basins, dividing the fat (after it has been scalded and boiled in some of the sauce) in equal quantities into each basin, as also some small *quenelles*, which are to be made with the fillets of hens reserved for that purpose, and in which, in addition to the usual ingredients in ordinary cases, put 6 yolks of eggs boiled hard. Mould these *quenelles* into small, round balls, to imitate turtles' eggs, roll them with the hand on a marble slab or table, with the aid of a little flour, and poach them in the usual way. When the turtle soup is wanted for use, warm it, and just before sending it to table add a small glass of Sherry or Madeira and the juice of one lemon to every four quarts of turtle. The second stock of the turtle *consommé* should be strained off after it has boiled for two hours, and immediately boiled down into a glaze very quickly and mixed in with the turtle soup previously to putting it away in the basins, or else it should be kept in reserve for the purpose of adding proportionate quantities in each tureen of turtle as it is served. [For this and several other receipts in fine cookery we are indebted to Francatelli.]

Mock Turtle Soup.

Procure a scalded calf's head, or as it is sometimes called, a turtle head, bone it in the following manner: Place the calf's head on the table with the front part of the head facing you, draw the sharp point of a knife from the back part of the head right down to the nose, making an incision down to the bone of the skull; then with the knife clear the scalp and cheeks from the bones right and left, always keeping the point of the knife close to the bone. Having boned the head put it into a large stewpan of cold water on the fire; as soon as it boils skim it well and let it continue to boil for ten minutes; take the calf's head out and put it into a pan full of cold water; then get a proper sized stockpot and after having buttered the bottom thereof, place in it 4 slices of raw ham, 2 large knuckles of veal, and an old hen partially roasted; moisten with 2 quarts of broth and put the stockpot on the stove fire to boil until the broth is reduced to a glaze, when instantly slacken the heat by covering the fire with ashes, and then leave the soup to color itself gradually. Allow the glaze at the bottom of the stewpan to be reduced to the same consistency as for brown sauce, and fill up the stockpot with water leaving room for the calf's head, which separate into two halves, and pare off all the rough cuticle about the inner parts of the mouth, then place it in the stock, and after setting it to boil and thoroughly skimming it garnish with the usual complement of vegetables, 6 cloves, 2 blades of mace, ¼ a pottle of mushrooms, 4 shallots, and a good bunch of parsley, green onions, thyme and bay leaf tied together, and a little salt. Set it by the fire to boil gently till the calf's head is done, then take the pieces of head out and place them on a dish to cool, afterward to be cut into squares and put into a basin till required for adding them to the soup. Strain the stock through a broth cloth and thicken it with some light colored browning to the consistency of thin brown sauce, let it boil and allow it to throw up all the butter and classify itself thoroughly, then add ¼ a bottle of Sherry, about ¼ a pint of *paste* of turtle herbs in which 6 anchovies have been mixed, a little Cayenne pepper, and the calf's head cut into squares, as also the tongue braized with it. Let these boil together for about ten minutes, then add 3 or 4 dozen small round *quenelles* and a little lemon juice and send to table.

Mock turtle Soup.

Scald a calf's head with the skin on, and take off

the horny part, which cut into two inch square pieces; clean and dry them well in a cloth, and put them into a stew-pan, with 4 quarts of water made as follows: Take 6 or 7 pounds of beef, a calf's foot, a shank of ham, an onion, 2 carrots, a turnip, a head of celery, some cloves and whole pepper, a bunch of sweet herbs, a little lemon-peel, and a few truffles. Put these into 8 quarts of water, and stew them gently till the liquid is reduced one half; then strain it off, and put into the stewpan with the horny parts of the calf's head. Add some knotted marjoram, savory, thyme, parsley chopped small, with some cloves and mace pounded, a little Cayenne pepper, some green onions, an eschalot cut fine, a few chopped mushrooms, and ½ pint Madeira wine. Stew these gently till the soup is reduced to 2 quarts, then heat a little broth. Mix some flour, smoothing it with the yolks of 2 eggs, and stir it over a gentle fire till it is near boiling. Add this to the soup; keep stirring as you pour it in, and continue stewing for another hour. When done, squeeze in the juice of half a lemon, half an orange, and throw in some boiled force-meat balls. Serve it up in a tureen hot. This soup is deliciously gratifying and nutritive.

Ox-tail Soup.

Procure 2 fresh ox tails, cut each joint after dividing them into inch lengths with a small meatsaw, steep them in water for two hours and then place them in a stewpan with 3 carrots, 3 turnips, 3 onions, 2 heads of celery, 4 cloves, and a blade of mace. Fill up the stewpan with broth from the boiling stockpot, boil this by the side of the stove fire till done, drain the pieces of ox tail on a large sieve, allow them to cool, trim them neatly, and place them in a soup pot. Clarify the broth the ox tails were boiled in, strain it through a napkin into a basin, and then pour it into the soup pot containing the trimmed pieces of ox tails, and also some small olive shaped pieces of carrot and turnip that have been boiled in a little of the broth, and a small lump of sugar; add a pinch of pepper, and previously to sending the soup to table let it boil gently by the side of the stove fire for a few minutes. This soup may be served also in various other ways, by adding thereto a purée of any sort of vegetables, such for instance as a purée of beans, carrots, turnips, celery, lentils.

Ox cheek Soup.

Procure a fresh ox cheek and put it to braize in a small stockpot with a knuckle of veal and some roast beef bones, fill the pot up from the boiling stockpot or with water, garnish with the same complement of stock vegetables used for ox tail soup, adding 6 cloves, a blade of mace, and a few peppercorns. As soon as the ox cheek is done take the meat off the cheek bone and put it in press between 2 dishes. Strain off the broth, adding to it a ladleful of gravy to color it, and proceed to clarify it with a couple of whites of eggs while the consommé is clarifying; trim the ox cheek and cut it into neat scallops 1 inch square and ¼ an inch thick; put them into a small soup pot and add to them some small carrots and turnips cut in fancy shapes and boiled in a little broth, a lump of sugar, and also 1½ dozen of very small white button onions. Strain the clarified consommé thus prepared into the soup pot, and having allowed the soup to boil a few minutes by the side of the stove fire, just before serving add 2 dozen blanched Brussels sprouts and a pinch of pepper, and send to table.

Bread Panada for Quenelles.

Take the crumb of 2 new French rolls, and steep it in tepid water for ten minutes; then put it into a napkin and wring it tightly, in order to remove the water from the bread. Put the crumb into a stewpan, with 2 ounces of fresh butter, a little salt, and 2 spoonfuls of white broth; put these on the stove fire, continuing to stir the panada the whole time with a wooden spoon, until it assumes the appearance of paste, and no longer adheres to the bottom of the stewpan; then add 3 yolks of eggs, and turn it out on a plate. Smoothe it over the surface with the blade of a knife, and, having covered it with a round piece of buttered paper, place it in the larder until required for use.

Pâte à Choux Panada.

To ½ pint of white chicken broth add 4 ounces of fresh butter and a little salt; put the stewpan containing these on the fire. As soon as it begins to simmer mix in with the aforementioned ingredients 5 ounces of sifted flour; and, by continuing to stir this batter on the fire for five minutes, it will become a delicately firm paste, which must be worked over the fire until it freely leaves the side of the pan; then take 3 yolks of eggs and quickly mix them in the batter; put it on a plate, cover it with a buttered paper, and keep it in the cool till wanted for use. This kind of panada is preferred by some cooks to bread panada, being considered by them more delicate, and less liable to produce fermentation in warm weather. However, bread panada has the advantage of not collapsing, as is the case with the pâte à choux panada, if prepared some time before the quenelle in which it is used be eaten.

Chicken Panada.

Roast off a young fowl, take all the white parts and pound them with the crumb of a French roll soaked in broth; dilute these with a little chicken broth (made from the remains of the roasted fowl) to the consistency of a soft butter or creamy substance, pass it through a tammy as in preparing any other purée.

Previously to serving this panada it should be moderately warmed and put into custard cups. In the composition of dietetic preparations for infants and invalids, it is necessary to avoid the use of herbs and spices.

Corn Oysters.

Take 6 ears of boiled corn, 4 eggs, 2 tablespoonsful of flour. Cut the corn off the cob, season it with pepper and salt, mix it with the yolks of the eggs beaten thoroughly, and add the flour. Whisk the whites to a stiff froth and stir them in; put a tablespoonful at a time in a pan of hot lard or butter and fry until they are a light brown color on both sides.

Egg Plants.

After paring cut them in slices as thin as possible, let them lie an hour in salt water; then season with pepper and salt, dredge fine powdered cracker or stale bread crumbs over each piece, beat up an egg as for veal cutlet and dip to each alternately and put in a pan with some hot butter or beef drippings. Fry slowly until quite soft, and a dark brown on both sides. Serve them up hot.

Potatoes, à la Maître d'Hôtel.

The small French kidney potatoes are best adapted for this purpose. Boil or steam them in the ordinary way and when done cut them into slices about the eighth of an inch thick, put them into a stewpan with a tablespoonful of white sauce or broth, 4 ounces of butter, some pepper and salt, chopped parsley and a little lemon juice; toss them over the stove fire until the butter, etc., is mixed in with the potatoes, then dish them up, either with or without croûtons round them, and serve.

New Potatoes a la Creme.

Cut some recently boiled new potatoes in slices, put them into a stewpan with a gill of cream, 4 ounces of fresh butter, a very little nutmeg, pepper and salt, and the juice of half a lemon; set them to boil on the stove fire, toss them well together, and dish them up with *croûtons*.

Green Peas, Plain.

Put the peas into boiling water, some salt, and a bunch of green mint; keep them boiling briskly for about twenty minutes, and when done, drain them in a colander, dish them up with chopped boiled mint on the top, and send some small pats of very fresh butter separately on a plate.

Stewed Peas.

Put 1 quart of young peas into a pan, with 4 ounces of butter, and plenty of cold water; rub the peas and butter together with the fingers, until well mixed, then pour off the water, and put the peas into a stewpan, with a couple of cabbage lettuces, shred small, a bunch of green onions and parsley, a dessertspoonful of pounded sugar, and a little salt; put the lid on, and set the peas to stew very gently over a slow fire for about half an hour; when done, if there appears to be much liquor, boil it down quickly over the fire. Next put about 2 ounces of fresh butter on a plate, with a dessertspoonful of flour, and knead them together; put this into the peas, and toss the whole together over the stove fire until well mixed; dish the peas up, garnished round with pastry, and serve.

Asparagus with White Sauce.

Pick the loose leaves from the heads, and scrape the stalks clean, wash them in a pan of cold water, tie them up in bundles of about 20 in each, keeping all the heads turned the same way; cut the stalks even, leaving them about 8 inches long. Put the asparagus in hot water with a small handful of salt in it, to boil for about twenty minutes, and when done, drain them carefully upon a napkin to avoid breaking off the heads; dish them up on a square thick piece of toasted bread dipped in the water they have been boiled in, and send to table with some white sauce, separately in a sauce-boat.

Spinach with Butter.

Pick all the stalks from the spinach, wash it in several waters, and drain it upon a sieve; throw it into a stewpan of hot water with a handful of salt, and keep it boiling until it becomes thoroughly tender and soft to the touch; then drain it in a colander, immerse it in cold water, and afterwards squeeze all the water from it. The spinach must next be carefully turned over with the point of a knife, to remove any straws or stalks that may have been overlooked; it should then be chopped or pounded in a mortar, rubbed through a coarse wire sieve, and placed in a stewpan with about 2 ounces of butter, a little salt, and grated nutmeg; stir the spinach over a stove fire with a wooden spoon until it becomes quite warm, then add a gravyspoonful of good sauce, a small piece of glaze, and about 4 ounces of fresh butter. Work the whole together, with a wooden spoon, until well mixed, then pile the spinach up in the centre of the dish, garnish it round with *croûtons*, and serve.

Macaroni à l'Italienne.

Break up the macaroni in 3-inch lengths, and put it on to boil in hot water, with a pat of butter, a little pepper and salt; when done, drain it on a napkin, and as soon as the moisture is absorbed, dish it up in the following manner: First, put 2 large tablespoonfuls of good tomato-sauce into a stewpan, and boil it over the stove fire; then add 2 pats of fresh butter with as much glaze, and work the whole well together; next, strew a layer of the macaroni on the bottom of the dish, then pour some of the sauce over it, and strew some grated Parmesan cheese over this; and so on, repeating the same until the dish is full enough; strew some grated cheese over the top, put the macaroni in the oven for five minutes, and then serve while it is quite hot.

Macaroni with Cream.

Boil 1 pound of macaroni, and when done, cut it up in three-inch lengths, and put it into a stewpan with 4 ounces of fresh butter, 4 ounces of grated Parmesan cheese, and a similar quantity of Gruyère cheese also grated, and 1 gill of good cream; season with pepper and salt, and toss the whole well together over the stove fire, until well mixed and quite hot, then shake it up for a few minutes to make the cheese spin, so as to give it a fibrous appearance, when drawn up with a fork. The macaroni, when dished up, may be garnished round the base with pastry, and then served.

Macaroni au Gratin.

Cut the macaroni up as above, put it into a stewpan with ¾ of a pound of grated cheese (Parmesan and Gruyère in equal quantities), 4 ounces of fresh butter, and 1 tablespoonful of good *Béchamel* sauce; season with pepper and salt, toss the whole together over the fire until well mixed, then pile it up in the centre of a border of a fried *croûtons* of bread (previously stuck round the bottom of the dish); strew the surface with fine bread-crumbs, and grated Parmesan cheese, in equal proportions; run a little melted butter through the holes of a spoon, over the top of the macaroni, and then put it into the oven to be baked of a bright yellow color; it should then be served quite hot.

Indian Sandwiches.

Cut the breast of a roast fowl or pheasant in very small, square, dice-like pieces, and place these on a plate; take about 4 ounces of red tongue or lean ham, and 4 anchovies (previously washed and filleted), cut these also in small dice, and place them with the chicken. Next, put 2 spoonsful of sauce, and a dessertspoonful of curry paste into a stewpan, boil them over the stove, stirring it meanwhile, until reduced to the consistency of a thick sauce; then add the chicken, etc., and the juice of ½ a lemon, mix the whole well together, and use this preparation in the following manner: Cut some thin slices of the crumb of a sandwich-loaf, and with a circular tin cutter, about an inch and a half in diameter, stamp out 24 *croûtons*; fry these in clarified butter to a bright yellow color, drain them on a napkin, and place one-half on a baking-sheet covered with clean paper; spread a thick layer of the above preparation on each of these, and then cover them with the remaining 12 *croûtons*. Next, grate 4 ounces of fresh Parmesan, and mix these with a pat of butter into a paste, divide it in 12 parts, roll each into a round ball, and place 1 of these on the top of each sandwich; about ten minutes before sending to table, put them in the oven to be warmed thoroughly, pass the red-hot salamander over them, to color them of a bright yellow; dish them up on a napkin, and serve.

Italian Salad.

Boil 2 heads of fine white cauliflower, a similar portion of asparagus-points, French beans, cut in diamonds, a few new potatoes (which after being boiled must be stamped out with a small vegetable cutter), ½ a pint of green peas and 3 artichoke-bottoms, also cut up in small fancy shapes when boiled. All these vegetables must be prepared with great attention, in order that they may retain their original color; the cauliflowers should be cut up in small buds or flowerets, and the whole, when done, put into a convenient-sized basin. Next, boil 2 large red beet-roots, 6 large new potatoes, and 20 large-sized heads of very green asparagus, or a similar quantity of French beans; cut the beet-roots and potatoes in two-inch lengths, and with a tin vegetable cutter, a quarter of an inch in diameter, punch out about two dozen small pillar-shaped pieces of each, and put these on a dish, with an equal quantity of asparagus-heads or French beans, cut to the same length. Then take a plain border-mould, and place the green vegetables in neat and close order all round the bottom of the mould; observing that a small quantity of jelly must be poured in the mould for the purpose of causing the pieces of French beans to hold together. Next, line the sides of the mould, by placing the pieces of beet-root and potatoes alternately, each of which must be first dipped in some bright jelly, previously to its being placed in the mould; when the whole is complete, fill the border up with jelly. Before placing the vegetables, the mould must be partially immersed in some pounded rough ice, contained in a basin or pan. When about to send this *entremêt* to table, turn the vegetable border out of the mould on to its dish; after the vegetables, before alluded to, have been seasoned, by adding to them a tablespoonful of jelly, 3 tablespoonfuls of oil, 1 of tarragon-vinegar, some pepper and salt; and when the whole have been gently tossed together, they should be neatly placed in the centre of the border, in a pyramidal form. Ornament the base of the *entremêts* with bold *croûtons* of bright jelly, and serve.

Sidney Smith's Recipe for Salad.

Two large potatoes passed through kitchen sieve,
Unwonted softness to the salad give;
Of mordant mustard add a single spoon —
Distrust the condiment which bites so soon
But deem it not, thou man of herbs, a fault
To add a double quantity of salt;
Three times the spoon with oil of Lucca crown
And once with vinegar procured from town
True flavor needs it, and your poet begs
The pounded yellow of two well-boiled eggs.
Let onion atoms lurk within the bowl,
And, scarce suspected, animate the whole;
And, lastly, on the flavored compound toss
A magic teaspoon of anchovy sauce.
Then, though green turtle fail, though venison's tough,
And ham and turkeys are not boiled enough,
Serenely full, the epicure may say —
Fate cannot harm me, I have dined to-day!

Chicken Salad.

Prepare the chickens as directed for a Mayonnaise. Pile the pieces of chicken up in the dish, upon a bed of seasoned shred lettuces, in a conical form; pour some white Mayonnaise sauce over the pieces, place a border of hard eggs cut in quarters, and hearts of cabbage-lettuce round the base; stick a white heart of a lettuce on the top, and serve.

Note. — Chicken-salad may also be ornamented and garnished with plover's eggs, decorated with truffles, and with eggs boiled hard cut in quarters, and ornamented either with their fillets of anchovies and capers, or colored butter, either lobster coral or green Ravigotte, or with tarragon, or chervil-leaves, laid flat on the eggs, or else stuck in the point.

Lobster Butter.

Procure some lobster spawn or coral, and pound it with twice as much butter, 1 anchovy and a little Cayenne pepper; rub it through a hair-sieve, collect it into a small basin, and keep it in a cool place till wanted for use.

Lobster Salad.

Break the shells, and remove the meat whole from the tails and claws of the lobsters; put this into a basin, with a little oil, vinegar, pepper and salt, and reserve the pith and coral to make some lobster-butter, which is to be thus used: First, spread a circular foundation of the lobster-butter upon the bottom of the dish, about seven inches in diameter, and the fourth part of an inch thick, then scoop out the centre, leaving a circular band. Drain the lobster on a cloth, cut the pieces in oval scallops, and with some of the butter (to stick the pieces firmly together), pile the lobster up in three successive rows, the centre being left hollow; fill this with shred lettuce, or salad of any kind, seasoned with oil, vinegar, pepper and salt; pour some scarlet Mayonnaise sauce over the salad, without mashing the pieces of lobster; garnish the base with a border of hearts of lettuces, divided in halves, and around these place a border of plover's eggs, having a small sprig of green tarragon stuck into the pointed end of each; place a white-heart of lettuce on the top, and serve.

Potted Lobster.

Lobsters for potting must be quite fresh. Take the meat, pith, and coral out of the shells, cut this up in slices, and put the whole into a stewpan with one-third part of clarified fresh butter, and to every pound of lobster add 4 whole anchovies (washed and wiped dry); season with mace, peppercorns, and a little salt, then put the lid on the stewpan, and set the lobster to simmer very gently over a slow fire for about a quarter of an hour. After this it must be thoroughly pounded in a mortar, rubbed through a sieve, put into small pots, steamed, and when cold should be pressed down with the bowl of a spoon, and the surface covered with a little clarified butter.

Mince-Meat.

Four pounds of beef and tongue mixed; 3 pounds of suet; 8 pounds of chopped apples; 3 pounds of currants (washed, dried, and picked); 3 pounds of seeded raisins; 6 pounds of *light* brown sugar; 2 pounds of citron cut into small thin pieces; the rind of 1 orange grated; 1 ounce of cinnamon; ¼ of an ounce of cloves; ¼ of an ounce of mace; ¼ of an ounce of allspice; 3 nutmegs grated; 1 quart of Madeira wine; 1 pint of Brandy. Boil the meat in salted water until tender; when cold chop it very fine. After freeing the suet from every particle of skin and chopping it fine, mix it through the meat with salt just sufficient to remove the fresh taste; to this add the apples, after which the sugar, fruit, spice, and other ingredients. Mix all well together and cover close. If too dry (before using) the quantity required may be moistened with a little sweet cider.

Note. — Mince-meat may be made *much* richer by using *uncooked* instead of cooked meat.

Mince-Meat.

Thoroughly cleanse 4 pounds of currants, and remove the stones from 4 pounds of raisins; cut up 2 pounds of candied citron, 1 pound of candied lemon, and 1 pound of orange-peel, into shreds, or very small dice; remove the skin, and then chop 4 pounds of fresh beef-suet, and place this with the currants and the candied peel in an earthern pan; next chop the raisins with 4 pounds of peeled apples, and add them to the other ingredients. Trim away all the sinewy parts from 8 pounds of roasted sirloin of beef, and chop all the lean of the meat quite fine; this will produce about 4 pounds, which must also be placed in the pan. To the foregoing must now be added 4 pounds of moist sugar, 4 ounces of ground spice—consisting of nutmegs, cloves, and cinnamon in equal proportions, with the grated rind of 12 oranges, and of the same number of lemons; the whole must then be thoroughly mixed together and pressed down to a level in the pan. Two bottles of brandy, and a like quantity of Madeira, sherry or port, should be poured into the mince-meat. Put the lid on the pan, place a cloth over it, and tie it down close, so as to exclude the air as much as possible, and also to prevent the evaporation of the brandy, etc. The mince-meat should be kept in a cool place, and will be fit for use a fortnight after it is made.

Cocoanut Cake, or Pudding.

A quarter of a pound of butter, 1 pound of sugar, 4 eggs, 1 cocoanut, 6 tablespoonfuls of flour. Cream the butter and sugar, and add to it the grated cocoanut, flour, and eggs. Bake forty minutes.

Cottage Pudding.

Take 3 tablespoonfuls of melted butter, with 1 cup of white sugar, 2 eggs beaten light, 1 pint of flour, 2 teaspoonfuls of cream of tartar sifted with the flour, and 1 teacup of milk with 2 teaspoonfuls of soda dissolved in it. This pudding may be either baked or boiled. Serve with wine sauce.

Patterdale Pudding.

Made at a celebrated inn in England. Three eggs and their weight in sugar, flour, and butter. Bake in small pans and eat with sauce.

Wedding-cake Pudding.

One cup of molasses, ½ cup of butter, 1 cup of sweet milk, 1 teaspoonful soda, 2 teaspoonfuls salt, 4 cups of flour, and 1 cup of raisins. Steam three hours in a bowl.

Sauce for the above.

One cup of powdered sugar, ½ cup of butter, beaten together to a cream; add 1 egg well beaten, 1 glass of wine, and 1 glass of boiling water. Steam five minutes.

Cocoanut Pudding.

A quarter of a pound of grated cocoanut, the same quantity of powdered loaf sugar, 3½ ounces of good butter, the whites of 6 eggs, and ¼ a glass of wine and brandy mixed, a teaspoonful of orange flower and rose-water—pour into your paste, and bake as above.

Mrs. Goodfellow's Lemon Pudding.

Take of butter (the very best) and loaf sugar, each ½ a pound, beat them to a froth as for poundcake, add 5 eggs, the juice of ½ of a large or the whole of a small lemon. Grate into it the outside yellow rind, but not an atom of the white—½ a glass of Madeira, ½ a glass of brandy, a teaspoonful of orange-flower water, pour it into your paste, and bake with a moderate oven.

Orange Custards.

Boil very tender the rind of half a Seville orange, and beat it in a mortar until it is very fine; put to it a teaspoonful of the best brandy, the juice of a Seville orange, 4 ounces of loaf sugar, and the yolk of 4 eggs. Beat them all together for ten minutes, and then pour in by degrees a pint of boiling cream; beat them until cold, then put them in custard cups, in a dish of hot water; let them stand till they are set, then take them out and stick preserved orange-peel on the top; this forms a fine flavored dish, and may be served up hot or cold.

Baked Custards.

Boil a pint of cream with some mace and cinnamon, and when it is cold, take 4 yolks of egg, a little rose-water, red wine, nutmeg, and sugar, to taste; mix them well and bake them.

Rice Custards.

Put a blade of mace and a quartered nutmeg into a quart of cream; boil and strain it, and add to it some boiled rice and a little brandy. Sweeten it to taste, stir it till it thickens, and serve it up in cups or in a dish; it may be used either hot or cold.

Almond Custards.

Blanch ¼ of a pound of almonds, beat them very fine, and then put them into a pint of cream, with 2 spoonfuls of rose-water; sweeten it, and put in the yolks of 4 eggs; stir them well together till the mixture becomes thick, and then pour it into cups.

Lemon Custards.

Take ½ a pound of double refined sugar, the juice of 2 lemons, the rind of 1 pared very thin, the inner rind of 1 boiled tender and rubbed through a sieve, and a pint of white wine; boil them for some time, then take out the peel and a little of the liquor; strain them into the dish, stir them well together and set them to cool.

Queen's Pudding.

Half pint of cream, 1 pint of milk, flavor with vanilla and white sugar to taste, and boil together for a quarter of an hour; add the yolks of 8 eggs, well beaten. Then place over the mass a piece of thin paper, and boil the pudding one hour. Serve it up with sauce made of 2 glasses of sherry, 1 pot of red-currant jelly, and white sugar mixed together, heated, and poured round the dish with the pudding.

Eve's Pudding.

Take ½ a pound of very finely grated breadcrumbs, ½ a pound of finely-chopped apples, ½ a pound of currants, ½ a pound of very fine suet, 6 ounces of sugar, 4 eggs, a little nutmeg, 2 ounces of citron and lemon-peel; butter the mould well and boil 3 hours.

Balloons.

One pint of milk, 3 eggs, 1 pint of flour. Beat the eggs light, and mix with the milk and stir into the flour gradually. Beat it well with 1 saltspoonful of salt; then butter small cups, fill them half full of the mixture and bake in a quick oven. When done turn them out of the cups, place them on a dish and send to table hot. Eat with wine sauce, or nun's butter.

Lemon Pudding.

Half a pound of butter, ½ a pound of sugar, 2 ounces of flour, 5 eggs, 2 tablespoonfuls of brandy, the gratings and juice of 1 lemon. Beat the butter and sugar very light, then add the flour; whisk the eggs until very thick, which stir in by degrees; lastly the lemon and brandy, alternately. Mix well without beating too much. This will make two puddings, soup-plate size. Line your plates with a rich paste and bake in a quick oven. When done and cool, sift white sugar over.

White Potato Pudding.

A quarter of a pound of butter, ½ a pound of sugar, 4 or 5 eggs, 1 pound of potatoes mashed exceedingly fine, with a little cream and salt through a colander; 2 tablespoonfuls of brandy, 1 grated nutmeg with ½ a teaspoonful of cinnamon. Beat the butter and sugar to a cream, then add the potato, eggs, brandy and spice. Line your plates with paste and bake in a quick oven. When done and cool, slip into plates suitable for the table, and sift white sugar over them.

Apple Pudding.

A quarter of a pound of butter, ½ a pound of sugar, 5 eggs, 4 large-sized tart apples, 2 ounces of currants, 2 tablespoonfuls of brandy, 1 teaspoonful of cinnamon and nutmeg mixed. Beat the butter and sugar to a cream, then whisk the eggs until thick and add to it. Pare the apples, grate and stir them into the mixture of eggs and sugar; then add the brandy, currants and spice. Stir the whole well together. This will be sufficient for two large-sized puddings. Line your plates with paste, put in the mixture and bake in a quick oven.

Rice Cups.

One quart of milk, 3 tablespoonfuls of rice boiled and stood to cool, 2 ounces of butter. Put on your milk to boil, mix the rice very smooth with some cold milk. As soon as the former begins to boil stir in the batter and let the whole boil twenty minutes. Whilst the rice is warm add the butter and a little salt. Rinse your custard cups with cold water; half fill them with the mixture; when it becomes cold they turn out of the cups and retain their forms. They are very ornamental to the table. To be eaten with cream and a little grated nutmeg.

Diavolini.

Eight ounces of ground rice, 4 ounces of sugar, a quart of milk, 2 ounces of butter, a teaspoonful of essence of ginger, 6 eggs, 1 pound of preserved ginger. Mix the rice, sugar, milk and butter together in a stewpan and stir the produce over a stove fire until it thickens; it must then be removed from the fire, and after being worked quite smooth and the lid being put on the stewpan, set it either in the oven or over a slow ash fire to finish doing; this will be effected in about half an hour. The rice must now be removed from the fire and the preserved ginger and the 6 yolks of eggs being added thereto, stir the whole over a quick fire until the eggs are set firm in the rice, and then turn out upon a clean dish or baking-sheet and spread equally to about a quarter of an inch in thickness, and when this has become cold it must be cut out in oblong shapes, which, after being first dipped in light frying batter, are to be fried crisp; then glaze with plain sugar and dish up on a napkin.

Brown-Bread Pudding.

Get ready the following ingredients: Twelve ounces of brown bread-crumbs, 6 ounces of pounded sugar, 6 eggs, ½ a pint of whipped cream, some grated lemon-rind, a little cinnamon-powder, 1 pound of morello cherries and a little salt. Mix the bread-crumbs, sugar, the yolks of eggs and whipped cream, the lemon, the cinnamon and the salt together in a large basin; then add the whipped whites of 6 eggs and set this aside. Next spread a plain mould with butter and strew it with brown bread-crumbs; then spread a large spoonful of the preparation at the bottom of the mould and arrange a layer of cherries (with the stones left in) upon it; cover this with some of the preparation, and upon it place more cherries, and so on until the mould is filled. The pudding must now be placed on a baking-sheet and put in the oven (moderately heated) to be baked for about an hour; when done turn it out of the mould on its dish, pour a *purée* of cherry-sauce round the base and serve. In Saxony it is customary to eat this kind of pudding as a cake when cold; in this case it should be entirely covered with sifted sugar, mixed with one-fourth part of cinnamon-powder.

Lemon Pudding.

The juice and grated rind (rubbed on sugar) of 6 lemons, 1 pint of cream, 6 ounces of bruised ratafias, 12 yolks and the whites of 4 eggs whipped, ½ a nutmeg grated, a little cinnamon-powder, 12 ounces of pounded sugar and a very little salt. Mix the above together in a large basin and work them with a whisk for about ten minutes. Next put a border of puff-paste round the edge of a tart dish, spread the dish with butter, pour the batter into it, strew some shred pistachio kernels on the top and bake it for about half an hour (at moderate heat). When done shake some sifted sugar over it, and serve.

Bread Pudding, Plain.

Twelve ounces of bread-crumbs, 6 ounces of sugar, 2 ounces of butter, a pint of milk, the rind of a lemon rubbed on a piece of sugar, 6 yolks of eggs and 2 whites whipped and a little salt. Put the bread-crumbs into a basin with the sugar, butter, lemon-sugar and salt; then pour in the milk boiling, cover up the whole and leave it to steep for about ten minutes; the eggs may then be added, and after the whole has been well mixed together pour the preparation into a mould or pudding basin previously spread with butter. Steam the pudding for about an hour, and when done dish it up with some arrow-root sauce made as follows: Mix a dessertspoonful of arrow-root with twice that quantity of sugar, half the juice of a lemon, a little nutmeg, and a gill of water, and stir this over the fire until it boils.

Plum Pudding.

Three-quarters of a pound of raisins, ¾ of a pound of currants, ½ a pound of candied orange, lemon and citron, 1¼ pounds of chopped beef suet, 1 pound of flour, ¾ of a pound of moist sugar, 4 eggs, about 3 gills of milk, the grated rind of 2 lemons, ½ an ounce of nutmeg, cinnamon and cloves (in powder), a glass of brandy and a very little salt. Mix the above ingredients thoroughly together in a large basin several hours before the pudding is to be boiled; pour them into a mould spread with butter, which should be tied up in a cloth. The pudding must then be boiled for four hours and a half; when done dish it up with sauce spread over it.

Tapioca Pudding.

Ten ounces of tapioca, 1 quart of milk, 6 ounces of sugar, 6 yolks of eggs and 2 whipped whites, the grated rind of a lemon, 2 ounces of butter, and a little salt. Put the tapioca, sugar, butter, salt, grated lemon, and the milk into a stewpan; stir this over the fire until it boils; then cover the stewpan with its lid, and set it on a very slow stove-fire (partially smothered with ashes), to continue gently simmering for a quarter of an hour. The tapioca should then be withdrawn from the fire, and after the 6 yolks and the 2 whipped whites of eggs have been thoroughly incorporated in it, pour the preparation into a mould or pudding-basin previously spread with butter; steam the pudding for about an hour and a half, and when done dish it up with either a plain arrow-root or custard sauce over it.

Rice Flummery.

Rice that is ground coarse, in a hand-mill, is much better for making flummery than the flour you buy. Put 1 quart of milk to boil; mix with water 5 tablespoonsful of ground rice, and stir it in the milk when it boils; while the milk is cold put in vanilla or lemon; wet your moulds with cold cream or water; keep stirring the rice till it is thick, when pour it out in the moulds; just before dinner turn them out on dishes. Have cream, sugar, and nutmeg mixed, to eat with it.

Rice Fritters.

Take 2 teacupfuls of boiled rice, cooled and mashed, 1 pint of milk, 1 egg, a handful of flour; season with a little salt. Have a pan of lard boiling hot; put them in and fry quickly.

Naples Biscuits.

Whisk 10 eggs till light; add to them 1 pound of dried flour and 1 of powdered sugar; beat all together till perfectly light; put in some rose-water and nutmeg, and bake in small shallow pans, in a moderately-heated oven.

Soft Gingerbread.

One pound of butter, ½ a pound of sugar, 10 eggs, 1 teaspoonful of cinnamon, 2 tablespoonfuls of ginger, 3 half pints of molasses, 1 gill of milk; 2 pounds of flour, 2 tablespoonfuls of saleratus. Beat the butter, sugar, ginger, and cinnamon together until light; then stir in one-fourth of the flour; whisk the eggs very thick, and add by degrees. Mix the milk and molasses together, which stir in gradually; then the remainder of the flour, half at a time. Beat all well together, then add the saleratus, mix, and bake.

French Loaf Cake.

One pound of sugar, ½ pound of butter, 1 pound of flour, 7 eggs, 1 cup of cream, the grating and juice of 1 lemon, ½ wineglass of brandy or Madeira, 1 teaspoonful of saleratus. Beat the butter and sugar very light, then stir in the cream; after which beat in one-fourth of the flour; whisk the eggs until very thick, which add by degrees, then the remainder of the flour, half at a time, alternately with the grating and juice of the lemon. After beating all well together, add the saleratus, after which beat but a few minutes. Line your pans (either square or round) with white paper, and bake in a moderate oven.

Madison Cake.

Half a pound of butter, ¾ of a pound of sugar, 1 pound of flour, 8 eggs, 1 gill of cream, 1 nutmeg, 1 pound of raisins chopped, ¾ of a pound of currants. Beat the butter and sugar until very light, to which add the cream; whisk the eggs until very thick, and stir in alternately with the flour. Beat all well together; then add the spice and fruit. Butter and paper your pans, put in the batter, spread it over smooth with a knife, and bake in a moderate oven.

Black Cake.

One pound of butter, 1 pound of sugar, 1 pound of flour, 10 eggs, 2 pounds of raisins (seeded and chopped), 2 pounds of currants (washed, dried, and picked), 1 pound of citron (cut thin and small), 1 wineglass of Madeira wine, 2 wineglasses of brandy, the grating of 1 large nutmeg, 2 teaspoonfuls of cinnamon, 1 teaspoonful of mace and cloves mixed. Beat the butter and sugar to a cream; then stir in one-fourth of the flour, whisk the eggs very thick, which add gradually; then the remainder of the flour, half at a time; after beating well, add the wine, brandy, and spice. Then mix all the fruit together, and add one-third at a time. Beat well. Then butter and line your pan with white paper, put in the mixture, smooth it with a knife, and bake in a moderate oven, about four hours.

Sponge Cake.

Twelve eggs and their weight in sugar, and the weight of 7 eggs in flour, and the peel and juice of 1 large lemon. Separate the eggs, beat the yolks, and then add sugar until thick and light. Whisk the whites until stiff and dry, and add with the flour. Stir sufficiently to mix the flour and whites through, but avoid beating as that will destroy the lightness. Grease your pan (either square or round) with fresh butter, and bake in a very moderate oven.

Macaroons.

One pound of pulverized sugar, the whites of 5 eggs, ½ a pound of sweet almonds, 1 ounce of bitter almonds. Mix the almonds, blanch and pound them quite fine; beat the eggs very dry, and add the sugar very gradually, then stir in the almonds lightly, put them on white paper with a teaspoon, about an inch apart. Bake them in a slack oven.

To make a rich Plum Cake.

Take 1 pound of fresh butter, 1 pound of sugar, 1¼ pounds of flour, 2 pounds of currants, a glass of brandy, 1 pound of sweetmeats, 2 ounces of sweet almonds, 10 eggs, ¼ of an ounce of allspice, and ¼ of an ounce of cinnamon.

Melt the butter to a cream and put in the sugar. Stir it till quite light, adding the allspice, and pounded cinnamon; in a quarter of an hour take the yolks of the eggs, and work them in, two or three at a time; and the whites of the same must by this time be beaten into a strong snow quite ready to work in; as the paste must not stand to chill the butter, or it will be heavy, work in the whites gradually; then add the orange-peel, lemon, and citron, cut in fine strips, and the currants, which must be mixed in well with the sweet almonds. Then add the sifted flour and glass of brandy. Bake this cake in a tin hoop in a hot oven for three hours, and put sheets of paper under it to keep it from burning.

To make a good Plain Cake.

The following is a receipt for making a good plain cake: Take as much dough as will make a quartern loaf (either made at home or procured at the baker's), work into this a quarter of a pound of butter, a quarter of a pound of moist sugar, and a handful of caraway seeds. When well worked together, pull into pieces the size of a golden pippin, and work it together again. This must be done three times, or it will be in lumps, and heavy when baked.

Rich Pudding Pound Cake.

Boil a teacup of rice in a pint and a half of water, pour over 1 quart of milk, beat the yolks of 5 eggs, add 5 tablespoonfuls of sugar, let it come to a simmer, then pour into a pudding dish and flavor; beat the whites of 5 eggs, 5 tablespoonfuls of sugar to an icing, spread it over the top of the pudding and brown it.

A rich Seed Cake.

Take 1¼ pounds of flour well dried, 1 pound of butter, 1 pound of loaf sugar, beat and sifted, 8 eggs, and 2 ounces of caraway seeds, 1 grated nutmeg, and its weight in cinnamon. Beat the butter into a cream, put in the sugar, beat the whites of the eggs and the yolks separately, then mix them with the butter and sugar. Beat in the flour, spices, and seed, a little before sending it away. Bake it two hours in a quick oven.

Ratafia Cakes.

Beat ½ a pound each of sweet and bitter almonds in fine orange, rose, or ratafia water, mix ½ a pound of fine pounded and sifted sugar with the same, add the whites of 4 eggs well beaten to it, set it over a moderate fire in a preserving-pan. Stir it one way until it is pretty hot, and when a little cool form it into small rolls, and cut it into thin cakes. Shake some flour lightly on them, give each a light tap, and put them on sugar papers, sift a little sugar on them, and put them into a thorough slack oven.

CAKES.

Queen Cakes.

Take a pound of sugar, beat and sift it, a pound of well dried flour, a pound of butter, 8 eggs, and ½ a pound of currants washed and picked; grate a nutmeg and an equal quantity of mace and cinnamon, work the butter to a cream, put in the sugar, beat the whites of the eggs twenty minutes, and mix them with the butter and sugar. Then beat the yolks for half an hour and put them to the butter. Beat the whole together, and when it is ready for the oven, put in the flour, spices, and currants; sift a little sugar over them, and bake them in tins.

Lemon Cakes.

Take 1 pound of sugar, ¾ of a pound of flour, 14 eggs, 2 tablespoonfuls of rose-water, the raspings and juice of 4 lemons; when the yolks are well beat up and separated, add the powdered sugar, the lemon raspings, the juice, and the rose-water; beat them well together in a pan with a round bottom, till it becomes quite light, for half an hour. Put the paste to the whites previously well whisked about, and mix it very light. When well mixed sift in the flour and knead it in with the paste, as light as possible; form the biscuits and bake them in small oval tins, with six sheets of paper under them, in a moderate heat. Butter the tins well or it will prove difficult to take out the biscuits, which will be exceedingly nice if well made. Ice them previous to baking, but very lightly and even.

Almond Cakes.

Take 6 ounces of sweet almonds, ½ a pound of powdered sugar, 7 eggs, 6 ounces of flour, and the raspings of 4 lemons. Pound the almonds very fine, with whole eggs, add the sugar and lemon raspings, and mix them well together in the mortar. Take it out, put it in a basin, stir it with the yolks of eggs, till it is white as a spongepaste; beat up the whites of the eggs to a strong snow, mix them very light with the paste, then take the flour and mix it as light as possible; on this the goodness of the cakes principally depends, as it is impossible to make a good cake with a a heavy paste; butter the mould, and bake in a slack oven for an hour, with ten sheets of paper under it and one on the top.

Fancy Biscuits.

Take 1 pound of almonds, 1 pound of sugar, and some orange-flower water. Pound the almonds very fine, and sprinkle them with orange-flower water: when they are perfectly smooth to the touch, put them in a small pan, with flour sifted through a silk sieve; put the pan on a slow fire, and dry the paste till it does not stick to the fingers; move it well from the bottom, to prevent its burning; then take it off, and roll it into small round fillets, to make knots, rings, etc., and cut it into various shapes; make an icing of different colors, dip one side of them in it, and set them on wire gratings to drain. They may be varied by strewing over them colored pistachios, or colored almonds, according to fancy.

Fine Cheesecakes.

Put a pint of warm cream into a saucepan over the fire, and when it is warm, add to it 5 quarts of new milk. Then put in some rennet, stir it, and when it is turned, put the curd into a linen cloth or bag. Let the whey drain from it, but do not squeeze it too much. Put it into a mortar, and pound it as fine as butter. Add ½ a pound of sweet almonds blanched, ½ a pound of macaroons, or Naples biscuits. Then add 9 well beaten yolks of eggs, a grated nutmeg, a little rose or orange-water, and ½ a pound of fine sugar. Mix all well together.

Almond Cheesecakes.

Put 4 ounces of blanched sweet almonds into cold water, and beat them in a marble mortar or wooden bowl, with some rose-water. Put to it 4 ounces of sugar, and the yolks of 4 eggs beat fine. Work it till it becomes white and frothy, and then make a rich puff-paste as follows: Take ½ a pound of flour, and ¼ of a pound of butter; rub a little of the butter into the flour, mix it stiff with a little cold water, and then roll out the paste. Strew on a little flour, and lay over it, in thin bits, one-third of the butter; throw a little more flour over the bottom, and do the like three different times. Put the paste into the tins, grate sugar over them, and bake them gently.

Brioche Paste.

One pound of flour, 10 ounces of butter, ½ an ounce of German yeast, a teaspoonful each of salt and sugar, about 7 eggs. Put ¼ part of the flour on a slab, spread it out to form a well, then place the yeast in the centre, and proceed to dissolve it with a little tepid water; when this is effected add sufficient water to mix the whole into a rather soft paste, knead this into the form of a round ball, put it into a stewpan capable of containing 3 times its quantity, score it round the sides with a knife, put the lid on and set it to rise in a rather warm place. In winter it may be put in the screen, but in hot weather the fermentation will proceed more satisfactorily if it is merely placed on the kitchen table or in some such place of moderate warmth. This part of the operation is termed setting the sponge. Next put the remainder of the flour on the slab and spread it out in the centre to form the well, then place the salt and sugar and a teaspoonful of water to dissolve these, after which the butter must be added; break in 6 eggs and work the whole together with the hands until well mixed; first working it between the hands and then rubbing it with both fists held flat on the slab and moving them to and fro, so as thoroughly to reduce any remaining lumps in the paste. By the time the paste is mixed the sponge will probably have risen sufficiently; to be perfect it must rise to 3 times its original size. When spread out on the paste prepared to receive it, it should present the appearance of a sponge, from which it takes its name. Both the above should be then gently, but thoroughly mixed. A napkin must be spread in a wooden bowl or a basin, some flour shaken over it, and the *brioche* paste lifted into it; then shake a little flour over the paste, and after throwing the ends of the napkin over all, set the bowl containing the paste in a cool place free from any current of air. It is usual to make this kind of paste late in the evening previously to the day on which it is required for use. The first thing on the following morning, the *brioche* paste must be turned off the napkin on to the slab, then shake some flour under and over it and fold the paste over half a dozen times, pressing it down with the knuckles each time; put the paste back again into the bowl in the same way as before, and about three hours afterwards knead it again in a similar manner previously to its being baked. If the paste when finished appears to be full of small globules of air, and is perfectly elastic to the touch, it is certain to be well made, and when baked will be both light and of a bright clear color.

If the paste is intended to be made into one *brioche* only, take five-sixths of it; mould this into the form of a round ball or cushion and place it in a plain mould or paper case (previously spread

15

with butter) with the smooth surface uppermost; press it down in the case with the knuckles, and after moulding the remaining piece of paste in a similar manner, first wet the surface of the other part over with the paste-brush dipped in water, and then after inserting the pointed end of this into the centre of that portion of the *brioche* which has been already placed in the case, press the head down upon it with the back of the hand; egg the *brioche* over with a paste-brush, score the sides slightly in a slanting direction, place it on a baking sheet and put it in the oven (at moderate heat). As soon as the *brioche* begins to rise and has acquired a slight degree of color, let it be covered over with a sheet of paper. About two hours will suffice to bake a large *brioche* of double the quantity of paste described in this article.

Note.—*Brioches* may be varied in their form when intended to be served as fancy bread for breakfast, etc.; in which case they should be moulded in the shape of twists, fingers, rings, etc. When served on the refreshment table at routs, public breakfasts, balls, etc., dried cherries, citron, candied orange or lemon-peel, pine-apple or angelica steeped in some kind of liqueur may be introduced. In either of these cases, previously to mixing in, the fruit part of the paste must be reserved, which after being rolled out must be used to inclose the other part of the *brioche*. This precaution is necessary to prevent the fruit from protruding through the paste, as it becomes calcined by the heat of the oven and gives an unsightly appearance to the sponge. When fruit has been mixed in a *brioche* it should be (when baked) glazed with fine sugar by the salamander. Gruyère and Parmesan cheese in equal proportions, are sometimes introduced into a *brioche* for a second course remove; the first should be cut up in dice, the latter grated. As in the above cases, this kind of *brioche* must be enclosed in a portion of the paste reserved for that purpose.

Scotch Bread.

One pound of flour, 1 pound of sugar, 1 pound of butter, 8 eggs, ½ a pound of candied lemon, orange and citron-peel in equal proportions, a gill of Cognac brandy, a very little salt, and 4 ounces of white comfits. Put the butter in a basin, work it with a wooden spoon until it presents the appearance of thick cream; then add the flour, sugar, eggs and salt, gradually throwing in a handful of each and two eggs at a time; when the whole is thoroughly mixed the candied peel (cut in shreds), also the brandy and the rind of two oranges or lemons (rubbed on sugar) must next be added. This paste should now be poured into tins of an oblong shape about 2 inches deep, spread with butter, and after the comfits have been strewn over the surface a little fine sugar should be shaken over the top previously to placing them in the oven on baking-sheets; they must be baked of a very light color.

Note.—This kind of cake is a *general* favorite in Scotland, being served on most occasions at breakfast, luncheon, or for casual refreshment, and also with the dessert.

Plain Seed-Cake.

One quartern of dough, 6 eggs, 8 ounces of sugar, 8 ounces of butter, ½ an ounce of caraway-seeds and a teaspoonful of salt. Spread the dough out on the pastry-slab, then add the whole of the above-named ingredients, work them well together with the hands so as thoroughly to incorporate them with the dough; the eggs should be added 2 at a time. When the paste is ready put it into a plain mould (previously spread with butter), and set it to rise in a warm place. As soon as the fermentation has taken place in a satisfactory manner, the cake should be immediately put into the oven and baked of a light color. When done serve it cold for luncheon or otherwise. This kind of cake may be varied by introducing raisins, currants, or candied orange or lemon-peel.

Brussels Biscuits, or Rusks.

One pound of flour, 10 ounces of butter, ½ an ounce of German yeast, 4 ounces of sugar, 4 whole eggs, 4 yolks, a teaspoonful of salt and a gill of cream. Set the sponge with one-fourth part of the flour and yeast in the usual way (as for *brioche*), and while it is rising prepare the paste as follows: Place the remainder of the flour on the slab, spread it out in the centre to form the well, place in this the salt and sugar (with a very little water to dissolve the salt), the butter and eggs; this must then be beaten with the hand on the slab until it presents an appearance of elasticity; then add the whipped cream and sponge after the whole has well worked once more; the paste must be placed in long narrow tins about 2 inches deep and of about the same width, preparatory to placing the paste in the moulds; these should be first well floured inside (to prevent the paste from sticking), then the paste rolled out to their own length and about one and a half inches thick dropped into them and set in a warm place to rise. When the paste has sufficiently risen it must be gently turned out on a baking-sheet previously spread with butter, then egged all over with a soft paste-brush and baked of a bright deep yellow color. When done cut them up in slices about one-quarter of an inch thick, place them flat on a baking-sheet and put them again in the oven to acquire a light yellow color on both sides. These form a superior kind of rusks, and are well adapted for the refreshment table at evening parties or for the breakfast table.

Note.—Rusks may also be made with *brioche* paste or pound cake.

Pound-Cake

One pound of butter, 1 pound of sugar, 8 eggs, 1 wineglass of wine and peach-water mixed, 1¼ pounds of flour, 1 nutmeg, 1 teaspoonful of cinnamon, 1 pound of dried currants. Carefully wash, dry and pick the currants. Beat the butter and sugar very light; then by degrees add the wine, spice, fruit and one-fourth of the flour. Whisk the eggs until very thick, which stir in the butter and sugar gradually, then add the remaining flour, one-third at a time. Beat all well together; line your pan with white paper, put in the batter, smooth the top with a knife and bake in a moderate oven about two hours and a half.

Duchess Loaves.

Half a pint of milk or water, 4 ounces of butter, 2 ounces of sugar, 5 ounces of flour, 3 eggs, a few drops of essence of orange and a very little salt. Put the water, butter, sugar and the salt into a stewpan on the fire, and as soon as these begin to boil withdraw the stewpan from the fire and add the flour; stir the whole well together with a wooden spoon over the stove fire for about three minutes, by which time the ingredients should present the appearance of a soft, compact paste. The essence of orange (or any other kind of flavor) should now be added, and also 1 egg; incorporate these with the paste, then mix in the other two eggs, and if the paste should be stiff another egg or a yolk only may be added. This must be laid on the pastry-slab in small pieces about the size of a pigeon's egg, then rolled out with a little flour in the form of a finger and placed in order upon a baking-sheet spread with butter; they should now be egged over and baked of a bright light color. Just before they are quite done shake some fine sifted sugar over them, set them back again in the oven until the sugar is nearly melted, and then pass the red-hot salamander over them to give them a bright, glossy appearance; the loaves must now be immediately withdrawn from the oven and allowed to cool. Just before sending this kind of pastry to table make an incision down the sides and fill the small loaves with apricot-jam; then dish them up in a pyramidal form on a napkin, and serve.

Almond Cakes.

Six ounces of flour, 8 ounces of sugar, 2 ounces of ground or finely-powdered almonds (with a few bitter almonds), 6 yolks of eggs, 2 whole eggs, 4 whites whipped, a glass of brandy, a little salt, 4 ounces of chopped almonds mixed with 2 ounces of sugar and half the white of an egg. First work the butter in a basin with a spoon until it presents a creamy appearance; next add the flour, sugar, almonds, brandy, eggs and salt gradually; then mix in the whipped whites of eggs lightly; pour this paste on a baking-sheet about an inch and a half deep (previously buttered), bake it of a light color. When the cake is nearly done spread the prepared chopped almonds over the top, and then put it back again into the oven to finish baking; when done the almonds should be of a light fawn color. Turn the cake out carefully, and when cold cut it up into bands about an inch and a half wide; then again divide them into diamond-shaped cakes and dish them up pyramidally. Some whipped cream may be placed in the centre of the dish and the cakes neatly dished up round it. Dried cherries, Sultana raisins, currants, any kind of candied peel, pistachios, or Spanish nuts, may be added. The cakes may also be flavored with any kind of essence or liqueur.

Meringues.

One pound of sifted sugar and 12 whites of eggs. Whisk the whites in an egg-bowl until they present the appearance of a perfectly white, smooth, substantial froth, resembling snow; then substitute a spoon for the whisk and proceed to mix in the whole of the sugar lightly; carefully avoid working the batter too much, for fear of rendering it soft, as in that case it becomes difficult to mould the *meringues;* they can never be so gracefully shaped as when it is kept firm. Next cut some stiff foolscap paper into bands about two inches wide; then take a tablespoon and gather it nearly full of the batter by working it up at the side of the bowl in the form of an egg, and drop this slopingly upon one of the bands of paper, at the same time drawing the edge of the spoon sharply round the outer base of the *meringue,* so as to give to it a smooth and rounded appearance, in order that it may exactly resemble an egg. Proceed in this manner until the band is full, keeping the *meringues* about two inches and a half apart from each other on the paper; as each band is filled, place them close beside each other on the slab or table, and when all the batter is used up, shake some rather coarse sifted sugar all over them and allow them to remain for about three minutes; then take hold of one of the bands at each end, shake off the loose sugar and place the band of *meringues* on the board, and so on with the other bands, which, when placed carefully on the boards closely side by side, must be put in the oven (at very moderate heat) and baked of a light fawn color. When done, each piece of *meringue* must be carefully removed from off the paper, the white part of the inside scooped out with a dessert-spoon and then nicely smoothed over; after this they must be placed in neat order on a baking-sheet and put back again in the oven to dry, taking particular care that they do not acquire any more color. When about to send the *meringues* to table, whip some double cream, season it with a little powdered sugar and either a glass of any kind of liqueur, a few drops of orange-flower-water, or some pounded vanilla; garnish each piece with a spoonful of this cream, join two together, dish them up in a pyramidal form on a napkin, and serve.

Note.—Meringues may be made of all sizes, and may also be shaped in the form of small bunches of grapes; for this purpose it is necessary to use a "*cornet*" or biscuit-forcer of paper to mould the berries. In order to vary their appearance, previously to shaking the sugar over them, some finely-shred pistachios or almonds, rough granite sugar, and small currants may be strewn over them. They may also be garnished with preserves, or any kind of iced creams.

Swedes.

One pound of pounded sugar, 12 ounces of finely-shred almonds, 4 ounces of flour, a stick of vanilla (pounded and sifted), and 1 whole egg and the white of another. Let the whole of the fore-named ingredients be well mixed together in a basin, and then with a tablespoon proceed to mould the preparation into round balls the size of a large walnut, which are to be placed on pieces of sheet-wafer previously cut to the size of half-crown pieces; these must now be placed on baking-sheets, and, after slightly shaking some fine sugar over them, are to be baked of a light color in a slack oven.

Chocolate Cream.

Put over the fire 1 quart of milk; when it comes to a boil add 3 tablespoonfuls of chocolate. Thicken with corn-starch, sweeten to the taste, and flavor with lemon or vanilla. Serve it up cold with cream.

Chocolate Glacés.

The foundation for these may be made either of poundcake, Genoese, or sponge-cake; the batter for making either of the foregoing may be first baked in a baking-sheet, and afterward cut out in shapes and sizes to suit taste or convenience, or otherwise may be baked in appropriate moulds or cases for the purpose; they must then be dipped in the following preparation:—First boil the sugar as directed in the foregoing article, and when it has reached its proper degree, add 6 ounces of chocolate dissolved with a wineglassful of water; work the whole well together, and use it while hot; but if it should become cold and set before the operation is terminated, the preparation may be easily liquefied by stirring it over the fire.

Cakes, both large and small, may be *glacés* or glazed in this manner in almost infinite variety, by using any kind of liquor, or a very strong infusion of tea or coffee instead of the chocolate here recommended.

Albert Biscuits.

Ten ounces of pounded sugar, 8 ounces of finely-chopped almonds, 6 ounces of flour, 12 yolks and 14 whites of eggs, 2 ounces of candied orange-peel shred fine, a teaspoonful of cinnamon-powder, half that quantity of ground cloves, and a little grated lemon-rind. Work the sugar and the almonds with the yolks and 2 whites of eggs for twenty minutes, then incorporate the remaining 12 whites firmly whisked together with the flour, candied peel and spices. Next pour the batter into a convenient-sized paper case, and bake it in a moderate oven; and when done and sufficiently cold, let it be cut up into thin slices for dishing up.

This preparation may also be baked in small

moulds, or forced out upon paper or baking-sheets previously buttered and floured for the purpose.

Charlotte de Russe.

Two quarts of cream, 2 ounces of isinglass, 1 pint of milk, 3 vanilla beans, the yolks of 4 eggs, 2 ounces of sugar. Put the isinglass in a saucepan, and pour over it one teacupful of boiling water, place it on the fire, and let it remain for one hour without boiling. Let the milk and vanilla boil together slowly until it is reduced to 1 gill; beat the eggs and stir them in the milk whilst it is on the fire; then add the isinglass and sugar, and keep stirring it until it is cooked about as much as custard; strain it through a fine sieve and set it in a cool place; when nearly cold add the cream and stir them well together; put the mixture in a dish or bowl, lined with sponge-cake.

Blanc-Mange.

Put into 1 quart of water an ounce of isinglass, and let it boil till it is reduced to a pint; then put in the whites of 4 eggs, with 2 tablespoonfuls of rice-water, and sweeten it to taste. Run it through a jelly-bag, and then put to it 2 ounces of sweet and 1 ounce of bitter almonds. Scald them in the jelly, and then run them through a hair sieve. Put it into a China bowl, and the next day turn it out. Garnish with flowers or green leaves, and stick all over the top blanched almonds cut lengthways.

Clear Blanc-Mange.

Skim off the fat, and strain a quart of strong calves'-foot jelly; add to the same the whites of 4 eggs well beaten; set it over the fire and stir it till it boils. Then pour it into a jelly-bag, and run it through several times till it is clear. Beat an ounce each of sweet and bitter almonds to a paste with a spoonful of rose-water strained through a cloth. Then mix it with the jelly, and add to it 3 spoonfuls of very good cream. Set it again over the fire, and stir it till it almost boils. Pour it into a bowl; then stir it often till almost cold, and then fill the moulds.

Blanc-Mange.

Parboil 12 ounces of Jordan and 2 ounces of bitter almonds in a quart of water for about two minutes; drain them on a sieve, remove the skins, and wash them in cold water; after they have been soaked in cold water for half an hour, pound them in a mortar with 4 ounces of sugar, until the whole presents the appearance of a soft paste. This must then be placed in a large basin, with 12 ounces of loaf sugar, and mixed with rather more than a pint of spring-water; cover the basin with a sheet of paper, twisted round the edges, and allow the preparation to stand in a cool place for about an hour, in order to extract the flavor of the almonds more effectually. The milk should then be strained off from the almonds through a napkin, with pressure, by wringing it at both ends. Add 2 ounces of clarified isinglass to the milk of almonds, pour the blanc-mange into a mould imbedded in rough ice, and when set quite firm turn it out on its dish with caution, after having first dipped the mould in warm water.

ORIGINAL RECEIPTS IN COOKERY AND PASTRY, ETC.

1. Shrewsbury Cake.

Sift 1 pound of sugar, some pounded cinnamon, and a nutmeg grated, into 3 pounds of flour. Add a little rose-water to 3 eggs well beaten, mix them with the flour, then pour in as much butter melted as will make it a good thickness to roll out.

2. Another.—Take 2 pounds of flour, 1 pound of sugar finely pounded; mix them together (take out ¼ of a pound to roll them in); ½ pound of butter, 4 eggs, 4 spoonsful of cream, and 2 of rose-water. Beat them well together, and mix them with the flour into a paste: roll them into thin cakes and bake them in a quick oven.

3. Macaroons.

Blanch 4 ounces of almonds, and pound them with 4 tablespoonfuls of orange-flower water; beat the whites of 4 eggs to a froth, mix it with a pound of sugar, sift the almonds into a paste, and lay it in different cakes on paper to bake.

4. Another.—Take 1 pound of almonds, blanch them and throw them into cold water, then rub them dry with a cloth, and pound them in a mortar; moisten them with orange-flower or rose-water, lest they turn to oil: then take 1 pound of fine loaf sugar, whisk the whites of 4 eggs; beat all well together, and shape them round with a spoon, on paper previously buttered and sugared, to prevent their burning; bake them in a gentle oven on tin plates.

5. Savoy Biscuit.

Take of sugar the weight of 12 eggs, of flour the weight of 7 eggs; beat the yellows and whites of 12 eggs separate; grate in the rind of 1 lemon; after being in the oven a few minutes, grate on some sugar. You may add peach-water or lemon-juice.

6. Jumbles.

Take 1½ pounds of flour, 1 pound of sugar, ¾ pound of butter, 4 yolks and 2 whites of eggs, with a wineglass of rose-water, roll them thick with fine powdered sugar, and bake on tins.

7. Almond Cake.

Take 1 pound of almonds blanched and beaten, 10 eggs well beaten, 1 pound of sugar, and ¾ pound of flour.

8. French Rolls.

Take 1 spoonful of lard or butter, 3 pints of flour, 1 cup of yeast, and as much milk as will work it up to the stiffness of bread; just before you take them from the oven, take a clean towel and wipe them over with milk.

9. Waffles.

To 1 quart of milk add 5 eggs, 1¼ pounds of flour, ½ pound of butter; beat them well together; when baked, sift sugar and cinnamon on them. If you make the waffles before it is time to bake them, add 1 spoonful of yeast.

10. Poundcake Gingerbread.

Six eggs, 1 pound of sugar, 1 pint of molasses, 1 teacupful of ginger, 1 teaspoonful of saleratus dissolved, a little mace, nutmeg, 1 pound of fresh butter creamed; after these ingredients are well mixed, beat in 2 pounds of flour. Fruit is an improvement.

11. Gingercake.

Three pounds of flour, 1 pound of sugar, 1 pound of butter rubbed in very fine, 2 ounces of ginger, a little nutmeg, 1 pint of molasses, 1 gill of cream; make them warm together, and bake them in a slack oven.

12. Gingerbread.

One pound and a half of flour, ¾ of a pound of sugar, and ½ a pound of butter, well rubbed together; 1 ounce of ginger, a few caraway seeds, 24 allspice, 12 cloves, a little cinnamon, 1 pint of molasses. Knead well.

13. Short Gingerbread.

One pound of sugar, ¾ pound of butter, 5 eggs, a little cream and saleratus, 1¾ pounds of flour, rolled hard. To be baked on tin sheets, marked ready to cut.

14. Calves'-foot Jelly.

Four calves'-feet well boiled, ½ pound of sugar, 1 pint of wine, 2 lemons, the whites of 4 eggs, and shells; boil all together about five minutes, then pour through a flannel bag to strain.

15. Apple Pudding.

Half the whites and all the yolks of 10 eggs, beat them very light, add 1 pint of apples, after they are stewed and put through a sifter, stir in ¼ pound of butter, the grated peel of 2 large lemons, and juice of one; sugar to taste. Mace and nutmeg are very good substitutes for lemon-juice.

16. Baked Apple Pudding.

Pare and quarter 4 large apples, boil them tender with the rind of a lemon in so little water that when done no water may remain, beat them quite fine in a mortar, add the crumb of a small roll, ¼ pound of butter melted, the yolks of 5 and whites of 3 eggs, juice of ½ a lemon, sugar to your taste; beat all well together, and bake it in a paste.

17. Lemon Blanc-Mange.

Pour 1 pint of hot water upon 1 ounce of isinglass, when it is dissolved add the juice of 3 lemons, the peel of one grated, 6 yolks of eggs beaten. ½ a pint of Lisbon wine, sweeten it to your taste; let it boil, then strain it, and put it in your moulds.

18. Mrs. Hoffmann's Blanc-Mange.

Take 2 ounces of isinglass, 1 quart of new milk, strain it and sweeten to your taste, add rose or peach-water, let it be only milk warm when you put it in the moulds; if you wish it particularly nice, blanch ½ pound almonds, beat them very fine in a mortar and stir in before you boil or strain.

19. Orange Pudding.

Take 1 pound of butter creamed, 1 pound of sugar, 10 eggs, the juice of 2 oranges; boil the peel, then pound it fine, and mix it with the juice; add the juice of one lemon, a wineglass of brandy, wine, and rose-water.

20. Hominy Pudding.

Take the hominy, warm it, and mash through a sifter until you get a pint, add ¼ of a pound of butter, melted, stir a teacup of cream into it, and let it cool; then add half the whites of 6 eggs; sugar, nutmeg, mace, and wine to your taste. Bake it.

21. Cocoanut Pudding.

To 1 large cocoanut, grated, add the whites of 8 eggs, ¼ pound of sugar, ¼ pound of butter, 2 tablespoonfuls of rose-water. Bake it in a paste.

22. Rice Pudding.

Take ½ pound of rice, tied in a cloth, boiled well, and then put through a sieve; add 1 quart of milk, and keep stirring until it thickens; then add 6 ounces of butter stirred into the rice, 12 yolks and 6 whites of eggs well beaten; mace, nutmeg, wine and sugar, to your taste. This quantity will make 2 large puddings. If you choose you may add currants or any other fruit.

23. Another.

Boil the rice very soft, dry from water, stir in a little butter, 1 pint of milk, and 3 eggs well beaten, sweeten to your taste, pour it in your dish, sprinkle flour on the top, put little bits of butter here and there on the top. Bake slowly.

24. Another, highly approved.

Take 2 tablespoonfuls of raw rice, 1 quart of new milk, a bit of butter the size of an egg, a little cinnamon, sweeten to your taste, put the pan in a slack oven after the bread is taken out; eat when cold.

25. Another.

Put in a deep pan ½ pound of rice washed and picked, 2 ounces of butter, 4 ounces of sugar, a few allspice pounded, and 2 quarts of milk. Bake in a slow oven.

26. Another.

Sweeten rice in milk, strain it off, and having pared and cored apples, put the rice around them, tying each in a cloth with a bit of lemon-peel, a clove, or cinnamon. Boil them well.

27. Ground Rice or Sago Pudding.

Boil a tablespoonful of it heaped, in a pint of new milk, with lemon-peel and cinnamon; when cold, add sugar, sugar, nutmeg, 2 eggs, well beaten.

28. Sweet Potato Pudding.

Take 5 eggs, ½ a pound of butter, ¼ of a pound of sugar, add as much sweet potato as will thicken it, the juice and grated peel of 1 lemon, beat it very light.

29. Potato Pudding.

Take ½ a pound of boiled potatoes, beat well in a mortar with ½ a pound each of sugar and butter, the yolks of 10 eggs, the whites of 4, well beaten, 2 Naples biscuit grated, and ½ a pint of cream; mix them well with the other ingredients, and pour it on a thin paste. Bake for half an hour.

30. Another.

Take 8 ounces of boiled potatoes, 2 ounces of butter, 2 eggs, ¼ of a pint of cream, 1 spoonful of white wine, a little salt, the juice and rind of a lemon, beat the whole to a froth, sugar to taste—a paste or not as you like. If you want it richer, put more butter, sweetmeats, and almonds, with another egg.

31. Citron Pudding.

Half a pound of sugar, ½ a pound of butter creamed, the yolks of 9 eggs, a wineglass of brandy, ½ a pound of citron chopped very fine.

32. Cream Pudding.

To 3 eggs beaten very light, stir in 1½ pints of flour, salt to your taste, mix a little milk, then put in 6 ounces of sugar, just before you put it in the oven add 1 pint of thick cream. Bake for three-quarters of an hour.

33. Custard Pudding.

One pint of milk, 3 spoonfuls of flour, 6 eggs, and salt to your taste. Sugar.

34. Wedding Cake.

Three pounds of flour, 3 pounds of butter, 3 pounds of sugar, 2 dozen of eggs, 3 pounds of raisins, 6 pounds of currants, 1 pound of citron, 1 ounce of mace, 1 ounce of cinnamon, 1 ounce of nutmegs, ½ an ounce of cloves, ½ a pint of brandy. Beat the butter with your hand to cream, then beat the sugar into the butter, add the froth of the yolks of the eggs after being well beaten, then the froth of the whites; mix fruit, spice, and flour together; then add them in with beating. Five or six hours' baking will answer for a large loaf.

35. Election Cake.

Five pounds of flour, 2 pounds of sugar, ¾ pound of butter, 5 eggs, yeast, 1 pint of milk, and spice as you please.

36. Indian Pudding.

Boil 1 spoonful of fine Indian flour well, then add 1 pint of milk, and let it all boil; when cool, beat in 2 eggs. Sweeten and season.

37. Baked Indian Pudding.

Eight ounces of mush, 6 ounces of butter, 6 ounces of sugar, the yolks of 6 eggs, and the white of 1; mix the butter in the mush when hot, beat the eggs and sugar together; add to the mush, when cool, nutmeg, mace, and wine to your taste; bake.

38. *Friend Wilson's Plum Pudding.*

Mix well together 1 pound of raisins, 1 pound of currants, the crumbs of ½ a loaf of bread, ¼ of a pound of flour, 1 pound of suet; stir in 6 eggs and 1 tumbler of porter; put in ½ of a nutmeg, ½ pound of citron and cinnamon; to give taste add 2 ounces of fine sugar. You may use, instead of porter, a small tea-cup of yeast. Before taking it out of the bag dip into cold water.

39. *Apple Custard.*

Take apples, pared, cored, and slightly stewed, sufficient to cover the dish, 6 eggs, 1 quart of milk; spice to your taste. Bake it one-third of an hour.

40. *Black Cake.*

One pound and three-quarters of flour, 1¾ pounds of brown sugar, 1 pound of butter, 1½ pounds of raisins, 1½ pounds of currants, ½ pound of lard, 4 eggs, 1 pint of milk, 1 nutmeg, and mace, 1 teaspoonful of baking powder. Wine and brandy.

41. *Tomato Catsup.*

Cut up the tomatoes, and between every layer sprinkle a layer of salt, let them stand a few hours before you boil them, which do very well: then strain them through a colander on some horse-radish, onions or garlic, mustard-seed, beaten ginger, pepper and mace; cover it close; let it stand a day or two, then bottle and seal it for use.

42. *Green Tomato Soy.*

To 1 peck of green tomatoes, sliced thin, add 1 pint of salt; stand twenty-four hours, then strain and put them on the fire, with 12 raw onions, 1 ounce of black pepper, 1 ounce of allspice, ¼ pound of ground mustard, ½ pound of white mustard-seed, and a little Cayenne pepper. Cover with vinegar, and boil until as thick as jam, stirring constantly to prevent burning.

43. *Puff-Paste.*

One pound and a quarter of flour, and 1 pound of butter; divide the butter into 4 equal parts; mix one fourth part of the butter with three-fourths of the flour; and work the remainder of the flour and butter in.

44. *Good Receipt for Paste (for Pies).*

To 1¼ pounds of sifted flour allow 1 pound of butter or half butter and half lard. Rub the lard and flour through your hands until thoroughly mixed, having first put aside 2 tablespoonfuls of flour to make out the paste with: then break up the butter in small pieces with your fingers with the flour and lard; moisten with cold water, and press it together lightly until it forms a mass, then flour the paste-board, lay the dough on it, and with the rolling-pin roll it lightly into a thick sheet. Sprinkle some of the flour on, cut it into fair pieces, and again proceed to roll as before; do this three times, then make the pies.

For plain home-made pies, to 2 pounds of flour ½ pound butter and ½ pound of lard, or all lard.

45. *Biddle Pudding.*

One pint of milk, 4 large tablespoonfuls of flour, 4 eggs. Butter the bake-dish. Put it in the oven when you are about to dish the dinner, allowing twenty-five minutes for baking; bring it directly from the oven to the table, or it falls.

Sauce for the above.—1 cup of brown sugar, 2 tablespoonfuls of cream, 1 ounce of butter. Stir the butter and sugar thoroughly, then add a little of the cream at a time, to keep from separating; add wine to the taste in the same manner (not quite a wineglass). Let the mixture melt; it will be a white froth when done. Enough for five persons.

46. *Meringue Pudding.*

One quart milk, 1 pint grated bread, the yolks of 4 eggs, the rind of 1 lemon grated; sweeten to taste. Bake to a custard, which will be in about half an hour, then take it from the oven. Beat the whites of the 4 eggs, 2 tablespoonsful of sugar, and the juice of the lemon, and put it on the top of the pudding. Set it in the oven again and let it brown lightly.

47. *Sponge Cake.*

Fourteen eggs, with their weight in sugar and half their weight in flour, the juice and peel of a lemon, and one nutmeg: beat the yolks and whites separately until stiff, add the sugar to the yolks, then add the whites; one minute before the oven is ready dredge in the flour. Bake in a quick oven half an hour.

48. *Lemon Cake.*

Twelve eggs, 1½ pounds sugar, ¾ pound flour; grate the outside of 2 lemons, with the inside of 1; or add 1 glass of wine, with 3 teaspoonsful of the essence of lemon.

49. *Sugar Cake.*

One pound flour, ¾ pound sugar, ½ pound butter, 5 eggs. Mix and drop them on tin, and put sugar sanded on them, just as you put them into the oven, or frost them.

50. *Cup Cake.*

Three cups of sugar, 1 cup of butter, 2 teaspoonfuls of saleratus, 3 eggs, 5 cups of flour; all beaten together with as much spice as you please.

51. *Cider Cake.*

Take 2 pounds flour, 1 pound sugar, ½ pound butter, 1 pint cider, cloves, and cinnamon, with or without fruit, 2 teaspoonfuls of saleratus.

52. *Whips.*

Two cups of cream, 1 of white wine, grate in the skin of a lemon, sweeten to your taste, the whites of 3 eggs; then whip it with a whisk; take off the froth; as it rises pour the froth into your jelly glasses.

53. *To make Venison Pasty.*

You must bone your venison and season it with 2 ounces of pepper, 1 nutmeg, mixed with salt; then mince 3 pounds of beef suet. Put it in the pan; it will take six hours' baking.

54. *To Dress a Turtle.*

Take a turtle of 8 pounds, cut off its head, cut it open, scald the fins and calipee or under-shell, skin them; then take out the guts, cut them open, and cleanse them well; take great care not to break the gall. Then take for the soup the guts and the fins, with a knuckle of veal, some sweet herbs, onions, and Cayenne pepper. Season the rest of the meat with the same seasoning, which put in the calipash, or upper-shell, and calipee, with some forcemeat balls, and bake it. When it is baked, take the yolks of 3 eggs to a turtle of 8 pounds, beat them well, pour in a little wine, take some of the soup, and brew it together very well, throw in a lump of butter rolled in flour, and put it into the calipash and calipee.

55. *To make Waffles the Dutch way.*

One quart of new milk, 1 penny loaf grated very fine, 10 eggs beaten with ¾ pound of sweet butter melted, a few cloves beaten, a little salt, fine flour enough to make a batter like a pancake, and 4 spoonsful of yeast. Mix them together and put them in an earthen pot covered, before the fire, to rise, for an hour; having your waffle-iron ready heated and buttered on both sides, put in the batter to bake. When done serve them hot, with sugar grated over them and cinnamon.

56. *A good Gravy, to be kept for any use.*

Burn 1 ounce of butter in the frying-pan, but

take care to do it at such a distance from the fire that, as you strew in the flour to the butter, it may brown but not blacken; put to it 2 pounds coarse lean beef, 1 quart water, ½ pint wine (red or white), 3 anchovies, 2 shallots, some whole pepper, cloves, and mace, 3 or 4 mushrooms or as many pickled walnuts. Let it stew gently one hour, then strain it. It will keep some time, and is proper for any savory dish.

57. *Federal Cake, or Bachelor's Loaf.*

Into a plateful of flour put a piece of butter not larger than a walnut, 2 eggs, 1 spoonful yeast; mix it either with milk or water, as you please; make it into a very stiff batter, so stiff you can scarce stir it with a spoon. Put it to rise in the same dish you wish to bake it in. It will take several hours to rise.

58. *Albany Cake.*

Take 1½ pounds of flour, 1 pound of sugar, ½ pound of butter, 1 tablespoonful of lard, 2 tablespoonfuls of rose-water, a little cinnamon, 1 egg, 1 teaspoonful of saleratus dissolved in a teacup of cream. Cut them out and bake them on tins.

59. *Black Cake that will keep for a year.*

One pound of sugar, the same of butter and flour, 10 eggs; beat them well together, and when light add 2 wineglasses of brandy, nutmeg, mace, and cloves. 2 pounds of raisins, and the same quantity of currants. It will take some hours to bake. A good deal of spice is necessary.

60. *To dress Calf's Head in imitation of Turtle.*

Take the calf's head when well soaked and washed, open it and boil it with the entrails until it is quite done; take part of the liver out when about half done for forcemeat balls. When it is all done strain the liquor, then cut off small pieces of the head in imitation of turtle; the small indifferent remainder chop up with the entrails; put in spice to your taste, a little savory herbs rubbed very fine, and a few little onions; some very small dumplings; season the forcemeat balls with spice and herbs to your taste, put a little parsley in them, and fry them in lard, and put them in your soup when you send it to table.

61. *Mock Turtle.*

Take a fine calf's head, cut the meat clean from the bones, then boil the bones in a quart of water until the liquor is reduced to a pint; then season it with Cayenne, nutmeg, and mace; pour into the gravy a pint of Madeira wine, a little parsley; thyme.

62. *Dr. Green's Bean Soup.*

Take a shin of beef, well cracked, and to every pound of beef add 1 quart of cold water; boil slowly until the meat is in shreds, only removing the lid to take off the scum. Having prepared your beans (one quart) the evening before, by washing well and soaking all night, boil them until soft enough to pass easily through a sieve; strain the soup, add the beans, give a boil-up together, season to the taste with pepper and salt, and just before serving add half a lemon cut in small pieces, a quarter of a grated nutmeg, and a teaspoonful of white sugar.

63. *Beef à la Mode.*

Choose a thick piece of flank of beef; cut some fat bacon in long slices; let each slice be near an inch thick; dip them in vinegar; then take seasoning of salt and pepper and cloves, mixed with parsley, thyme, and marjoram. Make holes in the meat to put in the larding; when you have put it in rub it over with the seasoning and bind it up with tape and set it in a pot over the fire. Three or four onions must be fried brown and put to the beef, with two or three carrots and a head of celery. Add a small quantity of water, and let it simmer ten or twelve hours, or until it is extremely tender, turning the meat twice; put the gravy into a pan, remove from it the fat; keep the beef covered; then put them together, add a glass of wine, remove the tape, and send it to table.

64. *Oyster Pie.*

Take 100 oysters and clean them well from the shell, put them into a kettle with their own liquor to plump them, then put them in a dish, and season them with 12 cloves and 3 blades of mace pounded fine; pepper to your taste; then lay crust around the edge of your dish. Take the yolks of 4 eggs boiled hard, with a handful of grated bread; sprinkle this over the top with a few pieces of butter; fill the dish nearly full; cover the pie over with a puff-paste.

65. *Damson Sauce.*

To 1 peck plums put 3 pounds brown sugar, ½ pint of vinegar, 2 ounces cloves, 1 ounce cinnamon, ½ ounce mace. Put it on the fire and boil until the fruit is soft and pulpy.

66. *Pickled Damson Plums.*

To 1 peck or 5 pounds of fruit put 3 pounds brown sugar, 1 quart vinegar, 2 ounces cloves, 1 ounce cinnamon, ½ ounce mace. Boil sugar and spices in the vinegar and pour it boiling on the fruit; when cold pour it off. Repeat for four or five mornings.

67. *Chicken Salad.*

Two large cold fowls, either boiled or roasted, the yolks of 9 hard-boiled eggs, ½ pint of sweet oil, ½ pint of vinegar, 1 gill of mixed mustard, 1 small teaspoonful of Cayenne pepper, 1 small teaspoonful of salt, 2 large heads, or 4 small ones, of fine celery. Cut the meat of the fowls from the bones, in small pieces. Cut the white part of the celery into pieces about an inch long. Mix the chicken and celery well together; cover them and set them away. With the back of a wooden spoon mash the yolks of eggs till they are a perfectly smooth paste. Mix them with the oil, vinegar, mustard, Cayenne, and salt. Stir them for a long time, till they are thoroughly mixed and quite smooth; the longer they are stirred the better. When this dressing is sufficiently mixed, cover it and set it away. Five minutes before the salad is to be eaten pour the dressing over the chicken and celery, and mix all well together.

68. *New mode of Cooking Egg Plant.*

Boil the plant *whole*. When tender cut it in half, mash the inside fine; mix in a dressing made of bread-crumbs with pepper and salt. Put in an oven and bake it.

69. *Chicken Soup without Chicken, for the Sick.*

Take 1 dessertspoonful of flour and rub smooth in 1 gill of milk; put 1 ounce of butter, and pepper and salt to suit the taste; pour in ½ pint of boiling water, boil ten minutes, and pour it over a slice of toasted or untoasted bread, as taste may direct. Use thyme or parsley, as is most agreeable. This receipt has been used in the hospitals, where chickens could not be had.

70. *Claret Punch.*

Into a large lunch-bowl capable of holding 2 gallons, pour 1 dozen bottles of claret; add 18 oranges and 6 lemons, cut into slices, rinds and all; 1 pound of white sugar (or more, to taste); and ½ a gallon of water, kept cold with ice.

71. *Paris Punch à la Nina.*

Equal portions of green tea, brandy, and water. Add cut lemons and sugar.

72. Brandy Peaches.

Pare the peaches, carefully removing all decay. Lay in a shallow dish and cover with white sugar. When a syrup has formed, remove the fruit and put into jars; put the syrup in a new tin pan, and place over the fire; when it comes to a boil, remove and pour into the jars hot, and fill up with the best white brandy. When cold seal up carefully.

73. Orange Marmalade.

One dozen good-sized oranges—those with the bitter skin are considered the best, or Sicily, if preferred; cut them in two, take off the peel, and boil it in water until tender enough to run a straw through; cut it up fine, add the pulp and juice of the oranges (carefully removing all the white skin), and the juice and grated skin of two lemons. Add the weight of the whole in white sugar, and boil for a short time till clear—say from twenty minutes to half an hour.

Eighteen good-sized Sicily oranges make about 4 quarts of marmalade.

74. Mock-Turtle Soup made of Beans.

Take 1 pint of black Mexican beans, wash them and put them to soak in some water over night. In the morning put them, with a bunch of potherbs and about 3 quarts of water into a pot, and boil till thoroughly done; strain through a colander into the liquor they were boiled in; let them simmer, add pepper and salt, with a lump of butter the size of an egg, 2 tablespoonfuls of walnut catsup; have ready 2 hard-boiled eggs chopped fine, put them into the tureen, and turn your soup over them; if you have some lemon or wine it will improve it.

75. J. R. K.'s Chicken Croquets.

Boil an ordinary-sized chicken, skin it and cut it up fine. Take a dessertspoonful of butter and the same of flour, mix well together and put into a saucepan with the yolk of an egg; add 3 spoonfuls of chicken broth and 3 of cream, and let it thicken to a boil; throw in the chicken, and after boiling a few moments put it away to cool. Roll out the croquets to the required size in egg and then in fine cracker, and fry in *very hot* lard.

76. Corn Bread.

To 1 quart of milk add 5 eggs beaten light, a small teaspoonful of baking soda, and a little salt; stir in sufficient corn meal to make a stiff batter, pour in a deep pan well greased, and bake; when done it should be two inches thick. Eat while hot.

77. Plain Corn Pone.

To a quart of white corn meal add a little salt and sufficient milk to make a dough, divide into two pones or loaves, making each an inch and a half thick, and bake in a quick oven.

78. Tapioca Pudding.

Take ½ a pound of tapioca, pour on 1½ pints of water, and let it soak over night; pare and core 10 apples, taking care not to break them, and place in a deep pan; sweeten and flavor the tapioca with wine or essence of vanilla, and pour it on the apples; if it does not cover them add a little more water; when the apples are cooked sufficiently the pudding is done. Eat with cream.

79. Currant Pudding.

To 3 cups of flour add 1½ cups of sugar, 2 eggs, ¼ a pound of suet cut fine, ½ a pound of currants, and nutmeg to suit the taste. Make in a stiff batter and boil in a bag two hours. To be eaten with butter sauce.

80. Italian Mode of Cooking Veal Cutlets.

For a cutlet weighing 1½ pounds take 2 onions, slice and parboil, pour off the water, and brown with butter; season and flour the cutlet and place in the pan with the onions, adding sufficient butter to fry nicely; slice 2 tomatoes, and when the cutlet is done place them under it, and let the whole remain over the fire until the tomatoes are well cooked, then remove the cutlet and tomatoes, and add to the gravy the juice of ½ a lemon and a little flour; after dishing the whole upon a meat dish, sprinkle a little parsley cut fine. This is a delicious way of cooking cutlets; beef can be done in the same manner.

81. To cook Frogs.

Put the hind legs in salt and water over night, wipe them dry with a cloth, pepper and salt them, then sprinkle a little flour over them, and fry in hot lard to a light brown.

CONFECTIONERY.

To prepare Sugar for Candying.

The first process is *clarifying*, which is done thus: Break the white of an egg into a preserving pan; put to it 4 quarts of water and beat it with a whisk to a froth. Then put in 12 pounds of sugar, mix all together and set it over the fire. When it boils put in a little cold water, and proceed as often as necessary till the scum rises thick on the top. Then remove it from the fire, and when it is settled take off the scum and pass it through a straining bag. If the sugar should not appear very fine, boil it again before straining it.

To Candy Sugar.

After having completed the above first process, put what quantity is wanted over the fire, and boil it till it is smooth enough. This is known by dipping the skimmer into the sugar and touching it between the forefinger and thumb, and immediately on opening them a small thread will be observed drawn between, which will crystallize and break, and remain in a drop on the thumb, which will be a sign of its gaining some degree of smoothness. Boil it again and it will draw into a larger string; it is now called *bloom sugar*, and must be boiled longer than in the former process. To try it forwardness, dip again the skimmer, shaking off the sugar into the pan; then blow with the mouth strongly through the holes, and if bubbles go through, it has acquired the second degree; to prove if the liquid has arrived at the state called *feathered sugar*, re-dip the skimmer and shake it over the pan, then give it a sudden flirt behind, and the sugar will fly off like feathers.

It now arrives at the state called *crackled sugar*, to obtain which the mass must be boiled longer than in the preceding degree; then dip a stick in it and put it directly into a pan of cold water, draw off the sugar which hangs to the stick in the water, and if it turns hard and snaps it has acquired the proper degree of crystallization; if otherwise, boil it again until it acquires that brittleness.

The last stage of refining this article is called *caramel sugar*, to obtain which it must be boiled longer than in any of the preceding methods; prove it by dipping a stick first into the sugar and then into cold water, and the moment it touches the latter it will, if matured, snap like glass. Be careful that the fire is not too fierce, as by flaming up the sides of the pan it will burn, discolor and spoil the sugar.

French Method.

Put into a pan syrup enough of clarified sugar to fill the mould; boil it until it comes to the state called *small feather;* skim it well; take the pan from the fire and pour it into a small quantity of spirits of wine, sufficient to make it sparkle; let it rest till the skin which is the candy rises on the surface; take it off with a skimmer and pour it directly into the mould, which keep in the stove at 90° heat for eight days; then strain the candy by a hole, slanting the mould on a basin or pan to receive the drainings; let it drain till it is perfectly dry, then loosen the paper by moistening it with warm water; warm it all round near the fire and turn the candy by striking it hard on the table. Put it on a sieve in the stove to finish drying it, but do not touch it while there, and keep up an equal heat, otherwise there will be only a mush instead of a candy. Spirits of wine will take off grease and not affect the candy, as it soon evaporates.

To make Barley Sugar.

Take a quantity of clarified sugar in that state that on dipping the finger into the pan the sugar which adheres to it will break with a slight noise; this is called *crack*. When the sugar is near this put in 2 or 3 drops of lemon-juice, or a little vinegar to prevent its graining. When it has come to the *crack* take it off instantly and dip the pan in cold water to prevent its burning; let it stand a little, and then pour it on a marble, which must be previously rubbed with oil. Cut the sugar into small pieces, when it will be ready for use. One drop of citron will flavor a considerable quantity.

Bonbons.

Provide leaden moulds, which must be of various shapes, and be oiled with oil of sweet almonds. Take a quantity of brown sugar syrup in proportion to their size, in that state called a *blow*, which may be known by dipping the skimmer into the sugar, shaking it and blowing through the holes, when gleams of light may be seen; add a drop of any esteemed essence. If the *bonbons* are preferred white, when the sugar has cooled a little, stir it round the pan, till it grains and shines on the surface; then pour it into a funnel and fill the little mould, when it will take a proper form and harden; as soon as it is cold take it from the moulds; dry it in two or three days and put it upon paper. If the *bonbons* are required to be colored, add the color just as the sugar is ready to be taken off the fire.

To Candy Ginger.

Put 1 ounce of race ginger grated fine, 1 pound of loaf sugar beaten fine, into a preserving pan, with as much water as will dissolve the sugar. Stir them well together over a slow fire till the sugar begins to boil; then stir in another pound of sugar beaten fine, and keep stirring till it grows thick; then take it off the fire and drop it in cakes upon earthen dishes. Set them in a warm place to dry, when they will become hard and brittle, and look white.

To Candy Hoarhound.

Boil it in water till the juice is extracted; then boil a sufficient quantity of sugar to a great height and add the juice to it; stir it with a spoon against the sides of the sugar pan, till it begins to grow thick; then pour it out into a paper case that is dusted with fine sugar and cut it into squares; dry the hoarhound and put it into the sugar finely powdered and sifted.

To make White Sugar Candy.

Sugar crystallized by the saturated syrup being left in a very warm place, from 90° to 100° Fahrenheit, and the shooting promoted by placing sticks or a net of threads at small distances from each other in the liquor; it is also deposited from compound syrup, and does not retain any of the foreign substances with which the syrup is loaded.

To Clarify Loaf Sugar.

Break the same into a copper pan, which will hold one-third more, put ½ a pint of water to each pound of sugar, mix 1 white of an egg to every 6 pounds; when it rises in boiling throw in a little cold water, which must be kept ready in case it should boil over; skim it the fourth time of rising, continue to throw in a little cold water each time till the scum ceases to rise, and strain it through a sieve, cloth or flannel bag. Save the scum, which, when a certain quantity is taken off, may be clarified. The latter skimming will do to add to fermented wines.

To Clarify Coarse Brown Sugar.

Put 50 pounds of coarse brown sugar into a pan which will contain one-third more; pour in 20 pints of water, well mixed with 5 whites of eggs; pound 5 pounds of small charcoal, mix it in the pan while on the fire, and boil it till it looks as black as ink. If it rises too fast, add cold water, strain it through a bag, and though at first it will be black, continue to strain it until it becomes quite clear, which may be seen by putting the syrup in a glass. Put it back until it comes out as fine as clarified loaf sugar.

To Improve and Increase Sugar.

To 5 pounds of coarse brown sugar add 1 pound of flour, and there will be obtained 6 pounds of sugar worth ten per cent. more in color and quality.

Starch Sugar.

Mix 100 parts of starch with 200 of water, and add to it gradually another 200 of water, previously mixed with as much of oil of vitriol, and brought to a boiling heat in a tinned copper vessel; keep the mixture boiling for 36 hours, and occasionally add water to keep up the original quantity; then add some powdered charcoal and also some chalk to get rid of the acid; strain and evaporate it by a gentle heat to the consistence of a syrup, and set by to crystallize.

Birch Sugar.

Wound the trees in the spring of the year by boring a hole under a large arm of the tree quite through the wood as far as the bark of the opposite side; collect the sap which flows from the wound and evaporate it to a proper consistence; these are the native sugars of cold countries, and might be made in England for all the purposes of home consumption.

To make Pear Sugar.

It is obtained by expressing the juice, adding chalk to remove the superabundant acid, and evaporating it to a due consistence; it does not crystallize and is a kind of white treacle. One hundred weight of pears yields about 84 pounds of this juice, which will produce nearly 12 pounds of this substance.

Grape Sugar.

The brown sugar obtained from grapes by the usual process, being previously freed from the acids and sulphate of lime that existed in the original juice, yields by refining 75 per cent. of a white granular sugar, 24 of a kind of treacle with a little gum and some malate of lime.

To Candy Orange-peel.

Soak the peels in cold water, which change frequently till they lose their bitterness; then put them into syrup till they become soft and transparent. Then they are to be taken out and drained.

Lemon-peel.

This is made by boiling lemon-peel with sugar, and then exposing to the air until the sugar crystallizes.

To Color Candied Sugar.

Red.—Boil an ounce of cochineal in half a pint of water for five minutes, add an ounce of cream of tartar, ¼ an ounce of pounded alum, and boil them on a slow fire ten minutes; if it shows the color clear on white paper, it is sufficient. Add 2 ounces of sugar, and bottle it for use.

Blue.—Put a little warm water on a plate, and rub an indigo-stone in it till the color has come to the tint required.

Yellow.—Rub with some water a little gamboge on a plate; or infuse the heart of a yellow lily flower with milk warm water.

Green.—Boil the leaves of spinach about a minute in a little water, and when strained bottle the liquor for use. In coloring refined sugars, taste and fancy must guide.

To make Devices in Sugar.

Steep gum tragacanth in rose-water, and with double refined sugar make it into a paste, and color and mould it to fancy.

Whipped Syllabub.

Rub a lump of loaf sugar on the outside of a lemon, and put it into a pint of thick cream, and sweeten it to taste. Squeeze in the juice of a lemon, and add a glass of Madeira wine, or French brandy. Mill it to a froth with a chocolate mill, take off the froth as it rises, and lay it in a hair sieve. Fill one-half of the glass with red wine, then lay the froth as high as possible, but take care that it is well drained in the sieve, otherwise it will mix with the wine, and the syllabub be spoiled.

Solid Syllabub.

To a quart of rich cream put a quart of white wine, the juice of 2 lemons, with the rind of 1 grated, and sweeten it to taste. Whip it up well, and take off the froth as it rises. Put it upon a hair sieve, and let it stand in a cool place till the next day. Then half fill the glasses with the scum, and heap up the froth as high as possible. The bottom will look clear and it will keep several days.

Snow Balls.

Pare and take out the cores of 5 large baking apples, and fill the holes with orange or quince marmalade. Then take some good hot paste, roll the apples in it, about the crust of an equal thickness; put them in a tin dripping-pan, bake them in a moderate oven, and when taken out, make icing for them; let the same be a quarter of an inch thick, and set them a good distance from the fire until they become hardened, but be cautious that they are not browned.

Capillaire.

Mix 6 eggs well beat up, with 14 pounds of loaf sugar, and 3 pounds of coarse sugar. Put them into 3 quarts of water, boil it twice, skim it well, and add a ¼ of a pint of orange-flower water; strain it through a jelly-bag, and put it into bottles for use. A spoonful or two of this syrup put into a draught of either cold or warm water, makes an exceedingly pleasant drink.

To make Confectionery Drops.

Take double-refined sugar, pound and sift it through a hair sieve, not too fine; and then sift it through a silk sieve, to take out all the fine dust, which would destroy the beauty of the drop. Put the sugar into a clean pan, and moisten it with any favorite aromatic; if rose-water, pour it in slowly, stirring it with a paddle, which the sugar will fall from, as soon as it is moist enough, without sticking. Color it with a small quantity of liquid carmine, or any other color ground fine. Take a small pan with a lip, fill it three parts with paste, place it on a small stove, the half hole being of the size of the pan, and stir the sugar with a little ivory or bone handle, until it becomes liquid. When it almost boils, take it from the fire and continue to stir it; if it be too moist take a little of the powdered sugar, and add a spoonful to the paste, and stir it till it is of such a consistence as to run without too much extension. Have a tin plate, very clean and smooth; take the little pan in the left hand, and hold in the right a bit of iron, copper, or silver wire, four inches long, to take off the drop from the lip of the pan, and let it fall regularly on the tin plate; two hours afterwards take off the drops with the blade of a knife.

Chocolate Drops.

Scrape the chocolate to powder, and put an ounce to each pound of sugar; moisten the paste with clear water, work it as above, only take care to use all the paste prepared, as, if it be put on the fire a second time, it greases, and the drop is not of the proper thickness.

Orange-flower Drops.

These are made as the sugar drops, only using orange-flower water; or instead of it, use the essence of neroli, which is the essential oil of that flower.

Coffee Drops.

An ounce of coffee to a pound of sugar will form a strong decoction; when cleared, use it to moisten the sugar, and then make the drops as above.

Peppermint Drops.

The only requisites to make these are, extreme cleanliness, the finest sugar, and a few drops of the essence of peppermint.

Clove Drops.

These are made as the peppermint drops, the cloves being pounded, or the essence used. Good cloves should be black, heavy, of a pungent smell, hot to the taste, and full of oil.

Ginger Drops.

Pound and sift through a silk sieve the required quantity of ginger, according to the strength wanted, and add to it the sugar with clear water. China ginger is best, being aromatic as well as hot and sharp-tasted.

Liquorice Lozenges.

Take of extract of liquorice, double-refined sugar, each 10 ounces; tragacanth, powdered, 3 ounces. Powder them thoroughly, and make them into lozenges with rose-water. These are agreeable pectorals, and may be used at pleasure in tickling coughs. The above receipt is the easiest and best mode of making these lozenges. Refined extract of liquorice should be used; and it is easily powdered in the cold, after it has been laid for some days in a dry and rather warm place.

Extract of Liquorice.

The liquorice root is to be boiled in eight times its weight of water, to one half; the liquor is then to be expressed, and after the fæces have subsided, to be filtered; it is then to be evaporated, with a heat between 200° and 212°, until it becomes thickish; and, lastly, it is to be evaporated with a heat less than 200°, and frequently stirred, until it acquires a consistence proper for forming pills. This is made into little pastils, or flat cakes, often bearing the impression of the places where they are made; and a bit now and then put into the mouth takes off the tickling of a cough. It should be dissolved slowly in the mouth to make it pleasant.

CONFECTIONERY.

To Prepare Liquorice Juice.

Take up the roots in July; clean them perfectly as soon as out of the earth, than hang them up in the air, till nearly dry; after this cut them into thin slices, and boil them in water till the decoction is extremely strong; then press it hard out to obtain all the juice from the roots. This decoction is left to settle a little, and when it has deposited its coarser parts, pour it off into vessels, evaporate it over a fire, strong first, but mild afterwards, till it becomes of a thick consistence; then let the fire go out, and when the extract is cool take out large parcels of it at a time, and work them well with the hands, forming them into cylindric masses, which cut into such lengths as required, roll them over half dried bay leaves, which adhere to their surfaces, and leave them exposed to the sun, till perfectly dried. Great nicety is to be observed at the end of the evaporation, to get the extract to a proper consistence without letting it burn.

Refined Liquorice.

That description of article which is vended in thin, rounded and glassed pieces about the thickness of a crow's quill, is chiefly prepared in England. The whole process consists in evaporating the liquorice-ball anew, and purifying it by rest, with the help of isinglass, etc.

To Candy Orange-Marmalade.

Cut the clearest Seville oranges into two, take out all the juice and pulp into a basin, and pick all the skins and seeds out of it. Boil the rinds in hard water till they become tender, and change the water two or three times while they are boiling. Then pound them in a marble mortar and add to it the juice and pulp; put them next into a preserving pan with double their weight in loaf sugar, and set it over a slow fire. Boil it rather more than half an hour, put it into pots; cover it with brandy-paper and tie it close down.

To make Transparent Marmalade.

Cut very pale Seville oranges into quarters, take out the pulp, put it into a basin and pick out the skins and seeds. Put the peels into a little salt and water and let them stand all night, then boil them in a good quantity of spring-water until they are tender, cut them in very thin slices and put them into the pulp. To every pound of marmalade put 1½ pounds of double-refined beaten sugar; boil them together gently for 20 minutes; if they are not transparent boil them a few minutes longer. Stir it gently all the time, and take care not to break the slices. When it is cold put it into jelly and sweetmeat glasses tied down tight.

Barberry Marmalade.

Mash the barberries in a little water on a warm stove; pass them through a hair sieve with a paddle; weigh the pulp and put it back on the fire; reduce it to ½, clarify a pound of sugar and boil it well; put in the pulp and boil it together for a few minutes.

Quince Marmalade.

Take quinces that are quite ripe, pare and cut them in quarters, take out the cores, put them in a stewpan with spring water, nearly enough to cover them, keep them closely covered and let them stew gently till they are quite soft and red, then mash and rub them through a hair sieve. Put them in a pan over a gentle fire, with as much thick clarified sugar as the weight of the quinces; boil them an hour and stir the whole time with a wooden spoon to prevent its sticking; put it into pots and when cold tie them down.

Scotch Marmalade.

Take of the juice of Seville oranges, 2 pints, yellow honey, 2 lbs. Boil to a proper consistence.

Hartshorn Jelly.

Boil ½ a pound of hartshorn in 3 quarts of water over a gentle fire till it becomes a jelly; when a little hangs on a spoon it is done enough. Strain it hot, put it into a well tinned saucepan, and add to it ½ a pint of Rhenish wine and ¼ of a pound of loaf sugar. Beat the whites of 4 eggs or more to a froth, stir it sufficiently for the whites to mix well with the jelly, and pour it in as if cooling it. Boil it two or three minutes, then put in the juice of 4 lemons, and let it boil two minutes longer. When it is finally curdled and of a pure white, pour it into a swan-skin jelly-bag over a China basin, and pour it back again until it becomes as clear as rock-water; set a very clean China basin under, fill the glasses, put some thin lemon-rind into the basin, and when the jelly is all run out of the bag, with a clean spoon fill the rest of the glasses, and they will look of a fine amber color. Put in lemon and sugar agreeable to the palate.

Whipped Cream.

Mix the whites of 8 eggs, a quart of thick cream, and ½ a pint of sack; sweeten them to taste with double refined sugar. It may be perfumed with a little musk or ambergris tied in a rag and steeped in a little cream. Whip it up with a whisk, and some lemon-peel tied in the middle of the whisk. Then lay the froth with a spoon in the glasses or basins.

Pistachio Cream.

Beat ½ a pound of pistachio nut kernels in a mortar with a spoonful of brandy. Put them into a pan with a pint of good cream and the yolks of 2 eggs beaten fine. Stir it gently over the fire till it grows thick, and then put it into a China sompplate. When it is cold stick it over with small pieces of the nuts and send it to table.

Ice Cream.

To a pound of any preserved fruit add a quart of good cream, squeeze the juice of 2 lemons into it and some sugar to taste. Let the whole be rubbed through a fine hair sieve, and if raspberry, strawberry, or any red fruit, add a little cochineal to heighten the color; have the freezing can nice and clean, put the cream into it and cover it, then put it into the tub with ice beat small, and some salt; turn the freezing can quickly, and as the cream sticks to the sides scrape it down with an ice spoon, and so on till it is frozen. The more the cream is worked to the side with the spoon, the smoother and better flavored it will be. After it is well frozen take it out and put it into ice-moulds with salt and ice; then carefully wash the moulds for fear of any salt adhering to them; dip them in lukewarm water and send them to table.

Another Method—(Water-Ice).

Bruise 1 quart of strawberries in a basin with ½ a pint of good cream, a little currant jelly, and some cold clarified sugar; rub this well through the tammy and put it into an ice can well covered; then set it in a tub of broken ice with plenty of salt; when it grows thick about the sides, stir it with a spoon and cover it close again till it is perfectly frozen through; cover it well with ice and salt both under and over, and when it is frozen change it into a mould and cover well with ice. Sweeten a little plain cream with sugar and orange-flower water, and treat it the same; likewise any other fruit, without cream, may be mixed as above. This is called water-ice.

Blackberry Brandy—U. S. Sanitary Commission Receipt.

Ten quarts of blackberries make 1 gallon of juice. To 1 gallon of juice add 4 pounds of white sugar. Boil and skim it. Add 1 ounce of cloves, 1 ounce of ground cinnamon, 10 grated nutmegs; boil again. When cool add 1 quart of best whiskey or brandy.

Blackberry Brandy.

To 1 quart of strained blackberry juice add 1 pound of white sugar, 1 teaspoonful of powdered allspice, 1 teaspoonful of ground cloves. Boil a few minutes, then remove from the fire, and add ½ a pint of fourth-proof brandy or good Monongahela whiskey. Bottle and cork close. It is fit for immediate use. On no account use inferior brandy.

Extract of Blackberries.

Fill a quart bottle half full of ripe berries, add 1 teaspoonful of whole allspice and a few cloves. Fill the bottle with best whiskey. At the end of a month it will be fit for use. In using mix with a little sugar and water.

Blackberry Cordial.

To 1 gallon of blackberry juice add 4 pounds of white sugar; boil and skim off, then add 1 ounce of cloves, 1 ounce of cinnamon, 10 grated nutmegs, and boil down till quite rich; then let it cool and settle, afterward drain off, and add 1 pint of good brandy or whiskey.

Blackberry Syrup.

Take 2 pounds of the smaller blackberry roots and 2 gallons of water, and boil them down to 3 quarts; add 5 pounds of crushed sugar and 1 pint of best brandy. To 60 gallons thus prepared add 3 pounds of allspice and 2 pounds each of cloves and cassia. The smaller roots are much better than the larger ones, on account of their possessing superior astringent qualities.

Another Recipe.

To 2 quarts of blackberry juice add ½ an ounce each of powdered nutmeg, cinnamon and allspice, and ¼ of an ounce of powdered cloves. Boil these together; and, while hot, add a pint of pure French brandy, and sweeten with loaf sugar.

Blackberry Wine.

The following is given by the *Tribune* as an excellent recipe: To 2 quarts of blackberry juice put 1¼ pounds of white sugar, ¼ an ounce of cinnamon, ½ an ounce of nutmeg, ½ an ounce of cloves, 1 ounce of allspice; let it boil a few minutes, and when cool add 1 pint of brandy.

Superior Receipt for Ice Cream.

One gallon of cream, 2 pounds of rolled loaf sugar, 1 teaspoonful of oil of lemon. If for vanilla cream, 2 eggs beaten and 1½ tablespoonfuls of tincture of vanilla should be used; mix well and freeze in the usual way. The vanilla or lemon should be *well* mixed with the *sugar*, before it is added to the cream; by this means the cream will all be flavored alike.

Freezing Ice Cream.

Take a bucket of ice and pound it fine; mix with it salt (2 quarts), place your cream in a freezer, cover it close, and put it in the bucket; draw the ice round it so as to touch every part in a few minutes, put in a spoon and stir it from the edge to the centre. When the cream is put in a mould, close it and move it in the ice, instead of using a spoon.

Lemon Ice Cream.

Roll 2 fresh lemons in as much powdered loaf sugar as will be sufficient to sweeten 1 quart of rich cream; if the juice is wished, you can put some in with more sugar; freeze it. A good plan is to rub the lemon on a large lump of sugar, and then use the sugar in sweetening the cream.

Ice Cream with Fruit.

Mix the juice of the fruit with the sugar *before* you add the cream, which need not be very rich.

Calf's-Foot Jelly.

Split the feet, and soak them in cold water four or five hours; wash them and boil in 6 quarts of water; when it is reduced one-half strain it through a colander, and skim off all the fat that is on the top; set it away to cool, and when the jelly is very stiff, wipe it with a towel, to take off any grease that should remain; cut it in pieces, and pare off all the dark parts; put it in your preserving kettle, with 3 gills of wine, the juice and peel of 2 lemons, sugar and mace to your taste, and the shells and whites of 6 eggs; after it has boiled twenty minutes, pour in some *cold* water to make it settle; if any scum arises, take it off; let it boil five minutes longer, and take it off the fire; keep it covered for about an hour; when done, strain it through a bag that has been dipped in hot water, and put it in your glasses.

Currant Jelly.

Take the juice of red currants, 1 pound; sugar, 6 ounces. Boil down.

Another Method.

Take the juice of red currants, add white sugar, equal quantities. Stir it gently and smoothly for three hours, put it into glasses, and in three days it will concrete into a firm jelly.

Black Currant Jelly.

Put to 10 quarts of ripe dry black currants, 1 quart of water; put them in a large stewpan, the paper close over them, and set them for two hours in a cool oven. Squeeze them through a fine cloth, and add to every quart of juice 1½ pounds of loaf sugar broken into small pieces. Stir it till the sugar is melted; when it boils, skim it quite clean. Boil it pretty quickly over a clear fire, till it jellies, which is known by dipping a skimmer into the jelly, and holding it in the air; when it hangs to the spoon in a drop it is done. If the jelly is boiled too long, it will lose its flavor and shrink very much. Pour it into pots, cover them with brandy papers, and keep them in a dry place. Red and white jellies are made in the same way.

Apple Jelly.

Take of apple juice strained, 4 pounds; sugar, 1 pound. Boil to a jelly.

Strawberry Jelly.

Take of the juice of strawberries, 4 pounds; sugar, 2 pounds. Boil down.

Gooseberry Jelly.

Dissolve sugar in about half its weight of water, and boil; it will be nearly solid when cold; to this syrup add an equal weight of gooseberry juice, and give it a boil, but not long; for otherwise it will not fix.

Raspberry Cream.

Rub 1 quart of raspberries through a hair sieve, and take out the seeds, and mix it well with cream; sweeten it with sugar to your taste, then put it into a stone jug, and raise a froth with a chocolate mill. As the froth arises, take it off with a spoon, and lay it upon a hair sieve. When there is as much froth as wanted, put what cream remains in a deep China dish, and pour the frothed cream upon it, as high as it will lie on.

CONFECTIONERY.

Raspberry Vinegar.

Pour 1 quart of vinegar on 1 quart of raspberries, the next day strain it upon another quart of the fruit, and repeat this every day for six days. Then add 1 pound of white sugar to every pint of the vinegar, and put it into a jar, which must be placed in a pot of boiling water to be scalded through.

Currant Wine.

To 1 quart of currant juice put 2 quarts of water and 1 pound of sugar. After mixing, let these stand twenty-four hours; then skim and put into a jug or barrel unstopped, and leave it to ferment in a cool place for a week or so. Then cork tightly, and bottle off when clear.

Raspberry Jam.

Mash a quantity of fine, ripe, dry raspberries, strew on them their own weight of loaf sugar, and half their weight of white currant juice. Boil them half an hour over a clear slow fire, skim them well, and put them into pots or glasses; tie them down with brandy papers, and keep them dry. Strew on the sugar as quick as possible after the berries are gathered, and in order to preserve their flavor they must not stand long before boiling them.

Strawberry Jam.

Bruise very fine some scarlet strawberries, gathered when quite ripe, and put to them a little juice of red currants. Beat and sift their weight in sugar, strew it over them, and put them into a preserving-pan. Set them over a clear slow fire, skim them, then boil them twenty minutes, and put them into glasses.

Raspberry Paste.

Mash 1 quart of raspberries, strain one-half, and put the juice to the other half; boil them a quarter of an hour, put to them a pint of red currant juice, and let them boil all together, till the raspberries are done enough. Then put 1½ pounds of double-refined sugar into a clean pan, with as much water as will dissolve it, boil it to a sugar again; then put in the raspberries and juice, scald and pour them into glasses. Put them into a stove to dry, and turn them when necessary.

Pineapple Jelly.

Peel a pineapple of about 1 pound weight, cut it into slices about a quarter of an inch thick, and put these into a basin. Clarify 1 pound of loaf sugar with 1 pint of spring-water, the juice of 2 lemons, and half the white of an egg whipped with a little water; when thoroughly skimmed, strain the syrup on to the pineapple, allow it to boil for three minutes, then cover it down with a sheet of paper twisted round the basin, and allow the infusion to stand for several hours in order to extract the flavor. When about to mix the jelly, strain the syrup through a napkin into a basin, and put the pieces of pineapple to drain upon a sieve; add 2 ounces of clarified isinglass to the pineapple syrup, and then pour the jelly into a mould previously imbedded in rough ice.

Currant and Raspberry Jelly.

Pick the stalks from 1 quart of red currants and 1 quart of raspberries; then put these into a large basin with ½ a pound of pounded sugar and a gill of spring-water; bruise them thoroughly by squeezing them with the back part of the bowl of a wooden spoon against the sides of the basin; then throw the whole into a beaver jelly-bag and filter the juice, pouring it back into the bag until it runs through perfectly bright; next add ½ a pint of clarified syrup and 2 ounces of clarified isinglass to the juice, and pour the jelly into a mould placed in rough ice to receive it.

Punch Jelly.

Put the prepared stock from 4 calves-feet into a stewpan to melt on the stove fire; then withdraw it, and add thereto the following ingredients: Two pounds of loaf-sugar, the juice of 6 lemons and 4 oranges, the rind of 1 Seville orange and of 4 lemons, ½ a nutmeg, 12 cloves and 2 sticks of cinnamon, a small cup of strong green tea, a pint of rum, and ½ a pint of brandy. Stir these well together, then add 6 whites and 2 whole eggs whipped up with a little Sherry and spring-water, and continue whisking the punch on a brisk stove fire until it begins to simmer; then set it down by the side of the fire and cover the stewpan with its lid containing some live embers of charcoal; about ten minutes after pour the jelly into a flannel or beaver filtering-bag; keep pouring the jelly back into the bag until it becomes quite clear and bright, and when the whole has been run through set it in a mould in ice in the usual way.

Coffee Cream.

Roast 8 ounces of Mocha coffee-berries in a small preserving pan over a stove fire, stirring it the whole time with a wooden spoon until it assumes a light brown color; then blow away the small burnt particles and throw the roasted coffee into a stewpan, and set it aside to allow the infusion to draw out the flavor of the coffee. Next strain this through a napkin into a stewpan containing 8 yolks of eggs and 12 ounces of sugar; add a very small pinch of salt, stir the cream over the stove fire until it begins to thicken; then quicken the motions of the spoon, and when the yolks of eggs are sufficiently set strain the cream through a tammy or sieve into a large basin. Mix ½ a pint of whipped cream and 1½ ounces of clarified isinglass in with this; pour the whole into a mould ready set in rough ice for the purpose, and when the cream has become firm dip the mould in warm water and turn the cream out on its dish.

Damson Cheese.

Boil the fruit in a sufficient quantity of water to cover it; strain the pulp through a very coarse sieve; to each pound add 4 ounces of sugar. Boil it till it begins to candy on the sides, then pour it into the moulds. Other kinds of plums may be treated in the same way, as also cherries, and several kinds of fruit.

An Omelette Soufflé.

Put 2 ounces of the powder of chestnuts into a skillet, then add 2 yolks of new-laid eggs, and dilute the whole with a little cream, or even a little water; when this is done and the ingredients well mixed, leaving no lumps, add a bit of the best fresh butter about the size of an egg and an equal quantity of powdered sugar; then put the skillet on the fire, and keep stirring the contents; when the cream is fixed and thick enough to adhere to the spoon, let it bubble up once or twice, and take it from the fire; then add ⅓ of the white of an egg to those you have already set aside, and whip them to the consistency of snow; then amalgamate the whipped whites of eggs and the cream, stirring them with a light and equal hand; pour the contents into a deep dish, sift over with double-refined sugar, and place the dish on a stove, with a fire over it as well as under, and in a quarter of an hour the cream will rise like an *omelette soufflé*; as soon as it rises about four inches it is fit to serve up.

Orgeat Paste.

Blanch and pound ¾ of a pound of sweet and a ¼ of a pound of bitter almonds; pound them in a mortar and wet them sufficiently with orange-flower water, that they may not oil. When they are pounded fine add ⅔ of a pound of finely powdered sugar to them and mix the whole in a stiff paste, which put into pods for use. It will keep six months; when wanted to be used take a piece about the size of an egg and mix it with ½ a pint of water and squeeze it through a napkin.

Pate de Guimauve.

Take of decoction of marshmallow roots 4 ounces; water 1 gallon. Boil down to 4 pints and strain; then add gum arabic ½ a pound, refined sugar 2 pounds. Evaporate to an extract; then take from the fire, stir it quickly with the whites of 12 eggs previously beaten to a froth; then add, while stirring, ½ ounce of orange-flower water.

Another.—Take of very white gum arabic and white sugar, each 2¼ pounds, with a sufficient quantity of boiling water. Dissolve, strain and evaporate without boiling to the consistency of honey; beat up the white of 6 eggs with 4 drachms of orange-flower water, which mix gradually with the paste, and evaporate over a slow fire, stirring it continually till it will not stick to the fingers, it should be very light, spongy and extremely white.

Pate de Jujubes.

Take of raisins, stoned, 1 pound; currants, picked, jujubes, opened, each 4 ounces; water, a sufficient quantity. Boil, strain with expression, add sugar 2½ pounds, gum arabic 2½ pounds, previously made into a mucilage with some water, and strain; evaporate gently, pour into moulds, finish by drying in a stove, and then divide it.

PICKLING.

This branch of domestic economy comprises a great variety of articles, which are essentially necessary to the convenience of families. It is at the same time too prevalent a practice to make use of brass utensils to give pickle a fine color. This pernicious custom is easily avoided by heating the liquor and keeping it in a proper degree of warmth before it is poured upon the pickle. Stone jars are the best adapted for sound keeping. Pickles should never be handled with the fingers, but by a spoon kept for the purpose.

To Pickle Onions.

Put a sufficient quantity into salt and water for nine days, observing to change the water every day; next put them into jars and pour fresh boiling salt and water over them; cover them close up till they are cold; then make a second decoction of salt and water, and pour it on boiling. When it is cold drain the onions on a hair sieve, and put them into wide-mouthed bottles; fill them up with distilled vinegar; put into every bottle a slice or two of ginger, a blade of mace and a teaspoonful of sweet oil, which will keep the onions white. Cork them up in a dry place.

To make Sour Krout.

Take a large, strong, wooden vessel or cask resembling a salt-beef cask, and capable of containing as much as is sufficient for the winter's consumption of a family. Gradually break down or chop the cabbages (deprived of outside green leaves) into very small pieces; begin with one or two cabbages at the bottom of the cask, and add others at intervals, pressing them by means of a wooden spade against the side of the cask until it is full. Then place a heavy weight upon the top of it, and allow it to stand near to a warm place for four or five days. By this time it will have undergone fermentation, and be ready for use. Whilst the cabbages are passing through the process of fermentation, a very disagreeable, fetid, acid smell is exhaled from them; now remove the cask to a cool situation, and keep it always covered up. Strew aniseeds among the layers of the cabbages during its preparation which communicates a peculiar flavor to the sour kraut at an after period.

In boiling it for the table, two hours is the period for it to be on the fire. It forms an excellent nutritious and antiscorbutic food for winter use.

Piccalilli—Indian method.

This consists of all kinds of pickles mixed and put into one large jar—sliced cucumbers, button onions, cauliflowers, broken in pieces. Salt them, or put them in a large hair sieve in the sun to dry for three days, then scald them in vinegar a few minutes; when cold put them together. Cut a large white cabbage in quarters, with the outside leaves taken off and at time; salt it, and put it in the sun to dry three or four days; then scald it in vinegar, the same as cauliflower; carrots, three parts, boiled in vinegar and a little bay salt. French beans, reddish pods, and nasturtiums all go through the same process as capsicums, etc. To 1 gallon of vinegar put 4 ounces of ginger bruised, 2 ounces of whole white pepper, 2 ounces of allspice, ½ ounce chillies bruised, 4 ounces of turmeric, 1 pound of the best mustard, ½ pound of shallots, 1 ounce of garlic, and ½ pound of bay salt. The vinegar, spice, and other ingredients, except the mustard, must boil half an hour; then strain it into a pan, put the mustard into a large basin, with a little vinegar; mix it quite fine and free from lumps, then add more. When well mixed put it into the vinegar just strained off, and when quite cold put the pickles into a large pan, and the liquor over them; stir them repeatedly, so as to mix them all. Finally, put them into a jar, and tie them over first with a bladder, and afterwards with leather. The capsicums want no preparation.

To Pickle Samphire.

Put the quantity wanted into a clean pan, throw over it two or three handsfuls of salt, and cover it with spring-water twenty-four hours; next put it into a clean saucepan, throw in a handful of salt, and cover it with good vinegar. Close the pan tight, set it over a slow fire, and let it stand till the samphire is green and crisp, then take it off instantly, for should it remain till it is soft it will be totally spoiled. Put it into the pickling-pot and cover it close; when it is quite cold tie it down with a bladder and leather, and set it by for use. Samphire may be preserved all the year by keeping it in a very strong brine of salt and water; and just before using it put it for a few minutes into some of the best vinegar.

Mushrooms.

Put the smallest that can be got into spring-water, and rub them with a piece of new flannel dipped in salt. Throw them into cold water as they are cleaned, which will make them keep their color; next put them into a saucepan with a handful of salt upon them. Cover them close, and set them over the fire four or five minutes, or till the heat draws the liquor from them; next lay them betwixt two dry cloths till they are cold; put them into glass bottles, and fill them up with distilled vinegar, with a blade of mace and a teaspoonful of sweet oil into every bottle; cork them up close and set them in a dry cool place. As a substitute for distilled vinegar, use white wine vinegar, or ale. Alegar will do, but it must be boiled with a little mace, salt, and a few slices of ginger, and it must be quite cold before it is poured upon the mushrooms.

Another Method.

Bruise a quantity of well-grown flaps of mushrooms with the hands, and then strew a fair proportion of salt over them; let them stand all night, and the next day put them into stewpans; set them in a quick oven for twelve hours, and strain them through a hair sieve. To every gallon of liquor put of cloves, black pepper, and ginger 1 ounce each, ½ pound of common salt; set it on a slow fire, and let it boil till half the liquor is wasted; then put it into a clean pot, and when cold bottle it for use.

Cucumbers.

Let them be as free from spots as possible. Take the smallest that can be got, put them into strong salt and water for nine days, till they become yellow; stir them at least twice a day; should they become perfectly yellow, pour the water off, and cover them with plenty of vine-leaves. Set the water over the fire, and when it boils, pour it over them, and set them upon the earth to keep warm. When the water is almost cold make it boil again, and pour it upon them; proceed thus till they are of a fine green, which they will be in four or five times; keep them well covered with vine-leaves, with a cloth and dish over the top to keep in the steam, which will help to green them.

When they are greened put them in a hair sieve to drain, and then to every 2 quarts of white-wine vinegar put ½ an ounce of mace, 10 or 12 cloves, 1 ounce of ginger cut into slices, 1 ounce of black pepper, and a handful of salt. Boil them all together for five minutes; pour it hot on the pickles, and tie them down for use. They may also be pickled with ale, ale vinegar, or distilled vinegar, and adding 3 or 4 cloves of garlic and shallots.

Walnuts White.

Pare green walnuts very thin till the white appears, then throw them into spring-water with a handful of salt; keep them under water six hours, then put them into a stewpan to simmer five minutes, but do not let them boil; take them out and put them in cold water and salt; they must be kept quite under the water with a board, otherwise they will not pickle white; then lay them on a cloth and cover them with another to dry; carefully rub them with a soft cloth, and put them into the jar, with some blades of mace and nutmeg sliced thin. Mix the spice between the nuts and pour distilled vinegar over them; when the jar is full of nuts pour mutton fat over them, and tie them close down with a bladder and leather, to keep out the air.

Artificial Anchovies.

To a peck of sprats put 2 pounds of salt, 3 ounces of bay salt, 1 pound of saltpetre, 2 ounces of prunella, and a few grains of cochineal; pound all in a mortar; put into a stone pan first a layer of sprats and then one of the compound, and so on alternately to the top. Press them down hard; cover them close for six months, and they will be fit for use, and will really produce a most excellent-flavored sauce.

Salmon.

Boil the fish gently till done, and then take it up, strain the liquor, add bay leaves, pepper corns, and salt; give these a boil, and when cold add the best vinegar to them; then put the whole sufficiently over the fish to cover it, and let it remain a month at least.

To Preserve Fish with Sugar.

Fish may be preserved in a dry state, and perfectly fresh, by means of sugar alone, and even with a very small quantity of it. Fresh fish may be kept in that state for some days, so as to be as good when boiled as if just caught. If dried, and kept free from mouldiness, there seems no limit to their preservation; and they are much better in this way than when salted. The sugar gives no disagreeable taste.

This process is particularly valuable in making what is called kippered salmon; and the fish preserved in this manner are far superior in quality and flavor to those which are salted or smoked. If desired, so much salt may be used as to give the taste that may be required; but this substance does not conduce to their preservation.

In the preservation it is hardly necessary to open the fish, and to apply the sugar to the muscular parts, placing it in a horizontal position for two or three days, that this substance may penetrate. After this it may be dried; and it is only further necessary to wipe and ventilate occasionally, to prevent mouldiness.

A tablespoonful of brown sugar is sufficient in this manner for a salmon of five or six pounds weight; and if salt is desired, a teaspoonful or more may be added. Saltpetre may be used instead, in the same proportion, if it is desired to make the kipper hard.

To Salt Hams.

For three hams pound and mix together ½ peck of salt, ½ ounce of salt prunella, 1½ ounces of saltpetre, and 4 pounds of coarse salt; rub the hams well with this, and lay what is to spare over them, let them lie three days, then hang them up. Take the pickle in which the hams were, put water enough to cover the hams with more common salt, till it will bear an egg, then boil and skim it well, put it in the salting tub, and the next morning put it to the hams; keep them down the same as pickled pork; in a fortnight take them out of the liquor, rub them well with brine, and hang them up to dry.

To Dry-salt Beef and Pork.

Lay the meat on a table or in a tub with a double bottom, that the brine may drain off as fast as it forms, rub the salt well in, and be careful to apply it in every niche; afterwards put it into either of the above utensils, when it must be frequently turned; after the brine has ceased running, it must be quite buried in salt, and kept closely packed. Meat which has had the bones taken out is the best for salting. In some places the salted meat is pressed by heavy weights or a screw, to extract the moisture sooner.

To Pickle in Brine.

A good brine is made of bay salt and water, thoroughly saturated, so that some of the salt remains undissolved; into this brine the substances to be preserved are plunged, and kept covered with it. Among vegetables, French beans, artichokes, olives, and the different sorts of samphire may be thus preserved, and among animals, herrings.

To Salt by another method.

Mix brown sugar, bay salt, common salt, each 2 pounds; saltpetre, 8 ounces; water, 2 gallons; this pickle gives meat a fine red color, while the sugar renders them mild and of excellent flavor. Large quantities are to be managed by the above proportions.

TO PRESERVE FRUITS.

Some rules are necessary to be observed in this branch of confectionery. In the first place, observe in making syrups that the sugar is well pounded and dissolved, before it is placed on the fire, otherwise their scum will not rise well, nor the fruit obtain its fine color. When stone fruit is preserved, cover them with mutton suet rendered, to exclude the air, which is sure to ruin them. All wet sweetmeats must be kept dry and cool to preserve them from mouldiness and damp. Dip a piece of writing paper in brandy, lay it close to the sweetmeats, cover them tight with paper, and they will keep well for any length of time; but will inevitably spoil without these precautions.

Another Method.

The fruit, if succulent, is first soaked for some hours in very hard water, or in a weak alum water, to harden it, and then to be drained from the fruit, either prepared or not; pour syrup, boiled to a candy height, and half cold; after some hours the syrup, weakened by the sauce of the fruit, is to be poured off, re-boiled, and poured on again, and this repent several times. When the syrup is judged to be no longer weakened, the fruit is to be taken out of it, and well drained.

To Bottle Damsons.

Put damsons, before they are too ripe, into wide-mouthed bottles, and cork them down tight; then put them into a moderately heated oven, and about three hours more will do them; observe that the oven is not too hot, otherwise it will make the fruit fly. All kinds of fruit that are bottled may be done in the same way, and they will keep two years; after they are done, they must be put away with the mouth downward, in a cool place, to keep them from fermenting.

To Preserve Barberries.

Set an equal quantity of barberries and sugar in a kettle of boiling water, till the sugar is melted, and the barberries quite soft; let them remain all night. Put them next day into a preserving-pan, and boil them fifteen minutes, then put them into jars, tie them close, and set them by for use.

To Preserve Grapes.

Take close bunches, whether white or red, not too ripe, and lay them in a jar. Put to them ¼ pound of sugar candy, and fill the jar with common brandy. Tie them up close with a bladder, and set them in a dry place.

To Dry Cherries.

Having stoned the desired number of morello cherries, put 1¼ pounds of fine sugar to every pound; beat and sift it over the cherries, and let them stand all night. Take them out of their sugar, and to every pound of sugar, put two spoonfuls of water. Boil and skim it well, and then put in the cherries; boil the sugar over them, and next morning strain them, and to every pound of syrup put ½ pound more sugar; boil it till it is a little thicker, then put in the cherries and let them boil gently. The next day strain them, put them in a stove, and turn them every day till they are dry.

To Clarify Honey.

The best kind is clarified by merely melting it in a water bath, and taking off the scum; the middling kind by dissolving it in water, adding the white of an egg to each pint of the solution, and boiling it down to its original consistence, skimming it from time to time. The inferior kind requires solution in water, boiling the solution with 1 pound of charcoal to 25 pounds of honey, adding, when an excess of acid is apprehended, a small quantity of chalk or oyster-shell powder; next by straining it several times through flannel, and reducing the solution to its original consistence by evaporation.

To Preserve Candied Orange-flowers.

Free them from their cups, stamina and pistils, put 4 ounces into 1 pound of sugar, boil to a candy height, and pour on a slab, so as to form them into cakes.

Fruits in Brandy or other Spirits.

Gather plums, apricots, cherries, peaches, and other juicy fruits, before they are perfectly ripe, and soak them for some hours in hard water to make them firm; as the moisture of the fruit weakens the spirit, it ought to be strong, therefore add 5 ounces of sugar to each quart of spirit.

Seville Oranges whole.

Cut a hole at the stem end of the oranges, the size of a five or ten cent piece, take out all the pulp, put the oranges in cold water for two days, changing it twice a day; boil them rather more than an hour, but do not cover them, as it will spoil the color; have ready a good syrup, into which put the oranges, and boil them till they look clear; then take out the seeds, skins, etc. from the pulp first taken out of the oranges, and add to it one of the whole oranges, previously boiled, with an equal weight of sugar to it and the pulp; boil this together till it looks clear, over a slow fire, and when cold fill the oranges with this marmalade, and put on the tops; cover them with syrup, and put brandy paper on the top of the jar. It is better to take out the inside at first, to preserve the fine flavor of the juice and pulp, which would be injured by boiling in the water.

Strawberries whole.

Take an equal weight of fruit and double-refined sugar, lay the former in a large dish, and sprinkle half the sugar in fine powder; give a gentle shake to the dish, that the sugar may touch the under side of the fruit. Next day make a thin syrup with the remainder of the sugar, and allow 1 pint of red currant-juice to every 3 pounds of strawberries; in this simmer them until sufficiently jellied. Choose the largest scarlets, and not dead ripe.

Apricots.

Infuse young apricots before their stones become hard into a pan of cold spring-water, with a plenty of vine leaves, set them over a slow fire until they are quite yellow, then take them out, and rub them with a flannel and salt to take off the lint; put them into a pan to the same water and leaves, cover them close at a distance from the fire, until they are a fine light green, then pick out all the bad ones. Boil the best gently two or three times in a thin syrup, and let them be quite cold each time before you boil them. When they look plump and clear make a syrup of double-refined sugar, but not too thick; give your apricots a gentle boil in it, and then put them into the pots or glasses. Dip a paper in brandy and lay it over them; tie them close, and keep them in a dry place.

To keep Fruit fresh without Sugar.

Air-tight cans are now made by which, with proper care, peaches, plums, cherries, tomatoes, or other fruit or vegetables may be kept for almost any length of time with all the qualities of the fresh article. All that is required is to heat the can containing the fruit sufficiently to drive out the air, and then seal it tightly. The following plan has also succeeded perfectly:

Cut the fresh peaches (always choosing the best varieties) in half, after paring them, and take the stones out. Put them in the can, which will generally hold a pint, and which should be entirely filled; and then solder the lid closely. Place the can in a kettle containing cold water enough to cover it, and bring the water to a boil. If there

WEIGHTS AND MEASURES.

Solids.

Butter, when soft, one pound is one quart.
Eggs, ten are one pound.
Flour, wheat, one pound is one quart.
Meal, Indian, one pound two ounces is one quart.
Sugar, best brown, one pound two ounces is one quart.
Sugar, loaf, broken, one pound is one quart.
Sugar, white, powdered, one pound one ounce is one quart.
Flour, four quarts are half a peck.
Flour, sixteen quarts are half a bushel.

Liquids.

Four tablespoonfuls are half a gill.
Eight spoonfuls are one gill.
Two gills, or sixteen spoonfuls, are half a pint.
Two pints are one quart.
Four quarts are one gallon.
Sixty drops are one teaspoonful.
Four tablespoonfuls are one wineglassful.
Twelve spoonfuls are one teacupful.
Sixteen spoonfuls, or half a pint, are one tumblerful.

THE ART OF CARVING.

Persons unaccustomed to serving at table will, with the help of the fleshy cuts, and the instructions accompanying them, soon be able to carve well: if, at the same time, they will, as occasion offers, take notice how a good carver proceeds when a joint or fowl is before him.

We will begin with those joints, etc., that are simple and easy to be carved, and afterwards proceed to such as are more complicate and difficult.

Leg of Mutton.

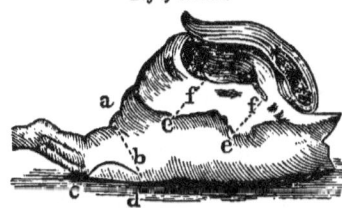

This cut represents a leg or *jigot* of boiled mutton; it should be served up in the dish as it lies, lying upon its back; but when roasted, the under side, as here represented by the letter *d*, should lie uppermost in the dish, as in a ham (which see); and in this case, as it will be necessary occasionally to turn it, so as to get readily at the under side, and cut it in the direction of *a b*, the shank, which is here broken and bent for the convenience of putting it into a less pot or vessel to boil it, is not broken or bent in a roasted joint, of course, should be wound round (after it is taken off the spit) with half a sheet of writing paper, and so sent up to table that a person carrying it may take hold of it without greasing his hands. Accordingly, when he wishes to cut it on the under side, it being too heavy a joint to be easily turned with a fork, the carver is to take hold of the shank with his left hand, and he will thus be able to turn it readily, so as to cut it where he pleases with his right.

A leg of wether mutton, which is by far the best flavored, may be readily known when bought, by the kernel, or little round lump of fat, just above the letters *a e*.

When a leg of mutton is first cut, the person carving should turn the joint towards him, and here lies, the shank to the left hand; then holding it steady with his fork, he should cut in deep on the fleshy part, in the hollow of the thigh, quite to the bone, in the direction *a b*. Thus will he cut right through the kernel of fat, called the *pope's eye*, which many are fond of. The most juicy parts of the leg are in the thick part of it, from the line *a b*, upwards towards *c*, but many prefer the drier part, which is about the shank or knuckles; this part is by far the coarser, but as I said, some prefer it, and call it the venison part, though it is less like venison than any other part of the joint. The fat of this joint lies chiefly on the ridge *e e*, and is to be cut in the direction *e f*.

In a leg of mutton there is but one bone readily to be got at, and that a small one; this is the *cramp-bone*, by some called the *gentleman's bone*, and is to be cut out by taking hold of the shank-bone with the left hand, and with a knife cutting down to the thigh-bone at the point *d*, then passing the knife under the cramp-bone, in the direction *d e*, it may easily be cut out.

A Shoulder of Mutton.—No. 1.

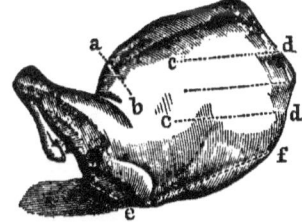

Figure 1 represents a shoulder of mutton, which is sometimes salted and boiled by fanciful people; but customarily served up roasted, and laid in a dish, with the back or upper side uppermost, as here represented.

When not over-roasted it is a joint very full of gravy, much more so than a leg, and as such by many preferred, and particularly as having many very good, delicate, and savory parts in it.

The shank-bone should be wound round with writing paper, as pointed out in the leg, that the person carving may take hold of it to turn it as, he wishes. Now, when it is first cut, it should be in the hollow part of it, in the direction *a b*, and the knife should be passed deep to the bone.

The gravy then runs fast into the dish, and the part cut opens wide enough to take many slices from it readily.

The best fat, that which is full of kernels and best flavored, lies on the outer edge, and is to be cut out in thin slices in the direction *e f*. If many are at table, and the hollow part, cut in the line *a b*, is all eaten, some very good and delicate slices may be cut out on each side of the ridge of the blade-bone, in the direction *c d*. The line between these two dotted lines is that in the direction of which the edge or ridge of the blade-bone lies, and cannot be cut across.

A Shoulder of Mutton—No. 2.

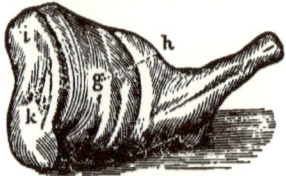

On the under side of the shoulder, as represented in figure 2, there are two parts very full of gravy, and such as many persons prefer to those of the upper side. One is a deep cut in the direction *g h*, accompanied with fat, and the other all lean in a line from *i* to *k*. The parts about the shank are coarse and dry, as about the knuckle in the leg, but yet some prefer this dry part, as being less rich or luscious, and of course less apt to cloy.

A shoulder of mutton over-roasted is spoiled.

A Leg of Pork,

Whether boiled or roasted, is sent up to table as a leg of mutton roasted, and cut up in the same manner; of course I shall refer you to what I have said on that joint, only that the close firm flesh about the knuckle is by many reckoned the best, which is not the case in a leg of mutton.

A Shoulder of Pork

Is never cut or sent to table as such, but the shank-bone, with some little meat annexed, is often served up boiled, and called a spring, and is very good eating.

Edge-Bone of Beef.

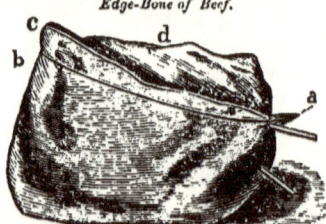

In carving it, as the outside suffers in its flavor from the water in which it is boiled, the dish should be turned towards the carver, as it is here represented, and a thick slice should be first cut off the whole length of the joint, beginning at *a* and cutting it all the way even and through the whole surface, from *a* to *b*.

The soft fat that resembles marrow lies on the back below the letter *d*, and the firm fat is to be cut in thin horizontal slices at the point *c*; but as some persons prefer the soft fat and others the firm, each should be asked what he likes.

The upper part, as here shown, is certainly the handsomest, fullest of gravy, most tender, and is encircled with fat; but there are still some who prefer a slice on the under side, which is quite lean. But as it is a heavy joint and very troublesome to turn, that person cannot have much good manners who requests it.

The skewer that keeps the meat together when boiling is here shown at *a*. It should be drawn out before the dish is served up to table, or if it be necessary to leave a skewer in, that skewer should be a silver one.

A Knuckle of Veal.

A knuckle of veal is always boiled, and is admired for the fat, sinewy tendons about the knuckle, which, if boiled tender, are much esteemed. A lean knuckle is not worth the dressing.

You cannot cut a handsome slice, but in the direction *a b*. The most delicate fat lies about the part *d*, and if cut in the line *d e*, you will divide two bones, between which lies plenty of fine, marrowy fat.

The several bones about the knuckle may be readily separated at the joints, and, as they are covered with tendons, a bone may be given to those who like it.

A Breast of Veal, Roasted.

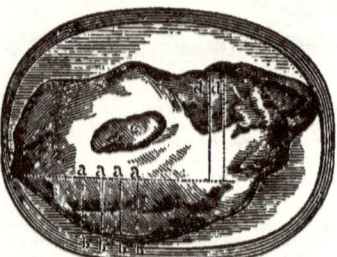

This is the best end of a breast of veal, with the sweetbread lying on it, and, when carved, should be first cut down quite through in the first line on the left, *d c*; it should next be cut across in the line *a c*; from *c* to the last *a* on the left, quite through divides the gristles from the rib-bones; this done, to those who like fat and gristle, the thick or gristly part should be cut into pieces as wanted, in the lines *a b*. When a breast of veal is cut into pieces and stewed, these gristles are very tender and eatable. To such persons as prefer a bone a rib should be cut or separated from the rest in the line *d c*, and with a part of the breast, a slice of the sweetbread, *e*, cut across the middle.

THE ART OF CARVING.

A Saddle of Mutton.

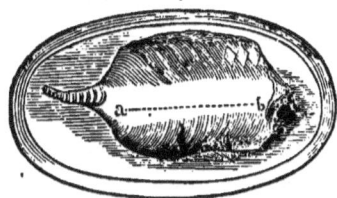

This is by some called a chine of mutton, the saddle being the two necks; but as the two necks are now seldom sent to table together, they call the two loins a saddle.

A saddle of mutton is a genteel and handsome dish; it consists of the two loins together, the back-bone running down the middle to the tail. Of course, when it is to be carved, you must cut a long slice in either of the fleshy parts on the side of the back-bone, in the direction *a b*.

There is seldom any great length of the tail left on, but if it is sent up with the tail many are fond of it, and it may readily be divided into several pieces by cutting between the joints of the tail, which are about the distance of one inch apart.

A saddle of venison is cut similarly to the above.

A Spare-Rib of Pork.

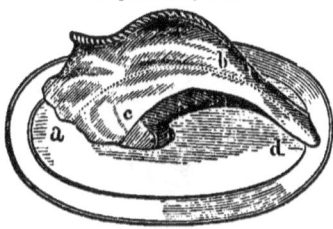

A spare-rib of pork is carved by cutting out a slice from the fleshy part in the line *a b*. This joint will afford many good cuts in this direction, with as much fat as people like to eat of such strong meat. When the fleshy part is cut away, a bone may be easily separated from the next to it in the line *d b c*, disjointing it at *c*.

Half a Calf's Head Boiled.

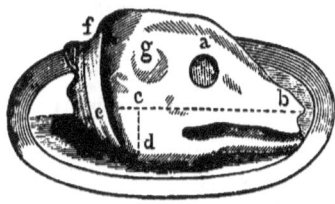

There are many delicate bits about a calf's head, and when young, perfectly white, fat and well-dressed, half a head is a genteel dish, if a small one.

When first cut it should be quite along the cheek bone, in the fleshy part, in the direction *c b*, where many handsome slices may be cut. In the fleshy part at the end of the jaw-bone, lies part of the throat sweetbread, which may be cut into in the line *c d*, and which is esteemed the best part in the head. Many like the eye, which is to be cut from its socket *a*, by forcing the point of a carving knife down to the bottom on one edge of the socket, and cutting quite round, keeping the point of the knife slanting towards the middle, so as to separate the meat from the bone. This piece is seldom divided, but if you wish to oblige two persons with it, it may be cut into two parts. The palate is also reckoned by some a delicate morsel. This is found on the under side of the roof of the mouth; it is a crinkled, white, thick skin, and may be easily separated from the bone by the knife by lifting the head up with your left hand.

There is also some good meat to be met with on the under side, covering the under jaw; and some nice gristly fat to be pared off about the ear, *g*.

There are scarcely any bones here to be separated, but one may be cut off at the neck, in the line *f e*, but this is a coarse part.

There is a tooth in the upper jaw, the last tooth behind, which, having several cells, and being full of jelly, is called the sweet tooth. Its delicacy is more in the name than in anything else. It is a double tooth, lies firm in its socket at the further end, but if the calf is a young one, may readily be taken out with the point of a knife.

A Ham.

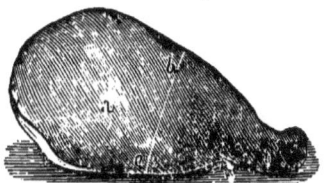

A ham is cut two ways; across, in the line *b c*, or with the point of a carving knife, in the circular line in the middle, taking out a small piece as at *a*, and cutting thin slices in a circular direction, thus enlarging it by degrees. This last method of cutting it is to preserve the gravy and keep it moist, which is thus prevented from running out.

A Haunch of Venison.

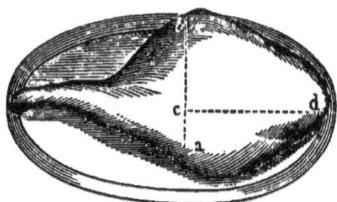

In carving a haunch of venison, first cut it across down to the bone, in the line *d e a*, then turn the dish with the end *a* towards you, put in the point of the knife at *c*, and cut it down as deep as you can in the direction *c b*; thus cut, you may take out as many slices as you please, on the right or left. As the fat lies deeper on the left, between *b* and *a*, to those who are fond of fat, as most venison eaters are, the best flavored and fattest slices will be found on the left of the line *c b*, supposing the end *a* turned towards you. Slices of venison should not be cut thick nor too thin; and plenty of gravy should be given with them.

An Ox Tongue.

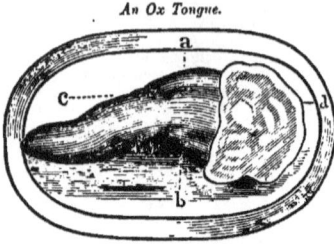

A tongue is to be cut across, in the line *a, b*, and a slice taken from thence. The most tender and juicy slices will be about the middle, or between the line *a b*, and the root. Towards the tip, the meat is closer and dryer. For the fat, and a kernel with that fat, cut off a slice of the root on the right of the letter *b*, at the bottom next the dish. A tongue is often cut lengthways, as from *c* to *d*. A tongue is generally eaten with white meat, veal, chicken, or turkey; and to those whom you serve with the latter, you should give of the former.

A Brisket of Beef.

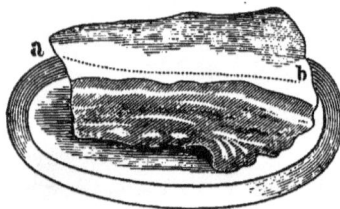

This is a part always boiled, and is to be cut in the direction of *a b*, quite down the bone, but never help any one to the outside slice, which should be taken off pretty thick. The fat cut with this slice is a firm gristly fat, but a softer fat will be found underneath, for those who prefer it.

A piece of Sirloin of Beef.

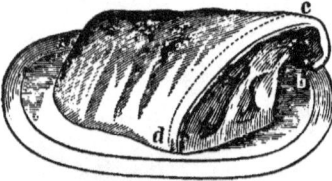

Whether the whole sirloin, or part of it only, be sent to table, is immaterial, with respect to carving it. The figure here represents part of the joint only, the whole being too large for families in general. It is drawn as standing up in the dish, in order to show the inside or under part; but when sent to table, it is always laid down, so as that the part described by the letter *c* lies close on the dish. The part *c d* then lies uppermost, and the line *a b* underneath.

The meat on the upper side of the ribs is firmer and of a closer texture than the fleshy part underneath, which is by far the most tender; of course, some prefer one part, and some another.

To those who like the upper side, and would rather not have the first cut or outside slice, that outside slice should be first cut off, quite down to the bone, in the direction *c d*. Plenty of soft, marrowy fat will be found underneath the ribs. If a person wishes to have a slice underneath, the joint must be turned up, by taking hold of the end of the ribs with the left hand, and raising it, until it is in the position as here represented. One slice or more may now be cut in the direction of the line *a b*, passing the knife down to the bone. The slices, whether on the upper or under side, should be cut thin, but not too much so.

A Buttock of Beef

Is always boiled, and requires no print to point out how it should be carved. A thick slice should be cut off all round the buttock, that your friends may be helped to the juicy and prime part of it. This cut into, thin slices may be cut from the top; but as it is a dish that is frequently brought to the table cold a second day, it should always be cut handsome and even. To those to whom a slice all round would be too much, a third of the round may be given, with a thin slice of fat. On one side there is a part whiter than ordinary, by some called the white muscle. A buttock is generally divided, and this white part sold separate as a delicacy, but it is by no means so, the meat being close and dry, whereas the darker colored parts, though apparently of a coarser grain, are of a looser texture, more tender, fuller of gravy, and better flavored; and men of discriminating palates ever prefer them.

A Fore-quarter of Lamb roasted.

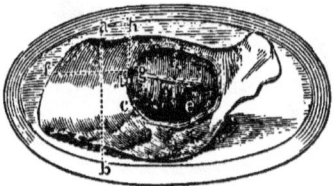

Before any one is helped to a part of this joint, the shoulder should be separated from the breast, or what is by some called the coast, by passing the knife under, in the direction *c g d e*. The shoulder being thus removed, a lemon or orange should be squeezed upon the part, and then sprinkled with salt where the shoulder joined it, and the shoulder should be laid on it again. The gristly part should next be separated from the ribs, in the line *f a*. It is now in readiness to be divided among the company. The ribs are generally most esteemed, and one or two may be separated from the rest, in the line *a b*; or, to those who prefer the gristly part, a piece or two, or more, may be cut off in the lines *h i*, etc. Though all parts of young lamb are nice, the shoulder of a fore-quarter is least thought of; it is not so rich.

If the fore-quarter is that of a grass lamb and large, the shoulder should be put into another dish when taken off; and it is carved as a shoulder of mutton, which see.

A Fillet of Veal,

Which is the thigh part, similar to a buttock of beef, is brought to table always in the same form, but roasted. The outside slice of the fillet is by many thought a delicacy, as being most savory; but it does not follow that every one likes it; each person should therefore be asked, what part he prefers. If not the outside, cut off a thin slice, and the second cut will be white meat, but cut it even and close to the bone. A fillet of veal is generally stuffed under the skirt or flap with a savory pudding, called forcemeat. This is to be cut deep into, in a line with the surface of the fillet, and a thin slice taken out; this, with a little fat cut from the skirt, should be given to each person present.

A Roasted Pig.

A roasted pig is seldom sent to table whole, the head is cut off by the cook, and the body slit down the back and served up as here represented; and the dish garnished with the chaps and ears.

Before any one is helped, the shoulder should be separated from the carcass, by passing the knife under it, in the circular direction; and the leg separated in the same manner, in the dotted lines $c\,d\,e$. The most delicate part in the whole pig is the triangular piece of the neck, which may be cut off in the line $f\,g$. The next best parts are the ribs, which may be divided in the line, $a\,b$, etc. Indeed, the bones of a pig of three weeks old are little less than gristle, and may be easily cut through; next to these, are pieces cut from the leg and shoulder. Some are fond of an ear, and others of a chap, and those persons may readily be gratified.

A Rabbit.

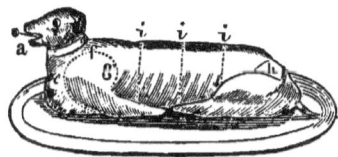

This is a rabbit, as trussed and sent up to table. After separating the legs, the shoulders or wings (which many prefer) are to be cut off in the circular dotted line $e\,f\,g$. The back is divided into two or three parts, in the lines $i\,k$, without dividing it from the belly, but cutting it in the line $g\,h$. The head may be given to any person who likes it, the ears being removed before the rabbit is served up.

A Goose,

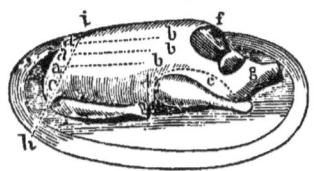

Like a turkey, is seldom quite dissected, unless the company is large; but when it is, the following is the method: Turn the neck towards you, and cut two or three long slices, on each side the breast, in the lines $a\,b$, quite to the bone. Cut those slices from the bone, which done, proceed to take off the leg, by turning the goose up on one side, putting the fork through the small end of the leg bone, pressing it close to the body, which, when the knife is entered at d, raises the joint from the body. The knife is then to be passed under the leg in the direction $d\,e$. If the leg hangs to the carcass at the joint e, turn it back with the fork, and it will readily separate if the goose is young; in old geese, it will require some strength to separate it. When the leg is off, proceed to take off the wing, by passing the fork through the small end of the pinion, pressing it close to the body, and entering the knife at the notch c, and passing it under the wing, in the direction c, d. It is a nice thing to hit this notch c, as it is not so visible in the bird as in the figure. If the knife is put into the notch above it, you cut upon the neck-bone, and not on the wing-joint. A little practice will soon teach the difference; and if the goose is young the trouble is not great, but very much otherwise if the bird is an old one.

When the leg and wing on one side are taken off, take them off on the other side; cut off the apron in the line $f\,e\,g$, and then take off the merry-thought in the line $i\,h$. The neck-bones are next to be separated as in a fowl, and all other parts divided as there directed, to which I refer you.

The best parts of a goose are in the following order: the breast slices; the fleshy part of the wing, which may be divided from the pinion; the thigh-bone, which may be easily divided in the joint from the leg-bone, or drumstick, as it is called; the pinion, and next the side-bones.

A Green Goose.

Is cut up in the same way, but the most delicate part is the breast and the gristle, at the lower part of it.

A Pheasant.

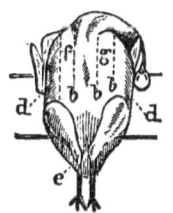

The pheasant, as here represented, is skewered and trussed for the spit, with the head tucked under one of the wings, but when sent to table the skewers are withdrawn.

In carving this bird, the fork should be fixed in the breast, in two dots there marked. You have then the command of the fowl, and can turn it as you please; slice down the breast in the lines $a\,b$, and then proceed to take off the leg on the outside, in the direction $d\,e$, or in the circular dotted line $b\,d$, as seen in the figure "a boiled fowl," next page. Then cut off the wing on the same side in the line $c\,d$, in the figure above, and $a\,h\,b$, in the figure at the bottom of this column, which is lying on one side, with its back towards us. Having separated the leg and wing on one side, do the same on the other, and then cut off or separate from the breast-bone on each side of the breast the parts you before sliced or cut down. In taking off the wing be attentive to cut it in the notch *a*, as seen in the print of the fowl, for if you cut too near the neck, as at *g*, you will find the neck-bone interfere. The wing is to be separated from the neck-bone. Next cut off the merry-thought in the line *f g*, by passing the knife under it towards the neck. The remaining parts are to be cut up, as is described in the fowl, which see.

A Partridge.

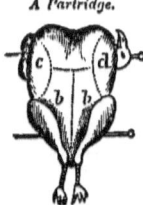

The partridge, like the pheasant, is here trussed for the spit; when served up the skewers are withdrawn. It is cut up like a fowl (which see), the wings taken off in the lines *a b*, and the merry-thought in the lines *c d*. Of a partridge the prime parts are the white ones, viz., the wings, breast, merry-thought. The wing is thought the best, the tip being reckoned the most delicate morsel of the whole.

A Fowl.

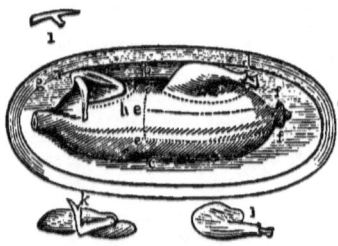

The fowl is here represented as lying on its side, with one of the legs, a wing and a neck-bone taken off. It is cut up the same way, whether it be roasted or boiled. A roasted fowl is sent to table trussed like a pheasant (which see), except that instead of the head being tucked under one of the wings, it is, in a fowl, cut off before it is dressed. A boiled fowl is represented below, the leg-bones of which are bent inwards and tucked in within the belly, but the skewers are withdrawn prior to its being sent to the table. In order to cut up a fowl, it is best to take it on your plate.

Having shown how to take off the legs, wings and merry-thought, when speaking of the pheasant, it remains only to show how the other parts are divided; *k* is the wing cut off, *i* the leg. When the leg, wing and merry-thought are removed, the next thing is to cut off the neck-bones described at *l*. This is done by putting in the knife at *g*, and passing it under the long, broad part of the bone in the line *g h*, then lifting it up and breaking off the end of the shorter part of the bone which cleaves to the breast-bone. All parts being thus separated from the carcass, divide the breast from the back by cutting through the tender-ribs on each side, from the neck quite down to the vent or tail. Then lay the back upwards on your plate, fix your fork under the rump, and laying the edge of your knife in the line *b e c*, and pressing it down lift up the tail or lower part of the back, and it will readily divide with the help of your knife in the line *b e c*. This done, lay the croup or lower part of the back upwards in your plate, with the rump from you, and with your knife cut off the side-bones by forcing the knife through the rump-bone in the lines *e f*, and the whole fowl is completely carved.

A Boiled Fowl.

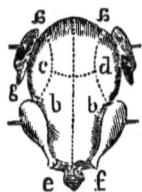

Of a fowl, the prime parts are the wings, breast and merry-thought, and next to these the neck-bones and side-bones; the legs are rather coarse; of a boiled fowl the legs are rather more tender, but of a chicken every part is juicy and good, and next to the breast the legs are certainly the fullest of gravy and the sweetest, and as the thigh-bones are very tender and easily broken with the teeth, the gristles and marrow render them a delicacy. Of the leg of a fowl the thigh is much the best, and when given to any one of your company it should be separated from the drum-stick at the joint *i* (see the cut, viz., "a fowl," preceding column), which is easily done if the knife is introduced underneath in the hollow, and the thigh-bone turned back from the leg-bone.

A Turkey,

Roasted or boiled, is trussed and sent up to table like a fowl, and cut up in every respect like a pheasant. The best parts are the white ones—the breast, wings and neck-bones. Merry-thought it has none; the neck is taken away, and the hollow part under the breast stuffed with force-meat, which is to be cut in thin slices in the direction from the rump to the neck and a slice given with each piece of turkey. It is customary not to cut up more than the breast of this bird, and, if any more is wanted, to take off one of the wings.

A Pigeon.

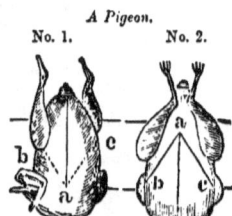

This is a representation of the back and breast of a pigeon. No. 1, the back; No. 2, the breast. It is sometimes cut up as a chicken, but as the croup, or lower part with the thigh, is most preferred, and as a pigeon is a small bird, and half a one not too much to serve at once, it is seldom carved now, otherwise than by fixing the fork at the point *a*, entering the knife just before it, and dividing the pigeon into two, cutting away in the lines *a b*, and *a c*, No. 1; at the same time bringing the knife out at the back in the direction *a b*, and *a c*, No. 2.

A Cod's Head.

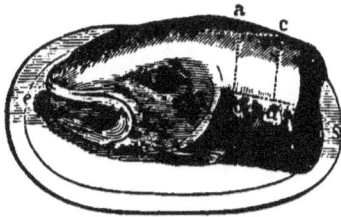

Fish, in general, requires very little carving; the middle or thickest part of the fish is generally esteemed the best, except in a carp, the most delicate part of which is the palate. This is seldom, however, taken out, but the whole head is given to those who like it. The thin part about the tail of a fish is generally least esteemed.

A cod's head and shoulders, if large and in season, is a very genteel and handsome dish, if nicely boiled. When cut, it should be done with a spoon or fish trowel. The parts about the back-bone, on the shoulders, are the most firm and best. Take off a piece quite down to the bone, in the direction *a b d c*, putting in the spoon at *a c*, and with each slice of fish give a piece of the sound, which lies underneath the back-bone and lines it, the meat of which is thin and a little darker colored than the body of the fish itself: this may be got by passing a knife or spoon underneath, in the direction *d s*.

There are a great many delicate parts about the head, some firm kernels, and a great deal of the jelly kind. The jelly parts lie about the jawbone, the firm parts within the head, which must be broken into with a spoon. Some like the palate and some the tongue, which likewise may be got by putting the spoon into the mouth, in the direction of the line *e s*. The green jelly of the eye is never given to any one.

A piece of Boiled Salmon.

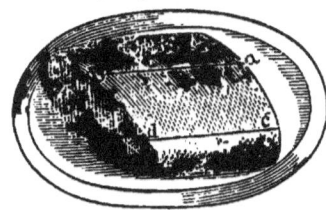

Of boiled salmon there is one part more fat and rich than the other. The belly part is the fattest of the two, and it is customary to give to those that like both a thin slice of each; for the one, cut it out of the belly part, in the direction *d c*; the other, out of the back, in the line *a b*. Those who are fond of salmon generally like the skin; of course, the slices are to be cut thin, skin and all.

There are but few directions necessary for cutting up and serving fish. In turbot the fish-knife or trowel is to be entered in the centre or middle, over the back-bone, and a piece of the flesh, as much as will lie on the trowel, to be taken off on one side close to the bones. The thickest part of the fish is always most esteemed, but not too near the head or tail; and when the meat on one side of the fish is removed close to the bones, the whole back-bone is to be raised with the knife and fork, and the under side is then to be divided among the company. Turbot eaters esteem the fins a delicate part.

The rock-fish and sheepshead are carved like the turbot. The latter is considered the most delicate fish of the Atlantic coast; and the former, though common, are highly esteemed, particularly those caught in fresh water.

The halibut is also frequently brought to market. The fins and parts lying near them are of a delicate texture and flavor; the remaining part of the fish is coarse.

Soles are generally sent to table two ways, some fried, others boiled; these are to be cut right through the middle, bone and all, and a piece of the fish, perhaps a third or fourth part, according to its size, given to each. The same may be done with other fishes, cutting them across, as may be seen in the cut of the mackerel, below *d e e b*.

A Mackerel.

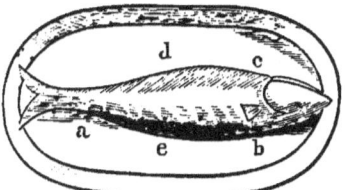

A mackerel is to be thus cut—Slit the fish all along the back with a knife, in the line *a e b*, and take off one whole side as far as the line *b c*, not too near the head, as the meat about the gills is generally black and ill flavored. The roe of a male fish is soft like the brain of a calf; the roe of the female fish is full of small eggs and hard. Some prefer one and some another, and part of such roe as your friend likes should be given to him.

The meat about the tail of all fish is generally thin and less esteemed, and few like the head of a fish, except it be that of a carp, the palate of which is esteemed the greatest delicacy of the whole.

Eels are cut into pieces through the bone, and the thickest part is reckoned the prime piece.

There is some art in dressing a lobster, but as this is seldom sent up to table whole, I will only say that the tail is reckoned the prime part, and next to this the claws.

THE CHOICE OF ANIMAL FOOD.

We conclude the foregoing treatise on the Art of Carving by the following instructions, intended to aid housekeepers in the purchase of the most common descriptions of meat for the table.

Beef.

If the flesh of ox-beef is young, it will have a fine smooth open grain, be of a good red, and feel tender. The fat should be white rather than yellow; for when that is of a deep color the meat is seldom good: beef fed by oil cakes is in general so, and the flesh is flabby. The grain of cow-beef is closer, and the fat whiter, than that of ox-beef, but the lean is not of so bright a red. The grain of bull-beef is closer still, the fat hard and skinny, the lean of a deep red and a stronger scent. Ox-beef is the reverse. Ox-beef is the richest and largest; but in small families and to some tastes, heifer-beef is better if finely fed. In old meat there is a streak of horn in the ribs of beef; the harder this is, the older, and the flesh is not finely flavored.

Veal.

The flesh of a bull calf is firmest, but not so white. The fillet of the cow-calf is generally preferred for the udder. The whitest is not the most juicy, having been made so by frequent bleeding, and having had whiting to lick. Choose the meat of which the kidney is well covered with white thick fat. If the bloody vein in the shoulder looks blue or of a bright red, it is newly killed; but any other color shows it stale. The other parts should be dry and white; if clammy or spotted the meat is stale and bad. The kidney turns first in the loin, and the suet will not then be firm.

Mutton.

Choose this by the fineness of its grain, good color, and firm white fat. It is not the better for being young; if of a good breed and well fed, it is better for age; but this only holds with wether mutton; the flesh of the ewe is paler, and the texture finer. Ram mutton is very strong flavored, the flesh is of a deep red, and the fat is spongy.

Lamb.

Observe the neck of a fore-quarter: if the vein is bluish it is fresh; if it has a green or yellow cast it is stale. In the hind-quarter if there is a faint smell under the kidney, and the knuckle is limp, the meat is stale. If the eyes are sunk, the head is not fresh. Grass-lamb comes into season in April or May, and continues till August. House-lamb may be had in great towns almost all the year, but is in highest perfection in December and January.

Pork.

Pinch the lean, and if young it will break. If the rind is tough, thick, and cannot easily be impressed by the finger, it is old. A thin rind is a merit in all pork. When fresh the flesh will be smooth and cool; if clammy it is tainted. What is called measly pork is very unwholesome, and may be known by the fat being full of kernels, which in good pork is never the case. Pork fed at still-houses does not answer for curing any way, the fat being spongy. Dairy-fed pork is the best.

A Turkey-Cock.

If young, has a smooth black leg, with a short spur. The eyes full and bright if fresh, and the feet supple and moist. If stale, the eyes will be sunk and the feet dry. A hen-turkey is known by the same rules, but if old her legs will be red and rough.

Fowls.

If a cock is young, his spurs will be short; but take care to see they have not been cut or pared, which is a trick often practised. If fresh the vent will be close and dark. Pullets are best just before they begin to lay and yet are full of eggs; if old hens, their combs and legs will be rough; if young, they will be smooth. A good capon has a thick belly and a large rump; there is a particular fat at his breast, and the comb is very pale. Black-legged fowls are most moist, if for roasting.

Geese.

The bill and feet of a young one will be yellow, and there will be but few hairs upon them; if old, they will be red; if fresh, the feet will be pliable, if stale, dry and stiff. Geese are called green till three or four months old. Green geese should be scalded; a stubble-goose should be picked dry.

Ducks.

Choose them by the same rules of having supple feet, and by their being hard and thick on the breast and belly. The feet of a tame duck are thick, and inclining to dusty yellow; a wild one has the feet reddish and smaller than the tame. They should be picked dry. Ducklings must be scalded.

Shad.

If good, they are white and thick. If too fresh they eat tough, but must not be kept above two days without salting.

Herrings.

If good, their gills are of a fine red, and the eyes bright, as is likewise the whole fish, which must be stiff and firm.

Lobsters.

If they have not been long taken the claws will have a strong motion when you put your finger on the eyes and press them. The heaviest are the best. The cock-lobster is known by the narrow back part of his tail, and the two uppermost fins within it are stiff and hard; but those of the hen are soft, and the tail broader. The male, though generally smaller, has the highest flavor, the flesh is firmer, and the color when boiled is a deeper red.

Crabs.

The heaviest are best, and those of a middling size are sweetest. If light they are watery; when in perfection the joints of the legs are stiff, and the body has a very agreeable smell. The eyes look dead and loose when stale.

Oysters.

When alive and strong the shell is close. They should be eaten as soon as opened, the flavor becoming poor otherwise.

The abundance and variety of fish daily brought to market in every seaport town of the United States, cannot be surpassed in any other part of the world.

QUALITIES OF THE ARTICLES OF FOOD IN COMMON USE.

Beef.

When this is the flesh of a bullock of middle age, it affords good and strong nourishment, and is peculiarly well adapted to those who labor or take much exercise. It will often sit easy upon stomachs that can digest no other kind of food; and its fat is almost as easily digested as that of veal.

Veal

Is not a proper food for persons suffering from indisposition, and should not be given to febrile patients. It affords less nourishment and is less digestible than the flesh of the same animal in a state of maturity. The fat of it is lighter than that of any other animal, and shows the least disposition to putrescency. Veal is a suitable food in costive habits; but of all meat it is the least calculated for removing acidity from the stomach.

Mutton,

From the age of four to six years, and fed on dry pasture, is an excellent meat. It is of a middle kind between the firmness of beef and the tenderness of veal. The lean part of mutton, however, is the most nourishing and conducive to health; the fat being hard of digestion. The head of the sheep, especially when divested of the skin, is very tender; and the feet, on account of the jelly they contain, are highly nutritive.

Lamb

Is not so nourishing as mutton; but it is light and extremely suitable to delicate stomachs.

Pork

Affords rich and substantial nourishment, and its juices are wholesome when properly fed, and when the animal enjoys pure air and exercise. But the flesh of hogs reared in towns is both hard of digestion and unwholesome. Pork is particularly improper for those who are liable to any foulness of the skin.

Smoked Hams

Are a strong kind of meat, and rather fit for a relish than for diet. It is the quality of all salted meat that the fibres become rigid, and therefore more difficult of digestion; and when to this is added smoking, the heat of the chimney occasions the salt to concentrate, and the fat between the muscles sometimes to become rancid.

Bacon

Is also of an indigestible quality, and is apt to turn rancid on weak stomachs; but for those in health it is an excellent food, especially when used with fowl or veal, or even eaten with peas, cabbages, or cauliflowers.

Goat's Flesh

Is hard and indigestible; but that of kids is tender as well as delicious, and affords good nourishment.

Venison,

Or the flesh of deer, and that of hares, is of a nourishing quality, but is liable to the inconvenience that though much disposed to putrescency of itself, it must be kept for a little time before it becomes tender.

The Blood of Animals

Is occasionally used as an aliment, but man could not long subsist upon it unless mixed with oatmeal, etc.; for it is not very soluble alone, by the digestive powers of the human stomach, and therefore cannot prove nourishing.

Milk

Is of very different consistence in different animals; but that of cows, being the kind used in diet, is at present the object of our attention. Milk, where it agrees with the stomach, affords excellent nourishment for those who are weak and cannot digest other aliments. It does not readily become putrid, but with some persons becomes sour on the stomach, and thence produces heartburn, or gripes, and in some constitutions a looseness. The best milk is from a cow at three or four years of age, about two months after producing a calf. It is lighter, but more watery than the milk of sheep and goats; while on the other hand it is more thick and heavy than the milk of asses and mares, which are next in consistence to human milk.

On account of the acid which is generated after digestion, milk coagulates in all stomachs; but the caseous or cheesy part is again dissolved by the digestive juices, and rendered fit for the purposes of nutrition. It is improper to eat acid substances with milk, as these would tend to prevent the due digestion of it.

Cream

Is very nourishing, but on account of its fatness is difficult to be digested in weak stomachs. Violent exercise after eating it will in a little time convert it into butter.

Butter.

Some writers inveigh against the use of butter as universally pernicious, but they might with equal reason condemn all vegetable oils, which form a considerable part of diet in southern climates, and seem to have been beneficially intended by nature for that purpose. Butter, like every other oily substance, has doubtless a relaxing quality, and if long retained in the stomach is liable to become rancid; but if eaten in moderation it will not produce those effects. It is, however, improper in bilious constitutions.

Cheese

Is likewise reprobated by many as extremely unwholesome. It is doubtless not easy of digestion, and when eaten in a great quantity may overload the stomach; but if taken sparingly its tenacity may be dissolved by the digestive juices, and it may yield a wholesome, nourishing chyle. Toasted cheese is agreeable to most palates, but it is rendered more indigestible by that process.

Fowls.

The flesh of birds differs in quality according to the food on which they live. Such as feed upon grain and berries afford, in general, good nourishment; geese and ducks are hard of digestion, especially the former. A young hen or chicken is tender and delicate food, and extremely well adapted to those in whom the digestive powers are weak. But of all tame fowls, the capon is the most nutritious.

Turkeys, etc.

Turkeys, as well as Guinea or India fowls, afford a substantial nutriment, but are not quite so easy of digestion as the common domestic fowls. In all birds those parts are the most firm which are most exercised; in the small birds, therefore, the wings, and in the larger birds the legs, are commonly the most difficult of digestion.

Wild Fowls.

The flesh of wild birds in general, though more easily digested, is less nourishing than that of quadrupeds, as being more dry on account of their almost constant exercise. Those birds are not wholesome which subsist upon worms, insects and fishes.

Eggs.

The eggs of birds are a simple and wholesome aliment. Those of the turkey are superior in all the qualifications of food. The white of eggs is by heat rendered tough and hard. The yolk contains much oil, and is highly nourishing, but has a strong tendency to putrefaction, on which account eggs are improper for people of weak stomachs, especially when they are not quite fresh. Eggs boiled hard or fried are difficult of digestion, and are rendered still more indigestible by the addition of butter. All eggs require a sufficient quantity of salt, to promote their solution in the stomach.

Fish,

Though some of them be light and easy of digestion, afford less nourishment than the flesh of quadrupeds, and are, of all the animal tribes, the most disposed to putrefaction. Salt water fish are, in general, the best; but when salted, though less disposed to putrescency, they become difficult of digestion. Whitings and flounders are the most easily digested. Acid sauces and pickles, by resisting putrefaction, are a proper addition to fish, both as they retard putrescency and correct the relaxing tendency of butter, so generally used with this kind of aliment.

Oysters and Cockles

Are eaten both raw and dressed. Oysters are very nourishing and easy of digestion.

QUALITIES OF FOOD.

Muscles and Periwinkles

Are far inferior to oysters, both in point of digestion and nutriment. Sea muscles are by some supposed to be of a poisonous nature, but though this opinion is not much countenanced by experience, the safest way is to eat them with vinegar, or some other vegetable acid.

Bread.

At the head of the vegetable class stands bread, that article of diet which, from general use, has received the name of the staff of life. Wheat is the grain chiefly used for the purpose in this country, and is the most nutritive of all the farinaceous kinds, as it contains a great deal of gluten and starch. Bread is very properly eaten with animal food, but is most expedient with such articles of diet as contain much nourishment in a small bulk, because it then serves to give the stomach a proper degree of expansion. To render bread easy of digestion it ought to be well fermented and baked, and it never should be used by dyspeptics till it has stood 24 hours after being taken out of the oven, otherwise it is apt to occasion various complaints in them, such as flatulence, heartburn, watchfulness, and the like. The custom of eating butter with bread, hot from the oven, is compatible only with strong digestive powers.

Pastry,

Especially when hot, has all the disadvantages of hot bread and butter; and still more so when it is tough and hard, or made with rancid butter or lard. Dry toast with butter is by far the most wholesome breakfast. Brown wheaten bread, in which there is a good deal of rye or bran, though not so nourishing as that made of fine flour, is both palatable and wholesome, but apt to become sour on weak stomachs.

Oats, Barley and Rice.

Oats, when deprived of the husk, and particularly barley, when properly prepared, are somewhat softening, and afford wholesome and cooling nourishment. Rice likewise contains a nutritious mucilage, and is less used than it deserves, both on account of its wholesomeness and economical utility. The notion of its being hurtful to the sight is a vulgar error. In some constitutions it tends to induce costiveness, but this seems to be owing chiefly to flatulence, and may be corrected by the addition of some spice, such as caraways, aniseed, and the like.

Potatoes

Are an agreeable and wholesome food, and yield nearly as much nourishment as any of the roots used in diet. The farinaceous or mealy kind is in general the most easy of digestion, and they are much improved by being roasted or baked. They ought always to be eaten with meat, and never without salt. The salt should be boiled with them.

Green Peas and Beans,

Boiled in their fresh state, are both agreeable to the taste and wholesome, being neither so flatulent nor so difficult of digestion as in their ripe state, in which they resemble the other leguminous vegetables. French beans possess much the same qualities, but yield a more watery juice, and have a greater disposition to produce flatulence.

Salads,

Being eaten raw, require good digestive powers, but the addition of oil and vinegar, qualified with mustard, renders the moderate use of them consistent even with a weak stomach.

Spinach

Affords a soft, lubricating aliment, but contains little nourishment. In weak stomachs it is apt to produce acidity, and frequently a looseness. To obviate these effects, it ought always to be well beaten, and have but little butter mixed with it.

Asparagus

Is a nourishing article in diet, and promotes the secretion of urine; but disposes a little to flatulence.

Artichokes

Resemble asparagus in their qualities, but seem to be more nutritive and less diuretic.

Cabbages

Do not afford much nourishment, but are an agreeable addition to animal food, and not quite so flatulent as the common greens. They are likewise diuretic, and somewhat laxative. Cabbage has a stronger tendency to putrefaction than most other vegetable substances; and, during its putrefying state, sends forth an offensive smell, much resembling that of putrefying animal bodies. So far, however, from promoting a putrid disposition in the human body, it is, on the contrary, a wholesome aliment in scurvy.

Beets,

When young and tender, are very digestible.

Indian Corn,

Before ripening, is wholesome for most persons when boiled upon the ear; and is very nourishing.

Turnips

Are a nutritious article of vegetable food, but not very easy of digestion, and are flatulent. This effect is in a good measure obviated by pressing the water out of them before they are eaten.

Carrots

Contain a considerable quantity of nutritious juice, but are among the most flatulent of vegetable productions.

Parsnips

Are more nourishing and less flatulent than carrots, which they also exceed in the sweetness of their mucilage. By boiling them in two different waters, they are rendered less flatulent, but their other qualities are thereby diminished in proportion.

Parsley

Is of a stimulating and aromatic nature, well calculated to make agreeable sauces. It is also a gentle diuretic, but preferable in all its qualities when boiled.

Celery

Affords a root both wholesome and fragrant, but is difficult of digestion in its raw state. It gives an agreeable taste to soups, as well as renders them diuretic.

Onions, Garlic, and Shallots

Are all of a stimulating nature, by which they assist digestion and expel flatulency. They are, however, most suitable to persons of a cold and phlegmatic constitution.

Radishes

Of all kinds, particularly the horse-radish, agree with the three preceding articles. They excite the discharge of air lodged in the intestines.

Tomatoes

Are generally considered the most wholesome of all vegetables.

Apples

Are a wholesome fruit; but, in general, they agree best with the stomach when eaten either roasted or boiled. The more aromatic kinds of apples are the fittest for eating raw.

Pears

Resemble much in their effects the sweet kind of apples, but have more of a laxative quality, and a greater tendency to flatulence.

Cherries

Are in general a wholesome fruit, when perfectly fresh, but not otherwise.

Plums

Are nourishing, but are apt to produce flatulence. If eaten fresh, and before they are ripe, especially in large quantities, they occasion colics, and other complaints of the bowels.

Peaches

Are of a nourishing quality, and they abound in juice; they are serviceable in bilious complaints.

Apricots

Are more pulpy than peaches, but are apt to ferment, and produce acidities in weak stomachs.

Gooseberries and Currants,

When ripe, are similar in their qualities to cherries, and when used in a green state they are agreeably cooling.

Strawberries

Are an agreeable, cooling aliment.

Cucumbers

Are cooling, and agreeable to the palate in hot weather; but to prevent them from proving hurtful to the stomach, the juice ought to be squeezed out after they are sliced, and vinegar, pepper and salt afterwards added.

Tea.

By some, the use of this exotic is condemned in terms the most vehement and unqualified, whilst others have either asserted its innocence, or gone so far as to ascribe to it salubrious, and even extraordinary, virtues. The truth seems to lie between these two extremes; there is however an essential difference in the effects of green tea and of black, or of bohea; the former of which is much more apt to affect the nerves than the latter, more especially when drunk without cream, and likewise without bread and butter. That, taken in a large quantity, or at a later hour than usual, tea often produces wakefulness, is a point that cannot be denied; but if used in moderation, and accompanied with the additions just now mentioned, it does not sensibly discover any hurtful effects, but greatly refreshes one who is fatigued, and abates a pain of the head. It ought always to be made of a moderate degree of strength; for if too weak it certainly relaxes the stomach. As it has an astringent taste, which seems not very consistent with a relaxing power, there is ground for ascribing this effect not so much to the herb itself as to the hot water, which not being impregnated with a sufficient quantity of tea, to correct its own emollient tendency, produces a relaxation, unjustly imputed to some noxious quality of the plant. But tea, like every other commodity, is liable to damage, and when this happens, it may produce effects not necessarily connected with its original qualities.

Coffee.

It is allowed that coffee promotes digestion, and exhilarates the animal spirits; besides which, various other qualities are ascribed to it, such as dispelling flatulency, removing dizziness of the head, attenuating viscid humors, increasing the circulation of the blood, and consequently perspiration; with a great many persons, even if not taken strong, it affects the nerves, occasions wakefulness, and tremor of the hands; though in some phlegmatic constitutions it is apt to produce sleep. Indeed, it is to persons of that habit that coffee is best accommodated; for to people of a thin and dry habit of body it seems to be especially injurious. Turkey coffee is greatly preferable in flavor to that of the West Indies. Drunk, only in the quantity of one dish, after dinner, to promote digestion, it answers best without either sugar or milk; but if taken at other times, it should have both; or rather in place of the latter, cream, which not only improves the beverage, but tends to mitigate the effect of coffee upon the nerves.

Chocolate

Is a nutritive and wholesome composition, if taken in a small quantity, and not repeated too often; but is sometimes hurtful to the stomach of those with whom a vegetable diet disagrees.

BREWING and DISTILLATION.

FERMENTATION.

Before proceeding to the consideration of the manufacture of wines, beer, and spirits, a general survey of the subject of fermentation will not be out of place.

Alcholic Beverages

May be divided into fermented drinks including beer and wines, and distilled drinks or spirits, which are obtained from the former by distillation. Spirits usually contain about fifty per cent. of alcohol, beer and wines from one to twenty per cent. The alcohol in all cases results from the breaking up of the sugar in the fermenting liquid.

Sugars.

Ordinary sugar, or cane sugar; uncrystallizable, or fruit sugar; and grape sugar, or glucose, are the three most important varieties. Fruit sugar exists in all the sub-acid fruits as grapes, currants, apples, peaches, etc. When these are dried, it changes to grape sugar forming the whitish grains which are seen on the outside of prunes, raisins, etc. Grape sugar is found to a limited extent in fruits associated with fruit sugar. Cane sugar is readily changed by the action of acids or ferments into fruit sugar, and the latter into grape sugar, but the process cannot be reversed. Grape sugar is the only fermentable variety, the others becoming changed into it before fermentation.

Transformation of Starch, etc.

Under the influence of acids, or *diastase*, a principle existing in germinating grains, starch is changed first into gum (dextrine) and afterwards into grape sugar. Hence one of our most important sources of alcohol is to be found in the starch of barley, corn, wheat, potatoes, etc. Wood may be converted into grape sugar by the action of strong sulphuric acid, which is afterwards neutralized. An attempt to produce alcohol in this way on a commercial scale was made in France, but was not successful.

Ferment.

A solution of pure sugar will remain unchanged

for an indefinite period of time. To induce fermentation, a portion of some nitrogenous body, itself undergoing decomposition, must be added. Such ferments are albumen (white of egg), fibrin (fibre of flesh), casein (basis of cheese), gluten (the pasty matter of flour). Yeast consists of vegetable egg-shaped cells, which is increased during its action as a ferment.

Circumstances influencing Fermentation.

In order that fermentation shall begin we require, besides the contact of the ferment, the *presence of air*. The most easily decomposed articles of food may be preserved for an indefinite period by hermetically sealing them in jars, after drawing out the air. When once begun, however, fermentation will go on, if the air be excluded. *Temperature* is important. The most favorable temperature is between 68° and 77° Fahr. At a low temperature fermentation is exceedingly slow. Bavarian or lager beer is brewed between 32° and 46½° Fahr. A boiling heat instantly stops fermentation, by killing the ferment.

To *check fermentation* we may remove the yeast by filtration. Hops, oil of mustard, sulphurous acid (from burning sulphur), the sulphites, sulphuric acid, check the process by killing the ferment.

Too much sugar is unfavorable to fermentation, the best strength for the syrup is ten parts of water to one of sugar.

Changes during Fermentation, etc.

The grape-sugar breaks up into carbonic acid which escapes as gas, alcohol and water which remain. In malting the grain is allowed to germinate, during which process the starch of the grain is changed into gum and sugar: the rootlets make their appearance at one end and the stalk or aerospire at the other. The germination is then checked by heating in a kiln; if allowed to proceed a certain portion of the sugar would be converted into woody matter, and lost.

In brewing the saccharine matter is extracted from the malt during the mashing. Yeast is added to cause fermentation; an infusion of hops afterwards, to add to the flavor and to check fermentation. In wine making there is sufficient albuminous matter in the grape to cause fermentation without the use of yeast.

Distillation separates the alcohol in great part from the water. Alcohol boils at 179° Fahr., and water at 212°. It is not possible, however, to separate entirely alcohol and water by distillation.

Acetic Fermentation.

Weak fermented liquors will become sour on exposure to the air. This is owing to the conversion of their alcohol into acetic acid (see Vinegar). This change is due to the absorption of the oxygen of the air, and is much promoted by the presence of a peculiar plant, the *mother* of vinegar. It is sometimes called the *acetous* fermentation.

Viscous Fermentation.

By the action of yeast on beet-sugar a peculiar fermentation is set up; but little alcohol is formed. The same gives ropiness to wines and beer. It is checked by vegetable astringents.

BREWING.

To fit up a small Brew-house.

Provide a copper holding full two-thirds of the quantity proposed to be brewed, with a gauge-stick to determine the number of gallons in the copper. A mash-tub, or tun, adapted to contain two-thirds of the quantity proposed to be brewed, and one or two tuns of equal size to ferment the wort; three or four shallow coolers; one or two wooden bowls; a thermometer; half a dozen casks of different sizes; a large funnel; two or three clean pails, and a hand-pump.

This proceeds on the supposition of two mashes for ale; but if only one mash is adapted for ale, with a view of making the table-beer better, then the copper and mash tun should hold one-third more than the quantity to be brewed.

The expenses of brewing depend on the price of malt and hops, and on the proposed strength of the article. One-quarter of good malt and eight pounds of good hops ought to make two barrels of good ale and one of table-beer. The other expenses consist of coal and labor.

Of public breweries, and their extensive utensils and machinery, we give no description, because books are not likely to be resorted to by the class of persons engaged in those extensive manufactories for information relative to their own particular business.

To choose Water for Brewing.

Soft water, or hard water softened by exposure to the air, is generally preferred, because it makes a stronger extract, and is more inclined to ferment; but hard water is better for keeping beer, and is less liable to turn sour. Some persons soften hard water by throwing a spoonful of soda into a barrel, and others do it with a handful of common salt mixed with an ounce of salt of tartar.

To make Malt.

Put about 6 quarters of good barley, newly threshed, etc., into a stone trough full of water, and let it steep till the water be of a bright reddish color, which will be in about 3 days, more or less, according to the moisture or dryness, smallness or bigness of the grain, the season of the year, or the temperature of the weather. In summer malt never makes well; in winter it requires longer steeping than in spring or autumn. It may be known when steeped enough by other marks besides the color of the water. The grains should be soft enough to be pierced with a needle, but not to be crushed between the nails. When sufficiently steeped take it out of the trough, and lay it in heaps, to let the water drain from it; then, after 2 or 3 hours, turn it over with a scoop, and lay it in a new heap, 20 or 24 inches deep. This is called the coming heap, in the right management of which lies the principal skill. In this heap it may lie 40 hours, more or less, according to the aforementioned qualities of the grain, etc., before it comes to the right temper of malt. While it lies it must be carefully looked to after the first 15 or 16 hours, for about that time the grains begin to put forth roots, which, when they have equally and fully done, the malt must, within an hour after, be turned over with a scoop; otherwise the grains will begin to put forth the blade and spire also, which must by all means be prevented. If all the malt do not come equally, but that which lies in the middle, being warmest, come the soonest, the whole must be turned, so that what was outmost may be inmost; and thus it is managed till it be all alike. As soon as the malt is sufficiently come, turn it over, and spread it to a depth not exceeding 5 or 6 inches; and by the time it is all spread out begin and turn it over again 3 or 4 times. Afterwards turn it over in like manner once in 4 or 5 hours, making the heap deeper by degrees, and continue to do so for the space of 48 hours at least. This cools, dries, and deadens the grain, so that it becomes mellow, melts easily in brewing, and separates entirely from the husk. Then throw up the malt into a heap as high as possible, where let it lie till it grows as hot as the hand can bear it, which usually

BREWING.

happens in about the space of 30 hours. This perfects the sweetness and mellowness of the malt. After being sufficiently heated, throw it abroad to cool, and turn it over again about 6 or 8 hours after; and then lay it on a kiln with a hair cloth or wire spread under it. After one fire, which must last 24 hours, give it another more slow, and afterwards, if need be, a third; for if the malt be not thoroughly dried, it cannot be well ground, neither will it dissolve well in the brewing; but the ale it makes will be red, bitter, and unfit for keeping.

To grind Malt.

To obtain the infusion of malt it is necessary to break it, for which purpose it is passed through stones placed at such distance, as that they may crush each grain without reducing it to powder: for if ground too small it makes the worts thick, while if not broken at all the extract is not obtained. In general, pale malts are ground larger than amber or brown malts.

Malt should be used within two or three days after it is ground, but in the London brew-houses it is generally ground one day and used the next. A quarter of malt ground should yield nine bushels, and sometimes ten. Crushing mills or iron rollers have lately been used in preference to stones which make a considerable grit with the malt. On a small scale, malt may be broken by wooden rollers, by the hands.

Steel mills like coffee mills have also been used for crushing malt with great success.

To determine the Qualities of Malt.

First, examine well if it has a round body, breaks soft, is full of flour all its length, smells well, and has a thin skin; next chew some of it, and if sweet and mellow, then it is good. If it is hard and steely, and retains something of a barley nature, it has not been rightly made, and will weigh heavier than that which has been properly malted.

Secondly, take a glass nearly full of water; put in some malt, and if it swims, it is good, but if any sinks to the bottom then it is not true malt.

Pale-malt is the slowest and least dried, producing more worts than high dried malt, and of better quality. Amber colored malt, or that between pale and brown, produces a flavor much admired in many malt liquors. Brown malt loses much of its nutritious qualities, but confers a peculiar flavor desired by many palates. Roasted malt, after the manner of coffee, is used by the best London brewers, to give color and flavor to porter, which in the first instance has been made from pale malt.

To choose Hops.

Rub them between the fingers or the palm of the hand, and if good, a rich glutinous substance will be felt, with a fragrant smell, and a fine yellow dust will appear. The best color is a fine olive green, but if too green, and the seeds are small and shrivelled, they have been picked too soon and will be deficient in flavor. If of a dusty brown color, they were picked too late, and should not be chosen. When a year old, they are considered as losing one-fourth in strength.

To determine the Proportion between the Liquor boiled and the Quantity produced.

From a single quarter, two barrels of liquor will produce but one barrel of wort. Three barrels will produce one barrel and three quarters. Four barrels will produce two barrels and a half. Five barrels will produce three barrels and a quarter. Six barrels will produce four barrels. Eight barrels will produce five barrels and a half, and ten barrels will produce seven barrels, and so on in proportion for other quantities.

To determine the Heats of the Liquor or Water for the First and Second Mashes on different kinds of Malt.

First Mash. — For very pale malt turn on the liquor at 176° Fahr. For pale and amber mixed, 172°; all amber, 170°; high-colored amber, 168°. An equal quantity of pale, amber, and brown, 160°. If the quantity of brown is very dark, or any part of the grains charred by the fire upon the kiln, 155°.

Second Mash. — For very pale malt turn on the liquor at 182°. For pale and amber mixed, 178°; all amber, 176°; high-colored amber, 172°. An equal quantity of pale, amber and brown, 166°. If the quantity of brown is very dark, or any part of the grains charred by the fire. 164°.

The heat should in some measure be regulated by the temperature of the atmosphere, and should be two or three degrees higher in cold than in warm weather.

The proper degree of heat will give the strongest wort and in the greatest quantity, for though the heat were greater and the strength of the wort thereby increased, yet a greater quantity of liquor would be retained in the malt; and again, if it were lower, it would produce more wort, but the strength of the extract would be deficient; the beer without spirit, and likely to turn sour.

To determine the Strength of the Worts.

To effect this a saccharometer is necessary, and may be purchased at any mathematical instrument maker's. It determines the relative gravity of wort to the water used, and the quantity of farinaceous matter contained in the wort. It is used in all public breweries after drawing off the wort from each mash, and regulates the heat and quantity of liquor turned on at each succeeding mash, that the ultimate strength may be equal though the quantity is less. This signifies little to the private, but it is of great consequence to the public brewer. Those who brew frequently and desire to introduce it will obtain printed tables and instructions with the instrument.

To proportion the Hops.

The usual quantity is a pound to the bushel of malt, or 8 lbs. to the quarter; but for keeping-beer, it should be extended to 10 or 12, and if for one or two years to 14 lbs. to the quarter. Small beer requires from 3 to 6 lbs. the quarter, and rather more when old hops are used.

Some persons, instead of boiling the hops with the wort, macerate them, and put the strong extract into the tun with the first wort, and make 2 or 3 extracts in like manner for the second and third worts

To Boil Worts.

The first wort should be sharply boiled for 1 hour, and the second for 2 hours; but if intended for beer of long-keeping, the time should be extended half an hour. The hops should be strained from each preceding wort, and returned into the copper with the succeeding one. Between the boilings the fires should be damped with wet cinders, and the copper door set open.

For small beer only half an hour is necessary for the first wort, 1 hour for the second, and 2 hours for the third. The diminution from boiling is from one-eighth to one-sixteenth.

To Cool the Wort.

Worts should be laid so shallow as to cool within 6 or 7 hours to the temperature of 60°. In warm weather the depth should not exceed 2 or 3 inches, but in cold weather it may be 5 inches. As soon as they have fallen to 60° they should instantly be tunned and yeasted.

To Choose Heats for Tunning.

In cold weather the heats in the coolers should be 5° or 6° higher than in mild and warm weather. For ale, in cold weather, it should be tunned as soon as it has fallen to 60° Fahr. in the coolers; for porter to 64°, and for table beer to 74°, and in warm weather strong beer should be 4° or 5° less, and table beer 7° or 8°. Care should also be taken that the worts do not get cold before the yeast is mixed to produce fermentation. The best rule for mixing the yeast is 1½ lbs. to every barrel of strong beer wort, and 1 lb. to every barrel of table beer wort.

To Mix the Yeast with the Worts.

Ale brewed for keeping in winter should be no more than blood warm when the yeast is put to it. If it is intended for immediate drinking, it may be yeasted a little warmer. The best method of mixing the yeast is to take 2 or 3 quarts of the hot water wort in a wooden bowl or pan, to which, when cool enough, put yeast enough to work the brewing, generally 1 or 2 quarts to the hogshead, according to its quality. In this bowl or pan the fermentation will commence while the rest of the worts are cooling, when the whole may be mixed together.

To Apportion Yeast and Apply it to the Worts.

The yeast of strong beer is preferable to that from small beer, and it should be fresh and good. The quantity should be diminished with the temperature at which the worts are tunned, and less in summer than in winter. For strong beer a quart of yeast per quarter will be sufficient at 58°, but less when the worts are higher and when the weather is hot. If estimated by the more accurate criterion of weight, 1½ lbs. should be used for a barrel of strong beer, and 1¼ lbs. for a barrel of small beer. If the fermentation does not commence add a little more yeast, and rouse the worts for some time. But if they get cold, and the fermentation is slow, fill a bottle with hot water and put it into the tun.

In cold weather small beer should be tunned at 70°, keeping beer at 50° and strong beer at 54°. In mild weather at 50° for each sort. The fermentation will increase the heat 10°.

To Manage the Fermentation.

A proportion of the yeast should be added to the first wort as soon as it is let down from the coolers, and the remainder as soon as the second wort is let down.

The commencement of fermentation is indicated by a line of small bubbles round the sides of the tun, which in a short time extends over the surface. A crusty head follows, and then a fine rocky one, followed by a light, frothy head. In the last stage the head assumes a yeasty appearance, and the color is yellow or brown, the smell of the tun becoming strongly vinous. As soon as this head begins to fall, the tun should be skimmed, and the skimming continued every 2 hours till no more yeast appears; this closes the operation, and it should then be put in casks, or, in technical language, cleansed. A minute attention to every stage of this process is necessary to secure fine flavored and brilliant beverage. Should the fermentation be unusually slow, it should be accelerated by stirring or rousing the whole. After the first skimming, a small quantity of salt and flour, well mixed, should be stirred in the tun. The fermentation will proceed in the casks, to encourage which the bung-hole should be placed a little aside, and the casks kept full by being filled up from time to time with old beer. When this fermentation has ceased the casks may be bunged up.

To Accelerate the Fermentation.

Spread some flour with the hand over the surface, and it will form a crust, and keep the worts warm, or throw in an ounce or two of powdered ginger, or fill a bottle with boiling water and sink it in the worts, or beat a small quantity of the worts and throw into the rest, or beat up the whites of two eggs with some brandy and threw it into the tun or cask, or tie up some bran in a coarse, thin cloth and put it into the vat, and above all things do not disturb the wort, as fermentation will not commence during any agitation of the wort.

To Check a Too Rapid Fermentation.

Mix some cold raw wort in the tun, or divide the whole between two tuns, where, by being in smaller body, the energy of the fermentation of the whole will be divided. Also open the doors and windows of the brew-house; but, if it still frets, sprinkle some cold water over it; or if it frets in the cask, put a mixture of a ¼ of a lb. of sugar with a handful of salt, to the hogshead.

To Brew Porter on the London System.

Thames or New River water is indifferently used, or hard water, raised into backs and exposed for a few days to the air.

Take a mixture of brown, amber and pale malts, in nearly equal quantities, and turn them into the mash-tub in this order. Turn on the first liquor at 165°, mash 1 hour and then coat the whole with dry malt. In 1 hour set the tap.

Mix 10 lbs. of brown hops to the quarter of malt, half old, half new; boil the first wort briskly with the hops for three-quarters of an hour, and after putting into the copper 1½ lbs. of sugar and 1½ lbs. of Legborn juice (extract of liquorice) to the barrel, turn the whole into the coolers, rousing the wort all the t me.

Turn on the second liquor at 174°, and in an hour set tap again. This second wort having run off, turn on again at 145°; mash for an hour and stand for the same, in the meantime boiling the second wort with the same hops for an hour. Turn these into the coolers as before, and let down into the tub at 64°, mixing the yeast as it comes down. Cleanse the second day at 80°, previously throwing in a mixture of flour and salt, and rousing thoroughly.

For private use, every quarter of malt ought to yield 2 barrels and a half, but brewers would run 3 barrels to a quarter.

To Brew three Barrels of Porter.

Take 1 sack of pale malt, ½ a sack of amber malt, and ½ a sack of brown malt.

Turn on 2 barrels for first mash at 165°; second mash, 1½ barrels at 172°; third mash, 2 barrels at 142°. Boil 10 lbs. of new and old hops, and 2 oz. of porter extract in the first wort. Cool, ferment, and cleanse according to the previous instructions.

Brown Stout.

The procedure is the same as in the preceding article, except that one-third or one-half the malt should be brown.

To brew Ale in Small Families.

A bushel and three-quarters of ground malt and a pound of hops are sufficient to make 18 gallons of good family ale. That the saccharine matter of the malt may be extracted by infusion, without the farina, the temperature of the water shou'd not exceed 155° or 160°. The quantity of water should be poured on the malt as speedily as possible, and the whole being well mixed together by active stirring, the vessel should be closely covered over for an hour; if the weather be cold, for an hour and a half. If hard water be employed it should be boiled, and the temperature allowed, by exposure to the atmosphere, to fall to 155° or 160°; but if rain water is used, it may be added to the malt as soon as it arrives to 155°. During the time this process is going on, the hops should be infused in a close vessel, in as much boiling water as will cover them, for 2 hours. The liquor may then be squeezed out, and kept closely covered.

The hops should then be boiled for about 10 minutes, in double the quantity of water obtained from the infused hops, and the strained liquor, when cold, may be added with the infusion to the wort, when it has fallen to the temperature of 70°. The object of infusing the hops in a close vessel previously to boiling, is to preserve the essential oil of hops, which renders it more sound, and at the same time more wholesome. A pint of good thick yeast should be well stirred into the mixture of wort and hops, and covered over in a place of the temperature of 65°; and when the fermentation is completed, the liquor may be drawn off into a clean cask previously rinsed with boiling water. When the slow fermentation which will ensue has ceased, the cask should be loosely bunged for two days, when, if the liquor be left quiet, the bung may be properly fastened. The pale malt is the best, because, when highly dried, it does not afford so much saccharine matter. If the malt be new, it should be exposed to the air, in a dry room, for 2 days previously to its being used; but if it be old, it may be used in 12 or 20 hours after it is ground. The great difference in the flavor of ale made by different brewers appears to arise from their employing different species of hops.

Another Method of Brewing Ale.

For 36 gallons, take of malt (usually pale), 2½ bushels; sugar, 3 lbs. just boiled to a color; hops, 2 lbs. 8 oz.; coriander seeds, 1 oz.; capsicum, ½ a drachm.

Work it 2 or 3 days, heating it well up once or twice a day; when it begins to fall, cleanse it by adding a handful of salt and some wheat flour.

Table Beer only, from Pale Malt.

The first mash should be at 170°, viz. 2 barrels per quarter; let it stand on the grains ¾ of an hour in hot weather, or 1 hour if cold. Second mash, 145° at 1½ barrels per quarter, stands ½ an hour. Third, 165°, 2 barrels per quarter, stands ½ an hour. Fourth, 130°, 3 barrels, stands 2 hours. The first wort to be boiled with 6 lbs. of hops per quarter for 1½ hours, the second wort to be boiled with the same hops 2 hours, and the remainder 3 hours. The whole is to be now heated as low as 55° if the weather permits, and put to work with about 5 pints of yeast per quarter; if the weather is too warm to get them down to 55°, a less proportion will be sufficient. The 8 barrels of liquor first used will be reduced to 6 of beer to each quarter; 1 barrel being left in the grains, and another evaporated in boiling, cooling and working.

Ale and Small Beer on Mr. Cobbett's Plan.
Utensils.

These are first, a copper that will contain at least 40 gallons. Second, a mashing-tub to contain 60 gallons; for the malt is to be in this along with the water. It must be a little broader at top than at bottom, and not quite so deep as it is wide across the bottom. In the middle of the bottom there is a hole about 2 inches over, to draw the wort off. Into this hole goes a stick a foot or two longer than the tub is high. This stick is to be about 2 inches through, and tapered for about 9 inches upwards, at the end that goes into the hole, which at last it fills up as closely as a cork. Before anything else is put into the tub, lay a little bundle of fine birch about half the bulk of a birch broom, and well tied at both ends. This being laid over the hole (to keep back the grains as the wort goes out), put the tapered end of the stick down through it into the hole, and thus cork the whole up. Then have something of weight sufficient to keep the birch steady at the bottom of the tub, with a hole through it to slip down the stick; the best thing for this purpose will be a *leaden collar* for the stick, with the hole large enough, and it should weigh 3 or 4 pounds.

Third, an underback or shallow tub, to go under the mash-tub for the wort to run into when drawn from the grains.

Fourth, a tun-tub that will contain 30 gallons, to put the ale into to work, the mash-tub serving as a tun-tub for the small beer. Besides these, a couple of coolers or shallow tubs, about a foot deep; or, if there are four it may be as well, in order to effect the cooling more quickly.

Process of Brewing the Ale.

Begin by filling the copper with water, and next by making the water boil. Then put into the mashing-tub water sufficient to stir and separate the malt. The degree of heat that the water is to be at, before the malt is put in, is 170° by the thermometer; but, without one, take this rule: when you can, looking down into the tub, see your face clearly in the water, the water is hot enough. Now put in the malt and stir it well in the water. In this state it should continue for about ¼ of an hour. In the meanwhile fill up the copper, and make it boil; and then put in boiling water sufficient to give 18 gallons of ale.

When the proper quantity of water is in stir the malt again well, and cover the mashing-tub over with sacks, and there let the mash stand for 2 hours; then draw off the wort. The mashing-tub is placed on a couple of stools, so as to be able to put the underback under it to receive the wort as it comes out of the hole. When the underback is put in its place, let out the wort by pulling up the stick that corks the hole. But observe, this stick (which goes 6 or 8 inches through the hole) must be raised by degrees, and the wort must be let out slowly in order to keep back the sediment. So that it is necessary to have something to keep the stick up at the point where it is to be raised, and fixed at for the time. To do this the simplest thing is a stick across the mashing-tub.

As the ale-wort is drawn off into the small underback, lade it out of that into the tun-tub; put the wort into the copper, and add 1½ pounds of good hops, well rubbed and separated as they are put in. Now make the copper boil, and keep it, with the lid off, at a good brisk boil for a full hour, or an hour and a half. When the boiling is done, put the liquor into the coolers, but strain out the hops in a small clothes-basket or wickerbasket. Now set the coolers in the most convenient place, in doors or out of doors, as most convenient.

The next stage is the tun-tub, where the liquor is set to work. A great point is, the degree of heat that the liquor is to be at, when it is set to work. The proper heat is 70°; so that a thermometer makes the matter sure. In the country they determine the degree of heat by merely putting a finger into the liquor.

When cooled to the proper heat, put it into the tun-tub, and put in about half a pint of good yeast. But the yeast should first be put into half a gallon of the liquor, and mixed well; stirring in with the yeast a handful of wheat or rye-flour. This mixture is then to be poured out clean into the tun-tub, and the mass of the liquor agitated well, till the yeast be well mixed with the whole. When the liquor is thus properly put into the tun-tub and set a working, cover over the top, by laying a sack or two across it.

The tun-tub should stand in a place neither too warm nor too cold. Any cool place in summer, and any warm place in winter, and if the weather be very cold, some cloths or sacks should be put round the tun-tub while the beer is working. In about 6 or 8 hours a frothy head will rise upon the liquor; and it will keep rising, more or less slowly, for 48 hours. The best way is to take off the froth, at the end of about 24 hours, with a common skimmer, and in 12 hours take it off again, and so on, till the liquor has done working, and sends up no more yeast. Then it is beer; and, when it is quite cold (for ale or strong beer), put it into the cask by means of a funnel. It must be cold before this is done, or it will be foxed; that is, have a rank and disagreeable taste.

The cask should lean a little on one side when filling it, because the beer will work again, and send more yeast out of the bung hole. Something will go off in this working, which may continue for 2 or 3 days, so that when the beer is being put in the cask, a gallon or two should be left, to keep filling up with as the working produces emptiness. At last when the working is completely over, block the cask up to its level. Put in a handful of fresh hops, fill the cask quite full, and bung it tight, with a bit of coarse linen round the bung.

When the cask is empty, great care must be taken to cork it tightly up, so that no air gets in; for, if so, the cask is moulded and spoilt for ever.

The Small Beer.

Thirty-six gallons of boiling water are to go into the mashing-tub; the grains are to be well stirred up, as before; the mashing-tub is to be covered over, and the mash is to stand in that state for an hour; then draw it off into the tun-tub.

By this time the copper will be empty again, by putting the ale liquor to cool. Now put the small beer wort into the copper with the hops used before, and with half a pound of fresh hops added o them; and boil this liquor briskly for an hour.

Take the grains and the sediment clean out of the mashing-tub, put the birch twigs in again, and put down the stick as before. Put the basket over, and take the liquor from the copper (putting the fire out first) and pour it into the mashing-tub through the basket. Take the basket away, throw the hops on the dunghill, and leave the small beer liquor to cool in the mashing-tub.

Here it is to remain to be set to working; only, more yeast will be wanted in proportion; and there should be for 36 galls. of small beer, 3 half pints of good yeast.

Proceed now as with the ale, only, in the case of the small beer it should be put into cask, not quite cold; or else it will not work in the barrel, as it ought to do. It will not work so strongly nor so long as ale; and may be put in the barrel much sooner, in general the next day after it is brewed.

All the utensils should be well cleaned and put away as soon as they are done with. "I am now," says Mr. Cobbet, "in a farm house, where the same set of utensils has been used for forty years; and the owner tells me, that they may last for forty years longer."

To Brew Ale and Porter from Sugar and Malt.

To every quarter of malt take 100 lbs. of brown sugar, and in the result, it will be found that the sugar is equal to the malt. The quarter of malt is to be brewed with the same proportions, as though it were 2 quarters; and sugar is to be put into the tun, and the first wort let down upon it, rousing the whole well together.

The other worts are then to be let down, and the fermentation and other processes carried on as in the brewing of malt.

To Brew Burton Ale.

Of this strong ale, only a barrel and a half is drawn from a quarter, at 180° for the first mash, and 190° for the second, followed by a gyle of table beer. It is tunned at 58°, and cleansed at 72°. The Burton brewers use the finest pale malt, and grind it a day or two before being used. They employ Kentish hops, from 6 to 8 lbs. per quarter.

To Brew Nottingham Ale in the small way.

The first copperful of boiling water is to be put into the mash-tub, there to lie a quarter of an hour, till the steam is far spent; or as soon as the hot water is put in, throw into it a pail or two of cold water, which will bring it at once to a proper temperature; then let 3 bus. of malt run leisurely into it, and stir or mash all the while, but no more than just to keep the malt from clotting or balling; when that is done, put 1 bu. of dry malt at the top, and let it stand covered 2 hours, or till the next copperful of water is boiled, then lade over the malt 3 handbowlsful at a time. These run off at the cock or tap by a very small stream before more is put on, which again must be returned into the mash-tub till it comes off exceedingly fine. This slow way takes 16 hours in brewing 4 bus. of malt. Between the ladings, put cold water into the copper to boil, while the other is running off; by this means, the copper is kept up nearly full, and the cock is kept running to the end of the brewing. Only 21 galls. must be saved of the first wort, which is reserved in a tub, wherein 4 oz. of hops are put, and then it is to be set by.

For the second wort there are 20 galls. of water in the copper boiling which must be laded over in the same manner as the former, but no cold water need be mixed. When half of this is run out into a tub, it must be directly put into the copper with half of the first wort, strained through the brewing sieve as it lies on a small loose wooden frame over the copper, in order to keep those hops that were first put in to preserve it, which is to make the first copper 21 galls. Then, upon its beginning to boil, put in 1 lb. of hops in 1 or 2 canvas bags, somewhat larger than will just contain the hops, that an* allowance may be given for their swell; this boil very briskly for ½ an hour, when take the hops out and continue boiling the wort by itself till it breaks into particles a little ragged; it is then done, and must be dispersed into the cooling tubs very shallow. Put the remainder of the first and second wort together, and boil it in the same manner, and with the same quantity of fresh hops, as the first.

By this method of brewing, ale may be made as strong or as small as is thought fit, and so may the small beer that comes after.

To brew Essex Ale.

Procure 2 mashing-tubs, 1 that will mash 4 bus., and the other 2 bus., and a copper that holds ½ a hogshead. The water, when boiled, is put into the largest tub, and a pail of cold water immediately on that; then put the malt in by a handbowlful at a time, stirring it all the while, and so on in a greater quantity by degrees (for the danger of balling is mostly at first), till at last ½ a bus. of dry malt is left for a top-cover; thus let it stand 3 hours. In the meanwhile, another copper of water is directly heated, and put as before into the other mash-tub, for mashing 2 bus. of malt, which stands that time. Then, after the wort of the 4 bus. is run off, let that also of the 2 bus. spend, and ladle it over the 4 bus., the cock running all the while, and it will make in all a copper and a half of wort, which is boiled twice; that is, when the first copper is boiled an hour, or till it breaks into large flakes; then take half out, and put the remaining raw wort to it, and boil it about ¼ an hour till it is broken. Now while the 2 worts are running off, a copper of water almost scalding hot is made ready, and put over the goods or grains of both tubs; after an hour's standing the cock is turned, and this second wort is boiled away, and put over the grains of both tubs to stand 1 hour; when off, it is put into the copper and boiled again, and then serves hot instead of the first water, for mashing 4 bus. of fresh malt; after it has again lain 3 hours, and is spent off, it is boiled; but while in the mash-tub, a copper of water is heated to put over the goods or grains, which stands 1 hour, and is then boiled for small beer. And thus may be brewed 10 bus. of malt with 2½ lbs. of hops for the whole.

To brew Edinburgh Ale.

Adopt the best pale malt.

1st. Mash two barrels per quarter, at 183° (170°); mash three-quarters of an hour, let it stand one hour, and allow half an hour to run off the wort.

2nd. Mash one barrel per quarter, at 190° (183°); mash three-quarters of an hour, let it stand three-quarters of an hour, and tap as before.

3rd. Mash one barrel per quarter, at 160°; mash half an hour, let it stand half an hour, and tap as before.

The first and second wort may be mixed together, boiling them about an hour or an hour and a quarter, with a quantity of hops proportioned to the time the beer is intended to be kept.

The two first may be mixed at the heat of 60° or 65° in the gyle-tun, and the second should be fermented separately for small beer.

Bavarian or Lager Beer.

The malt is first mixed with water of ordinary temperature; for 1 part of malt about 39 parts of water are employed. The whole is allowed to rest 6 or 8 hours, after which the mashing is begun by mixing the mass with 3 parts of boiling water added gradually during continual agitation, by which its temperature is raised to 106° Fahr. The thick part of the mash is then transferred to the copper and heated to boiling with constant agitation, and after an hour's boiling again returned to the mash-tun and mixed thoroughly with its liquid contents, by which the temperature in the mash-tun is raised to 133°. The thick part of the mash is once more transferred to the copper and boiled for an hour and returned to the mash-tun, by which the temperature is raised to 154°. The fluid part of the mash is then transferred to the copper and boiled for a quarter of an hour, and then poured back upon the mash in the tun, and mixed thoroughly with it. The temperature is thereby raised to from 167° to 180°. After agitation for a quarter of an hour the mash is left at rest for an hour or an hour and a half, after which the clear wort is drawn off.

The fermentation of lager is peculiar, it is performed very slowly, and at a temperature from 32° to 46½° Fahr. The yeast, instead of rising, falls to the bottom. The high temperature of the mash causes all albuminous matter to be coagulated, and much gummy matter remains unchanged. This, together with the bottom fermentation, carries off all nitrogenous matter; the beer is exceedingly clear. It is put in hogsheads lined with common rosin, and is preserved a long time in vaults or cellars before being used.

White Beer.

Boil enough ale wort, preferably pale, for 1 barrel, with 3 handsful of hops and 14 pounds of groats (hulled oats), until all the soluble matter is extracted from the latter. Strain, and when lukewarm add 2 pints of yeast, and when fermenting briskly bottle in strong stoneware bottles.

Cheap and Agreeable Table Beer.

Take 15 galls. of water and boil one-half, putting the other into a barrel; add the boiling water to the cold, with 1 gall. of molasses and a little yeast. Keep the bung-hole open till the fermentation is abated.

To make Sugar Beer.

Very excellent beer is made of sugar, and also of treacle. First boil a peck of bran in 10 galls. of water; strain the bran off, and mix with the branny water 3 pounds of sugar, first stirring it well. When cool enough add a teacupful of the best yeast, and a tablespoonful of flour to a bowl nearly full of the saccharine matter, which, when it has fermented for about an hour, is to be mixed with the remainder, and hopped with about ½ lb. hops; and the following day it may be put into the cask, to ferment further, which usually takes 3 days, when it is to be bunged, and it will be fit for drinking in a week. Treacle beer is made in the same way, 3 lbs. of it being used instead of 3 lbs. of sugar.

N. B.—This beer will not keep any length of time.

Spruce Beer

Boil 8 galls. of water, and when in a state of complete ebullition pour it into a beer barrel which contains 8 galls. more of cold water; then add 16 lbs. of molasses, with a few tablespoonfuls of the essence of spruce, stirring the whole well together; add half a pint of yeast, and keep it in a temperate situation, with the bung-hole open for two days till the fermentation is abated, when the bung may be put in and the beer bottled off. It is fit to drink in a day or two. If you can get no essence of spruce make a strong decoction of the small twigs and leaves of the spruce firs.

Another Receipt.

Take of oil of spruce, sassafras, and wintergreen, each 40 drops; pour 1 gall. of boiling water on the oils, then add 4 galls. of cold water, 3 pints of molasses, 1 pint of yeast. Let it stand for 2 hours and bottle.

Root Beer.

Take 3 galls. of molasses; add 10 galls. of water at 60° Fahr. Let this stand 2 hours, then pour into a barrel, and add powdered or bruised sassafras and wintergreen bark, each ½ lb., bruised sarsaparilla root ½ lb., yeast 1 pint, water enough to fill the barrel, say 25 galls. Ferment for 12 hours and bottle.

Ginger Pop.

Crushed white sugar 28 lbs, water 30 galls., yeast 1 pint, powdered ginger (best) 1 lb., essence of lemon ½ oz., essence of cloves ¼ oz. To the ginger pour half a gallon of boiling water and let it stand 15 or 20 minutes. Dissolve the sugar in 2 galls. of warm water, pour both into a barrel half filled with cold water, then add the essence and the yeast; let it stand half an hour, then fill up with cold water. Let it ferment 6 to 12 hours, and bottle.

Ginger Beer.

Take of good Jamaica ginger 2½ oz., moist sugar 3 lbs., cream of tartar 1 oz., the juice and peel of two middling-sized lemons, brandy ½ pint, good solid ale yeast ¼ pint, water 3½ galls. This will produce 4½ dozen of excellent ginger beer, which will keep 12 months. Bruise the ginger and sugar, and boil them for 20 or 25 minutes in the water; slice the lemon and put it and the cream of tartar into a large pan; pour the boiling liquor upon them, stir it well round, and when milk warm add the yeast. Cover it over, let it remain 2 or 3 days to work, skimming it frequently; then strain it through a jelly-bag into a cask, add the brandy, bung down very close, and at the end of a fortnight or 3 weeks draw it off and bottle, and cork very tight; tie the cork down with twine or wire. If it does not work well at first, add a little more yeast, but be careful not to add too much, lest it taste of it.

Mead.

Take of honey 3 galls., heat to the boiling point, taking great care that it does not boil over; pour this into a barrel half filled with cold water; let it stand 20 or 25 minutes, and add yeast 1 pint, oil nutmeg 1 tablespoonful, oil of lemon or orange 1 ounce. Fill the barrel with water, and let it ferment.

Sarsaparilla Beer, or Lisbon Diet Drink.

Take of compound syrup of sarsaparilla 1 pint, good pale ale 7 pints. Use no yeast.

Cheap Beer.

Pour 10 galls. of boiling water upon 1 peck of malt in a tub, stir it about well with a stick, let it stand about half an hour, and then draw off the wort; pour 10 galls. more of boiling water upon the malt, letting it remain another half hour, stirring it occasionally, then draw it off and put it to the former wort. When this is done, mix 4 oz. of hops with it, and boil it well; then strain the hops from it, and when the wort becomes milk warm put some yeast to it to make it ferment; when the fermentation is nearly over, put the liquor into a cask, and, as soon as the fermentation has perfectly subsided, bung it close down. The beer is then fit for use.

To make Beer and Ale from Pea-shells.

No production of this country abounds so much with vegetable saccharine matter as the shells of green peas. A strong decoction of them so much resembles, in odor and taste, an infusion of malt (termed wort) as to deceive a brewer. This decoction, rendered slightly bitter with the wood sage, and afterwards fermented with yeast, affords a very excellent beverage. The method employed is as follows:

Fill a boiler with the green shells of peas, pour on water till it rises half an inch above the shells, and simmer for three hours. Strain off the liquor, and add a strong decoction of the wood-sage, or the hop, so as to render it pleasantly bitter; then ferment in the usual manner. The wood-sage is the best substitute for hops, and, being free from any anodyne property, is entitled to a preference. By boiling a fresh quantity of shells in the decoction before it becomes cold, it may be so thoroughly impregnated with saccharine matter as to afford a liquor, when fermented, as strong as ale.

Required Time for Keeping Beer.

This depends on the temperature at which the malt has been made, thus:

Malt made at 110° will produce beer which may be drawn in a fortnight; at 124°, in a month; at 129°, in 3 months; at 134°, in 4 months; at 138°, in 6 months; at 143°, in 8 months; at 148° in 10 months; at 152°, in 15 months; at 157°, in 20 months; at 162°, in 24 months.

To give any required Brightness or Color to Beer.

This depends on the temperature at which the malt has been made, and on its color, thus:

Malt made at 119° produces a white; at 124°, a cream color; at 129°, a light yellow; at 134°, an amber color.

These, when properly brewed, become spontaneously fine, even as far as 138°. When brewed for amber, by repeated fermentations, they become pellucid. At 138°, a high amber; at 143°, a pale brown.

By precipitation, these grow bright in a short time. At 148°, a brown; at 152°, a high brown.

With precipitation these require 8 or 10 months to be bright. At 157°, a brown, inclining to black; at 162°, a brown speckled with black.

With precipitation these may be fined, but will never become bright. At 167°, a blackish brown speckled with black; at 171°, a color of burnt coffee; at 176°, a black.

These with difficulty can be brewed without setting the goods, and will by no means become bright, not even with the strongest acid menstruum.

To Brew Amber Beer.

Amber is now out of fashion, but formerly was drunk in great quantities in London, mixed with bitters, and called purl. The proportions of malt were 3 qrs. amber, and 1 qr. pale, with 6 lbs. of hops to the qr. The first liquor is usually tunned at 170°, and the second at 187°. The worts are boiled together for 2 hours. It is tunned at 64°, and after 24 hours roused every 2 hours till the heat is increased to 74°. It is then skimmed every hour for 6 hours and cleansed, and generally used as soon as it has done working in the barrels.

Another Method of Brewing Amber Beer, or Twopenny.

For 36 galls.: malt, 1½ bus.; hops, 1 lb.; liquorice root, 1 lb. 8 oz.; treacle, 5 lb.; Spanish liquorice, 2 oz.; capsicum, 2 drs. Frequently drunk the week after it is brewed; used in cold weather as a stimulant.

To make Molasses Beer.

For small beer, put 9 lbs. of molasses into a barrel-copper of cold water, first mixing it well, and boiling it briskly with ¼ lb. of hops or more 1 hour, so that it may come off 27 galls.

To Fine Beer.

To fine beer, should it be requisite, take an ounce of isinglass, cut small, and boil it in 3 qts. of beer, till completely dissolved; let it stand till quite cold, then put it into a cask, and stir it well with a stick or whisk; the beer so fined should be tapped soon, because the isinglass is apt to make it flat as well as fine.

Another Method.

Take a handful of salt, and the same quantity of chalk scraped fine and well dried; then take some isinglass, and dissolve it in some stale beer till it is about the consistence of syrup; strain it, and add about a quart to the salt and chalk, with 2 qts. of molasses. Mix them all well together, with a gallon of the beer, which must be drawn off; then put it into the cask, and take a stick or whisk, and stir it well till it ferments. When it has subsided, stop it up close, and in 2 days it may be tapped. This is sufficient for a butt.

Another.— Take 1 pt. of water, and ½ an oz. of unslaked lime, mix them well together, letting the mixture stand for 3 hours, that the lime may settle at the bottom. Then pour off the clear liquor, and mix with it ½ oz. of isinglass, cut small and boiled in a little water; pour it into the barrel, and in 5 or 6 hours the beer will become fine.

Another.—In general, it will become sufficiently fine by keeping; but fineness may be promoted by putting a handful of scalded hops into the cask. If the beer continues thick, it may then be fined by putting 1 pt. of the following preparation into the barrel:

Put as much isinglass into a vessel as will occupy ¼; then fill it up with old beer. When dissolved rub it through a sieve, and reduce it to the consistency of treacle with more beer. A pint of this put into the cask and gently stirred with a short stick, will fine the barrel in a few hours.

To Fine Cloudy Beer.

Rack off the cask, and boil 1 lb. of new hops in water, with coarse sugar, and when cold put in at the bung-hole.

Or, new hops soaked in beer, and squeezed, may be put into the cask.

Or, take 10 lbs. of baked pebblestone powder, with the whites of 6 eggs, and some powdered bay-salt, and mix them with 2 galls. of the beer. Pour in the whole into the casks, and in 3 or 4 days it will settle, and the beer be fine and agreeable.

To Recover Thick, Sour Malt Liquor.

Make strong hop tea with boiling water and salt of tartar, and pour it into the cask.

Or, rack the cask into 2 casks of equal size, and fill them up with new beer.

To Vamp Malt Liquors.

Old beer may be renewed by racking 1 cask into 2, and filling them from a new brewing, and in 3 weeks it will be a fine article.

To Restore Musty Beer.

Run it through some hops that have been boiled in strong wort, and afterwards work it with double the quantity of new malt liquor; or if the fault is in the cask, draw it off into a sweet cask, and having boiled ½ lb. of brown sugar in 1 qt. of water, add 1 or 2 spoonsful of yeast before it is quite cold, and when the mixture ferments, pour it into the cask.

To Enliven and Restore Dead Beer.

Boil some water and sugar, or water and treacle, together, and when cold add some new yeast; this will restore dead beer, or ripen bottled beer in 24 hours; and it will also make worts work in the tun if they are sluggish.

Or, a small teaspoonful of carbonate or soda may be mixed with a quart of it as it is drawn for drinking.

Or, boil for every gallon of the liquor 3 oz. of sugar in water; when cold add a little yeast, and put the fermenting mixture into the flat beer, whether it be a full cask or the bottom of the cask.

Or, beer may often be restored which has become flat or stale, by rolling and shaking the casks for a considerable time, which will create such a new fermentation as to render it necessary to open a vent-peg to prevent the cask from bursting.

A Speedy way of Fining and Preserving a Cask of Ale or Beer.

Take a handful of the hops boiled in the first wort, and dried; ½ lb. of loaf sugar dissolved in the beer; 1 lb. of chalk; and ¼ lb. of calcined oyster-shells. Put the whole in at the bung-hole, stirring them well and then rebunging. This preparation will also suit for racked beer; in putting in the hops it may be advisable to place them in a net with a small stone in the bottom so as to sink them, otherwise they will swim at the top.

To Prevent Beer Becoming Stale or Flat.—*First Method.*

To a quart of French brandy put as much wheat or bean flour as will make it into a dough, and put it in. in long pieces, at the bung-hole, letting it fall gently to the bottom. This will prevent the beer growing stale, keep it in a mellow state, and increase its strength.

Second Method.

To 1 lb. of treacle or honey add 1 lb. of the powder of dried oyster-shells, or of soft mellow chalk; mix these into a stiff paste and put it into the butt. This will preserve the beer in a soft and mellow state for a long time.

Third Method.

Dry a peck of egg-shells in an oven, break and mix them with 2 lbs. of soft mellow chalk, and then add some water wherein 4 lbs. of coarse sugar have been boiled, and put it into the cask. This will be enough for 1 butt.

Fourth Method.

In a cask containing 18 gals. of beer, put a pint of ground malt suspended in a bag, and close the bung perfectly; the beer will be improved during the whole time of drawing it for use.

Make use of any of these receipts most approved of, observing that the paste or dough must be put into the cask when the beer has done working, or soon after, and bunged down. At the end of 9 or 12 months tap it, and you will have a fine, generous, wholesome and agreeable liquor.

When the great quantity of sediment that lies at the bottom of the cask is neglected to be cleaned, this compound of malt, hops and yeast so affects the beer that it renders it prejudicial to health. On this account, during the whole process of brewing do not allow the least sediment to mix with the wort in removing it from one tub or cooler to the other; especially be careful, when tunning it into the cask, not to disturb the bottom of the working tub, which would prevent its ever being clear and fine. Again, by keeping it too long in the working tub, persons who make a profit of the yeast frequently promote an undue fermentation, and keep it constantly in that state for 5 or 6 days, which causes all the spirit that should keep the beer soft and mellow to evaporate; and it certainly will get stale and hard unless it has something wholesome to feed on.

It is the practice of some persons to beat in the yeast while the beer is working, for several days together, to make it strong and heady and to promote its sale. This is a pernicious custom. Therefore let the wort have a free, natural and light fermentation, and one day in the working tub will be long enough during cold weather; but turn it the second day at the farthest, throw out the whole brewing, and afterwards introduce no improper ingredients.

To Prevent and Cure Foxing in Malt Liquors.

Foxing, sometimes called bucking, is a disease of malt fermentation which taints the beer. It arises from dirty utensils, putting the separate worts together in vessels not deep enough, using bad malt; by turning on the liquors at too great heats, and brewing in too hot weather. It renders the beer ropy and viscid like treacle, and it soon turns sour. When there is danger of foxing, a handful of hops should be thrown into the raw worts while they are drawing off and before they are boiled, as foxing generally takes place when, from a scantiness of utensils, the worts are obliged to be kept some time before they are boiled. When there is a want of shallow coolers, it is a good precaution to put some fresh hops into the worts and work them with the yeast. If the brewing foxes in the tun while working, hops should then be put into it, and they will tend to restore it; and extra care ought to be taken to prevent the lees being transferred to the barrels.

Some persons sift quick-lime into the tun when the brewing appears to be foxed. If care is not taken to cleanse and scald the vessels after foxing, subsequent brewings may become tainted.

Other Methods of Curing Foxing.

Cut a handful of hyssop small; mix it with a handful of salt, and put it into the cask. Stir and stop close.

Or, infuse a handful of hops and a little salt of tartar in boiling water; when cold strain the liquor off and pour it into the cask, which stop close.

Or, mix 1 oz. of alum with 2 oz. of mustard-seed, and 1 oz. of ginger; stir them in the rack and stop close.

Or, in a fortnight, rack off the foxed beer, and hang 2 lbs. of bruised Malaga raisins in a bag within the cask, and put in a mixture of treacle, bean-flour, mustard-seed, and powdered alum.

To restore a Barrel of Ropy Beer.

Mix a handful of bean-flour with a handful of salt, and stir it in at the bung-hole; or take some well infused hops, and mix them in with some settlings of strong wort, and stir the mixture in at the bung-hole. Or, powder ½ oz. of alum very fine, and mix with a handful of bean-flour.

To make a Butt of Porter, Stout.

Insert 4 galls. of molasses and some finings; stir it well. In a week draw off the cask by a cock inserted half way down.

To restore Frosted Beer.

Such beer is usually sweet and foul, and will never recover of itself; but to remedy this, make a pailful of fresh wort, into which put a handful of rubbed hops, and boil them half an hour, so that it may be very bitter, and when almost cold, draw a pailful from the cask, and re-fill it with the bitter wort. Fermentation will re-commence, but when this is over bung it up for a month. If it is not then restored, rack it into another cask, and put into it ½ a peck of parched wheat, and 1 lb. of good hops, dried and rubbed, and tied up in a net. Bung it down, leaving the vent-hole open for a day or two, and in a month it will be fine liquor.

To give New Ale the Flavor of Old.

Take out the bung, and put into the cask a handful of pickled cucumbers; or a sliced Seville orange, and either mode will add an apparent six months to the age of the ale.

To give Beer a rich Flavor.

Put six sea-biscuits into a bag of hops, and put them into the cask.

To preserve Brewing Utensils.

In cleaning them before being put away, avoid the use of soap, or any greasy material, and use only a brush and scalding water, being particularly careful not to leave any yeast or fur on the sides.

To prevent their being tainted, take wood ashes and boil them to a strong lye, which spread over the bottoms of the vessels scalding, and then with the broom scrub the sides and other parts.

Or, take bay-salt, and spread it over the coolers, and strew some on their wet sides, turning in scalding water and scrubbing with a broom.

Or, throw some stone-lime into water in the vessel, and scrub over the bottom and sides, washing afterwards with clean water.

To sweeten Stinking or Musty Casks.

Make a strong lye of ash, beech, or other hard wood ashes, and pour it, boiling hot, into the bung-hole, repeating it as often as there is occasion.

Or, fill the cask with boiling water, and then put into it some pieces of unslaked lime, keeping up the ebullition for half an hour. Then hung it down, and let it remain until almost cold when turn it out.

Or, mix bay-salt with boiling water, and pour it into the cask, which bung down, and leave it to soak.

Or, if the copper be provided with a dome, and a steam-pipe from its top, pass the steam into the casks.

Or, unhead the cask, scrub it out, head it again; put some powdered charcoal into the bung-hole, and two quarts of a mixture of oil of vitriol and cold water. Then bung it tight, and roll and turn the cask for some time. Afterwards wash it well, and drain it dry.

Or, take out the head, and brush the inside with oil of vitriol, afterwards wash it, then burn a slip of brown paper steeped in brimstone within the bung-hole, and stop it close for two hours, when it should be well washed out with hot water.

Another Method.

Mix half a pint of the sulphuric acid (not the diluted) in an open vessel, with a quart of water, and whilst warm, put it into the cask, and roll it about in such a manner that the whole internal surface may be exposed to its action. The following day add about 1 lb. of chalk or sal soda, and bung it up for three or four days, when it may be washed out with boiling water. By this process a very musty cask may be rendered sweet.

For sweetening musty bottles, it will be only necessary to rinse the inside with the diluted sulphuric acid in the above-mentioned proportions. The addition of chalk, if it were immediately corked, would burst the bottle, and if the cask be old, it would be advisable to let a little of the gas escape before bunging it.

Another.—If a cask, after the beer is drunk out, be well stopped, to keep out the air, and the lees be suffered to remain in it till used again, scald it well, taking care that the hoops be well driven on, before filling; but should the air get into an empty cask, it will contract an ill scent, notwithstanding the scalding; in which case a handful of bruised pepper, boiled in the water, will remove it, though the surest way is to take out the head of the cask, that it may be shaved; then burn it a little, and scald it for use; if this cannot be conveniently done, get some limestone, put about 3 lbs. into a barrel (and in same proportion for larger or smaller vessels), put to it about 6 gall. of cold water, bung it up, shake it about for some time, and afterwards scald it well. Or, in lieu of lime, match it well and scald it. Then the smell will be entirely removed. If the casks be new, dig holes in the earth, and lay them in, to about half their depth, with their bung-holes downwards, for a week. After which scald them well, and they will be ready for use.

Another.—The process of charring fails only in the fire not being able to penetrate into the chasms or chinks of the cask, into which the coopers (to mend bad work) often insert strips of paper, or other substance, to make it water-tight, which in time become rotten and offensive; in order to remedy this, put into a cask containing a quantity of water (say about 2 gall. in a hogshead) 1-10th of its weight of sulphuric acid (oil of vitriol), and let this be shaken for some time; this is to be poured out, the cask well washed, and then rinsed with a few gallons of lime-water or sal soda. It is needless to say, that it ought likewise to be washed out.

The theory is, that sulphuric acid has the property, when used alone, of charring wood, and when diluted has sufficient strength to destroy must, etc., with the additional advantage of entering into every crevice. The lime in solution seizes any particle of acid which the first washing might leave, and converts it into an insoluble, inoffensive, neutral salt, such as, if left in the cask, would not in the least injure the most delicate liquor.

London Coopers' mode of Sweetening Casks.

It is their system to take out the head, place the cask over a brisk fire, and char the inside completely. The head is then put in again, and the cask, before used, is filled 2 or 3 times with hot liquor, bunged down and well shaken before it is used again.

Method of Seasoning New Casks.

Put the staves just cut and shaped, before they are worked into vessels, loose in a copper of cold water, and let them heat gradually so that they are well boiled, and in boiling take out a handbowl of water at a time, putting in fresh till all the redness is out of the liquor, and it becomes clear from a scum of filth that will arise from the sap so boiled out; also take care to turn the staves upside down, that all their parts may equally have the benefit of the hot water. Observe also that in a dry, sultry summer the sap is more strongly retained in the wood, than in a cool and moist one, and therefore must have the more boiling. Then, when the vessel is made, scald it twice with water and salt boiled together, and it may be readily filled with strong beer without fearing any twang from the wood.

Fermentation by Various Means.—First Substitute for Yeast.

Mix 2 quarts of water with wheat flour to the consistence of thick gruel; boil it gently for half an hour, and when almost cold stir into it ¼ lb. of sugar and 4 spoonfuls of good yeast. Put the whole into a large jug or earthen vessel with a narrow top, and place it before the fire, so that it may by a moderate heat ferment. The fermentation will throw up a thin liquor, which pour off and throw away; keep the remainder for use (in a cool place) in a bottle or jug tied over. The same quantity of this, as of common yeast, will suffice to bake or brew with. Four spoonfuls of this yeast will make a fresh quantity as before, and the stock may be always kept up by fermenting the new with the remainder of the former quantity.

Second Substitute.

Take 6 quarts of soft water and 2 handfuls of wheaten meal or barley; stir the latter in the water before the mixture is placed over the fire, where it must boil till two-thirds are evaporated. When this decoction becomes cool incorporate with it, by means of a whisk, 2 drachms of salt of tartar and 1 drachm of cream of tartar, previously mixed. The whole should be kept in a warm place. Thus a very strong yeast for brewing, distilling and baking may be obtained. For the last-mentioned purpose, however, it ought to be diluted with pure water, and passed through a sieve before it is kneaded with the dough, in order to deprive it of its alkaline taste.

In countries where yeast is scarce, it is a common practice to twist hazel twigs so as to be full of chinks, and then steep them in ale-yeast during fermentation. The twigs are then hung up to dry, and at the next brewing they are put into the wort instead of yeast. In Italy the chips are frequently put into turbid wine for the purpose of clearing it; this is effected in about 24 hours.

Third Substitute.

Take 1 lb. of fine flour, make it the thickness of gruel with boiling water, add to it ¼ a lb. of raw sugar. Mix them well together. Put 3 spoonfuls of well purified yeast into a large vessel, upon which put the above ingredients; they will soon ferment violently. Collect the yeast off the top and put it into a brown small-neck pot, and cover it up from the air; keep it in a dry and warmish place; when used in part, replace with flour made into a thin paste, and sugar in the former proportions. The above will be fit for use in five months, and no yeast is necessary except the first time.

Fourth Substitute.

Boil flour and water to the consistence of treacle, and when the mixture is cold saturate it with fixed air. Pour the mixture thus saturated into one or more large bottles or narrow-mouthed jars; cover it over loosely with paper, and upon that lay a slate or board with a weight to keep it steady. Place the vessel in a situation where the thermometer will stand from 70° to 80°, and stir up the mixture 2 or 3 times in the course of 24 hours. In about 2 days such a degree of fermentation will have taken place as to give the mixture the appearance of yeast. With the yeast in this state, and before it has acquired a thoroughly vinous smell, mix the quantity of flour intended for bread in the proportion of 6 lbs. of flour to a quart of the yeast, and a sufficient portion of warm water. Knead them well together in a proper vessel, and covering it with a cloth, let the dough stand for 12 hours, or till it appears to be sufficiently fermented in the forementioned degree of warmth. It is then to be formed into loaves and baked. The yeast would be more perfect if a decoction of malt were used instead of simple water.

Fifth Substitute.

A decoction of malt alone, without any addition, will produce a yeast proper enough for the purpose of brewing. This discovery was made by Joseph Senyor, and he received for it a reward of 20l. from the Society for Promoting Arts, Manufactures and Commerce. The process is as follows: Procure 3 earthen or wooden vessels of different sizes and apertures, one capable of holding 2 quarts, the other 3 or 4, and the third 5 or 6; boil ¼ of a peck of malt for about 8 or 10 minutes in 3 pints of water, and when a quart is poured off from the grains, let it stand in the first or smaller vessel in a cool place till not quite cold, but retaining that degree of heat which the brewers usually find to be proper when they begin to work their liquor. Then remove the vessel into some warm situation near a fire, where the thermometer stands between 70° and 80°, and there let it remain till the fermentation begins, which will be plainly perceived within 30 hours; add then 2 qts. more of a like decoction of malt, when cool as the first was, and mix the whole in the second or larger vessel, and stir it well in, which must be repeated in the usual way, as it rises from a common vat; then add a still greater quantity of the same decoction, to be worked in the largest vessel, which will produce yeast enough for a brewing of 40 gallons.

Sixth Substitute.

Boil 1 lb. of good flour, ¼ lb. of brown sugar, and a little salt in 2 galls. of water for 1 hour. When milk warm bottle it and cork it close. It will be fit for use in 24 hours. One pint of this will make 18 lbs. of bread.

Seventh Substitute.

To 1 lb. of mashed potatoes (mealy ones are best) add 2 oz. of brown sugar and 2 spoonfuls of common yeast; the potatoes first to be pulped through a colander, and mixed with warm water to a proper consistence. Thus a pound of potatoes will make a quart of good yeast. Keep it moderately warm while fermenting.

Eighth Substitute.

Infuse malt, and boil it as for beer; in the mean time soak isinglass, separated to fibres, in small-beer. Proportion the quantity of each, 1 oz. of isinglass to 2 qts. of beer. This would suffice for a hogshead of boiling wort, and the proportion may be diminished or increased accordingly. After soaking 5 minutes, set the beer and isinglass on the fire, stirring till it nearly boils; then turn it into a dish that will allow beating it up with a syllabub whisk to the consistence of yeast, and when almost cold put it to the wort.

Ninth Substitute.

Make a wort of the consistence of water-gruel, with either rye or malt, ground very fine; put 5 galls. of it into a vessel capable of holding a few gallons more; dissolve 1 lb. of leaven in a small portion of the wort, and add it to the remainder, with 2¼ lbs. of fine ground malt; mix the whole by agitation for some minutes, and in half an hour add 2 large spoonfuls of good yeast; incorporate it thoroughly with the mass, cover it close, and let it remain undisturbed for 48 hours in a moderate temperature. At the end of that period it will be found to be wholly converted into good yeast. It is requisite that the rye and malt should be fine, and the leaven completely dissolved before being put to the remaining wort, which, previous to the yeast being added, should be at about 100°.

To Preserve Yeast.

Common ale yeast may be kept fresh and fit for use several months by the following method: Put a quantity of it into a close canvas bag, and gently squeeze out the moisture in a screw-press till the remaining matter be as firm and stiff as clay. In this state it may be close-packed up in a tight cask, for securing it from the air, and will keep fresh, sound, and fit for use for a long time.

Another Method.

Stir a quantity of yeast and work it well with a whisk, till it seems liquid and thin; then get a large wooden dish or tub, clean and dry, and with a soft brush lay a thin layer of yeast thereon, turning the mouth downwards, to prevent its getting dusty, but so that the air may come to it to dry it. When that coat or crust is sufficiently dried, lay on another, which serve in the same manner and continue putting on others as they dry, till 2 or 3 inches thick, which will be useful on many occasions; but be sure the yeast in the vessel be dry before more be laid on. When wanted for use, cut a piece out, lay it in warm water, stir it together, and it will be fit for use. If for brewing, take a handful of birch tied together, dip it into the yeast, and hang it to dry, taking care to keep it free from dust. When the beer is fit to set to work, throw in one of these and it will work as well as fresh yeast. Whip it about in the wort and then let it lie. When the beer works well take out the broom, dry it again, and it will do for the next brewing.

To make Purl Bitters.

Take of Roman wormwood 2 doz. lbs., gentian root 6 lbs., calamus aromaticus (or the sweet-flag root) 2 pounds, snake-root 1 lb., horse radish 1 bunch, orange-peel dried and juniper-berries, each 2 lbs., seeds or kernels of Seville oranges cleaned and dried 2 lbs. Cut these and bruise them, and put them into a clean butt, and start some mild brown or pale beer upon them, so as to fill up the vessel, about the beginning of November, which let stand till the next season. If a pound or two of galanga root is added to it the composition will be better.

Cautions in the Use of Foreign Ingredients.

In general, the beer should be racked off first, because the sediments and lees will not accord with the foreign substances. Salt and alum in too large quantities induce staleness. The powder of soft stone, unburnt, should be avoided; too many whites of eggs are apt to make the beer ropy. The introduction of *cocculus indicus* confers a pernicious strength or headiness, which gratifies drunkards, but destroys the nervous system, and produces palsies and premature old age. It has been well remarked, that the brewer that uses this slow but certain poison, as a substitute for a due quantity of malt, ought to be boiled in his own copper.

Bitters are in like manner pernicious in many states of the stomach. When oyster-shells are used the bung should be left out to avoid bursting.

Use of Sugar in Brewing.

Families brewing their own malt liquor may use 32 lbs. of brown sugar with 2 bushels of malt, which will produce 50 galls. of ale, as good in every respect as if made from 6 bushels of malt. The sugar is mixed with the wort as it runs from the mash-tub.

To Close Casks without Bungs.

Some persons cover the bung-hole simply with brown paper, fastened at the sides, and covered with clay; others have found a single piece of bladder, well fixed at the edges, a complete and efficacious substitute for a bung. These methods at least prevent the bursting of the cask from changes of air.

To Bottle Porter, Ale, etc.

In the first place the bottles should be clean, sweet and dry, the corks sound and good, and the porter or ale fine. When the bottles are filled, if for home consumption, they should not be corked till the day following, and if for exportation to a hot climate, they must stand 3 days or more; if the liquor is new, it should be well corked and wired, but for a private family they may do without wiring, only they should be well packed in saw-dust, and stand upright. But if some ripe are wanted, keep a few packed on their sides, so that the liquor may touch the corks, and this will soon ripen, and make it fit for drinking.

To Remove Tartness.

Put a teaspoonful of carbonate of soda into a quart of tart beer, and it will be pleasant and wholesome.

To Bottle Malt Liquor.

It should be ripe, and not too young. Cork loose at first, and afterwards firm. For a day or two, keep the bottles in cold water, or in a cold place; or throw some cold water over them. Steep the corks in scalding water, to make them more elastic. Lay the bottles on their sides. When it is desired that the liquor should ripen soon, keep the bottles in a warmer place. October beer should not be bottled till midsummer; nor March beer till Christmas. If the ale is flat, or stale, put 3 horse-beans, or 3 raisins into each bottle, and to prevent the bottles' bursting, make a hole in the middle of the cork with an awl; or put into each bottle 1 or 2 peppercorns. If it is desired to ripen it quick, boil some coarse sugar in water, and when cold ferment it with yeast. Then put in 3 or 4 spoonsful of it, with 2 cloves, and if kept in a warm place it will be ripe the next day. When the ale is sour, put into it a little syrup of capillaire, and ferment it with yeast; when settled bottle it, and put a clove or two with a small lump of sugar into each bottle. It is also useful to put 2 or 3 pieces of chalk, or some powdered chalk into the barrel before bottling.

To Bottle Table Beer.

As soon as a cask of table beer is received into the house, it is drawn off into quart *stone* bottles, with a lump of white sugar in each, and securely corked. In three days it becomes brisk, is equal in strength to table ale, remarkably pleasant, very wholesome, and will keep many months.

To render Bottled Beer Ripe.

The following method is employed in Paris by some venders of bottled beer, to render it what they term ripe. It is merely by adding to each bottle 3 or 4 drops of yeast and a lump of sugar of the size of a large nutmeg. In the course of 24 hours, by this addition, stale or flat beer is rendered most agreeably brisk. In consequence of the fermentative process that takes place in it, a small deposit follows, and on this account the bottles should be kept in an erect position. By this means white wine may likewise be rendered brisk.

To Manage Ale in the Cellar.

In general nothing is more necessary than to keep it well stopped in a cool cellar, looking occasionally to see that there is no leakage, and to open the vent holes, if any oozings appear between the staves of the casks: but connoisseurs in malt liquor may adopt some of the following means: Leave the cock-hole of an upright cask, or the vent-hole of an horizontal one, open for 2 or 3 months; then rack off into another cask with 1 or 2 lbs. of new hops, and closely bung and stop down.

Or, leave the vent-holes open a month, then stop, and about a month before tapping draw off a little and mix it with 1 or 2 lbs. of new hops, which, having poured into the cask, it is again closely stopped.

Or, salt may be used with the hops, as it always gives beer the flavor of age.

To Keep Hops for Future Use.

Hops lose all their fine flavor by exposure to the air and damp. They should be kept in a dry, close place, and lightly packed.

TO MAKE CIDER.

After the apples are gathered from the trees they are ground into what is called *pommage*, either by means of a common pressing stone, with a circular trough, or by a cider mill, which is either driven by the hand, or by horse-power. When the pulp is thus reduced to a great degree of fineness, it is conveyed to the cider press, where it is formed by pressure into a kind of cake, which is called the *cheese*.

This is effected by placing clear, sweet straw or hair cloths between the layers of pommage till there is a pile of 10 or 12 layers. This pile is then subjected to different degrees of pressure in succession, till all the *must* or *juice* is squeezed from the pommage. This juice, after being strained in a coarse hair-sieve, is then put either into open vats or close casks, and the pressed pulp is either thrown away or made to yield a weak liquor called washings.

After the liquor has undergone the proper fermentation in these close vessels, which may be best effected in a temperature of from 40° to 60°, and which may be known by its appearing tolerably clear, and having a vinous sharpness upon the tongue, any further fermentation must be stopped by racking off the pure part into open vessels exposed for a day or two in a cool situation. After this the liquor must again be put into casks and kept in a cool place during winter. The proper time for racking may always be known by the brightness of the liquor, the discharge of the fixed air, and the appearance of a thick crust formed of fragments of the reduced pulp. The liquor should always be racked off anew, as often as a hissing noise is heard, or as it extinguishes a candle held to the bung-hole.

When a favorable vinous fermentation has been obtained, nothing more is required than to fill up the vessels every 2 or 3 weeks, to supply the waste by fermentation. On the beginning of March the liquor will be bright and pure and fit for final racking, which should be done in fair weather. When the bottles are filled they should be set by uncorked till morning, when the corks must be driven in tightly, secured by wire or twine or melted rosin, or any similar substance.

To make Devonshire Cider.

Prefer the bitter sweet apples, mixed with mild sour, in the proportion of one-third. Gather them when ripe, and lay them in heaps in the orchard. Then take them to the crushing engine, made of iron rollers at top and of stone underneath; after passing through which they are received into large tubs or sieves, and are then called pommage. They are afterwards laid on the vat in alternate layers of the pommage and clean straw, called reeds. They are then pressed, the juice running through a hair sieve. After the cider is pressed out it is put into hogsheads, where it remains for 2 or 3 days previously to fermenting. To stop the fermentation it is drawn off into a clean vessel, but if the fermentation be very strong, 2 or 3 cans of cider are put into a clean vessel, and a match of brimstone burnt in it; it is then agitated, by which the fermentation of that quantity is completely stopped. The vessel is then nearly filled, the fermentation of the whole is checked, and the cider becomes fine; but if, on the first operation, the fermentation is not checked, it is repeated till it is so, and continued from time to time till the cider is in a quiet state for drinking. Some persons, instead of deadening a small quantity with a match, as above directed, put from 1 to 2 pints of an article called *stum* (bought of the wine coopers) into each hogshead; but the system of racking as often as the fermentation appears, is generally preferred by the cider manufacturers of Devonshire, England.

About 6 sacks, or 24 bus., of apples, are used for a hogshead of 63 galls. During the process, if the weather is warm, it will be necessary to carry it on in the shade, in the open air, and by every means keep it as cool as possible.

In 9 months it will be in condition for bottling or drinking; if it continue thick, use some isinglass finings, and if at any time it ferments and threatens acidity, the cure is to rack it and leave the head and sediment.

Scotch Method.

The apples are reduced to mucilage, by beating

them in a stone trough (one of those used at pumps for watering horses) with pieces of ash-poles, used in the manner that potatoes are mashed. The press consists of a strong box, 3 feet square, and 20 inches deep, perforated on each side with small auger or gimblet holes. It is placed on a frame of wood, projecting 3 inches beyond the base of the box. A groove is cut in this projection 1¼ inches wide, and 1 inch deep, to convey the juice when pressed out of the box into a receiving pail. This operation is performed in the following manner: The box is filled alternately with strata of fresh straw and mashed fruit, in the proportion of 1 inch of straw to 2 inches of mucilage; these are piled up 1 foot higher than the top of the box; and care is taken in packing the box itself, to keep the fruit and straw about ½ inch from the sides of the box, which allows the juice to escape freely. A considerable quantity of the liquor will run off without any pressure. This must be applied gradually at first, and increased regularly towards the conclusion. A box of the above dimensions will require about 2 tons weight to render the residuum completely free from juice.

[The residuum is excellent food for pigs, and peculiarly acceptable to them.]

The necessary pressure is obtained very easily, and in a powerful manner, by the compound lever pressing upon a lid or sink made of wood, about 2 inches thick, and rendered sufficiently strong by 2 cross-bars. It is made to fit the opening of the box exactly; and as the levers force the lid down, they are occasionally slacked or taken off, and blocks of wood are placed on the top of the lid, to permit the levers to act, even after the lid has entered the box itself. Additional blocks are repeated, until the whole juice is extracted. The pressure may be increased more or less, by adding or diminishing the weight suspended at the extremity of the lever.

The liquor thus obtained is allowed to stand undisturbed 12 hours, in open vessels, to deposit sediment. The pure juice is then put into clean casks, and placed in a proper situation to ferment, the temperature being from 55° to 60°. The fermentation will commence sooner or later, depending chiefly on the temperature of the apartment where the liquor is kept; in most cases, during the first 3 or 4 days; but sometimes it will require more than a week to begin this process. If the fermentation begins early and proceeds rapidly, the liquor must be racked off, and put into fresh casks in 2 or 3 days; but if this does not take place at an early period, and proceeds slowly, 5 or 6 days may elapse before it is racked. In general, it is necessary to rack the liquor at least twice. If, notwithstanding, the fermentation continues briskly, the racking must be repeated; otherwise the vinous fermentation, by proceeding too far, may terminate in acetous fermentation, when vinegar would be the result.

In racking off the liquor it is necessary to keep it free of sediment, and the *scum* or yeast produced by the fermentation. A supply of spare liquor must be reserved to fill up the barrels occasionally, while the fermentation continues. As soon as this ceases, the barrels should be bunged up closely, and the bungs covered with rosin, to prevent the admission of air. If the cider is weak, it should remain in the cask about 9 months; if strong, 12 or 18 months is necessary before it should be bottled.

To Manage Cider and Perry.

To fine and improve the flavor of 1 hogshead, take 1 gal. of good French brandy, with ½ oz. of cochineal, 1 lb. of alum, and 3 lbs. sugar-candy; bruise them all well in a mortar, and infuse them in the brandy for a day or two; then mix the whole with the cider, and stop it close for 5 or 6 months. After which, if fine, bottle it off.

Cider or perry, when bottled in hot weather, should be left a day or two uncorked, that it may get flat; but if too flat in the cask, and soon wanted for use, put into each bottle a small lump or two of sugar-candy, 4 or 5 raisins, or a small piece of raw beef; any of which will much improve the liquor, and make it brisker.

Cider should be well corked and waxed, and packed upright in a cool place. A few bottles may always be kept in a warmer place to ripen and be ready for use.

To make Cheap Cider from Raisins.

Take 14 lbs. of raisins with the stalks; wash them out in 4 or 5 waters, till the water remains clear; then put them into a clean cask with the head out, and put 6 galls. of good water upon them; after which cover it well up, and let it stand 10 days. Then rack it off into another clean cask, which has a brass cock in it, and in 4 or 5 days' time it will be fit for bottling. When it has been in the bottles 7 or 8 days, it will be fit for use. A little coloring should be added when putting into the cask the second time. The raisins may afterwards be used for vinegar.

To make Perry.

Perry is made after the same manner as cider, only from pears, which must be quite dry. The best pears for this purpose are such as are least fit for eating, and the redder they are the better.

Observations on Cider.

From the great diversity of soil and climate in the United States, and the almost endless variety of its apples, it follows that much diversity of taste and flavor will necessarily be found in the cider that is made from them.

To make good cider the following general, but *important* rules should be attended to. They demand a little more trouble than the ordinary mode of collecting and mashing apples of all sorts, rotten and sound, sweet and sour, dirty and clean, from the tree and the soil, and the rest of the slovenly process usually employed; but in return they produce you a wholesome, high-flavored, sound, and palatable liquor, that always commands an adequate price, instead of a solution of "villainous compounds," in a poisonous and acid wash, that no man in his senses will drink.

General Rules for making Cider.

1. Always choose perfectly ripe and sound fruit.
2. Pick the apples by hand. An active boy, with a bag slung over his shoulders, will soon clear a tree. Apples that have lain any time on the soil contract an earthy taste, which will always be found in the cider.
3. After *sweating*, and before being ground, *wipe them dry*, and if any are found bruised or rotten, put them in a heap by themselves, for an inferior cider to make vinegar.
4. Always use hair-cloths instead of straws, to place between the layers of pommage. The straw when heated gives a disagreeable taste to the cider.
5. As the cider runs from the press, let it pass through a hair sieve into a large open vessel that will hold as much juice as can be expressed in one day. In a day, or sometimes less, the pumice will rise to the top, and in a short time grow very thick; when little white bubbles break through it, draw off the liquor by a spigot placed about three inches from the bottom, so that the lees may be left quietly behind.

6. The cider must be drawn off into very clean sweet casks, and closely watched. The moment the white bubbles before mentioned are perceived rising at the bung-hole, rack it again. When the fermentation is completely at an end, fill up the cask with cider, in all respects like that already contained in it, and bung it up tight; previous to which a tumbler of *sweet-oil* may be poured into the bung hole.

Sound, well made cider, that has been produced as described, and without any foreign mixtures, excepting always that of good cogniac brandy (which added to it in the proportion of 1 gal. to 30, greatly improves it), is a pleasant, cooling and useful beverage.

WINES.

American Wines.

The term wine is properly applied only to the fermented juice of the grape, but is popularly used in a more extended sense. What are termed domestic wines made from the currant, gooseberry, etc., are often supposed to be more wholesome and less intoxicating than the wine of the grape. This is an error; they are more acid than true wine, and have added to them sugar and spirits, neither of which are necessary with good grape juice. The culture of the grape and manufacture of wine have increased very rapidly in the United States of late years, and the time is not very distant when we shall be independent of foreign sources of supply.

The Vine.

The varieties of grape employed in wine-making, in the United States, are the Catawba, Delaware, Schuylkill (Cape), Isabella, and Scuppernong. In California, now so noted for its wine product, the vines are of Spanish origin. Of those named, the two first varieties are most prized. Vines require a dry, airy situation, preferably with a southern or eastern exposure.

Picking the Fruit.

The fruit should be allowed to stay on the vines until *fully* ripe. If any error is committed it should be that of allowing it to remain too long. A slight frost will not injure the grape for wine-making, but rather improve it. Remove all unripe and bad berries. In some cases the berries are detached from the stem, in others not; the latter method is most usual. All vessels and utensils used in wine-making, must be most *scrupulously clean* when used, and should be thoroughly cleansed after using. Without attention to this good wine cannot be made. Grapes should not be gathered in damp weather nor when the dew is on them.

Extracting the Juice.

The grapes are first crushed, the object being to break the skin and pulp, but not the seeds. This may be done in any of the ordinary cider-mills sold at the agricultural warehouses, or on the small scale by bruising in a mashing-tub. The juice is then expressed as directed in making cider. For extracting the juice of fruits on the small scale the ordinary clothes-wringer will be found very useful. The expressed juice is termed *must*, the remaining seeds, husks, etc., after being pressed, are put on the manure pile or used for making inferior brandy.

Fermenting the Must.

In this country the fermentation is performed in barrels; abroad vats are used. The barrels should, if new, be filled with pure water, and left to soak for 10 or 15 days; then well scalded out, and fumigated by means of a match made by dipping paper or rag into melted sulphur. When not in use they must be kept bunged, and each year they must be thoroughly cleansed or fumigated before using.

The barrels are to be filled within 5 or 6 inches of the top. The beginning of the fermentation is shown by a slight rise in temperature, this soon increases, the liquid froths, and carbonic acid gas escapes; in 2 or 3 weeks this ceases, the lees settle and the wine becomes clear. *Fermentation out of contact* of air is accomplished by having a bung fitted with a *tube* which dips under the surface of a pan of water. The gas escapes through the water, but the air cannot enter the cask. This is considered a great improvement by many. The bung should not be inserted until fermentation has begun. As soon as fermentation has ceased, fill up the cask and bung tightly. If you have not the same wine with which to fill the cask, put in enough well-washed flinty pebbles.

Racking.

The object of racking is to draw the wine from its lees, which contain various impurities, and the yeast is the fermentation. Some rack more than once, others but once. Rehfuss recommends to draw off the wine into fresh casks in December, and again in March or April, and again in the fall; after that only in the fall. Buchanan recommends one racking in March or April. It is objected to frequent racking that it injures the aroma of the wine, and renders it liable to become acid. The wine may be drawn off with the syphon or by the spigot; care being taken not to disturb the lees.

Spring Fermentation.

About the time that the vines begin to shoot the wine undergoes a second but moderate fermentation, after which it fines itself, and if kept well bunged will continue to improve by age. During the spring fermentation the bungs may be slightly loosened; otherwise the casks, if not strong, may burst, and the wine be lost. It is better kept in bottles. Wine may be bottled in a year after it is made, two years will be better. The bottles should be sealed and laid on their sides in a cool place.

Sparkling Wines.

The above directions will give a still wine of fine quality; no sugar, spirits or other addition is required. To make a sparkling wine is a matter of nicety, and requires considerable experience; and cellars, vaults and buildings especially adapted to the process. Abroad the wine is bottled during the first fermentation; although air is necessary to the beginning of fermentation, yet it will go on when once begun if air be excluded. The must continuing to ferment in the bottles, the gas generated is absorbed by the liquid under its own pressure. A very large percentage of bottles bursts.

Mr. Longworth's Process.

In the spring following the pressing of the grapes the wine is mixed with a small quantity of sugar, and put into strong bottles, the corks of which are well fastened with wire and twine. The spring fermentation is accelerated by the sugar, and the carbonic acid generated produces pressure enough to burst a considerable percentage of the bottles. At the end of a year the liquid has become clear. To get rid of the sediment the bottles are put in a rack with the necks inclining downward, and frequently shaken, the sediment deposits near and on the cork, and is blown out when the wires are cut. More sugar is added for sweetness; the bottles recorked, and in a few weeks the wine is ready for use.

Acidity of Wines.

The acidity of wine made from ripe grapes is due to cream of tartar or bitartrate of potassa. The grapes always contain a larger proportion than the wine, as much of it is deposited during fermentation, forming *Argols* of commerce. Tannic acid always present, giving, when in quantity, astringency or roughness. Citric acid is found in wine made from unripe grapes; malic and oxalic acids in those made from currants, rhubarb, etc. The cream of tartar gradually deposits as wine grows older, forming the crust or bees-wing. Hence wine of grape improves with age. Domestic wines do not deposit their acids, which have therefore to be disguised by the addition of sugar. Acetic acid is formed by the oxidation of the alcohol of wine. When considerable in quantity the wine is said to be "pricked." Moselle and Rhine wine are among the most acid, and Sherry and Port among the least so.

Sweet Wines.

Such as Malaga, are made by allowing the grapes to remain on the vine until partially dried. The must is also evaporated about one-third before fermentation. Wines, such as still Catawba, Claret, etc., which contain little or no sugar, are called *dry*.

Proportion of Alcohol in Wines.

The following gives the average proportion of absolute alcohol in 100 parts by measure: Port, Madeira, Sherry, 20; Claret, Catawba, Hock, and Champagne, 11; Domestic wines, 10 to 20; alcohol gives the *strength* or *body* to wine. It is often added to poor wines to make them keep, and to increase their intoxicating qualities.

Bottling and Corking.

Fine clear weather is best for bottling all sorts of wines, and much cleanliness is required. The first consideration, in bottling wines, is to examine and see if the wines are in a proper state. The wines should be fine and brilliant, or they will never brighten after.

The bottles must be all sound, clean and dry, with plenty of good sound corks.

The cork is to be put in with the hand, and then driven well in with a flat wooden mallet, the weight of which ought to be 1¼ lbs., but however, not to exceed 1½ lbs., for if the mallet be too light or too heavy it will not drive the cork in properly, and may break the bottle. The corks must so completely fill up the neck of each bottle as to render them air-tight, but leave a space of an inch between the wine and the neck.

When all the wine is bottled, it is to be stored in a cool cellar, and on no account on the bottles' bottoms, but on their sides and in saw-dust.

Mr. Carnell's Receipt for Red Gooseberry Wine.

Take cold soft water, 10 galls.; red gooseberries, 11 galls., and ferment. Now mix raw sugar, 16 lbs.; beet-root, sliced, 2 lbs.; and red tartar, in fine powder, 1 oz. Afterwards put in sassafras chips, 1 lb., and brandy, 1 gall., or less. This will make 18 galls.

Another.—When the weather is dry, gather gooseberries about the time they are half ripe; pick them clean, put the quantity of a cask into a convenient vessel, and bruise them with a piece of wood, taking as much care as possible to keep the seeds whole. Now having put the pulp into a canvas bag, press out all the juice; and to every gallon of the gooseberries add about 3 lbs. of fine loaf sugar; mix the whole together by stirring it with a stick, and as soon as the sugar is quite dissolved, pour it into a convenient cask, which will hold it exactly. If the quantity be about 8 or 9 galls., let it stand a fortnight; if 20 galls., 40 days, and so on in proportion taking care the place you set it in be cool. After standing the proper time, draw it off from the lees, and put it into another clean vessel of equal size, or into the same, after pouring the lees out, and making it clean; let a cask of 10 or 12 galls. stand for about 3 months, and 20 galls. for 5 months, after which it will be fit for bottling off.

Red and White Gooseberry Wine.

Take cold soft water, 3 galls ; red gooseberries, 1½ galls.; white gooseberries, 2 galls. Ferment.

Now mix raw sugar, 5 lbs.; honey, 1½ lbs.; tartar, in fine powder, 1 oz. Afterwards put in bitter almonds, 2 oz.; sweetbriar, 1 small handful; and brandy, 1 gall., or less. This will make 6 galls.

White Gooseberry or Champagne Wine.

Take cold soft water, 4½ galls.; white gooseberries, 5 galls. Ferment.

Now mix refined sugar, 6 lbs.; honey, 4 lbs.; white tartar, in fine powder, 1 oz. Put in orange and lemon-peel, 1 oz. dry, or 2 oz. fresh; and add white brandy, ½ gall. This will make 9 galls.

Gooseberry Wine of the Best Quality, resembling Champagne.

To each pint of full ripe gooseberries, mashed, add one pint of water, milk warm, in which has been dissolved one pound of single-refined sugar; stir the whole well, and cover up the tub with a blanket, to preserve the heat generated by the fermentation of the ingredients; let them remain in this vessel 3 days, stirring them twice or thrice a day; strain off the liquor through a sieve, afterwards through a coarse linen cloth; put it into the cask; it will ferment without yeast. Let the cask be kept full with some of the liquor reserved for the purpose. It will ferment for 10 days, sometimes for 3 weeks; when ceased, and only a hissing noise remains, draw off 2 or 3 bottles, according to the strength you wish it to have, from every 20 pint cask, and fill up the cask with brandy or whiskey; but brandy is preferable. To make it very good, and that it may keep well, add as much Sherry, together with ½ oz. of isinglass dissolved in water to make it quite liquid; stir the whole well. Bung the cask up, and surround the bung with clay; the closer it is bunged the better; a fortnight after, if it be clear at top, taste it; if not sweet enough, add more sugar; 22 lbs. is the just quantity in all for 20 pints of wine; leave the wine 6 months in the cask; but after being quite fine, the sooner it is bottled the more it will sparkle and resemble Champagne. The process should be carried on in a place where the heat is between 48° and 56° Fahr. Currant wine may be made in the same manner.

Gooseberry and Currant Wines.

The following method of making superior gooseberry and currant wines is recommended in a French work: For currant wine, 8 lbs. of honey are dissolved in 15 galls. of boiling water, to which, when clarified, is added the juice of 8 lbs. of red or white currants. It is then fermented for 24 hours, and 2 lbs. of sugar to every 2 galls. of water are added. The preparation is afterwards clarified with the whites of eggs and cream of tartar. For gooseberry wine, the fruit is gathered dry when about half ripe, and then pounded in a mortar. The juice, when properly strained through a canvas bag, is mixed with sugar, in the proportion of 3 lbs. to every 2 galls. of juice. It is then left in a quiet state for 15 days, at the expiration of which it is carefully poured off, and left to ferment for 3 months when the quantity is under 15 galls., and for 5 months when double that quantity. It is then bottled, and soon becomes fit for drinking.

Another.—Take cold soft water, 5½ galls.; gooseberries and currants, 4 galls. Ferment. Then add, raw sugar, 12½ lbs.; tartar, in fine powder, 1 oz.; ginger, in powder, 3 oz.; sweet marjoram, ½ a handful; whiskey, 1 qt. This will make 9 galls.

Red Currant Wine.

Take cold soft water, 11 galls.; red currants, 8 galls.; raspberries, 1 qt. Ferment. Mix, raw sugar, 20 lbs.; beet-root, sliced, 2 lbs.; and red tartar, in fine powder, 3 oz. Put in 1 nutmeg, in fine powder; add brandy, 1 gall. This will make 18 galls.

Another.—Put 5 qts. of currants and 1 pint of raspberries to every 2 galls. of water; let them soak a night; then squeeze and break them well. Next day rub them well through a fine sieve till the juice is expressed, washing the skins with some of the water; then, to every gallon, put 4 lbs. of the best sugar, put it into your barrel, and set the bung lightly in. In 2 or 3 days add a bottle of good Cogniac brandy to every 4 galls.; bung it close, but leave out the spigot for a few days. It is very good in 3 years, better in 4.

Another.—Boil 4 galls. of spring water, and stir into it 8 lbs. of honey; when thoroughly dissolved, take it off the fire; then stir it well in order to raise the scum, which take clean off, and cool the liquor.

When thus prepared, press out the same quantity of the juice of red currants moderately ripe, which being well strained, mix well with the water and honey, then put them into a cask or a large earthen vessel, and let them stand to ferment for 24 hours; then to every gallon add 2 lbs. of fine sugar, stir them well to raise the scum, and when well settled take it off, and add ½ an oz. of cream of tartar, with the whites of 2 or 3 eggs, to refine it. When the wine is well settled and clear draw it off into a small vessel, or bottle it up, keeping it in a cool place.

Of white currants a wine after the same manner may be made, that will equal in strength and pleasantness many sorts of white wine; but as for the black or Dutch currants, they are seldom used, except for the preparation of medicinal wines.

Another.—Gather the currants in dry weather, put them into a pan and bruise them with a wooden pestle; let them stand about 20 hours, after which strain through a sieve; add 3 lbs. of fine powdered sugar to each 4 quarts of the liquor, and after shaking it well fill the vessel, and put a quart of good brandy to every 7 gallons. In 4 weeks, if it does not prove quite clear, draw it off into another vessel, and let it stand previous to bottling it off about 10 days.

Red and White Currant Wine.

Take of cold soft water, 12 galls.; white currants, 4 galls.; red currants, 3 galls. Ferment. Mix, raw sugar, 25 lbs.; white tartar, in fine powder, 3 oz. Put in sweet-briar leaves, 1 handful; lavender leaves, 1 handful; then add spirits, 2 qts. or more. This will make 18 galls.

Dutch Currant Wine.

Take of cold soft water, 9 galls.; red currants, 10 galls. Ferment. Mix, raw sugar, 10 lbs.; beet-root, sliced, 2 lbs.; red tartar, in fine powder, 2 oz. Put in bitter almonds, 1 oz.; ginger, in powder, 2 oz.; then add brandy, 1 qt. This will make 18 galls.

Dutch Red Currant Wine.

Take of cold soft water, 11 galls.; red currants, 8 galls. Ferment. Mix, raw sugar, 12 lbs.; red tartar, in fine powder, 2 oz. Put in coriander seed, bruised, 2 oz.; then add whiskey, 2 qts. This will make 18 galls.

Mixed Berries from a Small Garden.

Take of cold soft water, 11 galls.; fruit, 8 galls. Ferment. Mix, treacle, 14 or 16 lbs.; tartar, in powder, 1 oz. Put in ginger, in powder, 4 oz.; sweet herbs, 2 handfuls; then add spirits, 1 or 2 qts. This will make 18 galls.

To make Compound Wine.

An excellent family wine may be made of equal parts of red, white and black currants, ripe cherries, and raspberries, well bruised, and mixed with soft water, in the proportion of 4 lbs. of fruit to 1 gall. of water. When strained and pressed, 3 lbs. of moist sugar are to be added to each gall. of liquid. After standing open for 3 days, during which it is to be stirred frequently, it is to be put into a barrel, and left for a fortnight to work, when a ninth part of brandy is to be added, and the whole bunged down. In a few months it will be a most excellent wine.

Other Mixed Fruits of the Berry kind.

Take of cold soft water, 2 galls.; fruit, 18 galls. Ferment. Honey, 6 lbs.; tartar, in fine powder, 2 oz. Put in peach leaves, 6 handfuls; then add brandy, 1 gall. This will make 18 galls.

White Currant Wine.

Take of cold soft water, 9 galls.; white currants, 9 galls.; white gooseberries, 1 gall. Ferment. Mix, refined sugar, 25 lbs.; white tartar, in powder, 1 oz.; clary seed, bruised, 2 oz.; or clary flowers or sorrel flowers, 4 handfuls; then add white brandy, 1 gall. This will make 18 galls.

Another.—Take of cold soft water, 10 galls.; white currants, 10 galls. Ferment. Mix, refined sugar, 25 lbs.; white tartar, in fine powder, 1 oz.; then add bitter almonds, 2 oz.; and white brandy, 1 gall. This will make 18 galls.

Black Currant Wine.

Take of cold soft water, 10 galls.; black currants, 6 galls.; strawberries, 3 galls. Ferment. Mix, raw sugar, 25 lbs.; red tartar, in fine powder, 6 oz.; orange-thyme, 2 handfuls; then add brandy, 2 or 3 qts. This will make 18 galls.

Another.—Take of cold soft water, 12 galls.; black currants, 5 galls.; white or red currants, or both, 3 galls. Ferment. Mix, raw sugar, 30 lbs. or less; red tartar, in fine powder, 5 oz.; ginger, in powder, 5 oz.; then add brandy, 1 gall. or less. This will make 18 galls.

Another, very fine.—To every 3 qts. of juice add as much of cold water, and to every 3 qts. of the mixture add 3 lbs. of good, pure sugar. Put it into a cask, reserving some to fill up. Set the cask in a warm, dry room, and it will ferment of itself. When this is over skim off the refuse, and fill up with what you have reserved for this purpose. When it has done working, add 3 qts. of brandy to 40 qts. of the wine. Bung it up close for 10 months, then bottle it. The thick part may be separated by straining, and the percolating liquor be bottled also. Keep it for 12 months.

Strawberry Wine.

Take of cold soft water, 7 galls.; cider, 6 galls.; strawberries, 6 galls. Ferment. Mix, raw sugar, 16 lbs.; red tartar, in fine powder, 3 oz.; the peel and juice of 2 lemons; then add brandy, 2 or 3 qts. This will make 18 galls.

Another.— Take of cold soft water, 10 galls.; strawberries, 9 galls. Ferment. Mix, raw sugar, 25 lbs.; red tartar, in fine powder, 3 oz.; 2 lemons and 2 oranges, peel and juice; then add brandy, 1 gall. This will make 18 galls.

Raspberry Wine.

Take of cold soft water, 6 galls.; cider, 4 galls.; raspberries, 6 galls.; any other fruit, 3 galls. Ferment. Mix, raw sugar, 18 or 20 lbs.; red tartar, in fine powder, 3 oz.; orange and lemon-peel, 2 oz. dry, or 4 oz. fresh; then add brandy, 3 qts. This will make 18 galls.

Another. — Gather the raspberries when ripe, husk them and bruise them; then strain them through a bag into jars or other vessels. Boil the juice, and to every gall. put 1½ lbs. of lump sugar. Now add whites of eggs, and let the whole boil for 15 minutes, skimming it as the froth rises. When cool and settled, decant the liquor into a cask, adding yeast to make it ferment. When this has taken place, add 1 pint of white wine, or ½ a pint of proof spirit to each gall. contained in the cask, and hang a bag in it containing 1 oz. of bruised mace. In 3 months, if kept in a cool place, it will be very excellent and delicious wine.

Mulberry Wine.

On a dry day gather mulberries, when they are just changed from redness to a shining black; spread them thinly on a fine cloth, or on a floor or table, for 24 hours, and then press them. Boil a gall. of water with each gall. of juice; putting to every gall. of water 1 oz. of cinnamon bark and 6 oz. of sugar candy finely powdered. Skim and strain the water when it is taken off and settled, and put to it the mulberry-juice. Now add to every gall. of the mixture a pint of white or Rhenish wine. Let the whole stand in a cask to ferment for 5 or 6 days. When settled, draw it off into bottles and keep it cool.

Elderberry Wine.

Take of cold soft water, 16 galls.; Malaga raisins, 50 lbs.; elderberries, 4 galls.; red tartar in fine powder, 4 oz. Mix ginger in powder, 5 oz.; cinnamon, cloves, and mace, of each 2 oz.; 3 oranges or lemons, peel and juice; then add 1 gall. of brandy. This will make 18 galls.

Another.—In making elder-juice let the berries be fully ripe, and all the stalks clean picked from them; then, have a press ready for drawing off all the juice, and 4 hair-cloths, somewhat broader than the press. Lay one layer above another, having a hair-cloth betwixt every layer, which must be laid very thin, and pressed a little at first, and then more till the press be drawn as close as possible. Now take out the berries, and press all the rest in the like manner; then take the pressed berries, break out all the lumps, put them into an open-headed vessel, and add as much liquor as will just cover them. Let them infuse so for 7 or 8 days; then put the best juice into a cask proper for it to be kept in, and add 1 gall. of malt spirits, not rectified, to every 20 galls. of elder-juice, which will effectually preserve it from becoming sour for two years at least.

Another.—Pick the berries when quite ripe, put them into a stone jar, and set them in an oven, or in a kettle of boiling water, till the jar is hot through; then take them out, and strain them through a coarse sieve. Squeeze the berries and put the juice into a clean kettle. To every quart of juice put 1 lb. of fine sugar; let it boil and skim it well. When clear and fine, pour it into a cask. To every 10 galls. of wine add 1 oz. of isinglass dissolved in cider, and 6 whole eggs. Close it up, let it stand 6 months, and then bottle it.

To make an Imitation of Cyprus Wine.

To 10 galls. of water put 10 qts. of the juice of white elderberries, pressed gently from the berries by the hand and passed through a sieve, without bruising the seeds; add to every gallon of liquor 3 lbs. of sugar, and to the whole quantity 2 oz. of ginger sliced, and 1 oz. of cloves. Boil this nearly an hour, taking off the scum as it rises, and pour the whole to cool, in an open tub, and work it with ale yeast, spread upon a toast of bread for 3 days. Then turn it into a vessel that will just hold it, adding about 1½ lbs. of bruised raisins, to lie in the liquor till drawn off, which should not be done till the wine is fine.

To make Elder-flower Wine, or English Frontignac.

Boil 18 lbs. of white powdered sugar in 6 galls. of water and 2 whites of eggs well beaten; skim it, and put in a quarter of a peck of elder-flowers; do not keep them on the fire. When cool stir it, and put in 6 spoonfuls of lemon juice, 4 or 5 of yeast, and beat well into the liquor; stir it well every day; put 6 lbs. of the best raisins, stoned, into the cask, and tun the wine. Stop it close, and bottle in 6 months. When well kept, this wine will pass very well for Frontignac.

Another.—To 6 galls. of spring-water put 6 lbs. of sun raisins cut small, and 12 lbs. of fine sugar. Boil the whole together for about an hour and a half. When the liquor is cold put half a peck of ripe elder-flowers in, with about a gill of lemon-juice, and half the quantity of ale yeast. Cover it up and, after standing 3 days, strain it off. Now pour it into a cask that is quite clean, and that will hold it with ease. When this is done, put a quart of Rhenish wine to every gallon; let the bung be slightly put in for 12 or 14 days, then stop it down fast, and put it in a cool, dry place for 4 or 5 months, till it be quite settled and fine; then bottle it off.

Imitation of Port Wine.

Take 6 galls. of good cider, 1¼ galls. of Port wine, 1½ galls. of the juice of elder-berries, 3 qts. of brandy, 1½ oz. of cochineal. This will produce 9½ galls.

Bruise the cochineal very fine, and put it with the brandy into a stone bottle; let it remain at least a fortnight, shaking it well once or twice every day. At the end of that time procure the cider, and put 5 galls. into a 9 gallon cask; add to it the elder-juice and Port wine, then the brandy and cochineal. Take the remaining gallon of cider to rinse out the bottle that contained the brandy; and, lastly, pour it into the cask, and bung it down very close, and in 6 weeks it will be ready for bottling.

It is, however, sometimes not quite so fine as could be wished: in that case add 2 oz. of isinglass, and let it remain a fortnight or 3 weeks longer, when it will be perfectly bright. It would not be amiss, perhaps, if the quantity of isinglass mentioned was added to the wine before it was bunged down; it will tend very considerably to improve the body of the wine. If it should not appear sufficiently rough flavored, add 1 oz. or 1½ oz. of roche-alum, which will, in most cases, impart a sufficient astringency.

After it is bottled it must be packed in as cool a place as possible. It will be fit for using in a few months, but if kept longer it will be greatly improved.

Whortleberry or Bilberry Wine.

Take of cold soft water 6 galls., cider 6 galls., berries 8 galls.; ferment. Mix raw sugar 20 lbs, tartar in fine powder 4 oz.; add ginger in powder 4 oz., lavender and rosemary leaves 2 handfuls, rum or British spirits 1 gall. This will make 18 galls.

Birch Wine.

The season for obtaining the liquor from birch-trees is in the latter end of February, or the beginning of March, before the leaves shoot out, and as the sap begins to rise; if the time is delayed the juice will grow too thick to be drawn out. It should be as thin and clear as possible. The method of procuring the juice is by boring holes in the trunk of the tree and fixing faucets of elder; but care should be taken not to tap it in too many places at once, for fear of injuring the tree. If the tree is large it may be bored in 5 or 6 places at once, and bottles are to be placed under the aperture for the sap to flow into. When 4 or 5 galls. have been extracted from different trees, cork the bottles very close, and wax them till the wine is to be made, which should be as soon as possible after the sap has been obtained. Boil the sap, and put 4 lbs. of loaf sugar to every gallon; also the peel of a lemon cut thin; then boil it again for nearly an hour, skimming it all the time. Now pour it into a tub and, as soon as it is almost cold, work it with a toast spread with yeast, and let it stand 5 or 6 days, stirring it twice or 3 times each day. Into a cask that will contain it put a lighted brimstone match, stop it up till the match is burnt out, and then pour the wine into it, putting the bung lightly in, till it has done working. Bung it very close for about 3 months, and then bottle it. It will be good in a week after it is put into the bottles.

Another.—Birch wine may be made with raisins in the following manner: To a hogshead of birch-water, take 400 Malaga raisins; pick them clean from the stalks and cut them small. Then boil the birch liquor for an hour at least, skim it well, and let it stand till it is no warmer than milk. Then put in the raisins and let it stand close covered, stirring it well 4 or 5 times every day. Boil all the stalks in a gallon or two of birch liquor, which, added to the other when almost cold, will give it an agreeable roughness. Let it stand 10 days, then put it in a cool cellar, and when it has done hissing in the vessel, stop it up close. It must stand at least 9 months before it is bottled.

Blackberry Wine.

Having procured berries that are fully ripe, put them into a large vessel of wood or stone with a cock in it, and pour upon them as much boiling water as will cover them. As soon as the heat will permit the hand to be put into the vessel, bruise them well till all the berries are broken. Then let them stand covered till the berries begin to rise towards the top, which they usually do in 3 or 4 days. Then draw off the clear into another vessel, and add to every 10 quarts of this liquor, 1 lb. of sugar. Stir it well and let it stand to work a week or 10 days in another vessel like the first. Then draw it off at the cock through a jelly-bag into a large vessel. Take 4 oz. of isinglass and lay it to steep 12 hours in a pint of white wine. The next morning boil it upon a slow fire till it is all dissolved. Then take 1 gallon of blackberry-juice, put it in the dissolved isinglass, give them a boil together, and pour all into the vessel. Let it stand a few days to purge and settle, then draw it off and keep it in a cool place.

Juniper-berry Wine.

Take of cold soft water, 18 galls., Malaga or Smyrna raisins, 35 lbs. juniper-berries, 9 quarts, red tartar, 4 oz., wormwood and sweet marjoram, each 2 handfuls, whiskey, 2 quarts or more. Ferment for 10 or 12 days. This will make 18 galls.

To make Damson Wine.

Take of cold soft water 11 galls., damsons, 8 galls. Ferment. Mix raw sugar, 30 lbs., red tartar, in fine powder, 6 oz. Add brandy, 1 gall. This will make 18 galls.

"When the *must*," says Mr. Carnell, "has fermented 2 days, (during which time it should be stirred up 2 or 3 times) take out of the vat about 2 or 3 quarts of the stones and break them and the kernels, and then return them into the vat again."

Another Method.

Take a considerable quantity of damsons and common plums inclining to ripeness; slit them in halves so that the stones may be taken out, then mash them gently and add a little water and honey. Add to every gallon of the pulp 1 gall. of spring-water, with a few bay-leaves and cloves; boil the mixture, and add as much sugar as will sweeten it; skim off the froth and let it cool. Now press the fruit, squeezing out the liquid part, strain all through a fine strainer, and put the water and juice together in a cask. Having allowed the whole to stand and ferment for 3 or 4 days, fine it with white sugar, flour, and white of eggs; draw it off into bottles, then cork it well. In 12 days it will be ripe, and will taste like weak Port, having the flavor of Canary.

Another.—Gather the damsons on a dry day, weigh them and then bruise them. Put them into a cask that has a cock in it, and to every 8 lbs. of fruit add 1 gall. of water. Boil the water, skim it and put it scalding hot to the fruit. Let it stand 2 days, then draw it off and put it into a vessel, and to every gallon of liquor put 2½ lbs. of fine sugar. Fill up the vessel and stop it close, and the longer it stands the better. Keep it for 12 months in the vessel, and then bottle, putting a lump of sugar into every bottle. The small damson is the best for this purpose.

Cherry Wine.

Take of soft cold water, 10 galls., cherries, 10 galls. Ferment. Mix raw sugar, 30 lbs., red tartar, in fine powder, 3 oz. Add brandy, 2 or 3 quarts. This will make 18 galls.

Two days after the cherries have been in the vat, take out about 3 quarts of the cherry-stones, break them and the kernels, and return them into the vat again.

Another.—Take cherries nearly ripe, of any red sort, clear them of the stalks and stones, then put them into a glazed earthen vessel and squeeze them to a pulp. Let them remain in this state for 12 hours to ferment, then put them into a linen cloth not too fine and press out the juice with a pressing-board, or any other convenient instrument. Now let the liquor stand till the scum rises, and with a ladle or skimmer take it clean off; then pour the clear part, by inclination, into a cask, where to each gallon put 1 lb. of the best loaf sugar, and let it ferment for 7 or 8 days. Draw it off, when clear, into lesser casks or bottles; keep it cool as other wines, and in 10 or 12 days it will be ripe.

To make Morella Wine.

Cleanse from the stalks 60 lbs. of Morella cherries, and bruise them so that the stones shall be broken. Now press out the juice and mix it with 6 galls. of Sherry wine, and 4 galls. of warm water. Having grossly powdered separate ounces of nutmeg, cinnamon and mace, hang them separately in small bags in the cask containing the mixture. Bung it down and in a few weeks it will become a deliciously flavored wine.

To make Peach Wine.

Take of cold soft water, 18 galls., refined sugar, 25 lbs., honey, 6 lbs., white tartar, in fine powder, 2 oz., peaches, 60 or 80 in number. Ferment. Then add 2 galls. of brandy. This will make 18 galls.

The *first division* is to be put into the vat, and the day after, *before* the peaches are put in, take the stones from them, break them and the kernels, then put them and the pulp into the vat and proceed with the general process.

Peach and Apricot Wine.

Take peaches, nectarines, etc.; pare them and take the stones out; then slice them thin and pour over them from 1 to 2 galls. of water and a quart of white wine. Place the whole on a fire to simmer gently for a considerable time, till the sliced fruit becomes soft; pour off the liquid part into another vessel containing more peaches that have been sliced but not heated; let them stand for 12 hours, then pour out the liquid part and press what remains through a fine hair bag. Let the whole be now put into a cask to ferment; add of loaf sugar 1½ lbs. to each gallon. Boil well 1 oz. of beaten cloves in a quart of white wine and add it to the above.

Apricot wine may be made by only bruising the fruit and pouring the hot liquor over it. This wine does not require so much sweetening. To give it a curious flavor, add 1 oz. of mace and ½ an oz. of nutmegs in 1 qt. of white wine; and when the wine is fermenting pour the liquid in hot. In about 20 days, or a month, these wines will be fit for bottling.

Lemon Wine.

Pare off the rinds of 6 large lemons, cut them, and squeeze out the juice. Steep the rinds in the juice, and put to it 1 qt. of brandy. Let it stand 3 days in an earthen pot close stopped; then squeeze 6 more, and mix with it 2 qts. of spring-water, and as much sugar as will sweeten the whole. Boil the water, lemons and sugar together, and let it stand till it is cool. Then add 1 qt. of white wine, and the other lemons and brandy; mix them together, and run it through a flannel bag into some vessel. Let it stand 3 months and then bottle it off. Cork the bottles well; keep it cool, and it will be fit to drink in a month or 6 weeks.

Another.—Pare 5 dozen of lemons very thin, put the peels into 5 qts. of French brandy, and let them stand 14 days. Then make the juice into a syrup with 3 lbs. of single-refined sugar, and when the peels are ready boil 15 galls. of water with 40 lbs. of single-refined sugar for ½ an hour. Then put it into a tub, and when cool add to it 1 spoonful of yeast, and let it work 2 days. Then tun it, and put in the brandy, peels and syrup. Stir them all together, and close up the cask. Let it stand 3 months, then bottle it, and it will be as pale and as fine as any citron-water.

Apple White Wine.

Take of cold soft water, 2 galls.; apples, well bruised, 3 bushels; honey, 10 lbs.; white tartar, 2 oz.; 1 nutmeg, in powder; rum, 3 qts. This will make 18 galls.

To make Apple Wine.

To every gall. of apple-juice, immediately as it comes from the press, add 2 lbs. of common loaf sugar; boil it as long as any scum rises, then strain it through a sieve, and let it cool; add some good yeast, and stir it well; let it work in the tub for 2 or 3 weeks, or till the head begins to flatten, then skim off the head, draw it clear off, and tun it. When made a year rack it off, and fine it with isinglass; then add ¼ a pt. of the best rectified spirit of wine, or a pt. of French brandy, to every 8 galls.

Apple Red Wine.

Take of cold soft water, 2 galls.; apples, well bruised, 3 bushels. Ferment. Mix, raw sugar, 15 lbs.; beet root, sliced, 4 lbs.; red tartar, in fine powder, 3 oz.; then add ginger, in powder, 3 oz.; rosemary and lavender leaves, of each 2 handfuls; whiskey, 2 quarts. This will make 18 galls.

To make Quince Wine.

Gather the quinces when pretty ripe, on a dry day, rub off the down with a linen cloth, then lay them in hay or straw for 10 days to *perspire*. Now cut them in quarters, take out the cores and bruise them well in a mashing-tub with a wooden pestle. Squeeze out the liquid part by pressing them in a hair bag by degrees, in a cider press; strain this liquor through a fine sieve, then warm it gently over a fire and skim it, but do not suffer it to boil. Now sprinkle into it some loaf sugar reduced to powder; then in a gall. of water and a qt. of white wine boil 12 or 14 large quinces, thinly sliced; add 2 lbs. of fine sugar, and then strain off the liquid part, and mingle it with the natural juice of the quinces; put this into a cask (not to fill it) and mix them well together; then let it stand to settle; put in 2 or 3 whites of eggs, then draw it off. If it be not sweet enough, add more sugar, and a qt. of the best Malmsey. To make it still better boil ¼ of a lb. of stoned raisins, and ½ an oz. of cinnamon bark in a qt. of the liquor, to the consumption of a third part, and straining it, put it into the cask when the wine is fermenting.

Another.—Take 20 large quinces, gathered when they are dry and full ripe. Wipe them clean with a coarse cloth, and grate them with a large grater or rasp as near the cores as possible; but do not touch the cores. Boil a gall. of spring-water, throw in the quinces, and let them boil softly about ¼ of an hour. Then strain them well into an earthen pan, on 2 lbs. of double-refined sugar. Pare the peel of 2 large lemons, throw them in, and squeeze the juice through a sieve. Stir it about till it is very cool, and then toast a thin bit of bread very brown, rub a little yeast on it, and let the whole stand close-covered 24 hours. Take out the toast and lemon, put the wine in a cask, keep it 3 months, and then bottle it. If a 20-gallon cask is wanted, let it stand 6 months before bottling it; and remember, when straining the quinces, to wring them hard in a coarse cloth.

Orange Wine.

Put 12 lbs. of powdered sugar, with the whites of 8 or 10 eggs well beaten, into 6 galls. of spring-water; boil them ¾ of an hour; when cold, put into it 6 spoonfuls of yeast and the juice of 12 lemons, which being pared, must stand with 2 lbs. of white sugar in a tankard, and in the morning skim off the top, and then put it into the water; add the juice and rinds of 50 oranges, but not the white or pithy parts of the rinds; let it work all together 2 days and 2 nights; then add

2 qts. of Rhenish or white wine, and put it into the vessel.

Another.—To 6 galls. of water put 15 lbs. of soft sugar; before it boils, add the whites of 6 eggs well beaten, and take off the scum as it rises; boil it ½ an hour; when cool add the juice of 50 oranges, and ¾ of the peels cut very thin, and immerse a toast covered with yeast. In a month after it has been in the cask, add a pt. of brandy and 2 qts. of Rhenish wine; it will be fit to bottle in 3 or 4 months, but it should remain in bottle for 12 months before it is drunk.

To make Parsnip Wine.

To 12 lbs. of parsnips, cut in slices, add 4 galls. of water; boil them till they become quite soft. Squeeze the liquor well out of them, run it through a sieve, and add to every gall. 3 lbs. of loaf sugar. Boil the whole three quarters of an hour, and when it is nearly cold add a little yeast. Let it stand for 10 days in a tub, stirring it every day from the bottom; then put it into a cask for 12 months; as it works over fill it up every day.

White Mead Wine.

Take of cold soft water 17 galls., white currants 6 qts. Ferment. Mix honey 30 lbs., white tartar in powder 3 oz. Add balm and sweetbriar, each 2 handfuls, white brandy 1 gall. This will make 18 galls.

Red Mead, or Metheglin Wine.

Take of cold water 17 galls., red currants 6 qts., black currants 2 qts. Ferment. Mix, honey 25 lbs. beet root sliced 1 lb., red tartar in fine powder 4 oz. Add cinnamon in powder 2 oz., brandy 1 gall. This will make 18 galls.

Another.—Fermented mead is made in the proportion of 1 lb. of honey to 3 pints of water; or, by boiling over a moderate fire, to two-thirds of the quantity, three parts water and one part honey. The liquor is then skimmed and casked, care being taken to keep the cask full while fermenting. During the fermenting process the cask is left unstopped and exposed to the sun, or in a warm room, until the working ceases. The cask is then bunged, and a few months in the cellar renders it pleasant, by the addition of cut raisins, or other fruits, boiled after the rate of ½ lb. of raisins to 6 lbs. of honey, with a toasted crust of bread; 1 oz. of salt of tartar in a glass of brandy being added to the liquor when casked, to which some add 5 or 6 drops of the essence of cinnamon; others, pieces of lemon-peel with various syrups.

Walnut Mead Wine.

To every gallon of water put 3½ lbs. of honey, and boil them together three-quarters of an hour. Then to every gallon of liquor put about 2 dozen of walnut leaves, pour the boiling liquor upon them and let them stand all night. Then take out the leaves, put in a spoonful of yeast, and let it work for 2 or 3 days. Then make it up, and after it has stood for 3 months bottle it.

To make American Honey Wine.

Put a quantity of the comb from which honey has been drained in a tub, and add a barrel of cider immediately from the press; this mixture stir and leave for one night. It is then strained before fermentation, and honey added until the specific gravity of the liquor is sufficient to bear an egg. It is then put into a barrel, and after the fermentation is commenced the cask is filled every day for 3 or 4 days, that the froth may work out of the bung-hole. When the fermentation moderates put the bung in loosely, lest stopping it tight might cause the cask to burst. At the end of 5 or 6 weeks the liquor is to be drawn off into a tub, and the whites of 8 eggs, well beaten up with a pint of clean sand, are to be put into it; then add 1 gall. of cider spirits, and after mixing the whole together, return it into the cask, which is to be well cleaned, bunged tight, and placed in a proper situation for racking off when fine. In the month of April following draw it off into kegs for use, and it will be equal to almost any foreign wine.

Cowslip Red Wine.

Take of cold soft water 18 galls.; Smyrna raisins 40 lbs. Ferment. Mixed beet-root, sliced, 3 lbs.; red tartar, in fine powder, 2 oz. Add cowslip-flowers, 14 lbs.; cloves and mace, in powder 1 oz. brandy, 1 gall. This will make 18 galls.

Cowslip White Wine.

Take of cold soft water, 18 galls.; Malaga raisins, 35 lbs.: white tartar, in fine powder, 2 oz. Ferment. Mix cowslip-flowers, 16 lbs. Add white brandy, 1 gall. This will make 18 galls.

Cowslip Mead.

Is made in this manner: To 15 galls. of water put 30 lbs. of honey, and boil it till 1 gall. be wasted. Skim it, take it off the fire, and have ready 16 lemons cut in halves. Take 1 gall. of the liquor and put it to the lemons. Put the rest of the liquor into a tub with 7 pecks of cowslips, and let them stand all night. Then put in the liquor with the lemons 8 spoonfuls of new yeast and a handful of sweetbriar. Stir them all well together, and let it work 3 or 4 days. Then strain it, put into the cask, and after it has stood 6 months bottle it off.

Cider White Wine.

Take of cold soft water, 2 qts.; cider, 9 galls.; honey, 8 lbs.; white tartar, in fine powder, 2 oz. Ferment. Mix cinnamon, cloves, and mace, 2 oz. Add rum, ½ gall. This will make 9 galls.

Cider Red Wine.

Take of cold soft water, 3 galls.; cider, 16 galls.; honey, 10 lbs. Ferment. Add raw sugar, 4 lbs.; beet-root, sliced, 4 lbs.; red tartar, in fine powder, 6 oz. Mix sweet marjoram and sweetbriar, 3 handfuls; rum. 1 gall. This will make 18 galls.

Cider Wine.

Take of cold soft water, 4 galls.; cider, 15 galls.; honey, 12 lbs.; tartar, in fine powder, 2 oz. Ferment. Mix ginger, in powder, 6 oz.; sage and mint, 2 handfuls. Add whiskey, 1 gall. This will make 18 galls.

To make Raisin Wine equal to Sherry.

Let the raisins be well washed and picked from the stalks; to every pound thus prepared and chopped, add 1 qt. of water which has been boiled and has stood till it is cold. Let the whole stand in the vessel for a month, being frequently stirred. Now let the raisins be taken from the cask, and let the liquor be closely stopped in the vessel. In the course of a month let it be racked into another vessel, leaving all the sediment behind, which must be repeated till it becomes fine, when add to every 10 galls. 6 lbs. of fine sugar, and 1 doz. of Seville oranges the rinds being pared very thin, and infused in 2 qts of brandy, which should be added to the liquor at its last racking. Let the whole stand 3 months in the cask, when it will be fit for bottling; it should remain in the bottle for a twelve-month.

To give it the flavor of Madeira, when it is in the cask, put in a couple of green citrons, and let them remain till the wine is bottled.

Another Raisin Wine.

Put 200 weight of raisins, with the stalks, into a hogshead, and fill it almost with spring-water;

let them steep for about 12 days, frequently stirring, and after pouring off the juice dress the raisins and mash them. The whole should then be put together into a very clean vessel that will exactly contain it. It will hiss for some time, during which it should not be stirred; but when the noise ceases it must be stopped close and stand for about 6 or 7 months, and then, if it prove fine and clear, rack it off into another vessel of the same size. Stop it up, and let it remain for 12 or 14 weeks longer, then bottle it off. If it should not prove clear fine it down with 3 oz. of isinglass, and ¼ lb. of sugar-candy dissolved in some of the wine.

Ginger Wine, excellent.

Put into a very nice boiler 10 galls. of water, 15 lbs. of lump sugar, with the whites of 6 or 8 eggs, well beaten and strained; mix all well while cold; when the liquor boils skim it, put in ½ a lb. of common white ginger, bruised, and boil it 20 minutes. Have ready the rinds (cut *very* thin) of 7 lemons, and pour the hot liquor on them; when cool put it into your cask, with 2 spoonfuls of yeast; put a quart of the warm liquor to 2 oz. isinglass *shavings*, *whisk* it well 3 or 4 times, and put all into the barrel. Next day stop it up, in 3 weeks bottle it, and in 3 months it will be a delicious and safe liquor.

Another.—Take of cold soft water, 19 galls.; Malaga raisins, 50 lbs.; white tartar, in powder, 4 oz. Ferment. Mix ginger, in powder or bruised 20 oz.; 18 lemons, peel and juice; add brandy, 2 qts. or more. This will make 18 galls.

Another.—Take 20 qts. of water; 5 lbs. of sugar; 3 oz. of white ginger; 1 oz. of stick liquorice. Boil them well together; when it is cold put a little new yeast upon it, but not too much; then put it into the barrel for 10 days, and after that bottle it putting a lump of white sugar into every bottle.

Another.—To 7 galls. of water put 19 lbs. of clayed sugar, and boil it for ½ an hour, taking off the scum as it rises; then take a small quantity of the liquor and add to it 9 oz. of the best ginger bruised. Now put it all together, and when nearly cold, chop 9 lbs. of raisins very small, and put them into an 8 gall. cask (beer measure), with 1 oz. of isinglass. Slice 4 lemons into the cask, taking out all the seeds, and yeast. Leave it unstopped for 3 weeks, and in about 3 months it will be fit for bottling.

There will be 1 gall. of the sugar and water more than the cask will hold at first; this must be kept to fill up as the liquor works off, as it is necessary that the cask should be kept full till it has done working. The raisins should be ⅔ Malaga, and ⅓ Muscadel. Spring and autumn are the best seasons for making this wine.

To make Koumiss, a Tartar Wine.

Take of fresh mare's milk any quantity; add to it ⅙ part of water, and pour the mixture into a wooden vessel. Use as a ferment ⅛ part of skimmed milk; but at any future preparation a small portion of old koumiss will answer better. Cover the vessel with a thick cloth, and set it in a place of moderate warmth; leaving it at rest for 24 hours; at the end of which time the milk will become sour, and a thick substance will be gathered on its top. Now, with a churn staff, beat it till the thick substance above-mentioned be blended intimately with the subjacent fluid. In this situation leave it at rest for 24 hours more; after which pour it into a higher and narrower vessel, resembling a churn, where the agitation must be repeated as before, till the liquor appears to be perfectly homogeneous. In this state it is called koumiss; of which the taste ought to be a pleasant mixture of sweet and sour. Agitation must be employed every time before it is used. Sometimes aromatic herbs, as Angelica, are infused in the liquor during fermentation.

To make Rhubarb Wine.

Take of sliced rhubarb, 2½ oz.; lesser cardamom seeds, bruised and husked, ½ oz.; saffron, 2 drs.; Spanish white wine, 2 pints; proof spirit, ½ pint. Digest for 10 days and strain. This is a warm, cordial, laxative medicine. It is used chiefly in weakness of the stomach and bowels, and some kinds of looseness. It may be given in doses of from ½ spoonful to 3 or 4 spoonfuls or more, according to the circumstances of the disorder and the strength of the patient.

To make Sage Wine.

Boil 26 quarts of spring-water ¼ of an hour, and when it is blood warm put 25 lbs. of Malaga raisins picked, rubbed and shred, into it, with almost ½ bushel of red sage shred, and a small pitcher of ale yeast; stir all well together and let it stand in a tub covered warm 6 or 7 days, stirring it once a day; then strain it off and put it in a runlet. Let it work 3 or 4 days, and then stop it up; when it has stood 6 or 7 days, put in a quart or two of Malaga Sherry, and when it is fine bottle it.

To make Turnip Wine.

Pare and slice a number of turnips, put them into a cider press and press out all the juice. To every gallon of the juice add 3 lbs. of lump sugar; have a vessel ready large enough to hold the juice, and put ½ pint of brandy to every gallon. Pour in the juice and lay something over the bung for a week, to see if it works; if it does, do not bung it down till it has done working; then stop it close for 3 months, and draw it off into another vessel. When it is fine bottle it off.

This is an excellent wine for gouty habits, and is much recommended in such cases in lieu of any other wine.

Rose Wine.

Take a well-glazed earthen vessel and put into it 3 galls. of rose-water drawn with a cold still. Put into that a sufficient quantity of rose-leaves, cover it close and set it for an hour in a kettle or copper of hot water, to take out the whole strength and tincture of the roses; and when it is cold press the rose-leaves hard into the liquor, and steep fresh ones in it, repeating it till the liquor has got the full strength of the roses. To every gallon of liquor put 3 lbs. of loaf sugar, and stir it well, that it may melt and disperse in every part. Then put it into a cask or other convenient vessel, to ferment, and put into it a piece of bread toasted hard and covered with yeast. Let it stand about 30 days, when it will be ripe and have a fine flavor, having the whole strength and scent of the roses in it; and it may be greatly improved by adding to it wine and spices. By this method of infusion, wine of carnations, clove gilliflowers, violets, primroses, or any other flower having a curious scent, may be made.

English Fig Wine.

Take the large blue figs when pretty ripe, and steep them in white wine, having made some slits in them, that they may swell and gather in the substance of the wine. Then slice some other figs and let them simmer over a fire in water until they are reduced to a kind of pulp. Then strain out the water, pressing the pulp hard, and pour it as hot as possible on the figs that are imbrued in the wine. Let the quantities be nearly equal, but the water somewhat more than the wine and figs. Let them stand 24 hours, mash them well together, and draw off what will run without squeezing. Then press the rest, and if not sweet enough add a sufficient quantity of sugar to make it so. Let it ferment, and add to it a little honey and sugarcandy; then fine it with the whites of eggs and a little isinglass, and draw it off for use.

Balm Wine.

Take 40 lbs. of sugar and 9 galls. of water, boil it gently for 2 hours, skim it well, and put it into a tub to cool. Take 2½ lbs. of the tops of balm, bruise them and put them into a barrel with a little new yeast, and when the liquor is cold pour it on the balm. Stir it well together and let it stand 24 hours, stirring it often. Then close it up, and let it stand 6 weeks. Then rack it off and put a lump of sugar into every bottle. Cork it well, and it will be better the second year than the first.

To make Scurvy-Grass Wine.

Take the best large scurvy-grass tops and leaves, in May, June, or July; bruise them well in a stone mortar, put them in a well-glazed earthen vessel and sprinkle them over with some powder of crystal of tartar; then smear them with virgin honey, and being covered close, let it stand 24 hours. Set water over a gentle fire, putting to every gallon 3 pints of honey, and when the scum rises take it off and let it cool; then put the stamped scurvy grass into a barrel, and pour the liquor to it, setting the vessel conveniently endways, with a tap at the bottom. When it has been infused 24 hours, draw off the liquor, strongly press the juice and moisture out of the herb into the barrel or vessel, and put the liquor up again; then put a little new yeast to it, and suffer it to ferment 3 days, covering the place of the bung or vent with a piece of bread spread over with mustard seed, downward, in a cool place, and let it continue till it is fine and drinks brisk. Draw off the finest part, leaving the dregs behind; afterwards add more herbs, and ferment it with whites of eggs, flour, and fixed nitre, verjuice, or the juice of green grapes, if they are to be had; to which add 6 lbs. of the syrup of mustard, all mixed and well beaten together, to refine it down, and it will drink brisk, but is not very pleasant; being here inserted among artificial wines rather for the sake of health, than for the delightfulness of its taste.

To make Cheap and Wholesome Claret.

Take a quart of fine draft Devonshire cider, and an equal quantity of good Port. Mix them, and shake them. Bottle them, and let them stand for a month.

To make Dry Wine.

Those who like a dry wine, should put into the vat, at the commencement of the vinous fermentation, an ounce or two of calcined gypsum, in fine powder.

MANAGEMENT OF DOMESTIC WINES.

To Guard against Unripe Fruit.

If the season proves bad so that some fruits are not sufficiently ripe, immediately after the vinous fermentation, and the must of such fruit is put into the cask, it is to be rolled 2 or 3 times a day for a week or two. A spirituous fermentation will soon commence, the bung of the cask must then be taken out, and the hole covered with a bit of light wood or canvas, and as any scum arises, it should be taken away. When the scum disappears, fill up the cask, and bung it up. But a vent hole must be left open for a week.

To Keep and Manage Wines.

Wines will diminish, therefore the cask must be kept filled up with some of the same wine, or some other that is as good or better.

They must at all times be kept in a cool cellar, if not, they will ferment. If wines are kept in a warm cellar, an acetous fermentation will soon commence, and the result consequently will be vinegar. The more a wine frets and ferments, the more it parts with its strength and goodness; when wines are found to work improperly in the cellar, the vent-peg must be taken out for a week or two.

If any wine ferments, after being perfected, draw off a quart and boil it, and pour it hot into the cask, add a pint or a quart of brandy, and bung up a day or two after.

Or, draw off the wine, and fumigate the cask, with 1 oz. of flower of brimstone, and ½ oz. of cinnamon, in powder. Mix the two together, and tie them up in a rag. Turn the bung-hole of the cask downwards, place the rag under the bunghole, and set fire to it, so that the gas ascends into the cask. As soon as it is burnt out, fill up the cask with wine, and bung it up tight.

To Sweeten a Foul Cask.

Set fire to 1 lb. or more of broken charcoal, put it into the cask, and immediately fill up the cask with boiling water. After this roll the cask once or twice a day for a week; then pour out the charcoal and water, wash out the cask with clean cold water, and expose it to the external air for some days.

To Improve Poor Wines.

Poor wines may be improved by being racked off, and returned to the cask again; and then putting into the wine about 1 lb. of jar or box raisins, bruised, and 1 quart of brandy.

Or, put into the wine 2 lbs. of honey, and a pint or two of brandy. The honey and brandy to be first mixed together.

Or, draw off 3 or 4 quarts of such wine and fill the cask up with strong wine.

To Improve Wine when Lowering or Decaying.

Take 1 oz. of alum, make it into powder; then draw out 4 galls. of wine, mix the powder with it, and beat it well for ½ an hour; then fill up the cask, and when fine (which will be in a week's time or little more), bottle it off. This will make it drink fine and nice.

To Restore Flat Wines.

Flat wines may be restored by 1 lb. of jar raisins, 1 lb. of honey, and ½ a pint of spirits of wine, beaten up in a mortar with some of the wine, and then the contents put into the cask.

To Remove a Musty or Disagreeable Taste in Wine.

Put into the cask 3 or 4 sticks of charcoal, and bung up the cask tight. In a month after take them out.

Or, cut two ripe medlars, put them in a gauze bag, and suspend them from the bung-hole into wine, and bung up the cask air-tight. A month after take them out, and bung up the cask again.

Or, mix ¼ lb. of bruised mustard-seed, with 1 pint or more of brandy, and stir it up in the wine; and 2 days after bung up the cask.

Another Mode.

At the finish of the process, when the brandy or spirit is put to the wine, it is particularly recommended that ¼ oz. of camphor, in the lump, be dropped into the bung-hole of each 18 galls. of wine.

Another Mode.

Oil poured upon wine, or any other liquor, will prevent it from growing musty, or turning corrupt.

To Take Away the Ill Scent of Wines.

Bake a long roller of dough, stuck well with cloves, and hang it in the cask.

To make Wine Sparkle like Champagne.

Take great care to rack off the wine well, and in March bottle it as quickly as possible. The bottles must be very clean and dry, and the corks of the best sort, made of velvet or white cork. In 2 months' after, the wine will be in a fine condition to drink.

To Clear Foul or Ropy Wines.

Take ½ oz. of chalk in powder, ½ oz. of burnt alum, the white of an egg, and 1 pint of spring-water.

Beat the whole up in a mortar, and pour it into the wine; after which, roll the cask 10 minutes; and then place it on the stand, leaving the bung out for a few days. As soon as the wine is fine, rack it off.

Or, take 1 oz. of ground rice, ½ oz. of burnt alum, and ½ oz. of hay-salt

Beat the whole up in a mortar, with 1 pint or more of the wine, pour it into the cask, and roll it 10 minutes. The cask must be bunged up for a few days. As soon as such wine becomes fine, rack it off.

Or, bring the cask of wine out of the cellar and place it in a shady situation to receive the circulation of the air, and take out the bung. In 3 weeks or a month rack it off into a sweet cask, which fill up, and put into the wine 1 oz. of cinnamon, in the stick; and bung it up tight.

Another Method.

Tap the cask, and put a piece of coarse linen cloth upon that end of the cock which goes to the inside of the cask; then rack it into a dry cask to 30 galls. of wine, and put in 5 oz. of powdered alum. Roll and shake them well together, and it will fine down, and prove a very clear and pleasant wine.

To Correct Green or Harsh Wines.

Take 1 oz. of salt, ½ oz. calcined gypsum, in powder, and 1 pt. of skimmed milk. Mix these up with a little of the wine, and then pour the mixture into the cask; put in a few lavender leaves, stir the wine with a stick, so as not to disturb the lees, and bung it up.

To Correct Sharp, Tart, Acid Wines.

Mix 1 oz. of calcined gypsum in powder and 2 lbs. of honey in 1 qt. of brandy; pour the mixture into the wine, and stir it so as not to disturb the lees; fill up the cask, and the following day bung it up. Rack this wine as soon as fine.

Or, mix ½ oz. of the salt of tartar ½ oz. of calcined gypsum, in powder, with a pint of the wine; pour it into the cask, and put an ounce of cinnamon in the stick; stir the wine without disturbing the lees, fill up the cask, and the day following bung it up.

Or, boil 3 oz. of rice; when cold put it into a gauze bag, and immerge it into the wine; put into the wine also a few sticks of cinnamon, and bung up the cask. In about a month after, take the rice out.

To Restore Sour Wines.

Take calcined gypsum in powder 1 oz., cream of tartar in powder 2 oz. Mix them in a pint or more of brandy; pour it into the cask; put in, also, a few sticks of cinnamon, and then stir the wine without disturbing the lees. Bung up the cask the next day.

Another Method.

Boil a gallon of wine with some beaten oyster-shells and crab's claws, burnt into powder, 1 oz. of each to every 10 galls. of wine; then strain out the liquor through a sieve, and when cold put it into wine of the same sort, and it will give it a pleasant lively taste. A lump of unslaked lime put into the cask will also keep wine from turning sour.

Fining.

Many wines require fining *before* they are racked, and the operation of fining is not always necessary. Most wines, well made, do not want fining; this may be ascertained by drawing a little into a glass from a peg-hole.

One of the best finings is as follows: Take 1 lb. of fresh marsh-mallow roots, washed clean, and cut into small pieces; macerate them in 2 qts. of soft water for 24 hours, then gently boil the liquor down to 3 half pints, strain it, and when cold mix with it ½ oz. of pipe-clay or chalk in powder; then pour the mucilage into the cask, and stir up the wine so as not to disturb the lees, and leave the vont-peg out for some days after.

Or, take boiled rice 2 tablespoonfuls, the white of 1 new egg, and ½ oz. of burnt alum, in powder. Mix with a pint or more of the wine, then pour the mucilage into the cask, and stir the wine with a stout stick, but not to agitate the lees.

Or, dissolve in a gentle heat ½ oz. of isinglass in a pint or more of the wine, then mix with it ½ oz. of chalk, in powder; when the two are well incorporated pour it into the cask, and stir the wine, so as not to disturb the lees.

Or, beat up the white of eggs, 1 egg to 6 galls.; draw the wine into the beaten egg, and keep stirring all the while, then return the wine and froth to the cask, and bung up.

To Check Fermentation.

It is in the first place necessary to consider whether the existing state of fermentation be the original or secondary stage of that process which comes on after the former has ceased for several days, and is indeed the commencement of acetous fermentation. That of the former kind rarely proceeds beyond what is necessary for the perfect decomposition of the saccharine and other parts of the vegetable substance necessary for the production of spirit, unless the liquor be kept too warm or is too weak, and left exposed to the air after the vinous fermentation is completed. The means to correct these circumstances are sufficiently obvious. The heat for spirituous fermentation should not be above 60°; when it is much above that point the liquor passes rapidly through the stage of vinous fermentation, and the acetous immediately commences. When too long continued fermentation arises from the liquor having been kept in a warm situation, it will be soon checked by bunging, after being removed into a cold place; the addition of a small proportion of spirits of wine or brandy, previously to closing it up, is also proper. A degree of cold, approaching to the freezing point, will check fermentation of whatever kind. Fermentation of this kind cannot be stopped by using a chemical agent, except such as would destroy the qualities of the liquor intended to be produced.

The secondary stage of fermentation, or the commencement of the acetous, may be stopped by removing the liquor to a cool situation; correcting the acid already formed; and if the liquor contain but little spirit, the addition of a proper proportion of brandy is requisite.

The operation of racking is also necessary to preserve liquor in a vinous state, and to render it clear. This process should be performed in a cool place.

FOREIGN WINES.

To Restore Pricked British Wines.

Rack the wines down to the lees into another cask, where the lees of good wines are fresh; then put a pint of strong aqua vitæ, and scrape ¼ lb. of yellow beeswax into it, which, by heating the spirit over a gentle fire, will melt; after which dip a piece of cloth into it, and when a little dry set it on fire with a brimstone match, put it into the bunghole, and stop it up close.

Another Method.

First prepare a fresh empty cask that has had the same kind of wine in which it is about to be racked; then match it, and rack off the wine, putting to every 10 galls. 2 oz. of oyster powder and ½ oz. of bay-salt; then get the staff and stir it well about, letting it stand till it is fine, which will be in a few days; after which rack it off into another cask previously matched, and if the lees of some wine of the same kind can be got, it will improve it much. Put likewise a quart of brandy to every 10 galls., and, if the cask has been emptied a long time, it will match better on that account; but, even if a new cask, the matching must not be omitted. A fresh empty cask is to be preferred. This method will answer for all made wines.

TO MANAGE FOREIGN WINE-VAULTS.

The principal object to be attended to in the management of foreign wine-vaults is to keep them of a temperate heat. Care must be taken, therefore, to close up every aperture or opening, that there may be no admission given to the external air. The floor of the vault should likewise be well covered with saw-dust, which must not be suffered to get too dry and dusty, but must receive now and then an addition of new, lest, when bottling or racking wine, some of the old dust should fly into it. At most vaults, in the winter, it is necessary to have a stove or chafing-dish, to keep up a proper degree of warmth. In the summer time it will be best to keep them as cool as possible.

To Fit Up a Cellar of Wines and Spirits.

Provide a good rope and tackling to let down the casks into the vaults or cellar, and a slide, ladder or pulley for the casks to slide or roll on; a pair of strong slings; a pair of can hooks and a pair of crate hooks; a block of wood to put under the pipes when topping them over in a narrow passage, or in casing them; a small valinch to taste wines; a crane, and a small copper pump to rack off; 2 or 3 gallon cans made of wood; a large wooden funnel; 2 or 3 copper funnels, from a quart to a gallon each; 2 racking cocks; 2 wine bottling-cocks; a brace and various bits; 2 small tubs; a square basket to hold the corks; 2 small tin funnels; a small strainer; 2 cork-screws; 2 or 3 baskets; a whisk to beat the finings; 2 flannel or linen bags; a strong iron screw to raise the bungs; a pair of pliers; bungs, corks, and vent-pegs; 2 frets or middle-sized gimblets; some sheet-lead and tacks to put on broken staves; brown paper to put round cocks and under the lead, when stopping leaks; a staff with a chain at one end to rumage the wines, etc.; shots and lead canister or bristle brush, and 2 cloths to wash bottles; 2 large tubs; some small racks that will hold 6 dozen each; a cooper's adze; an iron and a wooden driver to tighten hoops; 2 dozen of wooden bungs of different sizes; a thermometer, which is to be kept in the vault; a stove or chafingdish, to keep the heat of the vault at a known temperature; a few dozen of delph labels; a cupboard to hold all the tools; a spade; 2 good stiff birch brooms, and a rake to level the sawdust.

To make Port Wine.

The dark red port is made from grapes gathered indiscriminately and thrown into a cistern; they are then trodden, and their skins and stalks left in the mass, which separate during fermentation and form a dry head over the liquid. When the fermentation is completed, the liquor underneath is drawn out and casked. Before being exported it is mixed with one-third of brandy, to enable it to keep during the voyage; otherwise the carriage brings on the acetous fermentation, and the wine is converted into vinegar.

French Method of Making Wines.

In the southern parts of France their way is with red wines to tread or squeeze the grapes between the hands, and let the whole stand, juice and husks, till the tincture is to their liking; after which they press it. For white wines they press the grapes immediately, and when pressed they tun the must and stop up the vessel, leaving only the depth of a foot or more to give room for it to work. At the end of 10 days they fill this space with some other good wine that will not work it again.

To Rack Foreign Wines.

The vault or cellar should be of a temperate heat, and the casks sweet and clean. Should they have an acid or musty smell, it may be remedied by burning brimstone matches in them; and if not clean rinse them well out with cold water, and after draining, rinse with a quart of brandy, putting the brandy afterwards into the ullage cask. Then strain the lees or bottoms through a flannel or linen bag. But put the bottoms of Port into the ullage-cask without going through the filtering-bag. In racking wine that is not on the stillage, a wine-pump is desirable.

To Manage and Improve Poor Red Port.

If wanting in body, color and flavor, draw out 30 or 40 galls. and return the same quantity of young and rich wines. To a can of which put 3 gills of coloring, with a bottle of wine or brandy. Then whisk it well together and put it into the cask, stirring it well. If not bright in about a week or ten days, fine it for use; previous to which put in at different times a gallon of good brandy. If the wine is short of body put a gallon or two of brandy in each pipe, by a quart or two at a time, as it feeds the wine better than putting it in all at once. But if the wines are in a bonded cellar, procure a funnel that will go to the bottom of the cask, that the brandy may be completely incorporated with the wine.

To Manage Claret.

Claret is not a wine of a strong body, though it requires to be of a good age before it is used, and therefore it should be well managed; the best method is to feed it every 2 or 3 weeks with a pint or two of French brandy. Taste it frequently, to know what state it is in, and use the brandy accordingly; but never put much in at a time, while a little incorporates with the wine and feeds and mellows it.

If the claret is faint, rack it into a fresh emptied hogshead, upon the lees of good claret, and bung it up, putting the bottom downwards for two or three days, that the lees may run through it.

To Color Claret.

If the color be not yet perfect, rack it off again into a hogshead that has been newly drawn off, with the lees; then take 1 lb. of turnsole and put it into a gallon or two of wine; let it lie a day or two, and then put it into the vessel; after which lay the bung downwards for a night, and the next day roll it about.

Or, take any quantity of damsons or black sloes, and strew them with some of the deepest colored wine and as much sugar as will make it into a syrup. A pint of this will cover a hogshead of claret. It is also good for red Port wines, and may be kept ready for use in glass bottles.

To Restore Claret that Drinks Foul.

Rack it off from the dregs on some fresh lees of its own kind, and then take a dozen of new pippins, pare them and take away the cores or hearts; then put them in the hogshead, and if that is not sufficient, take a handful of the oak of Jerusalem and bruise it; then put it into the wine and stir it well.

To make Claret and Port Rough.

Put into 1 qt. of Claret or Port 2 qts. of sloes; bake them in a gentle oven, or over a slow fire, till a good part of their moisture is stewed out, then pour off the liquor, and squeeze out the rest. A pint of this will be sufficient for 30 or 40 galls.

To Manage Hermitage and Burgundy.

Red Hermitage must be managed in the same way as Claret, and the White likewise, except the coloring, which it does not require. Burgundy should be managed in the same manner as Red Hermitage.

To Manage Lisbon Wine.

If the Lisbon is dry, take out of the pipe 35 or 40 galls., and put in the same quantity of calcavella, stir it well about, and this will make a pipe of good mild Lisbon; or, if it be desired to convert mild into dry, take the same quantity out as above mentioned before, and fill the pipe with Malaga Sherry, stirring it about as the other. The same kind of fining used for Vidonia will answer for Lisbon wine; or it may be fined with the whites and shells of 16 eggs, and a small handful of salt; beat it together to a froth, and mix it with a little of the wine; then pour it into the pipe, stir it about, and let it have vent for 3 days; after which bung it up, and in a few days it will be fine. Lisbon, when bottled, should be packed either in saw-dust or leaths in a temperate place.

To Improve Sherry.

If the Sherry be new and hot, rack it off into a sweet cask, add 5 galls. of mellow Lisbon, which will take off the hot taste, then give it a head, take 1 qt. of honey, mix it with a can of wine, and put it into the cask when racking. By this method Sherry for present use will be greatly improved, having much the same effect upon it as age.

To Improve White Wine.

If the wine have an unpleasant taste, rack off one-half, and to the remainder add 1 gall. of new milk, a handful of bay-salt, and as much rice; after which take a staff, bent them well together for half an hour, and fill up the cask, and when rolled well about, stillage it, and in a few days it will be much improved.

If the white wine is foul and has lost its color, for a butt or pipe take 1 gall. of new milk, put it into the cask, and stir it well about with a staff; and when it has settled, put in 3 oz. of isinglass made into a jelly, with ¼ lb. of loaf sugar scraped fine, and stir it well about. On the day following, bung it up, and in a few days it will be fine, and have a good color.

To Improve Wine with Chalk.

Add a little chalk to the *must*, when it is somewhat sour; for the acidity arising from citric and tartaric acids, there is thus formed a precipitate of citrate and tartrate of lime, while the *must* becomes sweeter, and yields a much finer wine. Too much chalk may render the wine insipid, since it is proper to leave a little excess of acid in the *must*. Concentrate the *must* by boiling, and add the proper quantity of chalk to the liquor, while it is still hot. Even acid wine may be benefited by the addition of chalk. Oyster shells may be used with this view; and when calcined are a cleaner carbonate of lime than common chalk.

To Renovate Sick Wine.

Wines on the fret should be racked; if their own lee indicates decay they should be racked on the sound lee of another wine of similar but stronger quality, to protract their decline; if this be done at an early period, it may renovate the sick wine; on these occasions giving the sick wine a cooler place, will retard its progress to acidity: if convenient, such wines should be forced and bottled. Previous to bottling, or rather at the forcing, give it 1, 2, or 3 tablespoonfuls of calcined gypsum finely pulverized. This will check its tendency to acidity, without exciting much intumescence, without injuring the color of the red wine, and without retarding its coating to the bottle, which it rather promotes. The proper forcing for red wines are, the whites of 10 or 12 eggs, beat up with 1 or 2 teaspoonfuls of salt, per hogshead, and well worked into the wine with a forcing-rod; the gypsum should be first boiled in a little water.

To Mellow Wine.

Cover the orifices of the vessels containing it with bladder closely fastened instead of the usual materials, and an aqueous exhalation will pass through the bladder, leaving some fine crystallizations on the surface of the wine, which, when skimmed off, leaves the wine in a highly improved state of flavor. Remnants of wine covered in this manner, whether in bottles or casks, will not turn mouldy as when stopped in the usual way, but will be improved instead of being deteriorated.

German Method of restoring Sour Wines.

Put a small quantity of powdered charcoal in the wine, shake it, and after it has remained still for 48 hours decant steadily.

To Concentrate Wine by Cold.

If any kind of wine be exposed to a sufficient degree of cold in frosty weather, or be put into any place where ice continues all the year, as in ice-houses, and there suffered to freeze, the superfluous water contained in the wine will be frozen into ice, and will leave the proper and truly essential part of the wine unbroken, unless the degree of cold should be very intense, or the wine but weak and poor. When the frost is moderate, the experiment has no difficulty, because not above a third or a fourth part of the superfluous water will be frozen in a whole night; but if the cold be very intense, the best way is, at the end of a few hours, when a tolerable quantity of ice is formed, to pour out the remaining fluid liquor, and set it in another vessel to freeze again by itself.

The frozen part, or ice, consists only of the watery part of the wine, and may be thrown away, and the liquid part retains all the strength, and is to be preserved. This will never grow sour, musty, or mouldy, and may at any time be reduced to wine of the common strength, by adding to it as much water as will make it up the former quantity.

To Convert White Wine into Red.

Put 4 oz. of turnsole rags into an earthen vessel, and pour upon them a pint of boiling water; cover the vessel close, and leave it to cool; strain off the liquor, which will be of a fine deep red, inclining to purple. A small portion of this colors a large quantity of wine. This tincture may either be made in brandy, or mixed with it, or else made into a syrup, with sugar, for keeping.

In those countries which do not produce the tingeing grape which affords a blood-red juice, wherewith the wines of France are often stained, in defect of this the juice of elderberries is used, and sometimes logwood is used at Oporto.

To Force down the Finings of all White Wines, Arracks, and Small Spirits.

Put a few qts. of skimmed milk into the cask.

To render Red Wine White.

If a few quarts of well-skimmed milk be put to a hogshead of red wine, it will soon precipitate the greater part of the color, and leave the whole nearly white; and this is of known use in turning red wines, when pricked, into white; in which a small degree of acidity is not so much perceived.

Milk is, from this quality of discharging color from wines, of use also to the wine-coopers, for the whitening of wines that have acquired a brown color from the cask, or from having been hastily boiled before fermenting; for the addition of a little skimmed milk, in these cases, precipitates the brown color, and leaves the wines almost limpid, or of what they call a water whiteness, which is much coveted abroad in wines as well as in brandies.

To make Wine Settle Well.

Take a pint of wheat and boil it in a quart of water till it bursts and becomes soft; then squeeze through a linen cloth, and put a pint of the liquor into a hogshead of unsettled white wine; stir it well about, and it will become fine.

To make a Match for Sweetening Casks.

Melt some brimstone, and dip into it a piece of coarse linen cloth; of which, when cold, take a piece of about 1 inch broad and 5 inches long, and set fire to it, putting it into the bung-hole, with one end fastened under the bung, which must be driven in very tight. Let it remain a few hours before removing it out.

To make Oyster Powder.

Get some fresh oyster-shells, wash them, and scrape off the yellow part from the outside; lay them on a clear fire till they become red-hot; then lay them to cool, and take off the softest part, powder it, and sift it through a fine sieve; after which use it immediately, or keep it in bottles well corked up and laid in a dry place.

To make a Filtering Bag.

This bag is made of a yard of either linen or flannel, not too fine or close, and sloping, so as to have the bottom of it run to a point, and the top as broad as the cloth will allow. It must be well sewed up the side, and the upper part of it folded round a wooden hoop, and well fastened to it; then tie the hoop in three or four places with a cord to support it; and when used, put a can or pail under it to receive the liquor, filling the bag with the sediments; after it has ceased to run, wash out the bag in three or four clear waters, then hang it up to dry in an airy place, that it may not get musty. A wine-dealer should always have two bags by him, one for red and the other for white wines.

To Detect Alum in Wine.

Wine merchants add alum to red wine to communicate to it a rough taste and deeper color. For the discovery of the fraud in question adopt the following means:—The wine is to be discolored by means of a concentrated solution of chlorine; the mixture is to be evaporated until reduced to nearly the fourth of its original volume; the liquor is to be filtered; it then possesses the following properties when it contains alum:—1st, it has a sweetish, astringent taste; 2d, it furnishes a white precipitate (sulphate of baryta) with nitrate of baryta, insoluble in water and in nitric acid; 3d, caustic potash gives rise to a yellowish white precipitate of alumina, soluble in an excess of potash.

To Detect Metal in Wine.

Add a few drops of sulphydrate of ammonia. If a precipitate is formed the wine is impure. Lead is used by many wine merchants to give an astringency to port wine, that, like old port, it may appear rough to the tongue. Sometimes they hang a sheet of lead in the cask; at others they pour in a solution of acetate (sugar) of lead, for the purpose of sweetening, as they term it.

DISTILLATION.

The object of distillation is the preparation of alcohol or pure spirits, which is obtained from brandy, rum, arrack and whiskey, prepared from wine, sugar, rice and malt. It also includes compound spirits, or those which, in addition to alcohol, contain some volatile or pungent oil or essence, as gin, hollands, caraway and peppermint; the essential oils, as oil of cinnamon, oil of cloves, oil of peppermint, and otto of roses, and the simple distilled waters which retain the fragrant flavor of the particular herbs with which they have been distilled.

To manage Distillation.

Previous to distilling, the process of brewing and fermentation are necessary. The distiller, however, need not take the precautions of the brewer or wine-maker in moderating his fermentations so as to secure the good flavor and keeping qualities of the product. His object is to get as thorough a fermentation, and therefore as much alcohol, as possible. Hence large quantities of yeast are used, which is not skimmed off, but worked into the wort. He also mixes a quantity of raw grain with his malt in the mash, the diastase of the malt sufficing to convert all the starch of the raw grain into sugar. The quantity of raw grain may be twenty times that of the malt. All the saccharine matter cannot be converted into alcohol, the large quantity of alcohol formed towards the last of the process checking the fermentation. About one-fifth of all the saccharine matter remains in the grains. These are fed to cattle.

Utensils.

In a distillery are required a variety of utensils, such as still, worm-tub, pump, a water-cask, a strong press, hair-cloths, 3 or 4 iron-bound tubs capable of containing from a hogshead to a pipe of any liquor, 3 or 4 cans capable of holding from

2 to 6 galls. by measure, an iron-bound wooden funnel having a strong iron nosel or pipe, a pewter syphon about 6 feet long and 4 inches in circumference, flannel bags for refining the thick and feculent matter at the bottoms of the casks and other vessels.

Operation of the Still.

When the still is charged let the fire under it be lighted, and whilst it burns up the joints should be carefully luted.

By laying the hand on the still and capital, as the fire gains strength, the process of the operation will be ascertained; for whenever the head or capital feels hot, it is a proof that the volatile particles have arisen, and are about to enter the worm. When the still head is about to become hot, prepare a *damp*, made of the ashes under the grate, mixed with as much water as will properly wet them. This mixture is to be thrown upon the fire, to moderate its action, at the instant when distillation has commenced. Continue the heat as long as the distilled liquid is spirituous to the taste. When the distilled liquor carries with it any particular flavor, it should be re-distilled with essential oils, in order to convert it into a compound spirit, as gin, peppermint, and other cordials.

When all the spirituous fluid is drawn off, the still should be emptied by a cock in the side. The head, etc., should then be removed, and the several lutes taken clean off. The still may now be charged a second time, and luted. If the spirit or compound to be made is of a different nature or flavor from that procured by the last distillation, the still, capital and worm should be thoroughly cleaned by hot water, sand and a scrubbing brush, to remove the oily particles that adhere to their internal surfaces. The worm is best cleansed by passing hot water through it repeatedly, until the water flows out quite flavorless.

Great care should be taken that no grease, tallow, soap, or any other unctuous matter, fall into the tubs, pieces, rundlets, or cans. Above all things, lighted candles, torches, or papers should not be brought near any vessel containing spirits. The flue or chimney should be kept constantly clean.

To Use a Portable Furnace.

In the laboratories of experimental chemists, portable furnaces are employed. Charcoal is the only fuel that can be used in them, except the occasional use of the finer kinds of stone coal that yield a bright flame, and burn to a white ash without forming clinkers. When the fire is regulated by the admission of only the necessary quantity of air through the charcoal, and the whole heat of the fuel is directed upon the subject exposed to it, the expense is not so great as might be supposed, for no other fuel gives out so much heat. One lb. of charcoal will boil away 13 lbs. of water, whereas the same weight of Newcastle coal will boil away only 8 or 9 lbs. A pound of coke will only boil away 4 lbs. of water, and a pound of peat seldom more than 5 lbs., or, by a skilful mode of using it, at the utmost 10 lbs.

To Build Fixed Furnaces.

Fire bricks are generally used, as they may be cut as easily as chalk, and yet bear a violent heat without alteration; they must be set in clay of the same kind. The parts distant from the fire may be of common bricks set in mortar, but this mortar must be carefully removed before the other part is begun, as an accidental admixture of it with the clay would cause the latter to run into glass, and thus spoil the furnace. These furnaces are generally built as thin as possible, that they may take up the less room, and to save fuel in heating them, as they have seldom fire constantly in them; in this case they should be surrounded with iron braces, to prevent the alternate contraction and expansion destroying them as soon as they otherwise would.

To make a Portable Sand-pot.

For a portable one the ash pit may be an iron cylinder 17 inches in diameter and 8 deep, closed at bottom. In the front is cut a hole 3 inches high and 4 wide, with sliders to shut close. Three pins are riveted on the inside about an inch below the upper edge; these are to support the fire-place. The bottom of this ash pit is lined with clay, heat up with charcoal dust and formed into a kind of saucer. The fire-place is a small cylinder of nearly the same width, so as to fit easily into the top of the ash-pit, and rest on the three pins; its height is 15 inches, and it has a flat border at each end, leaving a circular opening of 10 inches in diameter. Around the lower border are riveted 3 screws, to which are fixed by nuts a grate. In the upper border, towards the circumference, and at equal distances from each other, are made 4 circular holes an inch over. The inside of the fire-place is lined with clay and charcoal, whose surface is adjusted to a core, made by drawing on a board an ellipsis, having its foci 15 inches asunder, and its semiordinates at the foci 5 inches, sawing off the board at each focus, and also down the greatest diameter, so that the internal cavity may represent an ellipsoid of those dimensions, cut off at the foci. A fire hole about 6 inches wide and 4½ high, with the lower limit about 3 inches above the grate, is left in the front to be closed with a lined stopper, both the fire-hole and stopper having a border to retain the lining. When the lining is dry, 4 openings are cut sloping through it, corresponding to the openings in the upper border, to serve as vents for the burnt air, and to regulate the fire by sliding pieces of tile more or less over them. In the central opening at the top of the fire-place is hung a cast-iron pot, either hemispherical, or, which is most usual, cylindrical, about 6 inches deep at the edge, with a rounded bottom, so that the axis is about an inch deeper. The common pots have only a reflected border, by which they hang, but the best kind have also an upright edge that rises an inch higher, to which a stone-ware head is fitted, and thus the pot serves for many distillations that require a strong fire. It is usual to cut a notch on one side of the top of the fire-place, sloping upwards to the edge of the pot, about 3 inches wide and 2 deep, to admit a low retort to be sunk deeper into the pot, by allowing a passage to its neck.

To make a Sand-heat Furnace.

A furnace of this kind may be stationary, and built of bricks that will stand the fire, and in this case the ash-pit is built about 12 inches high, and has an ash-door opening into it about 6 inches square; a grate is then laid, and a fire-door 6 inches by 8 opens immediately into the fire-place, even with the grate. The fire-place is made cylindrical, 2 inches wider than the sand pot, and about 8 inches deeper, the grate being a square whose side is about two-thirds the internal diameter of the sand-pot. This pot hangs by its border in an iron ring placed at the top of the furnace; we have not yet adopted Teichmeyer's method of sloping the pot. As stone coal is generally used in fixing furnaces, instead of the 4 register holes used as vents in the portable furnaces, only one opening, about as wide as the grate and 3 inches high, either in the back or on one side, is made to vent the burned air into the chimney. This, however, has the inconvenience of heating the pot unequally, the side next the vent becoming much the hottest, in spite of the endeavor to equalize the heat by bringing the fire from under the centre of the pot as forward as possible, by raising the wall opposite to the vent perpendicularly, and enlarging it only on the other three sides; sometimes with the same view several small vents are made round the pot, leading into the chimney. A notch for the neck of the retort is generally made on one side. As much heat passes through the vent, it is usual to cause the heated air to pass under a large cast-iron plate, placed on a border of bricks surrounding a platform of the same materials, and leaving a cavity of about 2½ inches deep, at the further end of which another opening leads into the chimney. On this iron plate sand is laid to form a sand heat, and thus several operations are carried on at the same time. If that in the sand-pot is finished, and it is desired to keep on those in the sand-heat without interruption, the vessel may be drawn out of the sand, some warm sand thrown on that remaining in the pot, and a fresh vessel with materials introduced. But if this new operation should require the heat to be more gradually exhibited, a pot of thin plate-iron, filled with cold sand, containing the vessel, may be partly slid into the heated sand-pot, and, being supported by pieces of brick placed under the edge or otherwise, kept there until it be necessary to increase the heat, when it may be slid down lower until at length it is permitted to reach the bottom of the sand-pot.

To make a Hot Still.

Portable hot stills should have an ash-pit and fire-place exactly similar in dimensions to those used with the sand-pot, or the same furnace may be used with a hot still, if economy and not convenience is the principal object. The copper or tin-plate cucurbite will, of course, be 10 inches wide and about 12 deep, and hang 7 inches within the fire-place. The mouth should be wide, that the water-bath to be occasionally hung within it so as to reach within 3 inches of the bottom, may be the larger. Between this wide neck and the circumference there should be a short pipe, through which the liquor left after distillation may be drawn off by a crane without unluting the vessels; fresh liquor added; or, in distilling with the water-bath, the steam may escape. This pipe has a ring round it, that the cork with which it is stopped may be firmly tied down, and like the other joinings be luted, for which purpose slips of paper smeared with flour and water, or common paste, are usually esteemed sufficient; but the best material is bladders rotted in water until they smell extremely offensive and adhere to the fingers when touched, and then worked between the hands into rolls, which are to be applied to the joinings. These small stills have usually a Moor's head that fits both the cucurbite and the waterbath, their necks being of equal diameter, and is furnished with a groove round the lower part on the inside to direct the condensed vapor to the nose of the alembic, and this head is surrounded by a refrigerator containing cold water, which is not so cumbersome as and less expensive than a worm and tub. But the most advantageous way of cooling the vapors is to use a Moor's head without a surrounding refrigerator, or only a plain bent tube, which should be at least 18 inches long, that the small globules of the boiling liquor which are thrown up near a foot high should not pass over and render the distilled liquor unfit for keeping. To this is to be adapted a pewter pipe about 8 feet long, if spirits of wine is to be distilled, or shorter for watery liquors, and in both cases ¾ of an inch in diameter on the inside, inclosed in a tinned plate tube with a funnel. With an adopter of this kind, and the consumption of 1½ pints of water in a minute, or about 9 galls. in an hour, spirits of wine may be distilled at the rate of a gallon by the hour from one of these portable stills. Another convenience of these straight pipes is, that they may be cleansed in the same manner as a fowling piece.

To make a Large Still.

If this furnace is fixed, and made of bricks, it may be constructed with a sand heat, like that annexed to the sand-pot; but this is seldom practised, although it would be advantageous for digestions and evaporations with a gentle heat, because the fire is generally kept up at an even height. If the cucurbite is not wanted for distilling, it may be used as a boiler to keep water ready heated for use, and to be drawn off when wanted by a syphon or crane. But these fixed stills are usually furnished with a pipe and cock on a level with the bottom, by which they can be emptied, and have almost always a worm and tub to cool the vapors. The head is usually of that kind which is called a swan's neck.

Astier's Improved Still.

It has been proved that as soon as a common still is in operation, the steam from the capital in the first turn of the worm is at a temperature of about 212° Fahr. Here *water only* condenses, and the alcohol in vapor passes into the *second* turn, where it condenses by the lowered temperature. If the condensed liquid is drawn off from the upper turn, it is mere phlegm, or water, while that from the second turn is alcohol or spirit. The mode of doing this is very simple, and can be applied to any old still; so that every advantage resulting from the most complicated and expensive stills can be obtained; that is to say, plain brandy, Dutch-proof, and even thirty-five and thirty-sixth proof. The alterations are effected as follows: Each turn of the worm is to be furnished with a very slender lateral pipe, ending in a faucet and tap. A crescent-shaped valve, placed just before the opening of the pipe into the worm, obliges the condensed liquid to trickle into the pipe, and a slight elbow above and below the pipe prevents any of the steam from running in the same direction. Each of these pipes follows the main worm in all its convolutions, comes out of the condenser at the same opening, and is led thence to its own receiver. The pipe of the first turn has also a second branch with a faucet, which lets out the phlegm (which is worthless) as fast as it is condensed. A prover indicates the moment when the feints should be separated, as simple brandy or proof-spirit is wanted. These feints are either detained in the boiler, or set aside for rectification, in all cases necessary, for the last spirit that comes over, without which it is worthless.

Besides producing more spirit, and saving three-fourths out of the feints, the worm prepared as above shortens the term of distillation by one-half, and consequently reduces the expense of fuel. In addition to this, and what is of more consequence, a sour wine may be distilled as well as any other, and without the least taint being perceptible in the brandy. The spirit is, of course, less in quantity, but whatever is obtained is good, and all the acid separates and flows out by the first pipe, which gives an opportunity of profiting by the acetous portion.

Column or Continuous Distillation.

A copper boiler is set in masonry, with a fire beneath: the mouth of the boiler is fitted with a tall copper cylinder, standing perpendicularly over the boiler and fitting closely. About half way up the height of this cylinder, and in its axis, a slender tube enters it and discharges a continual but small stream of the wine or wash to be distilled. The wine is prevented from falling down directly into the boiler beneath by means of a number of diaphragms, through which the wine percolates in streams like rain, whereby it presents a large extent of surface to the vapor which passes it in a different direction. In some cases the ascending vapors have to force their way at each diaphragm through a thin stratum of liquid, and they thus undergo a certain amount of pressure. The wine, when it enters the cylinder, is almost boiling, and, while it falls in small showers through the pierced shelves, a copious issue of watery vapor ascends from the boiling copper below. The watery vapor, at the temperature of boiling, comes in contact with the wine almost boiling: the latter, therefore, receives heat from the former, and by so doing there is a change of state; the watery vapor, losing heat, falls back as water; and the wine, acquiring heat, boils, and its alcohol, in a state of vapor, rises higher up in the cylinder, where, meeting with wine, it is absorbed, and a wine richer in alcohol is produced. This more alcoholic wine readily parts with its alcohol, in the form of vapor, by the action of heat continually carried up the cylinder. This vapor of alcohol, ascending higher, meets with more wine, is absorbed, and again set free in larger quantity. At length the portions of wine high up in the cylinder become highly charged with alcohol, and the alcoholic vapors, meeting with no more wine, pass on to a worm, where they are condensed into very strong spirit. The worm-tub is filled with wine, which in cooling the worm becomes heated itself, and this heated wine flows through the slender tube into the cylinder, where it is distilled as already explained. As this worm is never perfectly cold, the alcoholic vapor which escapes condensation is passed through a second worm, also surrounded by wine, which condenses it completely.

Should the watery vapor which ascends from the boiler into the cylinder, and becoming condensed, falls back into the boiler, carry any alcohol with it, the latter is again volatilized; so that the boiler contains nothing but water, derived from the wine; for, although the boiler had been filled with wine, it soon becomes water by parting with its alcohol. As fast as the boiler fills with water, it is emptied by a cock placed in the bottom. Two boilers are more efficient than one; and when arranged so that a tube proceeding from the head of one plunges to the bottom of the other, they act like two of the eggs in Adams's still.

The discharge of wine from the great reservoir is regulated by a ball-cock, and there is a constant supply of cold wine, first, to the two worms, for the purpose of cooling them (by which method of heating the wine fuel is economized); secondly, to the distillatory column. Having parted with its alcohol, the watery portion falls into the boilers, whence it is let off entirely deprived of alcohol. The flow of wine being thus perpetual, no time is lost by an interval of discharging and charging. It must also be noticed, that when the alcoholic vapors enter the first worm they are condensed; but as the weakest or most watery alcohol condenses in the first rounds of the worm, it is so contrived that this watery portion shall run back by small tubes into the cylinder, where it is redistilled. The worm at all its rounds is provided with cocks and tubes, by which the portions condensed in any part may be let back to be redistilled; or they may be all shut, or some may be left open, so as to return the whole or any part into the cylinder. In this way, by means of these cocks, alcohol of any required degree of condensation, within certain limits, can be obtained.

To Extinguish Fires in Distilleries.

A woollen blanket or rug, hung over a roller in a water-butt, is the readiest and best extinguisher.

To Dulcify Spirits.

In dulcifying, or sweetening the spirits, weigh the sugar, and dissolve it in one or more cans of the water with which the compound is to be made up: bruise the sugar, and stir it well till all is dissolved. Then empty it into the cask containing the spirits, mixing all together by drawing off several cans by the cock, and emptying them into the casks by the bung-holes. Now rummage all well together till they are perfectly compounded.

Spirits or compounds that are strong require no assistance in setting and becoming clear; but those that are weak must be refined by the addition of some other substance. To every hogshead of Geneva, or other spirituous compound, put 6 oz. of powdered alum, previously dissolved in 3 or 4 galls. of the compound: stir all well together. In the course of 24 hours the whole will be rendered completely clear.

It is a good practice to leave the bung-holes of casks (containing spirits or compounds newly made) open for several days. This improves their flavor, and renders them clear sooner than they would otherwise be.

Table-salt thrown into the still, in the proportion of 6 oz. to 10 galls. of any liquid to be distilled, will greatly improve the flavor, taste, and strength of the spirit. The viscid matter will be fixed by the salt, whilst the volatile matter ascends in a state of great purity.

The flavor of malt spirits is highly improved by putting 3½ oz. of finely-powdered charcoal, and 4½ oz. of ground rice into a quart of spirits, and letting it stand during 15 days, frequently stirring it; then let the liquor be strained, and it will be found of nearly the same flavor as brandy.

To make Charcoal.

This is usually manufactured from coppice wood, cut every 16 years; the fagots are made into a large conical pile, covered up with clods of earth, leaving circular rows of holes from top to bottom. The wood is then kindled, and as it becomes red the holes are regularly closed to stop the further combustion, and when the whole has been closed up, the pile is left to cool; when the black skeleton of the wood is left, which differs from the raw wood in burning without any smoke, and with little or no flame, yielding at the same time no soot, although some of the finer particles of the ashes are volatilized and adhere to the chimney. The air which passes through the burning charcoal has its oxygen converted into carbonic acid gas.

The air being thus rendered unfit for respiration, kills whatever animals or plants are confined in it. Numerous accidents have happened of persons being suffocated by sleeping in close rooms with a charcoal fire.

The charcoal for medical purposes should, like that for gunpowder, be made of soft woods, as willow, heated in iron retorts until no volatile matter is given out. Small quantities may be made by burying wood under sand in a covered crucible, and exposing the whole to fire.

To make Spirit of Wine.

Spirit of wine, as it is called, was formerly, and is still, in southern countries, obtained by distilling wire for its yield of brandy, and then slowly abstracting the more volatile part of the brandy, by a small fire and the use of tall vessels. In England, spirit of wine is, in general, obtained from ground meal, either of wheat, rye or barley, with from one-tenth to one-third of the same, or another grain, malted and ground, and then called malt spirit; or from treacle, and then called molasses spirit; some is also made from apples or cider-wash. In the United States, Indian corn is largely employed. The fermentation is carried on quicker and farther than in brewing or making cider, in order that all the sugar in the wash may be converted into spirit and water. The infusion of the malt and meal is made so strong that its specific gravity is from 1.083 to 1.14 (whereas that for strong ale is generally 1.06, and for small beer 1.015 to 1.04), and is mixed with a large quantity of yeast, added by successive portions, until, in about 10 days, the specific gravity is reduced to 1.002, when it is fit for the still. In general, a third part is drawn off at the first stilling, under the name of low wines, the specific gravity being about 0.975. On re-distilling the low wines, a fiery spirit, of a milky cast, comes over first, and is returned into the still; then follows the clean spirit; when it begins to grow too watery, the remaining spirit that comes over, as long as it will take fire, is kept apart, under the name of feints, and mixed with the next parcel of low wines. Instead of these trials the head of the still may have the bulb of a thermometer inserted into it, and by observing the temperature of the steam, an accurate judgment may be formed of the strength of the spirit that distills over. It is computed that 100 galls. of malt or corn wash will produce about 20 of spirit, containing about half its weight of water; molasses wash, 22 galls.; cider wash, 15 galls. The best French wines yield from 20 to 25 galls. The spirit thus obtained is for chemical and pharmaceutical purposes mixed with water, to separate the oil it contains, and redistilled several times in tall vessels, with a very gentle heat, until its specific gravity is reduced to 0.82; though that usually sold is only 0.837, at 60° Fahrenheit. By distilling spirit of wine with purified pearl ashes, salt of tartar, chloride of calcium, lime, or common salt, all previously heated to redness and cooled, its specific gravity may be reduced still lower, even as low as 0.792, at 68° Fahrenheit.

To make Ether.

The old chemists, after mixing spirit of wine with an equal weight of oil of vitriol, digested it for a long time, and then distilled the most volatile part, which was called the sweet oil of vitriol. At present the mixture, whose temperature is considerably increased, is placed in a heated sand-bath and distilled, without being suffered to cool until one-half the quantity of the spirit is come over; meanwhile, an inflammable gas also passes over. If the distillation is continued, sulphurous acid passes over, and a light yellow sweet oil of wine; then the black residuary sulphuric acid contains charcoal diffused through it, which may be separated by admixture with water and filtration. If fresh alcohol is poured on the residuum, more ether may be obtained by distillation. The unrectified ether, as the first product is called, contains both water and alcohol: dry salt of tartar separates the first, and then pouring off the upper liquid, and adding dry chloride of calcium in powder, this salt unites with the alcohol, and the ether swims on the solution.

The Continuous Ether Process.

This process is now generally followed. A vessel of alcohol is provided with a tube furnished with a stopcock, which tube dips to the bottom of a second vessel which contains sulphuric acid, and is provided with a thermometer. From the top of the second vessel a tube passes through a worm or condenser to the receiver. The alcohol is allowed to mix with the sulphuric acid until the boiling point of the mixture is 300° Fahr.; more alcohol will lower it, less raise it. The mixture is now kept boiling at 300°, fresh alcohol being steadily supplied. Ether and water distill, ever forming two layers, the ether on top. The sulphuric acid is unchanged, and the same quantity will convert an indefinite amount of alcohol into ether. If the alcohol contains oils, however, they will be charred and render the acid black.

To Purify Ether.

Agitate it well in a closed vessel with double its bulk of water to remove any alcohol. Decant the ether from the water on which it floats. Add quicklime to remove any water that may be left, and after it has slaked distill. The first third will be pure ether.

To Imitate Foreign Spirits.

A great desideratum among distillers, in this country, is to imitate foreign spirits, such as brandy, rum, Geneva, etc., to a tolerable degree of perfection; but, notwithstanding the many attempts that are daily made for this purpose, the success, in general, has been indifferent. The general method of distilling brandies in France differs in nothing from that practised here, with malt-wash or molasses; nor are the French distillers in the least more cleanly in their operations. Still, though brandy is distilled from wine, experience tells us that there is a great difference in the grapes from which the wine is made. Every soil, every climate, every kind of grape, varies with regard to the quantity and quality of the spirit distilled from them. A large quantity of brandy is distilled in France during the time of the vintage; for the poor grapes that prove unfit for wine, are usually first gathered, pressed, their juice fermented, and instantly distilled. It is a general rule with them, not to distill wine that will fetch any price *as wine*; for, in this state, the profits obtained are much greater than when the wine is reduced to brandies.

For a long time, this liquor was distilled only from spoiled wine, and afterwards from the dregs of beer and wine; and when, instead of these, the distillers employed rye, wheat and barley, it was considered as a wicked and unpardonable misuse of grain.

To Improve British Brandy.

Take 30 galls. of fine English brandy, 3 oz. of tincture Japonica, and 9 oz. of sweet spirit of nitre. Incorporate these with some of the spirit, and then put it into the rest of the liquor, and stir it well about. This will make 30 galls. of brandy, and if it be a good clean spirit, it will much resemble French brandy.

To prepare Tincture Japonica.

Take of the best English saffron, mace bruised, of each 1 oz.; infuse them in a pint of brandy till the whole tincture of the saffron is extracted, which will be in 7 or 8 days; then strain it through a linen cloth, and to the strained tincture add 2 oz. of terra Japonica powdered fine; let it infuse till the tincture is wholly impregnated.

To make Jamaica Rum.

This is obtained from the refuse of the raw sugar manufactories, by taking equal quantities of the skimmings of the sugar pans, of lees or returns as they are commonly called, and of water;

and to 100 galls. of this wash are added 10 galls. of molasses. This affords from 10 to 17 galls. of proof rum, and twice as much low wines; it is sometimes rectified to a strength approaching to spirit of wine, and is then called double distilled rum.

To Obtain Rum from Molasses.

Mix 2 or 3 galls. of water with 1 gall. of molasses, and to every 200 galls. of this mixture add a gallon of yeast. Once or twice a day the head as it rises is stirred in, and in 3 or 4 days 2 galls. more of water is added to each gallon of molasses originally used, and the same quantity of yeast as at first. Four, 5 or 6 days after this, a portion of yeast is added as before, and about 1 oz. of julap root powdered (or in winter 1½ oz.), on which the fermentation proceeds with great violence, and in 3 or 4 days the wash is fit for the still; 100 galls. of this wash is computed to yield 22 galls. of spirit from 1 to 10 over-proof. If the molasses spirit, brought to the common proof strength, is found not to have sufficient vinosity, it will be proper to add some sweet spirits of nitre; and if the spirit has been properly distilled by a gentle heat, it may, by this addition only, be made to pass with ordinary judges as French brandy. Great quantities of this spirit are used in adulterating foreign brandy, rum, and arrack. Much of it is also used alone in making cherry brandy and other cordials by infusion; in all which many prefer it to foreign brandies. Molasses, like all other spirits, is entirely colorless when first extracted; but distillers give it, as nearly as possible, the color of foreign spirits.

To Prepare Gin as in Holland.

The grist is composed of 10 qrs. of malt, ground considerably finer than malt distillers' barley grist, and 3 qrs. of rye-meal; or, more frequently, of 10 qrs. of rye and 2 qrs. of malt-meal. The 10 qrs. are first mashed with the least quantity of cold water it is possible to blend it with, and when uniformly incorporated, as much boiling water is added as forms it into a thin batter; it is then put into 1, 2, or more casks, or gyle-tuns, with a much less quantity of yeast than is usually employed by our distillers. Generally, on the third day, the Dutch distillers add the malt or rye-meal, prepared in a similar manner, but not before it comes to the temperature of the fermenting wash; at the same time adding as much yeast as at first.

The principal secret is the management of the mashing part of the business, in first thoroughly mixing the malt with the cold water, and in subsequently adding the due proportion of boiling water, that it may still remain sufficiently diluted after the addition of the fine meal; also in well rousing all together in the back, that the wash may be diluted enough for distilling without endangering its burning to the bottom.

Rectification into Holland Gin.

To every 20 galls. of spirit of the second extraction, about the strength of proof, take of juniper-berries, 3 lbs.; oil of juniper, 2 oz.; and distil with a slow fire until the feints begin to rise, then change the receiving can; this produces the best Rotterdam gin.

An inferior kind is made with a still less proportion of berries, sweet fennel seed, and Strasburg turpentine, with a drop of oil of juniper; and a better sort, but inferior to the Rotterdam, is made at Weesoppe. The distiller's wash at Schiedam and Rotterdam is lighter than at Weesoppe. Strasburg turpentine is of a yellowish-brown color, a very fragrant agreeable smell, yet the least acrid of the turpentines. The juniper-berries are so cheap in Holland, that they must have other reasons than mere cheapness for being so much more sparing of their consumption than our distillers.

To make Malt Spirit.

Mix 60 quarters of barley grist, ground low, and 20 quarters of coarse ground pale malt, with 250 barrels of water, at about 170°. Take out 30 barrels of the wort, and add to this 10 stone of fresh porter yeast, and when the remaining wort is cooled down to 55°, add 10 quarters more malt, previously mixed with 30 barrels of warm water; stir the whole well together, and put it to ferment along with the reserved yeasted wort; this wash will be found to weigh, by the saccharometer, from 28 to 32 lbs. per barrel, more than water. In the course of 12 or 14 days, the yeast head will fall quite flat, and the wash will have a vinous smell and taste, and not weigh more than from 2 to 4 lbs. per barrel more than water. Some now put 20 lbs. of common salt, and 30 lbs. of flour, and in 3 or 4 days put it into the still, previously stirring it well together. Every 6 galls. of this wash will produce 1 gall. of spirit, at from 1 to 10 over-proof; or 18 galls. of spirit from each quarter of grain.

English Geneva.

The best English Geneva is made as follows: Take of juniper-berries, 3 lbs.; proof spirit, 10 galls.; water, 4 galls. Draw off by a gentle fire, till the feint begins to rise, and make up the goods to the required strength with clear water.

To Distill Spirits from Carrots.

Take 1 ton and 8 stone of carrots, which, after being exposed a few days to dry, will weigh about 160 stone. The whole being cut, put one-third of the quantity into a copper, with 24 galls. of water, and after covering them up close, reduce the whole into a pulp. The other two-thirds are to be treated in the same manner, and as the pulp is taken from the copper, it is carried to the press, where the juice is extracted with great facility. The liquor obtained will amount to 200 galls., and will be of a rich sweet taste, resembling wort. It is then put into the copper with 1 lb. of hops, and suffered to boil about 5 hours, when it is put into the cooler, to remain till the heat comes down to 66°. From the cooler it is discharged from the vat, where 6 qts. of yeast are put to it, in the usual manner. Let it work 48 hours, or to 58°, when the yeast begins to fall. Then heat 12 galls. of unfermented juice, and put it to the liquor, and the heat will be raised to 60°. Work afresh for 24 hours longer, the liquor gradually lowering, as before from 66° to 58°. Tun the whole into half-hogsheads, to work from the bung. After standing 3 days in the cask, 50 galls. may be drawn off, which is rectified the next day without any additional substance. Twelve galls. of spirit will be obtained.

To make Arrack.

Arrack is no other than a spirit produced by distillation from a vegetable juice called toddy, which flows out of the cocoanut tree. The operator provides himself with a parcel of earthen pots, climbs up the trunk of a cocoa-tree; and when he comes to the boughs, he cuts off one of the small knot or buttons, and applies the mouth of a bottle to the wound, fastening it to the bough with a bandage; in the same manner he cuts off others, and proceeds till the whole number is employed; this done, he leaves them until the next morning, when he takes off the bottles, which are mostly filled, and empties the juice into the proper receptacle. When a sufficient quantity is produced, the whole put together, is left to ferment. When the fermentation is over, and the liquor is a little tart, it is put into the still, and fire being made, the still is suffered to work as long as that which comes off has any considerable taste of spirit. The liquor thus procured is the low wine of arrack; and is distilled again to separate some of its watery parts, and rectify it to that very weak kind of proof spirit in which state we find it.

Tungusian arrack is a spirituous liquor made by the Tartars of Tungusia, of mare's milk, left to sour, and afterwards distilled twice or thrice between two earthen pots closely stopped, whence the liquor runs through a small wooden pipe.

To Fine Spirits.

Mix a small quantity of wheat flour in water as if for making paste, and pour the same into the vessel. The whole is then to be well roused, and in a short time the contents will become bright.

To Extract Alcohol from Potatoes.

Take 100 lbs. of potatoes well washed, dress them by steam, and let them be bruised to powder with a roller, etc. In the meantime take 4 lbs. of ground malt, steep it in lukewarm water, and then pour into the fermenting back, and pour on it 12 qts. of boiling water; this water is stirred about, and the bruised potatoes thrown in, and well stirred about with wooden rakes, till every part of the potatoes is well saturated with the liquor.

Immediately 6 or 8 oz. of yeast is to be mixed with 28 galls. of water of a proper warmth to make the whole mass of the temperature of from 59° to 66°; there is to be added ½ a pt. to 1 pt. of good brandy.

The fermenting back must be placed in a room, to be kept by means of a stove at a temperature from 66° to 72°. The mixture must be left to remain at rest.

The back must be large enough to suffer the mass to rise 7 or 8 inches without running over. If, notwithstanding this precaution, it does so, some must be taken out, and returned when it falls a little; the back is then covered again, and the fermentation is suffered to finish without touching it — which takes place generally in 5 or 6 days. This is known by its being perceived that the liquor is quite clear, and the potatoes fallen to the bottom of the back. The fluid is decanted, and the potatoes pressed dry.

When the fermentation has been favorable, from every 100 lbs. of potatoes, 6 qts. and upwards of brandy, of 20° of the areometer are obtained. It contains much fusel oil, and is colored and sold as Marc brandy.

One thousand lbs. of potatoes at twice, gives 60 to 70 qts. of brandy. The residue of the distillation is used as food for stock.

Alcohol from Wood.

The wood is reduced to coarse saw-dust; in this state it is dried up to a temperature of 212°, so as to drive off the water which it contains, often amounting to one-half of its weight. The wood is then suffered to cool, and concentrated sulphuric acid is poured over it with great care, and very small quantities at a time, so as to prevent the materials from heating. The acid is mixed with the wood as it is poured, then for 12 hours the mixture is let alone; after that it is rubbed up with great care, until the mass, which is at first dry, becomes sufficiently liquid to run. This liquid, diluted with water, is brought to the boiling point: the acid is saturated with lime, and the liquid, after filtration, is fermented, and the alcohol distilled in the ordinary way. In this experiment, the sulphuric acid must be at least 110 per cent. of the weight of the dry wood.

Kirsch Wasser.

Spirits of cherry. Ripe cherries are crushed by hand in an inclined wooden trough; the juice is collected, the stones added, the liquid left to ferment, and is then distilled. It is not necessary to crack the stones.

Apple Brandy

Is distilled from cider. Generally the apples are crushed and allowed to ferment thoroughly, which takes from 6 to 10 days, and distilled. A better plan is to collect only the juice and ferment it. The former gives a larger yield, but the quality is not so good.

Peach Brandy.

The peaches are mashed with pestles in a trough, the juice pressed out, collected, fermented, and distilled. The pomace still contains considerable juice, it is therefore covered with water, and after fermentation, distilled.

Raisin Spirit,

Much used to give a vinous flavor to inferior spirits, is made by infusing the raisins in water, fermenting, and distilling with a quick fire. The quick fire is necessary in order to get all the flavor from the raisins.

Proof Spirit.

Contains half its weight of alcohol. Its specific gravity at 60° is .920. The strength, however, varies in different localities, and the idea is at best clumsy and antiquated.

To make Brandy from Beet-Root.

For the preparation of brandy, the water used in the first boiling of the roots, is boiled again, and poured out on the residuum from the first expression of the pounded roots; this must stand for a day or two, after which it is expressed, and the remaining dry pulp serves as a good food for cattle. The juice obtained in this way is mixed with the waste parts of the syrup and the mucilage which remains after the expression of the saccharine crystals, and all boiled together till half of it is evaporated. The liquor is then poured into a coop exposed to a temperature of 45°, and cooled to 65°. Having added a proportionate quantity of yeast, it is left to ferment, and in 3 or 4 days after the distillation may be undertaken.

To Obtain Sugar from Beet-Root.

The beet-roots best calculated for the extraction of sugar, are those which have a soft flesh, whitish towards the edges and not growing above ground. After being cleaned, they are boiled, cut into pieces and pounded in a wooden trough with wooden stampers, and afterwards pressed. The juice thus obtained is immediately put into a polished copper kettle and simmered, during which time the scum must continually be taken off. To 100 quarts of this juice add 2 oz. or less of slackened lime, diluted so as to have the appearance of milk, and continue the boiling till the juice is thickened to the half of it. Having strained it through a woollen cloth, thicken it to the consistency of a syrup, which afterwards is put into glass, stone, or wooden vessels. These being placed near a moderate fire, saccharine crystals appear, which being freed by expression from the mucilaginous juice, a very good raw sugar is obtained.

Fusel Oil

Is found in new whiskey, more especially from rye, corn, and potatoes. It is a nearly colorless liquid, of a powerful odor of new whiskey, causing irritation of the nostrils and fauces. It boils at 296° Fahr., and has a density of 0.818. In its solvent forms and chemical relation it resembles alcohol.

swallowed, it acts as an instant poison. When liquors containing it are long kept, it changes into ethers, and becomes innoxious. There are probably several bodies compounded together under the general name of fusel oil. It may be detected by adding to the suspected liquor in a glass some fused chloride of calcium. The oil, if present, will be liberated, and may be recognized by its smell.

To Remove Fusel Oil.

It may be separated by careful distillation, especially if some soft wood charcoal be introduced into the still. 2d. By filtering the whiskey through bone-black; this is termed by the dealers "rectifying," which is incorrect. 3d. Oils are added to the whiskey and the whole shaken up, the oil unites with the fusel oil and rises to the surface, and may be skimmed off.

LIQUEURS.

To make Ratafia d'Angelique.

Take of angelica seeds, 1 dr.; stalks of angelica, bitter almonds, blanched, each 4 oz.; proof spirit, 12 pts.; white sugar, 2 lbs. Digest, strain, and filter.

Anisette de Bourdeaux.

Take of sugar, 9 oz.; oil of aniseed, 6 drops. Rub them together, and add by degrees, spirit of wine, 2 pts.; water, 4 pts. Filter.

To make Real Creme des Barbades.

Take 2 doz. middling-sized lemons; 6 large citrons; loaf sugar, 28 lbs.; fresh balm leaves, ½ lb.; spirit of wine, 2½ galls.; water, 3½ galls. This will produce about 7 galls., full measure. Cut the lemons and citrons in thin slices, and put them into a cask; pour upon them the spirit of wine, bung down close, and let it stand 10 days or a fortnight, then break the sugar, and boil it for ½ an hour in the 3½ galls. of water, skimming it frequently; then chop the balm-leaves, put them into a large pan, and pour upon them the boiling liquor, and let it stand till quite cold; then strain it through a lawn sieve, and put it to the spirits, etc., in the cask; bung down close, and in a fortnight draw it off; strain it through a jelly bag, and let it remain to fine; then bottle it.

Eau de Barbades.

Take of fresh orange-peel, 1 oz.; fresh lemon-peel, 4 oz.; cloves, ½ dr.; coriander, 1 dr.; proof spirit, 4 pts. Distill in a bath heat and add white sugar in powder.

To make Ratafia de Cafe.

Take of roasted coffee, ground, 1 lb.; proof spirit, 1 gall.; sugar, 20 oz. Digest for a week.

Ratafia de Cassis.

Take of ripe black currants, 6 lbs.; cloves, ½ dr.; cinnamon, 1 dr.; proof spirit, 18 pts.; sugar, 3½ lbs. Digest for a fortnight.

Ratafia des Cerises.

Take of morello cherries, with their kernels, bruised, 8 lbs.; proof spirit, 8 pts. Digest for a month, strain with expression, and then add 1½ lbs. of sugar.

Ratafia de Chocolat.

Take of Caracca cocoanuts, roasted, 1 lb.; West India cocoanuts, roasted, ½ lb.; proof spirit, 1 gall. Digest for a fortnight, strain, and then add sugar, 1½ lbs.; tincture of vanilla, 30 drops.

Eau Divine.

Take of spirit of wine, 1 gall.; essence of lemons, and essence of bergamot, each 1 dr. Distill in a bath heat; add sugar, 4 lbs. dissolved in 2 galls. of pure water; and, lastly, orange-flower water, 5 oz.

Elephant's Milk.

Take of gum benzoin, 2 oz.; spirit of wine, 1 pt.; boiling water, 2½ pts. When cold, strain; and add sugar, 1½ lbs.

Ratafia de Grenoble.

Take of small wild black cherries, with their kernels, bruised, 12 lbs.; proof spirit, 6 galls. Digest for a month, strain, and then add 12 lbs. of sugar. A little citron peel may also be added at pleasure.

Marasquin de Groseilles.

Take of gooseberries, quite ripe, 102 lbs.; black cherry leaves, 12 lbs. Bruise and ferment; distill and rectify the spirits. To each pint of this spirit add as much distilled water, and sugar, 1 lb.

Huile de Venus.

Take of flowers of the wild carrot, picked, 6 oz.; spirit of wine, 10 pts. Distill in a bath heat. To the spirit add as much syrup of capillaire; it may be colored with cochineal.

Liquodilla.

Take the thin peel of 6 oranges and 6 lemons, steep them in a gallon of brandy or rum, close stopped for 2 or 3 days; then take 6 qts. of water, and 3 lbs. of loaf sugar clarified with the whites of 3 eggs. Let it boil ¼ of an hour, then strain it through a fine sieve, and let it stand till cold; strain the brandy from the peels, and add the juice of 5 oranges and 7 lemons to each gallon. Keep it close stopped up 6 weeks, then bottle it.

Ratafia de Brou de Noix.

Take of young walnuts, whose shells are not yet hardened, in number 60; brandy, 4 pts.; sugar, 12 oz.; mace, cinnamon, and cloves, each. 15 gr. Digest for 2 or 3 months, press out the liquor, filter, and keep it for 2 or 3 years.

Ratafia de Noyeau.

Take of peach or apricot kernels, with their shells bruised, in number 120; proof spirit, 4 pts.; sugar, 10 oz. Some reduce the spirit of wine to proof with the juice of apricots or peaches, to make this liqueur.

Creme de Noyeau de Martinique.

Take 20 lbs. of loaf sugar; 3 galls. of spirit of wine; 3 pts. of orange-flower water; 1½ lbs. of bitter almonds; 2 drs. of essence of lemon; and 4½ galls. of water. The produce will exceed 8 galls.

Put 2 lbs. of the loaf sugar into a jug or can, pour upon it the essence of lemon, and 1 qt. of the spirit of wine: stir it till the sugar is dissolved, and the essence completely incorporated. Bruise the almonds, and put them into a 4 gall. stone bottle or cask, add the remainder of the spirit of wine, and the mixture from the jug or can; let it stand a week or 10 days, shaking it frequently. Then add the remainder of the sugar, and boil it in the 4½ galls. of water for ¾ of an hour, taking off the scum as it rises. When cold, put it in a cask; add the spirit, almonds, etc., from the stone bottle; and lastly, the orange flower water. Bung it down close, and let it stand 3 weeks or a month; then strain it through a jelly bag, and when fine bottle it off. When the pink is wanted add cochineal, in powder, at the rate of ½ a dr., or 2 scr. to a qt.

Ratafia d'Ecorces d'Oranges.

Take of fresh peel of Seville oranges, 4 oz.; proof spirit, 1 gall.; sugar, 1 lb. Digest for 6 hours.

Ratafia de Fleurs d'Oranges.

Take of fresh flowers of orange-tree, 2 lbs.

proof spirit, 1 gall.; sugar, 1½ lbs. Digest for 6 hours.

Creme d'Orange of Superior Flavor.

Take 3 doz. middling sized oranges; orange-flower water, 2 qts.; loaf sugar, 18 lbs.; spirit of wine, 2 galls.; tincture of saffron, 1½ oz.; water, 4½ galls. This will produce 7½ galls.

Cut the oranges in slices, put them into a cask, add the spirit and orange-flower water, let it stand a fortnight, then boil the sugar in the water for ½ an hour, pour it out, and let it stand till cold, then add it to the mixture in the cask, and put in the tincture of saffron. Let it remain a fortnight longer; then strain, and proceed as directed in the receipt for *Cremes de Barbades*, and a very fine cordial will be produced.

Fine Brandy Shrub.

Take 8 oz. of citric acid; 1 gall. of porter; 3 galls. of raisin wine; 2 qts. of orange-flower water; 7 galls. of good brandy; 5 galls. of water. This will produce 16 galls. First, dissolve the citric acid in the water, then add to it the brandy; next, mix the raisin wine, porter, and orange-flower water together; and lastly, mix the whole; and in a week or 10 days it will be ready for drinking, and of a very mellow flavor.

Rum Shrub.

Leave out the brandy and porter, and add 1 gall. more raisin wine; 6 lbs. of honey; and 10 galls. of good flavored rum.

Currant Shrub.

Take white currants, when quite ripe, pick them off the stalks, and bruise them; strain out the juice through a cloth, and to 2 qts. of the juice put 2 lbs. of loaf sugar; when it is dissolved add to it 1 gall. of rum, then strain it through a flannel bag that will keep in the jelly, and it will run off clear; then bottle it for use.

Usquebaugh.

Usquebaugh is a strong compound liquor, chiefly taken by way of dram; it is made in the highest perfection at Drogheda, in Ireland. The following are the ingredients, and the proportions in which they are to be used:

Take of best brandy, 1 gall.; raisins, stoned, 1 lb.; cinnamon, cloves, nutmeg, and cardamoms, each 1 oz. crushed in a mortar; saffron, ½ oz.; rind of 1 Seville orange; and brown sugar candy, 1 lb. Shake these well every day, for at least 14 days, and it will at the expiration of that time be ready to be fined for use.

Another Method.

Take of nutmegs, cloves, and cinnamon, each 2 oz.; of the seeds of anise, caraway, and coriander, each 4 oz.; liquorice-root, sliced, ½ lb.; bruise the seeds and spices, and put them together with the liquorice, into the still with 11 galls. of proof spirit, and 2 galls. of water; distill with a pretty brisk fire. As soon as the still begins to work, fasten to the nozzle of the worm 2 oz. of English saffron, tied up in a cloth, that the liquor may run through it, and extract all its tincture. When the operation is finished, sweeten with fine sugar. This liqueur may be much improved by the following additions: Digest 4 lbs. of stoned raisins; 3 lbs. of dates; and 2 lbs. of sliced liquorice-root, in 2 galls. of water for 12 hours. When the liquor is strained off, and has deposited all sediment, decant it gently into the vessel containing the usquebaugh.

Ratafia a la Violette.

Take Florentine orris root 2 drachms, archol 1 oz., spirit of wine 4 pts. Digest, strain, and add sugar 4 lbs. Liqueurs are also made by adding Hungary-water, honey-water, eau de Cologne, and several other spirits to an equal quantity of simple syrup, or common capillaire.

COMPOUND SPIRITS, OR CORDIALS.

General Rules.

The perfection of this grand branch of distillery depends upon the observation of the following general rules, which are easy to be observed and practised: 1. The artist must always be careful to use a well-cleansed spirit, or one freed from its own essential oil; for as a compound cordial is nothing more than a spirit impregnated with the essential oil of the ingredients, it is necessary that the spirit should have deposited its own. 2. Let the time of previous digestion be proportioned to the tenacity of the ingredients, or the ponderosity of their oil. 3. Let the strength of the fire be proportioned to the ponderosity of the oil intended to be raised with the spirit. 4. Let a due proportion of the finest parts of the essential oil be united with the spirit; the grosser and less fragrant parts of the oil not giving the spirit so agreeable a flavor, and at the same time rendering it thick and unsightly. This may in a great measure be effected by leaving out the feints, and making up to proof with fine soft water in their stead.

A careful observation of these four rules will render this extensive part of distillation far more perfect than it is at present. Nor will there he any occasion for the use of burnt alum, white of eggs, isinglass, etc. to fine down the cordial waters, for they will presently be fine, sweet, and pleasant.

To make Aniseed Cordial.

Take aniseed, bruised, 2 lbs; proof spirit, 12½ galls.; water, 1 gall. Draw off 10 galls., with a moderate fire. This water should never be reduced below proof; because the large quantity of oil with which it is impregnated will render the goods milky and foul, when brought down below proof. But if there is a necessity for doing this, their transparency may be restored by filtration.

Strong Cinnamon Cordial.

Take 8 lbs. of fine cinnamon, bruised; 17 galls of clear rectified spirit, and 2 galls. of water. Put them into the still, and digest them 24 hours with a gentle heat; after which draw off 16 galls. by a pretty strong heat.

Caraway Cordial.

For 20 galls. Take ½ oz. of oil of caraway, 20 drops of cassia-lignea oil, 5 drops of essence of orange peel, 5 drops of the essence of lemons, 13 galls. of spirits, 1 in 5, and 8 lbs. of loaf sugar. Make it up and fine it down.

Cedrat Cordial.

The cedrat is a species of citron, and very highly esteemed in Italy, where it grows naturally. The fruit is difficult to be procured in this country; but, as the essential oil is often imported from Italy, it may be made with it as follows: Take of the finest loaf-sugar, powdered, ¾ lb. Put it into a glass mortar, with 120 drops of the essence of cedrat; rub them together with a glass pestle, and put them into a glass alembic, with a gallon of fine proof spirit and a quart of water. Place the alembic in a bath heat, and draw off 1 gall., or till the feints begin to rise; then dulcify with fine sugar This is considered the finest cordial yet known; it will therefore be necessary to be particularly careful that the spirit is perfectly clean, and, as much as possible, free from any flavor of its own.

Citron Cordial.

Take of dry yellow rinds of citrons, 3 lbs.; orange-peel, 2 lbs.; nutmegs, bruised, ¾ lb.; proof spirit, 10½ galls.; water, 1 gall. Digest with a gentle heat, then draw off 10 galls. in a bath heat, and dulcify with fine sugar.

Clove Cordial.

Take of cloves, bruised, 4 lbs.; pimento, or allspice, ½ lb.; proof spirit, 16 galls. Digest the mixture 12 hours in a gentle heat, and then draw off 15 galls. with a pretty brisk fire. The water may be colored red, either by a strong tincture of cochineal, alkanet, or corn poppy-flowers. It may be dulcified at pleasure with refined sugar.

Coriander Cordial.

For 3 galls. Take 7 qts. of spirits, 2 lbs. of coriander seed, 1 oz. of caraway seed, 6 drops of the oil of orange, and 2 lbs. of sugar. Fill up with water. The coriander seed must be bruised and steeped in the spirits for 10 or 12 days, and well stirred 2 or 3 times a day. Fine it the same as gin.

Eau de Bigarade.

Take the outer or yellow part of the peels of 14 bigarades (a kind of orange), ½ oz. of nutmegs, ¼ oz. of mace, 1 gall. of fine proof spirit, and 2 qts. of water. Digest all these together 2 days in a close vessel; after which draw off a gallon with a gentle fire, and dulcify with fine sugar.

Gold Cordial.

Take of the roots of angelica, sliced, 4 lbs.; raisins, stoned, 2 lbs.; coriander seeds, ½ lb.; caraway seeds and cinnamon, each ¼ lb.; cloves, 2 oz.; figs and liquorice root, sliced, each 1 lb.; proof spirit, 11 galls.; water, 2 galls. Digest 2 days, and draw off by a gentle heat, till the feints begin to rise; hanging in a piece of linen, fastened to the mouth of the worm, 1 oz. of English saffron. Then dissolve 8 lbs. of sugar in 3 qts. of rose-water, and add to it the distilled liquor.

The above cordial derives its name from a quantity of leaf gold being formerly added to it; but this is now generally disused.

Lovage Cordial.

For 20 galls. Take of the fresh roots of lovage, valerian, celery, and sweet fennel, each 4 oz.; essential oil of caraway and savin, each 1 oz.; spirit of wine, 1 pt.; proof spirit, 12 galls.; loaf sugar, 12 lbs. Steep the roots and seeds in the spirits for 14 days; then dissolve the oils in the spirit of wine, and add them to the undulcified cordial drawn off from the other ingredients; dissolve the sugar in the water for making up, and fine, if necessary, with alum.

Lemon Cordial.

Take of dried lemon-peel 4 lbs., proof spirit, 10½ galls., water 1 gall. Draw off 10 galls. by a gentle fire, and dulcify with fine sugar.

Nectar.

For 20 galls. Take 15 galls. of red ratafia, ¼ oz. of cassia-oil, and an equal quantity of the oil of caraway seeds. Dissolve in half a pint of spirit of wine, and make up with orange wine, so as to fill up the cask. Sweeten, if wanted, by adding a small lump of sugar in the glass.

Noyeau.

Take 1½ galls. of French brandy, 1 in 5, 6 oz. of the best French prunes, 2 oz. of celery, 3 oz. of the kernels of apricots, nectarines, and peaches, and 1 oz. of bitter almonds, all gently bruised, essence of orange-peel and essence of lemon-peel, of each 2 dwts., ½ lb. of loaf-sugar. Let the whole stand ten days or a fortnight; then draw off, and add to the clear noyeau as much rose-water as will make it up to 2 galls.

Orange Cordial.

Take of the yellow part of fresh orange-peel, 5 lbs., proof spirit, 10½ galls., water, 2 galls. Draw off 10 galls. with a gentle fire.

Peppermint Cordial.

For 20 galls. Take 13 galls. of rectified spirits, 1 in 5 under hydrometer proof, 12 lbs. of loaf-sugar, 1 pint of spirit of wine that will fire gunpowder, 15 dwts. (troy) of oil of peppermint, water, as much as will fill up the cask, which should be set up on end after the whole has been well roused, and a cock for drawing off placed in it.

Ratafia.

This a liquor prepared from different kinds of fruits, and is of different colors, according to the fruits made use of. These fruits should be gathered when in their greatest perfection, and the largest and most beautiful of them chosen for the purpose. The following is the method of making red ratafia, fine and soft: Take of the black-heart cherries, 24 lbs., black cherries, 4 lbs., raspberries and strawberries, each, 3 lbs. Pick the fruit from their stalks and bruise them, in which state let them continue 12 hours; then press out the juice, and to every pint of it add ¼ lb. of sugar. When the sugar is dissolved, run the whole through the filtering-bag and add to it 3 quarts of proof spirit. Then take of cinnamon, 4 oz., mace, 4 oz., and cloves, 2 drs. Bruise these spices, put them into an alembic with a gallon of proof spirit and 2 quarts of water, and draw off a gallon with a brisk fire. Add as much of this spicy spirit to the ratafia as will render it agreeable; about ¼ is the usual proportion.

Dry or Sharp Ratafia.

Take of cherries and gooseberries, each 30 lbs., mulberries, 7 lbs., raspberries, 10 lbs. Pick all these fruits clean from their stalks, etc., bruise them and let them stand 12 hours, but do not suffer them to ferment. Press out the juice, and to every pint add 3 oz. of sugar. When the sugar is dissolved, run it through the filtering-bag, and to every 5 pints of liquor add 4 pints of proof spirit, together with the same proportion of spirit drawn from spices.

Common Ratafia.

Take of nutmegs, 8 oz., bitter almonds, 10 lbs., Lisbon sugar, 8 lbs., ambergris, 10 grs. Infuse these ingredients three days in 10 galls. of proof spirit and filter it through a flannel bag for use. The nutmegs and bitter almonds must be bruised, and the ambergris rubbed with the Lisbon sugar in a marble mortar, before they are infused in the spirit.

Cherry-Brandy.

One of the best and most common ways of making cherry-brandy, is to put the cherries (being first clean-picked from the stalks) into a vessel till it be about half full; then fill up with rectified molasses-brandy, which is generally used for this compound; and when they have been infused 16 or 18 days draw off the liquor by degrees, as wanted; when drawn off, fill the vessel a second time nearly to the top, let it stand about a month, and then draw it off as there is occasion. The same cherries may be used a third time by covering them with over-proof brandy and letting it infuse for 6 or 7 weeks; when drawn off for use, as much water must be added as the brandy was over-proof, and the cherries must be afterwards pressed as long as any liquor remains in them, before being cast away.

When drawn off the second time the liquor will be somewhat inferior to the first, when more sugar, with ½ oz. of cinnamon and cloves beaten, may be added to 20 galls. of it; but there should only be half the quantity of cinnamon and cloves in each 20 galls. of the first infusion.

Another Method.

Take 72 lbs of cherries, half red and half black, mash or squeeze them to pieces with the hands, and add to them 3 galls. of brandy, letting them steep for 24 hours; then put the mashed cherries and liquor into a canvas bag, a little at a time, and press it as long as it will run. Sweeten it with loaf sugar and let it stand a month; then bottle it off, putting a lump of sugar into every bottle.

Another.—To every 4 qts. of brandy, put 4 lbs. of red cherries, 2 lbs. of black, 1 qt. of raspberries, with a few cloves, a stick of cinnamon, and a little orange peel; let these stand a month close stopped; then bottle it off, putting a lump of sugar into every bottle.

Black-Cherry Brandy.

Stone 8 lbs. of black cherries and put on them a gallon of brandy. Bruise the stones in a mortar, and then add them to the brandy. Cover them close, and let them stand a month or 6 weeks. Then pour it clear from the sediment and bottle it. Morello cherries, managed in this manner, make a fine rich cordial.

Caraway-Brandy.

Steep 1 oz. of caraway-seed and 6 oz. of loaf sugar, in 1 qt. of brandy; let it stand 9 days and then draw it off.

Lemon-Brandy.

Put 5 qts. of water to 1 gall. of brandy; take 2 doz. of lemons, 2 lbs. of the best sugar, and 3 pints of milk. Pare the lemons very thin and lay the peel to steep in the brandy 12 hours. Squeeze the lemons upon the sugar, then put the water to it, and mix all the ingredients together. Boil the milk and pour it in boiling. Let it stand 24 hours and then strain it.

Orange Brandy.

Put the chips of 18 Seville oranges in 3 qts. of brandy, and let them steep a fortnight in a stone bottle close stopped. Boil 2 qts. of spring-water with 1½ lbs. of the finest sugar, nearly an hour very gently. Clarify the water and sugar with the white of an egg, then strain it through a jelly-bag and boil it nearly half away. When it is cold, strain the brandy into the syrup.

Raspberry Brandy.

Take a pint of water and 2 qts. of brandy, and put them into a pitcher large enough to hold them and 4 pints of raspberries. Put in ½ lb. of loaf-sugar and let it remain for a week close covered. Then take a piece of flannel with a piece of holland over it, and let it run through by degrees. It may be racked into other bottles a week after, and then it will be perfectly fine.

Another Method.

Raspberry brandy is infused nearly after the same manner as cherry brandy, and drawn off with about the same addition of brandy to what is drawn off from the first, second and third infusion, and dulcified accordingly; first making it of a bright deep color, omitting cinnamon and cloves in the first, but not in the second and third infusion. The second infusion will be somewhat paler than the first, and must be heightened in color by adding cherry brandy, about 1 qt., with 10 or more galls. of raspberry brandy; and the third infusion will require more cherry brandy to color it. It may be flavored with the juice of the elderberry.

Whiskey Cordial.

Take of cinnamon, ginger, and coriander-seed, each 3 oz., mace, cloves, and cubebs, each 1½ oz. Add 11 galls. of proof spirit and 2 galls. of water, and distill; now tie up 5 oz. of English saffron; raisins (stoned), 4½ lbs.; dates. 3 lbs.; liquorice-root, 2 lbs. Let these stand 12 hours in 2 galls. of water; strain, and add it to the above. Dulcify the whole with fine sugar.

FACTITIOUS LIQUORS.

Much of the wine and spirits sold is factitious. In some cases the ingredients added are not inferior in their character; in others alcohol is replaced by poisonous bodies, some imitations containing absolutely no alcohol. The receipts given below are among the least injurious, although none are recommended.

Neutral Spirit,

Or sweet liquor, is made by filtering ordinary whiskey through bone-black, and afterwards through wood charcoal, to deprive it of all fusel oil, and other odorous matter.

Flavoring Materials.

These are acetic, butyric ethers, acetate of the oxyde of amyl (see CONFECTIONARY for Flavoring Extracts), sweet spirit of nitre, oil of bitter almonds, oil of cognac, light oil of wine, the various essential oils, tincture of benzoin, citric, tartaric, and sulphuric acid.

Nut kernels, mucilage of various kinds, slippery elm, almond oil, green tea, and sugar are used to give the appearance of age.

Cocculus indicus, Guinea pepper, mustard, horseradish, pellitory, are used to give pungency and intoxicating qualities.

Catechu, green tea, logwood, oak bark, etc., to give astringency and color.

Caramel and burned sugar to give color.

To Detect Adulterations.

The quantity of alcohol is determined by the hydrometer (see SPECIFIC GRAVITY). Should the liquor be much below proof, and still possess decidedly intoxicating qualities, cocculus indicus is to be suspected, but no good test for this substance is known. If, when the liquor be swallowed, it produces a burning sensation at the back of the throat, it is adulterated with pepper, etc.

The flavoring ethers may be separated by distillation, but as some of them exist in true wines and spirits, this cannot decide that the liquor is factitious.

If the liquor be cautiously evaporated to dryness, in a porcelain capsule, the extract will contain most of the adulterations, which can often be detected by the taste and smell.

If nitrate of baryta gives a precipitate with any spirit, the presence of acid artificially added may be suspected. This is not true of wines.

To detect *fusel oil,* put some fused chloride of calcium, broken into small pieces, into a glass; pour over it the suspected liquor, cover it with a glass plate, and let it stand aside for a short time. If fusel oil be present it will at once manifest itself by its smell. The smaller the quantity of fusel oil the longer must it stand before examination.

To Determine the Quantity of Alcohol in Wine, Beer, etc.

Distill carefully a small quantity of the liquid, until from ½ to ¾ have passed over, then add water enough to the distillate to make it up to its original bulk, put the mixture in a well-stopped bottle and shake well; let it stand aside for a day or two; its specific gravity may be then taken with the hydrometer, or specific gravity bottle.

To Determine the Strength of Spirits.

The simplest method and that generally adopted, is by the hydrometer. It consists of a cylinder, with a weighted bulb below to make it float upright, and a graduated stem. If it float with the bottom of the stem at the surface of pure water at 60° Fahr., it will sink deeper in a lighter liquid. The instrument of Tralles is so graduated as to indicate the percentage *by volume* of absolute alcohol in any mixture of alcohol and water. If the spirit be not at the temperature of 60°, it should be brought to that degree, or the temperature tested and allowance made by a table which is found in the chemical works. In introducing the instrument, care should be taken to avoid wetting the stem, as this would give a higher percentage than the truth. To convert volume percentage into that by weight, multiply the number of degrees on Tralles' scale by 0.794, and divide by the specific gravity of the liquid under trial. In case the Tralles' instrument is not at hand, take the specific gravity of the liquid by any of the methods given under that head. By means of tables to be found in the chemical works, the percentage of alcohol may be determined.

To Procure the Oil of Wine.

This oil should be distilled from the thick lees of French wines, because of the flavor, and when procured must be kept ready for use. It must be mixed with the purest spirits of wine, such as alcohol; by which means it may be preserved a long time. The bottle should be shaken before the oil is used.

When the flavor of the brandy is well imitated by a proper portion of the essential oil, and the whole reduced into one nature, yet other difficulties still exist; which are, the color, the softness, and the proof. The proof may be effected by using a spirit above proof, which after being mixed with the oil may be let down to any strength with water. The softness will be attained by getting a spirit that has been distilled by a slow fire; and the color may be regulated by the use of brandy coloring.

Preparation of Rum Ether.

Take black oxide of manganese, and sulphuric acid, each 12 lbs.; alcohol, 26 lbs.; strong acetic acid, 10 lbs.

The ether above prepared is the body to which rum owes its peculiar flavor; it is also used in making cheap brandy.

Artificial Fruit Essences.

The pine-apple flavor is butyrate of ethyloxide, or butyric ether; apple, valerianate of amyloxide; quince, pelargonate of ethyloxide; jargonelle pear, acetate of amyloxide; ordinary pear, acetate of amyloxide, with acetate of ethyloxide; melon flavor, cocinate of ethyloxide. Other flavors are made by using these in various proportions and different degrees of dilution with alcohol.

To make Butyric Acid.

Dissolve 6 lbs. of sugar and ½ oz. of tartaric acid in 26 lbs. of water. Let the solution stand for several days, add 8 oz. of putrid cheese, 3 lbs. skimmed and curdled sour milk, and 3 lbs. of levigated chalk. The mixture should be kept in a warm place, say 92° Fahr., and stirred from time to time. In about 6 weeks the sugar will have given rise to butyric acid, which unites with the lime of the chalk.

To separate the butyric acid, add hydrochloric (muriatic) acid and distill. It is well to neutralize the distillate with carbonate of soda and re-distill. Then saturate the distillate with fused chloride of calcium and re-distill.

To make Butyric Ether.

Take 3 oz. of butyric acid, 6 oz. alcohol, and 2 oz. of sulphuric acid. Distill in a glass retort. The distillate may be re-distilled over chloride of calcium.

This is the pine-apple oil. It is used to flavor syrup, creams, fruit-drops, and cheap brandy. It requires to be diluted with deodorized alcohol, in order to develop the true flavor.

To make Oil of Quince.

Pelargonic ether is made from oil of rue by treating with double its volume of dilute nitric acid, heating the mixture until it begins to boil. After some time two layers are seen. The lower one is separated with a pipette, and freed from nitric acid by evaporation in a chloride of zinc bath, it is then filtered mixed with deodorized alcohol, and digested at a gentle heat until the fruity odor is noticed.

This ether seems identical with the ethereal oil of wine, which gives the *bouquet*. It is sometimes sold as oil of Cognac.

Jargonelle Pear Oil

Is made from heavy fusel oil, that which comes over last in distillation. To purify the fusel oil wash with soda and water, and distill between 254° and 284° Fahr. Of this take 1 lb.; glacial acetic acid, 1 lb.; sulphuric acid, ½ lb. Digest for some hours at 254° Fahr. The ether separates upon the addition of water, and is purified by washing with soda and water. Mixed with 1-30th of acetic ether, and 7 parts of deodorized alcohol, it gives the essence of pears.

Apple Oil.

Mix cautiously 1 part of fusel oil, 3 parts of sulphuric acid, and 2 parts of water. Dissolve 2½ parts of bichromate of potash in 4½ parts of water, introduce this into a large tubulated retort, and gradually add the former liquid, so that the boiling continues very slowly. The distillate, which is principally valerianic acid, is saturated with carbonate of soda, and evaporated to dryness. Take of the valerianate of soda, thus formed, 1½ parts; fusel oil, 1 part; sulphuric acid, 1 part; mix cautiously, heat by a water bath, and mix with water; the impure valerianate of amyloxide will separate. It is washed several times with water, then with a solution of carbonate of soda, and finally with water. This is dissolved in from 6 to 8 parts of water.

To Improve the Flavor of Fruit Essences.

Add to the essence made by dissolving the oil in 6 or 8 parts of deodorized alcohol a small quantity of tartaric or citric acid. This will develop the flavor, and, when used in confectionary, imitate more closely the taste of the fruit.

Bead for Liquors.

Ether, 1 lb.; strong alcohol, 2 qts. Keep in a well-stopped bottle.

Jamaica Rum

Neutral spirits, 4 galls.; Jamaica rum, 1 gall.; sulphuric acid, ½ oz.; acetic ether, 4 oz.; burnt sugar coloring, 8 oz.

Pineapple Rum.

Neutral spirits, 4 galls.; honey, 5 pts.; water, to dissolve, 3 qts.; Jamaica rum, 1 gall.; sulphuric acid, 1 oz.; butyric ether, 2 oz.; tincture of cochineal, 3 oz.; burnt sugar, 2 oz.

Gin.

Aromatic Schiedam Schnapps.

Neutral spirits, 4 galls.; water, 4 pts., to dissolve honey, 4 pts.; oil of juniper, 15 drops, dissolved in nitric ether, 1 oz.

Curacoa.

Common whiskey, 5 galls ; fresh orange-peel, 4 lbs.; oil of bitter almonds, oil of cassia, of each, 1 dr.; oil of lemon, 2 drs.; oil of cinnamon, 50 drops; water, 5 qts., to dissolve refined sugar, 16 lbs.; tincture of cochineal, ½ a pt.; burnt sugar, 3 oz.; allow the above to digest for 5 days; the whole of the oils should be dissolved in ½ a glass of alcohol, and mix well.

BRANDIES.

Cognac Brandy.

Neutral spirits, 4 galls.; ½ a gall. of honey dissolved in water, 2 pts.; Jamaica rum, 1 gall.; catechu, ½ oz.; butyric ether, 1 oz. Mix.

Sarzerac Brandy.

Neutral spirits, 4 galls.; 3 pts. of water to dissolve honey, 4 pts.; rum, 3 qts.; porter, 3 pts.; infusion of almonds, ½ a pt.; oil of wine, 1 oz.; sugar coloring, 4 oz.; cochineal tincture, 1 oz.; then add the alcoholic solution of starch, 3 pts., and mix. This starch solution is made by infusing 1 qt. of wheat or rice flour in 1½ galls. of equal parts of clean spirit and water for 24 hours.

Cherry Brandy.

Neutral spirits, 4 galls.; refined sugar, 5 lbs.; water, to dissolve, 1 gall.; catechu, 1 oz.; infusion of bitter almonds, ½ a pt.; cloves, cassia, of each, ½ oz.; these are to be well bruised before adding tartaric acid, 4 oz., dissolved in 1 pt. of water; honey, 1 qt., dissolved in 1 pt. of water; 4 drops of oil of wintergreen, dissolved in 1 oz. of acetic ether, then color with 1 pt. of the tincture of cochineal; burnt sugar, 1 oz.

Peach Brandy.

Neutral spirits, 4 galls.; 3 pts. of honey, dissolved in 2 pts. of water; mix infusion of bitter almonds, 1 pt.; sulphuric acid, 80 drops; porter, 1 pt.; tincture of saffron, ½ a pt.: and flavor with oil of pears, 1 oz., dissolved in 2 oz. of alcohol, and acetic ether, ½ oz.

Old Apple Brandy.

Neutral spirits, 4 galls.; decoction of tea, 1 pt.; alcoholic solution of starch, 3 qts., sulphuric acid, ½ oz.; this is flavored with the oil of apples, 1 oz., dissolved in alcohol, 2 oz.; color with 4 oz. of sugar coloring; valerianate of amylic oxide is the chemical name for apple oil.

WHISKEYS.

Irish Whiskey.

Neutral spirits, 4 galls.; refined sugar, 3 lbs., in water, 4 qts.; creasote, 4 drops; color with 4 oz. of burnt sugar.

Scotch Whiskey.

Neutral spirits, 4 galls.; alcoholic solution of starch, 1 gall.; creasote, 5 drops; cochineal tincture, 4 wineglassfuls; burnt sugar coloring, ½ pt.

Old Bourbon Whiskey.

Neutral spirits, 4 galls; refined sugar, 3 lbs.; dissolved in water, 3 qts.; decoction of tea, 1 pt.; 3 drops of oil of wintergreen, dissolved in 1 oz. of alcohol; color with tincture of cochineal, 2 oz.; burnt sugar, 3 oz.

Monongahela Whiskey.

Neutral spirits, 4 galls.; honey, 3 pts., dissolved in water, 1 gall.; alcoholic solution of starch, 1 gall.; rum, ½ a gall.; nitric ether, ½ an ounce; this is to be colored to suit fancy.

Anisette de Bordeaux.

Whiskey, 2 galls.; 5 lbs. of refined sugar; water, to dissolve, 1½ galls.; 1 dr. oil of aniseed, dissolved in 1 oz. of alcohol, or well rubbed up in dry sugar, and added; if this is for white anisette, fine with ½ oz. of powdered alum; if it is for rose or pink anisette, color to suit taste.

Common rectified whiskey will answer in the above formula, or in any other in which a powerful aromatic is found necessary.

Maraschino.

Proof whiskey, 3 galls.; 6 qts. of water, to dissolve; sugar, 12 lbs.; oil of bergamot, and oil of cloves, of each, 1 dr.; oil of cinnamon, 5 drops; 2 oz. of nutmegs, bruised, 1 lb. of orange-peel, 3 oz. of bitter almonds, bruised; oil of lemon, 1 dr.; dissolve the oil in alcohol; color with cochineal and burnt sugar.

Sherry.

Cider, 10 galls.; bitter almonds, 4 oz.; honey, 1 gall.; mustard, 4 oz. Boil for 30 minutes, and strain, then add spirits of orris-root, ½ a pt.; essence of cassia, 2 oz.; and rum, 3 qts.

Port Wine.

Claret, 100 galls.; honey, strained, 12 galls.; red tartar, 1 lb.; powdered catechu, 12 oz.; wheat flour, made into a paste, 1 pt.; neutral spirits, 12 galls.: 2 oz. each of bruised ginger and cassia, 1 pt. of tincture of orris-root, and color with alkanet-root, or dissolve 16 oz. bruised cochineal in 1 gall. of the above spirit, and 1 pt. of burnt sugar; this will produce the desired shade of purple. For giving artificial strength, use tincture-grains of paradise, and the decoction of strong tea, in quantities to suit the palate.

If this is not perfectly transparent, fine with milk or isinglass.

Madeira Wine.

Water, 12 galls.; honey, 1 gall.; clean spirits, 5 qts.; hops, 5 oz.; bitter almonds, 3 oz. Boil for 25 minutes and allow it to ferment by the addition of 1 qt. of yeast; allow the fermentation to continue until the liquor tastes pleasantly acid, then fine with milk, and add 3 qts. of rum and 4 oz. of mustard. Allow it to stand for a few days; the mustard should be inclosed in a thin piece of muslin and be suspended in the wine.

Imitation Claret.

Boiled cider, 6 galls.; spirits, 2 galls.; clear water, 5 galls.; catechu, powdered, 2 oz. Color with red beets and tincture logwood to suit taste. When this is not sufficiently acid, add from 1 to 2 drops of sulphuric acid to the gallon, to suit taste.

Cheap Champagne.

Water, 50 galls.; honey, 2 galls.; bruised ginger, 5 oz.; ground mustard, 5 oz. Boil the mass for 30 minutes, and when quite cool add a quart of yeast. Ferment for 10 or 14 days; first add 6 oz. of bitter almonds, bruised; spirits, and grains of Paradise tincture, to suit convenience. The more spirit the Champagne possesses the greater will be its body. For coloring, use cochineal ½ oz. to 50 galls. The cheapest coloring is red beets, sliced, and added to the mass during fermentation. Five or 6 common-sized beets will color 50 galls. The best of this coloring will not compare with cochineal. A fine aroma is given to the champagne by adding 5 drops of spirits of orris, or 3 drops of essence of wintergreen, or essence of vanilla 4 drops; or dissolve 5 grs. of ambergris in ½ glass of pure alcohol; the alcohol should be kept hot for ½ an hour; this, when dissolved, should be added to 50 galls. of Champagne.

ESSENTIAL OILS.

General Directions.

The quantity of volatile oil yielded by a plant will depend upon the part employed, the season, and the period of growth. The drier the season and the warmer the climate, the richer are the plants in oils. They should be gathered, as a general rule, immediately after blossoming, and distilled, if possible, while fresh.

It is better to macerate the plants for one day before distilling. Roots, barks, etc., should be coarsely powdered. Parts which yield no oil, as the stems of mint, sage, etc., should be detached.

The larger the quantity operated on the better; the quantity of water should be sufficient to thoroughly cover the plant; too much water causes loss by dissolving a portion of the oil. When the plants are abundant the distillate should be returned to a fresh portion of the plant in a retort. It is a good plan to use the water of a previous distillation for the same plant, as it is already saturated with the oil.

If the oil is heavier than water, use a saturated solution of salt. If lighter, the Florentine receiver.

Solutions for the Water-bath.

Various salts dissolved in water materially raise the boiling point, and thus afford the means of obtaining a steady temperature at different degrees above 212°. The following are some of the most useful: A saturated solution of nitrate of soda boils at 246°; Rochelle salts at 240°; nitre at 238°; muriate of soda at 224°; sulphate of magnesia at 222°.

Oil of Aniseed.

One lb. of the seeds will yield 2 drs. It is congealed, except in warm weather; this oil is carminative, and poisonous to pigeons, if rubbed on their bills or head.

Oil of Ben, or Behen,

Is obtained by expression from the seeds of *Mohringa aptera*. It is insipid, inodorous, and does not become rancid. It is used in perfumery. Hazel-nut oil is sometimes substituted for it.

Birch Oil.

Obtained by distilling 20 parts of birch bark and 1 of *ledum palustre*, crammed in layers into an earthen pot, with a handful of tripoli between each layer; the mouth of the pot is closed with a perforated oak plug, and being inverted, it is luted to the mouth of another pot sunk in the ground; the pot being then surrounded with fire, a brown empyreumatic oil distils *per descensum* into the lower jar; an 8 gall. pot, properly filled, yields about 2 lbs. or 2½ lbs. of oil. In Siberia it is prepared without the ledum. This oil is liquid when fresh, but grows thick in time. It is used in Russia for currying leather, to which it gives a very peculiar smell, much disliked by insects.

Oil of Gum-benzoin.

Obtained by distilling the residuum left after making flowers of benjamin, by a strong fire. It is used instead of birch oil in making an imitation of Russia leather.

Cajeput Oil.

This is obtained from the leaves, which are imported from the East Indies, generally in large copper flasks; it is cooler than that of peppermint, but smells of turpentine. It is used externally in rheumatism.

Oil of Caraway.

This is obtained from the seeds; it is carminative; 2 lbs. will yield more than 1 oz., and 4 cwt. 83 oz.

Oil of Cloves.

This is obtained from a spice of that name; it is very heavy, acrimonious, and supposed to contain some part of the resin of the clove. One lb. of cloves will yield from 1½ to 2½ oz.; 7½ lbs. will yield 1 lb. of oil. It is also expressed from the cloves when ripe. Muller, by digesting ½ oz. of cloves in ether, and then mixing it with water, obtained 7 scruples of oil, greenish yellow, swimming upon water. Oil of cloves is imported from the spice islands; it is stimulant, and added to purgative pills to prevent griping; it is externally applied to aching teeth.

Oil of Cassia.

This is a common oil of cinnamon, and is obtained from the bark of inferior cinnamon, imported under the name of cassia. One lb. will yield from 1 to 1½ drs. It is stimulant and stomachic. Another oil is obtained from cassia buds.

Oil of Chamomile.

This is obtained from the flowers, and is stomachic. One lb. will yield a dr.; 82 lbs. will yield from 13 to 18 drs. It is of a fine blue, even if distilled in glass vessels.

Oil of Cinnamon.

This is obtained from the fresh bark, which is imported from Ceylon. De Guignes says the cinnamon from Cochin China is so full of essential oil that it may be pressed out by the fingers.

Essence of Cedrat.

This is obtained from the flowers of the citron tree; it is amber-colored and slightly fragrant; 60 lbs. yield 1 oz. It is also obtained from the yellow part of citron-peel; it is colorless, very thin, and fragrant. The second oil is obtained by the distillation of the yellow part of citron-peel, and is greenish; 100 citrons will yield 1 oz. of the white essence, and ½ oz. of this. It is likewise obtained from the yellow part of citron-peel by expression between two glass plates; also, from the cake left on squeezing citron-peel, by distillation with water. It is thick.

Common Essence of Cedrat.

This is obtained from the fæces left in the casks of citron-juice; clear, fragrant, greenish; 50 lbs. of fæces will yield, by distillation, 3 lbs. of essence.

Oil of Calamus.

The rhizoma of the *acorus calamus*, or swell flag, yields about 1 per cent. of oil. It is carminative, but little used. It is also employed in perfumery.

Oil of Cedar.

Obtained by distillation; is sometimes used in perfumery.

Camphor.

This is obtained from the roots and shoots of the *laurus camphora* and *laurus cinnamomum*, as also the *capura curundu*, by distillation with water. This crude camphor is refined by sublimation with one-sixteenth of its weight of lime in a very gentle heat.

Camphor from Essential Oils.

Obtained from the oils of the labiate plants by a careful distillation, without addition of ⅓ of the oil; the residuum will be found to contain crystals of camphor, on separating which and re-distilling the remaining oil 2 or 3 times, the whole of the camphor may be obtained. Oil of rosemary or of sweet marjoram yields about 1 oz. of camphor from 10 of oil; of the sage 1 oz. from 8, and of lavender 1 oz. from 4, or even less of oil; that from oil of marjoram is not volatile, and although it takes fire, it soon goes out. This resin, like the others from essential oils, may be obtained in a larger proportion if the oil is kept in slightly stopped bottles in a cool place.

ESSENTIAL OILS.

Dippel's Oil.

Obtained from hartshorn, distilled without addition, rectifying the oil, either by a slow distillation in a retort, etc., no bigger than is necessary, and saving only the first portion that comes over, or with water in a common still; it is very fine and thin, and must be kept in an opaque vessel, or in a drawer, or dark place, as it is quickly discolored by light. It is anti-spasmodic, anodyne, and diaphoretic, taken in doses of from 10 to 30 drops, in water.

Oil of Bitter Almonds

Is obtained by the distillation of the crushed kernels; at the same time hydrocyanic acid is formed and passes over with the oil. The crude oil is therefore poisonous. It is sometimes used in medicine for the hydrocyanic acid which it contains, but is uncertain. It is used in perfumery and confectionery. When cakes are flavored with it. the hydrocyanic acid can do little or no mischief, as it is driven off by the heat employed.

Artificial Oil of Bitter Almonds

Is made by action on true benzole (not that distilled from petroleum) of fuming nitric acid or a mixture of equal parts of ordinary nitric and sulphuric acids. It is of a yellowish color; is poisonous; is used for making aniline (see COAL TAR COLORS), and in perfumery. Its chemical name is nitro-benzole; it is sold as "Essence of Mirban." By heating benzoate of ammonia, an oily liquid having exactly the bitter almond smell, is obtained. It is not used. It is known in chemistry as benzonitrile.

Oil of Geranium,

From the leaves of the *Pelargonium odoratissimum*, is used in perfumery. It is adulterated with ginger-grass oil. It is used to adulterate attar of roses.

Artificial Oil of Geranium

May be obtained by distilling benzoate of copper. It has not come into practical use. Its chemical name is benzoxyl.

Krumholz' Oil.

Obtained by distillation from Hungarian balsam. It is distinguished from oil of turpentine, which is commonly sold for it, by its golden color, agreeable odor, and acid oiliness of taste.

Foreign Oil of Lavender.

This is the true oil of spike, and is obtained from the flowers and seeds of broad-leaved lavender, and more commonly those of French lavender, stoechas, with a quick fire. It is sweet-scented, but the oil of the narrow-leaved lavender, or English oil, is by far the finest.

Essence of Lavender.

The oil of the flowers of lavender is rendered more delicate in its odor by age; but to prevent its becoming glutinous by keeping, which it is very apt to do, draw it over in a water-bath, with a small quantity of alcohol, which is termed the essence, and which, after being kept closely corked for about 7 years, possesses a peculiarly fine delicate odor of lavender, entirely free from empyreuma.

Oil of Lemon

Is obtained by expression and distillation. It is used in confectionary and perfumery. When old it acquires the taste and smell of turpentine.

Oil of Lemon-grass.

Antropogon nargus, is a grass which grows in India, Ceylon, and the Moluccas. The oil is extensively used in perfumery.

Oil of Marjoram,

Origent majorana, is used in perfumery. The dried herb yields about 10 per cent. of oil.

Oil of Meadow Sweet.

The *Spiraea ulmaria* is sometimes used as a stimulant and in perfumery.

Artificial Oil of Meadow Sweet

Is made by distilling *salicin*, a crystalline, bitter principle, obtained from the leaves and young bark of the willow, with bichromate of potassa.

Oil of Mint.

Obtained from the dried plant. Six lbs. of fresh leaves will yield 3½ drs.; and 4 lbs. dried will yield 1½ oz. It is stimulant, carminative, and antispasmodic.

Essence of Neroli.

Obtained from the flowers of the orange tree. Six cwt. of flowers will yield only 1 oz. of oil. *Petits grains* is an inferior oil of neroli obtained in the same manner, but less care being taken in the selection of the flowers. Another essence is obtained from orange-peel, and is very fragrant. A third essence is obtained from unripe oranges, and is of a gold color.

Oil of Nutmegs.

Obtained from that spice; it is liquid, and of a pale yellow; a sebaceous insipid matter swims upon the water in the still.

Oil of Patchouly.

Obtained by distillation from the *Pogastemon patchouli*, a plant grown extensively in India and China. One cwt. of the herb yields about 23 oz. of essential oil. It is used in perfumery.

Oil of Peppermint.

Obtained from the dried plant. Four lbs. of the fresh herb will yield 3 drs. In general it requires rectification to render it bright and fine. It is stimulant and carminative.

Oil of Pennyroyal.

Obtained from the herb when in flower. Three lbs. will yield 6 drs. Emmenagogue.

Oil of Pimento.

Obtained from allspice. One oz. will yield 30 drops. It is stimulant.

Oil of Rhodium.

Obtained from the true *lignum rhodium*. Eighty lbs. will yield 9 drs., and in very resinous old wood 80 lbs. will yield 2 oz. It is light yellowish, but grows red by keeping. Another oil is obtained from the root of rose-wort, *rhodiola rosea*; it is yellowish, and has the smell and taste of that from the true *lignum rhodium*. One lb. will yield a drachm.

The True Riga Balsam.

Obtained from the shoots of the Aphernousti pine, *pinus cembra*, previously bruised and macerated for a month in water. It is pellucid, very liquid, whitish, and has the smell and taste of oil of juniper.

Butter of Roses.

Obtained from the flowers of damask roses, white, solid, separating slowly from the rose-water. It has little scent of its own, and is used to dilute the scent of musk, civet and ambergris. One cwt. of roses will yield from ½ an oz. to an oz.

Oil of Rosemary.

Obtained from the flowering tops; it is sweet-scented. One cwt. will yield 8 oz.; 1 lb. of dry leaves will yield from 1 to 3 drs.; 70 lbs. of fresh leaves will yield 5 oz.

Oil of Rue.

Obtained from the dried plant; it is carminative and antispasmodic. Ten lbs. of leaves will yield from 2 to 4 drs.; 4 lbs. in flower will yield 1 dr.; and 60 lbs. will yield 2½ oz.; 72 lbs., with the seeds, will yield 3 oz.

Oil of Sassafras.

Obtained from the sassafras root. Twenty-four lbs. will yield 9 oz.; 30 lbs. will yield 7 oz. and 1 dr.; and 6 lbs. will yield 2 oz.

Oil of Sandal Wood.

There are three kinds of sandal or santal wood, the white, yellow and red. The yellow is most used in perfumery. One cwt. of the wood will yield nearly 30 oz. of otto.

Oil of Spearmint,

Mentha viridis, is used in medicine as a carminative, and in perfumery.

Oil of Tar.

Obtained by distilling tar. It is highly valued by painters, varnishers, etc., on account of its drying qualities; it soon thickens of itself, almost to a balsam. The pyroligneous acid that comes over with it is useful for many purposes.

Oil of Thyme.

Obtained from the plant; 2 cwt. fresh will yield 5½ oz.; 3½ lbs., dried, will yield ½ a dr. It is stimulant and caustic; and used in toothache, applied to the tooth.

Oil of Tongua.

Obtained from the tongua, or tonka bean. *Dipterix odorata* is sometimes used in perfumery. The bean contains also a camphor-like body and benzoic acid.

Oil of Turpentine.

Distilled, in Europe, from common turpentine, with the addition of about 6 times as much water; but in America, where the operation is carried on upon a very large scale, no water is added, and its accidental presence is even dreaded, lest it should produce a disruption of the stilling apparatus.

To Rectify Oil of Turpentine.

Pour 3 parts of turpentine into a glass retort, capable of containing double the quantity of matter subjected to the experiment. Place this retort on a sand-bath, and having adapted to it a receiver 5 or 6 times as large, cement with paste made of flour and water, some bands of paper over the place where the 2 vessels are joined. If the receiver is not tubulated, make a small hole with a pin in the bands of cemented paper, to leave a free communication between the exterior and interior of the receiver; then place over the retort a dome of baked earth, and maintain the fire in such a manner as to make the essence and the water boil.

The receiver will become filled with abundance of vapors, composed of water and ethereous essence, which will condense the more readily if all the radiating heat of the furnace be intercepted by a plate of copper, or piece of board placed between the furnace and the receiver. When the mass of oil subjected to experiment has decreased nearly two-thirds, the distillation must be stopped. Then leave the product at rest to facilitate the separation of the ethereous oil, which is afterwards separated from the water, on which it floats, by means of a glass funnel, the beak of which is stopped by the finger.

This ethereous oil is often milky, or merely nebulous, by the interposition of some aqueous parts, from which it may be separated by a few days' rest. The essence, thus prepared, possesses a great degree of mobility, and is exceedingly limpid.

Another Method.

The apparatus employed in the preceding process may be used in the present case. Fill the retort ¾ with essence, and as the receiver is tubulated, apply to the tubular a small square of paper moistened with saliva, to afford a free passage to the vapors. Graduate the fire in such a manner as to carry on distillation very slowly, until a little more than ½ the oil contained in the retort is obtained. Separate from the product, a very small quantity of exceedingly acid and reddish water, which passes at the same time as the ethereous essence; by these means the operation is much shortened. The oil of turpentine which remains in the retort is highly colored, and thicker than the primitive essence. It may be used for extending fat, varnish, or for coarse oil painting.

Balsam of Turpentine, or Dutch-drops.

Obtained by distilling oil of turpentine in a glass retort, till a red balsam is left.

Or, by distilling resin and separating the oils as they come over; first a white oil, then yellow, lastly a thick red oil, which is the balsam. It is stimulant and diuretic.

Essence of Vitivert

Is obtained by distillation of the *kus-kus*, the rhizoma of an East Indian grass. Used in perfumery.

Oil of Wintergreen,

From the leaves of the *gaultheria procumbens*, is stimulant and carminative. Used in medicine, confectionary, and perfumery.

Oil of Wormwood.

Obtained from the herb; stomachic: 25 lbs. of green wormwood will yield from 6 to 10 drs. of oil; 4 lbs. of dry will yield 1 oz.; and 18 lbs. only 1½ troy oz.

Adulterations of Volatile Oils.

The most common are resinous matters, fixed oils. the cheaper volatile oils, and alcohol.

Resinous and fatty matters are left behind when the oil is evaporated; the latter communicate a greasy stain to paper which does not disappear with a gentle heat, and are comparatively insoluble in alcohol. Both are left behind when the oil is mixed with water and distilled.

The cheaper volatile oils are detected by the smell and taste, and specific gravity. Oil of turpentine (often used) may be detected by it being undissolved when the oil is treated with 4 times its volume of alcohol of a specific gravity of 0.84. Oil of geranium in oil of rose (a very common adulteration) is detected by sulphuric acid, which developes an unpleasant odor if the geranium oil be present, but has no effect upon pure oil of rose.

Alcohol is largely used in adulteration. Take some small pieces of fused chloride of calcium in the bottom of a test tube, add the oil to be examined, and heat gently to 212° Fahr. If much alcohol be present the chloride of calcium will be dissolved, if only a small quantity the fragments will fall together and form a pasty mass at the bottom of the tube.

DISTILLED WATERS.

Preservation of Flowers for Distillation.

Rub 3 lb. of rose-leaves for 2 or 3 minutes with 1 lb. of common salt. The flowers being bruised by the friction of the grains of salt, form a paste, which is to be put into an earthen jar, or into a water-tight barrel. The same process is to be repeated until the vessel is filled, so that all the roses may be equally salted. The vessel is then to be shut up and kept in a cool place until wanted.

For distillation, this aromatic paste is, at any season, to be put into the body of the still with twice its weight of water; and when heat is applied, the oil, or essential water, is to be obtained in the common way. Both the oil and water are in th... way produced in greater quantity than by using the leaves without the salt; besides, the preserved paste will keep its flavor and strength unimpaired for several years.

Other flowers, capable of affording essential oils, may also be treated in the above-mentioned way with economy and advantage; as there is thereby no occasion to carry on a hurried process in the heat of summer, when these are in perfection.

General Rules for the Distillation of Simple Waters.

1. Plants and their parts ought to be fresh gathered. When they are directed fresh, such only must be employed; but some are allowed to be used dry, as being easily procurable in this state at all times of the year, though rather more elegant waters might be obtained from them whilst green.

2. Having bruised the subjects a little, pour thereon thrice its quantity of spring-water. This quantity is to be diminished or increased according as the plants are more or less juicy than ordinary. When fresh and juicy herbs are to be distilled, thrice their weight of water will be sufficient; but dry ones require a much larger quantity. In general there should be so much water, that after all intended to be distilled has come over, there may be liquor enough to prevent the matter from burning to the still.

3. Formerly, some vegetables were slightly fermented with the addition of yeast, previous to the distillation.

4. If any drops of oil swim on the surface of the water, they are to be carefully taken off.

5. That the waters may be kept the better, about one-twentieth part of their weight of proof spirit may be added to each after they are distilled.

Stills for Simple Waters.

The instruments chiefly used in the distillation of simple waters are of two kinds, commonly called the hot still, or alembic, and the cold still. The waters drawn by the cold still from plants are much more fragrant, and more fully impregnated with their virtues, than those drawn by the hot still or alembic.

The method is this: A pewter body is suspended in the body of the alembic, and the head of the still fitted to the pewter body; into this body the ingredients to be distilled are put, the alembic filled with water, the still-head luted to the pewter body, and the nose luted to the worm of the refrigerator or worm. The same intention will be answered by putting the ingredients into a glass alembic and placing it in a bath heat, or balneum marœ.

The cold still is much the best adapted to draw off the virtues of simples which are valued for their fine flavor when green, which is subject to be lost in drying; for when we want to extract from plants a spirit so light and volatile as not to subsist in open air any longer than while the plant continues in its growth, it is certainly the best method to remove the plant from its native soil into some proper instrument where, as it dies, these volatile parts can be collected and preserved. And such an instrument is what we call the cold still, where the drying of the plant or flower is only forwarded by a moderate warmth, and all that rises is collected and preserved.

Expeditious Method of Distilling Simple Waters.

Tie a piece of muslin or gauze over a glazed earthen pot, whose mouth is just large enough to receive the bottom of a warming-pan; on this cloth lay the herb clipped; then place upon them the warming-pan with live coals in it, to cause heat just warm enough to prevent burning; by which means, as the steam issuing out of the herb cannot mount upwards, by reason of the bottom of the pan just fitting the brim of the vessel below it, it must necessarily descend and collect into water at the bottom of the receiver, and that strongly impregnated with the essential oil and the salt of the vegetable thus distilled; which, if wanted to make spirituous or compound water, is easily done by simply adding some good spirits or French brandy to it, which will keep good for a long time, and be much better than if the spirits had passed through a still, which must of necessity waste some of their strength. Care should be taken not to let the fire be too strong, lest it scorch the plants; and to be made of charcoal, for continuance and better regulation, which must be managed by lifting up and laying down the lid, as wanted to increase or decrease the degrees of heat. The deeper the earthen pan, the cooler the season, and the less fire at first (afterwards to be gradually raised), in the greater perfection will the distilled water be obtained.

As the more movable or volatile parts of vegetables are the aqueous, the oily, the gummy, the resinous, and the saline, these are to be expected in the waters of this process; the heat here employed being so great as to burst the vessels of the plants, some of which contain so large a quantity of oil that it may be seen swimming on the surface of the water.

Although a small quantity only of distilled waters can be obtained at a time by this confined operation, yet it compensates in strength what is deficient in quantity. Such liquors, if well corked up from the air, will keep a good long time, especially if about a twentieth part of any spirits be added, in order to preserve the same more effectually.

To make Rosemary Water.

As the method of performing the operation by the cold still is the very same, whatever plant or flower is used, the following instance of procuring a water from rosemary will be abundantly sufficient to instruct the young practitioner in the manner of conducting the process in all cases whatever.

Take rosemary fresh gathered in its perfection, with the morning dew upon it, and lay it lightly and unbruised upon the plate or bottom of the still; cover the plate with its conical head, and apply a glass receiver to the nose of it. Make a small fire of charcoal under the plate, continuing it as long as any liquor comes over into the receiver.

When nothing more comes over, take off the still head and remove the plant, putting fresh in its stead, and proceed as before; continue to repeat the operation successively, till a sufficient quantity of water is procured. Let this distilled water be kept at rest in clean bottles close stopped, for some days in a cold place; by this means it will, become limpid, and powerfully impregnated with the taste and smell of the plant.

Simple Alexetereal Waters.

Take of spearmint leaves, fresh, 1½ lbs.; sea wormwood tops, fresh, angelica leaves, fresh, each 1 lb.; water, as much as is sufficient to prevent burning. Draw off by distillation 3 galls. Or take of elder-flowers moderately dried, 2 lbs.; angelica leaves, fresh gathered, 1 lb.; water, a sufficient quantity. Distill off 3 galls.

Simple Pennyroyal Water.

Take of pennyroyal leaves, dry, 1½ lbs.; water as much as will prevent burning. Draw off by distillation 1 gall.

DISTILLATION.

Simple Spearmint Water.
Take of spearmint leaves, fresh, any quantity; water, 3 times as much. Distil as long as the liquor which comes over has a considerable taste or smell of the mint. Or, take spearmint leaves, dried, 1½ lbs., water as much as is sufficient to prevent burning. Draw off by distillation 1 gall.

Cinnamon Water.
Take of bruised cinnamon, 1 lb.; water, 2 galls. Simmer in a still for ½ an hour, put what comes over into the still again; when cold strain through flannel.

Eau Sans-Pareil.
Take 2 galls. of fine old honey-water, put it into a still capable of holding 4 galls., and add the thinly pared rinds of 6 or 8 fresh citrons, neither green nor mellow ripe. Then add 60 or 70 drops of fine Roman bergamot; and, having luted the apparatus well, let the whole digest in a moderate heat for 24 hours. Draw off, by a water-bath heat, about 1 gall.

Jessamine Water.
Take 6 lbs. of the white sweet almond cakes from which jessamine oil has been made abroad; beat and sift them to a fine powder, and put to it as much fresh oil of jessamine as will be required to make it into a stiff paste. Let this paste be dissolved in about 6 qts. of spring-water, which has been previously well boiled, and left until it has become about half cold. Stir and mix the whole well together; and when the oil and water have been well combined, let the whole stand until the powder has fallen to the bottom of the vessel. Now pour the liquid off gently, and filter it through cotton, in a large tin funnel, into the glass bottle in which it is to be kept for use. The powder or sediment which has been left at the bottom of the vessel, when dried by the heat of the sun, answers very well for making almond paste for the hands.

Jamaica Pepper Water.
Jamaica pepper is the fruit of a tall tree growing in the mountainous parts of Jamaica, where it is much cultivated because of the great profit arising from the cured fruit, sent in large quantities annually into Europe. Take of Jamaica pepper, ½ lb.; water, 2½ galls.; draw off 1 gall. with a pretty brisk fire. The oil of this fruit is very ponderous, and therefore this water is made in an alembic.

Myrtle Water.
Infuse 8 or 10 lbs. of the cuttings of green myrtle in nearly 20 galls of rum or river water, and add thereto a pint of fresh yeast, after it has stood for 24 hours. At the end of another day and night, put the whole into a still, with 1 lb. of bay-salt. Draw off the whole of the water, and next day infuse more myrtle leaves as before, and distil again. Repeat the same a third time.

Orange-flower Water.
Take 2 lbs. of orange-flowers, and 24 qts. of water, and draw over 3 pts. Or, take 12 lbs. of orange-flowers, and 16 qts. of water, and draw over 15 qts.

Orange-peel Water.
Take of the outward yellow rind of Seville oranges, 4 oz.; water, 3½ galls.; draw off 1 gall. by the alembic, with a brisk fire.

Peppermint Water.
Take of the herb of peppermint, dried, 1½ lbs.; water, as much as is sufficient to prevent burning. Distil off a gallon. This has been known to allay sickness when nothing else would succeed, and is used in flatulent colics. A wineglassful may be taken, and often repeated.

Another. — Take of oil of peppermint, 1 lb.; water, a sufficient quantity. Draw off 30 galls. This is stimulant and carminative, and covers disagreeable flavors.

Portugal and Angel Waters.
Take 1 pt. of orange-flower water; 1 pt. of rose-water; and ½ pt. of myrtle water; to these put a ¼ oz. of distilled spirit of musk, and an ounce of spirit of ambergris. Shake the whole well together, and the process will be finished.

Rose-water.
Take of the leaves of fresh damask-roses with the heels cut off, 6 lbs.; water, as much as to prevent burning. Distill off a gallon. The distilled water should be drawn from dried herbs, because the fresh cannot be got at all times in the year. Whenever the fresh are used the weights must be increased; but whether the fresh or dry are made use of, it is left to the judgment of the operator to vary the weight, according as the plants are in greater or less perfection, owing to the season in which they grew, or were collected.

Small Snail Water.
Take of balm, mint, hart's tongue, ground ivy; flowers of the dead nettle, mallow-flowers, elder-flowers, each a handful; snails freed from their shells, and whites of eggs, each 4 oz.; nutmegs, ½ oz.; milk, 1 gall. Distill in a water-bath to dryness.

Strawberry Water.
Take of the bruised fruit, 20 lbs.; water a sufficient quantity. Draw off 2½ galls.; this water is very fragrant.

Common Distilled Water.
Take of water, 10 galls. Distill. Throw away the first ½ gall. and draw off 4 galls., which keep in glass or stoneware. Distilled water is used in making medicine preparations when the salts contained in common water would decompose them.

COMPOUND DISTILLED WATERS.

General Rules for the Distillation of Spirituous Waters.

1. The plants and their parts ought to be moderately and newly dried, except such as are ordered to be fresh gathered.
2. After the ingredients have been steeped in the spirit for the time prescribed, add as much water as will be sufficient to prevent a burnt flavor, or rather more.
3. The liquor which comes over first in the distillation is by some kept by itself, under the title of spirit; and the other runnings, which prove milky, are fined down by art. But it is preferable to mix all the runnings together, without fining them, that the waters may possess the virtues of the plant entire.
4. In the distillation of these waters, the genuine brandy obtained from wine is directed. Where this is not to be procured take, instead of that proof spirit, half its quantity of a well-rectified spirit, prepared from any other fermented liquors. In this steep the ingredients, and then add spring-water enough both to make up the quantity ordered to be drawn off, and to prevent burning.

Bergamot Water.
Take of fine old French brandy 2 galls., or 1 gall. of highly rectified spirit of wine, and 1 gall. of spring-water. Put to the brandy, or diluted spirits ½ oz., or more, of true Roman oil of berga-

mot, whose parts have been previously well divided by trituration with lump-sugar, in a glass mortar. Now distill by a water heat, and draw off 6 qts. only. By this operation a most excellent bergamot water will be produced, which will remain good for 20 years.

Original Receipt for Hungary Water.

The original receipt for preparing this invaluable lotion is written in letters of gold in the hand-writing of Elizabeth, queen of Hungary. Take of aqua vitæ, four times distilled, 3 parts; the tops and flowers of rosemary, 2 parts. To be put together in a close-stopped vessel, and allowed to stand in a warm place during 50 hours, then to be distilled in an alembic, and of this, once every week, 1 dr. to be taken in the morning, either in the food or drink, and every morning the face and the diseased limb to be washed with it.

French Hungary Water.

The French Hungary water is made wholly from a wine spirit, and from rosemary flowers alone, which about Montpellier (the place from whence this commodity comes) grow in great plenty and perfection. The fragrancy of these flowers is so great as to render the waters made from them more excellent and valuable than anything of the kind made in England.

Best Hungary Water.

Take 30 galls. of spirit of wine: put to it, in a large still, 6 large bunches of fine green rosemary, when the flowers are white and in full bloom; 1 lb. of lavender flowers, and 4 oz. of true English oil of rosemary. The rosemary-leaves and flowers must be stripped from all their wood and green twigs. When the whole has been in a state of digestion for 24 hours, distill as before, drawing off about 25 or 26 galls., but no more. When distilled, stop it closely in a copper vessel, and keep it undisturbed for about a month.

Aqua Mellis, or the King's Honey-water.

First Distillation.

Take 28 lbs. of coriander seeds, ground small in the starch-mill; 28 common bunches of sweet marjoram, in flower, dried and stripped from the twigs; 1 lb. of calamus aromaticus; 1 lb. of yellow saunders; and 1 lb. of orange and lemon peel. Let the 3 last be separately beaten into gross powder. Mix the above ingredients, and put them into a 60 gall. copper still, and add to them 20 galls. of proof spirit, and the same quantity of rain or spring-water. Lute well all the junctures of the apparatus, and leave the ingredients in this state, without fire, for 48 hours. At the end of this time begin to distill by a very gentle heat, lest the flowers and seeds, which are very light, should rise suddenly in the still-head, stop up the worm, and endanger the whole work.

Increase the fire after the first half hour, and keep it regular till the termination of the process. Draw off about 26 or 27 galls., or continue so long as the spirit will burn by the application of a lighted paper to a small quantity of it in a saucer. Next day, when the still is perfectly cold, let it be well cleaned out. The ingredients should be immediately dried in the sun, otherwise they will become mouldy. When there is a considerable quantity from 3 or 4 makings it ought to be ground in a mill, and finely sifted. They will be found to be of great use in the making of ordinary brown wash-balls, and, with some additions of brown powders for the hair.

Second Distillation.

Now return the spirits drawn off into the still, and add 10 or 12 galls. of water; then put in the following ingredients, bruised and mixed: 14 oz. of nutmegs, 4 oz. of cloves, 12 oz. of cinnamon bark, 8 oz. of pimento, and 40 oz. of cassia-lignum. These are to be separately broken or bruised in an iron mortar, until they are about the size of small peas. If there be any dust, it must be sifted from them before they are used; then take 40 oz. of storax, 40 oz. of gum Benjamin, 44 oz. of lahdanum, and 40 vouellios.

Break and bruise the above also, but make as little dust as possible. Put the dust from these and the foregoing, together, into a coarse muslin bag, which is to be hung in the still, so that the liquor, during distillation, may extract all its virtues. The whole are then to remain in the liquor, in a cold state, for 48 hours, attention being still paid to luting and stopping close, as before. At the end of this time kindle the fire, and work off (slowly at first) until 26 galls. are distilled. Mix all the different runnings together in a copper vessel, kept for this purpose only.

Having drawn off, in this second distillation, 26 galls., mix together 10 oz. of spirit of musk, 10 oz. of spirit of ambergris, ½ oz. of true oil of lavender, ¼ oz. of essence of bergamot, and ½ oz. of oil of rhodium. Now add to it, in a copper vessel that will hold 40 galls., 6 galls. of orange-flower water, and 8 galls. of rose-water, recently made. When properly mixed, put all these into the copper vessel, and stir the whole well together. Add to all these a quart of milk, which has stood for a night, and which has had the cream taken clearly off; then agitate and mix the whole well together, and stop the vessel up close, until the time when it is to be used.

The jar ought to have a lock-cock soldered into it, to prevent accidents. This should be placed full two inches from the bottom, in order that the milk and other impurities may fall to the bottom.

If this honey-water be made in the spring, and if the weather be fair, it will be quite fined down in the course of a month, that is, if it be not opened or disturbed. When, by drawing off a little in a glass, the milk, etc., have fallen down to the bottom, draw the whole off into clean and well-seasoned stone or glass bottles, or into another copper jar. This composition ought never to be drawn off in rainy or cloudy weather, for then the milk is apt to rise. In warm weather it should be kept cool, and in winter as warm as possible. When distilled in the winter the jars ought to be warmed, or otherwise the honey-water will not be fined for 5 or 6 months.

This honey-water may keep 30 years.

The ingredients from the second distillation are of much greater value than those from the first, and therefore require more care in the drying. These are of great use for the best sort of gross powders, for sweet bags, etc.; and, if made into a fine powder, may be made use of with great success, in the best sort of brown perfumed balls.

The same powder, with fresh ingredients, makes excellent pastils, to burn; and may be further used in making spirit of Benjamin.

Compound Spirit of Juniper.

Take of juniper-berries, well bruised, 1 lb.; caraway seeds, and sweet fennel seeds, each, bruised, 1½ oz.; diluted alcohol, 1 gall. Macerate for two days, and having added as much water as will prevent empyreuma, draw off, by distillation, 1 gall.

Lavender Spirit.

Take 14 lbs. of lavender flowers, 10½ galls. of rectified spirit of wine, and 1 gall. of water, draw off 10 gall. by a gentle fire; or, which is much better, by a sand bath heat.

Lavender-water.

Take 30 galls. of the best wine spirit, pour it into a copper still, placed in a hot-water bath, over a clear but steady fire; put to it 6 lbs. of the largest and freshest lavender flowers, after having separated them from all stalks and green leaves, which give the lavender water a woody and faint smell. Put no water into the still; close all the junctures well, and let the spirits and flowers stand in a state of digestion for 24 hours; and then, with a gentle fire, draw off 25. or, at most, 26 galls. only, which, as soon as distilled, are to be poured into a copper vessel for keeping. Wooden vessels and cans are to be avoided, as the best parts of the oil and of the spirits will be absorbed by them, and consequently lost. When the distillation is over, draw out, or quench the fire, and let the remaining spirits and flowers continue in the still until the next day. When the above quantity of 25 or 26 galls. has stood for 4 or 5 days, put to it 10 oz. of true English oil of lavender. Mix the whole well in the jar, by drawing out 1 or 2 galls., and then returning them. Repeat this 10 or 12 times, then stop the vessel up close, and do not disturb it for a month at least.

Lavender-water of the Second Order.

To the 4 or 5 galls. of the spirits, and the lavender flowers left in the still, after the distillation mentioned in the last article, add 15 galls. of common proof spirit, 9 or 10 galls. of spring-water, 3 lbs. of lavender flowers, and 4 oz. o. oil of lavender, intimately mixed with loaf sugar, by powdering it in a glass mortar. Digest the whole, and draw off 25 galls., proceeding in every respect as before, except that, in this case, no oil is to be added; for, as there is so much water present, the addition of oil would be apt to turn the whole quantity muddy, or of a bluish or opaque color, which it cannot be easily freed from, without a second distillation.

Lavender-water for immediate use.

Mix with 1 gall. of proof spirit, 1¼ oz. of true English oil of lavender, which is all that will properly combine with the spirit, without injuring the color, by rendering it muddy. When the spirit and the oil are properly mixed, they are to be put into glass bottles, which are to be well stopped, and ought to be shaken before used.

Perfumed Lavender-water.

Distill by a gentle heat in a sand or water bath, or mix and shake frequently, during 14 days, the following ingredients: 1 oz. of foreign oil of lavender, ½ oz. of English lavender, ½ oz. of essence of ambergris, and 1 gall. of rectified spirit of wine.

Lemon-water.

The peel of the lemon, the part used in making this water, is a very grateful bitter aromatic, and, on that account, very serviceable in repairing and strengthening the stomach. - Take of dried lemon-peel, 4 lbs.; proof spirit, 10½ gall., and 1 gall. of water. Draw off 10 galls. by a gentle fire.

Spirit of Peppermint.

Take of the herb of peppermint, dried, 1½ lbs.; proof spirit, 1 gall.; water, sufficient to prevent burning. Distill off 1 gall.

Compound Gentian-water.

Take of gentian root, sliced, 3 lbs.; leaves and flowers of the lesser centaury, each 8 oz.; infuse the whole in 6 qts. of proof spirit and 1 qt. of water; and draw off the water till the feints begin to rise.

Spirit of Scurvy-Grass.

Take of scurvy-grass, fresh gathered and bruised, 15 lbs.; horseradish-root, 6 lbs.; rectified spirit of wine, 1 gall.; and water, 3 pts. Digest the whole in a close vessel 2 days, and draw off 1 gall. with a gentle fire.

Antiscorbutic Water.

Take of the leaves of water-cresses, garden and sea scurvy-grass, and brook-lime, each 20 handfuls; of pine-tops, germander, horehound, and the lesser centaury, each 16 handfuls; of the roots of bryony and sharp-pointed dock, each 6 lbs.; of mustard-seed, 1½ lbs. Digest the whole in 10 galls. of proof spirit, and 2 galls. of water, and draw off by a gentle fire.

ACID LIQUORS.

Vinegar. (Impure Dilute Acetic Acid.)

Vinegar is made by the oxidation of alcohol, either directly or through the medium of a ferment, or by the distillation of wood; the latter is known as pyroligneous acid. Any substance capable of fermentation or any containing alcohol is suitable for making vinegar. It is made in the slow way from wine, cider, beer, sugar, or honey and water, whiskey and water, juice of plants and vegetables; in the quick way from a spirit prepared for the purpose.

Slow Method of Making Vinegar.

This is the process usually adopted in the small scale. The "wash," as any weak alcoholic liquor is called, should be weak, from 5 to 10 per cent. of alcohol is best, too strong a liquor will ferment very slowly; the strength is best judged by the taste. The temperature should be from 74° to 86° Fahr. Sour beer, wine, or cider are better than good liquors. The addition of sugar, honey, or other sweet matter with a view of strengthening the vinegar is not to be recommended, as it renders the vinegar liable to spoil. Ordinary fermented liquors are quite alcoholic enough.

The best ferment is vinegar; an old cask in which good vinegar has been kept is the best to ferment in. Other ferments are used, as bread soaked in brewer's yeast, sour dough, dough of wheat and rye flour soaked in cream of tartar and vinegar; all these are used in small quantity, a few ounces to a barrel of wash. Vinegar made with them is more apt to spoil. The more ferment present the quicker the process.

The wash is put into the cask, which is best painted black in order to absorb the sun's rays when the weather is cool; the bung is left out, the bung-hole covered with a piece of slate, and in about 4 weeks the acetification is complete. The lower the temperature the slower the change.

To Purify Vinegar.

After all the mothers are deposited, draw it off into a vessel filled with beech shavings, and let it stand in a cool place until clear. Vinegar is apt to be infested with flies (*Musca cellaris*), and eels (*Vibrio aceti*). These may be killed by passing it through a coiled tube dipped in boiling water.

Vinegar (especially when weak) if exposed to the air becomes thick or mothery, and deposits a mucilaginous substance; the vinegar becomes weak and mouldy as this change goes on.

When vinegar is barrelled, a pint of spirits should be added to each barrel to secure its keeping. It should be kept in a cool place.

Varieties of Vinegar.

Wine Vinegar, made from wine, contains citric and tartaric acid, and a small portion of acetic ether, which communicates an agreeable flavor.

It is imitated by adding acetic ether and coloring matter to vinegar made from whiskey.

Cider Vinegar (which includes all fruit vinegars) contains malic acid.

Malt, or Corn Vinegar, made from weak worts, contains phosphates of lime and magnesia, gum, and extractive matter.

Wood Vinegar, or pyroligneous acid, when crude, contains tar and wood spirit.

Adulterations of Vinegar.

Sulphuric, nitric and muriatic acids, are used to give a false strength; burned sugar and acetic ether to give color and flavor. The latter cannot be considered as injurious. One one-thousandth of mineral acid is allowable, and tends to preserve the vinegar. This would be about four measured ounces to the barrel, or two to the ordinary half-barrel.

Sulphuric acid is detected by boiling with chloride of calcium; baryta is not admissible as a test for sulphuric acid in vinegar.

Muriatic acid gives a white, curdy precipitate, with a solution of nitrate of silver. This precipitate is soluble in ammonia, and blackens on exposure to light.

Nitric acid is detected by adding muriatic acid. If the solution will dissolve gold leaf, nitric acid is present.

To Strengthen Vinegar.

Freeze it and remove the ice which forms on the surface. The *water* of the vinegar alone freezes, leaving the acetic acid in solution in the remaining water.

To Determine the Strength of Vinegar.

The hydrometer (see SPECIFIC GRAVITY) is not to be much relied on in testing the strength of vinegar. The simplest test is to take a fragment of fine marble, weigh it and suspend it by a thread in a known measure of vinegar until all action ceases and the liquid has no longer a sour taste. Take out the marble, wash and dry it, and note the loss of weight it has sustained. Five-sixths of this is real (hydrated) acetic acid. An ounce of good vinegar should saturate from 30 to 32 grs. of pure and dry carbonate of soda; such vinegar contains about 5 per cent. of anhydrous (absolute) acetic acid. Vinegar above 30 per cent. of real acid will dissolve the essential oils and camphor.

Simple continuous Vinegar Process.

The following household vinegar method is to be recommended as simple, expeditious, and furnishing a constant supply of vinegar with scarcely any trouble, and at trifling cost: Two barrels are procured, one for making, the other for storing the vinegar. Those from which good vinegar has just been drawn are preferable. The storage barrel is kept always in the cellar, the generating one in the cellar or house, according to the season. In this latter barrel a small hole is bored, for the circulation of air, at the top of one of its heads. The barrels lie on their side, and contain each a wooden faucet. Of course their capacity is regulated by the yearly demand of vinegar.

We will suppose that the generator, filled to the level of the ventilating hole, contains 10 galls.; the manufacture will then be carried on in the following manner: Seven galls. of good vinegar are placed in it, and 3 galls. of a warm alcoholic mixture made in the following manner and added: If common whiskey (50 per cent.) be employed, have a small measure of 3 pts. and a large one (a bucket) of 3 galls. If 86 per cent. spirits are used, let the small measure be for 2 pts. Put a small measureful of the spirits in the large measure; fill quickly to the mark with boiling water, and pour by a funnel into the generator. Every 2 or 3 weeks 3 galls. of vinegar are withdrawn from the generator, added to the storage barrel, and 3 galls. of alcoholic mixture are placed in the generating barrel as before.

Another method of working the casks consists in half filling the generator with vinegar and adding every week so much of the alcoholic mixture that it fills the barrel in from 8 to 16 weeks, according to the season. Half the vinegar is then added to the storage cask, and the process recommenced in the generator. The warmer the season the more rapid may be the manufacture.—*Wetherill on the Manufacture of Vinegar.*

Vinegar without a Ferment (Döbereiner's Process).

The ferment used in the manufacture of vinegar is not necessary. Alcohol may be oxidized directly by the agency of finely divided platinum (platinum black); 10 per cent. alcohol placed in a close vessel with platinum black is rapidly converted into acetic acid. Dr. Ure estimates that with a box of 12 ft. cube and 6 to 8 oz. of strong platinum, 1 lb. of alcohol daily can be converted into acetic acid, and with from 20 to 30 lbs. we may obtain 300 lbs. of vinegar from the proportionate quantity of spirits. The same platinum black will last for an indefinite time, requiring only to be heated to redness from time to time, to restore it. This method is undoubtedly the most elegant one known of vinegar manufacture, and has been tried on a large scale in Germany. The objection to it is, however, the high cost of the platinum, in which a large amount of capital must necessarily be kept locked up.

The continuous Quick Vinegar Process.

This is the method almost universally adopted for manufacturing vinegar on the large scale. Common new whiskey makes excellent vinegar; the fusel oil becoming oxidized during the process, is converted into harmless, agreeable ether. It is diluted so as to form a wash of about 6 per cent. alcohol. Two tubs, or upright casks, are prepared as follows: A false top and bottom are inserted. In the false top are bored numerous holes one-tenth of an inch in diameter and 1¼ in. apart; the top is fixed water-tight about 6 to 8 in. from the top of the barrel. At from 8 to 14 in. above the bottom of the tube are bored ½ in. air-holes, inclining downwards, so that the liquid may not flow out. About 2 in. above the air-holes is placed the false bottom pierced with ½ in. or inch holes. The space between the false top and bottom is filled with closely-curled beech-shavings, or charcoal in lumps of the size of a walnut, sifted, washed and dried. The holes in the false top are filled with lamp-wick, and the space below the false bottom provided with a stop-cock, or goose-neck. There is also an inclined hole 6 in. below the false top for the insertion of a thermometer and hour-glass, or wood tubes are inserted into the false top, reaching nearly to the cover of the tub; these act as chimneys. The beech shavings are boiled in vinegar and pressed into their place until within 6 in. of the false top or sieve. Before starting the process the room and tubs are to be kept a day at a temperature of 75° to 80° Fahr.

The shavings at the thermometer hole, and at the lower ventilating holes, are then loosened by means of a stick thrust therein. A wash is now prepared which contains 1.5 vinegar and 4.5 of a 3 per cent. solution of alcohol; this heated to from 75° to 80°, is gradually poured through the hole in the cover of the generator, at the rate of 1 barrel in 24 hours. At the expiration of this time, warm the resulting vinegar if necessary, and having added enough alcohol to make the whole quantity taken thus far of 5 per cent. alcoholic strength, pour this through the generators as before. Repeat this operation on the third, and even on the fourth day if necessary. Investigate the temperature of the air escaping from the generator, and when it exceeds that of the wash which is running, it is a sign that the acetification has commenced. When it rises to a point between 98° and 104°, the generators are in a proper condition to commence the regular business of the manufacture; the fermentation has been properly established. We then daily pour through generator No. 1, a wash consisting of a certain quantity of spirits, vinegar, and water, heated to a temperature between 75° and 80° Fahr.; and through No. 2 the wash has passed through No. 1, to which has been added more spirits. We draw manufactured vinegar daily from generator No. 2. The vinegar resulting from setting the generators in action, though not prejudicial to health, is of inferior quality and bad flavor, from extractive matter from the shavings and tubs and from the iron cauldron. It may be added in very small quantity to the subsequent vinegar, if it be not thrown away.—*Wetherill on the manufacture of vinegar.*

To make Quass.

Mix rye flour and warm water together, and leave it till it has turned sour. This vinegar is much drunk in Russia; it looks thick and unpleasant at first, but becomes agreeable by use.

Distilled Vinegar.

This is obtained from vinegar by distillation, rejecting the fourth or eighth part that comes over first, and avoid its acquiring a burnt flavor.

Distilled vinegar is weaker than the common, but is used sometimes in pickles, where its want of color is an advantage.

To Deprive Vinegar and other Vegetable Liquids of their Color.

To take away the color of vinegar, a litre of red wine vinegar, cold, is mixed with 45 grammes of bone-charcoal, in a glass vessel. Shake this mixture from time to time, and in 2 or 3 days the color completely disappears. When the process is to be performed in the large way, throw the charcoal into a cask of vinegar, which must be stirred from time to time. The highest colored red wines treated in the same manner become perfectly limpid. Ivory-black possesses the same property as bone-black.

To Prepare the Charcoal.

Fill a crucible with the most compact parts of ox and sheep bones, lute the cover, carefully leaving only a small opening at the top, place the crucible on a forge fire, and heat it gradually till red; when the flame from the oily and gelatinous parts has ceased, diminish the opening and suddenly raise the fire; when cold, reduce the charcoal to fine powder.

To Procure Pyroligneous Acid.

This acid is procured from any kind of green wood (such as cord wood), used for making charcoal; a cord of wood will produce about 80 galls. It is obtained in the following manner: A brisk oven is filled with coal or wood, until it becomes sufficiently hot to heat an oven over it to that degree as to reduce green wood to a charcoal. The upper oven should be closely stopped except a tube at the top to carry off the steam or acid, which tube is passed through water, and the steam thus condensed forms the acid.

To Prepare the same.

Place a large cast-iron cylinder, or retort (similar to those used for the production of coal gas), in a furnace, so that it may receive as much heat, all round, as possible. One end of this cylinder must be so constructed as to open and shut, to admit wood, and exclude the air.

Oak, in pieces about 1 foot in length, is to be put into the cylinder, which is to be filled as full as possible, without being wedged, and the door must be shut close to exclude air; from the cylinder let a worm run through cold water to condense the acid; by this it is conveyed to a large cask placed on one end, where there is a pipe to carry it from that to 2 or 3 more; thus it is completely secured from flying off in the vaporous state. The fire is now to be raised to a great heat, sufficiently powerful to convert the wood completely into charcoal. When the acid ceases to come over, the fire is to be taken out, and the mass of wood left to cool in the confined state, when it becomes perfect charcoal. In the first cask, tar is chiefly contained with the acid, it precipitates to the bottom, and is drawn off by a cock; it is afterwards boiled in an iron boiler to evaporate the acid, before it is fit for use. If the acid is not strong enough, it is put into large square vats about 6 inches deep, for the purpose of making a large surface, to evaporate a part of the water contained in the acid, more especially by a slow heat. These vats are bedded on sand upon the top of a brick stove, where a gentle heat is applied; thus it may be procured in a pretty strong state.

This acid is a liquid of the color of white wine, possesses a strong acid and slightly astringent taste, combined with an empyreumatic smell. When allowed to remain in a state of rest for 8 or 10 days, tar of a black color subsides, and the acid is then comparatively transparent. To purify it further, it undergoes the process of distillation, by which it is freed from a still greater portion of the tar, with which it is combined, and is thus rendered still more transparent. But though the process of distillation be repeated without end, it will never be freed from the volatile oil with which it is combined, and which is the cause of empyreuma constantly attending it. In short, it contains the same properties for the preservation of animal matters from putrefaction as smoking them by wood does, which is practised at present by the most barbarous nations, and which has been handed down from the remotest ages of antiquity.

Glacial Acetic Acid (Ice Vinegar).

To 83 lbs. of fused acetate of soda add 100 lbs. of sulphuric acid and distill. Place the distillate in ice at 50° Fahr., it will become solid. Allow it to drain. It is the monohydrated acid.

Oil of Vitriol.

The strongest or Nordhausen or fuming acid is made by distilling green vitriol at a red heat. The residue is colcothar or crocus martis. It is used for dissolving indigo and other purposes where an acid of great strength is required. The ordinary sulphuric acid is made by causing vapors of sulphurous acid (from burning sulphur), nitric acid and water, to combine in a leaden chamber. The weak acid is concentrated in leaden pans, and afterwards in a platinum still.

Nitric Acid,

Or aqua fortis, may be made by distilling at a gentle heat in a glass retort, equal weights of saltpetre (nitrate of potassa), and sulphuric acid. The receiver should be kept cooled by a cloth dipped in water. To obtain it pure it must be redistilled over nitrate of silver.

Hydrochloric Acid,

Or muriatic acid (marine acid, spirit of salt).

Take 3 parts common salt, 5 of oil of vitriol, and 5 of water. Mix the oil of vitriol with 2 parts of water in a thin glass vessel, and allow the mixture to cool. Put the salt into a glass retort connected with a receiver containing the remaining 3 parts of water. Pour the mixture of sulphuric acid and water upon the salt, and distill with a gentle heat. To purify it, mix with an equal volume of water, and distill over chloride of barium.

Chlorine Water.

Pass a current of chlorine gas, made by the action of commercial muriatic acid upon black oxide of manganese, into a bottle half filled with water, shaking occasionally. Water will absorb twice its volume of this gas, acquires thereby a yellowish color, and the peculiar smell of chlorine. It is used in medicine and to bleach linen, take out fruit marks, etc. It should be kept in the dark, or in a bottle covered with blue paper.

Sulphurous Acid Water

Is made as above, using sulphurous acid instead of chlorine. This gas may be prepared by the action of sulphuric acid upon copper, charcoal, or sulphur. Water absorbs 50 volumes of the gas. The solution is used for bleaching purposes, in medicine, and to check fermentation.

TEST LIQUORS, TEST PAPERS, ETC.

Distilled water only should be used in these preparations. In preparing the papers the liquid should be placed in an earthenware plate or dish, and the paper carefully immersed in it so as to be uniformly wetted, then dried out of the reach of acid, ammoniacal, or other vapors likely to affect it; and afterwards kept in bottles, jars, or cases.

Brazil Paper.

Dip paper in a strong decoction of Brazil wood, and dry it. [It is rendered purple or violet by alkalies; generally yellow by acids.]

Cabbage Paper.

Make a strong infusion of red cabbage leaves, strain it, and evaporate it by a gentle heat till considerably reduced. Then dip the paper in it and dry it in the air. [This paper is of a grayish color; alkalies change it to green, acids to red. It is a very delicate test; if rendered slightly green by an alkali, carbonic acid will restore the color.]

Dahlia Paper.

From the petals of violet-dahlias, as cabbage paper.

Elderberry Paper.

This is merely paper stained with the juice of the berries. Its blue color is changed to red by acids, and to green by alkalies.

Indigo Paper.

Immerse paper in sulphate of indigo, wash it with water rendered slightly alkaline, then with pure water, and dry it in the air.

Iodide of Potassium and Starch Paper.

Mix starch paste with solution of iodide of potassium, and moisten bibulous paper with it. [It becomes blue when exposed to ozone. Chlorine has the same effect.]

Lead Paper.

Paper dipped in a solution of acetate of lead. [When moistened it detects sulphuretted hydrogen, which renders it black.]

Blue Litmus Paper.

Bruise 1 oz. of litmus in a mortar, and add boiling water; triturate together, put them in a flask and add boiling water to make up to half a pint; when cool strain it, and dip paper in it. More color may be extracted from the litmus by hot water, but the liquid will require to be concentrated by evaporation. [Acids change the color to red, but it does not become green with alkalies.]

Red Litmus Paper.

As the last, adding to the strained infusion a few drops of nitric acid, or of pure acetic acid.

Rose Paper.

Make a strong infusion of the petals of the red rose, and dip unsized paper in it. [Dipped in an alkaline solution so weak as not to affect turmeric paper, it assumes a bright green color.]

Manganese Paper.

Dip paper in a solution of sulphate of manganese. [It becomes black in an ozonized atmosphere.]

Rhubarb Paper.

Dip paper in a strong infusion of rhubarb, and dry it. [Alkalies render it brown. It is not, like turmeric paper, affected by boracic acid.]

Starch Paper.

This is merely paper imbued with starch paste. Cotton cord is sometimes used instead of paper. [As a test for iodine, which turns it blue.]

Turmeric Paper.

Boil 1 oz. of coarsely powdered turmeric-root in ½ a pint of water for ½ an hour, and strain; dip paper in the liquid and dry it. [It is rendered brown by alkalies, and also by boracic acid and borates.]

SALINE CARBONATED WATERS.

The following afford approximate imitations of these waters. The earthy salts, with salts of iron, should be dissolved together in the smallest quantity of water. The other ingredients to be dissolved in the larger portion of the water, and the solution impregnated with gas. The first solution may be then added, or be previously introduced into the bottles. The salts, unless otherwise stated, are to be crystallized.

Baden Water.

Chloride of magnesium, 2 grs.; chloride of calcium, 40 grs.; sesquichloride of iron, ¼ gr. (or 3 minims of the tincture); common salt, 30 grs.; sulphate of soda, 10 grs.; carbonate of soda, 1 gr.; water, 1 pt.; carbonic acid gas, 5 volumes.

Carlsbad Water.

Chloride of calcium, 8 grs.; tincture of chloride of iron, 1 drop; sulphate of soda, 50 grs.; carbonate of soda, 8 grs.; carbonated water, 1 pt.

Eger.

Carbonate of soda, 5 grs.; sulphate of soda, 4 scruples; chloride of sodium, 10 grs.; sulphate of magnesia, 3 grs.; chloride of calcium, 5 grs.; carbonated water, 1 pt. Or it may be made without the apparatus, thus:—Bicarbonate of soda, 30 grs.; chloride of sodium, 8 grs.; sulphate of magnesia, 3 grs.; water, 1 pt. Dissolve, and add a scruple of dry bisulphate of soda, and close the bottle immediately.

Ems.

Carbonate of soda, 2 scruples; sulphate of potash, 1 gr.; sulphate of magnesia, 5 grs.; common salt, 10 grs.; chloride of calcium, 3 grs.; carbonated water, 1 pt.

Pullna Water.

Sulphate of soda, 4 drs.; sulphate of magnesia, 4 drs.; sulphate of lime, 15 grs.; chloride of magnesium (dry), 1 scruple; common salt, 1 scruple; bicarbonate of soda, 10 grs.; water slightly carbonated, 1 pt. One of the most active of the purgative saline waters.

Pullna Water, without the Machine.

Bicarbonate of soda, 50 grs.; sulphate of magnesia, 4 drs.; sulphate of soda, 3 drs.; common salt, 1 scruple. Dissolve in a pint of water; add, lastly, 2 scruples of bisulphate of soda, and close the bottle immediately.

Salts for Making Pullna Water.

Dry bicarbonate of soda, 1 oz.; dried sulphate of soda, 2 oz.; dried sulphate of magnesia, 1½ oz.; dry common salt, 2 drs.; dry tartaric acid, ¾ oz. (or rather, dry bisulphate of soda, 1 oz.).

Seidlitz Water.

This is usually imitated by strongly aerating a solution of 2 drs. of sulphate of magnesia in a pint of water. It is also made with 4, 6, and 8 drs. of the salts to a pint of water.

Seidlitz Powder.

The common Seidlitz powders do not resemble the water. A closer imitation would be made by using effloresced sulphate of magnesia instead of the potassio-tartrate of soda. A still more exact compound will be the following:—Effloresced sulphate of magnesia, 2 oz.; bicarbonate of soda, ½ oz.; dry bisulphate of soda, ½ oz. Mix and keep in a close bottle.

Seltzer Water.

Chloride of calcium and chloride of magnesium, of each 4 grs. Dissolve these in a small quantity of water, and add it to a similar solution of 8 grs. bicarbonate of soda, 20 grs. common salt, and 2 grs. of phosphate of soda. Mix, and add a solution of ¼ of a gr. of sulphate of iron. Put the mixed solution into a 20-oz. bottle, and fill up with aerated water. But much of the Seltzer water sold is said to be nothing more than simple carbonated water. An imitation of Seltzer water is also made by putting into a stone Seltzer bottle, filled with water, 2 drs. bicarbonate of soda, and 2 drs. of citrate acid in crystals, corking the bottle immediately. Soda powders are sometimes sold as Seltzer powders.

Vichy Water.

Bicarbonate of soda, 1 dr.; common salt, 2 grs.; sulphate of soda, 8 grs.; sulphate of magnesia, 3 grs. tincture of chloride of iron, 2 drops; aerated water, 1 pt. Dorvault directs 75 grs. of bicarbonate of soda, 4 grs. of chloride of sodium, one-fifth of a gr. sulphate of iron, 10 grs. sulphate of soda, 3 grs. sulphate of magnesia, to 1 pt. of water. By adding 45 grs. (or less) of citric acid an effervescing water is obtained.

M. Soubeiran, relying on the analysis of Longchamps, imitates Vichy water by the following combination:—Bicarbonate of soda, 135 grs.; chloride of sodium, 2½ grs.; cryst. chloride of calcium, 12 grs.; sulphate of soda, 11½ grs.; sulphate of magnesia, 3¾ grs.; tartrate of iron and potash, ⅛ gr.; water, 2 and one-tenth pts. (1 litre); carbonic acid, 305 cubic inches (5 litres). Dissolve the salts of soda and iron in part of the water, dissolve and add the sulphate of magnesia, and then the chloride of calcium in the remaining water. Charge now with the carbonic acid gas under pressure.

Vichy Salts.

Bicarbonate of soda, 1½ oz.; common salt, 15 grs.; effloresced sulphate of soda, 1 dr.; effloresced sulphate of magnesia, 1 scruple; dry tartarized sulphate of iron, 1 gr.; dry tartaric acid, 1 oz. (or dry bisulphate of soda, 1 oz.). Mix the powders, previously dried, and keep them in a close bottle.

SULPHURETTED WATERS.

Simple Sulphuretted Water.

Pass sulphuretted hydrogen into cold water (previously deprived of air by boiling, and cooled in a closed vessel), till it ceases to be absorbed.

Aix-la-Chapelle Water.

Bicarbonate of soda, 12 grs.; common salt, 25 grs.; chloride of calcium, 3 grs.; sulphate of soda, 8 grs.; simple sulphuretted water, 2½ oz.; water slightly carbonated, 17½ oz.

Bareges Water.

Crystallized hydrosulphate of soda, crystallized carbonate of soda, and common salt, of each 2½ grs.; water (freed from air), 1 pt. A stronger solution for adding to baths is thus made:—Crystallized hydrosulphate of soda, crystallized carbonate of soda, and common salt, of each 2 oz.; water, 10 oz. Dissolve. To be added to a common bath at the time of using.

Naples Water.

Crystallized carbonate of soda, 15 grs.; fluid magnesia, 1 oz.; simple sulphuretted water, 2 oz.; aerated water, 16 oz. Introduce the sulphuretted water into the bottle last.

Harrowgate Water.

Common salt, 100 grs.; chloride of calcium, 10 grs.; chloride of magnesium, 6 grs.; bicarbonate of soda, 2 grs.; water, 18½ oz. Dissolve, and add simple sulphuretted water, 1½ oz.

CHALYBEATE WATERS.

Simple Chalybeate Water.

Water freed from air by boiling, 1 pt.; sulphate of iron, ½ gr.

Aerated Chalybeate Water.

Sulphate of iron, 1 gr.; carbonate of soda, 4 grs.; water deprived of air, and charged with carbonic acid gas, 1 pt. Dr. Pereira recommends 10 grs. each of sulphate of iron and bicarbonate of soda to be taken in a bottle of ordinary soda water. This is equivalent to 4 grs. of carbonate of iron.

Brighton Chalybeate.

Sulphate of iron, common salt, chloride of calcium, of each 2 grs.; carbonate of soda, 3 grs.; carbonated water, 1 pt.

Bussang, Forges, Provins,

And other similar waters, may be imitated by dissolving from ½ to ¾ of a gr. of sulphate of iron, 2 or 3 gr. of carbonate of soda, 1 gr. of sulphate of magnesia, and 1 of common salt, in a pint of aerated water.

Mont d'Or Water.

Bicarbonate of soda, 70 grs.; sulphate of iron, ⅜ gr.; common salt, 12 grs.; sulphate of soda, ½ gr.; chloride of calcium, 4 grs.; chloride of magnesium, 2 grs.; aerated water, 1 pt.

Passy Water.

Sulphate of iron, 2 grs.; chloride of sodium, 8 grs.; carbonate of soda, 4 grs.; chloride of magnesium, 2 grs.; aerated water, 1 pt.

Pyrmont Water.

Sulphate of magnesia, 20 grs.; chloride of magnesium, 4 grs.; common salt, 2 grs.; bicarbonate of soda, 16 grs.; sulphate of iron, 2 grs.; Carrara water, 1 pt.

Portable Lemonade.

Take of tartaric acid, ½ oz.; loaf sugar, 3 oz.; essence of lemon, ½ dr. Powder the tartaric acid and the sugar very fine, in a marble or wedgewood mortar (observe never to use a metal one), mix them together, and pour the essence of lemon upon them, by a few drops at a time, stirring the mixture after each addition, till the whole is added; then mix them thoroughly, and divide it into 12 equal parts, wrapping each up separately in a piece of white paper. When wanted for use, it is only necessary to dissolve it in a tumbler of cold water, and fine lemonade will be obtained, containing the flavor of the juice and peel of the lemon, and ready sweetened.

FIXED OILS.

To make Oil of Sweet Almonds.

It is usually made from bitter almonds for cheapness, or from old Jordan almonds, by heat, the oil from which soon grows rank, while that from fresh Barbary almonds, drawn cold, will keep good for some time. The almonds are sometimes blanched by dipping in boiling water, or by soaking some hours in cold water, so as to part with their skin easily; but are more usually ground to a paste, which is put into canvas bags, and pressed between iron plates in a screw press, or by means of a wedge; 1 cwt. of bitter almonds, unblanched, produces 46 lbs. of oil; the cake pays for pressing.

Nut Oil

Is obtained from the kernel of the hazelnut, and is very fine. As it will keep better than that of almonds, it has been proposed to be substituted for that oil. It is drunk with tea in China, probably in lieu of cream, and is used by painters, as a superior vehicle for their colors.

Oil of Mace

Is obtained from nutmegs by the press. It is buttery, having the smell and color of mace, but grows paler and harder by age; 2 lbs. of nutmegs in Europe will yield 6 oz. of this oil.

True Oil of Mace by Expression.

This oil is red, remains always liquid or soft, has a strong smell of mace, subacid taste, and is imported in jars or bottles, the lower part being rather thicker than the top; 1½ lbs. of mace will yield in Europe 1½ oz. troy of oil.

Olive, Salad, or Sweet Oil.

This is the most agreeable of all the oils; it is demulcent, emollient, gently laxative, and is also used as an emetic with warm water; dose, 1 oz. troy, or a large spoonful; also externally, when warm, to the bites of serpents, and, when cold, to tumors and dropsies. Rank oil is best for plasters, but fresh oil makes the best hard soap.

Castor Oil

Is made by pressing the beans, cold or slightly warmed. It may be rendered colorless and odorless by filtering through animal charcoal and magnesia. It is soluble in strong alcohol, and is used as the basis of many hair-oils. (See PERFUMERY.)

Oil of Croton.

This oil is extracted from Molucca grains, or purging nuts. In its chemical qualities it agrees with castor oil, but is considerably more active, as a single drop, when the oil is genuine, is a powerful cathartic.

Rape Oil.

This is made from rape-seed. It dries slowly, and makes but a softish soap, fit for ointments. The mucilage it contains may be got rid of, in a great measure, by adding ¼ ounce of oil of vitriol to 2 pts. of the oil.

To Purify Rape Oil.

The following is a simple method of rendering rape oil equal to spermaceti oil, for the purposes of illumination:

Begin by washing the oil with spring-water; which is effected by agitating the oil violently with a sixth part of the water. This separates the particles of the oil, and mixes those of the water intimately with them. After this operation it looks like the yolk of eggs beat up. In less than 48 hours they separate completely, the oil swimming at the top, the water, with all feculent and extraneous particles, subsiding to the bottom. This may be much improved, by substituting sea-water in the place of fresh-water.

By the process of washing the oil does not lose a hundredth part. The experiment can at all times be made in a glass decanter, or in a churn, with a cock at the bottom, the water to come up very near to the cock, by which all the oil can be drawn off, after it has deposited its impurities.

Another Method.

To 100 parts of oil add 1½ or 2 of concentrated sulphuric acid, and mix the whole well by agitation, when the oil will become turbid, and of a blackish-green color. In about three-quarters of an hour the coloring matter will begin to collect in clots; the agitation should then be discontinued, and clean water, twice the weight of the sulphuric acid, be added. To mix the water with the oil and acid, a further agitation of half an hour will be requisite. The mass may, afterwards, be left to clarify for 8 days, at the end of which time 3 separate fluids will be perceived in the vessel; the upper is the clear oil, the next is the sulphuric acid and water, and the lowest a black mud or fecula. Let the oil then be separated by a syphon from the acid and water, and filtrated through cotton or wool. It will be nearly without color, smell, or taste, and will burn clearly and quietly to the last drop.

To Purify Vegetable Oil.

To 100 lbs. of oil add 25 oz. of alum, and mix, dissolved in 9 lbs. of boiling water. After stirring it about half an hour, add 15 oz. of nitric acid, still continuing to stir it. Let it stand 48 hours, when the fine oil will swim on the surface, and then draw it off. Such oil is used all over the Continent, and an equal quantity yields double the light of whale and fish-oil, without its offensive odor.

To make Pumpkin Oil.

From the seeds of the pumpkin, which are generally thrown away, an abundance of an excellent oil may be extracted. When peeled they yield much more oil than an equal quantity of flax. This oil burns well, gives a lively light, lasts longer than other oils, and emits very little smoke. It has been used on the Continent for frying fish, etc. The cake remaining after the extraction of the oil may be given to cattle, who eat it with avidity.

Beech-nut Oil.

Beech-nuts are not only an excellent food for pigs, but they are known to yield an oil, fit for common purposes, by the usual methods of extraction.

ANIMAL OILS AND FATS.

Hog's Lard.

This is obtained like the rest of the animal fats, from the raw lard, by chopping it fine, or rather rolling it out, to break the cells in which the fat is lodged, and then melting the fat in a water-bath, or other gentle heat, and straining it while warm. Some boil them in water; but the fats thus obtained are apt to grow rank much sooner than when melted by themselves.

Neat's-foot, or Trotter Oil.

Obtained by boiling neat's-feet, tripe, etc. in

water. It is a coarse animal oil, very emollient, and much used to soften leather.

To Purify Trotter Oil.

Put 1 qt. of trotter oil into a vessel containing 1 qt. of rose-water, and set them over a fire till the oil melts and mixes with the rose-water. Stir well with a spoon. When properly combined take the vessel from the fire, and let it cool. Now take off the oil with a spoon, and add rose-water as before. When the oil is again separated and cleansed, set it in a cool place. The principal use of trotter oil is for the making of cold cream, in which its qualities exceed those of every other oil.

To Prepare Oil from Yolks of Eggs.

Boil the eggs hard, and after separating the whites break the yolks into 2 or 3 pieces, and roast them in a fryingpan till the oil begins to exude; then press them with very great force. Fifty eggs yield about 5 oz. of oil. Old eggs yield the greatest quantity.

Another Method.

Dilute the raw yolks with a large proportion of water, and add spirit of wine to separate the albumen, when the oil will rise on the top after standing some time, and thus may be separated by a funnel.

To Refine Spermaceti.

Spermaceti is usually brought home in casks, and in some cases has so little oil mixed with it as to obtain the denomination of *head matter*. It is of the consistence of a stiff ointment, of a yellowish color, and not tenacious. Besides the head matter, there is also a quantity of sperm obtained from the oil by filtration. Indeed, in all good spermaceti lamp oil, which is not transparent, particles of the sperm may be seen floating.

Having the head-matter, or filtered sperm, in order to purify it, first put it into hair-cloths, and with an iron plate between each cloth to the number of half a dozen or more, submit it to the action of an iron screw-press; and, as the oil does not separate very readily, it will in general be necessary to let the cakes of sperm be pressed three different times. The third time the cakes will become so dry that they may be broken in small pieces with little trouble, and then put in a furnace containing ½ water and ¾ cake. Let the fire be raised sufficiently under the furnace to melt the cake, which it will do before the water begins to boil; after which boil the whole together for about ½ an hour, taking off during the boiling what scum and other extraneous bodies rise to the top; then let the whole be dipped out into a tub or other coolers. After it is completely cold, take off the cake of spermaceti, which will be on the top of the water, and cut it into pieces. Suppose, for example, that the cake weighs 1 cwt., it will be necessary to have a furnace, or rather a movable kettle, where the light is thrown in such a way that the process can be observed. Having taken 1 cwt. of the unrefined spermaceti prepared as above, melt it together with about 3 galls. of water. As soon as it begins to boil, add from time to time small portions of the following liquor, say ½ pint at a time: Take of the alkaline salt, or potash, 7 lbs.; pour on it 2 galls. of water; let them stand together 24 hours, and from the top dip off the lye as wanted, adding more water occasionally, till the alkali is exhausted. After boiling the spermaceti for about 4 hours, having during the process taken off the scum as it arose, let the kettle be removed from the fire; and after remaining about ½ hour, dip off the spermaceti into suitable coolers. This process must in general be repeated 3 times. The third time, if the processes have been properly conducted, the spermaceti will be as clear as crystal; and then, after it is cool, the only thing necessary to make it fit for sale, is to cut it into moderately small pieces, when it will break into that flakey appearance which it has in the shops.

To Sweeten, Purify, and Refine Greenland Whale and Seal Oil.

The oil, in its raw state, is filtered through bags about 41 inches long, with circular mouths extended by a wooden hoop about 15 inches in diameter, fixed thereto. These bags are made of jean lined with flannel, between which jean and flannel powdered charcoal is placed, throughout, to a regular thickness of about ½ inch, for the purpose of retaining the glutinous particles of the oil and straining it from impurities; and the bags are quilted, to prevent the charcoal from becoming thicker in one part than another, and to keep the linings more compact. The oil is pumped into a large funnel made of tin, annexed to the pump through a perpendicular pipe, and passed from the funnel into another pipe placed over the bags horizontally, from whence it is introduced into them by cocks. The oil runs from the filtering-bags into a cistern about 8 feet long by 4 feet broad, and 4½ deep, made of wood and lined with lead, and containing water at the bottom about the depth of 5 or 6 inches, in which are dissolved about 8 oz. of blue vitriol, for the purpose of drawing down the glutinous and offensive particles of the oil which have escaped through the charcoal; and thereby rendering it clean and free from the unpleasant smell attendant upon the oil in the raw state; and in order to enable the oil thus to run from the bags, they are hung in a frame or rack made like a ladder, with the spokes or rails at sufficient distances to receive the hoop of the bag between two; and such frame or rack is placed in a horizontal position over the cistern. The oil is suffered to run into the cistern until it stands to the depth of about 2 feet in the water, and there to remain for 3 or 4 days, (according to the quality of the oil), and is then drawn off by a cock which is fixed in the cistern a little above the water, into a tub or other vessel, when it will be found to be considerably purified and refined; and the oil, after having undergone this operation, may be rendered still more pure by passing a second or third time through similar bags and cisterns. But the oil, after such second and third process, is drawn off into, and filtered through additional bags made of jean lined with flannel, inclosed in other bags made of jean, doubled, when the process is complete.

Clarifying Coal-Oils.

In a close vessel are placed 100 lbs. of crude coal-oil, 25 qts. of water, 1 lb. of chloride of lime, 1 lb. of soda, and ½ lb. of oxide of manganese. The mixture is violently agitated, and allowed to rest for 24 hours, when the clear oil is decanted and distilled. The 100 lbs. of coal-oil are to be mixed with 25 lbs. of resin-oil; this is one of the principal points in the manipulation; it removes the gummy parts from the oil, and renders them inodorous. The distillation spoken of may terminate the process, or the oils may be distilled before they are defecated and precipitated.

To Bleach and Purify Fixed Oils.

Fish and other fat oils are improved in smell and color by passing hot air or steam through them. Dunn's method is to heat the oil by steam to 170° or 200°, and force a current of air through it, under a chimney, till it is bleached and purified. Mr. Cameron's method of bleaching palm oil is to keep it at 230°, with continual agitation, by passing into it high pressure steam through leaden pipes of 2 inches diameter. Four tons of oil require 10 hours' straining. Palm oil is also bleached by chloride of lime. Take from 7 to 14 lbs. of chloride of lime, triturate in a mortar, adding gradually 12 times the quantity of water, so as to form a smooth cream. Liquefy 112 lbs. of palm oil, remove it from the fire, add the solution of chloride of lime, and stir well with a wooden stirrer. Allow it to cool, and when become solid, break it into small fragments, and expose it to the air for 2 or 3 weeks, then put into a cast-iron boiler lined with lead, diluted with 20 parts of water. Boil with a moderate heat till the oil drops clear from the stirrer; then let it cool. To remove the fœtor from fish oils, treat them in the same way (except the exposing to the air), using only 1 lb. of chloride of lime to 112 lbs. of oil. It does not remove the natural smell of the oil.

Calcined magnesia has been used to deprive oils of their rancidity.

Mr. Griseler finds that the addition of a few drops of nitric ether will prevent oils from becoming rancid.

Mr. Watt's patented method of bleaching oil is by chromic acid. For palm oil it is thus used: The oil is heated in a steam vessel, allowed to settle and cool down to 130° Fahr., then removed into wooden vessels, taking care that no water or sediment accompany it. For a ton of palm oil, make a saturated solution of 25 lbs. of bichromate of potash; add 8 lbs. of sulphuric acid, and 50 lbs. of muriatic acid (or an equivalent quantity of salt and sulphuric acid). Put the mixture into the oil, and let it be constantly stirred till it becomes of a light-green color. If not sufficiently decolored, add more of the mixture. Let the oil settle for half an hour, then pump it into a wooden vat, boil it for a few minutes with fresh water, by means of a steam pipe, and let it settle. For linseed, rape, and mustard oils a dilute solution of chromic acid is used, with a little muriatic acid; for olive, almond, and castor oils no muriatic acid is required. Fish oils and fats are first boiled in a steam-apparatus with a weak soda lye ($\frac{1}{2}$ lb. of soda for every ton of fat) for half an hour; then $\frac{1}{2}$ lb. of sulphuric acid, diluted with 3 lbs. of water, is added; the whole boiled for 15 minutes, and allowed to settle for an hour or more, when the water and sediment are drawn off, and the oil further bleached by a solution of 4 lbs. of bichromate of potash and 2 lbs. of sulphuric acid, properly diluted.

Mr. Davidson treats whale oil first with a solution of tan, next with water and chloride of lime, and lastly with diluted sulphuric acid and warm water. Rape and other seed oils are also refined by means of sulphuric acid and twice as much water. Mr. Gray directs 2 lbs. of oil of vitriol to 112 lbs. of oil. The oil should be carefully washed from the acid and filtered.

Mr. Bancroft's process for refining common olive oil, lard oil, etc., for lubricating purposes, is to agitate them with from $3\frac{1}{2}$ to 8 per cent. of caustic soda lye, of 1·2 specific gravity. If, on trial of a small quantity, the lye be found to settle clear at the bottom, enough has been added. The oil is allowed to rest for twenty-four hours, for the soapy matter to subside; the supernatant oil is then filtered.

Another plan of purifying oils (especially lamp oils) is to agitate them with a strong solution of common salt.

Purification of Castor Oil.

Mix 1000 parts of the oil with 25 parts of animal charcoal, and 10 parts of calcined magnesia, and leave them together for 3 days at a temperature of 68° to 78° Fahr., often stirring or shaking the mixture. The oil is then filtered off, and is found to be limpid, colorless, without taste, and easily soluble in alcohol. It congeals, too, at a lower temperature than before, and is in that respect superior to the ordinary oil.

Oil of Brick.

Used by lapidaries, is made by saturating fragments of brick with oil and distilling at a red heat.

Watchmaker's Oil.

1. Expose the finest porpoise oil to the lowest natural temperature attainable. It will separate into two portions, a thick, solid mass at the bottom, and a thin, oily supernatant liquid. This is to be poured off while at the low temperature named, and is then fit for use.

2. Put into a matrass or glass flask, a portion of any fine oil, with 7 or 8 times its weight of alcohol, and heat the mixture almost to boiling, decant the clear upper stratum of fluid, and suffer it to cool; a solid portion of fatty matter separates, which is to be removed, and then the alcoholic solution evaporated in a retort or basin, until reduced to one-fifth of its bulk. The fluid part of the oil will be deposited. It should be colorless and tasteless, almost free from smell, without action on infusion of litmus, having the consistence of white olive oil, and not easily congealable.

3. Take a white glass bottle of pure olive or almond oil, put into it a coiled strip of lead, and expose it to the sun's rays until a white curdy matter ceases to be deposited.

To Prevent Fats and Oils from becoming Rancid.

Heat the oil or melted fat for a few minutes with powdered slippery-elm bark, in the proportion of 1 dr. of the powder to 1 lb. of fat. The bark shrinks and gradually subsides, after which the fat is poured off. It communicates an odor like that of the hickory-nut. Butter thus treated has been kept unchanged for a year.

PERFUMERY.

Materials used.

The flowers, roots, and woods employed in perfumery are nearly all grown abroad, and even when raised in the United States are seldom used for perfumery.

Essential or volatile oils (p. 289) are obtained by distillation. In the case of delicate perfumes the flowers are macerated in warm oil or cold lard (*enfleurage*). From this grease the oil may be extracted by alcohol. Sometimes the flowers or other odorous bodies are macerated in alcohol.

Essences are solutions of volatile oils in alcohol. The term tincture is sometimes used to express the same idea.

The dried flowers and rasped woods or roots are used in the manufacture of *sachets*.

The following substances are obtained from the animal kingdom:—

Musk, a secretion of the Musk deer (*Moschus moschatus*), which inhabits Eastern Asia. There are three varieties. The Tonquin or Chinese is the finer, but is apt to be adulterated.

Civet, a secretion of the Civet cat (*Viverra civeta*), and

Castor, from the beaver (*Castor fiber*), are used in small quantities.

The *Essence of Mirbane* and flavoring ethers are obtained by the chemist.

Lard, suet, and the *fixed oils* are used as vehicles.

Alcohol employed in perfumery should be free from all smell of fusel or other oils. Atwood's (patent) alcohol is generally preferred. It is deodorized by distillation over permanganate of potassa.

Deodorizing Alcohol.

1. Spirit of wine, brandy, or alcohol distilled over soap lose their empyreumatic odors and tastes entirely. At about 215° the soap retains neither alcohol nor wood-spirit.

2. The empyreumatic oil, which remains in combination with the soap which forms the residuum of the distillation, is carried off at a higher temperature by the vapor of water, which is formed during a second distillation, the product of which is a soap free from empyreuma, and fit to be used again for similar purposes.

3. The concentration of the alcohol increases in this operation more than when soap is not employed, because this compound retains the water, and the alcoholic vapors which pass over are richer.

4. Thirty-three lbs. of soap is enough for 100 galls. of empyreumatic brandy, and direct experiments have shown that under the most favorable circumstances the soap can retain 20 per cent. of empyreumatic oil.

5. The soap employed should contain no potassa; it must be a hard or soda soap, and ought to be completely free from any excess of fat acids or fluids, otherwise it may render the product rancid and impure. Common soap, made with oleine and soda by the manufacture of stearine candles, has satisfied all the conditions in practice.

If this soap is employed, it will be better to add a little soda during the first distillation.

The hard soda-soaps, as exempt as possible from fluid fat-acids, remove completely the empyreumatic odor.

J. Maria Farina Cologne.

Benzoin dissolved in alcohol, 4 oz.; essence of lavender, 8 oz.; essence of rosemary, 4 oz.; alcohol at 75°, 325 qts. To this solution add successively neroli, 21 oz.; petit grain, 21 oz.; cedrat, 21 oz.; Portugal, 2½ lbs.; lemon, 2½ lbs.; alcoholic extract of geranium, 2½ lbs. Shake several times; leave 14 days, and bottle.

Fine Cologne Water.

Take alcohol at 85°, 10 qts.; dissolve in it essence of neroli petit grain, ½ oz.; essence of rosemary, 2½ drs.; essence of lavender, 1¼ drs.; essence of clove, ½ dr.; essence of peppermint, ½ dr.; essence of bergamot, 12½ drs.; lemon 12½ drs.; essence of Portugal, 7½ drs.; tincture of benzoin, 1¼ drs.

Ordinary Cologne.

Take alcohol at 85°, 10 qts.; essence of neroli, 1¼ drs.; essence of rosemary, 10 drs.; essence of lavender, 5 drs.; essence of thyme and clove, each ½ dr.: essence of lemon, 2 oz.; essence of peppermint, ¼ dr.; tincture of benzoin, 1¼ drs.; rose-water, 2 lbs.

Cheap Cologne.

Take alcohol at 85°, 10 qts.; essence of lemon, 5 oz.; essence of cedrat, 12½ drs.; essence of bergamot, 4 oz.; essence of lavender, 1 oz.; tincture of benzoin, 1 oz.

Recipes for Cologne Water, from Redwood Gray's Supplement.

1. Oil of neroli, 2 drs.; oil of orange-peel, ½ oz.; oil of citron, 1 dr.; oil of bergamot, 2 drs.; oil of lavender, oil of rosemary, each ½ dr.; oil of cinnamon, 1 scruple; cardamoms, powdered, balsam Peru, each 2 drs.; rectified spirits, 7 lbs. Macerate 10 days; then distill 6 pounds with a gentle heat.

2. Oil of bergamot, 3 oz.; oil of lemon, 2 oz.; oil of lavender, 3½ drs.; oil of neroli, 2½ drs.; oil of origanum, 2 drs.; oil of rosemary, 1 dr.: essence of vanilla, 2 drs.; musk, 10 grs.; rectified spirits, 13 pts.; rose-water, 1 qt.; orange-flower water, 1 pt. Mix the oils; dissolve them in 10 pts. of the spirits; then add the musk, and finally the waters, previously mixed with the remainder of the spirits, and, after standing 2 weeks, filter.

Florida Water.

Alcohol at 90°, 50 qts.; essence of lemon and Portugal, each 4 oz.; essence of lavender and clove, each 8 oz.; canella, ½ oz.; water, 20 qts.

Hungary Water.

Rectified alcohol, 1 gall.; oil of English rosemary, 2 oz.; oil of lemon-peel, 1 oz.; oil of balm (*melissa*) 1 oz.; oil of mint, ½ dr.; esprit de rose, 1 pt.; extract de fleur d'orange, 1 pt.

Extract of Verbena.

Rectified spirits, 1 pt.; oil of lemon-grass, 3 drs.; oil of lemon-peel, 2 oz.; oil of orange-peel, ½ oz. After standing together for a few hours, and then filtering, it is fit for sale. Another mixture of this kind, presumed by the public to be made from the same plant, but of a finer quality, is composed thus; it is sold under the title of

Extrait de Verveine.

Rectified spirits, 1 pt.; oil of orange-peel, 1 oz.; oil of lemon-peel, 2 oz.; oil of citron, 1 dr.; oil of lemon-grass, 2½ drs.; extrait de fleur d'orange, 7 oz.; extrait de tuberouse, 7 oz.: esprit de rose, ½ pt.

Imitation Essence of Wallflower.

Extrait fleur d'orange, 1 pt.; extract of vanilla, ½ pt.; esprit de rose, 1 pt.; extract of orris, ½ pt.; extract of cassia, ½ pt.; essential oil of almonds, ¼ dr. Allow this mixture to be made for 2 or 3 weeks prior to putting it up for sale.

Imitation Essence of Violet.

Extract of cassia, 1 pt.; extract of rose, tincture of orris, extract of tuberose, each ½ pint.

Fleur d'Italie, or Italian Nosegay.

Esprit de rose, from pomade, 2 pts.; esprit de rose, triple, 1 pt.; esprit de jasmin, esprit de violette, from pomade, each 1 pt.; extract of cassia, ½ pt.; extract of musk, extract of ambergris, each 2 oz.

Jockey Club Bouquet (English formula).

Extract of orris-root, 2 pts.; esprit de rose, triple, 1 pt.; esprit de rose de pomade, 1 pt.; extrait de cassia, extrait de tubereuse, de pomade, each ½ pt.; extrait de ambergris, ½ pt.; otto of bergamot, ½ oz.

Jockey Club Bouquet (French formula).

Esprit de rose, de pomade, 1 pt.; esprit de tubereuse, de pomade, 1 pt; esprit de cassia, de pomade, ½ pt.; esprit de jasmin, de pomade, ½ pt.; extract of civet, de pomade, 3 oz.

Kew Garden Nosegay.

Esprit de neroli (*Petale*), 1 pt.; esprit de cas

sie, esprit de tubereuse, esprit de jasmin, from pomade, each ½ pt.; esprit de geranium, ¼ pt.; esprit de musk, esprit de ambergris, each, 3 oz.

Eau de Millefleurs.

Esprit de rose, triple, 1 pt.; esprit de rose, esprit de tubereuse, esprit de jasmin, esprit de fleur d'orange, esprit de cassie, esprit de violette, esprit de reseda (mignonette), from pomade, each ½ pt.; esprit de vanilla, esprit de ambergris, esprit de musk, each 2 oz.; otto of almonds, otto of neroli, otto of cloves, each 10 drops; otto of bergamot, 1 oz. These ingredients are to remain together for at least a fortnight, then filtered prior to sale.

Essence of Rondeletia.

Spirits (brandy 60 o. p.), 1 gall., otto of lavender, 2 oz.; otto of cloves, 1 oz.; otto of rose, 3 drs.; otto of bergamot, 1 oz.; extract of musk, extract of vanilla, extract of ambergris, each ¼ pt. The mixture must be made at least a month before it is fit for sale. Very excellent rondeletia may also be made with whiskey.

Bouquet Royale.

Extract of rose (from pomade), 1 pt.; esprit de rose (triple), ½ pt.; extract of jasmin, extract of violet (from pomade), each ½ pt.; extract of verbena, extract of cassia, each 2½ oz.; otto of lemons, otto of bergamot, each ½ oz.; extract of musk, extract of ambergris, each 1 oz.

Suave.

Extract of tuberose, extract of jasmin, extract of cassin, extract of rose (from pomade), each 1 pt.; extract of vanilla, 5 oz.; extract of musk, extract of ambergris, each 2 oz.; otto of bergamot, otto of cloves, each 1 dr.

Spring Flowers.

Extract of rose, extract of violet (from pomade), each 1 pt.; extract of rose (triple), 2½ oz.; extract of cassia, 2½ oz.; otto of bergamot, 2 drs.; extract of ambergris, 1 oz.

Bouquet de Caroline, also called Bouquet des Delices.

Extrait de rose, extrait de violette, extrait de tubereuse (from pomade), each 1 pt.; extract of orris, extract of ambergris, each ½ pt.; otto of bergamot, otto of limette, otto of cedrat, each ¼ oz.

Esterhazy Bouquet

Extrait de fleur d'orange (from pomade), 1 pt.; esprit de rose (triple), 1 pt.; extract of vitivert, extract of vanilla, extract of orris, extract of tonquin, each 1 pt.; esprit de neroli, 1 pt.; extract of ambergris, ½ pt.; otto of santal, ¼ dr.; otto of cloves, ½ dr.

Essence of Bouquet.

Esprit de rose (triple), 1 pt.; extract of vanilla, 2 oz.; extract of orris, 8 oz.; otto of lemons, ¼ oz.; otto of bergamot, 1 oz.

American Shampoo Liquor.

Rum, 3 qts.; spirit of wine, 1 pt.; water, 1 pt.; tincture of cantharides, ½ oz.; carbonate of ammonia, ½ oz.; salt of tartar, 1 oz. Rub it on, and afterwards wash with water. By omitting the salt of tartar it nearly resembles Balm of Columbia.

Glycerine and Cantharides Lotion.

Rosemary water, 1 gall.; spirits of sal volatile, 1 oz.; tincture of cantharides, 2 oz.; glycerine, 4 oz. To be used with a sponge or soft brush twice a day when the hair is falling off.

Dupuytren's Pomade.

Tincture of cantharides (1 part flies to 8 of proof spirit), purified beef marrow, each 1 oz.; sugar of lead, 1 dr.; balsam of Peru, 3 drs.; oils of cloves and canella, each 15 drops. Used to prevent baldness, and restore the hair.

Eau Lustrale.

Castor oil (deodorized), 2½ lbs.; strongest alcobol (deodorized), 2½ lbs.; cantharides, in powder, ½ oz.; oil of bergamot, 2½ oz.; otto of roses, 20 drops. Mix; let them stand a few days, and filter. To soften the hair, and prevent baldness.

Honey-water for the Hair.

Honey, 4 lbs.; very dry sand, 5 lbs. Mix and put into a vessel that will hold 5 times as much; distill with a gentle heat a yellowish acid water.

Vegetable Hair Wash.

Southernwood 2 oz.; box-leaves, 6 oz.; water, 4 pts. Boil gently for ¼ of an hour; strain, and to each pint of the liquid add 2 oz. spirit of rosemary, and ½ dr. of salt of tartar, or 1 dr. of Naples soap.

Borax Hair Wash.

Borax, 1 oz.; camphor, ½ oz.; boiling water, 1 qt. When cold filter for use.

Excellent Hair Wash.

Sufficient liquid ammonia added to a pint of water to make the whole pungent. Be careful not to have it too strong. Afterwards wash with clean water.

To Cleanse Long Hair.

Beat up the yolk of an egg with a pint of softwater. Apply it warm, and afterwards wash it out with warm water.

Bandoline

Is usually made by infusing quince-seeds. It may also be made by boiling a tablespoonful of unbruised flaxseed in a pint of water for 5 minutes, and straining. It is sometimes made by dissolving gum arabic or gum tragacanth in water. About 4 oz. gum arabic or 1 oz. gum tragacanth to the pint.

Twiggs's Hair-Dye.

Sugar of lead, 1 dr.; milk of sulphur, 2 drs.; rose-water, 4 fl. oz.; glycerine, 1 fl. oz. Mix. This is the general composition of the various popular hair-dyes and restoratives, which contain a yellowish sediment and are not oily.

Silver Hair-Dye.

Nitrate of silver, 1 oz.; water, 9 oz., in blue bottle; sulphuret of potassium (fresh), 1 oz.; water, 8 oz., in white bottle. Moisten the hair first with the latter solution, and when dry add the silver solution.

Another.—Owing to the unpleasant smell of the mordant (white bottle) in the foregoing, a substitute is made by pouring boiling water, ½ pt., upon 3 oz. of bruised galls. When cold strain and bottle. For the blue bottle add to the solution, as above, ammonia, until the precipitate formed is redissolved.

Brown Dye.

To a saturated solution of sulphate of copper (blue vitriol), add ammonia until the precipitate which falls is redissolved. For a mordant, to be first applied, as above, use a saturated solution of ferrocyanide of potassium.

Orfila's Hair-Dye.

Take 3 parts of litharge and 2 of quicklime, mix thoroughly; keep in a well stopped bottle. When used mix with water or milk, apply to the hair, and envelope in an oil-skin cap for 5 or 6 hours.

To remove Superfluous Hair.

Take of quicklime, 16 parts; pearlash, 2 parts; liver of sulphur, 2 parts. Mix thoroughly, and keep in a tight bottle. When used mix to the consistence of a paste, and after it has remained on 2 or 3 minutes remove with a wooden knife.

Another.—The following is more efficient, but must be used with care as it contains arsenic.

Take of freshly slaked lime, 6 oz.; orpiment, ½ oz. Mix thoroughly, and keep in well closed bottles. When used apply as a paste with water until it begins to burn the skin, and shave off with an ordinary paper-knife. The time required will vary with different hair. Black hair takes longer than fair. All of the depilatories sold are founded upon the two foregoing receipts.

Toilet Powders

Are made of starch variously scented. Many of the powders and lotions sold contain bismuth, which will sometimes blacken.

Violet Powder.

Wheat-starch, 12 lbs.; powdered orris-root, 2½ lbs.; oil of lemon, ½ oz.; oil of bergamot, ¼ oz.; oil of cloves, 2 dr. Mix.

Bloom of Roses.

Dissolve ¼ oz. of cinnamon in ½ oz. of strong ammonia; after 2 days add 1 pt. rose-water, and ½ oz. Esprit de Rose (triple). Mix and set aside for a week. Then pour off the liquid from any sediment that may be present.

Pomade à la Rose.

Take white grease, 1 lb.; nut-oil, 3½ oz.; spermaceti, or white wax, 1½ oz. Melt together and add the oil. Pass the warm mixture through a clean cloth, and then stir it in a mortar till cold. If the pomade must be white, add no coloring matter; but if colored introduce the proper material. For red, soak ½ dr. of powdered alkanet in the oil previously warmed. For yellow, add ¼ or ½ dr. of annotto to the mixture of grease, when melted. Pass through a clean cloth, and perfume with essence of geranium, 1¼ dr.; essence of rose, ¾ dr.; essence of canella, 1-16 dr. Introduce the essences into the grease half fluid.

Economical Pomade.

Take white grease, 2 lbs.; essence of bergamot or lemon, 1½ dr.; essence of cloves, 1 dr. Color with alkanet or carmine lake.

Pomade of Bitter Almonds.

Take pure white grease, 2 lbs.; natural essence of bitter almonds, 1½ dr.; essence of lemon, cedrat, or Portugal, 1½ dr.

Pomade Canadienne.

Melt over a water-bath, 4 lbs. of bear's grease, and infuse 8 lbs. of rose leaves, as directed for the Pomade à la Rose. Then strain, and perfume with essence of mint, ½ oz.; essence of rose, 1 oz.; essence of vanilla, a few drops. Color rose with a little carmine.

Pomade Divine.

Beef marrow, 3 lbs.; put it into an earthen vessel and cover it with cold water, and change the water daily for a few days, using rose-water the last day. Pour off and press out the water; add to the marrow 4 oz. each of the styrax, benzoin, and Chio turpentine; 1 oz. orris powder; ½ oz. each of powdered cinnamon, cloves, and nutmeg. Set the vessel in hot water, and keep the water boiling for 3 hours; then strain.

Stick Pomatum.

This pomade is generally composed of mutton suets, but is sometimes made of hard body, to which is added, in summer, 1 oz. of wax for every pound of body. Lard body can also be used, but the proportion of wax must be increased. In this preparation always melt the least fusible body first. In moulding care must be taken not to run the pomade while too hot, as cavities will occur in the centre, rendering the sticks liable to break.

To perfume the usual odors are, for 1 lb. of pomade, essence of bergamot, lavender, thyme, orange peel, of each 1 dr. Color with annotto or saffron.

Another method of preparing this pomade, also called cosmetic, is by melting 2 parts of tallow and 1 part of wax, in sheet-iron moulds, the size desired for the stick, the mass having been perfumed and colored.

Philicomes and Cosmetics.

Philicomes and cosmetics are composed in winter, of equal parts of lard and earthnut oil, and in summer, of 2 parts of grease and 1 part oil. The greases are melted over a water-bath, and passed through a cloth. When the products begin to solidify the oils are added, and the mass is then run into jars or bottles. For the fine philicomes, the pommades à la rose, orange-flower, au bouquet, geranium, à la tubereuse, etc., are substituted for the lard.

Beef Marrow Philicome.

Take fat, 10 lbs.; pommade à la rose, aux millefleurs, 1 lb.; oil of cassia, 2 lbs.; oil of jasmine, 2 lbs.; spirit of roses 1¾ oz.; bergamot, 5 drs.; spirit of petit-grain, 2½ drs.; spirit of geranium, 2½ drs.; spirit of wintergreen, 4 drs.; infusion of cinchona, 5 drs.; pure rum, 10 drs.; essence of roses, 5 drops.

Macassar Oil.

Take oil of benzoin, 8 qts.; oil of noisette, 4 qts.; alcohol, 1 qt.; essence bergamot, 3 oz.; spirit of musk, 3 oz.; spirit of Portugal, 2 oz.; essence of roses, 2 drs. Mix, and keep the whole over a water-bath for 1 hour. Then digest for a week, stirring several times daily. Color with alkanet.

Amandine.

Mix in a mortar gum arabic, 2 oz.; white honey, 6 oz. Reduce to a thick mass and add 3 oz. of neutral white soap. This being gradually incorporated, add 2 oz. of fresh cold-pressed oil of sweet almonds, and finally, the yolks of 5 eggs.

The paste has a firm consistence, and is reduced by a thick milk of pistachio, made of fresh peeled pistach nuts, 4 oz.; distilled rose-water, 4 oz. Aromatize with ½ dr. of bitter almonds for 1 lb. of paste. A small portion, with a little warm water, produces a white lather of agreeable odor. This composition is used to whiten and soften the skin.

Cold Cream, No. 1.

Take of spermaceti and white wax, each 5 drs.; almond oil, 10 oz. Liquefy over a water-bath; pour into a marble mortar, heated by boiling water, stir quickly, and add 3½ oz. of rose-water. 15 grs. essence of roses, and a few drops of potash lye.

Camphor Cold Cream.

Take of almond oil and rose-water, each 1 lb.; wax and spermaceti, 1 oz.; camphor, 2 oz.; otto of rosemary, 1 dr.

Lotion for Freckles.

Take of corrosive sublimate, 5 grs.; muriatic acid, 30 drops; lump sugar, 1 oz.; alcohol, 2 oz.; rose-water, 7 oz. Agitate together till all is dissolved. Apply night and morning.

Another.—Take of sal ammoniac, 2 drs.; cologne water, 1 oz.; soft water, 1 pint. Mix.

Milk of Roses.

Melt together in a stoneware vessel over a water-bath, spermaceti, white wax, and soap, each 1 oz. Rub in a marble mortar bitter almonds, 2 oz.; sweet almonds, 1 lb. Take out ¾, and on the remaining ¼ pour the above mixture, and continue rubbing. Then add by degrees the other ¾ of the almonds, always pestling, so as to incorporate thoroughly. In a white glass bottle mix distilled water, 1 qt.; rose-water and spirit of rose, each, ½ pt. Reserve 1 pt., and gradually pour the mixture first made into the remainder.

Rub, and strain through a cloth, then return the residuum to the mortar, triturate it with the reserved mixture, strain, and mix with the other liquid.

Kalydor for the Complexion.

Take blanched bitter almonds, 1 part; rose-water, 16 parts. Mix and strain, then add 5 grs. of bichloride of mercury to every 8 oz. bottle of the mixture, and scent with rose or violet.

Pomade for Chapped Lips.

Take oxide of zinc, 1 oz.; lycopodium powder, 1 oz.; pomade rosat, 2 lbs. Mix, and make into a perfectly homogeneous pomade.

This is an excellent remedy for chapped lips, and is beneficial in cases of ulceration of the nails of the feet.

Heliotrope Sachet.

Powdered orris, 2 lbs.; Rose leaves, ground, 1 lb.; Tonqua beans, ground, ½ lb.; Vanilla beans, ¼ lb.; grain musk, ¼ oz.; otto of almonds, 5 drops. Well mix by sifting in a coarse sieve, it is fit for sale.

Lavender Sachet.

Lavender flowers, ground, 1 lb.; gum benzoin, in powder, ¼ lb.; otto of lavender, ¼ oz.

Millefleur Sachet.

Lavender flowers, ground, orris, rose leaves, benzoin, each, 1 lb.; cinnamon, allspice, each, 2 oz.; tonqua, vanilla, santal, each, ¼ lb.; musk and civet, each, 2 drs.; cloves, ground, ¼ lb.

Portugal Sachet.

Dried orange peel, 1 lb.; dried lemon-peel, ½ lb.; dried orris-root, ½ lb.; otto of orange-peel, 1 oz.; otto of neroli, ¼ dr.; otto of lemon-grass, ¼ dr.

Rose Sachet.

Rose heels, 1 lb.; santal wood, ground, ½ lb.; otto of roses, ¼ oz.

Santal Wood Sachet.

This is a good and economical sachet, and simply consists of the ground wood. Santal wood is to be purchased from some of the wholesale dry-salters; the drug-grinders are the people to reduce it to powder for you — any attempt to do so at home will be found unavailable, on account of its toughness.

Vervaine Sachet.

Lemon peel, dried and ground, 1 lb.; lemon thyme, ¼ lb.; otto of lemon-grass, 1 dr.; otto of lemon-peel, ½ oz.; otto of bergamot, 1 oz.

Violet Sachet.

Black-currant leaves, rose leaves, each, 1 lb.; powdered orris-root, 2 lbs.; oil of bitter almonds, ½ dr.: grain musk, 1 dr.; tonqua beans and gum benzoin, each, ½ lb. Mix thoroughly and keep together a week before offering for sale.

Perfume for Mouth Washes.

Asarum Canadense, orris root, each 1 oz.; strong alcohol, 1 pt. Make a tincture and add tincture of musk, 1 dr.; essence of millefleurs, ½ dr.; essence of patchouli, 20 drops.

A Superior Mouth Wash.

A close imitation of the popular sozodont. It cleanses the mouth thoroughly and is destructive to the parasites found in the deposits on the teeth. Add white castile soap, 2 drs.; alcohol, 3 fl. oz.; honey, 1 oz.; perfume as above, 4 fl. oz. Dissolve the soap in the alcohol, and add the honey and perfume.

Frangipanni Sachet.

Take orris-root and rose-leaves, each 1 lb.; sandal-wood ¼ lb.; Tonqua beans, ¼ lb.; musk, 1 dr.; civet, ¼ dr.; essence of roses, ½ dr. Triturate the musk, civet, and essence of roses, and mix with the other substances reduced to a powder.

Peau d'Espagne, or Spanish Skin,

Is merely highly-perfumed leather. Take of oil of rose, neroli, and santal, each ½ oz.; oil of lavender, verbena, bergamot, each ¼ oz.; oil of cloves and cinnamon, each 2 drs. In this dissolve 2 oz. of gum benzoin; in this steep good pieces of waste leather for a day or two, and dry it over a line. Prepare a paste by rubbing in a mortar 1 dr. of civet with 1 dr. of grain musk, and enough gum tragacanth mucilage to give a proper consistence. The leather is cut up into pieces about 4 inches square; two of these are pasted together with the above paste, placed between 2 pieces of paper, weighted or pressed until dry. It may then be inclosed in silk or satin. It gives off its odor for years; is much used for perfuming paper.

Indian or Yellow Pastils.

Santal-wood, in powder, 1 lb.; gum benzoin, 1½ lbs.; gum tolu, ¼ lb.; nitrate of potassa, 1½ lbs.; otto of santal, otto of cassia, otto of cloves, each 3 drs.; mucilage of tragacanth, q. s., to make the whole into a thick paste. The benzoin, santal-wood, and tolu are to be powdered and mixed by sifting them, adding the ottos. The nitre, being dissolved in the mucilage, is then added. After well beating in a mortar, the pastils are formed in shape with a pastil mould, and gradually dried.

The Chinese josticks are of a similar composition, but contain no tolu. Josticks are burned as incense in the temples of the Buddhist, in the Celestial Empire, and to such an extent as greatly to enhance the value of santal-wood.

Dr. Paris's Pastils.

Benzoin, cascarilla, each ½ lb.; myrrh, 1½ oz.; charcoal, 1½ lb.; otto of nutmegs, otto of cloves, each ¾ oz.; nitre, 2 oz. Mix as in the preceding.

Perfumer's Pastils.

Well-burned charcoal, 1 lb.; tolu, vanilla pods, cloves, each ½ lb.; benzoin, ¾ lb.; otto of santal, otto of neroli, each 2 drs.; nitre, 1½ oz; benzoin, ¾ lb.; otto of santal, otto of neroli, each 2 dr.; nitre, 1½ oz.; mucilage of tragacanth, q. s.

Piesse's Pastils.

Willow charcoal, ½ lb.; benzoic acid, 6 oz.; otto of thyme, otto of caraway, otto of rose, otto of lavender, otto of cloves, otto of santal, each ½ dr. Prior to mixing dissolve ¾ oz. nitre in ½ pt. of distilled or ordinary rose-water; with this solution thoroughly wet the charcoal, and then allow it to dry in a warm place. When the thus nitrated charcoal is quite dry, pour over it the mixed ottoes, and stir in the flowers of benzoin. When well mixed by sifting (the sieve is a better tool for mixing powders than the pestle and mortar), with enough mucilage to bind the whole together, and the less that is used the better.

Cachou Aromatisé.

Take of extract of liquorice and water, each 3½ oz.; dissolve by the heat of a water-bath, and add Bengal catechu, in powder, 462 grs.; gum arabic, in powder, 231 grs. Evaporate to the consistence of an extract, and then incorporate the following substances, previously reduced to fine powder: Mastic, cascarilla, charcoal, and orris-root, each 30 grs. Reduce the mass to a proper consistence, remove it from the fire, and then add English oil of peppermint, 30 drops; tincture of ambergris and tincture of musk, each 5 drops.; pour it on an oiled slab, and spread it out, by means of a roller, to the thickness of a sixpenny piece. After it has cooled, apply some folds of blotting-paper, to absorb any adhering oil, moisten the surface with water, and then cover it with the sheets of silver-leaf. It must now be allowed to dry, then cut into very thin strips, and these again divided into small pieces, about the size of a fenugreek seed.

SOAPS.

Hard soaps are made by boiling oils or fats with a lye of caustic soda. In soft soaps the lye is potash. Rosin is used in yellow soaps, as it saves fat. Silicate of soda is now frequently used instead; it gives a white soap, which has no offensive smell, and has not the stickiness of resin soap. Prentiss' Washing and Scouring Solution is pure silicate of soda. Besides refuse fat, the palm and cocoa-nut oils are largely used as a basis for soap. Castile soap is made from olive oil, and is mottled by iron.

Soft Soap.

Add 3 galls. of rain or other soft water to 1 lb. of saponified or concentrated lye; boil it and put into it 4 lbs. of tallow or soap-fat. When the solution becomes clear, add 12 galls. more of water. It is ready for use when cold.

Scented Soaps.

Cut the soap into thin shavings, and heat it with enough water until liquefied. Let it cool to 135° Fahr., and add the coloring matter and perfumes.

Almond Soap.

To 1 cwt. of the best hard curd soap add 20 of oz. oil of bitter almonds, or essence of Mirban (p. 291).

Rose Soap.

Put into a copper vessel, placed in boiling water, 20 lbs. of white curd soap and 30 lbs. of olive oil soap, both cut into thin shavings; add 5 lbs. of soft water, or rose-water; keep the heat below boiling until the soap is uniformly liquefied, and then add 12 oz. of finely-sifted vermilion, or enough to give the required color. Withdraw from the fire and, when sufficiently cool, add 3½ oz. otto of roses, ½ oz. oil of cloves, ½ oz. oil of cinnamon, and 2½ oz. oil of bergamot. For cheap soap use less perfume.

Honey Soap.

White curd soap, 1½ lbs.; Windsor soap, ½ lb. Cut into shavings and liquefy as before directed; then add 4 oz. of honey, and keep it melted until most of the water is evaporated. Perfume with any of the essential oils.

Floating Soaps

Are made by beating up soaps, liquefied as before directed, so as to incorporate a certain quantity of air.

Transparent Soaps

Are made by dissolving white soap in alcohol and evaporating. By the use of a still most of the alcohol may be recovered. They are made round by moulding with a drinking-glass, and then are known as wash-balls.

Glycerine Soap.

Cut the soap into fine shavings, dry, and powder it. Dissolve in a mixture of equal parts of alcohol and water by the aid of a water-bath. When the greater part of the alcohol has been evaporated, add a corresponding quantity of glycerine.

Windsor Soap.

White tallow scraps, 20 lbs.; essence of bergamot, oz.; carvi, 6 drs.; cloves, 4 drs.; thyme, ½ oz.

Saponaceous Cream of Almonds (Crême d'Amandes amerés.)

The preparation sold under this name is a potash soft soap, made with lard and perfumed with essential oil of almonds. It has a beautiful pearly appearance, and makes an excellent lather with a brush, and has met with an extensive demand as a shaving-soap, especially in Paris. It is prepared thus: Take of fine clarified lard, 7 lbs.; potash lye, containing about 26 per cent. of caustic potash, 3 lbs. 12 oz.; rectified spirit, 2 oz.; essential oil of almonds, 2 drs. Melt the lard in a porcelain vessel, by a salt-water bath or a steam-heat under 15 lbs. pressure, then run in the lye very slowly, agitating continually from right to left during the whole time; when about half the lye is run in the mixture begins to curdle; it will, however, finally become so firm and compact that it cannot be stirred, if the operation is successful. The soap is now finished, but is not pearly; it will, however, assume that appearance by long trituration in a mortar, gradually adding the alcohol, in which is previously dissolved the perfume.

Tooth Powder.

Take precipitated chalk and powdered orrisroot, each 1 lb.; carmine and powdered sugar, each 15 grs.; essence rose and essence neroli, each 60 grs.

Tooth Paste.

Honey, precipitated chalk, powdered orris-root, each 8 oz.; tincture of opium, tincture of myrrh, each 1¾ drs.; essence of rose, cloves, and nutmeg, each ½ dr.

Charcoal Tooth Powder.

Finely powdered charcoal, sugar, each 2 oz.; oil of cloves, 6 drops.

Another.—Finely powdered charcoal and red Peruvian bark, each 2 oz.; sugar, 1 oz.; oil of spearmint, 8 drops.

Charcoal Tooth Paste.

Finely powdered charcoal, white honey, and vanilla candy, each 2 oz.; red bark, 1 oz.; oil of rose or mint, 8 drops. Mix the whole into a paste.

AROMATIC VINEGARS.

In making these the vinegar known as No. 8 may be used. Vinegar of 25 to 30 per cent. is required to dissolve essential oils.

Tarragon (Estragon) Vinegar.

Tarragon (Artemesia dracunculus), 1 lb.; strong vinegar, 1 gal. The herb should be gathered before blossoming. This may be diluted when used.

Vinaigre aux fines herbes.

Tarragon, 12 oz.; basil, laurel leaves, each, 4 oz.; shallots, 2 oz.; strong vinegar, ½ gal. Let them soak for a week or two, and strain. It is too strong for use, but is added to table vinegar to improve its flavor.

Cologne Vinegar.

Add to each quart of cologne water, 1 oz. of No. 8 vinegar.

Aromatic Vinegar.

Concentrated acetic acid, 8 oz.; oil of English lavender, 2 drs.; oil of English rosemary, 1 dr.; oil cloves, 1 dr.; oil of camphor, 1 oz.

Henry's Vinegar.

Dried leaves of rosemary, rue, wormwood, sage, mint, and lavender flowers, each ½ oz.; bruised nutmeg, cloves, angelica root, and camphor, each, ¼ oz.; alcohol, rectified, 4 oz.; concentrated acetic acid, 16 oz. Macerate the materials for a day in the spirit; then add the acid, and digest for a week longer, at a temperature of about 70° Fahr. Finally, press out the now aromatized acid, and filter it.

Vinaigre des quatre Voleurs, or Four Thieves' Vinegar.

Take fresh tops of common wormwood, Roman

wormwood, rosemary, sage, mint, and rue, of each ¾ oz.; lavender flowers, 1 oz.; garlic, calamus aromaticus, cinnamon, cloves, and nutmeg, each 1 dr.; camphor, ½ oz.; alcohol, or brandy, 1 oz.; strong vinegar, 4 pts. Digest all the materials, except the camphor and spirit, in a closely covered vessel for a fortnight, at a summer heat; then express and filter the vinaigre produced, and add the camphor previously dissolved in the brandy or spirit.

Hygienic Vinegar.

Brandy, 1 pint; oil of cloves, 1 dr.; oil of lavender, 1 dr.; oil of marjoram, ½ dr.; gum benzoin, 1 oz. Macerate these together for a few hours,

then add brown vinegar, 2 pts.; and strain or filter, if requisite, to be bright.

Toilet Vinegar (à la Violette).

Extract of cassia, ¼ pt.; extract of orris, ¼ pt.; esprit de rose, triple, ¼ pt.; white wine vinegar, 2 pts.

Toilet Vinegar (à la Rose).

Dried rose leaves, 4 oz.; esprit de rose, triple, ½ pt.; white wine vinegar, 2 pts. Macerate in a close vessel for a fortnight, then filter and bottle for sale.

Camphorated Vinegar.

Camphor, 6 drs.; alcohol 2 oz.; strong vinegar, 1 lb. Powder the camphor, by the aid of the alcohol, in a mortar, and add the vinegar.

BLEACHING and SCOURING.

To Bleach Cloths, &c.

The mode of bleaching which least injures the texture of cloth formed of vegetable substances, is that effected by merely exposing it in a moistened state to the atmosphere, after having been steeped in a solution of potash or soda, but the length of time and other inconveniences attending this process, lead to the use of more active chemical operations.

It is by the combination of oxygen with the coloring matter of the cloth, that it is deprived of its hue, and the different processes employed must be adapted to prepare it for this combination, and render it as perfect as possible without destroying its texture, an effect which, however, must necessarily ensue in a greater or less degree from the union of oxygen with all bodies. The operation of bleaching requires 4 distinct processes. First, to remove the impurities, with which the threads are covered in the operation of spinning, which is called the weaver's dressing. This may be effected by soaking the cloth for some hours in warm water, and then boiling it in an alkaline lye, prepared with 20 parts of water, and 1 part of pearlash, rendered more active by being mixed with ⅓ of lime. After it has been boiled for some hours in this solution, it is to be well washed with water, and then exposed to the second process. The solution of chloride of lime must be of such strength as nearly to destroy the color of a solution of indigo in water, slightly acidulated with sulphuric acid. The cloth is to be alternately steeped in this liquor, and a solution (made as before directed), 4 or 5 times, using fresh liquor at each process. It is then to be well rubbed and washed with soft soap and water, which prepares it for the last process.

The steeping is in a weak solution of sulphuric acid, and from 60 to 100 parts of water, the strength being thus varied according to the texture of the cloth. This dissolves the remaining coloring matter which had resisted the action of alkali, and the chloride of lime, as well as a small quantity of iron contained in all vegetable matter. The cloth is then to be exposed to the air for some days, and watered, to carry off any remains of the acids, and remove the unpleasant odor it acquires from the chloride of lime and potash.

Bleaching Salt,

Commonly called chloride of lime, is made by passing chlorine gas over moistened lime. It is a moist greyish powder, soluble in 10 parts of water,

any excess of hydrate of lime remaining undissolved. It deteriorates by keeping; when freshly made it may contain 30 per cent. of chlorine, but often has less than 10 per cent. It is decomposed by acids, yielding chlorine. It consists of hypochlorite of lime and chloride of calcium, with water and excess of lime.

Chlorimetry.

The bleaching power of chloride of lime is often estimated, as above stated, by the quantity of a solution of sulphate of indigo, which a certain weight will deprive of its blue color. But as the indigo solution alters by keeping, this method is not unobjectionable.

Mr. Graham's test is founded on the fact that 10 grains of chlorine are capable of converting 77.9 grains of protosulphate of iron (copperas, green vitriol) into persulphate. Seventy-eight grains of green vitriol (powdered and dried by strong pressure between folds of cloth) are dissolved in about 2 oz. of water, which may be acidulated by a few drops of sulphuric or muriatic acid. Fifty grs. of the bleaching salt to be examined are dissolved in about 2 oz. of tepid water, by trituration in a mortar. This is transferred to a graduated glass vessel, which is filled to its 0 with pure water. The solution thus made is poured gradually into that of the iron, until it is entirely peroxidized. To test this we have a solution of ferricyanide of potassium (red prussiate of potash). This gives a precipitate only with the salts of the protoxide of iron. It is spattered in drops over the surface of a plate, and after each addition of the chlorine solution, a drop of the iron solution, on the end of a rod, is touched to the ferricyanide solution. When a deep blue precipitate is no longer formed, an amount of salt equal to 10 grains of chlorine has been used. By noting what portion of the whole solution has been employed, the percentage of chlorine may be determined.

To Bleach Cotton.

The first operation consists in scouring it in a slight alkaline solution; or what is better, by exposure to steam. It is afterwards put into a basket and rinsed in running water. The immersion of cotton in an alkaline ley, however it may be rinsed, always leaves with it an earthy deposit. It is well known that cotton bears the action of acids better than hemp or flax; that time is even necessary before the action of them can be prejudicial to it; and by taking advantage of this valuable property in regard to bleaching, means have been found to free it from the earthy deposit by pressing down the cotton in a very weak solution of sulphuric acid, and afterwards removing the acid by washing, lest too long remaining in it should destroy the cotton.

To Bleach Wool.

The first kind of bleaching to which wool is subjected, is to free it from grease. This operation is called scouring. In manufactories, it is generally performed by an ammoniacal lye, formed of 5 measures of river water and 1 of stale urine; the wool is immersed for about 20 minutes in a bath of this mixture heated to 56°; it is then taken out, suffered to drain, and then rinsed in running water. This manipulation softens the wool, and gives it the first degree of whiteness. It is then repeated a second, even a third time; after which the wool is fit to be employed. In some places, scouring is performed with water slightly impregnated with soap; and indeed, for valuable articles, this process is preferable; but it is too expensive for articles of less value. Bi-sulphide of carbon and benzine have been employed in cleansing wool. The fat may be saved by distilling off the solvent, which may be used over and over again.

Sulphurous acid gas unites very easily with water; and in this combination it may be employed for bleaching wool and silk.

To Prepare the Sulphurous Acid.

Sulphurous acid is used either as gas or in solution in water, which dissolves 50 times its volume of the gas. In the former case sulphur is burned in a close, moist room in which the stuffs (moistened) are hung. Two exposures, of 24 hours each, suffice for wool.

To get a solution of sulphurous acid, the cheapest and best plan is to heat in a glass retort 12 oz. sulphuric acid and 2 oz. of sulphur. The gas, which comes off quietly, is collected in a large bottle, partially filled with water; or better a series of bottles, so connected together that the gas must pass successively through the water contained in each.

To Full Cloths, Woollens, etc.

The method of fulling woollen stuffs with soap, is this: A colored cloth of about 45 ells, is to be laid in the usual manner in the trough of a fulling mill without first soaking it in water, as is commonly practised in many places. To full this trough of cloth, 15 lbs. of soap are required; ½ of which is to be melted in 2 pails of river or spring-water, made as hot as the hand can well bear it. This solution is to be poured by little and little upon the cloth, in proportion as it is laid in the trough; after which it is to be taken out and stretched. This done, the cloth is immediately returned into the same trough, without any new soap, and there fulled for 2 hours more. Then taken out, it is rung well, to express all the grease and filth. After the second fulling the remainder of the soap is dissolved in, as in the former, and cast 4 different times on the cloth, remembering to take out the cloth every two hours to stretch it, and undo the plaits and wrinkles it has acquired in the trough. When sufficiently fulled and brought to the quality and thickness required, scour it in hot water, keeping it in the trough till it is quite clean. As to white cloths, as these full more easily and in less time than colored ones, a third part of the soap may be spared.

To Bleach Silk.

Take a solution of caustic soda, so weak as to make only a fourth of a degree, at most, of the areometer for salts, and fill with it the boiler of the apparatus for bleaching with steam. Charge the frames with skeins of raw silk, and place them in the apparatus until it is full; then close the door and make the solution boil. Having continued the ebullition for 12 hours, slacken the fire and open the door of the apparatus. The heat of the steam, which is always above 250°, will have been sufficient to free the silk from the gum, and to scour it. Wash the skeins in warm water, and having wrung th m, place them again on the frames in the apparatus, to undergo a second boiling. Then wash them several times in water, and immerse them in water somewhat soapy, to give them a little softness. Notwithstanding the whiteness which silk acquires by these different operations, it must be carried to a higher degree of splendor by exposing it to the action of sulphurous acid gas, in a close chamber, or by immersing it in sulphurous acid, as before recommended in wool.

To Bleach Prints and Printed Books.

Simple immersion in chlorine gas, letting the article remain in it a longer or shorter space of time, according to the strength of the liquor, will be sufficient to whiten an engraving. If it is required to whiten the paper of a bound book, as it is necessary that all the leaves should be acted on by the gas, care must be taken to open the book well, and to make the boards rest on the edge of the vessel, in such a manner that the paper alone shall be dipped in the gas. The leaves must be separated from each other, in order that they may be equally acted on on both sides. Chlorine water, freshly made, will answer instead of the gas

Hare's Method of Bleaching Shell-lac.

Dissolve in an iron kettle 1 part of pearlash in about 8 parts of water, add 1 part of shell or seed-lac, and heat the whole to ebullition. When the lac is dissolved cool the solution and impregnate it with chlorine, till the lac is all precipitated.

To Wash Chintz.

Take 2 lbs. of rice, boil it in 2 galls. of water till soft; then pour the whole into a tub; let it stand till about the warmth in general used for colored linens; then put the chintz in, and use the rice instead of soap; wash it in this till the dirt appears to be out, then boil the same quantity as above, but strain the rice from the water, and mix it in warm clear water. Wash in this till quite clean; afterwards rinse it in the water which the rice has been boiled in, and this will answer the end of starch, and no dew will affect it. If a gown it must be taken to pieces, and when dried be careful to hang it as smooth as possible; after it is dry rub it with a sleek stone, but use no iron.

To Wash Fine Lace or Linen.

Take 1 gall. of furze blossoms and burn them to ashes, then boil them in 6 qts. of soft water; this, when fine, use in washing with the suds, as occasion requires, and the linen, etc., will not only be exceedingly white, but it is done with half the soap and little trouble.

To Clean Black and White Sarcenets.

Lay these smooth and even upon a board, spread a little soap over the dirty places; then make a lather with Castile soap, and with a common brush dip it in, pass it over the long way, and repeat it in this manner till one side is sufficiently scoured; use the other in the same manner; then put it into hot water, and there let it lie, till you have prepared some cold water, wherein a small quantity of gum arabic has been dissolved. Now rinse them well, take them out and fold them, pressing out the water with the hands on the board, and keeping them under the hands till they are dry; at which time have brimstone ready to dry them over, till they are ready for smoothing, which must be done on the right side, with a moderately hot iron.

To Wash and Stain Tiffanies.

Let the hems of the tiffanies be at first only a little soaped, then having a lather of soap, put them into it hot, and wash them very gently for fear they should be crumpled; and when they are clean rinse them in warm water, in which a little gum arabic has been dissolved, keeping them from the air as much as possible; then add a lump of starch, wet the tiffanies with a soft linen rag, and fold them up in a clean cloth, pressing them till they are nearly dry; after which put them near the fire, and finish the drying over brimstone; then shape them properly by gently ironing them.

To Wash and Starch Lawns.

Lawns may be done in the same manner as the former, only observe to iron them on the wrong side, and use gum arabic water instead of starch, and, according to what has been directed for sarcenets, any colored silks may be starched, abating or augmenting the gum-water as may be thought fit, according to the stiffness intended.

To Clean Buff-colored Cloth.

Take tobacco-pipe clay, and mix it with water till it is as thick as lime-water used for white-washing rooms; spread this over the cloth, and when it is dry rub it off with a brush, and the cloth will look extremely well.

To make Saponaceous Lye for Washing.

Boil together in a sufficient quantity of water, 1 gall. of good wood-ashes and 2 or 3 handfuls of fresh-burnt lime. Leave the lixivium at rest till the extraneous matters have been deposited at the bottom, or thrown to the surface to be skimmed off. Then draw off the pure lixivium, add to it oil, to about a thirtieth or fortieth part of its own quantity. The mixture will be a liquor white as milk, capable of frothing like soap-water, and in dilution with water perfectly fit to communicate sufficient whiteness to linen. This liquor may be prepared from wood-ashes of all sorts, and from rancid grease, oil or butter. It is therefore highly worthy the attention of the economist. When the ashes are suspected to be unusually deficient in alkali, a small addition of pulverized potash or soda may be made to the lixivium.

To Clean and Starch Point Lace.

Fix the lace in a prepared tent, draw it straight, make a warm lather of Castile soap, and, with a fine brush dipped in, rub over the point gently; and when it is clean on one side do the same to the other; then throw some clean water on it, in which a little alum has been dissolved, to take off the suds, and having some thin starch go over with the same on the wrong side, and iron it on the same side when dry, then open it with a bodkin and set it in order.

To clean point lace, if not very dirty, without washing, fix it in a tent as the former, and go over with fine bread, the crust being pared off, and when it is done dust out the crumbs, etc.

To Clean White Veils.

Put the veil in a solution of white soap, and let it simmer a quarter of an hour. Squeeze it in some warm water and soap till quite clean. Rinse it from soap, and then in clean cold water, in which is a drop of liquid blue. Then pour boiling water upon a teaspoonful of starch, run the veil through this, and clear it well by clapping it. Afterwards pin it out, keeping the edges straight and even.

To Clean Black Veils.

Pass them through a warm liquor of bullock's gall and water; rinse in cold water; then take a small piece of glue, pour boiling water on it, and pass the veil through it; clap it, and frame it to dry.

To Clean White Satin and Flowered Silks.

Mix sifted stale bread-crumbs with powder blue, and rub it thoroughly all over, then shake it well, and dust it with clean soft cloths. Afterwards, where there are any gold or silver flowers, take a piece of crimson ingrain velvet, rub the flowers with it, which will restore them to their original lustre.

Another Method.

Pass them through a solution of fine hard soap, at a hand heat, drawing them through the hand. Rinse in lukewarm water, dry and finish by pinning out. Brush the flossy or bright side with a clean clothes-brush the way of the nap. Finish them by dipping a sponge into a size, made by boiling isinglass in water, and rub the wrong side. Rinse out a second time, and brush and dry near a fire or in a warm room.

Silks may be treated in the same way, but not brushed. If the silks are for dyeing, instead of passing them through a solution of soap and water they must be boiled off; but if the silks are very stout, the water must only be of heat sufficient to extract the dirt, and when rinsed in warm water they are in a state for the dye.

Another Method.

Strew French chalk over them, and brush it off with a hard brush once or twice.

To Clean Colored Silks of all kinds.

Put some soft soap into boiling water, and beat it till dissolved in a strong lather. At a hand heat put in the article. If strong, it may be rubbed as in washing; rinse it quickly in warm water, and add oil of vitriol, sufficient to give another water a sourish taste, if for bright yellow, crimsons, maroons, and scarlets; but for oranges, fawns, browns, or their shades, use no acid. For bright scarlet, use a solution of tin. Gently squeeze and then roll it in a coarse sheet, and wring it. Hang it in a warm room to dry, and finish it by calendering or mangling.

For pinks, rose colors, and thin shades, etc., instead of oil of vitriol, or solution of tin, prefer lemon-juice, or white tartar, or vinegar.

For blues, purples, and their shades, add a small quantity of pearlash; it will restore the colors. Wash the articles like a linen garment, but instead of wringing gently squeeze and sheet them, and when dry finish them with fine gum-water or dissolved isinglass, to which add some pearlash, rubbed on the wrong side; then pin them out.

Blues of all shades are dyed with archil, and afterwards dipped in a vat; twice cleaning with pearlash restores the color. For olive greens, a small quantity of verdigris dissolved in water, or a solution of copper mixed with the water, will revive the color again. Grease spots may be removed by benzine.

To Clean Black Silks.

To bullock's gall add boiling water sufficient to make it warm, and with a clean sponge rub the silk well on both sides; squeeze it well out, and proceed again in like manner. Rinse it in spring-water, and change the water till perfectly clean; dry it in the air, and pin it out on a table; but first dip the sponge in glue-water, and rub it on the wrong side; then dry it before a fire.

To Dip Rusty Black Silks.

If it requires to be red dyed, boil logwood, and in half an hour put in the silk and let it simmer half an hour. Take it out, and dissolve a little blue vitriol and green copperas, cool the copper, let it simmer ½ hour, then dry it over a stick in the air. If not red dyed, pin it out, and rinse it in spring water, in which ½ teaspoonful of oil of vitriol has been put. Work it about 5 minutes, rinse it in cold water, and finish it by pinning and rubbing it with gum-water.

To Clean Silk Stockings.

Wash with soap and water, and simmer them in the same for 10 minutes, rinsing in cold water. For blue cast, put 1 drop of liquid blue into a pan of cold spring-water; run the stockings through this a minute or two, and dry them. For a pink cast, put 1 or 2 drops of saturated pink dye into cold water, and rinse them through this. For a flesh-color, add a little rose pink in a thin soap-liquor, rub them with clean flannel, and calender or mangle them.

To Extract Grease-spots from Silks and Colored Muslins, etc.

Scrape French chalk, put it on the grease-spot, and hold it near the fire, or over a warm iron, or water-plate, filled with boiling water. The grease will melt, and the French chalk absorb it; brush or rub it off. Repeat if necessary.

To take Stains out of Silk.

Mix together in a phial 2 oz. of essence of lemon, 1 oz. of oil of turpentine. Grease and other spots in silk are to be rubbed gently with a linen rag dipped in the above composition. Benzine may be used instead.

To Scour Yarn.

It should be laid in lukewarm water for 3 or 4 days, each day shifting it once, wringing it out, and laying it in another water of the same nature; then carry it to a well or brook, and rinse it till nothing comes from it but pure, clean water; that done, take a bucking-tub, and cover the bottom with very fine aspen ashes, and then having opened and spread the slippings, lay them on those ashes, and put some ashes above, and lay in more slippings, covering them with ashes as before; then lay one upon another till the yarn is put in; afterwards cover up the uppermost yarn with a bucking-cloth, and, in proportion to the size of the tub, lay in a peck or two more of ashes; this done, pour upon the uppermost cloth a great deal of warm water, till the tub can receive no more, and let it stand so all night. Next morning set a kettle of clean water on the fire, and when it is warm pull out the spigot of the bucking-tub to let the water run out of it into another clean vessel; as the bucking-tub wastes fill it up again with warm water on the fire, and as the water on the fire wastes so likewise fill up that with the lye that comes from the bucking-tub, ever observing to make the lye hotter and hotter, till it boils; then you must, as before, ply it with the boiling lye at least 4 hours together. For whitening, you must take off this bucking-cloth, then putting the yarn with the lye ashes into large tubs, with your hands labor the yarn, ashes and lye pretty well together; afterwards carry it to a well or river, and rinse it clean; then hang it upon poles in the air all day, and in the evening take the slippings down and lay them in water all night; the next day hang them up again, and throw water on them as they dry, observing to turn that side outermost which whitens slowest. After having done this for a week together, put all the yarn again into the bucking-tub without ashes, covering it as before with a bucking-cloth; lay thereon good store of fresh ashes, and drive that buck, as before, with a very strong boiling lye for half a day or more; then take it out and rinse it, hanging it up, as before, in the day-time, to dry, and laying it in water at night another week. Lastly, wash it over in fair water, and dry it.

To Scour Thick Cotton Counterpanes.

Cut 1 lb. of mottled soap into thin slices, and put it into a pan with ½ oz. of potash and 1 oz. of pearlash; pour a pail of boiling water on it and let it stand till dissolved; then pour hot and cold water in a scouring tub, with a bowl of the solution; put in the counterpane, beat it well, turn it often, and give it a second liquor as before; then rinse it in cold water; now put 3 teaspoonfuls of liquid blue into a thin liquor, stir it, and put in the counterpane; beat it about 5 minutes, and dry it in the air.

To Scour Undyed Woollens.

Cut ½ lb. of the best palm soap into thin slices, and pour such a quantity of boiling river-water on it as will dissolve the soap, and make it of the consistence of oil; cover the articles about 2 in. with water such as the hand can bear, and add a lump of pearlash and about ⅓ of the soap solution. Beat them till no head of lather rises on the water; throw away the dirty water and proceed as before with hotter water, without pearlash.

To Scour Clothes, Coats, Pelisses, etc.

If a black, blue, or brown coat, dry 2 oz. of fuller's earth, and pour on it sufficient boiling water to mix it, and plaster with it the spots of grease; take a pennyworth of bullock's gall, mix with it ½ a pt. of stale urine, and a little boiling water; with a hard brush dipped in this liquor, brush spotted places. Then dip the coat in a bucket of cold spring-water. When nearly dry, lay the nap right, and pass a drop of oil of olives over with a brush to finish it.

If gray, drab, fawns, or maroons, cut palm soap into thin slices, and pour water upon it to moisten it. Rub the greasy and dirty spots of the coat. Let it dry a little, and then brush it with warm water, repeating, if necessary, as at first, and use water a little hotter; rinse several times, in warm water, and finish as before.

To Scour Carpets, Hearth-Rugs, etc.

Rub a piece of soap on every spot of grease or dirt; then take a hard brush dipped in boiling water, and rub the spots well. If very dirty, a solution of soap must be put into a tub, with hot water, and the carpet well beat in it, rinsing it in several clean waters, putting in the last water a tablespoonful of oil of vitriol, to brighten the colors.

To Clean Cotton Gowns.

Make a solution of soap, put in the articles, and wash them in the usual way. If greens, reds, etc., run, add lemon-juice, vinegar, or oil of vitriol to the rinsing water.

To Clean Scarlet Cloth.

Dissolve the best white soap; and if black-looking spots appear, rub dry soap on them; while the other soap is dissolving, brush it off with hot water. If very dirty, immerse the article into the warm solution, and rub the stained parts. Dispatch it quickly, and as soon as the color begins to give, wring it out, and immerse it in a pan or pail of warm water; wring it again, and immerse it in cold spring-water, in which mix a tablespoonful of solution of tin. Stir it about, and in 10 minutes hang it to dry in the shade, and cold press it.

Another Method.

On ½ of a peck of wheaten bran pour boiling water in a hair sieve. In the bran-water, at a hand-heat, immerse the cloth, and rub it, looking through it to see the spots. To a second liquor, add nearly ½ oz. of white or crude tartar. If darkened, make a clean liquor of cold spring-water with a drop or two of solution of tin, soak it in 10 minutes, wring it, and hang it up to dry.

To Dip Scarlet Cloth.

After it has been thoroughly cleaned with soap, and rinsed in warm water, put into boiling spring-water ¼ lb. of young fustic or zant, 1 dr. of pounded and sifted cochineal, and an equal quantity of cream of tartar; boil 5 or 6 minutes, and cool by adding 1 or 2 pts. of cold spring-water, and 1 tablespoonful of the solution of tin. Stir the mixture, put in the cloth, boil it for 10 minutes, and when dry, cold press it.

To Raise the Nap on Cloth.

Soak in cold water for ½ an hour, then put on a board, and rub the thread-bare parts with a half-worn hatter's card, filled with flocks, or with a prickly thistle, until a nap is raised. Hang up to dry, and with a hard brush lay the nap the right way.

To Revive Faded Black Cloth.

Having cleaned it well, boil 2 or 3 oz. of logwood for ½ an hour. Dip it in warm water and squeeze it dry, then put it into the copper, and boil ¼ an hour. Take it out and add a small piece of green copperas, and boil it another ½ an hour. Hang it in the air for an hour or two, then rinse it in 2 or 3 cold waters, dry it, and let it be regularly brushed with a soft brush, over which 1 or 2 drops of oil of olives have been rubbed.

To Dry Clean Cloth.

Dip a brush in warm gall, and apply it to greasy places, rinse it off in cold water; dry by the fire, then lay the coat flat, strew damp sand over it, and with a brush beat the sand into the cloth; then brush it out with a hard brush, and the sand will bring away the dirt. Rub a drop of oil of olives over with a soft brush, to brighten the colors.

To Prevent Prints from Fading.

The dress should be washed in luther, and not by applying the soap in the usual way direct upon the muslin. Make a lather by boiling soap and water together; let it stand until it is sufficiently cool for use, and previously to putting the dress into it, throw in a handful of salt; rinse the dress without wringing it in clear, cold water, into which a little salt has been thrown; remove it and rinse it in a fresh supply of clear water and salt. Then wring the dress in a cloth and hang it to dry immediately, spreading as open as possible, so as to prevent one part lying over another. Should there be any white in the pattern, mix a little blue in the water.

To Bleach Wool, Silks, Straw Bonnets, etc.

Put a chafing-dish with some lighted charcoal into a close room, or large box; then strew 1 or 2 oz. of powdered brimstone on the hot coals. Hang the articles in the room or box, make the door fast, and let them hang some hours. Fine colored woollens are thus sulphured before dyed, and straw bonnets are thus bleached.

To take Iron-moulds out of Linen.

1. Hold the iron-mould on the cover of a tankard of boiling water, and rub on the spot a little oxalic acid, or salt of sorrel, and when the cloth has thoroughly imbibed the acid, wash it in lye.

2. Wet the spot wi h lemon-juice, sprinkle with salt, and lay in the sun until dry. Repeat the application until the stain is removed.

To make Breeches-Ball.

Mix 1 lb. of Bath brick, 2 lbs. of pipe-clay, 4 oz. of pumice-stone powder, and 6 oz. of ox-galls; color them with rose-pink, yellow ochre, umber, Irish slate, etc., to any desired shade.

Clothes' Ball.

1. Mix 2 lbs. of pipe-clay, 4 oz. of fuller's earth, 4 oz. of whiting, and ¼ of a pt. of ox-galls.

2. Portable balls, for removing spots from clothes, may be thus prepared: Fuller's earth, perfectly dried (so that it may crumble into a powder), is to be moistened with the clear juice of lemons, and a small quantity of pure pearlashes is to be added. Knead the whole carefully together, till it acquires the consistence of a thick elastic paste; form it into convenient small balls, and dry them in the sun. To be used, first moisten the spot on the clothes with water, then rub it with the ball, and let the spot dry in the sun; after having washed it with pure water, the spot will entirely disappear.

To take Grease out of Leather Breeches.

The white of an egg applied to the injured part and dried in the sun, will effectually answer this purpose.

Another Method.

To 2 tablespoonfuls of spirits of turpentine, put ½ an oz. of mealy potatoes, add some of the best Durham mustard, with a little vinegar; let them dry, and when well rubbed, the spots will be entirely removed.

To Cleanse Feathers from Animal Oil.

Mix well with 1 gall. of clear water, 1 lb. of quicklime; and, when the lime is precipitated in fine powder, pour off the clear lime-water for use, at the time it is wanted. Put the feathers to be cleaned in a tub, and add to them a sufficient quantity of the clear lime-water, so as to cover them about 3 inches. The feathers, when thoroughly moistened, will sink down, and should remain in the lime-water for 3 or 4 days; after which, the foul liquor should be separated.

Fuller's Purifier for Woollen Cloths.

Dry, pulverize, and sift the following ingredients:

Six lbs. of fuller's earth, 1 lb. of pipe clay, and 4 oz. of French chalk.

Make a paste of the above with the following: One oz. of rectified oil of turpentine, 2 oz. of spirit of wine, and 1½ lbs. of melted oil soap.

Make up the compound into six-penny or shilling cakes for sale. These cakes are to be kept in water, or in small wooden boxes.

To Clean all Sorts of Metal.

Mix ½ pt. of refined neat's-foot oil, and ½ a gill of spirit of turpentine. Scrape a little rottenstone; wet a woollen rag with the liquid, dip it into the scraped kernel, and rub the metal well. Wipe it off with a soft cloth, polish with dry leather, and use more of the kernel. In respect to steel, if it is very rusty, use a little powder of pumice with the liquid, on a separate woollen rag first.

To Take out Writing.

Wash by means of camel's hair pencils dipped alternately in solutions of cyanide of potassium and oxalic acid.

To take out Marking Ink.

Most indelible ink contains silver as a basis, and may be removed by a solution of cyanide of potassium. When the basis of the ink is carbon, however, this will fail. Chlorine will destroy all stains and markings dependent upon organic matters except the carbon ink.

To Restore Hangings, Carpets, Chairs, etc.

Beat the dust out of them as clean as possible, then rub them over with a dry brush, and make a good lather of Castile soap, and rub them well over with a hard brush, then take clean water and with it wash off the froth, make a water with alum, and wash them over with it, and when dry, most of the colors will be restored in a short time; and those that are yet too faint, must be touched up with a pencil dipped in suitable colors; it may be run all over in the same manner with water-colors mixed well with gum-water, and it will look at a distance like new.

To Clean Paper Hangings.

Cut into 8 half-quarters a stale quartern loaf; with one of these pieces, after having blown off all the dust from the paper to be cleaned by means of a good pair of bellows, begin at the top of the room, holding the crust in the hand, and wiping lightly downward with the crumb, about half a yard at each stroke, till the upper part of the hangings is completely cleaned all round; then go again round with the like sweeping stroke downward, always commencing each successive course a little higher than the upper stroke had extended, till the bottom be finished. This operation, if carefully performed, will frequently make very old paper look almost equal to new. Great caution must be used not by any means to rub the paper hard, nor to attempt cleaning it the cross or horizontal way. The dirty part of the bread too must be each time cut away, and the pieces renewed as soon as at all necessary.

To Clean Leather.

Take of French yellow ochre, 1 lb.; sweet oil, a dessertspoonful. Mix well together, so that the oil may not be seen; then take of pipe-clay 1 lb.; starch, ¼ lb. Mix with boiling water; when cold lay it on the leather. When dry rub and brush it well.

To Clean Marble.

Take verdigris and pumice-stone, well powdered, with lime newly slaked. Mix with soap lees, to the consistence of putty. Put it in a woollen rag, and rub the stains well one way. Wash off with soap and water. Repeat, if not removed. Or, cover the stains with fuller's earth or plaster of Paris, and when dry brush it off.

To take Stains out of Silver Plate.

Steep the plate in soap lyes for the space of 4 hours; then cover it over with whiting, wet with vinegar, so that it may stick thick upon it, and dry it by a fire; after which, rub off the whiting, and pass it over with dry bran, and the spots will not only disappear, but the plate will look exceedingly bright.

To take out Fruit Spots.

Let the spotted part of the cloth imbibe a little water without dipping, and hold the part over a lighted common brimstone match at a proper distance. The sulphurous acid gas, which is discharged, soon causes the spots to disappear. Or, wet the spot with chlorine water. [See page 436.]

To Clean Gold Lace and Embroidery.

For this purpose no alkaline liquors are to be used; for while they clean the gold they corrode the silk, and change or discharge its color. Soap also alters the shade, and even the species of certain colors. But spirit of wine may be used without any danger of its injuring either color or quality; and, in many cases, proves as effectual for restoring the lustre of the gold, as the corrosive detergents. But, though spirit of wine is the most innocent material employed for this purpose, it is not in all cases proper. The golden covering may be in some parts worn off; or the base metal, with which it has been alloyed, may be corroded by the air, so as to leave the particles of the gold disunited; while the silver underneath, tarnished to a yellow hue, may continue a tolerable color to the whole; so it is apparent that the removal of the tarnish would be prejudicial, and make the lace or embroidery less like gold than it was before.

To Remove Spots of Grease from Cloths.

Spots of grease may be removed by a diluted solution of potash, but this must be cautiously applied to prevent injury to the cloth. A better way is to lay a piece of brown or blotting-paper over the spot, and pass over it a hot iron. The grease is absorbed by the paper. Stains of white wax, which sometimes falls upon clothes from wax-candles, are removed by spirits of turpentine, sulphuric ether, or benzine. The marks of white paint may also be discharged by the above-mentioned agents.

To take Mildew out of Linen.

Rub it well with soap; then scrape some fine chalk and rub that also in the linen, lay it on the grass; as it dries, wet it a little, and it will come out after twice doing. [See page 437.]

To take out Spots of Ink.

As soon as the accident happens, wet the place with juice of sorrel or lemon, or with vinegar, and the best hard white soap. Oxalic acid in weak solution is more active, but must be used cautiously.

To take out Stains of Cloth or Silk.

Pound French chalk fine, mix with lavender-water to the thickness of mustard. Put on the stain; rub it soft with the finger or palm of the hand. Put a sheet of blotting and brown paper on the top, and smooth it with an iron, milk-warm.

To Remove Grease Spots from Paper.

Let the paper stained with grease, wax, oil, or any other fat body, be gently warmed, taking out as much as possible of it by blotting-paper. Dip a small brush in ether or benzine, and draw it gently over both sides of the paper, which must be carefully kept warm. Let this operation be repeated as many times as the quantity of the fat-body, imbibed by the paper, or the thickness of the paper may render it necessary. When the greasy substance is removed, to restore the paper to its former whiteness, dip another brush in highly rectified spirit of wine, and draw it, in like manner over the place; and particularly around the edges, to remove the border that would still present a stain. If the process has been employed on a part written on with common ink, or printed with printer's ink, it will experience no alteration.

Another.—Scrape finely some pipe-clay (the quantity will be easily determined on making the experiment); on this lay the sheet or leaf, and cover the spot, in like manner, with the clay. Cover the whole with a sheet of paper, and apply, for a few seconds, a heated iron-box, or any substitute adopted by laundresses. On using Indian rubber, to remove the dust taken up by the grease, the paper will be found restored to its original whiteness and opacity. This simple method has often proved much more effectual than turpentine, and was remarkably so, in an instance, where the folio of a ledger had exhibited the marks of candle-grease and the snuff for more than 12 months.

To Cleanse Gloves.

Benzine is the best material for cleaning gloves. It may be applied with a soft sponge or a piece of cloth.

To Clean Straw Hats.

Rub the soiled straw with a cut lemon, and wash off the juice with water. Stiffen with gum-water

---

DYEING, in all its Varieties.

PRELIMINARY REMARKS.

The art of dyeing has for its object the fixing permanently of a color of a definite shade upon stuffs. The stuffs are animal, as silk, wool, and feathers, or vegetable, as cotton and linen. The former take the colors much more readily, and they are more brilliant.

In some cases, as in dyeing silk and wool with coal-tar colors, the color at once unites with the fiber; generally, however, a process of preparation is necessary. In certain other cases, as in dyeing silk and wool yellow by nitric acid, the color is due to a change in the stuff, and is not properly dyeing.

Insoluble colors are managed by taking advantage of known chemical changes; thus chromate of lead (chrome yellow) is precipitated by dipping the stuff into solutions, first of acetate of lead, and then of bichromate of potassa.

Mordants (bindermittle, middle binder of the Germans) are bodies which, by their attraction for organic matter, adhere to the fibre of the stuff, and also to the coloring matter. They are applied first; but in domestic dyeing they are often mixed with the dye-stuff. By the use of a mordant, a dye which would wash out is rendered permanent.

Some mordants modify the color; thus alum brightens madder, giving a light-red, while iron darkens it, giving a purple.

MORDANTS.

The principal mordants are alum, cubic-alum, acetate of alumina, protochloride of tin, bichloride of tin, sulphate of iron, acetate of iron, tannin, stannate of soda.

DYE-STUFFS.

The materials used in dyeing are numerous; the following are the most important: Madder, indigo, logwood, quercitron or oak-bark, Brazil-wood, sumach, galls, weld, annato, turmeric, alkanet, red saunders, litmus or archil, cudbear, cochineal, lac; and the following mineral substances: ferrocyanide of potassium, bichromate of potash, cream of tartar, lime-water, and verdigris.

Coal-tar Colors

Are made under patents, and on the large scale. The receipts for their manufacture will, therefore, not be given; in many cases, indeed, they are kept secret. Especial instructions as to their use will be found at the end of the article.

Other Materials.

A bath of cow's dung is used after mordanting vegetable fibres, to remove the excess of mordant. A solution of silicate of soda has been lately used as a substitute.

Albumen, or gluten, is used to thicken the colors for printing, and sometimes to fix them. The colors are incorporated with the albumen applied to the stuff. By exposure to heat the albumen is coagulated and the color fixed.

Silicate of Soda, as a Means of Fixing Mordants.

The use of silicate of soda in calico printing has the advantage of rendering the colors deeper than when the dung-bath alone is used. In reference to the action of this salt, it is worthy of remark that alkaline silicates exist in cow-dung, which, according to Rogers, contains 17·5 per cent. of solid substances, 15 per cent. of this ash; so that the fresh dung contains 2·6 per cent. of ash, and the ash contains 62·5 per cent. of silica. A large portion of this silica is in the insoluble condition, but the quantity of soluble silica is not inconsiderable. The soluble portion of the ash amounts to 38 per cent., and of this 12 per. cent. is silica, and 10 per cent. potash and soda. There is, therefore, reason for regarding silicate of soda as the efficient ingredient of cow-dung.

Alum,

Used as mordant for silk and wool, is then dissolved in water. If it contain iron, reds will be injured. It is a sulphate of alumina combined with sulphate of potassa or ammonia. The alumina is the active mordant. Ammonia alum may be distinguished from potash alum by adding a little caustic potash to the powder; if ammonia exist it will be given off, and may be easily recognized by its pungent smell.

Cubic Alum

Is much used. It is made by adding carbonate of soda to alum until the precipitate, at first thrown down, is re-dissolved. If too much be added a permanent precipitate will be formed. It yields its alumina much more readily to organic matter than common alum.

Acetate of Alumina.

Used for COTTON and LINEN. When heated the acetic acid is driven off, and the alumina remains in the fibre. It is made by adding a solution of acetate (sugar) of lead to a solution of alum as long as any precipitate is formed; or take 8½ lbs. alum, 6½ lbs. sugar of lead; dissolve each in 2 galls. of boiling water. Mix and allow to settle.

Bichloride of Tin (Salt of Tin, Nitromuriate of Tin).

Take 4 lbs. of commercial nitric acid, ½ lb. sal ammoniac; put it in a stone vessel, and add ¼ lb. of pure granulated tin; or dissolve granulated tin in a mixture of 2 parts muriatic to 1 of nitric acid as long as any is taken up.

Protochloride of Tin.

Dissolve granulated tin in hot muriatic acid as long as any is taken up. Cream of tartar is generally added to the alum and tin bath.

Copperas.

Used for dyeing dark shades in wool. It is made by dissolving clean iron in dilute sulphuric acid and crystallizing. An inferior kind is made from pyrites. It contains iron in the form of protoxide. On exposure to the air, however, more oxygen is taken up, and, as in the case of all the salts of the protoxide of iron, sesquioxide is formed. This is a powerful mordant, as may be seen by the tenacity with which iron mould adheres to stuffs.

Acetate of Iron

Is made by dissolving iron scraps in acetic or pyroligneous acid. It is preferred for dyeing vegetable fibres.

Nitrate of Iron.

Take 10¼ lbs. each nitric and muriatic acids, and add little by little 72¼ lbs. of copperas dissolved in water.

Preparation for Dyeing.

Wool requires to be scoured; raw silk to be ungummed; cotton to be sheared, singed, and bleached. (See BLEACHING AND SCOURING.)

To Determine the Effects of Various Salts or Mordants on Colors.

The Dye of Madder.

For a madder red on woollens, the best quantity of madder is ½ of the weight of the woollens that are to be dyed; the best proportion of salts to be used, is 5 parts of alum and 1 of red tartar, for 16 parts of the stuff.

A variation in the proportions of the salts, wholly alters the color that the madder naturally gives. If the alum is lessened, and the tartar increased, the dye proves a red cinnamon. If the alum be entirely omitted, the red wholly disappears, and a durable tawny cinnamon is produced.

If woollens are boiled in weak pearlash and water, the greater part of the color is destroyed. A solution of soap discharges part of the color, and leaves the remaining more beautiful.

Volatile alkalies heighten the red color of the madder, but they make the dye fugitive.

To Dye Wool and Woollen Cloths of a Blue Color.

Dissolve 1 part of indigo in 4 parts of concentrated sulphuric acid; to the solution add 1 part of dry carbonate of potass, and then dilute it with 8 times its weight of water. The cloth must be boiled for an hour in a solution containing 5 parts of alum and 3 of tartar, for every 32 parts of cloth. It is then to be thrown into a waterbath, previously prepared, containing a greater or smaller proportion of diluted sulphate of indigo, according to the shade which the cloth is intended to receive. In this bath it must be boiled till it has acquired the wished-for color.

The only coloring matters employed in dyeing blue, are woad and indigo.

Indigo has a very strong affinity for wool, silk, cotton, and linen. Every kind of cloth, therefore, may be dyed with it without the assistance of any mordant whatever. The color thus induced is very permanent. But indigo can only be applied to cloth in a state of solution, and the only solvent known is sulphuric acid. The sulphate of indigo is often used to dye wool and silk blue, and is known by the name of saxon blue.

It is not the only solution of that pigment employed in dyeing. By far the most common method is, to deprive indigo of its blue color and reduce it to green, and then to dissolve it in water by means of alkalies. Two different methods are employed for this purpose. The first is, to mix with indigo a solution of green oxide of iron, and different metallic sulphurets. If therefore indigo, lime, and green sulphate of iron are mixed together in water, the indigo gradually loses its blue color, becomes green, and is dissolved. The second method is, to mix the indigo in water with certain vegetable substances which readily undergo fermentation; the indigo is dissolved by means of quicklime or alkali, which is added to the solution.

The *first* of these methods is usually followed by dyeing *cotton* and *linen;* the *second* in dyeing *wool* and *silk.*

In the dyeing of wool, woad and bran are commonly employed as vegetable ferments, and lime as the solvent of the green base of the indigo. Woad itself contains a coloring matter precisely similar to indigo; and by following the common process, indigo may be extracted from it. In the usual state of woad when purchased by the dyer, the indigo which it contains is probably not far from the state of green pollen. Its quantity in woad is but small, and it is mixed with a great proportion of other vegetable matter.

When the cloth is first taken out of the vat, it is of a green color; but it soons becomes blue. It ought to be carefully washed, to carry off the uncombined particles. This solution of indigo is liable to two inconveniences: first, it is apt sometimes to run too fast into the putrid fermentation; this may be known by the putrid vapors which it exhales, and by the disappearance of the green color. In this state it would soon destroy the indigo altogether. The inconvenience is remedied by adding more lime, which has the property of moderating the putrescent tendency. Secondly, sometimes the fermentation goes on too languidly. This defect is remedied by adding more bran or woad, in order to diminish the proportion of thick lime.

To make Chemic Blue and Green.

Chemic for light blues and greens, on silk, cotton or woollen, and for cleaning and whitening cottons, is made by the following process:

Take 1 lb. of the best oil of vitriol, which pour upon 1 oz. of the best indigo, well pounded and sifted; add to this after it has been well stirred, a small lump of common pearlash as big as a pea, or from that to the size of 2 peas; this will immediately raise a great fermentation, and cause the indigo to dissolve in minuter and finer particles than otherwise. As soon as this fermentation ceases, put it into a bottle tightly corked, and it may be used the next day. Observe, if more than the quantity prescribed of pearlash should be used, it will deaden and sully the color.

Chemic for green, as above for blue, is made by only adding one-fourth more of the oil of vitriol.

To Discharge Colors.

The dyers generally put all colored silks which are to be discharged, into a copper in which ½ a lb. or 1 lb. of white soap has been dissolved. They are then boiled off, and when the copper begins to be too full of color, the silks are taken out and rinsed in warm water. In the interim a fresh solution of soap is to be added to the copper, and then proceed as before till all the color is discharged. For those colors that are wanted to be effectually discharged, such as greys, cinnamons, etc., when soap does not do, tartar must be used. For slate colors, greenish drabs, olive drabs, etc., oil of vitriol in warm water must be used; if other colors, alum must be boiled in the copper, then cooled down and the silks entered and boiled off, recollecting to rinse them before they are again dyed. A small quantity of muriatic acid, diluted in warm water, must be used to discharge some fast colors; the goods must be afterwards well rinsed in warm and cold water to prevent any injury to the stalk.

To Discharge Cinnamons, Grays, etc., when Dyed Too Full.

Take some tartar, pounded in a mortar, sift it into a bucket, then pour over it some boiling water. The silks, etc., may then be run through the clear est of this liquor, which will discharge the color; but if the dye does not take on again evenly, more tartar may be added, and the goods run through as before.

To Re-Dye or Change the Color of Garments, etc.

The change of color depends upon the ingredients with which the garments have been dyed. Sometimes when these have been well cleaned, more dyeing stuff must be added, which will afford the color intended; and sometimes the color already on the cloth must be discharged and the article re-dyed.

Every color in nature will dye black, whether blue, yellow, red, or brown, and black will always dye black again. All colors will take the same color again which they already possess; and blues can be made green or black; green may be made brown, and brown green, and every color on re-dyeing will take a darker tint than at first.

Yellows, browns, and blues, are not easily discharged; maroons, reds of some kinds, olives, etc., may be discharged.

For maroons, a small quantity of alum may be boiled in a copper, and when it is dissolved, put in the goods, keep them boiling, and probably in a few minutes, enough of it will be discharged to take the color intended.

Olives, grays, etc., are discharged by putting in 2 or 3 tablespoonfuls, more or less, of oil of vitriol; then put in the garment, etc., and boil, and it will become white. If chemic green, either alum, pearlash, or soap will discharge it off to the yellow; this yellow may mostly be boiled off with soap, if it has received a preparation for taking the chemic blue. Muriatic acid used at a hand heat will discharge most colors. A black may be dyed maroon, claret, green, or a dark brown; and it often happens that black is dyed claret, green, or dark brown; but green is the principal color into which black is changed.

To Alum Silks.

Silk should be alumed cold, for when it is alumed hot, it is deprived of a great part of its lustre. The alum liquor should always be strong for silks, as they take the dye more readily afterwards.

To Dye Silk Blue.

Silk is dyed light blue by a ferment of 6 parts of bran, 6 of indigo, 6 of potassa, and 1 of madder. To dye it of a dark blue, it must previously receive what is called a *ground-color*; a red dye-stuff, called archil, is used for this purpose.

Prussian Blue.

A mordant is prepared of nitrate of iron, 1 pt.; 8 oz. of bichloride of tin crystals, ½ oz. of oil of vitriol, and 10 galls. of water. Another liquid is prepared by dissolving 4 oz. of red or yellow prussiate of potash, according to the shade desired. The silks are to be alternately handled in these for 10 minutes, 6 times. After each handling they are washed in cream of tartar water.

To Dye Cotton and Linen Blue.

Cotton and linen are dyed blue by a solution of 1 part of indigo, 1 part of green sulphate of iron, and 2 parts of quicklime.

Yellow Dyes.

The principal coloring matters for dyeing yellow, are weld, fustic, and quercitron bark. Yellow coloring matters have too weak an affinity for cloth, to produce permanent colors without the use of *mordants*. Cloth, therefore, before it is dyed yellow, is always prepared by soaking it in alumina. Oxide of tin is sometimes used when very fine yellows are wanting. Tan is often employed as subsidiary to alumina, and in order to fix it more copiously on cotton and linen. Tartar is also used as an auxiliary, to brighten the color; and muriate of soda, sulphate of lime, and even sulphate of iron, to render the shade deeper. The yellow dye by means of fustic is more permanent, but not so beautiful as that given by weld, or quercitron. As it is permanent, and not much injured by acids, it is often used in dyeing compound colors, where a yellow is required. The mordant is alumina. When the mordant is oxide of iron, fustic dyes a good permanent drab color. Weld and quercitron bark yield nearly the same kind of color; but the bark yields coloring matter in greater abundance and is cheaper than weld. The method of using each of these dye-stuffs is nearly the same.

To Dye Woollens Yellow.

Wool may be dyed yellow by the following process; let it be boiled for an hour, or more, with above 1-6 of its weight of alum, dissolved in a sufficient quantity of water as a mordant. It is then to be plunged, without being rinsed, into a bath of warm water, containing as much quercitron bark as equals the weight of the alum employed as a mordant. The cloth is to be turned through the boiling liquid, till it has acquired the intended color. Then, a quantity of clean powdered chalk, equal to the 100th part of the weight of the cloth, is to be stirred in, and the operation of dyeing continued for 8 or 10 minutes longer. By this method a pretty deep and lively yellow may be given.

For very bright orange, or golden yellow, it is necessary to use the oxide of tin as a mordant. For producing bright golden yellows, some alum must be added along with the tin. To give the yellow a delicate green shade, tartar must be added in different proportions, according to the shade.

To Dye Silks Yellow.

Silk may be dyed of different shades of yellow, either by weld or quercitron bark, but the last is the cheapest of the two. The proportion should be from 1 to 2 parts of bark, to 12 parts of silk, according to the shade. The bark, tied up in a bag, should be put in the dyeing vessel, whilst the water which it contains is cold; and when it has acquired the heat of about 100°, the silk, having been previously alumed, should be dipped in, and continued, till it has assumed the wished-for color. When the shade is required to be deep, a little chalk or pearlash should be added towards the end of the operation. Silk and wool may be dyed a fine yellow by picric acid; 15½ grains will color 2 lbs. of silk. No mordant is necessary. Various shades may be obtained by using solutions of different strength.

To Dye Cottons and Linens Yellow.

The mordant should be acetate of alumina, prepared by dissolving 1 part of acetate of lead, and 3 parts of alum, in a sufficient quantity of water. This solution should be heated to the temperature of 100°, the cloth should be soaked in it for 2 hours, then wrung out and dried. The soaking may be repeated, and the cloth again dried as before. It is then to be barely wetted with lime-water, and afterwards dried. The soaking in the acetate of alumina may be again repeated; and if the shade of yellow is required to be very bright and durable, the alternate wetting with lime-water and soaking in the mordant may be repeated 3 or 4 times.

The *dyeing-bath* is prepared by putting 12 or 18 parts of quercitron bark (according to the depth of the shade required), tied up in a bag, into a sufficient quantity of cold water. Into this bath the cloth is to be put, and turned in it for an hour, while its temperature is gradually raised to about 120°. It is then to be brought to a boiling heat, and the cloth allowed to remain in it only for a few minutes. If it is kept long at a boiling heat, the yellow acquires a shade of brown.

Golden (Chrome) Yellow on Cotton.

Heat till boiling, stirring all the time, 8½ oz. sugar of lead, 16¼ oz. litharge, 3 galls. of water. Keep boiling about 10 minutes; leave to settle, decant, and while warm, handle carefully in it the bleached cotton. When the cotton is thoroughly impregnated with the subacetate of lead of the bath, dry it by a gentle heat, and handle it in a bath of 8½ oz. bichromate of potassa and 4 oz. of nitric acid. Wash well with warm water. Afterwards dip it into a bath of 2 drs. saffron to 1 qt. of strong alcohol, until the desired tint is acquired.—*Ulrich.*

COAL-TAR AND OTHER NEW COLORS.

Coal-tar colors are made from aniline, carbolic or phenic acid and naphthaline, bodies obtained directly or indirectly from the distillation of coal. The following, among others, have been obtained from aniline, aniline purple, violine, rosein, bleu de Paris, magenta, mauve, fuchsine, Tyrian purple, night blue, aniline black, emeraldine. These may be divided into two groups: the reds as magenta, made by the action of bichlorides of carbon, tin or mercury on aniline, and the purples as mauve, made by the action of oxidizing agents, as bichromate of potassa.

Picric acid is obtained by the action of nitric acid upon phenic acid, the coal-tar creasote; it is a fine yellow. Artificial alzarin, carminaphtha, etc., obtained from naphthaline, are not employed practically in dyeing.

Chrysammic acid is made by the action of nitric acid on aloes; it gives blues, purples and greens, which are very solid.

Chinese Green, apparently identical with the lo-kao, is obtained from the bark of the *Rhamnus catharticus* (Buckthorn).

Murexide, a splendid purple, is obtained from guano by the action of nitric acid. It has been displaced by the aniline purples.

Molybdate of ammonia gives a magnificent and permanent blue to silks.

To Dye Silk and Wool with Coal-tar Colors.

Silk and wool can be dyed with all these colors, except the roseolates. Many of them, as aniline purple and violine, are taken from their solutions so perfectly as to leave the menstruum colorless. The coloring matters are generally dissolved in alcohol; for silks, this is diluted with eight times its bulk of hot water, slightly acidulated with tartaric acid; this is poured into the dye-bath, which consists of cold water, slightly acidulated. For wool, the solutions are cold, and acids are to be avoided as much as possible, as the colors are not so fine when they are used.

Red Dyes.

The coloring matters employed for dyeing red are archil, madder, carthamus, kermes, cochineal, and Brazil-wood.

To Dye Woollens Red, Crimson, and Scarlet.

Coarse woollen stuffs are dyed red with madder or archil, but fine cloth is almost exclusively dyed with cochineal, though the color which it receives from kermes is much more durable. Brazil-wood is scarcely used, except as an auxiliary, because the color which it imparts to wool is not permanent.

Wool is dyed crimson, by first impregnating it with alumine by means of an alum bath, and then boiling it in a decoction of cochineal till it has acquired the wished-for color. The crimson will be finer if the tin-mordant is substituted for alum; indeed, it is usual with dyers to add a little bichloride when they want fine crimsons. The addition of archil and potass to the cochineal both renders the crimson darker and gives it more bloom, but the bloom very soon vanishes. For paler crimsons, one-half of the cochineal is withdrawn, and madder substituted in its place.

Wool may be dyed scarlet by first boiling it in a solution of protochloride of tin, then dyeing it pale yellow with quercitron bark, and afterwards crimson with cochineal, for scarlet is a compound color, consisting of crimson mixed with a little yellow.

To Carry the Color into the Body of the Cloth.

Make the moistened cloth pass through between rollers placed within at the bottom of the dye-vat, so that the web passing from one windlass through the dye-vat, and being strongly compressed by the rollers in its passage to another windlass, all the remaining water is driven out, and is re-placed by the coloring liquid, so as to receive color into its very centre. The winding should be continued backwards and forwards from one windlass to the other, and through the rolling-press, till the dye is of sufficient intensity.

To Dye Silks Red, Crimson, etc.

Silk is usually dyed red with cochineal or carthamus, and sometimes with Brazil-wood. Kermes does not answer for silk; madder is scarcely ever used for that purpose, because it does not yield a color bright enough. Archil is employed to give silk a bloom, but it is scarcely ever used by itself, unless when the color wanted is lilac.

Silk may be dyed crimson by steeping it in a solution of alum, and then dyeing it in the usual way in a cochineal bath.

The colors known by the names of poppy, cherry, rose, and flesh-color, are given to silk by means of carthamus. The process consists merely in keeping the silk as long as it extracts any color in an alkaline solution of carthamus, into which as much lemon-juice as gives it a fine cherry-red color, has been poured.

Silk cannot be dyed a full scarlet, but a color approaching to scarlet may be given to it by first impregnating the stuff with protochloride of tin, and afterwards dyeing it in a bath composed of 4 parts of cochineal and 4 parts of quercitron bark. To give the color more body, both the mordant and the dye may be repeated.

A color approaching to scarlet may be given to silk by first dyeing it in crimson, then dyeing it with carthamus, and lastly yellow, without heat.

To Dye Linens and Cottons Red, Scarlet, etc.

Cotton and linen are dyed red with madder. The process was borrowed from the East; hence the color is often called Adrianople, or Turkey-red. The cloth is first impregnated with oil, then with galls, and lastly with alum. It is then boiled for an hour in a decoction of madder, which is commonly mixed with a quantity of blood. After the cloth is dyed it is plunged into a soda lye, in order to brighten the color. The red given by this process is very permanent, and when properly conducted it is exceedingly beautiful. The whole difficulty consists in the application of the mordant, which is by far the most complicated employed in the whole art of dyeing.

COMPOUND COLORS.

Solferino, aniline green, etc., are obtained from coal-tar. The silk is dyed without mordant.

Turkey-red on Cotton.

The cotton goods are cleaned regularly with soap made from cocoanut or palm oil, and a copper proportioned to the quantity of work: from 10 yds. to 100 yds. is made to boil, and when it boils the water is merely softened with pearlash, and then some of the palm-oil soap put in to make a soap liquor; put the cottons in this, boil ½ hour; have a tub with clean hot soap-liquor in it, handle the work well in this, wring it out and hang it up to ry. The next process is to bent up sheep and cow-dung, ash and water together until you have a paste; work this through a sieve into a clean copper, and put to it one-fourth of its bulk of sweet oil. Stir all together, with a fire under the copper, until a soap is formed. Add double its bulk of water. The cotton is well handled in this and allowed to dry overnight. In the morning it has a palm soap liquor, wrung out well and dried, and when dry is regularly cleaned in cocoanut-oil soap and dried again. Next give it a strong nut-gall liquor, and then a strong, hot alum; give it an hour in the alum, then return to the nut gall liquor again for an hour, and then another hour in the alum; wring it out and dry it. In a clean copper put for every 3 pails of water 1 lb. of the best madder and 1 qt. of horses', sheeps', pigs' or bullocks' blood; get the copper on to a scald, and handle in it, but do not boil; keep it in an hour, and then give it a good strong alum and hot water for ½ an hour; rinse in two waters and return to the blood and madder copper for half an hour; rinse dry and clean in very hot and strong soap liquors; dry; give them a weak starch for a finish.—*Love's Art of Dyeing*, etc.

Black Dyes.

The substance employed to give a black color to cloth. are red oxide of iron and tannin; also, bichromate of potassa and logwood. These substances have a strong affinity for each other, and when combined assume a deep black color, not liable to be destroyed by the action of air or light.

Logwood is usually employed as an auxiliary because it communicates lustre, and adds considerably to the fulness of the black. It is the wood of a tree which is a native of several of the West-India islands, and of that part of Mexico which surrounds the bay of Honduras. It yields its coloring matter to water. The decoction is at first a fine red, bordering on violet. but if left to itself it gradually assumes a black color. Acids give it a deep red color; alkalies, a deep violet, inclining to brown; sulphate of iron renders it as black as ink, and occasions a precipitate of the same color.

Cloth, before it receives a black color, is usually dyed blue; this renders the color much fuller and finer than it would otherwise be. If the cloth is coarse, the blue dye may be too expensive; in that case a brown color is given by means of walnut-peels.

To Dye Woollens Black.

Wool is dyed black by the following process: It is boiled for 2 hours in a decoction of nut-galls, and afterwards kept for 2 hours more in a bath composed of logwood and sulphate of iron, kept during the whole time at a scalding heat, but not boiling. During the operation it must be frequently exposed to the air, because the green oxide of iron of which the sulphate is composed must be converted into red oxide by absorbing oxygen before the cloth can acquire a proper color. The common proportions are 5 parts of galls, 5 of sulphate of iron and 30 of logwood for every 100 of cloth. A little acetate of copper is commonly added to the sulphate of iron, because it is thought to improve the color.

To Dye Wool a Chrome Black.

Having cleaned the wool with soap and cream of tartar, take 4 oz. each of bichromate of potash and crude tartar to a copper of water; put in the merino, boil for 40 minutes, and, after cooling, immerse in a bath made from 4 oz. logwood chips with one-fourth of fustic chips to a copper of water.

To Dye Silks Black.

Silk is dyed in nearly the same manner. It is capable of combining with a great deal of tan, the quantity given is varied at the pleasure of the artist, by allowing the silk to remain a longer or shorter time in the decoction.

To Dye Cottons and Linens Black.

The cloth, previously dyed blue, is steeped for 24 hours in a decoction of nut-galls. A bath is prepared containing acetate of iron, formed by saturating acetic acid with sesquioxide of iron; into this bath the cloth is put in small quantities at a time, wrought with the hand for a quarter of an hour; then wrung out and aired again, wrought in a fresh quantity of the bath, and afterwards aired. These alternate processes are repeated till the color wanted is given; a decoction of alder bark is usually mixed with the liquor containing the nut-galls.

To Dye Wool, etc., Brown.

Brown, or fawn color, though in fact a compound, is usually ranked among the simple colors because it is applied to cloth by a single process. Various substances are used for brown dyes.

Walnut-peels, or the green covering of the walnut, when first separated, are white internally, but soon assume a brown. or even a black color, on exposure to the air. They readily yield their coloring matter to water. They are usually kept in large casks, covered with water, for above a year before they are used. To dye wool brown with them, nothing more is necessary than to steep the cloth in a decoction of them till it has acquired the wished-for color. The depth of the shade is proportional to the strength of the decoction.

The root of the walnut-tree contains the same coloring matter, but in smaller quantity. The bark of the birch also, and many other trees, may be used for the same purpose.

To Dye Compound Colors.

Compound colors are produced by mixing together two simple ones; or, which is the same thing, by dyeing cloth first of the simple color, and then by another. These colors vary to infinity, according to the proportions of the ingredients employed.

From blue, red and yellow, *red olives* and *greenish grays* are made.

From blue, red and brown, *olives* are made from the lightest to the darkest shades; and by giving a greater shade of red, the *slated* and *lavender grays* are made.

From blue, red and black, *grays* of all shades are made, such as *sage*, *pigeon*, *slate* and *lead grays*. The king's or prince's color is duller than usual; this mixture produces a variety of hues, or colors almost to infinity.

From yellow, blue and brown, are made the *goose dung* and *olives* of all kinds.

From brown, blue and black, are produced *brown olives* and their shades.

From red, yellow and brown, are derived the

orange, gold color, feuille-mort or faded leaf, dead carnations, cinnamon, fawn and tobacco, by using 2 or 3 of the colors as required.

From yellow, red and black, *browns* of every shade are made.

From blue and yellow, *greens* of all shades.

From red and blue, *purples* of all kinds are formed.

To Dye Different Shades of Green.

Green is distinguishable by dyers into a variety of shades, according to the depth, or the prevalence of either of the component parts. Thus we have sea-green, grass-green, pea-green, etc.

Wool, silk, and linen, are usually dyed green by giving them first a blue color, and afterwards dyeing them yellow. When the *yellow* is first given, several inconveniences follow; the yellow partly separates again in the blue vat, and communicates a green color to it, thus rendering it useless for every other purpose except dyeing green. Any of the usual processes for dyeing blue and yellow may be followed, taking care to proportion the depth of the shades to that of the green required.

When sulphate of indigo is employed, it is usual to mix all the ingredients together, and to dye the cloth at once; this produces what is known by the name of Saxon or English green.

To Dye Violet, Purple and Lilac.

Wool is generally first dyed blue, and afterwards scarlet, in the usual manner. By means of cochineal mixed with sulphate of indigo, the process may be performed at once. Silk is first dyed crimson by means of cochineal, and then dipped into the indigo vat. Cotton and linen are first dyed blue, and then dipped in a decoction of logwood; but a more permanent color is given by means of oxide of iron.

To Dye Olive, Orange and Cinnamon.

When blue is combined with red and yellow on cloth, the resulting color is olive. Wool may be dyed orange by first dyeing it scarlet and then yellow. When it is dyed first with madder, the result is a cinnamon color.

Silk is dyed orange by means of carthamus; a cinnamon color by logwood, Brazil-wood and fustic, mixed together.

Cotton and linen receive a cinnamon color by means of weld and madder, and an olive color by being passed through a blue, yellow, and then a madder bath.

To Dye Gray, Drab and Dark Brown.

If cloth is previously mordanted with iron, and afterwards dyed yellow with quercitron bark, the result will be a drab of different shades, according to the proportion of mordant employed. When the proportion is small, the color inclines to olive, or yellow; on the contrary, the drab may be deepened, or *saddened*, as the dyers term it, by mixing a little sumach with the bark.

To Dye a Black upon Cotton, Linen and Mixed Goods.

Take tar iron liquor of the very best quality; add to each gall. thereof ¾ of a lb. of fine flour, and boil it to the consistency of a thin paste. Put the liquor or paste above-mentioned into a tub belonging to a machine used in the process. The goods intended to be dyed are wound upon a roller, and passed through the liquor or paste, betwixt the two rollers; thereby completely staining or dyeing the whole mass or body of the cloth. Pass them into a very hot stove or drying-house till dry, then take cow's dung, put it into a large copper of water about scalding hot, and mix it well together, through which pass the piece of cloth until it be thoroughly softened. Wash the goods, so dunged. extremely well in water. Take a quantity of madder, or logwood, or sumach, or all of them mixed together, as the strength of the cloth and nature of the color may require, and put them into a copper or tub of hot water, then enter the goods before mentioned in this liquor, and keep rinsing or moving them therein until they are brought up to the strength of color required. Have the goods again well washed and dried. For dyeing black, it will be proper to pass the goods a second time through the above operation, adding more or less of the dyeing-woods as before. If after the above operations the shade of color is too full, or too much upon the red hue, it will be necessary to give them a little sumach, and then run them through a liquor made from iron and owler, or alder-bark.

Another Method.

Take common iron liquor, and add ¾ of a lb. of fine flour, and by boiling bring it to the consistency of a thin paste; or instead of flour, add glue or linseed, or gum, or all of them mixed together, till it is brought to a proper thickness. Then pass the goods through the machine, and follow the before-mentioned operations.

To Dye Olives, Bottle-greens, Purples, Browns, Cinnamons or Snuffs.

Take common iron liquor, or common iron liquor with alum dissolved therein, in quantity of each according to the shade of color wanted, made into a paste or liquid by adding flour, gum, glue, linseed, or one or more of them as before. Then put the liquor or paste above mentioned into a tub belonging to the machine, and pass the goods so intended to be dyed through the machine. Take them from the machine, and hang them up in a very cool room, where they are to remain till thoroughly dry. Take cow's dung, put it into a large copper of hot water, and mix it well together; through which pass the cloth or goods until thoroughly softened, the quantity of dung and time required being proportioned as before.

The goods after this process being well washed, take a quantity of liquor made from madder, logwood, sumach, fustic, Brazil-wood, quercitron bark, peach-wood, or other woods, to produce the color wanted, or more of them; and if necessary dilute this liquor with water, according to the shade or fulness of color wanted to be dyed. Then work the goods through this liquor; after which pass them through cold or warm water, according to the color, the proper application of which is well known to dyers, adding a little alum, copperas or Roman vitriol, or two or more of them, first dissolved in water. Then wash them off in warm water and dry them. But if the color is not sufficiently full, repeat the same operations till it is brought to the shade required.

To Dye Crimson, Red, Orange, or Yellow.

Take red liquor, such as is generally made from alum, and dilute it with water according to the strength or shade of color wanted to dye, bringing it to the consistency of a paste or liquid, as before described. Then pass the cloth through the machine; which being dried in a cool room, pass it through the operations of dunging and washing as before. Take a quantity of liquor, made from cochineal, madder, peach-wood. Brazil, logwood, wonil, fustic, sumach, or any two or more of them proportioned in strength to the shade or color wanted to dye, and work the goods through this liquor till they are brought to the shade of color required; after which wash them in cold or warm water, and dry them.

Chevreul's Mode of Graduating Shades of Color from Prussian Blue.

Impregnate each parcel of silk to be dyed with a different proportion of the oxide of iron by immersing it in a solution, the strength of which has been regulated accordingly. For the deeper tones of color employ the acetate, and for the others the chloride or sulphate. After having properly rinsed (in separate water) each parcel, it is to be dipped into distinct baths of the prussiate of potash, the quantity of which has been made to correspond with the quantity of oxide of iron previously united to it. With these precautions all the desired shades may be obtained. Those which are light and have a greenish cast should be well washed in river water, which will soon produce the blue in its purity. If this does not happen, a very weak solution of muriatic acid will produce the effect to a certainty.

To Dye Wool a Permanent Blue Color.

Take 4 oz. of the best Indigo, reduce it to a very fine powder, and add 12 lbs. of wool in the grease; put the whole into a copper large enough to contain all the wool to be dyed. As soon as the requisite color is obtained, let the wool be well washed and dried. The liquor remaining may be again used to produce lighter blues. The color will be as beautiful and permanent as the finest blue produced by woad, and the wool, by this method, will lose less in weight than if it had been previously scoured.

To Dye Silks and Satins Brown in the small way.

Fill the copper with river-water, when it gently boils put in ¼ lb. of chipped fustic, 2 oz. of madder, 1 oz. of sumach, and ½ oz. of cam-wood; but if not required to be so red, the cam-wood may be omitted. These should boil at least from ½ an hour to 2 hours, that the ingredients may be well incorporated. The copper must then be cooled down by pouring in cold water; the goods may then be put in, and simmered gently from ½ an hour to 1 hour. If this color should appear to want darkening or saddening, it may be done by taking out the goods, and adding a small quantity of old black liquor; a small piece of green copperas may be used; rinse in 2 or 3 waters, and hang up to dry.

To Dye Silks of Fawn-color Drabs.

Boil 1 oz. of fustic, ½ oz. of alder bark, and 2 drs. of archil. From 1 to 2 drs. of the best crop madder must be added to a very small quantity of old black liquor, if it be required darker.

To Dye a Silk Shawl Scarlet.

First dissolve 2 oz. of white soap in boiling water, handle the shawl through this liquor, now and then rubbing such places with the hands as may appear dirty, till it is as clean as this water will make it. A second, or even a third liquor may be used, if required, the shawl must be rinsed out in warm water.

Then take ½ oz. of the best Spanish anatto, and dissolve it in hot water; pour this solution into a pan of warm water, and handle the shawl through this for ¼ of an hour; then take it out and rinse it in clean water. In the meanwhile dissolve a piece of alum of the size of a horse-bean in warm water, and let the shawl remain in this ½ an hour; take it out and rinse it in clear water. Then boil ¼ oz. of the best cochineal for 20 minutes, dip it out of the copper into a pan, and let the shawl remain in this from 20 minutes to ½ an hour, which will make it a full blood red. Then take out the shawl, and add to the liquor in the pan 1 qt. more of that out of the copper, if there is as much remaining, and about ⅛ a small wineglassful of the solution of tin; when cold; rinse it slightly but in spring-water.

To Dye a Silk Shawl Crimson.

Take about 1 tablespoonful of cud-bear, put it into a small pan, pour boiling water upon it, stir and let it stand a few minutes, then put in the silk, and turn it over a short time, and when the color is full enough take it out; but if it should require more violet or crimson, add 1 or 2 spoonfuls of purple archil to some warm water: and dry it within doors. To finish it, it must be mangled or calendered, and may be pressed, if such a convenience is at hand.

To Dye Silk Lilac.

For every pound of silk take 1½ lbs. of archil, mix it well with the liquor; make it boil ¼ of an hour, dip the silk quickly, then let it cool, and wash it in river-water, and a fine violet or lilac, more or less full, will be obtained.

To Dye thick Silks, Satins, Silk Stockings, etc., of a Flesh-color.

Wash the stockings clean in soap and water, then rinse them in hot water; if they should not then appear perfectly clear, cut ½ oz. of white soap into thin slices, and put it into a saucepan half-full of boiling water; when this soap is dissolved, cool the water in the pan, then put in the stockings, and simmer for 20 minutes; take them out, and rinse in hot water; in the interim pour 3 tablespoonfuls of purple archil into a washhand-basin half full of hot water; put the stockings in this dye-water, and when of the shade called half violet or lilac, take them from the dye-water, and slightly rinse them in cold; when dry hang them up in a close room in which sulphur is burnt; when they are evenly bleached to the shade required of flesh-color, take them from the sulphuring-room, and finish them by rubbing the right side with a clean flannel. Some persons calender them afterwards. Satins and silks are done the same way.

To Dye Silk Stockings Black.

These are dyed like other silks, excepting that they must be steeped a day or two in black liquor, before they are put into the black silk dye. At first they will look like an iron gray; but, to finish and black them, they must be put on wooden legs, laid on a table, and rubbed with the oily rubber or flannel, upon which is oil of olives, and then the more they are rubbed the better. Each pair of stockings will require ½ a tablespoonful of oil, at least, and ½ an hour's rubbing, to finish them well. Sweet oil is the best in this process, as it leaves no disagreeable smell.

To Dye Straw and Chip Bonnets Black.

Chip hats being composed of the shavings of wood, are stained black in various ways. First, by being boiled in strong logwood liquor 3 or 4 hours; they must be often taken out to cool in the air, and now and then a small quantity of green copperas must be added to the liquor, and this continued for several hours. The saucepan or kettle that they are dyed in may remain with the bonnets in it all night; the next morning they must be taken out and dried in the air, and brushed with a soft brush. Lastly, a sponge is dipped in oil, and squeezed almost to dryness; with this the bonnets are rubbed all over, both inside and out, and then sent to the blockers to be blocked. Others boil them in logwood; and instead of green copperas, use steel filings steeped in vinegar; after which they are finished as above.

To Dye Straw Bonnets Brown.

Take a sufficient quantity of Brazil-wood, sumach, bark, madder, and copperas, and sadden, according to the shade required.

To Remove the Stain of Light Colors from the Hands.

Wash the hands in soap and water in which some pearlash is dissolved, or wash in a paste of chloride of lime.

To Dye Black Cloth Green.

Clean the cloth well with bullock's gall and water, and rinse in warm water; then make a copper full of river water, boiling hot, and take from 1 to 1½ lbs. of fustic; put it in, and boil it 20 minutes, to which add a lump of alum of the size of a walnut; when this is dissolved in the copper, put in the coat, and boil it 20 minutes; then take it out, and add a small wineglass, three parts full, of chemic blue, and boil again from ½ an hour to 1 hour, and the cloth will be a beautiful dark-green; then wash out and dry.

To Dye Cotton with Coal-tar Colors.

The cotton is soaked in a decoction of galls, sumach, or other astringent matter, for an hour or two, then passed into a weak solution of stannate of soda, and worked in it for about an hour. It is then wrung out in a dilute acid liquor and rinsed in water. Cotton thus prepared is of a pale yellow color. The stannate of soda may be applied before the tannin, or alum may be substituted for it. The prepared cotton is immersed in a bath of the color slightly acidulated and worked. It will absorb all the coloring matter in time, leaving the bath colorless. Picric and rosalic acids are not adapted for dyeing cotton.

CALICO PRINTING.

This art consists in dyeing cloth with certain colors and figures upon a ground of a different hue; the colors, when they will not take hold of cloth readily, being fixed to them by means of mordants, as a preparation of alum, made by dissolving 3 lbs. of alum and 1 lb. of acetate of lead in 8 lbs. of warm water. There are added at the same time 2 oz. of potash, and 2 oz. of chalk.

Acetate of iron, also, is a mordant in frequent use in the printing of calicoes; but the simple mixture of alum and acetate of lead is found to answer best as a mordant.

To Apply the Mordants.

The mordants are applied to the cloth, either with a pencil or by means of blocks, or rollers, on which the pattern, according to which the cotton is to be printed, is cut. As they are applied only to particular parts of the cloth, care must be taken that none of them spread to the part of the cloth which is to be left white, and that they do not interfere with each other when several are applied; it is necessary, therefore, that the mordants should be of such a degree of consistence, that they will not spread beyond those parts of the cloth on which they are applied. This is done by thickening them with flour or starch, when they are to be applied by the block, and with gum arabic when they are to be put on with the pencil. The thickening should never be greater than is sufficient to prevent the spreading of the mordants; when carried too far, the cotton is apt not to be sufficiently saturated with the mordants, and of course the dye takes but imperfectly.

In order that the parts of the cloth impregnated with mordants may be distinguished by their color, it is usual to tinge the mordants with some coloring matter. The printers commonly use the decoction of Brazil-wood for this purpose. Sometimes, the two mordants are mixed together in different proportions; and sometimes one or both is mixed with an infusion of sumach, or of nut-galls. By these contrivances a great variety of colors are produced by the same dyestuff.

Process of Dyeing, etc.

After the mordants have been applied, the cloth must be completely dried. It is proper for this purpose to employ heat, which will contribute towards the separation of the acetic acid from its base, and towards its evaporation; by which means the mordant will combine in a greater proportion, and more intimately with the cloth.

When the cloth is sufficiently dried, it is to be washed with warm water and cow-dung, till the flour or gum employed to thicken the mordants, and all those parts of the mordants which are uncombined with the cloth, are removed. After this the cloth is to be thoroughly rinsed in clean water.

Dye-stuffs.

Almost the only dye-stuffs employed by calico-printers are indigo, madder, quercitron bark, or weld, and coal-tar colors; but weld is little used, except for delicate greenish yellows. The quercitron bark gives colors equally good; and is much cheaper and more convenient, not requiring so great a heat to fix it. Indigo, not requiring any mordant, is commonly applied at once, either by a block or by a pencil. It is prepared by boiling together indigo and potash, made caustic by quicklime and orpiment; the solution is afterwards thickened with gum. It must be carefully excluded from the air, otherwise the indigo would soon be regenerated, which would render the solution useless. Dr. Bancroft has proposed to substitute coarse brown sugar for orpiment; it is equally efficacious in decomposing the indigo, and rendering it soluble; while it likewise serves all the purposes of gum. Some calicoes are only printed of one color, others have two, and others three or more, even to the number of 8, 10, or 12. The smaller the number of colors, the fewer in general are the processes.

New Process to Separate the Red Coloring Principle of Madder.

For this purpose 3 tubs are necessary, say, A, B, C. The first, or A, sufficient for 55 lbs. of madder, is to be 2 feet 8 inches deep, and 2 feet 6 in diameter. The second, or B, is 5½ feet high and 3 feet in diameter. This tub is to be furnished with 3 cocks, the first placed at 2, the second at 3, and the third at 4 feet above its bottom. A serves as a fermenting tub; B, a washing vessel; and C, as a deposit. These tubs are placed near to each other, in the summer, in the open air, under a shed; in the winter, in a cellar kept at from 66° to 70°. To commence the process, put from 50 to 55 lbs. of ground madder into A, and add water, stirring the mixture continually, until the madder, when at rest, is covered with an inch and a half of water. In 36 or 48 hours (being at rest) fermentation takes place and raises a crust of madder to the surface. The mass is now to be transferred to the second tub or B, which is then to be filled with water, where it is to repose for 2 hours The uppermost cock is then opened, next the under one, and lastly the third. The liquor collected from the second and third cocks is carried to the tub C, where the precipitation of the madder that escaped from B, is completed. You may make repeated washings of the madder in B, until the water ceases to be colored. Care should be taken in summer to prevent the madder from fermenting a second time. The madder in C being washed and precipitated, is equally good with the other.

To Print Yellow.

For yellow, the block is besmeared with acetate of alumina. The cloth, after receiving this mordant, is dyed with quercitron bark, and is then bleached.

Nankeen Yellow.

One of the most common colors on cotton prints, is a kind of Nankeen yellow, of various shades down to a yellowish brown or drab. It is usually in stripes or spots. To produce it, the printers besmear the block, cut out into the figure of the print, with acetate of iron, thickened with gum or flour; and apply it to the cotton, which, after being dried and cleansed in the usual manner, is plunged into a potash lye. The quantity of acetate of iron is always proportioned to the depth of the shade.

Red.

Red is communicated by the same process, only madder is substituted for the bark.

Blue.

The fine light blues which appear so frequently on printed cottons, are produced by applying to the cloth a block besmeared with a composition, consisting partly of wax, which covers all those parts of the cloth which remain white. The cloth is then dyed in a cold indigo vat; and after it is dry, the wax composition is removed by hot water.

Lilac and Brown.

Lilac, flea brown, and blackish brown, are given by means of acetate of iron; the quantity of which is always proportioned to the depth of the shade. For very deep colors a little sumach is added. The cotton is afterwards dyed in the usual manner with madder and then bleached.

Green.

To 12 qts. of muriatic acid, add by degrees 1 qt. of nitric acid; saturate the whole with grain tin, and boil it in a proper vessel till two-thirds are evaporated.

To prepare the indigo for mixing with the solution, take 9 lbs. of indigo, ¼ pound of orange orpiment, and grind it in about 4 qts. of water; mix it well with the indigo, and grind it all in the usual way.

To Mix the Solution of Tin with Prepared Indigo.

Take 2 galls. of the indigo prepared as above; then stir into it, by degrees, 1 gall. of the solution of tin, neutralized by as much caustic alkali as can be added without precipitating the tin from the acids. For a lighter shade of green, less indigo will be necessary. The goods are to be dipped in the way of dipping China blues; they must not, however, be allowed to drain, but moved from one vat to another as quickly as possible. They are to be cleansed in the usual way, in a sour vat of about 150 galls. of water to 1 gall. of sulphuric acid; they are then to be well washed in decoctions of weld, and other yellow color drugs, and are to be branned or bleached till they become white in those parts which are required colorless.

To Print Dove-color and Drab.

Dove-color and drab are given by acetate of iron and quercitron bark; the cloth is afterwards prepared in the usual manner.

To Print different Colors.

When different colors are to appear in the same print, a greater number of operations is necessary. Two or more blocks or rollers are employed; upon each of which, that part of the print only is cut which is to be of some particular color. These are besmeared with different mordants and applied to the cloth, which is afterwards dyed as usual. Let us suppose, for instance, that these blocks are applied to cotton; one with acetate of alumina, another with acetate of iron, a third with a mixture of those two mordants, and that the cotton is then dyed with quercitron bark and bleached. The parts impregnated with the mordants would have the following colors:

Acetate of alumina, yellow; acetate of iron, olive, drab, dove. The mixture, olive green, olive.

If the part of the yellow is covered over with the indigo liquor applied with a pencil, it will be converted into *green*. By the same liquid, blue may be given to such parts of the print as require it.

If the cotton is dyed with madder, instead of quercitron bark, the print will exhibit the following colors:

Acetate of alumina, red; acetate of iron, brown, black. The mixture, purple.

When a greater number of colors is to appear —for instance, when those communicated by bark, and those by madder are wanted at the same time — mordants for parts of the pattern are to be applied. The cotton then is to be dyed in the madder bath and bleached; then the rest of the mordants to fill up the pattern, are added, and the cloth is again dyed with quercitron-bark, and bleached. The second dyeing does not much affect the madder colors, because the mordants, which render them permanent, are already saturated. The yellow tinge is easily removed by the subsequent bleaching. Sometimes a new mordant is also applied to some of the madder colors; in consequence of which, they receive a new permanent color from the bark. After the last bleaching, new colors may be added by means of the indigo liquor. The following table will give an idea of the colors which may be given to cotton by these processes.

I. *Madder dye.*—Acetate of alumina, red; acetate of iron, brown, black; acetate diluted, lilac. Both mixed, purple.

II. *Black dye.*—Acetate of alumina, yellow; acetate of iron, dove, drab; lilac and acetate of alumina, olive; red and acetate of alumina, orange.

III. *Indigo dye.*—Indigo, blue; indigo and yellow, green.

To Print in Coal-tar Colors.

The colors are mixed with albumen printed on the fibre; the albumen is then coagulated, and the color thus fixed. Another method consists in printing with tannin on the fabric, previously impregnated with stannate of soda, and then dyeing with a hot, dilute, acid bath. The color on the unmordanted parts, is easily discharged. This preparation is not necessary for silk and wool.

To Print Green with Aniline.

Print the design with a thickened solution of chlorate of potassa; pass through a solution of an aniline salt; in 2 or 3 days the green color will be developed. It may be changed to dark-blue by the use of soap or an alkaline liquid. Another method is to use alternately aniline blue and picric acid.

To Prepare a Substitute for Gum Used in Calico Printing.

Collect ½ a ton weight of scraps of pelts or skins, or pieces of rabbit or sheep-skins, and boil them together for 7 or 8 hours in 350 galls. of water, or until it becomes a strong size. Then draw it off, and when cold weigh it. Warm it again, and to every 1 cwt. add 4 galls. of the strongest sweet wort that can be made from malt or 20 lbs. weight of sugar. When incorporated, take it off and put it into a cask for use.

This substitute for gum may be used by calico printers in mixing up nearly all kinds of colors. By using a sixth part only of gum with it, it will also improve the gum. It will also improve and preserve the paste so much used by printers.

To Prepare Anatto for dyeing.

Anatto is a coloring fecula of a resinous nature, extracted from the seeds of a tree very common in the West Indies, and which in height never exceeds 15 feet.

The Indians employ two processes to obtain the red fecula of these seeds. They first pound them and mix them with a certain quantity of water, which in the course of 5 or 6 days favors the progress of fermentation. The liquid then becomes charged with the coloring part, and the superfluous moisture is afterwards separated by slow evaporation over the fire, or by the heat of the sun.

Another Method.

This consists in rubbing the seeds between the hands in a vessel filled with water. The coloring part is precipitated, and forms itself into a mass like a cake of wax; but if the red fecula thus detached, is much more beautiful than in the first process, it is less in quantity. Besides, as the splendor of it is too bright, the Indians are accustomed to weaken it by a mixture of red sandal wood.

Use of Anatto.

The natives of the East India islands used formerly to employ anatto for painting their bodies, etc. At present, it is employed in Europe for the purpose of dyeing. It is employed to give the first tint to woollen stuffs intended to be dyed red, blue, yellow and green, etc.

In the art of the varnisher it forms part of the composition of changing varnishes, to give a gold color to the metals to which these varnishes are applied.

To Choose Anatto.

It ought to be chosen of a flame color, brighter in the interior part than on the outside, soft to the touch and of a good consistence. The paste of anatto becomes hard in Europe, and it loses some of its odor, which approaches near to that of violets.

To Prepare Litmus.

The Canary and Cape de Verd islands produce a kind of lichen or moss, which yields a violet coloring part when exposed to the contact of ammonia disengaged from urine, in a state of putrefaction, by a mixture of lime. When the processes are finished, it is known by the name of litmus.

This article is prepared on a large scale at London, Paris, and Lyons. In the latter city another kind of lichen, which grows on the rocks like moss, is employed.

The ammonia joins the resinous part of the plant, develops its coloring part, and combines with it. In this state the lichen forms a paste of a violet-red color, interspersed with whitish spots, which give it a marble appearance.

Litmus is communicate in dyeing to communicate a violet color to silk and woollen. It is used also for coloring the liquor of thermometers, and as a test for acids and alkalies.

To Prepare Bastard Saffron.

The flowers of this plant contain two coloring parts: one soluble in water, and which is thrown away; the other soluble in alkaline liquors. The latter coloring part becomes the basis of various beautiful shades of cherry color, ponceau, rose color, etc. It is employed for dyeing feathers, and constitutes the vegetable red, or Spanish vermilion, employed by ladies to heighten their complexion.

Carthamus cannot furnish its resinous coloring part, provided with all its qualities, until it has been deprived of that which is soluble in water. For this purpose the dried flowers of the carthamus are enclosed in a linen bag, and the bag is placed in a stream of running water. A man with woollen shoes gets upon the bag every eight or ten hours, and treads it on the bank until the water expressed from it is colorless.

These moist flowers, after being strongly squeezed in the bag, are spread out on a piece of canvas extended on a frame, placed over a wooden box, and covered with 5 or 6 per cent. of their weight of carbonate of soda. Pure water is then poured over them; and this process is repeated several times, that the alkali may have leisure to become charged with the coloring part which it dissolves. The liquor, when filtered, is of a dirty red, and almost brown color. The coloring part, thus held in solution, cannot be employed for coloring bodies until it is free; and, to set it at liberty, the soda must be brought into contact with a body which has more affinity for it. It is on this precipitation, by an intermediate substance, that the process for making Spanish vermilion is founded, as well as all the results arising from the direct application of this coloring part, in the art of dyeing.

Utility of Sheep's Dung.

This article is used in dyeing for the purpose of preparing cotton and linen to receive certain colors, particularly the red madder and crosswort, which it performs by impregnating the stuffs with an animal mucilage, of which it contains a large quantity, and thus assimilating them to wool and silk.

To Prepare Woad.

This is effected from the leaves of the plant so called, by grinding them to a paste, of which balls are made, placed in heaps, and occasionally sprinkled with water to promote the fermentation. When this is finished the woad is allowed to fall into a coarse powder, used as a blue dye-stuff.

To Prepare Indigo.

This dye is derived from the leaves and the young shoots of several species of indigo plants, by soaking them either in cold water, or still better, in water kept warm, and at about 160°, till the liquor becomes a deep green; it is then drawn off and beat or churned till blue flakes appear, when lime-water is added, the yellow liquor drawn off, and the blue sediment dried and formed into lumps.

To Dye Hats.

The hats should be first strongly galled by boiling them a long time in a decoction of galls with a little logwood, that the dye may penetrate the better into their substance; after which a proper quantity of vitriol and decoction of logwood, with a little verdigris, are added, and the hats continued in this mixture for a considerable time. They are afterwards put into fresh liquor of logwood, galls, vitriol, and verdigris; and where the hats are of great price, or of a hair which with difficulty takes the dye, the same process is repeated a third time. For obtaining the most perfect color, the hair or wool is dyed blue previously to its being formed into hats.

Another Method.

Boil 100 lbs. of logwood, 12 lbs. of gum, and 6 lbs. of galls in a proper quantity of water for some hours; after which about 6 lbs. of verdigris and

10 of green vitriol are added, and the liquor kept just simmering, or of a heat little below boiling. Ten or 12 dozen of hats are immediately put in, each on its block, and kept down by cross-bars for about an hour and a half; they are then taken out and aired, and the same number of others put in their room. The two sets of hats are thus dipped and aired alternately 8 times each; the liquor being refreshed each time with more of the ingredients, but in less quantity than at first.

To Prove the Colors of Dyed Stuffs.

For crimson, scarlet, flesh-color, violet, peach-blossom, all shades of blue, and other colors bordering on these, dissolve half an ounce of *alum* in a pint of water, in an earthen vessel, and into this put the eighth of an ounce of the stuff or thread that is to be proved; boil the whole for five minutes, and wash it out in clean water.

For all sorts of yellow, green madder, red cinnamon, and similar colors, boil a quarter of an ounce of *soap* in a pint of water, put in the eighth of an ounce of the stuff to be tried, and boil for 5 minutes.

For hair-brown, etc. powder an ounce of tartar, and boil it in a pint of water, and boil ¼ of an ounce of the stuff or thread in the solution for 5 minutes.

MISCELLANEOUS RECEIPTS FOR DYEING, STAINING, ETC.

To Dye Bristles or Feathers Green.

Take of verdigris and verditer, each 1 oz.; gum-water, 1 pt. Mix them well, and dip the bristles or feathers (they having been first soaked in hot water) into the said mixture.

Blue.—Take of indigo and risse, each 1 oz., and a piece of alum the size of a hazelnut; put them into gum-water, and dip the materials into it hot; hang them up to dry, and clap them well that they may open; and, by changing the colors, the aforesaid materials may be in this manner, dyed of any color. For purple, use lake and indigo; for carnation, vermilion and smalt.

Red.—Take 1 oz. of Brazil-wood in powder, ½ oz. of alum, ¼ oz. of vermilion, and 1 pint of vinegar; boil them up to a moderate thickness, and dip the bristles or feathers (they having been first soaked in hot water) into the said mixture. Feathers may be dyed at once, of any shade, by means of coal-tar colors (p. 318).

To Dye or Color Horse-Hair.

Steep in water wherein a small quantity of turpentine has been boiled for the space of two hours; then, having prepared the colors very hot, boil the hair therein, and any color, black excepted, will take, but that will only take a dark-red or dark-blue, etc.

To Dye Gloves.

Take the color suitable for the occasion; if dark take Spanish brown and black earth; if lighter, yellow and whiting; and so on with other colors. Mix them with a moderate fire, daub the gloves over with the color wet, and let them hang till they are dry; then beat out the superfluity of the color, and smoothe them over with a stretching or sleeking stick, reducing them to their proper shape.

To Dye White Gloves Purple.

Boil 4 oz. of logwood and 2 oz. of roche-alum in 3 pts. of soft water till half wasted; let the liquor stand to cool after straining. Let the gloves be nicely mended; then, with a brush, rub them over, and when dry repeat. Twice is sufficient, unless the color is to be very dark. When dry, rub off the loose dye with a coarse cloth. Beat up the white of an egg, and with a sponge rub it over the leather. The dye will stain the hands; but wetting them with vinegar, before they are washed, will take it off.

To Dye Gloves resembling Limerick.

Brown or tan colors are readily imparted to leather gloves by the following simple process. Steep saffron in boiling soft water for about 12 hours; then, having slightly sewed up the tops of the gloves, to prevent the dye staining the insides, wet them over with a sponge or soft brush dipped into the liquid. The quantity of saffron as well as of water will of course depend on how much dye may be wanted, and their relative proportions on the depth of color required. A common teacup will contain sufficient in quantity for a single pair of gloves.

To Stain Bone or Ivory.

They may be stained with the ordinary dyeing materials. The body should first be steeped in the mordant, and then in a hot bath of coloring material. Bichloride of tin as a mordant will give red with Brazil-wood or cochineal, yellow with fustic, violet with logwood. Black is given by nitrate of silver; gilding by immersion in a fresh solution of copperas, and afterwards of chloride of gold; bleaching by a solution of sulphurous acid.

To Prepare Wood for Dyeing.

The wood mostly used to dye black is pear-tree, holly, and beech, all of which take a beautiful black color. Do not use wood that has been long cut, or aged, but let it be as fresh as possible. After the veneers have had 1 hour's boiling, and been taken out to cool, the color is always much stronger. When dyed, they should be dried in the air, and not by the fire, nor in a kiln of any kind, as artificial heat tends to destroy the color.

In order to dye blue, green, red or other colors, take clear holly. Put the veneers into a box or trough, with clear water, and let them remain 4 or 5 days, changing the water once or twice as occasion may require. The water will clear the wood of slime, etc. Let them dry about 12 hours before they are put into the dye; by observing this the color will strike quicker, and be of a brighter hue.

To Stain Oak a Mahogany Color.

Boil together Brazil-wood and alum, and before it is applied to the wood a little potash is to be added to it. A suitable varnish for wood, thus tinged, may be made by dissolving amber in oil of turpentine, mixed with a small portion of linseed oil.

Ebony black.—Steep the wood for 2 or 3 days in lukewarm water, in which a little alum has been dissolved; then put a handful of logwood, cut small, into a pint of water, and boil it down to less than ½ a pint. If a little indigo is added, the color will be more beautiful. Spread a layer of this liquor quite hot on the wood with a pencil, which will give it a violet color. When it is dry, spread on another layer; dry it again, and give it a third; then boil verdigris at discretion in its own vinegar, and spread a layer of it on the wood; when it is dry rub it with a brush, and then with oiled chamois skin. This gives a fine black, and imitates perfectly the color of ebony.

Another Method.

After forming the wood into the destined figure, rub it with aquafortis a little diluted. Small threads of wood will rise in the drying, which are to be rubbed off with pumice-stone. Repeat this process again, and then rub the wood with the following composition:—Put into a glazed earthen vessel 1 pint of strong vinegar, 2 oz. of fine iron filings, and ½ lb. of pounded galls, and allow them to infuse for 3 or 4 hours on hot cinders. At the end of this time augment the fire, and pour into the vessel 4 oz. of copperas (sulphate of iron), and a chopin of water having ½ oz. of borax and as much indigo dissolved in it; and make the whole boil till a froth rises. Rub several layers of this upon the wood; and, when it is dry, polish it with leather on which a little tripoli has been put.

Another. — Pour 2 qts. of boiling water over 1 oz. commercial extract of logwood, and when it is dissolved add 1 dr. of yellow chromate of potash, and stir well. This stain is cheap, keeps well, can be applied cold with a brush without any preparation.

To Stain Beech-wood a Mahogany Color.

Break 2 oz. of dragon's blood in pieces, and put them into a qt. of rectified spirit of wine; let the bottle stand in a warm place, and shake it frequently. When dissolved it is fit for use.

Another Method.

Boil 1 lb. of logwood in 4 qts. of water, and add a double handful of walnut-peeling. Boil it up again, take out the chips, add a pint of the best vinegar, and it will be fit for use.

To Stain Musical Instruments.

Crimson.—Boil 1 lb. of ground Brazil-wood in 3 qts. of water for an hour; strain it, and add ½ an oz. of cochineal; boil it again for ½ an hour gently, and it will be fit for use.

Purple.—Boil 1 lb. of chip logwood in 3 qts. of water for an hour; then add 4 oz. of pearlash and 2 oz. of indigo pounded.

To Stain Box-wood Brown.

Hold the work to the fire, that it may receive a gentle warmth; then take aquafortis, and with a feather pass it over the work till it changes to a fine brown. Then oil and polish it.

To Dye Wood a Silver Gray.

Let not the veneers be too dry; when put into the copper pour hot iron liquor (acetate of iron) over them, and add 1 lb. of chip logwood with 2 oz. of bruised nut-galls. Then boil up another pot of iron liquor to supply the copper, keeping the veneers covered and boiling 2 hours a day, until thoroughly penetrated.

Bright yellow. — A very small bit of aloes put into the varnish will make the wood of a good yellow color.

Another Method.

Reduce 4 lbs. of the roots of barberry, by sawing into dust, which put in a copper or brass pan, add 4 oz. of turmeric, to which put 4 galls. of water, then put in as many holly veneers as the liquor will well cover; boil them together for 3 hours, often turning them. When cool add 2 oz. of aquafortis, and the dye will strike through much sooner.

Bright green. — Proceed as before to produce a yellow; but instead of aquafortis add as much of the vitriolated indigo as will produce the desired color.

Another Method.

To 3 pts. of the strongest vinegar add 4 oz. of the best verdigris, ground fine, ½ oz. of sap green, and ½ oz. of indigo. Proceed in straining as before.

Bright red. — To 2 lbs. of genuine Brazil-dust add 4 galls. of water, put in as many veneers as the liquor will well cover, boil them for 3 hours, and let them cool; then add 2 oz. each of alum and aquafortis, and keep it lukewarm until it has struck through.

Purple.—To 2 lbs. of chip logwood and ½ lb. of Brazil-dust add 4 galls. of water. Put in the veneers, and boil them well; then add 6 oz. of pearlash and 2 oz. of alum; let them boil 2 or 3 hours every day, till the color has struck through.

Fine blue.—Into 1 lb. of oil of vitriol in a glass bottle put 4 oz. of indigo, and proceed as before directed.

To Stain Paper or Parchment.

Yellow.—Paper may be stained a beautiful yellow by the tincture of turmeric formed by infusing an oz. or more of the root, powdered, in a pint of spirit of wine. This may be made to give any tint of yellow, from the lightest straw to the full color, called French yellow, and will be equal in brightness even to the best dyed silks. If yellow be wanted of a warmer or redder cast, anatto or dragon's blood must be added. The best manner of using these, and the following tinctures, is to spread them even on the paper or parchment, by means of a broad brush, in the manner of varnish.

Crimson.—A very fine crimson stain may be given to paper by a tincture of the Indian lake, which may be made by infusing the lake some days in spirit of wine, and then pouring off the tincture from the dregs. It may be stained red by red ink. It may also be stained of a scarlet hue by the tincture of dragon's blood in spirit of wine, but this will not be bright.

Green. — Paper or parchment may be stained green by the solution of verdigris in vinegar, or by the crystals of verdigris dissolved in water.

Orange.—Stain the paper or parchment first of a full yellow by means of the tincture of turmeric, then brush it over with a solution of fixed alkaline salt, made by dissolving ½ an oz. of pearlash, or salt of tartar, in a quart of water, and filtering the solution.

Purple. — Paper or parchment may be stained purple by archil, or by the tincture of logwood. The juice of ripe privet-berries expressed will likewise give a purple dye.

The coal-tar colors are especially adapted to coloring paper.

To Marble the Edges of Books or Paper.

Dissolve 4 oz. of gum arabic in 2 qts. of clear water; then provide several colors mixed with water in pots or shells, and with pencils peculiar to each color, sprinkle them by way of intermixture upon the gum-water, which must be put into a trough, or some broad vessel, then with a stick curl them or draw them out in streaks to as much variety as required. Having done this, hold the book or books close together, and only dip the edges in on the top of the water and colors very lightly; which done, take them off, and the plain impression of the colors in mixture will be upon the leaves; doing as well the end as the front of the books in the same manner.

To Marble the Covers of Books.

This is performed by forming clouds with aquafortis, or oil of vitriol, mixed with ink, and afterwards glazing the covers.

To Color Vellum Green.

Take ½ pt. of the best white wine vinegar, 1 oz. of verdigris, and 1½ oz. of sap-green; dissolve them in the vinegar for a few days, having been heated by the fire. Shake the bottle frequently before it is used.

Wash the vellum over with weak potash water, and when dry color it with the green 3 or 4 times, till it has a good color; when dry wash it over with thin paste water to give the vellum a gloss.

To Black the Edges of Paper.

Mix black lead with ink, and when the paper is cut, color it thinly over with black ink, with a piece of fine cloth; rub on the black lead, covering every part; take the dog's-tooth and burnish the edge till it becomes well polished.

When the edge of the paper, after cutting, appears rather rough, scrape it over with a piece of glass or an iron scraper with a flat edge.

To Sprinkle the Edges of Books, etc.

The brushes used for book-edges must be made of Russia hogs' bristles, of good thickness, tied round with cord, glued at the thick end, and half covered with a piece of leather; when dry tie the brush again with waxed cord, within half an inch of the soft part of it, and cut it very smooth and even. Brushes made after this manner are preferable to those with a handle.

Prepare the color in a cup; dip in the brush till it is charged, and then press it out till it will drop no longer. The book must be screwed tight in the cutting press; hold the brush in the left hand, and, with a folding-stick in the right, rub it over the brush, which will cause the color to sprinkle finely on the edges. The brush must be moved up and down over the edge, as you sprinkle, to have it regular on every part. After the sprinkling is done, the brushes should be carefully washed in water, particularly after sprinkling blue, which will otherwise soon destroy the brush.

To Dye or Stain Horn Tortoise-shell Color.

The horn to be dyed must be first pressed into proper plates, scales, or other flat form, and the following mixture prepared: Take of quicklime two parts, and litharge one part, temper them together to the consistence of a soft paste, with soap lye. Put this paste over all the parts of the horn, except such as are proper to be left transparent, in order to give it a near resemblance to the tortoise-shell. The horn must remain in this manner, covered with the paste till it is thoroughly dry; when, the paste being brushed off, the horn will be found partly opaque and partly transparent, in the manner of tortoise-shell, and when put over a foil of the kind of lattern called orsedue, will be scarcely distinguishable from it. It requires some degree of fancy and judgment to dispose of the paste in such a manner as to form a variety of transparent parts, of different magnitudes and figures, to look like the effect of nature; and it will be an improvement to add semi-transparent parts, which may be done by mixing whiting with some of the paste, to weaken its operation in particular places, by which spots of a reddish-brown will be produced, which, if properly interspersed, especially on the edges of the dark parts, will greatly increase the beauty of the work, and its similitude to real tortoise-shell.

Another Method.

Take an equal quantity of quicklime and red-lead, and mix it up with strong soap lees. Lay it on the horn with a small brush, like the mottle in tortoise-shell. When dry repeat the same two or three times.

To Dye Horns of different Colors.

Black is performed by steeping brass in aquafortis till it is turned green; with this the horn is to be washed once or twice, and then put into a warmed decoction of logwood and water.

Green is begun by boiling it, etc., in alum-water, then with verdigris, ammoniac, and white wine vinegar, keeping it hot therein till sufficiently green.

Red is begun by boiling it in alum-water, then with verdigris, ammoniac, and finished by decoction in a liquor compounded of quicklime steeped in rain-water, strained, and to every pint an ounce of Brazil-wood added. In this decoction the horns are to be boiled till sufficiently red.

Horns receive a deep black stain from solution of nitrate of silver. It ought to be diluted to such a degree as not sensibly to corrode the substance, and applied 2 or 3 times if necessary, at considerable intervals, the matter being exposed as much as possible to the sun, to hasten the appearance and deepening of the color.

PAINTS and COLORS.

HOUSE PAINTING.

To Mix the Colors for House Painting.

All simple or compound colors, and all the shades of color which nature or art can produce, and which might be thought proper for the different kinds of painting, would form a very extensive catalogue, were we to take into consideration only certain external characters, or the intensity of their tint. But art, founded on the experience of several centuries, has prescribed bounds to the consumption of coloring substances, and to the application of them to particular purposes. To cause a substance to be admitted into the class of coloring bodies employed by painters, it is not sufficient for it to contain a color; to brightness and splendor it must also unite durability in the tint or color which it communicates.

To make Black Paint.

Usage requires attention in the choice of the matters destined for black. The following are their properties:

Black from peach-stones is dull.

Ivory-black is strong and beautiful when it has been well attenuated under the muller.

Black from the charcoal of beech-wood, ground on porphyry, has a bluish tone.

Lampblack may be rendered mellower by making it with black which has been kept an hour in a state of redness in a close crucible. It then loses the fat matter which accompanies this kind of soot.

Black furnished by the charcoal of vine-twigs, ground on porphyry, is weaker, and of a dirty gray color when coarse and alone, but it becomes blacker the more the charcoal has been divided. It then forms a black very much sought after, and which goes a great way.

To make Paints from Lampblack.

The consumption of lampblack is very extensive in common painting. It serves to modify the brightness of the tones of the other colors, or to facilitate the composition of secondary colors. The oil paint applied to iron grates and railing, and the paint applied to paper snuff-boxes, to those made of tin-plate, and to other articles with dark grounds, consume a very large quantity of this black. Great solidity may be given to works of this kind by covering them with several coatings of the fat turpentine, or golden varnish, which has been mixed with lampblack, washed in water, to separate the foreign bodies introduced into it by the negligence of the workmen who prepare it.

After the varnish is applied the articles are dried in a stove by exposing them to a heat somewhat greater than that employed for articles of paper. Naples yellow, which enters into the composition of black varnish, is the basis of the dark brown observed on tobacco-boxes of plate-iron, because this color changes to brown when dried with the varnish.

To make a Superior Lampblack.

Suspend over a lamp a funnel of tin plate, having above it a pipe to convey from the apartment the smoke which escapes from the lamp. Large mushrooms, of a very black, carbonaceous matter, and exceedingly light, will be formed at the summit of the cone. This carbonaceous part is carried to such a state of division as cannot be given to any other matter, by grinding it on a piece of porphyry.

This black goes a great way in every kind of painting. It may be rendered drier by calcination in close vessels.

The funnel ought to be united to the pipe, which conveys off the smoke, by means of wire, because solder would be melted by the flame of the lamp.

To make Black from Ground Pitcoal.

The best for this purpose is that which has a shining fracture. It affords, perhaps, the most useful brown the artist can place on his palet, being remarkably clear, not so warm as Vandyke brown, and serving as a shadow for blues, reds, or yellows, when glazed over them. It seems almost certain that Titian made large use of this material. Coal, when burnt to a white heat, then quenched in water, and ground down, gives an excellent blue black. This belongs to artists' colors.

To make Black from Wine-lees.

This black results from the calcination of winelees and tartar, and is manufactured on a large scale in some districts of Germany, in the environs of Mentz, and even in France. This operation is performed in large cylindric vessels, or in pots, having an aperture in the cover to afford a passage to the smoke, and to the acid and alkaline vapors which escape during the process. When no more smoke is observed, the operation is finished. The remaining matter, which is merely a mixture of salts and a carbonaceous part very much attenuated, is then washed several times in boiling water, and it is reduced to the proper degree of fineness by grinding it on porphyry.

If this black be extracted from dry lees, it is coarser than that obtained from tartar, because the lees contain earthy matters which are confounded with the carbonaceous part.

This black goes a great way, and has a velvety appearance. It is used chiefly by copper-plate printers.

Another.—Peach-stones, burnt in a close vessel, produce a charcoal, which, when ground on porphyry, is employed in painting to give an old gray.

Another.—Vine twigs reduced to charcoal give a bluish black, which goes a great way. When mixed with white it produces a silver white, which is not produced by other blacks; it has a pretty near resemblance to the black of peach stones, but to bring this color to the utmost degree of perfection, it must be carefully ground on porphyry.

To make Ivory and Boneblack.

Put into a crucible surrounded by burning coals, fragments or turnings of ivory, or of the osseous parts of animals, and cover it closely. The ivory or bones, by exposure to the heat, will be reduced to charcoal. When no more smoke is seen to pass through the joining of the cover, leave the crucible over the fire for half an hour or longer, or until it has completely cooled. There will then be found in it a hard carbonaceous matter, which, when pounded and ground on porphyry with water, is washed on a filter with warm water and then dried. Before it is used it must be again subjected to the matter.

Black furnished by bones is reddish. That produced by ivory is more beautiful. It is brighter than black obtained from peach-stones. When mixed in a proper dose with white oxide of lead, it forms a beautiful pearl gray. Ivory-black is richer. The Cologne and Cassel-black are formed from ivory.

Fine Black Color.

Take some camphor and set it on fire; from the flame will arise a very dense smoke, which may be collected on a common saucer by holding it over the flame. This black, mixed with gum arabic, is far superior to most India-ink.

Miniature painters, who use colors in small quantities, sometimes obtain a most beautiful and perfect black by using the buttons which form on the snuff of a candle when allowed to burn undisturbed. These are made to fall into a small thimble, or any other convenient vessel which can be immediately covered with the thumb, to exclude the air. This is found to be perfectly free from grease, and to possess every desirable quality.

To Paint in White Distemper.

Grind fine in water Bougival white, a kind of marl or chalky clay, and mix it with size. It may be brightened by a small quantity of indigo, or charcoal-black.

To make White Paint.

The White destined for varnish or oil requires a metallic oxide, which gives more body to the color. Take ceruse, reduced to powder, and grind it with oil of pinks and ¼ oz. of sulphate of zinc for each pound of oil. Apply the second coating without the sulphate of zinc, and suffer it to dry. Cover the whole with a stratum of sandarach varnish. This color is durable, brilliant and agreeable to the eye.

Boiled linseed oil might be employed instead of oil of pinks, but the color of it would in some degree injure the purity of the white.

Another.— White is prepared also with pure white oxide of lead, ground with a little essence, added to oil of pinks and mixed with gallipot varnish. The color may be mixed also with essence diluted with oil, and without varnish, which is reserved for the two last coatings. If for a lively white, the color is heightened with a little Prussian blue or indigo, or with a little prepared black. The latter gives it a gray cast. But pure white lead, the price of which is much higher than ceruse, is reserved for valuable articles. In this particular case, if a very fine durable white be required, grind it with a little essence, and mix it with sandarach or varnish.

To Paint in Light Gray and Distemper.

Ceruse, mixed with a small quantity of lampblack, composes a gray, more or less charged, according to the quantity of black. With this mat ter, therefore, mixed with black in different doses, a great variety of shades may be formed, from the lightest to the darkest gray.

If this color be destined for distemper, it is mixed with water; if intended for oil painting, it is ground with nut-oil, or oil of pinks; and with essence added to oil, if designed for varnish. This color is durable and very pure, if mixed with camphorated mastic varnish; the gallipot varnish renders it so solid that it can bear to be struck with a hammer, if, after the first stratum it has been applied with varnish, and without size. For the last coating sandarach varnish, and camphorated varnish are proper; and for the darkest gray, spirituous sandarac varnish.

To make Flaxen Gray.

Ceruse, or white lead, still predominates in this color, which is treated as the other grays, but with this difference, that it admits a mixture of lake instead of black. Take the quantity, therefore, of ceruse necessary, and grind it separately. Then mix it up, and add the lake and Prussian blue, also ground separately. The quantities of the last two colors ought to be proportioned to the tone of color required.

This color is proper for distemper, varnish, and oil painting. For varnish, grind it with mastic gallipot varnish, to which a little oil of pinks has been added, and then mix it up with common gallipot varnish. For oil painting, grind with unprepared oil of pinks, and mix up with resinous drying nut-oil. The painting is brilliant and solid.

When the artist piques himself upon carefully preparing those colors which have splendor, it will be proper, before he commences his labor, to stop up the holes formed by the heads of the nails in wainscoting with putty.

Every kind of sizing which, according to usual custom, precedes the application of varnish, ought to be proscribed as highly prejudicial, when the wainscoting consists of fir-wood. Sizing may be admitted for plaster, but without any mixture. A plain stratum of strong glue and water spread over it, is sufficient to fill up the pores to prevent any unnecessary consumption of the varnish.

The first stratum of color is ceruse without any mixture, ground with essence added to a little oil of pinks, and mixed up with essence. If any of the traces are uneven, rub it lightly, when dry, with pumice-stone. This operation contributes greatly to the beauty and elegance of the polish when the varnish is applied.

The second stratum is composed of ceruse changed to flaxen gray by the mixture of a little Cologne earth, as much English red or lake, and a particle of Prussian blue. First, so make the mixture with a small quantity of ceruse, that the result shall be a smoky gray, by the addition of the Cologne earth. The red, which is added, makes it incline to flesh-color, and the Prussian blue destroys the latter to form a dark flaxen gray. The addition of ceruse brightens the tone. This stratum and the next are ground, and mixed up with varnish as before.

This mixture of colors, which produces flaxen gray, has the advantage over pearl gray, as it defends the ceruse from the impression of the air and light, which makes it assume a yellowish tint. Flaxen gray, composed in this manner, is unalterable. Besides, the essence which forms the vehicle of the first stratum contributes to bring forth a color, the tone of which decreases a little by the effect of drying. This observation ought to serve as a guide to the artist, in regard to the tint, which is always stronger in a liquid mixture than when the matter composing it is extended in a thin stratum, or when it is dry.

To make Oak-wood Color.

The basis of this color is still formed of ceruse. Three-fourths of this oxide, and a fourth of ochre de rue, umber earth, and yellow de Berri; the last three ingredients being employed in proportions which lead to the required tint, give a matter equally proper for distemper, varnish, and oil.

To make Walnut-wood Color.

A given quantity of ceruse, half that quantity of ochre de rue, a little umber earth, red ochre, and yellow ochre de Berri; compose this color proper for distemper, varnish, and oil.

For varnish, grind with a little drying nut-oil, and mix up with the gallipot varnish.

For oil painting, grind with fat oil of pinks added to drying oil or essence, and mix up with plain drying oil, or with resinous drying oil.

To make Naples and Montpellier Yellow.

The composition of these is simple, yellow ochre mixed with ceruse, ground with water, if destined for distemper; or drying nut-oil and essence, in equal parts, if intended for varnish; and mixed up with camphorated mastic varnish; if for delicate objects, or with gallipot varnish, give a very fine color, the splendor of which depends on the doses of the ceruse; which must be varied according to the particular nature of the coloring matter employed. If the ground of the color is furnished by ochre, and if oil painting be intended, the grinding with oil added to essence may be omitted, as essence alone will be sufficient. Oil, however, gives more pliability and more body.

To make Jonquil.

This is employed only in distemper. It may, however, be used with varnish. A vegetable color serves as its base. It is made with Dutch pink and ceruse, and ground with mastic gallipot varnish, and mixed up with gallipot varnish.

To make Golden Yellow Color.

Cases often occur when it is necessary to produce a gold color without employing a metallic substance. A color capable of forming an illusion is then given to the composition, the greater part of which consists of yellow. This is accomplished by Naples or Montpellier yellow, brightened by Spanish white, or by white of Morat, mixed with ochre de Berri and realgar. The last substance, even in small quantity, gives to the mixture a color imitating gold, and which may be employed in distemper, varnish, or oil. When destined for oil, it is ground with drying or pure nut-oil, added to essence or mixed with drying oil.

To make Chamois and Buff Color.

Yellow is the foundation of chamois color, which is modified by a particle of minium, or what is better, cinnabar and ceruse in small quantity. This color may be employed in distemper, varnish, and oil. For varnish, it is ground with ½ common oil of pinks, and ½ of mastic gallipot varnish. It is mixed with common gallipot varnish. For oil painting, it is ground and mixed up with drying oil.

To make Olive Color for Oil and Varnish.

Olive color is a composition the shades of which may be diversified. Black and a little blue, mixed with yellow, will produce an olive color. Yellow de Berri, or d'Auvergne, with a little verdigris and charcoal, will also form this color.

It is ground and mixed up with mastic gallipot, and common gallipot varnishes. For oil painting, it is ground with oil added to essence, and mixed up with drying oil.

To make Olive Color for Distemper.

When intended for distemper, it will be necessary to make a change in the composition. The yellow above-mentioned, indigo, and ceruse, or Spanish white, are the new ingredients which must be employed.

To make Blue Colors.

Blue belongs to the order of vegetable substances, like indigo; or to that of metallic substances, like Prussian blue; or to that of stony mineral substances, as ultramarine; or to that of vitreous substances colored by a metallic oxide, as Saxon blue. Ultramarine is more particularly reserved for pictures. The same may, in some degree, be said of Saxon blue.

When prussiate of iron or indigo is employed without mixture, the color produced is too dark. It has no splendor, and very often the light makes it appear black; it is, therefore, usual to soften it with white.

To make Blue Distemper.

Grind with water as much ceruse as may be thought necessary for the whole of the intended work; and afterwards mix it with indigo, or Prussian blue.

This color produces very little effect in distemper; it is not very favorable to the play of the light; but it soon acquires brilliancy and splendor beneath the vitreous lamina of the varnish. Painting in distemper, when carefully varnished, produces a fine effect.

To make Prussian Blue Paint.

The ceruse is ground with oil, if for varnish, made with essence, or merely with essence, which is equally proper for oil painting; and a quantity of either of these blues sufficient to produce the required tone is added.

For varnish, the ceruse is generally ground with oil of pinks added to a little essence, and is mixed up with camphorated mastic varnish, if the color is destined for delicate objects; or with gallipot varnish if for wainscoting. This color, when ground and mixed up with drying oil, produces a fine effect, if covered by a solid varnish made with alcohol or essence.

If this oil color be destined for expensive articles, such as valuable furniture subject to friction, it may be glazed with the turpentine copal varnish.

Ultramarine.

A vitreous matter colored by oxide of cobalt, gives a tone of color different from that of the prussiate of iron and indigo. It is employed for sky-blues. The case is the same with blue verditer, a preparation made from oxide of copper and lime. Both these blues stand well in distemper, in varnish, and in oil.

Saxon blue requires to be ground with drying oil, and to be mixed with gallipot varnish. If intended for oil painting, it is to be mixed up with resinous drying oil, which gives body to this vitreous matter.

Blue Verditer

May be ground with pure alcoholic varnish added to a little essence, and may be mixed up with compound mastic varnish if the color is to be applied to delicate articles. Or mastic gallipot varnish, added to a little drying oil, may be used for grinding, and common gallipot varnish for mixing up, if the painting is intended for ceilings, wainscoting, etc. This color is soft and dull, and requires a varnish to heighten the tone of it, and give it play. Turpentine copal varnish is proper for this purpose, if the article has need of a durable varnish.

To make Green Color.

Every green color, simple or compound, when mixed up with a white ground, becomes soft, and gives a sea-green of greater or less strength, and more or less delicate, in the ratio of the respective quantities of the principal colors. Thus, green oxides of copper, such as chrome green, verdigris, dry crystallized acetate of copper, green composed with blue verditer, and the Dutch pink of Troyes, or any other yellow, will form, with a base of a white color, a sea-green, the intensity of which may be easily changed or modified. The white ground for painting in distemper is generally composed of Bougival white (white marl), or white of Troyes (chalk), or Spanish white (pure clay); but for varnish or oil painting, it is sought for in a metallic oxide. In this case, ceruse or pure white oxide of lead is employed.

To make Sea-Green for Distemper.

Grind separately with water, mountain-green and ceruse; and mix up with parchment size and water, adding ceruse in sufficient quantity to produce the degree of intensity required in the color. Watin recommends the use of Dutch pink of Troyes and white oxide of lead, in proportions pointed out by experience: because the color thence resulting is more durable.

In the case of a triple composition, begin to make the green by mixing Dutch pink with blue verditer, and then lower the color to sea-green, by the addition of ceruse ground with water.

To make Sea-Green for Varnish and Oils.

Varnish requires that this color should possess more body than it has in distemper; and this it acquires from the oil which is mixed with it. This addition gives it even more splendor. Besides, a green of a metallic nature is substituted for the green of the Dutch pink, which is of a vegetable nature.

A certain quantity of verdigris, pounded and sifted through a silk sieve, is ground separately with nut-oil, half drying and half fat; and if the color is intended for metallic surfaces, it must be diluted with camphorated mastic, or gallipot varnish.

On the other hand, the ceruse is ground with essence, or with oils to which ½ of essence has been added, and the two colors are mixed in proportions relative to the degree of intensity intended to be given to the mixture. It may readily be conceived that the principal part of this composition consists of ceruse.

If this color be destined for articles of a certain value, crystallized verdigris, dried and pulverized, ought to be substituted for common verdigris, and the painting must be covered with a stratum of the transparent or turpentine copal varnish.

The sea-greens, which admit into their composition metallic coloring parts, are durable and do not change.

The last compositions may be employed for sea-green in oil painting; but it will be proper to brighten the tone a little more than when varnish is used, because this color becomes darker by the addition of yellow, which the oil develops in the course of time.

To make Bright Red.

A mixture of lake with vermilion gives that beautiful bright red which painters employ for sanguine parts. This red is sometimes imitated for varnishing small appendages of the toilette. It ought to be ground with varnish and mixed up with the same, after which it is glazed and polished. The mastic gallipot varnish is used for grinding; gallipot varnish for mixing up, and camphorated mastic varnish for glazing.

To make Crimson, or Rose-color.

Carminated lake — that which is composed of alum charged with the coloring part of cochineal, ceruse, and carmine — forms a beautiful crimson. It requires a particle of vermilion and of white lead.

The use of this varnish is confined to valuable articles.

To make Violet-color.

Violet is made indifferently with red and black, or red and blue; and to render it more splendid, with red, white, and blue. To compose violet, therefore, applicable to varnish, take minium, or what is still better, vermilion, and grind it with the camphorated mastic varnish to which a fourth part of boiled oil and a little ceruse have been added; then add a little Prussian blue ground in oil. The proportions requisite for the degree of intensity to be given to the color will soon be found by experience. The white brightens the tint. The vermilion and Prussian blue, separated or mixed, give hard tones, which must be softened by an intermediate substance that modifies, to their advantage, the reflections of the light.

To make Chestnut-color.

This color is composed of red, yellow and black. The English red, or red ochre of Auvergne, ochre de rue and a little black, form a dark chestnut color. It is proper for painting of every kind. If English red, which is dryer than that of Auvergne, be employed, it will be proper, when the color is intended for varnish, to grind it with drying nut-oil. The ochre of Auvergne may be ground with the mastic gallipot, and mixed up with gallipot varnish.

The most experienced artists grind dark colors with linseed oil, when the situation will admit of its being used, because it is more drying. For articles without doors nut-oil is preferable. The colors of oak-wood, walnut-tree, chestnut, olive, and yellow, require the addition of a little litharge ground on porphyry; it hastens the desiccation of the color, and gives it body.

But if it is intended to cover these colors with varnish, as is generally done in wainscoting, they must be mixed up with essence, to which a little oil has been added. The color is then much better disposed to receive the varnish, under which it exhibits all the splendor it can derive from the reflection of the light.

To make a Dryer for Painting.

Vitreous oxide of lead (litharge), is of no other use in painting than to free oils from their greasy particles, for the purpose of communicating to them a drying quality. Red litharge, however, ought to be preferred to the greenish yellow; it is not so hard, and answers better for the purpose to which it is destined.

When painters wish to obtain a common color of the ochrey kind, and have no boiled oil by them, they may paint with linseed oil, not freed from its greasy particles, by mixing with the color about 2 or 3 parts of litharge, ground on a piece of porphyry with water, dried, and reduced to fine powder, for 16 parts of oil. The color has a great deal of body, and dries as speedily as if mixed with drying oil.

Siccitive Oil.

Boil together for 2 hours on a slow and equal fire, ¼ oz. of litharge, as much calcined ceruse, and the same of terre d'ombre and talc, with 1 lb. of linseed oil, carefully stirring the whole time. It must be carefully skimmed and clarified. The older it grows the better it is. A quarter of a pint of this dryer is required to every pound of color.

To Paint in Fresco.

It is performed with water-colors on fresh plaster, or a wall laid with mortar not dry. This sort of painting has a great advantage by its incorporating with the mortar, and drying along with it becomes very durable.

The ancients painted on stucco, and we may remark in Vitruvius what infinite care they took in making the plastering of their buildings, to render them beautiful and lasting, though the modern painters find a plaster of lime and sand preferable to it.

To Paint Fire-Places and Hearths.

The Genevese employ a kind of stone, known under the name of molasse, for constructing fire-places and stoves, after the German manner. This stone is brought from Saura, a village of Savoy, near Geneva. It has a greyish color, inclining to blue, which is very agreeable to the eye. This tint is similar to that communicated to common white-washing with lime, chalk, or gypsum, the dullness of which is corrected by a particle of blue extract of indigo, or by charcoal black.

To make Red Distemper for Tiles.

Dip a brush in water from a common lye, or in soapy water, or in water charged with a 20th part of the carbonate of potash (pearlash), and draw it over the tiles. This washing thoroughly cleanses them, and disposes all the parts of the pavement to receive the distemper.

When dry, dissolve in 8 pts. of water ½ lb. of Flanders glue; and while the mixture is boiling, add 2 lbs. of red ochre; mix the whole with great care. Then apply a stratum of this mixture to the pavement, and when dry apply a second stratum with drying linseed oil, and a third with the same red mixed up with size. When the whole is dry, rub it with wax.

To Distemper in Badigeon.

Badigeon is employed for giving an uniform tint to houses rendered brown by time, and to churches. Badigeon, in general, has a yellow tint. That which succeeds best is composed of the saw-dust or powder of the same kind of stone and slacked lime, mixed up in a bucket of water holding in solution 1 lb. of the sulphate of alumina (alum). It is applied with a brush.

At Paris, and in other parts of France, where the large edifices are constructed of a soft kind of stone, which is yellow, and sometimes white when it comes from the quarry, but which in time becomes brown, a little ochre de rue is substituted for the powder of the stone itself, and restores to the edifice its original tint.

To make a Composition for rendering Canvas, Linen, and Cloth durable, Pliable, and Waterproof.

To make it Black.

First, the canvas, linen, or cloth is to be washed with hot or cold water, the former preferable, so as to discharge the stiffening which all new canvas, linen, or cloth contains; when the stiffening is perfectly discharged, hang the canvas, linen, or cloth up to dry; when perfectly so, it must be constantly rubbed by the hand until it becomes supple; it must then be stretched in a hollow frame very tight, and the following ingredients are to be laid on with a brush for the first coat, viz., 8 qts. of boiled linseed oil, ½ oz. of burnt umber, ¼ oz. of sugar of lead, ¼ oz. of white vitriol, ¼ oz. of white lead.

The above ingredients, except the white lead, must be ground fine with a small quantity of the above-mentioned oil, on a stone and muller; then mix all the ingredients up with the oil, and add a oz. of lampblack, which must be put over a slow fire in an iron broad vessel, and kept stirred until the grease disappears. In consequence of the canvas being washed and then rubbed, it will appear rough and nappy; the following method must be taken with the second coat, viz., the same ingredients as before, except the white lead; this coat will set in a few hours, according to the weather; when set take a dry paint-brush and work it very hard with the grain of the canvas; this will cause the nap to lie smooth.

The third and last coat makes a complete jet-black, which continues its color: Take 3 galls. of boiled linseed oil, an ounce of burnt umber, ½ oz. of sugar of lead, ¼ oz. of white vitriol, ½ oz. of Prussian blue, and ¼ oz. of verdigris; this must be all ground very fine in a small quantity of the above oil, then add 4 oz. of lampblack, put through the same process of fire as the first coat. The above are to be laid on and used at discretion, in a similar way to paint. To make lead color, the same ingredients as before in making the black, with the addition of white lead in proportion to the color you wish to have, light or dark.

To make it Green.

Yellow ochre, 4 oz.; Prussian blue, ¾ oz.; white lead, 3 oz.; white vitriol, ½ oz.; sugar of lead ¼ oz.; good boiled linseed oil sufficient to make it of a thin quality, so as to go through the canvas.

To make it Yellow.

Yellow ochre, 4 oz.; burnt umber, ¼ oz.; white lead, 6 or 7 oz.; white vitriol, ½ oz.; sugar of lead, ¼ oz.; boiled linseed oil, as in green.

To make it Red.

Red lead, 4 oz.; vermilion 2 oz.; white vitriol, ¼ oz.; sugar of lead ¼ oz.; boiled linseed oil as before.

To make it Gray.

Take white lead, a little Prussian blue, according to the quality you want, which will turn it to a gray color; a proportion of sugar of lead and white vitriol, as mentioned in the other colors, boiled linseed oil sufficient to make it of a thin quality.

To make it White.

White lead, 4 lbs.; spirits of turpentine, ¼ pt.; white vitriol, ½ oz.; sugar of lead, ½ oz.; boiled oil sufficient to make it of a thin quality.

The above ingredients, of different colors, are calculated as near as possible; but, as one article may be stronger than another, which will soon be discovered in using, in that case the person working, the color may add a little, or diminish, as he may find necessary.

The same preparation for wood or iron, only reducing the oil about 3 qt. out of 8, and to be applied in the same manner as paint or varnish, with a brush.

ARTISTS' OIL COLORS.
On Coloring Materials.

The composition of colors as respects those leading tests of excellence, preservation of general tints, and permanency of brilliant hues, during their exposure for many centuries to the impairing assaults of the atmosphere, is a preparation in which the ancient preparers of these oily compounds, have very much excelled, in their skilfulness, the moderns. It is a fact, that the ancient painted walls, to be seen at Dendaras, although exposed for many ages to the open air, without any covering or protection, still possess a perfect brilliancy of color, as vivid as when painted, perhaps 2000 years ago. The Egyptians mixed their colors with some gummy substance, and applied them detached from each other, without any blending or mixture. They appeared to have used six colors, viz., white, black, blue, red, yellow, and green; they first covered the canvas entirely with white, upon which they traced the design in black, leaving out the lights of the ground color. They used minium for red, and generally of a dark tinge. Pliny mentions some painted ceilings in his day in the town of Ardea, which had been executed at a date prior to the foundation of Rome. He expresses great surprise and admiration at their freshness, after the lapse of so many centuries. These are, undoubtedly, evidences of the excellence of the ancients in their art of preparing colors. In the number of them there is, probably, not much difference between the ancient and modern knowledge. The ancients seem to have been possessed of some colors of which we are ignorant, while they were unacquainted, themselves, with some of those more recently discovered. The improvements of chemistry have, certainly, in later times, enriched painting with a profusion of tints, to which, in point of brilliancy at least, no combination of primitive colors known to the ancients could pretend; but the rapid fading in the colors of some of the most esteemed masters of the Modern School, proves at least there is something defective in their bases, or mode of preparing them. This fault is peculiarly evident in many of the productions from our esteemed master, Sir Joshua Reynolds, which, although they have not issued from his pallet more than 40 years, carry an impoverishment of surface, from the premature fading of their colors, so as almost to lose, in many instances, the identity of the subjects they represent. On this head (and a most important one it is), the superiority of the ancient compounders completely carries away the palm of merit.

To Prepare Ultramarine.

Separate from the stone the most apparent parts of the ultramarine; reduce them to the size of a pea, and, having brought them to a red heat in a crucible, throw them in that state into the strongest distilled vinegar. Then grind them with the vinegar, and reduce them to an impalpable powder; next take of wax, red colophonium, and lapis lazuli, an equal quantity, say ½ oz. of each of these three substances; melt the wax and the colophonium in a proper vessel, and add the powder to the melted matter, then pour the mass into cold water, and let it rest eight days. Next take two glass vessels filled with water, as hot as the hand can bear, knead the mass in the water, and when the purest part of the ultramarine has been extracted remove the resinous mass into the other vessels, where finish the kneading to separate the remainder; if the latter portion appears to be much inferior, and paler than the former, let it rest for 4 days, to facilitate the precipitation of the ultramarine, which extract by decantation, and wash it in fair water.

Ultramarine of four qualities may be separated by this process. The first separation gives the finest, and as the operation is repeated, the beauty of the powder decreases.

Kinckel considers immersion in vinegar as the essential part of the operation. It facilitates the division, and even the solution of the zeolitic and earthy particles soluble in that acid.

Another Method.

Separate the blue parts, and reduce them, on a piece of porphyry, to an impalpable powder, which besprinkle with linseed oil, then make a paste with equal parts of yellow wax, pine resin, and colophonium, say, 8 oz. of each; and add to this paste ½ oz. of linseed oil, 2 oz. of oil of turpentine, and as much more mastic.

Then take 4 parts of this mixture, and 1 of lapis lazuli, ground with oil on a piece of porphyry, mix the whole warm, and suffer it to digest for a month, at the end of which knead the mixture thoroughly in warm water, till the blue part separates from it, and at the end of some days decant the liquor. This ultramarine is exceedingly beautiful.

These two processes are nearly similar, if we except the preliminary preparation of Kinckel, which consists in bringing the lapis lazuli to a red heat and immersing it in vinegar. It may be readily seen, by the judicious observations of Morgraff on the nature of this coloring part, that this calcination may be hurtful to certain kinds of azure stone. This preliminary operation, however, is a test which ascertains the purity of the ultramarine.

To Extract the Remainder of Ultramarine.

As this matter is valuable, some portions of ultramarine may be extracted from the paste which has been kneaded in water; nothing is necessary but to mix it with four times its weight of linseed oil, to pour the matter into a glass of conical form, and to expose the vessel in the balneum marie of an alembic. The water of which must be kept in a state of ebullition for several hours. The liquidity of the mixture allows the ultramarine to separate itself, and the supernatant oil is decanted. The same immersion of the coloring matter in oil is repeated, to separate the rosinous parts which still adhere to it; and the operation is finished by boiling it in water to separate the oil. The deposit is ultramarine; but it is inferior to that separated by the first washing.

To Ascertain whether Ultramarine be Adulterated.

As the price of ultramarine, which is already very high, may become more so on account of the difficulty of obtaining lapis lazuli, it is of great importance that painters should be able to detect adulteration. Ultramarine is pure if, when brought to a red heat in a crucible, it stands that trial without changing its color; as small quantities only are subjected to this test, a comparison may be made, at very little expense, with the part which has not been exposed to the fire. If adulterated, it becomes blackish or paler.

This proof, however, may not always be conclusive. When ultramarine of the lowest quality is mixed with azure, it exhibits no more body than sand ground on porphyry would do; ultramarine treated with oil assumes a brown tint.

Another Method.

Ultramarine is extracted from lapis lazuli, or azure stone, a kind of heavy zeolite, which is so hard as to strike fire with steel, to cut glass, and to be susceptible of a fine polish. It is of a bright blue color, variegated with white or yellow veins, enriched with small metallic glands, and even veins of a gold color, which are only sulphurets of iron (martial pyrites); it breaks irregularly. The specimens most esteemed are those charged with the greatest quantity of blue.

Several artists have exercised their ingenuity on processes capable of extracting ultramarine in its greatest purity; some, however, are contented with separating the uncolored portions of the stone, reducing the colored part to an impalpable powder, and then grinding it for a long time with oil of poppies. But it is certain that, in consequence of this ineffectual method, the beauty of the color is injured by parts which are foreign to it; and that it does not produce the whole effect which ought to be expected from pure ultramarine.

It may be readily conceived that the eminent qualities of ultramarine must have induced those first acquainted with the processes proper for increasing the merit and value of it, to keep them a profound secret. This was indeed the case; ultramarine was prepared long before any account of the method of extracting and purifying it was known.

Artificial Ultramarine.

Sulphur, 2 parts; dry carbonate of soda, 1 part. Put them into a Hessian crucible, cover it up, and apply heat until the mass fuses; then sprinkle into it gradually a mixture of silicate of soda and aluminate of soda (the first containing 72 parts of silica, the second, 70 parts of alumina); lastly, calcine for 1 hour, and wash in pure water.

To Prepare Cobalt Blue.—Bleu de Thenard.

Having reduced the ore to powder, calcine it in a reverberatory furnace, stirring it frequently. The chimney of the furnace should have a strong draught, in order that the calcination may be perfect, and the arsenical and sulphurous acid vapors may be carried off. The calcination is to be continued until these vapors cease to be disengaged, which is easily ascertained by collecting in a ladle a little of the gas in the furnace; the presence or absence of the garlic odor determines the fact. When calcined, boil the result slightly in an excess of weak nitric acid, in a glass matrass, decant the supernatant liquor, and evaporate the solution thus obtained, nearly to dryness, in a capsule of platina or porcelain. This residuum is to be thrown into boiling water and filtered, and a solution of the subphosphate of soda to be poured into the clear liquor, which precipitates an insoluble phosphate of cobalt. After washing it well on a filter, collect it while yet in a gelatinous form, and mix it intimately, with eight times its weight of alumina, in the same state—if properly done, the paste will have a uniform tint, through its whole mass. This mixture is now to be spread on smooth plates and put into a stove; when dry and brittle, pound it in a mortar, enclosed in a covered earthen crucible, and heat it to a cherry-red for half an hour. On opening the crucible, if the operation has been carefully conducted, the beautiful and desired product will be found. Care should be taken that the alumina in the gelatinous form be precipitated from the alum by a sufficient excess of ammonia, and that it is completely purified by washing with water filtered through charcoal.

To make Artificial Saxon Blue.

Saxon blue may be successfully imitated by mixing with a divided earth prussiate of iron at the moment of its formation and precipitation.

Into a solution of 144 grs. of sulphate of iron pour a solution of yellow prussiate of potash.

At the time of the formation of iron add, in the same vessel, a solution of 2 oz. of alum, and pour in with it the solution of potash, just sufficient to decompose the sulphate of alumina, for a dose of alkali superabundant to the decomposition of that salt might alter the prussiate of iron. It will, therefore, be much better to leave a little alum, which may afterwards be carried off by washing.

As soon as the alkaline liquor is added, the alumina precipitated becomes exactly mixed with the prussiate of iron, the intensity of which it lessens by bringing it to the tone of common Saxon blue. The matter is then thrown on a filter, and, after being washed in clean water, is dried. This substance is a kind of blue verditer, the intensity of which may vary according to the greater or less quantity of the sulphate of alumina decomposed. It may be used for painting in distemper.

To make Blue Verditer.

Dissolve the copper, cold, in nitric acid (aquafortis), and produce a precipitation of it by means of quicklime, employed in such doses that it will be absorbed by the acid, in order that the precipitate may be pure oxide of copper, that is, without any mixture. When the liquor has been decanted, wash the precipitate and spread it out on a piece of linen cloth to drain. If a portion of this precipitate, which is green, be placed on a grinding-stone, and if a little quicklime, in powder, be added, the green color will be immediately changed into a beautiful blue. The proportion of the lime added is from 7 to 10 parts in 100. When the whole matter acquires the consistence of paste, desiccation soon takes place.

Blue verditer is proper for distemper, and for varnish, but it is not for oil painting, as the oil renders it very dark. If used it ought to be brightened with a great deal of white.

Chrome Yellow.

To a solution of bichromate of potassa add a solution of nitrate of lead as long as a precipitate falls. Wash and dry it.

Cadmium Yellow

Is a compound of cadmium and sulphur. It is obtained by precipitation from a salt of cadmium by a current of sulphuretted hydrogen gas, or by an alkaline sulphide.

Lemon Yellow (Steinbuhl Yellow)

Is a chromate of baryta, made by mixing hot saturated solutions of bichromate of potassa and nitrate of baryta. Wash and dry the precipitates. It is considered superior to chrome yellow.

To make Naples Yellow.

Twelve oz. of ceruse, 2 oz. of the sulphuret of antimony, ½ oz. of calcined alum, 1 oz. of sal ammoniac. Pulverize these ingredients, and having mixed them thoroughly, put them into a capsule or crucible of earth, and place over it a covering of the same substance. Expose it at first to a gentle heat, which must be gradually increased till the capsule is moderately red. The oxidation arising from this process requires, at least, 3 hours' exposure to heat before it is completed. The result of this calcination is Naples yellow, which is ground in water on a porphyry slab, with an ivory spatula, as iron alters the color. The paste is then dried and preserved for use. It is a yellow oxide of lead and antimony.

There is no necessity of adhering so strictly to the doses as to prevent their being varied. If a golden color be required in the yellow, the proportions of the sulphuret of antimony and muriate of ammonia must be increased. In like manner, if you wish it to be more fusible, increase the quantities of sulphuret of antimony and calcined sulphate of alumina.

To make Montpellier Yellow.

Take 4 lbs. of litharge, well sifted, divide it into 4 equal portions, and put it into as many glazed earthen vessels. Dissolve also 1 lb. of sea-salt in about 4 lbs. of water. Pour a fourth part of this solution into each of the 4 earthen vessels, to form a light paste; let the whole rest for some hours, and when the surface begins to grow white stir the mass with a strong wooden spatula. Without this motion it would acquire too great hardness, and a part of the salt would escape decomposition. As the consistence increases dilute the matter with a new quantity of the solution, and if this is not sufficient recourse must be had to simple water to maintain the same consistence. The paste will then be very white, and in the course of 24 hours becomes uniform and free from lumps; let it remain for the same space of time, but stir it at intervals to complete the decomposition of the salt. The paste is then well washed, to carry off the caustic soda (soda deprived of carbonic acid) which adheres to it; the mass is put into strong linen cloth and subjected to a press. The remaining paste is distributed in flat vessels, and these vessels are exposed to heat, in order to effect a proper oxidation (calcination), which converts it into a solid, yellow, brilliant matter, sometimes crystallized in transverse striæ.

This is Montpellier yellow, which may be applied to the same purposes as Naples yellow.

To prepare Carmine.

This kind of fecula, so fertile in gradation of tone by the effect of mixtures, and so grateful to the eye in all its shades, so useful to the painter, and so agreeable to the delicate beauty, is only the coloring part of a kind of dried insect known under the name of cochineal.

A mixture of 36 grs. of chosen seed, 18 grs. of autour bark, and as much alum thrown into a decoction of 5 grs. of pulverized cochineal, and 5 lbs. of water, gives, at the end of from 5 to 10 days, a red fecula, which, when dried, weighs from 40 to 48 grs. This fecula is carmine. The remaining decoction, which is still highly colored, is reserved for the preparation of carminated lakes.

Superfine Carmine of Amsterdam.

Heat 6 buckets of rain-water, and when it commences to boil throw in 2 lbs. of finely-powdered cochineal; continue boiling 2 hours, and then add 3 oz. of pure water, and immediately afterwards 4 oz. of binoxalate of potash. Boil again 1 minute, then remove the vessel from the fire, and let the decoction stand 4 hours. Draw off the supernatant liquid with a syphon into numerous basins, and put them aside upon a shelf for about 3 weeks, at the end of which time a mouldy pellicle will be formed, which is to be carefully removed with a whalebone, or by means of a small sponge attached to the end of a stick. The water is then run off through a syphon, which must reach to the bottom of the pans, the carmine being so compact that it adheres. This carmine is dried in the shade, and is of an intensely brilliant hue.

To prepare Dutch Pink from Wood.

Boil the stems of wood in alum-water, and then mix the liquor with clay, marl or chalk, which will become charged with the color of the decoction. When the earthy matter has acquired consistence, form it into small cakes and expose them to dry. It is under this form that the Dutch pinks are sold in the color shops.

Dutch Pink from Yellow Berries.

The small blackthorn produces a fruit which, when collected green, is called yellow berries. These seeds, when boiled in alum-water, form a Dutch pink superior to the former. A certain quantity of clay, or marl, is mixed with the decoction, by which means the coloring part of the berries unites with the earthy matter and communicates to it a beautiful yellow color.

Brownish Yellow Dutch Pink.

Boil for an hour in 12 lbs. of water 1 lb. of yellow berries, ½ lb. of the shavings of the wood of the Barberry shrub, and 1 lb. of wood-ashes. The decoction is strained through a piece of linen cloth. Pour into this mixture, warm, and at different times, a solution of 2 lbs. of the sulphate of alumina in 5 lbs. of water; a slight effervescence will take place, and the sulphate being decomposed, the alumina which is precipitated will seize on the coloring part. The liquor must then be filtered through a piece of close linen, and the paste which remains on the cloth, when divided into square pieces, is exposed on boards to dry. This is brown Dutch pink, because the clay in it is pure. The intensity of the color shows the quality of the pink, which is superior to that of the other compositions.

Dutch Pink for Oil Painting.

By substituting for clay a substance which presents a mixture of that earth and metallic oxide, the result will be Dutch pink of a very superior kind.

Boil separately 1 lb. of yellow-berries and 3 oz. of the sulphate of alumina in 12 lbs. of water, which must be reduced to 4 lbs. Strain the decoction through a piece of linen, and squeeze it strongly. Then mix up with it 2 lbs. of ceruse, finely ground on porphyry, and 1 lb. of pulverized Spanish white. Evaporate the mixture till the mass acquires the consistence of a paste; and, having formed it into small cakes, dry them in the shade.

When these cakes are dry, reduce them to powder, and mix them with a new decoction of yellow-berries. By repeating this process a third time a brown Dutch pink will be obtained.

In general the decoctions must be warm when mixed with the earth. They ought not to be long kept, as their color is speedily altered by the fermentation. Care must be taken also to use a wooden spatula for stirring the mixture.

When only one decoction of wood or yellow-berries is employed to color a given quantity of earth, the Dutch pink resulting from it is of a bright-yellow color, and is easily mixed for use. When the coloring part of several decoctions is absorbed the composition becomes brown, and is mixed with more difficulty, especially if the paste be argillaceous; for it is the property of this earth to unite with oily and resinous parts, adhere strongly to them, and incorporate with them. In the latter case the artist must not be satisfied with mixing the color; it ought to be ground, an operation equally proper for every kind of Dutch pink, and even the softest, when destined for oil painting.

To make Lake from Brazil-wood.

Boil 4 oz. of the raspings of Brazil-wood in 15 pts. of pure water till the liquor is reduced to 2 pts. It will be of a dark-red color, inclining to violet; but the addition of 4 or 5 oz. of alum will give it a hue inclining to rose-color. When the liquor has been strained through a piece of linen cloth, if 4 oz. of the carbonate of soda be added with caution, on account of the effervescence which takes place. the color, which by this addition is deprived of its mordant, will resume its former tint, and deposit a lake, which, when washed and properly dried, has an exceedingly rich and mellow violet-red color.

Another.—If only one-half of the dose of mineral alkali be employed for this precipitation, the tint of the lake becomes clearer, because the bath still retains the undecomposed aluminous mordant.

Another. — If the method employed for Dutch pinks be followed by mixing the aluminous decoction of Brazil-wood with pure clay, such as Spanish white and white of Morat, and if the mixture be deposited on a filter to receive the necessary washing, a lake of a very bright-dark rose-color will be obtained from the driers.

Lakes from other Coloring Substances.

By the same process a very beautiful lake may be extracted from a decoction of logwood. In general, lakes of all colors, and of all the shades of these colors, may be extracted from the substances which give up their coloring part to boiling water; because it is afterwards communicated by decomposition to the alumina precipitated from sulphate of alumina, by means of an alkali; or the tincture may be mixed with a pure and exceedingly white argillaceous substance, such as real Spanish white, or white of Morat.

To prepare Rouge.

Carmine united to talc, in different proportions, forms rouge employed for the toilette. Talc is distinguished also by the name of Briancon chalk. It is a substance composed in a great measure of clay, combined naturally with silex.

Carmine, as well as carminated lakes, the coloring part of which is borrowed from cochineal, is the most esteemed of all the compositions of this kind, because their coloring part maintains itself without degradation. There are even cases where the addition of caustic ammonia, which alters so many coloring matters, is employed to heighten its color. It is for this purpose that those who color prints employ it.

Pink Saucers

Are made with extract of safflower (carthamus), obtained by digesting it, after washing with cold water, in a solution of carbonate of soda, and precipitating by citric acid. It dyes silk and wool without a mordant. The extract is evaporated upon saucers as a dye-stuff, and, mixed with powdered talc, forms a variety of rouge.

Carminated Lake from Madder.

Boil 1 part of madder in from 12 to 15 pints of water, and continue the ebullition till it be reduced to about 2 lbs. Then strain the decoction through a piece of strong linen cloth, which must be well squeezed; and add to the decoction 4 oz. of alum. The tint will be a beautiful bright-red, which the matter will retain if it be mixed with proper clay. In this case, expose the thick liquor which is thus produced on a linen filter, and subject it to one washing, to remove the alum. The lake, when taken from the driers, will retain this bright primitive color given by the alum.

Another Method.

If, in the process for making this lake, decomposition be employed, by mixing with the bath an alkaline liquor, the alum, which is decomposed, deprives the bath of its mordant, and the lake, obtained after the subsequent washings, appears of the color of the madder bath, without any addition: it is of a reddish brown. In this operation 7 or 8 oz. of alum ought to be employed for each pound of madder.

This kind of lake is exceedingly fine, but a brighter red color may be given to it, by mixing the washed precipitate with alum-water, before drying.

Improvement on the above.

If the aluminated madder bath be sharpened with acetate of lead, or with arsenite of potash, the operator still obtains, by the addition of carbonate of soda, a rose-colored lake of greater or less strength.

To make Dark-Red.

Dragon's blood, infused warm in varnish, gives reds, more or less dark, according to the quantity of the coloring resin which combines with the varnish. The artist, therefore, has it in his power to vary the tones at pleasure.

Though cochineal, in a state of division, gives to essence very little color in comparison with that which it communicates to water, carmine may be introduced into the composition of varnish colored by dragon's blood. The result will be a purple red, from which various shades may be easily formed.

To Prepare Violet.

A mixture of carminated varnish and dragon's blood, added to that colored by prussiate of iron, produces violet.

To make a Fine Red Lake.

Boil stick-lac in water, filter the decoction, and evaporate the clear liquor to dryness over a gentle fire. The occasion of this easy separation is, that the beautiful red color here separated adheres only slightly to the outsides of the sticks broken off the trees along with the gum-lac, and readily communicates itself to boiling water. Some of this sticking matter also adhering to the gum itself, it is proper to boil the whole together; for the gum does not at all prejudice the color, nor dissolve in boiling water; so that after this operation the gum is as fit for making sealing-wax as before, and for all other uses which do not require its color.

To make a Beautiful Red Lake.

Take any quantity of cochineal, on which pour twice its weight of alcohol, and as much distilled water. Infuse for some days near a gentle fire, and then filter. To the filtered liquor add a few drops of the solution of tin, and a fine red precipitate will be formed. Continue to add a little solution of tin every 2 hours, till the whole of the coloring matter is precipitated. Lastly, edulcorate the precipitate by washing it in a large quantity of distilled water and then dry it.

To Prepare Florentine Lake.

The sediment of cochineal that remains in the bottom of the kettle in which carmine is made, may be boiled with about 4 qts. of water, and the red liquor left after the preparation of the carmine mixed with it, and the whole precipitated with the solution of tin. The red precipitate must be frequently washed over with water. Exclusively of this, 2 oz. of fresh cochineal, and 1 of crystals of tartar, are to be boiled with a sufficient quantity of water, poured off clear, and precipitated with the solution of tin, and the precipitate washed. At the same time 2 lbs. of alum are also to be dissolved in water, precipitated with a lixivium of potash, and the white earth repeatedly washed with boiling water. Finally, both precipitates are to be mixed together in their liquid state, put upon a filter and dried. For the preparation of a cheaper sort, instead of cochineal, 1 lb. of Brazil-wood may be employed in the preceding manner.

To make a Lake from Madder.

Inclose 2 oz. troy of the finest Dutch madder in a bag of fine and strong calico, large enough to hold three or four times as much. Put it into a large marble or porcelain mortar, and pour on it a pint of clear soft water cold. Press the bag in every direction, and pound and rub it about with a pestle, as much as can be done without tearing it, and when the water is loaded with color pour it off. Repeat this process till the water comes off but slightly tinged, for which about 5 pts. will be sufficient. Heat all the liquor in an earthen or silver vessel till it is near boiling, and then pour it into a large basin, into which 1 oz. of alum, dissolved in 1 pt. of boiling soft water, has been previously put; stir the mixture together, and while stirring pour in gently about 1½ oz. of a saturated solution of subcarbonate of potash; let it stand till cold to settle; pour off the clear yellow liquor; add to the precipitate a quart of boiling soft water, stirring it well; and when cold separate by filtration the lake, which should weigh ½ an oz. Fresh madder-root is superior to the dry.

To give Various Tones to Lake.

A beautiful tone of violet, red, and even of purple-red, may be communicated to the coloring part of cochineal by adding to the colored bath a solution of chloride of tin.

Another.—The addition of arseniate of potash (neutral arsenical salt), gives shades which would be sought for in vain with sulphate of alumina (alum).

To make a Carminated Lake by Extracting the Coloring Part from Scarlet Cloth.

To prepare a carminated lake without employing cochineal in a direct manner, by extracting the coloring matter from any substance impregnated with it, such as the shearings of scarlet cloth.

Put into a kettle 1 lb. of fine wood-ashes, with 40 lbs. of water, and subject the water to ebullition for ¼ of an hour; then filter the solution through a piece of linen cloth till the liquor passes through clear.

Place it on the fire; and having brought it to a state of ebullition, add 2 lbs. of the shearings or shreds of scarlet cloth, dyed with cochineal, which must be boiled till they become white; then filter the liquor again, and press the shreds to squeeze out all the coloring part.

Put the filtered liquor into a clean kettle, and place it over the fire. When it boils pour in a solution of 10 or 12 oz. of alum in 2 lbs. of filtered spring-water. Stir the whole with a wooden spatula till the froth that is formed is dissipated; and having mixed with it 2 lbs. of a strong decoction of Brazil-wood, pour it upon a filter. Afterwards wash the sediment with spring-water, and remove the cloth filter charged with it to plaster dryers, or to a bed of dry bricks. The result of this operation will be a beautiful lake, but it has not the soft velvety appearance of that obtained by the first method. Besides, the coloring part of the Brazil-wood which unites to that of the cochineal in the shreds of scarlet cloth, lessens in a relative proportion the unalterability of the coloring part of the cochineal. For this reason purified potash ought to be substituted for the wood-ashes.

To make a Red Lake.

Dissolve 1 lb. of the best pearlash in 2 qts. of water, and filter the liquor through paper; next add 2 more qts. of water and 1 lb. of clean scarlet shreds, boil them in a pewter boiler till the shreds have lost their scarlet color; take out the shreds and press them, and put the colored water yielded by them to the other. In the same solution boil another lb. of the shreds, proceeding in the same manner; and likewise a third and fourth pound. Whilst this is doing, dissolve 1½ lbs. of cuttle-fish bone in 1 lb. of strong aquafortis in a glass receiver; add more of the bone if it appear to produce any ebullition in the aquafortis, and pour this strained solution gradually into the other; but if any ebullition be occasioned, more of the cuttle-fish bone must be dissolved as before, and added till no ebullition appears in the mixture. The crimson sediment deposited by this liquor is the lake: pour off the water, and stir the lake in 2 galls. of hard spring-water, and pour the sediment in 2 galls. of fresh water; let this method be repeated 4 or 5 times. If no hard water can be procured, or the lake appears too purple, ¼ an oz. of alum should be added to each quantity of water before it is used. Having thus sufficiently freed the latter from the salts, drain off the water through a filter, covered with a worn linen cloth. When it has been drained to a proper dryness, let it be dropped through a proper funnel on clean boards, and the drops will become small cones or pyramids, in which form the lake must be dried, and the preparation is completed.

Another Method.

Boil 2 oz. of cochineal in 1 pt. of water; filter the solution through paper, and add 2 oz. of pearlash dissolved in ½ pint of warm water and filtered through paper. Make a solution of cuttlebone, as in the former process, and to 1 pt. of it add 2 oz. of alum dissolved in ½ pt. of water. Put this mixture gradually to the cochineal and pearlash as long as any ebullition arises, and proceed as above.

A beautiful lake may be prepared from Brazilwood, by boiling 3 lbs. of it for an hour in a solution of 3 lbs. of common salt in 3 galls. of water, and filtering the hot fluid through paper; add to this a solution of 5 lbs. of alum in 3 galls. of water. Dissolve 3 lbs. of the best pearlash in 1½ galls. of water, and purify it by filtering; put this gradually to the other till the whole of the color appears to be precipitated and the fluid is left clear and colorless. But if any appearance of purple be seen, add a fresh quantity of the solution of alum by degrees, till a scarlet hue is produced. Then pursue the directions given in the first process with regard to the sediment. If ½ lb. of seed-lac be added to the solution of pearlash, and dissolved in it before its purification by the filter, and 2 lbs. of the wood and a proportional quantity of common salt and water be used in the colored solution, a lake will be produced that will stand well in oil or water; but it is not so transparent in oil as without the seed-lac. The lake with Brazilwood may be also made by adding ½ oz. of anatto to each pound of the wood; but the anatto must be dissolved in the solution of pearlash.

After the operation, the dryers of plaster, or the bricks, which have extracted the moisture from the precipitate, are exposed to the sun, that they may be fitted for another operation.

To make Prussian Blue.

Dissolve sulphate of iron (copperas, green vitriol) in water; boil the solution. Add nitric acid until red fumes cease to come off, and enough sulphuric acid to render the liquor clear. This is the persulphate of iron. To this add a solution of ferrocyanide of potassium (yellow prussiate of potash), as long as any precipitate is produced. Wash this precipitate thoroughly with water acidulated with sulphuric acid, and dry in a warm place.

Soluble Prussian Blue.

Add ferrocyanide of potassium to a solution freshly made of green vitriol in water. The white precipitate which falls, becomes blue on exposure to the air, and is soluble in water.

Chrome Red.

Melt saltpetre in a crucible heated to dull redness, and throw in gradually chrome yellow until no more red fumes arise. Allow the mixture to settle; pour off the liquid portion, and wash rapidly the sediment. The liquid portion contains chromate of potash, and may be used to make chrome yellow.

To make Blue.

A diluted solution of sulphate of indigo.

To make Pink.

Cochineal boiled with bitartrate of potash and sulphate alumina, or a decoction of Brazil-wood with sulphate alumina; the color may be varied by the addition of carbonate potash.

To make Purple

A decoction of Brazil-wood and logwood affords, with carbonate of potash, a permanent purple.

To make Orange Lake.

Boil 4 oz. of the best anatto and 1 lb. of pearlash, ½ an hour, in 1 gall. of water, and strain the solution through paper. Mix gradually with this 1½ lbs. of alum, in another gallon of water, desisting when no ebullition attends the commixture. Treat the sediment in the manner already directed for other kinds of lake, and dry it in square bits or lozenges.

To make a Yellow Lake.

Take 1 lb. of turmeric-root, in fine powder, 3 pt. of water, and 1 oz. of salt of tartar; put all into a glazed earthen vessel, and boil them together over a clear gentle fire, till the water appears highly impregnated and stains a paper to a beautiful yellow. Filter this liquor, and gradually add to it a strong solution of alum, in water, till the yellow matter is all curdled and precipitated. After this, pour the whole into a filter of paper, and the water will run off, and leave the yellow matter behind. Wash it with fresh water till the water comes off insipid, and then is obtained the beautiful yellow called *lacque of turmeric*.

In this manner make a lake of any of the substances that are of a strong texture, as madder, logwood, etc., but it will not succeed in the more tender species, as the flowers of roses, violets, etc., as it destroys the nice arrangement of parts in those subjects on which the color depends.

To make another Yellow Lake.

Make a lye of potash and lime sufficiently strong; in this boil, gently, fresh broom-flowers till they are white; then take out the flowers, and put the lye to boil in earthen vessels over the fire; add as much alum as the liquor will dissolve; then empty this lye into a vessel of clean water, and it will give a yellow color at the bottom. Settle, and decant off the clear liquor. Wash this powder, which is found at the bottom, with more water, till all the salts of the lye are washed off; then separate the yellow matter, and dry it in the shade.

To Make a Yellow.

Gum guttæ and terra merita give very beautiful yellows, and readily communicate their color to copal varnish made with turpentine. Aloes give a varied and orange tint.

Chloride of lead tinges vitreous matters of a yellow color. Hence the beautiful glazing given to Queen's ware. It is composed of 80 lbs. of chloride of lead, and 20 lbs. of flints ground together very fine, and mixed with water till the whole becomes as thick as cream. The vessels to be glazed are dipped in the glaze and suffered to dry.

To make Chinese Yellow.

The acacia, an Egyptian thorn, is a species of minosa, from which the Chinese make that yellow which bears washing in their silks and stuffs, and appears with so much elegance in their painting on paper. The flowers are gathered before they are fully opened, and put into an earthen vessel over a gentle heat, being stirred continually until they are nearly dry, and of a yellow color: then to ½ lb. of the flowers a sufficient quantity of rain-water is added, to hold the flowers incorporated together. It is then to be boiled until it becomes thick, when it must be strained. To the liquor is added ½ oz. of common alum, and 1 oz. of calcined oyster-shells, reduced to a fine powder.

All these are mixed together into a mass. An addition of a proportion of the ripe seeds to the flowers renders the colors somewhat deeper. For making the deepest yellow add a small quantity of Brazil-wood.

Tunie White,

Largely used as a substitute for white lead, may be made by burning zinc, or by precipitating from a solution by caustic alkali. It is the oxide of the metal, and is not blackened by sulphuretted hydrogen.

To make a Pearl White.

Pour some distilled water into a solution of nitrate of bismuth as long as precipitation takes place; filter the solution, and wash the precipitate with distilled water as it lies on the filter. When properly dried, by a gentle heat, this powder is what is generally termed pearl white.

Chrome Green.

Mix bichromate of potash with half its weight of muriate of ammonia; heat the mixture to redness, and wash the mass with plenty of boiling water. Dry the residue thoroughly. It is a sesquioxide of chromium, and is the basis of the green ink used in bank-note printing.

Another. — Mix chrome yellow and Prussian blue.

Guignet's Chrome Green.

Mix 3 parts of boracic acid and 1 part of bichromate of potassa, heat to about redness. Oxygen gas and water are given off. The resulting salt when thrown into water is decomposed. The precipitate is collected and washed. This is a remarkably fine color, solid and brilliant even by artificial light.

To make Scheele's Green.

Dissolve 2 lbs. of blue vitriol in 6 lbs. of water in a copper vessel; and in another vessel dissolve 2 lbs. of dry white potash, and 11 oz. of white arsenic in 2 lbs. of water. When the solutions are perfect pour the arsenical lye into the other gradually, and about 1 lb. 6 oz. of good green precipitate will be obtained.

To make Green.

The acetic copper (verdigris) dissolved in acetic acid, forms an elegant green.

Brunswick Green.

This is obtained from the solution of a precipitate of copper in tartar and water, which, by evaporation, yields a transparent cuproous tartar, which is similar to the superfine Brunswick green.

Schweinfürth or Emerald Green Color.

Dissolve in a small quantity of hot water, 5 parts of sulphate of copper; in another part, boil 6 parts of oxide of arsenic with 8 parts of potash, until it throws out no more carbonic acid; mix by degrees this hot solution with the first, agitating continually until the effervescence has entirely ceased; these then form a precipitate of a dirty greenish yellow, very abundant; add to it about 3 parts of acetic acid, or such a quantity that there may be a slight excess perceptible to the smell after the mixture; by degrees the precipitate diminishes the bulk, and in a few hours there deposes spontaneously at the bottom of the liquor, entirely discolored, a powder of a contexture slightly crystalline, and of a very beautiful green; afterwards the floating liquor is separated.

Green Colors free from Arsenic.

Some green colors free from the objections which apply to the arsenical greens, are described by Elsner. The first, called "Elsner Green," is made by adding to a solution of sulphate of copper a decoction of fustic, previously clarified by a solution of gelatine; to this mixture is then added 10 or 11 per cent. of protochloride of tin, and lastly an excess of caustic potash soda. The precipitate is then washed and dried, whereupon it assumes a green color, with a tint of blue.

The "Tin-copper Green" is a stannate of copper, and possesses a color which Gentele states is not inferior to any of the greens free from arsenic. The cheapest way of making this is to heat 50 parts of tin in a Hessian crucible, with 100 parts of nitrate of soda, and dissolve the mass, when cold, in a caustic alkali. When clear, this solution is diluted with water, and a cold solution of sulphate of copper is added. A reddish yellow precipitate falls, which, on being washed and dried, becomes a beautiful green.

Titanium Green was first prepared by Elsner in 1846. It is made in the following way: Iserin (titaniferous iron) is fused in a Hessian crucible with 12 times its weight of sulphate of potash. When cold, the fused mass is treated with hydrochloric acid, heated to 50° C. and filtered hot; the filtrate is then evaporated until a drop placed on a glass plate solidifies. It is then allowed to cool, and when cold a concentrated solution of sal ammoniac is poured over the mass, which is well stirred and then filtered. The titanic acid which remains behind is digested at 50° or 70° with dilute hydrochloric acid, and the acid solution, after the addition of some solution of prussiate of potash, quickly heated to boiling. A green precipitate falls, which must be washed with water aciduated with hydrochloric acid, and then dried under 100° C. Titanium green then forms a beautiful dark green powder.

A Green Color which may be employed in Confectionary.

Infuse for 24 hours 0.32 grammes of saffron in 7 grammes of distilled water; take 0.26 grammes of carmine of indigo and infuse in 15.6 grammes of distilled water. On mixing the two liquids a beautiful green color is obtained, which is harmless. Ten parts will color 1000 parts of sugar. It may be preserved for a long time by evaporating the liquid to dryness, or making it into a syrup.

To mix the Mineral Substances in Linseed Oil.

Take 1 lb. of the genuine mineral green, prepared and well powdered, 1 lb. of the precipitate of copper, 1½ lbs. of refiners' blue verditer, 3 lbs. of white lead, dry powdered, 3 oz. of sugar of lead, powdered fine. Mix the whole of these ingredients in linseed oil, and grind them in a levigating mill, passing it through until quite fine; it will thereby produce a bright mineral pea-green paint, preserve a blue tint, and keep any length of time in any climate without injury, by putting oil or water over it.

To use this color for house or ship painting, take 1 lb. of the green color paint, with 1 gill of pale boiled oil; mix them well together, and this will produce a strong pea-green paint; the tint may be varied at pleasure by adding a further quantity of white lead ground in linseed oil. This color will stand the weather and resist salt water; it may also be used for flatting rooms, by adding 3 lbs. of white lead ground in half linseed oil and half turpentine, to 1 lb. of the green, then to be mixed up in turpentine spirits, fit for use. It may also be used for painting Venetian windowblinds, by adding to 1 lb. of the green paint 10 oz. of white lead, ground in turpentine, then to be mixed up in turpentine varnish for use. In all the aforesaid preparations it will retain a blue tint, which is very desirable. When used for blinds, a small quantity of Dutch pink may be put to the white lead if the color is required of a yellow cast.

To Imitate Flesh-color.

Mix a little white and yellow together, then add a little more red than yellow. These form an excellent imitation of the complexion.

A White for Painters, which may be Preserved Forever.

Put into a pan 3 qts. of linseed oil, with an equal quantity of brandy and 4 qts. of the best double-distilled vinegar, 3 doz. of whole new-laid eggs, 4 lbs. of mutton suet, chopped small; cover all with a lead plate and lute it well; lay this pan in the cellar for 3 weeks, then take skilfully the white off, and dry it. The dose of this composition is 6 oz. of white to 1 of bismuth.

To Clean Pictures.

Take the picture out of the frame, lay a coarse towel on it for 10 or 14 days; keep continually wetting it until it has drawn out all the filthiness from the picture; pass some linseed oil, which has been a long time seasoned in the sun, over it, to purify it, and the picture will become as lively on the surface as new.

Another Method.

Put into 2 qts. of the oldest lye ¼ lb. of Genoa soap, rasped very fine, with about a pint of spirit of wine, and boil all together; then strain it through a cloth, and let it cool. With a brush dipped in the composition rub the picture all over, and let it dry; repeat this process and let it dry again; then dip a little cotton in oil of nut, and pass it over its surface. When perfectly dry, rub it well over with a warm cloth, and it will appear of a beautiful freshness.

To Restore Discolored White.

In paintings, where the white has become blackened by sulphuretted hydrogen, the application of Thenard's oxygenated water will instantly restore it. Probably a solution of permanganate of potassa would have the same effect. (See Condy's Solution).

To Restore Paintings.

Prof. Pettenkoffer has shown that the change which takes place in old paintings, is the discontinuance of molecular cohesion, which, beginning on the surface in small fissures, penetrates to the very foundation. His process is to expose the picture in a tight box to the vapor of alcohol, ether, benzine, turpentine, or other similar solvent. The process has been successfully tried in several instances.

Compound for Receiving the Colors used in Encaustic Painting.

Dissolve 9 oz. of gum arabic in 1 pt. of water, add 14 oz. of finely powdered mastic and 10 oz. of white wax, cut in small pieces, and, whilst hot, add by degrees 2 pts. of cold spring-water; then strain the composition.

Another Method.

Mix 24 oz. of mastic with gum-water, leaving out the wax, and when sufficiently beaten and dissolved over the fire, add by degrees 1½ pts. of cold water, and strain.

Or, dissolve 9 oz. of gum arabic in 1½ pts. of water; then add 1 lb. of white wax. Boil them over a slow fire, pour them into a cold vessel, and beat them well together. When this is mixed with the colors, it will require more water than the others. This is used in painting, the colors being mixed with these compositions as with oil, adding water if necessary. When the painting is finished, melt some white wax, and with a hard brush varnish the painting, and, when cold, rub it to make it entirely smooth.

Grecian Method of Painting on Wax.

Take 1 oz. of white wax and 1 oz. of gum mastic, in drops, made into powder; put the wax into a glazed pan over a slow fire, and when melted add the mastic; then stir the same until they are both incorporated. Next throw the paste into water, and when hard take it out, wipe it dry, and beat it in a mortar; when dry pound it in a linen cloth till it is reduced to a fine powder. Make some strong gum-water, and when painting take a little of the powder, some color, and mix them all with the gum-water. Light colors require but a small quantity of the powder, but more must be put in proportion to the darkness of the colors, and to black there should be almost as much of the powder as of color.

Having mixed the colors, paint with water, as is practised in painting with water colors, a ground on the wood being first painted of some proper color, prepared as described for the picture. When the painting is quite dry, with a hard brush, passing it one way, varnish it with white wax, which is melted over a slow fire till the picture is varnished. Take care the wax does not boil. Afterwards hold the picture before a fire, near enough to melt the wax, but not to run, and when the varnish is entirely cold and hard, rub it gently with a linen cloth. Should the varnish blister, warm the picture again very slowly, and the bubbles will subside.

VARNISHES.

Solvents for India-Rubber and Gutta Percha.

1. *Benzine.* There are two bodies sold as benzine or benzole: one obtained by distilling coal or coal-tar—the true benzine—used in making coal-tar colors; the other, from petroleum, contains but little true benzine. They may be used instead of turpentine in mixing paints and the true benzine for varnishes. Commercial benzine will not generally do for varnishes; that from petroleum is much the cheaper. Either forms an excellent solvent for india-rubber.

2. *Bisulphide of Carbon* is an excellent rubber solvent; acts in the cold; is made by passing the vapor of sulphur over red-hot charcoal.

3. *Chloroform* is very good, but costly.

Turpentine acts slowly, and takes long to dry. India rubber should always be cut into fine strings or shreds before being submitted to the action of solvents.

Solvent for Old Paint or Putty.

Caustic soda, applied with a broom or brush made of vegetable matter. It is sold in the shops as concentrated lye.

To give a Drying Quality to Poppy Oil.

Into 3 lbs. of pure water put 1 oz. of sulphate of zinc (white vitriol), and mix the whole with 2 lbs. of oil of pinks, or poppy oil. Expose this mixture, in an earthen vessel capable of standing the fire, to a degree of heat sufficient to maintain it in a slight state of ebullition. When one-half or two-thirds of the water has evaporated, pour the whole into a large glass bottle or jar, and leave it at rest till the oil becomes clear. Decant the clearest part by means of a glass funnel, the beak of which is stopped with a piece of cork. When the separation of the oil from the water is effected, remove the cork stopper, and supply its place with the forefinger, which must be applied in such a manner as to suffer the water to escape, and to retain only the oil.

Poppy-oil, when prepared in this manner, becomes, after some weeks, exceedingly limpid and colorless.

To give a Drying Quality to Fat Oils.

Take of nut-oil, or linseed-oil, 8 lbs.; white lead, slightly calcined, yellow acetate of lead (sal saturni), also calcined, sulphate of zinc (white vitriol), each 1 oz.; vitreous oxide of lead (litharge), 12 oz.; a head of garlic, or a small onion.

When the dry substances are pulverized, mix them with the garlic and oil, over a fire capable of maintaining the oil in a slight state of ebullition. Continue it till the oil ceases to throw up scum, till it assumes a reddish color, and till the head of garlic becomes brown; a pellicle will then be soon formed on the oil, which indicates that the operation is completed. Take the vessel from the fire, and the pellicle, being precipitated by rest, will carry with it all the unctuous parts which rendered the oil fat. When the oil becomes clear, separate it from the deposit, and put it into wide-mouthed bottles, where it will completely clarify itself in time, and improve in quality.

Another Method.

Take of litharge, 1½ oz.; sulphate of zinc, ⅔ of an oz.; linseed or nut-oil, 16 oz. The operation must be conducted as in the preceding case.

The choice of the oil is not a matter of indifference. If it be destined for painting articles exposed to the impression of the external air, or for delicate painting, nut-oil or poppy-oil. Linseed-oil is used for coarse painting, and that sheltered from the effects of the rain and of the sun.

A little negligence in the management of the fire has often an influence on the color of the oil, to which a drying quality is communicated; in this case it is not proper for delicate painting. This inconvenience may be avoided by tying up the drying matters in a small bag; but the dose of the litharge must then be doubled. The bag must be suspended by a piece of packthread fastened to a stick, which is made to rest on the edges of the vessel in such a manner as to keep the bag at the distance of an inch from the bottom of the vessel. A pellicle will be formed as in the first operation, but it will be slower in making its appearance.

Another.—A drying quality may be communicated to oil by treating, in a heat capable of maintaining a slight ebullition, linseed or nut-oil, to each pound of which is added 3 oz. litharge, reduced to fine powder.

The preparation of floor-cloths, and all paintings of large figures or ornaments, in which argillaceous colors, such as yellow and red boles, Dutch pink, etc. are employed, require this kind of preparation, that the desiccation may not be too slow; but painting for which metallic oxides are used, such as preparations of lead, copper, etc., require only the doses before indicated, because these oxides contain a great deal of oxygen, and the oil, by their contact, acquires more of a drying quality.

Another.—Take of nut-oil, 2 lbs.; common water, 3 do.; sulphate of zinc, 2 oz.

Mix these matters, and subject them to a slight ebullition, till little water remains. Decant the oil, which will pass over with a small quantity of water, and separate the latter by means of a funnel. The oil remains nebulous for some time; after which it becomes clear, and seems to be very little colored.

Another.—Take of nut-oil, or linseed-oil, 6 lbs.; common water, 4 lbs.; sulphate of zinc, 1 oz.; garlic, 1 head.

Mix these matters in a large iron or copper pan; then place them over the fire, and maintain the mixture in a state of ebullition during the whole day. Boiling water must from time to time be added, to make up for the loss of that by evaporation. The garlic will assume a brown appearance. Take the pan from the fire, and having suffered a deposit to be formed, decant the oil, which will clarify itself in the vessel. By this process the drying oil is rendered somewhat more colored. It is reserved for delicate colors.

Preparation of a Drying Oil for Zinc Paint.

In order to avoid the use of oxide of lead in making drying oil for zinc paint, oxide of manganese has been proposed as a substitute. The process to be adopted is as follows:

The manganese is broken into pieces about the size of peas, dried, and the powder separated by means of a sieve. The fragments are then to be introduced into a bag made of iron-wire gauze. This is hung in the oil contained in an iron or copper vessel, and the whole heated gently for 24 or 36 hours. The oil must not be allowed to boil, in which case there is great danger of its running over. When the oil has acquired a reddish color, it is to be poured into an appropriate vessel to clear.

For 100 parts of oil 10 of oxide of manganese may be employed, which will serve for several operations when freshly broken and the dust separated. Experience has shown, that when fresh oxide of manganese is used it is better to introduce it into the oil upon the second day. The process likewise occupies a longer time with the fresh oxide. Very great care is requisite in this operation to prevent accident, and one of the principal points to be observed is that the oil is not overheated. If the boiling should render the oil too thick, this may be remedied by an addition of turpentine after it has thoroughly cooled.

On the Manufacture of Drying Linseed Oil without Heat.

When linseed-oil is carefully agitated with vinegar of lead (tribasic acetate of lead), and the mixture allowed to clear by settling, a copious white, cloudy precipitate forms, containing oxide of lead, whilst the raw oil is converted into a drying oil of a pale-straw color, forming an excellent varnish, which, when applied in thin layers, dries perfectly in 24 hours. It contains from 4 to 5 per cent. of oxide of lead in solution. The following proportions appear to be the most advantageous for its preparation:

In a bottle containing 4½ pts. of rain-water, 18 oz. of neutral acetate of lead are placed, and when the solution is complete, 18 oz. of litharge in a very fine powder are added; the whole is then allowed to stand in a moderately warm place, frequently agitating it to assist the solution of the litharge. This solution may be considered as complete when no more small scales are apparent. The deposit of a shining white color (sexbasic acetate of lead may be separated by filtration. This conversion of the neutral acetate of lead into vinegar of lead, by means of litharge and water, is effected in about a quarter of an hour, if the mixture be heated to ebullition. When heat is not applied, the process will usually take 3 or 4 days. The solution of vinegar of lead, or tribasic acetate of lead, thus formed, is sufficient for the preparation of 22 lbs. of drying oil. For this purpose the solution is diluted with an equal volume of rain-water, and to it is gradually added, with constant agitation, 22 lbs. of oil, with which 18 oz. of litharge have previously been mixed.

When the points of contact between the lead solution and the oil have been frequently renewed by agitation of the mixture 3 or 4 times a day, and the mixture allowed to settle in a warm place, the limpid straw-colored oil rises to the surface, leaving a copious white deposit. The watery solution, rendered clear by filtration, contains intact all the acetate of lead at first employed, and may be used in the next operation, after the addition to it as before, of 18 oz. of litharge.

By filtration through paper or cotton, the oil may be obtained as limpid as water, and by exposure to the light of the sun it may also be bleached.

Should a drying oil be required absolutely free from lead, it may be obtained by the addition of dilute sulphuric acid to the above, when, on being allowed to stand, a deposit of sulphate of lead will take place, and the clear oil may be obtained free from all trace of lead.

Resinous Drying Oil.

Take 10 lbs. of drying nut-oil, if the paint is destined for external articles, or 10 lbs. of drying linseed-oil if for internal; resin, 3 lbs.; turpentine, 6 oz.

Cause the resin to dissolve the oil by means of a gentle heat. When dissolved and incorporated with the oil, add the turpentine; leave the varnish at rest, by which means it will often deposit portions of resin and other impurities; and then preserve it in wide-mouthed bottles. It must be used fresh; when suffered to grow old it abandons some of its resin. If this resinous oil assumes too much consistence, dilute it with a little essence, if intended for articles sheltered from the sun, or with oil of poppies.

Fat Copal Varnish.

Take picked copal, 16 oz.; prepared linseed oil, or oil of poppies, 8 oz.; essence of turpentine, 16 oz.

Liquefy the copal in a matrass over a common fire, and then add the linseed oil, or oil of poppies, in a state of ebullition; when these matters are incorporated, take the matrass from the fire, stir the matter till the greatest heat is subsided, and then add the essence of turpentine warm. Strain the whole, while still warm, through a piece of linen, and put the varnish into a wide-mouthed bottle. Time contributes towards its clarification, and in this manner it acquires a better quality.

Varnish for Watch Cases in Imitation of Tortoise-shell.

Take copal of an amber color, 6 oz.; Venice turpentine, 1½ oz.; prepared linseed-oil, 24 oz.; essence of turpentine, 6 oz.

It is customary to place the turpentine over the copal, reduced to small fragments, in the bottom of an earthen or metal vessel, or in a matrass exposed to such a heat as to liquefy the copal; but it is more advantageous to liquefy the latter alone, to add the oil in a state of ebullition, then the turpentine liquefied, and in the last place the essence. If the varnish is too thick, some essence may be added. The latter liquor is a regulator for the consistence in the hands of an artist.

Gold-colored Copal Varnish.

Take copal in powder, 1 oz.; essential oil of lavender, 2 oz.; essence of turpentine, 6 oz.

Put the essential oil of lavender into a matrass of a proper size, placed on a sand-bath heated gently. Add to the oil while very warm, and at several times, the copal powder, and stir the mixture with a stick of white wood rounded at the end. When the copal has entirely disappeared, add at three different times the essence almost in a state of ebullition, and keep continually stirring the mixture. When the solution is completed, the result will be a varnish of a gold-color, exceedingly durable and brilliant.

Another Method.

To obtain this varnish colorless, it will be proper to rectify the essence of the shops, which is often highly colored, and to give it the necessary density by exposure to the sun in bottles closed with cork stoppers, leaving an interval of some inches between the stopper and the surface of the liquid. A few months are thus sufficient to communicate to it the required qualities. Besides, essence of the shops is rarely possessed of that state of consistence without having at the same time a strong amber color.

The varnish resulting from the solution of copal in oil of turpentine, brought to such a state as to produce the maximum of solution, is exceedingly durable and brilliant. It resists the shock of hard bodies much better than the enamel of toys, which often becomes scratched and whitened by the impression of repeated friction; it is susceptible also of a fine polish. It is applied with the greatest success to philosophical instruments, and the paintings with which vessels and other utensils of metal are decorated.

Camphorated Copal Varnish.

This varnish is destined for articles which require durability, pliableness, and transparency.

Take of pulverized copal, 2 oz.; essential oil of lavender, 6 oz.; camphor, ½ oz.; essence of turpentine, a sufficient quantity, according to the consistence required to be given to the varnish.

Put into a phial of thin glass, or into a small matrass, the essential oil of lavender and the camphor, and place the mixture on a moderately open fire, to bring the oil and the camphor to a slight state of ebullition; then add the copal powder in small portions, which must be renewed as they disappear in the liquid. Favor the solution, by continually stirring with a stick of white wood; and when the copal is incorporated with the oil, add the essence of turpentine boiling; but care must be taken to pour in, at first, only a small portion.

This varnish is a little colored, and by rest it acquires a transparency which, united to the solidity observed in almost every kind of copal varnish, renders it fit to be applied with great success in many cases.

Ethereal Copal Varnish.

Take of amberry copal, ½ oz.; ether, 2 oz.

Reduce the copal to a very fine powder, and introduce it by small portions into the flask which contains the ether; close the flask with a glass or a cork stopper, and having shaken the mixture for ½ an hour, leave it at rest till the next morning. In shaking the flask, if the sides become covered with small undulations, and if the liquor be not exceedingly clear, the solution is not complete. In this case add a little ether, and leave the mixture at rest. The varnish is of a white lemon-color. The largest quantity of copal united to ether may be a fourth, and the least a fifth. The use of copal varnish made with ether seems, by the expense attending it, to be confined to repairing those accidents which frequently happen to the enamel of toys, as it will supply the place of glass to the colored varnishes employed for mending fractures, or to restoring the smooth surface of paintings which have been cracked and shattered.

The great volatility of ether, and in particular its high price, do not allow the application of this varnish to be recommended, but for the purposes here indicated. It has been applied to wood with complete success, and the glazing it produced unites lustre to solidity. In consequence of the too speedy evaporation of the liquid, it often boils under the brush. Its evaporation, however, may be retarded, by spreading over the wood a light stratum of essential oil of rosemary or lavender, or even of turpentine, which may afterwards be removed by a piece of linen rag; what remains is sufficient to retard the evaporation of the ether.

Fat Amber or Copal Varnish.

Take of amber or copal of one fusion, 4 oz.; essence of turpentine, drying linseed oil, of each, 10 oz.

Put the whole into a pretty large matrass, and expose it to the heat of a balneum mariæ, or move it over the surface of an uncovered chafing-dish, but without flame, and at the distance from it of 2 or 3 inches. When the solution is completed, add still a little copal or amber to saturate the liquid; then pour the whole on a filter prepared with cotton, and leave it to clarify by rest. If the varnish is too thick, add a little warm essence to prevent the separation of any of the amber.

This varnish is colored, but far less so than those composed by the usual methods. When spread over white wood, without any preparation, it forms a solid glazing, and communicates a slight tint to the wood.

If it is required to charge this varnish with more copal, or prepared amber, the liquor must be composed of two parts of essence for one of oil.

To Apply Copal Varnish to the Reparation of Opake Enamels.

The properties manifested by these varnishes, and which render them proper for supplying the vitreous and transparent coating of enamel, by a covering equally brilliant, but more solid, and which adheres to vitreous compositions, and to metallic surfaces, admit of their being applied to other purposes besides those here enumerated.

By slight modifications they may be used also for the reparation of opake enamel which has been fractured. These kinds of enamel admit the use of cements colored throughout, or only superficially, by copal varnish charged with coloring parts. On this account they must be attended with less difficulty in the reparation than transparent enamel, because they do not require the same reflection of the light. Compositions of paste, therefore, the different grounds of which may always harmonize with the coloring ground of the pieces to be repaired, and which may be still strengthened by the same tint introduced into the solid varnish, with which the articles are glazed, will answer the views of the artist in a wonderful manner.

The base of the cement ought to be pure clay without color, and exceedingly dry. If solidity be required, ceruse is the only substance that can be substituted in its place. Drying oil of pinks will form an excellent excipient, and the consistence of the cement ought to be such that it can be easily extended by a knife or spatula, possessed of a moderate degree of flexibility. This sort of paste soon dries. It has the advantage also of presenting to the colors, applied to it with a brush, a kind of ground which contributes to their solidity. The compound mastic being exceedingly drying, the application of it will be proper in cases where speedy reparation of the damaged articles is required.

In more urgent cases, the paste may be composed with ceruse, and the turpentine copal varnishes, which dry more speedily than oil of pinks; and the colors may then be glazed with the ethereal copal varnish.

The application of the paste will be necessary only in cases when the accident, which has happened to the enamel, leaves too great a vacuity to be filled up by several strata, of colored varnish. But in all cases the varnish ought to be well dried, that it may acquire its full lustre by polishing.

To make White Copal Varnish.

White oxide of lead, ceruse, Spanish white, white clay. Such of these substances as are preferred ought to be carefully dried. Ceruse and clay obstinately retain a great deal of humidity, which would oppose their adhesion to drying oil or varnish. The cement then crumbles under the fingers, and does not assume a body.

Another.—On 16 oz. of melted copal, pour 4, 6, or 8 oz. of linseed-oil boiled, and quite free from grease. When well mixed by repeated stirrings, and after they are pretty cool, pour in 16 oz. of the essence of Venice turpentine. Pass the varnish through a cloth. Amber varnish is made the same way.

To make Black Copal Varnish.

Lampblack, made of burnt vine-twigs, or black of peach-stones. The lampblack must be carefully washed and afterwards dried. Washing carries off a great many of its impurities.

To make Yellow Copal Varnish.

Yellow oxide of lead, of Naples and Montpellier, both reduced to impalpable powder. These yellows are hurt by the contact of iron and steel; in mixing them up, therefore, a horn spatula with a glass mortar and pestle must be employed.

Gum guttæ, yellow ochre, or Dutch pink, according to the nature and tone of the color to be imitated.

To make Blue Copal Varnish.

Indigo, prussiate of iron (Prussian blue), blue verditer, and ultramarine. All these substances must be very much divided.

To make Green Copal Varnish.

Verdigris, crystallized verdigris, compound green (a mixture of yellow and blue). The first two require a mixture of white in proper proportions, from a fourth to two-thirds, according to the tint intended to be given. The white used for this purpose is ceruse, or the white oxide of lead, or Spanish white, which is less solid, or white of Moudon.

To make Red Copal Varnish.

Red sulphuretted oxide of mercury (cinnabar vermilion), red oxide of lead (minium), different red ochres, or Prussian reds, etc.

To make Purple Copal Varnish.

Cochineal, carmine, and carminated lakes, with ceruse and boiled oil.

Brick Red.

Dragon's blood.

VARNISHES. 343

Chamois Color.

Dragon's blood with a paste composed of flowers of zinc, or, what is still better, a little red vermilion.

Violet.

Cinnabar, mixed with lampblack, washed very dry, or with the black of burnt vine-twigs; and to render it mellower, a proper mixture of red, blue, and white.

Pearl Gray.

White and black; white and blue; for example, ceruse and lampblack; ceruse and indigo.

Flaxen Gray.

Ceruse, which forms the ground of the paste, mixed with a small quantity of Cologne earth, as much English red, or carminated lake, which is not so durable, and a particle of Prussian blue.

Brunswick Black Varnish.

Melt 4 lbs. of common asphalt, and add 2 pts. of boiled linseed-oil, and 1 gall. of oil of turpentine or coal-tar naphtha.

India-Rubber Varnish.

Four ounces india-rubber in fine shavings are dissolved in a covered jar, by means of a sand-bath, in 2 lbs. of crude benzole, and then mixed with 4 lbs. of hot linseed-oil varnish heated, and filtered. (See CEMENTS.)

To make Varnish for Silks, etc.

To 1 qt. of cold linseed-oil poured off from the lees (produced on the addition of unslaked lime, on which the oil has stood 8 or 10 days at the least, in order to communicate a drying quality, or brown umber burnt and powdered, which will have the like effect,) add ½ oz. of litharge; boil them for ½ hour, then add ½ oz. of the copal varnish. While the ingredients are on the fire, in a copper vessel, put in 1 oz. of chios turpentine or common resin, have a few drops of neat's-foot oil, and stir the whole with a knife; when cool it is ready for use. The neat's-foot oil prevents the varnish from being sticky or adhesive, and may be put into the linseed-oil at the same time with the lime or burnt umber. Resin or chios turpentine may be added till the varnish has attained the desired thickness.

The longer the raw linseed-oil remains on the unslaked lime or umber, the sooner will the oil dry after it is used; if some months, so much the better. Such varnish will set, that is to say, not run, but keep its place on the silk in four hours; the silk may then be turned and varnished on the other side.

Compound Mastic Varnish.

Take of pure alcohol, 32 oz.; purified mastic, 6 oz.; gum sandarac, 3 oz.; very clear Venice turpentine, 3 oz.; glass, coarsely pounded, 4 oz.

Reduce the mastic and sandarac to fine powder; mix this powder with white glass, from which the finest parts have been separated by means of a hair-sieve: put all the ingredients with alcohol into a short-necked matrass, and adapt to it a stick of white-wood, rounded at the end, and of a length proportioned to the height of the matrass, that it may be put in motion. Expose the matrass in a vessel filled with water, made at first a little warm; and which must afterwards be maintained in a state of ebullition for 1 or 2 hours. The matrass may be made fast to a ring of straw.

When the solution seems to be sufficiently extended, add the turpentine, which must be kept separately in a phial or pot, and which must be melted by immersing it for a moment in a balneum mariæ. The matrass must be still left in the water for ½ hour, at the end of which it is taken off, and the varnish is continually stirred till it is somewhat cool. Next day it is to be drawn off and filtered through cotton. By these means it will become exceedingly limpid.

The addition of glass may appear extraordinary; but this substance divides the parts of the mixture which have been made with the dry ingredients; and it retains the same quality when placed over the fire. It therefore obviates with success two inconveniences which are exceedingly troublesome to those who compose varnishes. In the first place, by dividing the matters, it facilitates the action of the alcohol; and in the second, its weight, which surpasses that of resins, prevents these resins from adhering to the bottom of the matrass, and also the coloration acquired by the varnish when a sand-bath is employed, as is commonly the case.

The application of this varnish is suited to articles belonging to the toilet, such as dressing-boxes, cut-paper works, etc. The following possess the same brilliancy and lustre, but they have more solidity, and are exceedingly drying.

Camphorated Mastic Varnish for Paintings.

Take of mastic, cleaned and washed, 12 oz.; pure turpentine, 1½ oz.; camphor, ½ oz.; white glass pounded, 5 oz.; essence of turpentine, 36 oz. Make the varnish according to the method indicated for Compound Mastic Varnish. The camphor is employed in pieces, and the turpentine is added when the solution of the resin is completed. But if the varnish is to be applied to old paintings, or paintings which have been already varnished, the turpentine may be suppressed; as this ingredient is here recommended only in cases of a first application to new paintings, and just freed from white-of-egg varnish.

The question by able masters respecting the kind of varnish proper to be employed for paintings, has never yet been determined. Some artists who have paid particular attention to this subject, make a mystery of the means they employ to obtain the desired effect. The real end may be accomplished by giving to the varnish destined for painting, pliability and softness, without being too solicitous in regard to what may add to its consistence or its solidity. The latter quality is particularly requisite in varnishes which are to be applied to articles much exposed to friction; such as boxes, furniture, etc.

Shaw's Mastic Varnish for Paintings.

Bruise the mastic with a muller on a painter's stone, which will detect the soft parts, or tears, which are to be taken out, and the remainder put into a clean bottle with *good* spirits of turpentine (twice distilled if you can get it); and dissolve the gum by shaking it in your hand for ½ hour, without heat. When dissolved, strain it through a piece of calico and place it in a bottle well corked, so that the light of the sun can strike it, for 2 or 3 weeks; which will cause a mucilaginous precipitate, leaving the remainder as transparent as water. It may then be carefully decanted into another bottle and put by for use. The proportions of gum and alcohol are: mastic, 6 oz.; turpentine, 14 oz. If found on trial to be too thick, thin it with turpentine.

To make Painter's Cream.

Painters who have long intervals between their periods of labor, are accustomed to cover the parts they have painted with a preparation which preserves the freshness of the colors, and which they can remove when they resume their work. This preparation is as follows:

Take of very clear nut-oil, 3 oz; mastic in tears,

pulverized, ¼ oz.; sal saturni, in powder (acetate of lead), ½ oz. Dissolve the mastic in oil over a gentle fire, and pour the mixture into a marble mortar, over the pounded salt of lead; stir it with a wooden pestle, and add water in small quantities till the matter assume the appearance and consistence of cream, and refuse to admit more water.

Sandarac Varnish.

Take of gum sandarac, 8 oz.; pounded mastic, 2 oz.; clear turpentine, 2½ oz.; pounded glass, 4 oz.; pure alcohol, 32 oz. Mix and dissolve as before.

Compound Sandarac Varnish.

Take of pounded copal, of an amber color, once liquefied, 3 oz.; gum sandarac, 6 oz.; mastic, cleaned, 3 oz.; clear turpentine, 3½ oz.; pounded glass, 4 oz.; pure alcohol, 32 oz. Mix these ingredients, and pursue the same method as above.

This varnish is destined for articles subject to friction; such as furniture, chairs, fan-sticks, mouldings, etc., and even metals; to which it may be applied with success. The sandarac gives it great durability.

Camphorated Sandarac Varnish for Cut-Paper Works, Dressing-Boxes, etc.

Take of gum sandarac, 6 oz.; gum elemi, 4 oz.; gum animi, 1 oz.; camphor, ½ oz.; pounded glass, 4 oz.; pure alcohol, 32 oz.

Make the varnish according to the directions already given. The soft resins must be pounded with the dry bodies. The camphor is to be added in pieces.

Another.—Take of gallipot or white incense, 6 oz.; gum animi, gum elemi, each 2 oz.; pounded glass, 4 oz.; alcohol, 32 oz.

Make the varnish with the precautions indicated for the compound mastic varnish.

The two last varnishes are to be used for ceilings and wainscots, colored or not colored. They may even be employed as a covering to parts painted with strong colors.

Spirituous Sandarac Varnish for Wainscoting small Articles of Furniture, Balustrades, Inside Railings.

Take gum sandarac, 6 oz.; shell-lac, 2 oz.; colophonium or resin, white glass pounded, clear turpentine, each 4 oz.; pure alcohol, 32 oz.

Dissolve the varnish according to the directions given for compound mastic varnish.

This varnish is sufficiently durable to be applied to articles destined to daily and continual use. Varnishes composed with copal, ought however, in these cases to be preferred.

Another.—There is another composition which, without forming part of the compound varnishes, is employed with success for giving a polish and lustre to furniture made of wood; wax forms the basis of it.

Many cabinet-makers are contented with waxing common furniture, such as tables, chests of drawers, etc. This covering, by means of repeated friction, soon acquires a polish and transparency which resembles those of varnish. Waxing seems to possess qualities peculiar to itself, but, like varnish, it is attended with inconveniences as well as advantages.

Varnish supplies better the part of glazing; it gives a lustre to the wood which it covers, and heightens the colors of that destined, in particular, for delicate articles. These real and valuable advantages are counterbalanced by its want of consistence; it yields too easily to the shrinking or swelling of the wood, and rises in scales or splits on being exposed to the slightest shock. These accidents can be repaired only by new strata of varnish, which render application to the varnisher necessary, and occasion trouble and expense.

Waxing stands shocks, but it does not possess in the same degree as varnish the property of giving lustre to the bodies on which it is applied, and of heightening their tints. The lustre it communicates is dull, but this inconvenience is compensated by the facility with which any accident that may have altered its polish can be repaired by rubbing it with a piece of fine cork. There are some circumstances, therefore, under which the application of wax ought to be preferred to that of varnish. This seems to be the case in particular with tables of walnut-tree wood, exposed to daily use, chairs, mouldings and for all small articles subject to constant employment.

But as it is of importance to make the stratum of wax as thin as possible in order that the veins of the wood may be more apparent, the following process will be acceptable to the reader:

Melt over a moderate fire in a very clean vessel 2 oz. of white or yellow wax, and when liquefied add 4 oz. of good essence of turpentine; stir the whole until it is entirely cool, and the result will be a kind of pomade fit for waxing furniture, and which must be rubbed over them according to the usual method. The essence of turpentine is soon dissipated, but the wax, which by its mixture is reduced to a state of very great division, may be extended with more ease and in a more uniform manner. The essence soon penetrates the pores of the wood, calls forth the color of it, causes the wax to adhere better, and the lustre which thence results is equal to that of varnish, without having any of its inconveniences.

Colored Varnish for Violins and other Stringed Instruments, also for Plum-tree, Mahogany and Rose-wood.

Gum sandarac, 4 oz.; seed-lac, 2 oz.; mastic, Benjamin, in tears, each 1 oz.; pounded glass, 4 oz.; Venice turpentine, 2 oz.; pure alcohol, 32 oz.

The gum sandarac and lac render this varnish durable; it may be colored with a little saffron or dragon's blood.

French Polish.

The varnish being prepared (shellac), the article to be polished being finished off as smoothly as possible with glass-paper, and your rubber being prepared as directed below, proceed to the operation as follows: The varnish, in a narrow-necked bottle, is to be applied to the *middle* of the flat face of the rubber, by laying the rubber on the mouth of the bottle and shaking up the varnish once, as by this means the rubber will imbibe the proper quantity to varnish a considerable extent of surface. The rubber is then to be enclosed in a soft linen cloth doubled, the rest of the cloth being gathered up at the back of the rubber to form a handle. Moisten the face of the linen with a little *raw* linseed-oil, applied with the finger to the middle of it. Placing your work opposite the light, pass your rubber *quickly* and *lightly* over its surface until the varnish becomes dry or nearly so; charge your rubber as before with varnish (omitting the oil), and repeat the rubbing until three coats are laid on, when a little oil may be applied to the rubber and two coats more given to it. Proceeding in this way until the varnish has acquired some thickness, wet the *inside* of the linen cloth, before applying the varnish, with alcohol, and rub quickly, lightly and uniformly the whole surface. Lastly, wet the linen cloth with a little oil and alcohol without varnish, and rub as before till dry.

To make the Rubber.

Roll up a strip of *thick* woolen cloth which has

been torn off so as to form a soft, elastic edge. It should form a coil from 1 to 3 inches in diameter, according to the size of the work.

Fat Varnish of a Gold-color.

Amber, 8 oz.; gum-lac, 2 oz.; drying linseed-oil, 8 oz.; essence of turpentine, 16 oz. Dissolve separately the gum-lac, and then add the amber, prepared and pulverized, with the linseed-oil and essence very warm. When the whole has lost a part of its heat, mix in relative proportions tincture of anatto, of terra merita, gum guttæ and dragon's blood. This varnish, when applied to white metals, gives them a gold color.

Fat Turpentine, or Golden Varnish, being a Mordant to Gold and Dark Colors.

Boiled linseed oil, 16 oz.; Venice turpentine, 8 oz.; Naples yellow, 5 oz. Heat the oil with the turpentine, and mix the Naples yellow pulverized.

Naples yellow is substituted here for resins, on account of its drying qualities, and in particular of its color, which resembles that of gold; great use is made of the varnish in applying gold leaf.

The yellow, however, may be omitted when this species of varnish is to be solid and colored coverings. In this case an ounce of litharge to each pound of composition may be substituted in its stead, without this mixture doing any injury to the color which is to constitute the ground.

To make Turners' Varnish for Boxwood.

Seed-lac, 5 oz.; gum sandarac, 2 oz.; gum elemi, 1½ oz.; Venice turpentine, 2 oz.; pounded glass, 5 oz.; pure alcohol, 24 oz.

Another. — Other turners employ the gum-lac united to a little elemi and turpentine digested some months in pure alcohol exposed to the sun. If this method be followed, it will be proper to substitute for the sandarac the same quantity of gum-lac reduced to powder, and not to add the turpentine to the alcohol, which ought to be exceedingly pure, till towards the end of the infusion.

Solar infusion requires care and attention. Vessels of a sufficient size to allow the spirituous vapors to circulate freely ought to be employed, because it is necessary that the vessels should be closely shut. Without this precaution the spirits would become weakened and abandon the resin which they laid hold of during the first day's exposure. This perfect obituration will not admit of the vessels being too full.

In general the varnishes applied to articles which may be put into the lathe acquire a great deal of brilliancy by polishing: a piece of woollen cloth is sufficient for the operation. If turpentine predominates too much in these compositions, the polish does not retain its lustre, because the heat of the hands is capable of softening the surface of the varnish, and in this state it readily tarnishes.

Loning's Colorless Varnish.

For this varnish a prize of 20 guineas was awarded by the Society of Arts, London. Dissolve 2½ oz. of shellac in a pint of alcohol; boil for a few minutes with 5 oz. of well washed and recently-heated animal charcoal. A small portion of the solution must then be filtered, and if not colorless more charcoal must be added. When all color is removed, press the liquid through a piece of silk, and afterwards filter through fine blotting-paper. This varnish should be used in a room of at least 60° Fahr., and free from dust. It dries in a few minutes, and is not liable afterwards to chill or bloom. It is particularly applicable to drawings and prints which have been sized, and may be advantageously used upon oil paintings, which are thoroughly hard and dry, as it brings out the colors with the purest effect. This quality renders it a valuable varnish for all kinds of leather, as it does not yield to the warmth of the hand and resists damp.

Dr. Hare's Colorless Varnish.

Dissolve in an iron kettle 1 part of pearlash in about 8 parts of water; add 1 part of seed or shellac, and heat to boiling. When the lac is dissolved impregnate the whole with chlorine (made by gently heating 1 part black oxide of manganese with 4 oz of muriatic acid) until the lac is all precipitated. Wash, dry, and dissolve in alcohol.

To Varnish Dressing-Boxes.

The most of spirit of wine varnishes are destined for covering preliminary preparations, which have a certain degree of lustre. They consist of cement, colored or not colored, charged with landscapes and figures cut out in paper, which produces an effect under the transparent varnish. Most of the dressing-boxes, and other small articles of the same kind, are covered with this particular composition, which, in general, consists of three or four coatings of Spanish white pounded in water, and mixed up with parchment glue. The first coating is smoothed with pumice-stone, and then polished with a piece of new linen and water. The coating in this state is fit to receive the destined color, after it has been ground with water and mixed with parchment glue diluted with water. The cut figures with which it is to be embellished are then applied, and a coating of gum or fish-glue is spread over them, to prevent the varnish from penetrating to the preparation, and from spoiling the figures. The operation is finished by applying 3 or 4 coatings of varnish, which when dry are polished with tripoli and water, by means of a piece of cloth. A lustre is then given to the surface with starch and a bit of doe-skin, or very soft cloth.

Gallipot Varnish.

Take of gallipot, or white incense, 12 oz.; white glass, pounded, 5 oz.; Venice turpentine, 2 oz.; essence of turpentine, 32 oz. Make the varnish after the white incense has been pounded with the glass.

Some authors recommend mastic or sandarac in the room of gallipot; but the varnish is neither more beautiful nor more durable. When the color is ground with the preceding varnish and mixed up with the latter, which, if too thick, is thinned with a little essence, and which is applied immediately, and without any sizing, to boxes and other articles, the coatings acquire sufficient strength to resist the blows of a mallet. But if the varnish be applied to a sized color it must be covered with a varnish of the first or second genus.

Varnish for Electrical Purposes.

Dissolve the best red sealing-wax in alcohol. Two or three coats will make a complete covering. It may be applied to wood or glass.

Mastic Gallipot Varnish, for Grinding Colors

Take of new gallipot, or white incense, 4 oz.; mastic, 2 oz.; Venice turpentine, 6 oz.; pounded glass, 4 oz.; essence of turpentine, 32 oz. When the varnish is made with the precautions already indicated, add prepared nut-oil or linseed-oil, 2 oz.

The matters ground with this varnish dry more slowly; they are then mixed up with the following varnish, if it be for common painting, or with particular varnishes destined for colors and for grounds.

Lacquer for Brass.

Take of seed-lac, 6 oz.; amber or copal, ground

or porphyry, 2 oz,; dragon's blood, 40 grs.; extract of red sandal-wood, obtained by water, 30 grs.; oriental saffron, 36 grs.; pounded glass, 4 oz.; very pure alcohol, 40 oz.

To apply this varnish to articles or ornaments of brass, expose them to a gentle heat, and dip them into varnish. Two or three coatings may be applied in this manner, if necessary. The varnish is durable and has a beautiful color. Articles varnished in this manner may be cleaned with water and a bit of dry rag.

Lacquer for Philosophical Instruments.

This lacquer or varnish is destined to change or to modify the color of those bodies to which it is applied.

Take of gum guttæ (gamboge), ¾ oz.; gum sandarac, gum elemi, each 2 oz.; dragon's blood, of the best quality, 1 oz.; seed-lac, 1 oz.; terra merita, ¾ oz.; oriental saffron, 2 grs.; pounded glass, 3 oz.; pure alcohol, 20 oz.

The tincture of saffron and of terra merita is first obtained by infusing them in alcohol for 24 hours, or exposing them to the heat of the sun in summer. The tincture must be strained through a piece of clean linen cloth, and ought to be strongly squeezed. This tincture is poured over the dragon's blood, the gum elemi, the seed-lac, and the gum guttæ, all pounded and mixed with the glass. The varnish is then made according to the directions before given.

It may be applied with great advantage to philosophical instruments. The use of it might be extended also to various cast or moulded articles with which furniture is ornamented.

If the dragon's blood be of the first quality it may give too high a color; in this case the dose may be lessened at pleasure, as well as that of the other coloring matters.

Gold-colored Lacquer for Brass Watch-cases, Watch-keys, etc.

Take of seed-lac, 6 oz.; amber, gum guttæ, each 2 oz.; extract of red sandal-wood in water, 24 grs.; dragon's blood, 60 grs.; oriental saffron, 36 grs.; pounded glass, 4 oz.; pure alcohol, 36 oz. Grind the amber, the seed-lac, gum guttæ, and dragon's blood on a piece of porphyry; then mix them with the pounded glass, and add the alcohol, after forming with it an infusion of the saffron and an extract of the sandal-wood. The varnish must then be completed as before. The metal articles destined to be covered by this varnish are heated, and those which will admit of it are immersed in packets. The tint of the varnish may be varied by modifying the doses of the coloring substances.

Lacquer of a Less Drying Quality.

Take of seed-lac, 4 oz.; sandarac, or mastic, 4 oz.; dragon's blood, ½ oz.; terra merita, gum guttæ, each 30 grs.; pounded glass, 5 oz.; clear turpentine, 8 oz.; essence of turpentine, 32 oz. Extract by infusion the tincture of the coloring substances, and then add the resinous bodies according to the directions for compound mastic varnish.

Lacquer or varnishes of this kind are called changing, because, when applied to metals, such as copper, brass, or hammered tin, or to wooden boxes and other furniture, they communicate to them a more agreeable color. Besides, by their contact with the common metals, they acquire a lustre which approaches that of the precious metals, and to which, in consequence of peculiar intrinsic qualities or certain laws of convention, a much greater value is attached. It is by means of these changing varnishes that artists are able to communicate to their leaves of silver and copper those shining colors observed in foils. This process of industry becomes a source of prosperity to the manufacturers of buttons and works formed with foil, which in the hands of the jeweller contributes with so much success to produce that reflection of the rays of light which doubles the lustre and sparkling quality of precious stones.

It is to varnish of this kind that we are indebted for the manufactory of gilt leather, which, taking refuge in England, has given place to that of papier-maché, which is employed for the decoration of palaces, theatres, etc.

In the last place, it is by the effect of a foreign tint, obtained from the coloring part of saffron, that the scales of silver disseminated in *confection d'hyacinthe* reflect a beautiful gold color.

The colors transmitted by different coloring substances, require tones suited to the objects for which they are destined. The artist has it in his own power to vary them at pleasure, by the addition of annatto to the mixture of dragon's blood, saffron, etc., or some changes in the doses of the mode intended to be made in colors. It is here impossible to give limited formulæ.

To make Lacquers of Various Tints.

There is one simple method by which artists may be enabled to obtain all the different tints they require. Infuse separately 4 oz. of gum guttæ in 32 oz. of essence of turpentine, and 4 oz. of dragon's blood, and 1 oz. of annatto also in separate doses of essence. These infusions may be easily made in the sun. After 15 days' exposure pour a certain quantity of these liquors into a flask, and by varying the doses different shades of color will be obtained.

These infusions may be employed also for changing alcoholic varnishes; but in this case the use of saffron, as well as that of red sandal-wood, which does not succeed with essence, will soon give the tone necessary for imitating with other tinctures the color of gold.

Mordant Varnish for Gilding.

Take of mastic, 1 oz.; gum sandarach, 1 oz.; gum guttæ, ½ oz.; turpentine, ¼ oz.; essence of turpentine, 6 oz.

Some artists, who make use of mordants, substitute for the turpentine 1 oz. of the essence of lavender, which renders this composition still less drying.

In general, the composition of mordants admits of modifications, according to the kind of work for which they are destined. The application of them, however, is confined chiefly to gold. When it is required to fill up a design with gold-leaf on any ground whatever, the composition, which is to serve as the means of union between the metal and the ground, ought to be neither too thick nor too fluid; because both these circumstances are equally injurious to delicacy in the strokes; it will be requisite also that the composition should not dry till the artist has completed his design

Other Mordants.

Some prepare their mordants with Jew's pitch and drying oil diluted with essence of turpentine. They employ it for gilding pale gold, or for bronzing.

Other artists imitate the Chinese, and mix with their mordants colors proper for assisting the tone which they are desirous of giving to the gold, such as yellow, red, etc.

Others employ merely fat varnish, to which they add a little red oxide of lead (minium).

Others make use of thick glue, in which they dissolve a little honey. This is what they call *batture*. When they are desirous of heightening the color of the gold, they employ this glue, to which the gold-leaf adheres exceedingly well.

Another.—The qualities of the following are fit for every kind of application, and particularly to metals: Expose boiled oil to a strong heat in a pan; when a black smoke is disengaged from it, set it on fire, and extinguish it a few moments after by putting on the cover of the pan. Then pour the matter still warm into a heated bottle, and add to it a little essence of turpentine. This mordant dries very speedily; it has body and adheres to, and strongly retains, gold-leaf, when applied to wood, metals, and other substances.

To Prepare a Composition for making Colored Drawings and Prints Resemble Paintings in Oil.

Take of Canada balsam, 1 oz.; spirit of turpentine, 2 oz.; mix them together. Before this composition is applied, the drawing or print should be sized with a solution of isinglass in water, and when dry, apply the varnish with a camel's-hair brush.

A Varnish to Color Baskets.

Take either red, black, or white sealing-wax. whichever color you wish to make; to every 2 oz. of sealing-wax, add 1 oz. of spirit of wine; pound the wax fine, then sift it through a fine lawn sieve, till you have made it extremely fine; put it into a large phial with the spirit of wine, shake it, let it stand near the fire 48 hours, shaking it often; then, with a little, brush the baskets all over with it; let them dry, and do them over a second time.

To Prepare Anti-attrition.

According to the specification of the patent, this mixture consists of 1 cwt. of plumbago, to 4 cwt. of hog's lard, or other grease; the two to be well incorporated. The application is to prevent the effects of friction in all descriptions of engines or machines; and a sufficient quantity must be rubbed over the surface of the axle, spindle, or other part where the bearing is.

Liard,

A French lubricating compound, is thus made: Into 50 parts of the finest rape-oil put 1 part of India-rubber, cut into strips, and apply a gentle heat until nearly dissolved.

Varnish for Pales and Coarse Wood-work.

Take any quantity of tar, and grind it with as much Spanish-brown as it will bear, without rendering it too thick to be used as a varnish or varnish, and then spread it on the pales, or other wood, as soon as convenient, for it quickly hardens by keeping.

This mixture must be laid on the wood to be varnished by a hard brush, or house-painter's tool; and the work should then be kept as free from dust and insects as possible, till the varnish is thoroughly dry. It will, if laid on smooth wood, have a very good gloss, and is an excellent preservative of it against moisture; on which account, as well as its being cheaper, it is far preferable to painting, not only for pales, but for weather-boarding, and all other kinds of woodwork for grosser purposes. Where the glossy brown color is not liked, the work may be made of a grayish-brown, by mixing a small proportion of white lead, or whiting and ivory black, with the Spanish-brown. Boiled coal-tar is extensively used for the same purpose.

A Black Varnish for Old Straw or Chip Hats.

Take of best black sealing-wax, ½ oz.; rectified spirit of wine, 2 oz.; powder the sealing-wax, and put it with the spirit of wine into a 4 oz. phial; digest them in a sand-heat, or near a fire, till the wax is dissolved; lay it on warm with a fine soft hair-brush, before a fire or in the sun. It gives a good stiffness to old straw hats, and a beautiful gloss, equal to new, and resists wet.

Flexible Paint.

Take of good yellow soap, cut into slices, 2¼ lbs.; boiling water, 1½ galls. Dissolve, and grind the solution while hot with 1¼ cwt. of good oil-paint. Used to paint on canvas.

Porous Water-proof Cloth.

This quality is given to cloth by simply passing it through a hot solution of weak glue and alum. To apply it to the cloth, make up a weak solution of glue, and while it is hot add a piece of alum (about 1 oz. to 2 qts.), and then brush it over the surface of the cloth while it is hot, and it is afterwards dried. Cloth in pieces may be run through this solution, and then run out of it and dried. By adding a few pieces of soap to the glue, the cloth will feel much softer. Goods in pieces may be run through a tubfull of weak glue, soap, and alum, and squeezed between rollers. This would be a cheap and expeditious mode of preparing them. Woollen goods are prepared by brushing them with the above mixture first in the inside, then with the grain or nap of the cloth; after which it is dried. It is the best to dry this first in the air, and then in a stove-room at a low heat; but allow the cloth to remain for a considerable time, to expel the moisture completely. This kind of cloth, while it is sufficiently water-proof to keep out the moisture and rain, being quite impervious to water, is pervious to the air.

To Thicken Linen Cloth for Screens and Bed-testers.

Grind whiting with zinc (white), and to prevent its cracking add a little honey to it; then take a soft brush and lay it upon the cloth, and so do 2 or 3 times, suffering it the meanwhile to dry between layings on; and for the last laying, smooth it over with Spanish white ground with linseed-oil; the oil being first heated and mixed with a small quantity of the litharge of gold, the better to endure the weather; and so it will be lasting.

Common Wax, or Varnished Cloth.

The manufacture of this kind of cloth is very simple. The cloth and linseed-oil are the principal articles required for the establishment. Common canvas, of an open and coarse texture, is extended on large frames placed under sheds, the sides of which are open, so as to afford a free passage to the external air. The manner in which the cloth is fastened to these frames is as follows: it is fixed to each side of the frame by hooks which catch the edge of the cloth, and by pieces of strong packthread passing through holes at the other extremity of the hooks, which are tied around movable pegs in the lower edge of the frame. The mechanism by which the strings of a violin are stretched or unstretched, will give some idea of the arrangement of the pegs employed for extending the cloth in this apparatus. By these means the cloth can be easily stretched or relaxed, when the oily varnish has exercised an action on its texture in the course of the operation. The whole being thus arranged, a liquid paste made with drying-oil, which may be varied at pleasure, is applied to the cloth.

To make Liquid Paste with Drying-oil.

Mix Spanish white. or tobacco-pipe clay, or any other argillaceous matter with water, and leave it at rest some hours; which will be sufficient to separate the argillaceous parts, and to produce a sediment. Stir the sediment with a broom, to complete the division of the earth; and after it has rested some seconds, decant the turbid water into an earthen or wooden vessel. By this process the earth will be separated from the sand and other foreign bodies, which are precipitated and which must be thrown away. If the earth has been washed by the same process on a large scale, it is divided by kneading it. The supernatant water is thrown aside and the sediment placed in sieves, on pieces of cloth, where it is suffered to drain; it is then mixed up with oil rendered drying by a large dose of litharge, that is about a fourth of the weight of the oil. That consistence of thin paste being given to the mixture, it is spread over the cloth by means of an iron spatula, the length of which is equal to that of the breadth of the cloth. This spatula performs the part of a knife, and pushes forward the excess of matter above the quantity sufficient to cover the cloth. When the first stratum is dry, a second is applied. The inequalities produced by the coarseness of the cloth, or by an unequal extension of the paste, are smoothed down with pumice-stone. The pumice-stone is reduced to powder and rubbed over the cloth with a piece of soft serge or cork dipped in water. The cloth must then be well washed in water to clean it; and after it is dried, a varnish of gum-lac dissolved in linseed-oil boiled with turpentine, is to be applied to it.

This preparation produces yellowish varnished cloth. When wanted black, mix lampblack with the Spanish white or tobacco-pipe clay, which forms the basis of the liquid paste. Various shades of gray may be obtained, according to the quantity of lampblack which is added. Umber, Cologne-earth, and different ochry argillaceous earths, may be used to vary the tints, without causing any addition to the expense.

To prepare Varnished Silk.

Varnished silk, for making umbrellas, capots, coverings for hats, etc., is prepared in the same manner as the varnished and polished cloths already described, but with some variation in the liquid paste or varnish.

If the surface of the silk be pretty large, it is made fast to a wooden frame furnished with hooks and movable pegs, such as that used in the manufacture of common varnished cloths. A soft paste, composed of linseed-oil boiled with a fourth part of litharge; tobacco-pipe clay, dried and sifted through a silk sieve, 16 parts; litharge, ground on porphyry with water, dried and sifted in the same manner, 3 parts, and lampblack, 1 part. This paste is then spread in a uniform manner over the surface of the silk by means of a long knife, having a handle at each extremity. In summer, 24 hours are sufficient for its desiccation. When dry, the knots produced by the inequalities of the silk are smoothed with pumice-stone. This operation is performed with water, and, when finished, the surface of the silk is washed. It is then suffered to dry, and fat copal varnish is applied.

If it be intended to polish this varnish, apply a second stratum, after which polish it with a ball of cloth and very fine tripoli. The varnished silk thus made is very black, exceedingly pliable, and has a fine polish. It may be rumpled a thousand ways without retaining any fold, or even the mark of one. It is light, and therefore proper for coverings to hats, and for making cloaks and caps so useful to travellers in wet weather.

Another Method.

A kind of varnished silk, which has only a yellowish color, and which suffers the texture of the stuff to appear, is prepared with a mixture of 3 parts boiled oil of pinks, or linseed-oil, and 1 part of fat copal varnish, which is extended with a coarse brush or knife. Two strata are sufficient when oil has been freed from its greasy particles over a slow fire, or when boiled with a fourth part of its weight of litharge.

The inequalities are removed by pumice-stone and water, after which the copal varnish is applied. This simple operation gives to white silk a yellow color, which arises from the boiled oil and the varnish.

This varnished silk possesses all those qualities ascribed to certain preparations of silk which are recommended to be worn as jackets by persons subject to rheumatism.

To Prepare Water-proof Boots.

1. Boots and shoes may be rendered impervious to water by the following composition: Take 3 oz. of spermaceti and melt it in a pipkin, or other earthen vessel, over a slow fire; add thereto 6 drs. of India-rubber, cut into slices, and these will presently dissolve. Then add, seriatim, of tallow, 8 oz.; hog's lard, 2 oz.; amber varnish, 4 oz. Mix, and it will be fit for use immediately. The boots or other material to be treated are to receive 2 or 3 coats with a common blacking-brush, and a fine polish is the result.

2. Half-pound of shoemaker's dubbing, ½ pt. of linseed-oil; ½ pt. of solution of India-rubber. Dissolve with a gentle heat (it is very inflammable), and rub on the boots. This will last for several months.

India-rubber Varnish.

Digest India-rubber, cut into small pieces, in benzine for several days, frequently shaking the bottle containing the materials. A jelly will be formed, which will separate from the benzine; this dissolved in the fixed and volatile oils, dries fast, does not crack or shine, unless mixed with some resinous substance.

On Chloroformic Solution of Gutta-percha.

Gutta-percha, in small slices, 1½ oz.; chloroform, 12 fluidounces. To 8 fluidounces of the chloroform contained in a bottle, add the gutta-percha, and shake occasionally till dissolved; then add the carbonate of lead, previously mixed smoothly with the remainder of the chloroform, and, having shaken the whole thoroughly together several times at intervals of ½ hour, set the mixture aside, and let it stand for 10 days, or until the insoluble matter has subsided, and the solution has become limpid, and either colorless or of a slight straw-color. Lastly, decant, and keep the solution in a glass-stopped bottle.

To make Black Japan.

Boiled oil, 1 gall.; umber, 8 oz.; asphaltum, 3 oz. oil of turpentine, as much as will reduce it to the thinness required.

To Preserve Tiles.

After the adoption of glazing, varnishing, etc., to increase the hardness of tiles, tarring has been found completely to stop their pores, and to render them impervious to water. This process is practicable, and not expensive. Lime and tar, whale-oil or dregs of oil, are equally adapted to the purpose, and still cheaper. Tarring is particularly efficacious when tiles are cracked by the frost. It is calculated that the expense of coal-tar for a roof of a middling extent, and supposing such a roof to require one hundredweight, would not exceed 15 dollars.

To Bronze Plaster Figures.

For the ground, after it has been sized and rubbed down, take Prussian blue, verditer and spruce ochre; grind them separately in water, turpentine, or oil, according to the work, and mix them in such proportions as will produce the color desired; then grind Dutch metal in a part of this composition, laying it with judgment on the prominent parts of the figure, which produces a grand effect.

To Polish Varnished Furniture.

Take 2 oz. of tripoli powdered, put it in an earthen pot with water to cover it; then take a piece of white flannel, lay it over a piece of cork or rubber, and proceed to polish the varnish, always wetting it with the tripoli and water. It will be known when the process is finished by wiping a part of the work with a sponge, and observing whether there is a fair even gloss. When this is the case, take a bit of mutton suet and fine flour and clean the work.

To Polish Wood.

Take a piece of pumice-stone and water, and pass regularly over the work until the rising of the grain is cut down; then take powdered tripoli and boiled linseed-oil, and polish the work to a bright surface.

To Polish Brass Ornaments inlaid in Wood.

File the brass very clean with a smooth file; then take some tripoli powdered very fine, and mix it with the linseed oil. Dip in this a rubber of felt, with which polish the work until the desired effect is obtained.

If the work is ebony, or black rosewood, take some elder coal powdered very fine, and apply it dry after you have done with the tripoli, and it will produce a superior polish.

The French mode of ornamenting with brass differs widely from ours; theirs being chiefly water-gilt (or-moulu), excepting the flutes of columns, etc., which are polished very high with rotten-stone, and finished with elder coal.

To Brown Iron and Steel Objects.

Dissolve 2 parts of crystallized chloride of iron, 2 parts of solid chloride of antimony, and 1 part of gallic acid in 4 or 5 parts of water. With this moisten a piece of sponge or cloth and apply to the object, a gun-barrel for instance. Let it dry in the air, and repeat the operation several times; then wash with water; dry, and rub with boiled linseed-oil. Objects browned in this way have a very agreeable dead gray appearance, and the shade deepens according to the number of times the operation is repeated.

To make Blacking.

Take of ivory black and treacle, each 12 oz.; spermaceti oil, 4 oz., white wine vinegar, 4 pts. Mix.

To make Liquid Blacking.

Take of vinegar, No. 18 (the common), 1 qt.; ivory-black and treacle, each 6 oz.; vitriolic acid and spermaceti (or common oil), each 1½ oz.

Mix the acid and oil first, afterwards add the other ingredients; if, when it is used, it does not dry quickly enough on the leather, add a little more of the vitriol, a little at a time, till it dries quickly enough. When there is too much of the vitriolic acid, which is various in its strength, the mixture will give it a brown color.

Vinegar is sold by numbers, viz., No. 18 (the weakest), 19, 20, 21, 22. The celebrated blacking is made with No. 18. When this mixture is properly finished, the ivory-black will be about one-third the contents of the bottle.

To make Bailey's Composition for Blacking-cakes.

Take gum tragacanth, 1 oz.; neat's-foot oil, superfine ivory-black, deep blue, prepared from iron and copper, each 2 oz.; brown sugar candy, river-water, each 4 oz. Having mixed well these ingredients, evaporate the water, and form your cakes.

To make Blacking Balls for Shoes.

Take mutton suet, 4 oz.; bees-wax, 1 oz.; sweet oil, 1 oz.; sugar candy and gum Arabic, 1 dr. each, in fine powder; melt these well together over a gentle fire, and add thereto about a spoonful of turpentine, and lampblack sufficient to give it a good black color. While hot enough to run, make it into a ball by pouring the liquor into a tin mould; or let it stand till almost cold; or it may be moulded by the hand.

To make Liquid Japan Blacking.

Take 3 oz. of ivory-black, 2 oz. of coarse sugar, 1 oz. of sulphuric acid, 1 oz. of muriatic acid, 1 tablespoonful of sweet oil and lemon acid, and 1 pt. of vinegar. First mix the ivory-black and sweet oil together, then the lemon and sugar, with a little vinegar to qualify the blacking; then add the sulphuric and muriatic acids, and mix them all well together.

Observation.—The sugar, oil, and vinegar, prevent the acids from injuring the leather, and add to the lustre of the blacking.

A Cheap Method.

Ivory-black, 2 oz.; brown sugar, 1½ oz.; and sweet oil, ¼ tablespoonful, Mix them well, and then gradually add ½ pt. of small beer.

Another Method.

A quarter lb. of ivory-black, ¼ lb. of moist sugar, a tablespoonful of flour, a piece of tallow about the size of a walnut, and a small piece of gum Arabic. Make a paste of the flour, and while hot put in the tallow, then the sugar, and afterwards mix the whole well together in a quart of water.

India Rubber Blacking (Patent.)

Ivory-black, 60 lbs.; treacle, 45 lbs.; vinegar (No. 24), 20 galls.; powdered gum, 1 lb.; India-rubber oil, 9 lbs. (The latter is made by dissolving by heat 18 oz. of India-rubber in 9 lbs. of rape-oil.) Grind the whole smooth in a paint-mill, then add by small quantities at a time 12 lbs. of oil of vitriol, stirring it strongly for ¼ an hour a day for a fortnight.

To render Leather Water-proof.

This is done by rubbing or brushing into the leather a mixture of drying oils, and any of the oxides of lead, copper, or iron; or by substituting any of the gummy resins in the room of the metallic oxides.

To make Varnish for Colored Drawings.

Take of Canada balsam, 1 oz.; spirit of turpentine, 2 oz. Mix them together. Before this composition is applied, the drawing or print should be sized with a solution of isinglass in water; and when dry apply the varnish with a camel's-hair brush.

To make Furniture Paste.

Scrape 4 oz. of beeswax into a basin, and add as much oil of turpentine as will moisten it through. Now powder a ¼ oz. of resin, and add as much Indian red as will bring it to a deep mahogany color. When the composition is properly stirred up, it will prove an excellent cement or paste for blemishes in mahogany and other furniture.

Another Method.

Scrape 4 oz. of beeswax as before. To a pint of oil of turpentine, in a glazed pipkin, add an ounce of alkanet-root. Cover it close and put it over a slow fire, attending it carefully that it may not boil over, or catch fire. When the liquid is of a deep red, add as much of it to the wax as will moisten it through, also a quarter of an ounce of powdered resin. Cover the whole close, and let it stand 6 hours, when it will be fit for use.

To make Furniture Oil.

Take linseed-oil, put it into a glazed pipkin with as much alkanet-root as it will cover. Let it boil gently, and it will become of a strong red color; when cool it will be fit for use.

To make Wash for Preserving Drawings made with a Black Lead Pencil.

A thin wash of isinglass will fix either black lead, or hard black chalk, so as to prevent their rubbing out; or the same effect may be produced by the simple application of skimmed milk, as has been proved by frequent trials. The best way of using the latter is to lay the drawing flat upon the surface of the milk; and then taking it up by one corner till it drains and dries. The milk must be perfectly free from cream, or it will grease the paper.

To make Varnish for Wood, which Resists the Action of Boiling Water.

Take 1½ lbs. of linseed-oil, and boil it in a red copper vessel, not tinned, holding suspended over it, in a small linen bag, 5 oz. of litharge and 3 oz. of pulverized minium; taking care that the bag does not touch the bottom of the vessel. Continue the ebullition until the oil acquires a deep brown color, then take away the bag and substitute another in its place, containing a clove of garlic; continue the ebullition and renew the clove of garlic 7 or 8 times, or rather put them all in at once.

Then throw into the vessel 1 lb. of yellow amber, after having melted it in the following manner: Add to the pound of amber, well pulverized, 2 oz. of linseed oil, and place the whole on a strong fire. When the fusion is complete, pour it boiling into the prepared linseed-oil, and continue to leave it boiling for 2 or 3 minutes, stirring the whole up well. It is then left to settle; the composition is decanted and preserved, when it becomes cold, in well-corked bottles.

After polishing the wood on which this varnish is to be applied, you give to the wood the color required; for instance, for walnut-wood, a slight coat of a mixture of soot with the essence of turpentine. When this color is perfectly dry, give it a coat of varnish with a fine sponge. In order to spread it very equally, repeat these coats four times, taking care always to let the preceding coat be dried.

To Restore the Blackness of old Leather Chairs, etc.

Many families, especially in the country, possess chairs, settees, etc. covered with black leather. These, impaired by long use, may be restored nearly to their original good color and gloss by the following easy and approved process: Take yolks of 2 newly-laid eggs and the white of one. Let these be well beaten up, and then shaken in a glass vessel or jug, to become like thick oil; dissolve in about a tablespoonful or less of geneva, an ordinary tea-lump of loaf-sugar; make this thick with ivory black, well worked up with a bit of stick; mix with the egg for use. Let this be laid on as blacking ordinarily is for shoes; after a very few minutes, polish with a soft, very clean brush, till completely dry and shining, then let it remain a day to harden.

The same process answers admirably for ladies' or gentlemen's dress-shoes, but with the following addition for protecting the stockings from soil. Let the white or glair of eggs be shaken in a large glass phial until it becomes a perfect oil, brush over the inner edges of the shoes with it, and when completely dry, it will prevent all soiling from the leather. This requires to be repeated.

Transparent Ivory.

The process for making ivory transparent and flexible is simply immersion in liquid phosphoric acid, and the change which it undergoes is owing to a partial neutralization of the basic phosphate of lime, of which it principally consists. The ivory is cut in pieces not thicker than the twentieth part of an inch, and placed in phosphoric acid of a specific gravity of 1.131, until it has become transparent, when it is taken from the bath, washed in water, and dried with a clean linen cloth. It becomes dry in the air without the application of heat, and softens again under warm water.

Bleaching of Ivory.

Ivory knife-handles which have become quite yellow from use, being left for from 2 to 4 hours in a watery solution of sulphurous acid, become quite white again. The acid in the gaseous form makes the ivory crack.

To Varnish Drawings and Card Work.

Boil some clear parchment cuttings in water, in a glazed pipkin, till they produce a very clear size. Strain it and keep it for use.

Give the work 2 coats of the size, passing the brush quickly over the work, not to disturb the colors.

To make Turpentine Varnish.

Mix 1 gall. of oil of turpentine and 5 lbs. of powdered resin; put it in a tin can, on a stove, and let it boil for ½ an hour. When cool it is fit for use.

Manufacture of Papier-Maché.

There are at present five principal varieties of papier-maché known in the trade, viz.: 1. Sheets of paper pasted together upon models. 2. Thick sheets or boards produced by pressing ordinary paper pulp between dies. 3. *Fibrous slab*, which is made of the coarse varieties of fibre only, mixed with some earthy matter, and certain chemical agents introduced for the purpose of rendering the mass incombustible. A cementing size is added, and the whole well kneaded together with the aid of steam. The kneaded mass is passed repeatedly through iron rollers, which squeeze it out to a perfectly uniform thickness. It is then dried at a proper temperature. 4. *Carton pierre*, which is made of pulp or paper mixed with whiting and glue, pressed into plaster piece-moulds, backed with paper, and, when sufficiently set, hardened by drying in a hot room. 5. *Martin's Ceramic Papier-Maché*, a new composition, patented in 1858, which consists of paper pulp, resin, glue, drying oil, and sugar of lead, mixed in certain fixed proportions and kneaded together. This composition is extremely plastic, and may be worked, pressed, or moulded into any required form. It may be preserved in this plastic condition for several months by keeping the air away, and occasionally kneading the mass.

The first-mentioned variety of *papier-maché* alone engages our attention here. A special kind of paper, of a porous texture, is manufactured for this purpose. An iron mould, of somewhat smaller size than the object required, is greased with Russian tallow. A sheet of the paper is laid on to the greased surface of the mould, and covered over with a coat of paste made of the best biscuit-flower and glue, which is spread evenly all over the sheet with the hands; another sheet is then laid on, and rubbed down evenly, so that the two sheets are closely pasted together at all points. After this the mould is taken to the drying chamber, where it is exposed to a temperature of about 120°. When quite dry, which it takes several hours to accomplish, it is carried back to the pasting-room, and another sheet is laid on, with another coat of paste, after which it is returned to the drying chamber; and the same operation is repeated over and over again, until a sufficient thickness is attained, which, for superior articles, such as are manufactured at these works, requires from 30 to 40 sheets of paper, and of course as many coats of paste between. The shell is then removed from the mould, and planed to shape with a carpenter's plane, after which it is dipped in linseed-oil and spirits of tar to harden it; this changes the color from gray to a dingy yellowish-brown tint. The article is then stoved, and 7 or 8 coats of varnish are laid on (with a stoving after each), which are cleared off each time, any equalities of surface being finally removed with pumice-stone. The number of drying processes the articles have to go through consume so much time, that it takes 3 or 4 weeks to fit them for ornamentation, which is applied in bronze-powder, gold, or color, and, for many articles, also in mother-of-pearl. The ornamentation of these articles is sometimes effected in the highest style of the painter's art.

The gold-leaf is laid on with a solution of isinglass in water, the design then pencilled on with asphaltum, the superfluous gold removed with a dossil of cotton dipped in water, which leaves intact the parts touched with asphaltum, and the latter finally removed with essence of turpentine.

After the application of every coat of color or varnish, the object so colored or varnished is dried in an oven or chamber, called a stove, and heated by flues to as high a temperature as can safely be employed without injuring the articles, or causing the varnish to blister.

For black grounds, drop ivory-black mixed with dark-colored anime varnish is used; for colored grounds, the ordinary painters' colors, ground with linseed-oil or turpentine, and mixed with anime varnish.

The colors are protected against atmospheric influences, and made to shine with greater brilliancy, by 2 or 3 coats of copal or anime varnish. Superior articles receive as many as 5 or 6 coats of varnish, and are finally polished.

The ornamentation of all such articles as come under the head of toilet wares is effected by the ordinary mode of painting with the camel's-hair pencil, or some fitting substitute; where imitation of woods or marble is intended, the ordinary grainers' tools are used. Many patterns are produced upon the various articles by "transfer printing." Designs in mother-of-pearl are laid on with black varnish; the article is then varnished all over, dried, then rubbed down over the design with pumice-stone; another coat of varnish is then laid on, dried, and the part covering the design again rubbed off with pumice-stone; and thus several coats are laid on, until all the surface is level with that of the design. Ornamental lines, writing, etc., are laid on with color. The inlaying with mother-of-pearl is a laborious business, owing to the small size of the pieces at the artist's disposal, and the necessity of attending to a proper distribution and fitting of lights and shades.

On a Black Varnish for Zinc.

M. Bœttger describes a process for covering zinc with a chemical, adherent, velvet-black varnish. Dissolve 2 parts by weight of nitrate of copper and 3 parts of crystallized chloride in 64 parts of distilled water; add 8 parts of hydrochloric acid of 1·10 density. Into this liquid plunge the zinc, previously scoured with fine sand; then wash the metal with water, and dry it rapidly.

Protection of Iron and Steel.

Moderately-heated benzine dissolves half its weight of wax; and if this solution be carefully applied to the tool with a brush, the evaporation leaves a very adhesive and permanent coating of wax, which will preserve the metal even from the action of acid vapors.

Varnish used for Indian Shields.

Shields made in Silhet, in Bengal, are noted throughout India, for the lustre and durability of the black varnish with which they are covered. Silhet shields constitute, therefore, no inconsiderable article of traffic, being in request among natives who carry arms, and retain the ancient predilection for the scimitar and buckler. The varnish is composed of the expressed juice of the marking-nut, *Semecarpus anacardium*, and that of another kindred fruit, *Holigarna longifolia*.

The shell of the *Semecarpus anacardium* contains between its integuments numerous cells, filled with a black, acrid, resinous juice, which likewise is found, though less abundantly, in the wood of the tree. It is commonly employed as an indelible ink, to mark all sorts of cotton cloth. The color is fixed with quicklime. The cortical part of the fruit of *Holigarna longifolia* likewise contains between its laminæ numerous cells, filled with a black, thick, acrid fluid. The natives of Malabar extract by incision, with which they varnish targets.

To prepare the varnish according to the method practised in Silhet, the nuts of the *Semecarpus anacardium*, and the berries of the *Holigarna longifolia*, having been steeped for a month in clear water, are cut transversely, and pressed in a mill. The expressed juice of each is kept for several months, taking off the scum from time to time. Afterwards the liquor is decanted, and two parts of the one are added to one part of the other, to be used as varnish. Other proportions of ingredients are sometimes employed, but in all the resinous juice of the *Semecarpus* predominates. The varnish is laid on like paint, and when dry is polished by rubbing it with an agate or smooth pebble. This varnish also prevents destruction of wood. etc. by the white ant.

To Varnish Silver Leaf like Gold.

Fix the leaf on the subject, similar to gold leaf, by the interposition of proper glutinous matters; spread the varnish upon the piece with a pencil. When the first coat is dry wash the piece again and again with the varnish till the color appears sufficiently deep. What is called gilt-leather, and many picture-frames, have no other than this gilding; washing them with a little rectified spirit of wine affords a proof of this, the spirit dissolving the varnish, and leaving the silver-leaf of its own whiteness. For plain frames thick tin-foil may be used instead of silver. The tin-leaf, fixed on the piece with glue, is to be burnished, then polished with emery and a fine linen cloth, and afterwards with putty applied in the same manner; being then lacquered over with varnish 5 or 6 times, it looks very nearly like burnished gold. The same varnish, made with a less proportion of coloring materials, is applied also on works of brass, both for heightening the color of the metal to a resemblance with that of gold, and for preserving it from being tarnished by the air.

To Recover Varnish.

Clear off the filth with a lye made of potash, and

the ashes of the lees of wine; then take 48 oz. of potash and 16 of the above mentioned ashes, and put them into 6 qts. of water, and this completes the lye.

To Polish Varnish.

This is effected with pumice-stone and tripoli earth. The pumice-stone must be reduced to an impalpable powder, and put upon a piece of serge moistened with water: with this rub lightly and equally the varnish substance. The tripoli must also be reduced to a very fine powder, and put upon a clean woollen cloth, moistened with olive-oil, with which the polishing is to be performed. The varnish is then to be wiped off with soft linen, and when quite dry cleaned with starch or Spanish white, and rubbed with the palm of the hand.

Process for giving various Objects a Pearly Lustre.

To produce the iridescence of mother-of-pearl on stone, glass, metal, resin, paper, silk, leather, etc., Reinsch adopts the following process: 2 parts of solution of copal, 2 parts of that of sandarac, and 4 parts of solution of Damara resin (equal parts of resin and absolute alcohol) are mixed with half their volume of oil of bergamot or rosemary. This mixture is to be evaporated to the thickness of castor-oil. If this varnish be then drawn, by means of a feather or brush, over the surface of some water, it will form a beautiful iridescent pellicle. This film is now to be applied to the objects which are to be rendered iridescent. The vessel in which the water is contained, on which the pellicle has been produced, must therefore be as large as or larger than these objects. The water should have about 5 per cent. of pure solution of lime added to it; its temperature should be kept at about 72°. The objects are dried in the air.

To Prevent the Formation of Fungi in Timber.

The following paint has been found successful: Flour of sulphur, 3088 grs.; common linseed-oil, 2084 grs.; refined oil of manganese, 463 grs.

Prevention of Rotting of Wood.

Take 50 parts of rosin, 40 of finely powdered chalk, 300 parts or less of fine, white, sharp sand, 4 parts of linseed-oil, 1 part of native red oxide of copper, and 1 part of sulphuric acid. First heat the rosin, chalk, sand and oil, in an iron boiler; then add the oxide, and, with care, the acid. Stir the composition carefully, and apply while hot. If too thick, add more oil. This coating, when cold and dry, forms a varnish hard as stone.

CEMENTS.

Hydraulic Mortar.

Slaked lime, 1 bu.; calcined clay, 1¼ bu.; washed sand, 1¼ bu.

Concrete.

Unslaked lime, 3 bu.; sand, 3 bu.; gravel, 2 bu.; broken stone, 4 bu.

Cement.

Hydraulic cement, 6 bu. (6-5 London, or 2 New York bbl.); sand, 6 bu. This amount will suffice to lay 1,000 bricks or 2 perches of stone.

Mortars.

1. Stone lime (unslaked), 1 bu.; sand, 3 bu.
2. Stone lime (unslaked), 1 bu.; gravel, 10 bu.

Beton

Is superior, in every respect, to concrete. It is made in the same way, using hydraulic instead of common mortar.

Mastic.

Sand, 100 lbs.; marble-dust, 100 lbs.; freestone, 100 lbs.; red lead (minium), 3 lbs.; litharge, 3 lbs.; linseed-oil, 21 pts.

Genuine Roman Cement,

Or pozzuolana, from the neighborhood of Vesuvius, is a peculiar mixture of silica, clay, and lime, which has been calcined by the volcano. It is used mixed with lime and sand. The following is the formula of Vitruvius: 12 parts pozzuolana well powdered, 6 sharp sand well washed, 9 rich lime, recently slaked. It has the power of rapidly hardening under water.

Artificial Portland Cement.

One hundred lbs. of pure, dry chalk is moistened and ground in a mill with excess of water; to this is added 137½ lbs. of pure alluvial clay, and the two are thoroughly incorporated. The mixture is made into balls, which are dried and calcined in an ordinary lime-kiln.

Rosendale Cement

Is made by calcining the limestone or cement-stone, found above the Potsdam sandstone and below the Utica slate of the New York survey. It consists of silica, magnesia, alumina, oxide of iron, with some salts of potash and soda. The stone is found in eastern New York, New Jersey, Pennsylvania and Virginia.

Artificial Hydraulic Cements

Are made 1, by combining thoroughly slaked lime with from 10 to 40 per cent. unburnt clay, and burning the mixture in a kiln; 2, by grinding clay and chalk as directed above for Portland Cement; 3, by making artificial pozzuolana from calcareous sand and clay, and calcining it; 4, by the use of silicate of soda: 8 or 10 per cent. of a solution of the consistence of thin syrup, is to be mixed with mortar of fat lime.

Cement for Rooms.

A coat of oxide of zinc (zinc white) mixed with size, is applied to the wall, ceiling or wainscot; over this, one of chloride of zinc, prepared in the same way. The two unite and form a cement smooth and polished as glass.

Parolic Cement.

Take unsalted curd of skimmed milk, press the whey out, dry and pulverize, and warm over a stove. Of this, 90 parts; caustic quicklime, in fine powder, 10 parts; powdered camphor, 1 part. Mix intimately and keep in small bottles corked perfectly tight. To use, mix the required amount with water with a palette-knife, and apply immediately.

To make Cement for Floors.

Earthen floors are commonly made of loam; and sometimes, especially to make malt on, of lime and brook-sand, and gun-dust or anvil-dust from the forge. The manner of making earthen floors for plain country habitations is as follows: take ⅔ lime and ⅓ coal-ashes well sifted, with a small quantity of loam clay; mix the whole together and temper it well with water, making it up into a heap; let it lie a week or 10 days and then temper it over again. After this, heap it up for 3 or 4 days, and repeat the tempering very high till it becomes smooth, yielding, tough and gluey. The ground being then levelled, lay the floor therewith about 2½ or 3 in. thick, making it smooth with a trowel. The hotter the season is, the better; and when it is thoroughly dried, it will make the best floor for houses, especially malt-houses.

Pew's Composition for Roofing Buildings.

Take the hardest and purest limestone (white marble is to be preferred), free from sand, clay or other matter; calcine it in a reverberatory furnace, pulverize and pass through a sieve. One part, by weight, is to be mixed with 2 parts of clay well baked and similarly pulverized, conducting the whole operation with great care. This forms the first powder. The second is to be made of 1 part of calcined and pulverized gypsum, to which is added 2 parts of clay baked and pulverized. These two powders are to be combined and intimately incorporated, so as to form a perfect mixture. When it is to be used, mix it with about ¼ part of its weight of water, added gradually, stirring the mass well the whole time, until it forms a thick paste, in which state it is to be spread like mortar upon the desired surface. It becomes in time as hard as stone, allows no moisture to penetrate, and is not cracked by heat. When well prepared it will last any length of time. When in its plastic or soft state, it may be colored of any desired tint.

Zeiodelite.

Zeiodelite is made by mixing together 19 lbs. of sulphur and 42 lbs. of pulverized stoneware and glass. The mixture is exposed to a gentle heat, which melts the sulphur, and then the mass is stirred till it becomes thoroughly homogeneous, when it is run into suitable moulds and allowed to cool. This preparation is proof against acids in general, whatever their degree of concentration, and will last an indefinite time. It melts at about 248°, and may be re-employed without loss of any of its qualities, whenever it is desirable to change the form of an apparatus, by melting at a gentle heat and operating as with asphalte. At 230° it becomes as compact as stone, and therefore preserves its solidity in boiling water. Slabs of zeiodelite may be joined by introducing between them some of the paste heated to 392°, which will melt the edges of the slabs, and when the whole becomes cold it will present one uniform piece. Chambers lined with zeiodelite, in place of lead, the inventor says, will enable manufacturers to produce acids free from nitrate and sulphate of lead. The cost will be only one-fifth the price of lead. The compound is also said to be superior to hydraulic lime for uniting stone and resisting the action of water.

To make Cement for Canals.

Take 1 part of iron filings, reduced to sifted powder, 3 parts of silica, 4 parts of red clay, the same quantity of pulverized brick, and 2 parts of hot lime; the whole measured by weight and not by bulk.

Put the mixture into a large wooden tub, in order that nothing foreign may be introduced into it. If sufficient water is poured out to extinguish the lime and give a degree of liquidness to the cement, and if all the component parts are briskly stirred, a great degree of heat will be emitted from the lime, and an intimate union formed by the heat.

Cement for Cast-Iron.

In mixing cement for cast-iron, put 1 oz. of sal ammoniac to each hundredweight of borings, and use it without allowing it to heat. Multiply the length of any joint in ft. by the breadth in in., by the thickness in eighths, and by 3; the product will be the weight of dry borings, in lbs. avoirdupois, required to make cement to fill that joint nearly.

Or, take of sal ammoniac, 2 oz.; flowers of sulphur, 1 oz.; clean cast-iron borings or filings, 16 oz.; mix them well in a mortar, and keep them dry. When required for use, take 1 part of this powder and 20 parts of clean iron borings or filings, mix thoroughly in a mortar, make the mixture into a stiff paste with a little water, and apply it between the joints, and screw them together. A little fine grindstone sand added improves the cement.

A mixture of white paint with red lead, spread on canvas or woollen, and placed between the joints, is best adapted for joints that require to be often separated.

In 100 lbs. of iron borings mix 1 oz. of flowers of sulphur, and add 1 oz. of sal ammoniac, dissolved in hot water.

To Preserve for Use.

Pack it close in an iron vessel, and cover with water.

For Mending Iron Retorts.

Fifteen lbs. fire-clay, 1 lb. saleratus, with water sufficient to make a thick paste. This mixture must be applied to the broken part of the retort when the retort is at a good working heat; after this has been done, cover it with fine coal dust, and charge the retort for working.

Cement for Rock-work and Reservoirs.

Where a great quantity of cement is wanted for coarser uses, the coal-ash mortar (or Welsh tarras) is the cheapest and best, and will hold extremely well, not only where it is constantly kept wet or dry, but even where it is sometimes dry and at others wet; but where it is liable to be exposed to wet and frost, this cement should, at its being laid on, be suffered to dry thoroughly before any moisture has access to it; and, in that case, it will likewise be a great improvement to temper it with the blood of any beast.

The mortar must be formed of 1 part lime and 2 parts of well-sifted coal-ashes, and they must be thoroughly mixed by being beaten together; for on the perfect commixture of the ingredients the goodness of the composition depends.

To make Mortar.

Mortar is composed of quicklime and sand, reduced to a paste with water. The lime ought to be pure, completely free from carbonic acid, and in the state of a very fine powder; the sand should be free from clay, partly in the state of fine sand, and partly in that of gravel; the water should be pure, and, if previously saturated with lime, so much the better. The best proportions are 3 parts of fine, and 4 parts of coarse sand, 1 part of quicklime, recently slaked, and as little water as possible. There should always be enough water added *at first*; if water is added after the slaking has begun, it will be chilled and the mortar lumpy.

The addition of burnt bones improves mortar by giving it tenacity and renders it less apt to crack in drying; but they ought never to exceed ¼ of the lime employed.

When a little manganese is added to mortar, it acquires the important property of hardening under water; so that it may be employed in constructing those edifices which are constantly exposed to the action of water. Limestone is often combined with manganese; in that case it becomes brown by calcination.

Tunisian Cement.

This is composed of 3 parts of lime, 1 of sand, and 2 of wood-ashes; these ingredients are mixed up with oil and water alternately, till they compose a paste of the desired consistency.

Water-cement, or Stucco.

Take 56 lbs. of pure coarse sand, 42 lbs. of pure fine sand; mix them together, and moisten them thoroughly with lime-water; to the wetted sand add 14 lbs. of pure fresh-burnt lime, and while beating them up together add, in successive portions, 14 lbs. of bone-ash. The quicker and more perfectly these materials are beaten together, and the sooner they are used, the better will be the cement; for some kinds of work it will be better to use fine sand alone, and for others coarse sand, remembering the finer the sand is the greater quantity of lime is to be employed.

To make a Fire and Water-proof Cement.

To ½ pt. of vinegar add the same quantity of milk; separate the curd, and mix the whey with the whites of 5 eggs; beat it well together, and sift into it a sufficient quantity of quicklime, to convert it to the consistency of a thick paste. Broken vessels mended with this cement never afterwards separate, for it resists the action of both fire and water.

Turkish Cement for Joining Metals, Glass, etc.

Dissolve mastic in as much spirit of wine as will suffice to render it liquid; in another vessel dissolve as much isinglass (which has been previously soaked in water till it is swollen and soft) in brandy as will make 2 oz. by measure of strong glue, and add two small bits of gum-galbanum or ammoniacum, which must be rubbed or ground till they are dissolved; then mix the whole with a sufficient heat; keep it in a phial stopped, and when it is to be used set it in hot water.

Solution of India-rubber.

A solution of caoutchouc, or India-rubber, for repairing india-rubber shoes, is prepared in the following manner: Cut 2 lbs. of caoutchouc into thin, small slices; put them in a vessel of tinned sheet-iron, and pour over 12 to 14 lbs. of sulphide of carbon. For the promotion of solution place the vessel in another containing water previously heated up to about 86° Fahr. The solution will take place promptly, but the fluid will thicken very soon, and thus render the application difficult, if not impossible. In order to prevent this thickening and difficulty, a solution of caoutchouc and rosin (colophony) in spirits of turpentine must be added to the solution of caoutchouc in sulphide of carbon, and in such quantity that the mixture obtains the consistency of a thin paste. The solution of caoutchouc and rosin in spirit of turpentine should be prepared as follows: Cut 1 lb. of caoutchouc into thin, small slices; beat them in a suitable vessel over a moderate coal fire, until the caoutchouc becomes fluid; then add ½ lb. of powdered rosin, and melt both materials at a moderate heat. When these materials are perfectly fluid, then gradually add 3 or 4 lbs. of spirit of turpentine in small portions, and stir well. By the addition of the last solution, the rapid thickening and hardening of the compound will be prevented, and a mixture obtained fully answering the purpose of gluing together rubber surfaces, etc.

Marine Glue.

Cut 3 parts India-rubber into small pieces, and dissolve it by heat and agitation in 34 parts of cold naphtha, chloroform, or benzine; add to this 64 parts of powdered shellac, and heat the whole with constant stirring until the shellac is dissolved; then pour it while hot on metal plates, to form sheets. When used it must be heated to 248° Fahr., and applied with a brush.

Water-proof Glue.

Fine shreds of India-rubber dissolved in warm copal varnish, make a water-proof cement for wood and leather.

Another.—Glue, 12 oz.; water, sufficient to dissolve it; add 3 oz. of rosin, melt them together, and add 4 parts of turpentine or benzine. This should be done in a carpenter's glue-pot, to avoid burning.

A New Cement.

M. Edmund Davy prepares a new cement, which is well spoken of, by melting in an iron vessel equal parts of common pitch and gutta-percha. It is kept either liquid under water, or solid to be melted when wanted. It is not attacked by water, and adheres firmly to wood, stone, glass, porcelain, ivory, leather, parchment-paper, feathers, wool, cotton, hemp, and linen fabrics, and even to varnish.

Aquaria Cement.

One part, by measure, of litharge; 1 part plaster of Paris; 1 part fine beach-sand; ½ part fine powdered rosin; mix all together. This may be kept for years, while dry, in a well-corked bottle; when used, make in a putty with boiled linseed-oil; a little patent dryer may be used; it will stand water at once, either salt or fresh.

New Gutta-percha Cements.

For uniting sheet gutta-percha to silk or other fabrics: Gutta-percha, 40 lbs.; caoutchouc, 3 lbs.; shellac, 3 lbs.; Canada balsam, or Venice turpentine, 14 lbs.; liquid styrax, 35 lbs.; gum mastic, 4 lbs.; oxide of lead, 1 lb.

For uniting sheet gutta-percha to leather, as soles of shoes, etc.: Gutta-percha, 50 lbs.; Venice turpentine, 40 lbs.; shellac, 4 lbs.; caoutchouc, 1 lb.; liquid styrax, 5 lbs.

Metallic Cement.

A metallic cement, which answers for all purposes and becomes hard in the heat, may be obtained in the following way: One hundred parts of oxide of zinc, with the same quantity of sulphate of lead, are triturated with 30 parts of linseed-oil, and then a mixture consisting of 100 parts of black oxide of manganese and 100 parts of peroxide of iron added until the mass forms a stiff dough. This is beaten in a mortar for 12 hours, during which the remainder of the above mixture of iron and manganese is added by degrees. The goodness of the cement may be recognized by its not crumbling when rolled out between the fingers.

Cement for Stoneware, by M. Heller.

Gelatine is allowed to swell in cold water, the jelly warmed, and so much recently-slaked lime added as is requisite to render the mass sufficiently thick for the purpose. A thin coating of this cement is spread while warm over the gently-heated surfaces of fracture of the articles, and let dry under a strong pressure. What oozes out is removed directly with a moist rag.

Yates' Water-proof Cement.

Take of the best glue 4 oz.; of isinglass, 2 oz., and dissolve them in mild ale over a slow fire, in a common glue-kettle, to the consistency of strong glue, when 1½ oz. of well boiled linseed-oil must be gradually added, and the whole be well mixed by stirring. When cold and made into cakes it

GLUE.

resembles India-rubber. When wanted for use, dissolve a piece of it in a proportionate quantity of ale. This cement is applicable to all joints of wood, to join earthenware, china, glass. It is an excellent cement for leather, for harness, bands for machinery, etc. The joints of these are to be prepared as if for sewing, the cement to be applied hot, laying a weight upon each joint as it is made, in which state it is to be left 6 hours, when the joints will be found nearly as firm as if they were of an entire piece. By adding a little tow to the above, you have an excellent cement for leaks in casks, etc., etc.

Common Cement for Joining Alabaster, Marble, Porphyry, and other Stones.

Take of beeswax 2 lbs., and of resin 1 lb.; melt them, and add 1½ lbs. of the same kind of matter, powdered, as the body to be cemented is composed of, strewing it into the melted mixture, and stirring them well together, and afterwards kneading the mass in water, that the powder may be thoroughly incorporated with the wax and resin. The proportion of the powdered matter may be varied where required, in order to bring the cement nearer to the color of the body on which it is employed.

This cement must be heated when applied, as also the parts of the subject to be cemented together, and care must be taken, likewise, that they may be thoroughly dry.

To make Lutes.

These are used for securing the juncture of vessels in distillations and sublimations. For the distillation of water, linen dipped in a thin paste of flour and water is sufficient. A lute of greater security is composed of quicklime, made into a paste with the whites of eggs. For the security of very corrosive vapors, clay finely powdered and sifted, made into a paste with boiled linseed-oil, must be applied to the juncture, which must be afterwards covered with slips of linen, dipped in the paste of quicklime and the whites of eggs. The lute must be perfectly dried before the vessels are used, or else the heat may cause the lute to dry too quickly, and thereby cause the lute to crack. If this be the case, it is repaired by applying fresh lute in the cracks, and suffering it to dry gradually. Vessels which are to be exposed to the naked fire are frequently coated to resist the effects of the heat, the best coating for which purpose consists in dissolving 2 oz. of borax in 1 pt. of boiling water, and adding to the solution as much slaked lime as is necessary to form a thick paste. The vessel must be covered all over with it by means of a painter's brush, and then suffered to dry. It must then be covered with a thin paste of linseed-oil and slaked lime, except the neck. In 2 or 3 days it will dry of itself, and the retort will then bear the greatest fire without cracking. The cracks of chemical vessels may be secured by the second lute.

To make Portable Glue.

Take 1 lb. of the best glue, boil and strain it very clear; boil likewise 4 oz. of isinglass, put it in a double glue-pot, with ½ lb. of fine brown sugar, and boil it pretty thick; then pour it into moulds; when cold, cut and dry them in small pieces. This glue is very useful to draughtsmen, architects, etc., as it immediately dilutes in warm water, and fastens the paper without the process of damping.

To make Glue that will Resist Moisture.

Dissolve gum sandarac and mastic, of each, 2 oz., in 1 pt. of spirit of wine, adding about 1 oz. of clear turpentine. Then take equal parts of isinglass and parchment glue, made according to the directions in the preceding article, and having beaten the isinglass into small bits, and reduced the glue to the same state, pour the solution of the gums upon them, and melt the whole in a vessel well covered, avoiding so great a heat as that of boiling water. When melted, strain the glue through a coarse linen cloth, and then put it again over the fire, adding about 1 oz. of powdered glass.

This preparation may be best managed by hanging the vessel in boiling water, which will prevent the matter burning to the vessel, or the spirit of wine from taking fire, and indeed it is better to use the same method for all the evaporation of nicer glues and sizes; but, in that case, less water than the proportion directed, should be added to the materials.

Another Method.

A very strong glue, that will resist water, may be also made by adding ½ lb. of common glue, or isinglass glue, to 2 qts. of skimmed milk, and then evaporating the mixture to the due consistence of the glue.

To make Parchment Glue.

Take 1 lb. of parchment, and boil it in 6 qts. of water, till the quantity be reduced to 1 qt.; strain off the fluid from the dregs, and then boil it again till it be of the consistence of glue.

The same may be done with glovers' cuttings of leather, which make a colorless glue, if not burnt in the evaporation of the water.

A very Strong Compound Glue.

Take common glue in very small or thin bits, and isinglass glue; infuse them in as much spirit of wine as will cover them, for at least 24 hours. Then melt the whole together, and, while they are over the fire, add as much powdered chalk as will render them an opake white.

The infusion in the spirit of wine has been directed in the recipes given for glue; but the remark on the use of it in one of the preceding articles will hold good also in this, and the mixture may be made with water only.

To make Compound Glue.

Take very fine flour, mix it with white of eggs, isinglass, and a little yeast; mingle the materials, beat them well together; spread them, the batter being made thin with gum-water, on even tin plates, and dry them in a stove, then cut them out for use. To color them, tinge the paste with Brazil, or vermilion for red; indigo or verditer, etc., for blue; saffron, turmeric, or gamboge, etc., for yellow.

To make Isinglass Glue.

This is made by dissolving beaten isinglass in water by boiling, and having strained it through a coarse linen cloth, evaporating it again to such a consistence, that, being cold, the glue will be perfectly hard and dry.

A great improvement is made in this glue by adding spirit of wine or brandy after it is strained, and then renewing the evaporation till it gains the due consistence.

To make Isinglass Size.

This may also be prepared in the manner above directed for the glue, by increasing the proportion of the water for dissolving it, and the same holds good of parchment size. A better sort of the common size may be likewise made by treated cuttings of glovers' leather in the same manner.

To make Flour Paste.

Paste is formed principally of wheaten flour boiled in water till it be of a glutinous or viscid consistence. It may be prepared with those ingredients simply for common purposes; but when it is used by bookbinders, or for paper-hangings to rooms, it is usual to mix a fourth, fifth, or sixth of the weight of the flour of powdered resin; and where it is wanted still more tenacious, gum arabic or any kind of size may be added.

To make Chinese Paste.

Mix together bullock's blood and quicklime, in the proportion of 1 lb. of the latter to 10 lbs. of the former. It becomes a stiff jelly, in which state it is sold to the consumers, who heat it down with an addition of water, into a state sufficiently fluid for use.

To Weld Tortoise-shell.

Provide a pair of pincers, the tongs of which will reach 4 inches beyond the rivet. Now file the tortoise-shell clean to a lap-joint, carefully observing that there be no grease about it. Wet the joint with water; apply the pincers hot, following them with water, and the shell will be found to be joined, as if it were originally one piece.

Gas-Fitters' Cement.

Rosin, 5 lbs.; beeswax, 1 lb.; red ochre, 1 lb.; plaster of Paris, 3 oz. Finely-powdered brickdust may be used instead of the red ochre and plaster.

Turners' Cement.

Soft rosin, 8 oz.; wax, 1 oz.; pitch, 1 oz.; red ochre, ½ oz.; hard shellac, 2 oz.; powdered pumice, 1 oz.

Opticians' Cement.

Sifted wood-ashes, 1 oz.; melted pitch, 3½ oz.

Lapidaries' Cement.

Rosin, 10 oz.; beeswax, 1 oz.; tallow, ¼ oz.; red ochre, ½ oz.

British Gum.

Take 1000 lbs. of starch, moisten with a mixture of 300 lbs. of water, and 2 lbs. of nitric acid, allow it to dry spontaneously, and heat for 1 or 2 hours in stoves, at a temperature of 212° to 230° Fahr.

Preparing Glue for Ready Use.

1. To any quantity of glue use common whiskey insteady of water. Put both together in a bottle, cork it tight, and set it for 3 or 4 days, when it will be fit for use without the application of heat. Glue thus prepared will keep for years, and is at all times fit for use, except in very cold weather, when it should be set in warm water before using. To obviate the difficulty of the stopper getting tight by the glue drying in the mouth of the vessel, use a tin vessel, with the cover fitting tight on the outside to prevent the escape of the spirit by evaporation. A strong solution of isinglass, made in the same manner, is an excellent cement for leather.

2. Take of best white glue, 16 oz.; white lead, dry, 4 oz.; rain-water, 2 pts.; alcohol, 4 oz. With constant stirring dissolve the glue and lead in the water by means of a water-bath. Add the alcohol, and continue the heat for a few minutes. Lastly, pour into bottles while it is still hot.

Liquid Glue.

Take 2 and 1-5th lbs. of glue, and dissolving it in 2 and 1-9th pts. of water in a glazed pot over a gentle fire, or, what is better, in the water-bath, stirring it from time to time. When all the glue is melted, 7 oz. Av. of nitric acid (spec. grav. 1·32) are to be poured in, in small quantities at a time. This addition produces an effervescence, owing to the disengagement of hyponitric acid. When all the acid is added, the vessel is to be taken from the fire, and left to cool.

Another. — Dissolve the best isinglass in the strongest (glacial) acetic acid.

Bottle Cement.

Resin, 15 parts; tallow, 4 (or wax, 3) parts; highly dried red ochre, 6 parts; or lampblack sufficient to give color.

Diamond Cement.

Isinglass, 1 oz.; distilled water, 5 oz.; dissolve and boil down to 3 oz.; add 1½ oz. of alcohol, boil for a minute or two. Strain, and while hot add ½ oz. of milky emulsion of gum ammoniac, and 5 drs. of tincture of mastic.

Oxychloride of Zinc Cement.

In liquid chloride of zinc, of 50° to 60° Beaumé, dissolve 3 per cent. of borax or sal ammoniac; add oxide of zinc (zinc white) until the mass is of proper consistence. This cement, when hard, becomes as firm as marble. It may be cast into moulds like plaster, as used in Mosaic work.

Bird Lime.

Boil the middle part of the holly 7 or 8 hours in water; drain it, and lay it in heaps in the ground, covered with stones, for 2 or 3 weeks, till reduced to a mucilage. Beat this in a mortar, wash it in rain-water, and knead it till free from extraneous matters. Put it into earthen pots, and in 4 or 5 days it will be fit for use. An inferior kind is made by boiling linseed-oil for some hours, until it becomes a viscid paste.

Transparent Cement.

Dissolve 75 parts India-rubber in 60 parts of chloroform or benzine, and add to the solution 15 parts of mastic.

Another. — Balsam of fir is a strong cement when not exposed to heat. It is to be warmed and applied to the glass, itself previously warmed. It is used for cementing lenses, mounting microscopic objects, etc., and does very well for broken glass when it is not to be washed in warm water. The thicker the balsam the stronger, when too thin it may be thickened by gentle evaporation.

To make Paper Water-proof.

Dissolve 8 oz. of alum and 3¾ oz. of white soap in 4 pints of water; in another vessel dissolve 2 oz. of gum Arabic and 4 oz. of glue in 4 pints or water. Mix the two solutions and make the mixture hot. Immerse the paper in the mixture, and then hang it up to dry or pass it between cylinders.

The alum, soap, glue, and gum form a sort of artificial covering which protects the surface of the paper from the action of water, and to a certain extent from fire. This paper will be very useful for packages which may be exposed to the inclemency of the weather.

New Applications for Gun-cotton.

In order to obtain cheap gun-cotton it may be made of rags instead of new cotton. It is first dissolved in any of its solvents, such as ether and alcohol, and becomes collodion. To this is now added any of the purest animal and vegetable oils, and it forms the new liquid which is to be used as a cement and vehicle. By adding to it gums and resins a cement is formed, which may be rolled out into sheets and stamped in dies into cups, fancy boxes, and various other articles. The oxide of copper imparts a green color to it, and the chloride of lime added renders it uninflammable. The addition of fine flax fibre, or the flocks of wool, renders it strong and flexible. It is stated to be an excellent compound for taking casts required for the purposes of dentistry, the models of jewellers, and other articles requiring sharp and smooth edges and sides.

The collodion oil-liquid, when very thin, may also be employed as a varnish for pictures, prints, etc.

Artificial Wood.

In one of his last lectures at the "Conservatoire des Arts et Métiers," M. Payen called the attention of his hearers to the process of making a kind of ebony or artificial wood, very hard, very heavy, and capable of receiving a very high polish and a brilliant varnish. M. Ladry, the inventor of this process, takes very fine saw-dust, mixes it with blood from the slaughter-houses, and submits the resulting paste to a very heavy pressure obtained by the hydraulic press. If the paste has been enclosed in moulds, it will take the form of the moulds, and resembles pieces of ebony carved by a skilful hand.

Another curious application of this paste consists in the formation of brushes; the bristles are arranged in the paste while yet soft; the paste is covered by a plate pierced with holes, through which the bristles pass; the pressure is then applied and brushes are obtained, made of a single piece cheaper and more lasting than the usual kind. This artificial wood of M. Ladry is much heavier than common woods.

Blood Cement for Coppersmiths.

A cement often used by coppersmiths to lay over the rivets and edges of the sheets of copper in large boilers, to serve as an additional security to the joinings, and to secure cocks, etc., from leaking, is made by mixing pounded quicklime with ox's blood. It must be applied fresh made, as it soon gets hard. If the properties of this cement were duly investigated, it would probably be found useful for many purposes to which it has never yet been applied. It is extremely cheap, and very durable.

Entomologist's Cement.

To a solution of gum ammoniac in proof spirit, add the best isinglass, and unite them with a gentle heat. The great value of this cement consists in the readiness with which it melts, and the little tendency it has to be affected by moisture. It is generally employed by entomologists in rejoining the dislocated parts of insects, for which it is very convenient.

Japanese Cement, or Rice Glue.

This elegant cement is made by mixing rice-flour intimately with cold water, and then gently boiling it; it is beautifully white, and dries almost transparent. Papers pasted together by means of this cement will sooner separate in their own substance than at the joining, which makes it useful in the preparation of curious paper articles, as tea-trays, ladies' dressing boxes, and other objects that require layers of paper to be cemented together.

SEALING-WAX.

Blue.

1. Shellac, 2 parts; dammar resin, 2 parts; Burgundy pitch, 1 part; Venice turpentine, 1 part; artificial ultramarine, 3 parts.
2. *Light Blue.* — As the last, with 1 part of dry sulphate of lead.
3. *Dark Blue.* — Venice turpentine, 3 oz.; finest shellac, 7 oz.; clear amber or black rosin, 1 oz.; Prussian blue, 1 oz.; carbonate of magnesia, 1½ dr. The last two to be made into a stiff paste with oil of turpentine and added to the melted shellac and Venice turpentine.

Black.

1. Venice turpentine, 4½ oz.; shellac, 9 oz.; colophony, ½ oz.; lampblack mixed to a paste with oil of turpentine, q. s.
2. *Inferior.* — Venice turpentine, 4 oz.; shellac, 8 oz.; 3 oz of colophony, and sufficient lampblack mixed with oil of turpentine to color it.
3. Shellac, 8 oz.; Venice turpentine, 4 oz.; lampblack, 6 oz.
4. *Common, for Bottles.* — Resin, 6 oz.; shellac, 2 oz.; Venice turpentine, 2 oz.; lampblack, q. s.

Brown.

1. *Light Brown.* — Venice turpentine, 4 oz.; shellac, 7½ oz.; brown earth (English umber), ½ oz.; cinnabar, ½ oz.; prepared chalk, ½ oz.; carbonate of magnesia, moistened with oil of turpentine, 1½ dr.
2. *Light Brown.—Second Quality.*—Venice turpentine, 4 oz.; shellac, 7 oz.; resin, 3 oz.; English umber 3 oz.; cinnabar, ¼ oz.; prepared chalk, 1 oz.; magnesia as the last.
3. *Dark Brown.*—Venice turpentine, 4 oz.; fine shellac, 7½ oz.; English umber, 1½ oz.; magnesia as before.
4. *Dark Brown.—Second Quality.*—Venice turpentine, 4 oz.; shellac, 7 oz.; colophony, 3 oz.; English umber, 1½ oz.; magnesia as before.

Green.

Venice turpentine, 2 oz.; shellac, 4 oz.; colophony, 1¼ oz.; King's yellow, ½ oz.; Prussian blue, ¼ oz.; magnesia as for brown.

Gold.

1. Venice turpentine 4 oz.; fine shellac, 8 oz.; leaf gold, 14 sheets; bronze powder, ½ oz.; magnesia (made into a paste with oil of turpentine), 1½ dr.
2. Use gold talc instead of gold leaf and bronze.

Marbled.

Melt each colored wax separately, and just as they begin to grow solid, mix together.

Red.

1. *Fine Carmine Wax.* — Venice turpentine, 2 oz.; finest shellac, 4 oz.; colophony, 1 oz.; English vermilion, 1½ oz.; magnesia (moistened with oil of turpentine), 1½ dr.
2. *Finest Red.*—Venice turpentine, 4 oz.; shellac, 7 oz.: cinnabar, 4 oz.; carbonate of magnesia (with oil of turpentine), 1½ dr;
3. As the last, with only 3½ oz. of cinnabar.
4. Venice turpentine, 4 oz.; shellac, 6½ oz.; colophony, 1 oz.; cinnabar, 2½ oz.; magnesia (with oil of turpentine), 1½ dr.
5. Venice turpentine, 4 oz.; shellac, 6 oz.; colophony, ¾ oz.; cinnabar, 1¾ oz.; magnesia as before.
6. As the last, but use colophony and cinnabar, each 1½ oz.
7. Venice turpentine, 4 oz.; shellac 5½ oz.; colophony, 1¼ oz.; cinnabar, 1¼ oz.; magnesia as before.
8. *English.*—Venice turpentine, 2 oz.; shellac, 3 oz.; vermilion, 1 oz.
9. *Spanish.*—Venice turpentine, 8 oz.; shellac, 2 oz.; colophony, 1 oz.; vermilion, 1 oz. Remove from the fire; and add ½ oz. rectified spirit.

Yellow.

Venice turpentine, 2 oz.; shellac, 4 oz.; colophony, 1¼ oz.; King's yellow, ¾ oz.; magnesia as before.

Perfumed Wax.

Add to any of the above a small quantity of fine benzoin.

Common Bottle Wax.

1. Dark resin, 18 oz.; shellac, 1 oz.; beeswax,

1 oz. Mix together and color with red-lead, Venitian-red or lampblack.

2. Resin, 19 oz.; beeswax, 1 oz.; color as before.

India-rubber Court-Plaster.

A stout frame of wood must be made, about 3 yards long and about 1¼ yards wide. Within this frame must be placed 2 sides of another frame, running longitudinally and across, so fixed in the outer frame that the 2 pieces may slide independently of each other backwards and forwards about 6 inches. Tapes of canvas must be tacked round the inside of the inner frame, so as to form a square for the material to be sewn in, which, when done, the two loop-frames must be drawn tightly to the outer by means of a twine passed round each, in order to stretch perfectly free from irregularities the silk or satin previous to laying on the composition.

To make the Plaster.

Dissolve India-rubber in naphtha or naphtha and turpentine; lay it on with a flat brush on the opposite side to that which is intended for the plaster. When the silk is perfectly dry, and the smell in a great measure dissipated, it will be ready for the adhesive material; to make which take equal parts of Salisbury or fine Russian glue and the best isinglass, dissolve in a sufficient quantity of water over a water-bath, and lay on with a flat hogtool while warm. It is requisite to use great caution to spread the plaster evenly and in one direction, and a sufficient number of coatings must be given to form a smooth surface, through which the texture of the fabric is not perceptible. Each coating should be perfectly dry before the succeeding one is given; after which the frame is to be placed in a situation free from dust, and where a draught of air would facilitate the drying. The quantity of water used and the weight of the two materials must be a little varied, according to the season and the gelatine strength they possess. Lastly, the plaster being ready to receive the polishing coat, which gives also the balsamic effect to it, a preparation is made in nearly the same manner as the compound tincture of benzoin, with the addition of more gums. This preparation must be laid on once only, and with a brush kept for the purpose. For making plasters on colored silk it is only necessary to select the silk a shade deeper than the colors required, as the plaster causes it to appear a little lighter.

Tooth Cements

Are only recommended when the decay has proceeded so far that the ordinary plugging is impossible. Those containing mercury are objected to by many. They consist of an amalgam of silver, gold, or tin, applied warm. The following have been used:

1. Anhydrous phosphoric acid, 12 grs.; pure caustic lime, 13 grs.; both finely powdered, and mixed rapidly in a mortar at the time of using. Smoothe off with the finger moistened with a drop of water.

2. Asbestos, or levigated quartz, made into a paste with mastic varnish.

Artificial Ivory for Photographers.

Tablets of gelatine or glue are immersed in a solution of alumina. When entirely penetrated by the alumina, the slabs are to be removed, dried, and polished like ivory.

INKS, etc.

PRELIMINARY REMARKS.

Ordinary black writing-ink contains a mixture of the tannates and gallates of the proto and sesquioxide of iron. These are insoluble in water, and are suspended by means of gum. Creosote or essential oils are added to prevent moulding.

Many receipts are given for inks; those found below are reliable. As a general rule, the use of vinegar, logwood, and salts of copper is not to be recommended. Inks so prepared are richer at first, but will fade and act on pens.

Most ink is pale when first written with, but becomes dark; this is owing to oxidation. Such ink lasts better than that which is very black.

When ink fades, it is from a decomposition of the organic matter; it may be restored by brushing over with infusion of galls or solution of ferrocyanide of potassium. The durability of any ink is impaired by the use of steel pens.

Writing Fluids.

Ink which is blue when first used (Stark's, Stephens's, Arnold's) contains sulphate of indigo, or soluble Prussian blue. It is an ink which is a true solution, and not merely a suspended precipitate. The same is true of Runge's Chrome Ink.

Marking Inks,

Containing nitrate of silver, are not indelible; they may be removed by cyanide of potassium.

Carbon inks, such as coal-tar diluted with naphtha, are indelible.

Aniline black is nearly indelible; it is turned yellowish, but not removed, by chlorine.

To make common Black Ink.

Pour 1 gall. of boiling soft water on 1 lb. of powdered galls, previously put into a proper vessel. Stop the mouth of the vessel, and set it in the sun in summer, or in winter where it may be warmed by any fire, and let it stand 2 or 3 days. Then add ½ lb. of green vitriol powdered, and, having stirred the mixture well together with a wooden spatula, let it stand again for 2 or 3 days, repeating the stirring, when add further to it 5 oz. of gum Arabic dissolved in a quart of boiling water; and, lastly, 2 oz. of alum; after which let the ink be strained through a coarse linen cloth for use.

Another. — A good and durable black ink may be made by the following directions: To 2 pts. of water add 3 oz. of the dark-colored, rough-skinned Aleppo galls in gross powder, and of rasped logwood, green vitriol, and gum arabic, each, 1 oz.

This mixture is to be put in a convenient vessel, and well shaken four or five times a day, for ten or twelve days, at the end of which time it will be fit for use, though it will improve by remaining longer on the ingredients.

Stark's Ink (Writing fluid).

Twelve oz. nut-galls, 8 oz. each, sulphate of indigo and copperas, a few cloves, 4 or 6 oz. of gum Arabic for a gallon of ink. The addition of the sulphate of indigo renders the ink more permanent and less liable to mould. It is blue when first written with, but soon becomes an intense black.

Chrome Ink (Runge's Ink).

This ink is of an excellent blue-black, does not fade, and, as it contains no gum, flows freely from the pen. It does not affect steel pens. Take 1 oz. extract of logwood, pour over it 2 qts. of boiling water, and, when the extract is dissolved, add 1 dr. of yellow chromate of potassa. This ink can be made for twenty-five cents a gallon. If put into an old inkstand, it must be thoroughly cleansed, as ordinary ink decomposes chrome ink.

Non-corrosive Writing Fluid.

Dissolve sulphate of indigo (chemic or Saxony blue) in twelve times its weight of water, add carbonate of soda as long as any precipitate falls, dissolve this in 150 parts of boiling water, let it settle and use the clear portion. It dries nearly black, flows very freely, and will not corrode pens or paper.

Alizarine Ink. Leonhardi.

Digest 24 parts Aleppo galls with 3 parts Dutch madder and 120 parts warm water. Filter. Mix 1.2 parts solution of indigo, 5.2 parts sulphate of iron, and 2 parts crude acetate of iron solution. This ink contains no gum, cannot get mouldy; the tannate of iron is prevented from separating by the sulphate of indigo. Alizarine ink may be evaporated to dryness and formed into cakes. One part with 6 parts hot water will then form an excellent writing fluid.

Indestructible Ink for Resisting the Action of Corrosive Substances.

On many occasions it is of importance to employ an ink indestructible by any process, and will not equally destroy the material on which it is applied. For black ink, 25 grs. of copal, in powder, are to be dissolved in 200 grs. of oil of lavender, by the assistance of a gentle heat, and are then to be mixed with 2½ grs. of lampblack and ½ gr. of indigo; for red ink use 120 grs. of oil of lavender, 17 grs. of Copal, and 60 grains of vermilion. A little oil of lavender or of turpentine may be added, if the ink be found too thick. A mixture of genuine asphaltum dissolved in oil of turpentine or benzine, amber varnish and lampblack, would be still superior.

This ink is particularly useful in labelling phials, etc. containing chemical or corrosive substances.

Ink Powder.

Take 4 oz. powdered galls, dried sulphate of iron, 1 oz.; powdered gum, 1 oz.; white sugar, ½ oz.; to make a quart of ink with water or beer.

MARKING INK.

Jules Guillier, who received five years' exclusive privilege in Paris for making marking inks, gives the following formulæ. But one preparation is required, and the inventor states that they will not wash out or fade.

No 1. Nitrate of silver, 11 parts; distilled water, 85 parts; powdered gum Arabic, 20 parts; arbonate of soda, 22 parts; solution of ammonia, .0 parts. Dissolve the carbonate of soda, and afterwards the gum (by trituration in a mortar) in the water, dissolve the nitrate of silver in the ammonia and add to the carbonate of soda solution. Heat gently to the boiling point; the ink at first turbid, becomes clear and very dark.

No. 2. Nitrate of silver, 5 parts; distilled water, 12 parts; powdered gum Arabic, 5 parts; carbonate of soda, 7 parts; solution of ammonia, 10 parts. Heat as before, and beat until it has a very dark color. This ink is very black and is suitable for marking by stamps.

A Purple-red Ink for Marking Linens.

The place where the linen is to be marked is first wetted with a solution consisting of 3 drs. of carbonate of soda, and 3 drs. of gum Arabic, dissolved in 1½ oz. of water, then dried and smoothed. The place is now to be written on with a solution composed of 1 dr. of chloride of platina dissolved in 2 oz. of distilled water, then allowed to dry. When quite dry, the writing is to be painted over with a goose's feather, moistened with a liquid consisting of one dr. of protochloride of tin dissolved in 2 oz. of distilled water.

Blue and Indelible Black Ink.

Take of iodide of potassium, 1 oz.; iodine, 6 drs.; water, 4 oz.; dissolve. Make a solution of 2 oz. of ferrocyanide of potassium in water. Add the iodine solution to the second. A blue precipitate will fall, which, after filtering, may be dissolved in water, forming a blue ink. This blue, added to common ink, renders it indelible.

Carmine Ink.

Dissolve 10 grs. of the best carmine in the least quantity possible of solution of ammonia. Let it stand for 24 hours, and add 2½ fl. oz. of distilled water.

To take out Spots of Ink.

As soon as the accident happens, wet the place with juice of sorrel or lemon, or with vinegar, and the best hard white soap, or use a weak solution of oxalic acid.

To take out Marking Ink.

Ordinary marking-ink is removed by wetting with a solution of cyanide of potassium, and afterwards washing with water. The cyanide must be carefully handled, as it is a violent poison.

To make New Writing look Old.

Take 1 dr. of saffron, and infuse it into ½ pt. of ink, and warm it over a gentle fire, and it will cause whatever is written with it to turn yellow, and appear as if of many years' standing.

To Write on Greasy Paper or Parchment.

Put to a bullock's gall 1 handful of salt, and ¼ pt. of vinegar, stir it until it is mixed well; when the paper or parchment is greasy, put 1 drop of the gall into the ink, and the difficulty will be instantly obviated.

To Restore Decayed Writings.

1. Cover the letters with solution of ferrocyanide of potassium, with the addition of a diluted mineral acid; upon the application of which, the letters change very speedily to a deep blue color, of great beauty and intensity. To prevent the spreading of the color, which, by blotting the parchment, detracts greatly from the legibility, the ferrocyanide should be put on first, and the diluted acid added upon it. The method found to answer best has been to spread the ferrocyanide thin with a feather or a bit of stick cut to a blunt point. Though the ferrocyanide should occasion no sensible change of color, yet the moment the acid comes upon it, every trace of a letter turns at once to a fine blue, which soon acquires its full intensity, and is beyond comparison stronger than the color of the original trace. If, then, the corner of a bit of blotting-paper be carefully and dexterously applied near the letters, so as to imbibe the superfluous liquor, the staining of the parchment may be in a great measure avoided; for it is this superfluous liquor which, absorbing part of the coloring matters from the letters, becomes a dye to whatever it touches. Care must be taken not to bring the blotting-paper in contact with the letters, because the coloring matter is soft

whilst wet, and may easily be rubbed off. The acid chiefly employed is the muriatic: but both the sulphuric and nitric succeed very well. They should be so far diluted as not to be liable to corrode the parchment, after which the degree of strength does not seem to be a matter of much nicety.

2. *Morid's Process.*— The paper or parchment written on is first left for some time in contact with distilled water. It is then placed for 5 seconds in a solution of oxalic acid (1 of acid to 100 of water); next, after washing it, it is put in a vessel containing a solution of gallic acid (10 grs. of acid to 300 of distilled water); and finally washed again and dried. The process should be carried forward with care and promptness, that any accidental discoloration of the paper may be avoided.

To take Impressions from Recent Manuscripts.

This is done by means of fusible metal. In order to show the application of it, paste a piece of paper on the bottom of a China saucer, and allow it to dry; then write upon it with a common writing ink, and sprinkle some finely powdered gum Arabic over the writing, which produces a slight relief. When it is well dried, and the adhering powder brushed off, the fusible metal is poured into the saucer, and is cooled rapidly, to prevent crystallization. The metal then takes a cast of the writing, and, when it is immersed in slightly warm water to remove adhering gum, impressions may be taken from it as from a copper-plate.

Another Method.

Put a little sugar into a common writing ink, and let the writing be executed with this upon common paper, sized as usual. When a copy is required, let unsized paper be taken and lightly moistened with a sponge. Then apply the wet paper to the writing, and passing lightly a flat-iron, of a moderate heat, such as is used by laundresses, over the unsized paper, the copy will be immediately produced. This method requires no machine or preparation, and may be employed in any situation.

To Produce a Fac-simile of any Writing.

The pen should be made of glass enamel; the point being small and finely polished; so that the part above the point may be large enough to hold as much ink as, or more than a common writing-pen.

A mixture of equal parts of Frankfort black, and fresh butter, is now to be smeared over sheets of paper, and rubbed off after a certain time. The paper, thus smeared, is to be pressed for some hours, taking care to have sheets of blotting-paper between each of the sheets of black paper. When fit for use, writing-paper is put between sheets of blackened paper, and the upper sheet is to be written on, with common writing-ink, by the glass or enamel pen. By this method, not only the copy is obtained on which the pen writes, but also two or more, made by means of the blackened paper.

Substitute for Copying Machines.

In the common ink used, dissolve lump sugar (1 dr. to 1 oz. of ink). Moisten the copying paper, and then put it in soft cap-paper to absorb the superfluous moisture. Put the moistened paper on the writing, place both between some soft paper, and either put the whole in the folds of a carpet, or roll upon a ruler 3 or 4 times.

To Copy Writings.

Take a piece of unsized paper exactly of the size of the paper to be copied; moisten it with water, or with the following liquid: Take of distilled vinegar, 2 lbs., dissolve it in 1 oz. of boracic acid; then take 4 oz. of oyster-shells calcined to whiteness, and carefully freed from their brown crust; put them into the vinegar, shake the mixture frequently for 24 hours, then let it stand till it deposits its sediment; filter the clear part through unsized paper into a glass vessel; then add 2 oz. of the best Aleppo galls bruised, and place the liquor in a warm place; shake it frequently for 24 hours, then filter the liquor again through unsized paper, and add to it after filtration, 1 qt., ale measure, of pure water. It must then stand 24 hours, and be filtered again, if it shows a disposition to deposit any sediment, which it generally does. When paper has been wet with this liquid, put it between 2 thick unsized papers to absorb the superfluous moisture; then lay it over the writing to be copied, and put a piece of clean writing-paper above it. Put the whole on the board of a rolling-press, and press them through the rolls, as is done in printing copper-plates, and a copy of the writing will appear on both sides of the thin moistened paper; on one side in a reversed order and direction, but on the other side in the natural order and direction of the lines.

COPPER-PLATE PRINTERS' INK.

Ink for the rolling-press is made of linseed-oil, burnt just as for common printing-ink, and is then mixed with Frankfort black, finely ground. There are no certain proportions, every workman adding oil or black to suit. Good ink depends most on the purity of the oil, and on its being thoroughly burned. Test it occasionally by cooling a drop on the inside of an oyster-shell; feel it between the thumb and finger, and if it draws out into threads, it is burnt enough. Weak oil well charged with black is called *stiff* ink. Oil fully burned and charged with as much black as it will take in, is termed *strong* ink. The character of the engraving to be printed determines which is suitable. It is cleaned out with spirits of turpentine.

Another Method.

Instead of Frankfort, or other kinds of black commonly used, the following composition may be substituted, and will form a much deeper and more beautiful black than can be obtained by any other method. Take of the deepest Prussian blue, 5 parts, and of the deepest colored lake and brown pink, each 1 part. Grind them well with oil of turpentine, and afterwards with the strong and weak oils in the manner and proportion above directed. The colors need not be bright for this purpose, but they should be the deepest of the kind, and perfectly transparent in oil, as the whole effect depends on that quality.

PRINTERS' INK.

Ten or 12 galls. of nut or linseed-oil are set over the fire in a large iron pot, and brought to boil. It is then stirred with an iron ladle; and whilst boiling, the inflammable vapor arising from it either takes fire of itself or is kindled, and is suffered to burn in this way for about ½ hour; the pot being partially covered so as to regulate the body of the flame, and consequently the heat communicated to the oil. It is frequently stirred during this time, that the whole may be heated equally; otherwise a part would be charred, and the rest left imperfect. The flame is then extinguished by entirely covering the pot. The oil, by this process, has much of its unctuous quality destroyed; and when cold is of the consistence of soft turpentine: it is then called varnish. After this, it is made into ink by mixture with the requisite quantity of lampblack, of which about 2½ oz. are sufficient for 16 oz. of the prepared oil. The oil loses by the boiling about ⅛ of its weight, and emits very offensive fumes. Several other additions are made to the oil during the boiling, such as crusts of bread, onions, and sometimes turpentine. These are kept secret by the preparers. The intention of them is more effectually to destroy part of the unctuous quality of oil, to give it more body, to enable it to adhere better to the wetted paper, and to spread on the types neatly and uniformly.

Besides these additions, others are made by the printers, of which the most important is a little fine indigo in powder, to improve the beauty of the color.

Another Method.

One pound of lampblack ground very fine or run through a lawn sieve; 2 oz. of Prussian blue ground very fine; 4 oz. of linseed-oil, well boiled and skimmed; 4 oz. of spirit of turpentine, very clear; 4 oz. of soft varnish, or neat's-foot oil. To be well boiled and skimmed; and while boiling the top burned off by several times applying lighted paper. Let these be well mixed; then put the whole in a jug, place that in a pan, and boil them very carefully 1 hour.

A Fine Black Printing-Ink.

Less turpentine and oil, without Prussian blue, for common ink.

Best Printing-Ink.

In a secured iron pot (fire outside when possible), boil 12 galls. of nut or linseed-oil; stir with iron ladle, long handle; while boiling put an iron cover partly over, set the vapor on fire by lighted paper often applied; keep stirring well, and on the fire 1 hour at least (or till the oily particles are burnt); then add 1 lb. of onions cut in pieces, and a few crusts of bread, to get out the residue of oil; also varnish, 16 oz.; fine lampblack, 3 oz.; ground indigo, ½ oz. Boil well 1 hour.

Good Common Printing-Ink.

Take 16 oz. of varnish, 4 oz. of linseed-oil well boiled, 4 oz. of clear oil of turpentine, 16 oz. of fine lampblack, 2 oz. of Prussian blue, fine, 1 oz. of indigo, fine. Boil 1 hour.

Printers' Red Ink.

Soft varnish and vermilion with white of eggs not very thick. Common varnish, red lead and orange. Colcothar is indelible.

Blue.

Prussian blue and a little ivory-black with varnish and eggs very thick. Common indigo and varnish; then wash off with boiling lees.

Green.

Sesquioxide of chromium (chrome green). This is the ink used in printing Greenbacks. It is indestructible, and cannot be photographed.

Perpetual Ink for Inscriptions on Tombstones, Marbles, etc.

This ink is formed by mixing about 3 parts of pitch with 1 part of lampblack, and making them incorporate by melting the pitch. With this composition, used in a melted state, the letters are filled, and will, without extraordinary violence, endure as long as the stone itself.

Ink for Writing on Zinc Labels.

Horticultural ink.—Dissolve 100 grs. of chloride of platinum in a pint of water. A little mucilage and lampblack may be added.

Another.—Mix thoroughly 2 parts (by weight) verdigris, 2 of sal ammoniac, 1 of lampblack, and 30 of water. Always shake well before using, and write with a quill pen. Writings made on zinc with this ink will keep many years.

Indian-ink.

Let ivory or lampblack be mixed with a small portion of Prussian blue or indigo, for a blue-black, and let the same blacks be united with raw or burnt umber, bistre, vandyke or any other brown, instead of the blue, for a brown-black. These should be mixed together in a weak gum-water (perhaps matt-work would answer the purpose better), first levigating them very fine, in common water, on a marble slab. When dried to the consistence of a paste, let the glutinous matter be well mixed with them; that will be found sufficiently strong, which binds the composition, so as to prevent rubbing off by the touch. Indian-ink drawings should be handled as lightly as possible. Too much gum in the composition will create an offensive gloss.

Another Method.

Isinglass, 6 oz., and 12 oz. of soft water; make into size; add 1 oz. of refined liquorice, ground up with 1 oz. of genuine ivory-black, and stir the whole well. Evaporate the water in balneum mariæ, and form the sticks or cakes.

A Substitute for Indian-ink.

Boil parchment slips or cuttings of glove-leather in water till it forms a size, which, when cool, becomes of the consistence of jelly; then, having blackened an earthen plate, by holding it over the flame of a candle, mix up, with a camel-hair pencil, the fine lampblack thus obtained with some of the above size, while the plate is still warm. This black requires no grinding, and produces an ink of the same color, which works as freely with the pencil, and is as perfectly transparent as the best Indian-ink.

SYMPATHETIC INKS.

Sympathetic inks are such as do not appear after they are written with, but which may be made to appear at pleasure by certain means to be used for that purpose. A variety of substances have been used as sympathetic inks, among which are the following:

Chloride of Gold and Tin.

Write with a solution of gold in aqua regia, and let the paper dry gently in the shade. Nothing will appear, but draw a sponge over it, wetted with a solution of tin in aqua regia, and the writing will immediately appear, of a purple color.

Starch and Iodine.

Write with weak boiled starch, and when the writing is required to appear, brush over with a weak solution of iodine; the letters will appear blue.

Chloride of Cobalt,

When pure, is invisible in dilute solution, but gives a blue when exposed to a gentle heat; if it contain (as it usually does) some nickel, the color will be green. A little common salt should be added to the solution, so that it will remain more on the paper. It can then be brought out and suffered to fade for many successive times.

Other Sympathetic Inks.

Write on paper with a solution of nitrate of bismuth, and smear the writing over by means of a feather with some infusion of galls. The letters, which were before invisible, will now appear of a brown color. If the previous use of nitrate of bismuth be concealed from the spectators, great surprise will be excited by the appearance of writing, merely by the dash of a feather. The same phenomenon will take place when infusion of galls is written with, and the salt of bismuth applied afterwards.

Another.—Write on a sheet of paper any sentence with a transparent infusion of nut-galls, and dip the paper in a transparent solution of the sulphate of iron. The writing, which was before invisible, will now, on a slight exposure to the air, turns quite black. A neater way of performing this experiment will be by smearing the written parts over with a feather dipped in the solution of the metallic salt; it may also be reversed, by writing with the salt and smearing with the infusion.

Another.—If a letter be written with a solution of sulphate of iron, the inscription will be invisible, but if it afterwards be rubbed over by a feather dipped in a solution of prussiate of potassa, it will appear of a beautiful blue color.

Another.—Write a letter with a solution of nitrate of bismuth. The letters will be invisible. If a feather be now dipped in a solution of the prussiate of potass, and rubbed over the paper, the writing will appear of a beautiful yellow color, occasioned by a formation of prussiate of bismuth.

Another.—Write with a solution of sugar of lead or tartar emetic; moisten the writing (or drawing) and expose to a current of sulphuretted hydrogen gas. The lead will turn black, and the antimony orange brown.

Chemical Landscapes.

These are drawn partly in Indian-ink and partly in sympathetic inks, which are only visible when gently heated. The picture represents ordinarily a winter scene, but when heated the sky becomes blue, the leaves green, and flowers and fruit are seen. The materials are as follows: *Green*, chloride of nickel; *blue*, pure chloride or acetate of cobalt; *yellow*, chloride of copper; *brown*, bromide of copper. If the picture is too highly heated it will not again fade.

COLORED INKS.

Gold Ink.

Mosaic gold, 2 parts, gum Arabic, 1 part, are rubbed up with water until reduced to a proper condition.

Silver Ink.

Triturate in a mortar equal parts of silver foil and sulphate of potassa, until reduced to a fine powder; then wash out the salt, and mix the residue with a mucilage of equal parts of gum Arabic and water.

Brown Ink.

Digest powdered catechu, 4 parts, with water, 60 parts, for some hours; filter, and add sufficient of a solution of bichromate of potassa, 1 part in 16 of water.

Yellow Ink.

Macerate gamboge, 1 part (or 1½); alum, ½ part; gum Arabic, 1 part, in acetic acid, 1 part, and water, 24 parts.

Blue Ink.

Triturate best Prussian blue, 6 parts, with a solution of 1 part of oxalic acid in 6 of water, and towards the end of ¼ of an hour or so add gradually gum Arabic, 18 parts, and water, 230. Pour off clear.

Red Inks.

1. Pernambuco-wood, 4 parts; alum and cream of tartar, each 1 part, with 30 of water; boil down to 16 parts, let stand, pour off, filter, and dissolve in the liquid gum Arabic, 1½ parts; white sugar, 1 part.

2. Digest powdered cochineal, 8 parts, and carbonate of potash, 16 parts, in 144 of water, for 24 hours; then boil up with powdered alum, 4 parts, and add 24 of cream of tartar, with 3 parts of tartaric acid, and, when effervescence has ceased, another part of the acid, or enough to produce the color; let cool, filter, and boil the residue on the filter with 12 parts of water; filter again, mix the liquids and dissolve in them 24 parts of gum Arabic, and lastly ⅛ part of oil of cloves. No iron vessels must be used in this process.

3. Digest powdered cochineal, 16 parts; oxalic acid, 2 parts; dilute acetic acid, 80 parts; distilled water, 40 parts, for 36 hours; then add powdered alum, 1 part; gum Arabic, 1 to 10; shake up, let stand for 12 hours, and strain.

4. Dissolve 1 part of carmine in 8 to 10 parts of aqua ammonia, and add mucilage of gum Arabic sufficient to reduce it properly.

Violet Ink.

Eight parts of logwood and 64 parts of water; boil down to one-half, then strain and add 1 part of chloride of tin.

Green Inks.

1. Digest 1 part of gamboge with from 7 to 10 parts of the blue ink.

2. To powdered bichromate of potassa, 8 parts, contained in a porcelain dish, add oil of vitriol, 8 parts, previously diluted with 64 of water; then heat, and, while evaporating, add gradually 24 parts of alcohol, and reduce to 56 parts, which filter, and in the clear liquor dissolve 8 parts of gum Arabic.

Crimson Ink.

A beautiful crimson ink is made by mixing red ink No. 1 with the violet ink; about equal parts will answer.

The parts given are those of weight, not measure. The mucilage of gum Arabic prevents the fine particles of color falling to the bottom in the form of a sediment. Sugar gives to inks a glossy appearance, but very little of it should be used, as it is liable to make the ink sticky.

METALLURGY.

ASSAYING OF METALLIC ORES.

Before metallic ores are worked upon in the large way, it will be necessary to inquire what sort of metal, and what portion of it, is to be found in a determinate quantity of the ore; to discover whether it will be worth while to extract it largely, and in what manner the process is to be conducted, so as to answer that purpose. The knowledge requisite for this is called the art of assaying.

Assay of Ores in the Dry Way.

The assaying of ores may be performed either in the dry or moist way; the first is the most ancient, and, in many respects the most advantageous, and consequently still continues to be mostly used.

Assays are made either in crucibles with the blast of the bellows, or in tests under a muffle.

Assay Weights.

The assay weights are always imaginary, sometimes an ounce represents a hundredweight on the large scale, and is subdivided into the same number of parts, as that hundredweight is in the great; so that the contents of the ore, obtained by the assay, shall accurately determine by such relative proportion the quantity to be expected from any weight of the ore on a larger scale.

Roasting the Ore.

In the lotting of the ores care should be taken to have small portions from different specimens, which should be pulverized, and well mixed in an iron or brass mortar. The proper quantity of the ore is now taken, and if it contain either sulphur or arsenic it is put into a crucible or test, and exposed to a moderate degree of heat, till no vapor arises from it. To assist this volatilization some add a small quantity of powdered charcoal.

Fluxes.

To assist the fusion of the ores, and to convert the extraneous matters connected with them into scoria, assayers use different kinds of fluxes. The most usual and efficacious materials for the composition of these are, borax, cream of tartar, nitre, sal ammoniac, common salt, glass, fluor-spar, charcoal powder, pitch, lime, litharge, etc., in different proportions.

As the whole process of which we are speaking is merely an experiment, made for the purpose of ascertaining what is the nature of the metal contained in the ore, and the proportion the former bears to the latter, the little additional expense incurred by employing *animal* instead of *vegetable* *charcoal* is not to be regarded, particularly when the increased fusibility of the ore, occasioned thereby is considered.

Crude or White Flux.

This consists of 1 part of nitre and 2 of cream of tartar, well mixed together.

Black Flux.

The above crude flux detonates by means of kindled charcoal, and if the detonation be effected in a mortar slightly covered it becomes black. It is a mixture of carbonate of potassa and charcoal.

Cornish Reducing Flux.

Mix well together 10 oz. of cream of tartar, 3 oz. and 6 drs. of nitre, and 3 oz. and 1 dr. of borax.

Cornish Refining Flux.

Deflagrate, and afterwards pulverize, 2 parts of nitre and 1 part of cream of tartar.

The above fluxes answer the purpose very well, provided the ores be deprived of all their sulphur, or if they contain much earthy matters; because, in the latter case, they unite with them, and convert them into a thin glass; but if any quantity of sulphur remain, these fluxes unite with it, and form a liver of sulphur, which has the power of destroying a portion of all the metals; consequently the assay under such circumstances must be very inaccurate. The principal difficulty in assaying appears to be in the appropriation of the proper fluxes to each particular ore, and it likewise appears that such a discriminating knowledge can only be acquired from an extensive practice, or from a knowledge of the chemical affinities and actions of different bodies upon each other.

In assaying we are at liberty to use the most expensive materials to effect our purpose, hence the use of different saline fluxes; but in the working at large such expensive means cannot be applied, as by such processes the inferior metals would be too much enhanced in value, especially in working very poor ores. In consequence of which in smelting works, where the object is the production of metals in the great way, cheaper additions are used, such as limestone, feldspar, fluor-spar, quartz, sand, slate, and slags. These are to be chosen according to the different views of the operator and the nature of the ores. Thus iron ores, on account of the argillaceous earth they contain, require calcareous additions, and the copper ores, rather slags or vitrescent stones, than calcareous earth.

Humid Assay of Metallic Ores.

The mode of assaying ores for their particular metals by the dry way is deficient, so far as relates to pointing out the different substances connected with them, because they are always destroyed by the process for obtaining the assay metal. The assay by the moist way is more correct, because the different substances can be accurately ascertained.

Dry Assay of Iron Ores.

Mix 100 grs. of the ore, thoroughly powdered, with from 30 to 100 grs. of calcined borax. The quality of the latter depends upon the quality of the ore, and is to be increased with the foreign matters. If the ore contains sulphur, it must first be roasted. The mixture is introduced into a crucible lined with charcoal, covered with powdered charcoal, on which is laid a piece of charcoal. The crucible is then closed, the cover luted on, and submitted to a white heat for an hour. The iron is found in the form of a button, and is not pure, but gives about the quality of the pig iron which will be obtained from the ore.

Humid Assay of Iron Ore.

Fuch's method is accurate, and determines the relative quantity of protoxide and peroxide in an ore, which is often desirable. The only ores to which it cannot be applied are those containing arsenious acid, and this is not a very common ingredient.

Dissolve the ore in muriatic acid, and filter. Put into a small round-bottomed flask, and cork tightly until ready to boil it. Immerse a clean, weighed strip of copper, and, removing the cork, boil until the copper is no longer attacked. It is then taken out, washed, well wiped, and weighed. To ascertain the amount of peroxide multiply this weight by 40 and divide by 31·7. The quotient gives the amount sought.

To know the whole amount of iron in the ore, another portion is weighed out—say 1 gramme (about 15 grs.)—and dissolved as before; it is then digested with chlorate of potassa, by which all the iron is converted into peroxide, after which copper will decompose the whole. Multiply the loss by 28 and divide by 31·7; the quotient will give the whole amount of iron in the ore.

The presence of copper in the ore will make it appear poorer than it really is.

Volumetric Assay of Iron Ore (Percy).

Heat 10 grs. of iron-ore, finely pulverized, with strong hydrochloric acid, for $\frac{1}{2}$ an hour, in a conical-shaped flask with a funnel inserted in the neck; when decomposition is complete dilute the solution with water acidulated with sulphuric acid, and add a few pieces of granulated zinc and boil until all traces of yellow color disappear, or the solution remains of a pale green tint, and free from fine particles of zinc. Transfer to a white porcelain dish, and dilute to 20 oz. with distilled water.

When cold it is ready for testing with the following solution.

Dissolve 50 grs. of crystallized permanganate of potassa in 20 oz. of distilled water, and keep it in a tightly corked bottle, marked "Standard Solution Permanganate of Potassa." To ascertain the standard of this solution, dissolve 10 grs. of iron piano wire in dilute hydrochloric acid in a narrow-mouth flask with gentle heat. Dilute to 10 oz. Take 1 oz. of the diluted iron solution and dilute to 20 oz. with distilled water in a white porcelain dish.

Allow the solution of permanganate to run slowly in from a graduated pipette, stirring constantly until the solution assumes a faint pink color. Record the amount used, this represents 1 gr. of metallic iron.

Proceed in the same manner to test the solution of ore first obtained, noting the amount required to produce the first tint of pink color. Divide this amount by the amounts required for 1 gr. of iron, and the result is the number of grains of metallic iron contained in the ore.

Tin Ores.

Mix a quintal of tin ore, previously washed, pulverized, and roasted till no arsenical vapor arises, with half a quintal of calcined borax, and the same quantity of pulverized pitch; these are to be put in a crucible lined with charcoal, which is placed in an air-furnace. After the pitch is burnt, give a violent heat for a quarter of an hour, and on withdrawing the crucible, the regulus will be found at the bottom. If the ore be not well washed from earthy matters, a larger quantity of borax will be requisite, with some powdered glass; and if the ore contain iron, some alkaline salt may be added.

In the Humid Way.

Dissolve the ore in hot muriatic acid, pass through the solution a current of sulphuretted hydrogen in large excess. Allow the precipitate to subside, add to it, with the aid of heat, nitric acid until no sulphuretted hydrogen is given off. This transforms the tin into stannic acid, wash carefully, dry, and weigh. Stannic acid contains 78.61 per cent. of tin.

Lead Ores.

As most of the lead ores contain either sulphur or arsenic, they require to be well roasted. Take a quintal of roasted ore, with the same quantity of calcined borax, ½ a quintal of fine powdered glass, ¼ of a quintal of pitch, and as much clean iron filings. Line the crucible with wetted charcoal-dust, and put the mixture into the crucible, and place it before the bellows of a forge-fire. When it is red hot, raise the fire for 15 or 20 minutes, then withdraw the crucible, and break it when cold.

In the Humid Way.

Powder the ore (Galena) finely. Moisten with fuming nitric acid and digest on the sand-bath. This converts the whole into sulphate of lead. Dilute with water and filter. The insoluble sulphate of lead will remain in the filter. Wash it thoroughly, dry it, and weigh — 100 parts of sulphate of lead contain 73.56 parts of oxide of lead and 68.286 of metallic lead.

Zinc Ores.

Take the assay weight of roasted ore, and mix it well with one-eighth part of charcoal-dust, put it into a strong luted earthen retort, to which must be fitted a receiver; place the retort in a furnace and raise the fire, and continue it in a violent heat for two hours; suffer it then to cool gradually, and the zinc will be found adhering to the neck of the retort in its metallic form.

In the Humid Way (Percy).

Take 20 grs. of the ore (finely pulverized) to be assayed. Digest it for 1 hour in nitric acid 1 part, water 2 parts, with a few drops of hydrochloric acid; add carbonate of ammonia dissolved in liquid ammonia until the reaction is strongly alkaline. Digest for half an hour, dilute with an equal bulk of distilled water; filter and mark the filtrate Sol. A.

Make a standard solution of zinc by dissolving 10 grs. of pure zinc in nitric acid and diluting to 10 oz. Sol. B.

Make a solution of sulphide of sodium, 1 oz. of saturated solution to 10 oz. of distilled water. Sol. C.

Take of solution chloride of iron, ½ oz.; distilled water, 5 oz.; add aqua ammonia; separate all of the iron. Shake. Sol. D.

Take of solution B, 1 oz.; dilute to 3 oz.; add of solution D, 1 oz.; take in a graduated pipette of solution C, and add gradually to the mixture of B and D (stirring rapidly all the while), until the flocculent iron begins to change color to grayish black. Make a memorandum of the number of graduations of solution C required. This is the amount of sulphide of sodium necessary to precipitate 1 gr. of metallic zinc.

Take ½ of solution A (diluted to 12 oz.) equal 6 oz.: add of solution D, 2 oz.; then with graduated pipette run in slowly the solution C until the flocculent iron begins to change color as before. The number of graduations required, divided by the number used in the former experiment, indicate the number of grains of metallic zinc in 10 grs. of the ore, and represent the per centage likewise.

Copper Ores.

Take an exact troyounce of the ore, previously pulverized, and calcine it well; stir it all the time with an iron rod without removing it from the crucible; after the calcination add an equal quantity of borax, ½ the quantity of fusible glass, ¼ the quantity of pitch, and a little charcoal-dust; rub the inner surface of the crucible with a paste composed of charcoal-dust, a little fine powdered clay, and water. Cover the mass with common salt, and put a lid upon the crucible, which is to be placed in a furnace; the fire is to be raised gradually till it burns briskly, and the crucible continued in it for ½ hour, stirring the metal frequently with an iron rod; and when the scoria which adheres to the rod appears clear, then the crucible must be taken out and suffered to cool; after which it must be broken and the regulus separated and weighed. This is called black copper; to refine which equal parts of common salt and nitre are to be well mixed together. The black copper is brought into fusion, and a teaspoonful of the flux is thrown upon it, which is repeated 3 or 4 times, when the metal is poured into an ingot mould and the button is found to be fine copper.

In the Humid Way.

Make a solution of vitreous copper ore in 5 times its weight of concentrated sulphuric acid, and boil it to dryness; add as much water as will dissolve the vitriol thus formed. To this solution add a clean bar of iron, which will precipitate the whole of the copper in its metallic form. If the solution be contaminated with iron, the copper must be re-dissolved in the same manner and precipitated again. The sulphur may be separated by filtration.

ASSAYING.

Volumetric Assay of Copper Ores. (*Percy.*)

Dissolve 10 grs. of the copper ore finely pulverized and moistened with strong sulphuric acid, in strong nitric acid, adding the acid gradually; and when the fumes of hyponitric acid cease to be evolved, add a small amount of water and boil for a few minutes. Dilute to 10 oz. and treat with ammonia in excess, and it will become of a deep blue color. Set aside to cool, and prepare the following solution: Dissolve 500 grs. of granulated cyanide of potassium in 20 oz. of distilled water, and keep in a tight-stoppered bottle in the dark. Mark "Standard Solution Cyanide of Potassium." To ascertain the standard of this solution, dissolve 10 grs. of electrotype copper in dilute nitric acid and boil to expel hyponitric acid fumes, and dilute to 10 oz. with distilled water. Take of this solution 1 oz. and dilute to 5 oz. with distilled water, and allow the standard cyanide solution to flow very slowly into it at intervals, from a graduated pipette, and note the amount used to render it nearly colorless. This process takes from $\frac{1}{2}$ to $\frac{3}{4}$ of an hour. Proceed in the same manner to test the solution of ore first obtained, noting the amount required to reduce the color to a faint lilac. Divide this amount by the amount found required for 1 gr. of metallic copper, and the result is the number of grains of metallic copper in the ore tested.

Bismuth Ores.

If the ore be mineralized by sulphur, or sulphur and iron, a previous roasting will be necessary. The strong ores require no roasting, but only to be reduced to a fine powder. Take the assay weight and mix it with half the quantity of calcined borax, and the same of pounded glass; line the crucible with charcoal, melt it as quickly as possible, and when well done, take out the crucible and let it cool gradually. The regulus will be found at the bottom.

In the Humid Way.

Bismuth is easily soluble in nitric acid or aqua regia. Its solution is colorless and is precipitated by the addition of pure water; 118 grs. of the precipitate from nitric acid, well washed and dried, are equal to 100 of bismuth in its metallic form.

Antimonial ores.

Take a common crucible, bore a number of small holes in the bottom, and place it in another crucible a size smaller, luting them well together; then put the proper quantity of ore in small lumps into the upper crucible, and lute thereon a cover; place these vessels on a hearth and surround them with stones about 6 in. distant from them; the intermediate space must be filled with ashes, so that the undermost crucible may be covered with them; but upon the upper charcoal must be laid, and the whole made red hot by the assistance of hand bellows. The antimony being of easy fusion is separated, and runs through the holes of the upper vessel into the inferior one, where it is collected.

Humid Assay of Arseniated Antimony.

Dissolve the ore in aqua regia; the sulphur is separated by filtration. Evaporate the solution to dryness and heat below redness until all the nitric acid is expelled. The resulting antimonic acid contains 76.33 per cent. of metallic antimony.

Manganese Ores.

The regulus is obtained by mixing the calx or ore of manganese with oil, making it into a ball, and putting it into a crucible lined with powdered charcoal 1-10th of an inch on the sides, and $\frac{1}{4}$ of an inch at bottom; then filling the empty space with charcoal-dust, covering the crucible with another inverted and luted on, and exposing it to the strongest heat of a forge for an hour or more. The ore is very difficult to reduce.

Arsenical Ores.

This assay is made by sublimation in close vessels. Beat the ore into small pieces and put them into a matrass, which place in a sand-pot with a proper degree of heat. The arsenic sublimes in this operation and adheres to the upper part of the vessel; when it must be carefully collected, with a view to ascertain its weight. A single sublimation will not be sufficient. It is better to perform the first sublimation with a moderate heat, and afterwards bruise the remainder and expose it to a stronger heat. The addition of charcoal is useful.

In the Humid Way.

Digest the ore in muriatic acid, adding nitric by degrees, to help the solution. The sulphur will be found on the filter; the arsenic will remain in the solution, and may be precipitated in its metallic form by boiling with a strip of copper.

Nickel Ore.

The ores must be well roasted to expel the sulphur and arsenic; the greener the calx proves during this torrefaction, the more it abounds in the nickel; but the redder it is, the more iron it contains. The proper quantity of this roasted ore is fused in an open crucible, with twice or thrice its weight of black flux, and the whole covered with common salt. By exposing the crucible to the strongest heat of a forge fire, and making the fusion complete, a regulus will be produced. This regulus is not pure, but contains a portion of arsenic, cobalt, and iron. Of the first it may be deprived by a fresh calcination, with the addition of powdered charcoal; and of the second by scorification. But it is with difficulty that it is entirely freed from the iron.

In the Humid Way.

By solution in nitric acid it is freed from its sulphur; and by adding water to the solution, bismuth, if any, may be precipitated; as may silver, if contained it, by muriatic acid; and copper, when any, by iron.

To separate cobalt from nickel, the two oxides are dissolved in muriatic acid; the solution diluted with distilled water. The liquor is saturated with chlorine, and when cold, an excess of precipitated carbonate of baryta added. It is then set aside for 18 hours, when the cobalt will be precipitated as sesquioxide, while the nickel will remain in solution.

Cobalt Ores.

Free them as much as possible from earthy matters by well washing, and from sulphur and arsenic by roasting. The ore thus prepared is to be mixed with 3 parts of black flux, and a little decrepitated sea-salt; put the mixture in a lined crucible, cover it, and place it in a forge-fire, or in a hot furnace, for this ore is very difficult of fusion.

When well fused, a metallic regulus will be found at the bottom, covered with a scoria of a deep blue color; as almost all cobalt ores contain bismuth, this is reduced by the same operation as the regulus of cobalt; but as they are incapable of chemically uniting together, they are always found distinct from each other in the crucible. The regulus of bismuth, having a greater specific gravity, is always at the bottom, and may be separated by a blow with a hammer.

In the Humid Way.

Make a solution of the ore in nitric acid, or

aqua regia, and evaporate to dryness; the residuum, treated with the acetic acid, will yield to it the cobalt; the arsenic should be first precipitated by the addition of water.

Mercurial Ores.

The calciform ores of mercury are easily reduced without any addition. A quintal of the ore is put into a retort, and a receiver luted on, containing some water; the retort is placed in a sand-bath, and a sufficient degree of heat given it, to force over the mercury which is condensed in the water of the receiver.

Sulphuretted Mercurial Ores.

The sulphurous ores are assayed by distillation in the manner above, only those ores require an equal weight of clean iron-filings to be mixed with them, to disengage the sulphur, while the heat volatilizes the mercury, and forces it into the receiver. These ores should likewise be tried for cinnabar, to know whether it will answer the purpose of extracting it from them; for this a determinate quantity of the ore is finely powdered and put into a glass vessel, which is exposed to a gentle heat at first, and gradually increased till nothing more is sublimed. By the quantity thus acquired, a judgment may be formed whether the process will answer. Sometimes this cinnabar is not of so lively a color as that which is used in trade; in this case it may be refined by a second sublimation, and if it be still of too dark a color, it may be brightened by the addition of a quantity of mercury, and subliming it again.

Humid Assay of Cinnabar.

The stony matrix should be dissolved in nitric acid, and the cinnabar being disengaged, should be boiled in 8 or 10 times its weight of aqua regia, composed of 3 parts of nitric, and 1 of muriatic acid. The mercury may be precipitated in the metallic form by zinc.

Silver Ores.

Take the assay quantity of the ore finely powdered, and roast it well in a proper degree of heat, frequently stirring it with an iron rod; then add to it about double the quantity of granulated lead, put it in a covered crucible, and place it in a furnace; raise the fire gently at first, and continue to increase it gradually, till the metal begins to work; if it should appear too thick, make it thinner by the addition of a little more lead; if the metal should boil too rapidly, the fire should be diminished. The surface will be covered by degrees with a mass of scoria, at which time the metal should be carefully stirred with an iron hook heated, especially towards the border, lest any of the ore should remain undissolved; and if what is adherent to the hook when raised from the crucible melts quickly again, and the extremity of the hook, after it is grown cold is covered with a thin, shining smooth crust, the scorification is perfect; but, on the contrary, if, while stirring it, any considerable clamminess is perceived in the scoria, and when it adheres to the book, though red hot, and appears unequally tinged, and seems dusty or rough, with grains interspersed here and there, the scorification is incomplete; in consequence of which the fire should be increased a little, and what adheres to the hook should be gently beaten off, and returned with a small ladle into the crucible again. When the scorification is perfect, the metal should be poured into a cone, previously rubbed with a little tallow, and when it becomes cold, the scoria may be separated by a few strokes of a hammer. The button is the produce of the assay.

By Cupellation.

Take the assay quantity of ore, roast and grind it with an equal portion of litharge, divide it into 2 or 3 parts, and wrap each up in a small piece of paper; put a cupel previously seasoned under a muffle, with about 6 times the quantity of lead upon it. When the lead begins to work, carefully put one of the papers upon it, and after :his is absorbed, put on a second, and so on till the whole quantity is introduced; then raise the fire, and as the scoria is formed it will be taken up by the cupel, and at last the silver will remain alone. This will be the produce of the assay, unless the lead contains a small portion of silver, which may be discovered by putting an equal quantity of the same lead on another cupel, and working it off at the same time; if any silver be produced it must be deducted from the assay. This is called the witness.

In the Humid Way — Gay Lussac's Method.

Dissolve the ore or coin in nitric acid. Prepare a standard solution of common salt; 542·74 of common salt will precipitate 1000 parts of silver. It is convenient to have, also, solutions of 1-10th the standard strength for the final precipitations. Add the solution until no precipitate appears. From the amount of solution, and consequently of salt used, the amount of silver is at once determined without further weighing. To correct the result a standard silver solution is used at the same time, and any correction it may require is applied to the rest of the assay.

To Assay the Value of Silver.

The general method of examining the purity of silver is by mixing it with a quantity of lead proportionate to the supposed portion of alloy; by testing this mixture, and afterwards weighing the remaining button of silver. This is the same process as refining silver by cupellation.

It is supposed that the mass of silver to be examined consists of 12 equal parts, called pennyweights; so that if an ingot weighs 1 oz., each of the parts will be 1-12th oz. Hence, if the mass of silver be pure, it is called silver of 12 dwts.; if it contain 1-12th of its weight of alloy, it is called silver of 11 dwts.; if 2-12ths of its weight be alloy, it is called silver of 10 dwts; which parts of pure silver are called 5 dwts. It must be observed here that assayers give the name dwt. to a weight equal to 24 real grs., which must not be confounded with their ideal weight. The assayers' grs. are called fine grs. An ingot of fine silver, or silver of 12 dwts., contains, then, 288 fine grs.; if this ingot contain 1-288th of alloy, it is said to be silver of 11 dwts. and 23 grs.; if it contain 4-288th of alloy, it is said to be 11 dwts., 20 grs., etc. Now a certain real weight must be taken to represent the assay-weights; for instance, 36 real grs. represent 12 fine dwts.; this is subdivided into a sufficient number of other smaller weights, which also represent fractions of fine dwts. and grs. Thus, 18 real grs. represent 6 fine dwts; 3 real grs. represent 1 fine dwt., or 24 grs; 1½ real grs. represent 12 grs.; 1-32d of a real gr. represents ¼ of a fine gr., which is only 1-752d part of a mass of 12 dwt.

Double Assay of Silver.

It is customary to make a double assay. The silver for the assay should be taken from opposite sides of the ingot, and tried on a touch stone. Assayers know pretty nearly the value of silver merely by the look of the ingot, and still better by the test of the touch-stone. The quantity of lead to be added is regulated by the portion of alloy, which being in general copper, will be nearly as follows:

Of silver

	dwt. gr.	dwt. gr.	Requires from	
From	11 6 to	— —	5 to 6	Times its weight of lead.
	0 12 to	— —	8 to 9	
	19 18 to	9 0	12 to 13	
	8 6 to	7 12	13 to 14	
	6 18 to	6 0	14 to 15	
	3 0 to	1 12	0 to 16	
	1 12 to	0 18	0 to 20	

The cupel must be heated red-hot for half an hour before any metal is put upon them, by which all moisture is expelled. When the cupel is almost white by heat the lead is put into it, and the fire increased till the lead becomes red-hot, smoking, and agitated by a motion of all its parts, called its circulation. Then the silver is to be put on the cupel, and the fire continued till the silver has entered the lead; and when the mass circulates well, the heat must be diminished by closing more or less the door of the assay furnace. The heat should be so regulated, that the metal on its surface may appear convex and ardent, while the cupel is less red; that the smoke shall rise to the roof of the muffle; that undulations shall be made in all directions; and that the middle of the metal shall appear smooth, with a small circle of litharge, which is continually imbibed by the cupel. By this treatment the lead and alloy will be entirely absorbed by the cupel, and the silver become bright and shining, when it is said to lighten; after which, if the operation has been well performed, the silver will be covered with rainbow colors, which quickly undulate and cross each other, and then the button becomes fixed and solid.

The diminution of weight shows the quantity of alloy. As all lead contains a small portion of silver, an equal weight with that used in the assay is tested off, and the product deducted from the assay-weight. This portion is called the witness. —*Richardson's Metallic Arts.*

By Specific Gravity.

The approximate weight of silver or gold in a nugget may be determined by calculation from its specific gravity. See MISCELLANEOUS.

Ores and Earths Containing Gold.

That which is now most generally used is by amalgamation. The proper quantity is taken and reduced to a powder; about one-tenth of its weight of pure quicksilver is added, and the whole triturated in an iron mortar. The attraction subsisting between the gold and quicksilver, quickly unites them in the form of an amalgam, which is pressed through shamoy leather; the gold is easily separated from this amalgam, by exposure to a proper degree of heat, which evaporates the quicksilver, and leaves the gold. This evaporation should be made with luted vessels.

This is the foundation of all the operations by which gold is obtained from the rich mines of Peru, in South America.

Another Method.

Take a quantity of the gold-sand and heat it red-hot; quench it in water; repeat this two or three times, and the color of the sand will become a reddish brown. Then mix it with twice its weight of litharge, and revive the litharge into lead, by adding a small portion of charcoal-dust, and exposing it to a proper degree of heat; when the lead revives, it separates the gold from the sand; and the freeing of the gold from the lead must be afterwards performed by cupellation.

Another.—Bergmann assayed metallic ores containing gold, by mixing 2 parts of the ore, well pounded and washed, with 1½ of litharge, and 3 of glass; covering the whole with common salt, and melting it in a smith's forge, in a covered crucible; he then opened the crucible, put a nail into it, and continued to do so till the iron was no longer attacked. The lead was thus precipitated which contained the gold, and was afterwards separated by cupellation.

Humid Assay of Gold mixed with Iron Pyrites.

Dissolve the ore in 12 times its weight of diluted nitric acid, gradually added; place it in a proper degree of heat; this takes up the soluble parts, and leaves the gold untouched, with the insoluble matrix, from which it may be separated by aqua regia. The gold may be again separated from the aqua regia by pouring ether upon it; the ether takes up the gold, and by being burnt off leaves it in its metallic state. The solution may contain iron, copper, manganese, calcareous earth, or argil; if it be evaporated to dryness, and the residuum heated to redness for ½ an hour, ammonia will extract the copper; fuming nitric acid the earths; the acetic acid the manganese; and the muriatic acid the oxide of iron. The sulphur floats on the first solution, from which it should be separated by filtration.

PARTING.

By this process gold and silver are separated from each other. These two metals equally resisting the action of fire and lead, must therefore be separated by other means. This is effected by different menstrua. Nitric acid, muriatic acid, and sulphur, which cannot attack gold, operate upon silver; and these are the principal agents employed in this process.

Parting by nitric acid is most convenient, consequently most used; indeed, it is the only one employed by goldsmiths. This is called simply parting.

That made by the muriatic acid is by cementation, and is called cemented parting; and parting by sulphur is made by fusion, and called dry parting.

Parting by Aqua-fortis.

This process cannot succeed unless we attend to some essential circumstances: 1st. The gold and silver must be in a proper proportion, viz. the silver ought to be three parts to one of gold; though a mass containing two parts of silver to one of gold may be parted. To judge of the quality of the metal to be parted, assayers make a comparison upon a touch-stone, between it and certain needles composed of gold and silver, in graduated proportions, and properly marked; which are called proof needles. If this trial shows that the silver is not to the gold as three to one, the mass is improper for the operation, unless more silver be added. And 2dly, that the parting may be exact, the aqua-fortis must be very pure, especially free from any mixture of the sulphuric or muriatic acid. For if this were not attended to, a quantity of silver proportional to these two foreign acids would be separated during the solution; and this quantity of silver would remain mingled with the gold, which consequently would not be entirely purified by the operation.

The gold and silver to be parted ought previously to be granulated by melting it in a crucible, and pouring it into a vessel of water, giving the water at the same time a rapid circular motion, by quickly stirring it round with a stick. The vessels generally used in this operation are called parting glasses, which ought to be very well annealed, and chosen free from flaws; as one of the chief inconveniences attending the operation is, that the glasses are apt to crack by exposure to cold, or even when touched by the hand. Some operators secure the bottom of the glasses by a coating composed of a mixture of new-slaked lime, with beer and whites of eggs, spread on a cloth, and wrapped round the glasses at the bottom; over which they apply a composition of clay and hair. The parting glasses should be placed in vessels containing water supported by trivets, with a fire under them; because if a glass should break, the contents are caught in the vessel of water. If the heat communicated to the water be too great, it may be properly regulated by pouring cold water gradually and carefully down the side of the vessel into a parting glass 15 inches high, and 10 or 12 inches wide at the bottom; placed in a copper pan 12 inches wide at bottom, 15 inches wide at top, and 10 inches high, there is usually put about 80 oz. of metal, with twice as much of aqua-fortis.

The nitric acid ought to be of 22° B., afterwards of 32° B. Little heat should be applied at first, as the liquor is apt to swell and rise over the vessel; but when the acid is nearly saturated, the heat may safely be increased. When the solution ceases, which is known by the effervescence discontinuing, the liquor is to be poured off; if any grains appear entire, more aqua-fortis must be added, till the silver is all dissolved. If the operation has been performed slowly, the remaining gold will have the form of distinct masses. The gold appears black after parting; its parts have no adhesion together, because the silver dissolved from it has left many interstices. To give them more solidity, and improve their color, they are put into a test under a muffle, and made red-hot, after which they contract and become more solid, and the gold resumes its color and lustre. It is then called grain gold. If the operation has been performed hastily, the gold will have the appearance of black mud or powder, which, after well washing, must be melted.

The silver is usually recovered by precipitating it from the aqua-fortis by means of pure copper, or by precipitation by muriatic acid and reduction. If the solution be perfectly saturated, no precipitation can take place till a few drops of aqua-fortis are added to the liquor. The precipitate of silver must be well washed with boiling water, and may be fused with nitre, or tested off with lead.

Parting by Cementation.

A cement is prepared, composed of 4 parts of bricks powdered and sifted; of 1 part of green vitriol calcined till it becomes red; and of 1 part of common salt. This is to be made into a firm paste with a little water. It is called the cement royal.

The gold to be cemented is reduced into plates as thin as money. At the bottom of the crucible or cementing pot, a stratum of cement, of the thickness of a finger, is put, which is covered with plates of gold; and so the strata are placed alternately. The whole is covered with a lid, which is luted with a mixture of clay and sand. This pot must be placed in a furnace or oven, heated gradually till it becomes red-hot, in which it must be continued during 24 hours. The heat must not melt the gold. The pot or crucible is then suffered to cool; and the gold carefully separated from the cement, and boiled at different times in a large quantity of pure water. It is then assayed upon a touch-stone, or otherwise; and if it be not sufficiently pure, it is cemented a second time. In this process the sulphuric acid of the calcined vitriol decomposes the common salt during the cementation, by uniting to its alkaline base, while the muriatic acid becomes concentrated by the heat and dissolves the silver alloyed with the gold. This is a very troublesome process, though it succeeds when the portion of silver is so small that it would be defended from the action of aqua-fortis by the superabundant gold; but is little used, except to extract silver, or base metals, from the surface of gold, and thus giving to an alloyed metal the color and appearance of pure gold.

Pattinson's Process.

For separating silver from lead ores, enables us to reduce profitably ores containing but 1 oz. of silver to the ton. It depends upon the fact that an alloy of lead and silver when cooled, with occasional stirring, to near the point of solidification, crystallizes in part, and these crystals are found to contain much less lead than the original fused mass. Eight or ten cast-iron pots are arranged in line and heated. Into the centre one a charge, say 5 tons, of the original alloy is put; as the crystals form they are removed by means of a perforated ladle, and put in the pot to the right until about four-fifths have been removed; the remaining enriched lead is transferred to the pot to the left. This process is continued with the remaining pots, thus gradually enriching to the left and becoming poorer to the right. The rich alloy, termed *lead riches*, is then cupelled.

ALLOYS, OR COMPOUND METALS.

Metals, in general, will unite with each other by fusion or amalgamation, and acquire new properties. Brass is a compound of copper and zinc; and possesses a different color to either of the component parts.

As metals fuse in different degrees of heat, care should be taken not to add those metals which fuse easily, to others which require a greater degree of heat, while they are too hot, because the former may evaporate and leave the compound imperfect. Or, if they are brought into fusion together, it should be under a flux to prevent the volatile metals from evaporating before the union is effected.

Or-moulu—Mosaic Gold.

Melt together equal parts of copper and zinc, *at the lowest temperature that will fuse the former*, stir them well to produce an intimate mixture of the metals, and add by degrees small quantities of zinc; the alloy first assumes a yellow color like brass, on adding a little more zinc it becomes purple, and lastly perfectly white, which is the proper appearance of the desired product when fused. The quantity of zinc to be used altogether, should be from 52 to 55 parts out of the hundred.

Talmi Gold.

A beautiful gold-colored alloy, sold under the above name, gives on analysis: Copper, 86.4; zinc, 12.2; tin, 1.1; iron, 0.3. The presence of the iron was probably accidental.

Queen's Metal.

Melt together 4½ lbs. of tin, ½ lb. of bismuth, ½ lb. of antimony, and ½ lb. of lead. A very excellent alloy will be formed by using these proportions; it is used for making tea-pots and other vessels which are required to imitate silver. They retain their brilliancy to the last.

Another. — A very fine silver-looking metal is composed of 100 lbs. of tin, 8 of regulus of antimony, 1 of bismuth, and 4 of copper.

Tombac.

Melt together 16 lbs. of copper, 1 lb. of tin, and 1 lb. of zinc.

ALLOYS.

Red Tombac.
Put into a crucible 5½ lbs. of copper; when fused add ½ lb. of zinc; these metals will combine, forming an alloy of a reddish color, but possessing more lustre than copper, and also greater durability.

White Tombac.
When copper is combined with arsenic, by melting them together in a close crucible, and covering the surface with common salt to prevent oxidation, a white brittle alloy is formed.

Common Pewter.
Melt in a crucible 7 lbs. of tin, and when fused throw in 1 lb. of lead, 6 oz. of copper and 2 oz. of zinc. This combination of metals will form an alloy of great durability and tenacity; also of considerable lustre.

Best Pewter.
The best sort of pewter consists of 100 parts of tin, and 17 of regulus of antimony.

Hard Pewter.
Melt together 12 lbs. of tin, 1 lb. of regulus of antimony, and 4 oz. of copper.

Common Solder.
Put into a crucible 2 lbs. of lead, and when melted throw in 1 lb. of tin. This alloy is that generally known by the name of solder. When heated by a hot iron and applied to tinned iron with powdered rosin, it acts as a cement or solder; it is also used to join leaden pipes, etc.

Hard Solder.
Melt together 2 lbs. of copper, and 1 lb of tin.

Soft Solder.
Melt together 2 lbs. of tin, and 1 of lead. The lining of tea chests makes a good solder for tin ware, being made of tin and lead in about the proper proportions.

Gold Solder
Consists of 24 parts gold, 2 silver, and 1 of copper.

Silver Solder.
Hard—4 parts of silver to 1 of copper. Soft—2 parts of silver to 1 of brass wire.

Shot Metal.
Lead, 1000 parts; metallic arsenic, 3 parts.

Printers' Types.
Put into a crucible 10 lbs. of lead, and when it is in a state of fusion, throw in 2 lbs. of antimony; these metals, in such proportions, form the alloy of which common printing types are made. The antimony gives a hardness to the lead, without which the type would speedily be rendered useless in a printing press. Different proportions of lead, copper, brass, and antimony, frequently constitute this metal. Every artist has his own proportions, so that the same composition cannot be obtained from different foundries; each boasts of the superiority of his own mixture.

Small Types and Stereotype Plates.
Melt 9 lbs. of lead, and throw into the crucible 2 lbs. of antimony and 1 lb. of bismuth; these metals will combine, forming an alloy of a peculiar quality. This quality is *expansion* as it cools, it is therefore well suited for the formation of small printing types (particularly when many are cast together to form stereotype plates), as the whole of the mould is accurately filled with the alloy; consequently there can be no blemish in the letters. If a metal or alloy liable to *contract* in cooling were to be used, the effect of course would be very different.

Another.—The proprietors of different foundries adopt different compositions for stereotype plates. Some form an alloy of 8 parts of lead, 2 parts of antimony, and ½ part of tin.

Mode of Casting.
For the manufacture of stereotype plates, plaster of Paris, of the consistence of a batter-pudding before baking, is poured over the letter-press page, and worked into the interstices of the types with a brush. It is then collected from the sides by a slip of iron or wood, so as to be smooth and compact. In about 2 minutes the whole mass is hardened into a solid cake. This cake, which is to serve as the matrix of the stereotype plate, is now put upon a rack in an oven, where it undergoes great heat, so as to drive off superfluous moisture. When ready for use, these moulds, according to their size, are placed in flat cast-iron pots, and are covered over by another piece of cast-iron perforated at each end to admit the metallic composition intended for the preparation of the stereotype plates. The flat cast-iron pots are now fastened in a crane, which carries them steadily to the metallic bath, or melting pot, where they are immersed and kept for a considerable time, until all the pores and crevices of the mould are completely and accurately filled. When this has taken place the pots are elevated from the bath by working the crane, and are placed over a water trough, to cool gradually. When cold the whole is turned out of the pots, and the plaster being separated by hammering and washing, the plates are ready for use; having received the most exact and perfect impression.

White Metal.
Melt together 10 oz. of lead, 5 oz. of bismuth, and 4 drs. of regulus of antimony.

Another.—Melt together 2 lbs. of regulus of antimony, 8 oz. of brass, and 10 oz. of tin.

Common Hard White Metal
Melt together 1 lb. of brass, 1½ oz. of spelter, and ½ oz. of tin.

Tutenag.
Melt together 2 parts of tin and 1 of bismuth.

Fusible Alloy.
Put into a crucible 4 oz. of bismuth, and when in a state of fusion throw in 2½ oz. of lead, and 1¼ oz. of tin; these metals will combine, forming an alloy fusible at the temperature of boiling water. Mould this alloy in bars, and take them to a silversmith's to be made into a half-a-dozen teaspoons. If one of these be given to a stranger to stir his tea, as soon as it is poured from the teapot, he will be not a little surprised to find the spoon melt in the tea-cup.

The fusibility of this alloy is certainly surprising, for the fusing temperature of each of its components, singly, is higher than twice that of boiling water. Bismuth fuses at 476°, lead at 612°, and tin at 442°; whilst water boils at 212°.

Another.—Melt together 1 oz. of zinc, 1 oz. of bismuth, and 1 oz. of lead. This alloy will be found to be remarkably fusible (although each of the metals, separately, requires considerable heat to melt it), and will melt even in hot water; it will likewise remain in a fused state on a sheet of paper, over the flame of a lamp or candle. Both of these alloys expand on cooling, and are well adapted for taking casts of medals, etc.

Wood's (patent) Fusible Metal
Melts between 150° and 160° Fahr. It consists of 3 parts cadmium, 4 tin, 8 lead, and 15 bismuth. It has a brilliant metallic lustre, and does not tarnish readily.

Casts from Fusible Metal.
A combination of 3 parts of lead, with 2 of tin

and 5 of bismuth, forms an alloy which melts at the temperature of 197° Fahr.

In making casts with this and similar alloys it is important to use the metal at a temperature as low as possible; as, if but a few degrees elevated, the water which adheres to the things from which casts are to be taken forms vapor, and produces bubbles. The fused metal must be allowed to cool in a teacup until just ready to set at the edges, and then pour it into the moulds, procuring in this way beautiful casts from moulds of wood, or of other similar substances. When taking impressions from gems, seals, etc. the fused alloy should be placed on paper or paste-board, and stirred about till it becomes pasty, from cooling, at which moment the gem, die, or seal should be suddenly stamped on it, and a very sharp impression will then be obtained.

Metallic Injection.

Melt together equal parts of bismuth, lead, and tin, with a sufficient quantity of quicksilver.

This composition, with the addition of a small proportion of mercury, is used for injecting the vessels of many anatomical preparations; also for taking correct casts of various cavities of the body, as those of the ear. The animal structure may be corroded and separated by means of a solution of potassa in water, and the metallic cast will be preserved in an isolated state.

For Cushions of Electrical Machines.

Melt together in a crucible 2 drs. of zinc and 1 of tin; when fused, pour them into a cold crucible, containing 5 drs. of mercury. The mercury will combine with those metals and form an alloy (or amalgam, as it is called) fit to be rubbed on the cushions which press the plate or cylinder of an electrical machine. Before the amalgam is applied it is proper to rub the cushion with a mixture of tallow and beeswax.

For Varnishing Figures.

Fuse ½ oz. of tin with the same quantity of bismuth in a crucible; when melted add ½ oz. of mercury. When perfectly combined take the mixture from the fire and cool it. This substance, mixed with the white of an egg, forms a very beautiful varnish for plaster figures, etc.

Moirée Metallique.—A Method of Ornamenting the Surface of Tin Plate by Acids.

The plates are washed by an alkaline solution, then in water, heated, and sponged or sprinkled with the acid solution. The appearance varies with the degree of heat and the nature and strength of the acids employed. The plates, after the application of the acids, are plunged into water slightly acidulated, dried, and covered with white or colored varnishes. The following are some of the acid mixtures used: Nitro-muriatic acid, in different degrees of dilution; sulphuric acid, with 5 parts of water; 1 part of sulphuric acid, 2 of muriatic acid, and 8 of water; a strong solution of citric acid; 1 part nitric acid, 2 sulphuric, and 18 of water. Solution of potash is also used.

To Plate Looking-glasses.

This art is erroneously termed *silvering*, for, as will be presently seen, there is not a particle of silver present in the whole composition.

On tin-foil, fitly disposed on a flat table, mercury is to be poured, and gently rubbed with a hare's-foot: it soon unites itself with the tin, which then becomes very splendid, or, as the workmen say, is *quickened*. A plate of glass is then cautiously to be slid upon the tin-leaf, in such a manner as to sweep off the redundant mercury which is not incorporated with the tin; leaden weights are then to be placed on the glass, and in a little time the quicksilvered tin foil adheres so firmly to the glass that the weights may be removed without any danger of its falling off. The glass thus coated is a common looking-glass. About 2 oz. of mercury are sufficient for covering 3 square feet of glass.

The success of this operation depends much on the clearness of the glass; and the least dirt or dust on its surface will prevent the adhesion of the amalgam or alloy.

Liquid Foil for Silvering Glass Globes.

Melt together 1 oz. of clean lead, and 1 oz. of fine tin, in a clean iron ladle; then immediately add 1 oz. of bismuth. Skim off the dross, remove the ladle from the fire, and before it sets add 10 oz. of quicksilver. Now stir the whole carefully together, taking care not to breathe over it, as the fumes of the mercury are very pernicious. Pour this through an earthen pipe into the glass globe, which turn repeatedly round.

Another.—To 4 oz. of quicksilver add as much tin-foil as will become barely fluid when mixed. Let the globe be clean and warm, and inject the quicksilver by means of a pipe at the aperture, turning it about till it is silvered all over. Let the remainder run out, and hang the globe up.

Another.—For this purpose 1 part of mercury and 4 of tin have been used; but if 2 parts of mercury, 1 of tin, 1 of lead, and 1 of bismuth are melted together, the compound which they form will answer the purpose better. Either of them must be made in an iron ladle, over a clear fire, and must be frequently stirred.

Martin's Process for Silvering Glass.

Prepare, 1. A solution of 10 grammes of nitrate of silver in 100 grammes of distilled water. 2. Take solution of ammonia of 13° Cartier's areometer. 3. A solution of 20 grammes of pure caustic soda in 500 grammes of distilled water. 4. A solution of 25 grammes of ordinary white sugar in 200 grammes of distilled water. Pour into this 1 cubic centimetre of nitric acid, of 36°, and boil for 20 minutes; then make up the volume of 500 cubic centimetres with distilled water and 50 cubic centimetres of alcohol at 36°. This done, prepare an argentiferous solution, by mixing in a flask 12 cubic centimetres of solution 1, then 8 cubic centimetres of solution 2, then 20 centimetres of solution 3; and, lastly, make up a volume of 100 centimetres by 60 centimetres of distilled water. If the directions have been properly observed the liquid will remain limpid, and a drop of solution of nitrate of silver will produce a permanent precipitate. After being left quiet for 24 hours the solution is ready for use. Clean the surface to be silvered with a cotton plug moistened with a few drops of nitric acid; then wash with distilled water, drain, and place it on supports on the surface of a bath composed of the argentiferous liquid, to which has been added 1-10th or 1-12th of the solution of sugar (4). Under the influence of diffused light the liquid becomes yellow, then brown, and, after from 2 to 5 minutes, the whole surface of the glass will have been silvered. After 10 or 15 minutes it will have attained the required thickness. Wash first with ordinary water, then with distilled water; drain, dry, and polish with rouge on chamois. (A table of French Weights and Measures will be found at the end of the volume.)

Mode of Repairing the Silvering of Looking-glasses.

Uncover and clean the damaged spot by very careful rubbing with fine cotton until there is no trace of grease or dust; then with the point of a

ALLOYS.

knife cut the size of the required piece on the silvering of another glass; a small globule of mercury (the size of a pin's hand for a surface the size of the finger nail) is dropped upon the cut piece. The mercury penetrates as far as the cut, and allows the piece to be removed. It is then gently pressed on the spot with a piece of cotton.

Bath-metal.

Melt together 1 lb. of brass and 4½ oz. of spelter.

Brass.

Put 4½ lbs. of copper into a crucible, expose it to heat in a furnace, and when perfectly fused add 1½ lbs. of zinc. The metals will combine, forming that generally used alloy called brass.

Another.—For brass which is to be cast into plates, from which pans and kettles are to be made, and wire is to be drawn, braziers use calamine of the finest sort instead of pure zinc, and in a greater proportion than when common brass is made; generally 56 lbs. of calamine to 34 lbs. of copper. Old brass, which has frequently been exposed to the action of the fire, when mixed with the copper and calamine, renders the brass far more ductile and fitter for the making of fine wire than it would be without it.

Pinchbeck.

Put into a crucible 5 oz. of pure copper; when it is in a state of fusion add 1 oz. of zinc. These metals combine, forming an alloy not unlike jeweller's gold; pour it into a mould of any shape. This alloy is used for inferior jewellery.

Some use only half this quantity of zinc, in which proportion the alloy is more easily worked, especially in the making of jewellery.

Another.—Melt together 1 oz. of brass with 1½ or 2 oz. of copper, fused under a coat of charcoal-dust.

Oréide, a New Brass.

M. M. Mourier and Vallent, of Paris, have succeeded in making an alloy which imitates gold sufficiently near to merit the name Oréide. The properties are as follows: Pure copper, 100 parts, by weight; zinc, 17; magnesia, 6; sal ammoniac, 3.6; quicklime, 1.80; tartar of commerce, 9. The copper is first melted, then the magnesia, sal ammoniac, lime and tartar in powder, little by little; the crucible is briskly stirred for about ½ an hour, so as to mix thoroughly, and then the zinc is added in small grains by throwing it on the surface and stirring until it is entirely fused; the crucible is then covered and fusion maintained for about 35 minutes; the crucible is then uncovered, skimmed carefully and the alloy cast in a mould of damp sand or metal. The oréide melts at a temperature low enough to allow its application to all kinds of ornamentation; it has a fine grain, is malleable, and capable of taking the most brilliant polish; when, after a time, it becomes tarnished from oxidation, its brilliancy may be restored by a little acidulated water. If the zinc is replaced by tin, the metal will be still more brilliant.

Prince's Metal.

Melt together 3 oz. of copper, and 1 oz. of zinc; or, 8 oz. of brass and 1 oz. of zinc.

Another.—Melt in a crucible 4 oz. of copper, and when fused, add 2 oz. of zinc; they will combine, and form a very beautiful and useful alloy, called Prince Rupert's metal.

Bronze.

Melt in a clean crucible 7 lbs. of pure copper; when fused, throw into it 3 lbs. of zinc and 2 lbs. of tin. These metals will combine, forming bronze, which, from the exactness of the impression which it takes from a mould, has, in ancient and modern times, been generally used in the formation of busts, medals and statues.

Specula of Telescopes.

Melt 7 lbs. of copper, and when fused add 3 lbs. of zinc and 4 lbs. of tin. These metals will combine to form a beautiful alloy of great lustre, and of a light yellow color, fitted to be made into specula for telescopes. Mr. Mudge used only copper and grain tin, in the proportion of 2 lbs. to 14½ oz.

Gun-metal.

Melt together 112 lbs. of Bristol brass, 14 lbs. of spelter, and 7 lbs. of block tin.

Another.—Melt together 9 parts of copper and 1 part of tin; the above compounds are those used in the manufacture of small and great brass guns, swivels, etc.

The pieces of ordnance used by the besiegers at the battle of Prague, were actually melted by the frequency of the firing; the mixture of which they were made contained a large portion of lead; it would have been less prone to melt, and consequently preferable, had it contained none. A mixture of copper and tin is preferred to pure copper, not only for the casting of cannon, but of statues, etc., for pure copper, in running through the various parts of the mould, would lose so much of its heat as to *set*, or become solid too soon.

Austrian Gun-metal (Aich's Metal),

Remarkable for great strength, being stronger than gun-metal or wrought-iron, consists of copper, 55.04; zinc, 42.36; tin, .83; iron, 1.77.

Aluminum Bronze

Resembles gold in appearance; is said to be twice as strong as the best gun-metal; as light as wrought-iron; is not easily tarnished. It is easily stamped and engraved. It is composed of 10 parts of aluminum and 90 of copper. It requires to be re-melted, as the first melting is brittle.

Babbitt's Anti-friction Metal.

Mix together 24 parts of copper, 24 of tin and 8 of antimony. The tin, best quality of Bancoa, is to be added gradually to the melted composition.

Bell-metal.

Melt together 6 parts of copper and 2 of tin. These proportions are the most approved for bells throughout Europe and in China.

Another.—Some bells are made in the proportion of 10 parts of copper to 2 of tin. It may be in general observed, that a less proportion of tin is used for making church bells than clock bells, and that a little zinc is added for the bells of repeating watches and other small bells.

Blanched Copper.

Melt together 8 oz. of copper and ½ oz. of neutral arsenical salt, fused together, under a flux composed of calcined borax, charcoal dust, and finely-powdered glass.

Composition of Ancient Statues.

According to Pliny, the metal used by the Romans for their statues, and for the plates on which they engraved inscriptions, was composed in the following manner: They first melted a quantity of copper, into which they put a third of its weight of old copper, which had been long in use; to every 100 lbs. weight of this mixture they added 12½ lbs. of an alloy composed of equal parts of lead and tin.

Muntz Metal

Can be rolled and worked at a red heat. It consists of 6 parts of copper and 4 of zinc.

Mock-platina.

Melt together 8 oz. of brass and 5 of spelter.

Fine Casting of Brass, etc.

The principal object in fine casting is to have a mould that shall receive a beautiful impression, and at the same time sufficiently adhesive to resist the force of the fluid metal, that shall neither wash nor be injured by the heat. The sand that covers or surrounds the model should be fine, close sand; after removing the mould, the model must be faced with burnt rotten-stone, and covered with loam, each dusted through a bag, and the mould laid down upon it; this facing may be repeated, the mould must be dried and smoked with a torch; in lieu of water, the sand is moistened with a solution of tartar, or the lees of wine, or with cream of tartar. Care must be taken to loosen the band quickly, viz.: loosen the first mould while the second is pouring, etc. On removing the work every particle of the facing should be carefully scraped from the mould and thrown away. Part the moulds with coal and black rosin.

Gilding-metal.

Melt together 4 parts of copper, 1 of Bristol old brass and 14 oz. of tin to every lb. of copper.

For Common Jewellery.

Melt together 3 parts of copper, 1 of Bristol old brass and 4 oz. of tin to every lb. of copper.

If this alloy is for fine polishing, the tin may be omitted, and a mixture of lead and antimony substituted. Paler polishing metal is made by reducing the copper to two or to one part.

Yellow Dipping-metal.

Melt together 2 parts of brass, 1 part of copper, with a little old brass, and ¼ oz. of tin to every lb. of copper. This alloy is almost of the color, etc., of gold coin.

Another.—Good dipping-metal may be made of 1 lb. of copper to 5 oz. of spelter; the copper should be tough cake, and not tile.

When antimony is used instead of tin, it should be in smaller quantity, or the metal will be brittle.

Imitation of Silver.

When copper is melted with tin, about ⅜ oz. of tin to 1 lb. of copper, will make a pale bell-metal; it will roll and ring very near to sterling silver.

Tutania or Britannia Metal.

Melt together 4 oz. of plate-brass and 4 oz. tin. When in fusion, add 4 oz. bismuth and 4 oz. regulus of antimony.

This is the hardening, which is to be added at discretion to melted tin, until it has the requisite color and hardness.

Another.—Melt together 2 lbs. of plate-brass, 2 lbs. of a mixture of copper and arsenic, either by cementing or melting, 2 lbs. of tin, 2 lbs. of bismuth and 2 lbs. regulus of antimony.

This is to be added at discretion to melted tin.

Another.—Melt together 1 lb. of copper, 1 lb. tin and 2 lbs. regulus of antimony, with or without a little bismuth.

Another.—Melt together 8 oz. Shruff brass, 2 lbs. regulus of antimony and 10 lbs. tin.

This is fit for use as Britannia metal.

German Tutania.

Melt together 2 drs. of copper, 1 oz. of regulus of antimony and 12 oz. of tin.

Spanish Tutania.

To 8 oz. of scrap-iron or steel, at a white heat, add 1 lb. of antimony in small portions, with 3 oz. of nitre. Melt and harden 1 lb. of tin with 2 oz. of this compound.

German Silver.

Melt together 20 parts of copper, 15.8 of nickel, 12.7 of zinc.

Another.—Melt together 4 oz. of antimony, 1 oz. arsenic, and 2 lbs. tin. This compound is ready for use. The first of these Spanish alloys would be a beautiful metal, if arsenic were added.

Engestroom Tutania.

Melt together 4 parts copper, 8 parts regulus of antimony, and 1 part bismuth.

When added to 100 parts of tin, this compound will be ready for use.

Kustitien's Metal for Tinning.

To 1 lb. of malleable iron, at a white heat, add 5 oz. regulus of antimony, and 24 lbs. of the purest Molucca tin.

This alloy polishes without the blue tint, and is free from lead or arsenic.

Solder for Steel Joints.

Take of fine silver, 19 dwts.; copper, 1 dwt.; and brass, 2 dwts. Melt these under a coat of charcoal-dust.

This solder possesses several advantages over the usual spelter solder, or brass, when employed in soldering cast-steel, etc., as it fuses with less heat, and its whiteness has a better appearance than brass.

Brass Solder for Iron.

Thin plates of brass are to be melted between the pieces that are to be joined. If the work be very fine, as when two leaves of a broken saw are to be brazed together, cover it with pulverized borax, melted with water, that it may incorporate with the brass powder which is added to it; the piece must be then exposed to the fire without touching the coals, and heated till the brass is seen to run.

Tungsten Steel.

Experiments have been made at Vienna, Dresden, and other places, in the use of tungsten or wolfram, in the alloying of steel, and some extraordinary results are stated to have been achieved. It is said that steel alloyed with 20 per cent. of tungsten produces a mixture, which, while it retains all the general qualities of steel, is so excessively hard, that tools made of it will cut, without difficulty, the hardest cast-steel.

A New Silver Alloy.

M. De Ruolz and De Fontenay, of France, have lately obtained, after several years' experiments, a new alloy, which may be very useful for small coin and for many industrial uses. It is composed of ⅓ silver, 25 to 30 per cent. of nickel, and from 37 to 50 per cent. of copper. Its inventors propose to call it tiers-argent, or tri-silver. Its preparation is said to be a triumph of metallurgical science. The 3 metals when simply melted together form a compound which is not homogeneous; and to make the compound perfect, its inventors have been compelled to use phosphorus and certain solvents which they have not yet specified. The alloy thus obtained is at first very brittle; it cannot be hammered or drawn, and lacks those properties which are essential in malleable metals. But after the phosphorus is eliminated, the alloy perfectly resembles a simple metal, and possesses, in a very high degree, the qualities to which the precious metals owe their superiority. In color it resembles platinum, and is susceptible of a very high polish. It possesses extreme hardness and tenacity. It is ductile, malleable, very easily fused, emits when struck a beautiful sound, is not affected by exposure to the atmosphere, or to any but the most powerful re-agents. It is without odor. Its specific gravity is a little less than that of silver. An alloy possessing these qualities must be very useful to gold and silversmiths. It can be supplied at a price 40 per cent. less than silver, and its greater hardness will give it a marked superiority. It may also serve as a substitute for gold-plated or silver-plated articles, which are now so common on account of their cheapness, but which will not bear replating more than a few times, and which are, in the long run, sometimes more expensive than the pure metal. The new alloy, however, will be most useful for small coin. Its preparation and coinage are so difficult that the coin made of it cannot easily be counterfeited. Its hardness would render it more durable than silver; and thus the expense of re-coining, and the heavy loss arising from the wearing of our silver coinage, would be greatly diminished.

Silver Test.

Silver coins, jewelry, or any other rich alloy, when moistened with a solution of chromic acid, or a mixture of bichromate of potassa and sulphuric acid, become covered with a red purple spot of bichromate of silver. This spot does not occur on poor alloys or metals imitating silver.

Useful Alloy of Gold with Platinum.

Put into a clean crucible 7½ drs. of pure gold, and when perfectly melted, throw in ¼ a dr. of platinum. The 2 metals will combine intimately, forming an alloy rather whiter than pure gold, but remarkably *ductile* and *elastic;* it is also less perishable than pure gold or jewellers' gold; but more readily fusible than that metal.

These excellent qualities must render this alloy an object of great interest to workers in metals. For *springs*, where steel cannot be used, it will prove exceedingly advantageous.

It is a curious circumstance, that the alloy of gold and platinum is soluble in nitric acid, which does not act on either of the metals in a separate state. It is remarkable, too, that the alloy has very nearly the color of platinum, even when composed of 11 parts of gold to 1 of the former metal.

Ring Gold.

Melt together of Spanish copper, 6 dwts. and 12 grs.; fine silver, 3 dwts. and 16 grs., to 1 oz. 5 dwts. of gold coin.

Gold from 35s to 40s per oz.

Melt together 8 oz. 8 dwts. of Spanish copper, 10 dwts. of fine silver, to 1 oz. of gold coin.

Manheim-Gold, or Similor.

Melt together 3½ oz. of copper, 1½ oz. of brass, and 15 grs. of pure gold.

PREPARATION OF FOILS.

Foils are thin plates or leaves of metal that are put under stones, or compositions in imitation of stones, when they are set.

The intention of foils is either to increase the lustre or play of the stones, or more generally to improve the color, by giving an additional force to the tinge, whether it be natural or artificial, by that of a ground of the same hue, which the foil is in this case made to be.

There are consequently two kinds of foils; the one is colorless, where the effect of giving lustre or play to the stone is produced by the polish of the surface, which makes it act as a mirror, and, by reflecting the light, prevents that deadness which attends the having a duller ground under the stone, and brings it by the double refraction of the light that is caused, nearer to the effect of the diamond. The other is colored with some pigment or stain of the same hue as the stone, or of some other which is intended to modify and change the hue of the stone in some degree; as, where a yellow foil may be put under green, which is too much inclined to the blue, or under crimson, where it is desired to have the appearance more orange or scarlet.

Foils may be made of copper or tin; and silver has been sometimes used, with which it has been advised, for some purposes, to mix gold; but the expense of either is needless, as copper may be made to answer the same end.

To Prepare Copper for Foils.

Where colored foils are wanted, copper may therefore be best used, and may be prepared for the purpose, by the following means:

Take copper plates beaten to a proper thickness, and pass them betwixt a pair of fine steel rollers very close set, and draw them as thin as is possible to retain a proper tenacity. Polish them with very fine whiting, or rotten-stone, till they shine, and have as much brightness as can be given them, and they will then be fit to receive the color.

To Whiten Foils.

Where the yellow, or rather orange-color of the ground would be injurious to the effect, as in the case of purples, or crimson red, the foils should be whitened, which may be done in the following manner:

Take a small quantity of silver and dissolve it in aqua-fortis, and then put bits of copper into the solution, and precipitate the silver; which being done the fluid must be poured off, and fresh water added to it, to wash away all the remainder of the first fluid; after which the silver must be dried, an equal weight of cream of tartar and common salt must then be ground with it, till the whole be reduced to a very fine powder; and with this mixture, the foils, being first slightly moistened, must be rubbed by the finger, or a bit of linen rag, till they be of the degree of whiteness desired; after which, if it appear to be wanted, the polish must be refreshed.

The tin foils are only used in the case of colorless stones, where quicksilver is employed; and they may be drawn out by the same rollers, but need not be further polished, as that effect is produced by other means in this case.

Foils for Crystals, Pebbles, or Paste, to give the Lustre and Play of Diamonds.

The manner of preparing foils, so as to give colorless stones the greatest degree of play and lustre, is by raising so high a polish or smoothness on the surface, as to give them the effect of a mirror, which can only be done, in a perfect manner, by the use of quicksilver, applied in the same general way as in the case of looking-glasses. The method by which it may be best performed is as follows:

Take leaves of tin, prepared in the same manner as for silvering looking-glasses, and cut them into small pieces of such size as to cover the surface of the sockets or the stones that are to be set. Lay three of these then, one upon another, and having moistened the inside of the socket with thin gum-water, and suffered it to become again so dry that only a slight stickiness remains, put the three pieces of leaves, lying on each other, into it, and adapt them to the surface in as even a manner as possible. When this is done, heat the socket and fill it with warm quicksilver, which must be suffered to continue in it 3 or 4 minutes, and then gently poured out. The stone must then be thrust into the socket, and closed with it, care having been taken to give such room for it that it may enter without stripping off the tin and quicksilver from any part of the furnace. The work should be well closed round the stone, to prevent the tin and quicksilver contained in the socket from being shaken out by any violence.

The lustre of stones set in this manner will continue longer than when they are set in the common way, as, the cavity round them being filled, there will be no passage found for moisture, which is so injurious to the wear of stones treated in any other way.

This kind of foil likewise gives some lustre to glass or other transparent matter, which has little of itself; but to stones or pastes that have some share of play it gives a most beautiful brilliance.

To Color Foils.

Two methods have been invented for coloring foils: the one by tingeing the surface of the copper of the color required by means of smoke, the other by staining or painting it with some pigment or other coloring substance.

The colors used for painting foils may be tempered with either oil, water rendered duly viscid by gum Arabic, size or varnish. Where deep colors are wanted, oil is most proper, because some pigments become wholly transparent in it, as lake, or Prussian blue; but yellow and green may be better laid on in varnish, as these colors may be had in perfection from a tinge wholly dissolved in spirit of wine, in the same manner as in the case of lacquers, and the most beautiful green is to be produced by distilled verdigris, which is apt to lose its color and turn black with oil. In common cases, however, any of the colors may be, with least trouble, laid on with isinglass size. in the same manner as the glazing colors used in miniature painting.

Ruby Colors.

For red, where the ruby is to be imitated, carmine, a little lake used in isinglass size, or shellac varnish is to be employed, if the glass or paste be of a full crimson, verging towards the purple; but if the glass incline to the scarlet or orange, very bright lake (that is, not purple) may be used alone in oil.

Garnet Red.

For the garnet red, dragon's blood dissolved in seed-lac varnish may be used; and for the vinegar garnet, the orange lake, tempered with shellac varnish, will be found excellent.

Amethyst.

For the amethyst, lake, with a little Prussian blue, used with oil, and very thinly spread on the foil, will completely answer the end.

Blue.

For blue, where a deep color, or the effect of the sapphire is wanted, Prussian blue, that is not too deep, should be used in oil, and it should be spread more or less thinly on the foil, according to the lightness or deepness of which the color is required to be.

Eagle Marine.

For the eagle marine, common verdigris with a little Prussian blue, tempered in shellac varnish, may be used.

Yellow.

Where a full yellow is desired, the foil may be colored with yellow lacquer, laid on as for other purposes: and for the slighter color of topazes the burnish and foil itself will be sufficiently strong without any addition.

Green.

For green, where a deep hue is required, the crystals of verdigris, tempered in shellac varnish, should be used, but where the emerald is to be imitated, a little yellow lacquer should be added to bring the color to a truer green, and less verging to the blue.

Other Colors.

The stones of more diluted color, such as the amethyst, topaz, vinegar-garnet and eagle-marine, may be very cheaply imitated by transparent white glass or paste, even without foils. This is to be done by tempering the colors above enumerated with turpentine and mastic, and painting the socket in which the counterfeit stone is to be set with the mixture, the socket and stone itself being previously heated. In this case, however, the stone should be immediately set, and the socket closed upon it before the mixture cools and grows hard. The orange lake above mentioned was invented for this purpose, in which it has a beautiful effect, and was used with great success by a considerable manufacturer. The color it produces is that of the vinegar-garnet, which it affords with great brightness. The colors before directed to be used in oil should be extremely well ground in oil of turpentine, and tempered with old nut or poppy-oil; or, if time can be given for the drying, with strong fat oil diluted with spirit of turpentine, which will gain a fine polish of itself.

The colors used in varnish should be likewise thoroughly well ground and mixed; and, in the case of the dragon's blood in the seed-lac varnish and the lacquer, the foils should be warmed before they are laid out. All the mixtures should be laid on the foils with a broad, soft brush, which must be passed from one end to the other, and no part should be crossed or twice gone over, or, at least, not till the first coat can be dry; when, if the color do not lie strong enough, a second coat may be given.

ELECTRO-METALLURGY.

Galvanoplasty or Electrotype, is the art of cold casting of metals by the agency of electricity. Its applications are extensive. It is used to multiply engravings and photographs; to cover the faces of types with harder metal; to deposit gold, silver, and alloys on other metals, etc. The process depends upon the fact that an electrical current passed through a metallic solution properly prepared, will cause a decomposition of the solution; the metal being deposited upon any conducting body attached to the negative pole (cathode) of a voltaic cell or battery. This is the pole attached to the zinc plate in all cases.

The Battery.

The term battery is properly applied to several voltaic cells united. Frequently, however, it is used to designate a single cell. The forms usually employed in practice are Smee's, Daniell's, and the nitric acid battery. In order to avoid confusion, the following points must be well understood. In all the batteries named, there are two plates and an exciting fluid. One of these plates is of zinc, which must be amalgamated by dipping it into weak sulphuric acid and rubbing the surface with mercury; or better still, immersing the whole plate in a bath of mercury. This must be repeated from time to time, when the battery is in use. This zinc plate is alone acted on by the exciting fluid. It is called the *positive* plate. Attached to it is a binding screw, by which a wire may be connected with the plate. This screw, or the end of the attached wire, is called the *pole* or *electrode*. The name of the pole is *opposite to that of the plate*. The positive pole or *anode* being attached to the negative plate, and the negative pole or *cathode* to the positive (zinc) plate.

The Decomposing Cell.

Usually the liquid to be decomposed (electrolyte) is kept in a separate vessel, and the current conveyed to it by wires. To the anode is usually attached a piece of metal of the same character as that to be deposited. This is gradually eaten away while the deposition is going on, on the cathode, and the solution thus kept of uniform strength. The current may be regulated by altering the distance between the poles. With the same battery power, the amount of electricity passing will be less as the distance of the poles in the electrolyte is greater. Too powerful a current must be avoided, as it renders the coating brittle and non-adherent. It should not be strong enough to cause bubbles of gas to arise from the object. A large number of objects can be plated by one battery if they are suspended on copper rods, the ends of which are connected with the pole.

Smee's Cell

Consists of two plates of amalgamated zinc, separated by a piece of baked and varnished wood, and between them a plate of silver having deposited on it by the electric current finely divided platinum; so as to roughen it and prevent the adhesion of hydrogen. The silver plate is fixed in the wood separating the zinc plates; to the zinc and to the silver plates are attached binding screws for the wires. The exciting fluid is dilute sulphuric acid; 1 part of acid to 20 of water, is strong enough. When more intensity is required, several cells are joined by passing wires from the anode of one cell to the cathode of the next. This form of battery is generally preferred on account of its simplicity, constancy, and ease of management.

Daniell's Cell.

In delicate operations, as in copying engraved plates, where great constancy is required, this form of cell is employed. It consists of a plate of amalgamated zinc, one of copper, generally of cylindrical form separated by a cell of porous earthenware (a flower-pot with the hole closed by a cork, makes a very good porous cell). The plates and cell are enclosed in a glass or earthenware vessel; the zinc is excited by dilute sulphuric acid; the copper is kept immersed in saturated solution of sulphate of copper (blue-stone). The solution of copper is gradually decomposed; the copper being deposited in the copper plate. Hence there should always be a quantity of crystals of the sulphate at the bottom of the cell, and the solution should be stirred from time to time; or the crystals may be suspended in a basket near the top of the solution.

Nitric Acid Batteries.

When great intensity is required, as in the deposition of copper on iron, and of certain alloys, the decomposition of fused chlorides for the purpose of obtaining certain metals, these batteries are used. In all cases the positive plate is of amalgamated zinc excited by dilute sulphuric acid; which may be as strong as 1 in 10 with 1-10th of nitric acid. This is separated by a porous cell from the negative plate, which may be of platinum (Grove), carbon (Bunsen), or passive iron (Callan). The negative plate is immersed in strong nitric acid. Iron may be rendered passive by dipping it once or twice into strong nitric acid, and then washing with water and carefully drying.

To Prepare Articles for Plating.

Wash in weak lye to remove grease. Dip into dilute nitric acid to remove oxide. Scour with a hard brush and fine sand. Then having fastened to a wire, dip in strong nitric acid and immerse in the electrolyte as quickly as possible.

Solution for Silvering.

Add to a solution of nitrate of silver (made by dissolving silver in pure nitric acid), a solution of cyanide of potassium until no further precipitate is formed; but not enough to re-dissolve the precipitate already thrown down. Pour off the supernatant liquid, wash with water, and then re-dissolve the precipitate in cyanide of potassium. The anode should be of silver. Should the solution change on keeping, add a little fresh cyanide. Use a moderate current. An ounce and a half of silver will give to a surface a foot square, a coating as thick as common writing-paper. And since silver is worth $1.25 per ounce, the value of the silver covering a foot square, would be about $1.87. At this rate, a well plated tea-pot or coffee-pot is plated at a cost in silver of not more than $1.50 to $2. The other expenses, including labor, would hardly be more than half that amount.

To Recover the Silver from a Bath.

Add muriatic acid, carefully avoiding the fumes which are given off. Dilute the liquid, decant from the precipitate formed, dry the precipitate, and reduce in a black lead crucible with carbonate of soda.

Solution for Gilding.

Electro-gilding is done in like manner. The gold is dissolved in nitro-hydrochloric acid, washed with boiling nitric acid, and then digested with calcined magnesia. The gold is deposited in the form of an oxide, which after being washed in boiling nitric acid, is dissolved in cyanide of potassium, in which solution the articles to be plated with gold, after due preparation, are placed. Iron, steel, lead, and some other metals that do not readily receive the gold deposit, require to be first lightly plated with copper, or dipped in a solution of nitrate of siver, 1 part; nitrate of mercury, 1 part; nitric acid (s. g. 1·384) 4 parts; water, 120 parts. The positive plate of the battery must be of gold, the other plate of iron or copper. The process is the same as that above described; use a feeble current.

The popular notion is, that genuine electro-gilding must necessarily add a good deal to the cost of the article plated. This is erroneous. A silver thimble may be so handsomely plated as to have the appearance of being all gold for 5 cents, a pencil-case for 20 cents, and a watch-case for 1 dollar. An estimate of the relative value of electro-gilding, as compared with silver-plating, considering the cost of material alone, is about 15 to 1.

To Deposit Brass.

Dissolve 5 oz. powdered acetate of copper in ½ gall. of water, add 1 pt. of solution of ammonia. Dissolve 10 oz. sulphate of zinc (white vitriol) in 1 gall. of water, at 180° Fahr., and when cool add 1 pt. of solution of ammonia. Dissolve 4½ lbs. potassa in 1 gall. of water. Lastly, dissolve 8 oz. cyanide of potassium in 1 gall. of hot water. Mix in the following order : add the copper solution to that of zinc, then the potash and cyanide, digest for an hour or so, and add water to make up 8 gall. Work with a brass anode and an active battery power, occasionally adding more ammonia and cyanide.

To Copy Medals.

Casts of the medals may be made in fusible metal, plaster, wax, etc. In case of a non-metallic mould it must have its face brushed over with black lead. The metallic mould is to be coated on the back with wax or varnish. The wire is usually attached to the edge by soldering or twisting. A decomposing cell is not necessary. A water-tight box is divided by a porous (plaster or leather) partition. On one side is a plate of zinc immersed in diluted, 1 to 20, sulphuric acid ; on the other a solution, kept saturated, of sulphate of copper. A wire from the zinc is attached to a copper rod, from which the medals are suspended, dipping into the copper solution.

To Bronze Copper Medals.

1. *Brown.* — Moisten the surface, well cleaned, with weak nitric acid, allow it to dry, and apply a gentle heat.

2. *Black.* — Use, instead of nitric acid, sulphydrate of ammonia or liver of sulphur.

3. *Green.* — Expose in a close box to the fumes of chloride of lime, or to the vapor of acetic or muriatic acid.

4. For bronzing all sorts of fine copper or brass work a weak solution of bichloride of platinum is used. By varying the temperature and color, between a steel gray and deep black may be obtained.

To Deposit Copper on Iron.

Prepare a solution of cyanide of copper, by dissolving oxide of copper in cyanide of potassium, or by adding cyanide of potassium to a solution of sulphate of copper, and re-dissolving the precipitate formed. Work with a strong battery power. The copper will not deposit unless the current be strong enough to evolve hydrogen at the cathode, which evolution should always be avoided in depositing the other metals.

Voltaic Protection of Metals.

When two metals are united and exposed to a corrosive agent, which would act unequally upon them if separate, the one which would be most acted on receives most of the force of the corrosion, while the other escapes. Thus iron coated with zinc (galvanized iron) will last for years exposed to the atmosphere. Copper points on lightning-rods remain bright for a long time, when screwed into a zinc ball.

Coating Electrotype-plates with Iron.

The following has been successfully employed in coating electrotype deposits with a coating of pure iron, thereby rendering them little inferior to steel-plate engravings as regards durability:—

Dissolve 1 lb. of sul ammoniac in 1 gall. of rain-water, then add 2 lbs. of neutral acetate of iron; boil the solution in an iron-kettle for 2 hours, replacing the water lost by evaporation; when cold, filter the solution, and keep it in close-covered vats (when not in use) to prevent oxidation.

The iron plate used in the decomposition-cell must be of the same surface as the plate to be coated with iron; a Smee's battery, of at least 3 cells, charged with 1 part sulphuric acid, and 60 parts water, being used for the decomposition.

To insure success the following rules must be observed: 1st. The plate must be thoroughly freed from any greasy matter by immersing it in a solution of caustic soda, then rinsed in clean cold rain-water, after which dip it in dilute acetic acid, and immediately transfer it to the solution of iron; this will insure perfect adhesion between the metals. 2nd. The solution must be filtered previous to use to remove the oxide of iron formed by exposure to the atmosphere. After the plates have been coated with iron they must be well rinsed in clear warm rain-water, then in a weak alkaline solution, well dried with a piece of clean soft cotton, and slightly oiled to prevent oxidation.

The coating of iron is very hard and brittle, resembling the white iron used by manufacturers of malleable iron. Should any of the surface be damaged, the whole coating of iron may be removed by immersion in dilute sulphuric acid, and re-coated again by the above process.

Copper Tubes made by Galvanic Process.

Le Génie Industrial publishes the details of a process for making copper-tubes without soldering, which consists simply in depositing copper upon lead patterns by the galvanic battery, and then melting out the lead. It is said to work perfectly, and of course tubes could be made of any desired form — straight, curved, or right-angled. This suggests the idea of forming tubes in the same manner with cores of wax or clay. The clay may be forced into the size of the pipe through a draw-plate, then allowed to harden slightly, when it may be covered with plumbago and an electro-deposit of copper made upon it with a galvanic battery. When the copper is deposited in sufficient thickness the clay may be removed from the interior by boiling the pipe in water. To conduct this manufacture it would require long depositing-troughs, and the expense would probably be too great for making straight copper-tubes; but for curved tubes, such as the worms of stills, it would perhaps pay. Curved copper-tubes are commonly made by filling straight tubes with hot resin, then twisting the entire tube into its curved form. When the resin becomes cool it is driven out by striking the pipe, which breaks the resin-core into small pieces.

GILDING, SILVERING, AND TINNING.

To Gild Glass and Porcelain.

Drinking and other glasses are sometimes gilt on their edges. This is done, either by an adhesive varnish, or by heat. The varnish is prepared by dissolving in boiled linseed-oil an equal weight either of copal or amber. This is to be diluted by a proper quantity of oil of turpentine, so as to be applied as thin as possible to the parts of the glass intended to be gilt. When this is done, which will be in about 24 hours, the glass is to be placed in a stove, till it is so warm as almost to burn the fingers when handled. At this temperature the varnish will become adhesive, and a piece of leaf-gold, applied in the usual way, will immediately stick. Sweep off the superfluous portions of the leaf; and when quite cold it may be burnished, taking care to interpose a piece of very thin paper (Indian paper) between the gold and the burnisher. If the varnish is very good, this is the best method of gilding glass, as the gold is thus fixed on more evenly than in any other way.

Another Method.

It often happens, when the varnish is but indifferent, that by repeated washing the gold wears off; on this account the practice of burning it in is sometimes had recourse to.

For this purpose some gold powder is ground with borax, and in this state applied to the clean surface of the glass by a camel's-hair pencil. When quite dry the glass is put into a stove heated to about the temperature of an annealing oven; the gum burns off, and the borax, by vitrefying, cements the gold with great firmness to the glass, after which it may be burnished. The gilding upon porcelain is in like manner fixed by heat and the use of borax; and this kind of ware being neither transparent nor liable to soften, and thus to be injured in its form, in a low red heat, is free from the risk and injury which the finer and more fusible kinds of glass are apt to sustain from such treatment. Porcelain and other wares may be platinized, silvered, tinned, and bronzed in a similar manner.

Preparation for Gilding Porcelain.

This preparation, the invention of the brothers Dutuste, is reported on by Salvétat. The peculiar advantage of it is, that after burning the gold is so bright as not to require polishing. Thirty-two grammes of gold are gently warmed with 128

GILDING, SILVERING, AND TINNING.

grammes of nitric acid and the same weight of hydrochloric acid. To the solution are added 1·2 grammes of tin and 1·2 grammes of butter of antimony, and, when all are dissolved, the solution is diluted with 500 grammes of water.

A mixture is now prepared by heating together 80 grammes of oil of turpentine, 16 grammes of sulphur, and 16 grammes of Venice turpentine. When the sulphur is dissolved 50 grammes of oil of lavender is added. The gold solution is now added, and the two are well stirred together, until the aqueous solution becomes decolorized, showing that all the gold has united with the balsam. The watery portion is then poured away, and the oily fluid is washed with warm water, and then heated. When the last trace of moisture has disappeared, 65 grammes more of lavender oil and 100 grammes of oil of turpentine are added, and the whole warmed to insure the perfect admixture. While quite fluid 5 grammes of subnitrate of bismuth are added. Afterwards the clear part is decanted from any reduced gold and other insoluble matter and the balsam is concentrated to a fit consistence for painting with. The balsam so prepared is a thick fluid, of a pale-green color, the gold being perfectly dissolved. When proper care is taken to remove all moisture this preparation never blisters in burning.

To Gild Leather.

In order to impress gilt figures, letters, and other marks upon leather, as on the covers of books, edgings for doors, etc., the leather must first be dusted over with very finely powdered yellow resin or mastic gum. The iron tools or stamps are now arranged on a rack before a clear fire, so as to be well heated, without becoming red hot. If the tools are *letters*, they have an alphabetical arrangement on the rack. Each letter or stamp must be tried, as to its heat, by imprinting its mark on the raw side of a piece of waste leather. A little practice will enable the workman to judge of the heat. The tool is now to be pressed downwards on the gold-leaf, which will of course be indented, and show the figure imprinted on it. The next letter or stamp is now to be taken and stamped in like manner, and so on with the others, taking care to keep the letters in an even line with each other, like those in a book. By this operation the resin is melted, consequently the gold adheres to the leather. The superfluous gold may then be rubbed off by a cloth, the gilded impressions remaining on the leather. In this, as in every other operation, adroitness is acquired by practice.

The cloth alluded to should be slightly greasy, to retain the gold wiped off (otherwise there will be great waste in a few months); the cloth will thus be soon completely saturated or loaded with the gold. When this is the case, these cloths are generally sold to the refiners, who burn them and recover the gold. Some of these afford so much gold by burning as to be worth from seven to ten dollars.

To Gild Writings, Drawings, etc. on Paper or Parchment.

Letters written on velum or paper are gilded in 3 ways: in the first, a little size is mixed with the ink, and the letters are written as usual; when they are dry, a slight degree of stickiness is produced by breathing on them, upon which the gold leaf is immediately applied, and by a little pressure may be made to adhere with sufficient firmness. In the second method, some white-lead or chalk is ground up with strong size, and the letters are made with this by means of a brush; when the mixture is almost dry the gold leaf may be laid on, and afterwards burnished. The last method is to mix up some gold powder with size, and to form the letters of this by means of a brush. It is supposed that this latter method was that used by the monks in illuminating their missals, psalters, and rubrics.

To Gild the Edges of Paper.

The edges of the leaves of books and letter paper are gilded whilst in a horizontal position in the bookbinder's press, by first applying a composition formed of four parts of Armenian bole, and one of candied sugar, ground together with water to a proper consistence, and laid on by a brush, with the white of an egg. This coating, when nearly dry, is smoothed by the burnisher, which is generally a crooked piece of agate, very smooth, and fixed in a handle. It is then slightly moistened by a sponge dipped in clean water, and squeezed in the hand. The gold-leaf is now taken upon a piece of cotton from the leathern cushion, and applied on the moistened surface. When dry it is to be burnished by rubbing the agate over it repeatedly from end to end, taking care not to wound the surface by the point of the burnisher. A piece of silk or India-paper is usually interposed between the gold and the burnisher.

Cotton-wool is generally used by bookbinders to take the leaf up from the cushion, being the best adapted for the purpose on account of its pliability, smoothness, softness, and slight moistness.

To Gild Silk, Satin, Ivory, etc., by Hydrogen Gas.

Immerse a piece of white satin, silk, or ivory in a solution of chloride of gold, in the proportion of 1 part of the chloride to 3 of distilled water. Whilst the substance to be gilded is still wet, immerse it in a jar of hydrogen gas; it will soon be covered by a complete coat of gold.

Another Method.

The foregoing experiment may be very prettily and advantageously varied as follows: Paint flowers or other ornaments with a very fine camel-hair pencil, dipped in the above-mentioned solution of gold, on pieces of silk, satin, etc., and hold them over a Florence flask, from which hydrogen gas is evolved, during the decomposition of the water by sulphuric acid and iron filings. The painted flowers, etc., in a few minutes, will shine with all the splendor of the purest gold. A coating of this kind will not tarnish on exposure to the air or in washing.

Oil Gilding on Wood.

The wood must first be covered, or primed, by 2 or 3 coatings of boiled linseed-oil and carbonate of lead, in order to fill up the pores and conceal the irregularities of the surface occasioned by the veins in the wood. When the priming is quite dry a thin coat of gold size must be laid on. This is prepared by grinding together some red oxide of lead with the thickest drying oil that can be procured, and the older the better. That it may work freely, it is to be mixed, previously to being used, with a little oil of turpentine, till it is brought to a proper consistence. If the gold-size is good it will be sufficiently dry in 12 hours, more or less, to allow the artist to proceed to the last part of the process, which is the application of the gold. For this purpose a leaf of gold is spread on a cushion (formed by a few folds of flannel secured on a piece of wood, about 8 inches square, by a tight covering of leather), and is cut into strips of a proper size by a blunt pallet-knife; each strip, being then taken upon the point of a fine brush, is applied to the part intended to be gilded, and is then gently pressed down by a ball of soft cotton. The gold immediately adheres to the sticky surface of the size, and, after a few minutes, the dexterous application of a large camel's-hair brush sweeps away the loose particles of the gold-leaf without disturbing the rest. In a day or two the size will be completely dried, and the operation will be finished.

The advantages of this method of gilding are that it is very simple, very durable, and not readily injured by changes of weather, even when exposed to the open air; and when soiled it may be cleaned by a little warm water and a soft brush. Its chief employment is in out-door work. Its disadvantage is that it cannot be burnished, and therefore wants the high lustre produced by the following method:

To Gild by Burnishing.

This operation is chiefly performed on picture frames, mouldings, beadings, and fine stucco-work. The surface to be gilt must be carefully covered with a strong size, made by boiling down pieces of white leather or clippings of parchment till they are reduced to a stiff jelly. This coating being dried, 8 or 10 more must be applied, consisting of the same size, mixed with fine Paris plaster or washed chalk. When a sufficient number of layers have been put on, varying according to the nature of the work, and the whole is become quite dry, a moderately thick layer must be applied, composed of size and Armenian bole, or yellow oxide of lead. While this last is yet moist the gold-leaf is to be put on in the usual manner. It will immediately adhere on being pressed by the cotton ball; and, before the size is become perfectly dry, those parts which are intended to be the most brilliant are to be carefully burnished by an agate or a dogs' tooth, fixed in a handle.

In order to save the labor of burnishing, it is a common, but bad practice, slightly to burnish the brilliant parts, and to deaden the rest by drawing a brush over them dipped in size; the required contrast between the polished and the unpolished gold is indeed thus obtained; but the general effect is much inferior to that produced in the regular way, and the smallest drop of water falling on the sized part occasions a stain. This kind of gilding can only be applied on in-door work; as rain, and even a considerable degree of dampness, will occasion the gold to peal off. When dirty it may be cleaned by a soft brush, with hot spirit of wine, or oil of turpentine.

Matting.

The parts to be burnished (in gilding on metals) being covered with the usual *guarding*, the piece is fastened by five iron wires to the end of an iron rod; it is then to be highly heated until the guarding becomes brown, when the gilding will be found to have acquired a fine gold color. It is now to be covered with a mixture of common salt, nitre, and alum, liquefied in the water of crystallization they contain; the piece to be carried again to the fire and heated until the saline coating is in a state of fusion and becomes nearly transparent, when it must be withdrawn and suddenly plunged into cold water, which removes both coating and guarding. Dip it afterwards in *very weak* nitric acid, and wash it repeatedly in several separate tubs of water. It may be dried either by exposure to air, or *gently* wiping it with clean, soft, dry linen.

To Gild Copper, etc., by Amalgam.

Immerse a very clean bright piece of copper in a diluted solution of nitrate of mercury. By the affinity of copper for nitric acid, the mercury will be precipitated; now spread the amalgam of gold rather thinly over the coat of mercury just given to the copper. This coat unites with the amalgam, but of course will remain on the copper. Now place the piece or pieces so operated on in a clean oven or furnace, where there is no smoke. If the heat is a little greater than 660°, the mercury of the amalgam will be volatilized, and the copper will be beautifully gilt.

In the large way of gilding, the furnaces are so contrived that the volatilized mercury is again condensed and preserved for further use, so that there is no loss in the operation. There is also a contrivance by which the volatile particles of mercury are prevented from injuring the gilders.

To Gild Steel.

Pour some of the ethereal solution of chloride of gold into a wineglass, and dip therein the blade of a new penknife, lancet, or razor; withdraw the instrument and allow the ether to evaporate. The blade will be found to be covered by a very beautiful coat of gold. A clean rag, or small piece of very dry sponge, may be dipped in the ether and used to moisten the blade with the same result.

In this case there is no occasion to pour the liquid into a glass, which must undoubtedly lose by evaporation; but the rag or sponge may be moistened by it by applying ether to the mouth of the phial. This coating of gold will remain on the steel for a great length of time, and will preserve it from rusting.

This is the way in which swords and other cutlery are ornamented. Lancets too are in this way gilded with great advantage to secure them from rust.

Gold Powder for Gilding.

Gold powder may be prepared in three different ways: Put into an earthen mortar some gold-leaf with a little honey or thick gum-water, and grind the mixture till the gold is reduced to extremely minute particles. When this is done, a little warm water will wash out the honey or gum, leaving the gold behind in a pulverulent state.

Another.—Another way is, to dissolve pure gold (or the leaf) in nitro-muriatic acid, and then to precipitate it by a piece of copper, or by a solution of sulphate of iron. The precipitate (if by copper) must be digested in distilled vinegar and then washed (by pouring water over it repeatedly) and dried. This precipitate will be in the form of a very fine powder; it works better and is more easily burnished than gold-leaf ground with honey as above.

Another.—The best method of preparing gold powder is by heating a prepared amalgam of gold in an open clean crucible, and continuing the strong heat until the whole of the mercury is evaporated; at the same time constantly stirring the amalgam with a glass rod. When the mercury has completely left the gold, the remaining powder is to be ground in a Wedgwood mortar, with a little water, and afterwards dried. It is then fit for use.

Although the last mode of operating has been here given, the operator cannot be too much reminded of the danger attending the sublimation of mercury. In the small way here described, it is impossible to operate without danger; it is therefore better to prepare it according to the former directions, than to risk the health by the latter.

To Cover Bars of Copper, etc., with Gold, so as to be Rolled out into Sheets.

This method of *gilding* was invented by Mr. Turner of Birmingham. Mr. Turner first prepares ingots or pieces of copper or brass, in convenient lengths and sizes. He then cleans them from impurity, and makes their surfaces level, and prepares plates of pure gold, or gold mixed with a portion of alloy, of the same size as the ingots of metal, and of suitable thickness. Having placed a piece of gold upon an ingot intended to be plated, he hammers and compresses them both together, so that they may have their surfaces as nearly equal to each other as possible; and then binds them together with wire, in order to keep them in the same position during the process required to attach them. Afterwards he takes silver-filings which he mixes with borax to assist the fusion of the silver. This mixture he lays upon the edge of the plate of gold, and next to the ingot of metal.

Having thus prepared the two bodies, he places them on a fire in a stove or furnace, where they remain until the silver and borax placed along the edges of the metals melt, and until the adhesion of the gold with the metal is perfect. He then takes the ingot carefully out of the stove. By this process the ingot is placed with gold, and prepared ready for rolling into sheets.

To Silver Copper Ingots.

The principal difficulties in plating copper ingots are, to bring the surfaces of the copper and silver into fusion at the same time; and to prevent the copper from scaling; for which purposes fluxes are used. The surface of the copper on which the silver is to be fixed must be made flat by filing, and should be left rough. The silver is first annealed, and afterwards pickled in weak muriatic acid: it is planished, and then scraped on the surface to be fitted on the copper. These prepared surfaces are anointed with a solution of borax, or strewed with fine powdered borax itself, and then confined in contact with each other, by binding wire. When they are exposed to a sufficient degree of heat, the flux causes the surfaces to fuse at the same time, and after they become cold they are found firmly united.

Copper may likewise be plated by heating it, and burnishing leaf-silver upon it; so may iron and brass. This process is called *French-plating*.

Grecian Gilding.

Equal parts of sal-ammoniac and corrosive sublimate, are dissolved in spirit of nitre, and a solution of gold made with this menstruum. The silver is brushed over with it, which is turned black, but on exposure to a red heat, it assumes the color of gold.

To Dissolve Gold in Aqua Regia.

Take an aqua regia, composed of 2 parts of nitric acid, and 1 of muriatic acid; let the gold be granulated, put into a sufficient quantity of this menstruum, and exposed to a moderate degree of heat. During the solution an effervescence takes place, and it acquires a beautiful yellow color, which becomes more and more intense, till it has a golden or even orange color. When the menstruum is saturated, it is very clear and transparent.

To Gild, by Dissolving Gold in Aqua Regia.

Fine linen rags are soaked in a saturated solution of gold in aqua regia, gently dried, and afterwards burnt to tinder. The substance to be gilt must be well polished; a piece of cork is first dipped into a solution of common salt in water, and afterwards into the tinder, which is well rubbed on the surface of the metal to be gilt, and the gold appears in all its metallic lustre.

Amalgam of Gold in the large way.

A quantity of quicksilver is put into a crucible or iron ladle, which is lined with clay and exposed to heat till it begins to smoke. The gold to be mixed should be previously granulated, and heated red hot, when it should be added to the quicksilver, and stirred about with an iron rod till it is perfectly dissolved. If there should be any superfluous mercury, it may be separated by passing it through clean soft leather; and the remaining amalgam will have the consistence of butter, and contain about 3 parts of mercury to 1 of gold.

To Gild by Amalgamation.

The metal to be gilt is previously well cleaned on its surface, by boiling it in a weak pickle, which is a very dilute nitrous acid. A quantity of aquafortis is poured into an earthen vessel, and quicksilver put therein; when a sufficient quantity of mercury is dissolved, the articles to be gilt are put into the solution, and stirred about with a brush till they become white. This is called quicking. But, as during quicking by this mode, a noxious vapor continually arises, which proves very injurious to the health of the workman, they have adopted another method, by which they, in a great measure, avoid that danger. They now dissolve the quicksilver in a bottle containing aqua-fortis, and leave it in the open air during the solution, so that the noxious vapor escapes into the air. Then a little of this solution is poured into a basin, and with a brush dipped therein, they stroke over the surface of the metal to be gilt, which immediately becomes quicked. The amalgam is now applied by one of the following methods, viz:

1st. By proportioning it to the quantity of articles to be gilt, and putting them into a white hat together, working them about with a soft brush, till the amalgam is uniformly spread.

Or, 2dly. By applying a portion of the amalgam upon one part, and spreading it on the surface, if flat, by working it about with a harder brush.

The work thus managed is put into a pan, and exposed to a gentle degree of heat; when it becomes hot, it is frequently put into a hat, and worked about with a painter's large brush, to prevent an irregular dissipation of the mercury, till at last the quicksilver is entirely dissipated by a repetition of the heat, and the gold is attached to the surface of the metal. This gilt surface is well cleaned by a wire brush, and then artists heighten the color of the gold by the application of various compositions, this part of the process is called *coloring*.

Silvering Powders.

For silvering copper, covering the worn parts of plated goods, etc.

1. Nitrate of silver, common salt, each 30 grs.; cream of tartar, 3½ drs. Mix. Moisten with cold water and rub on the article to be silvered.
2. Pure silver (precipitated from the nitrate by copper), 20 grs.; alum 30 grs.; cream of tartar, 2 drs.; salt, 2 drs.
3. Precipitated silver, ½ oz.; common salt, sal ammoniac, each 2 oz.; corrosive sublimate, 1 dr. Make into a paste with water. Copper utensils are previously boiled with cream of tartar and alum, rubbed with this paste made red hot and afterwards polished.
4. Nitrate of silver, 1 part; cyanide of potassium, 3 parts; water enough to make a paste.

Removing Silver from Injured Plated Ware.

Among the many branches of manufacturing at Nuremberg, in Germany, that of metals into various articles has obtained considerable importance. They include silver-plated ware of different styles and quality; which necessarily produce large quantities of spoiled materials and clippings, the recovery of which has hitherto been very imperfectly accomplished; thus causing annually a considerable loss. The reason of it was, the want of a method by which the silver might be removed without much expense, and the copper thus forced from its coating used again.

Repeated experiments have led to a very simple process, by the action of concentrated nitric acid on silver and copper when present together. If these metals are placed into common commercial acid, (sp. gr. 1·47) they will both be strongly acted on; but a separation of the two is unattainable, since the copper, so long as any remains undissolved, will precipitate the silver from its solution by galvanic action. Nitric acid of the highest specific gravity (1·5), however, acts on the silver, but not on the copper; it renders the copper more electro-negative than before, less oxidizable, and deprives it of the property of decomposing the acid, and precipitating the silver.

To produce this passive condition of copper, it is not absolutely necessary to employ directly acid of that specific gravity; for any concentrated nitric acid can be made to answer the purpose by the addition of a sufficient quantity of the oil of vitriol, which deprives it of a portion of its water, and thus contributes to make it stronger. A mixture of one volume of nitric acid (sp. gr. 1,47) and six of vitriol does not dissolve copper at the temperature of boiling water; but with a smaller proportion of sulphuric acid, evolution of nitrous acid takes place. The same end and much cheaper, is obtained by employing a mixture of oil of vitriol and nitrate of soda, which are the materials used in the practice. The following is the method now generally employed: Oil of vitriol, together with five per cent. of nitrate of soda, is heated in a cast-iron boiler; or better, a stoneware pan, to 212° Fahr. The silver-plated clippings are placed in a sheet-iron bucket or colander, which is fastened to a pulley that may be moved about in the acid. As soon as the silver is removed, the colander is raised, allowed to drain, then immersed in cold water and emptied, to be again used in the same manner. When the acid-bath is fresh, the desilvering proceeds very rapidly, and even with heavy plated ware takes but a few minutes; with the gradual saturation of the bath more time is required, and it is readily perceived when the acid must be renewed. The small amount of acid solution adhering to the copper, precipitates its silver when brought into the water. To obtain its complete removal, the clippings, when raised from the desilvering bath and before immersion in water, may be dipped into a second bath prepared in the same manner, which is afterwards to be used in place of the first.

The saturated bath, on cooling, congeals to a crystalline semi-fluid mass of sulphate of copper and of soda. The silver is removed by chloride of sodium, which is added in small portions at a time, while the solution is yet warm. The chloride of silver separates readily, and is washed and reduced in the usual manner. The acid solution contains but a very small portion of copper, hardly enough to pay for recovering.

Another Method.

This process is applied to recover the silver from the plated metal, which has been rolled down for buttons, toys, etc., without destroying any large portion of the copper. For this purpose, a menstruum is composed of 3 lbs. of oil of vitriol, 1½ oz. of nitre, and 1 lb. of water. The plated metal is boiled in it till the silver is dissolved, and then the silver is recovered by throwing common salt into the solution.

To Plate Iron.

Iron may be plated by three different modes.
1. By polishing the surface very clean and level with a burnisher, and afterwards by exposing it to a blueing heat, a leaf of silver is properly placed and carefully burnished down. This is repeated till a sufficient number of leaves are applied, to give the silver a proper body.
2. By the use of a solder; slips of thin solder are placed between the iron and silver, with a little flux, and secured together by binding wire. It is then placed in a clear fire, and continued in it till the solder melts; when it is taken out, and on cooling is found to adhere firmly.
3. By tinning the iron first, and uniting the silver by the intermedia of slips of rolled tin, brought into fusion in a gentle heat.

To Heighten the Color of Yellow Gold.

Take of saltpetre, 6 oz.; green copperas, 2 oz.; white vitriol and alum, of each, 1 oz.

If it be wanted redder, a small portion of blue vitriol must be added. These are to be well mixed, and dissolved in water as the color is wanted.

To Heighten the Color of Green Gold.

Take of saltpetre, 1 oz. 10 dwts.; sal ammoniac, 1 oz. 4 dwts.; Roman vitriol, 1 oz. 4 dwts.; verdigris, 18 dwts. Mix them well together and dissolve a portion in water, as occasion requires.

The work must be dipped in these compositions, applied to a proper heat to burn them off, and then quenched in water or vinegar.

To Heighten the Color of Red Gold.

To 4 oz. of melted yellow wax, add, in fine powder, 1½ oz. of red ochre, 1½ oz. of verdigris, calcined till it yield no fumes, and ½ oz. of calcined borax; mix them well together. It is necessary to calcine the verdigris, or else by the heat applied in burning the wax, the vinegar becomes so concentrated as to corrode the surface, and make it appear speckled.

To Separate Gold from Gilt, Copper and Silver.

Apply a solution of borax, in water, to the gilt surface, with a fine brush, and sprinkle over it some fine powdered sulphur. Make the piece red-hot, and quench it in water. The gold may be easily wiped off with a scratch-brush, and recovered by cupellation.

Gold is taken from the surface of silver by spreading over it a paste made of powdered sal ammoniac, with aqua-fortis, and heating it till the matter smokes, and is nearly dry, when the gold may be separated by rubbing it with a scratch-brush.

To Tin Copper and Brass.

Boil 6 lbs. of cream of tartar, 4 galls. of water, and 8 lbs. of grain-tin, or tin shavings. After the materials have boiled a sufficient time, the substance to be tinned is put therein and the boiling continued, when the tin is precipitated in its metallic form.

To Tin Iron or Copper-plate.

Iron which is to be tinned is first steeped in acid materials, such as sour whey, distillers' wash, etc., then scoured and dipped in melted tin, having been first rubbed over with a solution of sal ammoniac. The surface of the tin is prevented from calcining by covering it with a coat of fat. Copper vessels must be well cleansed, and then a sufficient quantity of tin with sal ammoniac is put therein and brought into fusion, and the copper vessel moved about. A little resin is sometimes added. The sal ammoniac prevents the copper from scaling, and causes the tin to be fixed wherever it touches.

To prepare the Leaden Tree.

Put ½ oz. of the sugar of lead, in powder, into a clear glass globe or wine decanter, filled to the bottom of the neck with distilled water and 10 drops of nitric acid, and shake the mixture well.

Prepare a rod of zinc with a hammer and file, so that it may be a quarter of an inch thick and 1 inch long, at the same time form notches in each side for a thread, by which it is to be suspended, and tie the thread so that the knot shall be uppermost when the metal hangs quite perpendicular. When it is tied, pass the two ends of the thread through a perforation in the cork, and let them be again tied over a small splinter of wood which may pass between them and the cork. When the string is tied, let the length between the cork and the zinc be such that the precipitant (the zinc) may be at equal distances from the sides, bottom and top of the vessel, when immersed in it. When all things are thus prepared, place the vessel in a place where it may not be disturbed, and introduce the zinc, at the same time fitting in the cork. The metal will very soon be covered with the lead, which it precipitates from the solution, and this will continue to take place until the whole be precipitated upon the zinc, which will assume the form of a tree or bush, the leaves and branches of which are laminal, or plates of a metallic lustre.

To prepare the Tin Tree.

Into the same, or a similar vessel to that used in the last experiment, pour distilled water as before, and put in 3 drs. of chloride of tin, adding 10 drops of nitric acid, and shake the vessel until the salt is completely dissolved. Replace the zinc (which must be cleared from the effects of the former experiment) as before, and set the whole aside to precipitate without disturbance. In a few hours the effect will be similar to the last, only that the tree of tin will have more lustre.

To prepare the Silver Tree.

Pour into a glass globe or decanter 4 drs. of nitrate of silver dissolved in a lb. or more of distilled water, and lay the vessel on the chimneypiece, or in some place where it may not be disturbed. Now pour in 4 drs. of mercury. In a short time the silver will be precipitated in the most beautiful arborescent form, resembling real vegetation. This has been termed the Arbor Dianæ.

Chinese Sheet-lead.

The operation is carried on by two men; one is seated on the floor with a large flat stone before him, and with a movable flat stone-stand at his side. His fellow-workman stands beside him with a crucible filled with melted lead, and having poured a certain quantity upon the stone, the other lifts the movable stone, and dashing it on the fluid lead presses it out into a flat and fine plate, which he instantly removes from the stone. A second quantity of lead is poured in a similar way, and a similar plate formed, the process being carried on with singular rapidity. The rough edges of the plates are then cut off, and they are soldered together for use.

IRON AND STEEL.

Expeditious Mode of Reducing Iron Ore into Malleable Iron.

The way of proceeding is by stamping, washing, etc., the calcine and materials, to separate the ore from extraneous matter; then fusing the prepared ore in an open furnace, and instead of casting it, to suffer it to remain at the bottom of the furnace till it becomes cold.

New Method of Shingling and Manufacturing Iron.

The ore being fused in a reverberating furnace, is conveyed, while fluid, into an air-furnace, where it is exposed to a strong heat till a bluish flame is observed on the surface, it is then agitated on the surface till it loses its fusibility and is collected into lumps called *loops*. These *loops* are then put into another air-furnace, brought to a white or welding heat, and then *shingled* into *half-blooms* or *slabs*. They are again exposed to the air-furnace, and the half-blooms taken out and forged into *anconies*, bars, *half-flats*, and rods for *wire ;* while the *slabes* are passed, when of a welding heat, through the grooved rollers. In this way of proceeding, it matters not whether the iron is prepared from *cold* or *hot-short* metal, nor is there any occasion for the use of finery, charcoal, coke, chafery or hollow-fire; or any blast by bellows or otherwise, or the use of fluxes in any part of the process.

Approved Method of Welding Iron.

This consists in the skilful *bundling* of the iron to be welded, in the use of an extraordinarily large forge-hammer, in employing a *balling-furnace*, instead of a *hollow-fire* or *chafery*, and in passing the iron, reduced to a melting heat, through grooved mill rollers of different shapes and sizes, as required.

Welding Steel, or Iron and Cast Steel.

Melt borax in an *earthen* vessel, and add 1-10th of pounded sal ammoniac. When well mixed, pour it out on an iron plate, and as soon as it is cold, pulverize and mix it with an equal quantity of unslaked lime. To proceed to the operation, the iron or steel must be first heated to a red heat, and the powder strewed over it; the pieces of metal thus prepared are to be again put in the fire, and raised to a heat *considerably lower* than the usual welding one, when it is to be withdrawn and well beaten by a hammer till the surfaces are perfectly united.

Welding by Pressure.

Soft metals can be welded cold by great pressure, and recently hydraulic pressure has been applied by M. Duportail to the welding of heated masses of iron. The advantage of pressure over hammering, is that it reaches the centre of the bar and produces a homogeneous weld.

Common Hardening.

Iron by being heated red-hot, and plunged into cold water, acquires a great degree of hardness. This proceeds from the coldness of the water which contracts the particles of the iron into less space.

Case-hardening.

Case-hardening is a superficial conversion of iron into steel by cementation. It is performed on small pieces of iron by enclosing them in an iron box containing burnt leather, bone-dust, or ferrocyanide of potassium, and exposing them for some hours to a red heat. The surface of the iron thus becomes perfectly hardened. Iron thus treated is susceptible of the finest polish.

To Convert Iron into Steel by Cementation.

The iron is formed into bars of a convenient size, and then placed in a cementing furnace with a sufficient quantity of cement, which is composed of coals of animal or vegetable substances, mixed with calcined bones, etc. The following are excellent cements: 1st, 1 part of powdered charcoal and $\frac{1}{2}$ a part of wood-ashes well mixed together; or, 2nd, 2 parts of charcoal, moderately powdered, 1 part of borax, horn, hair, or skins of animals, burnt in close vessels to blackness, and powdered, and $\frac{1}{2}$ a part of wood-ashes; mix them well together. The bars of iron converted into steel, are placed upon a stratum of cement, and covered all over with the same, and the vessel which contains them, closely luted, must be ex posed to a red heat for 8 or 10 hours, when the iron will be converted into steel.

Steel is prepared from bar-iron by fusion; which consists of plunging a bar into melted iron, and keeping it there for some time, by which process it is converted into good steel.

All iron which becomes harder by suddenly quenching in cold water is called steel; and that steel which in quenching acquires the greatest degree of hardness in the lowest degree of heat, and retains the greatest strength in and after induration, ought to be considered as the best.

Improved Process of Hardening Steel

Articles manufactured of steel for the purposes of cutting, are, almost without an exception, hardened from the anvil; in other words, they are taken from the forger to the hardener without undergoing any intermediate process; and such is the accustomed routine, that the mischief arising has escaped observation. The act of forging produces a strong scale or coating, which is spread over the whole of the blade; and to make the evil still more formidable, this scale or coating is unequal in substance, varying in proportion to the degree of heat communicated to the steel in forging; it is, partially, almost impenetrable to the action of water when immersed for the purpose of hardening. Hence it is that different degrees of hardness prevail in nearly every razor manufactured; this is evidently a positive defect; and so long as it continues to exist, great difference of temperature must exist likewise. Razor-blades not unfrequently exhibit the fact here stated in a very striking manner; what are termed clouds, or parts of unequal polish, derive their origin from this cause; and clearly and distinctly, or rather *distinctly* though not *clearly*, show how far this partial coating has extended, and where the action of the water has been yielded to, and where resisted. It certainly cannot be matter of astonishment, that so few improvements have been made in the hardening of steel, when the evil here complained of so universally obtains, as almost to warrant the supposition that no attempt has ever been made to remove it. The remedy, however, is easy and simple in the extreme, and so evidently efficient in its application, that it cannot but excite surprise, that, in the present highly improved state of our manufactures, such a communication should be made as a discovery entirely new.

Instead, therefore, of the customary mode of hardening the blade from the anvil, let it be passed immediately from the hands of the forger to the grinder; a slight application of the stone will remove the whole of the scale or coating, and the razor will then be properly prepared to undergo the operation of hardening with advantage. It will be easily ascertained, that steel in this state heats in the fire with greater regularity, and that when immersed, the obstacles being removed to the immediate action of the water on the body of the steel, the latter becomes equally hard from one extremity to the other. To this may be added, that, as *the lowest possible heat at which steel becomes hard is indubitably the best*, the mode here recommended will be found the only one by which the process of hardening can be effected with a less portion of fire than is, or can be, required in any other way. These observations are decisive, and will, in all probability, tend to establish in general use, what cannot but be regarded as a very important improvement in the manufacturing of edged steel instruments.—*Rhodes' Essay on the Manufacture of a Razor.*

Improved Mode of Hardening Steel by Hammering.

Gravers, axes, and in fact all steel instruments that require to be excessively hard, may be easily rendered so by heating them to the tempering degree and hammering them till cold. If a graver, it is to be heated to a straw-color, hammered on the acute edge of the belly, tempered to the straw-color again, ground and whetted to a proper shape. A graver thus prepared will cut into steel, without previous decarbonization. If the point should on trial be found not sufficiently hard, the operation of heating, hammering, and tempering, etc., may be repeated as often as necessary.

English Cast-Steel.

The finest of steel, called English cast-steel, is prepared by breaking to pieces blistered steel, and then melting it in a crucible with a flux composed of carbonaceous and vitrifiable ingredients. The vitrifiable ingredient is used only inasmuch as it is a fusible body, which flows over the surface of the metal in the crucibles, and prevents the access of the oxygen of the atmosphere. Broken glass is sometimes used for this purpose.

When thoroughly fused it is cast into ingots, which, by gentle heating and careful hammering, are tilted into bars. By this process the steel becomes more highly carbonized in proportion to the quantity of flux, and in consequence is more brittle and fusible than before. Hence it surpasses all other steel in uniformity of texture, hardness, and closeness of grain, and is the material employed in all the finest articles of English cutlery.

To make Edge-tools from Cast-Steel and Iron.

This method consists in fixing a clean piece of wrought iron, brought to a welding-heat, in the centre of a mould, and then pouring in melted steel, so as entirely to envelop the iron; and then forging the mass into the shape required

To Color Steel Blue.

The steel must be finely polished on its surface, and then exposed to a uniform degree of heat. Accordingly, there are three ways of coloring: first, by a flame producing no soot, as spirit of wine; secondly, by a hot plate of iron; and thirdly, by wood-ashes. As a very regular degree of heat is necessary, wood-ashes for fine work bears the preference. The work must be covered over with them, and carefully watched; when the color is sufficiently heightened, the work is perfect. This color is occasionally taken off with a very dilute muriatic acid.

To Distinguish Steel from Iron.

The principal characters by which steel may be distinguished from iron, are as follows:—

1. After being polished, steel appears of a whiter light gray hue, without the blue cast exhibited by iron. It also takes a higher polish.
2. The hardest steel, when not annealed, appears granulated, but dull, and without shining fibres.
3. When steeped in acids the harder the steel is, of a darker hue is its surface.
4. Steel is not so much inclined to rust as iron.
5. In general, steel has a greater specific gravity.
6. By being hardened and wrought, it may be rendered much more elastic than iron.
7. It is not attracted so strongly by the magnet as soft iron. It likewise acquires magnetic properties more slowly, but retains them longer; for which reason, steel is used in making needles for compasses and artificial magnets.
8. Steel is ignited sooner, and fuses with less degree of heat than malleable iron, which can scarcely be made to fuse without the addition of

powdered charcoal; by which it is converted into steel, and afterwards into crude iron.

9. Polished steel is sooner tinged by heat, and that with higher colors than iron.

10. In a calcining heat, it suffers less loss by burning than soft iron does in the same heat, and the same time. In calcination a light blue flame hovers over the steel, either with or without a sulphureous odor.

11. The scales of steel are harder and sharper than those of iron; and consequently more fit for polishing with.

12. In a white heat, when exposed to the blast of the bellows among the coals, it begins to sweat, wet, or melt, partly with light-colored and bright, and partly with red sparkles, but less crackling than those of iron. In a melting heat, too, it consumes faster.

13. In the sulphuric, nitric, and other acids, steel is violently attacked, but is longer in dissolving than iron. After maceration, according as it is softer or harder, it appears of a lighter or darker gray color; while iron on the other hand is white.

The Bessemer Process of Making Steel.

Hematite pig-iron smelted with coke and hot-blast has chiefly been used. The metal is melted in a reverberatory furnace, and is then run into a founder's ladle, and from thence it is transferred to the vessel in which its conversion into steel is to be effected. It is made of stout plate iron and lined with a powdered argillaceous stone found in this neighborhood below the coal, and known as ganister. The converting vessel is mounted on axes, which rest on stout iron standards, and by means of a wheel and handle it may be turned into any required position. There is an opening at the top for the inlet and pouring out of the metal, and at the lowest part are inserted 7 fire-clay tuyeres, each having five openings in them; these openings communicate at one end with the interior of the vessel, and at the other end with a box called the tuyere-box, into which a current of air from a suitable blast engine is conveyed under a pressure of about 14 lbs. to the square inch, a pressure more than sufficient to prevent the fluid metal from entering the tuyeres. Before commencing the first operation, the interior of the vessel is heated by coke, a blast through the tuyeres being used to urge the fire. When sufficiently heated, the vessel is turned upside down, and all the unburned coke is shaken out. The molten pig-iron is then run in from the ladle before referred to; the vessel, during the pouring in of the iron, is kept in such a position that the orifices of the tuyeres are at a higher level than the surface of the metal. When all the iron has run in the blast is turned on, and the vessel quickly moved round. The air then rushes upwards into fluid metal from each of the 35 small orifices of the tuyeres, producing a most violent agitation of the whole mass. The silicium, always present in greater or less quantities in pig-iron, is first attacked. It unites readily with the oxygen of the air, producing silicic acid; at the same time a small portion of the iron undergoes oxidation, hence a fluid silicate of the oxide of iron is formed, a little carbon being simultaneously eliminated. The heat is thus gradually increased until nearly the whole of the silicium is oxidized; this generally takes place in about 12 minutes from the commencement of the process. The carbon now begins to unite more freely with the oxygen of the air, producing at first a small flame, which rapidly increases, and in about three minutes from its first appearance we have a most intense combustion going on: the metal rises higher and higher in the vessel, sometimes occupying more than double its former space. The frothy liquid now presents an enormous surface to the action of the oxygen of the air, which unites rapidly with the carbon contained in the crude iron, and produces a most intense combustion, the whole, in fact, being a perfect mixture of metal and fire. The carbon is now eliminated so rapidly as to produce a series of harmless explosions, throwing out the fluid slags in great quantities, while the union of the gases is so perfect that a voluminous white flame rushes from the mouth of the vessel, illuminating the whole building, and indicating to the practised eye the precise condition of the metal inside. The workman may thus leave off whenever the number of minutes he has been blowing and the appearance of the flame indicate the required quality of the metal. This is the mode preferred in working the process in Sweden. But here we prefer to blow the metal until the flame suddenly stops, which it does just on the approach of the metal to the condition of malleable iron: a small quantity of charcoal pig-iron, containing a known quantity of carbon, is then added, and steel is produced of any desired degree of carburation, the process having occupied about 28 minutes from the commencement. The vessel is then turned, and the fluid steel is run into the casting ladle, which is provided with a plug rod covered with loam: the rod passes over the top of the ladle, and works in guides on the outside of it, so that, by means of a lever handle, the workmen may move it up and down as desired. The lower part of the plug, which occupies the interior of the ladle, has fitted to its lower end a fire-clay cone, which rests in a seating of the same material let into the bottom of the ladle, thus forming a cone valve, by means of which the fluid steel is run into different-sized moulds, as may be required, the stream of fluid steel being prevented by the valve plug from flowing during the movement of the casting ladle from one mould to another. By tapping the metal from below, no scoria or other extraneous floating matters are allowed to pass into the mould.

Uchatius Steel.

Pig-iron is first granulated by running it in a small stream into cold water kept constantly agitated. The granulated metal is mixed with sparry iron ore, and if necessary a small portion of manganese, and heated in crucibles in the ordinary cast-steel blast furnace.

PYROTECHNY, MATCHES, etc.

To make Gunpowder.

Take of refined nitre, 75 parts; sulphur, 10 parts; best refined willow charcoal, 15 parts. Powder each separately, and mix intimately with a little water in a mortar. The paste may be rolled out into thin rods, cut into grains and dried on a board in the sun. On the large scale the grains are made by forcing the paste through sieves, dried by steam-heat and polished by rolling against each other in a barrel. *Meal-powder* is ungrained powder.

To make Gun-cotton.

Immerse clean cotton wool in a mixture of equal parts of the strongest nitric and sulphuric acids, allowed to cool for one minute, wash in plenty of cold water, and dry in the sun or by a very gentle artificial heat. For *soluble* gun-cotton used in making *collodion*, see PHOTOGRAPHY.

Lenk's Gun-cotton.

This process gives a gun-cotton which is constant in composition, not liable to change, and of a moderate rapidity of explosiveness. It has been favorably reported on by the Imperial Commission. The following directions are extracted from the specifications of his patent:

First. The cotton or other vegetable fiber is first taken and spun into loose threads of sufficient strength to be easily handled.

Second. The cotton must then be thoroughly boiled in a solution of potash or of soda, in order to remove all greasy substances which the cotton may contain, and after thus boiled it may be exposed to the sun, or wind, or in a heated room, to dry.

Third. The cotton must now be taken into a room heated to 100° Fahr. in order to make it perfectly dry.

Fourth. A mixture is now made containing 1 part weight of nitric acid of 1.48 to 1.50 specific gravity, and 3 parts weight of common sulphuric acid. This mixture must stand in closed earthen or glass jars for several days, or until the two acids become fully mixed and cooled.

Fifth. This mixture of acids is now put into an apparatus containing three apartments, one for the main bulk of the acids, one for the immersion of the cotton, and one for receiving the cotton after being immersed. This apparatus may be made of cast-iron.

Sixth. The cotton is now taken and dipped in the acid-bath, in said apparatus, in such a manner that every 3 oz. of the cotton must come in contact with 60 lbs. of the mixture of acids, or in other words, the bath must contain fully 60 lbs. of the mixture while parcels of 3 oz. of cotton are being dipped. The parcels thus dipped must be gently pressed, and the acids allowed to flow back into the acid-bath, and the parcels are then put into the third apartment of the apparatus, where for every 1 lb. of cotton there must be 10½ lbs. of the said mixture of the acids. The cotton must remain in this state subject to the action of the acids for 48 hours, and the mixture must always have an equally strong concentration, and must be kept under a uniform temperature by a cooling process.

Seventh. The cotton is now taken out from the acids and pressed, and then put into a centrifugal machine to remove all surplus acids.

Eighth. The cotton is again put into another centrifugal machine, into which a constant stream of fresh water is admitted. This process is intended to remove the last particles of adherent acids.

Ninth. The cotton is now taken and put into a fume or trough, and secured in such a manner that a running stream of fresh water may pass through and over it; and the same must remain in this situation for at least 14 days. To lessen the time for this operation the cotton may be immersed or saturated in alcohol for the space of 24 hours. This process is also intended to extract all and the last particles of acids that may possibly adhere to the cotton.

Tenth. The cotton is now taken from the stream of water, or if from the alcohol it must be washed, and then boiled in a solution of common soap and again dried. This process is intended to restore the cotton to its original softness and appearance.

Eleventh. The cotton is now taken and immersed in a solution of water-glass of 1 lb. to 2 lbs. of soft water which must be 1.09 specific gravity of concentration. To 1 lb. of cotton 198-1000ths of a lb. of this solution of 46° Beaumé is required. The cotton is then taken out of this solution and exposed to the action of the atmosphere for at least 4 days. This process has the tendency to preserve the material, and also to make its explosive qualities less rapid.

Twelfth. The gun-cotton is again washed in soft water free from lime, dried, and then packed in wood or metal boxes for storage or exportation; and may be used for artillery, torpedoes, shells, mining, blasting, small arms, and for all purposes where explosive power is required.

Thirteenth. All other vegetable fibres may be treated and manufactured as herein stated, which process will make the same explosive, like the gun-cotton and adapted to the same purposes.

White Gunpowder (Angendre's).

Ferrocyanide of potassium, 28 parts; sugar, 23 parts; chlorate of potassa, 49 parts. This does not require granulating or glazing.

New Explosive Compound,

Invented by Reynaud de Net. It consists of nitrate of soda, 52.5; spent tan-bark, 27.5; pounded sulphur, 20. It is cheap, and applicable to working mines and quarries.

COLORED FIRES.

Red.

Sixty-one per cent. chlorate of potash, 16 sulphur, 23 carbonate of strontia.

Purple-red.

Sixty-one per cent. chlorate of potash, 16 sulphur, 23 chalk.

Rose-red.

Sixty-one per cent. chlorate of potash, 16 sulphur, 23 chloride of calcium.

Orange-red.

Ninety-two per cent. chlorate of potash, 14 sulphur, 34 chalk.

Yellow.

Sixty-one per cent. chlorate of potash, 16 sulphur, 23 dry soda.

Or. 50 per cent. nitre, 16 sulphur, 20 soda, 14 gunpowder.

Or, 61 per cent. nitre, 17½ sulphur, 20 soda, 1½ charcoal.

Light Blue.

Sixty-one per cent. chlorate of potash, 16 sulphur, 23 strongly-calcined alum.

Dark Blue.

Sixty per cent. chlorate of potash, 16 sulphur, 22 carbonate of copper, 12 alum.

Dark Violet.

Sixty per cent. chlorate of potash, 16 sulphur, 12 carbonate of potash, 12 alum.

Pale Violet.

Fifty-four per cent. chlorate of potash, 14 sulphur, 16 carbonate of potash, 16 alum.

Green.

Seventy-three per cent. chlorate of potash, 17 sulphur, 10 boracic acid.

Light Green.

Sixty per cent. chlorate of potash, 16 sulphur, 24 carbonate of baryta.

For Theatrical Illumination.—White.

Sixty-four per cent. nitre, 21 sulphur, 15 gunpowder.

Or, 76 per cent. nitre, 22 sulphur, 2 charcoal.

Red.

Fifty-six per cent. nitrate of strontia, 24 sulphur, 20 chlorate of potash.

Green.

Sixty per cent. nitrate of baryta, 22 sulphur, 18 chlorate of potash.

Pink.

Twenty per cent. sulphur, 32 nitre, 27 chlorate of potash, 20 chalk, 1 charcoal.

Blue.

Twenty-seven per cent. nitre, 28 chlorate of potash, 15 sulphur, 15 sulphate of potash, 15 ammonio-sulphate of copper.

The dark blue is rendered still darker by the addition of some sulphate of potash and ammonio-sulphate of copper. It must be borne in mind that the *red* and *purple* fires are liable to ignite spontaneously, and serious accidents have happened from this cause.

Sulphide of Cadmium in Fireworks.

In the following composition it is said that sulphide of cadmium gives a white flame, which is surrounded by a magnificent blue margin: Saltpetre, 20 parts; sulphur, 5; sulphide of cadmium, 4; powdered charcoal, 1.

Iron Sand.

Used to give corruscations in fireworks, is far better than iron or steel-filings. It is made by beating cast steel or iron into small pieces on an anvil. These are sifted into 4 sizes, the smallest for the smallest pieces; and vice versa. The corruscations produced by these are exceedingly brilliant. The sand should be kept in a dry place in a well-closed bottle, as any rust damages it. Fireworks containing it should not be made very long before using.

Touch-Paper.

Soak unglazed paper in a solution of nitre in vinegar or water. The stronger the solution, the faster will it burn. A good plan is to dip it in a weak solution, dry it, try it, and if it burns too slowly, make the solution stronger and dip it again.

25

Quick-Match

Is made by immersing lamp-wick in a solution of saltpetre with meal powder, winding it on a frame, and afterwards dusting with meal powder. To 1 lb. 12 oz. of cotton, take saltpetre, 1 lb.; alcohol, 2 qts.; water, 3 qts.; solution of isinglass (1 oz. to the pint), 3 galls.; mealed powder, 10 lbs.

Port Fires.

Take of sulphur, 2 parts; saltpetre, 6 parts; mealed powder, 1 part. This is rammed into cases of from 6 inches to 2 feet long, and ½ inch internal diameter. They should be lightly rammed. To give a brilliant flame, add 1 part of iron sand; for a dark flame, 1 part of powdered charcoal.

Stars.

Common.—Saltpetre, 1 lb.; sulphur, 4½ oz.; antimony, 4 oz.; isinglass, ½ oz.; camphor, ½ oz.; alcohol, ¾ oz.

White.—Mealed powder, 4 oz.; saltpetre, 12 oz.; sulphur, 6½ oz.; oil of spike, 2 oz.; camphor, 5 oz.

The above are to be made into balls, rolled in grained powder and dried in the sun. Used in Roman candles, rockets, etc.

Trailed Stars.

Saltpetre, 4 oz.; sulphur, 6 oz.; sulphate of antimony, 2 oz.; rosin, 4 oz.

With Sparks.—Mealed powder 1 oz.; saltpetre, 1 oz.; camphor, 2 oz.

Colored Stars

May be made by using any of the receipts for colored fires, with a solution of isinglass, ½ oz.; camphor, ½ oz.; and alcohol, ¾ oz. Make into balls of the requisite size, roll in gunpowder, dry in the sun.

Roman Candles.

Meal-powder, ½ lb.; saltpetre, 2½ lbs.; sulphur, glass dust, each, ½ lb. This is rammed in cases as follows: Put at the bottom of the case a small quantity of clay, then some gunpowder, then a wad of paper, then ⅛ of the height of the case of the composition, then a wad and powder and a star or ball, then more composition, and so on till the case is filled. The wads must be loose (only to prevent the mixing of the composition and gunpowder), and the ramming should not be begun until the case is ½ filled, and then should be gentle l[illegible]t the stars be broken.

Chinese Fire.

Red.—Saltpetre, 1 lb.; sulphur, 3 oz.; charcoal, 4 oz.; iron sand, 7 oz.

White.—Saltpetre, 1 lb.; mealed powder, 12 oz.; charcoal, 7½ oz.; iron sand, fine, 11 oz.

Golden Rain.

Mealed powder, 4 oz.; saltpetre, 1 lb.; sulphur, 4 oz.; brass-filings, 1 oz.; sawdust, 2¼ oz.; glass powder, 6 drs.

Silver Rain.

Mealed powder, 2 oz.; saltpetre, 4 oz.; sulphur, 1 oz.; steel-dust, ¾ oz.

Wheel Cases.

Mealed powder, 2 lbs.; saltpetre, 4 oz.; steel-filings, 6 oz.

For Rockets.

Four-Ounce.—Mealed powder, 1 lb.; charcoal, 1 oz.; saltpetre, 4 oz.

Eight-Ounce.—Mealed powder, 1 lb. 1 oz.; saltpetre, 4 oz.; sulphur, 3½ oz.; charcoal 1 oz.

One-Pound.—Mealed powder, 1 lb.; charcoal, 3 oz.; sulphur, 1 oz.

Two-Pound.—Mealed powder, 1 lb. 4 oz.; saltpetre, 2 oz.; charcoal, 3 oz.; sulphur, 1 oz.; iron-filings, 2 oz.

Four-Pound.—Mealed powder, ½ lb.; saltpetre, 15 lbs.; sulphur, 2 lbs.; charcoal, 6 lbs.

Matches for Instantaneous Light.

1. Chlorate matches, without sulphur. Chlorate of potash, separately powdered, 6 drs.; vermilion, 1 dr.; lycopodium, 1 dr.; fine flour, 2 drs.; mix carefully the chlorate with the flour and lycopodium, avoiding much friction, then add the vermilion, and mix the whole with a mucilage made with 1 dr. powdered gum Arabic, 10 grs. of tragacanth, 2 drs. of flour, and 4 oz. of hot water; mix, add sufficient water to bring it to a proper consistence, and dip in it the wood, previously dipped in a solution of 1 oz. of gum copal, and ½ oz. of camphor, in 6 oz. of oil of turpentine.

2. With sulphur. Chlorate of potash, 9 grs.; sulphur, 2 grs.; sugar, 3 grs.; vermilion, 1 gr.; flour, 2 grs.; spirit of wine, q. s. The chlorate of potash, etc., must be separately reduced to powder, and the whole mixed with as little friction as possible. The wood should be previously prepared as above, or with camphorated spirit. [These are ignited by dipping them in sulphuric acid, and instantly withdrawing them. The acid should be absorbed by asbestos.] They are now become obsolete having given place to

Lucifer Matches.

These contain phosphorus in a finely divided state, to which it is reduced by agitating it in some warm solution of gum or glue, then adding the other ingredients, so as to form a paste, into which the wood or card is dipped. It is said that urine and artificial urea have the property of readily dividing phosphorus when warmed and agitated together. The following are some of the published recipes:

1. Form 6 parts of glue into a smooth jelly, and rub with it 4 parts of phosphorus, at a temperature of 140° or 150° Fahr.; add 10 parts of nitro, 5 of red ochre, and 2 of fine smalts. The matches are dipped in melted wax to the depth of 1-10th of an inch, first rubbing their ends on a hot iron plate.

2. *Noiseless Congreves.*—Triturate 9 parts of phosphorus with a solution of 16 parts of gum, and add 14 parts of nitre and 16 of vermilion.

3. Glue, 6 parts; phosphorus, 4; nitre, 10; red lead, 5; smalts, 2; the glue is soaked in water for 24 hours, then liquefied in a warm mortar, and the phosphorus added, taking care that the temperature is not above 167° Fahr.

4. Glue, 21; phosphorus, 17; nitre, 38; red lead, 24; proceed as before.

Safety Matches.

Will only ignite upon the prepared surface. For the splints take of chlorate of potassa, 6 parts; sulphuret of antimony, 3 parts; glue, 1 part. For the friction surface, amorphous phosphorus, 10 parts; sulphuret of antimony, or black oxide of manganese, 8 parts; glue, 3 to 6 parts. Spread evenly upon the surface, previously made rough with glue and sand.

Matches without Phosphorus.

The dangers arising from the universal adoption of the common lucifer match have induced chemists to seek a substitute for it. M. Peitzer has recently proposed a compound which is obtained in the shape of a violet powder, by mixing together equal volumes of solutions of sulphate of copper, one of which is supersaturated with ammonia, and the other with hyposulphite of soda. A mixture of chlorate of potash and the above powder will catch fire by percussion or rubbing; it burns like gunpowder, leaving a black residue. M. Viederhold proposes a mixture of hyposulphite of lead or baryta, or chlorate of potash for matches without phosphorus. The only inconvenience of this compound is that it attracts moisture too easily.

TANNING.

The art of tanning is that by which animal skins are converted into leather, a product possessing certain properties differing from those of the raw material, and eminently adapted to the purposes for which it is employed. Chemically considered leather is a compound of tannin and gelatine, possessing the requisites of durability, pliability, insolubility in water, and great power of resisting the action of chemical reagents.

The name of tan is applied to coarsely powdered bark which is obtained mostly from oak and hemlock trees, although all barks contain more or less tannin, and in some countries the extract of others is used.

To tan a skin is to saturate it with tannin in such a manner as to promote the *slow* combination of this principle with the gelatine, albumen, and fibrine contained in the former.

The principal steps in the manufacture of leather are,

1. *The washing and soaking* in pure water, for the purpose of cleansing and softening the skins, and preparing them for

2. *The unhairing.*—This is effected by the use of lime, or by sweating the hides, which dissolves or softens the bulbous roots of the hairs, and thus facilitates their removal by more mechanical scraping with a blunt-edged knife.

When lime is employed, about 4 bus. are slacked and put into a large vat of clean water, capable of holding 40 hides or 2 hundred calf-skins; the lime is well mixed by a plunger, and the hides or skins are then put into it and allowed to remain from 7 to 10 days for the former, and 10 to 14 days for the latter, drawing them out daily to facilitate the process.

When the hair will slip they are taken out of the lime and plunged into clean water, from which they go to the beam where the hair is scraped off with a long curved blunt-edged knife; they are immersed in water again and taken back to the beam, and all the flesh removed from the inside of the hide or skin with a sharp knife similar in shape to the one used in unhairing, after which they are ready for

3. *Bating.*—As it is all important to have the skins soft and in a condition to absorb the tanning liquor readily; this is accomplished by put-

ting them in water impregnated with pigeon's-dung, 1 bu. being enough for the number of hides or skins above named. This is called a bate, and acts by means of the muriate of ammonia which it contains, the lime taking the acid becomes muriate of lime, which is soluble and easily worked and washed out of the skins, while the ammonia passes off in a gaseous state.

Hides intended for sole-leather should remain 24 hours in this bath, when they may be worked out and are ready for the bark extract; calf-skins, or other upper leather, should remain in the bate from 3 to 5 days, according to the weather (a longer time being required in cold than in hot weather), and during this time they are taken out 2 or 3 times and placed on the beam where they are scraped first on the grain side, and lastly on both flesh and grain with a worker similar to the one used in unhairing, after which they are ready for

4. *Tanning.*—When the hides or skins are taken from the beam-house they are put into vats containing a weak solution of ground bark, and should be handled two or three times a day until they are evenly colored, when they should go into a stronger liquor, or ooze, where they may remain a week, being taken out daily and allowed to drain off, at the same time strengthening the ooze. They may now be considered ready for laying away. For this purpose a vat is half filled with a very strong extract of bark, and the hides or skins are carefully laid in, one at a time, each being covered with finely-ground bark to the depth of half an inch, until all are thus laid away. About a foot in thickness of spent tan is put on for a heading, and the vat covered with boards.

The hides or skins may be allowed to remain in this their first layer for two weeks, at the expiration of which time they must be taken up, washed clean in the liquor, and the same process repeated, using a new liquor and fresh bark, as the strength has been absorbed from the other. As the tanning proceeds the extract is exhausted more slowly, and from 3 weeks to 1 month may be allowed for each successive layer, after the first—3 layers being enough for calfskins, and 4 to 6 for sole-leather, according to the thickness of the hides.

When the sole-leather is tanned it is taken out of the vats, washed clean, and hung up to dry in the rolling loft. When nearly dry it is rolled on the grain with a brass roller until it is quite smooth, hung up again, and thoroughly dried, and is ready for the market.

Currying or Finishing Calfskins.

When calfskins are sufficiently tanned they should be rinsed in the liquor in the vats, and hung over poles and slightly hardened, being careful not to expose them to the direct rays of the sun in the summer months. Put into piles, so that they will not dry out, dampening any part that may have become too dry. They are now shaved over a currier's beam, during which process the rough flesh is taken off, and the butts and heads are leveled and the rough edges trimmed off. The skins are then rinsed off, slicked on a marble table with a steel slicker and stiff brush on the flesh side, the dirt and coloring matter of the bark stoned, brushed, and slicked out on the grain side. They should then be hung up, by a loop cut in the head, for a few hours, that the water may be partially dried out of them; they must be then taken down and placed in a pile, and are ready for *stuffing.*

The grease called dubbing is composed of equal parts of cod-liver oil and melted tallow, and when ready the skin is laid on a wooden table and slicked on the flesh side. The stretch is in this manner taken out, and the skin should be perfectly smooth on the table before the dubbing is coated on; for which purpose a brush or pad is used, the quantity put on varying, according to the thickness of the skin. They are next hung up by the hind shanks, and allowed to dry. When entirely dry, they must be taken down, and piled flesh to flesh and grain to grain, and should remain for a week or two, so as to become an even color, and also to absorb the strength of the grease. When ready to finish the grease must be slicked off on a finishing table (made of cherry or mahogany wood), and the skins are softened by rolling them with a board having fine grooves cut in it. The surface of the flesh side is smoothed by shaving over it with a currier's knife which has a very fine and delicate edge turned on it, so that the smallest quantity only is taken off. This process is termed whitening. The skins are then stoned on the grain side, and all wrinkles and breaks taken out, and a fine grain is turned on them with a smooth board, or with very fine grooves cut in it. They are matched for size, laid down in a pile, the larger ones in the bottom, and blacked on the flesh side with a compound of lampblack, tanner's oil, and dubbing, and a small quantity of water, to prevent it striking through. As they are blacked they are laid over a strip. They must now be pasted, to prevent the black rubbing off. The paste is composed of wheat-flour and boiling water, stirring in a small quantity of soap and tallow, and is applied with a brush, coating them with as small a quantity as possible. They are hung up by the loop in the head and dried, then glassed with a polished glass slicker on the flesh side, and are ready for the last process, gumming. The gum used is gum tragacanth, dissolved in water, and is applied with a sponge, on the flesh side, hung up, and when thoroughly dry, they are ready for sale, or cutting into boots and shoes.

To Convert Sheep-skins into Leather.

Sheep-skins, which are used for a variety of purposes, such as gloves, book-covers, etc., and which, when dyed, are converted into mock Morocco leather, are dressed as follows: They are first to be soaked in water and handled, to separate all impurities, which may be scraped off by a blunt knife on a beam. They are then to be hung up in a close warm room to putrefy. This putrefaction loosens the wool, and causes the exudation of an oily and slimy matter, all which are to be removed by the knife. The skins are now to be steeped in milk of lime, to harden and thicken; here they remain for 1 month or 6 weeks, according to circumstances, and when taken out, they are to be smoothed on the fleshy side with a sharp knife. They are now to be steeped in a bath of bran and water, where they undergo a partial fermentation, and become thinner in their substance.

The skins, which are now called pelts, are to be immersed in a solution of alum and common salt in water; in the proportion of 120 skins to 3 lbs. of alum and 5 lbs. of salt. They are to be much agitated in this compound saline bath, in order to become firm and tough. From this bath they are to be removed to another, composed of bran and water, where they remain until quite pliant by a slight fermentation. To give their upper surfaces a gloss, they are to be trodden in a wooden tub, with a solution of yolks of eggs in water, previously well beaten up. When this solution has become transparent, it is a proof that the skins have absorbed the glazing matter. The pelt may now be said to be converted into leather, which is to be drained from moisture, hung upon hooks in a warm apartment to dry, and smoothed over with warm hand-irons.

Morocco.

The goat-skins being first dried in the air, are steeped in water 3 days and nights; then stretched on a tanner's horse, beaten with a large knife, and steeped afresh in water every day; they are then thrown into a large vat on the ground, full of water, where quicklime has been slaked, and there lie 15 days, whence they are taken, and again returned every night and morning. They are next thrown into a fresh vat of lime and water, and shifted night and morning for 15 days longer; then rinsed in clean water, and the hair taken off on the leg with the knife, returned into a third vat, and shifted as before for 18 days; steeped 12 hours in a river, taken out, rinsed, put in pails, where they are pounded with wooden pestles, changing the water twice; then laid on the horse, and the flesh taken off; returned into pails of new water, taken out, and the hair-side scraped; returned into fresh pails, taken out, and thrown into a pail of a particular form, having holes at bottom; here they are beaten for the space of an hour, and fresh water poured on from time to time; then being stretched on the leg, and scraped on either side, they are returned into pails of fresh water, taken out, stretched, and sewed up all round, in the manner of bags, leaving out the hinder legs, as an aperture for the conveyance of a mixture described below.

The skins thus sewed are put to luke-warm water, where dog's excrements have been dissolved. Here they are stirred with long poles for ¼ an hour, left at rest for 12 hours, taken out, rinsed in fresh water, and filled by a tunnel with a preparation of water and sumach, mixed and heated over the fire till ready to boil; and, as they are filled, the hind legs are sewed up to stop the passage. In this state they are let down into the vessel of water and sumach, and kept stirring for 4 hours successively; taken out and heaped on one another; after a little time their sides are changed, and thus they continue 1½ hours till drained. This done, they are loosened, and filled a second time with the same preparation, sewed up again, and kept stirring 2 hours, piled up and drained as before. This process is again repeated, with this difference, that they are then only stirred ¼ of an hour; after which they are left till next morning, when they are taken out, drained on a rack, unsewed, the sumach taken out, folded in two from head to tail, the hair-side outwards, laid over each other on the leg, to perfect their draining, stretched out and dried; then trampled under foot by two and two, stretched on a wooden table, what flesh and sumach remains scraped off, the hair-side rubbed over with oil, and that again with water.

They are then wrung with the hands, stretched, and pressed tight on the table with an iron instrument like that of a currier, the flesh-side uppermost; then turned, and the hair-side rubbed strongly over with a handful of rushes, to squeeze out as much of the oil remaining as possible. The first coat of black is now laid on the hair-side, by means of a lock of hair twisted and steeped in a kind of black dye, prepared of sour beer, wherein pieces of old rusty iron have been thrown. When half-dried in the air they are stretched on a table, rubbed over every way with a paumelle, or wooden-toothed instrument, to raise the grain, over which is passed a light couche of water, then sleeked by rubbing them with rushes prepared for the purpose. Thus sleeked, they have a second couche of black, then dried, laid on the table, rubbed over with a paumelle of cork, to raise the grain again; and after a light couche of water, sleeked over anew; and to raise the grain a third time, a paumelle of wood is used.

After the hair-side has received all its preparations, the flesh-side is pared with a sharp knife for the purpose; the hair-side is strongly rubbed over with a woollen cap, having before given it a gloss with barberries, citron or orange. The whole is finished by raising the grain lightly, for the last time, with the paumelle of cork; so that they are now fit for the market.

To Prepare Red Morocco.

After steeping, stretching, scraping, beating and rinsing the skins as before, they are at length wrung, stretched on the leg, and passed after each other into water where alum has been dissolved. Thus alumed, they are left to drain till morning, then wrung out, pulled on the leg, and folded from head to tail, the flesh inwards.

In this state they receive their first dye, by passing them after one another into a red liquor, described hereafter. This is repeated again and again, till the skins have got their first color; then they are rinsed in clean water, stretched on the leg, and left to drain 12 hours; thrown into water through a sieve, and stirred incessantly for a day with long poles; taken out, hung on a bar across the water all night, white against red, and red against white, and in the morning the water stirred up, and the skins returned into it for 24 hours.

Ingredients for the Red Color.

The following is the quantity and proportions of the ingredients required for the red color, for a parcel of 36 skins:

Cochineal, 130 drs.; ground suchet (crocus indicus), 45 drs.; gutta gamba, 15 drs.; gum Arabic, 10 drs.; white alum, pulverized, 10 drs.; bark of the pomegranate tree, 10 drs.; citron juice, 2 drs.; common water, 120 lbs.

The alum is gradually added to the other articles, and boiled in a copper for about 2 hours, till one-tenth part of the water is consumed.

To Manufacture Leather in Imitation of Morocco, from South American Horse Hides.

Soften the hide in water; then spread it on a tanner's beam, and let it be wrought with a knife on the flesh-side, and subjected to the action of lime-water. In the succeeding process it is treated as goat-skins for making morocco, i. e. put it into hot water, with dog's dung, to purify the animal juices; then let it be again wrought with a knife on both sides, on a tanner's beam; afterwards put it into blood-warm water with bran; and, finally, tan it with sumach.

To Manufacture Russia Leather.

Calf-skins steeped in a weak bath of carbonate of potass and water, are well cleaned and scraped, to have the hair, etc., removed. They are now immersed in another bath, containing dog and pigeon's dung in water. Being thus freed from the alkali, they are thrown into a mixture of oatmeal and water, to undergo a slight fermentation. To tan these hides, it is necessary to use birch bark instead of oak bark; and during the operation they are to be frequently handled or agitated. When tanned, and perfectly dry, they are made pliable by oil and much friction; they are then to be rubbed over gently with birch tar, which gives them that agreeable odor peculiar to this kind of leather, and which secures them against the attacks of moths and worms. This odor will preserve the leather for many years; and, on account of it,

Russia leather is much used in binding handsome and costly books. The marks, or intersecting lines on this leather, are given to it by passing over its grained surface a heavy iron cylinder, bound round by wires.

To Tan or Dress Skins in White for Gloves.

Clean the skins from wool or hair, by laying them in a vat of slaked lime-water for 5 or 6 weeks. During this operation the lime and water are to be twice changed, and the skins are to be shifted every day, and when taken out for good, they are to be laid all night in a running water, to clear them from the forcing qualities of the lime; next lay them on a wooden leg by sixes, to get the flesh off; then they are to be laid in a vat with a little water, and to be fulled with wooden pestles for a quarter of an hour, after which rinse them well in a full vat of water; place them next on a clean pavement to drain, and afterwards cast them into a fresh pit of water, rinse them again, and re-lay them on the wooden leg, with their hair outside, over which a whetstone is to be briskly rubbed, to fit them for further preparations. They are next to be put into a pit of water, mixed with wheaten bran, and stirred until the bran sticks to the wooden poles. They now arrive to a kind of fermentation, and as often as they rise on the top of the water, are to be plunged down at the same time the liquor, now highly fermented, is to be fined. When the skins have done rising, take them out, and scrape away the bran with a knife on the leg; when sufficiently drained give them their feeding. For 100 large sheep-skins, take 8 lbs. of alum, and 3 lbs. of sea-salt, and melt the whole with water in a vessel. Pour the solution out, while lukewarm, into a trough in which is 20 lbs. of the finest wheat flour, with the yolks of 8 dozen of eggs, of which mixed materials is formed a kind of paste, somewhat thicker than children's pap; next pour hot water into the trough where the paste was, mixing 2 spoonfuls of the paste with it, with a wooden spoon, which will contain a sufficiency for 12 skins, and when the whole is well incorporated, put 2 dozen of the skins into it, taking care that the water is not too hot. After they have been in some time, take them severally out of the trough, and stretch them twice well out. After they have absorbed the paste, put them into tubs, and full as before. Let them lie in a vat 6 days, and hang them out to dry; in fair weather, on cords or racks. When dry, put them into bundles, just dipped in clean water, and drained; throw them into an empty tub, and having lain some time they are to be taken out and trampled under foot; hang them up a second time on the cords to dry, and finally smooth them upon a table ready for sale.

To Prepare Sheep, Goat, or Kid Skins in Oil, in Imitation of Chamois.

Sheep Skins.

The skins, smeared with quicklime on the fleshy side, are folded lengthways, the wool outwards, and laid on heaps, to ferment 8 days; or if they had been left to dry after flaying, for 15 days.

Then they are washed out, drained, and half dried, laid on a wooden horse, the wool stripped off with a round staff for the purpose, and laid in a weak pit of slacked lime.

After 24 hours they are taken out, and left to drain 24 more; then put into another strong pit. Then they are taken out, drained, and put in again by turns; which begins to dispose them to take oil; and this practice is continued for 6 weeks in summer, or 3 months in winter; at the end whereof they are washed out, laid on the wooden horse, and the surface of the skin on the wool side peeled off, to render them the softer; then made into parcels, steeped a night in the river, in winter more; stretched 6 or 7, one over another on the wooden horse; and the knife passed strongly on the fleshy side, to take off anything superfluous, and render the skin smooth.

Then they are stretched, as before, in the river, and the same operation repeated on the wool side; then thrown into a tub of water and bran, which is brewed among the skins till the greater part sticks to them; and then separated into distinct tubs, till they swell, and rise of themselves above the water.

By these means, the remains of the lime are cleared out; they are then wrung out, hung up to dry on ropes, and sent to the mill, with the quantity of oil necessary to fill them; the best oil is that of cod-fish.

Here they are first thrown in bundles into the river for 12 hours, then laid in the mill-trough, and fulled without oil, till they are well softened; then oiled with the hand, one by one, and thus formed into parcels of 4 skins each, which are milled, and dried on cords a second time, then a third; then oiled again and dried.

This is repeated as often as necessary; when done, if any moisture remains they are dried in a stove, and made up in parcels wrapped up in wool; after some time they are opened to the air, but wrapped up again as before, till the oil seems to have lost all its force, which it ordinarily does in 24 hours.

To Scour the Skins.

The skins are now returned to the chamoiser, to be scoured, by putting them into a lixivium of wood-ashes, working and beating them in it with poles, and leaving them to steep till the lye has had its effect; then wrung out, steeped in another lixivium, wrung again, and this repeated till the grease and oil are purged out. They are then half-dried, and passed over a sharp-edged iron instrument, placed perpendicularly in a block, which opens and softens them; lastly, they are thoroughly dried, and passed over the same instrument again, which finishes the operation.

Kid and Goat Skins.

Kid, and goat skins, are chamoised in the same manner as those of sheep, excepting that the hair is taken off by heat; and that when brought from the mill they undergo a preparation called ramalling, the most difficult of all.

It consists in this, that as soon as brought from the mill they are steeped in a fit lixivium; taken out, stretched on a round wooden leg, and the hair scraped off with the knife; this makes them smooth, and in working cast a fine nap. The difficulty is scraping them evenly.

To Dress Hare, Mole, or Rabbit Skins.

Take a teaspoonful of alum, and 2 of saltpetre, both finely powdered; mix them well, sprinkle the powder on the flesh side of the skins, then lay the two salted sides together, leaving the fur outward; roll the skin exceedingly tight, and tie it round with pack-thread; hang it in a dry place for some days, then open it, and if sufficiently dry scrape it quite clean with a blunt knife, and keep it in a dry situation. This finishes the process.

It may not be generally known, that the bitter apple bruised and put into muslin bags, will effectually prevent furs from being destroyed by moths.

To make Parchment.

This article is manufactured from sheep skins, cleared from lime. The skin is stretched on a frame where the flesh is pared off with an iron circular knife; it is then moistened with a rag, and whiting spread over it; the workman then, with a large pumice-stone, flat at the bottom, rubs over the skin, and scours off the flesh. He next goes over it with the iron instrument as before, and rubs it carefully with the pumice-stone without chalk; this serves to smooth the flesh side. He drains it again by passing over it the iron instrument as before; he passes it over the wool side, then stretches it tight on a frame. He now throws more whiting and sweeps it over with a piece of woolly lamb-skin. It is now dried, and taken off the frame by cutting it all round. Thus prepared it is taken out of the skinner's hands by the parchment maker, who, while it is dry, pares it on a summer (which is a calf-skin stretched on a frame), with a sharper instrument than that used by the skinner, who, working it with the arm from the top to the bottom of the skin, takes away about half its substance, which leaves the parchment finished.

To Convert Old Parchment or Vellum into Leather.

Soak and wash the skins well and often in soft water for 24 hours; then remove them for the same period into a bath composed of 1½ lbs. of white vitriol, 1 lb. of cream of tartar, and 1 oz. of sal ammoniac, dissolved in 20 galls. of water. Next add 10 lbs. of vitriolic acid, 1 lb. of nitric acid, and 1 pt. of spirit of salt, in which steep the skins for a short time to purge away the old lime; next wash them clear of the acid, and rinse them as dry as possible, without damaging the skins. They are then to be put into a tanning liquor, composed of 20 lbs. of oak bark, 7 lbs. sumach, 5 lbs. of elm-bark, 3 lbs. of sassafras, and the same quantity of lignum vitæ shavings, portioned to 20 galls. of water, and previously warmed for 12 hours, and cooled down to a new-milk warmth, before the skins are immersed.

To make Vellum.

This is a species of parchment made of the skins of abortives, or sucking calves; it has a much finer grain, and is white and smoother than parchment, but is prepared in the same manner, except its not being passed through the lime-pit. The article is used for binding superior books, and covering of drum heads.

To Preserve Leather from Mould.

Pyroligneous acid may be used with success in preserving leather from the attacks of mould, and is serviceable in recovering it after it has received that species of damage, by passing it over the surface of the hide or skin, first taking due care to expunge the mouldy spots by the application of a dry cloth. This remedy will be of equal service if applied to boots, shoes, etc., when damaged in the same manner.

To Dye Morocco and Sheep Leather.

The following colors may be imparted to leather, according to the various uses for which it is intended.

Blue.

Blue is given by steeping the subject a day in urine and indigo, then boiling it with alum; or, it may be given by tempering the indigo with red wine, and washing the skins therewith.

Another.—Boil elderberries or dwarf elder, then smear and wash the skins therewith and wring them out; then boil the elderberries as before in a solution of alum-water, and wet the skins in the same manner once or twice; dry them, and they will be very blue.

Red.

Red is given by washing the skins and laying them 2 hours in galls, then wringing them out, dipping them in a liquor made with ligustrum, alum and verdigris; in water, and lastly in a dye made of Brazil-wood boiled with lye.

Purple.

Purple is given by wetting the skins with a solution of roche alum in warm water, and when dry, again rubbing them with the hand, with a decoction of log-wood in cold water.

Green.

Green is given by smearing the skin with sap-green and alum-water boiled.

Dark Green.

Dark green is given with steel-filings and sal ammoniac, steeped in urine till soft, then smeared over the skin, which is to be dried in the shade.

Yellow.

Yellow is given by smearing the skin over with aloes and linseed-oil, dissolved and strained, or by infusing it in weld.

Light Orange.

Orange color is given by smearing it with fustic berries boiled in alum-water, or, for a deep orange, with turmeric.

Sky-color.

Sky-color is given with indigo steeped in boiling water, and the next morning warmed and smeared over the skin.

ENAMELLING.

The art of enamelling consists in the application of a smooth coating of vitrified matter to a bright polished metallic surface. It is, therefore, a kind of varnish made of glass, and melted upon the substance to which it is applied; affording a fine uniform ground for an infinite variety of ornaments, which are also fixed by heat.

The only metals that are enamelled are gold and copper; and with the latter the opaque enamels only are used. Where the enamel is transparent and colored, the metal chosen should not only have its surface unalterable when fully red hot, but also be in no degree chemically altered by the close contact of melted glass, containing an abundance of some kind of metallic oxide. This is the chief reason why colored enamelling on silver is impracticable, though the brilliancy of its surface is not impaired by mere heat; for if an enamel, made yellow by oxide of lead or antimony, be laid on the surface of bright silver, and be kept melted on it for a certain time, the silver and the enamel act on each other so powerfully that the color soon changes from a yellow to an orange, and lastly to a dirty olive. Copper is equally altered by the colored enamels; so that gold is the only metal that can bear the long contact of the colored glass at a full red heat, without being altered by them.

To Enamel Dial-Plates.

A piece of thin sheet-copper, hammered to the requisite convexity, is first accurately cut out, a hole drilled in the middle for the axis of the

ENAMELLING. 391

hands, and both the surfaces made perfectly bright with a brush. A small rim is then made round the circumference with a thin brass band rising a little above the level, and a similar rim round the margin of the central hole. The use of these is to confine the enamel when in fusion, and to keep the edges of the plate quite neat and even. The substance of the enamel is a fine white opaque glass; this is bought in lump by the enamellers, and is first broken down with a hammer, then ground to a powder sufficiently fine with some water, in an agate mortar; the superfluous water being then poured off, the pulverized enamel remains of about the consistence of wetted sand, and is spread very evenly over the surface of the copper plate. In most enamellings, and especially on this, it is necessary also to counter enamel the under concave surface of the copper plate, to prevent its being drawn out of its true shape by the unequal shrinking of the metal and the enamel on cooling. For this kind of work, the counter-enamel is only about half the thickness on the concave, as on the convex side. For flat plates the thickness is the same on both sides.

The plate, covered with the moist enamel powder, is warmed and thoroughly dried, then gently set upon a thin earthen ring that supports it only by touching the outer rim, and put gradually into the red-hot muffle of the enameller's furnace. This furnace is constructed somewhat like the assay-furnace; but the upper part alone of the muffle is much heated, and some peculiarities are observed in the construction, to enable the artist to govern the fire more accurately.

The precise degree of heat to be given here, as in all enamelling, is that at which the particles of the enamel run together into a uniform pasty consistence and extend themselves evenly, showing a fine polished face; carefully avoiding on the other hand so great a heat as would endanger the melting of the thin metallic plate. When the enamel is thus seen to *sweat down*, as it were, to a uniform glossy glazing, the piece is gradually withdrawn and cooled; otherwise it would fly by the action of cold air.

A second coating of enamel is then laid on and fired as before; but this time the finest powder of enamel is taken, or that which remains suspended in the washings. It is then ready to receive the figures and division marks, which are made of a black enamel ground in an agate mortar to a most impalpable powder, worked up on a pallet with oil of lavender, and laid on with an extremely fine hair brush. The plate is then stoved to evaporate the essential oil, and the figure is burnt in as before. Polishing with tripoli, and minuter parts of the process, need not be here described.

To make the Purple Enamel used in the Mosaic Pictures of St. Peter's at Rome.

Take of sulphur, saltpetre, vitriol, antimony and oxide of tin, each, 1 lb.; minium, or oxide of lead, 60 lbs. Mix all together in a crucible and melt in a furnace; next take it out and wash it, to carry off the salts; after melting in the crucible, add 19 oz. of rose copper, ½ oz. of prepared zaffre, 1½ oz. of crocus martis, made with sulphur, 3 oz. of refined borax, and 1 lb. of a composition of gold, silver and mercury.

When all are well combined, the mass is to be stirred with a copper rod, and the fire gradually diminished, to prevent the metals from burning. The composition thus prepared is finally to be put into crucibles and placed in a reverberatory furnace, where they are to remain 24 hours. The same composition will answer for other colors, by merely changing the coloring matter. This composition has almost all the characters of real stone, and when broken exhibits a vitreous fracture.

To make White Enamel, for Porcelain.

Mix 100 parts of pure lead with from 20 to 25 of the best tin, and bring them to a low red heat in an open vessel. The mixture then burns nearly as rapidly as charcoal, and oxidizes very fast. Skim off the crusts of oxide successively formed, till the whole is thoroughly calcined. Then mix all the skimmings and again heat as before, till no flame arises from them, and the whole is of a uniform gray color. Take 100 parts of this oxide, 100 of white sand, and 25 or 30 of common salt, and melt the whole by a moderate heat. This gives a grayish mass, often porous and apparently imperfect; but which, however, runs to a good enamel when afterwards heated.

For Metals and Finer Work.

The sand is previously calcined in a very strong heat with a fourth of its weight; or if a more fusible compound is wanted, as much of the oxides of tin and lead as of salt are taken, and the whole is melted into a white porous mass. This is then employed instead of the rough sand, as in the preceding process.

The above proportions, however, are not invariable; for if more fusibility is wanted, the dose of oxide is increased, and that of the sand diminished; the quantity of common salt remaining the same. The sand employed in this process is not the common sort, however fine; but a micaceous sand, in which the mica forms about one-fourth of the mixture.

New Enamel for Porcelain.

Melt together pulverized feldspar, 27 parts; borax, 18 parts; sand, 4 parts; potash, nitre, and potter's earth, 3 parts each. Then add 3 parts of borax reduced to fine powder.

From the trial which the Society of Arts in London ordered to be made of this enamel, it has been found superior to any hitherto known. It is easily and uniformly applied, and spreads without producing bubbles or spoutings out; it neither covers nor impairs even the most delicate colors. It incorporates perfectly with them, and the porcelain which is covered over with it may pass a second time through the fire without this enamel cracking or breaking out.

Material for Opaque Enamels.

Neri, in his valuable treatise on glass making, has long ago given the following proportions for the common material of all the opaque enamels, which Kunckel and other practical chemists have confirmed: Calcine 30 parts of lead with 33 of tin, with the usual precautions. Then take of this calcined mixed oxide 50 lbs., and as much powdered flints (prepared by being thrown water when red-hot, and ground to powd 8 oz. of salt of tartar; melt the mixture i fire kept up for ten hours, after which   ae mass to powder.

To make it White.

Mix 6 lbs. of the compound with 4   if the best black oxide of manganese, and m-   a clear fire. When fully fused throw it into   d water; then re-melt and cool as before 2 or , .imes, till the enamel is quite white and fine.

Rich Red-colored Enamel.

The most beautiful and costly color known in enamelling is an exquisitely fine, rich red, with a purplish tinge, given by the salts and oxides of gold; especially by the purpl precipitate formed by tin in one form or other, and by nitromuriate of gold, and also by the fulminating gold. Thi•

beautiful color requires much skill in the artist, to be fully brought out. When most perfect it should come from the fire quite colorless, and afterwards receive its color by the flame of a candle.

Other and common reds are given by the oxide of iron, but this requires the mixture of alumina, or some other substance refractory in the fire, otherwise at a full red heat the color will degenerate into black.

To Prepare the Flux for Enamelling on Glass Vessels.

Take of *saturnus glorificatus*, 1 lb.; natural crystal, calcined to whiteness, ½ lb.; salt of pulverine, 1 lb. Mix them together, and bake in a slow heat for about 12 hours; then melt the mass, and pulverize the same in an agate mortar, or any other proper vessel, which is not capable of communicating any metallic or other impurity.

To Prepare Glorificatus.

Take litharge of white lead, put it in a pan, pour on distilled vinegar, stirring it well over a gentle fire till the vinegar becomes impregnated with the salt of the lead; evaporate half the vinegar, put it in a cool place to crystallize, and keep the crystals dry for use.

To make Green Enamel.

Take of copper-dust, 1 oz.; sand, 2 oz.; litharge, 1 oz.; nitre, ½ oz. Or, copper, 2 oz.; sand, 1 oz.; litharge, 2 oz.; nitre, 1½ oz.

Mix them with equal parts of flux, or vary the proportions of them as may be found necessary, according to the tint of color required.

Another. — Take of opaque or transparent enamel, 10 parts; oxide of chromium, 1 to 2 parts.

Black Enamel.

Take of calcined iron, cobalt, crude or prepared, each 1 oz. Or, zaffre, 2 oz.; manganese, 1 oz.

Mix them with equal parts of flux, by melting or grinding together.

Yellow Enamel.

Take of lead and tin ashes, litharge, antimony, and sand, each 1 oz.; nitre, 4 oz.

Calcine, or melt them together; pulverize, and mix them with a due proportion of flux, as the nature of the glass may require; or take more or less of any or all of the above, according to the depth of color desired. Or, opaque or transparent enamel, 6 parts; chloride of silver, 1 to 2 parts.

Blue Enamel.

Take of prepared cobalt, sand, red-lead, and nitre, each 1 oz.; flint-glass, 2 oz.

Melt them together by fire, pulverized and fluxed according to the degree of softness or strength of color required.

Olive Enamel.

Take of the blue, as prepared above, 1 oz.; black, ½ oz.; yellow, ½ oz. Grind them for use. If necessary add flux to make it softer.

White Enamel.

Take of tin, prepared by aqua-fortis, and red-lead, each 1 oz.; white pebble-stone, or natural crystal, 2 oz.; nitre, 1 oz.; arsenic, 1 dr., with equal parts of flux, or more or less, as the softness or opacity may require. Melt together, calcine, or use raw.

Purple Enamel.

Take of opaque or transparent enamel, 12 parts; purple of Cassius, 1 to 2 parts, regulated with sal ammoniac. Put it in a sand-heat for about 48 hours, to digest the gold. Collect the powder, grind it with 6 times its weight of sulphur; put it into a crucible on the fire till the sulphur is evaporated, then amalgamate the powder with twice its weight of mercury; put it into a mortar or other vessel, and rub it together for about 6 hours, with a small quantity of water in the mortar, which change frequently; evaporate the remaining mercury in a crucible, and add to the powder 10 times its weight of flux, or more or less, as the hardness or softness of the color may require.

Rose-colored Enamel.

Take purple as prepared above, mix it with 30 times its weight of flux, and 1-100th part of its weight of silver-leaf, or any preparation of silver, or vary the proportion of the flux and silver as the quality of the color may require; or any of the other preparations for purple will do, varying the proportions of the flux and silver as above; or any materials, from which purple can be produced, will, with the addition of silver and flux, answer.

Brown Enamel.

Take of red-lead, 1 oz.; calcined iron, 1 oz.; antimony, 2 oz.; litharge, 2 oz.; zaffre, 1 oz.; sand, 2 oz.

Calcine, or melt together, for use raw, as may be most expedient; or vary the proportions of any or all the above, as tint or quality may require.

Mode of Application.

The preceding colors may be applied to vessels of glass in the following manner, viz., by painting, printing, or transferring, dipping, floating, and grounding.

By Painting. — Mix the colors (when reduced by grinding to a fine powder) with spirits of turpentine, temper them with thick oil of turpentine, and apply them with camel-hair pencils, or any other proper instrument, or mix them with nut or spike oil, or any other essential or volatile oil, or with water, in which case use gum Arabic, or any other gum that will dissolve in water, or with spirits, varnishes, gums of every kind, waxes, or resins; but the first is conceived to be the best.

By Printing. — Take a glue-bat, full size for the subject, charge the copper plate with the oil or color, and take the impression with the bat from the plate, which impression transfer on the glass. If the impression is not strong enough, shake some dry color on it which will adhere to the moist color; or take any engraving, or etching, or stamp, or cast, and, having charged it with the oil or color, transfer it on the glass by means of prepared paper, vellum, leather, or any other substance that will answer; but the first is the best. Any engravings, etchings, stamps, casts, or devices may be charged with waters, oils, varnishes, or glutinous matters of any kind, reduced to a proper state, as is necessary in printing in general. Any or all of these may be used alone, or mixed with the colors. When used alone the color is to be applied in powder.

By Dipping. — Mix the color to about the consistency of a cream, with any of the ingredients used for printing, in which dip the glass vessel, and keep it in motion till smooth.

By Floating. — Mix the color with any of the ingredients used for printing, to a consistency according to the strength of the ground required, float it through a tube, or any other vessel, moving or shaking the piece of glass till the color is spread over the part required.

By Grounding. — First charge the glass vessel with oil of turpentine, with a camel-hair pencil, and while moist apply the color in a dry powder, which will adhere to the oil; or, instead of oil of turpentine, use any of the materials used for printing; but the first is the best.

Cautions to be Observed in making Colored Enamels.

In making these enamels, the following general

cautions are necessary to be observed. 1st. That the pots be glazed with white glass, and be such as will bear the fire.

2d. That the matter of enamels be very nicely mixed with the colors.

3d. When the enamel is good, and the color well incorporated, it must be taken from the fire with a pair of tongs.

General Method of making Colored Enamels.

Powder, sift, and grind all the colors very nicely, and first mix them with one another, and then with the common matter of enamels; then set them in pots in a furnace, and when they are well mixed and incorporated, cast them into water, and when dry set them in a furnace again to melt, and when melted take a proof of it. If too deep colored, add more of the common matter of enamels; and if too pale add more of the colors.

To Obtain Black Enamel with Platina.

Mix some chloride of platina, dissolved in water, with neutral nitrate of mercury, and expose the precipitate, which will be formed, to a heat simply sufficient to volatilize the proto-chloride of mercury; there will be obtained a black powder, which, applied with a flux, gives a beautiful black enamel.

To make Enamel, called Niello.

Take 1 part of pure silver, 2 of copper, and 3 of pure lead, fuse them together, and pour the amalgam into a long-necked earthenware matrass, half filled with levigated sulphur; let the mouth of the vessel be immediately closed, and the contents left to cool. The mass which results, when levigated and washed, is ready for the purposes of the artist. The cavities left by the fusion having been filled with it, the plate is to be held over a small furnace, fed with a mixture of charcoal and wood, taking care to distribute the enamel with the proper instrument. As soon as fusion has taken place, the plate is to be removed; and, when sufficiently cooled, is to be cleared by the file, and polished by fine pumice and tripoli.

To Paint in Enamel.

The enamel painter has to work, not with actual colors, but with mixtures, which he only knows from experience will produce certain colors after the delicate operation of the fire; and to the common skill of the painter, in the arrangement of his palette and choice of his colors, the enamelller has to add much practical knowledge of the chemical operation of one metallic oxide on another; the fusibility of his materials; and the utmost degree of heat at which they will retain, not only the accuracy of the figures which he has given, but the precise shade of color which he intends to lay on.

Painting in enamel requires a succession of firings; first of the ground which is to receive the design, and which itself requires two firings, and then of the different parts of the design itself. The ground is laid on in the same general way as the common watch-face enamelling. The colors are the different metallic oxides, melted with some vitrescent mixture, and ground to extreme fineness. These are worked up with an essential oil (that of spikenard is preferred, and next to it oil of lavender) to the proper consistence of oil colors, and are laid on with a very fine hair brush. The The essential oil should be very pure, and the use of this rather than of any fixed oil, is that the whole may evaporate completely in a moderate heat, and leave no carbonaceous matter in contact with the color when red hot, which might affect its degree of oxidation, and thence the shade of color which it is intended to produce. As the color of some vitrified metallic oxides (such as that of gold) will stand at a very moderate heat, whilst others will bear, and even require a higher temperature to be properly fixed, it forms a great part of the technical skill of the artist to supply the different colors in proper order; fixing first those shades which are produced by the colors that will endure the highest, and finishing with those that demand the least, heat. The outline of the design is first traced on the enamel, ground and burnt in; after which the parts are filled up gradually by repeated burnings, to the last and finest touches of the tenderest enamel.

Transparent enamels are scarcely ever laid upon any other metal than gold, on account of the discoloration produced by other metals. If, however, copper is the metal used, it is first covered with a thin enamel coating, over which gold-leaf is laid and burnt in, so that, in fact, it is still this metal that is the basis of the ornamental enamel.

To Manufacture Mosaic as at Rome.

Mosaic work consists of variously shaped pieces of colored glass enamel; and when these pieces are cemented together, they form those regular and other beautiful figures which constitute tessellated pavements.

The enamel, consisting of glass mixed with metallic coloring matter, is heated for 8 days in a glass-house, each color in a separate pot. The melted enamel is taken out with an iron spoon and poured on polished marble placed horizontally; and another flat marble slab is laid upon the surface, so that the enamel cools into the form of a round cake, of the thickness of three-tenths of an inch.

In order to divide the cake into smaller pieces, it is placed on a sharp steel anvil, called tagliulo, which has the edge uppermost; and a stroke of an edged hammer is given on the upper surface of the cake, which is thus divided into long parallelopipeds, or prisms, whose bases are three-tenths of an inch square. These parallelopipeds are again divided across their length by the tagliulo and hammer into pieces of the length of eight-tenths of an inch, to be used in the Mosaic pictures. Sometimes the cakes are made thicker and the pieces larger.

For smaller pictures, the enamel, whilst fused, is drawn into long parallelopipeds, or quadrangular sticks; and these are divided across by the tagliulo and hammer, or by a file; sometimes, also, these pieces are divided by a saw without teeth, consisting of a copper blade and emery; and the pieces are sometimes polished on a horizontal wheel of lead with emery.

Gilded Mosaic.

Gilded Mosaic is formed by applying the gold-leaf on the hot surface of a brown enamel, immediately after the enamel is taken from the furnace; the whole is put into the furnace again for a short time, and when it is taken out the gold is firmly fixed on the surface. In the gilded enamel, used in Mosaic at Rome, there is *a thin coat of transparent glass* over the gold.

On the Different Glazes used for Cooking Utensils.

The wrought and cast-iron vessels which are to be placed on the fire are often covered with enamel, which protects the liquid from metallic contact with the sides.

Two compositions are generally employed for this purpose, one having for its base silicate of lead, and the other boro-silicate of soda. These enamels are applied to the scoured surface of the metal in the form of a powder, which is fixed by heating it to a sufficiently high temperature to fuse it; it then spreads over and covers the metal with a vitreous varnish.

The boro-silicate of soda enamel possesses great superiority over that of silicate of lead, for it is unattacked by vinegar, marine salt, the greater number of acid or saline solutions, even when concentrated, and resists the action of the agents employed in cooking or chemical operations.

The silicate of lead enamel is whiter and more homogeneous, which explains the preference given to it by the public, but it gives up oxide of lead to vinegar or to common salt; it acts upon a great number of coloring matters, and it is attacked by nitric acid, which immediately communicates a dull appearance to it. On evaporation the liquid leaves a white crystalline residue of nitrate of lead. This enamel is instantly darkened by dissolved sulphides, and also by cooking food containing sulphur, such as cabbage, fish, and stale eggs.

It is very easy to distinguish these two enamels by means of a solution of sulphide of potassium, sodium, or ammonium. On allowing of one of these reagents to fall on the vessel to be tested, the lead enamel darkens in a few moments, whilst the boro-silicate of soda enamel retains its white color.

POTTERY.

To manufacture English Stoneware.

Tobacco-pipe clay from Dorsetshire is beaten much in water; by this process the finer parts of the clay remain suspended in the water, while the coarser sand and other impurities fall to the bottom. The thick liquid, consisting of water and the finer parts of clay, is further purified by passing it through hair and lawn sieves of different degrees of fineness. After this the liquor is mixed (in various proportions for various ware) with another liquor of the same density, and consisting of flints calcined, ground and suspended in water. The mixture is then dried in a kiln, and being afterwards beaten to a proper temper, it becomes fit for being formed at the wheel into dishes, plates, bowls, etc. When this ware is to be put into the furnace to be baked, the several pieces of it are placed in the cases made of clay, called seggars, which are piled one upon another, in the dome of the furnace; a fire is then lighted, when the ware is brought to a proper temper, which happens in about 48 hours, it is glazed by common salt. The salt is thrown into the furnace through holes in the upper part of it, by the heat of which it is instantly converted into a thick vapor, which, circulating through the furnace, enters the seggar through holes made in its side (the top being covered to prevent the salt from falling on the ware), and attaching itself to the surface of the ware, it forms that vitreous coat upon the surface which is called its glaze.

To make Yellow or Queensware.

This is made of the same materials as the flintware, but the proportion in which the materials are mixed is not the same, nor is the ware glazed in the same way. The flintware is generally made of 4 measures of liquid flint, and 18 of liquid clay; the yellowware has a greater proportion of clay in it. In some manufactories they mix 20, and in others 24 measures of clay with 4 of flint. The proportion for both sorts of ware depends very much upon the nature of the clay, which is very variable even in the same pit. Hence a previous trial must be made of the quality of the clay, by burning a kiln of the ware. If there be too much flint mixed with the clay, the ware, when exposed to the air after burning, is apt to crack, and if there be too little, the ware will not receive the proper glaze from the circulation of the salt vapor.

To manufacture English Porcelain.

The iron-stone, which contains a portion of argil and silex, is first roasted in a common biscuit-kiln, to facilitate its trituration, and to expel sulphur and other volatile ingredients which it may contain. A large earthen crucible is constructed after the exact model of an iron forge, a part of the bottom of which is filled with charcoal or cokes; these having been previously strewed with ore and about ⅓ part of lime, are raised to an intense heat by a strong blast of air, introduced under the cokes at the bottom. By this heat the ore is fused, and the fluid iron drops through the fuel to the bottom; then follows the scoria, which floats upon the top of the fluid iron. This latter scoria, or, as the workmen call it, slag, is the material used in the manufacture of china, and is much impregnated with iron, and of a compact and dense structure. The slag is next let off, by a hole through the forge, into a clean earthen vessel, where it cools. This last vessel is then broken, in order to detach the slag from it, with hammers. The scoria is next pounded into small pieces and ground in water to the consistence of a fine paste, at the flint-mills of the country. This paste is then evaporated to dryness on a slip-kiln, well known amongst potters. Thus evaporated to dryness, it is used with the other ingredients in the following proportions, viz.:

Prepared iron-stone, 3 cwt.; ground flint, 4 cwt.; ground Cornwall stone, 4 cwt.; Cornwall clay, 4 cwt.; blue oxide of cobalt, 1 lb.

These having been mixed together with water by the slip-maker, are again evaporated on the slip-kiln to the proper consistency for use. The clay, thus prepared, is of course used in the usual manner in the fabrication of the several kinds of vessels.

To make Porcelain, or China.

Porcelain, or china, is a semi-vitrified earthenware of an intermediate nature between common-ware and glass. Chinese porcelain is composed of two ingredients, of one of which is hard-stone, called petunse, which is carefully ground to a very fine powder, and the other, called kaolin, is a white earthy substance, which is intimately mixed with the ground stone.

Several compositions of mingled earth may yield a true porcelain by being burnt, and the porcelains of various countries differ in their mixtures. But the principal basis of any true porcelain is that kind of clay which becomes white by baking, and which, either by intermingled heterogeneous earth, or by particular additions, undergoes in the fire an incipient vitrification, in which the true nature of porcelain consists. Feldspar and gypsum, if added, may give that property to infusible clay.

When porcelain is to be made, the clay is properly selected, carefully washed from impurities, and again dried. It is then finely sifted, and most accurately mingled with quartz, ground very fine, to which then is added some burnt and finely-pulverized gypsum. This mass is worked with water to a paste and duly kneaded; it is usually suffered to lie in this state for years. The vessels and other goods formed of this mass are first moderately burnt in earthen pots, to receive a certain degree of compactness and to be ready for glazing. The glazing consists of an easily-melted mixture of some species of earths, as the petrosilex or chert, fragments of porcelain and gypsum, which, when fused together, produce a crystalline or vitreous mass, which, after cooling, is very finely ground, and suspended in a sufficient quantity of water. Into this fluid the rough ware is dipped, by which the glazing matter is deposited uniformly on every part of its surface. After drying, each article is thoroughly baked or burned in the violent heat of the porcelain furnace. It is usual to decorate porcelain by paintings, for which purpose enamels or pastes, colored by metallic oxides, are used, so easy of fusion as to run in a heat less intense than that in which the glazing of the ware melts.

To make Delftware.

This is a kind of pottery made of sand and clay, and but slightly baked, so that it resists sudden applications of heat. Articles made of this are glazed with an enamel, composed of common salt, sand ground fine, oxide of lead, and oxide of tin. The use of the latter is to give opacity to the glaze.

To make Chinaware.

The composition of the eastern or proper chinaware, according to accounts that have great marks of authenticity, is from two earths; one of which is, as was before mentioned, called petunse; the other a refractory earth, called kaolin.

The preparation of the petunse, or aluminous earth, is by pounding the stone till it is reduced to a very fine powder, and then washing it over to bring it to the most impalpable state, which is thus performed: After the stone is rendered as fine as it can be by pounding or grinding, the powder must be put into a large tub full of water, and, being stirred about, the upper part of the water must be laded out into another tub, by which means the finest particles of the powder will be carried into it. The water in the second tub must be then suffered to stand at rest till the powder has subsided, and as much as can be laded off clear must be put back into the first tub, and there being again stirred about, and loaded with a fresh quantity of the most subtle part of the powder, must be laded again into the second tub as before, and this must be repeated till none be left in the first tub but the grosser part of the stone, which, not being of a due fineness, must be again pounded, and treated as at first. The fine powder obtained in the second tub, must be then freed from the water, by lading off the clear part, and suffering what remains to exhale, till the matter becomes of the consistence of soft clay, when it will be fit to be commixed with the kaolin for use.

The kaolin is prepared in the same manner by washing over; but some specimens are so fine, that there is no occasion for this or any other purification.

From these two mixed together, the clay or paste is formed; but it is said that the proportion of the respective quantities is made to vary according to the intended goodness of the ware, the best being made from equal quantities, and the worst from two of the kaolin to one of the petunse.

To make Saxon or Dresden China.

The Saxon composition, of which the chinaware is formed, is greatly similar to that of the eastern. In the place of the petunse, a stone is used, which is improperly called in the German language, bleyspatt, or spar of lead. It is a stone of a very opposite nature, as spars are calcareous, and will, on calcining, become lime; on the other hand, this stone is of a vitreous nature. This spar is of a very hard texture, and of a light flesh-color, or pale whitish red. It is prepared by pounding and washing over, which may be done as above directed, and it is then ready for compounding with the mica. The mica is employed in the Saxon composition for the other ingredients; and is likewise prepared by grinding and washing over, when it is not in a perfect and pure state; but when it is entirely clean, it may be tempered with the texture, thoroughly broken, and it will be of the consistence of soft clay.

The two kinds of earth being prepared in the state of a soft paste, they are to be incorporated and blended into one mass, which is done by rolling and stirring them well after they are in the same vessel, and then kneading them with the feet till they are thoroughly united. When the compound mass is formed, it is made into cakes, or square pieces, and put by layers into cases of wood or stone, which must be placed in a moist situation, and left for 2 or 3 months; during which time a kind of ferment enters into the mixture, by which the parts of the different matter combine and form a substance with new qualities, unknown while separate. This change shows itself upon the whole mass by a fetid smell, and a greenish or bluish color, and a tenacity like that of clay, or the argillaceous moistened earths. If the time of keeping the paste in this condition be prolonged to a year or more, it will further improve its qualities, but great care must be taken to prevent its becoming dry; to prevent which, there may be occasion to water it. When, however, the described qualities are found in the matter, it is fit for use, and vessels, etc., may be wrought of it without any other preparation, the case below excepted.

Composition of English China.

The following composition will produce wares, which will possess the properties of the true china, if judiciously managed.

Mix the best white sand, or calcined flints, finely powdered, 20 lbs.; of very white pearlash, 5 lbs.; of white calcined bones, 2 lbs. Temper the whole with the gum Arabic or senegal, dissolved in water.

This requires a considerable force and continuance of heat to bring it to perfection, but it will be very white and good when it is properly treated. Where mica can be obtained, it is preferable to calcined bones, and as it will form a kind of paste for working, a weaker gum-water will answer the purpose.

To Bake Chinaware.

The furnace for this purpose may be constructed in the same manner as the potter's kilns usually are. The size of the furnace should be according to the quantity of ware required to be baked; but it must not be too small, lest the body of fire may not be sufficient to produce the requisite heat.

The caffettes, or coffins, to contain the pieces when placed in the furnace, are the most material utensils. They should be of good potter's clay, with a third of sand, and are generally made of a round form, with a flat bottom, the rim forming sides, being adapted to the height of the pieces to be inclosed.

The furnace and caffettes being prepared; the ware to be baked must be sorted in the caffettes in the most advantageous manner as to room, and as many caffettes must be set upon them as the furnace will conveniently contain, leaving space for the free passage of the fire betwixt the piles: take care to cover over the uppermost caffettes in each pile, then close the mouth of the furnace, and raise the fire so as to heat the caffettes red hot in every part, and keep them red hot for 12 or 14 hours. It is then to be extinguished, and the furnace left to cool gradually; and when little or no heat remains, the mouth may be opened, and the pieces taken out of the caffettes; when they will be in a condition to receive the glazing, or to be painted with such colors as are used under the glaze.

To make Tobacco-pipes.

These require a very fine, tenacious, and refractory clay, which is either naturally of a perfectly white color, or, if it have somewhat of a gray cast will necessarily burn white. A clay of this kind must contain no calcareous or ferruginous earth, and must also be carefully deprived of any sand it may contain by washing. It ought to possess, besides, the property of shrinking but little in the fire. If it should not prove sufficiently ductile, it may be meliorated by the admixture of another sort. Last of all, it is beaten, kneaded, ground, washed, and sifted, till it acquires the requisite degree of fineness and ductility. When, after this preparation, the clay has obtained a due degree of ductility, it is rolled out in small portions to the usual length of a pipe, perforated with the wire, and put, together with the wire, into a brass mould, rubbed over with oil, to give it its external form; after which it is fixed into a vice, and the hollow part of the bead formed with a stopper. The pipes, thus brought into form, are cleared of the redundant clay that adheres to the seams, a rim or border is made round the head, they are then marked with an iron stamp upon the heel, and the surfaces smoothed and polished. When they are well dried, they are put into boxes, and baked in a furnace.

To make White Glaze.

Take 26 parts of glass, 7 parts litharge, 3 parts nitre, 1 part arsenic, ½ part blue calx; either fritted in a glass oven or not.

Black Glazing.

Take 8 parts of red-lead, 3 parts of iron filings, 3 parts of calcined copper, and 2 parts of zaffre. This, when fused, will produce a brown-black; but if wanted a truer black color, the proportion of zaffre must be increased.

Silicious Glaze without Lead.

M. Hardsmith proposes the following in place of the ordinary lead glaze: Take boracic acid, 15 lbs.; calcareous spar, 5 lbs.; wood charcoal, 1 lb. Powder the mixture, and calcine to complete fusion; allow it to cool; powder again and apply it as the common lead glaze is applied.

To make China Glaze for Printing Blue Frit.

Take 10 parts of glass, 2 parts lead, and 3 or 3½ parts blue calx, as required.

To make White Frit.

Take 16 parts of glass, 5 parts lead, 1 part arsenic, 2½ parts nitre.

Take 11 parts white frit to the whole of blue frit, and grind them together. Then take of the mica frit, 8 parts of the above, 5 parts flint, 13 parts Cornish stone, 23 parts lead, and 6 oz. common salt.

To make Cream-colored Glaze.

Take 60 parts of Cornish stone, 20 parts flint, and 120 parts white-lead. Stained with 1 oz. of smalts, as above.

To form a Yellow Glaze.

Take 2 parts of litharge, 2 parts tin-ash, and 1 part antimony.

To prepare White Glaze.

Take 15 parts of Cornish stone, 10 parts flint glass, 5 parts mica flint, 5 parts nitre, 5 parts borax, 1 part common salt, and 1 part sal soda; fritted in a glass oven. Then add 2 parts frit, as above, to 1 part white-lead. Send to mill to grind very fine, and stain with 7 oz. blue calx.

To make a Mixture for Glaze.

Take 20 lbs. of white frit, 10 lbs. flint, 26 lbs. stone, 50 lbs. lead, and 4 oz. of blue.

To make a Mixture of Glaze for Printing Blue.

Take 6 parts of white frit, 5 parts flint, 13 parts stone, 25 parts lead, and 55 parts glass.

To make a Shining Black Glaze.

Take 100 parts of lead, 18 parts flint, and 40 parts manganese.

To make a Purple under Glaze.

Take ¼ oz. of fluxed blue, 1 oz. manganese, 1 oz. red-lead, and 1 oz. flint.

To prepare an Orange Sponge Dip.

Take 1 qt. of yellow slip, to 1 oz. zaffre.

To prepare a Brown under Glaze.

Take 8 oz. of glass antimony, 16 oz. litharge, 3 oz. manganese, and 4 drs. blue calx.

To prepare a China Glaze.

Take 42 parts of flint-glass, 3 oz. blue calx. Stain. 16 oz. flint-glass, 1 oz. red-lead, 1 oz. arsenic, and 1 oz. nitre.— White enamel. Run down in glass oven; then send with the above stain to the mill, 8 parts of white enamel, dry it and it will be fit for use. Eight parts of the above mixture (stain and white enamel), 6 parts dry flint, 14 parts Cornish stone, 24 parts white stone, which, when sifted, is fit for use.

To prepare a China Glaze for Flotts.

Take 27 parts of flint, 15 parts nitre, 4½ parts lime, 3½ parts stain. This run down in a glass oven, and, when sent to the mill, add 75 parts of glass, 15 parts lead, 10 parts white enamel; add 2 pailsful of lime, and when it comes from the mill, add 135 parts of lead. Stain to the above, 10 parts of glass, and 5 oz. of blue.

To prepare White Enamel.

Take 7 oz. of arsenic, 12 oz. potash, 6 oz. nitre, 5 oz. glass, 2 oz. flint, and 3 oz. white-lead.

To prepare China Glaze.

Take 56 parts of stone, 46 parts borax, 18 parts glass, 15 parts flint, and 40 parts lead.

To prepare Green Edge Glaze.

Take 20 parts of lead, 60 parts stone, 20 parts flint, and 10 parts ground glass.

To prepare Materials for Common Ware.

Take 25 parts of flint, 60 parts stone, 95 parts lead, and 8 parts frit.

To prepare Glaze for Green Edge.

Take 175 parts of lead, 100 parts stone, and 35 parts flint.

To prepare Fluxes for Blue Printing.

Take 5 parts of blue calx, 5½ parts coke stone, 1½ parts glass, and 1 part flint.

To prepare Flux for Black Printing.

Take 7½ parts of flint-glass, 2½ parts red-lead, and 2 parts borax.

To prepare Red Flux.

Take 5 parts of lead, 1 oz. of borax, and 12 oz. of glass.

To prepare Black for Printing.

Take 1 part of calcined copper, 1½ parts red flux. Passed through the enamel kiln, 1¾ of calx, sent to the mill for grinding.

To prepare Copper Black.

Take 1 lb. of calcined copper, pounded fine, and put into the enamel kiln, and it will come out black. Then 1½ oz. of red flux, put through the enamel kiln, second time; then 1 of the above, and 1¾ of flux, ground fine for use.

To prepare Red for Printing.

Take green copperas calcined to a fine powder, wash it well 10 or 12 days, and dry it (colcothar); 1 of the above to 6 of red flux.

To prepare Umber Black.

Take 5 oz. of umber, 2 oz. borax, 1 oz. blue calx. One of the above to 2 flux, as under; 7½ flint-glass, 2½ red-lead, and 2 borax.

To prepare Black.

Take 3 oz. of calcined umber, 1 oz. borax; run down together. This will fine with gold.

To prepare Oil for Black Printing.

Take ½ pt. of linseed-oil, boiled well until of a proper consistence, to which add a small quantity of Barbadoes tar, prepared the same way.

Another.—Take 1 qt. of linseed-oil, 4 oz. flowers of sulphur, 4 oz. balsam of sulphur, 8 oz. black rosin.

To Form a Stone Body.

Take 2 parts blue clay, 2 parts china clay, 4 parts composition.

To Form an Egyptian Black Body.

Take blue clay, 30 parts; black marl, 5 parts; calcined car, 25 parts; manganese, 2 parts.

Common Glazing for Earthenware.

Take of white sand, 40 lbs.; red-lead, 20 lbs.; pearlash, 20 lbs; common salt, 12 lbs. Powder this sand by grinding before it be mixed with the other ingredients, and then grind them together, after which, calcine them for some time with a moderate heat, which must be less than will make them melt and run to glass; and when the mixture is cold, grind it to powder again, and, when wanted, temper it with water, and it will then be fit for use.

The proportions of these ingredients may be varied occasionally, for, where the glazing can be fluxed conveniently with a very strong fire, the quantity of sand may be increased to 60 or 70 lbs., which not only renders the glazing stronger, but makes a saving in the expense. The proportion of pearl-ashes may likewise be diminished, or they may be wholly omitted where the ware is designed for very coarse purposes, and not for domestic uses, where the lead is very improper, being extremely apt to be corroded by acids, and to produce a very unwholesome substance. On this account, where good manufactories are established, the lead ought to be excluded from the composition of the glazings, and other fluxes used in its stead, as in the following:

Transparent Glazing for Earthenware.

Take of white sand, 40 lbs.; of pearlash, 21 lbs.; and of common salt, 15 lbs. Calcine, and proceed as above.

Where the expense is no object, this glazing may be improved by adding 1 or 2 lbs. of borax, and diminishing the pearlash, in the proportion of 6 lbs for 1 lb. of borax added, or 10 lbs. for 2; in the latter case, 2 lbs. of salt may be also kept out of the composition. The reason for this change is, that if the composition contain so large a proportion of salt, and the glazing be not fluxed for a long time after it is laid on the ware, it will be apt to be dissolved by boiling water, and peel off, if it be exposed to the action of it for any long time.

Another.—Take of sand, 40 lbs.; of wood-ashes, perfectly burnt, 50 lbs.; of pearlash, 10 lbs.; of common salt, 12 lbs.

This will make an admirable glazing, where the ashes are pure, and a strong fire can be given to flux it when laid on the ware. It will be perfectly free from the imperfection of the above, and will be very hard and glossy, and where the expense can be afforded, it may be made more yielding to the fire by the addition of borax, in which case no alteration need be made in the proportion of the other ingredients.

To Prepare Masticot used as the Ground of Glazing.

Take of clean sand, 1 cwt., of soda, 44 lbs., and pearlash, 30 lbs. Calcine the mixture.

Masticot for White Glazing.

Take of masticot, prepared as in the preceding, 100 lbs.; calx of tin, 80 lbs., and of common salt, 10 lbs. Calcine and powder this composition three several times.

The calx of tin is prepared and sold under the name of putty. Its goodness consists in its whiteness and purity; the first of which is easily known by comparing it with a specimen of any that is known to be good.

Another Preparation.

Take of mastic, 10 lbs.; red lead, 60 lbs.; calcined tin or putty, 20 lbs., and of common salt, 10 lbs. Mix them, and calcine and powder the mixture several times.

Another.—Take 2 lbs. of lead, and somewhat more than 1 lb. of tin. Calcine the two metals till reduced to a powder, by the means used by potters. Then take 2 parts of these ashes, 1 part of white sand, calcined flints or broken white glass, and ½ pint of common salt. Mix well together the several ingredients, and set the matter to bake in a proper furnace, and urge it at length to melt.

The trouble of calcining the tin and lead may be saved here, as well as on the occasions above-mentioned, by procuring them already reduced to a proper state.

Another.—Take 1½ lbs. of lead and 1 lb. of tin. Reduce them to the state of a calx, and then take of the calcined matter, 8 parts, and of calcined flints and common salt, each 4 parts. Bring the mixture, by heat, to a state of fusion.

Another.—Take of lead, 3 parts, and of tin, 1 part. Calcine them, and then take of this matter and of calcined flints and common salt, each, 2 parts. Fuse them as above.

Another.—Take of lead, 4 lbs.; tin, 1 lb. Calcine them, and take of the matter 8 parts; of calcined flints, 7 parts, and of common salt, 4 parts. Fuse them as the others.

White Glazing for Copper Vessels.

Take of lead, 4 lbs.; of tin, 1 lb.; of flints, 4 lbs.; of common salt, 1 lb., and of flint-glass, 1 lb. Melt the mixture, and it will be fit for use.

Another.—Take of lead, 4 lbs., and of tin, 1 lb. Calcine them, and take of the matter, 12 parts; of flints, 14 parts, and of common salt, 8 parts. Fuse them as the others.

Very fine White Glazing.

Take of lead, 2 parts, and of tin, 1 part. Calcine them, and take of the matter, 1 part; of flints and common salt, each, 1 part. Fuse the mixture.

Enamel for Earthenware.

Take of tin, any quantity, and enclose it in clay or loam and put it in a crucible. Place the crucible in a fire, that the tin may calcine, and then break it. There will be a pound of calx very white, and when it is used to paint with on a white ground, the color will come forth and be much whiter than that of the ground.

Yellow Glazing.

Take of tin and antimony, each 2 lbs.; of lead, 3 lbs.; or, according to some, equal quantities of all the three ingredients. Calcine the whole, and put them at last in fusion, that they may be vitrified. This glazing will run very soon, and be of a fine yellow color.

The calcining the tin, lead, and antimony together, as here directed, would be a very tedious operation. The calcined tin and red-lead should therefore be used, and the antimony calcined alone. But it is not to be understood that the antimony is to be calcined for this purpose to whiteness, or the state of a perfect calx; which is not easily practicable without nitre, and, if effected, would render the antimony incapable of producing any other color than white. The operation must therefore be performed with a slow fire, by roasting, as it were, the antimony till it loses its metallic appearance, and becomes a greenish powder; as is practised in making the glass of antimony.

Another.—Take 5 parts of red-lead, 2 parts of powdered bark, 1 part of sand, 1 part of any of the preceding white glazings, and 2 parts of antimony. This mixture must be calcined and then fused, and it will give a fine yellow glazing.

Another.—Take 7 parts of the mixture of the calxes of tin and lead, mentioned before in the recipe for preparing the masticot for a white glazing. Add 1 part of antimony, and fuse them together.

Another.—Take 4 parts of white glass, 1 part of antimony, 3 parts of red-lead, and 1 part of iron scales. Fuse the mixture.

Another.—Take 16 parts of flints, 1 part of filings of iron, and 24 parts of litharge. Fuse the mixture.

Lemon-colored Glazing.

Take of red-lead, 3 parts; of powdered bricks, very red, 3½ parts; and of antimony, 1 part. Calcine the mixture day and night, for the space of 4 days, in the ash-hole of a glass-house furnace. Urge it at last to fusion, and it will produce a very fine lemon-colored glazing.

The success of this operation depends greatly on the fineness of the color of the bricks that are powdered. Those which are of a fine red and very brittle, are the best; but such as are gray will not at all answer the end. The same attention should be paid to this matter wherever bricks are used in this kind of preparations.

Light Yellow Glazing.

Take of red-lead, 4 parts; of antimony, 3 parts; of the mixture of the calxes of lead and tin, before mentioned in the masticot for white glazing, 8 parts; and of glass, 3 parts.

When the red-lead and calx of tin are used, the proportion of the ingredients will be of red-lead, 10 parts; of antimony and glass, each, 3 parts; and of calcined tin, 2 parts.

Gold-colored Glazing.

Take of red-lead, 3 parts; of antimony, 2 parts; of colcothar, 1 part. Fuse the mixture; and, having powdered the mass, melt it again, and repeat this operation till the fourth time, and a fine gold-colored yellow will be produced.

Any preparation of the calcined iron may be used in the place of the colcothar: and the repeated fusions and levigations seem unnecessary.

Another.—Take of red lead and white flints, each, 12 parts; and of filings of iron, 1 part. Fuse them twice.

This glazing will be transparent. Care must therefore be taken what ground it be laid upon or it will not answer the end of a yellow, but combine with that of the ground; and, indeed, the body of color is too weak to produce any other than a faint yellowish cast, even on a pure white ground.

Green Glazing to be laid on a White Ground.

Take of calcined copper 1 part, and 2 parts of any of the preceding yellow glazings. Fuse them twice, but when the composition is used it must not be laid on too thick, for that would render the color too deep.

Fine Blue Glazing.

Take of red-lead, 1 lb.; powdered flints, 2 lbs.; common salt, 2 lbs.; tartar, 1 lb. Calcine till it is almost white. White flint-glass, ½ lb., and zaffre, ⅓ lb. Fuse the whole mixture, and quench the melted mass in water. Repeat the same operation several times. The same proceeding must be adhered to in all the compositions where the tartar enters, otherwise they would be too much charged with salt, and the color would not prove fine. It is proper, moreover, to calcine the mixture gently, day and night, for 48 hours, in a glass-house furnace.

Another.—Take 1 lb. of tartar, ¼ lb. of red-lead, ½ oz. of zaffre; and ¼ lb. of powdered flints. Fuse the whole, and proceed in the manner stated above.

Violet-blue Glazing.

Take 12 parts of tartar and an equal quantity of flints and zaffre. Proceed as with the above.

Another.—Take 4 oz. of tartar, 2 oz. of red-lead, 5 oz. of powdered flints, and ½ dr. of magnesia. Proceed as with the above.

Fine Red Glazing.

Take 3 lbs. of antimony, 3 lbs. of red-lead, and 1 lb. of colcothar. Grind the whole as fine as possible, and then paint with it.

Another.—Take 2 lbs. of antimony, 3 lbs. of red-lead, and 1 lb. of colcothar. Proceed as with the above.

To Prepare Varnish for Pottery Ware, free from Lead.

Melt and keep in fusion for 14 minutes a mixture of 1 oz. of fire-stone and glass, 2 drs. of salt, ½ oz. of pipe-clay, and 1½ oz. of borax. Varnish the pots over with this matter, after they have been in the fire, and put them again in it for about 18 hours.

Varnish for Earthenware.

This varnish is made of equal parts of white glass and soda, finely pulverized, carefully sifted, and mixed.

Chinese Mode of Glazing China.

They take the finest pieces of the petunse and treat them as before mentioned, by pounding and washing over, but extract, by repeated washings, over, the very finest part of the powder, which keeps so moist with the water that the mixture forms a liquid mass, which they call the oil of petunse. With this oil they mix an equal weight of borax; they then slake a quantity of quicklime and form layers of that and dried furze, which they set on fire. When they have raised a large heap, after the first one is burnt to ashes, they collect them and the lime, and form layers of them again, with a fresh quantity of the furze, which they burn as before, and they repeat this 5 or 6 times. They then put the ashes and lime into a vessel with water, adding some borax in the proportion of 1 lb. to 1 cwt. of the ashes; they next wash over the finer part of this mixture, and next off at last all fluid from the dregs, which they keep together with the solid part, washed over. They mix this composition of lime, ashes, and salts with the mixture above mentioned, of an equal quantity of the oil of petunse and borax, and this compound forms the matter for glazing the ware.

Instead of the petunse, the quartz used in the Saxon manufacture may be employed for forming a similar glazing, by treating it in the same manner; and it is said the glazing of the Dresden China is actually made in this way.

English Glazing for China.

Take of the finest white sand, or calcined flints, 20 lbs.; red-lead, 18 lbs.; pearlash, 10 lbs.; and common salt, decrepitated, 4 lbs. Levigate the sand or calcined flints and red-lead well together, and afterwards mix them thoroughly with the pearlash and common salt. Fuse the compound in the manner directed for the treatment of glass, till it be perfectly vitrified; then separate the fragments of the pot carefully from it, and reduce it in a flat agate or porphyry mortar to an impalpable powder. Finally, temper it with water to the proper consistence for painting or glazing.

Modification of the above.

When this glazing is used for embossed or other fine work it should be mixed with a third of its weight of the spar of lead, or other vitrescent earth, in lieu of the petunse, in the composition of the ware paste. Take care that this earth is formed of the best pieces of spar or other substance used, and that it is rendered to an extreme fineness, by washing it over. The design of this addition is to weaken the fluxing powder of the glaze, which, if used alone, would run the corners and edges of the smaller part and impair the sharpness and spirit of the work. It is necessary to pursue the same method with pieces that are to be painted with more delicate designs; for the glazing, melting otherwise again, in the burning in of the colors would become too fluid, and spread them so as to take away the effect of the fine touches.

To apply, on every kind of Ware, Colors which produce Herborizations.

Herborizations can be of all colors; but the most agreeable is that called bistre, which is composed in the following manner:

A pound of calcined manganese, 6 oz. of burnt-iron straw or 1 lb. of iron ore, and 3 oz. of flint powder.

The manganese and straw or iron ore must be pounded separately in a mortar, after which the whole is calcined together in an earthen pot. This mixture, thus prepared, is all pounded together, and then mixed in a small tub of water.

The blue, green, and other colors must be composed of the divers substances known to produce them, and mixed, calcined, and pounded in the same manner as for the bistres.

To make the application of these various colors to the pieces it is necessary, instead of diluting them with water, as is practised for ordinary painting, to make use of any kind of mordant. The most advantageous, and which are employed with the greatest success, are urine, and the essence of tobacco.

If the essence of tobacco is made use of, infuse 2 oz. of good tobacco, in leaves, during 12 hours, in a bottle of cold water, or very simply infuse the 2 oz. of tobacco in a bottle of hot water.

The pieces of clay, after taking a little consistency, are steeped in white or colored wormseed until the bath puts them in a state of moisture. To produce herborizations it will be sufficient, whilst the wormseed is still fresh, and at the moment when the piece is taken down from the tub to lay on slightly, and with a brush, one or several, drops of other colors. Each drop produces a tree more or less great, according as the workman has charged his brush with colors.

GLASS.

To Manufacture Glass.

Glass is a combination of sand, flint, spar, or some other silicious substances, with one or other of the fixed alkalies, and in some cases with a metallic oxide. Of the alkalies, soda is commonly preferred; and of the silicious substances, white sand is most in repute at present, as it requires no preparation for coarse goods, while mere washing in water is sufficient for those of a finer quality. The metallic oxide usually employed, is litharge, or some other preparation of lead. Iron is used in bottle-glass.

The silicious matter should be fused in contact with something called a flux. The substances proper for this purpose are lead, borax, arsenic, nitre, or any alkaline matter. The lead is used in the state of red-lead; and the alkalies are soda, pearlash, sea-salt, and wood-ashes. When red-lead is used alone, it gives the glass a yellow cast and requires the addition of nitre to correct it. Arsenic, in the same manner, if used in excess, is apt to render the glass milky. For a perfectly transparent glass, the pearlash is found much superior to lead; perhaps better than any other flux, except it be borax, which is too expensive to be used, except for experiments, or for the best looking-glasses.

The materials for making glass must first be reduced to powder, which is done in mortars or by horse mills. After sifting out the coarse parts, the proper proportions of silex and flux are mixed together, and put into the calcining furnace, where they are kept in a moderate heat for 5 or 6 hours, being frequently stirred about during the process. When taken out the matter is called frit. Frit is easily converted into glass by only pounding it, and vitrifying it in the melting pots of the glass furnace; but in making fine glass, it will sometimes require a small addition of flux to the frit to correct any fault. For, as the flux is the most expensive article, the manufacturer will rather put too little at first than otherwise, as he can remedy this defect in the melting pot. The heat in the furnace must be kept up until the glass is brought to a state of perfect fusion; and during this process any scum which arises must be removed by ladles. When the glass is perfectly melted, the glass-blowers commence their operations.

For the best flint-glass, 120 lbs. of white sand, 50 lbs. of red-lead, 40 lbs. of the best pearlash, 20 lbs. of nitre, and 5 oz. of manganese; if a pound or two of arsenic be added, the composition will fuse much quicker, and with a lower temperature.

For a cheaper flint-glass, take 120 lbs. of white sand, 35 lbs. of pearlash, 40 lbs. of red-lead, 13 lbs. of nitre, 6 lbs. of arsenic, and 4 oz. of magnesia.

This requires a long heating to make clear glass, and the heat should be brought on gradually, or the arsenic is in danger of subliming before the fusion commences. A still cheaper composition is made by omitting the arsenic in the foregoing, and substituting common sea-salt.

For the best German crystal-glass, take 120 lbs. of calcined flints or white sand, the best pearlash, 70 lbs.; saltpetre, 10 lbs.; arsenic, ½ lb.; and 5 oz. of manganese. Or, a cheaper composition for the same purpose is 120 lbs. of sand or flints, 46 lbs. of pearlash, 7 lbs of nitre, 6 lbs. of arsenic, and 5 oz. of manganese. This will require a long continuance in the furnace; as do all others where much of the arsenic is employed.

For looking-glass plates, washed white sand, 60 lbs.; purified pearlash, 25 lbs.; nitre, 15 lbs.; and 7 lbs. of borax. If properly managed, this glass will be colorless. But if it should be tinged by accident, a trifling quantity of arsenic, and an equal quantity of manganese, will correct it; an ounce of each may be tried first, and the quantity increased if necessary.

The ingredients for the best crown-glass must be prepared in the same manner as for looking-glasses, and mixed in the following proportions: 60 lbs. of white sand, 30 lbs. of pearlash, and 15 lbs. of nitre, 1 lb. of borax, and ½ lb. of arsenic.

The composition for common green window-glass is, 120 lbs. of white sand, 30 lbs. of unpurified pearlash; wood-ashes, well burnt and sifted, 60 lbs.; common salt, 20 lbs.; and 5 lbs. of arsenic.

Common green bottle-glass is made from 200 lbs. of wood-ashes, and 100 lbs. of sand; or 170 lbs. of ashes, 100 lbs. of sand, and 50 lbs. of the slag of an iron furnace; these materials must be well mixed.

The materials employed in the manufacture of glass, are by chemists reduced to three classes, namely, alkalies, earths, and metallic oxides.

The fixed alkalies may be employed indifferently; but soda is preferred in this country. The soda of commerce is usually mixed with common salt, and combined with carbonic acid. It is proper to purify it from both of these foreign bodies before using it. This, however, is seldom done.

The earths are silica (the basis of flints), lime, and sometimes a little alumina (the basis of clay). Silica constitutes the basis of glass. It is employed in the state of fine sand or flints; and sometimes for making very fine glass, rock crystal is employed. When sand is used, it ought, if possible, to be perfectly white, for when it is colored with metallic oxides, the transparency of the glass is injured. Such sand can only be employed for very coarse glasses. It is necessary to free the sand from all the loose earthy particles with which it may be mixed, which is done by washing it well with water.

Lime renders glass less brittle, and enables it to withstand better the action of the atmosphere. It ought in no case to exceed the 20th part of the silica employed, otherwise it corrodes the glass pots. This indeed may be prevented by throwing a little clay into the melted glass; but in that case a green glass only is obtained.

The metallic oxides employed are the red oxide of lead or litharge, and the white oxide of arsenic. The red oxide of lead, when added in sufficient quantity, enters into fusion with silica, and forms a milky hue like the dial-plate of a watch. When any combustible body is present, it is usual, in some manufactories, to add a little white oxide of arsenic. This supplying oxygen, the combustible is burnt, and flies off, while the revived arsenic is at the same time volatized.

There are several kinds of glass adapted to different uses. The best and most beautiful are the flint and the plate-glass. These, when well made, are perfectly transparent and colorless, heavy and brilliant. They are composed of fixed alkali, pure silicious sand, calcined flints and litharge, in different proportions. The flint glass contains a large quantity of oxide of lead, which by certain processes is easily separated. The plate glass is poured in the melted state upon a table covered with copper. The plate is cast ½ an inch thick or more, and is ground down to a proper degree of thickness, and then polished.

Crown-glass, that used for windows, is made without lead, chiefly of fixed alkali fused with silicious sand, to which is added some black oxide of manganese, which is apt to give the glass a tinge of purple.

Bottle-glass is the coarsest and cheapest kind, in this little or no fixed alkali enters the composition. It consists of alkaline earth and oxide of iron combined with alumina and silica. In this country it is composed of sand and the refuse of the soap-boiler, which consists of the lime employed in rendering this alkali caustic, and of the earthy matters with which the alkali was contaminated. The most fusible is flint-glass, and the least fusible is bottle-glass.

Glass for Looking-glass Plates, No. 1.

Take of white sand, cleansed, 60 lbs.; of purified pearlash, 25 lbs.; of saltpetre, 15 lbs; and of borax, 7 lbs.

This composition should be continued long in the fire, which should be for some time strong, and afterwards more moderate, that the glass may be entirely free from bubbles before it is worked. It will be entirely clear of all color, unless in case of some accident; but if any yellow tinge should, nevertheless, unfortunately infect it, there is no remedy except by adding a small proportion of manganese, which should be mixed with an equal quantity of arsenic, and after their being put into the glass, giving it a considerable heat again, and then suffering it to free itself from bubbles in a more moderate one, as before. If the tinge be slight, an ounce of manganese may be first tried, and if that prove insufficient, the quantity must be increased, but the glass will always be obscure in proportion to the quantity that is admitted.

Looking-glass Plates. No. 2

Take of the white sand, 60 lbs.; of pearlash, 20 lbs.; of common salt, 10 lbs.; of nitre, 7 lbs.; and of borax, 1 lb.

This glass will run with as little heat as the former, but it will be more brittle and refract the rays of the light in a greater degree.

Crown or Best Window-glass, No. 1.

Take of white sand, 60 lbs.; of purified pearlash, 30 lbs.; of saltpetre, 15 lbs,; of borax, 1 lb.; and of arsenic, ½ lb.

This will be very clear and colorless if the ingredients be good, and will not be very dear. It will run with a moderate heat; but if it be desired to be yet more fusible and soft, ½ a lb. or a pound more of arsenic may be added.

If the glass should prove yellow, the manganese must be used as above directed for the looking-glass.

Cheaper kind of Window-glass, No. 2.

Take of white sand, 60 lbs.; of unpurified pearlash, 25 lbs.; of common salt, 10 lbs.; of nitre, 5 lbs.; of arsenic, 2 lbs; and of manganese, 1½ oz.

This will be inferior to the above kind, but may be improved, where desired, by purifying the pearlash.

Common or Green Window-glass, No. 3.

Take of white sand, 60 lbs.; of unpurified pearlash, 30 lbs.; of common salt, 10 lbs.; of arsenic, 2 lbs.; and of manganese, 2 oz.

This is a cheap composition and will not appear too green nor be very deficient in transparency.

Common or Green Window-glass, No. 4.

Take of the cheapest kind of white sand, 120 lbs.; of unpurified pearlash, 30 lbs.; of wood-ashes, well burnt and sifted, 60 lbs.; of common salt, 20 lbs.; and of arsenic, 5 lbs.

This composition is very cheap, and will produce a good glass with a greenish cast.

Best Phial-glass, No. 1.

Take of white sand, 120 lbs.; of unpurified pearlash, 50 lbs.; of common salt, 10 lbs.; of arsenic, 5 lbs.; and of manganese, 5 oz.

This will be a very good glass for the purpose and will work with a moderate heat, but requires time to become clear, on account of the proportion of arsenic: when, however, it is once in good condition, it will come very near to the crystal glass.

Cheapest Green or Common Phial-glass, No. 2.

Take of the cheapest kind of white sand, 120 lbs.; of wood-ashes, well burnt and sifted, 80 lbs.; of pearlash, 20 lbs.; of common salt, 15 lbs; and of arsenic, 1 lb.

This will be green, but tolerably transparent and will work with a moderate fire, and vitrify quickly with a strong one.

Green or Bottle-glass.

Take of wood-ashes, 200 lbs.; and of sand, 100 lbs. Mix them thoroughly by grinding together.

This is the due proportion where the sand is good and the wood-ashes are used without any other addition.

The same, with the addition of scoria.

Take of wood-ashes, 170 lbs.; of sand 100 lbs.; and of scoria, or clinkers, 50 lbs. Mix the whole well by grinding them together.

The clinkers should be well ground before they are used, if they admit of it; but frequently they are too hard, and in that case they should be broken into as small bits as can be done conveniently and mixed with the other matter without any grinding. The harder they are, the less material will be the powdering of them as they will the sooner melt of themselves in the furnace, and consequently mix with the other ingredients.

The most Perfect kind of Flint-glass, No. 1.

Take of white sand, 120 lbs.; red-lead, 50 lbs.; the best pearlash, 40 lbs.; nitre, 20 lbs.; manganese, 5 oz.

If this composition be fused with a very strong fire, and time be given to it, a glass will be produced that will have the play of the best flint-glass, and yet be hard and strong. It is not so cheap as the compositions given below, where arsenic or common salt is introduced, or where more of the pearlash are used; in either of which cases, savings may be made by diminishing proportionably the quantities of nitre. But the qualities of this glass will be found to come nearer to the standard of perfection, which is to unite the lustre and hardness together in the greatest degree they are compatible with each other.

If this composition be, however, desired to flux with less heat, and quicker, a pound or two of arsenic may be added, which will be found effectually to answer the purpose.

Flint-glass, No. 2.

Take of sand, 120 lbs.; the best pearlash, 54 lbs.; red-lead, 36 lbs.; nitre, 12 lbs.; manganese, 6 oz.

This will require much the same heat as the other, but will be harder in its texture. If it be desired to be made more yielding to the fire, arsenic may be added, or the quantity of sand may be lessened. In these cases the glass will be softer and weaker.

White Flint-glass, No. 3.

Take of white sand, 120 lbs.; the best pearlash 35 lbs.; arsenic, 6 lbs.; manganese, 4 oz.

This glass will require a considerable time in the fire to become clear, and must not, if it can be avoided, be strongly urged at first. This glass will not be so hard as those of the above compositions, but it will be very clear, and may be employed for large vessels, where a sufficient thickness can be allowed to give it strength.

Cheaper Composition of Glass, No. 4.

Take the proportions of the other ingredients given in the last, and omitting the arsenic, add in its stead 15 lbs. of common salt.

This will be more brittle than the last, and therefore cannot be recommended, unless for the fabrication of such kind of vessels, or other pieces, where the strength is of little moment.

Cheapest Composition of White Flint-glass, No. 5.

Take of white sand, 120 lbs.; red-lead, 30 lbs.; the best pearlash, 20 lbs.; nitre, 10 lbs.; common salt, 15 lbs.; arsenic, 6 lbs.

This glass will fuse with a moderate heat, but requires time, like the last, to take off the milky appearance of the arsenic; it is yet softer than the last, and may therefore be deemed the worst kind of flint that can be made.

Best German Crystal-glass, No. 6.

Take of calcined flints, or white sand, 120 lbs.; the best pearlash, 70 lbs.; saltpetre, 10 lbs.; arsenic, ½ lb.; manganese, 5 oz.

If the pearlash be pure and good, this glass will equal the best of this kind that ever was made. Borax has been frequently used also in the compositions of this sort of glass, but its great price, without any equivalent advantage, will deter from the employing it in large manufactures, as there is no sort of transparent glass (plate excepted), that can bear the expense of it.

German Crystal-glass, No. 7.

Take of calcined flints, or white sand, 120 lbs.; pearlash, 46 lbs.; manganese, 5 oz.

This composition requires a long continuance of heat, on account of the arsenic, for the reason before given. It produces a glass equally or more transparent and colorless than the preceding, but somewhat more brittle. The arsenic is, however, so disagreeable an ingredient, from the deleterious qualities of the fumes, which will necessarily rise copiously till the fusion of the other ingredients check it, that, where the advantage is not more considerable than the saving arising from the difference of these two recipes, it is scarcely worth while to submit to the inconvenience of it.

To Anneal Glass.

"Nealing," as it is called by the workmen, is a process in the glass-houses, and consists in putting the glass vessels, as soon as they are formed, and while they are yet hot, into a furnace or an oven, not so hot as to re-melt them, and in which they are suffered to cool gradually. This is found to prevent their breaking easily, particularly on exposure to heat.

A similar process is used for rendering cast-iron vessels less brittle, and the effect depends on the same principles.

To Polish and Grind Glass.

To grind plate-glass, lay it horizontally upon a flat stone table, made of a very fine grained freestone; and for its greater security, plaster it down with mortar or stucco. The stone table is supported by a strong wooden frame, with a ledge all round its edges, rising about 2 inches above the glass. Upon the plate to be ground is laid another rough glass, not above half as big, and so loose as to slide upon the former; but cemented to a wooden plank, to guard it from the injury it must otherwise receive from the scraping of the wheel whereto the plank is fastened, and from the weights laid upon it to promote the triture or grinding of the glasses. The whole is covered with a wheel made of hard light wood, about 6 inches in diameter, by pulling of which backwards and forwards alternately, and sometimes turning it round, the workmen, who always stand opposite to each other, produce a constant attrition between the two glasses, and bring them to whatever degree of smoothness they please, by first pouring in water and coarse sand; after that, a finer sort of sand, as the work advances, till at last they pour in the powder of smalt. As the upper or incumbent glass becomes smooth, it must be removed, and another, from time to time, substituted for it.

The engine just described is called a mill by the workmen, and is employed only in grinding the largest-sized glasses. In grinding lesser glasses, they usually work without a wheel, having four wooden handles fastened to the corners of the stone that loads the upper plank, by which they work it about. The grinders' part done, the glass is turned over to the polisher, who, with fine powder of tripoli stone or emery, brings it to a perfect evenness and lustre. The instrument made use of in this branch, is a board furnished with a felt and small roller, which the workman moves by means of a double handle at both ends. The artist, in working this roller, is assisted by a wooden hoop or spring, to the end of which it is fixed; for the spring, by constantly bringing the roller back to the same points, facilitates the action of the workman's arm.

To make Frit.

Frit, in the glass manufacture, is the matter or ingredients of which glass is to be made, when they have been calcined or baked in a furnace. There are three kinds of frit: the first, crystal frit, or that for crystal or clear glass, is made with salt of pulverine and sand. The second and ordinary frit is made of the bare ashes of the pulverine or barilla, without extracting the salt from them. This makes the ordinary white or crystal-glass. The third is frit for green glasses, made of common ashes, without any preparation. This 'ast frit will require 10 or 12 hours' baking. The materials in each are to be finely powdered, washed and searced; then equally mixed, and frequently stirred together in the melting pot.

To bring Pearlash, or any other Fixed Alkaline Salt, to the Highest Degree of Purity.

Take of the best pearlash 3 lbs., and of saltpetre 6 oz. Pound them together in a glass or marble mortar, till they are thoroughly well mixed, and then put part of them into a large crucible, and set it in a furnace, where it may undergo a strong heat. When the part of the matter that was first put into the crucible is heated red hot, throw in the rest gradually, and if the crucible will not contain the whole, pour part of the melted matter out on a moistened stone, or marble, and having made room in the crucible, put in the rest, and let it continue there likewise till it be red hot. Pour it out then as the other, and afterwards put the whole into an earthen or very clean iron pot, with 10 pts. of water, and heat it over the fire, till the salts be entirely melted. Let it then be taken off the fire, stand till it is cold, and afterwards filter it through paper in a pewter colander. When it is filtered, return the fluid again into the pot, and evaporate the salt to dryness, which will then be as white as snow, the nitre having burnt all the combustible matter that remained in the pearlash after its former calcination.

To Polish Optical-glasses.

The operation of polishing optic-glasses, after being properly ground, is one of the most difficult points of the whole process. Before the polishing is begun, it is proper to stretch an even, well-wrought piece of linen over the tool, dusting upon it some very fine tripoli. Then taking the glass in the hand, run it round 40 or 50 times upon the tool, to take off the roughness of the glass about the border of it. This cloth is then to be removed, and the glass to be polished upon the naked tool, with a compound powder, made of four parts tripoli mixed with one of fine blue vitriol, 6 or 8 grains of which mixture are sufficient for a glass 5 in. broad. This powder must be wetted with 8 or 10 drops of clear vinegar in the middle of the tool, being first mixed and softened thoroughly with a very fine small muller. Then, with a nice brush, having spread this mixture thinly and equably upon the tool; take some very fine tripoli, and strew it thinly and equably upon the tool so prepared, after which take the glass to be polished, wiped very clean, and apply it on the tool, and move it gently twice or thrice in a straight line backwards and forwards; then take it off, and observe whether the marks of the tripoli, sticking to the glass, are equably spread over the whole surface; if not, it is a sign that either the tool or glass is too warm, in which case wait awhile and try it again, till the glass takes the tripoli everywhere alike. Then begin to polish boldly, there being no danger of spoiling the figure of the glass, which in the other case would infallibly happen.

To Purify Pearlash for the manufacture of Mirrors.

Take any quantity of the best pearlash, and dissolve it in 4 times its weight of water boiling, which operation may be best performed in a pot of cast iron. When they are dissolved, let the solution be put in a clean tub, and suffered to remain there 24 hours or longer. Let the clear part of the fluid be then decanted off from the dregs or sediment, and put back into the iron pot, in which the water must be evaporated away till the salts be left perfectly dry again. They should then, if not used immediately, be kept in stone jars, well secured from moisture and air, till such time as they are wanted.

Great care should be always taken in this treatment of the salts to keep the iron pot thoroughly clean from rust, which would give a yellow tinge to the glass, not to be removed without greatly injuring it.

To Ornament all kinds of Glass in Imitation of Engraving, etc.

The method heretofore known for engraving on glass, has been by means of a machine with wheels, of different substances, which have been employed with sand, etc., to grind off some parts of the surface of the glass which is to be engraved on, and then by means of grinding and polishing different parts on the rough surface, the different figures are formed according to the designs given. By this invention, instead of grinding or taking off any part of the surface of the glass, the patentee lays on an additional surface or coating of glass, prepared for the purpose, which, when subjected to a proper degree of heat, will incorporate with the glass to be operated upon, so as to produce an effect similar to that which has hitherto been obtained by means of grinding. When it is required to ornament glass, then, previously to the heat being applied, with an etching or engraving tool such parts are to be taken out as will produce the required effect, and that in a much superior way to the effect produced by the usual mode of grinding, polishing, etc. The materials used are to be melted in a crucible, or other pot, and they are to be made up in the same manner as if used for the making of the best flint glass, broken glass, or, as it is usually denominated, "cullitt," being the principal ingredient in it. Several mixtures are given, of which the first is 160 parts of cullitt, 10 of pearlash, 40 of red-lead, and 10 of arsenic.

The second is 120 parts of cullitt, 150 of red-lead, 60 of sand, and 60 of borax.

The third is 70 parts of red-lead, 22½ of sand, and 410 of calcined borax.

When these are subjected to such a heat as to be thereby completely fused, take equal parts of each mixture and grind them to an impalpable powder, for the purpose of being mixed with a menstruum proper for coating the glass.

The menstruum consists of 1 part of refined loaf sugar dissolved in 2 parts of pure water, to which is added, at the time of mixing the powder, about ¼ part of common writing-ink; the effect, we are told, produced by this addition of oxide of manganese, used in a small quantity by the glass makers in making their best flint-glass, because without such an addition the specimens would be of a cloudy or milky appearance. A quantity of this menstruum is used sufficient to render the ground mixture of a proper consistence for laying on with a thin, smooth surface. When the coating or mixture is thus prepared, the glass is to be coated by means of a camel's hair brush, or squirrel's foot, etc. It is then to be exposed to a heat sufficient to produce a semi-vitrification of the coaty surface, and to incorporate it with the substance or body of glass so coated. But the heat must not be carried higher than this, because in that case a complete vitrification would ensue, and the desired effect of having a surface in imitation of the rough surface produced by grinding would not be obtained; the article must, under such circumstances, be re-coated and submitted again to the fire. If, after the coating has been applied, any borders, cyphers, or other ornaments, are wanted to be executed thereon, then, previously to the heat being applied with an etching or engraving tool, such parts of the coated surface must be chased out as will produce the desired effect, after which the requisite degree of heat is to be applied.

This invention is not only applicable to all kinds of useful and ornamental articles of glassware on which the common methods of engraving have been practised, but may be applied to window glass and plate-glass of every description, in place of grinding for the purpose of making window-blinds. It is also said to be peculiarly adapted to produce beautiful specimens of art for the windows of altar-pieces, libraries, museums, coach-windows, and for the glass used in ornamental building of all descriptions. This invention has another advantage over the common method of the work wearing much cleaner than the work of ground glass, the surface of which being fractured by the action of the wheel, etc., is therefore liable to gather dirt on the rough, unpolished parts of the borders, etc.

To make the Bologna Phial.

The Bologna, or philosophical phial, is a small vessel of glass which has been suddenly cooled, open at the upper end, and rounded at the bottom. It is made so thick at the bottom that it will bear a smart blow against a hard body without breaking, but if a little pebble or piece of flint is let fall into it, it immediately cracks, and the bottom falls into pieces, but unless the pebble or flint is large and angular enough to scratch the surface of the glass, it will not break.

To make Prince Rupert's Drops.

Prince Rupert's drops are made by letting drops of melted glass fall into cold water; the drop assumes by that means an oval form, with a tail or neck resembling a retort. They possess this singular property, that if a small portion of the tail is broken off, the whole bursts into powder, with an explosion, and a considerable shock is communicated to the hand that grasps it.

To Break Glass in any Required Way.

In a piece of worsted thread in spirits of turpentine, wrap it round the glass in the direction required to be broken, and then set fire to the thread, or apply a red hot wire round the glass, and if it does not immediately crack, throw cold water on it while the wire remains hot. By this means glass that is broken may often be fashioned and rendered useful for a variety of purposes.

GLASS AND PASTES TO IMITATE PRECIOUS STONES.

The Best and Hardest Glass for Receiving Colors, No. 1.

Take of the best sand, cleansed by washing, 12 lbs.; of pearlash, or fixed alkaline salt, purified with nitre, 7 lbs.; of saltpetre, 1 lb.; and of borax, ½ lb.

The sand being first reduced to powder in a glass or flint mortar, the other ingredients and be put to it, and the whole well mixed by pounding them together.

Best Glass, but not so Hard, No. 2.

Take of the white sand, cleansed, 12 lbs.; of pearlash, purified with saltpetre, 7 lbs.; of nitre, 1 lb.; of borax, ½ lb.; and of arsenic, 4 oz.

Proceed as in the last; but if the glass be required to melt with yet less heat, 1 lb. of borax may be used instead of the ½ lb., and 1 lb. of common salt may be added. But this last is apt to make the glass more brittle, which is an injury done to such as is to be cut into very small pieces, and ground with so many angles in the figure, in imitation of jewels.

Soft Glass or Paste for Receiving Colors, No. 3.

Take of white sand, cleansed, 6 lbs.; of red lead, 3 lbs.; of purified pearlash, 2 lbs.; and of nitre, 1 lb.

Proceed with the mixture as with the foregoing.

Glass or Paste, Softer than the above, No. 4.

Take of white sand, cleansed, 6 lbs.; of red lead and purified pearlash, each 3 lbs.; of nitre, 1 lb.; of borax, ½ lb.; and of arsenic, 3 oz.

This is very soft and will fuse with a very gentle heat, but requires some time to become clear, on account of the arsenic. It may even be prepared and tinged in a common fire without a furnace, if the pots containing it can be surrounded by burning coals, without danger of their falling into it. The borax, being a more expensive ingredient than the others, may be omitted where a somewhat greater heat can be applied, and the glass is not intended for very nice purposes, or 1 lb. of common salt may be substituted in its place; but the glass will be more clear and perfect, and free itself much sooner from bubbles, where the borax is used.

This glass will be very soft, and will not bear much water, if employed for rings, buckles, or such imitations of stones as are exposed to much rubbing; but for ear-rings, ornaments worn on the breast, or such others as are but seldom put on, it may last a considerable time.

In all these soft compositions care should be taken that part of the sand be not left unvitrified in the bottom of the pot, as will sometimes happen, for in that case the glass, abounding too much with salt and lead, will not bear the air, but, being corroded by it, will soon contract a mistiness and specks in the surface, which will entirely efface all the lustre of the paste.

Hard Glass of a full Blue Color. No. 1.

Take of the composition of hard glass, No. 1 or 2, 10 lbs.; zaffre, 6 dr.; and of manganese, 2 dr. Proceed as with the above.

If this glass be of too deep a color, the proportion of the zaffre and manganese to the glass may be diminished; and if it verge too much on the purple, to which cast it will incline, the manganese should be omitted. If a very cool or pure blue be wanted, instead of the manganese, half an ounce of calcined copper may be used, and the proportion of zaffre diminished by one-half.

Paste of a Full Blue Color, No. 2.

Take of the composition for paste, No. 1 or 2, 10 lbs., and proceed as with the foregoing.

Hard Glass Resembling the Sapphire, No. 3.

Take of the composition for hard glass, No. 1 or 2, 10 lbs.; of zaffre, 3 drs. and 1 scr.; of purple of Cassius, 1 dr. Proceed as with the above.

Cheaper Hard Glass for Resembling the Sapphire, No. 4.

As the foregoing, only, instead of the purple of Cassius, use 2 drs. and 2 scr. of manganese.

If this be well managed, the color will be very good, and the glass, when set and cut, will not be easily distinguishable from the true sapphire; but the preceding will be a finer color, as there is a foulness in the tinge of the manganese, which will always diminish, in some degree, the effect of brighter colors, when with them.

Paste Resembling the Sapphire, No. 5.

Take of the composition for paste, No. 3 or 4, and proceed as with the foregoing.

It is not worth while to bestow the expense of coloring paste with the gold, and it is therefore more expedient, in the case of such, to use the other method.

Hard Glass and Paste for Sapphire, by means of Smalt, No. 6.

Take of the compositions for hard glass and paste, any quantity, and mix with them one-eighth of their weight of smalt, the brightest and most inclining to purple that can be procured.

If it be desirable to give a more purple tinge, manganese may be added in the proportion required.

Hard Glass Resembling Eagle Marine, No. 7.

Take of the composition for hard glass, No. 1 or 2, 10 lbs.; of oxide of copper, highly calcined with sulphur, 3 oz., and of zaffre, 1 scr. Proceed as with the foregoing.

Paste for Eagle Marine, No. 8.

Take of the composition for paste, No. 1 or 2, 10 lbs., and proceed as with the above.

Hard Glass of a Gold or Yellow Color, No. 1.

Take of the composition for hard glass, No. 1 or 2, 10 lbs., but omit the saltpetre, and for every pound add 1 oz. of calcined borax, or, if that do not render the glass sufficiently fusible. 2 oz.; of red tartar, the deepest color that can be procured, 10 oz.; of manganese, 2 oz.; of soft charcoal, 2 drs. Proceed as with the rest.

Paste of a Gold or Yellow Color, No. 2.

Take of the composition for paste, No. 3 or 4, prepared without the saltpetre, 10 lbs.; of colcothar, strongly calcined, 1½ oz. Proceed as with the others.

The crude tartar and the charcoal must not be used where lead enters into the composition of the glass, and the nitre may be spared, because the yellow tinge, given to the glass by the lead, on account of which the nitre is used, is no detriment in this case, but only adds to the proper color. This color may also be prepared by crude antimony, as well as the colcothar, but it is more difficult to be managed, and not superior in its effect.

Hard Glass Resembling the Topaz, No. 3.

Take of the composition for hard glass, No. 1 or 2, 10 lbs. and an equal quantity of the gold-colored hard glass. Powder and fuse them together.

As there is a great variety in the color of the topaz, some being a deeper yellow, and others slightly tinged, the proportions of the yellow glass to the white may be accordingly varied at pleasure the one here given being for the deepest.

Paste Resembling the Topaz, No. 4.

This may be done in the same manner as the preceding, but the saltpetre may be omitted in the original composition of the glass, and for the resemblance of the very slightly colored topazes neither the gold-colored paste nor any other tinging matter need be added, that of the lead being sufficient, when not destroyed by the nitre.

Glass Resembling the Chrysolite, No. 5.

Take of the composition for hard glass, No. 1 or 2, 10 lbs.; of colcothar, 6 drs. Proceed as with the above.

Paste Resembling the Chrysolite, No. 6.

Take of the composition for paste, No. 3 or 4, prepared without saltpetre, 10 lbs.; and of colcothar, 5 drs. Proceed as with the rest.

Hard Glass Resembling the Emerald, No. 1.

Take of the composition for hard glass, No. 1 or 2, 9 lbs.; of oxide of copper, 3 oz.; and of precipitated oxide of iron, 2 drs.

Paste Resembling the Emerald. No. 2.

Take of the composition for paste, No. 1 or 2, and proceed as with the above; but if the saltpetre be omitted in the preparation of the paste, a less proportion of the iron will serve.

Hard Glass of a Deep and very Bright Purple Color. No. 1.

Take of the composition for hard glass, No. 1 or 2, 10 lbs.; of zaffre, 6 drs.; of purple of Cassius, 1 dr. Proceed as with the rest.

Hard Glass of a Deep Purple Color, No. 2.

Take of the composition for hard glass, No. 1 or

2, 10 lbs.; of manganese, 1 oz.; and of zaffre, ½ oz. Proceed as with the other.

Paste of a Deep Purple Color, No. 3.

Take of the composition for pastes, No. 3 or 4, 10 lbs., and treat them as the foregoing.

Hard Glass of the Color of the Amethyst, No. 4.

Take of the composition of hard glass, No. 1 or 2, 10 lbs.; of manganese, 1½ oz.; and of zaffre, 1 dr. Proceed as with the rest.

Paste of the Color of the Amethyst, No. 5.

Take of the composition for paste, No. 1 or 2, 10 lbs., and treat it as the preceding.

Paste Resembling the Diamond.

Take of white sand, 6 lbs.; of red-lead, 4 lbs.; of pearlash, purified as above directed, 3 lbs.; of nitre, 2 lbs.; or arsenic, 5 oz.; and of manganese, 1 scr. Proceed as with the others, but continue the fusion for a considerable time on account of the large proportion of arsenic.

If this composition be thoroughly vitrified, and kept free from bubbles, it will be very white, and have a very great lustre; but if, on examination, it appears to incline to yellow, another scruple or more of the manganese may be added. It may be rendered harder by diminishing the proportion of lead, and increasing that of the salts, or fusing it with a very strong fire; but the diminution of the proportion of lead will make it have less of the lustre of the diamond.

Hard Glass, Perfectly Black.

Take of the composition for hard glass, No. 1 or 2, 10 lbs.; of zaffre, 1 oz.; of manganese and of colcothar, strongly calcined, each, 7 drs. Proceed as with the rest.

Paste, Perfectly Black.

Take of the composition for paste, No. 1 or 2, prepared with the saltpetre, 10 lbs.; of zaffre, 1 oz.; of manganese, 6 drs.; and of colcothar, 5 drs. Proceed as with the others.

White Opaque Glass, No. 1.

Take of the composition for hard glass, No. 1 or 2, 10 lbs.; of horn, ivory, or bone, calcined perfectly white, 1 lb. Proceed as with the others.

Paste of an Opaque Whiteness, No. 2.

Take of the composition No. 3 or 4, 10 lbs., and make the same addition as to the above.

Glass of an Opaque Whiteness Formed by Arsenic, No. 3.

Take of flint-glass 10 lbs., and of very white arsenic, 1 lb. Powder and mix them thoroughly, by grinding them together, and then fuse them with a moderate heat till they be well incorporated, but avoid liquefying them more than to make a perfect union.

This glass has been made in great quantities, and has not only been formed into a variety of different kinds of vessels, but, being very white and fusible with a moderate heat, has been much used, as a white ground, for enamel in dial-plates, and other pieces which have not occasion to go several times into the fire to be finished. It will not, however, bear repeated burnings, nor a strong heat continued for any length of time, when applied to this purpose, without becoming transparent, to which likewise the smoke of a coal fire will also greatly contribute; but it answers the end very well in many cases, though even in those, enamel of the same degree of whiteness would be preferable, as this is always brittle, and of less firm and tenacious texture.

Hard Glass, or Paste, Formed by Calx of Tin or Antimony, No. 4.

Take of any of the compositions for hard glass or pastes, 10 lbs; of oxide of tin (commonly called putty), or of antimony, or tin calcined by means of nitre, 1½ lbs.; mix them well by grinding them together, and then fuse them with a moderate heat.

The glass of this kind made with the composition for pastes, differs in nothing from white enamel, but in the proportion of the calx of tin and antimony.

Semi-transparent White Glass and Paste Resembling the Opal, No. 5.

Take of any of the compositions for hard glass or paste, 10 lbs.; of horn, bone, or ivory, calcined to a perfect whiteness, ½ lb. Proceed as with the rest.

This white hard glass is much the same with the German glass formerly brought here in porringers, cream pots, vinegar cruets, and other such pieces, of which we frequently meet with the remains.

Fine Red Glass Resembling the Ruby, No. 1.

Take of the hard glass, No. 1 or 2, 1 lb. of the purple of Cassius, 3 drs. Powder the glass, and grind the calx of gold afterwards with it in a glass, flint, or agate mortar, and then fuse them together.

This may be made of a stronger or more diluted color, by varying the proportion of the gold, in adjusting which proper regard should be had to the application of the glass when made; for where this glass is set in rings, bracelets, or other close work, where foils can be used, a great saving may be made with regard to the color of it, without much injury to the effect; but for ear-rings, or other purposes where the work is set transparent, a full strong color should be given, which may be effected by the proportions directed in the composition.

Paste Resembling the Ruby, No. 2.

Take of the paste No. 3 or 4, 1 lb. and of calx caffei, or precipitation of gold by tin, 2 drs. Proceed in the mixture as with the above.

This will be equally beautiful with the above, and defective only in softness; but as that greatly takes away the value for some purposes, such as is appropriated to them may be tinged in a cheaper manner by the following means.

A Cheaper Paste Resembling the Ruby, No. 3.

Take of the composition for paste, No. 3 or 4, of glass of antimony, each ½ lb., and of purple of Cassius, 1½ dr. Proceed as with the others.

This will be considerably cheaper, and will have much the same effect, except that it recedes more from the crimson to the orange.

Hard Glass Resembling the Garnet, No. 4.

Take of the composition for hard glass, No. 1 or 2, 2 lbs.; of glass of antimony, 1 lb.; of manganese, and of purple of Cassius, each 1 dr.

This composition is very beautiful, but too expensive, on account of the gold, for the imitation of garnets for common purposes; on which account the following may be substituted.

Hard Glass Resembling the Garnet, No. 5.

Take of the composition, No. 1 or 2, 2 lbs.; of the glass of antimony, 2 lbs.; and of manganese, 2 dr.

If the color be found too dark and purple in either this or the preceding composition, the proportion of manganese must be diminished.

Paste of the Color of Garnet, No. 6.

Take of the composition for paste, No. 1 or 2, and proceed as with the above.

Hard Glass Resembling the Vinegar Garnet, No. 7.

Take of the composition, No. 1 or 2, 2 lbs.; of glass of antimony, 1 lb.; of colcothar, ½ oz. Mix the colcothar with the uncolored glass, and fuse them together till the mass be perfectly transparent, then add the glass of antimony, powdered, stirring the mixture with the end of a tobacco-pipe, and continue them in the heat till the whole be perfectly incorporated.

Paste Resembling the Vinegar Garnet, No. 8.

Take of the composition for paste, No. 3 or 4, and proceed as with the foregoing.

Fictitious or Counterfeit Lapis Lazuli.

Take of any of the preceding compositions for hard glass, or paste, 10 lbs.; of calcined bones, horn, or ivory, ¾ lb.; of zaffre, 1 oz. Fuse the uncolored composition with the zaffre and manganese, till a very deep transparent blue glass be produced. The mass being cold, powder it, and mix it with the calcined matter, by grinding them together. After which fuse them with a moderate heat till they be thoroughly incorporated, and then form the melted mass into cakes, by pouring it on a clean bright plate of copper or iron.

Another.—If it be desired to have it veined with gold, it may be done by mixing the gold powder with an equal weight of calcined borax, and tempering them with oil of spike, by which mixture, the cakes being painted with such veins as are desired, they must be put into a furnace of a moderate heat, and the gold will be cemented in the glass as firmly as if the veins had been natural.

Another. — If the counterfeit lapis lazuli be desired of a lighter hue, the quantity of zaffre and manganese must be diminished; or, if it be required to be more transparent, that of the calcined horn, bone, or ivory, should be lessened.

To make Glass Resembling Red Cornelian.

Take of the composition for hard glass, No. 1 or 2, 2 lbs.; of glass of antimony, 1 lb.; of colcothar, 2 oz.; and of manganese, 1 dr.

Fuse the glass of antimony and manganese with the other glass first together, and then powder them well, and mix them with the colcothar, by grinding them together, and afterwards fuse the mixture with a gentle heat, till they are incorporated, but the heat must not be continued longer than is absolutely required to form them into a vitreous mass.

If it be desired to have the composition more transparent, part of the colcothar must be omitted.

Paste Resembling the Red Cornelian.

Take of the composition for paste, No. 1 or 2, 2 lbs.; and proceed as with the above.

Hard Glass Resembling White Cornelian.

Take of the composition for hard glass, No. 1 or 2, 2 lbs.; of yellow ochre, well washed, 2 dr.; and of calcined bones, each 1 oz. Mix them well by grinding them together, and fuse them with a gentle heat till the several ingredients be well incorporated in a vitreous mass.

Paste Resembling White Cornelian.

Take of the composition for pastes, No. 1 or 2, 1 lb., and proceed as with the foregoing.

Hard Glass or Paste Resembling the Turquoise Stone.

Take of the composition for blue glass or paste, No. 7 or 8 (being those resembling the eagle marine), 10 lbs.; of calcined bone, or ivory, ½ lb. Powder and mix them well, and then fuse them in a moderate heat till they are thoroughly incorporated.

If the color be not so deep as may be desired, a small proportion of smalt may be added.

Brown Venetian Glass with Gold Spangles.

Take of the composition for hard glass, No. 2, and the composition for paste, No. 1, each 5 lbs., and of colcothar, 1 oz. Mix them well, and fuse them till the iron be perfectly vitrified, and have tinged the glass of a deep transparent yellow brown color. Powder this glass, and add to it 2 lbs. of powdered glass of antimony, and mix them well by grinding them together. Take part of this mixture and rub into it 80 or 100 leaves of Dutch metal; and when the particles of the leaf seem sufficiently divided, mix the powder containing it with the other part of the glass. Fuse the whole then with a moderate heat till the powder runs into a vitreous mass, fit to be wrought into any of the figures or vessels into which it is usually formed; but avoid a perfect liquefaction, because that destroys, in a short time, the equal diffusion of the spangles, and vitrifies, at least, part of the matter of which they are composed, converting the whole into a kind of transparent olive-colored glass.

TO PAINT AND STAIN GLASS AND PORCELAIN.

To paint upon glass is an art which has generally appeared difficult; yet there is no representation more elegant than that of a mezzotinto painted in this manner, for it gives all the softness that can be desired in a picture, and is easy to work, as there are no outlines to draw, nor any shades to make.

The prints are those done in mezzotinto; for their shades being rubbed down on the glass, the several lines, which represent the shady part of any common print, are by this means blended together, and appear as soft and united as in any drawing of Indian-ink.

Provide such mezzotintos as are wanted; cut off the margin; then get a piece of fine crown-glass, the size of the print, and as flat and free from knots and scratches as possible; clean the glass, and lay some Venice turpentine, quite thin and smooth, on one side, with a brush of hog's hair. Lay the print flat in water, and let it remain on the surface till it sinks, it is then damp enough; take it carefully out, and dab it between some papers, that no water may be seen, yet so as to be damp.

Next lay the damp print with its face uppermost upon a flat table; then hold the glass over it, without touching the turpentine, till it is exactly even with the print, let it fall gently on it. Press the glass down carefully with the fingers in several parts, so that the turpentine may stick to the print; after which take it up, then holding the glass towards you, press the prints with the fingers, from the centre towards the edges, till no blisters remain.

When this is done, wet the back of the paint with a sponge, till the paper will rub off with the fingers; then rub it gently, and the white paper will roll off, leaving the impression only upon the glass; then let it dry, and, with a camel's hair pencil, dipped in oil of turpentine, wet it all over, and it will be perfectly transparent, and fit for painting.

Improved Method.

The first thing to be done, in order to paint, or stain glass in the modern way, is to design, and even color the whole subject on paper. Then choose such pieces of glass as are clear, even, and smooth, and proper to receive the several parts. Proceed to distribute the design itself, or the paper it is drawn on, into pieces suitable to those of the glass; always taking care that the glasses may join in the contours of the figures, and the folds of the draperies; that the carnations and other finer parts may not be impaired by the lead with which the pieces are to be joined together. The distribution being made, mark all the glasses, as well as papers, that they may be known again; which done, apply every part of the design upon the glass intended for it; and copy or transfer the design upon this glass with the black color diluted in gum-water, by tracing and following all the lines and strokes that appear through the glass, with the point of a pencil.

When these strokes are well dried, which will be in about 2 days (the work being only in black and white), give it a slight wash over with urine, gum-arabic, and a little black; and repeat this several times, according as the shades are desired to be heightened, with this precaution, never to apply a new wash till the former is sufficiently dried. This done, the lights and risings are given by rubbing off the color in the respective places with a wooden point, or by the handle of the pencil.

The colors are used with gum-water, the same as in painting in miniature, taking care to apply them lightly, for fear of effacing the outlines of the design; or even, for the greater security, to apply them on the other side; especially yellow, which is very pernicious to the other colors, by blending therewith. And here too, as in pieces of black and white, particular regard must always be had not to lay color on color, till such time as the former is well dried.

When the painting of all the pieces is finished, they are carried to the furnace to anneal, or to bake the colors.

Colors Proper to Paint with Upon Glass.

The several sorts of colors, ground in oil for this purpose, may be had at all the color-shops, etc.

Whites.—Flake white, podium.

Blacks.—Lampblack, ivory-black.

Browns.—Spanish brown, umber, spruce ochre, Dutch pink, orpiment.

Blues.—Blue bice, Prussian blue.

Reds.—Rose-pink, vermilion, red-lead, Indian-red, lake cinnabar.

Yellows.—English pink, masticot, English ochre, Saunders blue, smalt.

Greens.—Verdigris, terra vert, verditer.

The ultramarine for blue, and the carmine for red, are rather to be bought in powders, as in that state they are less apt to dry; and as the least tint of these will give the picture a cast, mix up what is wanted for present use with a drop or two of nut-oil upon the pallet with the pallet-knife.

Then lay a sheet of white paper on the table, and taking the picture in the left hand, with the turpentine side next you, hold it sloping (the bottom resting on the white paper), and all outlines and tints of the prints will be seen on the glass; and nothing remains but to lay on the colors proper for the different parts, as follows:

To Use the Colors.

As the lights and shades of the picture open, lay the lighter colors first on the lighter parts of the print, and the darker over the shaded parts; and having laid on the brighter colors, it is not material if the darker sorts are laid a little over them; for the first color will hide those laid on afterwards. For example:

Reds.—Lay on the first red-lead, and shade with lake or carmine.

Yellows.—The lightest yellow may be laid on first, and shaded with Dutch pink.

Blues.—Blue bice, or ultramarine, used for the lights, may be shaded with indigo.

Greens.—Lay on verdigris first, then a mixture of that and Dutch pink. This green may be lightened by an addition of Dutch pink.

When any of these are too strong, they may be lightened, by mixing white with them upon the pallet; or darken them as much as required by mixing them with a deeper shade of the same color.

The colors must not be laid on too thick; but if troublesome, thin them before using them, with a little turpentine oil.

Take care to have a pencil for each color, and never use that which has been used for green, with any other color without first washing it well with turpentine-oil, as that color is apt to appear predominant when the colors are dry.

Wash all the pencils, after using, in turpentine-oil.

The glass, when painted, must stand 3 or 4 days free from dust before it is framed.

To Draw on Glass.

Grind lampblack with gum-water and some common salt. With a pen or hair-pencil, draw the design on the glass, and afterwards shade and paint it with any of the following compositions:

Color for Grounds on Glass.

Take iron-filings and Dutch yellow beads, equal parts. If a little red cast is wanted, add a little copper filings. With a steel muller grind these together on a thick and strong copper plate, or on porphyry. Then add a little gum Arabic, borax, common salt, and clear water. Mix these with a little fluid, and put the composition in a phial for use.

When it is to be used there is nothing to do but, with a hair pencil, to lay it quite flat on the design drawn the day before; and having left this to dry also for another day, with the quill of a turkey, the nib unsplit, heighten the lights in the same manner as with crayons on blue paper. Whenever there are more coats of the above composition put one upon another, the shade will naturally be stronger; and when this is finished, lay the colors for garments and complexions.

To Prepare Lake for Glass.

Grind the lake with water impregnated with gum and salt; then make use of it with the brush. The shading is operated by laying a double, treble, or more coats of the color, where it is wanted darker.

Blue Purple for the same.

Make a compound of lake and indigo, ground together with gum and salt water, and use it as directed in the preceding article.

Green.

Mix with a proportionable quantity of gamboge ground together as above.

Yellow.

Grind gamboge with salt water only.

White.

Heighten much the white parts with a pen.

To Transfer Engravings on Glass.

Metallic colors prepared and mixed with fat oil, are applied to the stamp on the engraved plate. Wipe with the hand in the manner of the printers of colored plates; take a proof on a sheet of silver paper, which is immediately transferred on the tablet of glass destined to be painted, being careful to turn the colored side against the glass; it adheres to it, and as soon as the copy is quite dry, take off the superfluous paper by washing it with a sponge; there will remain only the color transferred to the glass; it is fixed by passing the glass through the ovens.

The bases of all the colors employed in painting on glass, are oxidized metallic substances.

In painting on glass, it is necessary that the matter should be very transparent.

To Prepare Metallic Oxides and Precipitates of Gold.

A solution of gold in aqua-regia, which is evaporated to dryness, leaves gold, which is used for glass, enamel, and porcelain gilding; or by precipitating the solution with green vitriol dissolved in water, a similar powder is produced. This powder is mixed with some essential oil, as oil of spike, and calcined borax, and the whole made to adhere *to the surface of the glass* by a solution of gum Arabic. It is then applied with a fine pencil, and burnt in under a muffle.

To Prepare Oxide of Cobalt.

When regulus of cobalt is exposed to a moderate fire in the open air, it calcines; and is reduced to a blackish powder.

This oxide vitrifies with vitrifiable matters and forms beautiful blue glasses. Cobalt is, at present, the only substance known which has the property of furnishing a very fine blue that is not changed by the most intense heat.

To Prepare Zaffre.

Zaffre is the oxide of cobalt, for painting pottery ware and porcelain of a blue color. Break the cobalt with hammers into pieces about the size of a hen's egg; and the stony gangue, with such other foreign matters, separate as much as possible. Pound the chosen mineral in stamping-mills, and sift it through brass-wire sieves. Wash off the lighter parts by water, and afterwards put it into a large flat-bottomed arched furnace resembling a baking-oven, where the flame of the wood reverberates upon the ore, which stir occasionally, and turn with long-handled iron hooks or rakes; and the process is to be continued till its fumes cease. The oven or furnace terminates by a long horizontal gallery, which serves for a chimney, in which the arsenic, naturally mixed with the ore, sublimes. If the ore contains a little bismuth, as this semi-metal is very fusible, collect it at the bottom of the furnace. The cobalt remains in the state of a dark gray oxide, and is called *zaffre*. This operation is continued four, or even nine hours, according to the quality of the ore. The roasted ore being taken out from the furnace, such parts as are concreted into lumps, pound and sift afresh. Zaffre, in commerce, is never pure, being mixed with two, or rather three parts of powdered flints. A proper quantity of the best sort of these, after being ignited in a furnace, are to be thrown into water, to render them friable and more easily reduced to powder; which, being sifted, is mixed with the zaffre, according to the before-mentioned dose; and the mixture is put into casks, after being moistened with water. This oxide, fused with 3 parts of sand and 1 of potassa, forms a blue glass which, when pounded, sifted, and ground in mills (included in large casks), forms *smalt*.

The blue of zaffre is the most solid and fixed of all the colors employed in vitrification. It suffers no change from the most violent fire. It is successfully employed to give shades of blue to enamels, and to crystal-glass made in imitation of opaque and transparent precious stones; as the lapis lazuli, the turquoise, the sapphire, and others.

Purple of Cassius.

Dissolve some pure gold in nitro-muriatic acid; add either acid or metal, until saturation takes place. Now dissolve some pure tin in the same kind of acid; observe the same point of saturation as with the gold, and pour it into the solution of gold. A purple powder will be precipitated, which must be collected and washed in distilled water.

This beautiful purple color, as before mentioned, is extremely useful to enamellers and to glass-stainers.

When brought into fusion with a clear, transparent glass, it tinges it of a purple, red, or violet color. Hence the method of making false rubies and garnets.

To Paint Colored Drawings on Glass.

This art is exercised two ways. 1. Plates of stained glass are cut into the shape of figures and joined by leaden outlines. On these plates a shading is afterwards traced by the painter, which gives features to the face and folds to the drapery. 2. Vitrifiable colors are attached to plates of white glass, which are afterwards placed in the oven, and thus converted into a transparent enamelling. The first sort is cheaper, but the shading wears off by the insensible corrosion of the atmosphere. The second sort defies every accident except fracture; but the color of the figures suffers in the oven. For small objects, the first sort, and for large objects, the second, as far as art is concerned, seems best adapted.

Flux for Staining Glass.

1. When the colors used are not affected by lead, 100 parts powdered quartz, 125 red-lead, 50 of bismuth.

2. When the flux is required free from lead, 100 parts quartz, 75 glass of borax, 12½ saltpetre, 12½ powdered statuary marble.

Colors for Staining Glass.

To 6 cwt. of flux or flint-glass are to be added as follows:

White (soft), 24 lbs. white arsenic, 6 lbs. antimony.

White (hard), 200 lbs. putty-powder.

Blue (transparent), 2 lbs oxide of cobalt.

Azure, 6 lbs. protoxide of copper.

Ruby, 4 oz. oxide of gold.

Amethyst, 20 lbs. oxide of manganese.

Common Orange, 12 lbs. iron ore, 4 lbs. oxide of manganese.

Emerald Green, 12 lbs. copper scales and 12 lbs. iron ore.

Gold Topaz (canary glass), 3 lbs. oxide of uranium.

The colors will vary with the degree of heat to which the glass is subjected. The whole glass may be colored, or the mixture of flux and oxide may be laid on the surface, and then vitrified.

PHOTOGRAPHY.

APOTHECARIES' weight is used throughout this article. In case of liquids the abbreviation oz. signifies fluidounce.

COTTON.

To make Pyroxyline or Gun-cotton, suitable for Photographic Collodion.

1. By nitre process: Oil of vitriol (s. g. 1·70), 6 oz,; dried nitrate of potash, 3½ oz.; water, 1 oz. Mix the acid and the water in a porcelain vessel, and add the pulverized nitre, gradually stirring with a glass rod until the lumps disappear and the mixture becomes transparent. Place a thermometer in the mixture, and when it indicates between 145° and 150° Fahr., the cotton should be immersed. Take 60 grs. of clean cotton, and separate it into 10 or 12 bolls, and immerse the bolls separately, and leaving the whole in the mixture for 10 minutes. Should the temperature fall to 140°, float the cup on boiling water, and maintain it between 140° and 150°. At the expiration of 10 minutes lift the cotton with glass rods, and squeeze out the acid quickly and dash the mass into a large vessel of clean, cold water, separating the mass so as to wash it thoroughly and quickly. Complete the washing by immersion for several hours in running water, then spread it out to dry spontaneously.

2. By mixed acids: Oil of vitriol (s. g. 1·845), 18 oz.; nitric acid (s. g. 1·457), 6 oz.; water, 5 oz. Mix the nitric acid and water in a porcelain vessel, then add the oil of vitriol and mix thoroughly and allow the mixture to cool to 150° Fahr., when immerse the cotton. Take 300 grs. of clean cotton, well loosened, and immerse piecemeal, so as to saturate thoroughly with the acids. Allow the whole to remain 7 minutes, after which time lift it out with the rods and wash it precisely as directed in last process.

Photographic Collodion.

Pure alcohol (s. g. ·805), 10 oz.; pure ether (s. g. 0·725), 20 oz.; prepared cotton, 300 grs. Pour the alcohol into a 40 oz. glass bottle, add the cotton, and shake until the cotton is thoroughly wetted; then add the ether, shake well and set away in a cool, dark place for several weeks to settle. Mark "*Plain Collodion.*" In very warm weather increase the proportion of alcohol by addition a day before use or at time of iodizing.

Iodizers for Photographic Collodion.

Iodide of ammonium, 90 grs.; iodide of cadmium, 90 grs.; bromide of ammonium, 40 grs.; alcohol (·810), 10 oz.

Or, iodide of magnesium, 200 grs.; bromide of cadmium, 50 grs.; alcohol (·810), 10 oz.

Pulverize the salts, and add gradually to the alcohol, commencing with the bromide; shake until completely dissolved, and set away in a dark place. Mark "*Iodizing Solution.*"

To Iodize Collodion.

Plain collodion, 3 oz.; iodizing solution, 1 oz. Mix and set away in a dark, cool place 12 hours before using.

Any of the ordinary iodides or bromides can be substituted in the above formulæ.

Sensitizing Baths.

For positives: Pure re-crystallized nitrate of silver (437 gr.), 1 oz.; pure nitric acid, 3 minims; alcohol, 2 drs.; distilled water, 10 oz.; iodide of potassium, 1 gr. Dissolve the nitrate of silver in 3 oz. of the distilled water, add the iodide of potassium, shake and allow to settle; test for acidity with blue litmus paper, and, if present, neutralize carefully with a solution of carbonate of soda. When neutral, add the remaining 7 oz. of distilled water, filter and add the alcohol and nitric acid, and the bath is ready for use.

For negatives: Pure re-crystallized nitrate of silver, 1 oz.; glacial acetic acid, 5 minims; alcohol, 3 drs.; iodide of potassium, 1 gr.; distilled water, 10 oz. Dissolve the silver in 3 oz., and treat precisely as for bath for negatives, observing that it is to be acidified with glacial acetic acid in place of nitric acid.

These baths should be kept in a dark place, and always show an acid test. When out of order, boil for a few minutes, add one-tenth volume of distilled water and restore to the original strength by adding strong solution of crystallized nitrate of silver in distilled water, and acidifying with the proper acids.

Developers.

For positives: 1. Pure sulphate of iron, 150 grs.; glacial acetic acid, 6 fl. drs.; water, 10 oz.; nitric acid, 2 minims. Dissolve the sulphate of iron in the water, and add the acetic and nitric acid and cork tightly.

2. Sulphate of iron, 480 grs.; nitrate of baryta, 320 grs.; alcohol, 1 oz.; nitric acid, 30 minims; water, 10 oz. Powder the nitrate of baryta and dissolve in the water warmed; when dissolved, add the powdered sulphate of iron, stirring for a few minutes; filter, and when the liquid becomes cold, add the nitric acid and alcohol separately. Bottle and cork tightly.

For negatives: 1. Pyrogallic acid, 10 grs.; glacial acetic acid, 3 drs.; distilled water, 10 oz. Dissolve the pyrogallic acid in the water, add the glacial acetic acid, cork tightly.

2. Sulphate of iron and ammonium, 2 oz., or sulphate of iron, 1½ oz.; glacial acetic acid, ½ oz., or acetic acid No. 8, 1½ oz.; alcohol, ½ oz.; distilled water, 10 oz. Add to the distilled water in the order indicated, the iron-salt to be first dissolved. In warm weather this developer requires dilution, and must be washed from the plate the instant the details appear.

Fixing Solutions.

For positives: Cyanide of potassium, 120 grs.; nitrate of silver, 6 grs.; water, 10 oz. When this solution requires more than a minute or two to clear the picture, add a small amount of cyanide of potassium.

[This solution is highly poisonous, and should not be allowed to touch unsound skin, nor should the fumes be breathed.]

For negatives: The above solution of cyanide of potassium answers very well, or hyposulphite of soda, 1 oz.; water, 10 oz.; ether, 30 minims.

Strengthening or Intensifying Solutions

Should be employed after the picture has been developed, fixed and carefully washed:

Nitrate of silver, 200 grs.; distilled water, 10 ounces.

Or, Bi-chloride of mercury, 30 grs.; distilled water, 40 oz.

Cleaning the Glass Plates.

Before washing the glasses, each square should be roughened on the edges and at the corners by means of a file, whetstone, or a sheet of emery-paper; or more simply by drawing the edges of two plates across each other.

A cream of Tripoli powder and spirits of wine, with a little ammonia added, is commonly employed. A tuft of cotton is to be dipped in this mixture and the glasses well rubbed with it for a few minutes.

After wiping the glass carefully, complete the process by polishing with an old silk handkerchief, avoiding contact with the skin of the hand. Leathers may be used instead of silk for the final polishing; they must be first beaten, then washed in pure water, dried in the sun and well pulled out until they are soft and yielding. Before deciding that the glass is clean, hold it in an angular position and breathe upon it.

Other modes of cleaning glasses have been recommended, of which, perhaps, the residues of collodion are the most simple. Add a fluidrachm of water to the ounce of collodion until the pyroxyline begins to form a white deposit not redissolved on agitation; this will prevent the collodion from evaporating too quickly. Then pour a little upon the glass and rub with a tuft of wool or piece of cambric. Clean off with a second piece, and finish with cloth and leathers as before; no water will be required.

New glass plates are frequently dotted on the surface with little gritty particles, which consist of carbonate of lime. They are not removed by potash or any alkali, but dissolve readily in a diluted acid, such as oil of vitriol, with about four parts of water added, or dilute nitric acid.

Lea's Cleaning Solution.

Water, 1 pt.; sulphuric acid, ½ oz.; bichromate potash, ½ oz. The glass plates, varnished or otherwise, are left, say 10 or 12 hours or as much longer as desired, in this solution, and then rinsed in clean water and wiped or rubbed dry with soft white paper. It removes nitrate of silver stains from the fingers.

Coating the Plate.

When the collodion is properly cleared from sediment, take a glass plate, previously cleaned, and wipe it gently with a broad camel's-hair brush, in order to remove any particles of dust which may have subsequently collected. If it be a plate of moderate size it may be held by the corners in a horizontal position, between the forefinger and thumb of the left hand. The collodion is to be poured on steadily until a circular pool is formed extending nearly to the edges of the glass,

By a slight inclination of the plate the fluid is made to flow towards the corner marked 1 in the above diagram, until it nearly touches the thumb by which the glass is held; from corner 1 it passes to corner 2, held by the forefinger; from 2 to 3, and lastly, the excess poured back into the bottle from the corner marked No. 4. It is next to be held over the bottle for a moment until it nearly ceases to drip, and then by raising the thumb a little the direction of the plate is changed so as to give a rocking movement, which makes the diagonal lines coalesce and produces a smooth surface.

The operation of coating a plate with collodion must not be done hurriedly, and nothing is required to ensure success but steadiness of hand and a sufficiency of the fluid poured in the first instance upon the plate.

With regard to the time which ought to elapse between coating and dipping, observe the following: After exposing a layer of collodion to the air for a short time, the greater part of the ether evaporates and leaves the pyroxyline in a state in which it is neither wet nor dry, but receives the impression of the finger without adhering to it. This is termed setting, and when it takes place, the time has come for submitting the plate to the action of the bath.

When the plate is ready, rest it upon the glass dipper, collodion side uppermost, and lower it into the solution by a slow and steady movement and let it remain until the oily appearance on the surface disappears.

Exposure.

After the plate has been taken out of the bath, it should be exposed and developed with all convenient despatch, otherwise the film will become partially dry, the developing solutions will not flow easily, and the negative will be weak and metallic.

Development.

The pyrogallic acid solution having been previously measured out (about 3 drs. for a stereoscopic plate or a plate 5×4, 1 oz. for a 9×7, and 12 drs. for a plate 10×8), hold the glass in the hand in the same manner as when coating it with collodion, and flow the liquid on evenly.

Development with Sulphate of Iron.

This reducing agent developes the picture so rapidly, when the collodion contains only iodide, that its employment requires care. The solution should be thrown on to the plate rather quickly, and with a sweep. In the course of a few seconds the image appears in all its parts, and the liquid on the film shows signs of commencing turbidity. When this happens, the developer must be poured off immediately, and the plate washed with water, otherwise the shadows will be misty from adherent particles of silver. Plates developed with sulphate of iron may be further blackened by washing the film and pouring over it a 20-gr. solution of nitrate of silver, followed by a second application of sulphate of iron. A better process, however, is to wash away all traces of the iron salt by a stream of water applied for a few seconds, and then to mix the ordinary solution of pyrogallic acid with nitrate of silver.

Fixing and Varnishing the Negative.

Wash the film gently with water, and pour the solution of hyposulphite on and off until the whole of the iodide has been cleared away. The solution of hyposulphite becomes nearly black after a time, but this is of no importance, some operators considering that even a preliminary washing to remove the pyrogallic acid solution is unnecessary. A thorough washing after the hyposulphite will be essential. After the negative has been washed flow it over with a solution of gum Arabic, stand it on clean blotting-paper to dry; otherwise dust will ascend the film by capillary action, and give an appearance as if impurities had drained down from above. It is important that the plate should be dried by artificial heat before varnishing, and the negative will also look more neat if a damp cloth be first run along the edge with the finger and thumb, so as to scrape away the collodion, and leave a clear margin of ⅛ to ¼ of an inch all round. After doing so remove with the nail or a camel's-hair brush any loose or detached particles of collodion, which otherwise might be washed on to the image by the varnish, and produce a spot.

To Adjust Camera for Chemical Focus.

Take a photograph of a printed sheet with the full aperture of the portrait lens, the central letters being carefully focussed as before. Then examine at what part of the plate the greatest amount of distinctness of outline is to be found. It will, sometimes, happen that whereas the exact centre was focussed visually, the letters on a spot midway between the centre and edge are the sharpest in the photograph. In that case the chemical focus is longer than the other, and by a distance equivalent to, but in the opposite direction of, the space through which the lens has to be moved, in order to define those particulars sharply to the eye.

Direct Positives on Glass.

In developing a glass positive, the solution of sulphate of iron should be flowed evenly over the film, and in some quantity, so as to wash off a portion of nitrate of silver into the sink.

Pyrogallic Acid Developer.

Forty grs. of pyrogallic acid being dissolved in 1 oz. of glacial acetic acid, and 20 minims added to 1 oz. of water when required for use. The strong solution becomes black from decomposition in the course of a few weeks, but when diluted it has only a faint yellow tint, and is tolerably effective in bringing out the image. In place of acetic acid strong alcohol may be used as a solvent, ½ a dr. of pyrogallic acid being dissolved in 1 oz. of spirit, and 20 minims of the resulting liquid added to each oz. of acidified water. No attempt must be made, however, to combine acetic acid and spirit in one solution, since abundance of acetic ether would be generated by so doing. These plans of preparing a concentrated developer are useful for a few weeks' keeping, but are not recommended for an unlimited time.

To Copy Engravings.

To photograph a full-sized steel engraving on a plate not larger than 7×6 or 5×4, is a very simple operation, and no special directions will be needed. Remove the engraving from its frame (the glass would cause irregular reflection), and suspend it vertically and in a reversed condition, in a good diffused light, placing a black cloth behind it, if any bright reflecting surface be presented to the lens. Point at it a camera mounted with a portrait-lens, and if the image upon the ground glass appears misty towards the edge, make a diaphragm, and place it in front of the anterior glass. Instead of a portrait-lens an ordinary view-lens may be used, and as the field to be covered is small, a comparatively large diaphragm will suffice.

Be careful not to over-expose the plate, develop with pyrogallic acid, and fix with hyposulphite.

Copying Prints.

The additional deposit obtained, as above described, will often be found sufficient, and when such is the case the method is to be preferred, because the half-tones of a photograph are easily obliterated by too much intensifying. In the case of large copies of maps taken with orthoscopic lenses of long focus, the iodine method proves insufficient, and the fine lines of the drawing become partly obliterated during the prolonged development. In such a case it is advised to develop the plate only partially in the first instance, and to fix it with cyanide of potassium; then to intensify twice with pyrogallic acid, citric acid, and nitrate of silver, and lastly to treat the plate with the two following liquids: No 1. Iodine, 6 grs.; iodide of potassium, 12 grs.; water, 6 oz. No. 2. Sulphide of potassium, 1 dr.; water, 6 oz.

Apply No. 1, either in the yellow room, or in the daylight, until the whole of the image is converted into iodide of silver, and the deposit appears yellow throughout. Then pour water on the image from a jug, and apply No. 2, which must be allowed to remain until the yellow color changes to a deep reddish-brown. Lastly, dry the plate, and varnish in the usual way.

Stereoscopic Pictures.

Photographs for the refracting stereoscope are taken with small lenses of about 4½ inches focus. For portraits a camera may advantageously be fitted with two double-combination lenses, of 1¾ inches diameter, exactly equal in focal length and in rapidity of action. The caps are removed simultaneously, and the pictures impressed at the same instant. The centres of the lenses may be separated by 3 inches, when the camera is placed at about 6 or 8 feet from the sitter. Pictures taken with binocular camera of this kind require to be mounted in a reversed position to that which they occupy on the glass, or a pseudoscopic effect will be produced. The negatives may be cut in half, the right half being printed on the left side, or the finished prints may be removed before mounting.

Stereoscopic Transparencies.

Sensitive films prepared by Russell's Tannin Process. Place the negative and the prepared plate in contact, and squeeze them together in an ordinary pressure-frame; not too strongly, however, or it will probably be found, after throwing off a few impressions, that the negative has been scratched. Lay a strip of black velvet behind the sensitive film to absorb stray light.

Fixing Bath.

Take of hyposulphite of soda, 1 oz.; water, 6 oz. Dissolve without filtering, and preserve the solution in a stock-bottle ready for use.

PAPER PRINTS.

Albuminized Paper.

Formula 1. — Take of chloride of ammonium, 200 grs.; water 5 oz.; albumen, 15 oz.

Chloride of barium is sometimes used in salting paper, instead of chloride of ammonium, but is contraindicated when the alkaline gold-toning process is adopted, since the carbonate of soda would throw down carbonate of baryta in the paper.

When pure albumen is used without water, from 5 to 8 grs. of salt to each ounce will be sufficient. The less the quantity of salt the warmer the color, but it must not be so far reduced as to injure the contrast and depth of shadow in the print.

If distilled water cannot be procured, rain-water, or even common spring-water, will often answer the purpose. For the albumen use eggs nearly fresh, and be careful that in opening the shell the yolk be not broken. Each egg will yield about one fluidounce of albumen.

When the ingredients are mixed, take a bundle of quills or a fork, and beat the whole into a perfect froth. As the froth forms it is to be skimmed off and placed in a flat dish to subside. The success of the operation depends very much upon this part of the process, for, if the albumen be not thoroughly beaten, flakes of animal membrane will be left in the liquid, and will cause streaks upon the paper. When the froth has partially subsided transfer the liquid part to a tall and narrow jar, and allow to stand for several hours, that the membranous shreds may settle to the bottom; then pour off the upper clear portion, which will be fit for use. Albuminous liquids are too glutinous to run well through a paper filter, and are better cleared by subsidence. Lower the paper on the liquid by one steady movement, since, if a pause be made, a line will be formed. Some papers are not readily wetted by the albumen, and when such is the case a few drops of spirituous solution of bile, or a fragment of the prepared oxgall sold by the artists' colormen, will be found a useful adjunct. Care must be taken, however, not to add an excess, or the albumen will be rendered too fluid, and will sink into the paper, leaving no gloss.

To render the Paper Sensitive.

This operation must be conducted by the light of a candle or by yellow light.

Take of nitrate of silver, 60 grs.; distilled water, 1 oz. Prepare a sufficient quantity of this solution, and pour it out into a porcelain dish. After it has been a short time in use, the albumen, dissolved out of the papers, will cause a greasy scum to form upon the liquid, which, if allowed to remain, produces marble stains upon the sensitive paper; it must therefore be removed by folding a strip of blotting-paper the exact breadth of the dish, and drawing it lightly along the surface; lay the sheet upon the solution in the same manner as above described for the albumen. Three minutes' contact will be sufficient with thin paper, but if a thick paper be used 4 or 5 minutes must be allowed for the decomposition. The papers are raised from the solution by a pair of bone forceps, or common tweezers tipped with sealing-wax; or a pin may be used to lift up the corner, which is to be held by the finger and thumb, and allowed to drain a little before again putting in the pin, otherwise a mark will be produced upon the paper, from decomposition of the nitrate of silver. When the sheet is hung up a small strip of blotting-paper, suspended from the lower edge of the paper, will serve to drain off the last drop of liquid.

Formula 2.—Preparation of Plain Paper.

Take of chloride of ammonium, 200 grs.; citrate of soda, 200 grs.; gelatine, 20 grs.; water, 20 oz. To prepare the citrate of soda dissolve 112 grs. of citric acid in 20 oz. of water, and add 133 grs. of the dried bicarbonate or sesquicarbonate of soda used for effervescing draughts. Supposing the citric acid to be adulterated with tartaric acid, the above quantity of carbonate of soda would be too great, and free alkaline carbonate would then remain in the liquid after the neutralization was complete. The size of the paper would be liable to suffer in such a case, and the print would not be clean and bright. Excess of citric acid, on the other hand, gives very clean pictures, but they are too pale and red, without depth of shadow. Amateurs, desirous of simplifying the formula, may substitute an equal weight of "Rochelle salt" for the citrate of soda. This substance is a tartrate of potash and soda, and is sold by druggists in large crystals. Both tartrates and citrates are used for the purpose of giving a red and warm tone to the prints.

Render sensitive by floating for 2 or 3 minutes upon the solution of nitrate of silver employed for the albuminized paper.

Formula 3.—Ammonio-Nitrate Paper.

This is always prepared without albumen, which is dissolved by ammonio-nitrate of silver.

Take of chloride of ammonium, 40 grs.; gelatine, 20 grs.; water, 20 oz. Dissolve by the aid of heat, and filter when cold.

Take 10 or 12 sheets of thin Saxe paper, and, having marked the right side, immerse them bodily in the liquid, 1 by 1, with care to remove air-bubbles; then turn the batch over, and remove them singly, beginning with the sheet first immersed. Each paper will thus be a similar length of time in the salting liquid.

This salting solution is very weak, but it must be borne in mind that the papers being immersed will take up a large quantity, and also that the ammonio-nitrate process requires less salt, inasmuch as the silver solution is to be laid on with a brush.

An ammonio-nitrate paper, yielding a very rich color, is made by salting Towgood's paper, or Papier Saxe, with a mixed chloride and citrate, in quantity exactly one-half of that advised in the last page, and afterwards sensitizing it with an 80 gr. solution of ammonio-nitrate.

Render sensitive by a solution of ammonio-nitrate of silver, 60 grs. to the oz. of water, prepared as follows: Dissolve the nitrate of silver in one-half of the total quantity of water; then take a pure solution of ammonia and drop it in carefully, stirring meanwhile with a glass rod. A brown precipitate of oxide of silver first forms, but on the addition of more ammonia it is redissolved. When the liquid appears to be clearing up, add the ammonia very cautiously, so as not to incur an excess. In order still further to secure the absence of free ammonia it is usual to direct that, when the liquid becomes perfectly clear, a drop or two of solution of nitrate of silver should be added until a slight turbidity is again produced. Lastly, dilute with water to the proper bulk. If the crystals of nitrate of silver employed contain a large excess of free nitric acid no precipitate will be formed on the first addition of ammonia; the free nitric acid, producing nitrate of ammonia with the alkali, keeps the oxide of silver in solution. From the presence of nitrate of ammonia, it is often useless to attempt to convert an old nitrate bath, already used for sensitizing, into ammonio-nitrate. Or, dissolve 60 grs. of nitrate of silver in ½ oz. of water, and drop in ammonia until the precipitated oxide of silver is exactly redissolved; then divide this solution of ammonio-nitrate of silver into 2 equal parts, to one of which add nitric acid cautiously, until a piece of immersed litmus-paper is reddened by an excess of the acid; them mix the two together, fill up to 1 oz. of water, and filter from the milky deposit of chloride or carbonate of silver, if any be formed.

Ammonio-nitrate of silver should be kept in a dark place, being more prone to reduction than the nitrate of silver.

To Apply the Liquid.

It is not usual to float the paper when the ammonio-nitrate of silver is used. Brushes are manufactured expressly for applying silver solutions, but the hair is soon destroyed unless the brush is kept scrupulously clean. Lay the salted sheet upon blotting-paper, and wet it thoroughly by drawing the brush first lengthwise and then across. Allow it to remain flat for a minute or so, in order that a sufficient quantity of the solution may be absorbed (you will see when it is evenly wet by looking along the surface), and then pin up by the corner in the usual way. If, on drying, white lines appear at the points last touched by the brush, it is probable that the paper was too highly salted, or that the ammonio-nitrate contained free ammonia.

Ammonio-nitrate paper is more prone to spontaneous decomposition than either albuminized or plain paper; hence it cannot be kept many hours after sensitizing without turning yellow.

Toning Bath.

No. 1. Solution of chloride of gold, 1 dr.; sesquicarbonate of soda, 10 grs.; distilled water, 6 oz. No. 2. Solution of chloride of gold, 1 dr.;

ordinary phosphate of soda, 20 grs.; distilled water, 2 oz.

Examine the chloride of gold, and if its solution immediately colors litmus-paper of a bright red, add to each grain a fragment of carbonate of soda about the size of a pin's head.

The solution of chloride of gold contains a grain to each fluidrachm of water, and will keep for an unlimited time without appreciable change, previously to the addition of the carbonate of soda. The toning baths, however, must not be kept ready mixed, since they gradually become colorless and eventually lose their toning properties in great measure. A useful simplification, substituting measure for weight, consists in having always on hand an aqueous solution of carbonate of soda containing 20 grs. to the oz.; or for the second formula, a solution of phosphate of soda containing 40 grs. to the oz. Half an oz. of the alkaline liquid would then in each case require a fluidrachm of the solution of chloride of gold, and a subsequent dilution with water to the full amount given in the formula.

PHOTOGRAPHIC PRINTING.

Sensitive papers ought not to be exposed in the frame until they are quite dry. The shutter at the back of the frame is removed, and the negative laid flat upon the glass, collodion-side uppermost. A sheet of sensitive paper is then placed upon the negative, sensitive-side downwards; next comes a layer of thick felt; and the whole is then tightly compressed by replacing and bolting down the shutter. The amount of pressure required is not very considerable, but if the springs of the frame become too weak after a time, a few pieces of mill-board may be placed beneath them.

The time of exposure to light varies much with the density of the negative and the power of the actinic rays, as influenced by the season of the year and weather.

If the exposure to light has been correct the print appears slightly darker than it is intended to remain. The toning bath dissolves away the lighter shades, and reduces the intensity, for which allowance is made in the exposure to light. A little experience soon teaches the proper point; but much will depend upon the state of the toning bath, and albuminized paper will require to be printed somewhat more deeply than plain paper. If, on removal from the printing-frame, a peculiar spotted appearance is seen, produced by unequal darkening of the chloride of silver, either the nitrate bath is too weak, the sheet removed from its surface too speedily, or the paper is of inferior quality.

If, in the exposure to ordinary diffused daylight, the shadows of the proof became very decidedly coppery before the lights are sufficiently printed, the negative is in fault. Ammonio-nitrate paper highly salted is particularly liable to this excess of reduction, and especially so if the light is powerful.

Toning.

The print should be first washed in common water until the soluble nitrate of silver is removed. This is known to be the case when the liquid flows away clear; the first milkiness being caused by the soluble carbonates and chlorides in the water precipitating the nitrate of silver. Ten minutes in water running slowly from a tap will be sufficient to cleanse a print from nitrate of silver; or three or four changes in a dish, pouring off quite dry between each change. It is an advantage to finish off with a solution of salt (2 grs. to the oz.) Pour the toning bath out into a flat dish, and put the prints into it 2 or 3 at a time, waving the dish meanwhile backwards and forwards to secure a constant movement. Continue to keep the prints moving, and watch the changes in color.

If the prints are removed as soon as the blue color of the gold is seen, they will usually change in the fixing bath to a warm shade of brown; but when left for 2 or 3 minutes longer in the toning bath, the darker tint becomes permanent.

Fixing.

One oz. of hyposulphite of soda dissolved in 6 oz. of water would fix two batches of stereoscopic prints, 20 in each batch. Allow the prints to remain in the fixing bath for 20 minutes, with occasional movement, after which they may be transferred to a dish of clean water.

Washing.

It is essential to wash out every trace of hyposulphite of soda from the print, if it is to be preserved from fading, and to do this properly requires care.

Always wash with running water when it can be obtained, and choose a large shallow vessel exposing a considerable surface in preference to one of lesser diameter. A constant dribbling of water must be maintained for 4 or 5 hours, and the prints should not lie together too closely, or the water will not find its way between them.

When the prints have been thoroughly washed, blot them off between sheets of porous paper and hang them up to dry.

Mounting.

Mount the proofs with a solution of gelatine in hot water, freshly made; gum-water, prepared from the finest commercial gum, and free from acidity, may also be used, but it should be made very thick, so as not to sink into the paper, or produce "cockling up" of the cardboard on drying.

Positive Printing by Development.

Negative printing processes will be found useful during the dull winter months, and at other times when the light is feeble, or where it is required to produce a large number of impressions from a negative in a short space of time. The proofs, however, as thus obtained, are not equal to direct sun-prints in beauty and gradation of tone.

Take of iodide of potassium, 120 grs.; bromide of ammonium, 30 grs.; water, 20 oz.

Float the paper on the iodizing bath until it ceases to curl up, and lies flat upon the liquid; then pin up to dry in the usual way.

Render sensitive upon a bath of aceto-nitrate of silver, containing 30 grs. of nitrate of silver with 30 minims of glacial acetic acid to each oz. of water.

Place the dried sheets in contact with the negative in a pressure frame, and expose to a *feeble light*. About 30 seconds will be an average time upon a dull winter's day, when it would be impossible to paint in the ordinary way. Develop by immersion in a saturated solution of gallic acid. After the picture is fully brought out, wash in cold and subsequently in warm water, to remove the gallic acid, which, if allowed to remain, would discolor the hyposulphite bath. Fix the print in a solution of hyposulphite of soda, one part to two of water, continuing the action until the yellow color of the iodide disappears. Wash thoroughly in plenty of water.

Negative Printing Process upon Chloride of Silver.

To salt the papers, prepare the following solution: Chloride of ammonium, 100 grs.; citric acid, 56 grs.; sesquicarbonate of soda, 66 grs.; gelatine, 40 grs.; distilled water, 20 oz. Float the sheets for 1 minute; render sensitive upon a bath of aceto-nitrate of silver. Take of nitrate of silver, 30 grs.; glacial acetic acid, 30 minims; water, 1 oz. Float the papers upon this bath for 3 minutes, and suspend them to dry. The exposure to light is conducted in the ordinary printing frame.

The developing solution is prepared as follows: Gallic acid, 2 grs.; water, 1 oz. Filter through blotting-paper, to remove floating particles, which would produce spots in this process; pour the solution of gallic acid into a flat dish, and immerse the prints, 2 or 3 at a time, moving them about, and using a glass rod to remove air-bubbles; wash the prints for several minutes in 1 or 2 changes of water, in order to extract the gallic acid; tone in bath of chloride of gold and phosphate of soda; fix in hyposulphite, and wash.

RUSSELL'S TANNIN PROCESS, MODIFIED.
Cleaning the Plate.

In order to clean the plates, make a stock solution of 2 oz. of bichromate of potash, 2 oz. of sulphuric acid, and 1 qt. of water (a green quart wine-bottle may be used). Pour the solution into a shallow tray; soak in it the plates to be cleansed, and afterwards wash the plates in water and dry them; then pour on each plate a small quantity of old collodion; rub it all over the plate with a tuft of cotton, and then clean it off with a dry linen cloth. It will perfect the cleaning if the plate be dipped in pure water and again dried with a clean linen cloth. The bichromate of potash solution may be filtered back into the bottle for future use.

To Coat the Plate.

1. Cover the plate with a bromised collodion. Take care, in all cases, gently to oscillate on running off the excess of collodion, or white marks, visible in a subsequent stage of the process, will be formed.
2. When the film is somewhat fixed, put the plate, by the aid of a dipper, in a well-bath of a 50 gr. nitrate of silver solution, and let it remain in the solution 10 minutes.
3. Put the plate in a well-bath of distilled water until what are called the "greasy" marks disappear.
4. Put the plate in a well-bath of a 10 gr. solution of bromide of ammonium, or cadmium, or magnesium, or of potassium. It may be best to adopt that bromide which enters into the preparation of the collodion. Let the plate remain in this solution about 1 minute. Occasionally filter this bath solution, in order to remove the excess of bromide of silver which is deposited in the bath. Keep a stock bottle of this bromide solution to supply the waste drippings.
5. Put the plate for a short time in a well-bath of distilled water.
6. Wipe the back of the plate, and let it drain for a short time, and then place it in a well-bath of 10 or 15 grs. of tannin to the oz. of distilled water; let the plate remain in this solution 4 or 5 minutes, and then, on removing it from this bath, let it rest on one end, to dry. When dry, it is ready for the camera, and it will keep a long time. It should be rapidly and evenly dried, and a stone bottle of hot water may be so used as to hasten the drying. Tannin which dissolves most easily in water, is to be preferred. Add to the tannin-bath 3 or 4 drops of creosote, and it will keep clear. A little experience will show how long a time the plate must be exposed to light in the camera. It will be best, in the beginning, not to make a very short exposure; harsh pictures are the result of long exposures, and soft pictures of short exposures to the light. These plates will bear a considerable amount of exposure in the camera without being fogged—even for 10 minutes.

Developing.

1. The film sometimes appears to be in a rotten state, and to crack up when water is poured on it. This will not happen if a small quantity of alcohol be added to the water solution first poured over it.
2. Take a solution of 2 grs. to the oz. of water of carbonate of ammonia; add to it some alcohol, and flush the plate with it; pour this off into a glass, and add to it from ½ gr. to 1 gr. of pyrogallic acid, in solution, and pour it back again on the plate. This picture will instantly appear, and the details may be allowed to come out well. The image will not be dark.
3. Pour off the alkaline pyro-solution, and gently wash the plate; add a few drops of citric acid (1 or two grs. of citric acid to the oz. of distilled water): pour it over the plate, and run off; or pour an acid pyro-solution over the plate instead of acid solution alone. Again gently pour distilled water on the plate, and run it off.
4. It will be found to be convenient to dissolve 1 dr. of pyrogallic acid in 1 oz. of alcohol, and to add to this 1 oz. of distilled water. Use 1 dr. graduate, and 16 minims of this solution will give 1 gr. of pyrogallic acid; also have a 2 oz. bottle of distilled water and dissolve in it 2 drs. of citric acid; 8 minims of this will be 1 gr. of citric acid. Have also an oz. bottle of a 10 gr. solution of nitrate of silver: and lastly, have at hand a pint bottle of distilled water, 1 or 2 glass oz. graduates, and 3 or 4 developing-glasses, which hold about a fluidounce.
5. The development of a plate is completed by solutions of ½ gr. to 1 gr. of pyrogallic acid, and 1 gr. or more of citric acid to the oz. of water, and the addition of 1 drop to 3, 4, or more of the 10 gr. nitrate of silver solution. If the picture is strongly out when the ammonia is washed off, let it be dosed with an excess of acid silver; if feeble, let an excess of pyrogallic acid be used. If there be a sign of fogging when pushing the development with an excess of nitrate of silver, immediately pour off the developer, gently wash the plate and flush it with the 8 gr. bromide solution. The image, as it at first shows its strength or weakness, very soon teaches the manner in which the plate is to be dealt with.

Lastly. Gently wash the plate, fix the image with a strong solution of hyposulphite of soda, and, when the picture is "cleared," wash it with distilled or common water, and dry it.

The three steps which have made the tannin process of Major Russell simple, clean, and certain, are: First, the use of the bromide bath; second, the use of the tannin bath, and third, the use of the acid solution, either alone or mixed with pyrogallic acid, after the alkaline solution of carbonate of ammonia has been washed off, not forgetting the mixture of some alcohol with the first application of water to the film on the development.

FOTHERGILL'S DRY PROCESS.

The directions for coating and dipping in the bath are the same as for "Russell's Process." After removing the stereoscopic plate from the nitrate bath, stand it vertically on blotting paper and allow it to drain as long as it would be required for a wet plate, wiping the back meanwhile in the usual manner.

Then take it in the left hand, either by one corner or with the pneumatic holder, and having arranged the yellow light so that it falls nicely upon the surface of the film, hold it quite level and pour on ½ oz. of water, waving it backwards and forwards. It should not be poured on entirely at one spot, or too much of the nitrate of silver would be displaced, producing a circular mark of imperfect development. As, however, a vacant space of a quarter of an inch in breadth is usually allowed at each end of a stereoscopic plate, this will be found convenient for pouring on the water, which must be allowed to run into each corner until greasiness has disappeared. It will probably touch the fingers by which the plate is held, and when they are not scrupulously clean, stains will, in consequence, result. After pouring away the water (which ought then to measure at least 3 drs. if the operation was well performed), drain the plate for an instant, and it will be ready for the albumen.

The Albumen Solution.

Take the white of a fresh egg and add to it 1 oz. of distilled water with 3 drops of strong ammonia. Shake for 10 minutes in a bottle, and pour out the liquid on a filter previously wetted. Apply the filtered albumen twice or thrice to the film in the same manner as collodion. Then pour water over the plate for a minute, in order to remove the excess of albumen, and afterwards rear the glass on end to drain upon blotting paper. When the plates are perfectly dry they are ready for exposure.

Development.

This process is not quick as regards development. When pyrogallic acid is used, each drachm of the liquid is previously mixed with about 5 minims of a solution of nitrate of silver, containing 20 grains to the oz. of water. The film is wetted and the mixed developer poured on and off from a glass measure.

Fix with hyposulphite of soda.

TAUPENOT'S COLLODIO-ALBUMEN PROCESS.

Cleaning the Glasses.

This part of the process must be conducted with care.

Sensitizing and Washing.

Employ 2 nitrate baths in this process, one for the collodion and the other for the second film, viz. the albumen. The albumen nitrate bath must contain free acetic acid, and therefore if one solution be employed for both films it should be a bath of aceto-nitrate.

Sensitize the collodion in the ordinary way, holding it rather longer than usual before dipping.

Having arranged 2 dishes of common water, side by side, lay the plate face uppermost in the first dish, and wave the water backwards and forwards for about 30 seconds. Then put the plate into the second dish and leave it whilst another glass is being coated and immersed in the sensitizing bath. Now drain plate No. 1 closely on blotting-paper, and it will be ready for the iodized albumen. Plate No. 2 remains in the sensitizing bath until the first glass has been coated with albumen and placed to dry.

Preparation of the Iodized Albumen.

Take of albumen, 3 oz.; distilled water, 1 oz.; strong ammonia, 10 minims; iodide of potassium, 10 grs.; bromide of ammonium, 10 grs.

First mix the ammonia and the water, then add the other ingredients and shake together in a bottle. Iodide of ammonium may be advantageously used.

To Apply the Albumen.

For a stereoscopic size, measure out 1 dr. of the albumen and pour it on and off twice to displace the surface water of the washed collodion film. Then apply a second quantity.

Stand the albuminized plates vertically on blotting-paper to drain and dry.

The Aceto-nitrate Bath.

Take an ordinary collodion negative bath and add to each fluidounce 30 minims of glacial acetic acid, keep it in glass or gutta percha and continue to use it until it has become blackened by the action of the albumen. The film of albumen must be rendered quite dry by holding it to the fire before it is dipped in the aceto-nitrate bath. Leave them in the bath any time between 30 seconds and 2 minutes, and then remove the wash with water. Use two dishes for washing and allow 20 or 30 seconds in each dish; then rear up again to dry, and the plates will be ready for exposure. Artificial heat may be used with advantage.

The most successful operators in Taupenot's process give a very long exposure.

Development.

Prepare a saturated solution of gallic acid in distilled water, adding 4 grs. to each oz. Filter this developer through paper.

The solution of nitrate of silver for use with the gallic acid may be made of the strength of 20 grs. to the ounce.

Add 15 minims to 1 oz. of gallic acid solution. Previous to the application of the developer the surface of the film must be moistened with water. From half an hour to an hour must be allowed for the full development with gallic acid. Fix with a saturated solution of hyposulphite.

PICTURES ON PORCELAIN.

The plates for these pictures are sold as porcelain, but are really an opaque white glass. The plate is coated with collodion, rendered sensitive in the usual way, and the image received from a negative adjusted as follows:

The negative is placed at one end of a box, the other end of which joins the front end of a camera having a quarter tube. The object of this box is to cut off extraneous light. The negative is placed toward the sun, or a piece of white paper placed in the sun. The image formed by the negative is focussed on the ground glass of the camera, in the usual manner. The box in front should admit of being varied in length, in order to alter the size of the picture, by changing the distance of the negative from the lens.

The white sensitive plate is then exposed and developed with the ordinary iron developer. After washing off with the developer, fix with a weak solution of cyanide of potassium.

The picture requires to be darkened with a weak solution of bichloride of mercury, chloride of gold, or chloride of platinum. As soon as the picture appears of the proper shade arrest the action of the strenghthening agent, by washing the plate under a copious stream of water.

THE WOTHLYTYPE PROCESS.

I. To Prepare the Uranic Salt.

Dissolve the ordinary commercial nitrate of uranium in distilled water; add ammonia till no more precipitate is formed. This precipitate is uranate of ammonia, insoluble in water. Wash in several waters, and then redissolve in nitric acid. The solution, crystallized and dried over a water-bath, constitutes the "uranammonium nitrium" of the specification, and is probably a double salt of uranium and ammonia. If it be very acid, dissolve in distilled water and again crystallize.

II. *The Sensitizing Liquor.*

To a saturated solution of the above salt in 6 oz. of distilled water add 220 grs. of nitrate of silver, previously dissolved in 1 oz. of distilled water, and intimately mix. This mixture, when crystallized over a water-bath, is the salt used to sensitize the collodion. It may be kept in a bottle, but not necessarily in a dark place, because it is only sensitive to light when brought into contact with organic substances.

Dissolve 3 oz. of this salt in 10 oz. of alcohol, to which 5 drs. of distilled water and a few drops of nitric acid have been added. This is the sensitizing liquor, and does not require to be kept in the dark.

III. *Preparation of the Resinized Collodion.*

The collodion may be the ordinary plain preparation, containing about 5½ grs. pyroxyline (not powdery) to the ounce of ether and alcohol, mixed in the proportion of 6 to 2; but, in order to give it an organic reaction with the sensitizing salt, it is necessary to add to each pint of the collodion about 10 drops of so-called "harz oel," which is thus prepared: Take equal parts of castor oil and Canada balsam; dissolve the latter in sufficient ether to enable it, when mixed with the castor oil, to pass through a filter. After filtration, evaporate the mixture over a water-bath till it is of the ordinary consistence of a fatty oil. The collodion is now ready for being sensitized.

IV. *To Sensitize the Resinized Collodion.*

To every 3 oz. of the collodion thus prepared add from 1 to 1½ oz. of the sensitizing solution, with a few drops of nitric acid, and intimately mix. The collodion is now sensitive to light, and must be kept in the dark.

V. *Sizing of the Paper.*

This is an important preliminary to prevent the image from sinking into the body of the paper. It is effected either by a tolerably strong solution of starch, Iceland or Irish moss, beaten up with about one-eighth its bulk of albumen and a few grains of acetate of lead. The paper may be floated on this in the usual way, and when dry is ready for the reception of the sensitive collodion.

VI. *Applying the Collodion.*

The paper is pinned down by 3 of its corners to a flat board, a little larger than the sheet to be collodionized. The collodion is poured on in the usual way, and the excess run off at the unpinned corner into the stock-bottle. This may be done with great deliberation, and more may be poured on to any part, where there is a deficiency, without much chance of its running in ridges, as would inevitably be the case if a glass plate were so treated. Hang up to dry in a dark room, and it is fit for the printing-frame.

VII. *Preliminary Fixing.*

When the picture is printed to the proper strength, that is to say, to the depth which it is wished finally to retain—for uranic-developed pictures lose very slightly in the toning and fixing process—place it in a bath containing distilled water 40 oz., acetic acid 1 oz., and hydrochloric acid 1 oz., for the space of 10 minutes. The object of this bath is to remove the uranic salts insoluble in water. The prints are afterwards washed in several waters before being placed in the toning solution.

VIII. *Toning the Pictures.*

The ordinary alkaline gold-bath answers very satisfactorily, and tones uranic prints much more rapidly than similar prints on chlorized paper.

IX. *Fixing the Proofs.*

If the picture be toned in hyposulphite of soda and gold no further fixing will be necessary; but if in the usual alkaline gold-bath, they will have to pass through a hyposulphite or sulphocyanide solution, to remove the silver salts insoluble in water. When thoroughly washed the process is complete.

PHOTOGRAPHY WITHOUT A NITRATE OF SILVER BATH. (*Sayce's process.*)

Preparation of Collodion.

Take of bromide of cadmium, 6 grs.; bromide of ammonium, 2 grs.; soluble cotton, 6 grs.; ether and alcohol, each, ½ oz. Mix, and after standing a week, filter. Then take 12 grs. cryst. nitrate of silver, in fine powder; add to it a drop or two of water, so as to produce a kind of pulp. Then in a chemically dark room, mix the collodion and silver, stirring as the mixture is poured into the bottle intended for its reception. Then shake up well, and allow it to stand.

To use the Collodion in the Wet State.

Take perfectly clean plate-glass, free from scratches; tip the edges for ⅛ of an inch with a solution of 1 gr. of India-rubber in 1 oz. of benzine. Then coat with the collodio-bromide of silver, allow it to set the usual time, and place it in a dish of water until the greasy appearance has vanished. Warm water is preferable when it can be procured. When the water flows freely over the film, take the plate out of the dish, wipe the back, and drain for a moment upon a piece of blotting-paper. Then place in the dark slide for exposure in the camera. Expose a little longer than wet collodion, with the nitrate-bath. Wet the film with a little water, and pour over it protosulphate of iron, 25 grs.; glacial acetic acid, 25 minims; water, 1 oz. To 3 drs. of which, 2 drops of a 20 gr. solution of nitrate of silver. Fix with cyanide of potassium, 20 grs. to the oz. Intensification may be accomplished by any of the means adapted to wet plates.

To use the Collodio-Bromide in the Preparation of Tannin Plates.

Coat the plates as directed in the last paragraph, and place them in a tank of water. Take the plates out of the tank in rotation, and place them in water as hot as the hand can bear, for about 30 seconds, and then into a bath of green solution of 15 grs. to the ounce of water well filtered. The following tannin solution is preferable: Tannin, 10 grs.; gallic acid, 5 grs.; water, 1 oz.; grape sugar, 5 grs.; alcohol, 10 minims. Dissolve the tannin in a portion of the water and filter; dissolve the gallic acid in another portion by the aid of heat, and filter; mix the two, add the grape sugar, and when dissolved, filter; then add the alcohol. If the plate be allowed to remain in the above solution three minutes, and is properly exposed, very little intensification will be necessary. Dry the plates evenly and quickly, and expose about half the usual time.

Development of the Dry Plates.

Prepare the following solutions: 1. Alcohol and water, each, ½ oz.
2. Carbonate of ammonia, 40 grs. to water, 20 oz.
3. Pyrogallic acid, 96 grs. to alcohol, 1 oz.
4. Bromide of potassium, 10 grs. to water, 1 oz.
5. Nitrate of silver, 30 grs.; citric acid, 15 grs.; distilled water, 1 oz.

Pour over the dry plate once or twice, enough of No. 1 to cover it, and return to the bottle for use in the next plate. Then place the plate in a dish of water until the greasy appearance has vanished. Then pour evenly, enough of No. 2 with a few drops of No. 3 and two drops of No. 4 added, and wave to and fro with a rocking motion.

The image should very soon appear, and may be developed until the shadows become slightly tinged. Then wash the surface and back of the plate freely with water, and rinse with a little very dilute acetic acid; suy 2 drops of glacial acid to the ounce. Wash again, and if any intensification is required, it may be accomplished by adding to 2 drs. of water 3 drops of No. 3 and 3 of No. 5 solution. When dense enough, wash and fix with cyanide, 20 grs. to the ounce of water.

FAILURES AND IMPERFECTIONS.
On Glass.

1. *Universal clouding* from over exposure or diffused light in preparation or development of the plate, or alkalinity of the bath, or too much nitric acid i'' bath, or organic matter in the bath, or the use t. colorless collodion; also vapors of ammonia or sulphuretted hydrogen. Such negatives may sometimes be recovered by the application of a weak solution of iodine, followed by hyposulphite of soda.

2. *Spots upon the plate* from excess of bromide of potassium in the collodion, impure nitrate of silver in the bath, super-saturation of the bath with iodide of silver, dust upon the glass or coating, the concentration of nitrate of silver by drying before exposure.

3. *Curtain-like marks* upon the edge, from the plate being too dry before dipping, not long enough in the bath to remove the greasy appearance.

4. *Wavy lines*, from the use of a glutinous, thick collodion from want of rocking when pouring off the collodion (common with cadmium sensitigus).

5. *Rottenness of film*, from bad cotton or dipping too soon after proving before properly set.

6. *Oily lines*, from the removal from the bath too soon.

7. *Curved lines*, from the developer not covering the whole plate immediately.

8. *Silver stains*, from reversing the plate between the bath and slide.

9. *Yellow patches*, imperfect removal of the iodide of silver in the fixing bath.

10. *Scum upon the surface* upon removal from the bath, over iodized collodion.

11. *Image black and white* without half tones, from under-exposure in the camera.

12. *Collodion curls from the glass* upon drying, from dirty glass, insufficient alcohol in the collodion, want of roughness of the edges of the glass.

13. *Blueness of film*, want of iodizer in collodion.

14. *Crystals on film* when dried, hyposulphite not washed entirely out.

15. *Developer flows greasily*, from want of alcohol in developer.

16. *Circular transparent spots* of large size, from pouring on the developer at one place.

On Paper.

1. *Marbling and spots*, from weak nitrate-bath.
2. *Marbling after toning*, from the prints overlying each other.
3. *Spots by transmitted light*, from imperfect removal of the silver salt.
4. *Cold and faded appearance*, from weakness of bath or excess of chloride in paper.
5. *Yellowness*, from acidity of bath.
6. *Bronzing* of deep shadows, negative is too transparent.

RECOVERY OF SILVER AND GOLD FROM WASTE SOLUTIONS.
Baths of Nitrate.

Throw down the silver as a chloride by muriatic acid; settle, pour off the clear part, and wash the precipitate; place the chloride in a dish, together with some bars of zinc, and pour over it sulphuric acid largely diluted with water (1 of acid to 60 of water). As soon as it ceases to give off gas add more acid until the zinc is entirely dissolved. Should any chloride remain add more zinc and acid. The gray powder is metallic silver, and may be run into a ingot in a crucible by mixing with twice its weight of carbonate of soda or borax.

Hyposulphite Baths.

Boil for several hours with a suspended bar of zinc, filter out the precipitate, and fuse with carbonate of soda or borax. The button contains silver and gold if the solution has been used to tone and fix prints.

Toning Baths (Alkaline).

Add a solution of sulphate of iron, filter out and wash the precipitate; digest with diluted nitric acid for several hours; filter out the residue, which is metallic gold.

All *waste solutions*, containing silver, in the laboratory should be run into a large vessel, and acidulated with muriatic acid every evening, and the clear liquid siphoned off in the morning; the precipitates will be principally chloride of silver, and when enough has accumulated it should be removed from the vessel, and reduced, as advised for baths of nitrate of silver.

Paper Clippings.

The clippings of sensitized paper should be preserved, and when a quantity has accumulated burned to ashes; the ashes to be in a crucible, mixed with twice their weight of a mixture of carbonate of soda and borax. If carefully brought to a full red heat, and allowed to cool, the silver will be found collected into an ingot at the bottom of the crucible. It is best to trim the prints before washing or toning, but the whole of the cuttings are worth saving.

Removal of Silver Stains.

1. By rubbing with a moistened lump of cyanide of potassium, and washing freely with water. This mode is dangerous, on account of the highly poisonous nature of the cyanide.

2. By rubbing the spot with moistened iodide of potassium, then with diluted nitric acid, and then with hyposulphite of soda, and washing with water.

3. Apply a paste of chloride of lime for a few minutes, wash thoroughly with water; rub with moistened iodide of potassium, and dissolve out the iodide of silver formed by hyposulphite of soda.

4. *For Linen or other Fabrics.*—Rub with solution : Cyanide of potassium, 100 grs.; iodine, 10 grs.; water, 1 oz.; (very poisonous;) and wash with large amount of water.

TOOVELY'S (PATENT) PHOTOLITHOGRAPHIC PROCESS.

From a negative on glass or paper a positive impression is taken on paper prepared in the following manner: Take sized paper, very smooth and even in texture, which coat with a solution of gum Arabic in pure water, saturated with bichromate of potash; it is known that bichromate of potash, in combination with an organic substance, such as gum, gelatine and starch, becomes insoluble in water after a certain exposure to light. The paper, prepared as above, is then exposed to light behind a negative, and when the photographic image is sufficiently developed, such parts of the gum impregnated with bichromate of potash as receive the rays of light become insoluble, or partly so, exactly according to the gradation of tone in the negative employed. The sheet of prepared paper, with the photographic image thus printed, is placed face downwards on a lithographic stone, grained very fine, or polished according to the nature of the image to be reproduced, and previously arranged in a percussion-press (it can be done in a lithographic press, but the result is uncertain). Place several sheets of damped paper upon the stone over the photographic proof, and apply a heavy pressure; the water contained in the damp paper is pressed through the photographic proof, and dissolves the parts of gum remaining at liberty; the dissolved gum attaches itself to the surface of the stone. When the stone has remained a certain length of time in the press, sufficient to allow the small quantity of soluble gum in the dark shadows to attach itself to the surface of the stone remove the pressure, and withdraw the photographic proof carefully from the stone; a negative image is then visible in gum on the stone, with all the gradations of tone. Dry the stone, either spontaneously or by gently warming it; when well dried, cover the whole surface of the stone with greasy ink, which may be applied with a roller or otherwise; the greasy ink is thus brought into contact with all the parts of the stone untouched by gum; the coating of ink is then removed by passing through the lithographic press, by spirits of turpentine or otherwise, and all the gum removed from the surface by washing. The stone is then rolled in with ordinary printing-ink, and the positive image appears in black; it is then printed as every lithographic drawing, but has the great peculiarity of requiring no etching, the gum having so far penetrated by pressure into the substance of the stone as to allow of a great number of impressions being taken off. Gum Arabic is preferable, but similar substances can be used instead, such as gelatine, dextrine, and mucilaginous solutions.

In photozincography proceed as above described, substituting a zinc plate for a lithographic stone.

In photographic engraving on copper, steel or other metal plates, the preliminary operations are the same as those employed for stone or zinc, excepting that a positive image on glass or paper should, in the first instance, be used instead of a negative. When the plate is withdrawn from the press, and the photographic proof detached from it, it should be well dried for the stone. The plate is then covered with a thin coating of varnish, and when dry may be soaked in water to remove the gum, or immediately plunged in a weak solution of acid, and etched in the usual way of etching on steel or copper.

Wherever the plate is protected from the varnish by the gum it will be attacked by the acid, and an engraving is produced, which is then printed as an ordinary etching on metal plate.

OSBORNE'S (PATENT) PHOTOLITHOGRAPHIC PROCESS.

Let us suppose that a map has been compiled and drawn with great care, and that it is desired to multiply copies of this original in the lithographic process. The first step in the process is to obtain a negative; for which purpose the map is placed upright upon a plane-board, and the camera opposite to it at such a distance as to give the desired ratio between original and copy. A negative is now taken on glass coated with collodion in the usual way, observing the greatest care to avoid distortion of all kinds, and to produce a negative of the highest excellence, success in which depends entirely upon the knowledge, judgment and experience of the operator. A sheet of plain, positive photographic paper is now coated on one side with a mixture, consisting of gelatine, softened and dissolved in water, to which a quantity of bichromate of potash and albumen has been added. The paper, evenly covered with this fluid, is dried in the dark, when it will be found possessed of a smooth glassy surface, and a bright yellow color. This surface is still further improved by passing it through the press in contact with a polished plate.

A suitable piece of positive photolithographic paper thus manufactured is now to be exposed to the action of the light under the negative of the map already described. This is accomplished in an ordinary pressure-frame, the time required varying from 10 to 15 seconds, or several minutes, according to the brightness of the weather. The positive thus obtained presents itself to the eye as a brown drawing upon the clear yellow of the sheet.

The exposed photographic copy of the original is covered all over, while dry, with transfer-ink, which is accomplished by running it through the press with its face in contact with a stone which has already received a coating of such ink. After it is separated from the blackened stone it will be found to have brought away with it an evenly distributed film of inky matter, forced by the pressure into intimate contact with the unexposed, as well as the exposed portion of the surface. This operation is known as "blacking" the positive print; that now to be described is called "congulation," its object being to effect a change of that nature upon the albumen contained in the coating of the organic matter. For this purpose moisture and heat are necessary, and both are applied very simply, by letting the blackened photographic copy swim upon the surface of boiling water with its inky side upwards, for it is important not to wet that with hot water. After the lapse of a certain period, determined by the experience of the operator, he proceeds to the next step in the process, that of "washing off." For this purpose the print is laid upon a smooth surface, such as a plate of glass or porcelain, and friction with a wet sponge, or other suitable material, is applied to the black inky coating, under which the photographic image still exists, and to develop which is now the object in view. The operator soon becomes aware that the moisture which percolated through the paper from the back, has exerted a softened or gelatinizing influence upon the gelatine in the sensitive coating; it has caused it to swell, and to let go its hold upon the ink. But this change does not extend to those parts of the coating which were acted on by light; in other words, to those places which were unprotected by the opacity of the negative; they remain intact, uninfluenced by the solvent or moistening effect of the water. Accordingly the operator finds a fac-simile of the original map gradually develop under his hand as he continues the friction. This process is proceeded with until all traces of ink are removed, save those required to form the picture, which must be clear and distinct in all its details. Abundance of hot water is then poured over it, so as to remove every particle of soluble matter, and it is then finally dried, which completes its preparation.

A stone to which a fine smooth surface has been imparted, is now slightly warmed, and put in the lithographic press; upon this is placed (inverted) the positive print, after it has been damped by lying between moist paper, and the whole is then passed repeatedly through the press. On examination the paper will now be found to have attached itself firmly to the stone, so that some force is required to separate the two. When the former is removed it brings with it its albuminous coating, which gives to it while damp a parchment-like appearance; but the ink is gone: it has left the paper for the stone, and on the latter we find a reversed drawing of the map, one which, after it has been properly "prepared," will print as well as if it had been drawn by hand.

PRETSCH'S PROCESS OF PHOTO-GALVANOGRAPHY.

Take a plate of glass, and spread on it ordinary glue, to which bichromate of potash and a small quantity of nitrate of silver has been added. For instance, take 2 or 3 solutions of glue, into one of which put a little nitrate of silver, into another bichromate of potash, and into another iodide of potassium. The silver and the iodide are for the purpose of producing a little iodide of silver on the sensitive film, so as to produce on the picture that grain which is necessary for holding the ink in the process of printing. Take the photographic picture obtained by any of the customary processes, and place it on the sensitive plate thus prepared and exposed to the action of the light. In the course of a short time (all those parts which are dark in the photograph, protecting the plate from change, and all those which are white, allowing the sunlight freely to pass through and the change to take place), we have a combination of bichromate of potash and gelatine in two different states, one soluble and the other insoluble. Consequently, when the plate is then put into water all the parts which remain soluble are dissolved out, whilst the other parts remain as they were, and we have the picture produced not only in different lights and shades, but also in different depths, the solution being eaten into by the process. When the plate is prepared to this point, there is poured upon it a preparation of gutta-percha, which, being kept under pressure for a short time, receives the reverse image of the photographic picture. This is now prepared for the voltaic battery by being simply rubbed over with fine black lead, and it being placed in connection with the trough, copper is precipitated on the plate, which receives an image the reverse of the mould. Then by the ordinary electrotype process another plate may be obtained, from which copies may be printed.

ENGRAVING.

The different modes of engraving are the following:

1. In strokes cut through a thin wax, laid upon the plate, with a point, and these strokes bitten or corroded into the plate with acid. This is called *etching*.
2. In strokes with the graver alone, unassisted by acid. In this instance, the design is traced with a sharp tool, called a *dry point*, upon the plate, and the strokes are cut or ploughed upon the copper with an instrument distinguished by the name of a *graver*.
3. In mezzotinto, which is performed by a dark ground raised uniformly upon the plate with a toothed tool.
4. In aquatinta, the outline is first etched, and afterwards a sort of wash is laid by the acid upon the plate, resembling drawings in Indian-ink, bistre, etc.
5. On wood.
6. Lithography.

Etching.

Etching is a method of working on copper or steel, wherein the lines or strokes, instead of being cut with a graver, are eaten with acid.

Materials, etc.

The principal materials for this art are, the copper or steel-plate, hard and soft ground (the first for winter, and the other for summer), a dabber, turpentine-varnish, lampblack, soft wax, and aqua-fortis.

The tools are an oil-rubber, a burnisher, a scraper, a hand-vice, etching-boards, etching-needles, an oil stone, and a parallel ruler.

LINE ENGRAVING.

So called because the result is produced by a combination of lines of various sizes, forms, lengths and textures, is the most beautiful and useful style of multiplying copies of works of art. All other modes are only efforts at lessening cost, not of excelling in quality. In producing a plate upon this principle, cutting with the graver, etching with the point, and biting or corroding with acids, are the ordinary means employed. This combination of chemical and mechanical together with the artistic, is universal in line engraving. Gravers are of various shapes; those most useful, however, are the lozenge and square. With lines laid in and cut up with this tool, it is useful to represent drapery, hair, flesh, in fact all that pertains to human figure, while with lines slightly cut into the metal through an etching ground, bitten with acid and finished with the assistance of the graver, that kind of line and character of manipulation best calculated to represent landscape, architecture, animals, etc., is obtained. As the steel point with which the etching is done is used much in the manner of a pen or lead-pencil, an ease, freedom and disposition of line is secured, which cannot result from the use of the graver alone. The burnisher is also an important tool, as by a skilled use of this instrument much of the delicacy and tenderness which characterizes a well finished line engraving, is obtained. The scraper is principally used to free the lines made by the other tools from the burr, or roughness which accompanies their application. It is intended in this article to treat of engraving on steel. Copper is now seldom used, but the remarks and instructions, except in so far as biting is concerned, are equally applicable to both. Nitrous acid diluted with water is the medium of corroding copper; nitric diluted with acetic, or even with water, is used for steel. The plates, properly prepared, can be obtained of the manufacturers.

Solid Etching-ground

Is composed of burgundy pitch, 3 parts; asphaltum, 3 parts; beeswax, 1½ parts. Increase the wax in proportion to the desired softness: when thoroughly melted by heat, pour into hot water, and work into balls of convenient size.

ENGRAVING.

Liquid Ground.

Take a ball of etching ground, break it in pieces of convenient size, place them in a bottle, and pour on sulphuric ether. If too thick, add ether; if too thin, take the cork out until it evaporates to proper consistency.

To Lay a Solid Ground.

Put a ball of ground into a piece of silk; make a dabber with a circular piece of pasteboard from 2 to 3 in. in diameter, and a pad of wadding on one surface about 1 inch in thickness, tied in a piece of kid-skin or good smooth silk, disposed evenly over this on the under side. Clean the surface of the plate thoroughly with whiting or air-slaked lime; attach in hand-vice; heat the plate until hot enough to boil spittle on the back; rub the ground evenly over the surface required, and use the dabber to distribute it smoothly. If the plate has cooled, heat again to former temperature, then turning the ground downwards, with a lighted candle or taper moved slowly back and forth, as near the surface as may be without touching the ground with the wick, smoke it till sufficiently black. Carefully avoid dust during the whole operation.

To lay Liquid Ground.

Clean the surface of the plate, first with turpentine, then a clean rag and whiting; take an ordinary etching dabber, or make a small ball with raw cotton, cover it with a piece of silk velvet, carefully drawn tight to avoid creases, then dip the dabber in the liquid or pour it on the plate and draw and streak it quickly and evenly; the evaporation of the ether leaves a clear, firm ground.

To Transfer the Outline to the Surface.

Various plans are used. If the design to be copied be the size to engrave, the outline may be traced with a pencil on a piece of oil-paper laid over it. This tracing may be transferred by laying it upon the ground, and while damp passing it through the printing press with a piece of damp printing paper laid over it. It may also be retraced upon the ground by laying between the tracing and plate a piece of thin paper, coated on the under side with vermilion or black-lead, and going carefully over the outline with a blunt point, or lead-pencil.

A better plan is to use gelatine paper. Trace the outline on this article with a sharp point, cutting into it; scrape off the raised edges from the lines with a smooth scraper; then fill the cuts with vermilion or black-lead; carefully wipe off the superfluous dust; lay in proper position, fix down with wax, and, while slightly damp, pass it through the printing press, or with the gelatine dry burnish over the back sufficiently firm to set off the outline, taking care not to break the ground. The best and most recent mode is to get a daguerreotype of the design, the requisite size; cut cleanly and smoothly with a sharp point into the copper over all the outline; this done, remove all the raised edges with the scraper, and get an impression from the copper. While this is still damp place it on the ground and pass it through the press. If the impression has been taken with red ink, the outline will at once appear; if in black, pass a hair-pencil dipped in vermilion lightly over the ground, which must be first freed from damp, so that the vermilion may adhere only to the oil from the impression.

Etching.

Fix down with wax, strips of wood or leather about ⅜ in. thick upon the margin. The best and most useful point, is a good stub small round file. Set it true in a tube, such as are used for handles for parasols; grind off the cutting, and smooth on an oil-stone. The point must be sharpened by rolling it between the palms of the hands, keeping the point on the stone; when once set, it can be easily put in order, by holding it in the right hand, and, while causing it to rotate between the thumb and second finger, draw it smoothly down upon a piece of fine emery paper until the point is perfectly round and sharp, extreme sharpness being undesirable. Hold the point nearly perpendicular between the finger and thumb, draw it without pressure, gently over the emery. The examination of a good specimen of the art will give the best idea of the necessary width, style, etc. As a general rule, the more distant parts are etched close, and the space between the lines should increase, as the approach is made forward. Sufficient pressure must be exerted to cut well into the steel, yet not enough to impede an easy motion. Cut with a steady and equal pressure, so that the lines may all present the same color to the eye, as all inequalities show when bitten.

Biting Hard Steel.

The etching completed, carefully cover the unetched surface of the plate with stopping-out varnish, composed of asphaltum dissolved in turpentine, or gum resins, or good sealing-wax, dissolved in alcohol. When dry, form a well around the work, of walling wax, composed of beeswax and burgundy pitch, equal parts dissolved together. Make a convenient spout by which to pour off the acid. The best acid for biting the steel in ordinary use is the commercial nitric, 1 part; acetic, 3 parts. For delicate tints, such as skies, distances, etc., this mixture may be diluted at pleasure with water to any extent, down to the sharpness of strong vinegar. Steel is acted upon by acid, with great rapidity as compared with copper; it must therefore be quickly put on, and quickly removed, and luke-warm water poured over the surface; blow dry with the bellows; the operation is much facilitated by heating both the plate and acid. Scrape off small portions of the ground on the lighter parts, to judge thereby of the quality of line, and stop out carefully all that may be considered dark enough. Continue this process until the stronger portions assume sufficient color for the first biting.

Biting Soft Steel.

The use of acids even on hard steel is uncertain and precarious, much more so on soft or partially decarbonized; on such nitric acid being unsatisfactory, resort is had to other materials in search of that success denied to the ordinary means.

1. Corrosive sublimate, ¼ oz.; alum, ¼ oz.; dissolved in a pint of warm water, bites a fair line. Keep sweeping off the sediment deposited during the process, with a hair-pencil or feather.

2. Spencer's, or magnetic acid; dissolve in ½ oz. of commercial nitric acid and the same quantity of water, and 1 oz. of fine silver. In the like proportions, of acid and water, dissolve 1 oz. of mercury. Then mix solution of silver and of mercury, each, 1 part; water, 25 parts; solution of nitric acid, ½ part.

This mixture bites very rapidly when once started; it will, however, lie perfectly inactive until some one of the following plans is used. 1. Heat a steel point by rapid friction or fire, and with it touch the steel through the acid and ground; a black deposit at once forms; sweep it off with a feather. 2. With a strip of zinc polished at both ends, touch with one end the acid, and with the other, a clear piece of steel. 3. Wet a part of the surface of the plate with spittle; this is a very ready means. 4. Dip a point in corrosive sublimate; this pressed into the steel will force action; or, 5. Put corrosive sublimate on for a moment, pour rapidly off, and as quickly put on the magnetic acid.

To Set and Use the Graver.

Lay the sides, the angles of which form the belly, on the oil-stone; rub gently, taking care to keep the part flat upon the stone, until the edge is sufficiently sharp; then, with the handle of the gravor in the hollow of the hand, and the forefinger on the belly, hold it at an angle of about 30 degrees, and rub the end till a good point is obtained. In *cutting*, hold the handle of the graver in the hollow of the hand, and the graver, between the forefinger and thumb, the plate lying solid upon the table, turning it as occasion may require. The outlines of figures are usually dotted in with the etching, slightly bitten, and stopped out, and the serious part of figure engraving now commences, by laying in the lines, according to the taste and skill of the workman, lightly at first, and gradually cutting deeper and broader into the darker parts. Sand-bags and oil-rubbers are exploded institutions.

Aquatint Engraving.

Etch the outline; bite slightly in the distance and light parts; more strongly those near at home. Clean the plate well to lay the ground, which is thus done: dissolve resin in proof alcohol; for distance, less resin is required. Increase the quantity for the nearest parts. Pour this mixture over the plate, run off the superfluous matter, and in drying it will form a granulation on the surface. This granulation is fine or coarse in proportion to the quantity, more or less, of resin contained in the alcohol. When the resin is in excess no granulation will form. Stop out, bite, and re-bite, as in etching.

MEZZOTINTO ENGRAVING.

So called from the circumstance that the subjects treated by this method in the earliest period after its invention, were such as admitted of a large amount of middle-tint or half-tone in the distribution of the masses of light and dark; it being then believed that such only were suited to this style of art. The process is of the utmost simplicity, and as the best general idea of it may be obtained from the anecdote related of what suggested the invention, it is perhaps advisable to begin by repeating the story, whether founded on fact or not.

Prince Rupert, to whom its origin is popularly attributed, is said to have taken the idea from observing a soldier in camp polishing a rusty sword. The rust had been, on some parts of the blade, entirely removed, while on others it remained in all its original roughness, and in some portions the polishing was half done. This accident suggested that a rapid and effective style of engraving might result, if a metal plate were roughened all over its surface by some means, so that it would take secure hold of a coating of plate-printers' ink when applied, and then, being again removed by grinding, or scraping, or burnishing wherever the middle tints and lights of the picture required, would thus retain the printers' ink just in proportion to the degree of such removal. Where the plate was polished bright, the ink would readily wipe clean away, and in printing leave the paper unstained, forming the high lights of the picture, while in the parts where the roughening was left the ink would refuse to wipe away, and thus would print the extreme darks of the picture. Such was the theory framed; the result of experiment proved it to have been well founded, and *mezzo-tinto*, a compound Italian term, signifying middle-tint, took a permanent and respected position among the arts.

So it is already seen that the operation of mezzotinto engraving is exactly the reverse of every other kind, being from dark to light; as in drawing a picture by means of white chalk on black paper, or by taking a panel of light-colored wood, and having charred with fire the whole surface to blackness, scrape this away again in various degrees of completeness in such manner as to present the lights and shadows of a picture.

The contrivance first used for producing the roughened surface on the copper-plate, termed the mezzotinto ground, was a wooden roller, in which were securely fixed multitudes of steel points, sharp ends outwards. This was rolled over the plate with moderate pressure, backwards and forwards in every direction, until no particle of the original polished surface remained unpunctured by a dot. But the difficulty presented itself of there being no means of sharpening the steel points when they broke off, or were worn dull by repeated use. Consequently there was substituted, in place of the roller, the instrument called the rocker, or cradle-tool, or more properly the *grounding* tool, which continues in use to the present day, notwithstanding its obvious imperfections, for it can easily be sharpened when dull, lasts a long time, and nothing better has yet been thought of.

The grounding tool is made in form like a broad chisel, two inches wide, cut all over one side with grooved straight lines parallel to each other, exactly equi-distant and of equal depth. These run lengthwise on the tool, so that when the end is sharpened to a bevel, they form a saw-like edge of teeth. The toothed edge being sharpened to a curved shape, the tool is held in a nearly upright position, its teeth resting on the plate, and is rocked from side to side, advancing forward with a slightly zigzag motion. The handle, attached to a shank at the upper end, is firmly grasped, the wrist being kept stiff. The elbow rests on the table as a pivot of the motion. Guide-lines are drawn on the plate with a pencil or charcoal against a ruler, parallel to each other, and not quite so wide apart as the breadth of the tool. The grounding tool is then held in the position described, not quite upright, but slightly inclined forwards, the middle of the tool midway between the lines, and the elbow in place so that an imaginary line between it and the tool is in the same direction as the pencil guide-lines on the plate. The rocking motion is then made with moderate pressure, stopping on each side as nearly on the guide-line as possible, great care being observed to avoid digging in the corner of the tool by rocking too wide a line, and also to avoid rocking repeatedly in the same place, thus making a deep irremediable cut. Having continued this operation until all the spaces between the lines have been rocked through, what is termed *one way* has been completed. Precisely the same operation is repeated with the guide-lines in another direction, and then in another, and so on until a full black ground has been produced, which is when every particle of the original polish has disappeared. It is well to make a scale to assist in varying the direction of the ways, such as a half circle of paper with lines drawn on it radiating to the circumference, like the spokes of a wheel; the straight edge of the paper being laid against the edge of the plate, the ruler is laid against one of the lines as a guide for the direction about to be worked.

The outline of the intended picture is then

made on the ground, either by sketching it delicately with the end of the burnisher, using it as a pencil, aided by division squares; or by transferring an outline previously drawn upon paper, on to the plate by means of the copper-plate roller press. The entire effect is next obtained by scraping away the ground to various degrees of lightness, scraping it entirely away only where the highest lights of the picture are, and leaving it totally unscraped only where the extreme darks are. All the sudden bright lights of the picture are made with the burnisher, and also the pure white lights are finished with it. The scraper used is a simple band of steel, about ¾ of an inch wide, and not quite thin enough to spring or bend in using, sharpened lancet-like towards the end where it is applied to the plate, both edges being used. It is, when new, 4 or 5 inches long, and is employed without a handle. A correct judgment of the progress of the work can only be had by occasionally procuring a proof of the plate from the printer, during the progress.

As the plate almost always yields an impression darker than would be expected, the engraver is not apt to scrape his tints too light, but if this should happen, the tint must be replaced by means of the grounding tool. To do this it is only necessary to lay what is termed a gauze ground over the part requiring renewal; that is, a ground composed of but from five to seven crossings, seldom more. Then scrape away again delicately to the proper degree of lightness. If a light form should have been inadvertently extended too far over on to its adjoining tint, the defect may be corrected by puncturing a few rows of dots by means of the rulette, a tool resembling a horseman's spur, only on a minute scale, and then delicately removing the burr raised with a very sharp scraper.

The foregoing description is of mezzotinto pure and simple, but it has become the practice of late years to aid and support it largely by a foundation of etching, in lines and dots. This is all done on the plate before commencing the mezzotinto ground. The process is described under its proper head. The drawing of the outline on the plate with the burnisher is then rendered unnecessary, as the etched forms are faintly visible through the ground.

The field of application of this style of engraving has been immensely widened since the introduction to the engravers' use of plates of annealed or softened steel, which occurred about the year 1820, or a little earlier. Previous to that, copper had been the metal in use from the time of Tomaso Finiguerra, the Florentine goldsmith, who, in 1460, invented the important art of plate-printing.

Mezzotinto engraving was invented in the earlier part of the seventeenth century, most probably by Ludwig von Siegen, an officer in the service of the Landgrave of Hesse. There is a portrait print by him in this style extant, of Amelia Elizabetha, Princess of Hesse, dated 1643.

TO ENGRAVE ON WOOD.

The block is commonly made of pear-tree or box, and differs in thickness according to its size. The surface for the engraving is on the transverse section of the wood; the subject is drawn upon it with a pen and Indian-ink, with all the finishing that is required to have in the impression. The spaces between the lines are cut away with knives, chisels, and gouges, leaving the lines that have been drawn with the ink.

The taking impressions from blocks of wood differs from that of copper-plate in this, that in the latter they are delivered from the incision, while in the wooden blocks they are delivered from the raised part.

To Prepare Box-wood for Engraving.

The wood being chosen, and cut into a proper form and size, it must be planed as evenly and truly as possible, and will be then ready to receive the drawing or chalking of the design to be engraved.

Now take white-lead and temper it with water, by grinding; then spread it first thinly on the surface by a brush pencil, and afterwards rub it well with a fine linen rag, while yet wet, and when it is dry, brush off any loose or powdery part by a soft pencil.

If the design be sketched on the wood by drawing, it may be done by Indian or common ink (but the first is far preferable), either by a pen or pencil, or by a black-lead pencil, though that scarcely marks strongly enough for finer work.

Chiar' Oscuro.

This method of engraving is performed with three blocks. The outline is cut in one, the deep shadows in a second, and the third gives a tint over the whole, except where the lights are cut away. These are substituted in their turn, each print receiving an impression from each block. This mode of engraving was designed to represent the drawings of the old masters.

To Secure Copper-plates from Corrosion.

Take equal parts of wax and turpentine and double the quantity of olive oil, with the same quantity of hog's lard. Melt the whole over the fire in an earthen vessel, taking care to mix the ingredients well, and leave them to boil some time, till they are well incorporated.

The advantage of this mixture is, that it may at any time, being warmed, be put with the finger on the places desired to be covered; by which means the further operation of the aqua-fortis on such places may be instantly prevented without any other trouble or preparation, or without interrupting or delaying the principal operation.

This mixture may be employed equally well with the hard as with the soft varnish. The intention of using such a composition is, that if any scratches or false strokes happen in the etching they are to be stopped out with a hair-pencil dipped in this composition, mixed with lampblack, previously to laying on the aqua-fortis, or, as it is called, biting in.

To Choose Copper for Engraving.

Plates intended for engraving ought to be of the best copper, which should be very malleable, firm, and with some degree of hardness, free from veins or specks. The redness of copper is a presumptive mark of its being good, but not an infallible one; for though it is, in general, a proof of the purity of the copper, yet it does not evince that the qualities may not have been injured by too frequent fusion.

Copper-plates may be had ready prepared in most large towns, but, when these cannot be had, procure a pretty thick sheet of copper, rather larger than the drawing, and let the brazier planish it well; then take a piece of pumice-stone, and with water rub it all one way, till it becomes tolerably smooth and level. A piece of charcoal is next used with water for polishing it still farther, and removing the deep scratches made by the pumice-stone, and it is then finished with a piece of charcoal of a finer grain, with a little oil.

To Etch upon Glass.

Procure several thick, clear pieces of crown-glass, and immerse them in melted wax, so that each may receive a complete coating, or pour over them a solution of wax in benzine. When perfectly cold draw on them, with a fine steel point, flowers, trees, houses, portraits, etc. Whatever parts of the drawing are intended to be corroded with the acid should be perfectly free from the least particle of wax. When all these drawings are finished the pieces of glass must be immersed one by one in a square leaden box or receiver, where they are to be submitted to the action of hydrofluoric acid gas, made by acting on powdered fluor spar by concentrated sulphuric acid.

When the glasses are sufficiently corroded they are to be taken out, and the wax is to be removed by first dipping them in warm and then in hot water, or by washing with turpentine or benzine. Various colors may be applied to the corroded parts of the glass, whereby a very fine painting may be executed. In the same manner sentences and initials of names may be etched on wineglasses, tumblers, etc.

Another Method.

Glass may also be etched by immersing it in liquid hydrofluoric acid, after having been coated with wax and drawn on, as in the last method. There is this difference, however, in the use of the liquid and the gas, that the former renders the etching *transparent*, whilst that produced by the gas is quite *opaque*.

In this method the potassa of the glass is set free, whilst the silex or sand is acted on, consequently no vessel of glass can ever be employed with safety to contain this acid in a liquid state, as it would soon be corroded into holes. It is, therefore, generally preserved in *leaden* bottles, on which it has no power to act.

Glass in Imitation of Muslin.

This is a simple and ingenious means of giving to glass the appearance of delicately-wrought muslin. The process, which comes to us from Germany, consists in spreading very smoothly a piece of lace or tulle and covering it with some fatty substance by means of a printer's roller. The glass being carefully cleaned, the cloth is laid upon it so as to leave in fat a print on the surface of all the threads of the fabric. The glass is then exposed about 5 minutes to the vapors of hydrofluoric acid, which roughens the spaces between the lines and leaves the polish on the surface under the fat.

A glass thus prepared becomes like a veil, protecting from exterior indiscretion persons who, from their apartment, desire to look commodiously outside.

To Transfer Engravings to Glass.

Fix the printed surface to the glass with ordinary paste. Etch with liquid hydrofluoric acid, s. g. 1·14. At the end of 3 or 4 minutes wash off the paper, and the design will be found reproduced upon the glass, the printers' ink having protected it. Mr. Napier, the patentee, prefers to have the glass ground enamelled or veneered beforehand, when the object stands out in relief. If the veneer or enamel is colored, of course the picture remains colored, while the body of the glass is white.

To Engrave on Precious Stones.

The first thing to be done in this branch of engraving is to cement two rough diamonds to the ends of two sticks large enough to hold them steady in the hand, and to rub or grind them against each other, till they be brought to the form desired. The dust or powder that is rubbed off serves afterwards to polish them, which is performed by a kind of mill that turns a wheel of soft iron. The diamond is fixed in a brass dish, and, thus applied to the wheel, is covered with diamond dust, mixed up with oil of olives; and when the diamond is to be cut facet-wise, first one face and then another is applied to the wheel. Rubies, sapphires, and topazes are cut and formed the same way on a copper wheel, and polished with tripoli diluted in water. Agates, amethysts, emeralds, hyacinths, granites, rubies, and others of the softer stones, are cut on a leaden wheel moistened with emery and water, and polished with tripoli on a pewter wheel. Lapis-lazuli, opal, etc. are polished on a wooden wheel.

To fashion and engrave vases of agate, crystal, lapis-lazuli, or the like, a kind of lathe is made use of, similar to that used by pewterers, to hold the vessels, which are to be wrought with proper tools. The engraver's lathe generally holds the tools, which are turned by a wheel, and the vessel cut and engraved, either in relievo or otherwise, the tools being moistened from time to time with diamond dust and oil, or at least emery and water. To engrave figures or devices on any of these stones, when polished, such as medals, seals, etc., a little iron wheel is used, the ends of whose axis are received within two pieces of iron, placed upright, as in the turner's lathe, and to be brought closer, or set further apart, at pleasure; at one end of the axis are fixed the proper tools, being kept tight by a screw. Lastly, the wheel is turned by the foot, and the stone applied by the hand to the tool, then shifted and conducted as occasion requires.

The tools are generally of iron, and sometimes of brass. Their form is various: some have small round heads, like buttons; others like ferrels, to take the pieces out, and others flat, etc. When the stone has been engraved it is polished on wheels of hair-brushes and tripoli.

CLEANING AND PRESERVATION OF ENGRAVINGS.

In commencing to restore an engraving, some attention must be given to the kind of injury it has suffered. A general brown color more or less deep, resulting from atmospheric action only, is the least possible change. Spots and stains, caused by ink, colored fluids, oil or insects, must be first treated, and all pencil marks removed by India-rubber or bread-crumbs. A fluid acid, obtained by dissolving 1 oz. of crystals of oxalic acid in ½ pt. of warm water, may be used for application to all stains, and the paper should be wet with it thoroughly where spots of any kind exist.

Excepting in a few cases, this acid will not cause the removal of stains immediately, but generally it combines with the bases of them, and they are removed by subsequent steps; the thorough wetting should be done a few hours before proceeding to clean the engraving. The engraving should be placed in a shallow tub or other vessel, and allowed to rest upon a piece of open cotton stuff, or millinet. This material of suitable dimensions, should have 2 rods or sticks sown to opposite edges. These sticks will hang over the sides of the vessel, and permit the prints to be withdrawn or moved without any risk of injury, and they should remain in soak with warm or cold water for 12 or 24 hours. When the prints no longer discolor the water on being agitated, the fluid should be withdrawn, and enough clean water added to cover them. Half a pound of chloride of lime should be made into a paste with cold water, and stirred up with 2 qts. of water, and allowed to settle for 6 hours. Part of the clear solution should be added to the bath till the smell of chlorine is perceived, and the prints should be moved to facilitate the action. In very bad cases, 1 oz. of muriatic acid mixed with a pint of water may be added, and when the bleaching is effected the prints should be well washed with fresh water and slowly dried.

On the first trial of this process, remarks Dr. Hayes, a degree of alarm will be felt in the case of a highly prized favorite at this seeming careless treatment; but it must be borne in mind that paper is a firmly felted mass of short fibres which may be soaked in various fluids for weeks, and resist all diluted acids and most chemical agents for a long time wet, if not exposed to mechanical abrasion by touch or rapid motion.

LITHOGRAPHY.

To Write and Engrave on Stone.

The stone used in lithography is a limestone (carbonate of limestone), of very hard and compact texture, admitting of being ground to a fine surface. There are three qualities recognized by dealers, which are called the blue, gray, and yellow stones, of which the blue is regarded as the best, and commands the highest price. The best lithographic stones are the production of a very limited district, in the kingdom of Bavaria. Several localities are known in the United States, and some years since it was reported that a quarry had been discovered in the State of Missouri, of very superior quality. The stone must have the qualities of imbibing both water and grease or oil; the crayon used in drawing upon it being composed of grease, wax, soap, shellac, and ivory-black, which is also the composition of the ink used in printing, with little variation.

The stone must be rubbed down with fine sand, to a perfect level, after which it is ready to receive the drawing; a weak solution of nitric acid should be thrown over the stone. This operation will slightly corrode its surface, and dispose it to imbibe moisture, with more facility. While the stone is still wet, a cylinder of about 3 inches in diameter, covered with common printer's ink, should be rolled over the whole surface of the stone. While the wet part refuses to take the ink, the chalk, being greasy, will take a portion of it from the roller. The stone is then ready for printing.

The press consists of a box drawn by a wheel, under a wooden scraper, pressing on it with great power. After the first impression, the stone must be wetted afresh, again rolled over with the cylinder, drawn under the scraper, and so on.

The same process is employed for ink drawings, except that the solution of nitric acid must be stronger, and the printing ink stiffer.

Imitations of wood-cuts are produced by covering the stone with lithographic ink, and scraping out the intended lights. As the finer touches may be added with a hair pencil, prints far superior to wood-cuts may be obtained, but the chief advantage of wood-cuts, that of printing them at the same time with the text of the book, is lost.

Within the last 20 years the art of engraving on stone has been brought to great perfection, and at this time nearly all maps used for school atlases, and by engineers, surveyors, etc., and nearly all bills of exchange, checks, drafts, and other blanks used for commercial purposes are thus engraved. The engraving is done with a pointed or sharp instrument, and is very similar to copper-plate engraving. The engraved stones are printed only when very small editions are required, transfers from these to other stones being much more easily printed.

The art of transferring and printing from transfers is now one of the most important and useful processes of lithography, and in the United States constitutes the greater part of the business of the lithographer. It is applicable to engravings on either stone or metal, and it is done from copperplates, to a considerable extent, in maps, charts, and other engravings, which consists mainly of lines and letters, without elaborate shading. This process was invented in Europe about 30 years since. An impression is taken from the engraved plate or stone with a greasy ink, and on paper having the surface prepared with a composition which is essentially albumen. This impression is carefully applied to the surface of another stone, and on removing the paper by dampening it, and with very careful manipulation, the impression in ink remains. It is then treated with diluted acid precisely as a drawing, and becomes *fixed*, as it is technically called, in relief on the stone, and can be printed from with entire facility. Much care is required in this process, and the method of doing it was for some years regarded as one of the most valuable secrets of the lithographic art. Engravings of any kind can, of course, be transferred, but in finely engraved pictures, or when there is much shading, the fine lines become massed together, or blurred in transferring. In printing small maps or other suitable descriptions of engravings, printing from transfers has a great advantage over plate-printing, in the fact that several copies of the same engraving can be put upon the stone at once, and thus printed much more rapidly and economically. Maps printed from well-prepared transfers can scarcely be distinguished from those printed from copper or steel-plates.

Laurent's Method of Drawing in Stone.

Take the outline of the original design upon transparent paper, by tracing all the lines of the original with a dry point; the outline is then glued by its edges on a board, and there is spread over it, with a piece of fine linen, a tolerably hard paste, formed of lithographic ink, dissolved in essence of turpentine. The outline is then rubbed hard with a piece of clean linen, until the linen ceases to have a black tint. The outline is then transferred to the stone by means of the press, placing in a vertical paper press the stone and the outline in contact, laying upon the latter 25 sheets of paper, wetted in water with some solutions of calcined muriate of lime. Upon these last sheets are placed large plates of paper, about 1 inch thick, to prevent injury from a thick and straight plank, which is to be laid over them. Pressure is now applied for 1 hour, when the outline will be found adhering to the stone. The paper is to be removed by hot water and the design will be left on the stone, which is now washed with cold water till no trace of the paper remains.

Thenard and Blainville's Lithographic Ink.

Soap, $\frac{1}{2}$; mutton-suet, $\frac{1}{2}$; yellow wax, 1 part; mastic in tears, $\frac{1}{2}$; and as much lampblack as necessary.

Three Different Methods of Printing from Stone.

In the chemical printing-office at Vienna, 3 different methods are employed, but that termed in relief. is most frequently used. This is the general mode of printing music.

The 2nd method is the sunk, which is preferred for prints.

The 3rd method is the flat, that is, neither raised nor sunk. This is useful for imitating drawings, particularly where the impression is intended to resemble crayons. For printing and engraving in this method, a block of marble is employed, or any other calcareous stone that is easily corroded, and will take a good polish. It should be 2½ inches thick, and of a size proportioned to the purpose for which it is intended. A close texture is considered as advantageous. When the stone is well polished and dry, the first step is to trace the drawing, notes, or letters to be printed with a pencil; the design is not very conspicuous, but it is rendered so by passing over the strokes of the pencil a particular ink, of which a great secret is made. This ink is made of a solution of lac in potash, colored with the soot from burning wax, and appears to be the most suitable black for the purpose. When the design has been gone over with this ink, it is left to dry about 2 hours. After it is dry, nitric acid, more or less diluted, according to the degree of relief desired, is poured on the stone, which corrodes every part of it, except when defended by the resinous ink. The block being washed with water, ink, similar to that commonly used for printing, is distributed over it by printer's balls; a sheet of paper disposed on a frame is laid on it, and this is pressed down by means of a copper roller or copper press.

The sunk or chalk method differs from that termed relief, only in having stone much more corroded by the nitric acid. In the flat method, less nitric acid is used. It is not to be supposed that the surface is quite plain in this way, but the lines are very little raised so that they can scarcely be perceived to stand above the ground, but by the finger.

To make Lithographic Pencils.

Mix the following ingredients: Soap, 3 oz.; tallow, 2 oz.; wax, 1 oz.

When melted smooth, add a sufficient quantity of lampblack, and pour it into moulds.

To take Impressions on Paper from Designs made in Stone.

The stone should be close grained, and the drawing or writing should be made with a pen dipped in ink, formed of a solution of lac in lyes of pure soda, to which some soap and lampblack should be added, for coloring. Leave it to harden for a few days; then take impressions in the following manner: Dip the surface in water, then dab it with printer's ink and printer's balls. The ink will stick to the design and not to the stone, and the impressions may be taken with wet paper, by a rolling or screw press, in the ordinary way. Several hundred copies may be taken from the same design, in this simple manner.

Cheap Substitute for Lithographic Stone.

Paste-board, or card-paper, covered with an argillo-calcareous mixture, has been employed with complete success, and effects a great saving. The material is to be reduced to a powder, and laid on wet; it sets, of course, immediately, and may be applied to a more substantial article than paper, and upon a more extensive scale than the inventor has yet carried it on. This coating receives the ink or crayon in the same way that the stone does, and furnishes impressions precisely in the same manner.

Another substitute for lithographic stone is zinc, which has been used to some extent lately for transfer-printing. The transfer is made on the surface from an engraving on metal or stone, and the method is nearly the same as that alluded to above.

Printing in colors is now much practised in Lithography, and quite attractive show-cards, lamp-shades, etc., are produced. Every color requires a separate design or drawing, and one color only is printed at a time. Skill and care is required in registering, as it is called, or in making the colors properly join together in the picture, and also in preparing the colors. Parts of pictures intended to be colored by hand in the usual manner, can frequently be printed more cheaply.

Photographing on stone is perhaps at present the most interesting of newly discovered processes in lithography. It is very useful in making either reductions or enlargements of drawings or engravings intended to be printed from stone, and is also applicable to obtaining and fixing figures of minute objects obtained by means of the microscope. The surface of the stone is prepared in a suitable manner, and the photograph made upon it; after which it is treated and printed as in other processes of this art. This method has at present the appearance of becoming very important and useful in lithography.

Process for Printing from Veneers.

A process of veneering by transfer is mentioned with approval in the French journals. The sheet of veneer or inlaying to be copied, is to be exposed for a few minutes to the vapor of hydro-chloric acid. This novel plate is then laid upon calico or paper, and impressions struck off with a printing-press. Heat is to be applied immediately after the sheet is printed, when a perfect impression of all the marks, figures, and convoluted lines of the veneer is said to be instantaneously produced. The process, it is affirmed, may be repeated for an almost indefinite number of times. The designs thus produced are said all to exhibit a general wood-like tint, most natural when oak, walnut, maple, and the light-colored woods have been employed.

New Tracing Paper.

Moisten a sheet of paper with benzine, by means of a sponge. The paper becomes temporarily transparent, and lines may be traced through it. In a few hours the benzine evaporates, and the paper becomes opaque as before.

Rapid Stereotyping.

The process now adopted by many newspapers is to take a cast of the form in a composition of strong glue, with alum and plaster of Paris. Into this the metal is poured. It requires only sixteen minutes to mould, cast, and finish the stereotype plate.

Autography.

On a plate of chalk or plaster, the artist sketches the design with a gummy ink (at present a secret). By means of a silk rag, the portions of the plate not protected by the ink are rubbed away. A copy is then obtained in fusible metal or by the electrotype.

NATURE PRINTING.

If the original be a plant, a flower, or an insect, a texture, or in short, any lifeless object whatever, it is passed between a copper plate and a lead plate, through two rollers that are closely screwed together. The original, by means of the pressure, leaves its image impressed with all its peculiar delicacies—with its whole surface, as it were—on the lead plate. If the colors are applied to this stamped lead plate, as in printing a copper plate, a copy in the most varying colors, bearing a striking resemblance to the original, is obtained by means of one single impression of each plate. If a great number of copies are required—which the lead form, on account of its softness, is not capable of furnishing — it is stereotyped, in case of being printed at a typographical press; or galvanized, in case of being worked at a copper-plate press, as many times as necessary; and the impressions are taken from the stereotyped or galvanized plate instead of from the lead plate. When a copy of a unique object, which cannot be subjected to pressure, is to be made, the original must be covered with dissolved gutta percha; which form of gutta percha, when removed from the original, is covered with a solution of silver, to render it available for a matrix for galvanic multiplication.

This process is also applicable to the purpose of obtaining impressions of fossils or of the structure of an agate or other stone. In all the varieties of agate, the various layers have different degrees of hardness. Therefore, if we take a section of an agate and expose it to the action of hydro-fluoric acid, some parts are corroded and others not. If ink is at once applied, very beautiful impressions can be at once obtained; but for printing any number, electrotype copies are obtained. These will have exactly the character of an etched plate, and are printed from in the ordinary manner. The silicious portions of fossil, and the stone in which they are imbedded, may in like manner be acted upon by acid; and from these, either stereotyped or electrotyped copies are obtained for printing from.

Dresser's Process of Nature Printing.

The process is one by which images of foliage may be taken by any who have leisure and choose to devote an hour or two to the registration of the beautiful forms of our leaves. The process, by its simplicity, commends itself; and the results gained are of the most charming character. The Vienna process of nature printing has achieved much, and produced results of the most admirable character; but the process necessitates the use of dried vegetable specimens, in order to the production of the image. While this is at least no drawback in the case of ferns, and is perhaps even an advantage, yet it strongly militates against the process in the case of many other plants. In order to meet this difficulty, Dr. Dresser suggested an "Improved Nature Printing" process which he patented, in conjunction with Dr. Lyon Playfair, in wh'ch impressions are taken from the living plant, and which may be substantially described as follows: A sheet of foolscap writing-paper should be provided, a handful of fine cotton-wool, a piece of muslin, one or more tubs of common oil-paint (according to the color required), a little sweet-oil, and a quantity of smooth, soft, cartridge-paper, or better, plate-paper. Having placed the sheet of foolscap-paper while doubled (the two thicknesses making it a little softer), on a smooth table, squeeze from the tube about as much oil-color as would cover a shilling, and place this on one corner of the sheet of foolscap; now form a "dabber" by enclosing a quantity of the cotton-wool in two thicknesses of muslin, and tying it up so as to give it roundness of form. Take up a portion of the oil-paint from the corner of the paper, with the dabber, and by dabbing give the central portion of the sheet of foolscap a coat of color. This dabbing may be continued for half an hour or more with advantage, taking a small quantity more color when the paper becomes dry; two or three drops of sweet-oil may now be added to the paper and distributed by the aid of the dabber, if the color is thick, when the paper will be fully prepared for use.

The paper may be left for an hour or two after being first coated with color without injury, and, indeed, this delay is favorable, for until the paper becomes impregnated with oil, the results desired are not so favorable as they become after the paper is more fully enriched with this material. While the color is soaking into the paper, a number of leaves should be gathered which are perfect in form and free from dust; and these can be kept fresh by placing them in an earthenware pan, the bottom of which is covered with a damp cloth, but it will be well to place a damp cloth over the orifice of the pan also. Selecting a woolly, hairy leaf, place it on the painted portion of the sheet of foolscap, and dab it with the dabber till it acquires the color of the paint used; this being done turn the leaf over and dab the other side; now lift it from the paint paper by the stalk, and place it with care between a folded portion of the "plate" or "cartridge" paper, and if the stalk of the leaf appears to be in the way, cut it off with a pair of scissors; now bring down the upper portion of the folded piece of paper upon the leaf, and rub the paper externally with the finger, or a soft rag, bringing the paper thus in contact with every portion of the leaf. If the paper is now opened, and the leaf removed, a beautiful impression of both sides of the leaf will be found remaining. In like manner, impressions of any tolerably flat leaves can be taken; but harsh leaves will be found most difficult, and should hence be avoided by the beginner. While the paper is yet rich in color, downy leaves should be chosen; but color may at any moment be added, care being always taken to distribute the paint evenly over the paper with the dabber before the latter is applied to the leaf, and the dabber is always removed from the painted paper till the color is exhausted, when the paper is again replenished from the reserve in the corner.

As the color on the paper becomes less and less in quantity, smoother leaves may be employed; and when the paper seems to be almost wholly without paint, the smoothest leaves will prove successful, for these require extremely little color. Should the natural color of the leaf be desired, it can be got by using paint of the color required; but, in many cases, purely artificial tints produce the most pleasing and artistic results; thus, burnt sienna gives a very pleasing red tint; and of all colors this will be found to work with the greatest ease.

By the process now described, the most beautiful results can be gained; but the effect will be better, if, when the impression is being rubbed off, the leaf, together with the paper in which it is enclosed, is placed on something soft, as half a quire of blotting paper. Should the first attempt not prove very satisfactory, a little experience will be found to be all that is required, and now the most common leaf will be seen to have a form of the most lovely character.

Collections of leaves of forest-trees will prove of the deepest interest, or of all the species which we have of any kind of plant; thus, if the leaves of the black, red, American, and golden currant be printed together with that of the gooseberry, all of which belong to one botanical genus or group, the variation or modification of the form will be seen to be of the deepest interest.

WEIGHTS AND MEASURES.

Troy Weight is used by jewellers and at the Mint. Its denominations are the pound, lb., = 12 ounces = 5,760 grains; ounce, oz., = 480 grains; and pennyweight, dwt., = 24 grains.

Apothecaries' Weight is used in prescribing and dispensing medicines, and in chemical and pharmaceutical operations generally. It is the official standard of the U. S. Pharmacopœia. The British Pharmacopœia uses the avoirdupois pound and ounce; hence the two agree only in the grain measure. The denominations of apothecaries' weight are the pound, lb., = 12 ounces = 5,760 grains; the ounce, ℥j, = 8 drachms = 480 grains; the drachm, ʒj, = 3 scruples = 60 grains; the scruple, ℈j, = 20 grains; and the grain, gr.

Avoirdupois Weight is the commercial weight, and is generally employed in the receipts in this volume. Its pound, lb., = 16 ounces, oz., = 7,000 grains. The ounce contains 437·5 grains. The apothecaries' or troy ounce contains 42½ grains *more* than the avoirdupois ounce, and the apothecaries' or troy pound contains 1·240 grains *less* than the commercial or avoirdupois pound. The troy pound contains 12 oz., the avoirdupois 16 oz.

RELATIVE VALUE OF TROY AND AVOIRDUPOIS WEIGHTS.

Useful in determining the troy weight of silver by ordinary weights.

1 lb. troy = 0·822857 lb. av. = 13 oz. 72·5 grs.
1 lb. avoirdupois = 1·215277 lb. troy = 1 lb. 2 oz. 280 grs.

UNITED STATES COINS

Are convenient standards of weight. Those of gold are to be preferred, and when new will rarely be found to vary more than the tenth of a grain from the following weights:

Double eagle, $20, weighs............. 516 grs.
Eagle, $10, "   .... 258 "
Half eagle, $5, "   .... 129 "
Quarter eagle, $2 50, "   .... 64½ "
Three dollar, $3, "   .... 77·4 "
One dollar, $1, "   .... 25·8 "

MEASURES OF CAPACITY FOR LIQUIDS.

In the United States the old wine gallon (Cong.), of 231 cubic inches = 58,328·8 grains of water at 60°, is used. In England the Imperial gallon of 277·274 cubic inches = 70,000 grains = 10 lb. av. is used. The *minim* of the former = ·95 gr., of the latter = ·91 gr. The former contains 16 fluidounces to the pint (O.), the latter 20. The following tables give the value of each in grains of pure water, at 60°.

Wine Measure, (*U. S. P.*)
60 minims = f℥j = ♏lx = 56·9 grs. water.
480 " = f℥j = f℥viii = 455·7 " "
7,680 " = Oj = f℥xvi = 7,291·2 " "
61,440 " = Cong j = Oviii = 58,328·8 " "

Imperial Measure, (*B. P.*)
60 minims = f℥j = ♏lx = 54·6 grs. water.
480 " = f℥j = f℥viii = 437·5 " "
9,600 " = Oj = f℥xx = 8,750 " "
76,800 " = Cong j = Oviii = 70,000 " "

To convert Imperial (*Br.*) *into Wine* (*U. S. P.*) *Measure.*

Imperial.		Wine or Apothecaries'.
1 gallon	=	6 pts., 13 fl. oz., 2 fl. drs., 23 minims.
1 pint	=	16 " 5 " 18 "
1 fluidounce	=	1 " 0 " 20 "
1 fluidrachm	=	1 " 2·5 "
1 minim	=	1·04 "

THE DECIMAL SYSTEM,

Adopted in France and on the Continent, is used in this country in scientific research. The standard of length is the metre ($\frac{1}{10,000,000}$ of a quadrant of the earth's meridian), which is equal (as corrected by Prof. Bache) to 39·36850535 inches, or, roughly, about 3¼ feet. This, as well as the measures of capacity and weight, is increased or divided decimally. The prefixes are *deca* (10 times), *hecto* (100 times), *kilo* (1000 times), and *myria* (10,000 times); *deci* ($\frac{1}{10}$), *centi* ($\frac{1}{100}$), *mille* ($\frac{1}{1000}$). The kilometre is equal to about two-thirds of a mile.

The cubic decimetre is the unit of capacity, and is called a litre, and is equal to 1·765 imperial pints, or 2·1135 wine pints (the latter are used in the United States). The weight of 1 litre of water, at 39·10°, is called a kilogramme, and that of a millilitre of water a gramme = 15·434 grains. The kilogramme is rather less than 2¼ lbs. avoirdupois. The metrical pound of France is half a kilogramme. One fluidounce equals in capacity 29·53 cubic centimetres.

Comparative Table of Decimal with Avoirdupois and Apothecaries' (*U. S.*) *Weights.*

Name.	Equivalent in Grammes.	Equivalent in Grains.	Equivalent in Avoirdupois.			Equivalent in Apothecaries' Weight, (U. S. P.)			
			lb.	oz.	gr.	lb.	oz.	dr.	gr.
Milligramme = ...	·001	·0154							
Centigramme = ...	·01	·1543							
Decigramme = ...	·1	1·5434							1·5
Gramme = ...	1·	15·4340							15·4
Decagramme = ...	10·	154·3402		0¼	·45			2	34·0
Hectogramme = ...	100·	1543·4023		3½	12·152		3	1	43·0
Kilogramme* = ...	1,000·	15434·0234	2	3¼	12·173	2	8	1	14·
Myriagramme = ...	10,000·	154340·2344	22	0¾	12·	26	9	4	20·

* Abbreviated *kilo*.

Comparison of Decimal Measures of Capacity with Wine (U. S. P.) and Imperial Measures.

Wine Measure.

	Eng. Cubic Inches.	Apothecaries' or Wine Measure.
Millilitre =	·061028 =	16·2318 minims.
Centilitre =	·610280 =	2·7053 fluidrachms.
Decilitre =	6·102800 =	3·3816 fluidounces.
Litre =	61·028000 =	2·1135 pints.
Decalitre =	610·280000 =	2·6419 gallons.
Hectolitre =	6102·800000	
Kilolitre =	61028·000000	

Imperial Measure.

1 litre = 0·22017 galls., 0·88066 qts., 1·76133 pts.
Stere (cubic metre) = 220·16643 galls.

CAPACITY OF BOXES.

Dry Measure.

A box 20 inches square, and 16$\frac{1}{8}$ inches deep, will contain 1 barrel (3 bushels).

A box 15 inches square, and 14$\frac{1}{3}$ inches deep, will contain half a barrel.

A box 17 inches by 14 inches, and 9 inches deep, will contain 1 bushel.

A box 10 inches by 12 inches, and 9 inches deep, will contain half a bushel.

A box 8 inches square, and 8$\frac{2}{5}$ inches deep, will contain 1 peck.

A box 8 inches square, and 4$\frac{3}{16}$ inches deep, will contain 1 gallon (dry) = $\frac{1}{8}$ bushel = 268$\frac{4}{5}$ cubic inches.

A box 4 inches square, and 4$\frac{3}{32}$ inches deep, will contain 1 quart.

LINEAR MEASUREMENT.

12 inches = 1 foot. 3 feet = 1 yard.
1 mile = 1760 yards = 5280 feet = 63,360 inches.

Inches expressed in Decimals of a Foot.

1 inch	= 0·08333 foot.	7 inches	= 0·58333 foot.
2 inches	= 0·16666 "	8 "	= 0·66666 "
3 "	= 0·25000 "	9 "	= 0·75000 "
4 "	= 0·33333 "	10 "	= 0·83333 "
5 "	= 0·41666 "	11 "	= 0·91666 "
6 "	= 0·50000 "	12 "	= 1·00000 "

Fractions of an Inch expressed in Decimals of an Inch, and in Decimals of a Foot.

Inch.	Dec. of an inch.	Dec. of a foot.	Inch.	Dec. of an inch.	Dec. of a foot.
$\frac{1}{16}$	= 0·0625	= 0·0052083	$\frac{9}{16}$	= 0·5625	= 0·0468747
$\frac{1}{8}$	= 0·1250	= 0·0104166	$\frac{5}{8}$	= 0·6250	= 0·0520833
$\frac{3}{16}$	= 0·1875	= 0·0156249	$\frac{11}{16}$	= 0·6875	= 0·0572913
$\frac{1}{4}$	= 0·2500	= 0·0288332	$\frac{3}{4}$	= 0·7500	= 0·0624996
$\frac{5}{16}$	= 0·3125	= 0·0260415	$\frac{13}{16}$	= 0·8125	= 0·0677079
$\frac{3}{8}$	= 0·3750	= 0·0312498	$\frac{7}{8}$	= 0·8750	= 0·0729162
$\frac{7}{16}$	= 0·4375	= 0·0364581	$\frac{15}{16}$	= 0·9375	= 0·0781245
$\frac{1}{2}$	= 0·5000	= 0·0416664	$\frac{16}{16}$	= 1·	= 0·0833328

1. In a *right-angled triangle* the sum of the squares of the two shorter sides = the square of the hypothenuse: the square of the hypothenuse less the square of one side = the square of the third side.

2. The diameter of a circle × 3·1416 = the circumference.

3. The circumference of a circle × 0·31831 = the diameter.

4. Given a chord and versed sine—to find the diameter of the circle. Divide the square of half the chord by the versed sine, and add the versed sine to the product = the diameter.

5. To find the length of an arc of a circle, when the cord of the whole arc and the chord of one-half of the arc are known, from 8 times the chord of one-half the arc, subtract the chord of the whole arc: one-third of the remainder will be the length of the arc nearly.

6. Periphery of an elipse. Multiply the square root of the sum of the squares of the axes by 2.22.

SURFACE MEASUREMENT.

Areas. — Product of two Linear Dimensions (proportioned to the squares of similar sides).

144 square inches = 1 square foot.
9 " feet = 1 " yard.

Acre = 43,560 square feet = 4480 yards = (660 × 66 feet).

Square mile = 640 acres.

1. *Parallelogram* (square, rectangular or rhomboidal) = the product of the length of one side × by perpendicular height.

2. *Triangle* = product of base × by one-half the perpendicular height.

3. *Triangle* — Area from 3 sides given. From the half sum of the three sides subtract each side separately; multiply the half sum and the three remainders together, and the square root of the product will be the area.

4. *Trapezoid* = the sum of the two parallel sides × by half the perpendicular height.

5. *Circle* = the square of the diameter × ·7854, or square of the circumference × ·07958.

6. *Sector of a Circle* = radius of the circle × by one-half the arc of the sector.

7. *Segment of a Circle.*—Find the area of a sector of a circle having the same arc, and deduct the triangle formed between the two radii and the chord of the arc.

Superficial Area of Solids.

8. Cube.
9. Parallelopipidon.
10. Prism.
} = { Sum of area of sides and bases.

11. Cylinder = circumference of base × height + area of bases.

12. Cone.
13. Pyramid.
} = { Circumference of bases × one-half slant height + area of base.

Sphere = square of diameter × 3.1416.

French square metre, 1550·85 square inches = 10·7698 square feet.

SOLID MEASUREMENT.

Cubic Content. — Product of three Linear Dimensions (proportional to cube of similar sides).

Cubic foot			= 1,728	cubic ins.
" yard	= 27	cubic ft.	= 46,656	"
Barrel	= 4·8125	"	= 8,316	"
Bushel	= 1·2438	"	= 2,150	"
Gallon (wine) =			= 231	"

Ton = 2240 lbs. avoirdupois.

1 gallon of water weighs 58,328·8 grains troy = 10·126 lbs. troy.

Cylindrical	inches	× ·0004546	=	cubic	feet.
"	feet	× ·02909	=	"	yards.
Cubic	inches	× ·00058	=	"	feet.
"	feet	× ·03704	=	"	yards.
"	feet	× 7·48	=	U. States	gallon.
"	inches	× ·004329	=	"	"
Cylindrical	feet	× 5·874	=	"	"
"	inches	× ·0034	=	"	"

Contents of Casks.—Add into one sum 39 times the square of the bung diameter, 25 times the square of the head diameter, and 26 times the product of the two diameters; then multiply the

SPECIFIC GRAVITY.

sum by the length, and the product again by 00924/3 for wine gallons.

General Rule for finding Cubic Content contained between two Parallel planes.

Let A and B be areas of ends of solids, and C the area of a section parallel to, and equidistant from the ends, and L the distance between the ends:

$$\text{Solidity} = \frac{A + B + 4C}{6} \times L.$$

1. *Cube* = side × side × side, or = area of base × perpendicular height.
2. *Parallelopipidon Prism Cylinder* } = { Area of base × by perpendicular height.
3. *Cone Pyramid* } = { Area of bases × by ⅓ the perpendicular height.
4. *Frustrum of Cone or Pyramid* = sum of the areas of the two ends + the square root of their product × by ⅓ of the perpendicular height.
5. *Sphere* = cube of the diameter × 0·5236.
6. *Spherical Segment* = 3 times the square of the radius of its base + the square of its height × the height × 0·5236.

MEASUREMENT OF STONE-WORK.

1 Perch, Masons' or Quarrymen's Measure.

16½ feet long,
16 inches wide, } = { 22 cubic feet. To be measured in wall.
12 " high,

16½ feet long,
18 inches wide, } = { 24·75 cubic feet. To be measured in pile.
12 " high,

1 cubic yard = 3 feet × 3 feet × 3 feet = 2 cubic feet.

The cubic yard has become the standard for all contract work of late years.

Stone walls less than 16 inches thick count as if 16 inches thick to mason; over 16 inches thick, each inch additional is measured.

Bricks required for Walls of various Thickness.— Number for each Square Foot of Face of Wall.

Thickness of Wall.		Thickness of Wall.	
4 inches	7½	24 inches	46
8 "	15	28 "	52½
12 "	22½	32 "	60
16 "	30	36 "	67½
20 "	37½	42 "	75

Cubic yard = 500 bricks in wall.
Perch (22 cubic feet) = 500 bricks in wall.
To pave 1 sq. yard on flat requires 41 bricks.
" " 1 " " edge " 68 "

BOARD MEASURE.

Boards are sold by superficial measure at so much per foot of 1 inch or less in thickness, adding one-fourth to the price for each quarter-inch thickness over an inch.

SPECIFIC GRAVITY.

In ordinary language the terms density and specific gravity (s. g.) are used to represent the relative weights of equal bulks or volumes of different substances. In order to compare these conveniently, pure water at 60° is taken as the standard. A cubic foot of water weighs 1000 oz., hence to determine the weight of a given bulk of any body the specific gravity of which is known, multiply the cubic content in feet by 1000, and this by the s. g., and the product will be the weight in ounces avoirdupois. Thus, the s. g. of cast-iron is 7.207, that is, it is 7.207 times heavier than an equal bulk of water. A cylinder of cast-iron 1 foot in diameter and 10 feet high, would contain 10 cubic feet, $10 \times 1000 \times 7.207 = 72.070$ oz. = 4500 lbs.

Specific Gravity of Solids.

1. *By the Pitcher.*—} 'll a pitcher, or similar vessel, brim full, put in the body, it will displace its own bulk of water; catch this water as it overflows and weigh it. Divide the weight of the body by that of the water displaced, the quotient will be its specific gravity. A very neat instrument for performing this process accurately has been contrived by Messrs. Eckfeldt and Dubois, of the United States Mint.

2. *By the Hydrostatic Balance.*—Weigh the body, fasten it, preferably by a horse-hair, immerse it in water, and note the *loss of weight*. The weight in air divided by the loss of weight in water = the s. g.

3. *When the Body is Lighter than Water.*—Attach to it some heavy body of known weight in air and water. Weigh the two together, first in air and then in water; note the loss. The loss of weight of the heavy body in water being known the difference between these losses divided *into* the weight of the light body in air, will give the specific gravity. Thus, a bit of wood weighed in air 200 grains, attached to a piece of copper the two weighed in air 2247 grains, and in water 1620 grains, suffering a loss of 627 grains, the copper alone loses in water 230 grains, $627 - 230 = 397$, the loss of the wood; $200 + 397 = .504$, s. g. of the wood.

When the Solid is Soluble in Water.

Take its s. g. in regard to some liquid which does not dissolve it, multiply this by the s. g. of the liquid.

Thus, a piece of sugar weighed in air 400 grs., it lost in oil of turpentine 217.5. $400 \div 217.5 = 1.84$. The s. g. of turpentine is .87; $1.84 \times .87 = 1.6$., s. g. of the sugar.

When the Body is in Powder.

Introduce it into a counterpoise bottle, of which the capacity is known. Fill the bottle with pure water at 60°. It will hold as much less as is equal to the bulk of the powder, and the weight of the powder in air divided by this difference will give the s. g.

Thus, the bottle holds 1000 grs. of water; 100 grs. of emery are introduced, and the bottle filled up with water. If no water were displaced the two should weigh 1100 grs., they really weigh 1070; the difference, 30 grs. = the weight of water displaced; $100 \div 30 = 3.333$, s. g of the emery.

When the Solid is Compound,

As a nugget of gold and quartz. Take the s. g. of the nugget, that of gold and quartz being known, then apply the following formula:

$$\frac{\text{s. g. nugget} - \text{s. g. quartz}}{\text{s. g. gold} - \text{s. g. quartz}} \times \frac{\text{s. g. gold}}{\text{s. g. nugget}} \times \text{weight}$$

of nugget = weight of gold in nugget.

$$\frac{\text{s. g. gold} - \text{s. g. nugget}}{\text{s. g. gold} - \text{s. g. quartz}} \times \frac{\text{s. g. quartz}}{\text{s. g. nugget}} \times \text{weight}$$

of nugget = weight of quartz in do.

This method will do approximately, but not accurately for alloys of metals generally.

SPECIFIC GRAVITY OF LIQUIDS.

By the Balance.

Take a bit of glass rod, note its loss when weighed in water and in the liquid under trial. Divide the latter by the former, the quotient will be the s. g. of the liquid. Thus a glass rod loses in water 171 grs., in alcohol, 143 grs. $143 \div 171 = .836$. s. g. of the alcohol.

Specific Gravity Bottles.

These are made to hold 100 or 1000 grs. of pure water at 60°, and are accompanied by a counterpoise. It is only necessary to fill the bottle with the liquid to be tested. Counterpoise and weigh; the weight in grains will be the s. g. Oily and viscous matter should never be introduced into the s. g. bottle. In case the s. g. bottle is not at hand any light flask will do. Make a file mark on the neck, counterpoise it, fill to the mark with pure water at 60°, note the weight of the water. Empty, dry thoroughly and fill with the liquid to be tested; the weight of this divided by that of the water = s. g.

Hydrometers

Are instruments for determining the specific gravity of liquids by noting the depth to which a stem sinks. They consist of a cylinder with a weight beneath it to make it float upright, and a graduated stem. When intended for liquids lighter than water, the 0 or point at which they float in pure water at 60° is at the lower point of the stem, and as the liquid is lighter they sink more deeply; for liquids heavier than water the 0 is at the top of the scale. Many are graduated according to their proposed use, as alcoholometers, lactometers, saccharometers. (See DISTILLATION). The graduation most employed is that of Beaumé. Excellent hydrometers with the degrees and the true s. g. on the same stem are made by Dr. W. H. Pile of Philadelphia.

To Convert Degrees Beaumé into Specific Gravity.

1. For liquids heavier than water—Subtract the degree B. from 145, and divide into 145, the quotient is the s. g.
2. For liquids lighter than water—Add the degree B. to 130, and divide it into 140. The quotient is the s. g.

To Convert Specific Gravity into Degrees Beaumé.

1. For liquids heavier than water.—Divide the s. g. into 145, and subtract from 145. The remainder is the degree B.
2. For liquids lighter than water.—Divide the s. g. into 140 and subtract 130 from the quotient. The remainder will be the degree B.

Table of Specific Gravity.

Mercury	13,600
Lead	11,325
Copper	9,000
Cast Brass	8,000
Steel	7,850
Wrought Iron	7,780
Cast Iron	7,207
Tin	7,300
Marble	2,690
Common Stone	2,520
Brick	1,800 @ 2,000
Soil	1,974
Coal, anthracite	1,436 @ 1,640
" bituminous	1,270
Sand	1,520
Sea-water	1,030
COMMON WATER	1,000
Oak, (dry)	925
Ash "	800
Maple "	755
Elm "	600
Yellow Pine, "	660
White Pine "	554
Cork	249
Carb. Acid	1·9
Air	1·25
Coal Gas	0·6
Hydrogen	0·0848

The specific gravity in table also represents the number of ounces in each substance in 1 cubic foot ÷ 16 = lbs.

1 cubic foot of Cast Iron	=	450	lbs.
1 " " White Pine	=	34·6	"
1 " " Water	=	62·5	"
10·9 cubic feet of Air	=	1	"
22 " " Coal Gas	=	1	"

GAS.

To Read the Gas Meter.

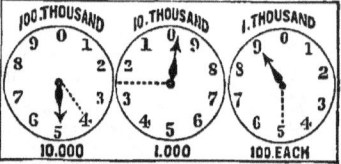

The figures on the index at the right hand denote even *hundreds*. When the hand completes the entire circle it denotes *ten hundred*, and is registered by the hand in the centre circle, pointing to one—each figure in the centre circle being a *thousand*—this entire circle being *ten thousand*, and is registered on the index of the left hand circle by the hand, there denoting by each figure, *ten thousand*.

The quantity of gas which passes through the meter, is ascertained by reading from the index at the time the amount is required to be known, and deducting therefrom the quantity shown by the index at a previous observation.
If the whole is registered by the hands on the three circles above, it indicates........ 49,900
Amount at previous observation, as shown by the dotted lines........................ 42,500

Shows amount which passed through since last taken off........................ 7,400
The register at all times shows the quantity that has passed through since the meter was first set, by deducting from which the amount that has been paid for (without any regard to the time when), shows that the difference remains unpaid.

To Avoid Waste of Gas.

Turn the gas partly off at the meter; much gas is burned to waste by too great pressure in certain localities. In buildings of any size a good regulator will soon pay for itself. Cresson's is the best.

Gas-burners.

The following are those in common use:

Batswing.—This has a single slit at the top of the burner. It is very steady; does not change its form under any pressure. It is, therefore, used in street lamps. It is not, however, economical.

Fish-tail.—This form is generally used in houses; it has two openings in the top, from which the jets of gas issue and form a flat flame, the plane of which is at right angles to that of the openings. When the pressure is too great the flame elongates and *sings*, thus calling attention to the waste. It is an economical burner, but flickers. This unsteadiness is trying to the eyes, and the fish-tail should never be used to read or write by.

Argand.—These are the steadiest and most economical burners, but require a chimney. The gas is allowed to escape by a ring of holes, and the air is admitted both inside and outside of this ring. In the patent Argand the outer ring of air passes through a series of small openings, and the inner ring is deflected into the flame by a button;

FOREIGN GOLD AND SILVER COINS.

It requires a swelled chimney. By cutting off the button a steadier light is obtained, and the economy is nearly the same; straight chimneys are more easily obtained than the others. The best flint-glass chimneys are in the end the cheapest; great loss of light ensues if they are not kept clean. But putting a chimney into hydrant-water, and gradually heating it, it may be cleaned safely; paper gives the best finish. The larger the burner the greater the relative economy.

Relative Light for Unit of Gas.

Batswing	consuming 5 feet,	1·000
Large patent Argand burner	"	6 "	2·880
Common Argand	"	5·4 "	2·132
Single jet	"	2·2 "	1·191
Fish-tail (Union jet)	"	4·5 "	1.513
Large Batswing	"	11·3 "	2·03
Wax candle, 4 to lb			0·143
Sperm " 6 "			0·111
Tallow " 5 "			0.1

Photometry.

1 wax candle, 4 to a lb. burns 13 hours.
1 spermaceti candle, 6 " " 8 "
1 Tallow " 6 " " 6 " 40 m.

A STATEMENT OF FOREIGN GOLD AND SILVER COINS, FROM THE ANNUAL REPORT OF THE DIRECTOR OF THE MINT.

Explanatory Remarks.

The first column embraces the names of the countries where the coins are issued; the second contains the names of the coin, only the principal denominations being given. The other sizes are proportional; and when this is not the case, the deviation is stated.

The third column expresses the weight of a single piece in fractions of the Troyounce, carried to the thousandth, and in a few cases to the ten thousandth, of an ounce. The method is preferable to expressing the weight in grains for commercial purposes, and corresponds better with the terms of the Mint. It may be readily transferred to weight in grains by the following rule: Remove the decimal point; from one-half deduct four per cent. of that half, and the remainder will be grains.

The fourth column expresses the fineness in thousands, *i. e.*, the number of parts of pure gold or silver in 1000 parts of the coin.

The fifth column expresses the valuation of coin The value of silver fluctuates.

Gold Coins.

Country.	Denominations.	Weight. Oz. Dec.	Fineness. Thous.	Value. 1864.
Australia	Pound of 1852	0·281	916.5	$ 5.32.37
"	Sovereign, 1855–60	0·256,5	916	4.85.59
Austria	Ducat	0·112	986	2.28.28
"	Souverain	0·363	900	6.75.35
"	New Union Crown (assumed)	0·357	900	6.64.19
Belgium	Twenty-five Francs	0·254	899	4.72.03
Bolivia	Doubloon	0·867	870	15.59.25
Brazil	Twenty Milreis	0·575	917.5	10.90.57
Central America	Two Escudos	0·209	853.5	3.68.75
Chili	Old Doubloon	0·867	870	15.59.26
"	Ten Pesos	0·492	900	9.15.35
Denmark	Ten Thaler	0·427	895	7.90.01
Ecuador	Four Escudos	0·433	844	7.55.46
England	Pound or Sovereign, new	0·256,7	916.5	4.86.34
"	Pound or Sovereign, average	0·256,2	916	4.84.92
France	Twenty Francs, new	0·207,5	899,5	3.85.83
"	Twenty Francs, average	0·207	899	3.84.69
Germany, North	Ten Thaler	0·427	995	7.90.01
" "	Ten Thaler, Prussian	0·427	903	7.97.07
" "	Krone (Crown)	0·357	900	6.64.20
Germany, South	Ducat	0·112	986	2.28.28
Greece	Twenty Drachms	0·185	900	3.44.19
Hindostan	Mohur	0·374	916	7.08.18
Italy	Twenty Lire	0·207	898	3.84.27
Japan	Old Cobang	0·362	568	4.44.0
"	New Cobang	0·289	572	3.57.6
Mexico	Doubloon, average	0·867.5	866	15.52.98
"	" new	0·867.5	870.5	15.61.05
Naples	Six Ducati, new	0·245	996	5.04.43
Netherland	Ten Guilders	0·215	899	3.99.56
New Granada	Old Doubloon, Bogota	0·868	870	15.61.06
" "	Old Doubloon, Popayan	0·867	858	15.37.75
" "	Ten Pesos, new	0·525	891.5	9.67.51
Peru	Old Doubloon	0·867	868	15.55.67
Portugal	Gold Crown	0·308	912	5.80.66
Prussia	New Union Crown (assumed)	0·357	900	6.64.19
Rome	Two and a half Scudi, new	0·140	900	2.60.47
Russia	Five Roubles	0·210	916	3.97.64
Spain	One Hundred Reals	0·268	896	4.96.39
"	Eighty Reals	0·215	869.5	3.86.44
Sweden	Ducat	0·111	975	2.23.72
Tunis	Twenty five Piastres	0·161	900	2.99.54
Turkey	One Hundred Piastres	0·231	915	4.36.93
Tuscany	Sequin	0·112	999	2.31.29

Silver Coins.

Country.	Denominations.	Weight. Oz. Dec.	Fineness. Thous.	Value. 1864.
Austria	Old Rix Dollar	0·902	833	$ 1.02.27
"	Old Scudo	0·836	902	1.02.64
"	Florin before 1858	0·451	833	51.14
"	New Florin	0·397	900	48.63
"	New Union Dollar	0·596	900	73.01
"	Maria Theresa Dollar, 1780	0·895	838	1.02.12
Belgium	Five Francs	0·803	897	98.04
Bolivia	New Dollar	0·643	903.5	79.07
"	Half Dollar	0·432	667	39.22
Brazil	Double Milreis	0·820	918.5	1.02.53
Canada	Twenty Cents	0·150	925	18.87
Central America	Dollar	0·866	850	1.00.19
Chili	Old Dollar	0·864	908	1.06.79
"	New Dollar	0·801	900.5	98.17
Denmark	Two Rigsdaler	0·927	877	1.10.65
England	Shilling, new	0·182.5	924.5	22.96
"	Shilling, average	0·178	925	22.41
France	Five Francs, average	0·800	900	98.00
Germany, North	Thaler, before 1857	0·712	750	72.67
" "	New Thaler	0·595	900	72.89
Germany, South	Florin, before 1857	0·340	900	41.65
" "	New Florin (assumed)	0·340	900	41.65
Greece	Five Drachms	0·719	900	88.08
Hindostan	Rupee	0·374	916	46.62
Japan	Itzebu	0·279	991	37.63
"	New Itzebu	0·279	890	33.80
Mexico	Dollar, new	0·867.5	903	1.06.62
"	Dollar, average	0·866	901	1.06.20
Naples	Scudo	0·844	830	95.34
Netherlands	Two and a half Guild	0·804	944	1.03.31
Norway	Specie Daler	0·927	877	1.10.65
New Granada	Dollar of 1857	0·803	896	97.92
Peru	Old Dollar	0·866	901	1.06.20
"	Dollar of 1858	0·766	909	94.77
"	Half Dollar, 1835–'38	0·433	650	38.31
Prussia	Thaler before 1857	0·712	750	72.68
"	New Thaler	0·595	900	72.89
Rome	Scudo	0·864	900	1.05.84
Russia	Rouble	0·667	875	79.44
Sardinia	Five Lire	0·800	900	98.00
Spain	New Pistareen	0·166	899	20.31
Sweden	Rix Dollar	1·092	750	1.11.48
Switzerland	Two Francs	0·323	899	39.52
Tunis	Five Piastres	0·511	898.5	62.49
Turkey	Twenty Piastres	0·770	830	86.93
Tuscany	Florin	0·220	925	27.60

CHEMICAL RECEIPTS.

TESTS FOR THE PRECIOUS METALS.

For Gold.

To a diluted colorless solution of chloride of gold, add a few drops of a solution of any salt of tin; or stir the solution of gold with a slip of metallic tin; in either case, the production of a beautiful purple or port wine color will be the immediate result. If the mixture is allowed to settle, it becomes colorless; a purple powder (which is an oxide of gold combined with a little tin) being precipitated. This powder is employed in the painting of china, and is called the purple precipitate of Cassius.

For Silver.

Let fall a drop of a solution of nitrate of silver into a glassful of water, and add to it a grain of common salt. Mutual decomposition of the salts will take place, and chloride of silver (in the form of a white powder) will be precipitated. This precipitate is soluble in ammonia, and blackens on exposure to light.

For Copper.

Add a few drops of a solution of nitrate of copper to a test glass of water; the mixture will be colorless; pour into it a little liquid ammonia. The mixture will then assume a fine deep blue color.

Another.—Ferrocyanide of potassium gives a dense brown precipitate with the salts of copper. This is very delicate.

BOILER INCRUSTATIONS.   433

To Detect Copper in Pickles or Green Tea.

Put a few leaves of the tea or some of the pickle, cut small, into a phial with 2 or 3 drs. of liquid ammonia, diluted with one-half the quantity of water. Shake the phial; when, if the most minute portion of copper be present, the liquid will assume a fine blue color. Or immerse a polished knife-blade; the copper will deposit upon it.

For Iron.

Infusion of galls gives a bluish black, and ferrocyanide of potassium a blue precipitate.

For Manganese.

Sulphydrate of ammonia (made by passing a current of sulphuretted hydrogen gas through solution of ammonia until no more is absorbed), gives a flesh-colored precipitate.

For Mercury.

Protochloride of tin gives a grayish precipitate. A piece of gold introduced into a solution containing mercury and touched with a piece of iron, has the mercury deposited upon it.

For Lead.

Sulphydrate of ammonia gives a black precipitate; chromate of potassa and iodide of potassium, yellow.

To make Oxygen.

Heat in a retort, flask, or test tube, finely powdered chlorate of potassa, mixed with about one-fourth its weight of black oxide of manganese. The gas must be collected by attaching a tube to the flask, the end of which dips under water; a jar full of water being inverted over the end of the delivering tube.

To make Hydrogen.

Act on zinc scraps with diluted sulphuric acid; say 1 part of acid to 10 of water. A common bottle with a perforated cork fitted with a glass tube or bit of pipe-stem, and another bottle to collect the gas, are all the apparatus required. In collecting the gas, the tube must reach quite to the top of the collecting vessel. Care must be taken that all the air has been driven out of each vessel before a light is applied, or an explosion will ensue.

To make Laughing Gas.

Heat gently in a flask or retort, nitrate of ammonia (made by adding carbonate of ammonia to nitric acid until no more gas comes off). It should be allowed to stand some time over water before being breathed.

To make Carbonic Acid.

Pour muriatic acid upon fragments of chalk or marble. The gas being heavy may be collected without the use of water, by simply allowing the delivery tube to pass to the bottom of the receiving vessel.

To make Chlorine.

Heat gently a mixture of muriatic acid and black oxide of manganese. It may be collected like carbonic acid. Care must be taken not to inhale it.

To make Sulphurous Acid.

To 12 oz. of sulphuric acid, in a glass retort, add 2 oz. of sulphur and apply a gentle heat. This is a cheap and easy process.

To make Sulphuretted Hydrogen.

Pour dilute sulphuric acid on sulphuret of iron. This is made by applying a roll of sulphur to a bar of iron heated white hot, or by heating in a crucible a mixture of 2 parts, by weight, of iron-filings and 1 of flowers of sulphur.

Gun-cotton as a Filter.

Gun-cotton, carefully prepared, is scarcely acted on by the most energetic chemical agents at ordinary temperatures. It may therefore be used as a filter for solutions containing strong acids, alkalies, etc.

To Determine whether Wheat Flour, or Bread be Adulterated with Chalk.

Mix with the flour to be tried, a little sulphuric acid; if chalk or whiting be present, an effervescence (arising from the discharge of the carbonic acid of the chalk) will take place; but if the flour be pure, no effervescence is produced.

Another Method.

Pour boiling water on some slices of bread, and then pour into the water some sulphuric acid; if there be any chalk in the bread, an effervescence will ensue as before; but if none be in it, no effervescence will take place.

To Prepare Soda Water.

Soda water is prepared (from powders) precisely in the same manner as ginger beer, except that, instead of the two powders there mentioned, the two following are used: For one glass, 30 grs. of carbonate of soda; for the other, 25 grs. of tartaric (or citric) acid.

To Prepare Ginger-Beer Powders.

Take 2 drs. of fine loaf sugar, 8 grs. of ginger, and 26 grs. of carbonate of potassa, all in fine powder; mix them intimately in a Wedgwood's ware mortar. Take also 27 grs. of citric or tartaric acid (the first is the pleasantest, but the last is the cheapest). The acid is to be kept separate from the mixture. The beer is prepared from the powders thus: Take two tumbler-glasses, each half filled with water; stir up the compound powder in one of them, and the acid powder in another, then mix the two liquors; an effervescence takes place, the beer is prepared and may be drunk off. The effervescence is occasioned by the discharge of the carbonic acid of the carbonate of potass. If the beer is allowed to stand for a few minutes it becomes flat; this is owing to its having lost all its carbonic acid. The cost of these powders is 20 cents a dozen sets.

To Determine whether Water be Hard or Soft.

To ascertain whether or not water be fit for domestic purposes, to a glassful of the water add a few drops of the solution of soap in alcohol. If the water be pure, it will continue limpid; if hard, white flakes will be formed.

To Preserve Phosphorus.

Keep it in places where neither light nor heat has access. It is obtained from druggists in rolls; these are put into a phial filled with cold water, which has been boiled to expel air from it, and the phial is enclosed in an opaque case.

Expeditious Method of Tinning.

Plates or vessels of brass or copper are rapidly and firmly coated with tin by boiling them with a solution of stannate of potassa, mixed with trimmings of tin, or by boiling them with tin-filings and caustic, potash or cream of tartar.

PREVENTING AND REMOVING BOILER INCRUSTATIONS.

The following substances have been used, with more or less success, in preventing and removing the incrustations which are formed by using hard water:—

Krause's Anti-incrustation Powder for Steam Boilers.

Powdered charcoal, sal soda, alum, each 1 lb. sawdust, 8 lbs. Mix. Most of the secret incrustation powders sold are but modifications of this.

Potatoes.

By using about 1-50th of potatoes to the weight of water in a boiler, scale will be prevented, but not removed. Their action is mechanical; they coat the calcareous particles in the water, and prevent them from adhering to the metal.

Extract of Oak Bark.

A mixture has been used of 12 parts of chloride of sodium, 2½ parts of caustic soda, ½ extract of oak bark, ½ of potash, for the boilers of stationary and locomotive engines. The principal agent in this case appears to be the tannin or the extract of oak bark.

Pieces of Oak Wood,

Suspended in the boiler and renewed monthly, prevent all deposit; even from water containing a large quantity of lime. The action depends principally upon the tannic acid.

Sawdust.

Mahogany and oak sawdust has been used to prevent and remove scale; but care must be exercised not to allow it to choke up pipes leading to and from the boiler. Catechu contains tannic acid, and has also been used satisfactorily for boilers. A very small quantity of free tannic acid will attack the iron; therefore, a very limited quantity of these substances should be employed.

Slippery-Elm Bark.

This article has also been used with some success in preventing and removing incrustations.

Soda.

The carbonate of soda has the sanction of Professors Kuhlman and Fresenius, of Germany, Grace Calvert, of England, and others. It is satisfactorily employed for the purpose.

Tin Salt.

The chloride of tin is equal to the muriate of ammonia, and is similar in its action in preventing scale.

Extract of Tobacco, and Spent Tanner's Bark

Have been employed with some degree of satisfaction. The sulphate, not the carbonate, of lime, is the chief agent in forming incrustations. By frequent blowing off, incrustations from carbonate of lime in water will be greatly prevented.

Ammonia.

The muriate of ammonia softens old incrustations. Its action is chemical; it decomposes the scale. About 2 oz. placed in a boiler, twice per week, have kept it clean, without attacking the metal.

Fatty Oils.

It is stated that oils and tallow in a boiler prevent incrustations. A mixture, composed of 3 parts of black-lead, and 18 parts of tallow, applied hot, in coating the interior of a boiler, has been found to prevent scale. It should be applied every few weeks.

Molasses.

About 13 lbs. of molasses, fed occasionally into a boiler of 8-horse power, has prevented incrustations for 6 months.

Curious Mode of Silvering Ivory.

Immerse a small slip of ivory in a weak solution of nitrate of silver, and let it remain till the solution has given it a deep yellow color; then take it out and immerse it in a tumbler of clear water, and expose it in the water to the rays of the sun. In about 3 hours the ivory acquires a black color; but the black surface on being rubbed, soon becomes changed to a brilliant silver.

Soluble Silica.

Add to soluble glass (water-glass) an excess of muriatic acid; put it into a box, the bottom of which is made of parchment-paper, afloat on the surface of water (dialysis); after a few days silica, combined with water, will be found in the box. It may be used for the preservation of building-stone, or to render wood fire and water proof.

Stoppers of Bottles for Chemical Re-agents.

Paraffine is the best material for lubricating the stoppers of bottles containing caustic alkali, as it is not acted upon by chemical agents under ordinary circumstances, and lubricates perfectly.

To Loosen Tight Stoppers.

1. Tap the stopper gently, upwards and sidewise, with a bit of wood.
2. Fasten the upper part of the stopper in the crack of a door or a drawer, and work the bottle gently from side to side.
3. Fasten a string firmly around the stopper (see KNOTS), attach it to a fixed body, and jerk the bottle suddenly downward.
4. When the stopper adheres on account of the solidification of matters dissolved in the liquid in the bottle, a little of the same liquid poured around the base of the stopper, and allowed to remain awhile will often dissolve the hardened matter, and free the stopper.
5. The most effectual way, but one requiring care, is to heat the neck of the bottle evenly and rapidly over an alcohol or gas-flame. The neck expands sooner than the stopper, and it is very rarely that any difficulty is found in the removal of the latter. If the bottle contain inflammable liquids, it is safer to wrap a cloth dipped in boiling water around the neck, instead of exposing it to the naked flame.

To Remove Ink from Paper.

Wash alternately, with a camel's-hair brush, dipped in a solution of oxalic acid and cyanide of potassium.

Artificial Tourmalines.

Dissolve 50 grains of disulphate of quinine in 2 fl. oz. of acetic acid, and 2 oz. of proof-spirit, warmed to 130° Fahr., in a very wide-mouthed flask or glass beaker; then slowly add 50 drops of a mixture of 40 grs. of iodine in 1 oz. of rectified spirits; agitate the mixture, and then set it carefully aside for 6 hours, in an apartment maintained at a temperature of about 50° Fahr. The utmost care must be taken to avoid any motion of the vessel; indeed, all accidental vibrations should be guarded against by suspending the vessel by a string, or by allowing it to rest on a mass of cotton and wool. If, in 6 hours, the large laminæ of the salt have not formed, warm the fluid with a spirit lamp, and when it has become clear, add a few drops of the solution of iodine in spirit. The large laminæ form on the top of the fluid, and should be removed carefully by gliding under one of them a circular piece of thin glass. The specimen should be drained by resting the edge of the glass on a piece of bibulous paper, but it must not be touched on account of its extreme fragility; if any small crystals adhere to its surface, they must be washed off by pouring over it a few drops of watery solution of iodine. When dry the specimen should be placed for a few minutes under a bell-glass by the side of a watch-glass, containing a few drops of tincture of iodine; and, lastly, a very little fluid Canada balsam should be dropped on it, and a thin glass cover applied without heat. Specimens may thus be obtained of extreme thinness, and ½ an inch in diameter, or even larger, possessing scarcely the slightest color, and yet completely polarizing transmitted light.

New Materials for Buttons.

Excellent buttons, and even handsome cameos,

may be made with talc or steatite, provided, after they are made, they be heated for several hours at a nearly white heat. By this strong calcination the steatite gets so hard that it strikes fire with flints, and resists the best tempered file. They may be polished by emery, tripoli, and jeweller's putty; and colored by mineral or organic matters; chloride of gold colors them purple; nitrate of silver, black; exposure to the reducing flame increases very much the brilliancy of the color.

ARTIFICIAL COLD.

When a solid body becomes liquid, a liquid vapor, or, when a gas or vapor expands, heat is abstracted from neighboring bodies, and the phenomena or sensation of cold is produced.

Evaporation produces cold, as is seen familiarly in the chilliness caused by a draught of air blowing on the moist skin. Water may be cooled to 60°, in warm climates, by keeping it in jars of porous earthenware; a flower-pot, moistened and kept in a draught of air, will keep butter, placed beneath it, hard in warm weather. In India water is exposed at night in shallow pans, placed on straw in trenches, and freezes even when the thermometer does not fall below 40° Water may be frozen by its own evaporation under the receiver of an air-pump over sulphuric acid; the process is a delicate one, and not adapted for use on the large scale.

Twining's ice-machine freezes water by the evaporation of ether, aided by the vacuum produced by a pump worked by a steam-engine. The same ether may be used over again indefinitely. The apparatus works well, but, in case of a leak, the ether vapor, mixed with air, would explode; there is always danger of fire.

Carré's Apparatus

Freezes by the evaporation of liquid ammonia, the ammoniacal gas produced being absorbed by water which will take up over 500 times its bulk of the ammonia, which it gives out again on heating. As liquid ammonia boils at 42° below zero, an intense cold is produced. This apparatus is efficient, but as the internal pressure rises sometimes to over 100 lbs. to the inch, it is not quite safe, although no accidents have yet been reported.

Compressed Air.

Air, when compressed, gives out heat which is re-absorbed when it is allowed to expand. By forcing the air into a strong receiver and carrying off the heat developed by a stream of water, it may, on expanding, re-absorb enough to reduce the temperature below 32°. It is thus used in the paraffine works in England, and would be an excellent method of at once ventilating and cooling large buildings.

Freezing Mixtures

Depend upon the conversion of solid bodies into liquids. There are two classes, those used without ice and those in which it is employed. Where extreme cold is required, the body to be frozen should be first cooled as much as possible by one portion of the mixture, and then by a succeeding one.

Without Ice.—Four oz. each of nitre and sal ammoniac in 8 of water will reduce the temperature from 50° to 10°.

Equal parts of nitrate of ammonia and water, from 50° to 4°. The salt may be recovered by evaporation and used over again.

Equal parts of water, crystallized nitrate of ammonia, carbonate of soda, crystallized and in powder, from 50° to 7°.

Five parts of commercial muriatic acid and 8 of Glauber's salt, in powder, from 50° to 0°.

With Ice.—Snow is always preferable. Ice is best powdered by shaving with a plane like a carpenter's, or it may be put into a canvas bag and beaten fine with a wooden mallet.

Equal parts of snow and common salt will produce a temperature of —4°, which may be maintained for hours. This is the best mixture for ordinary use.

Three parts of crystallized chloride of calcium and 2 of snow will produce a cold sufficient to freeze mercury, and to reduce a spirit thermometer from 32° to —50°. The chloride may be recovered by evaporation. There are many other freezing mixtures given in the books, but none are so cheap and efficient as the above.

ANTISEPTICS AND DISINFECTANTS.

Antiseptics are bodies which prevent or retard decay; disinfectants those which are supposed similarly to retard or prevent the spread of disease, whether epidemic or contagious. The latter term, however, is popularly applied to deodorizers or bodies which remove the offensive smell accompanying decaying organic matter.

Antiseptics.

Salt, spices and sugar are too well known to require comment. Professor Morgan's method of salting meat is to inject the brine into the aorta, or main artery; this process is highly recommended on the score of simplicity and economy. Alcohol and glycerine are used as preservative solutions. The latter does not shrink or alter the color of animal or vegetable substances preserved in it.

Gondby's Solutions.

1. (For ordinary use in preserving specimens.) Alum, 1 oz.; bay salt, 2 oz.; corrosive sublimate, 1 gr.; water, 1 pt. In very tender tissues, or where there is a tendency to mouldiness, use 2 grs. of corrosive sublimate.

2. (For objects containing carbonate of lime.) Bay salt, ¼ lb.; corrosive sublimate, 1 gr.; water, 1 pt.

3. (For old preparations.) Bay salt, ¼ lb.; arsenious acid (white arsenic), 10 grs.; water, 1 pt. Dissolve by the aid of heat. When there is a tendency to softening, add 1 gr. of corrosive sublimate.

Reboulet's Solution.

Nitre, 1 part; alum, 2 parts; chloride of lime, 4 parts; water, 16 or 20 parts; to be diluted as may be necessary. For pathological specimens.

Stapleton's Solution.

Alum, 2½ oz.; nitre, 1 dr.; water, 1 qt.

Burnett's Solution

Is made by adding scrap zinc to muriatic acid so long as any gas (hydrogen) is evolved. If it be required neutral, add carbonate of soda until a slight precipitate is seen. It is largely used in the preservation of timber, and in embalming, being in the latter case injected into the aorta.

Kyan's Solution

Is a strong solution of corrosive sublimate in water; used for the same purposes as Burnett's, but now generally superseded by the latter.

Coal Tar

Is used to preserve wood; it is boiled and applied as a paint, or forced into the pores of the wood under pressure.

Disinfectants.

The only true method to prevent the spread of contagious or epidemic diseases is thorough cleanliness. Abundance of air to dilute the poison, and the removal of organic effete matter by liberal use of water or soap and water, are effectual. Lime acts by destroying organic matter and absorbing certain offensive gases. Hence the use of white-washing. Sulphurous acid checks organic change or fermentation. A high temperature, say 240° Fahr., is useful in disinfecting clothes, letters, etc. Condy's Solution acts by destroying organic matter; solutions of chloride of zinc, corrosive sublimate, persulphate or perchloride of iron act by coagulating certain organic matters and preventing further decay; they also absorb sulphuretted hydrogen. Chloride of lime (bleaching salt), chlorine, nitrate of lead, and copperas are merely deodorizers. Pastils (see PERFUMERY), burned sugar, vinegar, and burning tar, merely disguise offensive odors.

Condy's Solution.

A saturated solution of permanganate of potassa is one of the most efficient and elegant of all disinfectants. A teaspoonful in a soup-plate of water, exposed in a room, quickly removes any offensive smell; when the pink color disappears more must be added. It has been used to remove the smell of bilge-water and guano from ships. It speedily cleanses foul water and makes it drinkable. A teaspoonful to a hogshead is generally enough, but more may be added, until the water retains a slight pinkish tint. This will disappear, by putting a stick into the water for a few minutes.

Ledoyen's Solution.

Litharge, 13½ oz.; nitric acid, s. g. 1·38, 12 oz., previously diluted with water, 6 pts. It contains nitrate of lead, and is merely a deodorizer.

Chlorine.

Free chlorine is seldom used, on acount of its offensive and suffocating qualities.

Chloride of lime contains hypochlorite of lime and chloride of calcium and lime. It is made into a paste with water; acids cause it to evolve chlorine.

Eau de Javelle is made by adding to chloride of lime 1 part, water 15 parts, and agitate at intervals for an hour; then dissolve 2 oz. carbonate of potassa in ¼ pint water. Mix the solutions, and when the mixture has settled pour off the clear part. Or, by passing a stream of chlorine through a solution of carbonate of potassa to saturation. It contains hypochlorite of potassa and chloride of potassium.

Labarraque's Solution.

Pass chlorine through a solution of carbonate of soda (1 lb. in water 1 qt.) to saturation; or, to a mixture of chloride of lime ½ lb., and water 3 pints, add 7 oz. crystallized carbonate of soda, in 1 pt. of water. Proceed in all respects as for Eau de Javelle. These solutions will remove fruit-stains from linen.

Iron Compounds.

Perchloride of Iron is made by dissolving iron in muriatic acid, and while boiling add nitric acid as long as red fumes are evolved. It is a powerful styptic.

Monsel's Solution, subsulphate of iron, is made by dissolving copperas 12 oz. (troy), in water 12 oz., adding sulphuric acid 510 grs., and then while boiling adding nitric acid as long as red fumes come off. It is much used as a styptic and astringent, and is a cheap and powerful deodorizer. *Copperas* mixed with ¼ its weight of lime is a cheap and popular agent in deodorizing sinks.

Carbolic Acid,

Or coal-tar creosote, coagulates organic matter; is a powerful antiseptic and deodorizer. It is used mixed with lime. Ridgewood's disinfecting powder contains 5 to 8 per cent. each of lime and of carbolic acid, and 70 to 80 per cent. of fuller's earth.

Charcoal

Is a useful deodorizer and purifier; it acts by its attraction for organic matter and gases. By condensing the latter as well as the oxygen of the air in its pores it causes rapid combination. Small animals buried in charcoal are rapidly converted into skeletons, while no offensive smell is noticed even in warm weather. Water is best kept in charred casks; foul water is purified by filtration through charcoal. Meat lightly tainted is restored by wrapping in powdered charcoal; animal charcoal is the best. Lampblack is nearly worthless for these purposes. Animal charcoal is an antidote to all animal and vegetable poisons; it rapidly removes organic coloring matters and also vegetable bitters from solution. Picric acid is not thus removed, and may in this way be detected when used instead of hops in brewing.

Noxious Vapors.

To prevent the effects of noxious vapors from wells, cellars, fermenting liquors, etc., procure a free circulation of air, either by ventilators, or opening the doors or windows where it is confined, or by keeping fires in the infected place; or throwing in lime, recently burnt or powdered.

Old wells, vaults, and sewers, which have been long shut up from the air, are generally occupied by vapors which soon prove fatal to persons breathing them. The property which these vapors have of extinguishing flame, affords the means of detecting their presence, and thereby avoiding the danger of an incautious exposure to them. When such places, therefore, are opened to be cleaned out or repaired, a lighted candle should be let down slowly by means of a cord, before any person is suffered to descend; and if it burns freely until it gets to the surface of the water, or other matter covering the bottom, the workmen may then venture down with safety. But, if without any accident, the candle is extinguished, and continues to be so on repeated trials, then the air of the place is highly noxious.

Parchment Paper

Is made by immersing unsized paper for a few seconds into a mixture (cold) of 2 parts, by measure, of commercial sulphuric acid, and 1 part of water; then washing in water, and afterwards in dilute solution of ammonia. It is water-proof, about 6 times as strong as paper, and may be used in all cases as a substitute for parchment, which it resembles. The same effect is produced by soaking paper in a solution of neutral chloride of zinc, s. g. 2100. It is then treated as before. This paper is used in Mr. Graham's process for dialysis.

New Mode of Preparing Paper for the Use of Draughtsmen, etc.

Reduce to a powder, and dissolve quickly in a glazed earthen vessel, containing cold water, some gum tragacanth, having been well worked with a wooden spatula, to free it from lumps. There must be a sufficient quantity of water, to give to this diluted gum the consistence of a jelly. Paper, and some sorts of stuffs, upon which, if this composition be smoothly applied, with a pencil or a brush, and dried before a gentle fire, will receive either water or oil colors; in using water colors, they must be mixed with a solution of the above gum. This cloth or paper, so prepared, will take any color except ink. When it is intended to retouch any particular part of the drawing, it should be washed with a sponge, or clean linen, or a pencil (containing some of the above-mentioned liquid); if the part is only small, it will then rise quickly, and appear as if repainted.

New Mode of Preserving Impressions in Sand, etc.

A sheet of thin iron-plate was placed over the marks made, and supported by an iron stand, at a distance of about 1½ inches from the surface of the ground; a quantity of lighted charcoal was then placed on the iron plate, which soon became red hot, and of course heated the spot over which it was placed. When the latter was raised to 100° Centigrade (212° Fahr.) the fire, together with the plate, was removed, and a quantity of finely-divided stearic acid was strewed over the impression by means of a sieve. The powder used was that of a common stearine candle, dissolved by heat in alcohol, and then thrown into a large quantity of cold water, when the stearine falls to the bottom in the form of a fine precipitate. This powder is so light and impalpable, that it is said it might be sifted over an impression in the dust of a common road, without, in the slightest degree, interfering with the faintest mark. The instant it touched the heated surface of the ground in question it melted, and, as it were, sealed the whole of the loose atoms into one compact mass. When a sufficient quantity of the stearine had been applied, the place was left until it had become completely cold; the surrounding earth was then dug out carefully at some little distance from the edges of the impression, and the portion containing this latter was lifted up in one entire block, and laid on a cloth several times doubled, the edges of which were raised up so as to form a kind of border, or rather framing, into which, and against the sides of the sandy earth containing the impression, plaster of Paris was poured; and when the latter was set, the whole could be handled without danger, and was firm enough to bear packing and carriage to any distance. It is evident, therefore, that if necessary it might also be used as a mould, from which casts in plaster could be obtained. The value of such a process, as an aid in criminal cases, is too self-evident to require demonstration; the production of the tell-tale impressions in a court of justice, where every mark can be conveniently exhibited and compared with the object by which it was produced, may be equally useful in the proof of guilt and of innocence, and it would be strange, indeed, if a use for such a process be not discovered in matters of scientific or practical interest.

To make Writing Indelible.

The following simple process will make lead-pencil writing or drawing as indelible as if done with ink. Lay the writing in a shallow dish, and pour skimmed milk upon it. Any spots not wet at first may have the milk placed upon them lightly with a feather. When the paper is all wet over with the milk take it up and let the milk drain off, and whip off with the feather the drops which collect on the lower edge. Dry it carefully, and it will be found to be perfectly indelible. It cannot be removed even with India-rubber. It is an old recipe and a good one.

To render Paper Fire-proof.

Whether the paper be plain, written, printed on, or even marbled, stained, or painted for hangings, dip it in a strong solution of alum-water, and then thoroughly dry it. In this state it will be fire-proof. This will be readily known by holding a slip thus prepared over a candle. Some paper requires to imbibe more of the solution than by a single immersion, in which case the dipping and drying must be repeated until it becomes fully saturated. Neither the color nor quality of the paper will be in the least affected by this process, but, on the contrary, will be improved.

A Composition to render Wood Fire-proof.

Glass made by heating sand with twice its weight of soda-ash or pearlash is soluble in boiling water, when finely powdered. Applied with a brush, it renders woodwork fire-proof, and when once dry is not affected by cold water.

To Render Dresses Incombustible.

Take of a solution of tungstate of soda, of a specific gravity 1·14, 100 parts; phosphate of soda, 3 parts. The articles are dipped in the solution, and allowed to dry before ironing. This solution keeps well, and is used in the Royal laundry.

How to Act when the Clothes take Fire.

Three persons out of 4 would rush right up to the burning individual, and begin to paw with their hands without any definite aim. It is useless to tell the victim to do this or that, or call for water. In fact, it is generally best to say not a word, but seize a blanket from a bed, or a cloak, or any woollen fabric—if none is at hand, take any woollen material—hold the corners as far apart as you can, stretch them out higher than your head, and, running boldly to the person, make a motion of clasping in the arms, most about the shoulders. This instantly smothers the fire, and saves the face. The next instant throw the unfortunate person on the floor. This is an additional safety to the face and breath, and any remnant of flame can be put out more leisurely. The next instant, immerse the burnt part in cold water, and all pain will cease with the rapidity of lightning. Next, get some common flour, remove from the water, and cover the burnt parts with an inch thickness of flour, if possible; put the patient to bed, and do all that is possible to soothe until the physician arrives. Let the flour remain until it falls off itself, when a beautiful new skin will be found. Unless the burns are deep, no other application is needed. The dry flour for burns is the most admirable remedy ever proposed, and the information ought to be imparted to all. The principle of its action is that, like the water, it causes instant and perfect relief from pain, by totally excluding the air from the injured parts. Spanish whiting and cold water, of a mushy consistency, are preferred by some. Dredge on the flour until no more will stick, and cover with cotton batting.

To Bleach Sponges.

Wash in hot dilute soda lye; then immerse in dilute muriatic acid, 1 part to 10 of water, until all gritty particles are removed, and no more gas arises; then immerse in a second bath of dilute muriatic acid, containing 3 per cent. of hyposulphite of soda, for 48 hours.

To take out Mildew.

Wet the linen where spotted in Labarraque's Solution (solution of chlorinated soda), or solution of chloride of lime (bleaching salt), or chlorine water; it will immediately disappear. Wash out at once with warm water. This is a better plan than that given in p. 314. Fruit and wine stains of all kinds may be removed in the same manner.

Simple Mode of Purifying Water.

A tablespoonful of pulverized alum sprinkled into a hogshead of water (the water stirred at the same time) will, after a few hours, by precipitating to the bottom the impure particles, so purify it that it will be found to possess nearly all the freshness and clearness of the finest spring-water. A pailful, containing 4 gallons, may be purified by a single teaspoonful of the alum.

Another.—Add to a hogshead of water a table-spoonful of a saturated solution of permanganate of potassa; this effectually destroys all organic matter. If the water retain a pink hue, put a stick or chip in it when the color will shortly disappear.

To Cure Dry-rot in Timber.

Saturate the wood in a weak solution of copperas, for joists, beams, rafters, and floorings; or, soak the wood in lime-water, suffering it to dry, and then apply water in which there is a weak solution of vitriolic acid; or wash it with a strong solution of potash, then with pyroligneous acid in which the oxide of lead or iron has been dissolved; and finally, with alum-water.

A current of air under a floor will always prevent the dry-rot, and stop it when it has commenced.

In boarding kitchens and other rooms on the basement story, the planks should be steeped in a strong solution of vitriol or alum, and when they are dried, the side next to the earth should receive a coat of tar or common paint.

Solutions used in Preserving Timber.

The following have been employed. They are forced into the pores of the wood by putting it into a close vessel, exhausting the air, and then allowing the liquid to flow in. In some cases the timber is merely immersed; in others the liquid flows in under heavy pressure. In Bouchérie's method the green tree is felled, the branches trimmed off, and a bag containing sulphate of copper or other antiseptic agent attached to the butt. The sap is gradually expelled by displacement, and flows from the free end of the log, the antiseptic solution taking its place.

These solutions probably act by coagulating the albuminous matters of the wood, and thus preventing the beginning of decay or dry-rot. They also prevent the attacks of insects. Corrosive sublimate (Kyan), chloride of zinc (Burnett), sulphate of copper (Bouchérie), chloride of calcium, followed by sulphate of iron (Payne), crude pyroligneous acid, saturated with iron scraps (Bethell), coal tar.

Prevention of Decay in Timber.

Well-seasoned timber may be preserved by charring the surface. The process adopted in the French dockyards is to use a jet of mixed coal-gas and air; the two being conveyed by India-rubber tubes, which unite at the jet. The air is forced in by a bellows worked by the foot of the operator. A slight previous coating of tar is useful for filling up cracks, and causing a uniformity of action of the flame.

To Check the Warping of Planks.

The face of the planks should be cut in the direction from east to west as the tree stood. The strongest side of a piece of timber is that which, in its natural position, faced the north.

To Get Oil out of Boards.

Mix together fuller's earth and soap lees, and rub it into the boards. Let it dry and then scour it off with some strong soft soap and sand, or use lees to scour it with. It should be put on hot, which may easily be done by heating the lees.

To Prevent the Splitting of Logs and Planks.

Logs and planks split at the ends because the exposed surface dries faster than the inside. Saturate muriatic acid with lime and apply like whitewash to the ends. The chloride of calcium formed attracts moisture from the air, and prevents the splitting.

Mode of Detecting Decay in Timber.

The Cosmos reports from the other journals a simple mode, said to have been adopted from immemorial times in the ship-yards of Venice, for ascertaining the fitness of timber for their constructions. "A person applies his ear to the middle of one of the ends of the timber, while another strikes upon the opposite end. If the wood is sound and of good quality, the blow is very distinctly heard, however long the beam may be. If the wood were disaggregated by decay or otherwise, the sound would be for the most part destroyed.

To Preserve Polished Irons from Rust.

Polished iron-work may be preserved from rust by a mixture not very expensive, consisting of copal varnish intimately mixed with as much olive-oil as will give it a degree of greasiness, adding thereto nearly as much spirit of turpentine as of varnish; or varnish with wax dissolved in benzine. The cast-iron work is best preserved by rubbing it with black-lead.

But where rust has begun to make its appearance on grates or fire-irons, apply a mixture of tripoli, with half its quantity of sulphur, intimately mingled on a marble slab and laid on with a piece of soft leather; or emery and oil may be applied with excellent effect; not laid on in the usual slovenly way, but with a spongy piece of the fig-tree fully saturated with the mixture. This will not only clean, but polish, and render the use of whiting unnecessary.

To Preserve Brass Ornaments.

Brass ornaments, when not gilt or lackered, may be cleaned in the same way, and a fine color may be given to them by two simple processes. The first is to beat sal ammoniac into a fine powder, then to moisten it with soft water, rubbing it on the ornaments; which must be heated over charcoal and rubbed dry with bran and whiting. The second is to wash the brass work with roche alum boiled in strong lye, in the proportion of an ounce to a pint. When dry it must be rubbed with fine tripoli. Either of these processes will give to brass the brilliancy of gold.

Easy Mode of Taking Impressions from Coins, etc.

A very easy and elegant way of taking the impressions of medals and coins, not generally known, is thus described by Dr. Shaw: Melt a little isinglass glue with brandy, and pour it thinly over the metal so as to cover its whole surface; let it remain on for a day or two, till it is thoroughly dried and hardened, and then taking it off it will be fine, clear, and as hard as a piece of Muscovy glass, and will have a very elegant impression of the coin. It will also resist the effects of damp air, which occasions all other kinds of glue to soften and bend if not prepared in this way.

Adamas.

A substitute for metal in the manufacture of gas-burners, journal bearings, taps, etc., is made of finely-powdered soapstone, pressed into moulds and annealed.

Soapstone Powder as a Lubricator.

Soapstone powder, in the form of dust, is proposed as a lubricant for the axles of machines. For this purpose it is prepared as follows: It is first reduced to the condition of very fine powder; then it is washed to remove all gritty particles; then it is steeped for a short period in dilute muriatic acid (about 1 qt. of acid to 20 of water), in which it is stirred until all particles of iron which it contains are dissolved. The powder is then washed in pure water again, to remove all traces of acid; then it is dried, and is the purified steatite powder used for lubrication. It is not used alone, but is mixed with oils and fats, in the proportion of about 35 per cent. of the powder, added to paraffine, rape, or other oil. This steatite powder, mixed with any of the soapy compounds, which are also now used, in many cases, for lubrication, also answers a good purpose. It is chiefly intended for heavy machinery, such as the journals of water-wheels, railway and other carriages.

Ransome's Artificial Stone.

Make sand or gravel into a paste with fluid silicate of soda (water-glass), mould it to the desired shape, and dip into a solution of chloride of calcium. This solution is made by neutralizing muriatic acid with lime, chalk, limestone, or marble. The mass becomes solid in a few minutes, and is exceedingly strong and durable.

To Imitate Ground Glass.

A ready way of imitating ground glass is to dissolve Epsom salts in beer, and apply with a brush. As it dries it crystallizes.

To Drill Glass.

Wet an ordinary drill with petroleum or benzine; turpentine will answer, but not so well; it will then bore common glass nearly as rapidly as steel. If it is intended to bore through, the glass should be first countersunk on each side with a drill dressed off so as to form a very flat three-sided pyramid. Flint and plate-glass are very difficult to bore.

A New Kind of Electric Machine.

The electro-magnetic coil has, in a great measure, superseded the electric machine; the latter, however, will never cease to be an object of interest; and, it is probable, will always be preferred for some purposes. The expense and difficulty of managing large plates and cylinders of glass have hitherto been obstacles to the use of large electric machines. These obstacles appear now removed — glass being rendered unnecessary by the discovery of a far more convenient and effective material. M. Edmond Bequerel exhibited to the Academy of Sciences on a recent occasion an electric machine, the plate of which was made of indurated red sulphur, the invention of a civil engineer. It was 80 centimetres in diameter, and afforded a spark 14 centimetres in length. No amalgamated cushions were required with it, the skin of a cat being quite sufficient to produce every desired effect. Sulphur undergoes extraordinary changes by successive fusions; becoming extremely hard and tenacious. After the third fusion it no longer acts on metals, or possesses its characteristic odor. The plate used by M. Bequerel was formed by fusing the sulphur 3 times in a cast-iron vessel, at a temperature between 250° and 300° Cent., and allowing it, after each fusion, to cool thoroughly. After the 1st and 2nd fusions it was crushed to a coarse powder; and, after the 3rd, it was poured into a plaster-mould. Plates, 4 metres in diameter, may easily be made in this way; they cost extremely little; and, besides being more efficient, are far less hygrometric than glass.

WEATHER PROGNOSTICS.

TO CONSTRUCT BAROMETERS.

The tubes intended for barometers ought to be sealed hermetically on both ends, immediately after they are made at the glass-house, and to be kept in this state until they are fitted up. Without this precaution they are apt to be sullied with dust, moisture, and other impurities, which it is afterwards almost impossible to remove on account of the smallness of their diameters. When they are opened, which may be done with a file, care should be taken not to breathe into them, nor to wash them with spirit of wine, or other fluid, experience having proved that in tubes so treated, the mercury always stands a little below its proper level; this is owing to the adhesion of a little of the spirit of wine to the sides of the tube. When cleaning is necessary, it must be done with a fine linen rag that has been previously well dried.

The tubes ought to be as perfectly cylindrical as possible, though, in some cases, this is not absolutely necessary. They should be about 33 inches in length, and the diameter of their bore should be at least 2 or 2½ lines, otherwise the friction, and the capillary action will be apt to affect the free motion of the mercury. The glass should not be very thick, as it is apt in that case to break; when the mercury is boiled in the tube half a line is sufficient.

The mercury ought to be perfectly pure and free from all foreign metals. The best is that which has been recently revived from cinnabar; the common mercury of the shops being often adulterated intentionally with tin, lead, and bismuth, stands at various heights in the tube, according to the nature and quantity of the foreign substances with which it is amalgamated.

To Obtain the Mercury Pure.

For this purpose take a pound of cinnabar and reduce it to powder; mix it well with 5 or 6 oz. of iron or steel filings; and, having put the mixture into an iron retort, expose the whole to the heat of a reverberatory furnace; the mercury will soon pass over in a state of great purity, and may be obtained by adapting to the retort an earthen receiver, which has been previously half filled with water. Commercial mercury may be purified by distilling it over a portion of cinnabar. These are put into an iron bottle with an iron tube attached; to the end of the iron tube is one made of leather or India-rubber which dips beneath the surface of water constantly renewed.

Process of Filling the Tube.

Before being introduced into the tube, the mercury ought to be well heated, or even boiled in a glazed earthen pipkin, in order to drive off any moisture which may adhere to it, but this will be unnecessary if the mercury has been recently reduced.

The mercury ought likewise to be boiled in the tube to expel any air or moisture which may still remain attached to it, or to the inside of the tube. This is done in the following manner: Pour as much mercury into the tube as will make it stand to the length of 3 or 4 inches; and introduce a long wire of iron to stir it during the boiling. Expose the mercury in the tube gradually to the heat of a chafing-dish of burning charcoal, or a well regulated gas flame; and when it begins to boil, stir it gently with the iron wire, to facilitate the disengagement of the bubbles of the air. When the first portion of the mercury has been sufficiently boiled, and all the air extricated, remove the tube from the chafing-dish and allow the whole to cool, taking care not to bring it into contact with any cold substance. Introduce an equal quantity of mercury, and treat it in the same manner, withdrawing the wire a little so that it may not reach below the upper part of the mercury already freed from air. The chafing-dish must also be placed immediately under the mercury which has been last poured in. Repeat the same process with each successive portion of mercury till the tube is filled, always applying the heat very cautiously; and be equally careful in allowing it to cool before a fresh portion of mercury is poured in.

The Aneroid Barometer

Consists of a brass-box partially exhausted of air with an elastic lid of corrugated brass. Changes of atmospheric pressure are indicated by the movements of the lid which are transmitted to an index hand. It is light, portable, contains no liquid, and is more sensitive than the mercurial barometer.

READING THE BAROMETER.

The following manual of the barometer has been compiled by Rear-Admiral Fitzroy, and published by the Board of Trade. It has been slightly altered to suit the climate of the United States.

Familiar as the practical use of weather-glasses is, at sea as well as on land, only those who have long watched their indications and compared them carefully, are really able to conclude more than that the rising glass usually foretells less wind or rain, a falling barometer more rain or wind, or both; a high one fine weather, and a low one the contrary. But useful as these general conclusions are in most cases, they are sometimes erroneous, and then remarks may be rather hastily made, tending to discourage the inexperienced.

By attention to the following observation (the results of many years' practice, and many persons' experience), any one not accustomed to use a barometer may do so without difficulty. The barometer shows whether the air is getting lighter or heavier, or is remaining in the same state. The quicksilver falls as the air becomes lighter, rises as it becomes heavier, and remains at rest in the glass tube while the air is unchanged in weight. Air presses upon everything within about 40 miles of the world's surface, like a much lighter ocean, at the bottom of which we live, not feeling its weight because our bodies are full of air, but feeling its currents, the winds. Towards any place from which the air has been drawn by suction, air presses with a force or weight of nearly 15 lbs. on a square inch of surface. Such a pressure holds the limpet to the rock when, by contracting itself, the fish has made a place without air under its shell. Another familiar instance is, that of the fly, which walks on the ceiling with feet that stick. The barometer tube, emptied of air and filled with pure mercury, is turned down into a cup or cistern containing the same fluid, which feeling the weight of air, is so pressed by it as to balance a column of about 30 inches (more or less) in the tube, where no air presses on the top of the column.

If a long pipe, closed at one end only, were emptied of air, filled with water, the open end kept in water, and the pipe held upright, the water would rise in it more than 30 feet. In this way water barometers have been made. A proof of this effect is shown by any well with a suckingpump, up which, as is commonly known, the water will rise nearly 30 feet by what is called suction, which is, in fact, the pressure of air towards an empty place.

The words on scales of barometers should not be so much regarded for weather indications as the rising or falling of the mercury, for if it stand at "changeable," and then rise towards "fair," it presages a change of wind or weather, though not so great as if the mercury had risen higher; and, on the contrary, if the mercury stand above "fair," and then fall, it presages a change, though not to so great a degree as if it had stood lower; besides which, the direction and force of the wind are not in any way noticed. It is not from the point at which the mercury may stand that we are alone to form a judgment of the state of the weather, but from its rising or falling, and from the movements of immediately preceding days, as well as hours, keeping in mind effects of change of direction and dryness or moisture, as well as alteration of force or strength of wind.

In this part of the world, towards the higher latitudes, the quicksilver ranges, or rises and falls, nearly three inches—namely, between about thirty inches and nine-tenths (30.9), and less than twenty-eight inches (28.0) on extraordinary occasions; but the usual range is from about thirty inches and a half (30.5) to about twenty-nine inches. Near the Line, or in equatorial places, the range is but a few tenths, except in storms, when it sometimes falls to twenty-seven inches.

The sliding scale (Vernier) divides the tenths into 10 parts each, or hundredths of an inch. The number of divisions on the Vernier exceeds that in an equal space of the fixed scale by one.

By a thermometer the weight of air is not shown. No air is within the tube, none can get in. But the bulb of the tube, is full of mercury which contracts by cold and swells by heat, according to which effect the thread of metal in the small tube is drawn down or pushed up so many degrees, and thus shows the temperature.

If a thermometer have a piece of linen round the bulb, wetted enough to keep it damp by a thread or wick dipping into a cup of water, it will show less heat than a dry one, in proportion to the dryness of the air and quickness of drying. In very damp weather, with or before rain, fog, or dew, a wet and dry bulb thermometer will be nearly alike.

For ascertaining the dryness or moisture of air, the readiest and surest method is the comparison of two thermometers, one dry, the other just moistened and kept so. Cooled by evaporation as much as the state of the air admits, the moist (or wet) bulb thermometer shows a temperature nearly equal to that of the other one, when the atmosphere is extremely damp or moist; but lower at other times in proportion to the dryness of air and consequent evaporation—as far as 12° or 15° in this climate, 20° or even more elsewhere. From 4° to 8° of difference is usual in England, and about 7° is considered healthy for inhabited rooms. The wet and dry bulb thermometer on the same frame, the water being supplied by a bird fountain, constitutes August's or Mason's hygrometers.

The thermometer fixed to a barometer intended to be used only as a weather-glass, shows the temperature of air about it, nearly, but does not show the temperature of mercury within, exactly. It does so, however, near enough for ordinary practical purposes, provided that no sun, nor fire, nor lamp heat is allowed to act on the instrument partially.

The mercury in the cistern and tube being affected by cold or heat, makes it advisable to consider this when endeavoring to foretell coming weather by the length of the column.

Briefly, the barometer shows weight or pressure of the air; the thermometer, heat and cold, or temperature; and the wet thermometer, compared with a dry one, the degree of moisture or dampness.

It should always be remembered that the state of the air foretells coming weather rather than shows the weather that is present—an invaluable fact too often overlooked; that the longer the time between the signs and the change foretold by them, the longer such altered weather will last, and, on the contrary, the less the time between a warning and a change, the shorter will be the continuance of such foretold weather.

To know the state of the air not only barometers and thermometers should be watched, but the appearance of the sky should be vigilantly noticed.

If the barometer has been about its ordinary height, say near 30 inches (at the sea level), and is steady, or rising while the thermometer falls, and dampness becomes less, northwesterly or northerly wind, or less wind, less rain or snow may be expected.

On the contrary, if a fall takes place with a rising thermometer and increased dampness, wind and rain may be expected from the south-eastward, southward or south-westward. A fall with a low thermometer foretells snow. A rise during frost indicates snow.

Exceptions to these rules occur when a north-easterly wind with wet (rain, hail or snow) is impending, before which the barometer often rises (on account of the direction of the coming wind alone) and deceives persons, who from that sign only (the rising) expect fair weather.

When the barometer is rather below its ordinary height, say down to near 29½ inches (at the sea level), a rise foretells less wind, or a change in its direction toward the northward, or less wet; but when it has been very low, about 29 inches, the first rising usually precedes or indicates strong wind; at times heavy squalls from the northwestward, northward or northeastward, after which violence a gradually rising glass foretells improving weather, if the thermometer falls; but if the warmth continue, probably the wind will back (shift against the sun's course) and more southerly or southwesterly wind will follow, especially if the barometer's rise is sudden.

The most dangerous shifts of wind or the heaviest northerly gales happen soon after the barometer first rises from a very low point, or if the wind veers gradually at some time afterwards.

Indications of approaching changes of weather and the direction and force of winds are shown less by the height of the barometer than by its falling or rising. Nevertheless, a height of more than thirty (30.0) inches (at the level of the sea) is indicative of fine weather and moderate winds, except from east to north occasionally or during frost, when northeast winds and snow are indicated.

The barometer is said to be falling when the mercury in the tube is sinking, at which time its upper surface is sometimes concave or hollow; or when the hand of the wheel barometer or Aneroid moves to the left. The barometer is rising when the mercurial column is lengthening, its upper surface being convex or rounded, or when the hand moves to the right.

A rapid rise of the barometer indicates unsettled weather, a slow movement the contrary; as likewise a steady barometer, which, when continued, and with dryness, foretells very fine weather.

The greatest depressions of the barometer are with gales from S.E., S., or S.W.; the greatest elevations, with wind from N.W., N., or N.E., or with calm.

Though the barometer generally falls with a southerly and rises with a northerly wind, the contrary sometimes occurs; in which cases, the southerly wind is usually dry with fine weather, or the northerly wind is violent and accompanied by rain, snow or hail; perhaps with lightning.

When the barometer sinks considerably, much wind, rain (perhaps with hail) or snow will follow; with or without lightning. The wind will be from the northward, if the thermometer is low, (for the season), from the southward if the thermometer is high. Occasionally a low glass is followed or attended by lightning only, while a storm is beyond the horizon.

A sudden fall of the barometer with a westerly wind, is sometimes followed by a violent storm from N.W., or N., or N.E.

If a gale sets in from the E. or S.E., and the wind veers by the S., the barometer will continue falling until the wind is near a marked change, when a lull may occur, after which the gale will soon be renewed, perhaps suddenly and violently, and the veering of the wind towards the N.W., N., or N.E., will be indicated by a rising of the barometer with a fall of the thermometer.

Three causes (at least) appear to affect a barometer:

1. The direction of the wind; the northeast wind tending to raise it the most, the southwest to lower it the most, and wind from points of the compass between them proportionally as they are nearer one or the other extreme point.

N.E. and S.W. may, therefore, be called the wind's extreme bearings.

The range or difference of height shown, due to change of direction only, from one of these bearings to the other (supposing strength or force and moisture to remain the same), amounts in these latitudes to about ½ an inch (as read off).

2. The amount taken by itself of vapor (moisture, wet, rain, or snow in the wind remaining the same), seems to cause a change amounting in an extreme case to about ½ an inch.

3. The strength or force alone of wind, from any quarter (moisture and direction being unchanged), is preceded or foretold by a fall or rise, according as the strength will be greater or less, ranging in extreme cases to more than 2 inches.

Hence, supposing three causes to act together, in extreme cases, the height would vary from near 31 in. (30·9) to about 27 in. (27·0), which has happened, though rarely (and even in tropical latitudes).

In general the three causes act much less strongly, and are less in accord, so that ordinary varieties of weather occur much more frequently than extreme changes.

Another general rule requires attention, which is, that the wind usually appears to veer, shift, or go round with the sun (right-handed, or from left to right), and that when it does not do so, or backs, more wind or bad weather may be expected, instead of improvement.

It is not by any means intended to discourage attention to what is usually called "weather wisdom." On the contrary, every prudent person will combine observation of the elements with such indications as he may obtain from instruments, and will find that the more accurately the two sources of foreknowledge are compared and combined, the more satisfactory their results will prove.

A barometer begins to rise considerably before the conclusion of a gale, sometimes even at its commencement. Although it falls lowest before high winds, it frequently sinks very much before heavy rain. The barometer falls, but not always, on the approach of thunder and lightning. Before and during the earlier part of settled weather it usually stands high and is stationary, the air being dry.

Instances of fine weather with a low glass occur, however, rarely, but they are always preludes to a duration of wind or rain, if not both.

After very warm and calm weather, a storm or squall, with rain, may follow; likewise at any time when the atmosphere is heated much above the usual temperature of the season.

Allowance should invariably be made for the previous state of the glasses during some days, as well as some hours, because their indications may be affected by distant causes, or by changes close at hand. Some of these changes may occur at a greater or less distance, influencing neighboring regions, but not visible to each observer whose barometer feels their effect.

There may be heavy rains or violent winds beyond the horizon, and the view of an observer, by which his instruments may be affected considerably, though no particular change of weather occurs in his immediate locality.

It may be repeated that the longer a change of wind or weather is foretold before it takes place, the longer the presaged weather will last, and conversely, the shorter the warning the less time, whatever causes the warning, whether wind or a fall of rain or snow, will continue.

Sometimes severe weather from the southward, not lasting long, may cause no great fall, because followed by a duration of wind from the northward, and at times the barometer may fall with northerly winds and fine weather, apparently against these rules, because a continuance of southerly wind is about to follow. By such changes as these one may be misled, and calamity may be the consequence if not duly forewarned.

A few of the more marked signs of weather, useful alike to seaman, farmer and gardener, are the following;

Whether clear or cloudy, a rosy sky at sunset presages fine weather; a red sky in the morning bad weather, or much wind (perhaps rain); a gray sky in the morning, fine weather; a high dawn, wind; a low dawn, fair weather.

Soft-looking or delicate clouds foretell fine weather, with moderate or light breezes; hard-edged, oily-looking clouds, wind. A dark, gloomy, blue sky is windy, but a light, bright, blue sky indicates fine weather. Generally, the softer clouds look, the less wind (but perhaps more rain) may be expected; and the harder, more "greasy," rolled, tufted, or ragged, the stronger the coming wind will prove. Also, a bright yellow sky at sunset presages wind; a pale yellow, wet; and thus by the prevalence of red, yellow, or gray tints, the coming weather may be foretold very nearly; indeed, if aided by instruments, almost exactly.

Small, inky-looking clouds foretell rain; light scud-clouds driving across heavy masses show wind and rain, but, if alone, may indicate wind only.

High, upper clouds crossing the sun, moon, or stars, in a direction different from that of the lower clouds, or the wind then felt below, foretell a change of wind.

After clear, fine weather, the first signs in the sky of a coming change are usually light streaks, curls, wisps, or mottled patches of white distant clouds, which increase and are followed by an overcasting of murky vapor that grows into cloudiness. This appearance, more or less oily, or watery, as wind or rain will prevail, is an infallible sign.

Usually the higher and more distant such clouds seem to be, the more gradual but general the coming change of weather will prove.

Light, delicate, quiet tints or colors, with soft, undefined forms of clouds, indicate and accompany fine weather, but gaudy or unusual hues, with hard, definitely outlined clouds, foretell rain, and probably strong wind.

Misty clouds forming or hanging on heights, show wind, if they remain, increase, or descend. If they rise or disperse, the weather will improve or become fine.

When sea-birds fly out early, and far to seaward, moderate wind and fair weather may be expected; when they hang about the land, or over it, sometimes flying inland, expect a strong wind with stormy weather. As many creatures besides birds are affected by the approach of rain or wind, such indications should not be slighted by an observer who wishes to foresee weather.

There are other signs of a coming change in the weather, known less generally than may be desirable, and therefore worth notice, such as when birds of long flight, rooks, swallows, or others, hang about home, and fly up and down, or low, rain or wind may be expected. Also, when animals seek sheltered places, instead of spreading over their usual range; when pigs carry straw to their styes; when smoke from chimneys does not ascend readily (or straight upwards during calm), an unfavorable change is probable.

Dew is an indication of fine weather; so is fog. Neither of these two formations occur under an overcast sky, or when there is much wind. One sees fog occasionally rolled away, as it were, by wind, but seldom or never formed while it is blowing.

Remarkable clearness of atmosphere near the horizon, distant objects, such as hills, usually visible, or raised (by refraction), and what is called "a good hearing day," may be mentioned among the signs of wet, if not wind, to be expected.

More than usual twinkling of the stars, indistinctness or apparent multiplication of the moon's horns, haloes, "wind-dogs," and the rainbow, are more or less significant of increasing wind, if not approaching rain, with or without wind.

Near land, in sheltered harbors, in valleys, or over low ground, there is usually a marked diminution of wind during part of the night, and a dispersion of clouds. At such times an eye on an overlooking height may see an extended body of vapor below (rendered visible by the cooling of night), which seems to check the wind.

Lastly, the dryness or dampness of the air and its temperature (for the season) should always be considered, with other indications of change, or continuance of wind and weather.

THERMOMETRIC SCALES.

The two natural points on the thermometric scale are the temperature of boiling water (at 30° in bar.), and that of melting ice. The latter is 0 on the Centigrade and Reaumur scale, 32° on Fahrenheit. The former is 100° on the Centigrade, 80° on Reaumur's, and 212° on Fahrenheit's. Hence 100° C. = 80° R. = 170° Fahr. To reduce Reaumur degrees to Fahrenheit, multiply by 9, divide by 4, and add 32. To reduce Centigrade to Fahrenheit, multiply by 9, divide by 5, and add 32.

FISH.

The Editor is indebted to Mr. Freas, editor of the Germantown Telegraph, for the following valuable articles:

ANGLING.

Among the lakes, rivers and brooks of our country, the lover of the "gentle art" has rare opportunities for indulging in his favorite amusement. Yet how few there are, comparatively speaking, that feel an interest in it. Considering that angling, and trout-fishing particularly, usually leads us among the wildest and most beautiful scenes of nature, it is, indeed, remarkable that this delightful recreation is not more generally indulged in. It is not our intention, however, to enter into a treatise upon this manly sport, but merely to embody within the limits of a single article information, that may be useful to an unpractised hand, in regard to fish which properly come under the angler's notice.

Salmon.

In the United States there is but one distinct species of the salmon. He is a bold biter, a sly and handsome fish, and, on account of his strength and build, possesses great leaping powers. He is a voracious feeder, and may be taken by the angler with his favorite food, minnows, the sea-sand eel, or any small and delicate fish, but the surest bait is the common red worm. The rivers of California, Oregon, and Washington Territory, are the only streams within the limits of the United States where the salmon is numerous, and the angler can have good sport. They may also be taken with rod and line in considerable numbers in nearly all the streams which flow into the St. Lawrence from the north, below Quebec, and those which empty into the Gulf of St. Lawrence and into the Atlantic, along the coast of Labrador. Anglers usually take the salmon with the artificial fly, and use an elastic pointed rod, about 18 feet in length, with reel capable of holding from 300 to 500 feet of twisted hair and silk line. The fishing season in Canada and New Brunswick commences about the 10th of June, and in Nova Scotia about one month earlier.

Trout.

This beautiful fish, with the exception of the salmon, is the most superb game-fish in the world. There are several species. In nearly all the pure cold-water streams of the Northern, Middle and Eastern States the speckled trout abounds. The best bait, in early spring, is the red dung-worm, but in June and July the fly is probably the most killing. In many of the States a very proper law is in force for the protection of the fish, allowing them to be taken only during the spring and summer months. Of the artificial flies the "red hackle" is usually preferred. The outfit of the trout angler should consist of a light, elastic rod and small reel, with 50 or 60 feet of plaited hair and silk line, and a silk worm "leader," 6 feet in length, attached. At the end of this, when bait is used, fasten a long-shanked Kirby hook of small size, and, if the current should be very swift, attach a split buck-shot to the leader about a foot above the hook. Put a whole live worm on the hook, allowing the head and tail to be free, so that it will make as natural an appearance as possible in the water. A small woollen bag pinned or buttoned to the pantaloons is the best receptacle for worms. As it is usually necessary to wade the streams, a large and easily-fitting pair of shoes, with nails projecting $\frac{1}{4}$ inch from the soles to prevent slipping, should be worn. Trout are usually found beneath falls, in eddies, or in portions of the brook where the current is not very swift. The stream should be waded very cautiously, and the fly or bait thrown as far as possible, as the trout is the most timid of all the finny tribes. When you feel the fish biting, draw the line slowly towards you 2 or 3 feet, and if it seems to be securely fastened draw him directly out of the water if small; when otherwise, allow him to remain in the water, giving him as much line as he desires until sufficiently exhausted to be drawn to the shore and lifted out. In Pennsylvania, New Jersey and Maryland trout are but seldom caught exceeding a pound in weight. In a day's sport in the most favored localities in these States, the weight of fish in the angler's reel would not exceed $\frac{1}{4}$ lb. each. In New York and the Eastern States the run of trout is much larger. In many of the lakes and tributaries of Maine they are exceedingly numerous and of very large size. On certain days they will not touch the most tempting bait, while at other times they rise savagely at any kind of artificial flies, and the angler frequently kills 3 at a cast weighing 2 or 3 lbs. each. They are often caught weighing as much as 8 lbs., and are most numerous in Maine, in Moosehead, Memfremagog, Mubagog and Schudic lakes, and their tributaries.

The most agreeable months to visit these lakes are August and September. Earlier in the season black flies, gnats and ticks are very annoying. Even early in the spring, before the snow has melted from the mountains, they trouble the angler. Insects of any kind, however, may be kept at a respectful distance by covering the hands and face with a preparation consisting of $\frac{1}{2}$ oil of pennyroyal and the remainder sweet oil.

The Salmon-trout is a fish of much larger growth than the speckled trout, and is less appreciated as an article of food, but nevertheless affords the angler capital sport. They are numerous in many of the lakes of New York and Maine, in Lake Superior and in the Straits of Mackinaw. The same tackle used for salmon fishing could be advantageously used for the salmon-trout or for the speckled trout in Maine.

Perch.

The white perch is a bold biter and a decidedly pretty fish. It is found in nearly all the rivers of the Atlantic coast, from Boston to Norfolk. In the Delaware, Susquehanna, and Potomac, they are particularly numerous, and give the angler rare sport. On the Delaware a contrivance for catching them called a bow-line or deepsea, is much used. Usually about eight small sized hooks are attached to it. It can be obtained at the fishing-tackle stores. This style of fishing requires no skill whatever, and is much less interesting than angling. Along the edge of the water-docks which skirt these rivers, or in among the leaves of the plants, when the tide is sufficiently high, fine sport may be had during the summer months with rod and line. Dung-worms are the best bait for white perch; but they are often caught of large size with the minnow. This fish, when cooked an hour or two after being taken, is our opinion, is unsurpassed in flavor by any, with the exception of the salmon and shad. It is but seldom killed in the rivers by anglers, exceeding a pound and a quarter in weight; although in ponds, canals, and inlets fed by the rivers, it frequently attains a much larger size. Like the salmon, shad, and herring, they are a migratory fish; and when enclosed in fresh water ponds they never propagate, and often become emaciated shortly after the migratory season. Those that survive the first year usually grow to a large size.

The yellow perch, although a pretty fish and a strong biter, is considered rather inferior as an esculent. It inhabits nearly all the rivers and large ponds of the Eastern and Middle States. They bite at almost anything. Indeed, we were informed by a fisherman residing in a cabin on the banks of a beautiful pond, in Pike County, Pennsylvania, that he has caught them with a whortleberry attached to a hook. This fish frequently attains a weight of from three to four pounds.

Black Bass.

This superb member of the finny tribe is peculiar to the West and South. It is found in the greatest numbers in the tributaries of the upper Mississippi, in nearly all the lakes of New York and Canada, including the great lakes, with the exception of Superior, and in the river St. Lawrence. He is a fierce biter, and, unlike the trout, is not a timid fish. He is particularly fond of romantic streams and dilapidated mill-dams. He bites freely at the red worm, rises readily at the fly or minnow, and may be taken as early as April and May, according to location.

Rock.

This superb game fish, also known as the Striped Bass, is found in all the rivers from the Penobscot to Savannah, but is most numerous along the shores of Connecticut, Rhode Island, Massachusetts, and Maine. Block Island, within four miles of the Rhode Island coast, is considered about the best locality. Just after a heavy gale is the most opportune time to troll for them, as the largest fish then come near to shore. Trolling from a boat with a rod, is the usual style of angling. For a bait, the skin of an eel attached to a "squid," is usually used. For still river fishing, minnows or the roe of any kind of fish, is most killing. The rock frequently attains a weight of 100 pounds.

Pike.

This savage creature is considered the longest lived of all fresh water fish. In this country, as in England, it is also known as the Pickerel, but reaches its greatest perfection here. A peculiarity of this fish is its great voraciousness, about which there are many anecdotes told. He is not very particular in regard to food, but it usually consists of fish and frogs. He inhabits nearly all the lakes and inland waters of the Northern and Middle States. A simple and good equipment for pike fishing is a stout rod and reel, a strong linen line, a brass leader, a sharp Kirby hook, and a small landing net. For still fishing a live minnow is excellent bait, and for trolling a small "shiner" should be used. In the winter, when the lakes and ponds are frozen, by making an opening in the ice very fine pike are frequently taken with live minnows. For this purpose the bait should be obtained in the summer or fall and kept alive in spring-water. Pike often attain the weight of from 50 to 60 pounds.

Muskalonge.

This fish belongs to the pike family, and usually weighs from 20 to 40 lbs. It is a favorite with anglers on the great lakes, the upper Mississippi, the St. Lawrence, and along the shores of the Ohio and the Tennessee. He is very fierce in his nature and attacks almost every species of the finny tribe. Small fish are excellent bait.

Catfish.

These well-known members of the fish family are, with one exception, fond of muddy waters, and are numerous North and South. There are several varieties. The white catfish when not exceeding a pound or two in weight is excellent eating. He is usually found in streams affected by the tides, and is fond of clear water. He can be propagated, however, in all the Northern streams and ponds. The yellow catfish, we believe, inhabits ponds, lakes, and rivers in every portion of the Union. In the Mississippi they grow to the weight of a hundred pounds, but elsewhere they don't often exceed ten pounds. They may be taken with various kinds of bait. The white catfish prefers a piece of minnow or the soft portion of clams.

Sunfish.

This beautifully colored fish is familiar to almost every school boy. They are usually found in shallow water, are very strong biters and tolerably good eating. They show great intelligence in constructing nests for the reception of their spawn. In the shallow streams of Maryland they can be taken in immense numbers. They are not very particular in regard to bait, but prefer either grasshoppers, crickets, or young bees. To catch them with the greatest satisfaction, a short rod, a light line with float, and small Kirby hook, are necessary. The sunfish but seldom exceeds a pound in weight. The largest are taken in August and September, and can be as readily captured with the artificial fly as with bait.

Eel.

This slippery fish inhabits nearly all the lakes, rivers and ponds of the United States. It is a singular fact, however, that the great Mississippi is destitute of it. When not exceeding 1 or 2 lbs. in weight they are capital eating. The most rapid way of catching them is with the "bob," composed of large earth-worms, strung together. For this purpose waxed homespun thread, with a long needle, should be used. Pass the needle and thread through the entire length of the worms, until a string about 6 feet in length is formed, which should be doubled up with loops a few inches in length, securely tied together, and fastened to a strong stick 5 or 6 feet in length—an old broomhandle would answer very well. Keep the worms on the bed of the stream, and when the eels pull at them quickly jerk them up into the boat, or upon the shore, wherever you may happen to be. Frequently 4 and 5 fish are taken at a single haul. With rod and line a piece of minnow is excellent bait. Young eels, a few inches in length, are a very killing bait for perch, pike and rock.

Chub.

Throughout the Eastern, Northern and Middle States this pretty fish is very numerous. He is a bold biter, and is often found in trout streams. He takes the fly readily, and is decidedly a game fish. Like the trout he is very shy, but for eating purposes is quite inferior. He sometimes weighs as much as 5 and 6 lbs.

Sucker.

Of this rather clumsy fish there appears to be two varieties. Those inhabiting cold water streams are more slender and more comely shaped than those found in rivers and ponds. The former are a better flavored fish than chub, and may be taken with the red worm in deep water at any season. They are poor biters, but often show considerable fight after being hooked. A full grown fish weighs from 3 to 4 lbs.

Herring.

This is the most numerous of all the migratory fish in the United States. He will take the red worm or shad-roe, and on clear days, with a southern wind, will jump at a gaudy fly or piece of red flannel fastened to a hook. For eating purposes, after going through a course of "curing," he is a very palatable fish. He don't often exceed a lb. in weight.

Roach.

This fish is found in nearly every portion of the United States; is a fair biter, but the poorest of all as an esculent, He don't usually exceed ½ lb. in weight, and may be taken at any season with a little piece of dough attached to a small hook.

Redfin.

This pretty little fish, we believe, is scarcely noticed in any of the works on angling. He frequents many of the streams in the northern and middle portions of the United States, but grows large in cold-water brooks, and is often taken alongside of the trout. He but seldom exceeds 7 or 8 inches in length, and is an excellent pan-fish. Very light tackle, small, long-shanked Kirby hook, and red worms for bait, should be used. He bites only during the spring months.

Salt-water Fish.

We have given a brief account of all the principal fresh-water fish of the United States that are of interest to the angler. Of the salt-water fish, those that are most fished for, are the sheepshead, Spanish mackerel, weakfish, bluefish, blackfish, croaker, flounder, porgy and sea-bass. Fishermen along the seaboard usually use the handline, but the true angler should fish with a strong rod with reel, and stout flax line with large hooks. The usual baits are soft-shell crabs and clams, large shrimps, fiddlers, young crabs and muscles. The fishing season extends from June to October.

THE CULTURE OF FISH.

Pisciculture

Is the name of a new and very important art destined, we believe, ere long, to hold a conspicuous place in human interests and pursuits. The extent to which Nature may be aided by artificial methods in the breeding of fishes, is a truly wonderful discovery. That eventually, and at no distant day, it will become the means of adding largely not only to the quantity but the variety also of those supplies for man's sustenance and luxury, admits scarcely of a doubt.

Fishes, whether in the freedom of nature or in artificial receptacles, show plainly enough the approach of spawning. The belly of the female becomes distended and yields readily to pressure. There is a fluctuation under the hand, which shows that the eggs are free from the ovary and easily displaced. This being the case, take up in your left hand a female fish, and hold it suspended by the head and thorax over a flat-bottomed vessel containing clear water. Then with the right hand passed from above, downwards, squeeze the loosened eggs through the anal opening. A male fish is then taken, and the milt is expressed in the same way, though often it flows by the mere act of suspending. This substance, white and cream-like, soon gives to the water the appearance of whey. To insure effectual fecundation, the mixture in this state should be gently stirred with the hand, or with a soft brush. It requires but 2 or 3 minutes to accomplish the fecundation.

The subsequent processes may be carried on upon the spot, or the impregnated eggs may, like those of the silk-worm, be packed and transported to other places, there to be hatched.

In the first case, the water with the eggs in it is poured immediately into the hatching apparatus. This may be very simple. Mr. Coste tells us that he has often used a long and narrow wooden box lined with zinc or lead, with a fish box of earthenware. In the laboratory of the colleges of France, the troughs used are of potter's enamelled ware. The eggs are spread upon a movable frame or grate composed of glass rods, about one-tenth of an inch apart. It seems to be a condition of Nature that this operation of hers, like the great water lily of the tropics, can go on well only in running-water. The water which supplies the hatching-trough must have a constant flow.

Double sieves of wire gauze set in floating frames, which keep them immersed, but near the surface, have been used for hatching fish in ponds and rivers; but the mud is apt to gather in them, incrusting the eggs and making it necessary to remove them for the purpose of cleaning. Such changes retard the process of incubation. Even after they are hatched, the young fish are apt to chafe the umbilical vesicle by coming in contact with the wire, an injury which generally proves fatal.

In preference to the above M. Coste recommends the use of a wooden box with hinged ends and cover, in all of which are openings for the water, protected by wire gauze, and containing also a fourfold frame of glass rods for the accommodation of the spawn.

In the course of a few hours after the process of fecundation, a change may be seen in the eggs. At first they become opaque, but soon resume their transparency. A small, round spot next appears, which gradually extends until one end takes the shape of a tail, and the other that of a spatula-shaped head. Two black points upon the sides presently turn into eyes. It is not long before the young animal gives sign of life by motion of the tail. As the eggs open the head and tail first emerge, and then the umbilical vesicle attached to the belly of the fish, and there retained for some time, as the only source of nutriment.

In case the eggs in the hatching-box become covered with film from the impurity of the water, they should be cleansed with a feather, or with a fine brush of badger's hair.

The eggs may be transferred from one vessel to another by means of a glass pipe, the stem of which is closed by the finger. The egg is made to enter the tube by removing the finger.

The young fish very soon displays differences of nature and instinct. Some, like the pike and perch, quickly free themselves from the umbilical vesicle and shoot about with great vivacity. Others, as the salmon and trout, retain their provision bags longer, seem more sluggish, and huddle together in dark corners. Some kinds are so bold and hardy that they require but little care. The pike, for instance, and the trout, may very soon be put into ponds and rivers, where they will look out for themselves. But others, more delicate and often more valuable, must be kept in artificial basins until they have acquired strength to resist the destructive agencies that await them in the ravenous waters.

In a box less than 2 feet long, 6 inches wide and 4 inches deep, Prof. Coste has sometimes reared to a sufficient size for removal, no less than 2000 salmon at a time.

The basin used at the College of France may serve as a model for the receptacles above named. It has different compartments for the fish of different ages. The wall is built waist-high, that the fish may be conveniently overlooked. Here and there, on the gravelly bed, are small heaps of rounded pebbles. Little shelters of earthenware are scattered about, that the fish may have dark places in which to hide and rest. A few aquatic plants are added to complete the conditions which would be found in nature.

The salmon, the trout and the eel, are fed upon boiled beef or horse-flesh, which is prepared for them by pounding in a mortar. These delicate morsels are eagerly seized by the young fish. After 8 or 10 days the boiled flesh is exchanged for raw, which is pounded and given in little pellets. At Huningue, salmon and trout are fed with the flesh of other and cheaper fish, which is prepared for them by pounding. Small earthworms and the minute crustacea of stagnant waters are sought with avidity by these young fry.

For the proper acclimation of fishes, and for other reasons, it is often desirable to transport the eggs to a considerable distance. When the eggs are free and separate, with a tough covering, as in the case with the salmon and the trout, pine boxes are used. These are filled with sand or moss, or fragments of sponge, or with some aquatic plant, in the moist folds of which the eggs are ranged in layers.

The eggs, which come in agglutinated clusters, with tender envelopes, such as the spawn of the carp, the roach, the perch, etc., cannot be conveyed so easily. The best method is to put them into jars three-quarters filled with water and containing some aquatic plant. There is another class of eggs which are deposited upon grass or small sticks. Let these, with the objects to which they adhere, be wrapped up in a wet cloth, and then be put into a box or basket.

The young fish also are often transported to great distances in bottles containing water and some living aquatic plants. The water must be renewed from time to time. To keep up the supply of air, which fishes must have, no less than animals which live in it, an ingenious apparatus has been devised by some fishermen of the Vosges. The vessel which holds the fish is swung at the back in the style of the rag-picker. A bellows, like that of the Scotch bagpipe, worked under the arm, sends at pleasure its current of air through the water that contains the fish. An occasional squeeze of the bellows keeps the fish in good breathing condition.

MISCELLANEOUS.

TO TIE KNOTS.

Few persons know how to tie a knot; even women with their neatness in all other matters tie very badly. It is as easy, indeed more easy, to make a neat, firm knot, easy to untie, as one clumsy, insecure, and readily jammed. In practising, it is better at first to use a coarse cord or fine rope. The knots given below can all be mastered in an hour's practice, and will be found of daily use.

Fig. 1.— *The Reefing Knot,*

Also called the flat knot, is the one best adapted for ordinary use in tying the two ends of a string. It is neat, flat, does not readily slip, and is easily untied. It is the same as is used in tying shoestrings and neck-ties, except that the ends are drawn through. It is essential that the two parts of each string should be on the *same* side or there will be formed a "granny" knot.

Fig. 2. — *The Sheet Bend,*

Also called the weavers' knot, is used where great firmness is required; it is small, cannot slip, and can be made when one end of the string is just long enough to make a loop. It is more liable to jam than the one last named. Bend one end of the cord into a loop, which hold in the left hand, pass the other end through the loop, around it and then under itself. A little practice will enable the learner to use both hands at once, in which case it can be tied very quickly. It is easily made after learning the flat knot, by passing one end across or under the loop instead of through it. It is obvious that in having the free end of the loop long it can be used instead of another end, and thus heavy bodies, as window-sash weights and clock weights are hung.

Fig. 3.— *The Binding Knot*

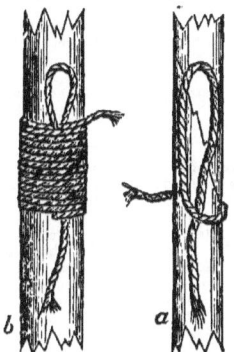

Is used for fastening broken sticks or rods after serving them with several turns of the cord which should never overlap. Before beginning the serving make a loop a little longer than the proposed extent of the turns (*a* Fig. 3). When the serving is finished pass the end of the cord through this loop, and by pulling in its free end the other is drawn within the serving and made secure (*b* Fig. 3).

Fig. 4.— *The Single Half-hitch*

Is made more quickly than any other tie, can be instantly undone, and is very secure. It is used to fasten ends of ropes in rings, etc., when they are to be quickly cast off, and may be used for slinging light bodies of small diameter. It is also put over the tops of bottles to fasten in the corks, and is then called the beer-knot: in this case the two ends are afterwards tied. By reversing it it becomes a running knot, or "sailor's knot." In practising, at first take the fixed or "standing" part of the line in the left hand, make a loop in it; then make a second loop in the right-hand part, and put it through the first (*a*, Fig. 4). Afterwards try it through rings, and around rods and small posts (*b*, Fig. 4). For large posts use the clove-hitch; the single half-hitch will slip. Remember that when it is to hold, the strain must come on the standing part. It differs but slightly from the common single bow-knot, and can be made as easily with a little practice.

Fig. 5.— *The Clove-hitch*.

One of the most useful of all fastenings; it is not properly a knot, for it is neither tied nor untied. It is largely employed on ship-board and in reducing dislocations, but opportunities for its use in ordinary life are of daily occurrence. In practising, take the fixed or standing part of the rope

in the left hand, turn the free end under it, and put it over the thumb; repeat this, and the hitch is made. (Fig. 5.) When the clove-hitch is made on the standing part of the rope, after it has passed around a post or box, it is called two half-hitches, and is the best method of fastening boxes or bundles. In this case it should never be fastened to the cord at right angles to its own, but that in a line with it. (Fig. 6.)

Fig. 6.

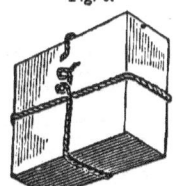

Fig. 7.— *The Bowline*

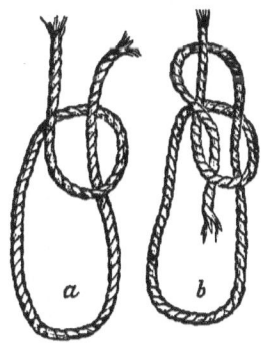

Is used in slinging heavy bodies; it cannot slip, and will never jam under the heaviest strain. It is difficult to understand at first, but with a little practice can be made very rapidly. Take the fixed or standing part of the rope in the left hand (this should be done in making *all* knots), lay the free end over it, and then by a twist of the wrist make a loop in the standing part which shall inclose the free end (*a*, Fig. 7); then carry the free end behind the standing part and through the loop, parallel with itself (*b*, Fig. 7). This knot will well repay the trouble spent in learning it.

KNITTING.

Shetland Wool Shawl (for the Centre).

Cast on 200 stitches on needles No. 7.

First Row.—Knit two; knit two together; thread forward; knit one; thread forward; knit two together; knit one; knit two together; thread forward; knit one; thread forward; knit two together; knit one.

Second Row.—Plain knitting.

Third Row.—Knit two together; knit one; thread forward; knit three; thread forward; knit three together; thread forward; knit three; thread forward; knit three together. At the end of this row plain knit the two last stitches.

Fourth Row.—Plain knitting.

Fifth Row.—Knit two; thread forward; knit two together; knit one; knit two together; thread forward; knit one; thread forward; knit two together; knit one; knit two together; thread forward; knit one.

Sixth Row.—Plain knitting.

Seventh Row.—Knit three; thread forward; knit three together; thread forward; knit three; thread forward; knit three together; thread forward. At the end of this row bring the thread forward; knit two.

Eighth Row.—Plain knitting.

These eight rows must be repeated until a square is knitted.

Border for the Shetland Wool Shawl—(This is for one-half.)

Cast on 600 stitches on needles No. 3.

First Row.—Knit two together four times; thread forward; knit one eight times; knit two together four times; purl one; knit two together four times; thread forward; knit one eight times; knit two together four times; purl one.

Second Row.—Purl knitting.

Third Row.—Plain knitting.

Fourth Row.—Purl; commence again as at first row. After having knitted a piece half a yard in depth, knit six rows plain and purled alternately; then six rows of holes, worked thus: one row plain, second row thread forward; knit two in one, and so on; third plain; then six rows of plain and purled. To form the corner two and three stitches must be knitted together in the centre and at the ends, commencing from the plain rows.

A Knitted Muff, in Imitation of Sable—pretty for Children.

Cast on 70 or 80 stitches.

First, Second, and Third Rows.—Plain knitting.

Fourth Row.—Bring the wool forward; knit two together, taken at the back; continue the same to the end of the row.

Repeat these 4 rows until the piece be about 18 inches long, admitting that the shading comes in correctly.

Two No. 19 needles are required, and double German wool, in 4 distinct shades, to match the color of sable. Commence with the lightest shade; then the second, third, and darkest, reversing them again to the lightest.

Another Muff.

Cast on 45 stitches.

Every row is worked the same, with a slip-stitch at the beginning; knit one; purl one; repeat to the end of the row.

It will require a piece of about 20 inches long to make a moderate-sized muff, which must be lined with silk, and stuffed with wool and a sufficient quantity of horse-hair to retain it in shape. Cord and tassels to match the color of the muff may be sewn at the ends, or it may be drawn up with ribbons.

CROCHETING.

A pretty Toilet Slipper.

Make a chain of fifteen stitches in single crochet; crochet two stitches in the middle stitch of every row, until you have completed twelve rows, which is sufficient for the front. Take up twelve stitches on one side; crochet thirty rows, and join them to the other side of the front; then catch the stitches up round the top, and crochet one row.

For the frill, crochet the stitches in every loop in single crochet, very loose, to form a full frill.

When finished, turn the slipper inside out, and sew in a cork sole; then pass the ribbon round under the frill and tie in front in a bow. The above is exceedingly pretty in shaded Berlin wool.

MANAGEMENT OF CANARY BIRDS

Breeding.

The breeding cage should have plenty of fine gravel or sea-sand at the bottom, and a lump of old mortar, for the birds to pick. Goats' hair must be supplied for the nest. The birds when put up should be fed on bread, the yolk of boiled eggs and a little sugar. Let them have fresh greens in moderation. The birds should not be allowed to breed more than twice or thrice a year. The period of incubation is 14 days; in very warm weather, 13. The last of March is early enough to put the birds in the breeding-cage.

If the hen *desert her eggs*, they are probably bad, and should be thrown out.

If the hen *eat her eggs*, feed her well very early in the morning, or late at night. If the male break the eggs, let him have two hens; these must not be allowed in the same cage, or they will fight.

If the hen *neglect to feed her young*, stir her out of the nest and supply her with an abundance of delicate food. As soon as the young are hatched, place beside the usual feeding-trough a cup containing finely grated hard-boiled egg and stale bread rubbed fine and soaked in milk; also, one containing crushed rape-seed, boiled and afterwards washed with fresh water.

The young may be placed in separate cages in about 4 weeks.

Feeding.

Canary-seed alone is sufficient, but usually a mixture of canary, hemp, millet and rape, known as bird-seed, is used. Each cage should have a piece of cuttle-fish bone. Food is best supplied in the evening, and all stale food and refuse of every kind should be removed daily. The bottom of the cage should be strewn with fine gravel or sand, fresh water supplied daily, and a saucer of water for bathing twice a week. Greens should be cautiously supplied.

To Distinguish the Sex.

The throat of the male vibrates while singing; this never happens with the hen. The males are larger, more yellow above the bill, under the throat and in the pinions of the wings. The body of the male is longer and more tapering.

Singing.

Birds with long, straight and tapering bodies are the best singers. By putting 2 or 3 birds together they will vie with each other.

Diseases.

Surfeit from improper or excessive food is shown by swelling of the belly, which, on blowing up the feathers, appears transparent and covered with little bloodvessels. In birds from 1 to 3 years old it shows itself in scabs and humors about the head. Take away canary-seed, and add some grits, which will purge; put a little saffron in the water. Anoint the affected parts with almond-oil.

Husk, from cold. It produces a dry, husky cough, and is difficult to cure. Give them some flaxseed mixed with the bird-seed and a little rock candy in the water, and for a few mornings a little boiled bread and milk.

Excessive perspiration from a warm season, confined locality, or sitting too closely on the nest. The feathers are ruffled and damp, and the bird feeble. Wash with salt and water for several mornings, or sprinkle a few drops of sherry over the bird, and put it in the sun to dry.

Egg-bound, from cold. Give the bird a little moist sugar, or anoint the abdomen with warm sweet oil; if these fail, give a drop of castor-oil.

Moulting.—Avoid cold, give sunshine, some bread and egg, with saffron in the water.

Sneezing is caused by obstruction of the nostril, which may be removed by a small quill.

Fits.—Plunge the bird suddenly into cold water, and cut two of its claws short enough for the blood to run.

Lice.—Allow the birds to bathe frequently; keep the cage very clean, with plenty of dry sand in the bottom. Put some hollow sticks in the cage; the lice will collect in them, and may be removed.

Drooping.—When a bird continues sickly without apparent cause, give a little powdered charcoal mixed with bread and egg.

Accidents.—For a broken leg or wing, put the bird in a cage without perches, and covered at the bottom with soft hay. Let its food be within easy reach, and keep the cage covered.

DOGS.

Of the Best Breed of Dogs for Shooting Game.

"The breed of dogs which I prefer, beyond all others, are those which are bred between a setter and a pointer, but not bred from those setters which have no natural point in them, for I have no idea of shooting to a dog which does not stop at birds the very first day he is taken into the field. I have not had a setter which was broken by force for above 20 years, nor ever will have one. Leave them at home only one week, for the next two days you must turn to dog-breaking, and not to shooting. I prefer those between a pointer and a setter, which take after the setter, for, generally speaking, they have better feet, which is a great point in a dog, for certain they have more hair on their feet, which is a great preservative to the foot, if it be kept clean. I never kept a cocker spaniel in my life; I always shoot to pointers, even in the strongest covers, with bells round their necks. I know, for certain, you will not find so much game, but then what you find you are sure to shoot at. Here is the great benefit of shooting to pointers: you may shoot every day in a wood, and not drive the game away. But, if you turn cocking spaniels into a wood, which quest, when they come on to the foot of a pheasant, in a very few days you will drive every pheasant out of the wood. A Newfoundland dog, tutored to keep behind you in the fields, and not to go above a dozen or twenty yards from you in a wood, is of wonderful utility in retrieving and bringing wounded game. I have had several that were uncommonly useful."

How to know the Age of a Dog until he is Six Years Old.

A dog has a very visible mark in his teeth, as well as a horse, which mark does not disappear totally until he is very near or full 6 years old. Look to the 4 front teeth, both in the upper and lower jaw, but particularly to the teeth in the upper jaw, for in those 4 front teeth the mark remains the longest. At 12 months old you will observe every one of the 4 front teeth, both in the upper and under jaw, jagged and uneven, nearly in the form of a *fleur de lis*, but not quite so pointed at the edges of the jags as a *fleur de lis* is. As the dog advances in age these marks will wear away, gradually decrease and grow smoother and less jagged every year. Between 3 and 4 years old these marks will be full half worn down, and when you observe all the 4 front teeth, both in the upper and lower jaw, quite worn smooth and even, and not in the least jagged, then you may conclude that the dog is nearly if not full 6 years old. When those marks are worn quite flat and even, and those teeth quite level and even, you can no longer judge the age of a dog. Many huntsmen and game-keepers ignorantly look at the side and eye-teeth of a dog; there are many dogs not 2 years old which have had the canker in the mouth, with hardly one sound tooth in their heads.

Distemper in Dogs

Is characterized by a running from the nose and eyes, and a short dry cough, followed by a wasting of the flesh, and loss of strength and spirits. At length the brain suffers, and fits, paralysis of the extremities, or convulsions come on. Give a teaspoonful of magnesia every other night, or the same quantity of washed flowers of sulphur.

Mange in Dogs

Is allied to the itch in man, and requires the same treatment. Wash with soft soap, and apply sulphur ointment.

Worms in Dogs

Are a frequent cause of fits, and when they get into the nostrils, windpipe, etc., generally cause death. For those in the bowels, Youatt recommends powdered glass made up into a roll with butter or lard. Cowhage (cow-itch, mucuna) is probably quite as effectual, and is safer. A teaspoonful may be given in lard, and repeated if necessary. Turpentine should not be given to dogs.

Sportsman's Beef.

Take a fine round of beef, 4 oz. of saltpetre, ½ of an oz. of allspice; rub it well on the beef, and let it stand 24 hours; then rub in as much common salt as will salt it. Lay it by 12 days, turning it every day; then put it into a pan, such as large pies are baked in, with 3 or 4 lbs. of beef-suet, some under, some over. Cover it with a thick crust, and bake it for 6 hours. It will keep for two months, and most excellent it is.

TO DESTROY INSECTS.

Persian Insect Powder

Is the *pyrethrum roseum Caucasicum*. The central or tubular florets are alone used. They are ground to powder. Although destructive to insect life it is harmless to man or domestic animals.

To Destroy Body Lice.

1. Mercurial ointment well rubbed on the infected part and washed off with warm water and soap. In the army a common practice was to wear a string saturated with the ointment around the waist as a means of protection. This might produce salivation.

2. Corrosive sublimate, 1 dr.; sal ammoniac, 2 drs.; water, 8 oz. This is to be used as the first; it is more cleanly.

3. *Cocculus indicus*, 1 oz.; boiling water, 1 pt.; use when cool.

To Destroy Fleas on Animals.

Wash with infusion of cocculus Indicus, or with coal-oil, and then with soap and warm water.

Chloride of Lime to Destroy Insects.

By scattering chloride of lime on a plank in a stable, biting fleas are driven away. Sprinkling beds of vegetables with a weak solution of this salt effectually preserves them from caterpillars, slugs, moths, etc. It has the same effect when sprinkled on fruit trees or shrubbery. Mixed in a paste with fatty matter and applied in a narrow band around the trees, it prevents insects from creeping up.

Coal-oil a Remedy for Insects.

At a late meeting of the Cincinnati Horticultural Society, Mr. Wells made the following statements:

He said he had found coal-oil a very effectual remedy for all insects, both on plants and trees. When he desired to rid his trees of the troublesome pests, as had been the case a year ago, when his plum crop threatened from their inroads to be a total failure, he had used with entire success the following truly valuable preparation: One pt. of soft soap mixed with half the quantity of coal-oil, the whole then being stirred into 7 or 8 galls. of rain-water. The application he had made with a powerful syringe, deluging the tops after the blossoming of the tree, and when the immature fruit began to fall, continuing the operation for 3 or 4 nights in succession, and afterwards once or twice a week.

He had also tried coal-oil on his cabbage plants, to prevent the depredations of the cut-worm, and had found the remedy uniformly successful. In this case he saturated the coarse chips from a planing-mill with undiluted oil, placing a handful of them, so prepared, around each plant.

He had tried experiments on plants, using different preventions with the following results: One hundred cabbage plants treated in the customary manner, with ashes, were still attacked by the worm, and suffered from the depredations of the louse. One hundred plants surrounded with common planing-mill chips — one plant slightly eaten; worm found dead beneath the leaves. One hundred plants surrounded with chips saturated with coal-oil — free from lice and untouched by the worm. He had been equally fortunate in his application of coal-oil to melon and other vines to prevent the inroads of the bugs.

To Destroy Slugs and Earthworms

Water the plants with a solution of carbonate of ammonia, 1 oz. to the gallon. They will come to the surface and perish. The ammonia will promote the growth of the plants.

Roach Poison.

Put a drachm of phosphorus in a flask with 2 oz. of water; plunge the flask into hot water, and when the phosphorus is melted, pour the contents into a mortar with 2 or 3 oz. of lard. Triturate briskly, adding water, and ¼ lb. of flour, with 1 or 2 oz. of brown sugar. Plaster of Paris, with oatmeal, is said to destroy roaches.

Roach Wafers.

These are made with flour, sugar, and red-lead, heated in wafer irons.

Ant-Trap.

Procure a large sponge, wash it well and press it dry, which will leave the cells quite open; then sprinkle it with fine white sugar, and place it near where the ants are troublesome. The ants will soon collect upon the sponge, and take up their abode in its cells. It is then only necessary to dip the sponge in boiling water when the ants will be destroyed, and it may be set over and over again. Cyanide of potassium is employed in Cuba, but is a violent poison and its use is not recommended.

To keep Ants out of Closets or Drawers.

Draw a line with a brush dipped in the following solution around the shelf to be protected. The ants will not cross it. Corrosive sublimate, 1 oz.; muriate of ammonia, 2 oz.; water, 1 pint. This solution may also be used to destroy bed-bugs by applying it to the cracks with a feather or brush.

Destruction of Insects in Grain.

In M. Louvel's plan the grain is put into a hollow cast-iron cylinder, from which the air is partially exhausted. No animal can there live, fermentation itself ceases as it has neither air nor moisture. On the large scale, the vacuum is created by filling a communicating cylinder with steam, which is then condensed. A vacuum of 20 inches is quite sufficient.

To Drive away Moths.

If the articles are to be wrapped up, enclose camphor, snuff, or Persian insect powder. Furs should be kept in cedar boxes, and opened out and beaten occasionally during the summer. It is stated that the Russians preserve furs by wrapping up with them a quill containing a small quantity of mercury and securely corked. In collections of birds open bottles of ether are placed in the cases; benzine is much cheaper and would probably answer. When articles become infested the surest remedy is to bake them in an oven at a temperature below that which would scorch them. Feathers may be preserved by dipping them in a solution of 16 grs. of strychnia in a pint of alcohol.

Bibron's Antidote for Snake-Bites.

Take of bromine, 2½ drs.; iodide of potassium, 2 grs.; corrosive sublimate, 1 gr.; diluted alcohol, 30 fl. drs. Dose, 1 fl. dr., in 1 tablespoonful of wine or brandy, to be repeated as required by the case.

For Bites and Stings of Small Reptiles and Insects.

The local pain produced by the bites and stings of reptiles and insects, in general, is greatly relieved by the following application: Make a lotion of 5 oz. of distilled water, and 1 oz. of tincture of opium. To be applied immediately.

Another. — Mix 5½ oz. of soft water, and ½ oz. of water of ammonia. Wash the part repeatedly with this lotion until the pain abates.

To Remove Bugs, etc.

The bedsteads ought to be taken down three or four times a year, the screws rubbed with pure oil, and a good manual cleaning given to all its parts. This plan, which has been slightly noticed under the general head of cleanliness, will render all poisonous mixtures unnecessary.

To Avoid Injury from Bees.

A wasp or bee swallowed may be killed before it can do harm by taking a teaspoonful of common salt dissolved in water. It kills the insect and cures the sting. Salt at all times is a good cure for external stings; sweet-oil, pounded mallows, or onions, powdered chalk made into a paste with water, or weak ammonia, are also efficacious.

If bees swarm upon the head, smoke tobacco and hold an empty hive over the head, and they will enter it.

PETROLEUM.

This name, meaning rock oil, is applied to certain bituminous fluids found in the earth. Solid bitumen, or asphalt, differs but little in chemical composition from petroleum, both being compounds of carbon and hydrogen.

Many varieties of petroleum, and perhaps all, become thicker by exposure to the air, and finally solid, resembling asphaltum. Bitumen, and doubtless petroleum also, was known from the earliest ages, being the "pitch" which Noah used in building the Ark, and the "slime" used for mortar in the Tower of Babel, being dug from pits in the Valley of Sodom, precisely as is done in the same region at the present day, where the Arabs annually extract considerable quantities.

The fluid petroleum has been collected in Burmah for at least 15 centuries. It is used by the inhabitants for light and fuel. The product obtained, at the present time, from 520 wells, is said to be 420,000 hogsheads annually. In the United States, petroleum is not, as many suppose, a new discovery. Years ago springs of it were known at many localities, but its use was very limited. No method of purifying it was known, so that it was looked upon as valueless, and several wells bored for salt water were abandoned on account of the oil rendering the salt impure. In 1861 it was purified, and introduced extensively as an illuminating oil, to take the place of burning fluid (camphene and alcohol), the price of which was greatly enhanced, and which, by the explosive qualities of its vapor, was causing many severe accidents. The trade increased, new wells were bored, and some of them yielding several hundred barrels a day, and making their possessors at once wealthy, started what has been known as the oil fever. Lands sold for fabulous prices, sometimes for 500 times as much as 2 or 3 years before.

Petroleum has probably been formed by a slow decomposition of organic matter under the earth's surface. It is found in cavities and crevices, and through the substance of the rock. In mining for it, a well 3 or 4 inches in diameter, and sometimes 700 or 800 feet deep, is bored by drills, generally by steam-power. When rock containing petroleum is being bored through, what is called "a show of oil" is found. The chips and water drawn up from the well show and smell of the oil, but, unless the drill strikes a cavity or crevice filled with oil, the well is not productive. This uncertainty is the most unfortunate peculiarity of oil-mining, and makes it, to a great extent, a lottery, for there are no surface indications by which these cavities can be discovered.

Petroleum is much lighter than water, of a dark green or black color, with a peculiar, and, to most persons, unpleasant odor. It is commercially divided into two kinds, the heavy, or lubricating oil, and the light oil. The former is more dense, and sometimes of the consistence of thin molasses. It is used, without preparation, for lubricating machinery, for which it is admirably suited. The light oil, before it can be used, is submitted to several purifying processes, the most important of which is distillation.

For this purpose the crude oil is pumped into stills holding from 200 to 1000 galls. each, and submitted to a gradually increasing heat, the vapors being passed through a worm immersed in cold water. At first there comes over a very light, mobile, and volatile liquid exceedingly inflammable. This is benzine, largely used as a cheap substitute for turpentine in painting, and as a solvent for India-rubber. It differs from benzole (obtained by distillation from coal-gas tar), and the beautiful colors obtained from the latter cannot be made from the benzine of Petroleum. The terms benzine and benzole are often confounded, and even used as synonyms, but the name benzole is properly applied only to one of the many substances contained in coal-tar, and from which the aniline colors are obtained.

Next, there condenses a less volatile and inflammable liquid, of greater specific gravity. This is the burning oil, and is generally the most abundant and valuable product. When the heat rises to near 500° Fahr., the oil that comes over is no longer suitable for burning, but is an excellent lubricant for light machinery. Finally, a substance (paraffine) solid at common temperatures, distils over, and there remains in the retort, as the heat has been less or greater, a thick tarry matter, or a porous coke. When the lubricating oil, just mentioned, is exposed to cold, a considerable portion of paraffine separates from it, and can be collected upon filters, purified, and used for candles, and for other purposes.

All these products, and especially the burning oil, require further purification after the distillation. This usually consists in agitation, first with water, followed by strong sulphuric acid, caustic soda, and finished with water. The effect of this is to render the oil colorless, and to diminish the odor.

The relative amount of these several products varies very greatly in different regions, and indeed in the oil of different wells in the same region. Thus, the oil from Canada contains little or no benzine, much burning oil, and much paraffine, while that from Ohio and Western Virginia contains much benzine, about the same amount of burning oil as the former, and but little paraffine.

Petroleum is found in many localities on this continent. Among these may be mentioned as the most important, Canada West, Pennsylvania, Ohio, Western Virginia, California, Kentucky, and Tennessee. The first four yield more than nine-tenths of all now obtained, but it is probable that other regions will yield equally well when as thoroughly explored.

To Test Burning Oil.

Burning oil is sometimes adulterated with benzine, or with the heavy oil. To detect the former, pour an ounce or two into a small tin cup, and put it on a stove or over a lamp, placing the bulb of a thermometer in the oil. Then as the temperature rises, try with a lighted taper when the oil gives off inflammable vapor. If this be below 100°—110° Fahr., the oil is dangerous to use, as its vapor becoming mixed with air in the lamp may take fire and explode. The adulteration with heavy oil is shown by dimness of the flame after having burned for some time, accompanied by a charring of the wick.

To Extinguish the Flame of Petroleum or Benzine.

Water, unless in overwhelming quantity, will not extinguish the flame of petroleum or benzine. It may, however, be speedily smothered by a woollen cloth, or carpet, or a wet muslin or linen cloth, or earth or sand being thrown over it. These act by excluding the air, without which combustion cannot be maintained.

ELECTRO-MAGNETIC TELEGRAPH.

This telegraph is based upon the principle that a magnet may be endowed and deprived at will with the peculiarity of attracting iron by connecting or disconnecting it with a galvanic battery; all magnetic telegraphs are based solely upon this principle. The telegraphs bearing the names of the several inventors, as Morse (who may be called the pioneer in this invention), House, Bain, etc., are simply modifications in the application of this great principle.

It is by breaking off the magnetic circuit, which is done near the battery, that certain marks are produced by means of a stylo or lever, which is depressed when the current is complete, and of the length of the interval of the breaking of this current, that signs of different appearances and lengths are produced and written out upon paper, making in themselves a hieroglyphic alphabet, readable to those who understand the key. This is the entire principle of electro-magnetic telegraphing.

It was formerly considered necessary to use a second wire to complete the magnetic circuit, now but one wire is used, and the earth is made to perform the office of the other.

Where the distance is great between the places to be communicated with a relay battery is necessary to increase the electric current, and in this manner lines of great length may be formed.

The House apparatus differs from the Morse only that by means of an instrument resembling a piano-forte, having a key for every letter, the operator, by pressing upon these keys, can reproduce these letters at the station at the other end of the line, and have them printed in ordinary printing type upon strips of paper, instead of the characters employed on the Morse instrument to represent these letters.

The Bain telegraph differs from either of the two preceding methods, simply in employing the ends of the wires themselves, without the means of a magnet or stylo to press upon the paper, the paper being first chemically prepared; so that when the circuit of electricity is complete, the current passes through the paper from the point of the wires, and decomposes a chemical compound, with which the paper is prepared, and leaves the necessary marks upon it. There is not the same need for relay batteries upon this line as upon the others.

The greatest and most important telegraphic attempt is the successful laying of the cable across the Atlantic Ocean, which was finally completed and open for business July 28th, 1866. The cable lost in mid-ocean in the unsuccessful attempt of the summer of 1865, has been recovered, and now forms the second cable laid, connecting the Eastern with the Western Continent.

The operation of telegraphing is very simple, and can easily be learned, being purely mechanical.

BOOK-KEEPING.

Double-entry book-keeping consists simply in this great principle — *that every debit must have a corresponding credit, and every credit a corresponding debit.* This simple rule is the whole theory of *Double-entry* book-keeping. For instance, you charge a person with $100 worth of merchandise. Merchandise must have a corresponding *credit* of $100 for *producing* this debit or charge; and the entry would read thus: — A. B. to Merchandise, Dr., $100; Merchandise, Cr. by A. B., $100; thus making an equalization in the two entries.

Two other short rules in book-keeping are important:

Debit, that which cost us value.
Credit, "   "   produces us value.

Merchandise in the case above cited, produced the charge to the individual, hence merchandise gets credit, and the party who receives gets the charge or debit.

The Day-Book

Is used to enter all daily transactions, as its name imports, excepting those belonging to Cash.

The Cash-Book,

For cash entries only. The left hand, or debit side, for receipts; the right hand, or credit side, for payments.

The Journal,

To arrange together in more convenient form for posting (or entering into the Ledger) the several entries in the Day-Book, Cash-Book, and such other books as may be kept.

The Ledger

Is to contain the *final* results of the preceding books, arranged under their proper heads. The left hand side, in individual accounts, shows all the party owes — the right hand side, his payments, or other credits due him.

The Editor of this work recommends the following (furnished by a practical printer, Mr. J. H. Morris) to the attention of authors, editors, and all those who write for the press:

ON PREPARING COPY AND MARKING PROOF.

Hints from a Typo.

As there are not a few who undertake to write for newspapers and to "make books," who do not appear to know how to prepare their copy, the writer of this article, who knows how copy *should be prepared*, respectfully offers a few suggestions:

A sentence, composed of fine, well-chosen words, may be so marred by inaccurate punctuation and arrangement, as to seem to an ordinary reader but a senseless string of words. Now, it is the interest of an author, as well as his duty, not only to select the words, but to arrange and punctuate them so that his meaning may be readily perceived by any reader possessed of common sense. This duty should not be forced upon the compositor. It is no part of a compositor's business to edit what he "sets up;" in fact, it is not generous, or even just, to expect him to lose time (*which to him is bread*) in "making sense" by punctuating, capitalizing, paragraphing, or otherwise arranging, his copy.

Copy should be written only on one side of each leaf, in a clear, legible hand, and, as far as possible, without erasures or interlineations; when these are unavoidable, they should be so marked as to leave no excuse for mistake. Proper names, technical or scientific terms, and all unusual words, should be so written as to show each letter distinctly. If the author wish a word emphasized by *Italics* or SMALL CAPITALS, he should underscore it, with one line for the former, and two lines for the latter; three lines under a word indicate that it is to be in CAPITALS. It is always safer to indicate where paragraphs are to be commenced by prefixing to the first word the paragraph mark, ¶. When a word is to have a capital initial letter, it is well to make three strokes under the letter, though this is unnecessary if the writer makes an unmistakable difference between his capitals and lower case or common letters. If cuts or engravings are to be inserted, they should all be ready before the copy is put in hand, and should be marked in just where the author wishes them inserted. If the work contain formulæ, algebraic problems, tables, or other peculiar matter, special care should be bestowed upon them, so as to have their arrangement clear to the compositor; it must be borne in mind that not every first-rate compositor understands the sciences and kindred subjects. The author should always make his commas, semi-colons, colons, periods, dashes, parentheses, etc., just where he wishes them to appear in print. If the work is to be set in different sizes or styles of type, the copy should be marked accordingly. Poetry should always be properly indented by the author.

In short, copy should be, in all respects, prepared as it is intended to appear in print, so that the author need see no proof, or if he desire, for any reason, to see proofs, it may be unnecessary for him to make alterations. It should be borne in mind that the making of alterations is charged extra by the compositor, and, in proportion as they are numerous, they entail a heavy extra outlay on the part of the publisher.

It was proposed to give some rules for punctuation, but to be reasonably exact in giving such rules would take up more space than such a work as this can spare; hence, I will only say that, as the object of punctuation is to make the meaning of the author clear to the reader, commas and other points should only be used where the sense would be obscure without them.

The following example of proof-marking, with the brief remarks appended, may be instructive to authors and others who are called upon to read proof, as well as interesting to the curious:

CASTING TYPES.

While there has been much diversity of opinion with respect to the name of the inventor (as well as the time of the invention) of Printing, there can be no question but that to Peter Schœffer of Gernsheim belongs the honor of originating the casting of metal letters, thus utilizing *the art of arts.*

He had learned from the world-renowned Guttembergs the art of cutting letters from wood. Not satisfied with this slow, tedious mode of making letters, he happily hit upon the expedient of cutting the characters each in a *matrix;* in this the letters might be cast, and thus many letters might be made in the same time that it had formerly taken, by the cutting method, to make each one.

Faust was so pleased with Schœffer's discovery, that he gave him his only daughter Christina in marriage.

Little did either anticipate the vast triumphs to be achieved through this discovery.

The caption to an article is sometimes run in before the first paragraph with a period and short dash, .— (in which case *Italics* or SMALL CAPITALS are generally used); but usually it is put above the article, in the *centre* of the line, in capitals, as in the example, or in some appropriate head-letter.

The marks above explain themselves, but, although, in my efforts to illustrate as many marks as possible, I have made the example *dirtier* than I should like to see the proof of any fellow-craftsman, I yet have been unable to show all the marks that are used in correcting proof. Two or three of the above marks need a word of explanation :

If a word or line, from any cause, is crooked, draw a line above and below, and two horizontal, parallel lines in the margin.

If a sentence or more than four words be left out, make a carat where the omission occurs, and on the margin write—Out,—see copy.

When the proof-reader doubts the correctness of a word, phrase, or anything else, he encircles or underscores it, and in the margin writes Qr., with or without a suggested correction, encircled. Should the author adopt the suggestion, he draws a line across only the Qr.; if he rejects it, he crosses also the correction. When the author, not having the copy at hand, suspects a deviation from copy, and wishes the copy literally followed, he encircles or underscores the doubtful word or phrase, and writes in the margin—Qr., see copy.

I might perhaps extend these remarks, but it is impossible to mention every supposable correction that can be made, and I think any author, with the above example and remarks and the exercise of his own common sense, should be able to mark a proof intelligibly.

THE ART OF ROWING.

Requisites for a Perfect Stroke.

1. Taking the whole reach forward, and falling back gradually a little past the perpendicular, preserving the shoulders throughout square, and the chest developed at the end.

2. Catching the water and beginning the stroke with a full tension on the arms at the instant of contact.

3. A horizontal and dashing pull through the water immediately the blade is covered, without deepening in the space subsequently traversed.

4. Rapid recovery after feathering by an elastic motion of the body from the hips, the arms being thrown forward perfectly straight simultaneously with the body, and the forward motion of each ceasing at the same time.

5. Lastly, equability in all the actions, preserving full strength without harsh, jerking, isolated and uncompensated movements in any single part of the frame.

Faults in Rowing.

The above laws are sinned against when the rower

1. Does not straighten both arms before him.
2. Keeps two convex wrists instead of the outside wrist flat.
3. Contrives to put his hands forward by a subsequent motion after the shoulders have attained their reach, which is getting the body forward without the arms.
4. Extends the arms without a corresponding bend on the part of the shoulders, which is getting the arms forward without the body.
5. Catches the water with unstraightened arms or arm, and a slackened tension as its consequence; thus time may be kept, but not stroke; keeping stroke always implying uniformity of work.
6. Hangs before dipping downwards to begin the stroke.
7. Does not cover the blade up to the shoulder.
8. Rows round and deep in the middle, with hands high and blade still sunken after the first contact.
9. Curves his back forward or aft.
10. Keeps one shoulder higher than the other.
11. Jerks.
12. Doubles forward and bends over the oar at the feather, bringing the body up to the handle, and not the handle up to the body.
13. Strikes the water at an obtuse angle, or rows the first part in the air.
14. Cuts short the end, prematurely slackening the arms.
15. Shivers out the feather, commencing it too soon and bringing the blade into a plane with the water while work may yet be done; thus the oar leaves the water in perfect time, but stroke is not kept. This and No. 5 are the most subtle faults in rowing, and involve the science of shirking.
16. Rolls backward, with an inclination towards the inside or outside of the boat.
17. Turns his elbows at the feather instead of bringing them sharp past the flanks.
18. Keeps the head depressed between the shoulders instead of erect.
19. Looks out of the boat instead of straight before him. (This almost inevitably rolls the boat.)
20. Throws up the water instead of turning it well aft off the lower angle of the blade. A wave thus created is extremely annoying to the oar further aft: there should be no wave travelling astern, but an eddy containing two small circling swirls.

MACADAMIZED ROADS.

Stone is to be procured in some form in almost every part of the country, and a road made of small broken stone to the depth of 10 inches, will be smooth, solid, and durable.

The size of stones for a road should be about that of a hen's egg. It must be in due proportion to the space occupied by a wheel of ordinary dimensions on a smooth level surface; this point of contact will be found to be longitudinally, about 1 inch; and every piece of stone put into a road, which exceeds 1 inch in any of its dimensions, is mischievous.

In repairing an old road no addition of materials is to be brought upon it, unless in any part it be found that there is not a quantity of clean stone equal to 10 inches in thickness.

The stone already in the road is to be loosened up. The road is then to be laid as flat as possible, a rise of 3 inches from the centre to the side is sufficient for a road 30 feet wide.

The stones when loosened in the road are to be gathered off by means of a strong heavy rake to the side of the road, and there broken.

When the large stones have been removed, the road is to be put in shape, and a rake employed to smooth the surface.

When the road is so prepared, the stones that have been broken by the side of the road are then to be carefully spread on it — not to be laid on it in shovelsful, but scattered over the surface, one shovelful following another, and spreading over a considerable space.

When additional stone is wanted on a road that has consolidated by use, the old hardened surface of the road is to be loosened with a pick, in order to make the fresh materials unite with the old.

Every road is to be made of broken stone, without mixture of earth, clay, chalk, or any other matter that will imbibe water and be affected with frost; nothing is to be laid on the clean stone on pretence of binding; broken stone will combine by its own angles into a smooth solid surface that cannot be affected by vicissitudes of weather, or displaced by the action of wheels, which will pass over without a jolt, and consequently without injury.

Flint makes an excellent road, if due attention be paid to the size; but, from want of that attention, many of the flint roads are rough, loose, and expensive.

Limestone, when properly prepared and applied, makes a smooth, solid road, and becomes consolidated sooner than any other material; but from its nature is not the most lasting.

To Manage Water-pipes in Winter.

When the frost begins to set in, cover the water-pipes with hay or straw bands, twisted tight round them. Let the cisterns and water-butts be washed out occasionally; this will keep the water pure and fresh.

In pumping up water into the cistern for the water-closet, be very particular, in winter time. Let all the water be let out of the pipe when done; but if this is forgotten, and it should be frozen, take a small gimblet and bore a hole in the pipe, a little distance from the place where it is let off, which will prevent its bursting. Put a peg into the hole when the water is let off.

To make an Æolian Harp.

Of very thin cedar, pine, or other soft wood make a box 5 or 6 inches deep, 7 or 8 inches wide, and of a length just equal to the width of the window in which it is to be placed. Across the top, near each end, glue a strip of wood half an inch high and a quarter of an inch thick, for bridges. Into the ends of the box insert wooden pins, like those of a violin, to wind the strings around, two pins in each end. Make a sound-hole in the middle of the top, and string the box with small catgut, or blue first-fiddle strings. Fastening one end of each string to a metallic pin in one end of the box, and, carrying it over the bridges, wind it around the turning-pin in the opposite end of the box. The ends of the box should be increased in thickness where the wooden pins enter, by a piece of wood glued upon the inside. Tune the strings in unison and place the box in the window. It is better to have four strings, as described, but a harp with a single string produces an exceedingly sweet melody of notes, which vary with the force of the wind.

To Cure Smoky Chimneys.

The common causes of smoky chimneys are either that the wind is too much let in above at the mouth of the shaft, or else that the smoke is stifled below. They may also proceed from there being too little room in the vent, particularly where several open into the same funnel. The situation of the house may likewise affect them, especially if backed by higher ground or higher buildings.

The best method of cure is to carry from the air a pipe under the floor and opening under the fire; or, when higher objects are the cause, to fix a movable cowl at the top of the chimney.

In regard to smoky chimneys, a few facts and cautions may be useful; and a very simple remedy may often render the calling in of masons and bricklayers unnecessary.

Observe that a northern aspect often produces a smoky chimney.

A single chimney is apter to smoke than when it forms part of a stack.

Straight funnels seldom draw well.

Large fire-places are apt to smoke, particularly when the aperture of the funnel does not correspond in size. For this a temporary remedy may be found in opening a door or window—a permanent cure by diminishing the lower aperture.

When a smoky chimney is so incorrigible as to require a constant admission of fresh air into the room, the best mode is to introduce a pipe, one of whose apertures shall be in the open air and the other under the grate; or openings may be made near the top of the apartment, if lofty, without any inconvenience even to persons sitting close by the fire.

This species of artificial ventilation will always be found necessary for comfort where gas is used internally, whether a fire is lighted or not.

Where a chimney only smokes when a fire is first lighted, this may be guarded against by allowing the fire to kindle gradually; or more promptly by laying any inflammable substance, such as shavings, on the top of the grate, the rapid combustion of which will warm the air in the chimney, and give it a tendency upwards, before any smoke is produced from the fire itself. If old stove-grates are apt to smoke, they may be improved by setting the stove further back. If that fails, contract the lower orifice.

In cottages, the shortness of the funnel or chimney may produce smoke; in which case the lower orifice must be contracted as small as possible by means of an upright register.

If a kitchen chimney overpowers that of the parlor, as is often the case in small houses, apply to each chimney a free admission of air, until the evil ceases.

When a chimney is filled with smoke, not of its own formation, but from the funnel next to it, an easy remedy offers, in covering each funnel with a conical top, or earthen crock, not cylindrical, but a frustum of a cone, by means of which the two openings are separated a few inches, and the cold air or the gust of wind no longer forces the smoke down with them.

If these remedies fail it will be generally found that the chimney only smokes when the wind is in a particular quarter, connected with the position of some higher building, or a hill, or a grove of trees. In such cases the common turncap, as made by tinmen and ironmongers, will generally be found fully adequate to the end proposed. A case has occurred of curing a smoky chimney exposed to the northwest wind, and commanded by a lofty building on the southeast, by the following contrivance.

A painted tin cap, of a conical form, was suspended by a ring and swivel, so as to swing over the mouth of the chimney-pot by means of an arched strap or bar of iron nailed on each side of the chimney. When a gust of wind laid this cap (which, from its resemblance in form and use to an umbrella, is called a paravent or wind-guard) close to the pot on one side, it opened a wider passage for the escape of the smoke on the opposite side, whichever way the wind came, while rain, hail, etc. were effectually prevented from descending the flue.

To Clean Chimneys.

The top of each chimney should be furnished with a pot somewhat in the shape of a bell, underneath the centre of which should be fixed a pulley, with a chain of sufficient length for both ends to be fastened, when not in use, to nails or pins in the chimney, out of sight, but within reach from below. One or both of these ends should be adapted to the reception of a brush of an appropriate construction; and thus chimneys may be swept as often as desired, by servants, with very little additional trouble.

To Extinguish a Chimney on Fire.

Shut the doors and windows, throw water on the fire in the grate, and then stop up the bottom of the chimney.

Another Method.

The gas produced by throwing a handful of flowers of sulphur on the burning coal, where a chimney is on fire, will immediately extinguish the flames.

To Clean Furniture.

Keep the paste or oil in a proper can or jar, that there may be no danger of upsetting when using it. Have two pieces of woollen cloth, one for rubbing it on, the other for rubbing it dry and polishing; also an old linen cloth to finish with, and a piece of smooth soft cork to rub out the stain. Use a brush if the paste be hard. Always dust the table well before the oil or paste is put on; and, if it should be stained, rub it with a damp sponge, and then with a dry cloth. If the stain does not disappear, rub it well with a cork or a brush the way the wood grows; for if rubbed cross-grained it will be sure to scratch it. Be careful to keep the cork and brush free from dust and dirt. When the dust is cleaned off and the stains have been got out, put on the oil or paste, but not too much at a time; rub it well into the wood. If oil, be as quick as possible in rubbing it over the table, and then polish it with another woollen cloth. If wax, put a little bit on the woollen cloth, with the finger or a small stick; rub it well with this till the table has a high polish, then have another cloth to finish it with. Be very careful to have the edges of the table well cleaned, and the oil and wax well rubbed off.

The furniture which is not in constant use will not require to be oiled above once a week; it ought, however, to be dusted every day and well rubbed. Tables which are used daily must be well rubbed every morning, and great care should be taken to remove all spots from them, particularly ink. This can very easily be done, if not left to dry long, by putting on a little salt of lemons with the finger.

When cleaning tables or chairs, be careful to remove them into the middle of the room, or at a distance from the wall. If the sideboard or sidetable is fixed to the wall, be still more careful in cleaning it, and roll up the woollen cloth tight in the hand, and into a small compass.

To Clean Looking-glasses, Mirrors, etc.

If they should be hung so high that they cannot

be conveniently reached, have a pair of steps to stand upon; but mind that they stand steady. Then take a piece of soft sponge, well washed and cleaned from everything gritty, just dip it into water and squeeze it out again, and then dip it into some spirit of wine. Rub it over the glass: dust it over with some powder blue, or whiting sifted through muslin; rub it lightly and quickly off again with a cloth; then take a clean cloth and rub it well again, and finish by rubbing it with a silk handkerchief.

If the glass be very large clean one half at a time, as otherwise the spirit of wine will dry before it can be rubbed off. If the frames are not varnished the greatest care is necessary to keep them quite dry, so as not to touch them with the sponge, as this will discolor or take off the gilding.

To clean the frames, take a little raw cotton in the state of wool, and rub the frames with it; this will take off all the dust and dirt without injuring the gilding. If the frames are well varnished rub them with spirit of wine, which will take out all spots and give them a fine polish. Varnished doors may be done in the same manner. Never use any cloth to frames, or drawings, or unvarnished oil-paintings, when cleaning and dusting them.

To Clean Knives and Forks.

Procure a smooth board, free from knots, or one covered with leather. If the latter, melt a sufficient quantity of mutton-suet, and put it hot upon the leather with a piece of flannel; then take two pieces of soft Bath brick, and rub them one against the other over the leather till it is covered with the powder, which rub in until no grease comes through when a knife is passed over the leather, which may easily be known by the knife keeping its polish.

If only a plain board, rub the Bath brick 2 or 3 times over it; for if too much be put on at once it will make the blades of the knives look rough and scratched. Let the board be of a proper height, and set so that the person may be a little on the stoop while cleaning the knives. Take a knife in each hand, holding them back to back; stand opposite the middle of the board; lay the knives flat upon it, and do not bear too hard upon them; by this method it will be easier to clean two knives at a time than one, and they will be less liable to be broken, for good knives will snap when pressed on too heavily. Many will say that they cannot clean two knives at once, or that they can get through them faster one by one; but if they will only try it a few times in the way recommended, they will find it not only much more expeditious, but easier.

Be careful in keeping a good edge on the knives. Carving-knives in particular ought to be kept sharp, which may easily be done by taking one in each hand, back to back when cleaning, scarcely letting them touch the board when expanding the arms, but when drawing the hands together again bearing a little hard on the edge of the knives; this will give them both a good edge and a fine polish, and is much better than sharpening them with a steel.

The best way to clean steel forks is to fill a small barrel with fine gravel, brick-dust, or sand, mixed with a little hay or moss; make it moderately damp, press it well down, and let it always be kept damp. By running the prongs of the steel forks a few times into this, all the stains on them will be removed. Then have a small stick, shaped like a knife, with leather round it, to polish between the prongs, having first carefully brushed off the dust from them as soon as they are taken out of the tub. A knife-board is often spoiled in cleaning forks upon it, and likewise the backs of the knives; to prevent this have a piece of old hat or leather put on the board where the forks and backs of the knives are cleaned.

Always turn the back of the knives towards the palm of the hand in wiping them, this will prevent all danger from cutting. In wiping the forks put the corner of the cloth between the prongs, to remove any dirt or dust that may not have been thoroughly brushed out; and if there should be silver ferules on the knives and forks, or silver handles, they must be rubbed with a piece of leather and plate powder, keeping the blades covered while the handles are cleaning.

Wipe the knives and forks as soon as possible after being used, as the longer they are left with grease and stains on them the harder they will be to clean; particularly if they have been used for acids, salads, tarts, etc., have then a jug of hot water ready to put them into as soon as done with, and wipe them as before directed.

In order to keep knives and forks in good condition when they are not in use, rub the steel part with a flannel dipped in oil; wipe the oil off after a few hours, as there is often water in it; or dust the blades and prongs with quicklime, finely powdered and kept in a muslin bag.

To Brush Clothes.

Have a wooden horse to put the clothes on, and a small cane to beat the dust out of them; also a board or table long enough for them to be put their whole length when brushing them. Have two brushes, one a hard bristle, the other soft; use the hardest for the great coats, and for the others when spotted with dirt. Fine cloth coats should never be brushed with too hard a brush, as this will take off the nap, and make them look bare in a little time. Be careful in the choice of the cane; do not have it too large, and be particular not to hit too hard. Be careful also not to hit the buttons, for it will scratch if not break them; therefore a small hand-whip is the best to beat with.

If a coat be wet and spotted with dirt, let it be quite dry before brushing it; then rub out the spots with the hands, taking care not to rumple it in so doing. If it want beating do it as before directed, then put the coat at its full length on a board; let the collar be towards the left hand and the brush in the right. Brush the back of the collar first, between the two shoulders next, and then the sleeves, etc., observing to brush the cloth the same way that the nap goes, which is towards the skirt of the coat. When both sides are properly done fold them together; then brush the inside, and last of all the collar.

To Clean a Hair-Brush.

Put a tablespoonful of spirits of hartshorn (aqua ammoniæ) in a pint of water and wash the brush in it; it will very quickly make the brush clean as new. This is also an excellent method of cleansing or shampooing the hair.

Japanning Old Tea-Trays.

First clean them thoroughly with soap and water and a little rotten-stone; then dry them by wiping and exposure at the fire. Now get some good copal varnish, mix with it some bronze powder, and apply with a brush to the denuded parts. After which set the tea-tray in an oven, at a heat of 212° and 300°, until the varnish is dry. Two coats will make it equal to new.

To Cleanse Silver.

Clean silver with hot water, followed by a solution of equal parts of spirits of ammonia and spirits of turpentine; and after this, if necessary, prepared chalk, whiting, magnesia, or rouge.

To Pack Glass or China.

Procure some soft straw or hay to pack them in, and, if they are to be sent a long way and are heavy, the hay or straw should be a little damp, which will prevent them slipping about. Let the largest and heaviest things be always put undermost in the box or hamper. Let there be plenty of straw, and pack the articles tight; but never attempt to pack up glass or China which is of much consequence, till it has been overlooked by some one used to the job. The expense will be but trifling to have a person to do it who understands it, and the loss may be great, if articles of such value are packed up in an improper manner.

To Clean China and Glass.

The best material for cleaning either porcelain or glassware is fuller's earth, but it must be beaten into a fine powder and carefully cleared from all rough or hard particles, which might endanger the polish of the brilliant surface.

To Clean Wine Decanters.

Cut some brown paper into very small bits, so as to go with ease into the decanters; then cut a few pieces of soap very small, and put some water, milk warm, into the decanters, upon the soap and paper; put in also a little pearlash. By well working this about in the decanters it will take off the crust of the wine and give the glass a fine polish. Where the decanters have been scratched, and the wine left to stand in them a long time, have a small cane, with a bit of sponge tied tight at one end; by putting this into the decanter any crust of the wine may be removed. When the decanters have been properly washed let them be thoroughly dried and turned down in a proper rack.

If the decanters have wine in them when put by, have some good corks always at hand to put in instead of stoppers; this will keep the wine much better.

To Decant Wine.

Be careful not to shake or disturb the crust when moving it about or drawing the cork, particularly Port wine. Never decant wine without a wine-strainer, with some fine cambric in it to prevent the crust and bits of cork going into the decanter. In decanting Port wine do not drain it too near; there are generally two-thirds of a wineglass of thick dregs in each bottle, which ought not to be put in; but in white wine there is not much settling. Pour it out, however, slowly, and raise the bottle up gradually. The wine should never be decanted in a hurry; therefore always do it before the family sits down to dinner. Do not jostle the decanters against each other when moving them about, as they easily break when full.

To Preserve Hats.

Hats require great care or they will soon look shabby. Brush them with a soft camel-hair brush; this will keep the fur smooth. Have a stick for each hat to keep it in its proper shape, especially if the hat has got wet. Put the stick in as soon as the hat is taken off, and when dry put it into a hat-box, particularly if not in constant use, as the air and dust soon turn hats brown. If the hat is very wet, handle it as lightly as possible; wipe it dry with a cloth or silk handkerchief, then brush it with the soft brush. If the nap sticks so close, when almost dry, that it cannot be got loose with the soft brushes, then use the hard ones; but if the nap still sticks, damp it a little with a sponge dipped in beer or vinegar; then brush it with a hard brush till dry.

To Clean Boots and Shoes.

Good brushes and blacking are indispensably necessary. First remove all the loose dirt with a wooden knife, and never use a sharp steel one, as the leather is too often cut, and the boots and shoes spoiled. Then take the hard brush and brush off the remainder, and all the dust; they must also be quite dry before blacking, or they will not shine. Do not put on too much blacking at a time, for if it dries before using the shining brush the leather will look brown instead of black. If there are boot-trees, never clean boots or shoes without them, but take care that the trees are always kept clean and free from dust. Never put one shoe within another, and when cleaning ladies' boots or shoes, be careful to have clean hands, that the linings may not get soiled. Always scrape off the dirt when wet from boots or shoes, but never place them too near the fire when dry, as that cracks the leather.

To Keep Up Sash Windows.

This is performed by means of cork, in the simplest manner, and with scarcely any expense. Bore 3 or 4 holes in the sides of the sash, into which insert common bottle-cork, projecting about the sixteenth part of an inch. These will press against the window frames along the usual groove, and by their elasticity support the sash at any height which may be required.

To Choose a Carpet.

Always select one the figures of which are small; for in this case the two webs in which the carpeting consists, are always much closer interwoven than in carpets where large figures upon ample grounds are represented.

Starch.

Use two kinds of clear starch in washing. For shirts and collars the pearl starch is preferred. It should be well boiled and smooth. To 1 qt. of starch put in a piece of spermaceti as large as a walnut; or dissolve 2 oz. of gum Arabic in 1 pint of water, and strain through a cloth; of this add a tablespoonful to each pint of starch. In bottling, a very little corrosive sublimate may be put with the gum to make it keep.

To Stain Floors.

To strong lye of wood-ashes add enough copperas for the required oak shade. Put this on with a mop, and varnish afterwards.

To Tell Good Eggs.

Put them into water; if the butt ends turn up they are not fresh. This is said to be a certain test.

Preservation of Eggs.

A writer says: The best method I know of to preserve eggs is to fill the pores of the shell with fresh, clean lard, so as to exclude all the air. It is my opinion that this simple and easy method is preferable to any now in use. Some put them in lime-water, some lay them down in salt, some put them in saw-dust. But the lime cooks them, so that they have a dried appearance; salt has a similar effect, while eggs saturated with lard (as far as my experience goes) open fresh and nice. In Paris, however, where they understand these things thoroughly, eggs are preserved by immersion in hot water, as follows: Water is made to boil in a kettle, a dozen eggs are put into a colander, which is plunged into the kettle, left there about a minute, and then withdrawn with the eggs. By this means a thin layer or yolk becomes coagulated, and forms in the interior surface of the shell a sort of coating, which opposes itself to the evaporation of the substance of the egg, and consequently to the contact of the air which rushes in to fill the void left by the evaporation.

A Method of Preserving Lime-Juice.

The juice, having been expressed from the fruit,

was strained and put into quart bottles; these having been carefully corked, were put into a pan of cold water, which was then by degrees raised to the boiling point. At that temperature it was kept for half an hour, and was then allowed to cool down to the temperature of the air. After being bottled for 8 months the juice was in the state of a whitish, turbid liquor, with the acidity and much of the flavor of the lime; nor did it appear to have undergone any alteration Some of the juice, which had been examined the year before, and which had since only been again heated and carefully bottled, was still in good condition, retaining much of the flavor of the recent juice. Hence it appears that, by the application of the above process, the addition of rum or other spirit to lime or lemon-juice, may be avoided, without rendering it at all more liable to spontaneous alteration.

To Preserve Milk.

Provide bottles, which must be perfectly clean, sweet, and dry. Draw the milk from the cow into the bottles, and, as they are filled, immediately cork them well up, and fasten the corks with pack-thread or wire. Then spread a little straw on the bottom of a boiler, on which place the bottles with straw between them, until the boiler contains a sufficient quantity. Fill it up with cold water; heat the water, and as soon as it begins to boil draw the fire, and let the whole gradually cool. When quite cold take out the bottles, and pack them with straw or saw-dust in hampers, and stow them in the coolest part of the house or ship. Milk preserved in this manner, although 18 months in the bottles, will be as sweet as when first milked from the cow.

To Preserve Cabbages and other Esculent Vegetables Fresh during a Sea Voyage or a Severe Winter.

Cut the cabbage so as to leave about 2 inches or more of the stem attached to it; after which scoop out the pith to about the depth of 1 inch, taking care not to wound or bruise the rind by the operation. Suspend the cabbage by means of a cord tied around the stem, so that that portion of it from which the pith is taken remains uppermost, which regularly fill every morning with fresh water. By this simple method cabbages, cauliflowers, brocoli, etc. may be preserved fresh during a long voyage, or in a severe winter, for domestic use.

Fish-House (State of Schuylkill) Punch.

One-third pt. of lemon-juice, ¾ lb. white sugar, ¼ pt. peach brandy, ¼ pint cogniac brandy, ¼ pt. Jamaica rum, no water, but a large lump of ice.

To Whitewash.

Put some lumps of quicklime into a bucket of cold water, and stir it about till dissolved and mixed, after which a brush with a large bead, and a long handle, to reach the ceiling of the room, is used to spread it thinly on the walls, etc. When dry, it is beautifully white, but its known cheapness has induced the plasterers to substitute a mixture of glue size and whiting for the houses of their opulent customers; and this, when once used, precludes the employment of limewashing ever after, for the latter, when laid on whiting, becomes yellow.

Whitewashing is an admirable manner of rendering the dwellings of the poor clean and wholesome.

First. For rough outside walls — those exposed to the weather — the best mixture is clear lime and water. Any animal or vegetable substance added diminishes the adhesion and durability of the wash.

Second. But if the wall is hard and smooth, the wash is improved by a mixture of very fine sand — as much as will mix and can be applied.

Third. For inside walls an addition of a little glue — say ¼ lb. to 3 pailfuls — increases the adhesion. If it is desired to have the walls very white, the whites of eggs may be used in the place of the glue.

To Prevent the Smoking of a Lamp.

Soak the wick in strong vinegar, and dry it well before you use it; it will then burn both sweet and pleasant, and give much satisfaction for the trifling trouble in preparing it.

Easy Method of Preserving Meat in the Country, for a Few Days, without Salt and without Ice.

Put the meat into the water running from a spring. It will sink — examine it daily — when it begins to rise from the bottom it must be used; it will be found perfectly sound and tender, and may be boiled or roasted. Meat may be preserved in this manner 3 or 4 days in summer-time, free from taint. The outside will appear somewhat whitened, but the flavor is not injured. It would be advisable to have a box or tub, with a cover, into and out of which the water shall have free passage, which may be put either inside or outside of the spring-house.

Ready Mode of Mending Cracks in Stoves, Pipes, and Iron Ovens, as Practised in Germany.

When a crack is discovered in a stove, through which the fire or smoke penetrates, the aperture may be completely closed in a moment with a composition consisting of wood-ashes and common salt, made up into paste with a little water, and plastered over the crack. The good effect is equally certain, whether the stove, etc., be cold or hot.

POTICHOMANIA;

Or, to make Glass Jars look like China.

After painting the figures, cut them out, so that none of the white of the paper remains, then take some thick gum Arabic water, pass it over all the figures, and place them on the inside of the glass to taste; let them stand to dry for 24 hours, then clean them well with a wet cloth betwixt the prints, and let them stand a few hours longer lest the water should move any of the edges, then take white wax and flake white, ground very fine, and melt them together; with a japanning-brush go over all the glass above the prints; done in this manner they will hold water; or, boil isinglass to a strong jelly, and mix it up with white lead, ground fine, and lay it on in the same manner; or use nut-oil and flake-white. For a blue ground, do it with white wax and Prussian blue, ground fine; for red, wax and vermilion, or carmine; for green, wax and verdigris; for a chocolate color, wax and burnt umber.

To make Grindstones without Moulds.

Take of river sand, 3 parts; of seed-lac, washed, 1 part. Mix them over a fire in a pot, and form the mass into the shape of a grindstone, having a square hole in the centre; fix it on an axis with liquefied lac, heat the stone moderately, and by turning the axis it may easily be formed into an exact circular shape. Polishing grindstones are made only of such sand as will pass easily through fine muslin in the proportion of 2 parts of sand to 1 of lac. This sand is found at Ragimaul. It is composed of small angular crystalline particles tinged red with iron; 2 parts to 1 of black magnetic sand. The stone-cutters, instead of sand, use the powder of a very hard granite called corune. These grindstones cut very fast. When they want to increase their power they throw sand upon them, or let them occasionally touch the edge of a vitri fied brick. The same composition is formed upon sticks for cutting stones, shells, etc., by the hand.

To make Wax Candles.

Place a dozen wicks on an iron circle, at equal distances, over a large copper vessel tinned and full of melted wax; pour a ladlefull of the wax on the tops of the wicks, one after another; what the wick does not take will drop into the vessel, which must be kept warm by a pan of coals; continue this process till the candles are as large as required. If they are wanted of a pyramidal form, let the first three ladlesful be poured on at the top of the wick, the fourth at the height of three-quarters, the fifth at half, and the sixth at a quarter; then take them down hot, and lay them beside each other in a feather-bed folded in two to preserve their warmth and keep the wax soft; then take them down and roll them one by one on a smooth table, and cut off the thick end as required.

To make Kitchen Vegetables Tender.

When peas, French beans, etc., do not boil easily, it has usually been imputed to the coolness of the season, or to the rains. This popular notion is erroneous. The difficulty of boiling them soft arises from an excess of gypsum imbibed during their growth. To correct this, throw a small quantity of carbonate of soda into the pot alone with the vegetables.

To Prevent Haystacks from Taking Fire.

When there is any reason to fear that the hay which is intended to be housed or stacked is not sufficiently dry, let a few handfuls of common salt be scattered between each layer. This, by absorbing the humidity of the hay, not only prevents the fermentation, and consequent inflammation of it, but adds a taste to it, which stimulates the appetites of cattle and preserves them from many diseases.

To Frame a Polygraph, or Instrument for Writing Two Letters at Once.

In this instrument, two pens, and even three, if necessary, are joined to each other by slips of wood acting upon the pivot; one of these pens cannot move without drawing the other to follow all its movements: the rules are inflexible, and they preserve in all their positions the parallelism which is given by uniting them. The movements of one of these pens are identically the same as those of the other; the characters traced by the first are the exact counterpart of those which the second has formed; if the one rise above the paper and cease to write, or rather, if it make a scratch, or advance towards the ink-bottle, the other, faithful to the movements which are transmitted to it by the species of light wood which directs it, either rises or scratches or draws ink, and that without having occasion to give any particular attention to it. The copy is made of itself, and without ever thinking of it.

The polygraph is not expensive; it is used without difficulty, and almost with the same facility as in ordinary writing. The construction is as simple as it is convenient; all the parts are collected so as to be taken to pieces, and put up again very easily. Its size admits of its taking every desirable position, horizontal, perpendicular, or oblique, according to the application which is made of it, and the piece of furniture to which it is to be adapted; for it may be fixed to a drawer, a desk, an inkstand, an easel, or simply laid upon the table; it is generally accompanied by a drawer, and a case of the form and bulk of an ordinary desk.

Castor Oil as a Dressing for Leather.

Castor oil, besides being an excellent dressing for leather, renders it vermin-proof; it should be mixed, say half and half, with tallow or other oil. Neither rats, roaches, nor other vermin will attack leather so prepared.

Substitute for a Corkscrew.

A convenient substitute for a corkscrew, when the latter is not at hand, may be found in the use of a common screw, with an attached string to pull the cork.

Another.—Stick two forks vertically into the cork on opposite sides, not too near the edge. Run the blade of a knife through the two, and give a twist.

Another.—Fill the hollow at the bottom of the bottle with a handkerchief or towel; grasp the neck with one hand, and strike firmly and steadily with the other upon the handkerchief.

To send Messages in Cypher.

Any document written in cypher, by which signs are substituted for letters, or even for words, is liable to be decyphered. The following plans are free from such objection: The correspondents select two copies of the same edition of a book, the word to be used is designated by figures referring to the page, line, and number of the word in the line: or the message may be written on a slip of paper wound spirally around a rod of wood; these can only be decyphered by bringing them into their original position, by wrapping around a second rod of the same size. [For SYMPATHETIC INKS, see INKS.]

Expectation of Life at any Age from Five to Sixty Years.

Every man, woman, and child has a property in life. What is the value of this property? Mr. Charles M. Willich has established an extremely easy rule for expressing this value—this "Expectation of Life" at any age from 5 to 60. His formula stand thus: $e = \frac{2}{3}(80-n)$; or, in plain words, the expectation of life is equal to two-thirds of the difference between the age of the party and 80. Thus, say a man is now 20 years old, between that age and 80 there are 60 years; two-thirds of 60 are 40; and this is the sum of his expectation of life. If a man be now 60 years, he will have an expectation of life nearly 14 years more. By the same rule, a child of 5 has a lien of life for 50 years. Every one can apply the rule to his own age. Mr. Willich's hypothesis may be as easily remembered as that by De Moivre in the last century, which has now become obsolete, from the greater accuracy of the mortality tables. The results obtained by the new law correspond very closely with those from Dr. Farr's English Life-Table, constructed with great care from an immense mass of returns.

Grafting Wax.

Five parts of rosin, 1 part of beeswax, 1 part of tallow. Melt these in a skillet, tin cup, or any metal vessel; the skillet being preferable, as it can be handled better, and the wax keeps warm longer in it. Mix these over the fire, and mix together well. When the scions are set — say as many as 20 or 30, or as few as wished — have the mixture ready and apply it warm with a small wooden paddle. See that every part is covered, and the air completely excluded. It requires no bandage. We have made the wax in different proportions to the above, but we find these to be best adapted to the purpose. The object to be attained is to have the wax of such consistency that it will not crack in the cold winds of March and April, nor run in the hot suns of summer.

To Prepare a cheap Hortus Siccus.

All the smaller plants should be expanded under water, in a plate, upon a piece of writing-paper sunk to the bottom. In this state they will assume their natural form and position. The paper, with the plant upon it, must be withdrawn from the water gently; and the plant and paper afterwards placed betwixt two or three sheets of blotting-paper and pressed with a book or flat board. It is then to be laid up in a quire of blotting paper, under pressure, for a day or two, when, if dry, it may be placed permanently upon writing-paper.

To make Artificial Red Coral Branches, for the Embellishment of Grottoes.

Take clear rosin, dissolve it in a brass pan; to every ounce of which add 2 drs. of the finest vermilion; when stirred well together, choose the twigs and branches, peeled and dried, then take a pencil and paint the branches all over whilst the composition is warm; afterwards shape them in imitation of natural coral. This done, hold the branches over a gentle coal fire, till all is smooth and even as if polished. In the same manner white coral may be prepared with white-lead, and black coral, with lampblack. A grotto may be built, with little expense, of glass, cinders, pebbles, pieces of large flint, shells, moss, stones, counterfeit coral, pieces of chalk, all bound or cemented together with the above described cement.

To Prevent Cold Feet at Night.

Draw off the stocking, just before undressing, and rub the ankles and feet with the hand as hard as can be borne for 5 or 10 minutes. This will diffuse a pleasurable glow, and those who do so will never have to complain of cold feet in bed. Frequent washing and rubbing them thoroughly dry with a linen cloth or flannel, is useful for the same purpose.

A Natural Dentifrice.

The common strawberry is a natural dentifrice, and its juice, without any preparation, dissolves the tartareous incrustations on the teeth, and makes the breath sweet and agreeable.

Fine Clay as a Dressing for Sores.

Dr. Schreber, of Leipzic, recommends the use of clay as the most "energetic, the most innocent, the most simple, and the most economical of palliative applications to surfaces yielding foul and moist discharges." He, moreover, considers that it has a specific action in accelerating the cure. Clay softened down in water, and freed from all gritty particles, is laid, layer by layer, over the affected part to the thickness of about a line. If it become dry and fall off, fresh layers are applied to the cleansed surface. The irritating secretion is rapidly absorbed by the clay, and the contact of air prevented. The cure thus goes on rapidly. This clay-ointment has a decisive action in cases of fœtid perspiration of the feet or arm-pits. A single layer applied in the morning will destroy all odor in the day. It remains a long time supple, and the pieces which fall off in fine powder produce no inconvenience.

To Prevent the Effects of Drinking Cold Liquors in Warm Weather, or when Heated by Exercise.

Avoid drinking water whilst warm, or drink only a small quantity at once, and let it remain a short time in the mouth before swallowing it, or wash the hands and face and rinse the mouth with cold water before drinking. If these precautions have been neglected, and the disorder incident to drinking cold water or eating ice when the body is heated, has been produced the first and in most instances the only remedy to be administered is 60 drops of laudanum in spirits and water, or warm drink of any kind.

If this should fail of giving relief, the same quantity may be given 20 minutes afterwards.

When laudanum cannot be obtained, rum and water, brandy and water, or even warm water alone, should be given.

To Remedy the Effects of Dram-drinking.

Whoever makes the attempt to abandon spirit-drinking, will find, from time to time, a rankling in the stomach, with a sensation of sinking, coldness and inexpressible anxiety. This may be relieved by taking often a cupful of an infusion of cloves made by steeping about an oz. of them in a pint of boiling water for 6 hours, and then straining off the liquor, or from a teaspoonful to a tablespoonful of elixir of valerianate of ammonia. In a state of permanent languor and debility, 1½ oz. of the cascarilla bark (being also first bruised in a mortar), should be added to the infusion. This mixture taken in the quantity above specified 3 times a day will be found a useful strengthener of the stomach and bowels when they have been disordered by frequent excess and intoxication.

The Portland Powder.

Take of aristolochia rotunda, or birthwort root, gentian root, tops and leaves, germander, tops and leaves, ground pine, tops and leaves, centaury, tops and leaves. Take of all these, well dried, powdered and sifted fine, equal weight; mix them well together, and take 1 dr. of this mixed powder every morning, fasting, in a cup of wine and water, broth, tea, or any other vehicle you like best; keep fasting 1½ hours after it; continue this for 3 months without interruption, then diminish the dose to ¾ dr. for 3 months longer, then to ½ dr. for 6 months more, taking it regularly every morning if possible; after the first year it will be sufficient to take ½ dr. every other day. As this medicine operates insensibly, it will perhaps take 2 years before you receive any great benefit, so you must not be discouraged, though you do not perceive at first any great amendment; it works slowly but surely; it does not confine the patient to any particular diet, so one lives soberly, and abstains from those meats and liquors that have always been accounted pernicious in the gout, as champagne, drams, high sauces, etc.

In rheumatism which is not habitual, a few of the drachm doses may do, but if habitual or of long duration, the powder must be taken as for the gout. The remedy requires patience, as it operates but slowly in both distempers.

Pradier's Cataplasm.

Pradier's remedy for the gout was purchased by the Emperor Napoleon, *pro bono publico*, for £2500. Take of balm of Mecca, 6 dr.; red bark, 1 oz.; saffron, ½ oz.; sarsaparilla, 1 oz.; sage, 1 oz.; rectified spirit of wine, 3 lbs. Dissolve separately the balm of Mecca in ½ of the spirit of wine: macerate the rest of the substances in the remainder for 48 hours; filter, and mix the two liquors for use; the tincture obtained is mixed with twice or thrice the quantity of lime-water; the bottle must be shaken in order to mix the precipitate settled at the bottom by standing.

Mode of Application.

The following is the mode of applying the remedy: A poultice must be prepared of linseed meal, which must be of good consistency and spread very hot of the thickness of a finger on a napkin, so as completely to surround the part affected; if it be required for both legs, from the feet to the knees, it will take about 3 qts. of linseed meal. When the poultice is prepared, and as hot as the patient can bear it, about 2 oz. of the prepared liquor must be poured equally over the whole of the surface of each, without its being imbibed; the part affected is then to be wrapped up in it, and bound up with flannel and bandages to preserve the heat. The poultice is generally changed every 24 hours, sometimes at the end of twelve.

Liebig's Soup for Invalids.

Take ½ lb. of newly-killed beef or fowl, chop it fine, add 1½ lbs. of distilled water, with 4 drops of pure muriatic acid, and 34 to 67 grains of common salt, and stir well together. After an hour the whole is to be thrown on a conical hair-sieve, and the fluid allowed to flow through without any pressure. The first thick portions which pass through are to be returned to the sieve, until the fluid runs off quite clear. Half a lb. of distilled water is to be poured, in small portions at a time, on the flesh residue in the sieve. There will be obtained in this way about 1 lb. of fluid (cold extract of flesh), of a red color, and having a pleasant taste of soup. The invalid is allowed to take it cold, a cupful at a time, at pleasure. It must not be heated, as it becomes muddy by heat, and deposits a thick coagulum of albumen and coloring matter of blood. In soup prepared in the usual way by boiling, all those constituents of flesh are wanting which are necessary for the formation of blood albumen; and the yolk of egg, which is added, is poor in those substances, for it contains in all 82½ per cent. of water and fat, and only 17½ per cent. of a substance, the same or very similar to albumen of egg. But whether it is equal in its power of nutrition to the albumen of flesh, is at least doubtful from the experiments of Magendie. Besides the albumen of flesh, the new soup contains a certain quantity of coloring matter of blood, and with it a much larger quantity of the necessary iron for the formation of the blood-corpuscles, and finally, the muriatic acid to assist digestion. A great obstacle to the use of this soup in summer is its liability to change in warm weather. It enters into fermentation like sugar with yeast, but without acquiring a bad odor. What may be the substance which gives rise to this fermentation is a question well worthy of being investigated. The extraction of the flesh must consequently be made with very cold water, and in a cool place. Iced water, and external cooling with ice, completely removes this difficulty. But the most important point to be attended to is to employ meat quite recently killed, and not several days old. The soup has been successfully employed in low fevers and the summer-complaint of children.

Liebig's Soup for Children.

With that remarkable estimation of the greatness of small things which is the most valuable of his many high intellectual qualities, and with a tender appreciation of the importance of small people, Baron Liebig devotes a special article in an English scientific periodical to the description of a new diet which he conceives to be the most fitting substitute for the natural nutriment of children robbed of their mother's milk. It is well known that the cow's milk does not adequately represent the milk of a healthy woman, and when wheaten flour is added, as it commonly is, Liebig points out that, although that starch be not unfitting for the nourishment of infants, the change of it into sugar in the stomach during digestion imposes an unnecessary labor on the organization, which will be spared it if the starch be changed into the soluble forms of sugar and dextrine. This he effects by adding to the wheaten flour a certain quantity of malt. As wheaten flour and malt flour contain less alkali than woman's milk he supplies this when preparing the soup. This soup may be shortly prepared, as follows: "Half an oz. of wheaten flour and an equal quantity of malt flour; 7½ grs. of bicarbonate of potash and 1 oz. of water are to be well mixed; 5 oz. of cow's milk are then to be added, and the whole put on a gentle fire; when the mixture begins to thicken it is removed from the fire, stirred during 5 minutes, heated and stirred again till it becomes fluid, and finally made to boil. After the separation of the bran by a sieve it is ready for use. By boiling it for a few minutes it loses all taste of the flour." The immediate inducement for Baron Liebig making this soup arose from the fact that one of his grandchildren could not be suckled by its mother, and that another required, besides his mother's milk, a more concentrated food. The soup proved an excellent food — the children thrived on it. Baron Liebig has himself used this soup with tea as a breakfast, and a most thoroughly nutritious meal it must be. The temperature before boiling should not exceed 148° Fahr.

To Write for the Use of the Blind.

Let an iron pen be used, the point of which is not split. Blind persons writing without ink, and pressing on a strong paper, will produce characters in relief, which they can immediately read by passing their fingers over the projecting characters on the opposite side of the paper, in the contrary direction.

On the Honing and Stropping of a Razor.

Let the hone be seldom and but sparingly resorted to, and never, unless by frequent and repeated stropping the edge of the razor is entirely destroyed; use the best pale oil, and be careful to preserve the hone clean and free from dust. Previously to the operation of shaving, it will be found of service, particularly to those who have a strong beard and a tender skin, to wash the face well with soap and water, and the more time is spent in lathering and moistening the beard, the easier will the process of shaving become. Dip the razor in hot water before applying it to the face; use the blade nearly flat, always taking care to give it a cutting instead of a scraping direction. Strop the razor immediately after using it, for the purpose of effectually removing any moisture that may remain upon the edge, and be careful not to employ a common strop, as the composition with which they are covered is invariably of a very inferior quality, and injurious to a razor. The strop should always be of the best manufacture, and when the composition is worn off it will be found particularly useful to rub it over, lightly, with a little clean tallow, and then put upon it the top part of the snuff of a candle, which, being a fine power, will admirably supply the place of the best composition ever used for the purpose. Another excellent mode of renovating a razor-strop is by rubbing it well with pewter, and impregnating the leather with the finest metallic particles.

Paste for Sharpening Razors.

Take oxide of tin levigated, vulgarly termed prepared putty, 1 oz.; saturated solution of oxalic acid, a sufficient quantity to form a paste. This composition is to be rubbed over the strop, and when dry a little water may be added. The oxalic acid having a great attachment for iron, a little friction with this powder gives a fine edge to the razor.

Horses Pulling at the Halter.

Many remedies have been proposed for curing this bad habit, but a simple and effective one is to discard the common halter, and get a broad, strong leather strap to buckle around the neck for a few inches below the ears. A horse may pull at this, but will soon give it up.

To Escape from or Go into a House on Fire.

Creep or crawl with your face near the ground, and although the room be full of smoke to suffocation, yet near the floor the air is pure, and may be breathed with safety. The best escape from upper windows is a knotted rope, but if a leap is unavoidable, then a bed should be thrown out first, or beds be placed by those outside for the purpose.

To Bring Horses out of a Stable on Fire.

Throw the harness or saddles to which they may have been accustomed, over the backs of the horses in this predicament, and they will come out of the stable as tractably as usual.

How to know whether a Horse has a Strong and Good Eye, or a Weak Eye, and likely to go Blind.

People generally turn a horse's head to a bright light to examine his eyes. You can know very little by this method what sort of an eye the horse has, unless it be a very defective one. You must examine the eye first, when the horse stands with his head to the manger. Look carefully at the pupil of the eye in a horse; it is of an oblong form; carry the size of the pupil in your mind, and turn the horse about, bring him to a bright light, and if in the bright light the pupil of the eye contracts and appears much smaller than it was in the darker light, then you may be sure the horse has a strong, good eye, but, provided the pupil remains nearly of the same size as it appeared in the darker light, the horse has a weak eye, therefore have nothing to do with him. There are contracting and dilating muscles in the eye, which will plainly show you in what state the eye is, whether it be a strong or a weak one.

How to Catch Wood-pigeons.

Wood-pigeons are very easily caught in hard weather, particularly when snow is on the ground. You have but to sweep the snow on one side for about a dozen yards long and about 3 feet broad. Lay about 20 small eel-hooks, fastened by a peg into the ground, and with a small bean on each; be sure you put the point of the hook only through the top of the bean and the barb standing quite out on the side, otherwise if the hook be totally buried in the bean, when the bird struggles he will pull the hook out of his throat.

I think as good a way as any is to punch 2 or 3 holes in horse-beans with an iron bodkin, and then boil them in some common gin; many will be so drunk that they cannot fly up; others will perch on the adjacent trees; watch them, and you will see them tumble down.

How to Catch Wild-fowl.

If you have a large pond or lake frequented by wild-fowl, in the shallow water, about 1 ft. deep, where you observe them feed, lay a few rabbit-traps, with a few beans on the bridge of the trap, under the water. This is a sure method of catching them. Where the water is about 2 ft. deep, put a stick in about 1 foot above the water; cut a slit at the top of the stick; tie a strong piece of pack-thread round a brick-bat, or to a large stone; let the string, after having tied it round the stone, be about a foot longer; to the other end fasten a small eel-hook, baited with a piece of bullock's lights, sheep's paunch, or a horse-bean; then about 3 or 4 in. from the brick-bat fasten a stick nearly as big as your little finger and about 4 in. long, tying the string with a single knot exactly to the centre of the stick; then place that part of the string which is between the brick-bat and the short stick into the notch at the top of the long stick which is stuck in the bottom of the pond. The short stick will prevent the weight of the brick-bat from drawing the string through the notch, and the hook will hang a few inches from the water and the brick-bat hung fast by the notch in the top of the stick. When the water-fowl takes the baited hook he pulls the stick and the brick-bat, and the latter pulls him under water and drowns him.

Assistance to a Person in Danger of Drowning.

If the spectator is unable to swim, and can make the sufferer hear, he ought to direct him to keep his hands and arms under water until assistance comes; in the mean time throw towards him a rope, a pole, or any thing that may help to bring him ashore, or on board; he will eagerly seize whatever is placed within his reach; thus he may, perhaps, be rescued from his perilous situation.

But this desirable object appears attainable by the proper use of a man's hat and pocket handkerchief, which, being all the apparatus necessary, is to be used thus: Spread the handkerchief on the ground, or deck, and place a stiff hat, with the brim downwards, on the middle of it; then tie the handkerchief round the hat, like a bundle, keeping the knots as near the centre of the crown as possible. Now, by seizing the knots in one hand, and keeping the opening of the hat upwards, a person without knowing how to swim, may fearlessly plunge into the water, with whatever may be necessary to save the life of a fellow creature.

The best manner in which an expert swimmer can lay hold of a person he wishes to save from sinking, is to grasp his arm firmly between the shoulder and the elbow; this will prevent him from clasping the swimmer in his arms, and thus forcing him under water, and, perhaps, causing him to sink with him.

To Estimate the Distance of a Thunder-cloud.

Sound travels at the rate of 1120 feet per second. Count the number of seconds between the flash and the thunder, and multiply by 1120. By this means the distance of a cannon or blast of rocks may also be estimated. The pulse of a healthy adult beats about 70 times a minute.

To Escape the Effects of Lightning.

When persons happen to be overtaken by a thunder-storm, although they may not be terrified by the lightning, yet they naturally wish for shelter from the rain which usually attends it; and, therefore, if no house be at hand, generally take refuge under the nearest tree they can find. But in doing this, they unknowingly expose themselves to a double danger; first, because their clothes being thus kept dry, their bodies are rendered more liable to injury — the lightning often passing harmless over a body whose surface is wet; and secondly, because a tree, or any elevated object, instead of warding off, serves to attract and conduct the lightning, which, in its passage to the ground, frequently rends the trunks or branches, and kills any person or animal who happens to be close to it at the time. Instead of seeking protection, then, by retiring under the shelter of a tree, hay-stack, pillar, wall, or hedge, the person should either pursue his way to the nearest house, or get to a part of the road or field which has no high object that can draw the lightning towards it, and remain there until the storm has subsided.

It is particularly dangerous to stand near leaden

spouts, iron gates, or palisadoes, at such times; metals of all kinds having so strong an attraction for lightning, as frequently to draw it out of the course which it would otherwise have taken.

When in a house, avoid sitting or standing near the window, door, or walls, during a thunderstorm. The nearer a person is to the middle of a room the better.

Means of Restoring Persons who have been Famished.

In our attempts to recover those who have suffered under the calamities of famine, great circumspection is required. Warmth, cordials, and food, are the means to be employed: but it is evident that these may prove too powerful in their operation, if not administered with caution and judgment. For the body, by long fasting, is reduced to a state of more than infantile debility; the minuter vessels of the brain, and of the other organs, collapse for want of food to distend them; the stomach and intestines shrink in their capacity; and the heart languidly vibrates, having scarcely sufficient energy to propel the scanty current of blood. Under such circumstances a proper application of heat seems an essential measure, and may be effected, by placing on each side, a healthy man in contact with the patent. Pediluvia, or fomentation of the feet, may also be used with advantage.

The temperature of these should be lower than that of the human body, and gradually increased according to the effects of their stimulus. New milk, weak broth, or water-gruel, ought to be employed, both for the one and the other; as nourishment may be conveyed into the system this way, by passages, properly the most pervious in a state of fasting, if not too long protracted.

It appears safer to advise the administration of cordials in very small doses, and, at first, considerably diluted with either wine or spirits; but slender wine whey will very well answer this purpose, and afford, at the same time, an easy and pleasant nourishment. When the stomach has been a little strengthened, an egg may be mixed with the whey, or administered under some other agreeable form. The yolk of one was, to Cornaro, sufficient for a meal; and the narrative of that noble Venetian, in whom a fever was excited by the addition of only two ounces of food to his daily allowance, shows, that the return to a full diet should be conducted with great caution, and by very slow gradations.

Welsh Rabbit.

Cut your cheese into small slips, if soft; if hard, grate it down. Have ready a spirit-of-wine lamp, etc., and deep block-tin dish; put in the cheese with a lump of butter, and set it over the lamp. Have ready the yolk of an egg whipped, with half a glass of Madeira, and as much ale or beer; stir your cheese when melted, till it is thoroughly mixed with the butter, then add gradually the egg and wine, keep stirring till it forms a smooth mass. Season with Cayenne and grated nutmeg. To be eaten with a thin hot toast.

Impromptu Chafing Dish.

It often happens that in travelling, the materials for a rabbit may be had when there is nothing else in the house the gourmand can eat. In this case, if there is no blazer, or chafing dish, an excellent substitute is formed in a moment by two soup plates, separated from each other by pieces of a bottle cork placed on the rim of the lower one, which should contain any kind of spirits. Put your cheese into the top one, fire the spirits with a slip of paper, and set your rabbit on the corks.; it answers as well as the most expensive heater in Christendom.

DIALYSIS

Is the term applied by Professor Graham to a process devised by him for separating bodies by taking advantage of their tendency to form crystals or to remain in the amorphous or glue-like condition.

It is well known that many bodies have a tendency to crystallize, such as salt, sugar and alum; others, as albumen (white of egg), glue and the like are never known to assume the crystalline form. Professor Graham has found that if a mixture of the former, which he terms *crystalloids*, with the latter (*colloids*), be placed in a vessel having its sides or bottom constructed of animal membrane or parchment paper (page 436) and floated or immersed in water, the crystalloid will pass through into the surrounding liquid, while the colloid will remain. This is not an action analogous to ordinary filtration, for the membrane is water-proof, but is of a more complex nature.

The dialyzer of Professor Graham consists of a hoop of wood having its bottom made of parchment-paper; it resembles, in fact, an ordinary tambourine. This is floated on the surface of a liquid and the mixture is poured into it. After a time the liquid gives on evaporation the crystalloid, salt, for instance, while the colloid, jelly, for instance, remains within the dialyzer.

Among the results of investigation with this apparatus have been the discovery of silica (sand, rock-crystal) in a soluble form (page 434) and the separation of crystalline poisons from organic matters in the stomach after death; many others will be found in the recent scientific journals.

Utilization of Brine.

Mr. A. Whitelaw has proposed to use the process of dialysis for obtaining the large amount of nutritious matter which exists in the brine of salted meats, and which is usually thrown away. According to Mr. W., 2 galls. of brine yield 1 lb. of solid extract, which makes a palatable and nutricious soup. It is only necessary to enclose the brine in bags of animal membrane, and immerse them in water; the salt passes through, and the albuminous and extractive matters remain.

To Freshen Salt Meat.

Another application of dialysis is that of rendering salt meat more juicy, tender and digestible. The meat is placed in a bag of untanned skin, which is nearly filled with brine from the beef-barrel. This is placed in sea-water for several days, when the brine, having lost its salt by dialysis, becomes reduced in strength to that of sea-water. The beef, which had been contracted by the action of the salt, gives up its salt to the brine in the bag, swells and absorbs part of the juice which it had given out to the brine. In this way no loss is sustained by steeping, and the brine left in the bags, after a nightly dialysis, may be used for soup.

Thoroughly salted meat without bone gradually takes up nearly ⅓ of its weight of juices from the brine. It becomes then somewhat like fresh meat, and may be cooked in a variety of ways which are inadmissible for salt meat.

RIDING.
Sitting a Horse.

The body of the rider is divided into three parts, of which two are movable and one immovable; one of the first consists of all the upper part of the body down to the waist, the other of the lower part of the legs, from the knee down; the immovable portion is from the waist to the knees. The rider should sit square on the middle of the saddle, the upper part of the body presenting a free and unconstrained appearance, the chest not much thrown forward, the ribs resting freely on the hips, the waist and loins not stiffened, and thus not exposed to tension or effort from the motions of the horse; the upper part of the body should lean slightly to the rear, rather than forward; the thighs, inclining a little forward, lie flat and firmly on the saddle, covering the surcingle, of which only a small part behind the knee, should be seen; the lower part of the leg, hanging vertically from the knees, touches the horse, but without the slightest pressure; the toes are pointed up without constraint, and on the same line with the knees, for if the toes are turned outward it not only causes the horse to be unnecessarily pricked by the spurs (if worn), but the firmness of the seat is lost; the heels should be seven-eighths of an inch below the toes, and the stirrups so adjusted that when the rider raises himself on them, there may be the breadth of 4 fingers between the crotch and the saddle; to make this adjustment, when the rider has acquired a firm and correct seat he should, without changing that seat, push the bottom of the stirrup to the hollow of the foot, and then, with the foot horizontal, feel a slight support from the stirrup; when this is accomplished he replaces the foot properly in the stirrup, and the heel will then be seven-eighths of an inch below the toes.

To give the rider a correct seat, the instructor, having caused him to mount, seizes the lower part of his leg, and stretches it straight toward the fore-quarters of the horse, so as to bring the buttocks of the rider square on the saddle; then, resting one hand on the man's knee, he seizes the lower part of the leg with the other, and carries back the thigh and knee so as to bring the crotch square on the saddle, the thighs covering the surcingle, the lower part of the leg, from the knee down, also over the surcingle, and sees that the rider does not sit too much on his crotch, but has his buttocks well under him. He then explains to the rider that the firmness of the seat consists in this : that the rider grasps the horse with his legs; that both thighs press equally upon the saddle, in conformity with the movements of the body, and that the general movements of the body and thighs must conform to those of the horse. He should be taught, too, how to hold the feet, without allowing him to place them in the stirrups, for this is one of the most essential conditions for a good seat.

Dough-nuts.

Take two deep dishes, and sift ¾ of a pound of flour into each. Make a hole in the centre of one of them, and pour in a wineglassful of the best brewer's yeast; mix the flour gradually into it, netting it with lukewarm water; cover it, and set it by the fire to raise for two hours. In the meantime, cut up 5 oz. of butter into the other dish of flour, and rub it fine with your hands; add ½ lb. of powdered sugar, a teaspoonful of powdered cinnamon, a grated nutmeg, a tablespoonful of rose-water, and ½ pint of milk. Beat 3 eggs very light, and stir them hard into the mixture. Then, when the sponge is perfectly light, add it to the other ingredients, mixing them all thoroughly with a knife. Cover it, and set it by the fire for another hour. When it is quite light, flour your paste-board, turn out the lump of dough, and cut it into thick diamond or round shape cakes. If you find the dough so soft as to be unmanagable, mix in a little more flour. Have ready a skillet of boiling lard, put the dough nuts into it, and fry them brown.

Crullers.

One and a half lbs. of flour, 5 eggs, ¾ of a lb. of sugar, 6 oz. of butter, 1 teaspoonful of cinnamon and nutmeg mixed, 1 wineglassful of rose-water, 1 tablespoonful of saleratus. Rub the butter, sugar, and flour together, add the spice, rose-water, and saleratus. Beat the eggs very light, mix all into a dough, knead it well, and roll it out an inch thick. Cut it into slips, twist them into various forms, fry in hot lard until they are of a light brown. When cold, sift sugar over them.

How to make Otto of Roses.

Gather the leaves of the hundred-leaved rose (*rosa centifolia*), put them in a large jar or cask, with just sufficient water to cover them; then put the vessel to stand in the sun, and in about a week afterward the otto (a butyraceous oil) will form a scum on the surface, which should be removed by the aid of a piece of cotton.

How to Keep Fresh Fish.

Draw the fish and remove the gills, then insert a piece of charcoal in their mouths, and two or three pieces in their bellies. If they are to be conveyed any distance, wrap each fish separately in paper and place them in a box. Fish thus preserved will keep fresh for several days.

To Varnish Articles of Iron and Steel.

Dissolve 10 parts clear grains of mastic, 5 parts camphor, 15 grs. sandarac, and 5 parts elemi, in a sufficient quantity of alcohol, and apply this varnish without heat. The articles will not only be preserved from rust, but the varnish will retain its transparency, and the metallic brilliancy of the articles will not be impaired.

To Keep Water Pure in Iron Kettles.

Keep an oyster-shell in the bottom of the kettle, this will prevent the iron from rusting and keep the water clear.

To Wash Flannels.

Wash first in warm soap-suds and rinse them in warm water, having the water neither too hot nor too cold.

Pharaoh's Serpent's Eggs.

These are little cones of sulphocyanide of mercury, which, when lighted, give forth a long, serpent-like, yellowish-brown body.

Prepare nitrate of mercury by dissolving red precipitate in strong nitric acid as long as it is taken up. Prepare also sulphocyanide of ammonium by mixing one volume of bisulphide of carbon, four of strong solution of ammonia, and four of alcohol. This mixture is to be frequently shaken. In the course of about 2 hours the bisulphide will have dissolved, forming a deep red solution. Boil this until the red color disappears and the solution becomes of a light yellow color. This is to be evaporated at about 80° Fahr. until it crystallizes. Add little by little the sulphocyanide to the mercury solution. The sulphocyanide of mercury will precipitate; the supernatent liquid may be poured off, and the mass made into cones about half an inch in height. The powder of the sulphocyanide is very irritating to the air passages, and the vapors from the burning cones should be avoided as much as possible. To ignite, set them on a plate or the like, and light them at the apex of the cone. The result is certainly most remarkable; the fiery vapors, winding and twisting in the strangest fashion, render them objects of curiosity and astonishment to all who witness their performance.

DECALCOMANIA,

Or the Art of Ornamenting China, Glass, Earthenware, Woodenware, Fancy Boxes, Ivory, and Paper Maché Goods, Japannedware, Binding of Books, Fans, Leather Work, etc., etc.

Directions.—Cover the picture entirely (taking care not to go beyond the outlines) with a slight coat of fixing varnish; then put the picture on the object to be ornamented, being careful to place it properly at once, in order not to spoil it by moving. The varnish newly applied being too liquid, the picture should be left to dry eight or ten minutes, and placed on the object to be ornamented, when just damp enough to be still adherent; this done, cover the back of the picture with a piece of cloth steeped in water, then, by means of a knife or pen-holder, rub it all over, so as to fix every part of it; then remove the piece of cloth and rinse the paper with a paint-brush steeped in water; at the end of a few minutes the paper will come off, leaving the painting transferred.

Care must be taken that the piece of cloth, without being too wet, should be sufficiently so for the paper to be entirely saturated. The picture must now be washed with a wet paint-brush, and dried very lightly with some blotting paper. The ornamented article should, after this, be put near the stove or any other warm place, to make it dry well and to improve the adhesiveness of the pictures. The polishing varnish should not be applied until the next day, keeping the pictures in the meantime carefully out of the dust. The latter varnish should be put on as lightly as possible.

If dark-colored objects are to be ornamented, such as bindings of books, Russian leather, leather bags, &c., the picture must first be covered with a mixture of white lead and turpentine, following the outlines of the design and covering it entirely. When this coat is perfectly dry, proceed according to the above instructions.

To print on silk, paper, or materials that cannot bear washing after the process, proceed as follows: Cover the picture entirely with a light coat of fixing varnish and let it dry for an hour or two; then pass a sponge, lightly damped, over the whole surface of the paper, in order to take away the composition which is on it in the blank parts, and which often cleans the material.

When the paper is dry, re-varnish the picture, and transfer it on to the material by means of a paper cutter, avoiding to employ the piece of cloth or anything damp; then, with a paint-brush slightly steeped in water, wet the paper lightly, and leave it a full quarter of an hour on the object before removing it.

To remove a spoiled print, rub it with a soft rag imbibed in turpentine.

Our readers will at once appreciate the merits of this invention; the facility with which it can be applied, also its numerous applications.

Cosmetic for the Complexion.

Mix glycerine with water, together with a small quantity of alcohol, add Cologne, or other perfume, and you have a preparation closely resembling the celebrated *Email de Paris*. This preparation is said to impart a soft, white, and elegant skin of the texture and color of polished ivory, and to remove all discolorations, black worm specks, and roughness of the skin, and smooths out the marks of small-pox.

Cheap Outside Paint.

Take 2 parts (in bulk) of water-lime ground fine, 1 part (in bulk) of white lead ground in oil. Mix them thoroughly, by adding best boiled linseed-oil enough to prepare it to pass through a paint-mill, after which temper with oil till it can be applied with a common paint-brush. Make any color to suit. It will last three times as long as lead paint, is superior, and cost not one-fourth as much.

Brilliant Whitewash, closely resembling Paint.

Many have heard of the brilliant stucco whitewash on the east end of the President's house at Washington. The following is a receipt for it:

Take ½ bushel nice unslaked lime, slake it with boiling water, cover it during the process to keep in the steam. Strain the liquid through a fine sieve or strainer, and add to it a peck of salt, previously well dissolved in warm water, 3 lbs. ground rice, boiled to a thin paste, and stirred in boiling hot, ½ lb. powdered Spanish whiting, and 1 lb. of clean glue, which has been previously dissolved by soaking it well, and then hang it over a slow fire, in a small kettle within a large one filled with water. Add 5 galls. of hot water to the mixture, stir it well, and let it stand a few days, covered from the dirt. It should be put on right hot: for this purpose, it can be kept in a kettle on a portable furnace. It is said that about a pint of this mixture will cover a square yard upon the outside of a house, if properly applied. Brushes more or less may be used, according to the neatness of the job required. It answers as well as oil-paint for wood, brick, or stone, and is cheaper. It retains its brilliancy for many years. There is nothing of the kind that will compare with it, either for inside or outside walls. Coloring-matter may be put in, and made of any shade you like. Spanish-brown stirred in will make red pink, more or less deep, according to the quantity. A delicate tinge of this is very pretty for inside walls. Finely pulverized common clay, well mixed with Spanish-brown, makes a reddish stone-color. Yellow ochre stirred in makes yellow-wash; but crome goes further, and makes a color generally esteemed prettier. In all these cases the darkness of the shades, of course, is determined by the quantity of coloring used. It is difficult to make rules, because tastes are different; it would be best to try experiments on a shingle, and let it dry. Green must not be mixed with lime; it destroys the color, and the color has an effect on the whitewash which makes it crack and peel. When walls have been badly smoked, and you wish to have them a clean white, it is well to squeeze indigo plentifully through a bag into the water you use, before it is stirred in the whole mixture, or add a little blue stone. If a larger quantity than 5 galls. be wanted, the same proportion should be observed.

To render Gunpowder Incombustible and Combustible at pleasure.

It has been recently announced that a plan has been discovered by which gunpowder may be rendered non-explosive at pleasure, and afterwards restored to its former condition of combustibility. This remarkable discovery was lately announced to have been made in England, but it seemed so improbable that little attention was paid to it. By experiments made during October of this year (1865), at Jersey City, New Jersey, under the charge of Mr. Handel Cossham, one of the party of English railway capitalists accompanying Sir Morton Peto to this country, the matter has been clearly demonstrated to be possible. At this experiment, common gunpowder was first exploded in the ordinary manner. *Ground glass* was then mixed with it, in proportion of two parts of gunpowder to one of ground glass. This mixture then refused to explode under the stimulation of red-hot pokers, matches, fuses, and lighted paper. It took fire and burned slowly, but it would not explode. After these tests the remains of the same powder were sifted, and the glass cleared from it, when, at the slightest touch of a match, the whole compound went off at a flash. But the most remarkable of the experiments was the placing of a four-pound keg of prepared gunpowder on the top of a small portable furnace, in full process of ignition. Under ordinary circumstances, such an attempt would have produced a terrible explosion; but here in a very few minutes it was seen to be perfectly harmless. The hoops of the keg soon fell apart and the powder dropped in the fire, almost extinguishing it.

The addition of ground glass has no chemical effect, but it acts mechanically. The glass separates the grains of powder, and prevents continuous combustion. Each grain is consumed by itself, and does not communicate sufficient force to its neighbor to render the latter dangerous. Mixed in heavier proportions, the gunpowder will scarcely burn; and by uniting four parts of ground glass with one of gunpowder, the latter is rendered as incombustible as a stone.

The importance of this discovery can scarcely be estimated. It is one of the greatest safeguards of human life ever discovered. It will render the powder magazine harmless, and prevent those frequent and terrible events resulting in the loss of life, which have sent misery and woe through many communities. This discovery was made by Mr. James Gale, of Plymouth, England, a blind man, who, in happier days, ere vision was denied him, had been extensively engaged in scientific pursuits.

To prevent and correct Rancidity in Vegetable and Animal Oils.

A small quantity of nitric ether ("sweet spirits of nitre") mixed with the crude oil, carries off all the disagreeable odor of rancidity, whilst by subsequently warming the oil so treated, the spirituous ingredient is removed and the oil becomes sweet and limpid. A few drops of nitric ether added to a bottle of oil when first opened serves as a constant preventive to rancidity.

Fatty bodies in a globular state may be kept a long time without becoming rancid. This peculiar state can be imparted to fatty matters by melting them at 130° Fahr. and adding a small quantity of yolk of egg, or bile, or albuminous substances, or best, a solution of alkali, composed of 5 to 10 parts for every 100 of oil, at the same temperature. The whole is then agitated for some time to bring the fatty matter into a globular condition.

A New Hydraulic Cement.

At a sitting of the Academy of Sciences at Paris, December 4, 1865, it was announced that a very valuable hydraulic cement may be obtained by heating dolomite, commonly known as "magnesian limestone," to between 575° and 750° Fahr., or *below a dull redness*, powdering the calcined mass, and making it into a paste with water. This forms under water a stone of extraordinary hardness, which, when once set, is not affected in the slightest degree either by fresh or sea-water. He also found that a mixture of magnesia with powdered chalk or marble-dust forms with water a plastic mass, which, by exposure in water for some time, becomes converted into a kind of extremely hard artificial marble.

Clay for Modelling and Luting.

The clay is first well dried, and then rendered plastic by admixture with glycerine. It retains its plasticity for months, and is capable of being used over and over again just like wax, with the advantage of always retaining the same consistence of plasticity, being neither hardened by cold nor softened by heat.

Another. — A cheaper method than the above, available for modelling and luting, is to make a mixture of pipe-clay with a solution of chloride of calcium of the specific gravity of 1·35. This retains its plasticity for more than a year, and makes a capital luting.

A New Artificial Light.

Possessing a very high degree of actinic power, has been discovered by M. Sayes, of Paris. It is produced by the combustion of a mixture of 24 parts of well-dried and pulverized nitre with 7 parts of flour of sulphur and 6 of realgar. This mixture does not cost more than 10 cents per pound, and its light is therefore cheaper than the magnesium, to which it is only very slightly deficient in actinic energy. It is not, however, suitable for in-door photography.

New Waterproofing Material.

Paraffin is melted with 5 per cent. of linseed-oil and run into cakes for use. When needed it is melted, and the mixture spread with a brush over the cloth, leather, stone, iron, etc.

The above is also used as a good insulator for electric telegraph wires.

To imitate Meerschaum.

Mix 1 part of casein, or curds of milk, with 6 parts of calcined magnesia and 1 part of oxide of zinc, and a sufficient quantity of water to form a pasty mass, which is left to solidify, and when dry it is extremely hard, susceptible of receiving a high polish, and is sold as a substitute for meerschaum.

To clean Silver or Plated Ware.

Plunge the article in this solution: Hyposulphite of soda, 1 lb.; sal-ammoniac, 8 oz.; solution of ammonia, 4 oz.; cyanide of potassium, 4 oz. Let it remain ½ hour, wash, and rub with buckskin. The cyanide of potassium is very poisonous. It may be omitted, but then the solution is not so active. No powder is necessary in polishing.

Estimate of Farm Seeds for an Acre.

Wheat, broadcast,	1¾ to 2 bushels.
" drilled,	1½ "
Rye, broadcast,	1¾ "
" drilled,	1½ to 1¾ "
Barley, broadcast,	2 to 2½ "
" drilled,	1¾ to 2 "
Oats, broadcast,	2 to 3 "
" drilled,	2 "
Timothy, { When sown with grain in autumn, to be followed by clover in spring. }	1¼ to 2 galls.
RedClover, { Sown on grain in spring in connection with Timothy (without Timothy double quantity). }	1½ to 2 galls.
Herbs, or Red Top,	1 to 1½ bushels of 14 lbs.
Kentucky Blue Grass,	1 to 1½ " " 14 "
Lucerne, drilled,	10 "
Dutch White Clover, broadcast,	8 "
" " " drilled,	6 "
Lawn Grass,	2 to 2½ bushels of 15 "
Millet,	¾ to 1 bushel.
Corn, in hills,	1 to 1½ gallons
Sorghum, or Chinese sugar cane,	2 to 3 quarts.
Buckwheat,	1 bushel.
Beets and Mangel-Wurzel,	4 to 6 lbs.
Carrots,	2 to 3 lbs.
Turnips and Ruta Baga,	1 lb.
Parsnips,	4 to 6 lbs.
Beans, in drills, 2½ feet apart,	1½ bushels.
Potatoes,	12 "

THE CATTLE PLAGUE, OR RINDERPEST.[*]

The following comprehensive article on the Cattle Disease has been prepared from the best English authorities on the subject, by a prominent physician of Philadelphia.

The wide-spread interest at present felt in the serious disorder which is now prevailing in England and other parts of Europe, under the name of the "Cattle Plague," and which it may justly be feared is destined also to afflict the United States, renders it desirable to furnish, in a condensed and popular form, such information as can be relied on, as the result of the studies of scientific men.

In 1865, a most valuable treatise "On the Cattle Plague; or, the Contagious Typhus of Horned Cattle, its History, Origin, Description, etc.," was published by H. Bourguignon, Doctor of the Faculty of Paris, etc., etc. From it much of the following account has been condensed.

DURATION OF THE DISEASE.

The duration of the cattle plague, when it passes through all its phases, up to the death of the animal, consists of from ten to twelve days. In this time there are usually four stages, each of these averaging three or four days. First. A period of incubation, during which the blood and humors of the animal are poisoned by noxious exhalations, and undergo important changes. Second. A febrile stage. Third. A revulsion, inducing *stupor*. Fourth. Characterized by free discharges from all the mucous membranes, as the nostrils, lungs, bowels, etc., ending in extreme prostration and death.

This typhus is a virulent, contagious, febrile, and non-recurring disease, to regulate which, it is all-important *that every means should be employed to prevent its extension, not only to animals, but also to man*, especially those who, having a slight sore or abrasion of the skin, come in contact with the diseased animals.

MEASURES TO PREVENT ITS EXTENSION.

Various measures have been taken in England to prevent the spread of the contagion, among the most prominent of which is "the removal and destruction by burning or burying of all matters capable of reproducing the disease;" hence all articles which have been in contact with a diseased animal or any of its discharges, especially its dung, must be regarded as "infectious." Animals diseased had better be at once killed and *deeply* buried. In order to maintain or restore the health of cattle, there should be furnished *abundance of pure air*, dry, clean, well ventilated sheds, plenty of *pure water*, clean and dry meadows or pasture, frequent *currying* and washing of the skin, proper food at proper intervals, protection from inclement weather, the utmost cleanliness in the removal of manure, with its storage at a great *distance from the cattle shed*.

SYMPTOMS OF THE DISEASE.

It is highly important to be able to recognize the "ox typhus fever," that the necessary measures may be taken to prevent contagion, and that the proper treatment may be pursued.

Symptoms. — When the contagious typhus is raging, keep a watchful eye on your cattle. If you notice in their gait, their looks, or about their ears, any unusual signs; if they seem less eager, less active, less vigilant; if they leave part of their food when in the stables, or if, when in the fields, they no longer browse with continued alacrity, — be upon your guard. If to these changes of minor importance is added an appetite really less acute, if the rumination is less regular, if the animal looks sad and dispirited, if he exhibits an unwonted look of gloom, if his leaden eye seems fixed and astonished, be assured that this cruel distemper is spreading through his frame.

By-and-by the animal loses his appetite more and more, rumination is shorter and less frequent. He holds his head down, his ears sink and fall, and he grinds his teeth. Then, as to the cows, their milk, which was already diminished, suddenly dries up altogether, and the lowness of spirits which had been visible for some days before, passes into stupor. If at this time you touch their horns, their extremities, or their hide in any part, you will find that all these different parts are sometimes warm and sometimes cold. From this day forward you will witness a succession of disorders, such as shiverings at the attachments of the fore and hind legs, loud, panting breathing, with slight cough, scanty and thick urine, with hard and constipated droppings, and finally generally excessive warmth. If the back is now pressed, it will cause pain, and all the signs of intense fever will be manifest.

Already these indications have divulged the nature of the malady you have to deal with, but others more significant succeed them, and will remove every doubt.

The breathing now becomes more hurried and oppressed, and more puffy; from the eyes, nostrils, and mouth there issues a discharge which is at first thin and irritating, but soon becomes thick and purulent, and of a fetid smell; diarrhœa takes the place of constipation; the cattle grow leaner, and some will die at this period: if they still hold out, the diarrhœa becomes more frequent, more fetid, and sometimes bloody; gases are developed under the skin along the spine, and form wide, flat tumors, which crackle when pressed upon; — finally, the mucus which runs from the head becomes still thicker and more fetid; a glutinous foam stops up the mouth; the eyes, filled with humor, sink in the orbits; the bodily warmth decreases; the animal sways his head from right to left, becoming insensible and cold; his head lolls on one side, and he dies, panting from exhaustion and asphyxia, on the tenth or twelfth day after the disease has been confirmed.

The carcass exhibits a repulsive appearance; the hide is dry and cracked: it sticks to the bones, which show the form of the skeleton, and the putrid decomposition which had already set in before death, seizes rapidly on all the tissues.

The course of the disease is not always the same. Sometimes the animal is agitated at first, and all the functions of life are so disturbed that death comes on in two or three days. At times the lungs are more affected than the other internal organs; the cough is more intense, and the breath hurried and obstructed.

TO DISTINGUISH FROM PLEURO-PNEUMONIA.

When once seen, it is impossible to mistake this disease (ox typhus — cattle plague) for any other, unless it be the chest complaint, called *peri-pneumonia*, which is likewise contagious; but in peri- or pleuro-pneumonia the attack is generally insidious, — the eyes preserve their vivacity, and the appetite is not lost until towards the close. In this disorder (pleuro-pneumonia) a short, dry cough shows itself from the outbreak, and persists; the breathing is frequent and painful; and the sides of the chest, when struck with the fingers, give out the hard, solid sound of a full barrel (flatness), this percussion being painful. The eyes, nose, and mouth do not discharge those purulent secretions seen in typhus, and the diarrhœa only comes on at the end, being less

---

[*] In a letter received from the publisher from Hon. J. Brownell, Chairman of the House Committee on Agriculture, dated July 14, 1866, he states that the Committee intend recommending the publication by Congress of an important English discovery for the cure of Rinderpest and other kindred diseases. So soon as the pamphlet is issued, we will insert the information in our next edition of this work. We are reliably informed, however, that the following are the diseases cured and treatment: Rinderpest, pleuro-pneumonia, mange, ringworm, and grease-heel in barn-yard animals and horses, and the relief of phthisis and tubercular affections of the lungs in the human patient. A small

frequent and fetid. In the milch cows the milk decreases, but is not quite suppressed.

The heat of the horns and lower extremities is retained, and the pneumonia runs its course more regularly, the animal dying about the *fourth week.* Thus it will be seen that the two distempers widely differ in their symptoms.

The cattle plague (ox typhus) is by far the most formidable malady which can attack animals. When left to itself, or treated without judgment, it carries off ninety cattle out of a hundred. In prior visitations, and especially in 1750, when six millions of horned cattle were swept off in Europe. England lost from three to four hundred thousand, and the number of cattle which have perished in England from June to October, 1865, exceeds sixty thousand.

PREVENTION AND TREATMENT OF THE CATTLE PLAGUE.

Every farmer who keeps many cattle should divide them into several classes; thus:— First. The sound and healthy that have had no direct or indirect intercourse with tainted cattle, and these must be kept carefully isolated. Second. Cattle which, though unaffected, have been exposed in cars, ships, or markets. These are to be made the subject of treatment the moment the first sign of the disease shows itself. Third. Cattle actually smitten with the plague, to be treated according to each stage of the disease.

The healthy cattle must be removed from the farm, or, if they remain at the rack, must be taken out twice daily for the twofold purpose of taking wholesome exercise and allowing their stalls and sheds to be thoroughly cleaned. Their feeding should also be carefully watched, and the following provisions added to their daily supplies:

Pounded oats . . . . 4 pounds.
Pounded juniper berries 1 pound.
Powdered gentian . . 1 ounce.
Sulphate of iron . . . 2 drachms.
Carbonate of soda . . 2 drachms.

Whilst in the fields, the cattle should not be allowed to drink out of ponds or at any stagnant or muddy water.

Cattle belonging to our second class (having been exposed to infection) must receive the same strengthening and tonic ration in the morning, and twice every day take the following *anti-contagious* preparation:

Chlorate of potash . . 2 drachms.
Water . . . . . . ½ pint.

Dissolve and mix with one gallon sage or hysop tea; to be given when drink is given them.

The use of this *anti-contagious drink* is of the highest importance. It should be continued even after the plague has broken out.

During the absence of those cattle which are undergoing the preventive treatment, let the healthy condition of their stalls and sheds be looked to.

Be careful to take out the litter every day; wash the floor and cleanse it thoroughly; ventilate the place well; fumigate it with burnt sulphur or dried juniper berries, sage and rosemary, salted with saltpetre, and a little arsenic. This will burn readily if placed on a pan of coals. At night, tar, creosote, benzine, petroleum or iodine may be left in the stable, to diffuse their vapors and modify the air.

As the cattle plague, or ox typhus, when once developed in the ox, cow, or sheep, usually pursues its course, the various functions of the body are so changed that they vary during the different stages of the disorder, the latter at first producing excitement, but in the latter stages great exhaustion. Hence it requires a high degree of skill, practical experience, and vigilance. During the disorder the ox undergoes in two weeks all the feverish commotion which a man laboring under typhoid fever would be subject to in a month.

The phenomena succeed each other with terrific swiftness, leaving barely time for the medicines to act.

At the outbreak of the disorder, abolish solid feeding. This is easily done, as the animal has lost his appetite. Give him, instead, half a pailful of soaked hay, adding to it a sprinkling of salt; or give water, whitened with bran and flour, with a little vinegar, three or four times daily. When the animal coughs and his breathing is oppressed, give him warm drinks, such as steamed barley and oats, or a hot mash, and cover him well with blankets, *but don't exclude the fresh air."*

The following "hygienic measures" are to be taken against the extension of the plague:

DISINFECTION.

The contagious matters are all kinds of cattle of the ox tribe, and also hides, hair, horns, and hoofs of those killed or dead with the plague.

The intestinal discharges are the principal agents that spread the disorder.

Hence all articles that have been in contact with a diseased animal or any of its discharges, are capable of carrying the infection for an indefinite time, as racks of wood, or iron cribs, or mangers of wood, iron, or stone; collars, straps, ropes, chains, harness, carts, wagons, or carriages, which they have touched; gutters or drains in which their urine has flowed; all implements for removing manure; the manure heap; the ground on which they have stood; paths and roads on which diseased cattle have walked or been drawn, etc., etc.;— to all and any of which, disinfectants must be applied.

Burying deeply in dry ground is the quickest, cheapest, and most certain way of disinfecting an animal dead from the plague.

The droppings, straw, and all other matters contaminated should also be buried, so that they cannot be disturbed for a long time.

Manure heaps and down-trodden manure of cattle yards, if infected by even a small quantity of the droppings of a diseased animal, should be removed to a suitable place, and covered with a layer of earth.

Floors of any shed or stable in which diseased cattle have stood, if not formed of water-tight and impenetrable material, must be assumed to be infected to the depth of six inches. Half rotten wood is an especially favorable carrier of infection. Any lining of a pen where a diseased animal has stood, should be broken out and burned.

All infected articles, as racks of wood or iron, etc., can be disinfected by exposing them to a heat which will char wood, and all such of iron should then be galvanized.

Chloride of Lime is among the cheapest and most powerful of artificial disinfectants, and should be applied as much as possible in solution. It is not applicable to large quantities of manure, or to matters rich in ammonia, as putrid urine. One pound of chloride of lime to one gallon of water can be distributed by a garden engine, or by a watering-pot, after a thorough scrubbing and scraping of stalls, etc. All brooms and other implements, or persons stepping from a dirty or partially cleaned place to a clean one, may suffice to bring back infection. Workmen must also be careful to wash their own bodies and hair with

---

crucible is set in hot ashes, and a piece of stick sulphur of the size of a man's thumb dropped into it. The sulphurous acid gas thus generated is sufficient to fumigate thoroughly a large cattle-shed in about twenty minutes. The process which, by the way, the cattle are said to like, must be repeated four or five times a day, and the disease is soon got under.

January 28, 1867.— We have just received the pamphlet alluded to, and find this foot-note to contain the essence of the information. — PUBLISHER.

soap, and to destroy such clothing as is of little value, or have the other disinfected in chloride-of-lime water.

Despatches received by the Department of State from the United-States consul at Liverpool, under date of March 12, 1866, give the following remedies now in use, said to be very effective:

1 oz. of Peruvian bark, 1 oz. of gentian, 1 oz. of ground ginger, 2 drs. of sulphate of iron, 4 table-spoonfuls of molasses, and 1 glass of brandy or whisky. Dose, once a day.

The other prescription is:—1 lb. of onions, small and strong; 1 lb. of garlic, 1 lb. of ground ginger, ¾ lb. of asafœtida; to be covered with water and stirred on the fire till in a milky pulp; then put over the other articles; add of rice-water 3 pints for every 2 of the mixture. Dose for a cow—1 pint a day.

To keep Milk.

Among the many methods adopted to preserve milk for a lengthened period, is that of M. Pasteur. He has found that if milk be heated to 212°, the boiling-point of water, it will remain sweet for a few days; if heated to 220° (under pressure, of course), it will remain sweet for several weeks; but if heated to 250°, the milk will keep for any number of years.

To detect Watered Milk.

The cheapest and easiest method of adulterating milk is by adding water, and we may readily ascertain the exact extent of adulteration by the following plan. If a glass tube, divided into 100 parts, be filled with milk and left standing for 24 hours, the cream will rise to the upper part of the tube, and occupy from 11 to 13 divisions, if the milk is genuine.

To preserve Milk.

Milk becomes sour by the formation of lactic acid, which is rapidly developed at a temperature of 70° to 90°. The best way to preserve milk sweet for domestic purposes, is to add to it every day a few grains of carbonate of soda per pint, to keep the milk alkaline.

TRICHINÆ.

The following account of this disease has been condensed from a report made in April, 1866, by a commission of scientific and medical men, appointed by the Chicago Academy of Sciences, and may be regarded as thoroughly reliable:

Trichina is the term applied to a minute animal (parasite) known for some time to have existed in the muscles of man, and which could be bred in the muscles of some other mammals by feeding them with it. More recently it has been discovered to occur naturally in the muscles of swine. It is a minute, slender, and transparent worm, scarcely 1-20th of an inch in length. After this animal becomes introduced into the stomach of man, or other animals susceptible to its ravages, and which may feed upon flesh infected with it, the worms become freed from their capsules by the action of the digestive fluid, and range freely in the stomach and intestines of the custodian. Their development proceeds rapidly, and procreation takes place within 4 or 5 days; each female gives birth to from 60 to 100 young, and dies soon after. The young thread-like worm remains for a short time within the lining membrane of the intestines, causing irritation, diarrhœa, and sometimes death if present in sufficient numbers. After attaining a proper size and strength, these young trichinæ begin to penetrate the walls of the intestines, and make their way toward their proper homes, the voluntary muscles. In traversing the muscles they do not seem to penetrate the fibre of the muscle, but to wind their way between them. At this time they cause to those afflicted great muscular pain and soreness, cramps, and even tetanic symptoms. After about 4 weeks migration they commence to encyst themselves in the muscular fibre, none having ever been found encysted in fat or the other tissues. They perforate the walls of the fibre selected as their abode, pass into it, and fasten themselves in the space so made. The worm then secretes a delicate membranous sac, which finally becomes calcareous by still further secretions. It is only in man, however, that these calcareous cysts have been observed, hogs being usually killed long before time has elapsed for the accumulation of sufficient lime. The young trichina having now reached its torpid stage, it will so remain during the lifetime of its custodian. It feeds no longer, but goes on slowly in development until it has reached the condition of puberty, and then awaits its chances of freedom to "commence its cycle." They can breed but once in the body of one and the same animal. They have been known to cause partial paralysis of certain muscles by the great number embedded in them. So much now for the history of this animal and its mode of life, and cause of disease. Now to what extent does this parasite exist in this country?

An examination of this medical commission made in Chicago, Ill., during the spring of 1866, of 1394 hogs, 28 of them, or 1 in 48, were found to contain trichinæ, and numbering in each hog from 48 to 18,000 trichinæ to a cubic inch.

HOW TO PREVENT TRICHINÆ.

As no trichina nor germ of trichina has ever been found in vegetable food, the parasite must inevitably come through the eating of flesh of some kind. A strict attention to the feeding of hogs and their confinement in pens where no animal food is accessible, is an infallible preventative against Trichiniasis. As the disease cannot be detected by external appearance, no farmer can tell if the disease exists among his animals, nor should he be blamed if he sells animals found to be affected with trichinæ. The use of the microscope will effectually tell if the muscles of the hog be free from this parasite.

HOW TO KILL THE PARASITES.

To do this it is simply necessary to *thoroughly* cook the pork, so that every portion of the meat shall have experienced a temperature of at least 160° Fahr. This is of the utmost importance; it is owing to eating pork uncooked that has occasioned such loss of life among the poorer classes in Germany. Again, by properly salting and smoking the meat for at least 10 days, the trichinæ, should they exist, will be certainly killed. Simple desiccation of the meat, if continued for a period of sufficient length, will also kill them; as for instance they will never be found in old hams; mere pickling, however, does not appear to have any effect upon these worms. When we reflect, then that but 1 hog out of 48 of the 1394 examined was found to contain trichinæ at all, and but one in 300 was found to contain them in sufficient number to cause considerable danger, and that even in these cases the worms are rendered inocuous by proper smoking, drying, or cooking, we cannot see that the popular panic which now exists should be permitted to continue among intelligent persons, and thus deprive nine-tenths of our agricultural population of one of their chief articles of food.

IMPLEMENTS OF AGRICULTURE.

MOWERS AND REAPERS.

The Great National Field Trial of Mowers and Reapers held at Auburn, N. Y., in July, 1866, under the patronage of the Legislature and supervision of the New York State Agricultural Society, was the most thorough and extensive ever held in this country. Fifty-nine machines were entered for competition, and over two weeks occupied in subjecting the machines to every variety of severe tests. The Legislature of the State appropriated $5000 towards the expenses and premiums.

The Committee of Judges was composed of practical and scientific agriculturists,* and included some of the first men of the State. The following synopsis of their report will be found to embody the main results of their investigation, and cannot fail of being of great use to Farmers. Invitations were extended to all the prominent Agricultural Implement Makers of the country. The following points were to be considered and determined by the Committee on trial.

1. Which is the cheapest machine.
2. The most simple in its construction.
3. The most durable.
4. Which requires the least power.
5. Which has the least side-draught.

All of which is to be determined, and the capacity to perform a given amount of work in a workmanlike manner, in a given time, in the most economical way.

6. Which does the most work in the least time.
7. Which does the best work.
8. Which is managed with the most facility.

When the Judges have determined the above questions, they will proceed to decide which of the machines is best adapted to the use of the farmer, by having the greatest number of merits and the fewest defects.

No exhibitor shall furnish other machines for trial than those which they habitually furnish from their shops to their customers.

The following were the class divisions for entry of MOWERS and REAPERS.

No. 1. Mowing machine for two horses.
No. 2. Reaping machines, (hand-rakers.)
No. 2½. Self-rakers.
No. 3. Combined mowers and reapers, (hand-rakers.)
No. 4. Combined reapers, with self-raking or dropping attachment.
No. 5. Combined reapers for use as self-rakers, or hand-rakers, as may be preferred.
No. 6. One-horse mowers.

ENTRIES UNDER THE ABOVE, AND RESULT.

The Society's large gold medal (costing $75 or more) as first premium. For the second premium, a cash prize of $25.

The mowing and reaping fields were each of one acre in extent, and to be chosen by lot.

Explanation.— Assuming that 40 to represent the best work that can be done; No. 30, as representing the best work that can be done with a hand-scythe; No. 20, as inferior work to any that would be tolerated by a respectable farmer. The gradations of work to be expressed by numbers intermediate to these. Standard speed, one hour per acre.

ENTRY, AND RESULT.

CLASS 1.— TWO-HORSE MOWERS.

D. M. Osborne & Co., Auburn, New York. No. 1 Mower.
"Cut uneven and not very close." Time, 54 minutes; quality mark, 33.

D. M. Osborne & Co. Entry No. 2. One mower, (large,) entered also as No. 27, 37, 48, and 19. Lot No. 7, hilly; time, 50 minutes; quality, 37. "Worked smoothly and well."
No. 48, hilly; time, 48 minutes; quality, 32.

C. C. Bradley & Son, Syracuse. Entry No. 3. One "Hubbard" mower, "well done;" time, 61 min.; quality, 37.

E. F. Herrington, Valley Falls, N. Y. No. 4. One Eagle mower. Same as entry No. 29. Lot No. 20, stony and weedy; cut close; time, 58 minutes; quality, 38.

J. D. Wilber, Poughkeepsie. No. 5. One Eureka mower; cut well *against* the lay of the clover; not well with it; time, 44½ minutes; quality mark, 25.

J. D. Wilber. No. 6. One Eureka mower, (large;) time, 35 minutes; mark, 20; joints hot.

Peekskill Manufacturing Co. No. 7. One Clipper mower, (invented by R. Dutton.) Cut uneven, but well laid; time 43 minutes; quality, 30.

Walter A. Wood, Hoosick Falls. No. 8. One mower. Lot bad to cut, stony, clover tall; cut tolerably well; time, 49½ minutes; quality mark, 29.

Dow & Fowler, Fowlersville. No. 9. One Yankee mower. Cutting uneven, noisy, and bearings hot; time, 46 minutes; quality, 28.

Adriance, Platt & Co., Poughkeepsie. No. 10. One No. 2 Buckeye mower. Lot much trodden down; time, 55½ minutes; cut even and neatly; quality, 40.

American Agricultural Works, New York. No. 11. One Columbian Junior Mower. Lot easy to cut; time, 66 minutes; quality, 37; very noisy.

Dodge & Stevenson, Manufacturing Co., Auburn. No. 12. One No. 2 Iron Mower, Ohio and Buckeye Patents combined. (Dodge's Patent.) Time, 61½ minutes; quality, 29; cutting irregular.

C. A. Wheeler, Jr., Auburn. No. 13. One mower, (A); No. 14. One mower, (B); No. 15. One mower, (C); No. 16. One mower (D).
No. 13, (A,) cut well but not close; time 44 min.; quality, 32.
No. 14, (B,) cutting irregular; time, 48½ min.; quality, 37.
No. 15, (C,) cutting fair; time, 44 min; quality, 36.
No. 16, (D,) cutting good; time, 44½ min.; quality, 35.

W. H. Halladay, Auburn. No. 17. One American Mower; cut close; time, 68 minutes; quality, 33.

Rhode Island Clipper Mower Co., Newport. No. 18. One two-horse Harvest Clipper Mower, (invented by R. Dutton.) Stubble long; time 55 minutes; quality, 32; bearings cool.

C. R. Brinckerhoff. No. 18½. One mower, cutting bad; time, 53; quality, 22.

---

* For full details of this trial of Implements, we would call attention to the valuable report of John Stanton Gould, Esq., President N. Y. State Agricultural Society, and Chairman Committee of Judges, from whose report this article is condensed.

IMPLEMENTS OF AGRICULTURE. 471

CLASS 2. — REAPERS (HAND-RAKES).

D. M. Osborne & Co., Auburn, No. 19. One Reaper (hand-rake); "work good, not a fault to be found;" ten sheaves were bound in 4 min.; time 64 min.; quality, 40.

C. Wheeler, jr., Auburn. No. 20. One Reaper (hand-rake).

CLASS 2½. — REAPER (SELF-RAKE).

C. R. Brinckerhoff, Rochester. No. 21. One Reaper (self-rake).

C. C. Bradley & Son, Syracuse. No. 22. One Syracuse (self-raking) Reaper, time 48 min.; mark 39.

Walter A. Wood, Hoosick Falls. No. 23. One Reaper, self-raking (chain-rake). No. 24. One Reaper (sweep-rake); same entry as No. 40.

No. 23. Not cut close; time 47 and 55 min.; quality, 28 and 35.

No. 24. Field good; tolerably well cut; time 48 min.; quality, 35.

Stephen Hull, Poughkeepsie. No. 25. One Reaper (self-rake); withdrawn.

N. A. Dederer Greene. No. 26. One Reaper (self-raker); did not arrive.

D. M. Osborne & Co., Auburn. No. 27. One Reaper (self-rake).

Seymour, Morgan & Allen. No. 27½. One Reaper (self-rake).

CLASS 3. — COMBINED MOWERS AND REAPERS.

D. M. Osborne & Co., No. 28. One combined Mower and Reaper; time 55 min.; quality, 36.

E. F. Herrington, Valley Falls, N. Y. No. 29. One Eagle Combined Machine; same as entry No. 40, except that it now has a pinion changed; stubble long, bearings cool; time 62 min.; quality, 35.

Walter A. Wood, Hoosick Falls. No. 30. One Combined Mower and Reaper (hand-rake); field good, stubbles left high; time 46 min.; quality, 19.

Adriance, Platt & Co., Poughkeepsie. No. 31. One No. 1 Buckeye combined. Cutting bad; time 51 min.; quality, 30. Driver unskilful.

Aultman, Miller & Co., Akron, O., No. 32. One Buckeye combined. Lot bad to cut, machine noisy and imperfectly geared; time 51 min.; quality, 38. Bearings cool.

Dodge & Stevenson Manufacturing Co., Auburn. No. 33. One Combined Machine (Dodge pat.) No. 2, wood frame.

C. Wheeler, jr., Auburn. No. 34. One Combined Machine (hand-rake). G. No. 35. One Combined (hand-rake) H. No. 34 G. time 39 min.; quality 35.

No. 35 H. Field stony and bad; cutting even; time 45 min.; quality, 36.

CLASS 4. — COMBINED (SELF-RAKING).

D. M. Osborne & Co., Auburn, No. 36. One Combined Machine. Field rough, stubble even; time 46 min.; quality, 35.

Walter A. Wood, Hoosick Falls. No. 39. One Combined Machine (self-rake.) No. 40. One Combined Machine (self-rake.)

Aultman, Miller & Co., Akron, O. No. 41. One Buckeye combined (self-rake.) Good field, cutting good; time 65 min.; quality, 38. All the Buckeyes leave the grass in good condition for drying.

Williams, Wallace & Co., Syracuse. No. 42. One No. 1 Hubbard Machine (Syracuse self-rake) No. 43. One No. 2 Hubbard Machine (Syracuse self-rake).

No. 43, work good; time 57 min.; quality, 38; bearings cool; good mower in all respects.

Seymour, Morgan & Allen, Brockport. No. 44. One New York Combined Machine (self-rake.) Field good, cutting irregular; time 38; quality 35.

C. Wheeler, jr., Auburn. No. 45. One Combined Machine (self-raking attachment). No. 46. One Combined Machine (dropping attachment.)

Entry No. 45, I. Cayuga Chief, not closely cut; time 48 min.; quality 34; journal cool.

No. 46, Cayuga Chief, J. A bad field to cut; time 37 min.; quality 30; bearings hot.

W. H. Halliday, Auburn. No. 47. One Marsh's Combined Machine (self-rake). No. 47½, Marsh's Valley Chief.

No. 47. Field stony; cut uneven; time 46 min.; quality 28.

CLASS 5. — COMBINED REAPERS, (SELF OR HAND-RAKE).

D. M. Osborne & Co., Auburn. No. 48. One Combined Machine. No. 49. One Combined. No. 50. One Combined.

American Agricultural Works, N. Y. No. 51, one Columbian Machine (hand and self-raker). Field bad, cutting very bad; time 57 minutes; quality, 26.

Dodge & Stevenson Manufacturing Co., Auburn. No. 52, one Dodge's patent combined Machine (self or hand-raker), wood frame, No. 1. No. 53, one Dodge's patent combined Machine (self or hand-rake), iron frame, No. 1.

No. 52, stubble not well cut, time 56 min.; quality, 29. No. 53, field good, time 43 min.; quality, 32.

The above machines unite the patents of the Buckeye and the Ohio mowers, having the gearing of the former and the movable shoe of the latter. Both well approved machines everywhere, and have done good work. It is strange that machines combining the best features of both patents should make so poor a record as these have done upon this field.

C. Wheeler, Jr., No. 54, one combined machine, self or hand-rake, (K.) No. 55, the combined machine as dropper or hand-rake, (L.)

No. 54. Cayuga Chief, K. Cutting not good; time 54 min.; quality 30.

No. 55, Cayuga Chief, L. Field rocky; time 43 min.; quality, 30.

Twelve of the Cayuga Chiefs were entered; all agreeing in general structure though, not in minor details, they attracted much attention, but as a whole they did not appear well in the clover lots.

CLASS 6. — ONE-HORSE MOWERS.

D. M. Osborne & Co., Auburn, No. 56, (one-horse mower.) Field good, well cut; time 64 minutes; quality, 35.

The work done by the machine of D. M. Osborne & Co., was done with tolerable uniformity, the average mark for quality of work being 34–36. The average time exclusive of the one-horse Machine was 51 minutes. The machines were all remarkable for the steadiness of their motion and freedom from noise.

R. L. Allen, N. Y. No. 57, one one-horse mower.

C. Wheeler, jr., Auburn, N. Y., No. 58, one one-horse Mower, F, Cayuga Chief, cutting good; time 30 min.; quality, 34.

Pony Clipper (invented by R. Dutton.)

R. Dutton, Brooklyn, No. 59, one one-horse gleaner mower (invented by R. Dutton.)

Trial of July 20th. — (*Same Machines.*)

Twenty machines made a trial upon lots of very irregular surface, which had not been ploughed for many years; the general surface was level, but broken up with many deep hollows and having a thick growth of sedges and rushes. The prevailing herbage was red top, blue-grass, and fowl meadow; it was the hardest test for action in rough ground that could be found in the vicinity. The following is the result; the marks for quality of work were 1 to 40, the latter number indicating perfect work.

	Quality of work.
Seymour, Morgan & Allen, No. 44	39

The divider of this machine pressed down the grass, some of which was not cut off at the next round.

Cayuga Chief, D, No. 16	37
Cayuga Chief, A, No. 13	37
Dodge, Stevenson & Co., No. 52 (wood)	37
Dodge, Stevenson & Co., No. 53 (iron)	37

A spike projecting from the ground was half severed by this machine.

D. M. Osborne & Co.,	37
C. C. Bradley & Son, No. 3	38
Williams, Wallace & Co., No. 43	38
Walter A. Wood, No. 8	40
E. F. Herrington, No. 4	37

Herrington's Eagle was remarkable for its easy adaptation of its bar to the steep sides of hollows, in one case mowing with it sloping downward at an angle of 40 degrees.

Rhode Island Clipper, No. 18	40
Adriance, Platt & Co., No. 10	40
Dow & Fowler, No. 9	31
Aultman, Miller & Co., No. 32	38
Wm. H. Halladay, No. 17	37

Some dry grass caught on the ends of his fingers which prevented him from cutting clean for about 20 rods.

R. L. Allen, Pony Clipper, No. 57	36
James S. Marsh, No. 47½	38
J. D. Wilber, No. 6	30

"Those who had been present at the former great trials, held by the society were astonished at the general perfection which had been attained by the manufacturers of mowing-machines. Every machine, with two exceptions, did good work, which would be acceptable to any farmer, and the appearance of the whole meadow after it had been raked over, was as good as it could be, and vastly better than the average mowing of the best farmers in the State, notwithstanding the great difficulties which they had to encounter. At previous trials most of the machines would clog more or less, and some of them so frequently that they were of no practical value. At this trial, not a single instance of clogging was observed either in clover or fine grass.

"At previous trials, very few machines could stop in the grass and start without backing for a fresh start. At the present trial every machine stopped in the grass and started again without backing, without any difficulty, and without leaving any perceptible ridge to mark the place where it occurred. We look upon these facts with pride and pleasure, as showing the great success which has attended the efforts of our mechanics to meet the requirements of the farmer, and we have good reason to believe that the experiments made at Auburn will lead to still greater advances in the path of progress.

"Four machines were allowed to work at once, marked stakes being driven down at their entrance; they cut entirely around the lot, passing through all the different kinds of bottom and of grass, and into all the gullies and hollows. Then four more succeeded them, and so on in groups of four, until all had gone round. Then each machine cut a double swath across the lot. After this the whole number of machines were put in motion at once, until both meadows were cut down. In this way the path of each machine could be traced without difficulty through its entire length, and the work of each, under very different circumstances, could be accurately compared."

REAPING TRIALS.

The wheat field was divided into thirty lots, of one acre each, the bottom generally smooth, tolerably level, and the grain (Mediterranean) stood up very well.

Walter A. Wood, entry No. 30, with a hand-raker. The gavels were twisted at the bottom from the left-hand corner towards the right. The binders bound ten of these gavels in 5 minutes. Time of cutting 49 minutes. Mark for quality of work, 33.

D. M. Osborne, No. 27, using a reel and sweep rake. There is a want of a proper divider. The rake draws forwards some of the last cut straw, and in its next\sweep this is twisted in raking. The twist is from the left-hand corner towards the right, and in the lower part of the gavel the twist is less than on the top, but what there is, is in the opposite direction. The binders bound ten bundles in 4 minutes. Time of cutting 53½ minutes. Mark for quality of work, 33.

Cayuga Chief, J, No. 46, with a dropping attachment. The lower part of the gavel is drawn forward and somewhat twisted as it falls. It requires six men to keep up with the machine, who occasionally fall behind with their work in bad places. The binders bound ten of these sheaves in 5 minutes. Time of cutting, 57 min. Mark for quality of work, 32.

D. M. Osborne & Co., No. 19, hand-raker. The work is as good as can be done. Not a fault could be found with it in any way. Ten sheaves were bound in 4 minutes, 3 seconds. Time of cutting 64½ minutes. Quality of work, 40.

Lot No. 5 was cut by Dodge, Stevenson & Co., No. 33, (wood), hand raker. The grain in this lot was lodged in one or two places. One man drove and raked, the sickle being set almost low enough for mowing. The gavels are crossed, the bottom towards the right and the top towards the left. Ten bundles bound in 5 minutes. Time 66½ minutes. Quality of work, 30.

Lot No. 6 was not a good one for reaping. It was cut by Adriance, Platt & Co., No. 31, hand raker. It was cut the wrong way and a good deal of the lodged was left upon the ground. It was thrown off the platform with a fork instead of a rake. The gavels were not very good. Time 47 minutes. Quality of work, 31.

D. M. Osborne & Co., No. 36, with reel and sweep rake. Time 53½ minutes. Work, 34.

Aultman, Miller & Co., with a dropper. The gavels unevenly laid. Ten sheaves bound in 5 minutes. Time, 58 minutes. Quality of work, 32.

D. M. Osborne & Co., No. 37, with the combined rake and reel, or Burdick self-rake. The gavels were rather better than those made by his sweep rake. Time, 68½ minutes. Work, 34.

W. A. Wood, No. 23, with a chain rake. The gavels were tolerably well laid. Time, 47 minutes. Work, 35. Binders were four minutes in binding ten sheaves.

D. M. Osborne, No. 48, with a hand rake. The work excellent in all respects. Time, 39½ minutes. Work, 40.

W. A. Wood, No. 40, with a sweep rake. The cutting was very good, but the gavels not as well laid as the chain rake. Time, 52 minutes. Work, 35.

Mr. Osborne and other exhibitors protest against W. A. Wood's chain and sweep rake being admitted into the class of combined machines, on the ground that they are never sold or used as such.

IMPLEMENTS OF AGRICULTURE. 473

D. M. Osborne & Co., No. 36, with the same that cut No. 11, now working with a *sweep rake* and a reel. Time, 53 minutes. Work, 34.

Dodge, Stevenson & Co., No. 53, with iron frame and combined rake and reel, or *Marsh's self-rake*. He came in collision with a stump and bent the guard finger. The gavels are badly scattered in front of the platform; the gavel does not all drop at once, but is dragged forward. Time, 53 minutes. Work, 34.

W. A. Wood's *revolving rake*, No. 24. Binders make ten sheaves in 4 minutes, 20 seconds. Gavels very large. Time, 57½ minutes. Work, 36.

Williams, Wallace & Co's Hubbard Machine, No. 42, with *Johnson's rake*. Gavels laid straight and compact; no scattering; the swath between the gavels very clean. The binders make ten of the sheaves in 4 minutes, 12 seconds. Time, 52½ minutes. Work, 39.

C. Wheeler, Jr., Cayuga Chief, K, No. 54. Half the lot as a *hand-raker*, and the other half as a *self-raker*. The gavels were badly twisted and the straw was scattered between the gavels. Time, 56 minutes, 32 seconds. Work, 28.

Columbian machine, *self rake*, No. 51. There was some lodged grain in the lot which it cut very well, but the gavels were strangely twisted, and the work as a whole was poor. Time, 57 minutes. Work, 31.

C. C. Bradley & Son, No. 22, with *Johnson's rake*. The gavels admirably laid. Time, 48½ minutes. Quality of work, 39.

C. Wheeler, Jr., Cayuga Chief, G, No. 34. *Hand rake*. Time, 48 minutes. Quality of work, 31.

Dodge, Stevenson & Co., No. 12, iron frame. *Hand rake*. Gavels very well laid. Time, 37 minutes. Work, 32.

Seymour, Morgan & Allen, No. 44, with their *sweep rake*. Gavels very well laid, and all the work was very well done. Time, 62 minutes. Work, 38.

C. Wheeler, Jr., Cayuga Chief, L, No. 55. Half the lot as a *dropper*, and the other half as a *hand rake*. Time, 59 minutes. Work, 32.

D. M. Osborne & Co., No. 37, with *Burdick rake*. There was a very bad, rocky place at the end of this lot which he cut over very well with the wind against him. Time, 68½ minutes. Work, 34.

Aultman, Miller & Co., Buckeye, senior, No. 41. *Self rake*. The gavels crossed and dragged. Time, 50½ minutes. Work, 30.

Wm. H. Halladay, No. 47, with *Marsh's rake*. Machine left-handed. There was some lodged wheat in the lot which he cut very closely, and the gavels were in general very well laid, but occasionally he would make a very bad one; this want of uniformity reduced his mark. Time, 54 minutes. Mark for quality of work, 37.

C. Wheeler, Jr., Cayuga Chief, II, No. 35. *Hand rake*. There was a fast rock in his swath 18 inches high. The driver, without any deviation from his line, drove over it, dropping the whole height perpendicularly, demonstrating at the same time his own skill as a driver and the great strength of the machine. Although much of the ground was stony, the work was the best done by any of the Cayuga Chiefs. Time, 53 minutes. Work, 36.

E. F. Herrington, No. 29, hand rake. The cutting was very fine, but the gavels were not well laid. Time not noted.

Dodge, Stevenson & Co. Wood frame, No. 52, Marsh's rake. Gavels laid square and handsome, without scattering. Time, 60 minutes. Work, 37.

Seymour, Morgan & Allen, No. 27½, self-rake. Time, 51 minutes. Work, 30.

The average time of all the machines, in cutting an acre, was 53 minutes.

The longest time was made by D. M. Osborne. The shortest time made by any hand rake was D. M. Osborne. The shortest made by a self-rake, was by Walter A. Wood.

The average of the marks for quality of work in reaping, is 34.3.

RESULT TRIAL IN 22 ACRE LOT, GRAIN BADLY LODGED.

Quality of work.
Cayuga Chief, II, entry No. 35 30
D. M. Osborne, Burdick rake, entry No. 48 . 32
D. M. Osborne, sweep rake, entry No. 2 . . 33
Seymour & Morgan, entry No. 44 38
Cayuga Chief, entry No. 54 32
Dodge, Stevenson & Co., Marsh rake, entry No. 52 32
Williams, Wallace & Co., Johnson rake, entry No. 43 36
Buckeye, jr., dropper, entry No. 32 . . . 30
W. A. Wood, hand rake, entry No. 3 . . 32
Dodge, Stevenson & Co., Marsh rake, entry No. 53 34
Columbian revolving rake, entry No. 51 . . 30
Walter A. Wood, sweep rake, entry No. 40 . 34
C. C. Bradley & Son, Johnson rake, entry No. 22 37
Walter A. Wood, chain rake, entry No. 23 . 33
Cayuga Chief, G, entry No. 34 35
Cayuga Chief, L, entry No. 55 31
Wm. H. Halladay, entry No. 47 40
Dodge, Stevenson & Co., entry No. 52 . . 35
Eagle combined hand rake, entry No. 29 . . 35
Brinckerhoff, entry No. 21 31

RYE LOT.

Quality of work.
C. Brinckerhoff, No. 21 31
C. C. Bradley & Son, No. 22 37
Seymour, Morgan & Allen, No. 27½ . . . 40
Aultman & Miller, Buckeye, jr., dropper, No. 32 35
Wm. H. Halladay, No. 47 38
Dodge, Stevenson & Co., No. 53 29
Cayuga, L, dropper, No. 55 34

BARLEY LOT.

On the same day, after the rye was cut, the machines were tried in the barley lot, which was on rolling ground, the barley varying very greatly in the length of the straw, some of it being not more than 18 inches high, while in some parts it was 4 feet long. The following table shows the record of the machines:

Quality of work.
Brinckerhoff, No. 21 35
C. C. Bradley & Son, No. 22 39
Seymour, Morgan & Allen, No. 27½ . . . 40
Aultman & Miller, No. 32 36
Wm. H. Halladay, No. 47 38
Valley Chief, No. 47½ 36
Dodge, Stevenson & Co., No. 53 37
Cayuga Chief, L, No. 55 34

AWARD, CLASS 1. (MOWERS).

Three machines seem to claim special consideration with regard to award of premiums, each having received the mark of 40, indicating perfect work. These machines were Buckeye, entry No. 10; Rhode Island Clipper, entry No. 18; and

Wood's Mower, entry No. 8. Of these, the stubble of the two first were slightly the shortest, but the cutting in other respects was about the same, and was all that could be desired. The Buckeye, however, is the only one which received the perfect number (40) in both fields. We are constrained then by these facts to give the preference to the Buckeye for *quality of work*, so also as to *ease of draft, side-draft*, and *durability*. As to *simplicity*, the Committee were unable to discover much difference, though they gave to the Buckeye the preference as to *portability* and *general ease of management*. In view of these superiorities the Committee awarded the premium of the gold Medal in the first class to Adriance, Platt & Co., for their Buckeye Mower, entry No. 10.

Class 2. — Hand-Rakes.

But two entries in this class, Osborne & Co's, No. 19, and C. Wheeler, jr., No. 20. D. M. Osborne & Co., entry No. 19, having the most good points, the gold Medal was awarded to them.

Class 2½. — Self-Raker.

Five competitors here. Medal awarded to Seymour, Morgan & Allen, New York, entry No. 27½. The committee, however, strongly recommend C. C. Bradley & Son, entry No. 22.

Class 3. — Combined Mower and Reaper, Hand-Rakes.

The claims in this class rested between Cayuga Chief, H, entry No. 35, Eagle No. 29, and W. A. Wood, entry No. 30; all of them had special advantages. The medal was awarded, however, to W. A. Wood, entry No. 30.

Class 4. — Combined Reaper with self-raking or dropping attachments.

Ten competitors in this class. Medal awarded to Williams, Wallace & Co., entry 42.

Class 5. — Combined Reaper, Self and Hand-Rakes.

As desired. No award.

Class 6. — One-Horse Mower.

Award to R. L. Allen, Medal, entry No. 57.

SECOND PREMIUMS OF $25.

Class 1. — R. J. Clipper, entry No. 18, as coming so near to first premium.
Class 2. — C. Wheeler, jr., entry No. 20, G.
Class 2½. — C. C. Bradley & Son, entry No. 2.
Class 3. — E. F. Herrington, entry No. 29.
Class 4. — Seymour, Morgan & Allen.
Class 5. — No second premium.
Class 6. — D. M. Osborne one-horse mower, entry No. 56.
Class 13. — Horse-Rake. First premium to Wanzer & Cromwell, Chicago, Ill. Sulky Horse Rake.
Second premium, A. B. Sprout, Muncy, Pa. Steel-tooth horse rake.
Special recommendation, H. N. Tracy, Burlington, Vt., and P. S. Carver, Honeoye Falls, N. Y., for improvements in Revolving rake, with and without Sulky attachment.

Class 15. — Horse-Power Hay-Fork.

Six entries. Gold Medal to J. L. Mansfield & Co., Clockville, for Gladding's long-handled self-sustaining; weight, 24 lbs. Price, $11.00, and capable of pitching 2000 lbs. of hay in 13 pitches in 3 minutes.
Second premium to Chapman, Hauley & Co., Utica, N. Y., for Raymond's Hay-Fork; weight, 22 lbs. Price, $20; pitches 2720 lbs. in 13 pitches in 5 minutes; can be used for barley and oats also.
Special recommendation to A. B. Sprout, Muncy, Pa., for Hay-Fork and Knife.

After using all Mowers, Reapers, and the like, the journals should be carefully wiped, all dust removed, the machine placed under cover in a level position where no part is subjected to a strain.

INDEX TO MACKENZIE.

INDEX.

Abscess, 142
   in the Horse, 106
ACCIDENTS, 143
   Compound, 149
Acetate of Ammonia, 176
ACIDS, 296, 433
   Acetic, 296
   Carbazotic, 318
   Carbolic, 436
   Carbonic, 433
   Chrysammic, 318
   Hydrochloric, 298
   Muriatic, 298
   Nitric, 298
   Nitromuriatic, 379
   Poisoning by, 151
   Pyroligneous, 298
   Sulphhydric, 433
   Sulphuric, 298
   Sulphurous, 433
Adamas, 438
Adhesive Plaster, 175
Adulteration in Bread, 98
   Flour, 433
   Spirits, 287
   Wine, 277
Æolian Harp, to make, 454
Age of Cattle, 121
   Dog, 449
   Horse, 104
AGRICULTURE, 9, 470
Ague, 123
   Cake, 129
Ailanthus Silk Worm, 59
Air, Fresh, Importance of, 184
   in Buildings, to cool, 435
   to purify, 163
Aix la Chapelle Water, 300
ALCOHOL, 283
   to make, 280
   from Potatoes, 283
   from Wood, 283
   Proportions of, in Wine, etc., 287
   to Deodorize, 304
ALE, London, to Brew, 254
   from Sugar and Malt, 256
   on Mr. Cobbett's Plan, 255
   Posset, 200
   Table, 255
   to Brew, in small Families, 254
   to Brew, Burton, Nottingham, Essex, Edinburgh, 256, 257
   to Fine and Preserve, 258, 259
   to Bottle, 262
   to Ripen, if Flat, when Bottled, 263
   to Manage in the Cellar, 263
Alexiterial Water, 293
Alkalies, Poisoning by, 152
ALLOYS, 363
Almonds, Artificial, 291
   Bitter, Oil of, 291
   Milk of, 308

Almonds, Oil of, 301
Alum, Cubic, 315
Alumina, Acetate of, 315
Aluminum Bronze, 371
Amalgam, for Electrical Machines, 370
Amandine, 306
Ammonia, Acetate, 176
   Molybdate of, 313
   Water of, 176
AMPUTATION, 149, 151
Anatto, 324
Anbury, or Wart in the Horse, 106
Anchovies, Artificial, 239
Aneurism, 141
Angina Pectoris, 137
ANGLING, 443
Animal Food, 247
Animals, Bites and Stings of, 145, 450
Animation, Suspended, 151
Aniseed Cordial, 285
   Oil of, 290
Anisette de Bordeaux, 289
Annuals, for the Garden, 89
Anti-attrition, 347
   Incrustation Powder, 433
Antimony, Ores of, 365
   Poisoning by, 152
Antiscorbutic Water, 296
ANTISEPTICS, 435
Ants, to Prevent and Destroy, 450
Aperient Pills, 160
Apiary, 100
Apoplexy, 136
Appetite, to Improve, 161
Apple, Culture of, 68, 75, 76, 77
   Brandy, 283, 289
   Tapioca, 196
Apricots, to Preserve, 240
Aqua Mellis, 295
   Regia, 379
Aquaria Cement, 354
Aquatint, 421
Arrack, 282
Arrow-root, 196
Arsenical Ores, 365
Artichokes, 250
Artificial Cold, 435
   Liquors, 287
   Oils, 291
   Stone, 439
   Wood, 357
ARTISTS' COLORS, 331
Ascarides, or Seatworm, 160
Asparagus, to Cultivate, 81, 82
   Qualities of, 250
   Ragout, 213, 220
Assafœtida, Pills of, 161,
ASSAYING, 363
Asthma, 127
Asthmatic People, to Prevent Lamp Smoke from Affecting, 185
Astringent Injections, 166

(476)

INDEX. 477

Astringent Mixture, 124
    Pills, 166
Attrition, Anti-, 347
Autography, 425

Babbitt's Metal, 371
Bacon, 249
Baden Water, 299
Balling in Horses, 114
Balloons, 222
Balsam, Godbold's, 176
    of Honey, 175
    Riga, 291
    Tolu, 175
Bareges Water, 300
Barley, 31, 466
BAROMETERS, to Construct, 439
    to Read, 440
Basilicon Ointment, 174
Bath Metal, 371
Bathing, 183
Batteries, Electrical, 374
Bavarian Beer, 257
Bead for Liquors, 288
Beans, to Cultivate, 33, 466
    String, 195
Bee Flowers, to Cultivate, 100
BEEF, à la Mode, 205, 231
    to Choose, 248
    and Pork, to Salt, 239
    Braized, 207
    Collops, 211
    Corned, 190
    Dried, 190
    en Daube, 205
    Essence, 178
    Hashed, 207
    Potted, 190
    Qualities of, 249
    Salt, and Cabbage, 208
    Sanders, 206
    Sportsman's, 449
    Steak, 206, 207
    Tea, 178
    Tongue, 205
BEER, Amber, or Two-penny, to Brew, 258
    to Bottle, 263
    Cheap, 257
    Dead, to Enliven, 259
    Flat, to Recover, 259
    from Pea-shells, to Brew, 258
    from Sugar, 256
    Frosted, to Restore, 260
    Foxing, to Cure, etc., 259
    Ginger, 258
    Lager, 257
    Molasses, to make, 258
    Musty, to Restore. 259
    on Mr. Cobbett's Plan, 255
    Poultice, 156
    Required Time for Keeping, 258
    Root, 257
    Sarsaparilla, 257
    Spruce, 257
    Stale or Sour, to Restore, 259
    Table, to Brew from Pale Malt, 255
    to Fine, 258, 259
    to Fine and Preserve a Cask of, 25
    to give a Rich Flavor to, 260
    to Prevent becoming Stale and Flat, 259
    White, 257
    to determine Quantity of Alcohol in, 287
BEES, Flowers best for, 100
    in Straw Hives, 99
    Italian, 104
    Management of, 98, 102, 104
    to Avoid Injury from, 450

Bees, to Feed, 101
    to Hive, 101
    to Swarm, 100
Beet Brandy, 283
    Sugar, 53, 283
Bell Metal, 371
Belly, Wounds of, 145
Benzoin, Tincture of, 176
Bergamot, Essence of, 160
    Water, 294
Bibron's Antidote for Snake-bites, 450
Biennials, 89
Biles, 141
Bilious Fever, 123
Birch Oil, 290
Bird-lime, 356
Birds, Canary, 448
    Useful to Farmers, 3
Biscuit, Albert, 227
    Fancy, 225
    Naples, 224
    Savoy, 228
    Sponge, 202
    Sugar, 201
Bismuth Ores, to Assay, 365
Bites and Stings of Noxious Animals, 145, 450
Blacking, 349
Blackberry Brandy, 236
    Cordial, 236
    Culture of, 69
    Extract, 236
    Mush, 197
    Syrup, 236
    Wine, 236, 269
Black Drop, 175
Bladder, Inflamed, 132
    in the Horse, 106
    Stone in, 132
Blanc Mange, 228, 229, 288
BLEACHING AND SCOURING, 309
Bleeding, after Extraction of Teeth, 157
    Directions for, 153
    from the Nose, 125
    from Wounds, 144
    in the Horse, 114
Blight in Fruit Trees, 77
    in Wheat, 29
Blind, to Write for the, 461
Blistering in the Horse, 106
Blood, as Food, 249
    Spitting of, 127
    Vomiting of, 128
Blotched Face, 140
Blubber as Manure, 26
Blue, Prussian, 333, 337
    Saxon or Chemic, 316
    Thenard's, 333
    Ultramarine, 332
Board Measure, 429
Boat, Upsetting of, 180
Boerhaave's Rules for Health, 184
Bog Spavin, 106
Bone, to Stain, 325
BOILERS, INCRUSTATIONS IN, TO PREVENT, 44
Boils, 141
Bologna Sausage, 190
    Vials, 403
Bonbons, 233
BOOK-KEEPING, 452
Books, Covers, to Marble, 326
    Edges of, to Sprinkle, 327
    to Gild, 377
    Printed, to Bleach, 310
Boots, to Clean, 457
    Water-proof, 348
Bots, 106
Bottle Stoppers, 434

Bougies, to Pass, 153
Bouillien Matelote, 191, 205
Bouquet de Caroline, 305
 Essence of, 305
 Esterhazy, 305
Bowels, Inflammation of, 129
 in the Horse, 107
Boxes, Capacity of, 428
Brain, Compression of, 144
 Concussion of, 143
 Inflammation of, 125
Bran Bread, 97
Brandy, Apple, 289
 Blackberry, 236
 British, 281
 Cherry, 286
 Imitation, 289
 Peach, 289
 Peaches, 232
 to Preserve Fruits in, 240
 from Root Beer, 283
Brass, 371
 and Copper, to Tin Rapidly, 433
 Ornaments, to Preserve, 438
 to Polish, 349
Brazil Paper, 299
Bread, Adulterated, to detect, 98, 433
 of Iceland Moss and Flour, 98
 on Cobbett's Plan, 98
 Qualities of, 250
Bread, Scotch, 226
 to make, 90, 97, 98
Breasts, Inflamed, 168
Breeches Ball, 313
Brew, to, Ale in Small Families, 254
 Amber Beer, 258
 Beer and Ale from Pea-Shells, 258
 Brown Stout, 254
 Burton, Edinburgh, Essex, and Nottingham Ale, 256, 257
 Lager, 257
 London Ale, 254
 Molasses Beer, 258
 Porter on the London Plan, 254
 Root Beer, 257
 Spruce Beer, 257
 Table Beer from Pale Malt, 255
  from Sugar and treacle, 255
 White Beer, 257
Brew-House, to fit up a Small, 252
BREWING, 251
 to choose Water for, 252
 to cool Worts in, 253
 Utensils, to preserve, 260
Brine, to Utilize, 463
Bristles, to Dye, 325
Britannia Metal, 372
British Gum, 356
Broiling, 190
Bronze, 371
 Aluminum, 371
 Gun Barrels, to, 349
 Plaster Figures, 348
Broth, Chicken, 113
 Jelly, 216
 Liebig's, 216, 461
 Mutton, 193
 Scotch, 193, 217
Brown Stout, to Brew, 254
Brushes in one piece, 357
 Hair, to Clean, 456
Bubo, 133
Buckwheat, 46, 466
 Cakes, 201
Budding, 63
Bugs, to Prevent, etc., 450
Bulbous Roots, to hasten, 84

Buns, Common, 201
 Cross, 201
Burgundy Pitch Plaster, 174
Burnett's Antiseptic Fluid, 435
Burnishing, to Gild by, 37
Burns and Scalds, 153
Butter, to Cure, 96
 to Remove Turnip Flavor from, 96
 Drawn, 194
 Dumbarton Mode, 96
 Maitre d'Hotel, 214
 Nuns', 194
 to make, 91
Buttons, New Material for, 434
Butyric Acid, 288
 Ether, 288

Cabbages, Qualities of, 249
 to Keep Caterpillars from, 83
 to Preserve for Sea-Voyages, 458
Cachou Aromatisé, 307
Cadmium, Yellow, 334
 in Fireworks, 385
CAKES, 200
 Albany, 231
 Almond, 225, 227, 228
  Cheese, 225
 Apple, 202
 Banbury, 201
 Bath, 200
 Black, 224, 230, 231
 Bread, 202
 Cheap Fruit, 202
 Cheese, Bread, 202
 Cheese, Rice, 202
 Cider, 230
 Cocoanut, 222
 Cream, 201
 Cup, 230
 Election, 229
 Federal, 231
 Fine Cheese, 225
 Flannel, 201
 French Loaf, 224
 Fruit, Plain, 202
 Good Plain, 224
 Lemon, 225, 230
 Madison, 224
 Plain Seed, 226
 Plain, 224
 Portugal, 200
 Pound, 226
 Pudding Pound, 224
 Queen, 225
 Ratafia, 224
 Rice, 200
 Rich Plum, 224
 Rich Seed, 224
 Savoy, 200
 Shrewsbury, 200, 226
 Sponge, 224, 230
 Sugar, 230
 Swedes, 227
 Wedding, 229
CALICO PRINTING, 322
Callan's Battery, 375
Calves' Head, to Dress, 231
 Foot Jelley, 229
 to Rear, 91, 92
Camphor, 290
 Mixture, 124
CANARY BIRDS, 448
Cancer, 135
Cancerous Ulcers, Lotion for, 154
Candied Sugar, 232
 to Color, 234
 Lemon Peel, 233

INDEX. 479

Candied Oranges, 235
    Orange Peel, 233
Candles, Substitute for, 94
    Wax, to make, 458
Canker in the Horse, 107–115
    in Trees, 77
CANNING FRUIT, 240
Cantharides, Poisoning by, 152
Canvas, to Waterproof, 347
Caoutchouc Varnish, 348
Capacity of Boxes, 428
Capsicum, to Raise, 82
Caraway Cordial, 285
    Oil, 290
Carbazotic Acid, 318
Carbolic Acid, 436
Carbonic Acid, 433
Carbuncle, 141
Carlsbad Water, 299
Carpets, to choose, 457
    to Restore, 311
    to Scour, 312
Carré's Apparatus, 435
Carrots, to Cultivate, 40
Cartilages, Displaced, 135
CARVING, ART OF, 241
Case Hardening, 381
Casks, Musty, to Sweeten, 260, 273
    New, to Season, 261
    to close without Bungs, &c., 261, 262
Cassia Oil, to Obtain, 290
Castor Oil, 301
    as a Dressing for Leather, 459
    Clyster, 158
Cast Steel, 382
Casts from Fusible Metal, 370
Cataplasms, Cold, 154
Cataract in the Horse, 108
Catarrh, or Cold, 126
Caterpillars on Gooseberries, to Remove, 76
    on Shrubs, Plants, etc., 83
Catheter, Directions for Passing the, 153
Catsup for Sea Stores, 194
    Tomato, to make, 194, 214, 230
    Mushroom, 214
Cattle, Age of, 121
    Colds in, 120
    Distemper in, 116
    Frenzy in, 120
    Garget in, 116
    Hoven or Blown in, 121
    Jaundice in, 120
    Lung Fever in, 116
    Paunching in, 121
    Purging Drink for, 120
    Rinderpest in, 467; Red Water in, 116
    Scouring in, 116
    Swelling with Food, 116
    Swimming in the Head in, 121
    Tar-water for, 116
    Treatment of, 116
    Wounds in, 105
Caustic, Lunar, Poisoning by, 152
Cayenne Pepper, to Raise, 82
Cautions, Salutary, 178, 180
    to Painters and Glaziers, 164
Cedrat Cordial, to make, 285
    Essence, 290
Celery, Qualities of, 250
CEMENTS, 352
Cerate of Spanish Flies, 174
    Turner's, 174
Chafing Dish, Impromptu, 463
Chalk Mixture, 130
Chalybeate Draughts, 166
    Pills, 166
    Water, 300

Chalybeate Wine, 160
Champagne, 289
Chancres, 133
Chapped Hocks, 107
    Skin, 156, 306
Charcoal, Animal, 298
    as a Deodorizer, 436
    as a Purifier, 178
    Poultice, 155
    to make, 280
    to Protect from the Effects of, 185
Charlotte Russe, 228
Cheese Cakes, 202, 225
    Cheshire, 96
    Cottage, 214
    Damson, 237
    Green Gooseberry, 199
    Hogshead, 190
    Qualities of, 249
Chemic Blue, 316
CHEMICAL RECEIPTS, 432
    Landscapes, 362
Cherries, to Dry, 240
Cherry Brandy, 286
Chestnuts, to Keep, 97
Chest, Dropsy of, 127
    Wounds in the, 145
Chicken, Fricassee, with Mushrooms, 209
    Broth, 194
    Pie, 196, 210
    Pox, 138
    Salad, 231,
    Stewed, with Corn, 210
Chickens, to Hatch, 93
    to Manage, 93, 116
Chilblains, 156
Children, Management and Diseases of, 169
Chills and Fever, 123
Chimneys on Fire, to Extinguish, 460
    Smoky, to Cure, 455
    to Clean, 455
China-ware, to Manufacture, 394
    and Glass, to Clean and Pack, 457
    to Clean, 457
Chinese Sheet-lead, to make, 381
    Fire, 385
Chintz, to Wash, 310
Chloride of Lime, 436
    to Destroy Insects, 450
Chlorine, 433, 436
    Water, 299
Chlorimetry, 309
Chlorosis, 166
Chocolate, 200
    Cream, 227
    Glacé, 227
    Qualities of, 251
Choice of Animal Food, 247
    Plants, 69
Choking, 153
CHOLERA, 162
Cholera Morbus, 129
Chowder, 192
Chrome Green, 338
    to Dye, 318
    Vermilion, 337
    Yellow, 334
Chrysammic Acid, 318
Cider, Cheap, from Raisins, 264
    Devonshire, 263
    General Rules for Making, 264
    Scotch, 263
    to make, 263
    to Manage, 264
    from Pears, 264
Cinnabar, Humid Assay of, 365
Cinnamon, Cordial, to make, 285

480 INDEX.

Cinnamon, Oil of, to Obtain, 289
 Water, to make, 294
Citrate of Magnesia, 175
Citron Cordial, to make, 285
Clam Soups, 193
Clap, 133
Claret Punch, 231
Claret Wine, to Imitate, 289 [Luting, 466
Clarifying Honey, 240; Clay for Modelling and
Clay, Burning, Mr. Craig's Method, 24
 Lands, to Underdrain, 49, 50
Cleaning Water Casks, 95
Climate, Effect of, 78
Climbing Shrubs, 88
Cloth, Buff-colored, to Clean, 311
 Faded Black, to Revive, 313
 Scarlet, to Clean and Dip, 313
 the Nap on, to Raise, 313
 to Bleach, 310
 to Dry Clean, 313
 to Dye, 317
 to Full, 310
 to render Waterproof, 331, 347
 to Take Out Fruit-stains from, 314
 to Take Spots of Paint from, 314
 to Take Spots of Grease from, 314
Clothes Ball, to make, 313
 Incombustible, 437
 on Fire, How to Act, 437
 to Brush, 456
 to Scour, 312
 to take Grease from, 314
CLOTHING, 184
Clove Cordial, to make, 286
Cloves, Oil of, 290
Coal-oil, 302, 450, 451
 to Destroy Insects, 450
Coal-tar, 318, 435
 Ashes as Manure, 24
 Colors, 318
Coats, to Scour, 313
Cobalt Ores, to Assay, 365
Cocoa, 200
Cocoanut-cake, 222
 Pudding, 222
Codfish-cakes, 191
Coffee, 200, 202
 Qualities of, 251
 Tree, to Engraft, 75
Coins, 427
 Easy Mode of Taking Impressions from, 438
 Relative Value of American and Foreign, 431
Cold Cream, 306
 Artificial, 435
 Drinks, Prevent Effects of, 460
 Suspended Animation from, 151
Colds, Gargles for, 159
 in the Head, 126
 in the Horse, 107
Cole Slaw, 195
Colic, 130
 Painter's, 131
Collar-bone, Fractures of, 146
 Dislocation of, 148
Collodion, 409
Collyria, or Eye-washes, 157
Colocynth Pills of, 158
Cologne-water, 304
COLORS, Chevreul's Method of Graduating, 321
 Coal-tar, 318
 Compound, 310
 to Discharge, 316
 for Confectionery, 338
 Oil, 332
Composition, Water-proof, 331
Composts, 21, 61
Compression of the Brain, 144

Concrete, 352
Concussion of the Brain, 143
Condy's Disinfecting Solution, 436
CONFECTIONERY, 232
 Colors for, 338
Conservatory, to make, 61
Consumption, 127
Contusions, 143, 145
Convalescents, Soup for, 178
Convulsions in Pregnancy, 168
 in Children, 171
 in the Horse, 107, 111
COOKERY, 188
Cook's, Captain, Rules for Seamen
Copal Varnish, 341, 343
Copper, Assay of, 364
 in Pickles or Tea, 433
 Foils, 373
 Plates, Secure from Corrosion, 422
 Poisoning by, 152
 Test for, 432
 Tubes, 376
 on Iron, 376
Copy, on Preparing, for the Printer, 452
Coral Branches, Artificial, 460
CORDIALS OR COMPOUND SPIRITS, 285
 Anise-seed, Caraway, Cedrat, Cinnamon, Strong Cinnamon, Citron, Clove, Coriander, Eau de Bigarrade, Gold, Lemon, Lovage, Nectar, Noyau, Orange, Peppermint, Ratafia, Dry Ratafia, Whiskey 285—287
Cork-screw, Substitute for, 459
Corn, Indian, to Cultivate, 29
 Oysters, 219
 to Dry, 88, 219
Corn-bread, 232
Corned Beef, 190
Corns, 156
 in the Horse, 107
Cosmetic for Complexion, 465
Cosmetics, 306
Costiveness, 158, 161, 167
Cottage Cheese, 214
Cotton, 53
Coughs and Colds, 158, 159
 in the Horse, 107
Court-plaster, 175, 358
Cow Feeder, Directions to the, 91
 Milch, to Choose, 92
 to Keep, 92
 Pox, 138
Crabs, to Choose, 248
 to Pot, 190
Cracked Heels in the Horse, 107
Cracks in Stoves, 458
Cramp in the Stomach, 161
Cramps, 168
 in Bathing, 183
Cranberry, Culture of, 69
Cream, Coffee, 237
 Ice, 235
 Painter's, 343
 Pistachio, 235
 Qualities of, 249
 Raspberry, 236
 Substitute for, 96
Creme de Barbades, Real, 284
 de Noyeau de Martinique, 284
 d'Orange, 285
Crocheting, 448
Crops, Rotation of, 10, 26, 27
Croquets, Chicken, 232
Croup, 173
Crows, to Banish, 40, 90
Crullers, to make, 464
Crumpets, 201

INDEX.

Crust, Short, 198
Cucumbers, to Cultivate, 77, 78, 79
    to Pickle, 239
CULINARY ARTS, 188
Curacoa, 289
Currants, Culture of, 69
    Qualities of, 251
Currant Jelly, 215, 235
    Wine, 236, 267
Currying Leather, 387
Curry, 216
    Indian Sauce, 214
    Maloy's, 116
    Powder, 216
    Salmon, 210
Custards, Almond, 222
    Apple, 230
    Baked, 222
    Boiled, 199
    Cold, 199
    Lemon, 222
    Orange, 222
    Rice, 222
Cutlets, Lamb, with Peas, 208
    Mutton, 208
    Pork, 208
    Veal, 206, 232
Cuts, Treatment of, 144
Cuttings, for Plants, 65
Cypher, writing in, 459

Dahlia-paper, 299
Dairy, to Manage, 91
Damson Cheese, 237
    Plums, Pickled, 231
    to Bottle, 239
Damsons, to Preserve, 240
Dance of St. Vitus, 137
Decalcomania, 465
Decanters, to Clean, 457
Dentrifice, 308, 460
DEODORIZATION, 164, 435
Depilatories, 305
Devils, Dry, 205
Diabetes, 132
    in the Horse, 108
DIALYSIS, 463
Diamond Cement, 356
    to Imitate, 373
Diarrhœa, 130, 162, 171
Diavolini, 223
DIET, 247
Digestion, to Improve, 128, 161
Diphtheria, 126
Dippel's Oil, to Obtain, 291
DISEASES OF CHILDREN, 169
    General Rules for Treating, 122
    PECULIAR TO FEMALES, 165
    of Wheat, 29
DISINFECTANTS, 164, 184, 185, 436
Disinfection, 185
DISLOCATIONS, 148
Distemper, 328, 331
    in Dogs, 115, 449
DISTILLATION, 277
    of Compound Spirits, 285
    of Compound Waters, 292, 294
    of Essential and other Oils, 289
    General Rules for, simple waters, 293
    to Preserve Flowers for, 292
Distilleries, Fires in, to Extinguish, 280
Diuretic Balls, 113
DOGS, Best Breed of, for Shooting Game, 449
    Distemper in, 115, 449
    Mange in, 115, 449
    Purging Ball for, 115
    to know the Age of, to six years, 449

DOMESTIC ECONOMY, 90
    Medicines, 173
Dough-nuts, 464
Doses, Medicinal, 188, 241
Dover's Powders, 173
Dram-Drinking, to Remedy Effects of, 460
Draining Land, 49, 50
Drawings, Lead Pencil, to Preserve, 350
    to Varnish, 350
Drawn Butter, 194
Dresden China, 395
Dresses, Incombustible, 437
Drier for Paints, 331
Drilling Glass, 439
    Wheat, 28
Drop, Black, 175
Drops, Chocolate, 234
    Clove, 234
    Coffee, 234
    Confectionery, to make, 234
    Ginger, 234
    Orange-Flower, 234
    Peppermint, 234
Dropsy of the Bag, 134
    Belly, 132
    Chest, 127
    Knee, 135
    Medicines for, 167
Drowning, 151, 180, 181, 182
    Assistance in, Danger of, 462
Drying Herbs, Roots, etc., 85
    Oils, 340
Dry-rot, 352, 432, 438
Duchess Loaves, 226
Duck, Wild, Salmis, 209
    to Choose, 248
Duffy's Elixir, 175
Dumplings, Apple, 199
    Raspberry, 198
Dung Beds, to form, 60
Dutch Drops, 292
    Pink, 334
DYEING, 315
    of Leather, 390
Dysentery, 130
Dyspepsia, 129

Ear, Extraneous Bodies in the, to Extract, 187
    Inflammation of, 125
    Wounds of, 145
Eau de Barbade, 284
    de Bouquet, 304
    de Cologne, 304,
    de Javelle, 436
    de Luce, 173
    de Millefleurs, 305
    Divine, 284
    Lustrale, 305
    Sans Pareil, 294
ECONOMY, RURAL AND DOMESTIC, 90
Eels, to Pot, 190
Eger Water, 299
Eggs, à la Dauphin, 213
    au Gratin, 212
    to Choose, as Food, 249, 457
    to Preserve, 95, 96, 457
    with Wine, 200
Egg-Plant, to Cook, 219, 231
Elbow, Dislocations of, 149
Elderberry Wine, 268
    Paper, 299
Electric Machines, New, 435
Electrical Machine, Alloy for, 370
ELECTRO-PLATING, 374
Elephant's Milk, 284
Elixir, Duffy's, 175
Elm Trees, 77

482　INDEX.

Email de Paris, 465
Embrocation for Rheumatism and Sprains, 154
Embroidery, to Clean, 314
Emissions, Involuntary, 133
Ems Water, 299
Enamel for Cooking Utensils, 393, 398
　to Paint in, 393
ENAMELLING, 390
　Varnish for, 341
Engrave, to, in Aquatinta, 421
　in Mezzotinto, 421
　on Chiar' Oscuro, 422
　on Precious Stones, 423
　on Steel, 420
　on Stone, 423
　on Wood, 422
ENGRAVING, 419
　from Photographs, 418
Engravings, Cleaning and Preservation of, 426
　on Glass, to Transfer, 407, 423
Enlargement of Spermatic Vein, 134
　Tonsil, 126
　Uvula, 126
Eolian Harp, to make, 454
Epilepsy, 136
Erysipelas, 138
Essence of Cedrat, 290
　Lavender, 291
　Neroli, 291
　Petits Grains, 291
Essential Oils, 289
ETCHING, 419, 422
Ether, to make, 281
　to Purify, 281
Evil, the King's, 135
Exercise, 185
Expectation of Life, 459
Expectorant Pills, 159
Extracts, Toilet, 304
Eye Waters, 157
　Inflammation of the, 125
Eyelids, Inflamed, Remedy for, 157
Eyes of the Horse, 108, 114
Eyesight, to Preserve the, 186

Fac Similes, 360
FACTITIOUS LIQUORS, 287
Failures in Photography, 417
Fainting, 136
Fallow, to Conduct a, 15
Famished Persons, to Restore, 463
Fans for Cleaning Grain, 18
Farcy, 108
FARRIERY, 104
Fattening Hogs, 92
　Poultry, 92
Feathers, to Cleanse, 313
　Dye, 325
　Preserve, 450
Feet, to Keep Dry, 186
　Disease of in the Horse, 113
Felon, 142, 155,
FEMALES, DISEASES OF, 165
FERMENTATION, 251, 254, 261, 262
Fertilizers, 11
FEVER, Bilious, 123
　Hectic, 124
　Intermittent, 123
　Milk, 168
　Puerperal, 168
　Remittent, 123
　Scarlet, 137
　Simple, Inflammatory, 123
　Typhoid, 124
　Typhus, 124
Filberts, to Keep, 87
Film, or Cataract in the Horse, 108

Filter, for Corrosive Liquids, 433
Fining of Spirits, 285
　Wines, 274
Finings, to make and Apply, 274
　of Wines and Spirits, to Force down the, 277
Fires,
　Colored, 384
　in Distilleries, to Extinguish, 280
　in Hay-stacks, to prevent, 459
　to Escape from, 462
　to Extinguish in Chimneys, 460
Fireproof Dresses, 437
　Paper, 437
　Wood, 437
FIREWORKS, 384
FISHING, 443
Fish Bones, to Extract, when swallowed, 153
　Culture, 445
　to Cure, 94
　Poisonous, 153
　Qualities of, 249
　to Cook, 191, 206
　to Preserve with Sugar, 239
　to Keep Fresh, 464
Fistula, 142
Fits in Children, 171
Fixed Oils, 301
Flannel Cakes, 201
Flannels, to Wash, 464
Flatulence, 161, 170
Flavorings for Imitated Wines, 287
Flax, to Cultivate, Dress, etc., 42, 43
Fleas, to Destroy, 450
Fleur d'Italie, 304
Flies, to Remove from Rooms, 96
　Stables, 450
Floors, to Stain, 457
　Cement for, 352
Florida Water, 304
Flounders, to Cook, 191
Flour, Chalk in, to Detect, 433
　to Improve, 86, 96
　to Preserve, 96
Flower Gardening, 84, 88
Flowers, Bulbous, to Accelerate, 67
　Faded, to Restore, 84
　to Dry, 84
　for Distillation, 292
　to Grow in Winter, 82, 83
　to Preserve, 87
Fluor Albus, 166
Flux, 130
Fluxes, 363
Foils, 373
Fomentations, 154
FOOD, QUALITIES OF, 247, 251
　of Plants, 9
Forcemeat, 216
Foreign Spirits, to Imitate, 281
Foretelling the Weather, 439
Forges, Water, 300
Fothergill Process, 414
Foul Air, Suspended Animation from, 151
Foul Rooms, to Ventilate, 164
Foundered Feet, 108
Fowls, Qualities of, 249
　Choice of, 248
　Treatment of, 93, 116
　Wild, to Catch, 462
FRACTURES, 146
Frangipani, Toilet, 307
Freckles, 306
FREEZING MIXTURES, 435
French Polish, 344
　Rolls, 228
Fresco, 331
Fresh Water from Salt, 179

INDEX. 483

Fricassee, 209
Friction for Rheumatism, etc., 162, 185
   to lessen, 347, 438
Fritters, 199
Frogs, to Cook, 232
Frostbite, 151
   in Fruit Trees, 75
   in Potatoes, 35
Fruit Essences, 288
   to Protect, from Insects, 71, 450
   Trees, 67, 69, 70, 75, 76, 77
   Spots, to Remove, 314
   Stains, to Remove, 314, 436
Fruits, 85, 86, 87, 88
   to Preserve, 86–88, 240
      without Sugar, 240, 246
   Qualities of, 250, 251
   to Pack, 87
Frumenty, 197
Frying, 190
Fuel, Cheap, 95
Fulling Cloths, etc., 310
Fumigation, 163, 164, 436
Fundament, Falling of, 171
Furnace, Sand-heat, to make a, 278
Furnaces, Portable, 278
Furniture, Oil, 350
   Paste, to make, 349
   to Clean, 455
   Varnished, to Polish, 349
Furs, to Preserve, 450
Fusel Oil, 283
Fusible Metal, 369

Gallipot Mastic, for Grinding Colors, 345
   Varnish, to make, 345
Ganglion, 141
Gardeners, Practical Directions to, 90
GARDENING, 60, 66, 98
Gargle for Thrush, 159
   Sore Throat, 159
Gas Burners, 430
   Meter, to Read, 430
   to Save, 430
Geese, to Choose, 243
Gems, Artificial, 403
Gems, to Engrave, 423
Geneva, English, to make, 282
Gentian Water, 296
   Wine, 160
Geraniums, 89
German Silver, 372
Gild by Burnishing, 378
   Edges of Paper, 377
   Glass and Porcelain, to, 376
   Leather, 377
   on Wood, with Oil, 377
   Silk, Satin, Ivory, etc, by Hydrogen Gas, 377
Gilding, 376–379
   Electro-, 375
   Fire, 379
   Jewellery, 379
   Solution, 375
Gilders, Cautions to, 185
   Varnish for, 346
Gin, to Prepare, as in Holland, 282
   to Imitate, 288
Ginger Beer, 258
   Nuts, 202
   Pop, 257
   Powders, 433
   Syrup, 176
   to Candy, 233
Gingerbread, Plain, 200, 228
   Poundcake, 200, 228
   Short, 228
   Soft, 224

Gingerbread, without Butter, 200
Glands, Inflamed, 135
Glanders, 115
GLASS, 399
   to Anneal, 401
   and Porcelain, to Paint and Stain, 406, 408
   to Draw on, 407
   Globes, Liquid Foils for Silvering, 370
   Ground, to Imitate, 409
   in Imitation of Muslin, 423
      " " Precious Stones, 403
   Powdered, Poisoning by, 152
   to Break, in any Required Way, 403
   to Clean, 409
   to Drill, 439
   to Etch upon, 422
   Stoppers, to Loosen, 434
   to Ornament, in Imitation of Engraving, 402, 407
   to Pack, 457
   to Polish and Grind, 402
   to Silver, 370
   Jars, like China, to make, 458
Glaziers, Caution to, 164
Glazings for Earthenware, etc., 396, 398
Gleet, 133
Gloves, to Cleanse, 315
   to Dye, 325
   to Prepare Skin for, 389
Glue, 354, 355
   Liquid, 356
   Marine, 354
Goadby's Solution, 435
Goat's Flesh, Qualities of, 249
   Skins, 389
Godbold's Balsam, 176
Godfrey's Cordial, 175
Goitre, 136
Gold, Amalgam of, in the Large Way, 379
   Assay, 367
   Lace, to Clean, 314
   Ores and Earths containing, 367
   Poisoning by, 152
   Powder, 378
   Solder, to Prepare, 369
   Test for, 433
   to Dissolve in Aqua Regia, 379
   to Separate from Gilt, Copper, and Silver, 380
   Varnish, 351
Gonorrhœa, 133
Goodfellow's, Mrs., Lemon Pudding, 222
Goose, Choice of, 242
Gooseberries, Culture of, 69, 76
Gooseberry Cheese, Green, 199
Gout, 134, 162
   Chelsea Pensioner's Remedy for, 161
   Cordial, to make, 161
   Lotion, 134
   Portland Powder for, 460
   Pradier's Cataplasm for, 459
   Rheumatic, 134
Grafting, 63, 65
   Wax, 459
Grain, Damaged, to Correct, 96
   to Preserve from Vermin, 96
   Reaping before Ripe, 31
Grapes, to Cultivate, 73
   to Keep, 88
   Sugar from, 233
Gravel, 131
   Remedies for the, 131
   Walks, to make, 60
Gravy, 215, 230
   Cakes, 194
Grease, in Horses, 108, 115
   Spots, 312, 314, 438

INDEX.

Grecian Painting, 339
Green, Chrome, 338
    Colors free from Arsenic, 338
    House, to make, 61
    Scheele's, 338
    Schweinfürth, 338
    Sickness, 166
Grindstones, to make, 458
Gripes in the Horse, 108
Grip ng in Children, 170
Grottoes, to Embellish, 460
Gruel, to make, 177
Guano, 10, 11
Gum Benzoin, Oil of, to obtain, 290
    Elastic, to Dissolve, 339, 354
    the Yellow, 170
Gun Barrels, to Brown, 349
    Cotton, 356
        as a Filter, 433
        Cement, 356
        Explosive, 384
            Link's, 384
        Soluble, 409
    Metal, 371
    Powder, 384
        to render Incombustible at pleasure, 465
        White, 384
Gutta-percha, Solution of, 348, 354
    Solvents for, 339

Hair Brush, to Clean, 456
    Dyes, 305
    Honey-water for the, 305
    Superfluous, to Remove, 305
    Washes, etc., 305
Hams, Qualities of, 248
    to Cure, 91
    to Cook, 207
    to Salt, 239
Hanging, Suspended Animation from, 151
Hangings, Paper, to Restore, 314
Hare, Roast, 209
Harrowgate Water, 300
Harrows, 16
Hartshorn Jelly, to make, 235
Hash of Beef, 206
Hats, to Dye, 324
    Straw, to Clean, 315
    to Preserve, 457
Hay Making, 46
    Stacks, to Save from Fire, 459
Headache, to Relieve, 125
HEALTH, PRESERVATION OF, 183
Heartburn, 128, 161
Heart, Palpitation of, 127
Hearths, to Paint, 331
Heat, Excessive, to Guard Against, 136
Hectic Fever, 124
Hedge-hog, Usefulness of the, 29
Hedges, Thorn, 51
Heels, Cracked, 107
Heliotrope, 89
Hemorrhage after Pulling Teeth, 157
Hemp, to Cultivate, 40, 41
    Process of Grassing, 41
Herbs, to Propagate, 76, 83
    to Dry, 85
Herpes, 139
Herrings, to Cure, 94
    to Choose, 248
Hiccup, 128
    in Children, 170
Hiera Picra, 158
Hip-joint Disease, 135
Hives, Cobbett's, 104
    Langstroth's, 104

Hives, Thorley's, 103
Hoarhound, to Candy, 233
Hocks, Chapped, 107
Hodge-Podge, 215, 217
Hog Cholera, 117
Hogs, to Fatten, 92
Hogs, 116, 121
Hogshead Cheese, 190
Hominy, 98
Honey, to Clarify, 240
    to Manage, 102
    Water, 295, 305
Hoof-bound, 108
Hooping-cough, 172, 173
Hops, to Cultivate, etc., 43, **44, 45**
    to Choose, 253
    to Keep, 263
Horn, to Dye Various Colors, 327
HORSE, Abscesses in, 106
    Anbury, or Wart in, 106
    Balling with Snow, 114
    Balls for, 106
    Bladder, Inflamed, in, 106
    Bleeding in, 110
    Bleeding, to Stop, in, 114
    Blistering Ointment for, 106
    Bog Spavin in, 106
    Bone Spavin in, 106
    Bots in, 106
    Broken Knees in, 107
    Broken Wind in, 107, 111
    Burns or Scalds in, 107
    Canker in, 107
    Cataract in, 108
    Chapped Hocks in, 107
    Cold in, 107
    Convulsions in, 107, 111
    Corns in, 107
    Cough in, 107, 110
    Cracked Heels in, 107
    Curb in, 107
    Diabetes in, 108
    Disease of Feet in, 113
    Diuretic Balls for, 113
    Drink for, 110
    Dysentery, 109
    Eyes of, 108, 114, 462
    Farcy in, 108
    Fever in, 111
    Foundered Feet in, 108
    Glanders, 115
    Grease, 108, 115
    Green Ointment, 106
    Gripes, 108, 112
    Hoof Bound, 108
    Inflamed Bowels, 106
    Inflamed Lungs, 108, 110, **114**
    Jaundice, 111
    Lameness, 114
    Lampas in, 108
    Laxity in, 108
    Lock-Jaw, 115
    Looseness in, 110
    Mallenders, 108
    Mange, 108, 111, 114
    Molten Grease, 109
    Ointment, 105
    Poll Evil, 109
    Pulling at the Halter, **461**
    Purging, 108, 110
    Purging Ball, 108, 110
    Quittor, 109
    Ring-Bone, 109
    Rupture, 115
    Sallenders, 109
    Sand-Crack, 109
    Scratched Heels, 114

INDEX.

Horse, Shoeing in Winter, 114
   Sitting a, 463
   Sit-fasts, 109
   Sores and Bruises, 105
   Spavin, 106
   Staggers, 109
   Staling Profusely, 111
   Strains, 109, 114, 115
   Strangles, 109
   Strangury, 109
   Surfeit, 111
   Teeth, 104
   Tetanus, or Lock-jaw, 115
   Thrush, 109, 114
   to Take out of a Stable on Fire, 462
   Unsoundness, 105
   Vives, 109
   Wart, 106
   Wind-galls, 109
   Worms, 106, 111
   Wounds, 105, 109
HORTICULTURE, 60
Hot-houses, 67
Hot-beds, 60
Hortus Siccus, 459
Houses on Fire, How to Escape from, 462
   Painting, 327
Hoven in Cattle, 121
Humus, 9
Hunger and Thirst, to Restore Famished Persons, 463
Hungary Waters, 295, 304
HUSBANDRY, 9
   Implements of, 15, 470
Huxham's Tincture of Peruvian Bark, 176
Hydraulic Cement, 352, 466
Hydrogen, 433
Hydrometers, 430
Hydrophobia, 145
Hysteric Fits, 165, 167

Ice, to make, 95, 435
   to Extricate Persons from Broken, 181
   from a Powder, to Procure, 95, 435
   Cream, Water-Ice, 235, 236, 237
   House, Portable, 94
   for Culinary Purposes, to Produce, 95
Icing for Cakes, 200
Iceland Moss Bread, 98
Impotency, 134
Inclosures, to Form, 51
In-arching, 62
Incombustible Wood, 437
   Dresses, 437
Incontinence of Urine, 132
Indelible Writing, 437
Indian Shields, to Prepare Varnish for, 351
Indigo, for Dyeing, to prepare, 316
   Paper, 299
   Solution of, 316
Inflammation of the Bladder, 132
   to Diminish, 154
   Brain, 125
   Ear, 125
   Eye, 125
   Glands, 135
   Intestines, 129
   Kidneys, 131
   Liver, 128
   Stomach, 128
   Throat, 126
India-rubber, Solvents for, 339
   Varnish, 343, 348
   Blacking, 349
   Cement, 354
   Solutions of, 354
Indian-corn, 29, 466

Indian-corn, Pone, 197
Indigestion, 128
   Medicines for, 160, 161
Injection, Laxative, 158
Instruments, Musical, to Stain, 326
INKS and Writing-fluids, 358
Ink, Indelible, 358, 359
   Perpetual, for Writing on Tombs, etc., 361
   Powder, 359
   Printers', 360
   Marking, to Take Out, 359
   Horticultural, 361
   for Zinc Labels, 361
   Indian, to make, 36 /
      Substitute for, 361
   Permanent, for Marking Linen, 359
   Sympathetic, 361
   to Write on Greasy Paper or Parchment, 359
   to Restore Decayed Writings, 359
   to Take Out Writing, 313
   Spots, to Take Out, 314, 434
Insects on Plants, etc., 38, 39, 71, 72, 76, 79, 83, 84, 90, 449
   to Destroy, 449
   Persian Powder for, 449
   Stings and Bites, 145, 173
Intermittent Fever, 123
Intestines, Inflammation of, 129
Intoxication, 179
Iodine, Tincture of, 167
Irish Whiskey, to Imitate, 289
Iron, Acetate of, 316
   Nitrate of, 316
   Ores, to Assay, 363
   and Steel, to Brown, 349
      to protect, 351
   Cast, Cement for, 353
   Polished, to Preserve, 438
   to Plate, 380
   Vessels, to Tin, 380
      to Keep from Rust, 464
   Ore, to Reduce into Malleable, 381
   to Shingle and Manufacture, New Way, 381
   to Weld, 381
   Hardening of, 381
   to Convert into Steel, 381
   to Deposit Copper on, 376
   Test for, 433
   Mould, to Remove, 313
   Varnish for, 464
Isinglass-jelly, to make, 178
Itch, 139, 156
Itching, 167
Ivory, to Gild, 377
   to Bleach, 350
   Artificial, 353
   to Dye Various Colors, 325
   Mode of Silvering, 434
   Transparent, 350
   Jelly, 171

Jam, Raspberry, to make, 237
   Strawberry, 237
Japan-black, 348
Japanning Old Tea Trays, 456
Jaundice, 129
   in the Horse, 111
Jessamine-water, to Prepare, 294
Jelly, Isinglass, 178
   Apple, 236
   Hartshorn, Currant, etc., etc., 235—237
   Calves'-foot, 229, 236
   Gooseberry, 236
   Ivory, 171
   Pineapple, 237
   Punch, 237
   Raspberry, 237

Jelly, Strawberry, 236
Jewelry, Metal for Common, 372
　　Paste for, 403
Jockey-Club, 304
Joints, Cartilage in, 135
　Wounds of, 146
Jujube Paste, 238
Jumbles, 202, 228
Juniper, Compound Spirit of, 295

Kali, Sea, to Cultivate, 82
Kalydor, 307
Kettles, Iron, to Keep from Rust, 464
Kew-garden Nosegay, 304
Kidneys, Inflammation of, 131
　to Cook, 204, 206
Kid-Skins, 389
Kirchwasser, 283
Kitchener's Pudding, 196
King's Evil, 135
Knee-joint, Dropsy of, 135
Knives and Forks, to Clean, 456
Knife-handles, Ivory, to Bleach, 350
KNITTING, 448
KNOTS, TO TIE, 446
Krumholz' Oil, to Procure, 291
Kustitlen's Metal for Tinning, 372
Kyan's Antiseptic Fluid, 435

Labdanum Plaster, 174, 176
Labarraque's Solution, 436
Lace, to Wash, 310
　Veils, White, to Clean, 311
　　Black, to Clean, 311
　Point, to Clean and Starch, 311
　Gold and Embroidery, to Clean, 314
Lackers of Various Tints, to make, 345, 346
Lacquer, for Brass, 345
LACQUERS, 345
Lakes, 335, 336
Lager Beer, 257
Lamb, Qualities of, 247
　Cutlets, 208
　Kidneys, 204
Lampas, 108
Lamps, to Prevent being Pernicious to Asthmatic persons, 185
　to Prevent Smoking, 458
Lampblack, 328
Land, Arable, Management of, 9
Lands, Clay, to Underdrain, 49, 50
Landscape, Chemical, 362
Lard, 301
Laudanum, Poisoning by, 152
Laughing-gas, 433
Lavender, Oil of (Foreign), to obtain, 291
　Spirit, 166, 295
　Water, to Prepare, 176, 296
　for Immediate Use, 296
Lawns, to Wash and Starch, 311
Lax, 130
Laxative Solutions, 158, 175
Layering, 62
Lead Ores, to Assay, 364
　Tests for, 433
　Chinese Sheet, to Prepare, 381
　Chromate of, 334
　Paper, 299
　Pencil Drawings, etc., to Preserve, 350
　Colic, 131
　Poisoning by, 152
　Water, 156
　Tree, to Prepare the, 380
Leather, to Gild, 377
　Dressing for, 459
　to Clean, 314
　to Render Water-proof, 348, 349

Leather Chairs, to Restore the Blackness of, 350
　Sheep, to Prepare, 387
　Morocco, to Manufacture, 388
　to Convert Old Parchment into, 390
　to Preserve from Mould, 390
　Morocco and Sheep, to Dye, 388, 390
　Russia, to Manufacture, 388
　to Color, 390
Leaven, Bread, 97
Ledoyen's Disinfecting Solution, 164, 436
Leeches, Application of, 156
Lemonade, Portable, 300
Lemon Cordial, to make, 286
　Juice, Preservation of, 457
　Peel, to Candy, 234
　Water, to Prepare, 296
Leprosy, Lotion for, 156
Leprous Affections, 156
Letters, to Disinfect, of the Plague, 164
Leucorrhœa, 166
Liard, for Lubricating, 347
Lice, to Destroy, 449
Liebig's Soup and Broth, 461
Life, Expectation of, 459
Life-boat, 181; Light, Artificial, 466
Lightning, to Guard Against, 462
Lime as a Manure, 22
　to Burn, Without Kilns, 24
　Juice, to Preserve, 457
Line Engraving, 419
Linear Measurement, 428
Linen, to Render Water-proof, 347
　Cloth for Screens, etc., to Thicken, 347
　to Remove Iron-moulds from, 313
　Mildew on, to Take Out, 314
　Fire-proof, 437
　and Cotton, to Dye, 320
Liniment, Compound Soap, 173,
　of Ammonia, 173
Linseed Poultice, 154
Lip-salve, 174
LIQUEURS, to make, 284
Liquid Manure, 25
　Paste, with Drying-oil, to make, 347
Liquorice, Extract of, to make, 234
　Juice, to make, 235
　Lozenges, 234
　Refined, to Prepare, 235
Liquors, Factitious, 287
　Bead for, 288
Lisbon Diet-drink, 258
LITHOGRAPHY, 423
Lithographic Ink, 424
　Pencils, 425
Litmus, for Dyeing, 324
　Paper, 299
Liver, Inflammation of the, 128
Lock-jaw, 137
Looking-glass Plates, 400
Looking-glasses, to Plate, 370, 402
　to Repair, 370
　etc., to Clean, 455
Lobsters, to Pot, 190, 221
　to Boil, 191
　to Choose, 248
Lobster Butter, 221
　Salad, 221
Looseness, to Check, 130
Lovage Cordial, to make, 286
Lozenges, Liquorice, 234
　Black Pectoral, 176
　White Pectoral, 176
Lubricating Compound, 347, 438
Lumbago, 162
Lung-fever in the Horse, 108
Lutes, to make, 355
Luting for Grafting, 459; Luting Clay, 466

INDEX.

Lye, to make, 311

Macadamized Roads, 454
Macaroni. 195, 206
  a l'Italienne, 220
  au Gratin, 220
  with Cream, 220
Macaroons, 224, 228
  English, 202
Macassar Oil, 306
Mackerel, etc., to Cure, 94
Madder, to Cultivate, 45
  Red. 319
  Use of, 46
Mad-dog. Bite of, 145
Madeira Wine, 289
Magnesia, Citrate of, 175
Mahogany, to Take Stains out of, 315
Male Fern, Remedy for Worms, 159
Mallenders, 108
Malt, 252, 253
  Poultice, 155
Manganese Ore, to Assay, 365
  Test for, 433
Mange. 108, 111, 114, 115, 449
Manheim Gold, 373
Manure, 10, 18, 22-26
  Bone, 25
  for a Garden, 60
  Liquid, 25
  Mineral, 11
  Organic, 11
  Plaster, 25
  Solid, 10
  Spreading of 19, 20
Manuscripts, to Renovate, 359
Maple Sugar, 52
Maraschino Cordial, 289
Marble, to Clean, 314
  Cements for, etc., 355
Marine Glue, 354
Marking Inks, 359
  to take out, 314
  Proof, 452
Marl, 22, 23
Marmalade, 232, 235
Mastic, 352
Matches, 384
Matting, Gold, 378
Mayonnaise, 210
  Sauce, 215
Mead, 258
Meadows, to Water, 51
Mealy-bug, 90
Measles, 138
MEASURES, 427
Measuring-glasses, 188, 241
  of Boards, 429
  of Stonework, 429
Meats, to Cook, 188, 190
  to Preserve without Ice, 458
  Salt to Freshen, 463
  Qualities of, 248, 249
Medals, to Copy, 375
  to Bronze, 376
MEDICINE, 122
Medicines, Domestic, 173
Medlars, to Preserve, 87; Meerschaum, 466
Melons, irregular Growth of, to Prevent, 79
Menses, the, 166, 167, 173
MENSURATION, 428
Mercurial Ointment, 174
  Ores, 366
Mercury, Poisoning by, 152
  to Purify, 439, 440
  Test for, 433
  to Protect Gilders from Effects of, 185

Meringues, 227
METALLURGY, 362
Metallic Injection, 370
Metals, Voltaic, Protection of, 376
  to Clean all sorts of, 311
Mezzotint, 421
Mildew, 29
  to Remove, 314, 437
  on Fruit Trees, 77
Milk, Qualities of, 249; Watered, to detect, 469
  and Cream, Substitutes for, 96
  to free from Turnip Flavor, 96
  of Roses, 306
  Fever, 168
  Punch, 200
  to Preserve, 458, 469
Mince Meat, 221,
  Pies, 198
MINERAL WATERS, 300
Mint, Oil of, 291
MISCELLANEOUS RECEIPTS, 446
Mock Turtle, 218, 231, 232
Moirée Metallique, 370
Molybdate of Ammonia, 318
Mont d'Or Water, 300
Monthly Sickness, 166
Montpellier Yellow, 334
Morocco, 388, 390
Mordants, 315, 345
Mortars, 352, 353
Mortification, 153
Mosaic Gold, 368, 393
  to make, 393
Moss, as Manure, 21, 22, 25
  Land to Improve, 23
  on Trees, to Destroy, 76
Moths, to Drive away, 450
Mother of Pearl, to Imitate, 352
Mouth Wash, 307
MUCILAGINOUS OR FIXED OILS, 301
Muffins, 201
Mulberry Tree, to Cultivate, 59
Munro's Cough Mixture, 159
Muntz Metal, 371
Muroxide, 318
Muriatic Acid, 298
Mussels and Periwinkles as food, 250
Mushrooms, 79, 196
  Catsup, 214
Mush, 197
Musk Mixture, 124
Mustard, to Cultivate, 94
Musical Instruments, to Stain, 326
Mutton, Qualities of, 248
  Broth, 194
  Cutlets, 207
  Leg of, 206
  Shoulder of, 204
  to Choose, 248
  à l'Anglaise, 206
Myrtle Water, 294

Napoleon's Pectoral Pills, 159
Naples Water, 300
  Yellow, 334
Nature Printing, 425
Neat's-foot Oil, 301
Nectar, 202
Nettle-rash, 139
Neuralgia, 137, 162
Neutral Spirit, 287
Nickel Ore, to Assay, 365
Nightmare, 161
Nipples, Sore, 168
Nitrous Oxide, 433
Noodles, 193
Nose, bleeding of, 125

Nose, Injuries of, 145
Noxious Vapors, 184, 436
Noyeau, 286
Nutmegs, Oil of, 291
Nut Oil, 301

Oak, to Dye, 326
Oaks, to Raise, 52
Oats, 32, 466
    Qualities of, 250
Oatmeal Gruel, 196
Odors, Unpleasant, to Remove, 185, 435
Oil and Water Colors (see COLORS), 332
    Artificial, of Quince, 288
        Wine, 288
        Apple, 278
        Jargonelle Pear, 288
        Bitter Almonds, 291
        Geranium, 291
    Macassar, 306
OILS, ESSENTIAL, ETC., 289
    Adulterations of, 292
    Siccitive, 331, 340
    Furniture, to make, 350
    Fixed, 301
    of Sweet Almonds, 301
    Beech-nut, 301
    Brick, 303
    Hazel-nut, 301
    Mace, 301
    Olives, Salad, or Sweet, 301
    Castor, 301
        to Purify, 303
        Mixture, 129
    Croton, 301
    Rape, 301
        to Purify, 301
    Vegetable, to Purify, 301
    Watchmaker's, 303
    Coal, to Clarify, 302
        to Test, 451,
    Drying, 331, 340
    Pumpkin, to make, 301
    Animal, and Fat, etc., 301
    Hog's Lard, 302
        to Purify and Bleach, 302
    Spermaceti, to Refine, 302
    Trotter, or Neat's-foot, 302
    Greenland Whale and Seal, to Refine, 302
    to Extract from Stone or Marble, 314
    out of Boards, 433
    Fish, to Purify, and Apply the Refuse to Useful Purposes, 302
    to Prevent becoming Rancid, 303, 466
    for making Hard Soap, to prepare, 302
Ointments, 174
Olio Broth, to make, 205
Omelette, 212
    Soufflé, 237
Onions, to Cultivate, 81
Opodeldoc, 173
Opium, Poisoning by, 152
Optical Glasses, to Polish, 402
Oreide, a New Brass, 371
Ores to Assay, 363
    and Earths containing Gold, 367
Ormolu, or Mosaic Gold, 368
Orange Cordial, to make, 286
    Marmalade, 232
    Flower Water, 294
        Drops, 234
        Paste for Hands, 303
    to Candy, 233, 235
Orchards, to Manage, 69, 70
Orfila's Hair Dye, 305
Osborn's Photographic Process, 418
Otto of Roses, 464

Oxygen, 433
Oxymel of Squills, 177
Oysters, to Fry, 191
    to Choose, 248
    Corn and, 219
    Pan, 191
    Pickle, 191
    Roast, 191
    Scollop, 191
    Spice, 191
    to Stew, 191
    and Cockles, Qualities of, 249
Ozone, Tests for, 299

Paint, Cheap, for Outside Work, 465
Painter's Cream, to make, 343
    Colic, 131
PAINTING, 327, 465
    on Glass, etc., 406
Paintings, to Clean and Restore, 339
Paints, 327, 465
    Old, Solvents for, 339
    Flexible, 347
    for Coarse Wood-work, 347
Palpitation, 127
Palsy, 136
Panada, 177, 219
Pancakes, 199
Paper, to Gild the Edges of, 377
    Fire-proof, 437
    to Remove Spots of Grease from, 314
    Hangings, to Clean, 314
    Water-Proof, 356
    Parchment, 436
    for Draughtsmen, 436
    Tracing, 425
Papier-Maché, 350
Parchment, Old, to Convert into Leather, 390
    to make, 389
    to Dye, various Colors, 326
    Paper, 436
Paregoric, 158
Parsley, Qualities of, 250
Parsnips, Mode of Cultivating in Guernsey, 40, 250
Parting, Process of, 367
Passy Water, 300
Paste, Liquid, to make, 355
    Brioche, 225
    Chinese, to make, 356
    for Artificial Gems, 403
    Ward's, for the Piles, 157
    Furniture, 349
    Orgeat, 237
    Puff, 198, 230
    Raspberry, 237
    Short, 230
    for Tarts, etc., 198
Pastils, 307
PASTRY, ETC., Qualities of, 250
Patchouli, Oil of, 291
Pâte de Guimauve, 238
    de Jujube, 238
Pattinson's Process, 368
Paunching in Cattle, 116
Peach, Culture of, 68, 77
    Brandy, 283, 289
Peaches, Brandy, 232
Pearlash, to Purify, 402
    Powder for the Face, 337
Pearly Lustre, to Produce, 352
Pears, Culture of, 68
Peas, to Raise, 34, 80
    to Keep from Mice, 80
    to Boil, 195, 220
    to Steam, 220
    Qualities of, 250
    and Bacon, to Cook, 191

Peat, as Manure, 24
Pents, 95
Pectoral Lozenges, 176
Pelisses, to Scour, 312
Pencil Drawings and Writings, to Preserve, 250
Pennyroyal, Oil of, to Obtain, 291
Peppermint, Spirit, 296
 Water, Simple, to make, 293
 Oil of, to Procure, 291
 Water, to Prepare, 293
Pepperpot, 193
Perennials, 89
PERFUMERY, 303
Perry, to make, 264
Peruvian Bark, Tincture of, 175
PETROLEUM, 451
Pewter, 369; Pharaoh's Serpent's Eggs, 464
Pheasants, to Breed, 92
 Roast, 210
Phial, Bologna, to make, 403
Philicomes, 306
Philip's Rules for Health, 183
Philosophical Instruments, Lacker for, 346
Phosphorus, to Preserve, 433
 Poisoning by, 153
Photogalvanography, 419
Photographs, to Engrave from, 418
 on Porcelain, 415
PHOTOGRAPHY, 409
 Failures and Imperfections, 417
Photolithography, 417
Photozincography, 418
Piccalilli, 238
PICKLING, 238
 Artificial Anchovies, 239
 Cucumbers, 239
 in Brine, 239
 Mushrooms, 238
 Onions, 238
 Piccalilli, 238
 Salmon, 239
 Samphire, 238
 Sour-krout, 238
 Seed-wheat, 28
 to Detect Copper in, 433
 Walnuts, White, 239
Pictures, to Clean, 339
 to Restore, 339
 to Preserve, 339
 Ancient, to Restore the White of, 339
 on Wax, 339
Pies, Beefsteak and Oyster, 211
 Chicken, 211, 212
 Crust, 198
 Giblet, 210
 Mince, 198
 Oyster, 231
 Perigord, 211
 Pigeon, 210
 Rabbit, 211
 Raised, French, 211
 Raised Ham, 211
 Raised Pork, 211
 Rhubarb, 199
 Rumpsteak, 211
Pig, Age of, 121
 Roasted, 206
Pigeon, à la Gauthier 209
 to Catch, 462
 Boiled, 210
 Roasted, 210
 Pie, 210
Pilchards, to Cure, 94
Piles, 142, 157, 158, 162, 167
 Ointments for, 142
 Ward's Paste for, 157
 Electuary for, 158

Pills, Aperient, 160, 161
 Chalybeate, 166
 Compound Aloetic, 158, 173
 Aloetic and Myrrh, 173
 Assafœtida, 173
 Plummer's, 173
 Compound Colocynth, 158
 Aloetic, 158, 173
 Compound Rhubarb, 158
 Expectorant, 159
 Napoleon's Pectoral, 159
 Anti-hysteric, 173
Pimento, Oil of, to Procure, 291
Pinchbeck, 371
Pineapple Rum, 239
 Jelly, 237
 to Raise, 71, 72
Pinery, to Manage a, 71, 72
Pink Saucers, 335
Pinks, 89
Pipings, a Mode of Cultivating Plants by Cutting, 65
Pippins, 75
Pismires, in Grass, to Prevent, 38
PISCICULTURE, 445
Pistachio, Cream, 235
Pitch Plaster, 174
Plague, to Disinfect Substances of the, 164
Plant, to, Shrubs and Trees, 66, 68
Plants, to Accelerate, in Hot-houses, 67
 to Choose, 69
 Insects on, to Destroy, 38, 39, 71, 72, 76, 79, 83, 84, 90, 449
 to Preserve from Frosts, 75
 to Preserve from Slugs, 450
Plaster, of Spanish Flies, 174
 Compound Burgundy Pitch, 174
 Lubdanum, 174
 Adhesive, 175
 Court, 353
 for Rooms, 352
 of Paris, as manure, 25
Plate, to, Looking-glasses, 370
 to Clean, 313, 466
Plated Copper, from, to Obtain Silver, 379
Platina, Mock, to Prepare, 371
PLATING, 375
 Electro, 376
 Silver Solder for, 369
Pleurisy, 127
Plumbers, Painters, and Glaziers, Cautions to, 164
Plums, Culture of, 62
 Pickled, 231
Poisoned Wounds, 145
 Bibron's Antidote for, 450
Poisonous Fish, 153
POISONS, 151–153
 from Acids, 151
 Alkalies, 152
 Arsenic, 152
 Antimony, 152
 Copper, 152
 Hemlock, 153
 Laudanum, 152
 Lead, 152
 Lunar Caustic, 152
 Mercury, 152
 Nightshade, 153
 Opium, 152
 Phosphorus, 152
 Powdered Glass, 152
 Sal Ammoniac, 152
 Saltpetre, 152
 Salts of Tin, 152
 Salts of Bismuth, Gold, and Zinc, 153
 Spanish Flies, 152
 Spurred Rye, 153

Poisons, Toadstools, 153
    Tobacco, 153
Polish, to, Varnish, 352
    French, 344
    Varnished Furniture, 349
    Wood, 349
    Brass Ornaments Inlaid in Wood, 349
Poll Evil, 109
Polygraph, an Instrument for Writing Two Letters at Once, 459
Polypus, 135
Pomatum, 306
Pomade, Divine, 306
    Dupuytren, 305
    à la Rose, 306
    of Bitter Almonds, 306
    Stick, 306
Pone, 197, 232
Porcelain, to Manufacture, 394
    to Gild, 376
    Enamel for, 391
    New Enamel for, 391
    to Paint on, 406
    Photographs on, 415
Pork, Qualities of, 249
    Pies, 211
    to Salt, 239
    Choice of, 242, 243
    Cutlets, 208
Port Wine, 289
Portable Lemonade, 300
Porter, to Brew, London System, 254
    Three Barrels of, 254
    from Sugar and Malt, 255
    to make a Butt of Stout, 260
    to Bottle, 262
    to Ripen, if Flat, when Bottled, 263
Portland Cement, 352
    Powder for the Gout, 460
Portugal Water, to Prepare, 294
Posset, Ale, 200
Potatoes, Culture of, 34, 36, 79, 466
    à la Crême, 220
    à la Maitre d'Hôtel, 219
    and Greens, 195
    Balls, 195
    Bread from, to make,
    Boiled, 195
    Cold, Fried, 195
    Early, to Produce, in Great Quantity, 36
    Escaloped, 195
    Fourteen Ways of Dressing, 195
    Fried in Slices, 195
        Mashed, 195
        with Onions, 195
        Whole, 195
    Frosted, to Use, 36, 196
        to make Starch of, 36
    Irish Method of Cultivating, 36
    Mode of Taking up and Stirring the Crop, 36
    Mashed, 195
    Pie, 195
    Qualities of, 250
    Quantity of Seed for, 34
    Roasted, 195
    Snow, 195
    for Sea Provisions, to Keep, 196
    to Boil, Mealy, 195
    to Cultivate, 34
    to Extract Alcohol from, 283
    to Grow Constantly on the Same Piece of Ground, 36
    to Prepare the Ground for, 34
    to Preserve from Frost, 35
    to Preserve, 36
    to Raise, Advantageous Method, 35

Potatoes, to Remove Frost from, 35
    to Steam, 196
Potichomania, 458
Pot-pie, 196
Potted Beef, 190
    Lobster, 190
    Shad, 190
POTTERY, 394
    English Stoneware, to Manufacture, 394
    Yellow, or Queensware, 394
Poultices, Various, 154
Poultry, to fatten, etc., 92, 94
Poundcake, Plain, 200
    Gingerbread, 200
Powders, Seidletz, 178
    Portland, 460
    Dover, 173
    Alvotic, with Iron, 173
    for Gilding, 378
    Ginger Beer, 433
    Toilet, 306
Pox, 133
Pradier's Cataplasm for Gout, 460
Precious Stones, to Imitate, 374, 403
    to Engrave on, 423
Pregnancy, Diseases of, 167
Prescriptions, Various, 154
PRESERVING, 239
Pretsch's Process, 419
Prince Ruperts' Drops, 403
Princes' Metal, 371
Printing, Photographic, 413
    Ink, 360
    Nature, 425
Prints, to Bleach, 310
    to Wash without Fading, 313
    to make, Resemble Paintings, 347
Privies, to Deodorize, 164
Proof Marking, 452
Provisions, Salt, to Freshen, 463
Prussian-Blue, to make, 330, 337
    Soluble, 337, 380
    to Dye, 317
    to Paint, 330
Psoas Abscess, 142
Pudding, Apple, 223, 229
    Baked Apple, 229
    Indian, 229
    Batter, 198
    Beefsteak and Oyster, 212
    Biddle, 230
    Boiled, 199
    Bread, 198, 223
    Brown-bread, 223
    Carrot, 197
    Cheshire, 197
    Citron, 229
    Cocoanut, 222, 229
    Cottage, 222
    Cream, 229
    Currant, 232
    Custard, 199, 222, 229
    Dutch, 197
    Eve's, 222
    Friend Wilson's Plum, 230
    Hominy, 229
    Indian, 199, 229
    Kidney, 212
    Kitchener's 196
    Lemon, 198, 222, 223
        Goodfellow's, 222
    Meringue, 198, 230
    Newcastle, 198
    Newmarket, 198
    Nottingham, 197
    Oldbury, 198
    Orange, 229

Pudding, Patterdale, 222
   Plain, 197
      Rice, 197, 229
   Plum, 223
   Potato, 197, 229
   Potato Rice, 197
   Pumpkin, 199
   Queen's, 222
   Quince, 198
   Rice, 197, 229
   Sago, 229,
   Suet, 199
   Sweet Potato, 229
   Swiss, 197
   Tapioca, 223, 232
   Transparent, 197
   Vermicelli, 198
   Wedding Cake, 222
   Wedding, 229
   Windsor, 197
   White Potato, 222
   Yorkshire, 197
Puerperal Fever, 168
Puff Paste, 198, 230
Pullna Water, 299
Pulse, the, 122
Pumps, Temporary, at Sea, 182
Punch, 202
   Milk, 200, 202
   Claret, 231
   Fish-House, 458
   Paris à la Nina, 231
Purgatives, 158, 175
Purification of Water by Charcoal, 178
Purple of Cassius, 408
Putrid Sore Throat, 126
Putty, Old, to Soften, 339
Pyrmont Water, 300
Pyroligneous Acid, 298
PYROTECHNY, 384

Quass, to make, 298
Queen's Metal, 368
Quince, Marmalade, to make, 235 .
   to Keep, 87
Quinine Mixture, 124
Quittor, 109

Rabbit Pie, 209
Rabbits, à la Bourguingnonne, 209
Radishes at all seasons, 82
Ragout of Asparagus, to make, 213
   Mushrooms, to make, 213
   Artichokes, to make, 213
   Calves' Sweet-bread, to make, 214
   with Roots, to make, 214
Raisin Spirits, 283
Raspberry, to Cultivate, 69
   Brandy, 287
   Cream, to make, 236
   Dumplings, 198
   Jam, to make, 237
   Paste, to make, 237
   Vinegar, 237
Ratafia, 284, 285, 286
Rattlesnake Bites, 145
   Bibron's Antidote for, 450
Razors, to Hone, Strop, etc., 461
   Paste for Sharpening, 461
Reading Proof, 453
Reapers, 17, 470
Reaping Unripe Grain, 31
Reboulet's Antiseptic Fluid, 435
Red Spider, 83, 90
Refrigerant Lotion, 154
   Mixtures, 123
Retention of Urine, 132

Rheumatism, 135
   Medicine for, 177
   Pills, etc., for, 162
   Portland Powders for, 460
Rhodium, Oil of, 291
Rhubarb, to Cultivate, 80
   Pills, 158
   Tincture of, 175
Rice Cups, 223
   Diavolini, 223
   Flummery, 223
   Fritters, 223
   Pudding, 197, 229
Rickets, 172
Ridgwood's Disinfectant, 164
RIDING, 463
Riga Balsam, 291
RINDERPEST, 467; Ringbone, 109
Ringworm, 139, 156, 172
Roach Poison, 450
Roads, to make, 454
Rockets, 385
Rollers, for Land, 16
Rolls, French, 228
Roman Cement, 352
   Candles, 385
Roofing, Composition for, 353
Rooms, Cement for, 352
Root Beer, 257
Roots, to Preserve and Pack, 70, 85
Rosemary, Oil of, 291
Rosendale Cement, 352
   Water of, 293
Roses, 88
   Butter of 291
   Milk of, 306
   Otto of, 464
Rot, Dry, 352, 432, 438
Rotation of Crops, 26
Rouge, 335
   Jeweller's, 397
ROWING, THE ART OF, 453
Rue, Oil of, 291
Rugs, to Scour, 312
Rum, Jamaica, 281
   to Imitate, 288
   from Molasses, 282
   Shrub, 285
   Ether, 288
Ruperts' Drops, 403
Ruptures, 140
   in the Hog, 117
   Horse, 115
RURAL AND DOMESTIC ECONOMY, 90
Rusks, 201, 202, 226
Russell's Tannin Process, 414
Russia Leather, 388
Rust, to Prevent, 30, 351, 438
   in Kettles, 464
Rutabaga Turnips, 38
Rye, 33, 466

Sachets, Toilet, 307
Safety-matches, 386
Saffron, Bastard, 324
Sail-cloth, Water-proof, 347
Salads, 220, 221, 231
Sallenders, 109
Sally Lunn, 202
Salmis of Wild Duck, 209
Salmon, to Pickle, 239
   Curry, 210
Salt, Spirit of, 298
Salt Meat, to Freshen, 463
Salting of Meats, 239
Salutary Cautions, 178-180
Samphire, to Pickle, 238

492 INDEX.

Sand pot, Portable, 298
    Crack, 109
    Impressions in, to Preserve, 437
Sandwiches, 220
Sanfoin, 39
Sarsaparilla, 177
    Beer, 258
Sarsenets, to Clean, 310
Sassafras, Oil of, 292
Satins, to Gild, 377
Sauce, Apple, 194
    Béchamel, 213
    Boar's Head, 215
    Brown, 194
    Brown Oyster, 214
    Caper, 215
    Cherry, 215
    Common, 194
    Cream, for a Hare, 194
    Cream, Béchamel, 214
    Currant-jelly, 215
    Curry, 215
    Damson, 231
    Fish, 194
    for Veal, 213
    Fried Bread, 215
    German Sweet, 214
    Indian Curry, 214
    Italienne, 213
    Kitchener's Superlative, 213
    Mayonnaise, 215
    Miser's, 194
    Nivernoise, 194
    Nonpareil, 194
    Nun's, 213
    Parson's, 194
    Piquante, 213
    Plain Curry, 215
    Poivrade, 214
    Pontiff's, 213
    Poor Man's, 214
    Queen's, 194
    Sailor's, 194
    Sweet, 194
    Wine, 214
Sausages, 190
Saxon or Chemic Blue, 316
    Artificial, 333
Sayce's Photographic Process, 416
Scald Head, 139, 156, 172
Scalds, 153
Scale on Plants, 90
    Boiler, 433
Scalp, Wounds of, 145
Scarlet-fever, 137
Schnapps, to Imitate, 288
Sciatica, 162
Scions, to Choose, 65
Scirrhus, 135
Scorbutic Eruptions, 154
SCOURING, 312
Scrapple, 191
Scrofula, 135
Scurvy, 140
    Grass, Spirit of
Sea Bathing, Substitute for, 183
    Kail, to Cultivate, 82
    Voyages, 178
    Water, to Render Fit for Washing, 180
        to Drink, 180
    Weed as Manure, 23
Sealing-wax, 357
Seamen, 178
    Health of, to Preserve, 180
Seatworms, 160
Sedative Lotion, 154
    Cataplasm, 154

Seeds, to Sow, 66, 466
    Farm, Estimate, per Acre, 466
    to Preserve, 84
    to Improve All Sorts of, 31
Seed-wheat, to Pickle, 28
Seidlitz Powders, to Prepare, 178
    Water, 300
Seltzer-water, 300
Senna, as a Laxative, 158
Serpents, Bites of, 145
Shad, to Pot, 190
    to Choose, 248
Shampoo Liquor, 305
Shawls, Silk, to Dye, 321
Sheep, Foot-rot in, 117
    Age of, 121
    Maggots in, 117
    Scab in, 117, 118
    Skins, to Prepare, 387, 389
    to Prevent Catching Cold after Shearing,117
    Water in the Heads of, to Cure, 118, 119
Sheeps' Tongues, 204
Shellac, to Bleach, 300
Sherry Wine, 289
Shield-budding, 63
Ships, Health on Board of, to Preserve, 178, 180
    Hints on board, 180
    to Fumigate, 179
    to Render Sinking Impossible, 182
Shipwrecks, Preservation in case of, 182
Shoes, to Render Water-proof, 348
Shot Metal, 369
Shower-bath, 183
Shrubbery, 88
Shrubs, Brandy, to make, 285
    Rum and Currant, 285
    to Plant, 66
Sick Rooms, 164
Sight, Weak, Remedy for, 157
    Dimness of, 125
Silica, Soluble, 434
Silk, to Gild, 377
    to Clean, 311
    to Extract Grease-spots from, 312
Silks, to Clean, 312
    to Bleach, 310
    to Dye, 317
    to Varnish, 348
    Varnish for, 343
SILKWORMS, 53-59
    Ailanthus, 59
Silver, Test for, 432
    Imitation of, 372
    Plate, to take Stains out of, 314
    Plate, 379
    Plating, 375
    Solder, 369
    Solutions, 375
    Tree, to Prepare the, 381
    to Clean, 456, 466
    to Recover, from Baths, 375, 417
        Plate, 380
Silvering Glass Globes, Liquid Foil for, 370
    Copper Ingots, 379
    Electro, 376
    Glass, 370
    Powders, 379
Similor, or Manheim Gold, 373
Sitfasts, 109
Size, Isinglass, to make, 355
Skin, Eruptions, 156, 171
Small-beer, to Brew, 256
Small-pox, 139
    Vaccination, 138
Smee's Battery, 375
Smoky Chimneys, to Cure, 455
Smut, 30, 31

INDEX. 493

Snail-water, Small, to make, 294
Snake-bites, 450
    Bibron's Antidote for, 450
Soap-liniment, 173
SOAPS, 308
Soapstone as a lubricator, 438
Soda-water, to Prepare, 433
Soil for a Garden, 60
    for Window-gardening, 90
Soiling, 21
Soils, Constituents of, 12–14
Solid Measurement, 428
Solder, 369, 372
    Brass, for Iron, 372
    for Steel Joints, 372
    Gold, 369
    Hard, 369
    Soft, 369
    Silver for Jewellers, 369
Soleil, Coup de, 136
Soluble Silica, 434
Sore Legs, 155
    Nipples, 168
    Throat, 159
Sores, Dressing for, 460
    Clay as a Dressing for, 460
Sorghum, 29, 466
SOUP, Asparagus, 192
    Beef-gravy, 192
    Charitable, 192
    Cheap, 193
    Chicken, 193
    Chicken, without Chicken, 231
    Clam, 193
    Corn, 193
    Dr. Green's Bean, 231
    for Convalescents, 178
    Giblet, 192
    Herring, 193
    Hodge-podge, 215, 217
    Julienne, 217
    Letuce and Pea, 217
    Liebig's, 216, 461
    Maigre, 192
    Mock-turtle, 218
    Mullaga-tawny, 215
    Noodle, 193
    Nutritious, 193
    Ox-cheek, 219
    Ox-tail, 219
    Oyster, 193
    Pea, 193
    Pepperpot, 193
    Portable, 192
    Rice and Meat, 192
    Scotch Broth, 193
    Spring, 217
    Turtle, 217
    Veal-gravy, 192
    Vegetable, 193
    Vermicelli and Vegetable, 216
    White, 216
    Winter, 215
Sour-krout, 238
Soy, Tomato, 230
Sozodont, 307
Spanish Flies, Ointment of, 174
Spavin, 106
Spearmint-water, Simple, 294
SPECIFIC GRAVITY, 429
Spectacles, Use of, 156
Specula, for Telescopes, 371
Spermaceti, to Refine, 362
Spinach, 219, 250
Spine, Crooked, 172
Spirits, to Distil, from Carrots, 282
    to Dulcify, 280

Spirits, to Fine, 283
    of Nutmeg, 176
    of Salt, or Marine Acid, 298
    of Wine, to make, 280
    Foreign, to Imitate, 287
    Proof, 283
Spleen, Enlarged, 129
Sponge, to Bleach, 437
Sportsman's Beef, 449
Sprains, 143, 154
Spruce-beer, Brown and White, 257
Squills, Oxymel of, 177
    Syrup of, 176
    Vinegar of, 177
Staggers, 109
Staining Wood, etc., 325
St. Anthony's Fire, 138
Stapleton's Antiseptic Fluid, 435
Starch, 457
    from Frosted Potatoes, 37
Starvation, Effects of, 463
Statues, Ancient, Composition of, 371
Steak à la Soyer, 206
    Française, 207
    Plain Rump, 207
Steel, 382
    Bessemer Process for, 383
    Goods, to Preserve, 351
    Improved Mode of Hardening, 382
    Tungsten, 372
    to Color Blue, 382
    to Distinguish from Iron, 382
    to Engrave on, 420
    to Gild, 376
    Uchatius, 383
    Varnish for, 464
Steinbuhl Yellow, 334
Stereoscopic Pictures, 411
Stereotype Plates, 369
Stereotyping, Rapid, 425
Stews, 191
Still, Hot, to make a, 279
    Large, to make a, 279
    New Worm for, 279
    for Simple Waters, 293
Stings and Bites, 145
Stockings, Silk, to Clean, 312
    to Dye, 321
Stomach, Inflamed, 128
    Cramp in, 128
Stomachic Pills, 160
Stone in the Bladder, 132
    Artificial, 439
Stoneware, 394
Stonework, Measurement of, 430
Stoppers, Chemical, to Prevent Sticking, 434
    to Loosen, 434
Stoves, Cracks in, to Mend, 353
    Cement for, 458
Strangury, 133
    in the Horse, 109
Strangles, 109
Straw Hats to Clean, 313, 315
    to Dye, 321
    Importance of, 46, 49
Strawberry Water, 294
    Jelly, to make, 236
    Jam, 237
    to Cultivate, 69, 82
    Qualities of the, 248
    to Preserve the, Whole, 240
Strictures, 133
Stucco, 353
St. Vitus' Dance, 137
Styes, 158
Suffocation, by Noxious Vapors, 151
    by Hanging, 151

494　　　　　　　　　　INDEX.

Suffocation, Drowning, 151
  by Strangling, 153
Sugar, 232, 233, 234
  Brown, to Clarify, 233
  Candy, to make, 233
  Cane, 52
  to Obtain from Beets, 283
            Birch, 233
            Grapes, 233
            Pears, 233
            Starch, 233
  to make Devices in, 234
  Ornaments in, 234
Sulphur in Electrical Machines, 439
Sulphuretted Hydrogen, 433
Sulphurous Acid, 310, 433
Sunflower, the, 83
Sunstroke, 136
Suppuration, 154
Surface Measurement, 428
Sweetbreads, 206, 208
Swelling, White, 135
  of the Feet, 167
Swimming, Art of, 183
Swine, Age of, 121
    Cholera in, 117
    to Fatten, 92
    Kidney Worm in, 116
    Measles, etc., in, 116, 117
    Rupture in, 117
    TRICHINÆ, 469; Sore Throat in, 117
Syllabub, Whipped, to make, 234
  Solid, to make, 234
Syphilis, 133
Syrup of Ginger, 176
  Poppies, 177
  Squills, 177
  Violets, 177

Table Beer, 257
Talmi Gold, 368
TANNING, AND THE TREATMENT OF LEATHER, 386
Tape Worm, 160
Tapioca, 196, 223, 232
Tar, Oil of, to Procure, 292
  Water, to Prepare, 177
Tartar Emetic, Poisoning by, 152
Tarts, 198
  Paste for, 198
Taupenot's Collodio—Albumen Process, 415
Tea, Beef, to make, 178
  Qualities of, 251
  Trays, to Clean, 456
Teeth, Cutting the, 171
  Cements for, 358
  Diseases of the, Remedies for, 157
  Extraction of, to Check Hemorrhage in, 157
  Preservation of, 186
  Remedies for, 157, 187
Telegraph, Electric, 451
Telescopes, Specula for, 371
Tendons, Wounds of, 146
Tepid Bath, 183
Terrapins, 210
Test Papers, 299
Testicle, Cancer of, 134
Tests, Chemical, 432
  for Gold, Silver, and Copper, 432
  Iron, Lead, Manganese, 433
  Liquors, 299
  Mercury, 433
Tetanus, 137
  in the Horse, 115
Tetter, 139
Thermometers, 442
    Thenard bleu de, 333
Thorn-hedges, 51

Threshing Machines, 17
Throat, Wounds in, 145
  Foreign Bodies in, 153
  Gargle for, 126, 159
  Inflammatory, 126, 159
  Putrid, 126, 159
  Strictures in, 126
  Ulcerated, 159
Thrush in Children, Remedies for, 159, 171
  Gargles for, 159
  in the Horse, 109, 114
Thunder, etc., 462
Thyme, Oil of, 292
Tic Douloureux, 137
Tiffanies, to Wash and Stain, 311
Tiles, Red Distemper for, 331
  to Preserve, 348
Tillage, 14
Timber, to Preserve, 352, 438
  to Prevent from Splitting, 438
  to Detect Decay in, 438
  Measure, 429
Timothy, 466
Tincture of Benzoin, 176
  Catechu, 176
  Ginger, 175
  Guaiacum, 176
  Japonica, to Prepare, 281
  Peruvian Bark, 176
  Rhubarb, 175
  Senna, 175
  of Tolu, 175
Tin Ores, to Assay, 364
  to Ornament Surface of, 370
  Tree, to Prepare the, 381
Tinning, 376
  Brass and Copper, Rapid, 380, 433
  Rustition's Metal for, 372
Tobacco, 53
  Poisoning by, 153
  Pipes, 396
Toadstools, Poisoning by, 153
Toilet Powders, 306
Tomato Catsup, 194, 214, 230
  to Bake, 196
  to Broil, 196
  Soy, 230
Tombac, to Prepare, 368, 369
Tonsils, Swollen, 126
Tongues, Sheeps', 204
  Beef and Champagne, 205
Tonics, 160, 166
Toothache, 187
  Powders and Pastes, 308
  Cements, 358
  Remedies for the, 187
Toovely's Photolithographic Process, 417
Tortoise Shell, to Weld, 356
Tourmaline, Artificial, 434
Tracing Paper, 425
Trees, to Graft, 64; to Force, 68
  to Pack for Exportation, 88
  to Plant, 66, 68
  to Protect from Hares, 76
  to Transplant, 67, 83
TRICHINÆ IN SWINE, 469
Tropical Climate, Cautions when in, 179
Tubes, Copper, by Electrotype, 376
Tumors, 140, 141
Tunisian Cement, 354
Turkeys, Qualities of, 249
  Choice of, 242
  Dropsy in the Crops of, 119
  Roast, 207
Turmeric Paper, 299
Turner's Cerate, 174
Turnips, to Cultivate, 37, 466

INDEX. 495

Turnips, Flavor of, in Butter, 96
   Insects in, 38
   Qualities of, 249
   Ruta-baga, 38
   to Remove Taste from Butter, 96
Turnsole, or Litmus Blue, for Dyeing, 324
Turpentine, Oil of, 292
Turtle, to Dress, 290, 230
   to Dress Calf's Head like, 231
Tutania, or Britannia Metal, 372
Tutenag, to Prepare, 369
Twiggs' Hair Dye, 305
Twining's Ice Machine, 435
Tying Knots, 446
Tympany, 133
Type Metal, 369
Typhoid Fever, 124
Typhus Fever, 124

Ulcers, 126, 142, 143, 154, 155
   and Pimples on the Tongue, 154
Ultramarine, 332
   Artificial, 333
Underdraining, 49
Unventilated Places, to Explore, 436
Urine, Incontinence of, 132, 168
   Difficulty of, 132
   Suppression of, 132
Usquebaugh, 285
Uvula, Enlarged, 126

Vaccination, 138
VARNISHES, 339, 464
   to Polish, 352
Veal, Qualities of, 249
   Breast, Glacée, 204
   Cake, to make, 205
   Cutlet, 206, 232
   Ragout, 205
   Savory, Dish of, to make, 204
   Shoulder, en Galantine, 204
   to Choose, 248
Vegetables, to Propagate; 62
   Qualities of, 250
   to make Tender, 459
   to Preserve, 85
   to Protect, 67
Veils, to Clean, 311
Veins, Enlarged, Spermatic, 134, 168
Vellum, to make, 390
   Artificial, 436
   to Stain, Green, 326
Veneers, to Print from, 425
Venereal Warts, 134
Venison Chops, 209
   Pastry, 230
   Scallops, 208
Ventilation, 163, 184
Verbenas, 89
Verbena, Extract of, 304
Verditer, 334
Vermin, 38, 39, 98
Vichy Water, 300
Vinegar, to make, 296
   Adulteration, 296
   Aromatic, 164, 308
   Ice or Glacial, 298
   of Squills, 177
   Quass, to make, 298
   Raspberry, 237
   Strength of, to Determine, 296
   Tarragon, 308
   to Deprive of Color, 298
   to Purify, 296
   to Strengthen, 297
Vines, Culture of, 73, 74, 265
Vinous Fermentation, 251

Violets, Essence of, 304
Vives, 109
Vol-au-Vent, to make, 211
Vomiting in Pregnancy, 167
   in Children, 170

Waffles, 202, 228, 230
Walks, Gravel, to make, 60
Wallflower, Essence of, 304
Wall Trees, 66, 71
Walnuts, to Pickle, 239
   to Keep, 87
Ward's Paste for Piles, 157
Warping of Planks, 438
Warts, Common, 157
   in the Horse, 106
   Venereal, 134
Watch, Works, Oil for, 303
Water, Casks, to Clean, 95
   Distilled, 294
   Fresh, from Sea, to Obtain, 179
   Gruel, 177
   Pipes, to Manage, in Winter, 454
   Sea, to Render Fit for Washing, 180
   Soda, 433
   to Determine if Hard or Soft, 433
   to Keep Pure in Iron Kettles, 404
   to Purify, 437
Water-bath, Solutions for, 290
Watering Gardens, 66
   Meadows, 51
   Wall Trees, 66
Water-proof Cloth, 347; Water-proofing, 466
   Boots, 348
   Leather, 349
   Paper, 356
Waters, Simple, Rules for Distilling, 492
   Aerated, 299
   Chalybeate, 300
   Compound Distilled, 294
   Medicinal, 299
   Stills for, 293
   to Purify, 438
Wax, Sealing, to make, 357
   Bordering, for Engravers, 420
   Candles, to make, 459
   Painting on, 339
Weather, to Foretell, 187, 420
Weeds, to Destroy, 39
   to Prevent Growth of, 76
WEIGHTS AND MEASURES, 241, 427
Welding, 381
Welsh Rabbit, 463
Wheat, to Cultivate, 27, 28, 466
   Diseases of, 29, 30
   to Preserve, 96
Whips, 230
Whiskey, Factitious, 288, 289
White Beer, 257
   Metal, 369
   Swelling, 155
Whites in Women, 166
Whitewash, to, 458, 465
   Resembling Paint, 465
Whitlow, Treatment of, 142, 155
Wild-Fowls as Food, 249
   en Salmis, 210
   to Capture, 462
Wind Broken, 107
   Galls, 109
Window Glass, 400
Windows, to Keep up, 457
Wine Gardening, 90
   Vaults, to Manage, 275
   Whey, 178, 200
WINES, AMERICAN, 265
   American honey, 271

Wines, Port, to make Rough, 276
    and Spirits, Collar of, to fit up, 275
    Apricot, 270
    Balm, 273
    Blackberry, 269
    Bottling and Corking, 266
    Claret, 289
    Cherry, 269
    Currant red, 267
        Black, 267
        Dutch, 267
        White, 267
    Domestic, Management of, 266, 273
    Elderberry, 268
    Fining, 274
    Foul, to Restore, 276
    Ginger, 272
    Gooseberry, 266
        and Currant, 267
    Honey, 269
    Ill Scent of, 274
    Juniperberry, 269
    Lemon, 269
    Madeira, 289
    Mead, 271
    Mulberry, 268
    other Mixed Berries, 268
    Peach, 270
    Port, to Imitate, 268, 269
    Raspberry, 268
    Red into White, 277
    Rhubarb, 272
    Sherry, 289
    Strawberry, 268
    to Check the Fermentation of, 274
    to Decant, 457
    to Determine Quantity of Alcohol in, 287
    to make Sparkling, 266
    Various Kinds, 271-273, 289
    White, to Convert into Red, 276
    Whortle, or Bilberry, 269
Wintergreen, Oil of, 292
Woad for Dyeing, to Prepare, 324
Wood, to Preserve, 84, 347, 352
    Artificial, 357
    Decoction of, 178
    for Dyeing, to Prepare, 325
    Oil Gilding on, 377
    to Dye Various Colors, 325
    to Engrave on, 422
    to Render Incombustible, 437

Wood, to Polish, 349
Wool, to Dye, 316
    to Bleach, 310
Woollens, Undyed, to Scour, 310
    Fuller's Purifier for, 313
    to Dye, 316
    to Full, 310
Worms, 131, 132, 158, 159
    in Dogs, 444
    in the Horse, 106
    Medicines for, 159, 160
Wormwood, Oil of, to Procure, 292
Worthlytype Process, for Photography, 415
Worts, to Boil, 254
    to Cool, 254
    to Determine the Strength of, 253
    to Mix the Yeast with the, 254
Wounds, 144
    in Trees, 76
Writing, Fluids, 356, 360
    for the Blind, 461
    in Cypher, 459
    on Greasy Paper, 359
    to Gild, 377
    to make New look Old, 359
    to Produce Fac Simile of, 360
    to take out, 313
Writings, Decayed, to Restore, 359
    to Copy, 360

Yarn, to Scour, 312
Yeast Poultices, 155
    Substitutes for, 261
    to Keep, 262
Yellow Fever, 123
    Cadmium, 334
    Chrome, 334
    Gum, in Children, 170
    Montpellier, 334
    Naples, 334
    Steinbuhl, 334

Zaffre, 408
Zeiodolite, 353
Zinc Ores, to Assay, 366
    Black Varnish for, 351
    Poisoning by, 152
    Paint, Drying Oil for, 340
        Dryer for, 340
        White, 338

www.ingramcontent.com/pod-product-compliance
Lightning Source LLC
Chambersburg PA
CBHW020831020526
44114CB00040B/503